MEDIEVAL LITERATURE IN ENGLISH

The study of medieval literature has experienced a revolution in the last two decades, which has reinvigorated many parts of the discipline and changed the shape of the subject in relation to the scholarship of the previous generation. 'New' texts (laws and penitentials, women's writing, drama records), innovative fields and objects of study (the history of the book, the study of space and the body, medieval masculinities), and original ways of studying them (the Sociology of the Text, performance studies) have emerged. This has brought fresh vigour and impetus to medieval studies, and impacted significantly on cognate periods and areas. *The Oxford Handbook of Medieval Literature in English* brings together the insights of these new fields and approaches with those of more familiar texts and methods of study, to provide a comprehensive overview of the state of medieval literature today. It also returns to first principles in posing fundamental questions about the nature, scope, and significance of the discipline, and the directions that it might take in the next decade.

The *Handbook* contains 44 newly commissioned essays from both world-leading scholars and exciting new scholarly voices. Topics covered range from the canonical genres of Saints' lives, sermons, romance, lyric poetry, and heroic poetry; major themes including monstrosity and marginality, patronage and literary politics, manuscript studies and vernacularity are investigated; and there are close readings of key texts, such as *Beowulf, Wulf and Eadwacer,* and *Ancrene Wisse* and key authors from Ælfric to Geoffrey Chaucer, Langland, and the *Gawain* Poet.

Elaine Treharne is Roberta Bowman Denning Professor of Humanities and Professor of English at Stanford University. She has published extensively on Old and Middle English literature and particularly religious prose, and she works on medieval manuscripts and their contents, focusing recently on the architextuality of early books. Her current projects include *The Ideology of Early English* and *The Sensual Book, 800–1300*. She is a Fellow of the Society of Antiquaries, a Fellow of the Royal Historical Society, and a Honorary Fellow of the English Association.

Greg Walker is Regius Chair of Rhetoric and English Literature at the University of Edinburgh. He has published widely on the history, literature, and drama of the late-medieval and Renaissance periods in England and Scotland. Among his more recent publications are *Writing Under Tyranny: English Literature and the Henrician Reformation* (OUP, 2005) and *Imagining Spectatorship from The Mysteries to The Shakespearean Stage* (OUP, 2016), co-written with John J. McGavin. He is a Fellow of the Royal Society of Edinburgh, the Royal Historical Society, the Society of Antiquaries, and the English Association.

THE OXFORD HANDBOOK OF

MEDIEVAL LITERATURE IN ENGLISH

Edited by

ELAINE TREHARNE

and

GREG WALKER

with the assistance of

WILLIAM GREEN

OXFORD

UNIVERSITY PRESS

OXFORD
UNIVERSITY PRESS

Great Clarendon Street, Oxford, OX2 6DP,
United Kingdom

Oxford University Press is a department of the University of Oxford.
It furthers the University's objective of excellence in research, scholarship,
and education by publishing worldwide. Oxford is a registered trade mark of
Oxford University Press in the UK and in certain other countries

First published 2010
First published in paperback 2017

Published in the United States of America by Oxford University Press
198 Madison Avenue, New York, NY 10016, United States of America

British Library Cataloguing in Publication Data
Data available

Library of Congress Cataloging in Publication Data
Data available

ISBN 978–0–19–922912–3 (Hbk.)
ISBN 978–0–19–879808–8 (Pbk.)

PREFACE

The Oxford Handbook to Medieval Literature aims to provide advanced Medieval undergraduates and graduate students with an accessible set of scholarly essays on key themes, written by leading scholars. The editors thank all the contributors for making their job so enjoyable and free of problems.

We should also like to thank William Green, who has ably assisted us in the editing process, Kate Lechler for the Manuscript Index and Andrew McNeillie who contracted us to undertake this project for OUP and has kept a benevolent eye upon our progress ever since.

Finally, Greg Walker would like to thank Randall Stevenson, Sarah Carpenter, David Salter, Sarah Dunnigan, John J. McGavin, the Southampton Cavaliers cricket team, Sharon, Matthew, David and Tessa and, of course, his esteemed co-editor; while Elaine Treharne wishes to thank *her* venerable co-editor, and to say how grateful she is to Andy, Joffy, and Izzy as always.

CONTENTS

PART III   LITERATURE, CLERICAL AND LAY

PART IV   LITERARY REALITIES

PART V COMPLEX IDENTITIES

PART VI LITERARY PLACE, SPACE, AND TIME

PART VII LITERARY JOURNEYS

EPILOGUE

LIST OF ILLUSTRATIONS

LIST OF CONTRIBUTORS

Daniel Anlezark is Associate Professor of English at the University of Sydney.

Anke Bernau is Senior Lecturer in Medieval Literature and Culture at the University of Manchester.

Alcuin Blamires is Professor of English Literature at Goldsmiths College, University of London.

Mishtooni Bose is Professor, and Christopher Tower Official Student in Medieval Poetry in English, Corpus Christi College, University of Oxford.

Thomas Bredehoft is an Independent Scholar.

Mary Baine Campbell is Professor of English and American Literature at Brandeis University.

Jayne Carroll is Associate Professor of English and Director of the Institute of Name Studies at the University of Nottingham.

Jeffrey Jerome Cohen is Professor and Chair of English at George Washington University.

Orietta Da Rold is University Lecturer in English and Fellow of St John's College at the University of Cambridge.

Elisabeth Dutton is Associate Professor at the University of Fribourg.

Siân Echard is Professor of English at the University of British Columbia.

A. S. G. Edwards is Professor of Medieval Manuscripts Studies at the University of Kent.

Elizabeth Elliott is Lecturer in English Literature at the University of Aberdeen.

Elizabeth Evenden-Kenyon is Senior Lecturer in English at Brunel University.

Jacqueline Fay is Associate Professor of English at the University of Texas at Arlington.

Helen Fulton is Professor of Medieval Literature at the University of Bristol.

Andrew Galloway is Professor of English at Cornell University.

Ralph Hanna is Professor Emeritus of Palaeography at Keble College, University of Oxford.

Alfred Hiatt is Reader in Medieval English Literature at Queen Mary, University of London.

Simon Horobin is Professor of English Language and Literature and Tutorial Fellow at Magdalen College, University of Oxford.

Stephen Kelly is Lecturer in English at Queen's University Belfast.

Kathryn Kerby-Fulton is Notre Dame Professor of English at the University of Notre Dame.

Susan M. Kim is Professor of English at Illinois State University.

Kathy Lavezzo is Associate Professor of English at the University of Iowa.

Nicola McDonald is Senior Lecturer in English at the University of York.

John J. McGavin is Professor Emeritus of Medieval Literature and Culture in the School of Humanities at the University of Southampton.

Bella Millett is Professor Emeritus of Medieval Literature in the School of Humanities at the University of Southampton.

Asa Simon Mittman is Professor of Art History at California State University, Chico.

Nicholas Perkins is CUF Associate Professor and Tutorial Fellow at St Hugh's College, University of Oxford.

Andrew Prescott is Professor of Digital Humanities at the University of Glasgow.

Gillian Rudd is Professor of English at the University of Liverpool.

Wendy Scase is Geoffrey Shepherd Professor of Medieval English Literature at the University of Birmingham.

Elaine Treharne is Roberta Bowman Denning Professor of Humanities and Professor of English at Stanford University.

Thorlac Turville-Petre is Professor Emeritus of Medieval English Literature at the University of Nottingham.

Greg Walker is Regius Professor of Rhetoric and English Literature at the University of Edinburgh.

Diane Watt is Professor of Medieval Literature at the University of Surrey.

Alison Wiggins is Senior Lecturer in English Language and Literature at the University of Glasgow.

Samantha Zacher is Professor of English and Medieval Studies at Cornell University.

PROLOGUE

....

SPEAKING OF THE MEDIEVAL

....

ELAINE TREHARNE

THIS extensive volume covers by far the longest single literary period in English: from Old to Early Modern English, a thousand years of textual production from the seventh to the sixteenth centuries, from the Classical era to the Renaissance. During this vast stretch of time, many great works of English literature were created, some by authors we know a reasonable amount about, like Geoffrey Chaucer or Wulfstan, archbishop of York, or Margery Kempe; others—the majority—by anonymous writers placing themselves in the same tradition of the *auctor*, the 'author', the authority, by engaging in the practice of textual dissemination, at a time when 'the word' was so often equated with permanence, with scripture, and with an explicit self-authentication.

This book, and in miniature, this chapter, seeks to provide a taste of the medieval for students, to show what the excitement is all about, to highlight major new trends in scholarship, and to confirm positions of preeminence for the startlingly brilliant work of so many of these early authors. Each newly commissioned chapter takes as its starting point a range of material addressing a specific genre, theme, or issue. Sections are themed, but each of the essays is permeable, boundless in the literary aspects discussed by the contributors. Thus, the chapter 'Secular Drama' might as easily have been in the section 'Literature, Clerical and Lay' as 'Literary Realities'; 'Scottish Writing' is as much a part of 'Complex Identities' as it is of 'Literary Place, Space, and Time'. Indeed, there is room for debate over the validity of the section titles at all, and particularly the unfortunate boundaries that such organization can imply, and readers are encouraged to mull over these categories in their search for the full interpretative potential of the medieval texts discussed here.

All the chapters, then, focus on a number of case studies, anchoring the essay writer's approach to examples that illustrate major issues and concerns in the discipline today. Readers should also be encouraged to find their own textual examples and test out the applicability of the kinds of theories that abound in this volume. Thus, when reading the chapters in the section 'Complex Identities', one might ponder the place of poems such as the Old English *Wife's Lament* or *Wulf and Eadwacer*, texts that seem to evince the subjective self speaking of some dire situation in each case: the 'I' of the poems illustrates how desperate circumstances affecting the individual can be transformed into riddlic, and arguably, resigned acceptance. In the case of *Wulf and Eadwacer*, a poem found in the Exeter Book datable to *c*.970, its utterance is opaque and context-less, and scholars have offered numerous proposals seeking to unravel its complexity. Comprised of only nineteen lines in a modern edition, it is worth a close look, because in every respect, its existence can speak to each of the section titles chosen for the structure of this volume.

The manuscript of this poem, Exeter Cathedral Library 3501, contains the largest number of extant Old English poems. The unique poem known to scholars as *Wulf and Eadwacer* is written by one scribe, and his work includes well over a hundred religious, elegiac, and riddlic verses, all laid out in long lines as if they were composed in prose. Lacking systematic punctuation as we would recognize it now, and, significantly, lacking titles in the manuscript, these poems are very open to interpretation, and the more so because of the difficulties modern scholars have in accessing the precise meaning of particular words and phrases. In every sense, though, this makes the student's task of critical construal immensely challenging and enjoyable; careful scrutiny of the Old English can yield new meaning and an equally valid reading.

UTTERING THE UNUTTERABLE

Leodum is minum   swylce him mon lac gife;
willað hy hine aþecgan   gif he on þreat cymeð.
Ungelic is us.
Wulf is on iege,   Ic on oþerre.
5   Fæst is þæt eglond,   fenne biworpen.
Sindon wælreowe weras   þær on ige;
willað hy hine aþecgan   gif he on þreat cymeð.
Ungelice is us.
Wulfes Ic mines widlastum   wenum dogode:
10   þonne hit wæs renig weder,   ond Ic reotugu sæt,
þonne mec se beaducafa   bogum bilegde:
Wæs me wyn to þon;   wæs me hwæþre eac lað.
Wulf, min Wulf,   wena me þine
seoce gedydon,   þine seldcymas,

15   murnende mod,   nales meteliste.
    Gehyrest þu, eadwacer?   Uncerne earmne hwelp
        bireð Wulf to wuda.
    Þæt mon eaþe tosliteð   þætte næfre gesomnad wæs,
        uncer giedd geador.[1]

For my tribe it's like being given a tribute;
they'll consume him if he comes on that crowd.
It's not like that for us.
Wulf's on one island, I'm on the other.

5   Fast-bound is that island, surrounded by fen.
Death-crazed men are there on the island;
they'll consume him if he comes on that crowd.
That's unlikely for us.
I traced the wide travels of Wulf in my wonderings:

10   when it was rainy weather, and I sat weeping,
then battle-hardened, he clasped arms about me.
That meant pleasure for me; still, there was pain for me too.
Wulf, my Wulf, my wonderings of you
made me sick—your seldom comings,
my mourning mind—not the absence of meals.
Can you hear, you watcher of property? Wulf carries our
wretched whelp to the woods.
That may easily be split apart what was never spliced,
the riddle of us both together.

This poem rather startlingly demonstrates both the flexibility of early English verse and simultaneously its boundedness. From a lexical point of view, much of the vocabulary in this riddle-like narration is polysemous, individual words like 'lac' in the first line might potentially mean a multitude of things: 'gift', 'offering', 'sacrifice', 'reward', 'message', or 'favour'. The first line alone could thus be translated in myriad ways which might set the tone for what follows as deeply threatening ('It's as if to my people someone might give them a sacrifice'), or positive ('It's as if for my people someone gave them a gift'), and whereas one might expect this opening to be clarified by the succeeding line, line 2, in fact, deepens the mystery. It, too, is replete with ambiguity: 'on þreat cymeð' might mean 'comes into their troop', or 'comes upon their army', or 'comes with force'; 'aþecgan', for its part, could mean 'consume', 'receive', 'kill', or 'take'. What is clear is that by the end of the second line, the speaker is noting that something potentially hostile might happen to a male person, whose identity is never revealed, but who is clearly of significance for the 'us'—the two who are bound by the close physical and emotional relationship at the core of this poem.

    Crucially, the speaker of this poem is female, since the adjective 'reotugu', which occurs nowhere else in the corpus of Old English, has a feminine inflection. This rare, first-person, highly individuated narration thus gradually reveals a tale of sorrow and separation, even though we do not know what the circumstances surrounding this outcome might be. While the precise events are not known, the woman's profound

---

[1] Based on Treharne (2009), but with a new translation here and some revised punctuation.

dismay is evinced in her outbursts to this person 'Wulf' and to the 'eadwacer' ('guardian of property', or, perhaps Eadwacer, a person). The diction enhances the sense of loss and apprehensiveness from her 'wonderings' ('wenum', which can also mean 'hopes', 'thoughts', 'expectations') to her 'weeping', her reminiscences of embracing a lover, her mourning mind. The framework for the poem is the Germanic Heroic world, evocatively discussed in Jayne Carroll's chapter in this volume. The 'army' or 'troop', the 'battle-hardy' man, are metonyms of a warrior society, a culture underpinned by the lord and his *comitatus*, where loyalty, bravery in battle, and reward for courageous deeds, both reflect and contribute to this social code, idealized in the verse that commemorates it.

Despite the unfamiliarity of the social context from which this poem seems to emerge, and despite the poem's mediation through the edition of a scribe in a monastery somewhere in the south-west of England, there is, nevertheless, a great deal of the present in this manifestation of the past. What is beyond doubt is the pain of the speaker, who can reveal only circumspectly the details of her situation. This interiorizing of fact, and lack of revelation even through explicit utterance, is resonant of trauma and the silence that follows. This whole monologue, perhaps spoken only in the mind, is permeated with images of containment: from being surrounded by a crowd, to being fixed in isolation, to being pinned down in an embrace, and then guarded over, this speaker is fastened securely in private, endless, anguish from which there seems to be no escape. Even with these constraints, plus those imposed by the formulaic nature of Old English alliterative verse with its metrical rules, this poet manages to break free, uttering hypermetric verse-lines and making use of the short refrain, rare in poetry at this time. And so it is that, despite readers knowing nothing about the back-story of this poem, the emotive depth of these few lines is easily acknowledged.

The Meaning of Life

The only escape, presumably, from misery in this temporal life is to be sought in the release of death and the hope afforded by the afterlife. This theme is relatively common in medieval (and later) literature and lends itself to reflection on life and its meaning. Among many Old English poems, *The Wanderer, The Seafarer, Resignation, The Dream of the Rood*, and *The Fates of the Apostles*, together with a great many homilies and other prose pieces, use textual space to reflect on our place in the world; on the transience of worldly things; and on the role of the Christian as he or she makes their way through the pilgrimage of life. This focus, tracked through great works of literature from *Piers Plowman* to *Pilgrim's Progress*, takes us into another great utterance from medieval literature—*Poema Morale*. This almost four-hundred-line poem, which might be thought of more accurately as a verse sermon than a moral ode, survives in seven manuscript copies, the earliest of which is late twelfth century. It was probably written in the second half of the twelfth century, and is included in manuscripts most often containing homilies, so it seems an appropriate generic fit.

Where it differs from so many sermons is that it is a first-person monologue, a confessional text, in which the speaker—an old man—is both repenting of his own misdeeds and urging others to do the same. The old man who has gained wisdom, is, of course, a *senex*, a common topos in literature, but the detail of this poem brings this archetypal character to life in a way that is highly engaging. The opening lines of the text lay out his message, greatly amplified in the lines that follow:

> Ich am nu elder þan Ich was a wintre and a lore.
> Ich wealde more þan I dude; mi wit oh to be more.
> To longe Ich habbe child iben a worde and a dade;
> Þeih I bie a winter eald, to jung Ich am on rade.
> 5 Unnet lif Ich habbe ilad and ʒiet me þincheð ilade;
> Þan I biðenche me þar on wel, sore I me adrade.
> Mast al Ich habbe idon is idelnesse and chilce.
> Wel late Ich habbe me biþoht, bute me God do milce.
> Fele idel word Ich habbe ispeken seðen Ich speken cuðe,
> 10 And fele ʒeunge dade idon, þe me ofdinkeð nuðe.
> Al to lome Ich habbe igult a werke and a worde;
> Al to muchel Ic habbe ispend, to litel ileid on horde.
> Mast al þat me liked ar, nu hit me mislicað:
> Þe michel folʒed his iwil himselfen he biswicað.
> 15 Ich mihte habben bet idon, hadde Ich þo iselðe.
> Nu Ich wolde, ac I ne mai for elde and for unhalðe:
> Elde me is bistolen on ar Ich hit iwiste;
> Ne mai Ich isien bifore me for smeche ne for miste.
> Are we beð to don god; to ivel al to þriste.
> 20 More eie stondeð man of man þan him do of Criste.
> Þe wel ne deð þe hwile he mai wel ofte hit sal him rewen,
> Þan alle men sulle ripen þat hi ear sewen.
> Do al to Gode þat he muʒe ech, þe hwile he beð alive.[2]

> I am now older than I was in years and in learning.
> I own more than I did; my wit ought to be more.
> Too long I've been a child in words and in deeds;
> Though I may be old in years, I'm too young in wisdom.
> 5 An idle life I've led, and still seem to lead;
> When I reflect on it, I am very afraid for myself.
> Most of all I've done is idleness and childish.
> I have meditated on this late, but God have mercy on me.
> Many idle words I've spoken since I was able to speak,
> 10 And I've done many childish deeds, which I regret now.
> All too often I've sinned in deeds and in words;
> I have spent far too much, too little laid aside.

---

[2] Based on Treharne (2003), but with a new translation here and some revised punctuation.

Most of which pleased me before now offends me:
The ones who follow their desire deceive themselves.
15   I might have done better, had I had the good sense.
Now I'd like to, but I can't because of age and ill-health:
Old age has stolen up on me before I knew it;
I can't see in front of me because of smoke and mist.
We are too cowardly to do good; to do evil, all too bold.
20   More men stand in awe of men than they do of Christ.
Those who don't do well while they can, shall regret it very often,
When all men shall reap what they have sown before.
Everyone should do all they can for God, while they are alive.

Through this carefully constructed sequence of antitheses—old age versus youth, wisdom versus ignorance, action versus idleness, thrift versus profligacy—the speaker is able to elucidate both negative and positive examples of behaviour. The author's aim is clearly didactic; namely, to teach what is required to lead a proper Christian life, and thus assist in assuring salvation for listeners. All the elements of the text assist in ensuring the message is successful, and thus repetition is employed in various guises: at lines 3, 7, 9, 10, 11, and 21, the emphasis on words and deeds illustrates that the two major, external facets of the good Christian's efforts to live faithfully are how they act and what they say. This is underscored by the third aspect of the triad, 'thought', and clearly, the consequences of the speaker's careful meditation are the keen sensibility that there is much to regret and seek forgiveness for. So it is that within these first twenty lines, the speaker enunciates the complete taxonomy of sin, which for the great church father St Augustine, in his *Enchiridion* or *Handbook of Faith, Hope, and Charity*, would be sins of thought (or desire), word, and deed. This taxonomy, illustrated in *Poema Morale* by first-hand example, provides the driving force for the remaining lengthy exposition of its reflecting subject. Apparently personal touches bring the text to life, from the misty, failing eyes of the old man, mentioned at line 18 (perhaps alluding to spiritual blindness, as much as physical impairment) to the poet's condemnation of sheriffs and reeves, late twelfth-century officials, often depicted as corrupt.

The long poem draws readers in, and through its rhyming couplets, maintains a rhythmic beat as it marches through the whole of salvation history, pausing lengthily to dwell on what the damned will participate in (no rest, boiling pitch for souls to live in, extreme heat and cold, eternal thirst, adders, snakes, lizards, and frogs) and ending the poem with what the saved will find once they are released from the fetters of the body (wealth, rest, bliss, joy). All of the major techniques and themes of the typical medieval sermon appear, encouraging reflection, contrition, repentance, and faithful living. Moreover, typical of didactic literature in this period are biblical allusions, authorizing the validity of the text, like that at line 12 referring to Matthew 6: 19–20,[3] as well as numerous proverbial and idiomatic phrases making the delivery of the text lively and accessible.

---

[3] 'Lay not up to yourselves treasure on earth . . . but lay up to yourselves treasure in heaven.'

THE LONG AND THE SHORT OF IT

Perhaps at least as lively, but a good deal briefer, is a lyric that shares many features of *Poema Morale*, the most notable of which is the age and penitential attitude of the speaker. *An Old Man's Prayer* is contained in the fourteenth-century manuscript, London, British Library, Harley 2253, among the most famous books that survive from late medieval England.[4] This one-hundred-line lyric movingly recounts the life of the elderly man, and how he idled away his youth in pursuit of gluttony, lechery, and other sinful fun. He tells us that in his contemplations he is called 'fulleflet' ('floor-filler') and 'waynoun wayteglede' ('good-for-nothing fire-gazer'), scorned by those around him, who know no better. Previously a lover of the high life, he can no longer bend his fingers; from behaving like a young buck, he now suffers from gout. His life has taught him that everything in this world—from buildings to bodies—is transient, and the only genuine remedy is to seek salvation with God.

This lyric, sharing the struggles of the individual, albeit an individual who represents the whole of sinful humanity, jostles in the manuscript, Harley 2253, alongside numerous other lyrics, fabliaux (bawdy tales of lust), histories, romances, and hagiographies, or saints' lives. This collection is itself representative of the ways in which medieval manuscript compilers were entirely satisfied to draw up large gatherings of texts reflecting contemporary life in general—compendia of knowledge, reflection, wisdom, and entertainment. In this, the later medieval manuscripts like Harley 2253 or London, British Library, Harley 978 (mostly in Latin and French), or Oxford, Jesus College, 29, all datable to the thirteenth and fourteenth centuries, have a great deal in common with much earlier Old English manuscript collections, like Cambridge, Corpus Christi College 201 or London, British Library, Cotton Tiberius A. iii, both dated to the eleventh century. Within the latter manuscript, for example, the *Life of St Margaret* occurs in between Christian commonplaces about the size of Noah's ark and a homily for Palm Sunday; earlier in the manuscript, there is a monastic rule, and elsewhere within it, a lapidary and colloquy add to the educative and encyclopædic nature of the book. This manuscript was made in Christ Church, Canterbury, and is therefore a monastic production. As with most other surviving books from Anglo-Saxon England, it seems to have belonged to a senior ecclesiastical figure.

Corpus 201 offers broadly similar information about itself. It contains law-codes, religious poetry, sermons, and perhaps most famously, the first romance in English, *Apollonius of Tyre*. This text is based on a classical exemplar and is the same legend that formed the source for Shakespeare's *Pericles*. The Old English prose text is a compelling telling of the romance, detailing the displaced young prince and his search to regain the kingdom which is his birthright. Within the narrative, we encounter incest, murder, exile and return, disguise and revelation, the loss and regaining of relatives and land, and, of course, love and loyalty. There are moments of vivid character delineation, as in

---

[4] Treharne (2009).

the depiction of the charming and chatty heroine, Arcestrate, who marries Apollonius, after he is shipwrecked in her father's kingdom. It is possible also to see the narration of the legend as a *speculum princeps*, 'a mirror for princes', acting as an exemplar for the noble audience, who might once have listened to it being read from Corpus 201, by the manuscript's (presumably clerical) owner.

Such a didactic and, simultaneously, entertaining impetus seems also to have been behind the creation of most vernacular literature throughout this period. While law-codes, prognostications, and confessional texts might not seem the most engaging reading for any audience, they are irrefutably educational, essential texts for running a Christian kingdom, and supervising the moral well-being of all subjects. The institutionalization of law, the significant increases in administration, bureaucracy, and literacy in the twelfth and thirteenth centuries saw notable shifts in the nature of some manuscript anthologies, such that, even by the twelfth century, one would find law-codes literally codified in their own right; canon law collected and dispersed with commentaries; and scholastic texts being copied in great numbers for study by university students in Oxford, Cambridge, and on the European mainland. But in the extensive manuscript compendia, owned by senior clergy (like William of Winchester, a monk who owned London, British Library, Harley 978[5]) or noble families or mercantile households, one will find treatises on hunting intermingled with sacred music, profane fabliaux, and fables (Harley 978). And more commonly, one will find collections put together with a historical and religious focus, like London, British Library, Egerton 613, a trilingual manuscript from the south of England, containing verse and prose, some of which is macaronic, and another copy of *Poema Morale*, the verse sermon discussed above.

In general, though, it should be clear that the generic divisions and textual categories so dear to modern scholars (delineation of form—drama, novel, poetry; delineation of type—fiction, non-fiction, verse; and delineation of genre—romance, tragedy, history, pastoral, elegy, chick lit) are not so clear-cut from the medieval perspective. This is not to say that genre did not exist, but simply to suggest that a fluidity of genre is insisted upon by the inclusion of many different kinds of texts within one manuscript book, and by the deliberate use and manipulation of common features of one genre within another, which should alert readers to the exploitation of convention evinced in medieval texts of all kinds.

Saint, Sinner, Hero, Victim

A text exemplifying this fluidity of genre is *Sir Orfeo*. All of the structural and thematic elements of the romance, outlined very briefly above in relation to

---

[5] Taylor (2003: 93).

Apollonius of Tyre, are witnessed in the Breton Lay, *Sir Orfeo*. A Breton Lay, a term originating in the work of Marie de France in the twelfth century, is a short romance, containing not only the themes of exile and return or disguise and revelation, but also 'supernatural' episodes and characters. Surviving in three manuscript versions, dating from the fourteenth to the fifteenth century, *Sir Orfeo* shows perfectly the nature of manuscript transmission, and the multivalent potential of romance.

Each of the three English *Sir Orfeo* poems relates a recontextualized narrative of Ovid's episode of Orpheus and Eurydice from his *Metamorphoses* in which the hero loses his wife to the king of the Underworld. This Underworld is transformed into a faery Otherworld in the medieval version, a malevolent parallel kingdom, into which Herodis, wife of Orfeo, is taken by the faery king, and kept, suspended in a quasi-limbo, other than at those times when she is released to engage in courtly pursuits with the faeries. Orfeo abandons his kingdom to live the life of a hermit in the woods, taking only his harp with him, and charming the wild birds and animals with his playing. He sees his wife one day while she is out hawking with the faeries, and he follows them, managing to reclaim her from the faery king, because of his superlative harping prowess. He leads his wife to safety and regains his kingdom after a ten-year absence, during which time his faithful steward has looked after his kingdom. This happy outcome is in significant contrast to the classical legend where Eurydice is lost to Orpheus as he looks backwards over his shoulder when leading her out of the Underworld. The tale, one should note, also underwent substantial interpretative revision at the hands of Boethius in his *Consolation of Philosophy*, and then again by the late ninth-century Anglo-Saxon king, Alfred, in his Old English adaptation of the Boethian legend. Here, an allegorical reading of the denouement is dominant: that the loss of Eurydice proves it is harmful to keep one's eyes fixed on the things of this world, instead of focusing attention heavenwards.[6]

Sir Orfeo occurs in the Auchinleck manuscript—Edinburgh, National Library of Scotland, Advocates 19. 2. 1, dating to *c*.1330—and in two other manuscripts: London, British Library, Harley 3810, a text dated to the fifteenth century, and Oxford, Bodleian Library, Ashmole 61, a late fifteenth-century volume. The issues involved in studying any of the three Middle English texts of *Sir Orfeo*, then, revolve around the kinds of variations introduced into this Breton Lay, when compared with earlier versions of the text, because any such variations illustrate the specific cultural moment in which a work is produced. The authors of the medieval *Sir Orfeo* were keen to contemporize this version, choosing to adapt the legendary Otherworld of Celtic myth, and to create it as a virtual parallel world with Sir Orfeo's kingdom. This parallelism is shown through the repetition of shared description; both kingdoms are described in identical terms. We are told that when Sir Orfeo has given up his entire kingdom that 'He . . . hadde had castels and tours / River, forest, friþ wiþ flours' (ll. 245–6); and when Herodis is returned by the faery king the first time he has

---

6 Treharne (2009).

captured her, she tells Orfeo he took her to his kingdom, 'And shewed me castels and tours, / Rivers, forestes, friþ wiþ flours' (ll. 159–60). The implications of this virtual replication are quite sinister, inasmuch as the faery king might appear as Orfeo's malevolent doppelgänger, and it warns us, in this Middle English version, that appearances are painfully deceptive.

The three English *Sir Orfeo* texts are certainly true to the romance tradition in narrating a story of love and loyalty, with an ostensibly happy ending (though, one should note, the faeries are still on the loose, and liable to snatch unsuspecting humans at any point—this rather usurps our expectations of the traditional joyful resolution demanded by the conventions of romance). Intermingled with the traditional themes of the genre (concerned with courtliness, kingship and nobility, love and beauty) are possible allusions to the hagiographic genre, the writing of saints' lives. Both romance and hagiography tend to share narratological features in relation to the telling of a story focused on a heroic individual, the one a noble knight who pursues an individual goal on a quest, or fights for the love of king or lady; the other, a noble Christian who pursues salvation through resistance to pagan persecutors and/or abstinence from sin. Sir Orfeo in his penitent garb, dressed as a pilgrim with only his harp as a reminder of his days as king, seems deliberately to seek a life of asceticism after losing his wife. He is distinctly reminiscent of a hermit, voluntarily undergoing hardship in a penitential act:

Al his kingdom he forsoke,	
Bot a sclavin on him he toke:	Only; pilgrim's mantle
He no hadde kirtel° no hode,	short coat
No schert, no noþer° gode;	other
Bot his harp he tok algate°	at any rate
And dede him barfot out atte ȝate (ll. 237–42)[7]	went; barefoot; gate

His redemption comes in his harrowing of the Otherworld, where the exploitation of his natural gift of music wins him back his wife. These potential allusions (and that is all they are, allusive resonances) add another dimension to the text, insisting that the audience focus for a moment on the example of leadership and nobility offered by Orfeo himself. It may be that these apparent Christian allusions (or even Christ-like allusions) are ironic, since this is a king who ignobly abandons his kingdom and who, in assuming he can protect his wife with a thousand knights, fails to understand the futility of temporal might in the face of an otherworldly threat.

As a character, he differs somewhat in each retelling of the poem, and the two fifteenth-century *Sir Orfeo* texts are not identical with the Auchinleck version. Moreover, since it is unclear which best represents the 'original', ideally each should be read in its own right.[8]

---

[7] Treharne (2009).
[8] Bliss (1966) publishes all three texts in tandem. The predominance of the Auchinleck version is made visually apparent by being in the upper register on the page, and in a larger font size.

Complicating the interpretation of these texts somewhat are the manuscript contexts in which they survive. These three versions of the story exist in their manuscripts, alongside a variety of other vernacular verse pieces. The earliest surviving text is included in the famous extensive collection known as the Auchinleck manuscript. In this codex, *Sir Orfeo* is contiguous with *Sir Tristrem* and *The Four Foes of Mankind*. The former relates, at great length, the deeds of Tristan, while the latter is a short poem detailing the battle that Christians face against death, the devil, the world, and the flesh, and is, essentially, a penitential and admonitory text. *The Four Foes* was added to the manuscript to fill in the blank column next to *Sir Orfeo*, and the following blank verso at the end of a quire. It is therefore easily dismissed as of tangential interest, particularly if one is seeking to determine thematic unification within the manuscript, or sections of the manuscript.

The scribe who added *The Four Foes*, though, is the same scribe who copied *Sir Orfeo* and a large number of the other texts in the manuscript. It is possible that this scribe was the compiler of the manuscript's contents, the supervisor of its production. In this case, there could be no firmer indication that *Four Foes* was considered an appropriate *sequitur* to *Sir Orfeo*. The potential thematic link that might conceivably be inferred between these two texts would involve an admonition as a response to *Sir Orfeo*'s closing lines:

Þat lay 'Orfeo' is yhote—	called
Gode is þe lay, swete is þe note.	good
Þus com Sir Orfeo out of his care:	sorrow
God graunt ous alle wele to fare! Amen (ll. 601–4)[9]	

In response to the request that 'God grant us all a safe farewell', *The Four Foes* swiftly reminds the audience how the faithful can seek to ensure the sentiment of this parting prayer by being on guard themselves against the enemies of mankind. It may be possible, therefore, to regard *Four Foes* as a comment on the fragility of human happiness so emotively illustrated in *Sir Orfeo*, recasting the Breton Lay in an explicitly religious light.

While this is a speculative interpretation of *Sir Orfeo*, dependent on the thin threads of evidence yielded by the manuscript context, it is one that is substantially reinforced by the physical setting of the other two texts of the poem. In both the later manuscripts, copied in the fifteenth century, *Sir Orfeo* has been recontextualized by the manuscripts' directors to emphasize the didactic elements of the text at the expense of the supernatural, faery features. The allegorical potential of the poem thus comes to the fore, and has to be regarded as the main way in which audiences that were much closer to the texts' creation than we are read the verse narratives. In Harley 3810, for example, which is a shorter text than that in Auchinleck, the faery elements are excised, and the poem closes with a five-line prayer:

---

[9] Treharne (2009).

>Þus cam þey out of care: sorrow
>God ȝeve us grace wele to fare,
>And all þat have herde þis talking,
>In heven-blys be his wonyng.   dwelling
>Amen, Amen, for charyte,   charity
>Lord us graunt þat it so be.[10]

Not only is this possible evidence of a more pious interpretation of the text on the part of the compiler, but it also functions as excellent self-promotion, since it seeks a blessing for those who have listened to the poem (with the corollary that listeners do not end up in the horrors of the Otherworld, presumably). The apotropaic function of the text is witnessed by the end of the Ashmole version too, which notably asks that,

>God grante us all hys blyssing
>And all þat þys wyll here or rede
>God forgyff þem þer mysded
>To the blysse of Heuyn þat þei may com...[11]

Here, there is clearly a reading audience as well as a listening one, whose participation in the text's performance earns them a specific request for the forgiveness of their sins. The purgative potential of these texts, their inherent redemptory qualities, unequivocally demonstrate the overwhelming Christian context of *Sir Orfeo* within these later manifestations.

Further evidence for this reading is provided by analysis of the contents of the manuscripts, which include devotional and religious legendary materials. In both Harley 3810 and Ashmole 61, *Sir Orfeo* is surrounded by other edifying narratives. Harley 3810 is a composite manuscript containing texts in English and Latin, and while medical recipes immediately follow *Sir Orfeo*, after these are Penitential Psalms, and *St Gregory's Trental*. In the case of Ashmole 61, *Sir Orfeo* is surrounded by another forty texts, all of which are romances or hagiographies, and other religious works. As is the case with Harley 3810, the potential for a pious reading of the poem is significantly greater than a purely secular interpretation.

A core part of medieval literature is its variety, then, and not just in terms of genre and form, but variety even within what modern scholarship traditionally thinks of as a single text. Textual *mouvance* in manuscript culture means no two versions of a work will be the same, and that texts continued to change according to the preferences of manuscript compilers and scribes, the latter often functioning more as editors. Examining the physical context of production also yields potentially interesting evidence for the links between contiguous texts or groups of texts discernible to a manuscript compiler, if no longer evident to us, and also suggests something of the many ways in which these texts might have been received by their multiple audiences in this period.

[10] Bliss (1966: 50; ll. 504–10), with small changes and added glosses here.
[11] Bliss (1966: 51; ll. 597–600).

CLOSING WORDS

In 'Speaking of the Medieval', some of the key issues of textual production have been touched upon, while moving freely to and fro within this lengthy and extraordinary period. In the three dozen essays that follow, many of these issues will be revisited in different guises and with different referents. What this volume hopes to show the reader are the continuities and innovations in medieval literature; some of the significant moments in English literary history; but most of all, the challenges and excitement generated by working with engaging and demanding works of art, crafted by wordsmiths centuries before many students might even imagine such vernacular literature could exist.

BIBLIOGRAPHY

AUCHINLECK MANUSCRIPT, ed. David Burnley and Alison Wiggins, National Library of Scotland <http://www.nls.uk/auchinleck/>.

AUGUSTINE (1978), *Faith, Hope and Charity (Enchiridion De Fide, Spe et Caritate)*, ed. and tr. J. Kuasten and Louis A. Arand (Ancient Christian Writers; New York: Broadway).

BELANOFF, PATRICIA A. (1990), 'Woman's Song, Women's Language: Wulf and Eadwacer and The Wife's Lament', in Helen Damico and Alexandra Hennessy Olsen (eds.), *New Readings on Women in Old English Literature* (Bloomington, Ind.: Indiana University Press), 193–203.

CERQUIGLINI, B. (1989), *In Praise of the Variant: A Critical History of Philology*, tr. Betsy Wing (Baltimore, Md.: Johns Hopkins University Press).

FEIN, SUSANNA (ed.) (2000), *Studies in the Harley Manuscript: The Scribes, Contents, and Social Contexts of British Library MS Harley 2253* (Kalamazoo, Mich.: Medieval Institute Publications).

FRANKIS, JOHN (1986), 'The Social Context of Vernacular Writing in the Thirteenth Century: The Evidence of the Manuscripts', in P. R. J. Coss and Simon D. Lloyd (eds.), *Thirteenth-Century England*, (Woodbridge: Boydell & Brewer), i. 175–84.

KER, NEIL R. (1957), *Catalogue of Manuscripts Containing Anglo-Saxon* (Oxford: Oxford University Press; repr. with supplement, 1991).

LAING, MARGARET (1993), *Catalogue of Sources for a Linguistic Atlas of Early Medieval English* (Cambridge: Cambridge University Press).

LIUZZA, ROY MICHAEL (1991), '*Sir Orfeo*: Sources, Traditions, and the Poetics of Performance', *Journal of Medieval and Renaissance Studies*, 21: 269–84.

SPEARING, A. C. (1987), *Readings in Medieval Poetry* (Cambridge: Cambridge University Press).

TAYLOR, ANDREW (2002), *Textual Situations: Three Medieval Manuscripts and their Readers* (Philadelphia: University of Pennsylvania Press)

TREHARNE, ELAINE ((ed.) (2009), *Old and Middle English: An Anthology, 800–1450* (3rd edn. Oxford: Oxford University Press).

PART I

LITERARY PRODUCTION

....

CHAPTER 1

BOOKS AND MANUSCRIPTS

....

A. S. G. EDWARDS

Textual Transmission

....

This chapter is concerned with modes of vernacular, chiefly Middle English, literary production during the Middle Ages in Britain. The use of the plural 'modes' requires immediate clarification. It was only at the very end of the Middle Ages, in about 1476, that William Caxton set up the first printing shop in England, at Westminster, thereby making it possible to produce books from movable type in this country (as it had been in Europe from the 1450s). Before this the only durable form of literary production had been the various forms of the book copied by hand, that is, the manuscript.

Manuscript production and circulation will be central to this chapter. But it is necessary to remember that copying by hand was not the only way texts were transmitted during the Middle Ages in England. It is clear, from a variety of evidence, that some works were often subject to forms of oral or memorial transmission. That is, a text would not be written down at every stage in its textual history, but would on occasions be memorized and transmitted from speaker to speaker by word of mouth before being written down again, possibly at a considerable interval after its original composition and after having been adapted for specific circumstances of local delivery. There is evidence that this practice could occur even with lengthy texts.

Oral or memorial transmission appears to have been a factor in the circulation of various Old English works and is clearly demonstrable in Middle English metrical and alliterative romances and ballads, where performers, possibly minstrels, like most performers, had to recite their repertoire without direct access to a written text. Such transmission is demonstrable as well as in shorter gnomic verse texts of various kinds, often surviving as 'flyleaf poems' because their easily memorizable form led to their copying in informal manuscript contexts on flyleaves; a popular example is a single stanza often extracted from John Lydgate's long poem, *The Fall of Princes*. It begins 'Deceit deceiveth and shall be deceived', an aphoristic formulation that a number of readers felt worthy of excerption.

In the case of longer works oral transmission tends to leave clear stylistic traces of its presence, most often through a tendency to formulaic expression, the use of stock phrases or clichés the stock in trade of an extempore performer, that often tends to a level of stylistic banality of the kind satirized by Chaucer in *Sir Thopas*, his hilarious parody of romance idiom. It is also reflected in the striking variations in content that can occur, for example, in the often marked textual differences between surviving texts of the same romance, as a text becomes, like any script, adapted over time and by circumstance—cut, expanded, modified for particular audiences most likely to listen to rather than read the work in question. The variant versions of the Middle English romances *Lybeaus Desconus* or *Bevis of Hampton* provide examples of these tendencies to create essentially unstable textual forms.[1] In general terms, the role of memory in the circulation of literary works in the medieval period is unquantifiable but very probably pervasive.[2] It is best to be properly conscious of its potential implications for the study of a number of medieval works.

The evidence of oral transmission is linked to the creation of manuscripts because at some stage or stages in their textual history works were actually written down and thus become linked to the manuscript culture that forms the central focus of this chapter. The history of the development of the industry for manuscript production in England can be sketched as it relates to specifically literary works.

EARLY MEDIEVAL MANUSCRIPT CULTURE

A manuscript culture depends on the existence of various material resources: tools for writing and materials for writing on, exemplars to be copied and trained personnel to copy them, scribes, working in a relatively fixed and stable environment, with adequate warmth, light, and appropriate furniture. In certain circumstances, such an environment might be termed a scriptorium, a space dedicated to and equipped specifically for the copying of books by a trained staff. But not all manuscript production took place in highly organized scriptoria. The equipment and material circumstances enumerated above could be obtained by any individual with proficiency as a copyist, access to the

---

[1] See Edwards (1991).
[2] See Carruthers (1990).

necessary materials, and with a market for his work. Nor were all scriptoria organized for the same purposes: some had a primarily administrative function, for example, to support the activities of bureaucracy, a function that steadily developed over time, or to serve other administrative functions for either Church or State. As we will see, links sometimes developed between those who worked for such bureaucracies and other forms of literary production.

In the earlier Middle Ages in England religious institutions were the most stable locations for literary manuscript production. A number of monasteries or cathedral towns seem to have had their own scriptoria to produce books for their own libraries and/or for those of other religious houses. As sites of education, with relative affluence and access to the institutional resources of the Church, their importance was clear. Before the Norman Conquest, some of these houses had established their own organizations for manuscript production with trained scribes and with access to other artisans, like decorators and illustrators, in such centres as Wearmouth Jarrow, Winchester, Exeter, Salisbury, and Canterbury.[3]

It was almost certainly within such religious houses that the earliest surviving major literary manuscripts of the Old English period were prepared. These are the four substantial collections of Old English poetry, the Exeter Book (Exeter Cathedral Library 3501), the Vercelli Book (Vercelli, Italy, Cathedral Library CXVII), the Junius Manuscript (Oxford, Bodleian Library, Junius 11) and the *Beowulf* manuscript (London, British Library, Cotton Vitellius A. xv). The primary historical importance of these manuscripts is the often unique copies of Old English verse texts they contain (they also include prose works) and the indications they reveal of a vital vernacular literary culture. Although it is not possible to identify exact sites of production for any of these manuscripts, it seems certain they were produced in monastic environments, as was almost all of the surviving Old English literary corpus.[4]

And it was monasteries and other religious sites that seem to have been the means of both preserving the Old English literary past after the Norman Conquest in 1066 and of providing links to the emergent early Middle English culture in the following generations, particularly houses on the geographical and cultural periphery of what quickly became primarily an Anglo-Norman culture. The relative remoteness of the West Midlands and East Anglia provided the environments most conducive to the nurturing of an emergent native literary activity.

Worcester Cathedral Priory maintained a tradition of copying Old English down to the early thirteenth century, evidenced in part in the activities of the copyist of the so-called 'Tremulous Hand' of Worcester, who also copied the now fragmentary Middle English *Soul's Address to the Body*.[5] It was also at Worcester where what are possibly the earliest surviving Middle English secular lyrics were copied.[6] Worcester is associated dialectally with at least one substantial thirteenth-century multilingual

---

[3] For an overview see Ker (1960).
[4] On the provenance of Old English manuscripts see Ker (1957).
[5] See Franzen (1991).
[6] Brown (1932), p. xii.

devotional collection, Cambridge, Trinity College, B.14.39, with London, British Library, Cotton Caligula A. ix, one of two extant manuscripts of Layamon's *Brut*, the earliest surviving long Middle English verse work, and with another trilingual manuscript of the thirteenth century, Oxford, Bodleian Library, Digby 86, which includes a number of mainly religious lyrics, as well as some longer didactic works, and the earliest English fabliau, *Dame Sirith*.[7] These manuscripts indicate the range of literary materials available in a region remote from the Anglo-Norman culture imposed on England after the Norman Conquest.

Other early Middle English works seem to have been produced on the outer edges of Norman control and cultural influence, under similar auspices. Cambridge, Corpus Christi College 402, possibly the earliest manuscript of the Middle English prose devotional work, the *Ancrene Wisse*, originally composed for an audience of female anchoresses, was copied in western England, possibly Herefordshire.[8] It is written in a standardized literary dialect, notable for its highly consistent orthography, which was also used in other vernacular devotional texts of the thirteenth century, the so-called 'AB' language.[9]

There is also evidence of substantial English literary activity at the eastern extent of Norman influence, within East Anglia. Two of the manuscripts of one of the earliest surviving Middle English romances, *Havelok the Dane*, Cambridge University Library, Additional 4407 and Oxford, Bodleian Library, Laud Misc. 108, were produced in Norfolk; the latter also includes the romance *King Horn*. The Laud manuscript is early fourteenth century, the Cambridge one towards the end of that century.[10] Other English manuscripts were also produced in this region in the earlier part of the century, especially in Norfolk; one example is London, British Library, Arundel 292, a manuscript that includes the *Bestiary* and other poems.[11]

Circumstantial evidence suggests again that religious houses had an important role in the production of these vernacular manuscripts. The site of production for the *Ancrene Wisse* was, very probably, an Augustinian house. Wigmore Abbey in Herefordshire is certainly a contender for localizing *Ancrene Wisse*.[12] Arundel 292 was owned, if not demonstrably produced by, the Benedictine Cathedral Priory in Norwich. It may also be suggestive that the two romances in Laud 108 were, early in their history, joined to a separate manuscript containing the religious verse *South English Legendary*, an extremely popular and widely circulating collection of saints' lives, possibly originally composed in a religious house in the Worcester region. Where manuscripts of the *South English Legendary* have an early provenance, it is in religious and monastic houses.[13]

This fact is one indication of the literary importance of such monastic houses as catalysts in the transition from Old to Middle English. Early long poems like Layamon's *Brut* and Robert of Gloucester's *Chronicle*, as well as such collections as

---

[7] See Parkes and Tschann (1996).
[8] See Dobson (1977).   [9] See Tolkien (1929).
[10] See McIntosh (1976).   [11] See Beadle (1991).
[12] See Brewer (1956); Dobson (1977).
[13] Görlach (1974: 45–54).

the *South English Legendary*, were probably produced under their auspices. Their preservation at such sites was probably an important factor in the origins of the so-called 'alliterative revival' in the West Midlands in the fourteenth century, where poets seem to have looked backwards to earlier literary models like these to establish new verse models based on forms of the alliterative line.[14]

This is not to say that there may not have been local secular environments in which literary works may have been produced. One notable indication of this comes once again from the geographic periphery with London, British Library, Harley 2253,[15] the manuscript of the famous Harley lyrics.[16] This manuscript was apparently made in Ludlow by a scribe who copied a large number of legal documents. He also copied a large part of at least one other literary manuscript in French and Latin.[17] Other manuscripts may have originated in comparable provincial environments. This may have been the case with the unique copy of the famous romance *Sir Gawain and the Green Knight*, which survives, with other alliterative poems (also unique) in London, British Library, Cotton Nero A. x. The manuscript is clearly northern in derivation and may reflect the activities of some local household alert to its regional cultural implications[18] seeking to offer some provincial version of a 'courtly' environment. Such attempts stand in contrast to the recurrent literary testimony to the inferior cultural status of English between the twelfth and the fourteenth centuries and the perceived superiority of a French speaking elite.[19]

LATER MEDIEVAL MANUSCRIPT CULTURE

Rather surprisingly we lack much clear evidence of sustained English literary production in the London area until the mid-fourteenth century. However, the first evidence we have of such activity is dramatic in its scale and form. The 'Auchinleck' manuscript, now Edinburgh, National Library of Scotland 19.2.1, is a very large manuscript, written almost entirely in Middle English verse by six different scribes, and originally extensively illustrated.[20] The contents of the manuscript chiefly comprise a large number of romances, many unique, although there is some religious narrative and didactic verse. The logistics of assembling and organizing so many different scribes and exemplars and coordinating the activities of copying, decoration,

---

[14] See Pearsall (1981).   [15] For facsimile see Ker (1965).

[16] See Brook (1984); it also contains other works in Middle English verse, including the romance of *King Horn*, as well as items in French and Latin in both verse and prose.

[17] See Revard (2000).

[18] Bennett (1983).

[19] See Boffey and Edwards (2008: 381–2).

[20] For facsimile see Pearsall and Cunningham (1977); originally there were probably about thirty-seven pictures; only six now survive; a significant number of leaves containing miniatures have now been excised.

and assemblage must have been considerable. The manuscript suggests both a market for English works and the resources to meet such a demand on an unprecedented scale within the metropolitan area.

But the Auchinleck manuscript has no parallels, in London or elsewhere, until the very end of the fourteenth century in terms of vernacular manuscript production. And the parallels that survive involve primarily vernacular religious works. The greatest of these, in every sense of the word, is the Vernon manuscript (Oxford, Bodleian Library, Eng. poet a. 1).[21] This huge compilation (it weighs over 40 pounds and originally comprised more than 420 very large leaves) was prepared in the Midlands, probably in the 1390s. It is copied largely in triple columns by two main scribes and is very elaborately decorated and illuminated by a number of artists. It contained an assemblage of over 400 separate items, chiefly of Middle English works, in both verse and prose, works so numerous that the assemblage of exemplars itself must have been a complex and extended process.

The site of production of the Vernon manuscript is not clear but the available evidence suggests that it was produced for some Midlands religious community, possibly a Cistercian house. Bordesley Abbey in Warwickshire seems the likely place of origin since it was clearly a site well-equipped for the production of such large vernacular religious books. The main scribe of Vernon was also one of the scribes of another originally very large collection (a number of leaves have been lost), the Simeon manuscript. Now London, British Library, Add. 22283, it shares a significant number of the contents of Vernon in the same order. The preparation of the Vernon and Simeon manuscripts constitutes the zenith of vernacular religious book production in England. Indeed, the extent of the effort they represent is without parallel in the investment of time, money, and other resources involved in their preparation.

Such a level of organization does not seem to have been replicated elsewhere within orthodox religious communities after the end of the fourteenth century. A significant factor in this decline was doubtless the promulgation of Archbishop Arundel's Constitutions in 1409 that led to growing restrictions on the circulation of vernacular religious works.[22] This was a response to the developing efforts of followers of John Wyclif (d. 1384), the Wycliffites or Lollards, to disseminate their own forms of devotional or instructional writing in English. Their efforts were evidently remarkably successful as the large numbers (over 250) of surviving manuscripts of the Wyclif translations of the Bible demonstrate. These manuscripts often demonstrate high standards of production and indicate the extent to which, by the early fifteenth century, it was possible to draw on considerable skilled resources to produce multiple copies of the same text, even in an officially hostile environment. Other Wycliffite texts also demonstrate similar indications of organized book production.

---

[21] For facsimile see Doyle (1987).
[22] See Watson (1995).

THE COMMERCIALIZATION
OF BOOK PRODUCTION

Other forms of organization of manuscript production begin to emerge in the early fifteenth century, of less clandestine kinds and seemingly more fluid in structure, particularly in London. The metropolis clearly offered the largest pool of resources for such production, scribes, illuminators, parchmenters, artists, and binders, and also gave access to the largest and some of the wealthiest potential markets.[23]

At the centre of this nexus of commercial potential lies the scribe. It is largely through the evidence of scribal hands recurring in different manuscripts that it is possible to build up a picture of patterns of secular, commercial book production in this period. The ground-breaking research of A. I. Doyle and Malcolm Parkes identified various scribes producing manuscripts of Chaucer's *Canterbury Tales*, Gower's *Confessio Amantis*, and other substantial vernacular works in London at the beginning of the fifteenth century.[24] Their work suggested that the crucial figure in the patterns of organization for book production was the scribe, who tended to develop loose and shifting patterns of relationship with other artisans of the book trade. And it seems likely that the scribe remained the central figure in the London book-producing nexus throughout most of the century.[25]

An illustration of these patterns of relationship identified by Doyle and Parkes is the figure of Thomas Hoccleve (*c.*1367–1426), a poet who also worked as a clerk of the Privy Seal. In the latter capacity he was employed as a professional scribe writing government letters and documents; and his own model letter book for his correspondence survives. But Hoccleve also employed his scribal skills elsewhere. His hand has been identified in a manuscript of Gower's *Confessio Amantis* in a manuscript otherwise copied by scribes who seem to been producing commercial literary manuscripts on some scale. Clearly Hoccleve found scope for some kind of part-time activity that enabled him to use his professional scribal skills in different ways. He demonstrates the social interconnectedness that must have existed within circles of trained scribes in London that made such occasional moonlighting possible.

Behind the scribe and other artisans of the book trade lies a less definable figure, the stationer, whose existence is inferred from the larger circumstances of book production. There had to be someone to organize the logistics of production, to make contact with the potential purchaser and establish his/her specific needs, to purchase the materials, paper, or parchment, to obtain an exemplar to be copied, and arrange the decoration that might follow transcription, and, of course, to arrange payment. No records indicate clearly how stationers undertook such roles, but in

[23] See Christianson (1989).
[24] See Doyle and Parkes (1977).
[25] See further Edwards and Pearsall (1989).

what was essentially a bespoke trade such entrepreneurial presences were clearly an important aspect of the book trade. They were the crucial middle men.

London was the chief site for the production of high-quality manuscripts, but there were others that, at different periods, seem to have been capable of producing manuscripts to a high standard. One of the most elaborate surviving Middle English verse manuscripts is London, British Library, Harley 2278, the *Lives of SS Edmund and Fremund*, verse saints' lives by John Lydgate (1370–1449). This was clearly produced in Bury St Edmunds, Suffolk, where Lydgate was a member of the Benedictine Abbey, for presentation to the young Henry VI to commemorate his visit to the Abbey in 1433–4. It contains nearly 120 narrative miniatures.[26] Some of the artists involved in producing this manuscript may have been involved in the production of a second *de luxe* manuscript of another of Lydgate's works, the *Fall of Princes*, at about the same time; this manuscript is now divided between Huntington Library California HM 268 and London, British Library, Sloane 2452. And, a little later in the fifteenth century, a related group of manuscripts, chiefly of Lydgate's works, linked to each other by scribe and/or decoration, seem also to have been produced at Bury.[27]

These manuscripts are one aspect of the emergence of East Anglia as a significant region for the production of Middle English manuscripts in the first half of the fifteenth century. John Capgrave (1393–1464), Augustinian friar at King's Lynn, Norfolk, illustrates this phenomenon in a particularly striking way through the extent of his direct involvement in copying manuscripts of his own works in both verse and prose (see Lucas). And it is clear that there were sufficient, logistical, scribal, and artistic resources to enable the production of manuscripts often of extensive content and elaborate form, like the extremely large Chaucer collection that is now Cambridge University Library Gg.4.27, which originally included extensive illustration and other decoration and was made in Norfolk,[28] or the illustrated copy of the translation of Deguileville's *Pilgrimage of the Soul*, made in eastern England c.1430 that is now New York Public Library Spenser 19.[29]

VARIATION IN MANUSCRIPT PRODUCTION

These manuscripts just discussed all indicate the high end of the provincial manuscript market for vernacular literary production. The resources, material and artistic, for such elaborate manuscripts were infrequent, either in London or

[26] For a facsimile see Edwards (2004*b*).
[27] See Scott (1982).
[28] For a facsimile see Parkes and Beadle (1980).
[29] See Scott (1996), ii. 217–19.

outside it. These manuscripts may be balanced by a very different kind of compilation, London, British Library Add. 37049, probably produced for, if not in, a Carthusian house in the north of England. This is a vernacular collection of chiefly religious verse and prose accompanied by a considerable number of crude illustrations seemingly designed to provide some visual gloss or commentary to aid understanding of the text. The ambition of this manuscript in its attempt to link verbal and visual elements is not matched by the quality of its execution; the illustrations demonstrate the limited artistic resources available to those preparing this collection.[30]

Indeed, extended illustration remains infrequent throughout the period in Middle English manuscripts. The general range of scale of production is conveniently demonstrated by briefly considering the relative levels of elaborateness of the three manuscripts of the so-called 'Oxford Group' all of which share significant common content, particularly of Chaucer's shorter poems. These manuscripts are Oxford, Bodleian Library, Fairfax 16,[31] Tanner 346, and Bodley 638. The Fairfax manuscript is a well-produced manuscript, with an elaborate full-page pictorial frontispiece illustrating the first poem, Chaucer's 'Complaints of Mars and Venus', and a professional, consistent level of textual decoration throughout its over 300 vellum leaves.

In contrast to this manuscript is Bodley 638 (for a facsimile see Robinson 1982), a smaller manuscript (219 leaves), mainly of paper, copied by a competent, if undistinguished scribe named 'Lyty,' and without any illustration. And between these extremes is Tanner 346,[32] a much smaller vellum manuscript (119 leaves), but copied by three quite accomplished scribes, with limited, but consistent decoration.

These three manuscripts and the range of production models they embody demonstrate the diversity of fifteenth-century production possibilities and the range of audiences for which they had come to cater, even within the same place of production. Thus, it seems most likely that Fairfax, copied by a single scribe, was prepared in London, given its access to a high-quality illustrator. And the collaboration of three trained scribes in Tanner again also suggests a metropolitan origin. On the other hand, the Bodley manuscript, produced late in the century, seems much less accomplished in terms of layout and its rather crude scribal decoration.[33] Its place of production is unclear, but was again probably London, if, as seems to have been the case, it was used as setting copy by an early sixteenth-century printer.[34]

---

[30] See Brantley (2007).
[31] For a facsimile see Norton-Smith (1979).
[32] For a facsimile see Robinson (1980).
[33] See Robinson (1982), p. xxxvii.
[34] See Erler (1999).

PROFESSIONALIZATION OF MANUSCRIPT PRODUCTION

Indeed, one aspect of fifteenth-century manuscript production is the blurring of the distinction between professional and amateur manuscript production, both within London and elsewhere. During the course of the century, private individuals at some distance from London showed themselves capable of creating substantial volumes by ambitious programmes of assembling and transcribing texts. One of the most remarkable of these collector/copyists was Robert Thornton who, in the north of England in the middle of the century, produced single-handedly two very large collections of Middle English verse and prose, one now Lincoln Cathedral Library 91,[35] the other London, British Library, Add. 31042.[36] These manuscripts contain religious and secular works, in both verse and prose, amounting to over 450 large leaves. The difficulty of assembling and transcribing so many different exemplars is testimony to the scale of Thornton's activities. The motivation for his endeavours remains less clear. He is generally viewed as an 'antiquarian' enthusiast, but his manuscripts are organized and transcribed very competently, in ways that cannot be readily distinguished from the work of demonstrably professional copyists.

Similar difficulties of interpretation relate to another prolific copyist John Shirley (c.1366–1456) who, in the later years of his very long life, copied a number of manuscripts, chiefly of Middle English works in verse and prose, particularly those of Lydgate and Chaucer.[37] In addition, there is evidence which suggests that he copied a number of other manuscripts that no longer survive and also that he hired a professional scribe. Whether Shirley was an enthusiastic amateur, the provider of a 'lending library' to a coterie of associates or was engaged in the commercial book trade are questions that cannot be confidently resolved. Certainly his activities, like those of Robert Thornton, point to a determination to disseminate vernacular texts on a large scale.

The motives of a number of copyists fall into this penumbral category in the fifteenth century in ways that suggest that clear distinctions between amateur and professional copyists may not be useful or possible. Little is known about 'Rate' who added his name at a number of points in Oxford, Bodleian Library, Ashmole 61. This is a collection primarily of verse narrative works, both secular and religious including a number of romances, but also satire, burlesque, exempla, and saints' lives.[38] Rate was clearly able to draw on a wide range of material somewhere in north-west England and able to impose his own identity on the finished product both by the recurrent use of his own name and of drawings of fishes and flowers. It seems likely

---

[35] For a facsimile see Brewer and Owen (1977).

[36] Described by Stern (1976) and discussed by Thompson (1987).

[37] He preserves a number of unique copies of lyrics by the latter; see Connolly (1998) for the fullest account of his activities.

[38] For a description see Blanchfield (1996).

that he was a professional scribe, but one who served markets satisfied with modestly produced manuscripts.

Much the same points can be made about the scribe Heege, who compiled the manuscript that is now Edinburgh, National Library of Scotland 19.3.1, a paper manuscript of the late fifteenth century.[39] Once again the contents are largely English verse but not as variegated in their range as in the collections of Thornton and Shirley. The contents are predominantly religious: some pious romances, *Sir Gowther* and *Sir Isumbras*, part of Lydgate's *Life of Our Lady*, and William Lichfield's *Complaint of God* are among the longer works included. But the manuscript is undecorated and in a competent but undistinguished hand that shows little concern with careful layout. It suggests a level of utilitarian production that caters to a growing demand for vernacular manuscripts of a functional kind to meet the demands of a widening readership.

We may feel on firmer ground in making the distinction between professional and amateur production with the 'Findern' manuscript (Cambridge University Library Ff. 1.6).[40] This manuscript was compiled over several generations in Derbyshire, chiefly by members of the Findern family. The contents reflect the range of their reading, which included Chaucer, Gower, Hoccleve, and Lydgate, metrical romance, as well as a large number of unique lyrics, some seemingly composed by members of the family themselves. There are over thirty different hands in the manuscript, an indication of the degree of domestic collaboration that went on over time to enlarge it. But its private, amateur form also reveals connections, however vestigial, with the wider ramifications of the metropolitan professional book trade. A number of the texts of works in Findern that circulated before and beyond it can be shown to have links to commercially produced manuscripts including those of the Oxford Group.[41] In this respect Findern points to the ramifications of manuscript transmission of texts through which, over time, professionally circulated texts could be assimilated into amateur forms of manuscript production.

PROVINCIAL PRODUCTIONS

A number of other important fifteenth-century manuscripts were produced under various auspices in non-metropolitan environments. Some of these were almost certainly associated by virtue of their authorship with various religious houses. The various poems associated with John Audelay (d. c.1427) survive uniquely in Oxford, Bodleian Library, Douce 302, a manuscript that was certainly owned and possibly

---

[39] For a facsimile see Hardman (2000).
[40] For a facsimile see Beadle and Owen (1977).
[41] See Harris (1983: 307–12).

produced at the Augustinian Priory of Launde in Leicestershire. Although not all the poems in this manuscript are by Audelay, it indicates the way in which a single local figure can become the focus around which a collection is assembled. In contrast, the 'book of hymns and songs' in Cambridge University Library Ee. 1.12 contains only the poems, chiefly carols, of James Ryman, copied in the 1490s, probably in Canterbury at the Franciscan Friary with which he was associated. Both these collections demonstrate the ways in which particular individuals contribute to the creation of what were probably forms of vernacular production designed for local consumption.

Compilations like the Douce and Cambridge manuscripts show that it was clearly possible in the fifteenth century to produce reasonable-quality manuscripts drawing on such local resources outside of major urban areas in England. That more complex negotiations were possible over time and distance involving the marshalling of the resources of scribes, decorators, and multiple exemplars is demonstrated by Oxford, Bodleian Library, Arch. Selden. B. 24. This manuscript was produced at either the very end of the fifteenth century or the beginning of the sixteenth century in Edinburgh. It is the last major manuscript collection of Chaucer's works; it includes *Troilus & Criseyde*, the *Legend of Good Women, Parliament of Fowls*, as well as other poems by Lydgate, Hoccleve, Clanvowe, and Walton, some erroneously ascribed to Chaucer. Its contents are wholly in verse; it also contains a collection of Scottish poems, including *The Kingis Quair*, most of them unique.[42] The manuscript was produced, in more than one stage, for Henry, Lord Sinclair, a Scottish nobleman, who at some stage in its preparation had the manuscript decorated, with borders, illuminated initials, and an opening historiated initial.

The Selden manuscript is clearly an ambitious compilation, one that demonstrates the range of the circulation of exemplars of popular work and also the efforts that might be made to ensure local accessibility. The Middle English poems in it have all been translated in various degrees into Scottish dialect.[43] It is hard to establish with any confidence how many intervening stages of translation lie behind the Selden texts, but such activity demonstrates the efforts of a market-sensitive manuscript industry committed to ensuring the local accessibility of its products.

The Selden manuscript is interesting in other respects. Print first appeared in Scotland shortly after it was copied. John Chepman and Andrew Myllar set up the first printing press in Scotland in 1507/8[44] and the works they printed—all in the vernacular—included a couple that appear in Selden that seem textually linked to it. In this respect the Selden manuscript can be seen as a transitional collection, one that is linked to the emergence of print as the primary means for the transmission of literary culture.[45]

---

[42] For a facsimile see Boffey *et al.* (1997).
[43] See Boffey and Edwards (1999).
[44] See Beattie (1950).
[45] See Edwards (1996).

FROM SCRIPT TO PRINT

This move from manuscript to printed book seems to have been a surprisingly rapid one. Certainly within twenty years of Caxton establishing his first shop in Westminster in about 1476 there were complaints by London stationers that the trade in manuscripts was destroyed.[46] And the manuscript circulation of literary works in the first half of the sixteenth century seems to have been highly unsystematic, where it was not nonexistent. The copying of manuscripts of earlier works, those of Chaucer, Gower, and Lydgate, for example, seems to have swiftly dried up. By the early sixteenth century, a significant number of works by these three were available in print, some in multiple editions, and this availability was significantly increased by William Thynne's 1532 edition of Chaucer's *Works*, which made available not just a comprehensive Chaucer canon, but also a substantial number of other Middle English works associated with Chaucer. Later collected editions of Chaucer, by John Stow (1561) and Thomas Speght (1598, 1602), further enlarged the corpus of Middle English works in print.

The effect of print on more contemporary writers reveals a diversity of responses. The works of some early sixteenth-century poets like Thomas Wyatt and Henry Howard, Earl of Surrey,[47] did continue to circulate almost wholly in manuscript during their lifetimes. For others, like John Skelton, the issue is more complex. He seems to have quite precise discriminations between the audiences for various of his works and chosen the appropriate medium, manuscript or print, accordingly.[48] For yet others, like Stephen Hawes and Alexander Barclay, print was virtually their sole means of transmission.[49] There was a fundamental split between general and coterie audiences for the different media.

As print developed large chunks of the literary past were left behind, particularly from the earlier periods of English literature. Old English verse texts were not printed until the nineteenth century and only occasional prose works from this period before that. Nor did early Middle English fare much better. The list of works that failed to achieve print from this period is a long one and includes such works of manifest popularity in manuscript, as the *South English Legendary*, the *Northern Homily Cycle*, and the *Prick of Conscience* and most of the surviving lyrics and many metrical romances—although *Guy of Warwick*, *Bevis of Hampton*, *Eglamour of Artois* were among those printed by Wynkyn de Worde and William Copland. Some prose works had better luck, thanks in important measure again to de Worde: he printed parts of the corpora of Walter Hilton and Richard Rolle, as well as some of the *Ancrene Riwle* and other devotional writings.

---

[46] See Christianson (1987).
[47] See Edwards (2004*a*).
[48] See Edwards (2008).
[49] See Edwards (1980), Carlson (1995).

From the later Middle English period, some forms of prose evidently had an enduring audience. Malory's *Morte Darthur*, for example, was regularly reprinted between its first publication by Caxton in 1485 and Thomas East's edition in 1634. The printing of such prose devotional writings as Nicholas Love's *Mirror of the Blessed Life of Christ*, and John Myrk's *Festial* (the latter the single most popular Middle English printed work before 1500; there are fourteen editions) all indicate that in some respects manuscript popularity could be replicated in print. But there are some surprising indications of the failure of works popular in later manuscripts to get any purchase on the sensibilities of print audiences. Most obviously, Thomas Hoccleve's *Regement of Princes*, extant in fifty manuscripts, was not printed until the nineteenth century.

Literary manuscript culture did not, however, die out with the invention of printing. It continued to exist in parallel to it through the sixteenth and seventeenth centuries. In part this was a function of class sensibility. Poets like Surrey, Wyatt, and Sidney in the sixteenth were doubtless conscious of the stigma of print that had the potential to expose their writings to a wider, far less defined audience than they envisage for their works. Such discriminating reticence did not survive their deaths, when their writings swiftly found print publishers, but it does testify to some awareness on their parts of a direct connection between the poet and those to whom he addressed his works. In the seventeenth century, Jonson, Donne, Herbert, Oldham, and Rochester exemplify in different ways the idea of coterie poetry, circulating within limited circles and hence in manuscript. It was not until the end of the seventeenth century that print finally stifled manuscript culture.

BIBLIOGRAPHY

BEADLE, R. (1991), 'Prolegomena to a Literary Geography of Later Medieval Norfolk', in Felicity Riddy (ed.), *Regionalism in Late Medieval Manuscripts and Texts* (Cambridge: D. S. Brewer), 89–108.

——and A. E. B. OWEN (1977), *The Findern Manuscript: Cambridge University Library MS. Ff. 1. 6* (London: Scolar Press).

BEATTIE, W. (1950), *The Chepman and Myllar Prints: A Facsimile* (Edinburgh: Edinburgh Bibliographical Society).

BENNETT, M. J. (1983), *Community, Class and Careerism: Cheshire and Lancashire Society in the Age of Sir Gawain and the Green Knight* (Cambridge: Cambridge University Press).

BLANCHFIELD, LYNNE S. (1996), 'Rate Revisited: The Compilation of the Narrative Works in MS Ashmole 61', in Jennifer Fellows, Rosalind Field, Gillian Roger, and Judith Weiss (eds.), *Romance Reading on the Book: Essays on Medieval Literature Presented to Maldwyn Mills* (Cardiff: University of Wales Press), 208–20.

BOFFEY, JULIA and A. S. G. EDWARDS (2008), 'Middle English Literary Writings, 1150–1400', in N. J. Morgan and R. Thomson (eds.), *Cambridge History of the Book*, ii (Cambridge: Cambridge University Press), 380–90.

——(1999), 'Middle English Texts in Scottish Dress', in T. Prendergast and B. Kline (eds.), *ReWriting Chaucer* (Columbus, Ohio: Ohio State University Press), 166–85.

——and JOHN J. THOMPSON (1989), 'Anthologies and Miscellanies: Production and the Choice of Texts', in Jeremy Griffiths and Derek Pearsall (eds.), *Book Production and Publishing in Britain 1375–1475* (Cambridge: Cambridge University Press), 279–315.

——A. S. G. EDWARDS, and B. C. BARKER-BENFIELD (introd.) (1997), *The Works of Geoffrey Chaucer and the Kingis Quair: A Facsimile of Bodleian Library, Oxford, MS Arch. Selden. B. 24* (Cambridge: D. S. Brewer).

BRANTLEY, JESSICA (2007), *Reading in the Wilderness: Private Devotion and Public Performance in Late Medieval England* (Chicago: University of Chicago Press).

BREWER, DEREK S. (1956), 'Two Notes on the Augustinian, Possibly West Midlands Origin of the Ancrene Riwle', *Notes and Queries*, NS 3: 232–5.

——and A. E. B. OWEN (1977), *The Thornton Manuscript (Lincoln Cathedral MS. 91)* (London: Scolar Press).

BROOK, G. L. (ed.) (1984), *The Harley Lyrics* (3rd edn. Manchester: Manchester University Press).

BROWN, CARLETON (ed.) (1932), *English Lyrics of the XIIIth Century* (Oxford: Clarendon Press).

CARLSON, D. R. (1995), 'Alexander Barclay and Richard Pynson: A Tudor Printer and his Writer', *Anglia*, 113: 283–302.

CARRUTHERS, MARY (1990), *The Book of Memory* (Cambridge: Cambridge University Press).

CHRISTIANSON, C. PAUL (1987), 'An Early Tudor Stationer and the "prynters of bokes"', *The Library*, 6th ser. 9: 259–62.

——(1989), 'Evidence for the Study of London's Late Medieval Manuscript-Book Trade', in Jeremy Griffiths and Derek Pearsall (eds.), *Book Production and Publishing in Britain 1375–1475* (Cambridge: Cambridge University Press), 87–108.

CONNOLLY, MARGARET C. (1998), *John Shirley: Book Production and the Noble Household in Fifteenth-Century England* (Aldershot: Ashgate).

DOBSON, E. J. (1977), *The Origins of Ancrene Wisse* (Oxford: Clarendon Press).

DOYLE, A. I. (introd.) (1987), *The Vernon Manuscript: A Facsimile of Bodleian Library, Oxford MS Eng. poet. a.1* (Cambridge: D. S. Brewer).

——and M. B. PARKES (1977), 'The Production of Copies of the *Canterbury Tales* and the *Confession Amantis* in the Early Fifteenth Century', in M. B. Parkes and A. G. Watson (eds.), *Medieval Scribes, Manuscripts and Libraries: Essays Presented to N. R. Ker* (London: Scolar Press), 163–210.

EDWARDS, A. S. G. (1980), 'Poet and Printer in Sixteenth Century England: Stephen Hawes and Wynkyn de Worde', *Gutenberg Jahrbuch*, 82–8.

——(1991), 'Middle English Romance: The Limits of Editing, the Limits of Criticism', in T. W. Machan (ed.), *Medieval Literature: Text and Interpretation* (Binghamton, NY: Medieval and Renaissance Texts and Studies), 91–104.

——(1996), 'Bodleian Library MS. Arch. Selden B. 24: A "Transitional" Collection', in Stephen G. Nichols and Siegfried Wenzel (eds.), *The Whole Book* (Ann Arbor: University of Michigan Press), 53–68.

——(2004a), 'Manuscripts of the Verse of Henry Howard, Earl of Surrey', *Huntington Library Quarterly*, 67: 283–93.

——(introd.) (2004b), *The Life of St Edmund King and Martyr: A Facsimile of British Library MS Harley 2278* (London: British Library).

——(2008), 'Skelton's English Poems in Manuscript and Print', in D. R. Carlson (ed.), *John Skelton and Early Modern Culture* (Tempe, Ariz.: Medieval and Renaissance Texts and Studies), 85–94.

——and DEREK PEARSALL (1989), 'The Manuscripts of the Major English Poetic Texts', in Jeremy Griffiths and Derek Pearsall (eds.), *Book Production and Publishing in Britain 1375–1475* (Cambridge: Cambridge University Press), 257–69.

ERLER, MARY (1999), 'Printers' Copy: MS Bodley 638 and *The Parliament of Fowls*', *Chaucer Review*, 33: 221–9.

FRANZEN, CHRISTINE (1991), *The Tremulous Hand of Worcester: A Study of Old English in the Thirteenth Century* (Oxford: Oxford University Press).

GÖRLACH, MANFRED (1974), *The Textual Tradition of the South English Legendary* (Leeds: University of Leeds School of English).

GRIFFITHS, JEREMY, and DEREK PEARSALL (1989), *Book Production and Publishing in Britain 1375–1475* (Cambridge: Cambridge University Press).

HARDMAN, PHILLIPA M. (introd.) (2000), *The Heege Manuscript: A facsimile of National Library of Scotland MS Advocates 19.3.1* (Leeds Texts and Monographs, NS 16; Leeds: Leeds School of English).

HARRIS, KATE (1983), 'The Origins and Make-Up of Cambridge University Library MS Ff. 1. 6', *Transactions of the Cambridge Bibliographical Society*, 8: 299–333.

KER, N. R. (1957), *Catalogue of Manuscripts Containing Anglo-Saxon* (Oxford: Clarendon Press).

——(1960), *English Manuscripts in the Century after the Norman Conquest* (Oxford: Clarendon Press).

——(introd.) (1965), *Facsimile of British Museum MS. Harley 2253* (EETS OS 255; London: Oxford University Press for the Early English Text Society).

LUCAS, P. J. (1997), *From Author to Audience: John Capgrave and Medieval Publication* (Dublin: University College Dublin Press).

MCINTOSH, ANGUS (1976), 'The Language of the Extant Versions of *Havelok the Dane*', *Medium Ævum*, 45: 36–49.

NORTON-SMITH, J. (introd.) (1979), *Bodleian Library MS Fairfax 16* (London: Scolar Press).

PARKES, M. B., and J. TSCHANN (introd.) (1996), *Facsimile of Oxford, Bodleian Library MS Digby 86* (EETS SS 16; Oxford: Oxford University Press).

——and R. BEADLE (introd.) (1980), *Poetical Works of Geoffrey Chaucer: Cambridge University Library MS Gg. 4. 27* (3 vols. Cambridge: Boydell & Brewer).

PEARSALL, DEREK (1981), 'The Origins of the Alliterative Revival', in Bernard S. Levy and Paul Szarmach (eds.), *The Alliterative Tradition in the Fourteenth Century* (Kent, Ohio: Kent State University Press), 1–24.

——and I. C. CUNNINGHAM (1977), *The Auchinleck Manuscript* (London: Scolar Press).

REVARD, CARTER (2000), 'Scribes and Provenance', in Susanna Fein (ed.), *Studies in the Harley Manuscript: The Scribes, Contents, and Social Contexts of British Library MS Harley 2253* (Kalamazoo, Mich.: Medieval Institute, Western Michigan University), 21–109.

ROBINSON, P. R. (introd.) (1980), *Manuscript Tanner 346: A Facsimile* (Norman, Okla.: Pilgrim Books).

——(introd.) (1982), *Manuscript Bodley 638: A Facsimile* (Norman, Okla.: Pilgrim Books).

SCOTT, KATHLEEN L. (1982), 'Lydgate's Lives of Saints Edmund and Fremund: A Newly Located Manuscript in Arundel Castle', *Viator*, 13: 335–66.

——(1996), *Later Gothic Manuscripts 1390–1490* (2 vols. London: Harvey Miller).

STERN, K. (1976), 'The London "Thornton" Miscellany', *Scriptorium*, 30: 26–37, 201–18.

THOMPSON, J. J. (1987), *Robert Thornton and the London Thornton Manuscript* (Cambridge: D. S. Brewer).

TOLKIEN, J. R. R. (1929), '*Ancrene Wisse* and *Hali Meihad*', in H. W. Garrod (ed.), *Essays and Studies*, xiv (Oxford: Clarendon Press), 104–26.

WATSON, NICHOLAS (1995), 'Censorship and Cultural Change in Late Medieval England: Vernacular Theology, the Oxford Translation Debate, and Arundel's Constitutions of 1409', *Speculum*, 70: 822–64.

CHAPTER 2

....

TEXTUAL COPYING
AND
TRANSMISSION

....

ORIETTA DA ROLD

DISSEMINATING TEXTS
....

The question of medieval textual copying and transmission is multifaceted. It hinges on a handwritten culture whose protagonists are those individuals who nurture manuscript production for entertainment, administrative, educational, and religious purposes. The chain of transmission evinces a varied and diverse book culture, whether it is interpreted diachronically or synchronically, which witnesses a continuously renewed interest in medieval texts. These texts are known to us because they were written, copied, altered, or translated at a certain point in history to satisfy a changing demand and intellectual curiosity. Although some works survive in only one manuscript and others are fragmentary, the number of surviving manuscripts offers important evidence to think about who copied them, for whom, and for what reason.

This chapter will discuss the transmission of medieval texts in their manuscript culture.[1] It will consider the complicated process of the making of a manuscript from several perspectives: it will look at the difficult relationship between scribes and authors; it will evaluate the different writing environments in which manuscripts

---

[1] I would like to thank Mary Swan, Andrew Merrills, and the editors for reading a draft of the essay and offering valuable suggestions.

were copied and circulated, and it will in particular assess the difficulties associated with the transmission of the texts of two medieval authors, who are situated at the opposite ends of the medieval period: Ælfric in the tenth century and Chaucer in the fourteenth. These two authors were writing four centuries apart and yet have many textual problems and scribal solutions in common. A close look at the making of the manuscripts which transmitted their works will not only shed new light on our understanding of how texts were transmitted, but will also make us reflect on other significant issues such as textual integrity, functionality, and usage.

It is customary to consider the complex associations of the agencies which are involved in the development of the transmission of texts by processing and explaining textual traditions through editorial practices and textual criticism.[2] The debate on editorial practices is mainly divided into two main schools of thought.[3] On the one hand, we have editors who firmly believe that the text they edit should be as close as possible to the version the author intended to publish.[4] Thorpe explains: 'The process of the transmission of a text is full of chance for error at every step of the way . . . the history of the transmission of a text is one of progressive degeneration';[5] thus, it is the editor's task to recover the 'original text' by correcting these mistakes.[6] On the other hand, work on reception theory and scribal activities has encouraged a different approach to the task of an editor. Variance and mouvance are two terms which encourage the reader to think about the text as a flexible entity and thus to re-evaluate the work of a scribe within a different production milieu, the one of the scribe rather than the editor.[7]

During the 1980s and the 1990s numerous publications appeared considering how these two approaches could contribute to the editing of Old and Middle English texts.[8] It is not the scope of this article to judge whether the debate was successful or not, it suffices to say that no consensus was reached and amongst editors there is still

---

[2] Greetham (1994).

[3] For a recent and thorough overview on the issue and a clear explanation on the main steps towards the establishment of a text following these two different schools see Cole (forthcoming).

[4] Reynolds and Wilson (1968); Bowers (1975); Tanselle (1990); Thorpe (1972).

[5] Thorpe (1972: 51).

[6] 'Textual criticism is the process of ascertaining and reproducing what an author wrote . . . And because copyists are human, they are prone to make errors of many kinds in copying – involuntary errors of omission (caused by eye-skip provoked by homoeoteleuton, etc.) or addition (dittography), of miscomprehension of unfamiliar words and names, or voluntary errors caused by deliberate scribal interference (interpolation, emendation, and so on). Textual criticism therefore becomes, in A. E. Housman's memorable phrase, "the science of discovering error in texts and the art of removing it". It need hardly to be stressed that the detection of error is facilitated by thorough understanding of the habits and practices of the scribes who copied manuscripts, whereas the correction of error requires a thorough familiarity with the particular author's style, language and subject-matter, as well as a gift for guessing (the technical term is "conjecturing") what the author might have written in cases where error in the transmitted text has been detected.' Lapidge (2003: 107–8).

[7] For an overview see the excellent introduction by Millet (2002). On reception theory see Jauss (1982); Zumthor (1972); Cerquiglini (1989).

[8] I include here some examples, which could be representative: Beit-Arié (1992); Edwards (1987); Frank (1993); Keefer and O'Keeffe (1998); Lerer (1996); Machan (1994); McCarren and Moffat (1998); Pearsall (1994); Scragg and Szarmach (1994).

much variation of opinions and methodologies. These discussions by their own nature focus on the text and its author: the work of the individuals who made the transmission of the text possible is judged in the light of the text itself.

The work of a scribe in a book can be explained from several different angles, but in essence scholars focus on two main aspects; namely, their palaeographical skills and their abilities to copy faithfully an exemplar.[9] This last approach, in particular, represents only one aspect of the consumption and circulation of medieval texts. In an influential essay Robert Darton argues that it is important to look at 'a general model for analysing the way books come into being and spread through society'.[10] His Communication Circuit is a very famous model, which represents in abstract form the intricate aspects pertaining to book production, circulation and use. The originator of the circuit is the author, who publishes via a publisher. Printers set the text for publication and give the book to a shipper who will get copies to booksellers and thus they will be accessible by a reader. The reader ultimately will feed back to the author, who will reinitiate the cycle. This is only a synopsis of the circuit, which Darton successfully used to explain the production and circulation of books in eighteenth-century France. It was devised to consider the communication process as a whole and as Darton explains: 'With minor adjustments, it should apply to all periods in the history of the printed book (manuscript books and book illustrations will have to be considered elsewhere).'[11] We do not have as far as I am aware a similar model to understand the production, circulation, and consumption of medieval manuscripts, although Wilcox briefly explored it for the copying of Anglo-Saxon books using Darton's model.[12] It is difficult to superimpose a schema which was prepared for printed book culture onto manuscripts, because of the condition of the medieval book market, which is often anonymous. The absence of recognizable agencies (anonymity in authorship, copying, and use), the diversity of linguistic and textual communities, the numerous writing environments, the varied circumstances of production and use also complicate matters despite identifiable and localizable examples.[13]

Bibliographers of printed books have argued that the transmission of texts can be explicated 'by explaining the process of book production'.[14] The tool for such an investigation is the application of analytical bibliography to the printed books.[15] By similar means scholars working on manuscript culture can use the large corpus of manuscripts to discuss not only the transmission of the text, but also the complex dynamics which the communication circuit entails in the middle ages. The bibliographer of the manuscript books can use codicological, linguistic, and palaeographical tools and methodologies to elucidate such a cycle. Thus, it is possible to filter the communication circuit through the known evidence and divide it in a tripartite

---

[9] Maniaci *et al.* (2002: 121).   [10] Darton (2002: 10).

[11] Ibid. 11.   [12] Wilcox (2001: 67–8).

[13] Griffiths and Pearsall (1989); Da Rold (2006); Hanna (2001, 2004); Morgan and Thomson (2008).

[14] Gaskell (1972), preface; McKerrow (1927).

[15] Bowers (1994).

relationship among authors, those individuals who transmitted and/or read the texts, and editors as mediators. By transmission I do not only mean copying; transmission can also be understood as usage, because scribes did not only disseminate work, they also perpetuated and altered what they had available. For the purpose of this article I will focus on the relationship between authors and scribes and scribes and authors.

AUTHORS AND THEIR SCRIBES

Ælfric concludes his 'Preface' to the *Catholic Homilies*, first series, with a seemingly informed judgement on textual copying and scribal activity:

Nu bydde ic 7 halsige on godes naman gif hwá þas bóc awritan wylle þæt hé hí geornlice gerihte be ðære bysene. þy læs ðe we ðurh gymelease writeras geleahtrode beon; Mycel yfel deð se ðe leas writ. buton he hit gerihte. swylce he gebringe þa soðan lare to leasum gedwylde. for ði sceal gehwa gerihtlæcan þæt þæt he ær to woge gebigde gif hé on godes dome unscyldig beon wile.[16]

Almost four hundred years later Chaucer writes:

> Adam scryveyn, if ever it thee byfalle
> Boece or Troylus for to wryten newe,
> Under thy long lokkes thou most have the scalle
> But after my makyng thow wryte more trewe!
> So ofte a daye I mot thy werke renewe
> It to corecte and eke to rubbe and scrape;
> And al is thorugh thy neglygence and rape.[17]

Examples such as these do not abound in English literature,[18] but they offer an opportunity to reflect on the role of the author and the scribe in the transmission of medieval texts. Both Ælfric and Chaucer are preoccupied with the state of their text after scribal copying. Mize scrutinizes these literary examples to respond to scholars who believe that medieval authors did not have real expectations about the fixed nature of their texts,[19] and demonstrates that: 'medieval authors had a sense of their works' formal intactness, though they might not always have defined it exactly as we would, and they cared about it'.[20] Indeed Ælfric and Chaucer imply that copying a text will inevitably bring alteration and corruption to their works and by contrast they affirm the importance of authorial intention. However, one cannot fail to notice

---

[16] Clemoes (1997: ll. 128–34; italics mine): 'Now I pray and entreat in god's name, that if anyone wishes to copy this book, he earnestly correct it by the exemplar, lest we be blamed because of careless scribes. He who writes falsely does great evil unless he corrects it, so that he brings the true teaching to false heresy; therefore, each one should put right what he previously distorted with error if he wishes to be blameless at God's judgment.' Tr. Treharne (2004: 121).

[17] Benson (1988: 650).   [18] Hanna (1991).

[19] Machan (1991).   [20] Mize (2001: 353).

that this form can also be interpreted as a well-established literary trope that Staley Johnson defines as 'the trope of the scribe' and analyses within the context of a scribal metaphor which is used by authors such as Hildegard of Bingen, Christine de Pisan, Julian of Norwich, and Margery Kempe to validate their authority and textual assertiveness.[21] The trope of the careless scribe can, however, be traced from antiquity to modern times and it is not confined to the manuscript culture. Strabo, Cicero, Jerome, and Petrarch, for instance, complain in their letters to friends and family of the inaccuracy of published books, which are full of mistakes.[22] In this sense Chaucer and Ælfric may perpetuate a literary form which was well established. However, the two authors do not illustrate the same attitude towards their works, though they share a similar attitude towards their preservation. It will be useful, therefore, to look closely at these two texts, trying to set them in their literary context.

Ælfric's anxiety with the preservation of authorial intention is a concern in most of his prefatory works and letters. He often uses the formula 'gif hwá þas bóc awritan wylle' (that if anyone wishes to copy this book) to sign off his compositions: in the Old English preface to the first series and to the second series of the *Catholic Homilies*; in the Old English preface to *Grammar*; in the translation of *Genesis*, and in the Old English preface to *Lives of Saints*.[23] It is remarkable that none of the prefatory or adjoining materials in Latin carries a similar formula.[24]

Scholars have commented on Ælfric's short-lived desire to preserve the textual integrity of his work.[25] The manuscript context of both the *Catholic Homilies* and the *Lives* witnesses a high degree of textual variation and alteration. Manuscripts do not retain the uniformity of the collection as dictated by the author, resulting in a variety of compilations which show no uniform line of descent.[26] Only one copy of the first series of the *Catholic Homilies* survives in its integrity with authorial annotations— London, British Library, Royal 7. c. xii; all the other manuscripts are fragmentary or composite.[27] As Hill puts it: 'The appropriation common to a manuscript culture prevailed almost immediately'[28] after Ælfric releases his work and it started to be dismembered and copied with other texts in manuscripts. Thus, as Swan comments, 'authorial identity in a manuscript culture, then, is essentially unstable and usually unfixable'.[29]

---

[21] Staley Johnson explains: 'writers ... did not simply employ scribes as copyists: they elaborated upon the figurative language associated with the book as a symbol and incorporated scribes into their texts as tropes'; Staley Johnson (1991: 820).

[22] Root (1913); Scattergood (1990).

[23] Wilcox (1994); Hill (1994: 180–1).

[24] There is only one exception, in the Latin preface to the first series of *Catholic Homilies* Ælfric asks: 'Tatum obsecro ne pervertat nostrum interpretationem, quamspe[ra]mus ex Dei Gratia, non causa iactantiae, nos studiose sicuti valuimus interpretari.' (But I entreat him not to pervert our version which we hope that we translate accurately, as far as we have been able, by God's grace and not through vainglory); Wilcox (1994: 107–8, 128).

[25] Hill (1997, 2003); Wilcox (2001); Swan (2001).

[26] Skeat (1881–1900); Clemoes (1997).   [27] Clemoes and Eliason (1966).

[28] Hill (1997: 408).   [29] Swan (2001: 79).

Textual fixity, however, is an established anxiety which goes back to the Fathers of the Church and probably to texts that Ælfric read. In the Latin preface to the first series of *Catholic Homilies*, which is only witnessed in one manuscript, Cambridge University Library, Gg. 3. 28, Ælfric acknowledges his debts to the Patristic tradition: Augustine of Hippo, Jerome, Bede, Gregory, and Smaragdus are all authors whose expositions he followed.[30] Jerome criticizes those who copy his texts for their lack of attention and unwillingness to correct them by comparing their copies with his originals.[31] In the *Decem Libri Historiarum*, Gregory of Tours pleads for his work not to be miscopied, misrepresented, or dismembered.[32]

The preoccupation with defacing the true appearance and meaning of words is also present in one of the letters of Gregory the Great's *Registrum Epistolarum*. Gregory writes to John, Subdeacon of Ravenna, regarding the appointment of a new abbot to the monastery of a student of his Claudius, who was the late abbot of this monastery. In his letter Gregory explains that he would like to have back the notes that Claudius

---

[30] Wilcox (1994); Hill (2003). 'Hos namque auctores in hac explanation sumus secuti, videlicet Augustinum [Ypponiensem], Hieronimum, Bedam, Gregorium, Smaragdum, et aliquando [Hæg]monem, horum denique auctoritas ab amnibus catholicis libentissime suscipitur' (For, indeed, we have followed these authors in this exposition: namely, Augustine of Hippo, Jerome, Bede, Gregory, Smaragdus, and sometimes Haymo, for the authority of these is most willingly acknowledged by all the orthodox—Wilcox 1994: 107, 127).

[31] Jerome, 'Epistola LXXXI, Ad Lucinium', 'Opuscula mea, quae non sui merito, sed bonitate tua desiderare te dicis, ad describendum hominibus tuis dedi, et descripta vidi in chartaceis codicibus: ac frequenter admonui, ut conferrent diligentius, et emendarent. Ego enim tanta volumina prae frequentia commeantium et peregrinorum turbis relegere non potui, et ut ipsi probavere praesentes, longo tentus incommodo, vix diebus Quadragesimae, quibus ipsi proficiscebantur, respirare coepi. Unde si paragrammata repereris, vel minus aliqua descripta sunt, quae sensum legentis impediant, non mihi debes imputare, sed tuis, et imperitiae notariorum librariorumque incuriae, qui scribunt non quod inveniunt, sed quod intelligunt; et dum alienos errores emendare nituntur, ostendunt suos'; Migne (1844–55 and 1862–5), xxii, coll. 0672, para. 5. 'As for my works which from no merits of theirs but simply from your own kindness you say that you desire to have; I have given them to your servants to transcribe, I have seen the paper-copies made by them, and I have repeatedly ordered them to correct them by a diligent comparison with the originals. For so many are the pilgrims passing to and fro that I have been unable to read so many volumes. They have found me also troubled by a long illness from which this Lent I am slowly recovering as they are leaving me. If then you find errors or omissions which interfere with the sense, these you must impute not to me but to your own servants; they are due to the ignorance or carelessness of the copyists, who write down not what they find but what they take to be the meaning, and do but expose their own mistakes when they try to correct those of others.' Schaff and Wace (1892), vi. 153–4.

[32] 'Quos libros licet stile rusticiori conscripserim tamen coniuro omnes sacerdotes Domini, qui post me humilem ecclesiam Turonicam sunt recturi, per adventum domini nostri Iesu Christi ac terribilem reis omnibus iudicii diem, sic numquam confuse de ipso iudicio discedentes cum diabolo condempnemini, ut numquam libros hos aboleri faciatis aut rescribi, quasi quaedam eligentes et quaedam praetermittentes, sed ita omnia vobiscum integra inlibataque permaneant, sicut a nobis relicta sunt' (Gregory of Tours 1885: 10. 31). 'I know very well that my style in these books is lacking in polish. Nevertheless I conjure you all, you Bishop of the Lord who will have charge of Tours cathedral after my unworthy self, I conjure you all, I say, by the coming of our Lord Jesus Christ and by the Judgment Day feared by all sinners, that you never permit these books to be destroyed, or to be rewritten, or to be reproduced in part only with sections omitted, for otherwise when you emerge in confusion from this Judgement Day you will be condemned with the Devil. Keep them in your possession, intact, with no amendments and just as I have left them to you.' Thorpe (1974: 603).

took when he heard Gregory's lectures on the scriptures. Gregory is concerned that the meaning of his words is misrepresented in these notes. Therefore he must recover the writings in order to correct and recover the true sense of what he had originally intended. Gregory's main anxiety does not focus on scribal activities or copying of his writings, but on note taking. He is anxious about the incorrect transmission of his words, because they may provide incorrect interpretation of the scriptures and this is not acceptable.[33]

Ælfric is the first author in English to show a preoccupation with the transmission of his work. He is happy for people to copy his book, but begs for accurate writing 'gerihte be ðære bysene'. He does not wish to be blamed for any mistakes due to careless scribes 'gymelease writeras', albeit correcting mistakes is acceptable. Accurate copying and correct preservations of his words are essential concerns in his concluding remarks and the significance of these sentences can be interpreted in several directions.

They could be understood as an insight on the state of the transmission of texts in the early medieval period. On a superficial level it could be understood that scribes are generally careless in their job and therefore correcting books was extremely important. But Ælfric's directions contextualize a book culture in which variation and differentiation is expected, although uniformity is what an author wishes for. This, of course, implies that preserving an author's words is equivalent to maintaining the true meaning of Ælfric's texts, which ought to be theologically upheld. Checking and correcting copies become an essential process to the recovery of authorial intention. To err in copying a text is to misrepresent, in Ælfric's case, the scriptures for which the author is ultimately accountable. Therefore, it is essential that scribes are aware of the importance of keeping to the author's words. As Swan observed, Ælfric's concluding remarks in his prefaces are 'an assertion of doctrinal rather than authorial identity',[34] which is still an identity to be preserved. In the Latin prefatory remarks to both the first and the second series of the *Catholic Homilies*, Ælfric elects Archbishop Sigeric as his censor. He asks Sigeric to correct any mistakes in the translation from his authority.[35] By doing this, Ælfric is also publishing his own works in what he thinks will be a finished stage. Of course, he will revise his work and issue different editions of the *Catholic Homilies*,[36] but nevertheless he still publishes his work as a complete finished product. Chaucer, despite similar claims

---

[33] 'Furthermore, forasmuch as my late most dear son Claudius had heard me speak something about the Proverbs, the Song of Songs, the Prophets, and also about the Books of Kings and the Heptateuch, which on account of my infirmity I was unable to commit to writing, and he himself had dictated them for transcription according to his own understanding of their meaning, lest they should be forgotten, and in order that he might bring them to me at a suitable time, so that they might be more correctly dictated (for, when he read to me what he had written, I found the sense of what I had said had been altered very disadvantageously), it is hence necessary that your Experience, avoiding all excuse or delay, should go to his monastery, and assemble the brethren, and that they should produce fully and truly whatsoever papers on various Scriptures he had brought thither; which do take, and transmit them to me with all possible speed'; Gregory I (1898: book 12, letter 24).

[34] Swan (2001: 79).   [35] Wilcox (1994: 108, 111).   [36] Clemoes and Eliason (1966).

about scribal attitude towards texts, does not. This is an important issue to bear in mind in our discussion of the 'communication circuit' in medieval textual production.

Scholars have commented on *Adam Scriveyn* on several occasions. The most famous case in the history of manuscript studies was the discovery of Adam Pynkhust, a member of the London scribal community of the fourteenth century, as the possible addressee of the poem.[37] This discovery carries a number of textual and historical implications which still remain to be fully explored.[38] The interpretation of the poem as a piece of literature, however, opens a number of possible investigations. Olson reads it within the context of the 'Book curse' in which 'Chaucer reveals both his independence from scribes—his superiority to them—and his indebtedness to them'.[39] Root places it within the complaint genre.[40] Scattergood follows this suggestion and argues that the poem 'is a complaint by a creative literary artist against the transmitter of his art' and he associates this genre to the complaint literature from twelfth- and thirteenth-century Provence, the *sirventes joglare*. In this literary tradition the poet would complain against jongleurs, who would deliver poems orally without keeping faith to the copy.[41]

It seems clear that as a literary trope Chaucer was not influenced by the writings of the Fathers of the Church, but most probably by a different set of continental influences. Petrarch and the Italian tradition are remarked upon as historical comparative material. In particular the letter regarding the copying of Petrarch's *The Life of Solitude* is often cited.[42] In this letter, Petrarch complains about scribes and their luck of accuracy; he is often vociferous about this by his own admission.[43] He is also generally concerned with the scarcity of copyists and remarks in another letter to a friend that it is almost impossible to find reliable scribes who will transcribe Cicero adequately. He claims that professional scribes satisfactorily trained to copy literary works are hard to come by. Training he recognizes is essential. Having undertaken the task of copying the book himself, he realizes that perhaps the task is too great for him to complete as he is not trained to do this job.[44] Petrarch's dissatisfaction with scribes

---

[37] Mooney (2006).   [38] Da Rold (2007: 409–10); Gillespie (2008).   [39] Olson (2008: 290).
[40] Root (1922: 69–70). See, in particular Root (1913), his early essay on publication of texts before printing. De Bury in his *Philobiblion* talks about 'treacherous scribes' 'Alas! how ye commit us to treacherous copyists to be written, how corruptly ye read us and kill us by medication, while ye supposed ye were correcting us with pious zeal. Oftentimes we have to endure barbarous interpreters, and those who are ignorant of foreign idioms presume to translate us from one language into another; and thus all propriety of speech is lost and our sense is shamefully mutilated contrary to the meaning of the author! Truly noble would have been the condition of books if it had not been for the presumption of the tower of Babel, if but one kind of speech had been transmitted by the whole human race' (de Bury 1907: 32). De Bury is here concerned with the inability of certain scribes to copy ancient texts, because they cannot understand the language. It is not a judgement on scribes in general.
[41] Scattergood (1990: 501); Minnis, Scattergood, and Smith (1995).
[42] Root (1922: 69–70); Scattergood (1990: 501).
[43] Robinson (1898: 27).
[44] 'Your Cicero has been in my possession four years and more. There is a good reason, though, for so long a delay; namely, the great scarcity of copyists who understand such work. It is a state of affairs that has resulted in an incredible loss to scholarship. Books that by their nature are a little hard to understand are no longer multiplied, and have ceased to be generally intelligible, and so have sunk into utter neglect, and in the end have perished . . . But I must return to your Cicero. I could not do without

goes beyond the accuracy of their work. In a letter to Boccaccio, he disapproves of the type of script that scribes adopt. He dislikes their pompous style and points out that a more legible script is preferable.[45]

Petrarch's correspondence tells us the story of an author who is deeply troubled by the state of his text and the quality of his publication. The surviving manuscripts, which are annotated by Petrarch, confirm the view that as an author he was constantly striving for perfection and as a humanist he was a keen annotator and collector.[46]

Unfortunately we do not have the same evidence for Chaucer. Comparing Chaucer to Petrarch's textual practices is unfair; we simply do not have the same textual and manuscript evidence to rely upon. There is no large collection of letters to draw from and most of the textual evidence is incomplete. Chaucer shows similar concerns to Petrarch and Ælfric on the orthodoxy of the texts in his poem to Adam, but it may not be reasonable to take this poem as an example of the relationship between Chaucer and his texts. Chaucer does not constantly plead with his audience to correct his texts as Ælfric and Petrarch do. In *Troilus and Criseyde*, Chaucer expresses a certain concern about the state of his text, but he takes this concern to a different level.

> Go, litel boke, go, litel myn tragedye . . .
> . . . And for ther is so gret diversite
> In Englissh and in writyng of oure tonge,
> So prey I God that non myswrite the,
> Ne the mysmetre for defaute of tonge.
> And red wherso thow be, or elles songe,
> That thow be understonde, God I biseche!
> But yet to purpos of my rather speche:[47]

The appeal here is traditional, as the *Riverside Chaucer* points out.[48] However, there is no criticism towards scribes and their work. Chaucer expresses uneasiness with the linguistic context in which his work will be copied. He talks about a recognized variety in English and thus worries about possible errors which might lead scribes to

it, and the incompetence of the copyists would not let me possess it. What was left for me but to rely upon my own resources, and press these weary fingers and this worn and ragged pen into the service? . . . And yet I must confess that I did finally reach a point in my copying where I was overcome by weariness; not mental, for how unlikely that would be where Cicero was concerned, but the sort of fatigue that springs from excessive manual labour. I began to feel doubtful about this plan that I was following, and to regret having undertaken a task for which I had not been trained . . .'; Robinson (1898: 275–7).

[45] Petrarch talks about a young man who is helping him to compile his letters into a publishable book and comments on his handwriting: 'You will not find the ill-defined though sumptuous penmanship affected by our copyists, or rather painters, of to-day, which delights us at a distance, but, as if invented for any other purpose than to be read, strains and tires the eyes when we look at it intently, thus belying the saying of the prince of grammarians that the word letter comes from *legere*, to read. This youth's characters are, on the contrary, compressed and clear, carrying the eye with them, nor will you discover any faults of orthography or grammatical errors'; Robinson (1898: 151).

[46] Petrucci (1967); Mann (1975).

[47] Benson (1988: ll. 1786–99).   [48] Ibid. (1056).

'myswrite' or 'mysmetre' his book. Chaucer does not talk about incompetent scribes or about scribal practices, but points out that copying a text in a country which speaks and writes in different dialects could be problematic. Chaucer is certainly a poet aware of dialectal variation which he uses for dramatic effect in the *Reeve's Tale*.[49] It is not possible from these textual examples to infer that Chaucer was an author who took the transmission of his texts to heart. Blake commented that: 'All we know about Chaucer himself suggests that he may well have been far more casual about the text of his works than these lines suggest.'[50] Despite recent research[51] on the possibility that National Library of Wales, Aberystwyth, Peniarth 392 D (Hengwrt), and Oxford, Corpus Christi College, 198, could be earlier copies of the *Canterbury Tales* validated by Chaucer, there is no firm evidence that Chaucer published his own works. No surviving manuscripts of Chaucer's work—with the exception of Cambridge, Corpus Christi College 61, containing *Troilus and Criseyde* and dated 1398[52]—are firmly dated to the fourteenth century. No manuscripts survive with Chaucer's own corrections. All this makes it doubtful that Chaucer was interested in the transmission of his texts to the same extent that Ælfric was.

SCRIBES AND AUTHORS

Authors, as we have seen, discuss the copying and transmission of their texts by focusing on the inability of scribes to copy accurately. Scribes do not complain about their authors. Some grumble about their hard job; for example, Hoccleve[53] and others plead for their work to be paid. William Ebesham 'beseeches' Sir John Paston to pay him for his work.[54] The job of a scribe is a hard and unforgiving one, and anonymous in England more than on the Continent. Apart from famous examples, some of which I have mentioned above, most English book production is anonymous, and there are no registered contracts from which we can write a prosopography of scribes in medieval England.[55]

There is also no overall historiography of scribal culture in England during the Middle Ages to help provide an overall picture of the period and many questions still

---

[49] See Blake (1979); Horobin (2001, 2002); Tolkien (1934).   [50] Blake (1998: 65).
[51] Blake (1997); Stubbs (2007).   [52] Seymour (1995).
[53] Knapp (2001); Burrow and Doyle (2002).   [54] Davis (1971).
[55] In Bologna 'writing contracts' were registered with the city authority, this type of evidence has provided precious information on the type of copyist, their training, the type of work they were copying, their identity and their clientele, and of course the time spent copying books (Murano 2006); a similar study has appeared for 15th-cent. Rome (Caldelli 2006). On occasions we stumble upon precentors' accounts on the expenses incurred in producing books in monasteries and cathedrals, e.g. from Ely (Gullick 1985) and Norwich (Ker 1949–53), but these are exceptions rather than the rule and more work needs to be done in this field. Despite the lack of information on English scribes, numerous scholars have published on anonymous or named scribes; for an overview see Moffat and McCarren (1998: 54–7); Parkes (2008); Thomson (2006).

remain to be answered. How can we find out more about these scribes? Is it correct to use the term 'scribe' to talk about those individuals who help perpetuate medieval manuscript culture? Who are these individuals? Richard de Bury writes, 'we had always in our different manors no small multitude of copyists and scribes, of binders, correctors, illuminators, and generally of all who could usefully labour in the service of books'.[56] How does his notion of people who produced books fit our own understanding? Can we talk about scribes, copyists, clerks, scriveners, monks, notaries, school masters, or scholars? Crucially for our discussion, what type of relationship do these copyists establish with the author they copy? What is their role in the communication circuit? The answers are not easy to find, but they must be asked. Information is often fragmentary; however, by looking closely at the evidence that manuscripts reveal, we can advance some suggestions. Those individuals who copied Ælfric and Chaucer are not, however, uniformly distributed in localizable spaces despite recognizable patterns.

Scribes and Ælfric

Clemoes in his introduction to the EETS edition of Ælfric's first series of *Catholic Homilies* has demonstrated how a close analysis of the manuscripts which survive can offer interesting evidence for the state of the text, the stages of its development, and tentative information about the localization of the manuscripts.[57] According to Clemoes, the extant copies of the *Catholic Homilies* descend from manuscripts written in Ælfric's scriptorium at Cerne; for instance, London, British Library, Royal 7 C.xii and at least three other copies including the manuscript prepared for Archbishop Sigeric. These are the origin of the tradition. From this origin Clemoes reconstructed six main phases in the development of Ælfric's text. Using a stemmatic approach, he was also able to re-enact the manuscripts' evidence for each phase, explaining the existence of missing witnesses and their influence on the existing evidence. His explanation of the movement of the exemplars in relationship to localizable religious institutions places a great emphasis on Canterbury, the West Midlands and Worcester, Rochester and Exeter. Canterbury, according to Clemoes, has an important function in the dissemination of Ælfric's text. For example, Cambridge, Corpus Christi College 162, pp. 1–38 and 161–564, and Cambridge, Trinity College B.15.34 were probably written there. Worcester has also a significant role in the distribution of the first series of the *Catholic Homilies* in the West Midlands. This confirms the relationship between Ælfric and Wulfstan, as corroborated in surviving letters, that Ælfric may have sent material to Worcester.[58] Examples of manuscripts

---

[56] De Bury (1907).   [57] Clemoes (1997: 64–168).
[58] See Hill (1994); Treharne (2007).

localized to the West Midlands are, for instance, Oxford, Bodleian Library, Hatton 116, and Oxford, Bodleian Library, Bodley 343. Other manuscripts which have strong connections to Worcester are Cambridge, Corpus Christi College 178, pp. 1–270, and Cambridge, Corpus Christi College 162, pp. 139–60; Oxford, Bodleian Library, Hatton 113 and 114 and Junius 121. Rochester, however, also seems to have received material from the first series of the *Catholic Homilies* for Cambridge, Corpus Christi College 303, and Oxford, Bodleian Library, Bodley 340 and 342 are localizable to this Benedictine cathedral. Ælfric's text also travels south to Exeter, since the distinctive hand of Leofric's scriptorium is recognizable in London, British Library, Cotton Cleopatra B. xii and London, Lambeth Palace 489.[59] This is just a sketchy summary of the intricate relationships that Clemoes has traced in his introduction and by his admission evidence does not seem to suggest the assignment of manuscripts to other religious institutions.[60]

The communication circuit for the transmission of Ælfric's first series of the *Catholic Homilies* needs further analysis. Swan questions 'Worcester's centripetal force' which 'seems to function as the default location for modern scholars wishing to identify a West Midlands place of production for a given manuscript'.[61] Treharne has demonstrated that bishops such as Wulfstan and Leofric 'seem to have placed very great importance on acquiring vernacular religious materials for the successful completion of their own duties'.[62] Therefore, on the one hand, there is a desire amongst scholars to find recognizable patterns to write secure histories, and on the other important agencies influence the production of manuscripts to shape their own agenda. Thus we have the fragmentation of text and the deliberate adaptation of a text to create a new work. The main protagonists of this process are the individuals who write the text. Unfortunately this type of relationship is missing from textual histories, and the study of the manufacture of the medieval book, which will help us to understand the process of the making of the book, has not been fully investigated.

The very important work by Clemoes has advanced our knowledge of the textual transmission of Ælfric's homilies by looking to establish a stemmatic relationship between manuscripts based on the study of significant variations. This work has helped us to understand how one text relates to another and consequently editors are able to establish a scholarly edition which we all use as a point of reference all the time. This valuable approach opens a number of other questions about things which affect a text's interpretation. Scribes not only wrote down a text, they mapped the text onto the page. How did they do this? What comprised the exemplar? What did the text in front of them look like? How did texts circulate physically: in books or in codicological units? After the influential work by Pamela Robinson, the concept of booklets has been widely accepted and, indeed, there is some evidence of this practice.[63] However, by looking at the textual tradition of Ælfric's works what is remarkable is the fragmentation of the collections. A glance at the 'Manuscript

---

[59] For an overview on Leofric's scriptorium see Treharne (2003, 2007).
[60] Clemoes (1997: 168).   [61] Swan (2007: 30).
[62] Treharne (2007: 27).   [63] Robinson (1980).

distribution of individual homilies' in Clemoes's edition of the *Catholic Homilies* shows that there is very little manuscript evidence for booklets, and, yet, there is also no concept of consistent textual unity beyond Royal 7 c.xii. The manuscript tradition of this text is made up of several different parts, but no diachronic or even synchronic textual unity is apparent. It is therefore important to understand how the scribe conceives his work on the manuscript page. This question can be answered only by remapping the text to the smallest codicological unit—the quire. I will now try to explain what I mean and suggest a new methodology to look at the making of the book and the mapping of the text.

Mapping the Text

Cambridge University Library Ii.1.33 contains a collection of Ælfric's homilies and saints' lives. It also includes other penitential material: three anonymous texts and a translation of Alcuin's *De uirtutibus et uitiis*, chapters 1–13. Several items have interlineata and marginalia in English, Latin, and French. It was copied by two scribes during the second half of the twelfth century. The manuscript has been associated with Christ Church Canterbury and Ely.[64] Clemoes describes the manuscript as:

A collection mainly of saints' narrative taken from CH I and II and Ælfric's Lives of Saints, not ordered according to the sequence of the church year, but not without some features of arrangement: a Christmas homily (CH I. II) heads the main run of contents (if we take that to begin with the fifth quire . . .); then follow items concerning St Æthelthryth and St Benedic; the (after a loss of unknown extent) a run of items (twelve in Ker's numbering) concerned with apostles. The different origins of the texts seem to have had an influence on the order.[65]

Codicologically the manuscript combines various quiring, ruling, and pricking techniques some of which are characteristic of the late twelfth century. The manuscript offers an irregular make-up of the sequence of the quires, with gaps and codicological incongruities, which demonstrate that the manuscript was assembled over time.

Scribe 1 prepares quires 6 and 15, folios 37–120^v, with no indication of quire boundaries in quires 6 and 7. However, he regularly signs his quires from .i. to .viii. and these correspond to quires 8 to 15 (folios 53–120^v). Scribe 2 copies folios 2–36^v and 120^v–227^v using a mixed quiring technique: catchwords and signatures in quires 1–5, but catchwords only in quires 16–27. This scribe also copied Cambridge, Corpus Christi College 367.[66] It is likely that those quires that now make up the beginning of

---

[64] For a description of the manuscript and an overview of the literature, see Da Rold (2007).
[65] Clemoes (1997: 25–6).   [66] Treharne (2003).

the manuscript were not the initial ones, but were moved to their present position when the manuscript was rebound in the sixteenth century. Although it is not possible to say which quire was the first one, the possible candidate is quire 5. The thirteenth/fourteenth-century note on the top margin on folio 29[r]. commenting on the nature of the language of the texts in the manuscript, may suggest that once the manuscript started with this folio.[67]

The layout and the ruling of the quires are irregular. Scribe 2 alternates techniques, and the ruling symmetry is often out of sequence; the alternation between double and single and single and double bounding lines appears on the 'wrong side of the frame'. Scribe 1 uses a varying technique, and the double pricking of the ruling of the lines in the final quires of the manuscript is the same as the one used on Cambridge, Corpus Christi College 367, and this suggests that this was a technique used by the scribe himself.

The scribes who copied this book seem to have difficulties in mapping the text onto the quires and then in assembling the book itself. Looking at the manuscript diagrammatically,[68] it seems clear that the two scribes did not conceive of the book as a uniform textual unit. Quire 5, which is usually considered the first one in the sequence of 26, could easily be a self-contained unit, copied by scribe 2 and then inserted in Ii.1.33. It starts on folio 29[r] with Ælfric's *Catholic Homilies*, first series, II, *Christmas Day* and finishes at folio 36[v] with Ælfric's *Lives of Saints*, XX, *St Æthelthryth*. There are no signatures or catchwords, which may connect this quire to the rest of the manuscript. A diagram also shows that these two scribes are skilful book makers. They use a specific way of mapping the text to the quires and to add or replace text *ad infinitum*. Quire 10, which sits well into the sequence created by scribe 2, is signed .iii. and has been expanded by adding four half sheets: folios 71, 72, 73, 75. This expansion allows for Ælfric's *Catholic Homilies*, first series, IV, *St John* to be inserted with only three final lines running onto folio 79[r] (the beginning of quire 11). Similar examples can be found in quires 1, 20, and 26. It seems obvious that the codicology of this manuscript begs a number of questions; for instance, how did scribes 1 and 2 obtain their exemplars and from where did they come. It also makes one wonder about the use of this book and who these scribes were. The number of revisions in the manuscript gives the impression of scribes who were also scholars. Their annotations have clear functions; they may correct, clarify, or augment the item under discussion.[69] But as well as scholars they were book makers. They collaborated to give uniformity to a collection of texts which did not appear as such, and thus the care in compiling the book compensates for the fragmentary nature of the text.

---

[67] Traxel (2004: 131–4).
[68] For a diagram of the manuscript see Da Rold (2007).
[69] Da Rold and Swan (forthcoming).

SCRIBES AND CHAUCER

Chaucer's texts survive in a large number of manuscripts. A perusal of catalogues shows up to about 150 artefacts, which were produced from the end of the fourteenth century to the end of the fifteenth century.[70] The production of Chaucer's books is mainly a fifteenth-century phenomenon and some of the scribes who contributed to the dissemination and transmission of these manuscripts are well known. The Hammond scribe,[71] the 'hooked-g' scribe,[72] the scribe of HM 114,[73] scribe D,[74] John Shirley,[75] and Adam Pinkhurst[76] are some of the most famous examples. They all contributed to the copying of Chaucer's texts, and to their publishing. They may have responded to the text they read, changing and altering what they had in front of them, as Windeatt demonstrates working on the manuscripts of *Troylus*.[77] However, in many instances they were just trying to get their job done and a close look at the *Canterbury Tales* will help to expound this point.

The *Canterbury Tales* is a complicated text. A major problem about its tradition is what constitutes the text. The poem is unfinished, and in each manuscript there are discrepancies in the number of *Tales*, their order, and their text. Therefore, what constitutes the complete poem is arbitrary and is left to the judgement of each editor.[78] Some manuscripts contain Chaucer's 'Retraction', in which the poet takes his leave from the reader and repents for some of his writings: 'Thilke that sownen into synne'.[79] Thus an argument can be made that Chaucer had finished with this poem. Indeed, we read the Benson's edition of the *Canterbury Tales* and accept that both the content and the order of the tales reflect what Chaucer's had intended.

The crux is the authorial order of the text, which is an ongoing debate amongst critics and of great importance to editors. On the one hand, scholars such as Manly and Rickert[80] believe that Chaucer cannot be held responsible for any of the arrangements extant in the manuscript tradition. On the other hand, scholars argue that not only did Chaucer have a plan, which he changed over time, but also his intentions are possible to detect from the text. Geographical and temporal references within the tales and links have been used as an argument to support these hypotheses.[81] Benson argues that Chaucer completed the *Canterbury Tales* and set an order to the text, although the poem is unfinished.[82] Blake opposes this view and points out that Chaucer started to arrange some sections of the poem, but died

[70] Seymour (1995, 1997); Manly and Rickert (1940); Boffey and Edwards (2005).
[71] Mooney (1996); (2000, 2001). [72] Horobin (1998).
[73] Hanna (1989). [74] Doyle and Parkes (1978).
[75] Connolly (1998). [76] Mooney (2006).
[77] Windeatt (1979). [78] Ruggiers (1984).
[79] Benson (1988). [80] Manly and Rickert (1940: ii. 475).
[81] This was the main argument ever after Furnivall's *Preface* (Furnivall 1868). The literature is vast and the debate is still open. For an overview see also Pratt (1951), Donaldson (1970), Cohen (1974–5), and Owen (1977).
[82] Benson (1981).

before finishing the poem. Chaucer's 'retraction' cannot be used as proof that Chaucer had done with the poem.[83]

There is no easy solution to this debate, because unlike Ælfric there is no extant manuscript from which we can deduce authorial intention. In fact there is now a well-established belief amongst scholars that no extant manuscripts of the *Canterbury Tales* can be dated to before Chaucer's death, although pre-circulation of booklets may have been possible and this would explain the highly fragmented textual tradition of the poem.[84] Different views and tentative arguments have been put forward that Chaucer was involved in the production of Aberystwyth, National Library of Wales, Peniarth 392 D (Hengwrt); perhaps Oxford, Corpus Christi College 198 (Corpus) was also a very early copy datable to pre-1400.[85] The order of these two manuscripts is not regarded as the 'best order' for it seems to be recognized that California, San Marino, Huntington Library, El. 26 C 9 (Ellesmere) contains the most authoritative sequence of text. This sequence is referred to as the *a*-El order. As Pratt suggests this order reflects Chaucer's arrangement of his pile of papers: 'The scribe of El and *a* knew the authentic "Chaucerian" tradition of the order of the tales, slightly damaged (presumably in 1400) by the accidental misplacement of Fragment VII.'[86] Benson subsequently supported this theory arguing that only Chaucer could have arranged the *Tales* in this way: 'The creator of the Type *a* order had an intimate knowledge of the contents of the tales, by which he knew that D, E, and F came in that order.'[87] Cooper agrees, but concludes:

Whoever put the various exemplars of the tales, links, and fragments in order for Ellesmere did not have any manuscript consensus to work from, and indeed, they have helped create such consensus as there is . . . and the end result is more likely than any other to represent Chaucer's own scheme . . . The Ellesmere order may not be fully authorial; it mirrors the unfinished state of the work and so can be no better than provisional.[88]

Cooper's observation brings the scribe into the foreground of our discussion. Scholars have commented extensively on the role of the scribes in establishing the order of Chaucer's *Canterbury Tales*, and have particularly argued that the *a*-Ellesmere arrangement is a development of the Hengwrt order, after scribes realized that certain parts could have been misplaced.[89] Textual discrepancies in the copying of the *Canterbury Tales* are frequently commented upon and this is how traditionally the textual affiliation of the poem has been studied.[90]

There has not been enough effort to understand how the manuscripts of this tradition are actually copied and what this process will reveal about the ability of scribes to do their job. A close look at the manuscript tradition reveals that all manuscripts carried uncertainties and codicological ambiguities. The earliest exemplars show just how difficult it is for scribes to copy texts which do not seem to be available in one complete version. Scribes' ingenuity as book makers is challenged,

---

[83] Blake (1985*b*).   [84] Manly and Rickert (1940); Owen (1991).
[85] Hanna (1989); Blake (1997); Stubbs (2007).   [86] Pratt (1951: 1165).
[87] Benson (1981: 111).   [88] Cooper (1995: 257).
[89] Dempster (1949); Blake (1985*a*).   [90] Manly and Rickert (1940); Blake (1985).

but often with rather interesting results. Recent research has shown that scribes had to work with uneven numbers of quires, correct the sequence of the text by replacing paper or parchment, and look for exemplars which were not always readily available. Stubbs highlights that the scribe who copied Corpus, known as scribe D, does not have access to a uniform type of parchment while preparing the manuscript. Quires 8, 11, 12, and 13, for example, are made up of heavy parchment in their outer leaves—a different type of membrane from the one which makes up the majority of the quires. Quire 26 is not made up of four bifolia, as would be most common, but four single leaves have been inserted to contain *Pardoner's Prologue* and part of his *Tale* (VI. 329–968 (C)).[91] The luxurious and apparently smoothly produced Ellesmere also contains a number of codicological incongruities on those leaves which contain the same text. Similar difficulties in Ellesmere are also particularly evident in those texts which link, for instance, *Lenvoye de Chaucer* (IV. 1170–1212 (E)) to the Clerk's End-Link (IV. 1212a–g (E)).[92]

The Hengwrt manuscript, which is copied by the same scribe who copied Ellesmere, the now famous Adam Pinkhurst, also contains a number of quires which are made up of uneven leaves. For instance, quires 6 and 7 which contain the 'Miller's Tale' (I. 3187–3720 (A)) are created by a single bifolium and three bifolia respectively.[93] This text is traditionally considered a stable text within Fragment I of the *Canterbury Tales*. It is therefore interesting to see that the quires are so small. Hanna explains this anomaly by suggesting that Hengwrt is built by a series of booklets bound together.[94] This anomaly, however, is present in another early manuscript, Cambridge University Library Dd 4.24 (Dd). Dd is dated to the first decades of the fifteenth century, and the scribe who copied it, known as Wytton, has a similar problem to Adam and scribe D with the sequence of the text. Wytton replaced a leaf in quire 5 to adjust the sequence from the *Clerk's Tale* to the *Merchant's Tale* and shows hesitation in the organization of his work in several other quires.[95] Estelle Stubbs has eloquently demonstrated that 'Scribe D's work in Corpus appears closely linked with Adam's copying of Hengwrt, and Harley 4 and Ellesmere share codicological irregularities in some places which are difficult to account for unless each scribe was acquiring material and information at more or less the same time'.[96] Moreover, Wytton was most probably working close to them too.[97]

What these scribes did to the physical arrangement of the manuscripts can be interpreted in two ways: it can be argued that scribes were not skilful copyists and made mistakes in copying the sequences of text, then had to emend their errors by substituting leaves and correcting the content of the text. However, the consistent replacements of material at crucial points in the textual sequence, the absence of mistakes in other codicological units, and the professional approach to the writing of the text argue against this hypothesis. These early scribes of Chaucer's texts were skilful book makers, who were trained not only in the art of writing

[91] Stubbs (2007).   [92] Stubbs (2006).
[93] Doyle and Parkes (1979); Stubbs (2000).   [94] Hanna (1989).
[95] Da Rold (2003).   [96] Stubbs (2007: 133).   [97] Da Rold (2007).

books, but also in making them. They understood how to map the text they were given onto a page and a quire. They could acquire exemplars and could make corrections to their sequence fairly easily and they must have worked in an environment which was conducive to developing this type of relationship. Adam Pinkhurst, a Londoner, was well connected with the administration of the City and the London Guilds. Chaucer was not just a Londoner, he was also a public servant and as such I would not doubt that he met a number of scribes who could have easily been supplied with the material he wrote. Adam, Scribe D, Wytton, and many others are probably part of the same 'communication circuit' to which Chaucer belongs.

Clemoes in establishing his textual relationship for the manuscripts of Ælfric's *Catholic Homilies* was able to trace possible connections between manuscripts and places of production. No work such as this has been thoroughly done for Chaucer and the manuscripts of his works. Scholars, with a few exceptions,[98] have been generally preoccupied with the debate about the recovery of Chaucer's authorial intention, but after the discovery of Adam, it may just be possible to start thinking about scribes and their role in the dissemination of Chaucer's works within specific production milieux. It is accepted that the interplay between the circulation of Chaucer's text and these scribes is not always clear. But new research is now under way by Estelle Stubbs, Simon Horobin, and Linne Mooney on an AHRC-funded research project 'The identification of the scribes responsible for copying major works of Middle English literature', which, no doubt, will assist in furthering our knowledge on the manuscript 'communication circuit' in the late medieval period.

CONCLUSIONS

The aim of this article has been to demonstrate and discuss how the process of copying and transmission of medieval texts is influenced by a variety of forces. The hermeneutic approach to the relationship between authors and scribes has demonstrated that comments on textual variations and preservation of authorial intention are a trope which is very common in medieval literature. This is often associated with the anxiety of the author to be perceived as writing the 'truth'. Both Ælfric and Chaucer share the same anxieties regarding scribes, but they are part of a different book culture. The relationship of the scribes with their texts is, however, similar and different at the same time. As Gillespie argues there is a very close relationship between form and meaning: 'The very word "book" in the Middle Ages recognizes the interesting ways in which the voice of the text and the shape of the object that bears it are involved in the production of meaning.'[99] Ælfric's text was to be

---

[98] Hanna (1995).   [99] Gillespie (2007: 276).

fragmented by scribes almost immediately after its creation, and within a culture which perhaps required his text, but not as a single unit. The text did not have a function as a whole, but it became part of many others because of the real or projected use of these texts. Eleventh- and twelfth-century scribes developed practical techniques to create composite manuscripts with textual units which would fit their use.

Chaucer's text, meanwhile, was unfinished and fragmented; scribes used similar techniques to the early medieval copyists to put these fragments together to make the *Canterbury Tales* a finished work. It is still debatable whether this finished work is actually finished, but they tried to make the text on the page look as polished as possible. In this article I have not discussed the role of many other manuscripts that constitute the earlier and the later manuscript culture of the Middle Ages. Indeed, more work is needed on the association of these specific examples within the wider book culture for other known and anonymous authors across the Middle Ages, so that Darton's communication circuit can be suitably applied, modified, and understood for the history of the medieval book and its literary milieux.

BIBLIOGRAPHY

BEIT-ARIÉ, MALACHI (1992), 'Trasmission de textes par scribes et copistes: Interférences inconscientes et critiques', in J. Hamesse (ed.), *Les Problèmes posés par l'édition critique des textes anciens et medievaux* (Louvain-la-Neuve: Universite Catholique de Louvain).

BENSON, LARRY D. (1981), 'The Order of the *Canterbury Tales*', *Studies in the Age of Chaucer*, 3: 77–120.

——(ed.) (1988), *The Riverside Chaucer* (Oxford: Oxford University Press).

BLAKE, N. F. (1979), 'The Northernisms in "The Reeve's Tale"', *Lore and Language*, 3: 1–8.

——(1985a), 'The Debate on the Order of the *Canterbury Tales*', *Revista Canaria de Studios Ingleses*, 10: 31–41.

——(1985b), *The Textual Tradition of the 'Canterbury Tales'* (London: Edward Arnold).

——(1997), 'Geoffrey Chaucer and the Manuscripts of the *Canterbury Tales*', *Journal of the Early Book Society for the Study of Manuscripts and Printing*, 1: 95–122.

——(1998), 'Reflections on the Editing of Middle English Texts', in V. P. McCarren and D. Moffat (eds.), *A Guide to Editing Middle English* (Ann Arbor: University of Michigan Press).

BOFFEY, JULIA, and A. S. G. EDWARDS (2005), *A New Index of Middle English Verse* (London: British Library).

BOWERS, FREDSON (1975), *Essays in Bibliography, Text, and Editing* (Charlottesville, Va.: published for the Bibliographical Society of the University of Virginia by the University Press of Virginia).

——(1994), *Principles of Bibliographical Description*, introd. by G. Thomas Tanselle (Winchester: St Paul's Bibliographies; New Castle, Del.: Oak Knoall Press).

BURROW, J. A., and A. I. DOYLE (eds.) (2002), *Thomas Hoccleve: A Facsimile of the Autograph Verse Manuscripts* (EETS SS 19; Oxford: Oxford University Press).

DE BURY, RICHARD (1907), *The Love of Books, the Philobiblon, of Richard de Bury,* tr. E. C. Thomas (London: Chatto & Windus).

CALDELLI, ELISABETTA (2006), *Copisti a Roma nel Quattrocento* (Scritture e libri del medioevo, 4; Roma: Viella).

CERQUIGLINI, BERNARD (1989), *Éloge de la variante: Histoire critique de la philologie* (Paris: Seuil).

CLEMOES, PETER (ed.) (1997), *Ælfric's Catholic Homilies: The First Series. Text* (EETS SS 17; London: Published for the EETS by the Oxford University Press).

——and NORMAN ELLSWORTH ELIASON (eds.) (1966), *Ælfric's First Series of Catholic Homilies: British Museum, Royal 7.C.XII, fols. 4–218. Early English Manuscripts in Facsimile* (Copenhagen: Rosenkilde & Bagger).

COHEN, E. S. (1974), 'The Sequence of the Canterbury Tales', *Chaucer Review,* 9: 190–5.

COLE, GAVIN (forthcoming), 'The Criticism of Middle English Textual Traditions', *Literature Compass* (2009).

CONNOLLY, MARGARET (1998), *John Shirley: Book Production and the Noble Household in Fifteenth-Century England* (Aldershot and Brookfield, Vt.: Ashgate).

DA ROLD, ORIETTA (2003), 'The Quiring System in Cambridge University Library MS Dd.4.24 of Chaucer's *Canterbury Tales', The Library,* 4(2): 107–28.

——(2006), 'English Manuscripts 1060 to 1220 and the Making of a Re-source', *Literature Compass,* 3: 750–66.

——(2007), 'Homilies and Lives of Saints: Cambridge, University Library, Ii. 1. 33', *The Production and Use of English Manuscripts 1060 to 1220,* http://www.le.ac.uk/english/em1060to1220/mss/CUL.Ii.1.33.htm.

——(2007), 'The Significance of Scribal Corrections in Cambridge University Library, MS Dd.4.24', *Chaucer Review,* 41: 393–436.

——and MARY SWAN (forthcoming), 'Linguistic Contiguities: English Manuscripts 1060–1220', in E. Tyler (ed.), *Conceptualizing Multilingualism in England, 800–1250* (Turnhout: Brepols).

DARTON, ROBERT (2002), 'What is the History of Books?', in D. Finkelstein and A. McCleery (eds.), *The Book History Reader* (London: Routledge; 1st publ. *Daedalus* (Summer 1982), 65–83).

DAVIS, NORMAN (1971), *Paston Letters and Papers of the Fifteenth Century, in Three Parts* (Oxford: Clarendon Press).

DONALDSON, E. T. (1970), 'The Ordering of the Canterbury Tales', in B. A. Rosenberg and J. Mandel (eds.), *Medieval Literature and Folklore Studies: Essays in Honor of Francis Lee Utley* (New Brunswick, NJ: Rutgers University Press).

DOYLE, A. I., and M. B. PARKES (1979), 'A Paleographical Introduction', in P. G. Ruggiers (ed.), *The Canterbury Tales: A Facsimile and Transcription of the Hengwrt Manuscript with Variants from the Ellesmere Manuscript* (Norman, Okla.: University of Oklahoma Press).

——and ——(1978), 'The Production of Copies of the "Canterbury Tales" and the "Confessio Amantis" in the Early Fifteenth Century', in M. B. Parkes and A. G. Watson (eds.), *Medieval Scribes, Manuscripts and Libraries: Essays Presented to N. R. Ker* (London: Scolar Press).

EDWARDS, A. S. G. (1987), 'Observations on the History of Middle English Editing', in D. PEARSALL (ed.), *Manuscripts and Texts: Editorial Problems in Later Middle English Literature. Essays from the 1985 Conference at the University of York* (Cambridge: D. S. Brewer).

FRANK, ROBERTA (ed.) (1993), *The Politics of Editing Medieval Texts: Papers Given at the Twenty-Seventh Annual Conference on Editorial Problems, University of Toronto, 1–2 November 1991* (New York: AMS Press).

FURNIVALL, FREDERICK JAMES (ed.) (1868), *A temporary preface to the six-text ed. of Chaucer's Canterbury Tales, part 1. Attempting to show the true order of the tales, and the days and stages of the pilgrimage, etc. etc.* (Publications of the Chaucer Society, 2nd ser. 3; London: N. Trubuner & Co. for the Chaucer Society).

GASKELL, PHILIP (1972), *A New Introduction to Bibliography* (Oxford: Oxford University Press).

GILLESPIE, ALEXANDRA (2007), 'The History of the Book', in D. Lawton, W. Scase, and R. COPELAND (eds.), *New Medieval Literatures*, 9 (Turnhout: Brepols), 245–86.

——(2008), 'Reading Chaucer's Words to Adam', *Chaucer Review*, 42: 269–83.

GREETHAM, D. C. (1994), *Textual Scholarship: An Introduction* (New York and London: Garland Publishing).

Gregorius, Bishop of Tours (1885), 'Gregorii Turonensis Opera', in W. Arndt, B. Krusch, and M. Bonnet (eds.), *Monumenta Germaniae historica: Scriptorum rerum Merovingicarum*, 1 (Hanover: Impensis bibliopolii Hahniani).

GREGORY I, POPE (1898), 'Selected Epistles of Gregory the Great', trans. J. Barmby, *A Select Library of Nicene and Post-Nicene Fathers of the Christian Church*, 2nd ser., XIII (Oxford: James Parker & Co.).

GRIFFITHS, JEREMY, and DEREK PEARSALL (eds.) (1989), *Book Production and Publishing in Britain 1375–1475* (Cambridge: Cambridge University Press).

GULLICK, MICHAEL (1985), *Extracts from The Precentors' Accounts Concerning Books and Bookmaking of Ely Cathedral Priory* (Hitchin: Camberwell Press; London: Red Gull Press).

HANNA, RALPH (1989), 'The Hengwrt Manuscript and the Canon of the "Canterbury Tales"', *English Manuscript Studies 1100–1700*, 1: 64–84.

——(1989), 'The Scribe of Huntington HM 114', *Studies in Bibliography*, 42: 120–33.

——(1991), 'Presenting Chaucer as Author', in T. W. Machan (ed.), *Medieval Literature: Texts and Interpretation* (Binghamton, NY: Medieval and Renaissance Texts & Studies).

——(1995), '(The) Editing (of) the Ellesmere Text', in M. Stevens and D. Woodward (eds.), *The Ellesmere Chaucer: Essays in Interpretation* (San Marino, Calif.: Huntington Library).

——(2001), 'Analytical Survey 4: Middle English Manuscripts and the Study of Literature', in R. Copeland, D. A. Lawton, and W. Scase (eds.), *New Medieval Literatures*, 4 (Oxford: Clarendon Press), 243–64.

——(2004), 'Middle English Books and Middle English Literary History', *Modern Philology*, 102: 157–78.

HILL, JOYCE (1994), 'Ælfric, Authorial Identity and the Changing Text', in D. G. Scragg and P. E. Szarmach (eds.), *The Editing of Old English: Papers from the 1990 Manchester Conference* (Woodbridge and New York: D. S. Brewer).

——(1997), 'The Preservation and Transmission of Ælfric's Saints' Lives: Reader-Reception and Reader-Response in the Early Middle Ages', in P. E. Szarmach and J. T. Rosenthal (eds.), *The Preservation and Transmission of Anglo-Saxon Culture: Selected Papers from the 1991 Meeting of the International Society of Anglo-Saxonists* (Studies in Medieval Culture, 40; Kalamazoo, Mich.: Medieval Institute Publications, Western Michigan University), 405–30.

——(2003), 'Translating the Tradition: Manuscripts, Models and Methodologies in the Composition of Ælfric's Catholic Homilies' in D. G. Scragg (ed.), *Textual and Material Culture in Anglo-Saxon England* (Woodbridge: D. S. Brewer), 241–59.

HOROBIN, SIMON (1998), 'The "Hooked G" Scribe and his Work in Three Manuscripts of the Canterbury Tales', *Neuphilologische Mitteilungen*, 99: 411–17.

——(2001), 'J. R. R. Tolkien as a Philologist: A Reconsideration of the Northernisms in Chaucer's Reeve's Tale', *English Studies*, 82: 97–105.

——(2002), 'Chaucer's Norfolk Reeve', *Neophilologus*, 86: 609–12.

JAUSS, HANS ROBERT (1982), *Toward an Aesthetic of Reception* (Brighton: Harvester).

KEEFER, SARAH LARRATT, and KATHERINE O'BRIEN O'KEEFFE (1998), *New Approaches to Editing Old English Verse* (Woodbridge: D. S. Brewer).

KER, N. R. (1949–53), 'Medieval Manuscripts from Norwich Cathedral Priory', *Transaction of Cambridge Bibliographical Society*, 1: 1–28.

KNAPP, ETHAM (2001), *The Bureaucratic Muse: Thomas Hoccleve and the Literature of the Late Medieval Period* (Pennsylvania: Pennsylvania University Press).

LAPIDGE, MICHAEL (2003), 'Textual Criticism and the Literature of Anglo-Saxon England', in D. G. Scragg (ed.), *Textual and Material Culture in Anglo-Saxon England* (Woodbridge: D. S. Brewer).

LERER, SETH (1996), *Readings from the Margins: Textual Studies, Chaucer, and Medieval Literature* (San Marino, Calif.: Huntington Library Press).

MCCARREN, VINCENT P., and DOUGLAS MOFFAT (eds.) (1998), *A Guide to Editing Middle English* (Ann Arbor: University of Michigan Press).

MACHAN, TIM WILLIAM (1994), *Textual Criticism and Middle English Texts* (Charlottesville, Va., and London: University Press of Virginia).

——(ed.) (1991), *Medieval Literature: Texts and Interpretation* (Binghamton, NY: Medieval and Renaissance Texts and Studies).

MCKERROW, RONALD (1927), *An Introduction to Bibliography for Literary Students* (Oxford: Clarendon Press).

MANIACI, MARILENA, CARLO FEDERICI, and EZIO ORNATO (2002), *Archeologia del manoscritto: Metodi, problemi, bibliografia recente* (Rome: Viella).

MANLY, JOHN MATTHEWS, and EDITH RICKERT (eds.) (1940), *The Text of the Canterbury Tales: Studied on the Basis of All Known Manuscripts* (8 vols. Chicago: University of Chicago Press).

MANN, NICHOLAS (1975), *Petrarch Manuscripts in the British Isles: Censimento dei codici petrarcheschi* (Padua: Antenore).

MIGNE, J. P. (1844–55 and 1862–5), *Patrologiae Latina* (217 vols. Paris: Migne).

MILLET, BELLA (2002), 'What is Mouvance?', *Wessex Parallel WebTexts project*, http://www.soton.ac.uk/~wpwt/mouvance/mouvance.htm.

MINNIS, A. J., V. J. SCATTERGOOD, and J. J. SMITH (1995), *Oxford Guides to Chaucer: The Shorter Poems* (Oxford: Clarendon Press).

MIZE, BRITT (2001), 'Adam, And Chaucer's Words unto Him', *Chaucer Review*, 35: 351–77.

MOFFAT, DOUGLAS, and VINCENT P. MCCARREN (1998), 'A Bibliographical Essay on Editing Methods and Authorial and Scribal Intention', in V. P. McCarren and D. Moffat (eds.), *A Guide to Editing Middle English* (Ann Arbor: University of Michigan Press), 25–60.

MOONEY, L. R. (1996), 'More Manuscripts Written by a Chaucer Scribe', *Chaucer Review*, 30: 401–7.

——(2000), 'A New Manuscript by the Hammond Scribe: Discovered by Jeremy Griffiths', in A. S. G. Edwards, V. Gillespie, and R. I. Hanna (eds.), *The English Medieval Book: Studies in Memory of Jeremy Griffiths* (London: British Library), 113–23.

——(2001), 'Scribes and Booklets of Trinity College, Cambridge, MSS R.3.19 and R.3.21', in A. J. Minnis (ed.), *Middle English Poetry: Texts and Traditions. Essays in Honour of Derek Pearsall* (Woodbridge: York Medieval Press), 241–66.

——(2006), 'Chaucer's Scribe', *Speculum*, 81: 96–138.

MORGAN, NIGEL J., and RODNEY M. THOMSON (eds.) (2008), *The Cambridge History of the Book in Britain* (Cambridge: Cambridge University Press).

MURANO, GIOVANNA (2006), *Copisti a Bologna (1265–1270)* (Turnhout: Brepols).

OLSON, GLENDING (2008), 'Author, Scribe, and Curse: The Genre of Adam Scriveyn', *Chaucer Review*, 42: 284–97.

OWEN, CHARLES A., JR. (1977), *Pilgrimage and Storytelling in the Canterbury Tales: The Dialectic of 'Ernest' and 'Game'* (Norman, Okla.: University of Oklahoma Press).

——(1991), *The Manuscripts of the Canterbury Tales* (Chaucer Studies, 17; Cambridge: D. S. Brewer).

PARKES, M. B. (2008), *Their Hands Before our Eyes: A Closer Look at Scribes. The Lyell Lectures Delivered in the University of Oxford, 1999* (Aldershot: Ashgate).

PEARSALL, D. (1994), 'Theory and Practice in Middle English Editing', *Text*, 7: 107–27.

PETRUCCI, A. (1967), *La scrittura di Francesco Petrarca* (Vatican City: Biblioteca Apostolica Vaticana).

PRATT, ROBERT A. (1951), 'The Order of the Canterbury Tales', *PMLA* 66: 1141–67.

REYNOLDS, L. D., and N. G. WILSON (1968), *Scribes and Scholars: A Guide to the Transmission of Greek and Latin Literature* (Oxford: Clarendon Press).

ROBINSON, JAMES HARVEY (1898), *Petrarch: The First Modern Scholar and Man of Letters* (New York and London: Putnam).

ROBINSON, PAMELA (1980), 'The Booklet: A Self-Contained Unit in Composite Manuscripts', *Codicologica*, 3: 46–69.

ROOT, R. K. (1913), 'Publication before Printing', *Publications of the Modern Language Association*, 28: 417–31.

——(1922), *The Poetry of Chaucer: A Guide to its Study and Appreciation* (Boston: Houghton Mifflin).

RUGGIERS, PAUL G. (ed.) (1984), *Editing Chaucer: The Great Tradition* (Norman, Okla.: Pilgrim Books).

SCATTERGOOD, JOHN (1990), 'The Jongleur, the Copyist, and the Printer: The Tradition of Chaucer's Wordes unto Adam, His Own Scriveyn', in K. Busby and E. Kooper (eds.), *Courtly Literature: Culture and Context. Selected Papers from the 5th Triennial Congress of the International Courtly Literature Society, Dalfsen, the Netherlands, 9–16 August, 1986* (Amsterdam and Philadelphia: J. Benjamins), 499–508.

SCHAFF, P., and HENRY WACE (eds.) (1892), 'Jerome: Letters and Select Works', in *A Select Library of Nicene and Post-Nicene Fathers of the Christian Church*, 2nd ser., tr. into English with prolegomena and notes (Mich.: Eerdmans).

SCRAGG, D. G., and PAUL E. SZARMACH (eds.) (1994), *The Editing of Old English: Papers from the 1990 Manchester Conference* (Woodbridge and New York: D. S. Brewer).

SEYMOUR, M. C. (1995), *A Catalogue of Chaucer Manuscripts: Works before the Canterbury Tales* (Aldershot: Scolar Press), i.

——(1997), *A Catalogue of Chaucer Manuscripts: The Canterbury Tales* (Aldershot: Scolar Press), ii.

SKEAT, W. W. (ed.) (1881–1900), *Ælfric's Lives of Saints* (EETS OS 76, 82, 94, 114; London and Oxford: Oxford University Press for the Early English Text Society).

STALEY JOHNSON, LYNN (1991), 'The Trope of the Scribe and the Question of Literary Authority in the Works of Julian of Norwich and Margery Kempe', *Speculum*, 66: 820–38.

STUBBS, E. (ed.) (2000), *The Hengwrt Chaucer Digital Facsimile*, ed. N. F. Blake and P. Robinson (Leicester: Scholarly Digital Editions).

——(2006), 'A Study of the Codicology of Four Early Manuscripts of the Canterbury Tales; Aberystwyth, National Library of Wales MS. Peniarth 392D (Hengwrt), Oxford, Corpus Christi College, MS. 198 (Corpus), London, British Library MS. Harley 7334 (Harley 4), and California, San Marino, Huntington Library MS. El. 26 C 9 (Ellesmere)', The School of English: Department of English Language and Linguistics, University of Sheffield.

——(2007), '"Here's One I Prepared Earlier": The Work of Scribe D on Oxford, Corpus Christi College, MS 198', *Review of English Studies*, 58: 133–53.

SWAN, MARY (2001), 'Authorship and Anonymity', in P. Pulsiano and E. M. Treharne (eds.), *A Companion to Anglo-Saxon Literature* (Oxford: Blackwell), 71–83.

——(2007), 'Mobile Libraries: Old English Manuscript Production in Worcester and the West Midlands, 1090–1215', in W. Scase (ed.), *Vernacular Manuscript Books of the English West Midlands from the Conquest to the Sixteenth Century* (Turnhout: Brepols).

TANSELLE, G. THOMAS (1990), *Textual Criticism and Scholarly Editing* (Charlottesville, Va., and London: Published for the Bibliographical Society of the University of Virginia by the University Press of Virginia).

THOMSON, R. M. (2006), *Books and Learning in Twelfth-Century England: The Ending of 'Alter Orbis'. Lyell Lectures 2000–2001* (Walkern, Herts.: Red Gull Press).

THORPE, JAMES (1972), *Principles of Textual Criticism* (San Marino, Calif.: Huntington Library).

THORPE, LEWIS G. M. (ed.) (1974), *A History of the Franks* (Harmondsworth: Penguin).

TOLKIEN, J. R. R. (1934), 'Chaucer as Philologist: The Reeve's Tale', *Transactions of the Philological Society*, 1–70.

TRAXEL, OLIVER M. (2004), *Language Change, Writing and Textual Interference in Post-Conquest Old English Manuscripts: The Evidence of Cambridge, University Library, Ii.1.33* (Münchener Universitätsschriften: Texte und Untersuchungen zur englischen Philologie, 32; Frankfurt am Main: Peter Lang).

TREHARNE, ELAINE M. (2003), 'Cambridge, Corpus Christi College 367', in T. Graham, R. J. S. Grant, P. J. Lucas, and E. M. Treharne (eds.), *Anglo-Saxon Manuscripts in Microfiche Facsimile* (Tempe, Ariz.: Medieval and Renaissance Texts and Studies).

——(2003), 'Producing a Library in Late Anglo-Saxon England: Exeter, 1050–1072', *Review of English Studies*, 54: 155–72.

——(ed.) (2004), *Old and Middle English c.890–c.1400: An Anthology* (2nd edn. Oxford: Blackwell).

——(2007), 'Bishops and their Texts in the Later Eleventh Century: Worcester and Exeter', in W. Scase (ed.), *Essays in Manuscript Geography: Vernacular Manuscripts of the English West Midlands from the Conquest to the Sixteenth Century* (Turnhout: Brepols).

——(ed.) (1994), *Ælfric's Prefaces* (Durham: Durham Medieval Texts).

WILCOX, JONATHAN (2001), 'Transmission of Literature and Learning: Anglo-Saxon Scribal Culture', in P. Pulsiano and E. M. Treharne (eds.), *A Companion to Anglo-Saxon Literature* (Oxford: Blackwell), 50–70.

WINDEATT, B. A. (1979), 'The Scribes as Chaucer's Early Critics', *Studies in the Age of Chaucer*, 1: 119–41.

ZUMTHOR, PAUL (1972), *Essai de poétique médiévale* (Paris: Éditions du Seuil).

CHAPTER 3

THE PROFESSION-ALIZATION OF WRITING

SIMON HOROBIN

PRODUCING VERNACULAR TEXTS

Our knowledge of the scribes responsible for copying the manuscripts of medieval English literature has expanded considerably in recent years, so that we are now in a much better position to chart the professionalization of the book trade than previous generations of scholars. The stereotypical view of medieval book production is of a medieval monk sitting in a monastic scriptorium silently copying books as a means of filling the long hours between regular devotions. While, like most stereotypes, there may be some truth in this image, this is far from capturing the diversity of institutional situations and locations within which medieval books were produced.

The fifteenth century witnessed a huge increase in the production of manuscripts containing vernacular literary texts and numerous copies of the works of Chaucer, Gower, Langland, Lydgate, and others were produced during this century. The turn of the century seems to have represented something of a watershed: there are very few surviving manuscripts containing works by vernacular authors that can be shown to have been copied before 1400. This may be simple chance: all the pre-1400 copies may be lost. But the complete absence of early copies of texts composed in the 1350s and 1360s, such as the works of Richard Rolle, the A-text of *Piers Plowman* and Chaucer's *House of Fame*, *Book of the Duchess*, and *Parliament of Fowls*, seems to indicate that the mechanisms for the production of books were considerably more developed after

1400, and that far more books were made in the fifteenth century than had been in the previous century.

Fourteenth-century manuscripts containing vernacular literary texts are few in number and as a consequence it is difficult to assess how representative they are of manuscript culture of this period. Are these manuscripts the relics of a vibrant and developed industry producing multiple similar copies of vernacular works, or do they represent the isolated and independent efforts of particular individuals? London, British Library, Harley 2253, is a good example of this difficulty. This manuscript, as mentioned by A. S. G. Edwards above, contains a substantial collection of vernacular lyrics, alongside other works in French and Latin, and was copied around 1330 in the Ludlow area of Shropshire.[1] Despite being a product of the West Midlands, Harley 2253 contains lyrics that were composed throughout the country, many of which do not survive in any other collection. The evidence of the Harley manuscript is thus difficult to assess: is it the sole survivor of a number of similar anthologies containing parallel collections of lyrics, or does it represent a unique and unprecedented attempt to gather together the vernacular lyrics of medieval England into a single written anthology?[2] Nor is it possible to determine whether the volume represents the personal collection of its scribe designed for his own pleasure, or a commission intended for the use of a wealthy patron. Thanks to the indefatigable researches of Carter Revard we now know a considerable amount about the scribe of the Harley manuscript, whose hand has been identified in numerous legal documents produced in the Ludlow area from 1314 to 1349.[3] These documents indicate that the scribe of the Harley manuscript worked as a professional scribe, copying legal charters for members of the local gentry. However this discovery does not help us determine whether the scribe was commissioned to compile and copy the Harley manuscript by a wealthy patron, or whether it was his personal compilation. This example is thus useful in highlighting the difficulties involved in applying labels like professional and amateur to medieval scribes.

Similar problems apply to our understanding of a contemporary collection of vernacular romances, now known as the Auchinleck manuscript and housed in the National Library of Scotland. This manuscript contains numerous romances, many of which do not survive in any other manuscript witness. The manuscript was copied by five or six scribes working in London, although the dialect of several of the scribes implies that they were not of London origins. The collaborative nature of the enterprise led Laura Loomis to hypothesize the existence of a London bookshop routinely producing books of this kind, of which the Auchinleck manuscript was the sole survivor.[4] That there were other vernacular books on this scale seems unlikely and it is more likely that the Auchinleck manuscript is a one-off production. While the presence of five or six hands in the manuscript might be taken to indicate collaborative production in a bookshop, the majority of the text, as well as the rubrics and catchwords, is in the hand of Scribe 1, who seems to have been the

---

[1] Ker (1965).   [2] Turville-Petre (1996).
[3] Revard (2000).   [4] Loomis (1942).

major figure responsible for producing the book. Rather than seeing the Auchinleck manuscript as the product of a London bookshop specializing in the copying of vernacular romance, we should probably consider it an unusual commission placed with a professional scribe who called upon several of his colleagues to help him complete the job. But while these scribes were probably not employed in a bookshop producing manuscripts of vernacular literature, the quality of the product testifies to their professional status. As with the Harley scribe, the Auchinleck scribes were presumably full-time scriveners whose main business involved copying non-literary manuscripts, including collections of statutes such as the *Liber Horn*, an anthology of texts concerning the City of London compiled between 1310 and 1320 and donated to the Guildhall by Andrew Horn, Chamberlain from 1320–8.[5]

THE NATURE OF BOOK PRODUCTION
IN THE FIFTEENTH CENTURY

If we turn now to the beginning of the fifteenth century we find a similar situation. Doyle and Parkes's landmark study of the five scribes who contributed to a single manuscript of Gower's *Confessio Amantis* showed that, while the scribes were evidently professional copyists, they were not working together in a single location such as a bookshop.[6] In order to speed up the production of this manuscript of Gower's *Confessio Amantis*, now Cambridge, Trinity College, R.3.2, the text was divided up into sections and parcelled out to five different scribes so that these separate sections could be copied simultaneously. Given the considerable amount of time it must have taken to copy out lengthy works like the *Confessio*, this would have been a useful means of speeding up the production process. In the case of the Trinity Gower the distribution of labour was strangely uneven: Scribe D contributed six quires (booklets comprising eight leaves), Scribe B copied three quires, while Scribe E was responsible for a mere two and a half leaves. For this method to work it was necessary for each scribe to be given the correct amount of text in advance and for each of them to employ the same format when reproducing their exemplar. In this particular instance the scribes were instructed to copy the text in two columns of forty-six lines per page, a layout found in numerous surviving copies of Gower's work. As long as each scribe stuck to this format there would be no problem when the finished booklets were reunited to form the finished product. Unfortunately, in the case of Trinity R.3.2 the system was disrupted by one of the scribes, Scribe B, who ruled his third and final quire with forty-four lines per column instead of the requisite forty-six, so that when he had filled this quire he still had sixty-four lines of text remaining.

5 Hanna (2005).   6 Doyle and Parkes (1978).

This meant that, when the booklets were assembled to be stitched together, there was a gap of sixty-four missing lines between the sections copied by scribes B and C. This problem was remedied by the insertion of an extra leaf containing the missing sixty-four lines, copied by Scribe C, into B's final quire.

This simple practical problem and its solution provide some fascinating insights into the nature of the book trade in this period. It is apparent that the various stints were being copied simultaneously, otherwise once Scribe B had finished and noticed his error, Scribe C could have simply started copying sixty-four lines earlier and so on. Evidently by the time Scribe B had finished his stint and noticed his error, it was too late to change the copying of the later portions. This also suggests that the two scribes were working independently of each other. Once Scribe B had noticed the mistake he evidently did not alert Scribe C to the problem; he may have been unaware that Scribe C was already copying the next section or perhaps he was unable to make contact with him. It is clear that these scribes could not have been working in close collaboration, or in close physical proximity, in a bookshop or scriptorium, otherwise this problem could have been solved more smoothly. The fact that it was Scribe C who supplied the sixty-four lines omitted by Scribe B also highlights the *ad hoc* nature of their interaction, as do the abrupt transitions between the scribes. This is particularly apparent in the switch from Scribe A to Scribe D in quire 14, which occurs not at the beginning of a folio as we might expect, but at the third word of line 15. This suggests that Scribe A rather abruptly gave up work on the book before finishing his stint, leaving Scribe D to clear up after him. The uneven size of their contributions, the obvious differences in the styles of handwriting they employ, the lack of coordination and collaboration between the individual scribes, all suggest that the scribes who were employed to produce Trinity R.3.2 were independent professionals contributing to this commission on a freelance basis. While it is likely that a single individual was responsible for accepting the commission and for organizing and overseeing the book's production, there is no evidence that any of the scribes acted in this capacity. Each scribe appears to have checked his own work and there are few signs of any of the scribes correcting the work of their fellow contributors.

Trinity R.3.2 is just one manuscript among many copies of vernacular literary works produced in the early fifteenth century, and we do not know how typical this method of book production was, although there is evidence of a similar 'leapfrogging' production process in other copies of Gower's *Confessio Amantis*. But the most important evidence for the centrality of this manuscript to the London book trade concerns the appearance of the same scribal hands in many of the most important vernacular manuscripts of this period. Doyle and Parkes identified Scribe B as the copyist of the Hengwrt and Ellesmere manuscripts of the *Canterbury Tales*, the earliest and most authoritative copies of Chaucer's work, as well as fragments of another *Canterbury Tales* manuscript and of Chaucer's *Troilus and Criseyde*.[7] Since

---

[7] Doyle and Parkes (1978).

Doyle and Parkes's article copies of Chaucer's *Boece* and the B version of Langland's *Piers Plowman* have been added to the scribe's curriculum vitae.[8] Most recently Linne Mooney has identified Scribe B as the professional London scrivener Adam Pinkhurst, through comparison of the hand of his signature and oath copied into the Common Paper of the Scriveners' Company.[9] Mooney also argued that Pinkhurst was responsible for copying the Petition of the Mercers' Company of 1387/8 and entries in their accounts book from 1391. The picture of Adam Pinkhurst that emerges from these various identifications is of a busy freelance professional who undertook a variety of copying commissions encompassing legal documents, account books, and literary works by Chaucer, Gower, and Langland. The correspondence between Pinkhurst's first name, Adam, and the 'Adam scriveyn' addressed in a poem by Chaucer in which the poet complains about the amount of correction that is required on account of the scribe's 'negligence and rape' led Mooney to conclude that the poem was addressed to Pinkhurst himself. While this seems a reasonable deduction we must be careful not to make the assumption that Pinkhurst was employed by Chaucer as his personal copyist. While there is considerable evidence of Pinkhurst's involvement in copying Chaucer's works, he also copied the works of the other Ricardian authors as well as a range of non-literary texts too. Just as Chaucer did not make his living from his poetry, so Pinkhurst could not have relied entirely upon Chaucer for his livelihood. A professional scribe in this period would have sought commissions from a range of different employers requiring copies comprising a variety of different types of text.

SCRIBES AND THEIR WORK

While Adam Pinkhurst was evidently a major figure on the early fifteenth-century London scribal scene, he was no less prominent than the fourth contributor to the Trinity Gower manuscript, Scribe D. This scribe has been identified in a total of eight copies of Gower's *Confessio Amantis*, two copies of the *Canterbury Tales*, and single copies of Langland's *Piers Plowman* and Trevisa's translation of *De Proprietatibus Rerum*. While the large number of Gower manuscripts copied by this scribe suggests a particular specialism in this work, and perhaps an association with Gower himself, the variety of other texts in his hand shows that, like Pinkhurst, he was not dependent on a single author, or a single text for his livelihood. Presumably Scribe D, like Pinkhurst, was also a freelance professional who made his living by copying a range of types of text of which literary copying was merely one aspect.

Another fascinating aspect of the Trinity Gower manuscript is the presence of the hand of the poet and Privy Seal clerk Thomas Hoccleve, whom Doyle and Parkes

---

[8] Stubbs (2002); Horobin and Mooney (2004).   [9] Mooney (2006).

identified as Scribe E. Hoccleve's contribution was considerably smaller than the others, comprising a mere two and a half folios. Hoccleve was a professional scribe whose full-time occupation was based in the Privy Seal, therefore it is not particularly surprising to find him supplementing his meagre income in this way. But given Hoccleve's literary interests and his supposed connections with Chaucer himself, his association with Pinkhurst on Trinity R.3.2 is intriguing. As Pinkhurst was probably the scribe responsible for assembling the earliest copies of the *Canterbury Tales* from the papers left behind by Chaucer at his death in 1400, it seems possible that Hoccleve might have had some input into the production of these manuscripts too. The unfinished nature of the *Canterbury Tales*, and the inconsistencies and contradictions left unresolved by Chaucer at the time of his death, posed considerable difficulties for the scribe who was responsible for assembling a complete and coherent copy of the work. It would be natural for Pinkhurst to turn to a fellow scrivener like Hoccleve, with known literary interests, for help in making sense of Chaucer's foul papers. The possibility that Hoccleve contributed to the production of the first of these attempts, the Hengwrt manuscript, is further strengthened by Doyle and Parkes's suggestion that Hoccleve's hand appears in the Hengwrt manuscript as one of the supplementary scribes who filled in some of the lines left blank by Pinkhurst.[10] But we must remain cautious in our interpretation of this evidence. While the Trinity Gower implies some kind of association between Pinkhurst and Hoccleve, and the presence of his hand in Hengwrt appears to indicate that he was involved in the completion of the manuscript, we must not conclude that Hoccleve had a major role in supervising the production of the book. All of the additions made in this hand are spurious, suggesting someone composing lines to fill gaps rather than checking the original scribe's work against his exemplar. The process of checking the copied text against the exemplar seems to have been carried out by Pinkhurst himself and there are a number of corrections of basic errors in his own hand. Given the possible identification of Pinkhurst as Chaucer's 'Adam scriveyn', we might have hoped to find evidence of the author correcting the scribe's work, a process alluded to in that poem. But there are no such indications in any of the surviving manuscripts in Pinkhurst's hand, and the likelihood is that they were all produced after Chaucer's death.

Hoccleve provides an interesting contrast to Chaucer in that he produced several 'holograph' manuscripts: copies of his poetry in his own hand.[11] There are three surviving holograph copies of Hoccleve's poems, all of which are anthologies of his shorter verse, compiled towards the end of his life. It is probable that he also produced a holograph copy of his long poem, the *Regiment of Princes*, for John Duke of Bedford, although this is now lost.[12] The survival of a ballad to Edward Duke of York, probably intended to accompany a presentation manuscript containing a selection of Hoccleve's short poems, may indicate that a further holograph manuscript

---

[10] Doyle and Parkes (1979).   [11] Burrow and Doyle (2002).   [12] Burrow (1994: 17).

has been lost. Hoccleve did not rely exclusively on this method of copying, but seems also to have commissioned other scribes to produce copies of his work; there are a total of forty-three surviving copies of the *Regiment*, none of which is in Hoccleve's own hand. The two earliest and best copies of the *Regiment*, London, British Library, Arundel 38, and Harley 4866, designed for presentation to noble patrons, are not holograph copies but were copied by contemporary professionals, perhaps colleagues in the Privy Seal. Although Hoccleve was clearly engaged in the production and dissemination of copies of his own works, it is difficult to assess how active a member of the London book trade he was. The two and a half leaves he contributed to the Trinity Gower and the few lines he added to the Hengwrt manuscript are the only instances so far identified of Hoccleve contributing to the copying of literary works by other writers. It may be that his full-time employment in the Privy Seal meant that there were comparatively few such opportunities, although, like Pinkhurst, Hoccleve was also commissioned to copy a petition. Although the petition itself does not survive, the accounts of the Earl Marshal, John Mowbray, for 1423 record the payment of two marks to Hoccleve for writing a petition to the council on Mowbray's behalf and for writing and sealing the consequent Privy Seal warrant.[13] Mowbray's connection with Hoccleve may, however, stem from an enthusiasm for his poetry: Mowbray was likely the patron for whom one of the presentation copies of the *Regiment* (now London, British Library, Arundel 38) was produced.[14]

The evidence provided by the Trinity manuscript of *Confessio Amantis* and the interaction between the contributing scribes, as well as the evidence of their other copying activities, suggests that the London book trade in this period relied on a small number of freelance professionals who made their living by copying a variety of different copying commissions. Some, like Adam Pinkhurst, were members of the Scriveners' Company, while others, like Hoccleve, were full-time scribes working in government offices like the Privy Seal, the Chancery, and Signet offices. The lack of evidence of consistent and organized collaboration and cooperation between these scribes implies that they were independent practitioners rather than members of established bookshops or scriptoria. The independence of their work is also implied by the lack of uniformity and standardization in the books that they produced. Both Pinkhurst and Scribe D, for instance, copied Chaucer's *Canterbury Tales*, but used exemplars belonging to different textual traditions and produced copies of the poem using contrasting tale orders and with different contents. Both scribes copied Langland's *Piers Plowman*, although Pinkhurst's manuscript contains the B text while Scribe D's is a witness to the C text. So, despite the fact that both scribes were working at the same time and copying a similar range of texts, they appear to have made few efforts to pool their resources. If these scribes were working in a bookshop then we would surely expect greater evidence of collaboration by more than one copyist on a single manuscript, the reuse of exemplars to produce multiple copies of a single text, adoption of a standardized format and the use of a set script. The only evidence that

<hr>

13 Ibid.   14 Harris (1984).

Doyle and Parkes offer for the adoption of a similar script is the palaeographical similarities between Scribe D and a contemporary whom they label Scribe Delta, who produced three copies of Trevisa's *Polychronicon*, one copy of the *Confessio Amantis*, and single copies of Nicholas Love's *Mirror of the Blessed Life of Jesus Christ* and Guy de Chauliac's *Cyrurgie*. But, while there are indeed similarities between the hands of these two scribes, they are by no means identical. If these two scribes had been taught to write in a similar way within a bookshop, then we would expect to find manuscripts where the two scribes share the copying, but there are no such examples. Rather than see the similarity between these two scribal hands as evidence of a bookshop's house style, the more likely explanation is that the two scribes independently adopted similar hands.

THE LATER FIFTEENTH CENTURY

Turning from the early fifteenth century to the period around 1450 we begin to find evidence pointing to the emergence of bookshops and the greater professionalization of the vernacular book trade. This process may be observed in the group of manuscripts containing the works of Chaucer, Gower, and Lydgate attributed to the hooked-g scribe and his associates. The hooked-g scribe, so-called because of a distinctive hook on the tail of his g, appears in a number of manuscripts, often in conjunction with other scribes with very similar handwriting.[15] These palaeographical similarities provide an important contrast with the more obvious differences observed in the hands of the scribes who contributed to the Trinity Gower. In addition to the shared handwriting conventions, these scribes also employ strikingly similar spelling habits and methods of *ordinatio* and layout. An example of a distinctive feature of layout employed by these scribes is the use of the larger, more formal, textura semi-quadrata script (book hands of considerable formality) for the opening line of a section of text, often requiring a line of poetry to be split over two lines. It is hard to imagine that such a feature could have been developed independently; it is more likely that the conventions of writing, spelling, and layout shared by these manuscripts are the result of common training and employment. Another important development registered in these manuscripts is the reuse of an exemplar, indicating that scribes or stationers were retaining exemplars of popular works in the anticipation of further demand. Two copies of Gower's *Confessio Amantis* belonging to this group, Oxford, Magdalen College 213, and London, British Library, Harley 7184, were copied from the same exemplar; as were Oxford, Bodleian Library, Rawlinson Poetry 223, and Cambridge, Trinity College, R.3.3, containing Chaucer's *Canterbury Tales*; as well as London, British Library, Royal 18. D. vi, and Oxford, Exeter College,

---

[15] Mooney and Mosser (2004).

129, of Lydgate's *Troy Book*. Similarities in decoration and illumination also found among these manuscripts point to the repeated use of a single limner or group of limners, further supporting the theory that these manuscripts were produced in a bookshop specializing in high-grade copies of prominent literary works.

The appearance of examples like this should not be taken to imply the demise of the independent freelance scrivener. The evidence of manuscripts produced after 1450 indicates that such professionals continued to exist, copying literary works alongside a range of more utilitarian texts. An example of such is the 'Hammond scribe', first identified by the Chaucerian scholar Eleanor Hammond.[16] His hand appears in several important anthologies of Chaucerian and Lydgatean minor verse, as well as two copies of the *Canterbury Tales* and Hoccleve's *Regiment of Princes*. While it is possible that he was working in a bookshop, the range of other non-literary texts identified in his hand implies that he was a freelance scribe. Among the many different types of text copied by the Hammond scribe are collections of medical texts, heraldic texts, religious works, London charters, and Statutes of the Realm.[17] A parallel example is the expert scribe, possibly of French origin, Ricardus Franciscus.[18] In addition to luxurious copies of literary works in his hand, including copies of Lydgate's *Fall of Princes* and Gower's *Confessio Amantis*, his surviving output includes a grant of arms to the London Tallow Chandlers' Company, a cartulary for St Bartholomew's Hospital and a copy of the statutes of the Archdeaconry of London. Some of Ricardus's commissions are signed by the scribe himself, perhaps indicative of the increased status accorded to expert practitioners of this period.

The proliferation of scribal copyists and the establishment of bookshops in the period post-1450 should not be taken as evidence that the age of the monastic scribe had passed. Books continued to be copied in monastic environments, as may be seen from the œuvre of a prolific scribe belonging to the Carthusian order, Stephen Dodesham.[19] Dodesham seems to have received his training among the scribes of the Chancery and his earliest literary productions, including three copies of Lydgate's *Siege of Thebes*, were probably undertaken as freelance commissions during a period of secular employment. Unlike the hooked-g scribe and his colleagues, Dodesham used different exemplars of this text and various models of *ordinatio*, suggesting that these manuscripts were produced in an *ad hoc* manner rather than in a bookshop, where we might have expected the use of a single exemplar and a standard format.[20] However, Dodesham's vocation changed radically in the late 1460s when he became a Carthusian monk and member of the Carthusian house at Witham, Somerset. A subsequent record of 1471 describes him as a professed monk of the house at Sheen, indicating that he had by this date moved to the Surrey house, where he died in 1481–2. A number of his copying commissions can be associated with his period as a Carthusian, including a copy of the pseudo-Augustine *Sermones morales ad fratres suos in heremo* copied while at Witham, a Latin choir Psalter containing a Carthusian liturgical calendar, and at least one of his three surviving copies of Nicholas Love's

---

[16] Hammond (1929–30).   [17] Mooney (1996); (2000).   [18] Hamer (1983).
[19] Doyle (1997).   [20] Edwards (1991).

Mirror of the Blessed Life of Jesus Christ, Glasgow, Glasgow University Library, Hunterian MS T.3.15 (77). The example of Stephen Dodesham indicates the survival of the monastic copyist alongside the professionalization of the London book trade in the second half of the fifteenth century. While there was likely a distinction between the types of copying carried out in London workshops and in the cloister, as witnessed in Dodesham's own copying career, the distinction between secular and religious books is not always clear cut. While the Hunterian copy of Love's *Mirror* was evidently produced at Sheen Charterhouse, the breadth of appeal and readership of this work mean that the two further deluxe copies of the work in Dodesham's hand could have been copied during his period of lay or monastic employment.

The evidence for the professionalization of the copying of literary texts in the medieval period is thus complex and contradictory. Scribes gained employment in a variety of institutions, secular and monastic, and copied a wide range of texts for a diversity of patrons. The fifteenth century appears to have seen a considerable increase in the number of books being produced, although it is not until the period after 1450 that we see the establishment of bookshops employing groups of scribes collaborating on the production of copies of literary texts. While this change was likely linked to an increase in the resources available for producing books, it was also stimulated by a greater demand for copies from the buying public. Prior to this period books were copied on a bespoke basis, that is, they were produced to order rather than speculatively. After 1450 there is greater evidence for the production of books 'on spec', in a range of styles and formats, catering for a variety of readers. This increased demand inevitably led to a need for quicker methods of production, leading to the establishment of the scribal bookshops witnessed in the work of the hooked-g scribe and his associates.

BIBLIOGRAPHY

BURROW, J. A. (1994), *Thomas Hoccleve* (Authors of the Middle Ages, 4; Aldershot: Variorum).
——and A. I. DOYLE (eds.) (2000), *Thomas Hoccleve: A Facsimile of the Autograph Verse Manuscripts* (EETS supplementary series, 19; Oxford: Oxford University Press for the Early English Text Society).
DOYLE, A. I. (1997), 'Stephen Dodesham of Witham and Sheen', in P. R. Robinson and Rivkah Zim (eds.), *Of the Making of Books: Medieval Manuscripts, their Scribes and Readers: Essays Presented to M. B. Parkes* (Aldershot: Scolar), 94–115.
——and M. B. PARKES (1978), 'The Production of Copies of the *Canterbury Tales* and the *Confessio Amantis* in the Early Fifteenth Century', in M. B. Parkes and A. G. Watson (eds.), *Medieval Scribes, Manuscripts, and Libraries: Essays Presented to N. R. Ker* (London: Scolar Press), 163–210.
——and——(1979), 'Paleographical Introduction', in Paul G. Ruggiers (ed.), *A Facsimile and Transcription of the Hengwrt Manuscript, with Variants from the Ellesmere Manuscript* (Norman, Okla.: University of Oklahoma Press), pp. xix–xlix.
EDWARDS, A. S. G. (1991), 'Beinecke MS 661 and Early Fifteenth-Century English Manuscript Production', *Yale University Library Gazette*, 66 (suppl.): 181–96.

HAMER, RICHARD (1983), 'Spellings of the Fifteenth-Century Scribe Ricardus Franciscus', in E. G. Stanley and D. Gray (eds.), *Five Hundred Years of Words and Sounds: A Festschrift for Eric Dobson* (Cambridge: D. S. Brewer), 63–73.

HAMMOND, ELEANOR PRESCOTT (1929–30), 'A Scribe of Chaucer', *Modern Philology*, 27: 27–30.

HANNA, RALPH (2005), *London Literature 1300–1380* (Cambridge: Cambridge University Press).

HARRIS, KATE (1984), 'The Patron of British Library MS. Arundel 38', *Notes and Queries*, NS 31: 462–3.

HOROBIN, SIMON, and LINNE R. MOONEY (2004), 'A *Piers Plowman* Manuscript by the Hengwrt/ Ellesmere Scribe and its Implications for London Standard English', *Studies in the Age of Chaucer*, 26: 65–112.

KER, N. R. (1965), *Facsimile of British Museum MS Harley 2253* (EETS, OS 255; London: Oxford University Press).

LOOMIS, LAURA HIBBARD (1942), 'The Auchinleck Manuscript and a Possible London Bookshop of 1330–1340', *PMLA* 57: 595–627.

STUBBS, ESTELLE (2002), 'A New Manuscript by the Hengwrt/Ellesmere Scribe? Aberystwyth, National Library of Wales, MS. Peniarth 393D', *Journal of the Early Book Society*, 5: 161–7.

MOONEY, LINNE R. (2006), 'Chaucer's Scribe', *Speculum*, 81: 97–138.

——(2000), 'A New Manuscript by the Hammond Scribe Discovered by Jeremy Griffiths', in A. S. G. Edwards, Ralph Hanna, and Vincent Gillespie (eds.), *The English Medieval Book: Essays in Memory of Jeremy Griffiths* (London: British Library), 113–23.

——(1996), 'More Manuscripts Written by a Chaucer Scribe', *Chaucer Review*, 30(4): 82–7.

——and DANIEL W. MOSSER (2004), 'The Hooked-G Scribe and Takamiya Manuscripts', in Takami Matsuda, Richard Linenthal, and John Scahill (eds.), *The Medieval Book and a Modern Collector: Essays in Honour of Toshiyuki Takamiya* (Cambridge: D. S. Brewer), 179–96.

REVARD, CARTER (2000), 'Scribe and Provenance', in Susanna Fein (ed.), *Studies in the Harley Manuscript: The Scribes, Contents, and Social Contexts of British Library MS Harley 2253* (Kalamazoo, Mich.: Medieval Institute Publications), 21–109.

TURVILLE-PETRE, THORLAC (1996), *England the Nation: Language, Literature, and National Identity, 1290–1340* (Oxford: Oxford University Press).

CHAPTER 4

....

WRITING, AUTHORITY, AND BUREAUCRACY

....

NICHOLAS PERKINS

CONTEXTS

....

On 16 October 1834, the Clerk of Works at the Palace of Westminster disposed of bundles of wooden tally sticks by burning them in a cellar stove, which overheated.[1] The resultant fire destroyed the medieval and later buildings of the royal palace, home to governmental offices and a venue for dispensing justice and taking counsel since the eleventh century. The palace was, of course, rebuilt in a medievalist Gothic style that asserts continuity between parliamentary democracy and the administrative institutions of pre-modern England. At the same time, foundational scholarly projects on those institutions were being undertaken, such as the publications of the Camden Society (1838 onwards) and the Rolls Series (1857 onwards), while in 1857 that ultimate bureaucrat-writer Anthony Trollope published *The Three Clerks*, an affectionately satirical novel set in the Weights and Measures Office, whose historically resonant protagonists include Harry Norman and Alaric Tudor.

Those combustible tally sticks cluttering the Westminster storerooms were not, however, nostalgic remnants of a long-vanished regime; rather, their fate provides compelling evidence of the complexity and continuities of medieval forms of

....

[1] Translations of primary texts are based on the cited edns. where available, but have sometimes been adapted. I am very grateful to Helen Barr for helpful comments on this essay in draft form.

authority, writing, and bureaucracy. Tally sticks had been issued by the royal Treasury perhaps since before the Norman Conquest to record debts or payments, and were still used into the nineteenth century. Small notches cut into a stick indicated an amount paid or owed, while other details were written along its length. It was then split lengthways, each party keeping one half as a secure record which could be matched up, like a chirograph document, in case of disputes.[2] The practicality of this system, its use of writing in conjunction with other physical marks, and the symbolic function of the divided object/text, are all important for the three terms in this chapter's title.

I shall return to Westminster, but wish to stress at the outset the variety of interactions between authoritative discourses, institutions, and individuals or groups in the Middle Ages; the way that writing (on single sheets or rolls of parchment, on wax tablets, on wood, or pressed onto sealing wax) acted alongside other forms of representation and (re)counting to survey people and livestock, record tax payments, confirm grants of land or office, or sue for redress; and the numerous small-scale systems of record that operated. In that sense, 'bureaucracy', both as a back-formation from modern institutions and as a singular noun, might seem to misrepresent the patchwork and personal nature of many medieval institutions and jurisdictions—ecclesiastical, royal, lordly, urban, familial—and their varied relationships with 'authority' or 'writing'.[3] Nevertheless, there is evidence for sophisticated and robust medieval administrations: one influential account even states that 'the country was dominated by a centralizing royal bureaucracy' in the period 1066–1307.[4] Here it would be impossible adequately to survey medieval administrative practices,[5] or the intertwined histories of ecclesiastical and common law administrations.[6] Instead, I shall explore how relationships of power are staged or created in the productive interplay between bureaucratic repetition and the imagination, or between authoritative forms and the 'practice of everyday life', which generates opportunities for parasitic adaptations or unlooked-for co-options of text and object at moments of performance.[7] Such relations between form and moment, discipline and pleasure, give energy to many kinds of medieval writing emerging from or responding to bureaucratic textuality, and are still at the centre of debates around the literary as a category.

---

[2] Campbell (1986: 175–6); Clanchy (1993: 123–4 and pl. VIII).
[3] The classic discussion of bureaucracy is in Weber (1948: 196–244); see also Albrow (1970).
[4] Clanchy, (1993: 5).
[5] See e.g. the magisterial Tout (1920–33); Brown (1971); Loyn (1984); Given-Wilson (1986); Brown (1989); Clanchy (1993); Harriss (1993); Woolgar (1992); Richardson (1999); Bartlett (2000: 121–201); Mason (2003); Prestwich (2005: 55–77); Harriss (2005: 41–92).
[6] Helmholz (2004); Wormald (1999); Brand (1992a); Brand (1992b).
[7] On theories of practice, see Bourdieu (1977) and de Certeau (1984); on authority and writing, see Galloway (2000); Steiner (2007).

EARLY ADMINISTRATION

The earliest substantial English text to survive is the law-code of King Æthelberht of Kent (d. 616). Alongside law-codes, other documents such as charters (usually in Latin), writs, manumissions, and wills all provide information about administrative organization in Anglo-Saxon England and about the relationships between spoken and written languages, authoritative structures and religious practice.[8] The law-code, or *Domboc*, of King Alfred the Great incorporates parts of Mosaic law and clearly acts as a statement about the binding together of royal and Christian ideology. As Patrick Wormald comments: 'Alfred's code need no longer be understood as a primarily legislative instrument. It neither made nor codified law . . . Instead, it said something of immense symbolic moment about the law of Wessex.'[9] Likewise, the formulaic wording and layout of many Anglo-Saxon charters appear initially to show how written authority and bureaucratic procedures have established themselves over a 'prior' oral culture. Charters are, however, more aptly thought of as part of a 'performance of authority' that relies on and at the same time reproduces the originating presence of the grantor (usually the king) and the invocation of a speaking voice; rather than replacing a personal grant, they record and interact with it.[10] Oral, aural, and written forms are mutually reinforcing, and the charters' prayerful formulae also invoke a cosmic perspective on the disposition of land and rights.[11] The personal marks recorded alongside charter witness lists, ceremonial actions such as the placing of a sod of earth (or the charter) on an altar, and the authority and authenticity provided by a seal give a rich context to the power of performative utterance in Anglo-Saxon texts, underlining their concern with symbolic action alongside authoritative speech and their mingling of the language of regnal and divine authority.

A similar mixture of written and oral tradition and ideological work can be discerned in Anglo-Saxon royal genealogies which, with their frequent inclusion of Germanic gods or biblical ancestors, act both as a document of royal history and as a current or future claim to superlative power: 'Encapsulated in verse (particularly praise poems), in heroic tales, and in the less literary genealogical records . . . dynastic propaganda could be broadcast via the learned classes whose responsibility it was to maintain "knowledge" of this type.'[12] Old English poetry can embed or scrutinize such claims in subtle ways, as in the opening passage of *Beowulf*, which describes the arrival of Scyld Scefing and the founding of the dynasty to which Hrothgar is heir, before apposing this genealogy with the biblical creation myth through the prism of a poet's song in the newly constructed but proleptically doomed hall Heorot. The

---

[8] Loyn (1984: 106–30); Wormald (1999); many documents are translated in Whitelock (1979).
[9] Wormald (1999: 429); see also Pratt (2007: 214–41).
[10] Kelly (1990); Keynes (1990); Foot (2006).
[11] Fell (1991: 173–4).
[12] Dumville (1977: 83); see also Davis (1992).

Creation also implies the Fall, however, and another genealogical record immediately replayed in a darker key is the descent of Grendel from the first murderer, Cain:

> fifelcynnes eard
> wonsæli wer   weardode hwile,
> siþðan him Scyppend   forscrifen hæfde
> in Caines cynne.[13]

The verb *forscrifan*, meaning 'judge' or 'proscribe', can also imply physical marking or writing, and confirms Grendel's place as a legal exile outlawed by God's *dom* (judgement). The recollection of genealogies, vengeful repayments, and disposal of property are all woven into the poem's narrative and its perspective on final judgement. *Beowulf*'s readers have sometimes attempted to localize or date it by its genealogical connections, linking epic verse to the concerns of royal legitimacy or ethnic continuity.[14] Such attempts have mostly been suggestive rather than definitive, but do remind us of how discourses of authority and record emerge in linguistic forms in varying combinations; to adapt Foucault's term, we might think of a 'bureaucratic function', differently individuated and disposed amongst texts in different cultural conditions.[15] It may seem perversely oblique to read *Beowulf* through its relationship with bureaucracy, but the poem contains rich moments of reflection on processes of recording, defining, and judging; turning the tables, we find that legal or administrative productions from Anglo-Saxon royal courts are also claims about history, mythology, and continuity with pre-Christian tribes, both Germanic and Israelite.

Despite controversy about the development of a royal 'chancery' under the West Saxon dynasty,[16] and about King Alfred the Great's personal role in a programme of education and literary production at the end of the ninth century,[17] the reigns of Alfred and his successors did establish the conditions necessary for secure record keeping and the written standard form of Late West Saxon used both for administrative documents and for religious texts, especially those connected to the monastic reforms of the tenth century.[18] Monastic centres such as Winchester and Canterbury were important not only in ecclesiastical organization and scholarly activity, but also in providing education, administrative services, and the safe storage of documents for often itinerant kings; throughout the Middle Ages, of course, clerics were also clerks for royal and aristocratic households. The homilist Archbishop Wulfstan of York, for example, was responsible for several law-codes, culminating in a code for promulgation by King Cnut in 1020 or 1021 'as a foundation for a regime that would now earn God's favour rather than his wrath',[19] while his *Sermo Lupi ad Anglos*[20] targets breaches of the law and of oaths as a marker of political and moral collapse under the Danish attacks: for Wulfstan the two spheres are not

---

13 Lines 104–7, in Jack (1994: 34): 'the unblessed being dwelt for a time in the land of the monstrous race, after the Creator had condemned him amongst Cain's kin'.
14 Newton (1993: 54–76).   15 See Foucault (1979) for the 'author function'.
16 Lapidge *et al.* (1999: 94–5).   17 Godden (2007).
18 Gneuss (1972).   19 Wormald (2004).
20 *Sermon of the Wolf to the English*, in Treharne (2000: 226–33).

distinguishable. Such thoroughgoing use of a standardized written vernacular for bureaucratic, religious, and secular texts was unique for this period; as Clanchy notes, in 1066 'Norman administrators probably had less experience than Anglo-Saxon ones of written records... There was nothing in Normandy comparable with the *Anglo-Saxon Chronicle* and the law codes.'[21] The *Anglo-Saxon Chronicle*, and the translation of other philosophical, historical, and spiritual texts in the late ninth or early tenth century testify to the connections envisaged between the development of authority by good governance and its passing on through written learning. The personal involvement of the king in translating and writing is not, then, as important as the authoritative voice on which these texts rely to create their model of religious and secular governance. The preface to the Alfredian translation of Gregory's *Cura pastoralis* (*Pastoral Care*), which begins in a language of command comparable to that of royal writs,[22] imagines a golden age in which there is no gap between military, administrative, and philosophical/religious activity: each generates and supports the other, and the availability of written texts is central to this enterprise. Kings in those days

ægðer ge hiora sibbe ge hiora siodo ge hiora onweald innanbordes gehioldon, ond eac ut hiora eðel gerymdon; ond... him ða speow ægðer ge mid wige ge mid wisdome.[23]

The task imagined by the preface is to re-establish that power through educating the governing class and translating books 'most necessary for all men to know'.[24] One such translation, which provided a powerful aetiology both for the conversion of Anglo-Saxon peoples to Christianity and for their absorption of Latin literacy, is the Old English version of Bede's *Historia ecclesiastica gentis Anglorum* (*Ecclesiastical History of the English People*). In book 5, a narrative occurs that places authority, writing, and forms of reckoning or accounting in troubling relation. The second of three monitory visions, it concerns a Mercian layman whom King Coenred has repeatedly advised to change the dissolute habits of his private life. The man is suddenly taken ill and relates a terrifying vision to the king:

Ær hwene ðu come, eode inn on þis hus to me twegen geonge men fægre & beorhte, & gesæton æt me, oðer æt minum heafde, oðer æt minum fotum. Ða teah heora oðer forð fægre boc & swiðe medmicle & me sealde to rædanne. Ða ic ða boc sceawade, þa mette ic ðær awriten ealle ða god ða ic æfre gedyde. Ah ða wæron swiðe feawe & medmicle. Ða noman heo eft ða boc æt me & me noht to cwædon.

Ða com her sæmninga micel weorud werigra gasta, & wæron swiðe ongrislicum heowe & ondwliotan... Ða teah he forð boc ongryslicre gesihðe & unmættre micelnisse & lytesne unabeorendlic byrdenne; sealde ða anum his geferena & heht me beran to rædanne. Mid ðy ic ða þa boc rædde, ða gemette ic on hiere sweartum stafum & atolecum sweotole awritene eall

[21] Clanchy (1993: 27).   [22] Loyn (1984: 115).
[23] Treharne (2000: 10); 'both maintained their peace and their morality and their authority internally, and also extended their territory outwards; and... they prospered both in warfare and in wisdom'.
[24] Ibid. 13.

ða man ðe ic æfre gefremede; & nales ðæt an þæt ic on weorce & on worde, & eac hwylce þæt ic on þæm medmestan geðohte gesyngode, ealle ða wæron ðær on awritene.[25]

Accepting that he belongs to the devils, the angels vanish. Two devils then wound the man with knives, one at the head and one at the feet—wounds that are working their way into his body. When they meet, he tells the king, he will die and be carried to hell.

This striking story—what we might call a 'text of account'—has a context in visionary literature, the *exemplum* tradition, and in the Anglo-Saxons' fascination with the demonic otherworld, but central is the image of authoritative writing. Oral counsel, even from the king, has little sway over this sinner. Instead, the books recording good and bad deeds trump royal, lay, and oral authority and accurately predict, indeed prescribe, the future.[26] The man relates his vision to the king in a reversal of authoritative positions, but the inexorable power of the books, 'fægre' and 'ongryslicre', looms over the story and binds together processes of word, action, thought, and *dom*. The books allude to God as divine *auctor* of the universe,[27] but more specifically recall the book of Revelation 3: 5, in which John relates the promise that 'He that overcometh, the same shall be clothed in white raiment; and I will not blot out his name out of the book of life'; the angel with a 'little book open' in 10: 2 (a passage evoking hidden knowledge, prophecy and judgement); and 20: 12–13, in which 'the books were opened: and another book was opened, which is the book of life: and the dead were judged out of those things which were written in the books, according to their works'. In Anglo-Saxon England, a book of life, or *liber vitae*, was also the name given to a book in which religious houses customarily recorded the patronage of their prominent supporters, with the expectation that this public declaration of their generosity and piety would help to ensure their place in heaven. Such a document is also centrally a text of account, part of a ubiquitous medieval understanding of Christianity as an economic system in which bureaucratic processes such as record keeping, payment, and reciprocal service were fundamental operations.

One of the most splendid pre-Conquest *libri vitae* is from New Minster, Winchester, initially written by the monk Ælfsige in 1031.[28] Ælfsige's list of patrons is continued and surrounded on folio 28ᵛ by a swarm of later names, which seem to borrow power from their proximity to the original list, as well as having the practical purpose of using the blank marginal space. This spiritual account book tells us much

---

[25] Miller (1890–8: i. 438–40); 'A little before you arrived, there came into this house to me two young men, beautiful and radiant, and they sat down beside me, one at my head, the other at my feet. Then one brought out a beautiful but very small book and gave it to me to read. When I examined the book, I found written all the good deeds that I had ever done, but they were very few and trifling. They took the book back and said nothing to me. // Then came here suddenly a great troop of evil spirits, terrible in shape and appearance . . . He [the chief devil] brought out a book, horrible in appearance and of immense size and of almost unbearable weight; he gave it to one of his fellows and ordered him to bring it to me to read. When I read the book I found there, written clearly in black and dreadful letters all the sins that I had ever committed—and not only in deed and word, but even in the slightest thought: all were written there.'

[26] See Lerer (1991: 30–60).

[27] Gellrich (1985: 39–44); Minnis (1988: 94–103).

[28] London, British Library, MS Stowe 944.

about political affiliations, family histories, and the ongoing institutional development of the New Minster and Hyde Abbey, Winchester, amidst the changing circumstances of the eleventh century, but I shall focus here on two pictures towards the start of the manuscript. Folio 6ʳ shows the Golden Cross of Winchester, grasped by King Cnut on the right, with Queen Ælfgifu (Emma) on the left.[29] Above them, Christ sits in majesty, a golden book open on his knee, while the Virgin Mary gestures with her left hand and holds a scroll in her right. To the right of Christ, St Peter holds enormous keys, emphasizing this book's importance in opening the gates to heaven. In the *bas-de-page*, a group of monks in an ecclesiastically columned space look up, perhaps singing the liturgy, the central monk holding an open book, which mirrors Christ's Book of Life. The manuscript's next opening portrays the Last Judgement, and on folio 7ʳ, the central panel depicts St Peter struggling for a soul against a clawed devil, whom he shoves in the face with his keys. Both the devil and St Peter's angelic secretary hold open volumes symbolizing the eternal register of good and bad deeds: this particular battle of the books again mingles writing, authority, and bureaucratic forms in a vital narrative that is both personal and apocalyptic, involving dispassionate record keeping and the most visceral of rewards and punishments. The documentary record of sins becomes a commonplace of medieval Judgement Day imagery, as in the *ars moriendi* tradition[30] or alongside the weighing of souls, as in the Doom painting at St Peter's Church, Wenhaston, Suffolk.

In Bede's Mercian story, the doomed man is wounded with pointed instruments or knives to mark his impending death and damnation, while we are reminded that deeds and thoughts 'nales on þiosne wind in idelnesse toflowenne, ah to dome þæs hean deman ealle gehaldene beon'.[31] The *Historia ecclesistica* explains the two books by saying that the man's wickedness had obscured (*obnubilauit*)[32] his earlier good deeds. The Old English version renders this as 'aðeostrade & fordilegade' ('obscured and blotted out'),[33] strengthening the Latin verb with another that connotes both the utter destruction of an enemy and manuscript deletion. Indeed, it may refer directly to Revelation 3: 5, a promise not to 'blot out' from the Book of Life (*non delebo* in the Vulgate) the name of someone who has won through. Like Grendel's monstrous body, which paradoxically both records and justifies God's marking him out amongst the damned, the text of account here can itself be a human body, whose history and final chapter are inscribed—in this case by the devils' eloquent knives—on its own flesh.

These pre-Conquest texts and images richly suggest the interlinked relationships of authority with writing and bureaucratic processes in early English contexts, where accounting is a telling metaphor for judgement and authoritative discourse (the meanings of both Germanic 'tell' and Latinate 'account' encompass economic and narrative processes). Nor does writing simply take over as the medium of account.

[29] Keynes (1996); Parker (2002).   [30] Duffy (1992: pl. 117).
[31] Miller (1890–8: i. 440); 'do not drift away idly in the wind, but are all preserved for the judgement of the supreme judge'.
[32] Bede (1969: 502).   [33] Miller (1890–8: i. 442).

While writing's connection with authoritative utterance may be stressed in a story like that of the Mercian nobleman, spoken utterance, the powerful presence of a ruler, and the physicality of documents or signs are all figured or imagined into legal and administrative processes in Anglo-Saxon documents and poetry, especially those invoking royal or divine *dom*.

RECORDING AUTHORITY

Given the associations between bureaucratic record-keeping and God's judgement, it is little wonder that one of the most ambitious bureaucratic projects of the Middle Ages was known as Domesday Book. Writing in the 1170s or 1180s, about a hundred years after its compilation, the king's Treasurer Richard FitzNigel explains in his *Dialogus de Scaccario* (Dialogue of the Exchequer) that

Hic liber ab indigenis 'Domesdei' nuncupatur, id est dies iudicii per metaphoram. Sicut enim districti et terribilis examinis illius nouissimi sententia nulla tergiuersationis arte ualet eludi, sic cum orta fuerit in regno contentio de his rebus que illic annotantur, cum uentum fuerit ad librum, sententia eius infatuari non potest uel impune declinari.[34]

As with many Anglo-Saxon documents, Domesday Book was perhaps more important as a political statement of William the Conqueror's power than for its immediate practical purpose.[35] Richard FitzNigel's discussion in his guide to Exchequer practice is framed by Domesday Book's metaphorical power and theoretical authority as a final arbiter. Nevertheless, along with Magna Carta, it still symbolizes the centripetal force of Norman and Angevin rule and the attempts of other groups to define their legal rights in response.[36] Domesday Book and Magna Carta are still the most widely known documents from medieval England, although expanding groups of professionally trained administrators were a conduit for the power play conducted through other legal and documentary moments or developments.[37] These included the so-called Barons' War of the mid-thirteenth century;[38] Edward I's ambitious ownership survey in 1279 prior to the *quo warranto* prosecutions;[39] and, in the longer term, the petty assizes of novel disseisin and mort d'ancestor, the former allowing those dispossessed of property to apply quickly for restoration pending full investigation,

---

[34] Amt and Church (2007: 96–8); 'The native people call this book "Domesday", that is, metaphorically, the day of judgement. For, just as no judgement of that final severe and terrible trial can be evaded by any subterfuge, so when any controversy arises in the kingdom concerning the matters contained in the book, and recourse is made to the book, its word cannot be denied or set aside without penalty.'

[35] Clanchy (1993: 32–5).   [36] Holt (1992).

[37] Turner (1988); Brand (1992a); Baswell (1999: 137–40).   [38] Machan (2003: 21–69).

[39] Clanchy (1993: 35–43).

and the latter establishing an initial inheritance claim.[40] Legal compendia such as Glanvill and Bracton are part of this movement towards professionalization and the codifying of procedure.[41]

FitzNigel's *Dialogus* testifies to the growth of written procedure in the royal administration, but is also a fascinating work of 'imaginative bureaucracy', premised on a fictional dialogue between teacher and student, incorporating biblical wisdom, historical mythology and discussions of rhetorical tropes. The chapter describing Danegeld (heregeld) begins with three Latin verses on the self-sufficient abundance of *Insula nostra* ('our island').[42] Having cited Seneca it describes the attacks of 'robbers from the surrounding islands' ('*Circumiacentium . . . insularum pre-dones*')[43]—especially the Danes, and the voice of the Magister directs the Discipulus (and us) to '*Britonum . . . historia*' ('the history of the Britons')[44] for more details. He then describes Danegeld as a tax to fund the defence of the kingdom and states that it was collected annually up to the time of William I, as if it successfully overcame some irritating criminality, rather than faced full-scale takeover by a Scandinavian dynasty and all the other upheavals of the eleventh century. Under King William, the Danes and others 'scripture est "Cum fortis armatus custodit atrium suum, in pace sunt ea que predones hostiles cohibebant incursus, scientes uerum esse quod possidet"'.[45]

FitzNigel's text, then, is fascinatingly poised between spoken and written, the authority of documents and the continuity of memorial traditions, and between practical guidebook and moral treatise—comparable to the mingling of political theory, everyday advice, and ethics in texts such as John of Salisbury's *Policraticus* and other mirrors for princes. Elsewhere in the *Dialogus*, the Magister describes the Exchequer itself as an event, an institution, and a place. Its sittings feature a repeated performance of authority at which county sheriffs settle their account with the royal Treasurer, the money being counted out on a chequered tablecloth (hence the name Exchequer) with a group of other officials acting as umpires, recorders, and spectators. The analogy between the Exchequer table and a chessboard invites this extended simile:

sicut enim in scaccario lusili quidam ordines sunt pugnatorum et certis legibus uel limitibus procedunt uel subsistunt, presidentibus aliis et aliis precedentibus, sic in hoc quidam president quidam assident ex officio, et non est cuiquam liberum leges constitutas excedere, quod erit ex consequentibus manifestum. Item, sicut in lusili pugna committitur inter reges, sic in hoc inter duos principaliter conflictus est et pugna committitur, thesaurarium scilicet et uicecomitem qui assidet ad compotum residentibus aliis tanquam iudicibus ut uideant et iudicent.[46]

---

[40] Sutherland (1973); Baker (2002: 223–37), and, more broadly, Harding (2002).

[41] Hall (1965); Bracton, (1968–77).

[42] Amt and Church (2007: 84).

[43] Ibid.

[44] Ibid.

[45] Ibid. citing Luke 11: 21, 'ceased their hostile attacks, knowing the truth of the Scripture: "When a strong armed man guards his hall, his possessions are left in peace"'.

[46] Ibid. 10; 'For just as in a chess game the pieces have a certain order and move or stand still according to certain laws and within certain parameters, some ranking higher and some leading the way; in the same way, at the exchequer, some preside and others have seats because of their official positions, and no one is free to act outside the established rules, as will be clear from what is to follow. Also, just as, in chess,

This portrayal of the Exchequer as a sporting contest that sublimates the potentially violent conflict between different interest groups has strong affiliations with certain narrative forms in twelfth- and thirteenth-century England, including romance and debate writing. Of course, debate has its own generic history and institutional contexts, especially in university disputation, but as I have noted, the worlds of the noble household, monastery, and university are permeable, and texts that emerge from them can share the references and prejudices of a male clerical cadre, whether at administrative work or goliardic play.[47] A thirteenth-century poem that invokes these contexts is *The Owl and the Nightingale*.[48] Written in English but using French-derived octosyllabic couplets and permeated by clerical vocabulary amongst its brilliantly demotic voices, this poem exemplifies the multi- and inter-lingual environment of post-Conquest culture. Its two manuscripts testify to this linguistic and generic plurality. London, British Library, Cotton Caligula A. ix includes saints' lives and a debate poem (the *Petit Plet*) in French; English religious lyrics; a prose chronicle in Anglo-Norman French and Layamon's English version of the *Brut*, in alliterative verse. The other manuscript, Oxford, Jesus College 29 (II), includes further English religious lyrics; a debate between the four daughters of God from Guillaume le Clerc's French version of the book of Tobit; *The Proverbs of Alfred* in English; a text on morals and manners by Sauvage d'Arras, and two administrative texts: 'The Shires and Hundreds of England' (English), and the *Assisa panis Anglie* (Latin), a record of prices for bread announced in 1256. As Cartlidge suggests, these manuscripts may have been produced in a religious institution, but could also have served a lay household.[49]

The eponymous female antagonists are apparently aligned with nature and English vernacular orality against Latin and French bureaucratic textuality, and the *auctoritates* on which each draws to promote the value of her song include proverbial wisdom and personal experience, with violent emotions threatening to spill over into a real fight. A key element of the poem's architecture, however, is a linguistically regulated framework for dispute resolution that might defer or deflect violence, as the Nightingale suggests:

> 'Ac lete we awei þos cheste,
> Vor suiche wordes boþ unwreste,
> & fo we on mid riȝte dome,
> Mid faire worde & mid ysome.
> Þeȝ we ne bo at one acorde,
> We muȝe bet mid fayre worde,
> Witute cheste & bute fiȝte,
> Plaidi mid foȝe & mid riȝte;

battle is joined between the kings, so at the exchequer there is basically a competition and struggle between two individuals, namely the treasurer and the sheriff who makes his account to the others sitting there as arbiters, so that they may see and judge.' See also pp. xx–xxv, and, for chess as a metaphor, Adams (2006).

47 Mann (1980).   48 Cartlidge (2001).   49 Ibid. pp. xxvii–xxxi.

> & mai hure eiþer wat hi wile,
> Mid riȝt segge & mid sckile.'
> Þo quaþ þe Hule, 'Wu schal us seme
> Þat kunne & wille riȝt us deme?'[50]

The vocabulary here—'cheste', 'dome', 'Plaidi', 'riȝte', 'sckile', 'seme', 'deme'—is steeped in ethical, intellectual, but also legal and bureaucratic discourse.[51] The Nightingale nominates Nicholas of Guildford as judge, and the Owl readily agrees: 'Ich granti wel þat he us deme' (201). In a text that itself delights in the serious play of institutions, rhetoric, and authoritative positioning, the Owl claims that Nicholas 'Nu him ne lust na more pleie' (213). Finally, a wren arrives to warn the disputants not to breach the king's peace, and recapitulates the call for arbitration:

> 'Hwat! Wulle ȝe þis pes tobreke
> An do þanne kinge swuch schame?
> Ȝe, nis he nouþer ded ne lame!
> Ȝunke schal itide harm & schonde,
> Ȝef ȝe doþ griþbruche on his londe.
> Lateþ beo & beoþ isome,
> An fareþ riht to ower dome:
> An lateþ dom þis plaid tobreke
> Al swo hit was erur bispeke!'[52]

This intervention helps to bring the debate and the poem to a pre-emptory end, but not before a satirical reference to Nicholas of Guildford's lack of sufficient preferment amidst the corrupt administration of ecclesiastical offices. Finally, the poem dissolves the tension between written record and oral performance in the claim by the Owl that 'al ende of orde / Telle ich con word after worde' (1785–6). Her *litteratim* memory takes the place of a court or exchequer roll and imaginatively fuses the energy of oral debate about birdsong (and much more) with writing's claim to permanence. It also leaves us with a question: have we been 'listening' to the oral debate, or 'reading' the record of it, and which is more authentic?

I noted earlier that the birds cite proverbs as a form of authoritative utterance. The figure to whom they appeal as the fount of proverbial wisdom is frequently King Alfred (for example, at ll. 685, 697). Alfred's reputation for authoritative wisdom and legal judgement is confirmed not only by the *Proverbs of Alfred*, ascribed to him and appearing in the Jesus manuscript, but also by the way that institutions—the

---

[50] Ibid. 6, ll. 177–88: 'But let's leave off this quarrelling, for this kind of language is worthless. We should adopt some proper procedure, using fair and peaceable words. Even though we don't agree with each other, we can better plead our cases in decent language with propriety and decorum, than with bickering and fighting. Then each of us can rightfully and reasonably say whatever we might wish.' Then the Owl said, 'But who should arbitrate between us? Who'd be ready and able to give us a fair decision?'

[51] Holsinger (2002).

[52] Cartlidge (2001: ll. 1730–8); 'Listen!...do you want to break this peace and so then disgrace the King? Well, you won't find him dead or crippled! If you commit a breach of the peace in his land, you'll both suffer injury and dishonour. Now stop all this, call a truce and go straight off to hear the verdict upon you: and let arbitration bring this dispute to an end, just as it was previously agreed!'

University of Oxford, for example—claimed him as a founding figure and thus guarantor of their privileges. Many apparently Alfredian charters or traditions copied into documents and chronicles are post-Conquest compositions, examples of imaginative and sometimes highly skilled reconstruction; likewise facsimiles or verbatim copies of administrative documents are frequently embedded in medieval institutional and personal narratives.[53] The birds' contestive retelling of proverbs and exemplary narratives shows that these kinds of authority too have a wax nose, but also reminds us that authority is not separable from the forms in which it is exercised or debated; it often moves amongst various symbolic as well as literal modes, and speakers, listeners, readers, and writers were often acutely tuned to the contingent, explosive potential of performances of authority, as in *Piers Plowman*, when Piers 'for pure tene' tears the bureaucratically framed, morally provocative pardon from Truth.[54]

The dangers of the document—its capacity to lie as well as record the facts—are suggested in an episode from *Chronicle of the Abbey of Bury St Edmunds* by Jocelin of Brakelond (*fl.* 1173–*c.*1215). Jocelin describes a dispute over church patronage between Abbot Hugh and Robert de Ulmo. The Abbot upped the stakes by asking Robert to swear on oath that he was in the right, but the knight refused, possibly fearing divine displeasure if he swore falsely. After a jury of local citizens has consulted their collective memory and found in favour of Hugh, a cleric named Jordan de Ros 'sprang up, holding out two charters, one from Abbot Hugh and the other from Robert de Ulmo, so that whichever party won the case, he would get the parsonage'.[55] In this narrative, memorial tradition is reliable, and the written document easily manufactured, forged, doubled.[56] Medieval romances, whose plots often turn on moments of recognition, memory, or sudden news, similarly explore this ambivalence towards the documentary text as opposed to the symbolic object or readable body. In *Emaré* (based on the 'Constance' story which also appears in Chaucer's *Man of Law's Tale*) the long-suffering protagonist is cast out to sea when she refuses her father's incestuous desires. She eventually marries a king, but her mother-in-law hates her. After giving birth to a healthy boy, the letter reporting the good news is doctored by the dowager queen so that Emaré's husband reads that the baby is a monster. His loving reply is likewise changed on the messenger's return trip by the 'false qwene' (584),[57] and now commands that Emaré be cast adrift with her child. The boy, once grown, provokes recognition from his father, acting like an unfalsifiable document that records the stamp of its originator. Distrust of written documents, court functionaries (the steward, the chamberlain), and non-personal processes of legitimization is not at a constant level in medieval texts: certain genres, story patterns, or historical moments carry different inflections of the power of documentary and bureaucratic procedure as against the (precisely) unpredictable force of personal identity, and narratives of the written word's frailty exist alongside

---

[53] Hiatt (2004).   [54] B VII. l. 115, in Langland (1995: 118); Steiner (2003: 93–142).
[55] Jocelin (1989: 55).   [56] Hughes (1992); Clanchy (1993: 260–6).   [57] Mills (1973: 62).

increasing reliance on writing for a wider range of tasks.[58] These developments meant, for example, that a range of noble and gentry households employed administrators who also wrote 'literature', increasingly in English and exploring what Vance Smith has termed the 'household imaginary'.[59] Literate, or functionally literate, groups also included some who resisted the oppressive labour conditions underwritten by administrative documents such as manorial rolls. Many such records were destroyed in the revolt of 1381,[60] but rebel groups could also use ancient custom and record in astute ways to try to protect their rights.[61]

By the late fourteenth century, conditions were in place for a particularly close engagement between bureaucratic practice, forms of written authority and imaginative work, especially in London and Westminster, where royal and urban administrations, mercantile and ecclesiastical institutions, and a developing quarter of legal services and clerkly training all coexisted, operating in a variety of languages, engaging in political, military, intellectual, and other commerce with continental Europe and beyond.[62] This 'bureaupolitan' network of interlocking institutions supported a significant number of clerks, bureaucrats, and professional writers who also composed, compiled, and/or copied literary texts, including Geoffrey Chaucer, John Gower, William Langland, Thomas Usk, Thomas Hoccleve, the authors of *Richard the Redeless* and *Mum and the Soothsegger*, Adam Pinkhurst (who copied manuscripts of Chaucer, Gower, and Langland), Adam Usk, and other chronicle writers. Much recent work has studied these literate and political cultures, especially the relations between professional writing and forms of script, the development of English as a literary and administrative language, and the imaginative reach of late-medieval literature.[63] I cannot hope to survey all these, let alone other centres such as the Scottish court, or later bureaucrat-writers such as John Shirley and George Ashby; instead, in the last parts of this chapter I shall trace two elements of this imaginative environment: the bureaucracy of love, and the physicality of scribal labour.

The Bureaucracy of Love

Late-medieval royal administration, finances, and law-making were fuelled by the circulation of bills and petitions: typically small strips of parchment inscribed with a lack, complaint, or request that deserved attention from someone in authority.[64] In 1398 Geoffrey Chaucer petitioned Richard II for letters patent to confirm an annual grant of wine:

[58] Clanchy (1993); Green (1999).   [59] Smith (2003).   [60] Crane (1992); Justice (1994).
[61] Galloway (2001); Müller (2003).   [62] Nightingale (1995); Barron (2004); Hanna (2005).
[63] See e.g. Strohm (1992); Barr (1993); Kerby-Fulton and Justice (1998); Knapp (2001); Perkins (2001); Steiner (2003); Mooney (2006); Giancarlo (2007); Nuttall (2007); Mead (2007); Mooney (2007); Turner (2007); Scase (2007). Also see Chapter 2 in this volume.
[64] Harriss (1993); Perkins (2001: 34–8).

Plese a nostre tressoverain seignur le roy granter a vostre humble lige Geffrey Chaucer voz gracieuses lettres patentes desouz vostre grand seal pur prendre un tonel de vin chescun an durante sa vie en port de [vostre] citee de Londres par les mains de vostre chief butiller . . . pur Dieu et en oevre de charitee.[65]

An added note in Latin confirms that this *billa* was granted, converting it into a warrant; two days later, a Privy Seal warrant orders the letters patent to be issued; the order was then recorded on the Patent Roll in Latin, beginning 'Pro Galfrido Chaucer. Rex omnibus ad quos etc. salutem'.[66] Chaucer later resorted to a playful but tense petitionary poem, the *Complaint to his Purse*, to nudge the incoming Henry IV into remembering him.[67] The combination of nagging lack, rhetorical superfluity, and duplicatory process in petitions and complaints is also at work in many texts that imagine a court of Love or Fortune, including Charles of Orleans's poetic sequence and James I of Scotland's *Kingis Quair*. Another such is Chaucer's *Complaint unto Pity*, which begins as if addressing Pity directly, but soon becomes mired in syntactical indirection and political instability:

> Pite, that I have sought so yore agoo
> With herte soore and ful of besy peyne,
> That in this world was never wight so woo
> Withoute deth—and yf I shal not feyne,
> My purpos was to Pite to compleyne
> Upon the crueltee and tirannye
> Of Love, that for my trouthe doth me dye.[68]

The poem moves through a tortuous series of allegorical scenarios in which, having summoned up the courage 'be lengthe of certeyne yeres'[69] to speak directly to Pity, the poem's persona finds her 'ded, and buried in an herte'.[70] In this self-fashioning, self-cancelling world, Pity (the quality that allows someone to accept a lover's suit) is both the addressee of the petition and a prerequisite for any reader/lover to engage with the text. Her 'death' thus places both the suit itself and the allegorical process at an impasse, in a court full of backbiting and false 'companye',[71] a dark counterpart to the socially inclusive if potentially rivalrous pilgrim 'compaignye' of *The Canterbury Tales*:

> A compleynt had I, writen in myn hond,
> For to have put to Pite as a bille;
> But when I al this companye ther fond,
> That rather wolden al my cause spille
> Then do me help, I held my pleynte stille,
> For to that folk, withouten any fayle,
> Withoute Pitee ther may no bille availe.[72]

---

[65] Crow and Olson (1966: 116–17); 'May it please our most mighty lord the King to grant to your humble servant Geoffrey Chaucer your gracious letters patent under your great seal to take a tun of wine each year of his life in the port of your city of London from the hands of your chief butler . . . for God and as a work of charity.'

[66] Ibid. 117.   [67] Chaucer (1988: 656).   [68] Ibid. 640–1 ll. 1–7.   [69] Ibid. l. 8.

[70] Ibid. l. 14.   [71] Ibid. l. 45.   [72] Ibid. ll. 43–9.

The speaker dares not present his bill, but still reveals its 'effect'[73] in nine highly wrought stanzas laced with the rhetorical deployments of legal and court process:[74] addressing Pity as 'highest of reverence',[75] calling on her to 'breke that perilouse alliaunce'[76] of Cruelty and others, and repeating his claim to undying service in the face of his own death and that of his addressee.

> This is to seyne I wol be youres evere,
> Though ye me slee by Crueltee your foo,
> Algate my spirit shal never dissevere
> Fro youre servise for any peyne or woo.
> Sith ye be ded—allas that hyt is soo—
> Thus for your dethe I may wel wepe and pleyne
> With herte sore and ful of besy peyne.[77]

In the final rhyme of 'pleyne' and 'peyne', the speaker draws together the dual processes of writing and loving, the rhetorical shape of suffering with its physical source and bodily manifestation, and makes a case for the particularity of complaint, its singular emotional force which also constitutes a claim to selfhood amidst the interchangeability of bureaucratic formulations.[78]

SCRIBAL LABOUR

Thomas Hoccleve (c.1367–1426), who knew and admired Chaucer, worked as a clerk in the Privy Seal office, a writing office that had developed out of the king's need to issue orders when travelling away from the Great Seal in Chancery. By Hoccleve's time this role had been taken by the Signet, with the Privy Seal settling in Westminster and acting as a conduit for much government correspondence and business.[79] Descriptions of the Privy Seal can seem reminiscent of the Department of Administrative Affairs in the classic television satire *Yes, Minister*, and Gerald Harriss has described Hoccleve's career as 'a lifetime's employment in a dead-end job',[80] though the significant growth in government business made such a secretariat a vital part of the royal administration. Hoccleve himself wrote a lengthy manuscript containing sample Privy Seal documents (the 'Formulary', London, British Library, Additional 24062). Amidst the otherwise anonymized or historically important documents, however, there is a sequence of letters into which Hoccleve has inserted his initials, 'TH', planting small moments of particularity within the general or the repeatable, and providing suggestive analogies with his poetic self-revelation: 'for Hoccleve,

---

[73] Ibid. l. 56.   [74] Nolan (1979).   [75] Chaucer (1988: 640–1, l. 57).
[76] Ibid. l. 83.   [77] Ibid. ll. 113–19.   [78] Burrow (1981).
[79] Tout (1920–33: v. 1–110); Brown (1971); Catto (1985); Burrow (1994); Harriss (2005: 42–5); Mooney (2007).
[80] Harriss (2005: 44).

autobiography begins its history in the wake of the bureaucratic document'.[81] Hoccleve's poetry is extremely sensitized to the relations between the specifics of scribal
labour and authoritative power of documents on the one hand, and persuasive,
sometimes marginal voices on the other.[82] In *The Letter of Cupid*, which mimics the
form of a royal letter to play with the feminist/antifeminist debate, Hoccleve ends with
a dating formula typical of a bureaucratic document: 'Writen . . . In our Paleys . . . /
The yeer of grace ioieful & iocunde, / .M CCCC. and secunde'.[83] In a holograph
manuscript of the poem (San Marino, Huntington Library, MS HM 744) Hoccleve
writes a Latin *explicit*, and then a French *incipit* to the next poem: an encomiastic
balade addressed to King Henry V. Next comes a complaint to 'Lady moneye' and her
scornful reply. This manuscript, along with its partner HM 111, in some ways provides
a poetic counterpart to Hoccleve's Formulary, not only in his inhabiting of bureaucratic forms, but also because by collecting his own poems together he seems to be
'enrolling' them in a more permanent documentary form as a way to preserve them.[84]
In its mobility between familiar bureaucratic formulations, three languages of record,
speech, and writing, between complaints to contemporary authoritative figures and
figments of Hoccleve's imaginary polities at the courts of England and of Love, MS
HM 744 provides a fascinating record of the entanglements of this chapter's topic. The
leaf on which Hoccleve ends *The Letter of Cupid* and begins the subsequent balade has
indeed been trimmed at the bottom, removing a strip of parchment about the right
size to write a note, petition, or bill. The quires in which Hoccleve copied his poems
have been sandwiched inside other pages containing religious and catechetical texts
and notes relating to a fifteenth-century family called Filer from Little Baddow in
Essex, including an inventory of household items and versions of a merchant's mark.[85]
Here, the accretive layering of the 'literary' and 'bureaucratic' both within and
between texts make those terms increasingly unstable as separable forms of writing
or thinking. Hoccleve's longest poem, *The Regiment of Princes*, presses this point when
it moves from an apparently artless 'spoken' conversation between Hoccleve and an
Old Man towards the authoritative 'written' address to the future King Henry V,
meanwhile airing the lack of payment for Hoccleve 'in th'eschequer',[86] and the closing
of the loophole which might have seen him remunerated instead via the Hanaper
(a department of the Chancery that paid for the enrolment of charters). Hoccleve's
poetic voice is one expertly modulated through bureaucratic processes, but nevertheless constructing a claim to individual recognition and recompense. The ventriloquism shared between poetic and bureaucratic practice helps him to assume the voice
of authoritative counsellor in the *Regiment* proper, yet insist on the physical cost
of scribal labour in its Dialogue, where he reminds the Old Man, and us:

> What man that three and twenti yeer and more
> In wrytynge hath continued, as have I,

---

[81] Knapp (2001: 35); see also Perkins (2001: 36).   [82] Perkins (2007).
[83] Hoccleve (1970: 308, ll. 475–6).   [84] See Bowers (1989).
[85] Hoccleve (2002: p. xxvi).   [86] Hoccleve (1999: 93, l. 1877).

I dar wel seyn, it smertith him ful sore
In every veyne and place of his body.[87]

As with Chaucer's rhyming 'pleyne' and 'peyne', Hoccleve's bureaucratic forms do not prevent him from (re)marking the cost of such labour on fragile bodies.[88] In this sense, the wounded hearts of Love's servants and the sore limbs and eyes of King Henry IV's clerks share an ethical space with Bede's Mercian nobleman, a sinner whose body becomes the most telling documentary evidence of a final accounting return. The late-medieval texts known as the 'Charters of Christ' give a gruesome inflection to this tradition: whereas in Bede the wages of sin are projected onto a fallen human body, here, a charter of human salvation is inscribed on Christ's sinless flesh, with his blood as ink, the nails as pens, and the authorizing seal formed by the Sacred Heart.[89] The version in London, British Library, MS Additional 37049 depicts a bloody Christ holding out the charter, which in effect merges with his body to form the text's written space.[90] This is another document that relies on repeated written instantiations, but also embodies the performative speaking voice of a king.

In his outstanding book, M. T. Clanchy argues that 'lay literacy grew out of bureaucracy, rather than from any abstract desire for education or literature'.[91] This statement is an important reminder to scholars working in departments of English literature to be wary of literary teleologies that render the bulk of medieval written production invisible or shapeless. However, Clanchy's opposition between bureaucracy on the one hand, and abstract desire, education, and literature on the other, is open to modification. Texts of account can operate across generic boundaries; bureaucratic texts can make space for the imagination (the claim to biblical precedent, the voice of the king, the metaphors of the Exchequer); and medieval literature often revels in mingling pragmatic and imaginative forms or desires. Medieval practices of bureaucracy, then, can help us to ask certain questions. What does it matter who is writing and/or speaking? What relationships are performed by this text, and which are hidden? How does the physical form of this document relate to its linguistic or rhetorical forms? They might also help us to ask analogous questions of texts across traditional period boundaries. Continuities between King Alfred the Great in the ninth century and Sir Thomas More in the sixteenth used to be predicated on the modulations of their literary prose and the permanent qualities of the English spirit. Perhaps a more productive set of analogies might be found in the interlinked discourses of authority, ethics, and governance which each of their situations required them to confront. In a kingdom whose precocious royal administration was soon to dismantle and reform the institutions of the English Church, filling the royal Treasury but destroying books and lives on all sides, the future chancellor More imagined his alter ego in *Utopia* as a royal functionary, abroad on some business or other, whose brief moment of *otium* unfolds into a seriously playful

[87] Ibid. ll. 1023–6.   [88] Knapp (2001: 77–106); Justice and Kerby-Fulton (1997).
[89] Spalding (1914); Steiner (2003: 193–228).   [90] Brantley (2007: 189–92).
[91] Clanchy, (1993: 19).

reflection on authority, writing, and the bureaucracies of England and of the mind. As a late-medieval engagement with the medieval cultures of authority and account, More's telling work gains much of its ambivalent power from the ideas and relationships that we have touched on in this chapter.

BIBLIOGRAPHY

ADAMS, J. (2006), *Power Play: The Literature and Politics of Chess in the Middle Ages* (Philadelphia: University of Pennsylvania Press).

ALBROW, M. (1970), *Bureaucracy* (Basingstoke: Macmillan).

AMT, E., and S. CHURCH (ed. and tr.) (2007), *Richard FitzNigel, 'Dialogus de Scaccario': 'The Dialogue of the Exchequer'; and 'Constitutio Domus Regis': 'Disposition of the King's Household'* (Oxford: Clarendon Press).

BAKER, J. (2002), *An Introduction to English Legal History* (4th edn. London: Butterworths Tolley).

BARR, H. (ed.) (1993), *The Piers Plowman Tradition* (London: Dent).

BARRON, C. (2004), *London in the Later Middle Ages: Government and People, 1200–1500* (Oxford: Oxford University Press).

BARTLETT, R. (2000), *England under the Norman and Angevin Kings, 1075–1225* (Oxford: Clarendon Press).

BASWELL, C. (1999), 'Latinitas', in D. Wallace (ed.), *The Cambridge History of Medieval English Literature* (Cambridge: Cambridge University Press), 122–51.

BEDE (1969), *Bede's 'Ecclesiastical History of the English People'*, ed. B. Colgrave and R. Mynors (Oxford: Clarendon Press).

BOURDIEU, P. (1977), *Outline of a Theory of Practice*, tr. Richard Nice (Cambridge: Cambridge University Press).

BOWERS, J. (1989), 'Hoccleve's Huntington Holographs: The First "Collected Poems" in English', *Fifteenth Century Studies*, 15: 27–51.

BRACTON, H. (1968–77), *De Legibus et Consuetudinibus Angliae: Bracton on the Laws and Customs of England*, ed. and tr. G. Woodbine and S. Thorne (4 vols. Cambridge, Mass.: Belknap Press).

BRAND, P. (1992a), *The Origins of the English Legal Profession* (Oxford: Blackwell).

——(1992b), *The Making of the Common Law* (London: Hambledon Press).

BRANTLEY, J. (2007), *Reading in the Wilderness: Private Devotion and Public Performance in Late Medieval England* (Chicago: University of Chicago Press).

BROWN, A. (1971), 'The Privy Seal Clerks in the Early Fifteenth Century', in D. Bullough and R. Storey (eds.), *The Study of Medieval Records: Essays in Honour of Kathleen Major* (Oxford: Clarendon Press), 260–81.

——(1989), *The Governance of Late Medieval England: 1272–1461* (London: Edward Arnold).

BURROW, J. (1981), 'The Poet as Petitioner', *Studies in the Age of Chaucer*, 3: 61–75.

——(1994), *Thomas Hoccleve* (Aldershot: Ashgate).

CAMPBELL, J. (1986), *Essays in Anglo-Saxon History* (London: Hambledon Press).

CARTLIDGE, N. (ed. and tr.) (2001), *The Owl and the Nightingale* (Exeter: Exeter University Press).

CATTO, J. (1985), 'The King's Servants', in G. Harriss (ed.), *Henry V: The Practice of Kingship* (Oxford: Oxford University Press), 75–95.

CHAUCER, G. (1988), *The Riverside Chaucer*, gen. ed. L. Benson (Oxford: Oxford University Press).

CLANCHY, M. (1993), *From Memory to Written Record: England 1066–1307* (2nd edn. Oxford: Blackwell).

CRANE, S. (1992), 'The Writing Lesson of 1381', in B. Hanawalt (ed.), *Chaucer's England: Literature in Historical Context* (Minneapolis: University of Minnesota Press), 201–21.

CROW, M., and C. OLSON (eds.) (1966), *Chaucer Life-Records* (Oxford: Clarendon Press).

DAVIS, C. (1992), 'Cultural Assimilation in the Anglo-Saxon Royal Genealogies', *Anglo-Saxon England*, 21: 23–36.

DE CERTEAU, M. (1984), *The Practice of Everyday Life*, tr. S. Rendall (Berkeley and Los Angeles: University of California Press).

DUFFY, E. (1992), *The Stripping of the Altars: Traditional Religion in England c.1400–c.1580* (New Haven: Yale University Press).

DUMVILLE, D. (1977), 'Kingship, Genealogies and Regnal Lists', in P. Sawyer and I. Wood (eds.), *Early Medieval Kingship* (Leeds: School of History, University of Leeds), 72–104.

FELL, C. (1991), 'Perceptions of Transience', in M. Godden and M. Lapidge (eds.), *The Cambridge Companion to Old English Literature* (Cambridge: Cambridge University Press), 172–89.

FOOT, S. (2006), 'Reading Anglo-Saxon Charters: Memory, Record, or Story?', in E. Tyler and R. Balzaretti (eds.), *Narrative and History in the Early Medieval West* (Turnhout: Brepols), 39–65.

FOUCAULT, M. (1979), 'What is an Author?', tr. J. Harari, in J. Harari (ed.), *Textual Strategies: Perspectives in Post-Structuralist Criticism* (Ithaca, NY: Cornell University Press), 141–60.

GALLOWAY, A. (2000), 'Authority', in P. Brown (ed.), *A Companion to Chaucer* (Oxford: Blackwell), 23–39.

——(2001), 'Making History Legal: *Piers Plowman* and the Rebels of Fourteenth-Century England', in K. Hewett-Smith (ed.), *William Langland's 'Piers Plowman': A Book of Essays* (London: Routledge), 7–39.

GELLRICH, J. (1985), *The Idea of the Book in the Middle Ages: Language Theory, Mythology, and Fiction* (Ithaca, NY: Cornell University Press).

GIANCARLO, M. (2007), *Parliament and Literature in Late Medieval England* (Cambridge: Cambridge University Press).

GIVEN-WILSON, C. (1986), *The Royal Household and the King's Affinity: Service, Politics and Finance in England, 1360–1413* (New Haven: Yale University Press).

GNEUSS, H. (1972), 'The Origin of Standard Old English and Æthelwold's School at Winchester', *Anglo-Saxon England*, 1: 63–83.

GODDEN, M. (2007), 'Did King Alfred Write Anything?', *Medium Ævum*, 76: 1–23.

GREEN, R. (1999), *A Crisis of Truth: Literature and Law in Ricardian England* (Philadelphia: University of Pennsylvania Press).

HALL, G. (ed.) (1965), *The Treatise on the Laws and Customs of the Realm of England Commonly Called Glanvill* (London: Nelson).

HANNA, R. (2005), *London Literature, 1300–1380* (Cambridge: Cambridge University Press).

HARDING, A. (2002), *Medieval Law and the Foundations of the State* (Oxford: Oxford University Press).

HARRISS, G. (1993), 'Political Society and the Growth of Government in Late Medieval England', *Past and Present*, 138: 28–57.

——(2005), *Shaping the Nation: England 1360–1461* (Oxford: Clarendon Press).

HELMHOLZ, R. (2004), *The Canon Law and Ecclesiastical Jurisdiction from 597 to the 1640s* (Oxford: Oxford University Press).

HIATT, A. (2004), *The Making of Medieval Forgeries: False Documents in Fifteenth-Century England* (London: British Library and Toronto University Press).

HOCCLEVE, T. (1970), *Hoccleve's Works: The Minor Poems*, ed. F. Furnivall and I. Gollancz, rev. J. Mitchell and A. Doyle (EETS extra ser. 61 and 73; London: Oxford University Press).

——(1999), *The Regiment of Princes*, ed. C. Blyth (Kalamazoo, Mich.: Medieval Institute Publications).

——(2002), *Thomas Hoccleve: A Facsimile of the Autograph Verse Manuscripts*, ed. J. Burrow and A. Doyle (EETS suppl. ser. 19; Oxford: Oxford University Press).

HOLSINGER, B. (2002), 'Vernacular Legality: The English Jurisdictions of *The Owl and the Nightingale*', in E. Steiner and C. Barrington (eds.), *The Letter of the Law: Legal Practice and Literary Production in Medieval England* (Ithaca, NY: Cornell University Press), 154–84.

HOLT, J. (1992), *Magna Carta* (2nd edn. Cambridge: Cambridge University Press).

HUGHES, J. (1992), ' "The Feffement that fals hath ymaked": A Study of the Image of the Document in *Piers Plowman* and Some Literary Analogues', *Neuphilologische Mitteilungen*, 93: 125–33.

JACK, G. (ed.) (1994), *'Beowulf': A Student Edition* (Oxford: Oxford University Press).

JOCELIN OF BRAKELOND (1989), *Chronicle of the Abbey of Bury St Edmunds*, tr. D. Greenaway and J. Sayers (Oxford: Oxford University Press).

JUSTICE, S. (1994), *Writing and Rebellion: England in 1381* (Berkeley, Calif.: University of California Press).

——and K. KERBY-FULTON (eds.) (1997), *Written Work: Langland, Labor, and Authorship* (Philadelphia: University of Pennsylvania Press).

KELLY, S. (1990), 'Anglo-Saxon Lay Society and the Written Word', in R. McKitterick (ed.), *The Uses of Literacy in Early Medieval Europe* (Cambridge: Cambridge University Press), 36–62.

KERBY-FULTON, K., and S. JUSTICE (1998), 'Langlandian Reading Circles and the Civil Service in London and Dublin, 1380–1427', *New Medieval Literatures*, 1: 59–83.

KEYNES, S. (1990), 'Royal Government and the Written Word in Late Anglo-Saxon England', in R. McKitterick (ed.), *The Uses of Literacy in Early Medieval Europe* (Cambridge: Cambridge University Press), 226–57.

——(ed.) (1996), *The Liber vitae of the New Minster and Hyde Abbey, Winchester: British Library Stowe 944. Together with Leaves from British Library Cotton Vespasian A. VIII and British Library Cotton Titus D. XXVII* (Copenhagen: Rosenkilde & Bagger).

KNAPP, E. (2001), *The Bureaucratic Muse: Thomas Hoccleve and the Literature of Late Medieval England* (University Park, Pa.: Pennsylvania State University Press).

LANGLAND, W. (1995), *The Vision of Piers Plowman*, ed. A. Schmidt (2nd edn. London: Dent).

LAPIDGE, M. *et al.* (eds.) (1999), *The Blackwell Encyclopaedia of Anglo-Saxon England* (Oxford: Blackwell).

LERER, S. (1991), *Literacy and Power in Anglo-Saxon Literature* (Lincoln, Neb.: University of Nebraska Press).

LOYN, H. (1984), *The Governance of Anglo-Saxon England, 500–1087* (London: Edward Arnold).

MACHAN, T. (2003), *English in the Middle Ages* (Oxford: Oxford University Press).

MANN, J. (1980), 'Satiric Subject and Satiric Object in Goliardic Literature', *Mittellateinisches Jahrbuch*, 15: 63–86.

MASON, E. (2003), 'Administration and Government', in C. Harper-Bill and E. van Houts (eds.), *A Companion to the Anglo-Norman World* (Woodbridge: Boydell Press), 135–64.

MEAD, J. (2007), 'Chaucer and the Subject of Bureaucracy', *Exemplaria*, 19: 39–66.

MILLER, T. (ed. and tr.) (1890–8), *The Old English Version of Bede's 'Ecclesiastical History'* (2 vols. EETS original series 95–6, 110–11; London: N. Trübner & Co.).

MILLS, M. (ed.) (1973), *Six Middle English Romances* (London: Dent).

MINNIS, A. (1988), *Medieval Theory of Authorship: Scholastic Literary Attitudes in the Later Middle Ages* (2nd edn. Aldershot: Scolar Press).

MOONEY, L. (2006), 'Chaucer's Scribe', *Speculum*, 81: 97–138.

——(2007), 'Some New Light on Thomas Hoccleve', *Studies in the Age of Chaucer*, 29: 293–340.

MÜLLER, M. (2003), 'The Aims and Organisation of a Peasant Revolt in Early Fourteenth-Century Wiltshire', *Rural History*, 14: 1–20.

NEWTON, S. (1993), *The Origins of 'Beowulf' and the Pre-Viking Kingdom of East Anglia* (Cambridge: D. S. Brewer).

NIGHTINGALE, P. (1995), *A Medieval Mercantile Community: The Grocers' Company and the Politics and Trade of London, 1000–1485* (New Haven: Yale University Press).

NOLAN, C. (1979), 'Structural Sophistication in the "Complaint unto Pity"', *Chaucer Review*, 13: 363–72.

NUTTALL, J. (2007), *The Creation of Lancastrian Kingship: Literature, Language and Politics in Late Medieval England* (Cambridge: Cambridge University Press).

PARKER, E. (2002), 'The Gift of the Cross in the New Minster Liber Vitae', in E. Sears and T. Thomas (eds.), *Reading Medieval Images: The Art Historian and the Object* (Ann Arbor: University of Michigan Press), 176–86.

PERKINS, N. (2001), *Hoccleve's 'Regiment of Princes': Counsel and Constraint* (Cambridge: D. S. Brewer).

——(2007), 'Thomas Hoccleve: *La Male Regle*', in P. Brown (ed.), *A Companion to Medieval English Literature and Culture, c.1350–c.1500* (Oxford: Blackwell), 585–603.

PRATT, D. (2007), *The Political Thought of King Alfred the Great* (Cambridge: Cambridge University Press).

PRESTWICH, M. (2005), *Plantagenet England, 1225–1360* (Oxford: Clarendon Press).

RICHARDSON, M. (1999), *The Medieval Chancery under Henry V* (Kew: List and Index Society).

SCASE, W. (2007), *Literature and Complaint in England, 1272–1553* (Oxford: Oxford University Press).

SMITH, D. (2003), *Arts of Possession: The Middle English Household Imaginary* (Minneapolis: University of Minnesota Press).

SPALDING, M. (1914), *The Middle English Charters of Christ* (Bryn Mawr, Pa.: Bryn Mawr College).

STEINER, E. (2003), *Documentary Culture and the Making of Medieval English Literature* (Cambridge: Cambridge University Press).

——(2007), 'Authority', in P. Strohm (ed.), *Middle English* (Oxford: Oxford University Press), 142–59.

STROHM, P. (1992), *Hochon's Arrow: The Social Imagination of Fourteenth-Century Texts* (Princeton: Princeton University Press).

SUTHERLAND, D. (1973), *The Assize of Novel Disseisin* (Oxford: Clarendon Press).

TOUT, T. (1920–33), *Chapters in the Administrative History of Mediaeval England: The Wardrobe, the Chamber and the Small Seals* (6 vols. Manchester: Manchester University Press).

TREHARNE, E. (ed.) (2000), *Old and Middle English: An Anthology* (Oxford: Blackwell).

TURNER, M. (2007), *Chaucerian Conflict: Languages of Antagonism in Late Fourteenth-Century London* (Oxford: Clarendon Press).

TURNER, R. (1988), *Men Raised from the Dust: Administrative Service and Upward Mobility in Angevin England* (Philadelphia: University of Pennsylvania Press).

WEBER, M. (1948), *From Max Weber: Essays in Sociology*, ed. H. Gerth and C. Wright Mills (London: Routledge & Kegan Paul).

WHITELOCK, D. (ed.) (1979), *English Historical Documents, c.500–1042* (2nd edn. London: Eyre & Spottiswoode).

WOOLGAR, C. (1992), *Household Accounts from Medieval England* (2 vols. Oxford: Oxford University Press/British Academy).

WORMALD, P. (1999), *The Making of English Law: King Alfred to the Twelfth Century*, i. *Legislation and its Limits* (Oxford: Blackwell).

——(2004), 'Wulfstan (d. 1023)', in *The Oxford Dictionary of National Biography* (Oxford: Oxford University Press), http://www.oxforddnb.com/view/article/30098 (accessed Aug. 2008).

CHAPTER 5

....

THE IMPACT
OF PRINT

THE PERCEIVED WORTH
OF THE PRINTED BOOK
IN ENGLAND, 1476–1575

....

ELIZABETH EVENDEN-KENYON

THE BOOK: WRITTEN AND PRINTED

....

Students who first turn their attention to the study of book production often come with the erroneous belief that the invention of the book was synonymous with the invention of printing.[1] They might assume that the production of such an end-product only came about once the system of producing a text by mechanical means came to fruition. In part, this is because we tend to refer to any text produced by hand as a 'manuscript'; even the earliest printed books do not tend to be categorized as 'books', but go under a different name: incunabula. Students are often aware that academics go to libraries to look at books, archives to look at manuscripts.[2] But the

[1] I am grateful to the British Academy for providing me with a Small Research Grant to complete research for this chapter in a number of libraries across North America. I would also like to thank Bruce Janacek for all his help and support.

[2] David McKitterick has likewise recently noted that, even in the early 21st century, 'there remains too much of a division in historians' minds between manuscript and print' (McKitterick 2003: 11). There are also problems inherent in academic fields of study, which can then be passed on to students; e.g. an

truth of the matter is not so simple. Manuscript books did—do—exist. And the earliest printed books—incunabula—were made to *look* like manuscript books. They were merely using a new means to produce the same product.

This essay will examine the first hundred years of printed book production in England—from the first text printed in England by William Caxton to the death of one of England's most prolific collectors of English manuscripts, incunabula, and early printed books: Elizabeth I's archbishop of Canterbury, Matthew Parker. Though there is not room enough to cover all of the areas here, what this chapter aims to show is that, in the space of almost one hundred years, 1476–1576, the invention of printing had an impact in many areas of book production and dissemination, and upon the trade in new and old texts as a whole. The power of the press to circulate the content of earlier manuscripts will be examined in order to exemplify the impact of dissemination by print; it will also explore the ways in which those in the book trade, those supporting it, and the English reading public perceived the value (not just in fiscal terms) of both the texts themselves and the artefacts—books—that divulged these many and varied texts.

The book—or 'codex'—had been the most popular format for the production of text in the West since around AD 400. It had existed prior to then, battling for supremacy over alternative formats: the 'roll' and, to a lesser extent, the tablet. But the popularity and ultimate endurance of the codex was the result of a number of factors, not least because it was easier to handle, easier to store, easier to move back and forth in, and could potentially accommodate more texts than the alternatives. The codex was adopted quickly by the early Christians, and spread to the West with comparable ease. A thousand years later, by 1400, manuscript books proliferated in the religious institutions of England and beyond.[3]

With the rise of scholasticism and its intellectual explorations in the written, rather than purely oral, word, the need for—and interaction with—texts became increasingly sophisticated. Books were being 'read' silently, rather than 'heard', as never before. As a result, the texts produced as the period progressed reflect these changes. Chapter divisions became increasingly common, as did the use of other textual apparatus to assist the 'reader' of these texts, such as running heads, diagrams, marginal notes, as well as new forms of punctuation, even the inclusion of coloured paragraph marks to help quickly identify different portions of texts. The inclusion of new signs, symbols, and of colours in such texts, it should be noted, provides us with

over-simplification in the use of the crude distinction between the two periods of history described as the 'Middle Ages' and the 'early modern period'. They can seem to be two very distinct periods of study and of experience: the 'Middle Ages', a period of manuscript and oral communication; the 'early modern period', the period of print, where texts were proliferated as a result of the Reformation and Renaissance. We all run the risk of thinking that manuscript and oral dissemination ceased to exist at this point. Crick and Walsham warn us of the problems caused by such a 'paradigm devised to justify a major historical rupture', noting that recent scholarship is at least going some way to emphasizing the crucial importance of manuscript and oral communication during the 16th century and beyond. (See Crick and Walsham 2004: 24.)

[3] See Diringer (1982); Hurtado (1986); Roberts and Skeat (1987).

internal evidence of how books were increasingly produced to be read by individual readers, rather than to be read to an audience. Such apparatus were included to help the reader navigate the text.

Across much of Europe, during the later Middle Ages, the script used to produce these texts for readers was usually a Gothic cursive script, since it could be written legibly at a relatively quick pace. It allowed the books to be produced quickly, thus potentially allowing more copies of the same text to be produced with relative speed, as reader demand began to challenge supply. During the thirteenth century, paper began to be more readily available, and thus the possibilities of producing less costly, although still time-consuming, codices was also becoming possible. By the fourteenth century, paper was accessible across much of Europe and book production was increasing significantly.[4]

As lay literacy began to increase during the late Middle Ages, so too did the demand for specific types of books. Demand increased for works of popular literature, such as romance and poetry, as well as for technical handbooks. Perhaps just as significant was the rise in requests for books specifically in the vernacular. The production of such texts—in large quantities—was initially confined predominantly to continental Europe and its languages. Although there was a demand from readers in England, it lagged behind its continental counterparts in the number of scriptoria available to undertake such orders. It appears that many of the English scribes and rubricators producing such multiple manuscripts worked across a number of locations, each production-base struggling to meet demand. Lay book producers were particularly rare in England so the numbers of production staff available to manufacture books were fewer in number than in other countries. But in all countries, the process was essentially the same.[5]

MAKING THE BOOK

To produce a book first of all an adequate amount of parchment or paper would be acquired, folded at least once, with one sheet folded inside the other (usually in fours) to create a booklet or 'quire'. This was the easiest method to produce large books. For smaller books the sheets would be folded again and again (if necessary) to produce smaller pages, which then would need to be cut to open up the pages. Once the text was completed by the scribe, it would sometimes be checked for errors by a corrector. Any errors could be excised by removing the ink with a knife or by applying a light acidic solution that could loosen the ink. The correction would

---

[4] On the manufacture of paper see Gaskell (1995: 57–77). On early paper mills in England, see Febvre and Martin (1976: 29–44); Lyall (2007).

[5] For the production of manuscript books and the transition to print also see: Goldschmidt (1943); Hindman and Farquhar (1977: 11–99); Ker (1985, 1960).

then be filled in. If this more time-consuming method was not applied, the scribe would simply cross out the erroneous text and add the correction where possible.

The next stage was to add rubrication, which, as its name suggests (from 'rubrica', meaning red earth) was usually completed in red. Chapter headings or key words, capital letters, and paragraph marks would frequently be rubricated. Sometimes, the text would receive further attention in the form of decoration. Usually this involved the decoration of painted capitals but additional illumination and gilding could also be applied.[6] Although significant numbers of texts were rubricated, decoration and illumination were still reserved for specific clientele who could afford such adornments and were prepared to wait while the additional work was undertaken.

By the fifteenth century those producing books were under increasing pressure to produce multiple copies of new and popular texts with relative speed. Scriptoria and ateliers (where artists worked) found themselves struggling to meet demand. Across all of Europe, the time was right for an alternative, speedier mode of book production to be invented, to meet consumer demand. In the West, it is perhaps no surprise that it came to continental Europe first. Johann Gutenberg, a goldsmith from Mainz, invented the manufacture and use of movable type in around 1439.[7] As for the printing presses that would use Gutenberg's great invention, they were adaptations of the common screw press, which had been in existence for centuries, first used to press oil from olives, juice from grapes, and, subsequently, water out of paper.[8]

The art of printing spread quickly across Europe and by the 1470s there were presses in many of the countries of western Europe.[9] The bulk of material they produced was significant: it has been estimated that in continental Europe 'by 1472 at the latest, the number of printed pages produced exceeded the number of pages written by scribes'.[10] The books produced in the later Middle Ages differed little in their appearance from the manuscript books that preceded them. Indeed, the first printed texts were intended to look the same; printing was merely a cheaper and quicker method of producing the same product. The typefaces used were modelled on the regional scripts.[11] The use of signatures, foliation, and catchwords were all first used in manuscript books and then continued in their printed counterparts, so that early printed books emulated the visual features of manuscript books; at first glance, indeed, some printed books can look just like manuscripts.[12]

Sometimes scribes would identify themselves on the copy of a book they had worked on; printers, however, went further, including a 'device' that would identify

---

[6] See Alexander (1978, 1994, 1999); de Hamel (1997); Scott et al. (2007).

[7] On Gutenberg see: Füssel (2005); McMurtrie (1941); Needham (1983).

[8] See Moran (1973: 17–48); Gaskell (1995: 118–24).

[9] The spread of printing across Europe is too complex and voluminous a topic to cover here but for discussions of the early years of printing in continental Europe see, by way of example: Steinberg (1996: 17–53); Balsamo (1975–6); Carter (1969); Gerulaitis (1976); Hellinga-Querido (1971); Hirsch (1974); Pettas (1973); Rhodes (1949); Trapp (1983); Witten (1959).

[10] See Flood (2003: 139).

[11] On early type design see Steinberg (1996: 9–17); Gaskell (1995: 9–39).

[12] See Gaskell (1995: 5–8).

them as the creator of the printed book. They included woodblock images, which would act as advertising symbols for their printing house, making their work instantly recognizable by its inclusion, usually at the end of the book.[13] Some printers, particularly the Parisians, included large woodblock images, which were difficult to include at the end of the book. Consequently, they put their device at the front of the book; a decision that, over time, contributed to the rise of the title-page in printed books.[14] Printers increasingly included details of their location—where the text was printed and where it could be purchased. The advertising of the printer's name and location quickly began to appear, as a marketing strategy to assist sales.

Although the appearance of books changed little with the arrival of the printing press, the book trade itself changed substantially. The greatest initial impact of the arrival of mechanized production in the book trade was on its personnel: scribes were theoretically no longer in demand. Some were able to adapt to the changing market and become printers, others found work in chanceries and as notaries, while some managed, nonetheless, to continue as scribes, but for a diminished market in manuscript books.[15] Those whose role it was to illuminate and decorate books could still find work, since many books, for elite clientele, continued to be coloured well into the next century. Once books began to be produced on a press, print runs of texts, needless to say, increased dramatically, and printers found themselves more than capable of meeting the demand for books—so much so that the cost of books initially decreased significantly, although they remained expensive goods despite this reduction in cost to the consumer. With an increase in copies available for sale came the rise of the independent bookseller.

THE BOOK TRADE

Although there remained a market for bespoke manuscript books, the potential for fiscal return brought about by the new technology was enough to ensure that printing houses began to proliferate across Europe. This increase in the numbers of printing houses and booksellers to disperse their wares exemplifies one of the biggest impacts printing had on the book trade: it had become a financially speculative business venture, moved firmly into the realm of the laity. As purely commercial enterprises, many printing centres founded their businesses and focused their attention on building up clientele in the great commercial centres across Europe, where they could potentially reach significant numbers of customers. These mercantile

[13] Johann Fust and Peter Schoeffer used the first such device in 1462. At first the device was placed at the end of the book below the colophon.
[14] See Smith (2000).
[15] Manuscript books continued to be produced long after the period studied here. See Love (1993); Beal (1998).

centres also offered the attractive possibility of reaching a wide range of customers from across Europe—so long as readers could understand the language of the text. Hence Latin texts could be—and were—transported across Europe in vast numbers, while vernacular texts were produced closer to home, for an internal market. As the use of the vernacular began to regain authority in England, English readers increasingly sought texts in their mother tongue. The time was right for someone to step into the breach and fill this gap in the English consumer market.

William Caxton was the man to do exactly that. Born in Kent at some point between 1415 and 1424, Caxton was apprenticed to a mercer, Robert Large, when he was around 14 years old.[16] By 1449 he was in Bruges, a hub for merchants travelling all across Europe; it is likely that he earned his way trading not only cloths but also manuscripts—a not uncommon practice for the time. In 1462 Caxton became the governor of the English Merchant Adventurers in the city. By 1469 he had decided to engage in book production, with the English market in mind, and began translating texts, such as the *History of Troy* from French into English. Although civil war led him to delay his plans, he finished the translation, moving to Cologne to finally learn the art of printing, where he met many aspiring printers, including the young Wynkyn de Worde. Caxton printed his own translation of the *Recuyell of the Historyes of Troye* in Bruges for his first literary patron, Margaret of Burgundy, at some point between 1473 and 1474.[17] Within two years he had moved his business to England. In 1476 his name appeared on an account roll of John Estency, Sacrist of Westminster Abbey; he paid a year's rent in advance for premises in which to set up the first printing press in England.[18] Westminster was a calculated choice; he could find plenty of customers among the merchants, clerics, and lower gentry there. The abbey and its cathedral precincts had long been associated with scribes and stationers.

Caxton's first known production on this Westminster press, at the sign of the Red Pale, was a Letter of Indulgence by John Sant, abbot of Abingdon, dated 13 December 1476 and presented to Henry and Katherine Langley.[19] Indulgences and pardons were cheap to produce and brought in a steady income for a printer.[20] A sound financial income was necessary, since Caxton needed to raise capital to fund larger projects that would take some time to make it through the press. Like Gutenberg before him, Caxton quickly learnt that by producing cheap printed works for the authorities, such as indulgences and primers, he could generate an income for himself while working on more substantial projects, upon which he could build his reputation as a quality printer. Such a strategy would become the foundation stone of all successful printing businesses in the coming century and beyond.[21]

---

[16] For a comprehensive account of the life of William Caxton, see the entry by N. F. Blake in the *Oxford Dictionary of National Biography*.

[17] See Blake (1978).

[18] On Caxton's property and its use after his death, see Nixon (1976).

[19] The National Archives, E 135/6/56.

[20] See Füssel (2005: 68); Swanson (2007: 85, 249, 253); Carlson (2006).

[21] For a discussion of the necessity of gaining the rights to produce cheap, small books to fund bigger projects see Evenden (2008: *passim*).

PRINT IN ENGLAND

Among the earliest books produced by Caxton during this period, funded by the production of small, ephemeral texts, was *The dictes or sayengis of the philosophers*, which he completed on 18 November 1477.[22] Like many of his productions, this was a translation of a French text (Guillaume de Tignoville's *Les ditz moraulz des philoso-phers*). Although Caxton translated many texts himself, this text was translated by another patron, Anthony Woodville, second Earl Rivers, brother-in-law of Edward IV. Copies of this work certainly provide ample evidence of how the earliest printed books looked very much like manuscripts—the font used is particularly hard to distinguish from manuscript hand.[23] It contains little in the way of punctuation and has many rubricated initials.

In 1481 Caxton produced the first illustrated book in England, the *myrrour of the world*.[24] The text was a translation by Caxton of *L'image du Monde*, an introduction to the history of science, covering a number of subjects, such as geography, cosmology, zoology, as well as economics and music. Caxton included thirty-eight woodcuts, which depict a variety of scenes, including a globe, a compass, a tutor with his pupils, and a musician, to accompany his text in Gothic typeface. He produced a second edition nine years later. In his preface to the work, Caxton asserts that the commissioning of diagrammatic illustrations for inclusion was necessary, since 'without whiche it may not lightly be understande'.[25] The other illustrations included, such as the illustration of the tutor at work, were added for their aesthetic appeal to the reader, an aspect of book production and marketing that will be explored further below.

But perhaps the books considered in modern times to be the most famous of Caxton's productions on the first printing press in England are his editions of *The Canterbury Tales*, a work which had proven immensely popular in manuscript. His first printed edition appeared in 1477.[26] The layout of the pages is very basic (no borders or headers), in Gothic typeface, and has rubricated initials throughout, not all of which have director letters in place to confirm which letter needs to be rubricated. Six years later Caxton produced a second edition. In the preface to this edition Caxton explains that a dissatisfied customer, who had purchased a first edition and noted many errors in the printing, brought to him a manuscript version 'by whiche I have corrected my book'.[27] Yet this 'corrected' edition went further than

---

[22] *The dictes or sayengis of the philosophers* (1477).

[23] Indeed, a copy in the Pierpont-Morgan Library, New York, contains manuscript marginal notes, which closely resemble the typeface of the text (ChL 1759a; see e.g. fo. 49^v).

[24] Gossuin of Metze (1481, tr. Caxton).

[25] Ibid., sig.A4^v. It should be noted that printing also speeded up the process of illustration. Once a woodblock had been cut, the printer could reproduce its images quickly, each imprint of it being an exact replica of the last.

[26] Chaucer (1477).

[27] Chaucer (1483), sig. A2^v.

merely correcting the text. It improved on its visual appearance also: Caxton introduced twenty-two woodcuts into this edition: images of the pilgrims on horseback, plus one of them at dinner in the Tabard Inn. Caxton was listening to customer feedback and improving on his art.[28] He was also doing something more in these editions: both printing *and* editing these works, he was significantly shaping the text.[29]

By his death in 1492, Caxton had produced around one hundred works, had himself translated around a quarter of these texts, and had personally edited most of them. What is noticeable from even a glance at the list of titles he produced is his awareness of what was popular with the reading public: romances, poetry, and various texts of devotion. He was also aware of the importance of financial backing for his ventures: twenty-three of the seventy-seven original works produced by Caxton (nearly 30 per cent) were assured financial support before he commenced work on them. Caxton clearly realized the fiscal volatility of the printing trade. After all, printing was a front-loading business; he needed capital up-front to survive.

BOOK PRODUCTION IN THE SIXTEENTH CENTURY

A greater level of experimentation with layout and illustration came with Wynkyn de Worde and his London contemporaries. Having taken over Caxton's business, De Worde moved to the sign of the Sun in Fleet Street in 1500.[30] Such a move emphasizes the growing market for books among the merchants of the City of London, which had seen a steady increase in demand over the previous century.[31] Indeed the trade in books had increased in organization considerably. There had been a mistery (or fellowship) of limners and writers of script since at least 1357; in 1403 a mistery comprising of 'limners, scriveners, and textwriters, together with binders and sellers of books' was established.[32] With the arrival of printing in the capital, an increase in demand for their trade soon meant that competition began to open up, with more and more printers setting up business in the capital, some providing not only the texts that they produced themselves but also a significant number of imported books.[33] There was also a healthy trade in second-hand books and manuscripts.[34]

---

[28] It is important to note that these early printed texts, like the manuscript versions before them, did not emblazon the author's name on the opening page. Rather, in these early edns. of the *Canterbury Tales*, Chaucer's name is 'embedded ambiguously within the text'. See Gillespie (2006: 56).

[29] See Hellinga (1983).

[30] On Wynkyn de Worde, see the entry by N. F. Blake in the *ODNB*; Hellinga (2003); Plomer (1925); Moran (2003); Blayney (2003).

[31] A rival printer, William de Machlinia, also moved to Fleet Street, from Dowgate, prior to De Worde's move there. See Raven (2007: 14).

[32] Ibid. 12.

[33] On the early London book trade see Christianson (1999); Raven (2007: 12–45).

[34] See Christianson (1999: 132–3).

But it should not be assumed that the scribe became defunct in the book trade. It continued as an independent role, diversifying and adapting to consumer tastes. Indeed, even after the arrival and initial spread of printing in England, print did not automatically become the medium of choice for writers of the period. Some, such as the poet John Skelton, made deliberate choices between manuscript and print, depending on the motivations that lay behind the production of their text.[35] Skelton was having his works printed as early as 1499 but it was not always his first choice of medium, being very much dependent upon the target audience for his writings. In 1509, for example, he wrote a poem on Henry VIII's coronation, *A Lawde and Prayse Made for our Sovereigne Lord the Kyng*, which he presented in manuscript to the King, presumably in the hope of patronage.[36] At other times, when later professing his support for Henry, however, Skelton chose to publicize his work to a wider reader-ship by disseminating it in print: his *A Ballade of the Scottysshe Kynge*, about the Battle of Flodden, for example, was printed in September 1513.[37] The coexistence of print and manuscript presented writers with tactical choices.

This ability to choose to 'publish' ideas and opinions in print *or* manuscript continued well into the sixteenth century and beyond.[38] Such a choice ultimately had an effect on how manuscript could be perceived. Once the option to print was firmly established and was in general the medium of choice, books in manuscript often developed 'an aura of forbidden knowledge' or one of 'privileged secrecy'.[39] To have a text printed gave its contents a form of legitimacy, an air of orthodoxy. Manuscript allowed authors far more freedom of expression and, potentially, let them be more subversive. Increasingly, the printed word gained authority, prestige, and stories or accounts that remained purely in the oral realm ran a danger of being dismissed as merely unreliable and lacking in substantiating proof. In such instances, manuscript was likely to be favoured above the purely oral, since it was considered that documentary evidence was of more authority. Words on a page then—preferably a printed one—were perceived to be of greater value than word of mouth. Certainly by the end of the period in question this had become true for many. In the 1570s, for example, the oral testimonies of witnesses remained important in his accounts of the Marian martyrs, but John Foxe nonetheless favoured written testimony and manu-script accounts as narrative sources above those delivered to him orally.[40] The written

---

[35] For the career of John Skelton, see the entry by John Scattergood in the *ODNB*; Walker (1988).

[36] The autograph copy survives at TNA, E 36/228. Skelton presented the king with other manuscripts. See Corpus Christi College, Cambridge, 432, a 13th-cent. copy of the *Chroniques de Rains*. Skelton's autograph appears on fo. iv.

[37] Skelton (1513).

[38] Recent scholarship has acknowledged the problems surrounding the use of the term 'publication'. Most recently, Crick and Walsham (2004) have pointed to the erroneous use of the term as 'synonymous with printing, without thought for how texts reached the reading public... before 1500, where it was often equated with the act of presenting a work to a patron'. 'Publishing', like 'uttering', was a term whose use had its roots firmly in oral dissemination. Early printers referred to the selling of their wares as the 'uttering' of books. (See the entries on 'publish' and 'utter' in the *Oxford English Dictionary*.)

[39] Love (1993: 107, 111).

[40] For evidence of this practice see Evenden (2009).

word was perceived by Foxe to be worth more to him than evidence provided by word of mouth.

Foxe, like many writers and compilers of editions, often commented on the salvaging aspect of their work. So too did printers. In their prefaces, many of the early printers voiced the claim that by printing certain texts they had acquired in manuscript form they were rescuing their contents from the brink of oblivion. In 1530, Robert Copland, himself a poet and printer, penned some additional verses for Wynkyn de Worde's edition of Chaucer's *The assemblie of foules*, claiming, in a poem at the close of the book that the manuscript:

> Layde upon shelfe / in leves all to torne
> With letters dymme / almost defaced clene
> Thy hyllynge rotte / with wormes all to worne
> Thou lay / that pyte was to sene
> Bounde with olde quayres / for aege all hoore and grene
> Thy mater endormed / for lacke of they presence
> But nowe thou arte losed / go shewe forth thy sente[n]ce

> And where thou become so ordre thy language
> That in excuse thy prynter loke thou have
> Whiche hathe the kepte frome ruynous domage
> In snoweswyte paper / thy mater for to save
> With thylke same langage that Chaucer to the gave
> In termes olde / of sentence clered newe
> Tha[n] methe moche sweter / who ca[n] his my[n]de avewe ...[41]

Copland was aware of both the market for such texts and of consumer tastes in general, claiming in his opening poem that *The assemblie of foules* would appeal to customers, unlike, he bemoaned, some of his other stock: 'Olde morall bokes stonde styll upon the shelfe / I am in fere they wyll never be bought'.[42] If texts were withering out of existence in manuscript, then those not committed to any sort of paper were in even greater danger of disappearing. Chaucer himself had conceded as much (albeit partly as a marketing strategy for his own writings) in his verse rendition of the tale of Anelida and Arcite. In the opening of the work Chaucer notes how the passage of time can 'frete and byte ... many a noble storye' out of memory.[43] Caxton's marketing strategy was both astute and accurate: texts were more likely to live on if put on paper and not just spoken.

Equally, the new technology gave a fresh lease of life to many texts that had been in manuscript for generations, if not longer, thus allowing readers to access copies for the first time or replace an earlier, manuscript copy. Yet it should also be noted that this was an astute, fairly safe, business move by these early English printers. If a book had sold well in manuscript, it was likely to prove just as popular in printed form. It is perhaps therefore unsurprising that, as Martha Driver has observed of the first fifty

---

[41] Chaucer (1530), sig. B6ᵛ.   [42] Ibid. sig. A2ʳ.
[43] Chaucer (1477?), sig. A1ʳ. The title of the book is taken from the first line of text.

years of printing in western Europe, 'very little appeared in print that had not previously appeared in manuscript'.[44]

Jacobus de Voragine's *Legenda sanctorum* (more popularly known in the *Legenda aurea* or *Golden Legend* in English and containing lives of the saints) is one such example. This hagiographic bestseller, written by de Voragine, a Dominican friar, in around 1266, was highly popular in manuscript. It still survives today in more than 900 manuscripts, not only in the original Latin but in a number of European languages also. The text was first printed in Basle in 1470 and it was not long after setting up business in the precinct of Westminster Abbey that Caxton set to work on production of his own translation into English from the French of Jean de Vignay.[45] After Caxton's death in 1492, his former business partner, Wynkyn de Worde, continued to produce copies of the *Golden Legend*. This proved a wise commercial venture, since the book continued to sell well; between 1470 and 1530 it was amongst the most popularly printed books across Europe.[46] After the Reformation, its popularity in print dwindled to the extent that, after 1613, only one edition was printed in the next 230 years.

USERS OF BOOKS

Surviving copies of the *Golden Legend* often provide evidence of how readers interacted with the printed texts they owned. In modern times, we have a tendency to venerate printed texts in the sense that many of us leave no trace of our thoughts on the pages of books. After all, we have been taught for generations not to write on library books. Our awareness of the high cost of books (academic books in particular) leaves us often reluctant to write, even in pencil, in books that we own. The potential for the book to be sold on, after we no longer need it, makes us want to leave the pages pristine; it is worth more on the second-hand market if we have left well alone. Similarly, we tend to feel that the book just looks better without a wealth of notes inside; most readers respect its white spaces.

This reverence (whether enforced or for pecuniary or aesthetic reasons) was not a sentiment shared by readers of the period in question here. As Bill Sherman has recently researched, in his seminal study, *Used Books: Marking Readers in Renaissance England*, fifteenth- and sixteenth-century printed books, like contemporary and earlier manuscripts, were frequently used by readers to leave their mark. They did this for a multitude of reasons.[47] In his detailed survey of early printed books in the

---

[44] Driver (2004: 5–6).
[45] Jacobus (1483, tr. Caxton). A 2nd edn. appeared from Caxton's press around 1487.
[46] De Worde produced at least six further edns. of the *Golden Legend* during his career. See the entry on Jacobus de Voraigne in Short Title Catalogue.
[47] Sherman (2008).

Huntington Library, Sherman discovered a wealth of manuscript manicules (point-ing hands), hederas (ivy leaves), doodles, and writings of various sorts within the collection. The perceived worth of the pages of these books for these readers was very different in many ways to that which we hold today. These books are valuable items, now accessible only for specialized study. For their earliest readers, they were costly commodities, whose contents provided a wealth of valuable information.

The paper surrounding the text was also valuable in the sense that it provided space for personal writings. These might be notes or glosses on the text being read or references to other works read but, as Sherman notes, they could also be nothing to do with the text they accompanied. Paper was still a valuable commodity and not to be wasted. Readers (or, indeed, younger members of their household) might choose to practise penmanship in the available spaces, to work out financial accounts, preserve a recipe, or simply to acknowledge their ownership of the text. Just as generations of readers before them had done with manuscripts, printed book owners continued to see available space as valuable for a multitude of reasons.

As with signing one's name, or practising one's signature, the nature of the markings could, at times, be highly personal. Reading books could not only offer information to improve knowledge, but also consolation to a troubled spirit. By way of example, a copy of Wynkyn de Worde's 1521 edition of the *Legenda aurea*, now in the Pierpont Morgan Library, New York, had multiple owners who made their mark upon its pages.[48] The most poignant of these marks are the writings of Ursula Stafford, wife of Henry Stafford, first Baron Stafford, and daughter of Sir Richard Pole of Ellesborough, in Buckinghamshire, and sister to Reginald Pole, who would become cardinal and archbishop of Canterbury under Mary Tudor. Her eldest son, Thomas, rebelled against Mary at Scarborough, was caught, and subse-quently executed for High Treason in May 1557.[49] Ursula appears to have used this text for consolation, writing a number of manuscript notes within it, suggestive of her state of mind while she perused its pages, such as 'Jesus sende me grace. And in heaven a place. Amo. Ursula Stafford I live devoyde of love.'[50] She later passed the book on to her fourth son, whose only marks were acknowledgement of his subsequent ownership of the text: 'Edward Stafford o[n]eth this boocke. god profese his life. Amen.'[51]

If the Stafford family used their copy of the *Golden Legend* for spiritual consola-tion, other families did not. A family of the name of Goodin once owned a copy of Wynkyn de Worde's 1521 edition now housed in Cambridge University Library. While family members practised their signature in the volume, one member expressed his perceived worth of its contents in its margins: this reader clearly disagreed with much of the contents. Prayers to the saints are identified as blasphemy and damnable.[52] In the life of St Agathon, they have added a manicule to mark the passage: 'he answered / I trow there be no laboure so grete as to praye to god / for the sende laboureth alway to breke his prayer and in other laboures a man hath some reste / he [tha]t

---

[48] Call number W 16C.   [49] See Bindoff (1982: iii. 363–4; Loades (1991: 304–8).
[50] Sig. E2ʳ.   [51] Sig. q3ᵛ.   [52] Cambridge University Library, shelfmark: Sel.3.54.

prayeth hath alwaye need of grete stryfe'. In response to this passage is the manuscript note: 'I think that that is one of the truest things in this book: whether Agathon spake yt or noe'.[53]

Like many Reformation readers, this person believed that such early printed religious texts contained false, or at the very least potentially misleading, material. Martha Driver has noted that this led them 'to censor, deface and gloss late medieval manuscripts, printed books and indulgence texts that contained material that they found objectionable'. It is important to note that such readers did not destroy such books; they merely erased the objectionable, leaving intact any content that they considered 'was still, from their point of view, instructive and spiritually elevating'.[54]

Many incunables and early printed books, like many medieval manuscripts, were deemed worth holding on to, even though they contained material considered offensive to reformed readers. It is this very method of censorship, rather than destruction, that modern readers have to thank for the survival of these texts today. After the break with Rome, such a method of censorship, rather than destruction, was central to English reform; the authorities were aware of the amount of potentially offensive printed material already out there in the hands of a reading public. In 1542 Thomas Cranmer, archbishop of Canterbury, successfully passed an order through convocation that 'all manner of mention of the bishop of Rome's name, [be removed] from all apocrypha, feigned legends, superstitious orations, collects, versicles and responses'.[55]

Surviving printed texts suggest that many individual readers followed the order. Again, copies of Caxton's *Golden Legend* can provide us with such examples of censorship. A copy now housed in the Rare Book Room of New York Public Library has all the references to the Pope in it crossed out. There are also a number of cross-hatchings throughout various lives of the saints.[56] Similarly, Missals often came in for the same treatment: a copy of the Sarum Missal, printed by Richard Pynson in 1520 and now housed in the Pierpont Morgan Library has all instances of the word 'pope' crossed out also.[57] In the same library, a copy of Wynkyn de Worde's 1502 edition of the *Ordynarye of Crystante of crysten men* has also received the same treatment.[58] Indeed, numerous examples survive in the major collections of Britain and North America, where references to the papacy and to saints have been defaced, while other portions of the text remain untouched.

This is one of the key points of impact that the Reformation had on books and the book trade: titles once deemed bestsellers and a guaranteed source of income for printers were swept away from the shelves of the book stores, not to be reprinted. What is particularly interesting is that individual readers were not so much expected

---

[53] Sig. 2y1ᵛ. The words 'one of' are an interlinear addition. The word 'only' is crossed out before the word 'truest'. Clearly the reader was modifying his opinion whilst in the act of writing his comments.

[54] Driver (2004: 185).

[55] Ibid. 200.

[56] It is noteworthy that these references to the Pope in the Goodin family copy remain untouched.

[57] Call number E1 03B.

[58] Call number W 16A.

to remove these texts from their own bookshelves, but more to be mindful that some of their contents might now be deemed, at best, inappropriate or, at worst, false doctrine. This form of censorship and of selective reading was propounded at every level under Protestant rule. It left readers mindful of what could or should be trusted in medieval manuscripts and incunabula.

THE INFLUENCE OF BOOKS

Under the Protestant Elizabeth I, this questioning of earlier writings took on new meaning and this process of selection became an essential tool for the regime in its defence of the English Church. In order to prove itself the True Church and show Catholic doctrine as false, the Elizabethan authorities needed to show that the English Church was purging itself of corruptions and returning to its pristine state; rather than corruptors, the English aimed to prove themselves as having once been corrupted; the English Protestants were merely returning religious practice to its original state. In order to do this, they not only purged the manuscripts and printed texts already in existence, they looked back to earlier texts for evidence of a true doctrine in England, prior to its corruption by the papacy.

The central figure in this strategy was Matthew Parker (1504–75), Elizabeth's archbishop of Canterbury. Parker commissioned a great 'searching out of books', in order to recover books lost as a result of the Dissolution of the Monasteries in the late 1530s and early 1540s and the subsequent dispersal of their manuscripts across the country.[59] Parker believed that manuscripts would provide the evidence he required to prove the 'pedigree' of the English Church. Thousands of manuscripts were recovered; some of those that proved beneficial to his argument, Parker decided to have printed. He turned to print for a number of reasons. First, by the 1560s, the impact that a printed text could have in the cross-confessional arguments of the day had become clear. Texts could be copied quickly in print and circulated in great numbers, not just in England but also to continental detractors if so required. Like the early printers, Parker was selecting the manuscripts that would be of most use to him. He was also replicating the printers' motives and claims in that he was preserving texts that had been in real danger of being lost for all time. But he was *only* putting into print texts that were useful to him.

Parker turned to the printing press to replicate and disseminate early English documents, such as the writings of the Old English homilist Ælfric (including his sermons on the Eucharist) and Anglo-Saxon settings of the Lord's Prayer and Creed. These particular texts were in fact printed together in one volume, whose title left the

---

[59] See Evenden (2008: 81).

reader in no doubt of Parker's agenda in having them printed: *A testimonie of antiquitie shewing the auncient faith in the Church of England touching the sacrament of the body and bloude of the Lord here publikely preached, and also receaued in the Saxons tyme, abt 600. yeares agoe.*[60] This was the first time that any printer had attempted to replicate the contents of an Anglo-Saxon text. For decades printers had used Gothic typeface and roman type (which replicated the hand used for Latin scripts and which was beginning to be favoured by printers and their clientele above the Gothic typefaces). But here the printer chosen by Parker for the task, John Day, was entering new territory. Day had to commission a new typeface to replicate the special insular characters of the Anglo-Saxon script and its alphabet, which were not found in the Latin alphabet. This was a costly venture, which the printer wisely insisted was paid for by the Archbishop.[61]

Parker knew that the printing press was a powerful weapon in his defence of Protestantism against Catholic attacks. He also knew that a faulty weapon could be dangerous. His opponents would seize on any errors they found in the text and be likely to print their objections. Evidence survives in the printed texts themselves to show that Parker took great pains to ensure that texts such as *A testimonie of antiquitie* were printed accurately, in an attempt to avoid such attacks. The first edition of the text survives in two states, the latter of which includes changes in punctuation, corrections to minor errors, but also the inclusion of additional supporting material.[62] Clearly the printed text was being corrected during the proofing stage. A second edition occurred soon afterwards, which contained even more corrections to the text of the first.[63]

Further works followed from Day's presses, including an Anglo-Saxon/English parallel text of the Gospels. In a foreword to this book, the martyrologist John Foxe attacked those he claimed 'have judged our native tongue unmeete to expresse Gods high secret mysteries', noting that the scriptures had been translated into English many times before the arrival of printing: 'the divers tra[n]slations wherof, and in divers ages, be yet extant to be seen'.[64] These were the manuscripts that had so nearly been lost but which had resurfaced, thanks to the efforts of Matthew Parker and those who assisted him in his search for manuscripts.[65]

The reproduction of these manuscripts in printed format leads us to an important point about the impact of printing. There has not been space here to discuss

---

[60] Ælfric (1566?). For a discussion of this text see Evenden (2008: 80–4).

[61] For a detailed analysis of the career of John Day see Evenden (2008). Discussion of this Anglo-Saxon typeface occurs on pp. 82–3; see also Lucas (1999).

[62] The manuscripts used by Parker to produce *A testimonie of antiquitie* are Corpus Christi College, Cambridge, 198, and London, British Library, Cotton Faustina A.IX.

[63] See Evenden (2008: 83).

[64] Foxe (1571: sig. A3ʳ). The manuscripts used to produce this printed edn. were Oxford, Bodleian Library, Bodley 441, with some corrections from Cambridge University Library, Ii. 2. 11.

[65] On Parker's response to the dissemination of monastic collections and the actions of the Parker circle in acquiring texts, see Summit (2008: 101–35).

the collection of manuscripts into personal or institutional collections. But what should be noted is that, unlike monastic collections whose contents had 'upheld the authority of a church whose head was based in Rome', post-Reformation, Protestant collections 'were not meant simply to contain and preserve the past; rather, the books and written materials that they contained were deliberately selected and in some cases literally remade in order to strengthen' the authority of the Protestant monarch and the Protestant Church.[66] When considering the great collections of the early modern period, we must be aware of not only what they include but also consider what they left out. And much of this is left to speculation. Vast numbers of texts have been lost to us over time either through 'neglect or intentional destruction', particularly that of the later sixteenth century.[67]

THE VALUE OF EARLY BOOKS

Matthew Parker died in 1575. In just one century, English printing had turned from a small-scale, speculative trade into one whose wares proliferated across the realm, into Europe and beyond, to the New World. Each text in its own way is a priceless insight into the period of its production. The earliest of these printed texts, incunabula, now regularly make high prices at auction. It should be remembered that the term is applied to books printed prior to 1500, a way of classifying those texts produced in the earliest years of European printing. It also identifies their perceived worth to modern collectors. The directors and curators of the Huntington Library, San Marino, California, have recently acknowledged the disparate price tags on books from either side of 1500 auctioned recently, noting that 'a book published in 1501 might today be valued at only two-thirds the price of a similar book printed in the previous year'.[68] The cost of these early productions from Europe's printing presses has a considerable impact on a library's ability to purchase such tomes today. All too frequently now do librarians and academics bemoan the price tags that risk a book's disappearance into a private collection, with no access for scholars.

Yet their worth should not be considered purely in pecuniary terms. As artefacts they provide us with invaluable insights into early printing practices and consumer tastes of their day. To their contemporary readers their worth could certainly be variable. They could be seen as commercial commodities for sale at a particular price, but they could also be family heirlooms, artefacts of great personal worth, beyond that of their commercial value. A book could be an invaluable source of Truth or the

[66] Ibid. 3.   [67] Ibid.   [68] Huntington Library (2004: 71).

worthless provider of false doctrine. But whatever they sell for in auctions today, books produced from the 1470s through to the 1570s provide those of us fortunate enough to examine them with precious insights into the religious, political, cultural, and personal passions of those who wrote them, printed them, read them, and even wrote *in* them.

BIBLIOGRAPHY

ÆLFRIC (1566?), *A testimonie of antiquitie* (London, STC 159).

ALEXANDER, J. J. G. (1978), *The Decorated Letter* (New York: Braziller).

——(1994), *Medieval Illuminators and their Methods of Work* (New Haven: Yale University Press).

——(1999), 'Foreign Illuminators and Illuminated Manuscripts', in L. Hellinga and J. B. Trapp (eds.), *The Cambridge History of the Book in Britain*, iii. *1400–1557* (Cambridge: Cambridge University Press), 47–64.

BALSAMO, LUIGI (1975–6), 'The Origins of Printing in Italy and England', *Journal of the Printing Historical Society*, 11: 48–63.

BEAL, P. (1998), *In Praise of Scribes: Manuscripts and their Makers in Seventeenth-Century England* (Oxford: Oxford University Press).

BINDOFF, S. T. (ed.) (1982), *The House of Commons 1509–1558* (3 vols. London: Secker & Warburg).

BLAKE, NORMAN F. (1978), 'Dating the First Book Printed in English', *Gutenberg Jahrbuch*, 43–50.

BLAYNEY, PETER W. M. (2003), 'The Site of the Sign of the Sun', in Robin Myers, Michael Harris, and Giles Mandelbrote (eds.), *The London Book Trade: Topographies of Print in the Metropolis from the Sixteenth Century* (London: British Library; New Castle, Del.: Oak Knoll), 1–20.

CARLSON, DAVID R. (2006), 'A Theory of the Early English Printing Firm', in W. Kushin (ed.), *Caxton's Trace: Studies in the History of English Printing* (Notre Dame, Ind.: University of Notre Dame Press), 35–68.

CARTER, HARRY (1969), *A View of Early Typography up to about 1600* (Oxford: Clarendon Press).

CHAUCER, GEOFFREY (1477?), *Thou fiers god of armes, mars the rede . . .* (Westminster, STC 5090).

——(1477), *Canterbury Tales* (Westminster, STC 5082).

——(1483), *Canterbury Tales* (Westminster, STC 5083).

——(1530), *The assemblie of foules . . .* (London, STC 132.13).

CHRISTIANSON, C. PAUL (1999), 'The Rise of London's Book-Trade', in L. Hellinga and J. B. Trapp (eds.), *The Cambridge History of the Book in Britain*, iii. *1400–1557* (Cambridge: Cambridge University Press), 128–47.

CRICK, JULIA C., and ALEXANDRA WALSHAM (2004), *The Uses of Script and Print, 1300–1700* (Cambridge: Cambridge University Press).

The dictes or sayengis of the philosophers (1477) (London, STC 6830).

DIRINGER, DAVID (1982), *The Book Before Printing: Ancient, Medieval and Oriental* (New York: Courier Dover Publications).

DRIVER, MARTHA W. (2004), *The Image in Print: Book Illustration in Late Medieval England and its Sources* (London: British Library).

EVENDEN, ELIZABETH (2008), *Patents, Pictures and Patronage* (Aldershot: Ashgate).

——(2009), 'Closing the Books: The Problematic Printing of John Foxe's Histories of Henry VII and Henry VIII in his "Book of Martyrs" (1570)', in J. N. King (ed.), *Tudor Books and*

Readers: Materiality and the Construction of Meaning (Cambridge: Cambridge University Press).

FEBVRE, LUCIEN, and HENRI-JEAN MARTIN (1976), *The Coming of the Book: The Impact of Printing 1450–1800*, tr. David Gerard (London and New York: NLB).

FLOOD, JOHN L. (2003), '"Volentes Sibi Comparare Infrascriptos Libros Impressos . . .": Printed Books as a Commercial Commodity in the Fifteenth Century', in Kristian Jensen (ed.), *Incunabula and their Readers* (London: British Library), 139–51.

FOXE, JOHN (1571), *The Gospel of the fower Evangelistes translted into vulgare toung of the Saxons, newly collected out of auncient Monumentes of the sayd Saxons, and now published for testimonie of the same* (London, STC 2961).

FÜSSEL, STEPHEN (2005), *Gutenberg and the Impact of Printing*, tr. Douglas Martin (Aldershot: Ashgate).

GASKELL, PHILIP (1995), *A New Introduction to Bibliography* (2nd edn. New Castle, DE: Oak Knoll; Winchester: St Paul's Bibliographies).

GERULAITIS, L. V. (1976), *Printing and Publishing in Fifteenth Century Venice* (Chicago: American Library Association).

GILLESPIE, ALEXANDRA (2006), *Print Culture and the Medieval Author: Chaucer, Lydgate and their Books, 1473–1577* (Oxford: Oxford University Press).

GOLDSCHMIDT, E. P. (1943), *Medieval Texts and their First Appearance in Print* (London: Bibliographical Society).

Gossuin of Metze (1481), *Hier begynneth the book callid the myrrour of the worlde . . .*, tr. William Caxton (Westminster, STC 1588.01).

DE HAMEL, CHRISTOPHER (1997), *A History of Illuminated Manuscripts* (London: Phaidon).

HELLINGA-QUERIDI, LOTTE (1971), 'Early Printing in the Low Countries: Its Survival and Importance', *Delta*, 14: 24–43.

HELLINGA, LOTTE (1983), 'Manuscripts in the Hands of Printers', in J. B. Trapp (ed.), *Manuscripts in the Fifty Years after the Invention of Printing* (London: Warburg Institute, University of London), 3–11.

——(2003), 'Tradition and Renewal: Establishing the Chronology of Wynkyn de Worde's Early Work', in K. Jensen (ed.), *Incunabula and their Readers: Printing, Selling and Using Books in the Fifteenth Century* (London: British Library), 13–30.

HINDMAN, SANDRA, and JAMES DOUGLAS FARQUHAR (1977), *Pen to Press: Illustrated Manuscripts and Printed Books in the First Century of Printing* (College Park, Md.: University of Maryland).

HIRSCH, RUDOLPH (1974), *Printing, Selling and Reading, 1450–1550* (Wiesbaden: Otto Harrassowitz).

Huntington Library (2004), *The Huntington Library: Treasures from Ten Centuries* (San Marino, Calif.: Huntington Library; London: Scala).

HURTADO, L. W. (1986), *The Earliest Christian Artifacts: Manuscripts and Christian Origins* (Cambridge: Cambridge University Press).

JACOBUS DE VORAIGNE (1483), *Legenda aurea*, tr. William Caxton (Westminster, STC 24873; 2nd edn. 1487, STC 24874).

KER, N. R. (1960), *English Manuscripts in the Century after the Norman Conquest* (Oxford: Clarendon Press).

——(1985), *Books, Collectors, and Libraries: Studies in the Medieval Heritage*, ed. Andrew G. Watson (London: Hambledon Press).

LOADES, DAVID (1991), *The Reign of Mary Tudor: Politics, Government and Religion in England 1553–1558* (2nd edn. Harlow: Longman).

LOVE, HAROLD (1993), *Scribal Publication in Seventeenth-Century England* (Oxford: Oxford University Press).

LUCAS, PETER (1999), 'Parker, Lambarde and the Provision of Special Sorts for Printing Anglo-Saxon in the Sixteenth Century', *Journal of the Printing Historical Society*, 28: 41–69.

LYALL, R. J. (2007), 'Materials: The Paper Revolution', in Jeremy Griffiths and Derek Albert Pearsall (eds.), *Book Production and Publishing in Britain, 1375–1475* (Cambridge: Cambridge University Press), 11–29.

McKITTERICK, DAVID (2003), *Print, Manuscript and the Search for Order, 1450–1830* (Cambridge: Cambridge University Press).

McMURTRIE, DOUGLAS C. (tr.) (1941), *The Gutenberg Documents, with Translations of the Texts into English* (New York: Oxford University Press).

MORAN, JAMES (1973), *Printing Presses: History and Development from the Fifteenth Century to Modern Times* (London: Faber & Faber).

——(2003), *Wynkyn de Worde: Father of Fleet Street* (London: British Library; New Castle, Del.: Oak Knoll).

NEEDHAM, PAUL (1983), 'The Compositor's Hand in the Gutenberg Bible: A Review of the Todd Thesis', *Papers of the Bibliographical Society of America*, 77: 341–71.

NIXON, HOWARD M. (1976), 'Caxton, his Contemporaries and his Successors in the Book Trade from Westminster Documents', *The Library*, 5th ser. 31: 305–26.

PETTAS, WILLIAM (1973), 'The Cost of Printing a Florentine Incunable', *La bibliofilia*, 75: 67–85.

PLOMER, HENRY R. (1925), *Wynkyn de Worde and his Contemporaries from the Death of Caxton to 1535: A Chapter in English Printing* (London: Grafton & Co).

RAVEN, JAMES (2007), *The Business of Books: Booksellers and the English Book Trade 1450–1850* (New Haven and London: Yale University Press).

RHODES, DENNIS (1982), *Studies in Early Italian Printing* (London: Pindar).

ROBERTS, COLIN H., and T. C. SKEAT (1987), *The Birth of the Codex* (Oxford: Oxford University Press).

SCHOLDERER, VICTOR (1949), 'The Beginnings of Printing at Basel', *The Library*, 5th ser. 3: 50–4.

SCOTT, KATHLEEN L., MARTHA W. DRIVER, and MICHAEL T. ORR (eds.) (2007), *An Index of Images of English Manuscripts from the Time of Chaucer to Henry VIII, c.1380–c.1509* (London: Harvey Miller Publishers).

SHERMAN, WILLIAM H. (2008), *Used Books: Marking Readers in Renaissance England* (Philadelphia: University of Pennsylvania Press).

SKELTON, JOHN (1513), *A Ballade of the Scottysshe Kynge* (London, STC 22593).

SMITH, MARGARET M. (2000), *The Title-Page: Its Early Development, 1460–1510* (London: British Library; New Castle, Del.: Oak Knoll).

STEINBERG, S. H. (1996), *Five Hundred Years of Printing* (London: British Library; New Haven: Oak Knoll).

SUMMIT, JENNIFER (2008), *Memory's Library: Medieval Books in Early Modern England* (Chicago and London: University of Chicago Press).

SWANSON, R. N. (2007), *Indulgences in Late Medieval England: Passports to Paradise?* (Cambridge: Cambridge University Press).

TRAPP, J. B. (ed.) (1983), *Manuscripts in the Fifty Years after the Invention of Printing* (London: Warburg Institute, University of London).

WITTEN, LAURENCE (1959), 'The Earliest Books Printed in Spain', *Papers of the Bibliographical Society of America*, 53: 91–113.

WALKER, GREG (1988), *John Skelton and the Politics of the 1520s* (Cambridge: Cambridge University Press).

PART II

....

LITERARY
CONSUMPTION

....

CHAPTER 6

LITERATURE AND THE CULTURAL ELITES

RALPH HANNA

DEFINING THE ELITE

The title of this chapter presents a tautology and something of a challenge in terms of a long-standing Whig/progressivist model of medieval, especially late medieval, culture. In such a history, one emphasizes the developing spread of literacy, and most particularly English literacy, during the period—and within such an account, the development of sophisticated middle-class literacy looms large. In contrast, any definition of a 'cultural elite' must emphasize exclusivity, rather than the demotic. Moreover, such a group has always been defined by its artistic involvement, and among such interests, literature plainly should have prominent position. Whatever the nature of general literate culture, the 'literary' involves a particularly sophisticated, elite stripe of textual engagement, well beyond 'pragmatic' uses most normally associated with the idea of being literate, the actual thrust of the Whig argument.[1]

The topic turns out to be extremely broad. Engagement with objects that could be taken as 'literary' reflects behaviours remarkably diverse and potentially highly variegated. In the Middle Ages, the most obvious cultural elite could be described rather broadly as 'clerical'. This is comprised of persons given professionally to some form of religious life (and including enclosed women living under rule). This group

---

[1] See the standard discussions of Clanchy (1993); Parkes (1991: 275–97).

included the most sophisticated of all medieval literates, those committed to a life of the mind, whether conceived as rarefied university training in disciplines like law or theology (both succeeding a training in 'arts'), or as the regimen associated with elaborate forms of spiritual and devotional self-improvement, or as that dispersed 'teaching and preaching' that comprised the medieval cure of souls. 'Literature', for such individuals will have been based upon texts communicated in Latin or French (frequently Anglo-Norman). But simultaneously, a foretaste of the argument below, increasingly visible among such spiritual professionals are a quite substantial number of authors, among them Richard Rolle, Walter Hilton, and Nicholas Love, who choose to transfer skills acquired in different languages to a broader, English-reading audience.

A second site of elite literacy might be described as 'magnatial culture'. This would encompass that broad and variegated group that governed medieval England, one most particularly responsible for defence of the realm and the internal administration of law and justice. Yet 'magnatial culture' encompasses a wide range of various experiences. At the social pinnacle, it includes royalty and its dependants, both those related by blood and those in some form of retinue service. But magnates might run well down the social scale, through lords mainly capable of exercising local influence (the parliamentary 'barons' and those called to Westminster as 'knights of the shire') to prosperous yeomen, major property owners in a locale. At the upper reaches, this group has been quite extensively treated.[2] Like clerical intellectuals, relatively little of these persons' literary activity appears to have gone on in English, and well into the early Tudor period, such readers, particularly at the upper end, appear most stimulated by works in Latin and French (in the latter case, frequently continental luxury products). Later in the chapter I will consider more fully some lower, 'gentry' endeavours, in which increasingly, English comes to share a prominent place with literature in England's other languages.

Magnates, of whatever stripe, are most commonly associated with the administration of rural, agricultural properties. But from the late twelfth century, they were in competition with a further elite, in this case distinguished by neither blood nor extensive landholdings, but by wealth. These individuals represented urban professional classes, perhaps especially prominent merchant entrepreneurs from (and in individual cases, frequently engaged in) a variety of trades, and, in a nation with a staunch legal tradition (and a concomitant plethora of litigation), lawyers. Perhaps most visibly present through a book like the Auchinleck manuscript (Edinburgh, National Library of Scotland, Advocates' 19.1.2), produced in London, c. 1330, this group, like the lower gentry, were eventually to become prominent users of English materials. At least in part, this occurred through the activity of metropolitan local authors, like Chaucer, Gower, Hoccleve, and Lydgate. But throughout the Middle Ages, mercantile accounts are customarily trilingual, and lawyers needed both Latin

---

[2] Among the many examples of such studies, see Doyle (1983); Cavanaugh (1988); the three richly referenced chapters, by Jenny Stratford, Janet Backhouse, and James P. Carley, in Hellinga and Trapp (1999: 255–81), supplemented e.g. by Carley (2000).

and Anglo-Norman for professional purposes.[3] As a result, these people could scarcely be described as monolingual, and their book use was just as varied as the activities of those groups I have already described.

The rather bare confirmations of interests I have sketched above would tend to suggest that distinguishing components among a single elite literary audience is a matter of some difficulty. Indeed, even trying to offer three distinct, yet varied, groups of readers, as I have done in the last paragraphs, ignores significant and continuous overlaps of acquaintance, business and professional dealings, and, with them, what one might assume to be cultural interchanges.

The most ambitious and highly literate clerics, for example, seem generally to have ignored the most ubiquitous duty of their social order, that of teaching and preaching. The road to clerical success led, not through the parish or the chantry, but through administrative or bureaucratic employment. Much of this may have been ecclesiastical, service in a bishop's *familia* or retinue, but far from all of it was, and intelligent men in orders, up to the rank of bishop, frequently pursued careers as powerful (and indispensable) royal administrators. In such a context, their lives were scarcely sheltered ones, and their daily duties would have included constant interchanges with other administrators with courtly connections, as well as a large group of royal contractors, provisioners, and servants.[4]

Similarly, although those groups one might consider 'magnatial' or 'aristocratic' cover a wide range of individuals, all the way from a nationally prominent individual like John of Gaunt to local lords of considerably lesser means, but considerable intellectual pretensions, distinguishing these ranks absolutely would be extremely difficult. People of this stripe were expected to achieve notoriety through war-service and to govern a locality through domestic service in such institutions as commissions of justices of the peace. In both these procedures, given that great lords exercised their influence by building up extensive retinues, men of rather lowly station had ample opportunity to associate with and experience the splendour associated with their social 'betters'—and to set about emulating it, as far as they could.[5] And given the tenacity of English administration, both groups had ample opportunity to associate with learned clerical cadres.

---

[3] On mercantile language-use, see Laura Wright's various studies, conveniently grouped at 'Bills, Accounts, Inventories: Everyday Trilingual Activities in the Business World of Late Medieval England', in Trotter (2000: 149–56, at 151–2, n. 5); on 'The Languages of the Law in Later Medieval England', see Brand, ibid. 63–76.

[4] Pantin (1955: 9–14) traces the rise of administrator-bishops. On clerics in royal service, see Grassi (1970: 12–33), her narrative continued by Hughes (1988). Although it is easy to dismiss the literacy of parish and chantry clergy, one Geoffrey de Lawath MA, a London rector in the late 13th cent., left a list of 48 vols., all inferentially his; see James (1905: 158–9). Probably a great deal more typical is the 'perpetual library' established by a York priest, described by Moran (1984).

[5] See e.g. Keen's (2005) modelling of the 'rise of gentry culture'; or the detailed case studies provided by Walker (1990). One might well consider the sophistication exhibited by someone like Sir Geoffrey Luttrell: like many East Anglian landlords, he had produced for his use an early 14th-cent. psalter, London, British Library, MS Additional 42130, yet was scarcely a person of any special prominence. See further Camille (1998).

Nor can the most prominent urban elites be excluded from this kind of levelling contact. London merchants, for example, made their largest profits by supplying aristocratic households with sumptuary goods of all sorts, from spices and wines to tapestries to tournament saddles. Moreover, they were immediately useful to aristocracy for other purposes, as moneylenders, suppliers of capital. And throughout the period, one commonplace goal of mercantile investment was to escape urban status altogether, to acquire a country estate and live, like the 'gentry', as a gentleman. (Lawyers, of course, always follow money and prefer clients richer, rather than otherwise; most large households will have required several of them, on some form of retainer.)[6] Indeed, it is very hard to see how a medieval English literary elite might be thoroughly compartmentalized, other than to note different emphases in the reading habits we can uncover: sophisticated theology more apt to appear in clerical contexts than in lay ones, sophisticated imported continental French literature more apt to appear in magnate contexts than associated with lesser persons, for example.

But it was not simple proximity that produced some blurring of elite literary tastes. After all, one can admire one's betters' possessions, cultural and otherwise, but one requires resources to acquire them and the tools to use them. Leaving aside differentials of social status, one can say that the tools for elite or sophisticated literacy were widely available, at low cost, and that they appear to have been remarkably homogeneous from c. 1180 to c. 1350, and probably so for a generation or two later.

This is because learning to read in a sophisticated fashion is an acquired 'art', not one innate, and the accepted parameters of instruction in grammar were well fixed in English culture. The grammar taught was Latin, and with it came a panoply of set teaching texts, and set methods of instruction in reading them (how to recognize figures of speech, for example). Moreover, until the mid-fourteenth century, the language of instruction was not everyone's vernacular, English, but Anglo-Norman. (Indeed, grammar students were customarily forbidden to use English at school.) As a result, everyone had a fairly fixed notion of what it meant to be seriously 'literate' (in upper forms of grammar school, dragged through Claudian's brief epic, *De raptu Proserpinae*, for example). But in addition, they had acquired, through classroom reliance on Anglo-Norman, a polylingual competence that could serve them in other contexts than the schoolroom, and the potential to engage literarily in much broader riches than those ever available in English in the Middle Ages.[7]

---

[6] See Keene (1989, 1990, 1999). On the career of one great merchant lender, see Fryde (1988). On rural retirement as culmination of a mercantile career, see Thrupp (1948: 226–87); O'Connor (1994*a*, 1994*b*).

[7] For the best (and quite extensive) survey of the early evidence, see Hunt (1991); and for extensive discussion, Orme (1973), as well as Orme's subsequent contributions. Rickert (1932) discusses a sophisticated grammar-master's library.

RECONSTRUCTING THE EVIDENCE

Instantiating these quite general, social history predicated remarks involves considerable difficulties, however. First of all, our knowledge of medieval books and their use is extremely limited, mainly owing to sixteenth-century disruptions, as Evenden has outlined in her chapter above. Henry VIII's monastic dissolution destroyed and (if it did not do so thoroughly) scattered the largest libraries of the kingdom. This destruction was intensified by contemporary theological and intellectual developments. These rendered both specifically Catholic materials and the common forms of medieval intellectual and imaginative pursuit passé—and thus easily discarded.

Moreover, leaving book survival aside, the surviving records are excessively fragmentary and often opaque about the information they provide. Surviving volumes seldom come with clear indications of ownership (and even more infrequently, notice of an original owner). Even those survivors with clear medieval provenances typically fail to answer basic questions like, 'How was this book used?', or even 'Was this book ever read?' The most commonplace surviving information about book ownership comes from wills, but these form notoriously limited sources of information. Typically, they include special bequests only, the core library probably having passed silently with the residue of the estate; they tend to describe books by their major content (when they do not just note the colour of the binding) and thus obscure smaller material; for example, short texts and lyric verse. Further, as is apparent from some comments above, any individual's 'own books' will fail to exhaust their literary knowledge or interests. This remains especially true in a situation where literature was routinely communicated in public reading and books might be loaned among circles of individuals; many wills, for example, bequeath someone a book acknowledged as already in their possession. In the following pages, I do the best I can to describe elite literary engagement in the face of this evidentiary gap; most of my analysis depends on legal records with some purport to completeness in describing one or another collection.[8]

There are a couple of further immediate caveats. For medieval book owners, the primary (and most necessary) book investment was not what we should consider literary at all. In the Middle Ages, whether one was 'elite' or not, one's primary responsibility in this life was saving one's soul; thus, everyone's first purchase (and probably a continuing drain on any book-budget) must have been volumes that would help do this. Further, from a book perspective, much of this spiritual 'investment' (and potentially a more expensive part of it) will go unnoted, among expenditure upon things like clerical costume and equipment (candlesticks, patens, chalices), provisions to support clerics who would aid in the process.

---

[8] See particularly the seminal and thought-provoking essays of Kate Harris and Carol Meale in Griffiths and Pearsall (1989: 163–238). The most extensive collection of evidence, although limited to printed sources and ending c.1450, is Cavanaugh (1980).

TYPES OF BOOKS

The most common surviving type of medieval book is the private prayer-book or devotional volume. Such volumes are often those most marked as 'elite' expenditure, whatever the social status of the owner/patron, with elaborate ornament and painted illustration. Most usually these books fall into the category described as *Horae* ('hours') or 'primers', centring in, but not limited to, 'the little office of the Blessed Virgin', a set of psalms and prayers divided into sections to be said at various hours of the day. If not totally Latinate, even down to the Reformation they were very nearly so.[9]

But having a prayer-book for personal use would scarcely have been sufficient for many of the 'cultural elite'. These people expressed their power and sophistication in religious, every bit as much as social, display. Most of them would not have been content with simply a prayer-book, but would have purchased further items for their spiritual self-improvement. Moreover, many of them had private chapels in their homes, or enthusiastically patronized the local church (for which they often had the right of 'advowson', the power to appoint the rector). This would have involved them in quite extensive purchases, to ensure a full range of books for 'their priests' to use in suitably impressive liturgical offices. Simply one example will illustrate this (and this is one to which I will return): when royal clerks went to inventory the possessions of the attainted Thomas of Woodstock, duke of Gloucester in 1397, they found about ninety books in his library, but also about half that number as part of the chapel 'furnishings'. Moreover, Thomas had married into the Bohun family, famous book patrons—but virtually all whose surviving volumes are opulently decorated liturgical books.[10]

Liturgical volumes particularly raise a further issue. It is a good deal too easy to assimilate medieval book acquisition to our own. We wander into the local Borders or Waterstones bookshops and pick up a new copy of whatever interests us. While we are aware that books were not quite so readily available in the Middle Ages, we most easily imagine what certainly did happen in the period, the equivalent of our 'placing a special order': consumers arrange to be provided with a new copy of what they need.

While such activity did go on (and probably inspires a too excessive interest in book owners as book patrons, commissioning new volumes to accord with personal taste and specification), it is far from the normal case, and liturgical books provide great examples of this custom. There were certainly booksellers ('stationers' or *stationarii*, those with fixed shops), and they certainly knew how to facilitate the

---

[9] For a fine introduction to such volumes, see Wieck (1988: esp. pp. 149–67).

[10] Such liturgical interests underwrite some famous and very opulent books, the so-called 'East Anglian Psalters' of the early 14th cent. (of which Geoffrey Luttrell's, mentioned n. 5 above, is a splendid example). For Thomas of Woodstock's inventory, see most conveniently, Cavanaugh (1980: 844–51); for his predecessors, the Bohuns, and theirs, Sandler (2004).

production of new volumes to order. But until the 1450s, there is very little evidence that they actually could survive in trade on such a basis.

Rather, stationers' 'standing stock', what one could see as one came in the door, was used books—and especially used devotional and service books, for which book dealers knew there was a ready demand. Thus, excepting the translated Wycliffite version, there are almost no surviving medieval Bibles produced in the fourteenth or fifteenth centuries. Thirteenth-century Parisian book-producers had developed (then mass-produced) a revolutionary one-volume packaging of the full text, which was then imitated across Europe. These books were simply recycled, passed on as gifts and bequests, resold second-hand, throughout the remainder of the period. Again, the University of Oxford had an official University Stationer, but the most extensively recorded function of these individuals in the fifteenth century was appraising used volumes, whether as part of probate proceedings or to assess the item as security for a loan. (One assumes the prices the stationers fixed were those at which they were prepared to purchase the volume for resale, and that they were consciously measuring demand).

PRIVATE BOOK COLLECTORS

Medieval private collections might be perceived as mirroring features of this trade. Like geological sediments, they reflected sequences of acquisition, only a small part of them actually 'John Smith's books', in the sense that they had been prepared for the current owner. Some may have been in the family for generations, if not centuries. Some will have come as gifts or bequests (with their own quite separate histories). Only a few will actually reflect the precise tastes of the library 'owner'; trying to unpack such documents as we have will be perpetually complicated by such processes of admixture. And, of course, such an experience is nearly completely foreign to modern practice, where executors impatiently seek to translate whole libraries into a cash payout from the neighbourhood used bookshop.

I offer a single example, from a well-documented and ostentatious fifteenth-century gentry book-collector. Sir Edmund Rede of Borstall, Buckinghamshire (1413–89), specifically mentions about two dozen books in his will.[11] Four of these survive; in three cases, they are quite opulently ornamented volumes, including an outsized copy of Gower's *Confessio Amantis* that Rede had produced to his specifications by Oxford craftsmen, *c.*1445–55. But the fourth example, now Oxford, Christ Church, manuscript 98, which Rede certainly used and valued, is quite different. This, as perhaps the preceding discussion might lead one to expect, is a liturgical volume: a Psalter, the basic biblical book of private devotion (the whole text

---

[11] See the elaborately documented account, Pearsall (2000).

conventionally recited once a week in church services). One cannot be certain where Rede got it, but he certainly bought it second-hand, and probably for its exceedingly pleasant design, including its elegant script and fine, often lively, painted illustration. The book had originally been made in the late thirteenth century, in the vicinity of St-Omer, in northern France. In the will, in which the book was left to his male heir, Rede indicates that the Psalter was intended to form part of an ongoing family liturgical collection. Indeed, he had expended considerable cash assimilating the volume to the remainder of his collection with an opulent binding consonant with that on some other books.[12] Moreover, the will describes 'duo psalteria mea cum duobus clapsis de argento et deauratum pounced cum capitibus unicornum'.[13] The unicorn heads, mentioned at the end, were the device of Rede's mother's family, the Jameses, and thus this, like all Rede's other surviving books, provides an ornate reminder of the ancestry that underwrote his claim to the estate at Boarstall. Such concerns of lineage are indicated, too, by Rede's entry of the anniversary of Christine James Rede's death in 1435 in the liturgical calendar at the front of the volume.

MEDIEVAL BOOK USERS

At this point, I turn to examine some examples of medieval book use. About the only sensible way of doing this, in gross, is to enter what I have already described as a particularly troubled area, to survey what one can know of a few full libraries. I draw my evidence, whatever the wise caveats I have noted above, primarily from inventories (which offer some hope of being complete records), secondarily from wills and booklists usually scribbled on endleaves (which are certainly not so; do the informal lists describe any library at all?). I want to adopt a rather polyform argument: first, to examine evidence among members of the several groups of elite readers I have singled out above; second, to perturb somewhat the boundaries between them.

The Clerical Book Owner

I begin with the largest surviving well-documented clerical library, that of John Erghome, an Oxford MA and eventually a regent master of his religious order, the

---

[12] For the book, see Alexander and Temple (1985: no. 702 (70) and pl. xl—even at 33% reproduction, one gets a brilliant sense of the volume's quality). The current binding is 18th-cent. with a gold-stamped armorial (continuing assimilation, now antiquarian, of used volumes to a private collection).

[13] H. E. Salter, *The Boarstall Cartulary* (Oxford Historical Society, 88; Oxford, 1930), 286–95.

heremitic friars of St Augustine.[14] The record of his books is datable to 1372 (with later additions) and reveals a huge, and thus wildly atypical, collection, perhaps 225 volumes in all. But it is also a helpful collection, in its breadth of intellectual engagement. A great many private clerical libraries, at least in the way we know them, often appear vastly too focused on topics of utilitarian professional use; for instance, the extensive collections of canon law bequeathed by Bishop William Rede of Chichester to various Oxford colleges.[15]

Erghome's library testifies to a well-funded intellectual omnivore. The friary of the York Augustinians, who received his collection, divided their books among an unusually profuse twenty-four categories (most Oxford colleges were content with only four), and Erghome owned items representing sixteen of these. His collection covers all the topics one might expect of a learned man: the Bible and commentators on it, liturgy, the various laws (an extensive twenty-three-volume collection, nos. 406–28, 103–6), university Aristotelian philosophy, and theology. However, except for the last subject I mention—an extremely impressive thirty volumes of 'questiones et quodlibeta'—the proportions each contributes to the total collection are decidedly skewed. The heft of Erghome's library falls in unexpected areas, subjects which were, one imagines, the owner's special penchants. Thus the York Augustinians list as his books twenty-seven volumes of astronomy, most of them large collections including numerous titles—as well as a set of seven instruments for pursuing the study (which the friary sold; nos. 369–94, 90–101).

Amid such riches, I choose to examine only a small, but rather unusual, portion, the forty-three books catalogued with the overtly literary title, 'Grammatica' (catalogue items 475–517, 117–30). Like all Erghome's collections, this group, entirely in Latin, has at its centre the most basic encyclopedic tools of the discipline, here Priscian and his commentators, as well as those authors considered in the later Middle Ages fundamental to grammatical knowledge. These include figures like Éverard de Bethune, Alexander de Villa Dei, and John of Garland, all responsible for basic handbooks in verse. In addition, there are several dictionaries. But these foundational materials scarcely prepare one for the literary riches at Erghome's disposal. As I have noted above, schoolboys were expected to know the late Roman poet Claudian, through his short epic De raptu Proserpinae (on which Chaucer draws in 'The Merchant's Tale'); of course, Erghome had two copies of this. But he had two further Claudian manuscripts, as well, and these gave him access to the poet's entire corpus.

That single fact will provide some idea of the comprehensiveness of Erghome's 'grammatical' collection. He had extensive, usually multiple-copy, access to a grand

---

[14] Given the tenor of the following discussion, it is worth noting here that works in medieval England's 'other languages' probably have been subjected to more comprehensive and careful bibliographical study than works in Middle English. See Sharpe (1997); Dean (1999). As Sharpe's title indicates, he treats named insular authors only.

[15] For Erghome's Library, see Humphreys (1990: 11–154 passim). He takes his name from Argam, a locale near Bridlington, and he was probably the uncle of another figure who will appear later in my discussion, Thomas Cumberworth. For Rede's various bequests, see Cavanaugh (1980: 689–714).

run of Latin verse, from the classics all the way through those works considered central to post-1300 collections. For many of these authors, he owned the standard commentaries (Servius on all the works of Virgil, for example) as well. And the library included not just Virgil, but Ovid, Horace, Statius, Martial, Juvenal, Terence, at least one tragedy of Seneca the younger—the list runs on. Erghome could also consult the run of Christian Latin poets from late antiquity, including Prudentius, Sedulius, and Arator.

Moreover, he owned copies of numerous works that, whatever the paucity of their record elsewhere, were widely available enough to become inspirations for later poets writing in English.[16] Langland persistently refers to Matthew of Vendôme's epic life of Tobit (and a copy appears as early as 1294 in a list of books confiscated, not from a scholar, but a London lawyer), and he certainly knew a range of 'goliardic', often Anglo-Latin, verse, both sets of texts represented here.[17] Chaucer's 'Parliament of Fowls' explicitly draws on Alan of Lille's *De planctu naturae*, and the Wife of Bath castigates her fifth husband for his dabbling in Walter Map's popular *Epistola Valerii*, both books to be found in the collection. And like Chaucer, an assiduous student of Trojan lore, Erghome could read both a Latinized version of Homer's *Iliad* and the prose account ascribed to 'Dares the Phrygian'. Like everything about Erghome's collection, this was encyclopedic access, here to the wealth of *litteratura*, a purely Latinate tradition. But it is a tradition shared with a limited, highly literate cadre, and in time its study ceased to be 'grammatical' and was overtaken by the concerns of early modern 'civic humanism'.

The Noble Book Owner

As an example of a magnatial library, I offer a brief survey of Thomas of Woodstock's books. This collection is well known and certainly exemplifies materials in use at this level well into the sixteenth century.[18] As I have already indicated, this was a quite extensive collection: forty-seven chapel books and just over eighty volumes in a 'library'. Quite surprisingly, this did include English books, four of them, but all of them testimony to a quite unusual enthusiasm of the collector. The clerks who prepared the inventory found:

Un bible en Engleys en ij. grantz livres coverez de rouge quyr
Un livre d'Engleis de les evangelies coverez de quyr rouge
Un novel livre de les evangelies glosez en Engleis.

---

[16] For the inspirational force of these texts, see the fine companion essays, Michael Lapidge, 'Versifying the Bible in the Middle Ages', and Jill Mann, ' "He Knew Nat Catoun": Medieval School-Texts and Middle English Literature', in Mann and Nolan (2006: 11–74).
[17] For the lawyer's *Tobias*, see Whitwell (1905).
[18] See the studies referred to in n. 2 above.

All three of these represent one form or another of English Wycliffite scripture, the last entry the so-called 'glossed gospels'. The first item cited above still survives, the great two-volume Bible now London, British Library, Egerton 617 and 618.

Extant record certainly allows us to associate an early interest in English scripture—and its provocations—with Duke Thomas. Dublin, Trinity College, 244, folios 212^v–219 contain a text introduced:

Moost worschipfulleste and gentilleste lord, duke of Glowcestre, I ȝoure seruaunt sendiþ ȝou disputusun writen þat was bifore ȝow bitwixe a frere and a seculer, ȝoure clerk.

Although the announced proposition is 'þat frere prechouris haueþ no possessioun in Engeland' the confrontation wanders through a number of conventional Wycliffite propositions, broadly centred about clerical possession. Thomas belonged to a royal court party whose flirtations with Lollards are reported to have aroused Richard II's animosity. And he apparently saw such ideas as intriguing enough to watch directed discussions of their implications.[19]

But the remainder of Thomas's recorded library offers no real surprises, unless it is the opulence of many of the volumes, sumptuously decorated—and a very great many of them apparently of continental manufacture. The royal clerks' title for the collection, 'rymances et estories', is pretty descriptive—and just what one would expect, at a guess, a great lord to have read. Still, there was a considerable amount of fairly sophisticated Latin theology; for example, Gregory's *Pastoral Care*, a quire of Augustine *On the Trinity*, an unidentifiable work by Isidore of Seville, and a fragment of a glossed Job. But there were also Latin questions de Divinite, and the basic text of university-level theology, Peter Lombard's *Sentences*.

In addition to these materials, Thomas, in spite of his Lollard flirtations, could read a great deal of orthodox devotional material, in Latin and especially French. Here one could single out two copies of 'the Apocalypse', conventionally hyper-illustrated exegetical volumes in either Latin or Anglo-Norman and popular in aristocratic circles, particularly c.1250–1320.[20] His one bow to science was Bartholomaeus's Latin encyclopedia, *De proprietatibus rerum*. Thomas was interested enough in political theory to have two manuals of statecraft: Brunetto Latini's French *Trésor*, a demi-encyclopedia popularizing Aristotelian ethical ideas (his book now survives as Oxford, Bodleian Library, Douce 319) and the considerably more sophisticated Latin *De regimine principum* by the Augustinian friar Giles of Rome.

The interest in 'good governance' draws attention to one practical (and polylingual) feature of the collection. For many people, like Thomas, there would have been a second drain on a book-budget before one ever approached anything smacking of the literary. Legal books were necessary to any lord with property and a considerable

---

[19] For an image of the quite elegant Egerton MS, see McKendrick and Doyle (2007: 139 (no. 126)). On the glossed gospels, see Hudson (1988: 249–57 and *passim*); and on records of courtly support for Lollardy, ibid. 110–14.

[20] Frequently viewed as exercises in 'biblicized chivalry'; see Morgan's (2006) recent illustration and discussion of an example prepared for Edward I.

clerical establishment. Moreover, in the English situation, this had to be a varied collection, and Thomas had precisely one copy each of the basic texts necessary to operate in any of the three laws: Roman civil, canon law, or common law. And as a great lord, with continental holdings, he had a Statutes of France to boot.

While the 'chronicle' part of the collection was heavily Latinate, the 'romance', and a good deal more, was resolutely French. There were at least three books of Arthuriana, four or five accounts of Troy, and four more of Alexander the Great (one of these perhaps the hyper-illustrated Oxford, Bodleian Library, Bodley 264). But Thomas also appears devoted to the equally genteel pursuit of 'courtesy', and the library included a *Roman de la rose* (now London, British Library, Royal 19 B. iii), as well as 'j. large livre de tretes amireux et moralitez et de caroll' fraunceis bien eslumines' (of course!), a common enough kind of continental French book with dream-visions and lyric poetry.[21]

Much of this material was very cosmopolitan indeed, as one might expect. But Thomas's library also included a quite substantial Anglo-Norman contribution, testimony to the continuing appeal of locally produced French literature. While much of this material was 'romance', including a copy of the now lost *Fouke Fitz Waryn*, there were diverse (and more commonplace) items; for example, Pierre d'Abernon of Fetcham's *Lumière as lais* and a French copy of *Mandeville's Travels*. This is, as I say, although extensive, comfortably conventional—and one should notice the Anglo-Norman element, which conventional literary historical accounts, probably incorrectly, tend to describe as old-fashioned and on the verge of becoming extinct.

The Lawyer Book Owner

Rather than analysing an exemplary London mercantile library, I choose one of a comparable urban professional, a lawyer. This is another well-known example, a man named Thomas Kebell, who was, among other things, administrator as clerk of works for Lady Margaret Beaufort. When Kebell died in 1500, his house at Humberstone, Leicestershire, was inventoried for probate. The investigation revealed a collection of thirty-six volumes, a mixture of handwritten and early print books, a pretty substantial haul.[22]

The gross parameters of Kebell's library strike me as immediately revelatory. In terms of distribution by language, it offers no real surprises; even in 1500, exactly two-thirds of the volumes were in Latin, and, among the remainder, there were twice as many French books (eight) as English (four). Of the thirty-six volumes, twenty utilized the new medium of print. Here one interesting observation might be made, for while the Latin and English show generally similar ratios of manuscript to print

---

[21] See Huot (1987).
[22] See Ives (1983), relevant portions of the inventory at pp. 436, 444–6, discussion at pp. 362–7, 426–7.

(eight of twenty Latin books, one of four English ones), the French was overwhelmingly in manuscript (seven of the eight titles).

There are at least a couple of immediate inferences to draw from these raw figures. First of all, Kebell was considerably less thoroughly engaged with contemporary (printed) materials in French than with those in the other languages. Indeed, his only printed French book was a 'professional' volume, a collection of 'yearbooks', records of court pleadings. Actually, legal volumes comprise half the French in his collection. The remainder, so far as identifiable, was a literary collection, by this date perhaps a little passé; it included a copy of Froissart's *Chronicles* (perhaps instructively, bequeathed in Kebell's will to an aristocratic woman, Lady Hungerford) and a 'Boccaccio' (Laurent de Premierfait's translation of *De casibus virorum illustrium*). I would consider this showing a sign that one might, at this date, be well on the way to Thomas Cromwell's observation in 1537 that far too few Englishmen any longer were competent at French. This marks the full reversal of the complaint customary in English writings of *c*.1300, that the French language—and texts in it—are far too ubiquitous in 'English' culture.

Kebell's twenty-four Latin books form quite an intriguing collection. At its core, of course, were the Bible, liturgical texts, and an impressive array of supporting aids, two volumes of printed sermons, for example. The Bible—four printed volumes—also included the standard late medieval commentary, by the early fourteenth-century Norman scholar Nicholas of Lyra, and there were several comparable aids to understanding scripture. Kebell's library included, for example, a manuscript of Peter Comestor (an early twelfth-century paraphrase of biblical history) and a text very popular in early print (as here), Ludolph of Saxony's *Vita Christi*. This relatively learned inquisitive address of the biblical text, and the acting out of its injunctions in formal Christian prayer account for fourteen of the Latin volumes.[23]

The remaining Latin books are a great deal more interesting. Although these include (as did Thomas of Woodstock's library) a print of the standard late medieval compendium of all needful knowledge, Bartholomaeus's *De proprietatibus rerum*, other volumes reveal Kebell as an incipiently 'humanist' reader of Latin classics. He had copies of Seneca the elder's *Declamationes*, Cicero's *De officiis*, and Boethius's *Consolatio* (only the first in manuscript). There is, from the remaining Latin volumes, every evidence that Kebell was as seriously committed to this study as he was to the text of scripture. Yet the shape of the remaining collection might imply that pursuing Latin literature was, for him, even a more demanding task than reading biblical literature.

For both the volumes themselves, as well as Kebell's remaining collection, Latin and English, contain a variously elaborate apparatus for approaching sophisticated Latin. Two of the texts were explicitly glossed versions (the Seneca with the commentary of the early fourteenth-century English friar Nicholas Trivet), and it is hard

---

[23] This number includes 'a litell prynted boke called *Cursus mundi*', an error for 'Cursus hinc inde collecti', less likely 'Cursus virginis', but in either case *Horae* (or excerpts therefrom, customarily produced in small formats). For Ludolph of Saxony, see Zeeman-Salter (1957).

to believe that the Boethius was not as well. In addition, Kebell had a ready supply of basic, yet sophisticated aids for getting at Latin vocabulary and grammar: two printed dictionaries (the late medieval standard, Johannes Balbus's *Catholicon*; and Johann Reuchlin), as well as a manuscript table to Isidore of Seville's *Etymologies*, which will have offered further lexical aid.

Moreover, he improved his access to the originals through supportive help-texts. In addition to the genuine Ciceronian item, for example, Kebell owned a manuscript of its Christian imitation, Ambrose's *De officiis ministrorum*, which, through its revisions, reveals a good deal about the sense of its classical model. And he had a ready guide to Ciceronian idiom and its comprehension in one of the four English books, Caxton's 1481 print of two mid-fifteenth-century translations of Cicero's great dialogues on friendship and old age (STC 5293).[24] Similarly, Kebell could approach his Boethius through English, as well as the original, since one of the remaining four English books was Caxton's 1478(?) rendition of Chaucer's translation (STC 3199). Just as with Kebell's preparations to understand Christian scripture, the collection testifies to impressive intellectual commitment, as well as, in this case, perhaps the lawyer's awareness of his abilities being a bit more modest than his aspirations.

The Gentry Book Owner

Although still extensive, studies have been less concentrated in what one might take to be 'gentry'. These persons were usually armigerous, yet not within the reaches of parliamentary nobility. They might have extensive property holdings (often over several locales) and, often, extensive local service as officials. Although they were certainly drawn to London for various purposes, including governmental service, their careers were more usually provincially dispersed. The long-time litmus for their activities has always been the gentryman/book producer Robert Thornton of East Newton (North Riding, Yorkshire).[25]

Perhaps only the wide dispersal of such individuals and the frequently fragmentary nature of their remains have induced scholars to de-emphasize such literary sites. But after all, they are writ large in any history of 'English literature'. Those early landmarks of literary culture, Oxford, Bodleian Library, Digby 86 (late thirteenth century) and London, British Library, Harley 2253 (second quarter of the fourteenth century), emanate from such locales.[26] These books are strikingly trilingual in their contents,

---

[24] On these texts and comparable efforts, see Wakelin (2007). The two English books that remain undiscussed were probably a printed Mandeville (Pollard and Redgrave 1976–91: 17246 or 17247) and 'a litell old boke', likely to have been some form of Middle English devotional anthology.

[25] For Thornton and his context, see Keiser (1979, 1983); as well as Thompson's (1987) account of his book making. In the years since Keiser wrote, studies like these have proliferated. A list exemplary, rather than exclusive, would include items like Wilson (1979); Boffey and Edwards (2000); Hanna (2002).

[26] For the first of these, see Tschann and Parkes (1996), esp. pp. lvi–ix; and for the second, Revard (2000: esp. pp. 74–86). On trilingual miscellanies, see Hunt (1999).

the English appearing along with a mass of Latin and French, which is not all of insular origins. Such a juxtaposition is conventionally associated with 'clerical' culture; for example, the similar Cambridge, Trinity College, B.14.39 (dated to the third quarter of the thirteenth century and perhaps originating with the Worcester Franciscans) and London, British Library, Additional 46919 (an early fourteenth-century volume of the Hereford Franciscans), but, as I hope succeeding discussion will show, this juxtaposition is a continuing strain of gentry reading habits as well.[27]

I want to examine and extrapolate from the surviving evidence the book activities of four mid-fifteenth-century gentlemen. All of them, more or less well-known, were locally prominent in parts of the north-east Midlands. One was nominally a parliamentary baron but with only localized influence, and one I include largely because his library, at least inferentially, was heavily dependent on that of one of my central figures. My central exhibits include Sir Thomas Cumberworth of Somerby/Someretby (near Brigg, Lindsey, d. 1450), Sir Thomas Chaworth of Wiverton (south-eastern Nottinghamshire, d. 1459), and Lionel, Lord Welles (of Well, Lindsey, d. 1461). To these I add one of Chaworth's executors, Richard Willoughby of Wollaton (now within the City of Nottingham, d. 1471), whose collection partly depended upon Chaworth's.[28] I join the four, and treat the evidence together, as if a combined single specimen of book use, simply as a way of averting the limitations of the evidence. Cumberworth and Chaworth we know only through specific bequests in their wills; Lord Welles, by a list of titles which may or may not reflect the contents of his library; and the Willoughbys, only through collection procedures that may have gone on for as long as a century, into the age of Elizabeth. Together, the four will give, I hope, an extensive idea of what English gentlemen in a fairly small area of the north-east Midlands were reading in the mid and later fifteenth centuries. And one must immediately insist upon the continuing trilingual nature of book ownership in these contexts. Although I have deliberately chosen what are, in the context, lists with heavy concentrations of English texts, this material sits within a surround already familiar from other sources.

The Latin immediately identifiable here could be described as pre-eminently 'utilitarian'. A great deal of it was liturgical in the broad sense. It included both personal prayer books (the eight items, quite circumstantially described, that Chaworth set aside for his son as a way of memorializing the family line, for example) and the quite customary involvement in domestic chapels and local churches, used, to some extent, as private spiritual sites. For example, Cumberworth had both his local chantry and another in Launde priory, Leicestershire, where he was buried; the Willoughbys were very active patrons of Wollaton church.[29]

---

[27] For these two books, see Reichl (1973); Reimer (1987).

[28] See, for Cumberworth, Clark (1914: 45–57); for Chaworth, *Testamenta Eboracensia* (1845), pp. 220–9; and for Welles, Hamel (1990). The library eventually constructed by the Willoughbys is described in detail by Stevenson (1911: esp. pp. 196–269, 283, 621–2); see further Turville-Petre and Johnson (1996).

[29] Indeed, Chaworth's Willoughby executor probably provided both the connections and the funds to purchase from the estate for Wollaton church one of the largest surviving books from the English Middle Ages (an enormous 585 mm × 390 mm; Chaworth seems to have loved outsized books). This is

The other intense focus of the Latin is also purely instrumental, legal materials. This is insurance expenditure, associated with protection of the household and securing property rights. One should include here both Chaworth's 'notes of fines' (probably a Latin/Anglo-Norman mixture), as well as the Welles's book of civil law, paralleled in a similar printed volume the Willoughbys may have acquired in the 1490s. Although limited, there is some evidence for an interest in Latin literature. Chaworth bequeathed a copy of the standard late medieval national and world history, Ranulph Higden's *Polychronicon*, and he had an English version as well.

But this attenuated showing may be more apparent than real—a failure of the record. The Willoughbys may have been acquiring printed books from the 1490s; among the earliest volumes are, like Thomas Kebell's library, Latin classics: a Cicero and an Ovid. Their early purchases also included a printed version of Ludolph of Saxony's *Vita Christi*, again a book that Kebell owned, and an item (here in manuscript) bequeathed in Cumberworth's will.[30] Although there is no overt reference to 'theology', sophisticated Latin material, around 1561, the Willoughbys were using pristine leaves from a copy of Peter Lombard's *Sentences* (recall that the book also appeared in Thomas of Woodstock's library), to bind estate records, now the manuscript Nottingham University Library, Mi A 28.

French materials do appear to be distinctly on the wane, support for arguments I have ventured above in the case of Thomas Kebell. But there is still a substantial amount on view, the greater part of it Anglo-Norman. The Welles family booklist appears on a flyleaf in a typically aristocratic book I have already mentioned in the collection of Thomas of Woodstock. This surviving Apocalypse, also including another Anglo-Norman devotional text, is now London, British Library, Royal 15 D. ii. In addition, the Welleses had a French bestiary, more antiquated (and extra-illustrated) aristocratic reading, probably an early thirteenth-century book. Their roll-chronicle, a common type of monarch-centred history of England, also appears to have been in local French. Outside this list, one can point to two surviving Willoughby volumes of Anglo-Norman instructional verse, one with William of Waddington's *Manuel des péches*; Waddington was an early thirteenth-century secular servant of the archbishops of York. Adjoining this text, and independently in another volume, the Willoughbys also could consult Robert of Gretham's *Miroir*, an Anglo-Norman annual cycle of sermons in verse; their two copies represent one-third of the total survival of the text, and the family's extensive holdings may have brought Robert's works to their attention as something of a 'local author'.

But the libraries of these individuals are mainly given over to English books, and the gentry would seem to be the true growth area of literary interest in English during

---

'The Wollaton Antiphonal', now Nottingham, University of Nottingham Library, 250, and was only one of four—all presumably for chapel or parochial use—that Chaworth's will mentions. In his will of 1471, Richard Willougby, the executor, bequeathed the church another six liturgical volumes; see *Testamenta Eboracensia* 3 (1865), pp. 170–2.

[30] The Willoughbys disposed of their print book collection (as well as a few MSS) in a Christie's auction, 15–18 June 1925, and the collection has to be reconstructed from the sale catalogue.

the later Middle Ages, as the thirteenth-century examples I cited a page or so ago might have predicted. Indeed, the efflorescence of English writing in the late four-teenth-century might specifically be identified with such baronial (alternatively, upper gentry) sites. Chaucer's immediate audience, after all, was not royal, although centred in the king's court; it was apparently composed of country gentlemen with continuing roles as minor officials.[31] Similar backgrounds might be adduced for such central literary figures as the gentryman John Gower, and the royal clerk Thomas Hoccleve.

But equally productively, one could also cite the example of Thomas IV, Lord Berkeley.[32] His family had long been ensconced as barons in the area surrounding Bristol, and, given the absence of greater lords in the vicinity, he may have been the most powerful man in Gloucestershire in the later fourteenth century. But the Berkeleys' national visibility was negligible (although Thomas himself had a promi-nent role in 'the revolution of 1399'). But Berkeley was a sort of national model in one respect, as a person who not only read books, but also instigated literary efforts—and efforts engaged in providing acknowledged (Latin) 'classics' in a form more broadly legible. He patronized local translators, pre-eminent among them his parish priest, John Trevisa (d. 1402), to render these into English prose. These works—as well as a long string of similar items, the sources of Kebell's anglicized Cicero, for example—were both staples and models of gentry reading into the early modern period, and often, indeed, they drew the attention of early printers.

In the fictionalized conversation that forms 'The Dialogue of a Lord and a Clerk', Berkeley, while admitting his status in general social terms as fully Latin-literate, tells 'his clerk' Trevisa: 'þer ys moche Latyn in þeus bokes þat Y can noȝt vnderstonde, noþer þou, wiþoute studyinge and auysement and lokyng of oþer bokes'. Whatever their impressive degrees of Latin literacy, not just Thomas Kebell found sophisticated Latin more difficult to construe than he would have wished (and had a number of those 'other books' to help him out). Berkeley took the extra step to aid those without 'other books', or the inclination to use them. For example, I have twice cited owners of Bartholomaeus' encyclopedia; Trevisa finished his translation of it for Berkeley in 1398 (and de Worde was to print it in 1495, STC 1536). Both works Berkeley patronized, and analogous offerings found a ready audience among people of his ilk.

Between them, London writing and Berkeley translation provide a literary core to the gentry libraries I am describing. Both Cumberworth and Welles owned *The Canterbury Tales*, the most widely circulating Chaucer text. The Willoughby copy of Gower's *Confessio*, still in the Nottingham University Library collection, may have been prepared for the family in the 1480s. Chaworth's grand(iose) copy of Trevisa's *Properties of Things* (not mentioned in the will), after more than four centuries in the Willoughbys' collection, is now Columbia University Library, Plimpton 263. Cha-worth's copy of another Berkeley-patronized work, Trevisa's translation of Higden's

---

[31] See Strohm (1977).   [32] See Waldron (1988), Hanna (1989).

Polychronicon, mentioned in the will, has vanished; but the Willoughbys had acquired another by about 1540 (now the manuscript, Tokyo, Senshu University
Library, 1).

Moreover, secular literature in these libraries was filled out by reliance upon the
imitators of fourteenth-century innovation. Cumberworth owned 'Gras dew of the
sowde', a prose translation of Guillaume de Deguilleville's allegory of the fate of the
soul after death, made in 1413, probably in London. His copy survives as New York
Public Library, Spencer 19. Chaworth probably also owned a copy of this text, and the
Welles 'pilgrimage de vita humana' may well have been its probable companion work,
The Mirror of the Life of the Manhood, again a translation into prose of a Deguilleville
allegorical poem.[33]

The grand inheritor of Chaucerian London culture in the middle fifteenth-century
was, of course, John Lydgate. The libraries analysed here speak to his widespread
dispersal—and eager gentry reading public. Chaworth mentions a book beginning
with his life of saints Alban and Amphibel, and his gigantic *Troy Book*, unmentioned
in the will, is now London, British Library, Cotton Augustus A. iv. The Welles list
includes a copy of *The Life of Our Lady*, and the Willoughby copy of *The Fall of
Princes* (certainly in the library before 1528) now is Princeton University Library,
Taylor 2.

One notable omission from some lists is a genre usually taken as almost *de rigueur*
reading for gentry, romance. In part, this perception relies upon Robert Thornton's
long-time centrality to the topic. (He has been known as a romance-collector since
the dawn of Middle English Studies in 1865.) Here, interest in this subject seems
negligible, outside of the Welles collection. But one should, in fairness, notice that the
Willoughbys had two such volumes (date of acquisition uncertain), but in both cases,
sophisticated *French* romance communicated in thirteenth-century volumes
prepared on the Continent and one of them quite nicely illustrated.

Much more prominent than any interest in texts of chivalry is a further area of
innovation: investment in up-to-date English devotional material. Some of the
collections, however, are resolute in their preservation of fourteenth-century classics.
Cumberworth's 'gret boke of Dauid sauter' was surely a copy of Richard Rolle's
English commented version, surprisingly widely distributed, given the bulk of the
text. A second volume he calls 'gras dew' in the will might have been an anthology
headed by the Rollean 'Holy Book *Gracia Dei*'. Similarly, the Willoughbys had, quite
early on, a copy of a very popular (but not so much as *The Prick of Conscience*, with a
circulation half again as large as *The Canterbury Tales*) fourteenth-century Yorkshire
poem of spiritual instruction. Their *Speculum Vitae* will have fitted in very well with
the Anglo-Norman instructional verse I have already mentioned. Both Cumberworth
and the Welles list also mention works that sound like Walter Hilton's popular
treatise, *Medled Lyf*, if so, again heading some variety of devotional anthology.

---

[33] For these two works, see Guillame de Deguilleville (1985–8, 1990).

Two lists provide further references to what are probably similar volumes, in each instance headed with the same text, an English translation of Heinrich Suso on dying well.[34] These belonged to Chaworth and the Welles family. Indeed, the latter list might be perceived as more engaged with devotional innovation than with romance, for it also includes the early fifteenth-century manual, *Dives and Pauper* (focused as a discussion of the Ten Commandments), as well as a volume of saints' lives. Cumberworth also bequeathed another *Latin* devotional text already noted in a non-gentry collection, Ludolph of Saxony's *Vita Christi*. One can conclude the survey by noting two of the Willoughbys' early printed book purchases. Like Cumberworth, they owned a 1502 Paris Ludolph, but also, analogous to the Welles family, Julian Notary's 1503 anglicized *Golden Legend* (STC 24877). Apparently, this last purchase encouraged the family in feeling that an earlier collection of saints' lives in the library was expendable, good only for patching pages in other books; this was a very early manuscript of *The South English Legendary* dating from the 1310s.

Obviously, a Whig narrative would privilege collections like these I last describe. Cumberworth, Chaworth, Welles, and Willoughby all look forward to a conception of 'English studies' as English only—and generally confined to imaginative works in English. But such a view is largely a product of the 1580s and later. Further, this survey has sought to indicate the continuity between these collections and earlier, more ubiquitous polylingual tendencies in English culture. Equally, it has suggested the relative isolation, until a fairly late date, of any such vernacular enthusiasms in sophisticated English cultural sites. In the Middle Ages, literary engagement was a far richer and more diverse thing than any modern English-literature syllabus would be prepared to allow.

BIBLIOGRAPHY

ALEXANDER, J. J. G., and ELŻBIETA TEMPLE (1985), *Illuminated Manuscripts in Oxford College Libraries, the University Archives and the Taylor Institution* (Oxford: Clarendon Press).

BOFFEY, JULIA, and A. S. G. EDWARDS (2000), 'Books Connected with Henry Parker, Lord Morley, and his Family', in Marie Axton and James P. Carley (eds.), *Triumphs of English: Henry Parker, Lord Morley, Translator to the Tudor Court* (London: British Library), 69–75.

CAMILLE, MICHAEL (1998), *Mirror in Parchment: The Luttrell Psalter and the Making of Medieval England* (London: Reakton Books).

CARLEY, JAMES P. (2000), *The Libraries of King Henry VIII* (Corpus of British Medieval Library Catalogues, 7; London: British Library in association with the British Academy).

CAVANAUGH, SUSAN H. (1980), 'A Study of Books Privately Owned in England: 1300–1450', Ph.D. dissertation, Philadelphia: University of Pennsylvania.

---

[34] Two famous late 15th-cent. vols. are focused near their openings around this text, Oxford, Bodleian Library, MS Douce 322 (produced for a gentryman, for use of his niece, a Dominican nun); and London, British Library, MS Harley 1706 (I). But the Suso translation, excerpts from it, or comparable materials on 'holy dying' form a textual focus in a wide range of English devotional books.

CAVANAUGH, SUSAN H. (1988), 'Royal Books: King John to Richard II', *The Library*, 6th ser. 10: 304–16.

CLANCHY, M. T. (1993), *From Memory to Written Record* (2nd edn. Oxford: Blackwell).

CLARK, ANDREW (ed.) (1914), *Lincoln Diocese Documents, 1450–1544* (Early English Text Society OS 149; London: K. Paul, Trench, Trübner & Co. and Oxford University Press for the Early English Text Society).

DEAN, RUTH J. (1999), *Anglo-Norman Literature: A Guide to Texts and Manuscripts* (Anglo-Norman Text Society occasional publications, 3; London: Anglo-Norman Text Society).

DOYLE, A. I. (1983), 'English Books In and Out of Court from Edward III to Henry VII', in V. J. Scattergood and J. W. Sherborne (eds.), *English Court Culture in the Later Middle Ages* (London: Duckworth), 164–81.

FRYDE, E. B. (1988), *William de la Pole, Merchant and King's Banker (1366)* (London: Hambledon).

GRASSI, J. L. (1970), 'Royal Clerks from the Archdiocese of York in the Fourteenth Century', *Northern History*, 5: 12–33.

GRIFFITHS, JEREMY, and DEREK PEARSALL (eds.) (1989), *Book Production and Publishing in Britain 1375–1475* (Cambridge: Cambridge University Press).

GUILLAME DE DEGUILLEVILLE (1985–8), *The Pilgrimage of the Lyfe of the Manhode*, ed. Avril Henry (Early English Text Society, 288, 292; London: Oxford University Press for the Early English Text Society).

——(1990), *The Pilgrimage of the Soul: A Critical Edition of the Middle English Dream Vision*, ed. Rosemarie P. McGerr (New York: Garland).

HAMEL, MARY (1990), 'Arthurian Romance in Fifteenth-Century Lincolnshire: The Books of the Lords Welles', *Modern Language Quarterly*, 51: 341–61.

HANNA, RALPH (1989), 'Sir Thomas Berkeley and his Patronage', *Speculum*, 64: 878–916.

——(2002), 'Two New (?) Lost Piers Manuscripts(?)', *Yearbook of Langland Studies*, 16: 169–77.

HELLINGA, LOTTE, and J. B. TRAPP (eds.) (1999), *The Cambridge History of the Book in Britain, iii. 1400–1557* (Cambridge, Cambridge University Press).

HUDSON, ANNE (1988), *The Premature Reformation: Wycliffite Texts and Lollard History* (Oxford: Clarendon Press).

HUGHES, JONATHAN (1988), *Pastors and Visionaries: Religion and Secular Life in Late Medieval Yorkshire* (Woodbridge: Boydell Press).

HUMPHREYS, K. W. (1990), *The Friars' Libraries* (Corpus of British Medieval Library Catalogues, 1; London: British Library in association with the British Academy).

HUNT, TONY (1991), *Teaching and Learning Latin in Thirteenth-Century England* (3 vols. Cambridge: D. S. Brewer).

——(1999), 'Insular Trilingual Compilations', in R. Jansen-Sieben and H. van Dijk (eds.), *Codices Miscellanearum* (Archives et Bibliothèques de Belgique, numéro spécial, 60; Brussels: Bibliothèque Royale de Belgique), 51–70.

HUOT, SYLVIA (1987), *From Song to Book: The Poetics of Writing in Old French Lyric and Lyrical Narrative Poetry* (Ithaca, NY: Cornell University Press).

IVES, E. W. (1983), *The Common Lawyers of Pre-Reformation England: Thomas Kebell. A Case Study* (Cambridge: Cambridge University Press).

JAMES, MONTAGUE R. (1905), *A Descriptive Catalogue of the Manuscripts in the Library of Pembroke College, Cambridge* (Cambridge: Cambridge University Press).

KEEN, MAURICE (2005), 'Chivalry', in Raluca Radelescu and Alison Truelove (eds.), *Gentry Culture in Late Medieval England* (Manchester: Manchester University Press), 35–49.

KEENE, DEREK (1989), 'Medieval London and its Region', *London Journal*, 14: 99–111.

——(1990), 'Shops and Shopping in Medieval London', in Lindy Grant (ed.), *Medieval Art, Architecture and Archaeology in London* (British Archaeological Association conference transactions for the year 1984 (vol. 10); Oxford: British Archaeological Association), 29–46.

——(1999), 'Wardrobes in the City: Houses of Consumption, Finance and Power', *Thirteenth-Century England*, 7: 103–15.

KEISER, GEORGE (1979), 'Lincoln Cathedral MS. 91: Life and Milieu of the Scribe', *Studies in Bibliography*, 32: 158–79.

——(1983), 'More Light on the Life and Milieu of Robert Thornton', *Studies in Bibliography*, 36: 111–19.

MCKENDRICK, SCOT, and KATHLEEN DOYLE (2007), *Bible Manuscripts: 1400 Years of Scribes and Scripture* (London: British Library).

MANN, JILL, and MAURA NOLAN (eds.) (2006), *The Text in the Community: Essays on Medieval Works, Manuscripts, Authors, and Readers* (Notre Dame, Ind.: University of Notre Dame Press).

MORAN, JO ANN H. (1984), 'A "Common Profit" Library in Fifteenth-Century England and Other Books for Chaplains', *Manuscripta*, 28: 17–25.

MORGAN, NIGEL (2006), *The Douce Apocalypse: Picturing the End of the World in the Middle Ages* (Oxford: Bodleian Library).

O'CONNOR, STEPHEN (1994a), 'Adam Fraunceys and John Pyel: Perception of Status among Merchants in Fourteenth-Century London', in Dorothy J. Clayton and Peter McNiven (eds.), *Trade, Devotion and Governance: Papers in Later Medieval History* (Stroud, Glos.: Phoenix Mill), 17–35.

——(1994b), 'Finance, Diplomacy and Politics: Royal Service by Two London Merchants in the Reign of Edward III', *Historical Research*, 67: 18–39.

ORME, NICHOLAS (1973), *English Schools in the Middle Ages* (London: Methuen).

PANTIN, W. A. (1955), *The English Church in the Fourteenth Century* (Cambridge: Cambridge University Press).

PARKES, MALCOLM B. (1991), 'The Literacy of the Laity', in *Scribes, Scripts, and Readers* (London: Hambledon Press) 275–97.

PEARSALL, DEREK (2000), 'The Rede (Boarstall) Gower: British Library, MS Harley 3490', in A. S. G. Edwards, Vincent Gillespie, and Ralph Hanna (eds.), *The English Medieval Book: Studies in Memory of Jeremy Griffiths* (London: British Library), 87–99.

POLLARD, A. W., and G. R. REDGRAVE (1976–91), *A Short-Title Catalogue of Brooks Printed 1475–1640* (2nd edn. 3 vols. London: Bibliographical Society).

REICHL, KARL (1973), *Religiöse Dichtung im englischen Hochmittelalter: Untersuchung und Edition der Handschrift B. 14. 39 des Trinity College in Cambridge* (Munich: Wilhelm Fink Verlag).

REIMER, STEPHEN R. (1987), *The Works of William Herebert, OFM* (Studies and Texts, 81; Toronto: Pontifical Institute of Medieval Studies).

REVARD, CARTER (2000), 'Scribe and Provenance', in Susannah Fein (ed.), *Studies in the Harley Manuscript: The Scribes, Contents, and Social Contexts of British Library MS Harley 2253* (Kalamazoo, Mich.: Medieval Institute Publications), 21–109.

RICKERT, EDITH (1932), 'Chaucer at School', *Modern Philology*, 29: 257–74.

SALTER, H. E., (1930), *The Boarstall Cartulary* (Oxford Historical Society, 88; Oxford: Oxford University Press).

SANDLER, LUCY F. (2004), *The Lichtenthal Psalter and the Manuscript Patronage of the Bohun Family* (London: Harvey Miller).

SHARPE, RICHARD (1997), *A Handlist of the Latin Writers of Great Britain and Ireland before 1540* (Publications of the Journal of Medieval Latin, 1; Turnhout: Brepols).

STEVENSON, W. H. (1911), *Report on the Manuscripts of Lord Middleton Preserved at Wollaton Hall, Nottinghamshire* (Historical Manuscripts Commission reports, 69; London: The Hereford Times for HM Stationery Office).

STROHM, PAUL (1977), 'Chaucer's Audience', *Literature and History*, 5: 26–41.

Testamenta Eboracensia 2 (1845), Publications of the Surtees Society, 30 (Durham: Surtees Society).

Testamenta Eboracensia 3 (1865), Publications of the Surtees Society, 45 (Durham: Surtees Society).

THOMPSON, JOHN (1987), *Robert Thornton and the London Thornton Manuscript: British Library MS Additional 31042* (Cambridge: D. S. Brewer).

THRUPP, SYLVIA (1948), *The Merchant Class of Medieval London, 1300–1500* (Chicago: University of Chicago Press).

TROTTER, D. A. (ed.) (2000), *Multilingualism in Later Medieval Britain* (Cambridge: Brewer).

TSCHANN, JUDITH, and M. B. PARKES (eds.) (1996), *Facsimile of Oxford, Bodleian Library, MS Digby 86* (Early English Text Society suppl. ser. 16; Oxford: Oxford University Press for the Early English Text Society).

TURVILLE-PETRE, THORLAC, and DOROTHY JOHNSON (1996), *Image and Text: Medieval Manuscripts at the University of Nottingham* (Nottingham: Djanogly Art Gallery, University of Nottingham Arts Centre).

WAKELIN, DANIEL (2007), *Humanism, Reading, and English Literature, 1430–1530* (Oxford: Oxford University Press).

WALDRON, RONALD (1988), 'Trevisa's Original Prefaces on Translation: A Critical Edition', in Edward D. Kennedy, Ronald Waldron, and Joseph S. Wittig (eds.), *Medieval English Studies Presented to George Kane* (Woodbridge: D. S. Brewer), 285–99.

WALKER, SIMON (1990), *The Lancastrian Affinity 1361–1399* (Oxford Historical Monographs; Oxford: Clarendon Press).

WHITWELL, ROBERT J. (1905), 'The Libraries of a Civilian and Canonist and of a Common Lawyer, an. 1294', *Law Quarterly Review*, 21: 393–400.

WIECK, ROGER S. (1988, repr. 2001), *Time Sanctified: The Book of Hours in Medieval Art and Life* (New York: George Braziller).

WILSON, EDWARD (1979), 'Sir Gawain and the Green Knight and the Stanley Family of Stanley, Storeton and Hooton', *Review of English Studies*, 30: 308–16.

ZEEMAN-SALTER, ELIZABETH (1957), 'Continuity and Change in Middle English Versions of the *Meditationes Vitae Christi*', *Medium Ævum*, 26: 25–31.

....

CHAPTER 7

THE VERSE OF
HEROES

....

JAYNE CARROLL

INTRODUCTION

....

Old English literature is customarily categorized in a variety of ways: prose as opposed to verse; religious as opposed to secular; or by perceived theme or genre. These categories are in almost all cases the results of judgements made by readers who are temporally and culturally distant from the original audiences of the texts under consideration. The only textual organization which we can safely attribute to the Anglo-Saxons themselves is that of the manuscripts they have bequeathed to us, and their principles of compilation are rarely transparent. Nevertheless, for various pragmatic, intellectual, and aesthetic purposes, we continue to dissect the Old English corpus and then to label and discuss it. The category under discussion here is that of 'heroic' verse. This has tended to loom large in discussions of Old English literature, despite the roll-call of so-called heroic poems being rather short. Typically in scholarly literature, there are just five poems discussed under the umbrella heading of heroic poetry: *Widsith, Deor, Waldere, The Finnsburh Fragment*, and *Beowulf*.[1] The last of these is, of course, the longest and best known of all Old English poems, which

---

[1] See e.g. Hill 1994, 1999; Bremmer 2005 ('Old English traditional heroic poetry'); North 2007. Edns. of the first four poems can be found together and accessibly presented with notes and glossary in both Hill 1994 and Muir 1989. They also exist in separate edns.: Malone 1962, 1977; Fry 1974. Quotations in this chapter are taken from Hill 1994, except for those from *Deor*, which are from Klinck 1992. There are numerous edns. of *Beowulf*. Fulk *et al.* 2008 is a recent and scholarly revised version of Klaeber's standard edn. and is used here. All translations are my own.

contributes considerably to the skewing of the record. These five poems take as their subject figures, historical or imagined, from the time of the Germanic migrations (*Völkerwanderungszeit*), or 'heroic age':[2] that period from the fourth to sixth centuries characterized by the movement of various peoples into areas which were previously under Roman control. It is in this rather narrow sense that they can be labelled 'heroic'. This period was characterized by the dominance of competing aristocratic warrior groups. As depicted in (non-contemporaneous) texts,[3] these groups practised what has become known as the 'heroic ethos' or, more commonly, the 'heroic code'. That is, a mode of societal organization whose cohesion and success depends upon the loyalty of the groups of warriors ('retainers') for their lord, for whom they fight and defend to the last. The retainers' loyalty is gained and rewarded through the provision of feasts (which take place in the mead-hall, a potent symbol of the heroic community) and gifts, usually treasure, weapons, or horses, as well as the protection afforded by membership of a group. The martial deeds of such leaders and their men were celebrated by court poets, whose praise poems ensure the lasting fame and glory of the warrior-kings.

By the time Old English texts came to be written down, this mode would have been a literary ideal rather than an actual way of life (and it is difficult to say, strictly speaking, whether it ever was an actual way of life), but it nevertheless finds expression both in evocations of the heroic age itself, and in texts which yoke the code somewhat anachronistically to their contemporary situation for political or ideological gain. In fact, such is the hold that it had on the Anglo-Saxon literary imagination that it penetrates to varying degrees almost all kinds of Old English literature, from the maximic to the religious.[4] Glory, vengeance, and the conflicting demands of tribal and familial allegiances are central issues in Old English texts which espouse or engage with the code, and the choice between honourable action which may result in death or a shameful act of self-preservation is seen by many to be *the* fundamental concern of heroic literature.[5]

The code, as understood in this way, is male, aristocratic, and idealized, and little time is given over to anyone other than warrior leaders: women are sidelined, children are occasionally seen but never heard, and the lower echelons of society are entirely absent. Such an understanding undoubtedly goes some way towards helping a reader traverse the literary landscape of late Anglo-Saxon England, but it nevertheless obscures several important features of so-called heroic verse, not least

---

[2] Thus labelled—most famously—in Chadwick 1912 (following Ker 1908: 1–14), and many times subsequently.

[3] Tacitus's account of 1st-cent. 'Germanic' tribes (tr. Rives 1999) was for many years the starting point for scholars interested in the 'heroic' aspects of Anglo-Saxon society. It is only in relatively recent times that the viability of applying a propagandistic, albeit anthropological, 1st-cent. account to explain the functioning of a much later and very different society has been questioned.

[4] So, for instance, '[i]t is perhaps the Christian Poetry of saints' lives and biblical heroes and heroines that best illustrates what we call the heroic spirit' (Caie 1994: 80).

[5] It is Busse and Holtei's 'characteristic feature of a definition of heroism' (1981: 615), and Hill's 'traditional choice of heroic poetry' (1994: 32).

because this catch-all label suggests generic similarity, an affinity in form, content, and preoccupations. This is deceptive. Not all of the so-called heroic poems are straightforward expressions of this ethos, or even about acts of heroism worthy of celebration (at least not as we would understand them); they are disparate in form, content, and preoccupations, even when they treat of the same underlying story, and the focus is by no means exclusively male: women feature to a very significant extent. In fact the use of figures well-known to several different Germanic-language cultures, who have their origins in historical figures of the heroic age, or who were imagined to have lived during that period, is the only thing common to the five heroic poems. These figures are sometimes—and traditionally—thought to be part of the common inheritance of the cultures who share them; it is assumed that these cultures took care to preserve them in art and literature for centuries after the original migrations from the continental homelands to new settlements, including those on the island of Britain. Alternatively, their appearance in Old English texts may be attributed to later contacts (after c.800) between the Continent and England, and a political desire to manufacture 'ancestral' links between their cultures (Frank 1991: 93–5). Either way, these figures loom large in the Anglo-Saxon imaginative reconstruction of past times, and whether they arrived with the Angles, Saxons, and Jutes, or were appropriated when it was politically expedient to have continental ancestry, they are made to do good service as the traditional, literary 'heroes' of the late Anglo-Saxon period: male—and occasionally female—figures who surface repeatedly, albeit sometimes only fleetingly, in different texts and with different functions.

The aim of what follows is to give a sense of each of the five poems which depict in various ways heroic-age figures and events; but also, and perhaps more importantly, to show how extraordinarily varied the creative responses of different individuals to this subject-matter could be. Anglo-Saxon poets—and indeed poets from other related cultures—used the same well-known stories, with their (usually well-born) characters, for very different purposes. They moulded them so that they reflected and commented upon the literary and philosophical preoccupations explored in different genres, from the mutedly elegiac to the explicitly celebratory. Where the verse does engage directly with the heroic code and its stringent demands, with its concern for honour, vengeance, and long-lasting fame, it evidences widely divergent attitudes and modes of presentation. Parts of what follows are therefore overtly comparative. The first and most substantial section examines the figure of Weland, the mythical smith of Germanic legend, as he and his story appear in *Deor*, other Old English texts, and in the Old Norse-Icelandic *Vǫlundarkviða*, in order to show how poets from different times and places, working within different literary traditions, make significantly different choices in presenting the same basic material. A later section examines the radically different treatment of Finn and Hengest in two Old English texts, *Beowulf* and the *Finnsburh Fragment*. The examination of the fragmentary *Waldere* is focused in such a way as to highlight the potential importance of the role that women were imagined to play in reinforcing ideals of heroic behaviour. The concluding section focuses upon the perceived fruits of living up to these ideals: long-lasting, preferably immortal fame, achieved by the repeated recital of poems which praise heroic behaviour.

WELAND AND VQLUNDR, BEADOHILD AND BQÐVILDR

The figure of Weland the Smith seems to have been well-known throughout Anglo-Saxon England, surfacing not only in poetry but also in prose texts and in sculpture. His earliest appearance is on the front panel of the Franks Casket, an eighth-century whalebone box probably made in Northumbria, where he features alongside the Adoration of the Magi, an iconographical juxtaposition long puzzled over by art historians. He finds his way into King Alfred's translation of Boethius's *De consolatione philosophiae*, in which the king substitutes 'Where now are the bones of the famous and wise goldsmith Weland?'[6] for Boethius's 'Where now are the bones of good Fabricius?'[7] Weland would undoubtedly have been more familiar to Alfred's ninth-century audience than Fabricius, a Roman general and consul in the third century BCE, famed for his integrity.[8] He appears in three of the poems which make up our small heroic corpus. In *Waldere* and *Beowulf*, the smith's name is mentioned only in passing, as the father of Widia (*Waldere*, II, l. 9), or attached to pieces of outstanding workmanship (Waldere's sword, Mimming, in *Waldere*, I, l. 2; Beowulf's corselet in *Beowulf*, l. 455). His most significant role is in *Deor*, a stanzaic poem of forty-two lines preserved in the late tenth-century Exeter Book. Even here, however, the narrative is brief and enigmatic—a six-line stanza describing his suffering which heads four further short stanzaic narratives of misfortune, each punctuated by the refrain, *Þæs ofereode; þisses swa mæg* ('That passed over; so can this'):

> Welund him be wurman   wræces cunnade,
> anhydig eorl,   earfoþa dreag;
> hæfde him to gesiþþe   sorge ond longaþ,
> wintercealde wræce,   wean oft onfond,
> siþþan hine Niðhad on   nede legde,
> swoncre seonobende   on syllan monn.
> Þæs ofereode;   þisses swa mæg!
> *(Deor, ll. 1–7)*

---

[6] 'Hwær synt nu þæs foremæran [ond] þæs wisan goldsmiððes ban Welondes?' (Sedgefield 1899: 46). Alfred's lengthier excursus on Weland, in the *Meters of Boethius*, is discussed below, p. 140–41.

[7] *Ubi nunc fidelis ossa Fabricii manent?* (Boethius 1973: 222).

[8] The appearance of 'Weland's Smithy' in a 10th-cent. charter ([*be eastan*] *welandes smiððan*; Sawyer 564), referring to the megalithic tomb on the Berkshire Downs, shows that in some form Weland's fame extended beyond the realms of the purely literary and aristocratic milieux of Anglo-Saxon England (Gelling 1974: 347). The Franks Casket's depiction of the scene of Weland's revenge is not labelled—all its other scenes are—which may also suggest that the story was very well-known.

Weland, resolute warrior, experienced torment among snakes,[9] suffered hardships, had sorrow and longing as company for himself, winter-cold suffering; he often experienced woes after Nithhad laid him in fetters, supple sinew-bonds on the better man. That passed over; so can this.

The characteristics recorded in the first stanza of *Deor* do not fit well with notions of heroic behaviour held by a twenty-first-century audience. Our modern-day fictional heroes tend not to be celebrated for stalwart suffering and endurance, but for action, usually in a good cause. Nor can we easily reconcile this account with what we know about the idealized heroic code: where are the 'mighty deeds of heroes' (Hill 1999: 236) supposedly common to heroic poetry? Our opinion of the smith may fall further when we learn that the second stanza of *Deor*, with its grieving female figure who is bereft of brothers and paralysed by the fact of her own unwanted pregnancy, is telling the story, in the poem's characteristically oblique style, of one of Weland's victims:

> Beadohilde ne wæs   hyre broþra deaþ
> on sefan swa sar   swa hyre sylfre þing,
> þæt heo gearolice   ongieten hæfde
> þæt heo eacen wæs;   æfre ne meahte
> þriste geþencan   hu ymb þæt sceolde.
> Þæs ofereode;   þisses swa mæg!
> *(Deor, ll. 8–13)*

To Beadohild the death of her brothers was not as painful as her own situation, in that she had clearly realized that she was pregnant; she could never confidently perceive what she should do about that. That passed; so can this.

To understand how the stories of Beadohild and Weland are linked, we must turn to texts written down several centuries later than *Deor*, and outside England. *Vǫlundarkviða* ('The Lay of Vǫlundr [Weland]'), an Old Norse-Icelandic poem preserved in the thirteenth-century Icelandic manuscript known as the Codex Regius, gives a relatively full account of Vǫlundr's story.[10] There, we learn of the marriages of three beautiful swan-maidens to three men, Egill, Slagfiðr, and Vǫlundr. Eight years later the swan-maidens abandon their husbands. Egill and Slagfiðr seek their lost wives, but Vǫlundr stays at home, forging wondrous rings in red-gold for his unnamed loved one. The smith's troubles increase: he is captured and imprisoned by the evil king Níðuðr (OE Nithhad), who takes Vǫlundr's own sword for himself and gives one of the swan-maiden's gold rings to his daughter, Bǫðvildr (OE Beadohil). Níðuðr's queen, wary of Vǫlundr, has him hamstrung. Lame and fettered, he embarks upon the production of all kinds of treasure for his captors. To this point,

---

[9] *Be wurman* 'among snakes' is obscure. Various explanations have been offered; these are outlined in Klinck 1992: 158–9.

[10] Dronke 1997: 243–54. Elsewhere, the smith is mentioned fleetingly in *Waltharius*, a Latin text from Germany, possibly from as early as the 9th cent., and a version of his story (different in a number of respects from *Vǫlundarkviða*) is told at length in *Velents þáttr*, one of the narratives which make up the Old Norse Þiðreks saga, first preserved in a defective manuscript of the 13th cent. and then in a 17th-cent. Icelandic paper manuscript, and perhaps Norwegian in origin (Dronke 1997: 273–4).

our sympathy lies with the unfortunate smith, but this sympathy must surely disappear when the Old Icelandic poem explains in horrifying detail what *Deor* refers to only obliquely: Vǫlundr beheads the king's young sons and creates treasures of their facial features for their parents and sister. Bǫðvildr does not escape the smith's wrath, although the description of her role in his revenge is more circumspect:

> Bar hann hana bióri,
> þvíat hann betr kunni,
> svá at hón í sessi
> um sofnaði.
> > (*Vkv*, st. 28, ll. 1–4)

> He bemused her with beer,
> for he was more knowing than she,
> so that on the couch
> she fell asleep.

Raped or seduced, and certainly befuddled with alcohol, Bǫðvildr is left pregnant, a fact with which Vǫlundr taunts his former oppressors, before escaping into the sky:[11]

> 'Nú gengr Bǫðvildr
> barni aukin,
> einga dóttir
> ykkor beggia.'
> > (*Vkv*, st. 36, ll. 1–4)

> 'Now Bǫðvildr goes
> with child,
> the only daughter
> of the two of you.'

Vǫlundarkviða's final stanza ends with Bǫðvildr confessing all to her father.

We cannot know whether the version of the Weland–Beadohild story narrated by *Vǫlundarkviða* is exactly the one known to *Deor*'s audience, and at first glance the two accounts are dissimilar. In particular there are no details of Weland's circumstances before his capture by Nithhad, and no trace of his swan-maiden wife is found in *Deor*, or in other Anglo-Saxon sources.[12] However, scholars generally agree that *Vǫlundarkviða* represents 'an amalgam of two different types of story' (Larrington 1992: 146). These stories are held to be 'virtually independent of each other' (Dronke 1997: 255), with the swan-maiden episode a recognizable folk- or fairy-tale motif, and possibly 'an artistic expansion and adaptation of the fairy-tale theme to another older

---

[11] The poem's description of his flight, *hófz at lofti* ('raised himself into the air') is ambiguous; scholars have debated whether Vǫlundr's smithing has provided him with wings to escape or whether he has the shamanic gift of flight.

[12] Unless we accept the argument that *Vǫlundarkviða* in its entirety is the product of England's Danelaw areas (McKinnell 2001), an argument that relies upon the premise that English linguistic influence implies English provenance.

tale of the smith's revenge' (Grimstad 1983: 188 and references therein).[13] The swan-maiden episode has an obvious structural and thematic function within *Vǫlundarkviða*: the maidens' confinement and eventual flight mirrors that of Vǫlundr later in the poem. Its absence from *Deor* should therefore not trouble us unduly, and the 'smith's revenge' as narrated in *Vǫlundarkviða* elucidates both the account given in *Deor* and the portrayal of the Weland on the Franks Casket, which focuses upon this revenge, depicting him holding the head of one of the princes and offering a cup to Beadohild.[14] We can therefore think of two different poets sharing the same basic material and story-shape, making individual choices in how to present it.[15] In *Deor*, Weland and Beadohild are enlisted in an allusive roll-call of figures who exemplify loss and hardship in their—presumably well-known—situations.[16] Each situation is described obliquely, and punctuated with a refrain. Despite the oblique mode of presentation, Weland's state of isolation, physical hardship, and longing, coupled with the poem's consolatory refrain, clearly align him with the central figures of what is commonly called Old English elegiac verse. Some of the particulars of the smith's situation are highly reminiscent of other examples of the genre. The *wræces* (l. 1) that he experiences is translated above as 'torment', but it can also mean 'exile', the usual state for an elegiac figure in Old English verse; his *wintercealde wræce* 'winter-cold suffering' (l. 4) echoes the *wintercearig* 'winter-sad' central figure of *The Wanderer* (*Wan*, l. 24) and the ice-bound narrator of *The Seafarer* (*Seaf*, ll. 8–19); his confinement, described in terms that can be understood both literally and metaphorically,[17] recalls that of the Wanderer, who has had to constrain his heart in fetters (*feterum sælan*; *Wan*, l. 21), and who repeatedly refers to 'binding' as a condition experienced by the solitary man (*Wan*, ll. 13, 18, 40); Weland's grim companions, sorrow and longing (*sorge ond longaþ*; *Deor*, l. 3), are recognized as cruel by the Wanderer (ll. 29–31).[18]

It is crucial for the successful presentation of Weland as elegiac protagonist that *Deor* remains silent on the smith's active role in Beadohild's tragic predicament. The poem does not make explicit the connection between them, and the element of harsh vengeance so prominent in *Vǫlundarkviða* (and on the Franks Casket) is absent, lost or suppressed in the silent link between the two stanzas, sublimated into the higher

[13] Hatto 1980 (repr. from 1961): 267–97. For a concise summary of the main characteristics of the swan-maiden motif, see Dronke 1997: 258.

[14] Excellent photographs of the Franks Casket can be found in Wilson 1980: 30–1.

[15] The exact nature of the relationship between the poems is not investigated here. For that, see Dronke (1997: 276–80) and McKinnell (2001: 331–3).

[16] The other legendary figures are: Mæðhild, otherwise unknown; Đeodric, most probably the Ostrogothic ruler (493–526); and Eormanric, the Gothic tyrant (d. *c.*375). In the case of Eormanric, and possibly also Đeodric, it is the imposition of hardship that they exemplify. For a brief summary of the roles these figures play in the poem, see Fulk and Cain 2003: 216–17.

[17] He is placed *on nede* (*Deor*, l. 5), often translated as 'in fetters', but perhaps more accurately rendered as 'in constraints' (Hill 1994: 29–30 n. 5); these are then specified as *swoncre seonobende* 'supple sinew-bonds' (l. 6), which is simultaneously more particular and yet still ambiguous, referring either to the hamstringing reported in *Vǫlundarkviða* or to the specific character of the bonds themselves.

[18] Edns. of *The Wanderer*, *The Seafarer*, and *The Wife's Lament* can be found in Klinck 1992.

cause of reconciling the endurance of hardship with the promise of future consolation. The subject of the Beadohild stanza is the woman's inner turmoil and mental anguish. In describing her solipsistic focus on her own particular situation rather than on the murder of her two brothers, the poet depicts the bereft girl in a psychologically astute way and at the same time sets her apart from her family, and in particular from her parents, of whom there is no mention. She is thus dissociated from the cruelty of her parents' treatment of Weland, and the link between the two individuals is further obscured, or at least reconfigured, as both emerge as tragic figures in the elegiac mode. Beadohild's inability to find resolution, to 'perceive what she should do about that' (Deor, l. 12) evokes the hinterland of Old English elegiac poetry in the same way that Weland's chill isolation does. She brings to mind the female speaker of the Wife's Lament, whose repetition of key lexical items suggests a mind unable to move on from fruitless contemplation of the past and its resultant misery (Renoir 1977: 4–19). Both Beadohild and the 'wife' display in adversity a 'debilitating egocentricity' (Boran 1975: 268).

In Deor, the figures of both Weland and Beadohild are, through lexis, theme, and preoccupation, thoroughly assimilated into the elegiac mode, a mode central to much Old English literature. The narrative outline provided by a synopsis of Vǫlundarkviða may not immediately suggest elegiac subject-matter to us, but the surviving evidence may nevertheless imply that Weland's story was commonly found in Old English elegiac tradition, or that an earlier Old English poem explored his predicament at greater length in elegiac style.[19] In fact, it was probably not only Weland's widespread fame that prompted King Alfred's mind to skip to him from Fabricius.[20] Fame may be the one obvious thing that the incorruptible, successful Roman and the vengeful, embittered smith have in common, but it is probable that Alfred, in referring to Weland, was adding a further dimension to Boethius's illustration of death as supreme leveller, as well as offering a native 'gloss' on Fabricius for an Anglo-Saxon audience. The themes of eternity, mutability and transience, death and suffering were central both to Old English elegy and to Boethius's philosophical narrative. This, together with the Latin author's use of the Ubi sunt? ('Where are they?') motif, also found in Old English elegy,[21] evoked in Alfred an explicitly elegiac response, clear in his second, poetic translation of the text, The Meters of Boethius, and it is unlikely to be happy coincidence that it is Weland, rather than some other famous figure, who is depicted with elegiac topoi:

---

[19] It is possible that the poets of Deor and Vǫlundarkviða both drew upon such a poem: shared (cognate) vocabulary (nede, Deor (l. 5) and nauðir, Vkv (12/6); eacen, Deor (l. 11) and barna aukin, Vkv (36/2)) and English linguistic influence on Vǫlundarkviða may suggest such a relationship.

[20] Further suggestions on the 'link' between the two figures are the similarity between Fabricius's name and the Latin for smith (faber), and a particular association between Weland and the grave (Ellis Davison: 1958).

[21] Most famously in The Wanderer, ll. 92–3: 'Hwær cwom mearg? Hwær cwom mago? Hwær cwom maþþumgyfa? / Hwær cwom symbla gesetu? Hwær sindon seledreamas?' ('Where has the horse gone? Where has the man gone? Where have the treasure-givers gone? / Where have the seats of feasts gone? Where are the joys of the hall?')

Hwær sint nu þæs wisan   Welandes ban,
þæs goldsmiðes,   þe wæs geo mærost?
Forþy ic cwæð þæs wisan   Welandes ban,
forðy ængum ne mæg   eorðbuendra
se cræft losian   þe him on Crist onlænð.
Ne mæg mon æfre þy eð   ænne wræccan
his cræftes beniman,   þe mon oncerran mæg
sunnan onswifan   ond ðisne swiftan rodor
of his rihtryne   rinca ænig.
(Meters of Boethius, 10, ll. 33–41[22])

Where now are the bones of wise Weland,
the goldsmith who was most famous, long ago?
I said the bones of wise Weland,
because from no man among earth-dwellers may
the skill be lost which Christ lends him.
No man can more easily take from an exile
his skill than can one
turn the sun and this swift sky from its right course.

Here, Weland is *ænne wræccan* 'an exile', aligned once again with the Wanderer, who treads *wræclastas* 'paths of exile' (*Wan*, l. 5), with the Seafarer, who spends a winter *wræccan lastum* 'on paths of exile' (*Sea*, l. 15), and with the female narrator of *The Wife's Lament*, who experiences *wonn... wræcsiþa* 'torment of exile' (*Wife's Lament*, l. 5). Alfred's poetic text discusses Weland within an explicitly Christian context: his skills are lent by Christ and therefore immutable, regardless of earthly circumstances. For Alfred, the kind of cruel vengeance exacted by Weland had no place within a society governed by Christian principles, even if it had been a dominant feature of heroic literary tradition and a governing principle of the culture of the Heroic Age, as imagined by its post-migration descendants.[23] The structure of *Deor* perhaps suggests a similar unease with the explicitly vengeful: its elliptical narrative style may not have been the only reason for the silencing of Weland's dark side, and towards the end of the poem the varied stories of the first five stanzas are subsumed under a generalized Christian narrative of suffering and relief:

Siteð sorgcearig   sælum bidæled,
on sefan sweorceð,   sylfum þinceð
þæt sy endeleas   *earfoða* deal.

---

[22] Krapp 1993: 166.

[23] Attempts to curb the bloodfeud are found in the very earliest preserved law-codes (Æthelberht of Kent, r. 602–3). The most extensive reforms to the existing regulations were made by Alfred and Edmund. Alfred's laws show his desire to ensure that all potential bloodfeuds were settled by the payment of *wergild* rather than blood-vengeance (Attenborough 1922: 62–93). That he was not successful is demonstrated by Edmund's subsequent and more detailed code concerning the bloodfeud (Robertson 1925: 8–11).

Mæg þonne geþencan   þæt geond þas woruld
witig dryhten   wendeþ geneahhe,
eorle monegum   are gesceawað,
wislicne blæd,   sumum weana dæl.

(Deor, ll. 28–34)

He sits, troubled with sorrow, deprived of joys,
darkens in spirit; it seems to him
that his share of hardships is endless.
Then he can consider that throughout this world
the wise Lord often brings about change,
shows favour to many men,
a certain happiness, to some a share of woes.

The narrator's specific reason for intense interest in the consolations offered by Christian belief, and what exactly it is that he hopes might pass over, are finally detailed in the poem's final eight lines:

Þæt ic bi me sylfum   secgan wille,
þæt ic hwile wæs   Heodeninga scop,
dryhtne dyre;   me wæs Deor noma.
Ahte fela wintra   folgað tilne,
holdne hlaford,   oþþæt Heorrenda nu,
leoðcræftig monn,   londryht geþah
þæt me eorla hleo   ær gesealde.
Þæs ofereode;   þisses swa mæg!

(Deor, ll. 35–42)

I wish to reveal about myself
that I for a while was poet to the Heodenings,
dear to my lord; my name was Deor.
For many winters I held a good position,
a loyal lord, until now Heorrenda,
a man skilled in verse, has received the land-rights
that the protector of men previously afforded me.
That passed over; so can this.

Deor was a court poet, now usurped by another man, Heorrenda, from both position and attendant land-rights. Deor's attitude seems not to be marked by bitterness: Heorrenda is *leoðcræftig* 'skilled in verse' and the lord is labelled *holdne* 'loyal'. The depiction of a man waiting patiently, if wearily, for reversal of fortune or heavenly grace would be complete were it not for the intrusion of a possible bathetic element. The juxtaposition of semi-historical, heroic-mythical events which resound throughout the literary traditions of a number of related cultures with Deor's personal misfortune serves either to put that misfortune into perspective, or to lace the poem with the spirit of irony. The application of the recurrent refrain to this situation, too, sits rather oddly here: is it Heorrenda's new-found wealth and security that Deor imagines passing over, or simply its effects on him? If the final lines of the poem prompt us towards an ironic reading, we return to the Weland and Beadohild stanzas with the sense that the underlying narrative of cruel vengeance is more important than is immediately apparent, and that it may work to undermine, rather than support, the ostensible message of consolation.

There is, however, nothing ironic in Alfred's description of Weland as wise, and this informs us that Weland, as noble and tragic figure, *anhydig eorl* ('resolute warrior'; *Deor*, l. 2) and *syllan monn* ('better man'; *Deor*, l. 6), was readily available for use by Old English authors of an elegiac bent; the Franks Casket is the only Anglo-Saxon source which convincingly informs us that his darker side was an appropriate subject for art.

And although there are aspects of *Vǫlundarkviða* that can be described as elegiac, 'vengeance is [its] supreme value' (Fidjestøl 1997: 318), not consolation. While the Eddic poet shares not only the same basic plot but also certain thematic preoccupations with the *Deor* poet, these are explored in quite different ways, ways which reflect the development of medieval Scandinavian literary tradition, a tradition to which feud and revenge were central, if complex, concerns.[24] Where vengeance is largely written out of the Old English record of Weland, in *Vǫlundarkviða* the matching of wrong with vengeful wrong is glaringly clear from the moment in the poem that Vǫlundr speaks. The smith's words, when after his capture he first responds to Níðuðr's taunts about his hoard of treasure, foreshadow the punishment he will mete out in return for the treatment he receives at the king's hand:

> 'Man ek at vér meiri
> mæti áttom,
> er vér heil hiú
> heima vórom.'
> (*Vkv*, st. 15, ll. 1–4)

> 'I remember that we owned
> a greater treasure
> when we were a whole family
> in our home.'

Vǫlundr's harking back to his lost, happy existence alongside his swan-maiden wife undoubtedly augurs the destruction which awaits Níðuðr's family, a fact recognized by Níðuðr's *kunnig kván* ('cunning wife', *Vkv*, 16/1–2), whose prescient words should alert us to his evil intent:

> 'Tenn hánom teygiaz,
> er hánom er tét sverð,
> ok hann Bǫðvildar

---

[24] Most medieval Scandinavian literature comes from, or at least was preserved in, Iceland. There are, accordingly, many studies of feuding and vengeance in Icelandic literature and culture, including two book-length studies, Byock 1982 and Miller 1990.

baug um þekkir!
Ámon eru augo
ormi þeim enom frána.'
            (*Vkv*, st. 17, ll. 1–6)

'He shows his teeth
when the sword is shown to him,
and he recognizes
Bǫðvildr's ring!
His eyes are like
those of the glittering serpent.'

Her words, too, in their focus upon Vǫlundr's eyes anticipate the terrible fate to be meted out to her sons:

En ór augom
iarknasteina
sendi hann kunnigri
kono Níðaðar.
            (*Vkv*, st. 25, ll. 9–12)

And from the eyes
gem-stones
he sent to the cunning
wife of Níðuðr.

Her cunning, while it alerts her to the danger Vǫlundr poses, does not enable her to recognize her sons' eyes, magically transformed into jewels, until the cruel smith reveals their provenance (35/5–8).

Time and again, one act is specifically pitched against another. Vǫlundr discovers that Bǫðvildr wears the rings he fashioned for his swan-bride:

'Nú berr Bǫðvildr
brúðar minnar—
bíðka ek þess bót—
bauga rauða.'
            (*Vkv*, st. 18, ll. 11–14)

'Now Bǫðvildr wears
my bride's red rings—
I shall not be
compensated for this.'

The *bót* 'compensation, redress' he eventually does exact for this is to make Bǫðvildr a bride of sorts, through their union and her resulting pregnancy. He refers to her as his wife and bride in his curiously touching attempt to secure her safety before revealing all to her father:

'Eiða skaltu mér áðr
alla vinna,

      . . .

at þú kveliat

> kván Vǫlundar,
> né brúði minni
> at bana verðir.'
> (*Vkv*, st. 33, ll. 1–2, 7–10)

> 'First you must swear to me
> every oath,
> . . .
> that you shall not harm
> Vǫlundr's wife,
> nor put to death
> my bride.'

This recalls the poet's description of the weeping Bǫðvildr, who *tregði fǫr friðils* 'grieved over the departure of [her] lover' (*Vkv*, 29/9), rather than for any wrong he might have done her.

Any sympathy that Vǫlundr's concern for the girl might evoke in the poem's audience is promptly dashed when he goes on to reveal in detail to Níðuðr what he has done to the king's three children. Sympathy must be reserved for Bǫðvildr, whose words we are left with at the end of the poem:

> 'Satt er þat, Níðaðr,
> er sagði þér;
> sát vit Vǫlundr
> saman í hólmi
> —eina ǫgurstund—
> æva skyldi!
> Ek vætr hánom
> [vinna] kunnak,
> ek vætr hánom
> vinna máttak.'
>   (*Vkv*, st. 41)

> 'It is true, Níðuðr,
> what he said to you;
> Vǫlundr and I sat
> together on the island
> —for a tide's turning only—
> it should not have happened!
> I did not know at all
> how to resist him,
> I was in no way able
> to resist him.'

Unlike her *kunnig* mother, Bǫðvildr is ignorant (*ek . . . kunnak* 'I did not know how'), and it is this which renders her most vulnerable to the plotting smith. Unlike in *Deor*, there is no sense of future relief from suffering, only of the stark consequences of cruelty and revenge.[25] Christianity is nowhere to be seen, despite—or more probably

---

[25] It is possible that *Vǫlundarkviða*'s medieval audience was aware of a version of the story which sees the smith and the girl reunited and married (*Velents þáttr*, see above, n. 10), and it is probable that it

because of—the thirteenth-century date of *Vǫlundarkviða*'s preservation, although we may choose to divine it in our interpretations of the poet's attitude towards the heroic 'ideal' of vengeance. The Old English and Old Norse-Icelandic poems work their common storyline to radically different effect: the 'hero' Weland/Vǫlundr proves malleable, an effective conduit for the rather different preoccupations and motifs of two related but separately developed literary cultures.[26]

WALDERE AND HILDEGYTH—BEHIND EVERY GOOD MAN

Beadohild/Bǫðvildr is the victim of an ethos which demands that vengeful action is taken to 'right' wrongs, and female victim-figures are familiar to us from a number of Old English poems.[27] However, it is not the only role assigned to women within the workings of this ethos. The 'whetting' woman, who encourages her menfolk by fair or foul means to gird their loins for battle, murder, revenge, and other masculine adventures, is a commonplace of Norse-Icelandic literature (Níðuðr's queen, with her 'cold counsel' to her husband, is one, minor, example),[28] but her Anglo-Saxon cousin is harder to find. It is probable that we have a good example in one of the two fragments surviving from the poem known as *Waldere*, an Old English version of the story of Walter of Aquitaine (a putatively fifth-century figure).[29] Three other versions of this story survive intact, two in Latin (*Waltharius*, a tenth-century Frankish verse epic, and a prose narrative from thirteenth- or fourteenth-century Poland) and one in Old Norse (preserved, like *Velents þáttr*, in the thirteenth-century *Þiðreks saga*). The Old English fragments are usually explained with recourse to the plot of *Waltharius*, which runs as follows. Two royal hostages are sent by their fathers to Attila the Hun (OE Ætla), who has defeated their kingdoms in war. They are the Aquitainian prince Walter (OE *Waldere*) and the Burgundian princess Hildgunt (OE

knew that tradition had it that their son was the hero Viðga (OE Widia). Widia may be the literary reflex of the Gothic warrior mentioned by Jordanes in his mid-5th-cent. history of the Goths (Hill 1994: 4).

[26] Dance 2004 is a concise, accessible, and judicious guide to possible links between Old English and Old Norse-Icelandic literatures.

[27] Hill 1990 assesses the various tragic female figures found in the heroic corpus.

[28] Níðuðr's words, *kǫld ero mér ráð þín* 'cold are your counsels to me' (*Vkv*, 31/6), are found elsewhere in the Old Norse-Icelandic corpus, usually with a sense of impending disaster related to the matter of feuding, where women's words are held to have had disastrous consequences (Anderson 2002: pp. xi–xvi).

[29] These fragments are single leaves from an Old English MS, *c*.1000. The order of the two portions of text is not established beyond doubt. Hill (1994: 2–3) outlines the difficulties. It is impossible to assess how many lines a fully preserved *Waldere* would run to, but Hill (1994: 11) estimates 'at least' 1,000, and Robinson (2001: 285) suggests that it would have been 'a full-blown epic poem . . . to compare with *Beowulf*'; see also Campbell (1962: 15), where *Waldere*, along with *Beowulf*, is 'direct proof of the existence of epics on heroic themes'.

*Hildegyth),[30] whose families intend them to become betrothed. Hagano (OE Hagena), a Frankish noble, is also sent to Attila, but later escapes and returns home, where Guntharius (OE Guthhere, Burgundian rather than Frankish in the Anglo-Saxon tradition, and therefore related to Hildegyth) is now king. At Attila's court, Waltharius becomes a mighty warrior, and Attila's queen attempts to secure his loyalty and attendance at Attila's court by engineering a marriage with a Hunnish woman. In response, Waltharius and Hildgunt flee, only to encounter Guntharius and a band of men, which includes Hagano, who refuses to fight his former companion. On the first day of battle, Waltharius kills eleven of Guntharius's men, including Hagano's nephew; when, on the second day of fighting, Waltharius cuts off Guntharius's leg, Hagano joins in. He cuts off Waltharius's hand, and in return loses an eye and six teeth. These injuries, coupled with the men's breathlessness, prompt them to cease fighting, and, somewhat improbably, they engage in cheery banter while Hildgunt dresses their wounds.

One fragment of *Waldere*, traditionally labelled Fragment I, appears to comprise part of a speech by Hildegyth, although she is not named, in which she employs a range of conventional heroic motifs to spur her lover on at what appears to be a point some way through the battle, when a number of Waldere's enemies lie dead. She presents him with the time-honoured heroic choice, death or glory:

> ***** [nu] is se dæg cumen,
> þæt ðu scealt aninga   oðer twega,
> lif forleosan   oððe lang[n]e dom
> agan mid eldum,   Ælfheres sunu.
> (*Waldere*, I, ll. 8–11)

***** [now] the day has come when you, son of Ælfhere, must surely do one of two things, lose your life or achieve long-lasting glory among men.

The auxiliary verb *sculan* does not admit of doubt, and Hildegyth's use of *Ælfheres sunu* to describe her lover implies that it is not only personal, but also family honour at stake. It is possible to imagine that such encouragement, while highly conventional, might also be necessary if, as has been suggested, Hildegyth is here encouraging Waldere to fight his former companion Hagena.[31] Hildegyth vividly sketches out the alternatives of shame or glory in her flattering description of Waldere's warrior attributes: shirking battle, fleeing slaughter, and preserving body (*wig forbugan oððe on weal fleon, / lice beorgan*; *Wald*, I, ll. 15–16) represent the disgrace (*edwitscype*, *Wald*, I, l. 14) to which he has not stooped and will not, while the reckless disregard for personal safety (*to fyrenlice feohtan*; *Wald*, I, l. 21) she has witnessed brings honour and hero-status 'though many enemies were hacking at your mailcoat with swords' (*Wald*, I, ll. 16–17). Her speech refers to the outstanding weapon which is

---

[30] Hildegyth is not named in *Waldere*: her Old English name is a reconstructed cognate of Hildgunt, hence the starred form.

[31] It is not only Waldere but also Hildegyth who is involved in a clash of loyalties: in the Old English tradition, Guthhere is of Burgundian royal stock, just as she is.

conventionally carried by the warrior-hero (Weland's sword, Mimming), to the proud boast (*beot*) which conventionally precedes battle (here, Guthhere's rather than Waldere's), and to the treasure which can never belong to the vanquished, who must remain ringless (*beaga leas*; *Wald*, I, l. 29). In short, Hildegyth's speech is packed with the commonplaces of the heroic literary mode, 'as comprehensive an evocation of the determinants of male heroism as one could hope to find' (Hill 1990: 244), rendered splendidly vivid by the poet.

Fragment II brings us the voice of the hero himself, but its first ten lines, which start in the middle of a speech, have been variously attributed to each of the three main male characters, and indeed to Hildegyth. What is preserved of this speech is entirely given over to lauding an outstanding sword, either Mimming or a different weapon, whose history is rehearsed over six leisurely lines which take in some of the foremost figures of the Heroic Age: the sword seems to have been in the possession of Theodoric the Goth, who sent it Widia, Weland's son, as a reward. More than half of the fragment (ll. 14–32) is certainly the formal speech of Waldere, addressed to Guthhere, *wine Burgenda* 'friend of the Burgundians' (*Waldere*, II, l. 14). Again, a good deal of it is given over to the trappings of battle, in this case the mailcoat Waldere has inherited from his father (*Waldere*, II, ll. 19–22), and to the treasure-distributing power of the victor (*Waldere*, II, ll. 30–1), but Waldere's brief but telling reference to Hagena effectively highlights the conflict of loyalties which is central to the episode:

> 'Hwæt, ðu huru wendest,   wine Burgenda,
> þæt me Hagenan hand   hilde gefremede
> ond getwæmde feðewigges.'
> > (*Wald*, II, ll. 14–16)

'Indeed, you expected, friend of the Burgundians, that Hagena's hand would do battle with me and put a stop to the combat on foot.'

Waldere's taunting belongs to the tradition of verbal duelling, or flyting, allied with the heroic 'boast', where a hero demonstrates his verbal dexterity in advance of his outstanding martial abilities. Old English literature is rich with examples which demonstrate the importance of rhetorical, as well as literal, battle in establishing the credentials of its hero-figures.[32] Here, as elsewhere, this strand of the heroic tradition is given a subtle Christian gloss in the hands of its Old English poet, as Waldere anachronistically places his faith in the final judgement of a recognizably Christian God:[33]

> 'Ðeah meag sige syllan   se ðe symle byð
> recon ond rædfest   ryhta gehwilces;
> se ðe him to ðam Halgan   helpe gelifeð,

---

[32] Beowulf's crushing of Unferth (*Beowulf*, ll. 499–606) is probably the best-known Old English example. For more on the flyting traditions, see Parks 1987, 1990.

[33] More explicitly Christianized flyting can be found in poems as various as *The Battle of Maldon* and Cynewulf's *Juliana*, both of which draw upon the traditions of the heroic ethos.

> to Gode gioce,   he þær gearo findeð,
> gif ða earnunga   ær geðenceð.'
>
> (*Wald*, II, ll. 25–9)

'Yet he can give victory, who is always prompt and resolute in every right thing; he who trusts to the holy one for help, to God for support, he readily finds it there, if he first considers how he will deserve it.'

What we have of *Waldere* celebrates the exploits of its reckless hero and the literary tenets of the heroic ethos with very little in the way of ambivalence (and with Waldere seemingly drawing upon the support of the Christian God), and for this reason it has been called 'straightforwardly heroic' (Fulk and Cain 2003: 216). However, fifty-nine of the surviving sixty-three lines are speeches, rather than the words of the narrator or poet. It is impossible to say whether the celebratory viewpoint conveyed in the fragments would be found throughout the whole poem, had it survived. We know from the evidence presented by *Beowulf* that widely divergent views can be represented by different voices in a single poem, and a fully preserved *Waldere* may have been rather more dialogic than the surviving text suggests.

BEOWULF, THE FINNSBURH FRAGMENT, AND THE HEROES OF OLD

The *Beowulf*-poet was fully conversant with a range of stories relating to the exploits of Heroic Age figures, and, judging by the allusive style in which many of their stories are mentioned in the poem, he expected the same of his audience.[34] Part of one of the poet's stories, that of Finn and Hengest at Finnsburh, survives elsewhere, in George Hickes's 1705 edition from a transcription of a single manuscript leaf, now lost.[35] Its text is known as the Finnsburh Fragment. The information from the Finnsburh Episode (*Beowulf*, ll. 1063–1159) and, to a lesser degree, from this Fragment has been pieced together to suggest the following plot outline:[36] Hnæf, leader of the Danes, and his retinue visit his sister, Hildeburh, and her Frisian husband, Finn, at Finnsburh. For some reason, the Danes are attacked and Hnæf is killed.[37] Hengest takes

---

[34] These include the stories of Ingeld (*Beowulf*, ll. 82–5, 2020–69), Sigemund the dragon-slayer (ll. 874–900), Heremod (ll. 901–15), Finn and Hengest (ll. 1063–1159), Hama and Eormanric the Goth (ll. 1198–1201), Offa (ll. 1931–62), and Heoroweard and Hrothulf (ll. 2160–9).

[35] It seems to have been part of Lambeth Palace Library, MS 487, or at least inserted as a loose leaf into this MS.

[36] Tolkien's reconstruction (1962: 159–62), in all but minor hypothetical details, remains the most widely accepted explanation of events.

[37] Many critics suspect that a pre-existing feud between the Danes and Frisians, possibly settled—at least temporarily—by Hildeburh's marriage to Finn, has been reawakened during the Danes' visit.

over as leader, but the remaining days of battle—more than five—prove inconclusive, and an uneasy truce is established whereby the Danes agree to follow Finn provided that the Frisians do not mention his killing of their former lord. The code of honour embraced by literary Heroic Age figures dictates that this truce will not hold. In the spring, the Danes exact their vengeance: they kill Finn and depart for Denmark with Hildeburh and Finn's treasure-hoard.

It is generally agreed that the forty-eight surviving lines of the Fragment are concerned with the first of the two Finnsburh battles: that in which Hnæf is killed. Like *Waldere*, the Fragment is speech-heavy, in parts runs at a similarly leisurely pace,[38] and hosts an abundance of motifs found elsewhere. The ten-line speech of the *heorogeong cyning* 'battle-young king' (*Finnsburh*, l. 2), later revealed to be the doomed Hnæf, gives a taste both of the poem's statelier mode and of its use of topoi:

'Ne ðis ne dagað eastan,   ne her draca ne fleogeð,
ne her ðisse healle   hornas ne byrnað;
ac her forþ berað,   fugelas singað,
gylleð græghama,   guðwudu hlynneð,
scyld scefte oncwyð.   Nu scyneð þes mona
waðol under wolcnum;   nu arisað weadæda
ðe ðisne folces nið   fremman willað.
Ac onwacnigeað nu,   wigend mine,
habbað eowre linda,   hicgeaþ on ellen,
windað on orde,   wesað onmode.'
(*Finnsburh*, ll. 3–12)

'It does not dawn from the east, nor does a dragon fly here, nor here in this hall are the gables burning; but here [weapons] are carried forth, birds sing, the grey-coated one howls, battle-wood rattles, shield answers shaft. Now the moon shines, wandering under the clouds; now deeds of woe will arise, which will bring strife to this people. But now rouse yourselves, my warriors, take your shields, think on courage, make your way to the front and be resolute.'

The speech's highly rhetorical opening, with its series of negative statements and repeated use of 'here', ratchets up the audience's expectation of some significant development,[39] as well as establishing Hnæf's oratory credentials. The traditional beasts of battle, here the wolf and raven,[40] are 'a compulsory element of battle narration' for an Old English poet (Griffiths 1993: 184), and their exulting voices, which anticipate the corpse-carrion they are to enjoy when Hnæf's prophetic words are confirmed (*Finnsburh*, l. 34), are as formulaic as their appearance. They are as much a part of the trappings of war as the *guðwudu* (lit. 'battlewood', hence spear or shield) and *scyld* ('shield') whose sounds they forestall or echo, and with which they

---

[38] In general critics tend towards the view that it is part of a 'lay' (Hill 1994: 15 suggests 200–300 lines) rather than a long narrative poem, but there is no compelling evidence either way—parts of the Fragment are leisurely, others move briskly.

[39] Similar narrative devices are found elsewhere in Irish and Welsh literature. See Sims-Williams 1976–8.

[40] *Græghama* 'grey-coated one' unambiguously signifies a wolf; the 'birds' are specified later in the poem as *hræfen . . . sweart and sealobrun* 'the raven . . . dark and dusky' (*Finnsburh*, ll. 34–5).

are thereby linked.[41] The elaborate rhetorical patterning continues: the thrice-sounded *her* of lines 3–5 is matched with three instances of *nu*, with the third *nu* ('now rouse yourselves') answering the third *her* ('here [weapons] are carried forth') as Hnæf details the appropriate response to the perceived attack.

Five Danish warriors are named in the response to Hnæf's call to arms, and their unanimous and valorous willing is implicitly contrasted with the mixed response of their enemies, as one of the Frisians urges another to desist from attacking *forman siþe* 'to start with' (*Finnsburh*, l. 19) in order to preserve life. Here, the poet softly voices the heroic choice, by implying that withdrawal rather than honourable—though ultimately disastrous—action is a possibility. Both the Danes and the Frisians opt for glory in the face of death, and Sigeferth's verbal preamble to the fight not only incorporates the standard genealogical information and claim to experience found in such pre-battle boasts,[42] but again alludes to the death/honour opposition in what is 'destined' (*witod*) for his opponent:

> 'Sigeferþ is min nama,' cweþ he,[43] 'ic eom Secgena leod,
> wreccea wide cuð;   fæla ic weana gebad,
> heordra hilda.   Ðe is gyt her witod
> swæþer ðu sylf to me   secean wylle.'
> *(Finnsburh*, ll. 24–7)

'My name is Sigeferth,' he said, 'I am prince of the Secgan,[44] a well known adventurer; I have experienced many trials, hard battles. It is already destined, which of two things you wish to seek from me.'

The naming of five of Hnæf's retainers serves to suggest a personal relationship between the Danish men and Hnæf, their leader, and to summon up images of hand-to-hand combat and individual heroism. Later in the Fragment, the relationship between Hnæf and his warriors is framed in terms of the conventional lord–retainer bond:

> Ne gefrægn ic næfre wurþlicor   æt wera hilde
> sixtig sigebeorna   sel gebæran,
> ne nefre swanas hwitne medo   sel forgyldan
> ðonne Hnæfe guldan   his hægstealdas.
> *(Finnsburh*, ll. 37–40)

I have never heard of sixty victory-warriors behave better, more honourably, in battle; nor did retainers ever repay better the white mead, than when his young men repaid Hnæf.

---

[41] Elsewhere in the OE poetic corpus, the links between beast, warrior, and weapon are underlined to an even greater extent. See Griffiths (1993: 189–91).

[42] *The Battle of Maldon* provides a range of examples in the speeches of Ælfwine, Offa, Leofsunu, and Dunnere (ll. 209–59).

[43] *Cweþ he* is extra-metrical; some editors omit it or mark it as intrusive.

[44] The *Secgan* are referred to in *Widsith* (ll. 31, 62) but otherwise unknown; they are presumably a tribe allied with the Danes.

The mead previously enjoyed by Hnæf's men functions almost metonymically, standing not only for the range of material comforts and rewards traditionally provided by the hero-leader, but also for the community and conviviality of the mead-hall, the site where declarations of loyalty are traditionally made (cf. *Beowulf*, ll. 480–3, 628–38; *The Battle of Maldon*, ll. 212–15). The comradeship forged in happier times, it is implied, lies behind this exemplary behaviour.

As with *Waldere*, there is little that implies criticism or even ambivalence in the Fragment's presentation of heroic action, with its focus upon close combat and the opportunities it presents for deeds of valour. If we look determinedly, we may find something in Hnæf's reference to the 'deeds of woe' (*weadæda*; *Finnsburh*, l. 8) which will cause strife, and in Sigeferth's equation of 'hard battle' (*heordra hilda*) with 'woes' (*weana*; *Finnsburh*, ll. 25–26). However, the option of reading this as 'the grim admiration of sublime suffering' (Fulk and Cain 2003: 217) said to be characteristic of the heroic mode is also open to us. The account of the same events in *Beowulf* (the Finnsburh Episode), on the other hand, largely ignores the combat and the opportunities it presents for describing valorous deeds, vaunting words, and attendant beasts; it focuses instead upon its causes, aftermath, and far-reaching consequences. The Episode is a poem within a poem, presented as the work of a fictional *scop*, or court poet. It is recited at the court of Hrothgar, the Danish king, as part of the festivities which mark Beowulf's killing of the cannibalistic monster, Grendel, who has plagued Hrothgar's people for twelve long years before being despatched in one night by the visiting Geatish warrior.[45] In this account of the events at Finnsburh, the plight of Hildeburh, sister to Hnæf and wife to Finn, looms as large as the conduct of the warriors, upon which it must surely be commenting. At the Episode's start, Hnæf's death is described in a cursory three lines (*Beowulf*, ll. 1068–70) before we are invited to consider it at greater length from the perspective of his bereft sister, robbed of both brother and sons:

> Ne huru Hildeburh   herian þorfte
> Eotena treowe;   unsynnum wearð
> beloren leofum   æt þam *li*ndplegan
> bearnum ond broðrum;   hie on gebyrd hruron
> gare wunde;   þæt wæs geomuru ides!
> Nalles holinga   Hoces dohtor
> meotodsceaft bemearn,   syþðan morgen com,
> ða heo under swegle   geseon meahte
> morþorbealo maga,   þær he[o] ær mæste heold
> worolde wynne.
>
> (*Beowulf*, ll. 1071–80)

Nor indeed did Hildeburh need to praise the good faith of the Jutes; blameless, she was bereft of beloved sons and brothers at the spear-play; they perished as decreed, wounded by spear; that was a sad woman! Not at all without cause did Hoc's daughter mourn fate's decree, when

---

[45] The Geats lived in what is now the southerly half of Sweden. Beowulf is not a historical figure.

morning came, when under the heavens she was able to see the terrible slaughter of kinsmen, where she previously had joy in the world.

The poet returns to her twice. The first time sees her committing her beloved dead to the funeral pyre, as *hire selfre sunu* 'her own sons' are burnt *eame on eaxle* 'alongside their uncle' (lit. 'at [their] uncle's shoulder') (*Beowulf*, ll. 1115–17). 'The woman lamented, mourned in songs', we are told, as well she might. Finally, we see her summarily returned to her Danish homeland:

> ond seo cwen numen.
> Sceotend Scyldinga   to scypon feredon
> eal ingesteald   eorðcyninges,
> swylce hie æt Finnes ham   findan meahton
> sigla searogimma.   Hie on sælade
> drihtlice wif   to Denum feredon,
> læddon to leodum.
>
> (*Beowulf*, ll. 1153–9)

. . . and the queen taken. The Scylding [Danish] archers ferried to their ships all the belongings of the king that they were able to find, all the precious jewels and ornaments from Finn's homestead. They ferried the noble woman on the sea-journey to the Danes, led her to her people.

The juxtaposition of Hildeburh with Finn's material wealth, and the telling use of the same verb, *ferian*, to describe the transport of both, has often been remarked. Hildeburh's will and emotions, those elements which make her a sentient being, are highlighted by the poet, who sees Hnæf off in two lines but takes ten to describe his sister's grief. They are, however, of no concern to those who treat her exactly as they treat the spoils of war. The attitude of the poet and the attitude he appears to bestow upon his warrior-creations could hardly be more different here.

The *Beowulf*-poet's interest in the psychological aspects of this story is by no means evident only in the portrait of Hildeburh. It is evident, too, in the lengthy description of the flawed peace-terms worked out between the Danes and Frisians after Hnæf's death (*Beowulf*, ll. 1085–1106), and in the convincing picture of the workings of Hengest's agonized mind, sketched in detail over twenty-seven lines (*Beowulf*, ll. 1125–51). Here, we learn of his intense yearning for his homeland, vividly evoked in the language of elegy and exile, and the even more powerful desire to avenge Hnæf's death. Hengest's feelings are matched by those of his retainers, one of whom places in his lap a sword, 'battle-bright, best of blades' (*hildeleoman / billa selest*) with, we surmise, the unvoiced stipulation that vengeance against Finn be taken.[46] This vengeance is dealt with in three swift and impressionistic lines:

> Ða wæs heal roden
> feonda feorum,   swilce Fin slægen,
> cyning on corþre,   ond seo cwen numen.
>
> (*Beowulf*, ll. 1151–3)

---

[46] *Lines* 1142–4 are extremely difficult; the reading outlined above has gone further towards achieving critical consensus than any of the other possible interpretations.

Then was the hall reddened with the lives of the enemies, and Finn—the king amongst his troop—slain, and the queen taken.

The 'heroic' elements of the story—the lord–retainer loyalty, the difficult choice, the physical aggression, the weaponry, the treasure—are no less present in the Episode than in the Fragment, but they are framed in tragic, rather than celebratory terms. Hengest can hardly be accused of the reckless bravery said to be characteristic of poetic heroes, given that his action seems finally to be determined as much by pressure from his followers as by his own need for vengeance. The *Beowulf*-poet seems rather less interested in the heroic deeds themselves than in motivation and consequence. That the entire Finnsburh Episode is framed with the experiences of Hildeburh, the suffering, innocent woman, tells us that he was thoroughly familiar with that seemingly modern concept, collateral damage. This should probably not surprise us: whether our poet belonged to the eighth century or to the eleventh, he would have had some experience of warfare, or at least of its consequences. That he chose to highlight it in this striking manner, however, is worthy of note and is directly related to his treatment of Wealhtheow, wife of Hrothgar and the most prominent female figure of the main narrative (excluding the monstrous mother of Grendel), and her concerns.

When the *scop*'s tale of internecine warfare is done, Wealhtheow steps forward to where her husband and his nephew, Hrothulf, sit: 'then the peace between them was still intact, each true to the other' (*þa gyt wæs hiera sib ætgædere, æghwylc oðrum trywe*; *Beowulf*, ll. 1164–5). Unferth, the victim of Beowulf's sharp wit earlier in the poem, is also seated by Hrothgar, 'though he had not been fast in honour to his kinsmen at play of swords' (*þeah þe he his magum nære arfæst æt ecga gelacum*; *Beowulf*, ll. 1167–8). It is thus made abundantly clear that Hrothgar's taste in feasting companions is questionable. Wealhtheow offers her husband advice: in the first of her two mead-hall speeches, she indicates that he should leave his kingdom and belongings to his sons, and not to the foreign Beowulf. Hrothulf, who is to be entrusted with the regency of the kingdom if the boys are too young to rule, is reminded of the goodness shown to him by his aunt and uncle, in a thinly disguised attempt to secure the future safety of the young boys. Wealhtheow's voice is left to echo around the walls of Heorot, unanswered by husband or nephew, as she turns to Beowulf. *Se goda* 'the good man' (*Beowulf*, l. 1190) is seated between her young sons, away from Hrothgar's untrustworthy attendants. The implication is none too subtle: Hrothulf is a poor choice of future guardian; Beowulf would have made a far better one. The fictional smoke from Finnsburh's 'greatest of battle-corpse fires' (*wælfyra mæst*; *Beowulf*, l. 1119), which swallowed the bodies of another uncle and his nephews, hangs threateningly over the mead-hall celebrations. Wealhtheow's fate is to suffer: this is the inevitable conclusion suggested by the narration of the Finnsburh Episode within this context. The *Beowulf*-poet has introduced a celebrated episode not for its own sake but to gloss events within his main narrative, events which are thus subtly revealed as deeply sinister.

GUARDIANS OF GLORY: REPRESENTING THE HEROIC AGE *SCOP*

In Wealhtheow's second speech, addressed directly to Beowulf, she tells him that,

> 'Hafast þu gefered   þæt ðe feor ond neah
> ealne wideferhþ   weras ehtigað,
> efne swa side   swa sæ bebugeð,
> windgeard, weallas.'
>
> (*Beowulf*, ll. 1221–4)

'You have brought it about that far and near, for all time, men will praise you, even as widely as the sea, home of the winds, encompasses the cliffs [lit. walls].'

A thousand years or so after the poem made its way into British Library manuscript Cotton Vitellius A.xv, Wealhtheow's words remain true, but it was not through the written word that sixth-century queens imagined the exploits of their warrior-heroes to be lauded. Such praise was the work of the *scop*—the professional court poet, who worked for his patron as a public relations guru *avant la lettre*. Beowulf is indeed lauded within Hrothgar's court, after his defeat of Grendel:

> Hwilum cyninges þegn
> guma gilphlæden,   gidda gemyndig,
> se ðe ealfela   ealdgesegena
> worn gemunde,   word oþer fand
> soðe gebunden;   secg eft ongan
> sið Beowulfes   snyttrum styrian
> ond on sped wrecan   spel gerade,
> wordum wrixlan.
>
> (*Beowulf*, ll. 867–74)

Sometimes a king's retainer, a proud man, mindful of songs, he who remembered a great number of old stories, devised words truthfully put together; the man afterwards began to narrate wisely the exploit of Beowulf and to recite with expertise the skilful tale, to render it in words.

It seems, however, that a considerable part of the man's poem concerns Beowulf only through analogy: the deeds of the heroes Heremod and especially Sigemund are rehearsed and the analogy is then made explicit (*Beowulf*, ll. 913–15).[47] Although the idea of the spontaneous eulogy, uttered in the mead-hall in the presence of the praisee, features in the *Beowulf*-poet's imagination, it is not fully realized. Instead, Hrothgar's retainer recalls one of his 'great number of old stories' (*ealdgesegena worn*), and an opportunity is created for including more of the digressive, legendary material which, like the Finnsburh Episode, pertains indirectly to the events in hand.

---

[47] Sigemund, like Beowulf, is a famed dragon-slayer; Heremod was a valiant warrior who became a (poor) Danish king.

Again, the *Beowulf*-poet manipulates our understanding of the main narrative through recourse to Heroic Age stories, and at the same time gives voice to the *scop*'s role as repository of the stock of narratives which shaped his culture's image and identity. His role as praise poet is of secondary concern to the *Beowulf*-poet, as it is in *Deor*. *Widsith*, the final poem to be discussed from our small heroic corpus, has as its central concern the role and the art of the poet, yet in even this text the fictional poet's business of praise seems to function primarily as a framework for the elliptical narration of historical-legendary material.

Widsith's editorial title, the poem's first word, is the name of this fictional poet, and means 'far-traveller'. Of the poem's 143 lines 125 are the words of Widsith, and these are liberally sprinkled with names, many of which are those of well-known Heroic Age figures and tribes, others either lost to us or, just possibly, invented by the poet. Widsith's catalogue is divided into three: the first section comprises a list of rulers and their tribes ('Attila ruled the Huns, Eormanric the Goths, Becca the Banings...'); the second details peoples among whom Widsith appears to have plied his poetic trade ('I was with the Huns and with the Ostrogoths, with the Swedes and with the Geats...'); and the third section lists those rulers and peoples with whom Widsith has stayed on his travels, but seems not to have served ('I sought Hehca and Beadeca and the Herelingas...'). Widsith has indeed travelled widely, both in space and time: he claims to have visited lands as far-flung as India and Pictland (northern Scotland), and to have served leaders who lived variously from the fourth to the sixth centuries.

Widsith's lengthy mental inventory, although in part impenetrable for a twenty-first-century audience, nevertheless conveys very effectively the extent to which a poet was expected to store and pass on the traditional narratives which were drawn upon for such widely different purposes. It has been suggested that the poem as a whole has a largely mnemonic function (e.g. Caie 1994: 82): that in effect it is a series of poetic prompts, a key to an underlying hoard of lengthier accounts of Hrothgar and Hrothulf, Hagena and Guthhere, a 'poetic encyclopedia' of continental migration-age heroes (Howe 1985: 169), and thus a clue to the repertoire expected of an Anglo-Saxon *scop*. We learn little of the heroes themselves, however, other than the odd brief note of their generosity or martial prowess, and in this sense the praising role of the poet is sidelined. What we do glean from the account is an idealized picture of the *scop*'s role, and the few relatively expansive passages which punctuate Widsith's list place him at the heart of the heroic community—in the mead-hall (*Widsith*, ll. 3–4, 54–6)—and make much of the treasure-distributing duties of the praiseworthy leaders of the Heroic Age and their female companions (*Widsith*, ll. 3–4, 56, 66–67, 90–92, 97–103). The poem ends with a neat summary of the praising role of the *scop*: through the repeated recitals of songs, he ensures the immortality of

> sumne ...
> gydda gleawne,   geofum unhneawne,
> se þe fore duguþe wile   dom aræran
> eorlscipe æfnan,   oþ þæt eal scæceð,

> leoht ond lif somod;   lof se gewyrceð,
> hafað under heofonum   heahfæstne dom.
> (*Widsith*, ll. 138–43)

a certain one appreciative of verse and unstinting of gifts, he who before the troop wishes to acclaim his glory, enact his nobility, until all departs, light and life together; he achieves praise and has under the heavens lasting glory.

In this particular context, the poet–patron relationship is exactly parallel to that of retainer and lord, and it is therefore appropriate that, ultimately, Widsith's loyalty is to one man, Eadgils, ruler of the Myrgingas (*Widsith*, ll. 93–6).

It is clear that, for the poets of *Deor*, *Widsith*, and *Beowulf*—poets whose works are preserved in the manuscripts of late Anglo-Saxon England—*scops* were as integral a part of the imagined heroic community as warriors were; they were necessary to ensure that the ultimate aim of heroic behaviour, long-lasting glory, was achieved through the dissemination of praise poetry. Such later poets seem not have been interested, however, in recreating eulogies as they might have been recited, or if they did indeed recreate them, these poetic products did not find their way into the surviving manuscripts. Instead, the Heroic Age *scop* bequeathed to those Anglo-Saxon disciples who recreated him in their own verse his role as guardian of the cultural capital from which was forged an English identity with a proud continental past. These disciples then recycled 'his' tales of Finn and Hildeburh, Weland and Beadohild, for their varying purposes, and these purposes are indeed various: subsuming the surviving verse under the heading 'heroic' risks ironing out the generic, thematic, and indeed structural variety to be found even in such a small corpus. It seems a relatively safe assumption that a greater number of such stories circulated, and that these figures were popular subjects for creative activity in pre-Conquest England. The shift in 'English' identity occasioned by the Norman Conquest appears to have brought an end to this popularity: these Heroic Age figures disappear from the textual record. Thereafter, an alternative set of ancestral myths took precedence: those expounded first in Geoffrey of Monmouth's Latin *Historia regum Britanniae* (History of the Kings of Britain) and thence in the Middle English *Brut* chronicles. In these texts, Brutus, great-grandson of Aeneas, is celebrated as Britain's founder, and Arthur, scourge of the Saxons, comes to the fore.

BIBLIOGRAPHY

ANDERSON, S. M. (2002), 'Introduction: "og eru kvöld kvenna ráð"', in S. M. Anderson with K. Swenson (eds.), *Cold Counsel: Women in Old Norse Literature and Mythology* (New York and London: Routledge), pp. xi–xvi.

ATTENBOROUGH, F. L. (ed.) (1922), *The Laws of the Earliest English Kings* (Cambridge: Cambridge University Press).

BOETHIUS (1973), *The Theological Tractates and The Consolation of Philosophy*, ed. and tr. H. F. Stewart, E. K. Rand, and S. J. Tester (Loeb Classical Library; London: Heinemann; Cambridge, Mass.: Harvard University Press).

BORAN, J. L. (1975), 'The Design of the Old English Deor', in L. E. Nicholson and D. W. Frese (eds.), *Anglo-Saxon Poetry: Essays in Appreciation* (Notre Dame, Ind., and London: University of Notre Dame Press), 264–76.

BREMMER, R. (2005), 'Old English Heroic Literature', in D. Johnson and E. Treharne (eds.), *Readings in Medieval Texts: Interpreting Old and Middle English Literature* (Oxford: Oxford University Press), 75–90.

BUSSE, W. G., and R. HOLTEI (1981), '*The Battle of Maldon*: A Historical, Heroic and Political Poem', *Neophilologus*, 65: 614–21.

BYOCK, J. (1982), *Feud in the Icelandic Saga* (Berkeley, Calif., and London: University of California Press).

CAIE, G. (1994), 'The Shorter Heroic Verse', in H. Aertsen and R. H. Bremmer Jr (eds.), *Companion to Old English Poetry* (Amsterdam: VU University Press), 79–94.

CAMPBELL, A. (1962), 'The Old English Epic Style', in N. Davis and C. L. Wrenn (eds.), *English and Medieval Studies Presented to J. R. R. Tolkien* (London: George Allen & Unwin), 13–26.

CHADWICK, H. M. (1912), *The Heroic Age* (Cambridge: Cambridge University Press).

DANCE, R. (2004), 'North Sea Currents: Old English–Old Norse Relations, Literary and Linguistic', *Literature Compass* 1 (ME 117): 1–10.

DRONKE, U. ed. and tr. (1997), *The Poetic Edda*, ii. *Mythological Poems* (Oxford: Clarendon).

ELLIS DAVIDSON, H. (1958) 'Weland the Smith', *Folklore*, 69: 145–59.

FIDJESTØL, B. (1997 [1976]), 'Norse-Icelandic Composition in the Oral Period', in his *Selected Papers*, ed. O. E. Haugen and E. Mundal, tr. P. Foote (The Viking Collection, Studies in Northern Civilization, 9; Odense: Odense University Press), 303–32.

FRANK, R. (1991), 'Germanic Legend in Old English Literature', in M. Godden and M. Lapidge (eds.), *The Cambridge Companion to Old English Literature* (Cambridge: Cambridge University Press), 88–106.

FRY, D. K. ed. (1974), *The Finnsburh Fragment and Episode* (London: Methuen).

FULK, R. D., and C. M. CAIN (2003), *A History of Old English Literature* (Malden, Mass., and Oxford: Blackwell).

——R. E. BJORK, and J. D. NILES (eds.) (2008), *Klaeber's Beowulf and the Fight at Finnsburh* (4th edn. Toronto and London: University of Toronto Press).

GELLING, M. (1974), *The Place-Names of Berkshire*, part ii (Cambridge: English Place-Name Society).

GRIFFITHS, M. S. (1993), 'Convention and Originality in the Old English "Beasts of Battle" Typescene', *Anglo-Saxon England*, 22: 179–99.

GRIMSTAD, K. (1983), 'The Revenge of Vǫlundr', in R. J. Glendinning and Haraldur Bessason (eds.), *Edda: A Collection of Essays* ([Winnipeg]: University of Manitoba Press), 187–209.

HATTO, A. T. (1980 [1961]), 'The Swan-Maiden: A Folk-Tale of North Eurasian Origin?', in his *Essays on Medieval German and Other Poetry* (Cambridge: Cambridge University Press), 267–97.

HILL, J. (1990), ' "Þæt wæs geomuru ides!" A Female Stereotype Examined', in H. Damico and A. H. Olsen (eds.), *New Readings on Women in Old English Literature* (Bloomington, Ind., and Indianapolis: Indiana University Press), 235–47.

——(ed.) (1994), *Old English Minor Heroic Poems* (rev. edn. Durham: Durham Medieval Texts).

——(1999), 'Heroic Poetry', in M. Lapidge, John Blair, Simon Keynes, and Donald Scragg. (eds.), *The Blackwell Encyclopaedia of Anglo-Saxon England* (Malden, MA: Blackwell), 236–7.

HOLMSTRÖM, H. (1919), *Studier över svanjungfrumotivet i Volundarkvida och annorstades* (Malmö: Maiander).

HOWE, N. (1985), *The Old English Catalogue Poems* (Copenhagen: Rosenkilde & Bagger).

KER, W. P. (1908), *Epic and Romance: Essays on Medieval Literature* (2nd edn. London: Macmillan).

KLINCK, A. L. (1992), *The Old English Elegies: A Critical Edition and Genre Study* (Montreal and Kingston: McGill-Queen's University Press).

KRAPP, G. P. (ed.) (1933), *The Paris Psalter and the Meters of Boethius* (Anglo-Saxon Poetic Records, 5; London: Routledge).

LARRINGTON, C. (1992). 'Scandinavia', in C. Larrington (ed.), *The Feminist Companion to Mythology* (London: Pandora), 146.

McKINNELL, J. (2001), 'Eddic Poetry in Anglo-Scandinavian Northern England', in J. Graham-Campbell, Richard Hall, Judith Jesch, and David N. Parsons (eds.), *Vikings and the Danelaw: Select Papers from the Proceedings of the Thirteenth Viking Congress, Nottingham and York, 21–30 August 1997* (Oxford: Oxbow), 327–44.

MALONE, K. (1962), *Widsith* (rev. edn. Copenhagen: Rosenkilde & Bagger).

——(1977), *Deor* (rev. edn. Exeter: University of Exeter Press).

MILLER, W. I. (1990), *Bloodtaking and Peacemaking: Feud, Law, and Society in Saga Iceland* (Chicago: University of Chicago Press).

MUIR, B. J. (ed.) (1989), *Leoð: Six Old English Poems. A Handbook* (New York: Gordon & Breach).

NORTH, R. (2007), 'Old English Minor Heroic Poems', in R. North and J. Allard (eds.), *Beowulf and Other Stories: A New Introduction to Old English, Old Icelandic and Anglo-Norman Literatures* (Harlow: Pearson Education), 95–129.

PARKS, W. W. (1987), 'The Flyting Speech in Traditional Heroic Narrative', *Neophilologus*, 71/2: 285–95.

——(1990), *Verbal Dueling in Heroic Narrative: The Homeric and Old English Traditions* (Princeton: Princeton University Press).

RENOIR, A. (1977), 'A Reading of *The Wife's Lament*', *English Studies*, 58: 4–19.

RIVES, J. B. (tr.) (1999), *Tacitus: Germania* (Oxford: Clarendon).

ROBERTSON, A. J. (ed.) (1925), *The Laws of the Kings of English from Edmund to Henry I* (Cambridge: Cambridge University Press).

ROBINSON, F. C. (2001), 'Secular Poetry', in P. Pulsiano and E. Treharne (eds.), *A Companion to Anglo-Saxon Literature* (Oxford: Blackwell).

Sawyer: *The Electronic Sawyer; an online version of Sawyer's* Anglo-Saxon Charters section one [S11602], prepared by S. E. Kelly and adapted for the WWW by S. M. Miller [www.trin.ac.uk/chartwww/eSawyer.99/eSawyer2. html].

SEDGEFIELD, W. J. (ed.) (1899), *King Alfred's Version of Boethius*, De consolatione Philosophiae (Oxford: Clarendon).

SIMS-WILLIAMS, P. (1976–8), ' "Is it Fog or Smoke or Warriors Fighting?": Irish and Welsh Parallels to the *Finnsburg Fragment*', *Bulletin of the Board of Celtic Studies*, 27: 505–14.

TOLKIEN, J. R. R. (1962), *Finn and Hengest: The Fragment and the Episode*, ed. A. Bliss (London: George Allen & Unwin).

WILSON, D. (ed.) (1980), *The Northern World: The History and Heritage of Northern Europe AD 400–1100* (New York: H. N. Abrams), 30–1.

CHAPTER 8

INSULAR ROMANCE

SIÂN ECHARD

THE term romance instantly troubles a handbook focused on medieval English literature, for romance is, etymologically speaking, a recognition of non-English origins, a name for works whose origins are *en romanz*; that is, in the romance languages which developed from Vulgar Latin. In medieval England, works *en romanz* were in the mother tongue (French and Norman French) for some audiences, while for others they were linguistically foreign and required further translation, a situation whose class-sensitive reality is reflected in Robert Mannyng's preface to his *Brut* chronicle of about 1338, in which he offers:

> Alle þe story of Inglande
> Als Robert Mannyng wryten it fand,
> And on Inglysch has it schewed,
> Not for þe lerid bot for the lewed,
> For þo þat in þis land won
> þat þe Latyn no Frankys kon.[1]

As for chronicle, so for romance: many (though by no means all) English romances are adaptations or translations from French originals, and many vernacular chronicles in both French and English, themselves a ground for romance, depend on Latin material.

Romance is a word that is capacious in generic as well as linguistic terms, encompassing Arthurian romance, chronicle romance, hagiographic romance, friendship romance, family romance, and fairy romance, among others. Formal descriptions

---

[1] Mannyng (1996: ll. 3–8).

often attach themselves to the word: there are tail-rhyme romances and alliterative romances, for example, both highly characteristic English forms. Romances may be in prose or verse, short or long; some were widely read, translated, and adapted, while others survive in single copies, uncertain as to both origin and audience. Romance is simultaneously a quintessential medieval genre and a genre that both pre- and post-dates the Middle Ages.[2] Attempts to define the term more closely tend to founder on the rocks of these various complexities. Some definitions have concentrated on the ethos of romance, often identifying elements of fantasy, escapism, and inwardness as central to the operation of the genre. Others have looked to the incidents, characters, and what we might think of as the 'furniture' of romance: quests, knights and ladies, forests, castles, monsters, and supernatural adventures. Often attempts to define romance pull in two contradictory directions. Some aim to discover the description which will encompass as many examples of the genre as possible, and one is often left with little more than is suggested by the title of Erich Auerbach's famous chapter in *Mimesis*, 'The Knight Sets Forth'.[3] Others make efforts to describe the genre more closely, thus creating a plethora of sub-types which offer precision for particular texts but do less to link those texts to others.[4] Noting the 'heroic labours' of one such critic, Ralph Hanna has nevertheless recently suggested 'one might profitably attend to the expansive fuzzy-edgedness of this discourse',[5] thus pointing to another trend in critical attempts to grapple with the genre; that is, a willingness to observe how romance melts into, or enters into exchanges with, contiguous genres such as chronicle history or hagiography.

Jehan Bodel's medieval classification by 'matters' is another starting-point for many approaches to the problem of romance classification. In the late twelfth century, Bodel described the Matters of Rome (stories of classical antiquity), of France (stories of Charlemagne), and of Britain (stories about King Arthur). The scheme is not particularly useful, oddly enough, when it comes to Britain, for while there are examples of all of Bodel's matters in the languages of the island, there are many other texts that defy Bodel's divisions, a situation which led W. R. J. Barron to suggest that we add 'the matter of romance'.[6] Writing specifically about English romance, Barron noted that 'The emergence of literature in the vernacular, providing a medium in which the ideals and social concerns of the secular aristocracy could find expression, allowed the evolution of a genre which ultimately pre-empted the description "romance".'[7] Writing at almost the same time as Barron, and in response to a similar recognition of the political and cultural work performed by romance, Susan Crane coined the phrase 'insular romance', in a study that explored the continuity between Anglo-Norman and Middle English romance in terms of the

---

2 For a recent representation of the range of the term, see the contents of Saunders (2004).
3 Auerbach (1953: 123–42).
4 Good examples of this sort of classification include Mehl (1968); Finlayson (1980).
5 Hanna (2005: 97). Hanna is responding to Finlayson (1980).
6 Barron (1987); the term is a title for a chapter, pp. 177–207.
7 Ibid. 177.

political and social concerns of the baronial class.[8] Several of Crane's Anglo-Norman/ Middle English pairings will be discussed below, but I use the term 'insular' here somewhat more broadly, in order to open the consideration of texts fitting the romance category, in a range of languages, produced and read in the British Isles during the Middle Ages.[9]

PROLOGUE I: LANGUAGES

[Britain] has five languages, just as the divine law is written in five books. These are the English, Welsh, Irish, Pictish, and Latin languages: all are devoted to examining and setting forth the knowledge of the highest truth and of true sublimity—but Latin, by means of the study of scriptures, has become common to all.[10]

> This land is born of varied stock, and blood
> And war and slaughter hold it in their grip.
> The fields, deformed, give bitter wormwood birth,
> And by this fruit the land's harsh savour's shown.
> Yet if true love was found among these men,
> I think there'd be no finer race on earth.[11]

I begin with two reflections of Britain's linguistic diversity, separated by some 650 years and a world of tone. Neither refers to romance; both reflect a reality that any essay on insular romance must immediately acknowledge. The first is the Venerable Bede, opening his *Ecclesiastical History* with a description of the range of tongues on the island of Britain, a potential cacophony here managed by the harmonious tuning of all to the pursuit of divine scripture, and particularly by the beneficent hegemony of Latin. The second, like Bede's remarks written in that highest tongue, comes near the end of the first book of John Gower's *Vox clamantis*, a book which reflects the speaker's revulsion at the events of the (very vernacular) Peasants' Revolt. In the lines

---

[8] See Crane (1986). Most of Crane's subject romances were those with both Anglo-Norman and Middle English survivals—the stories of Horn, Havelok, Bevis, Guy, Fouke, Amis, and Amiloun, among others.

[9] Field (1999) similarly stretches both the time-frame and linguistic co-ordinates of Crane's seminal study, though like her work it concentrates on the Anglo-Norman/Middle English pairings. The essays in part II of the volume in which her essay appears (Wallace 1999), under the title 'Writing in the British Isles', suggest even more of the linguistic diversity I comment on below.

[10] Bede (1969: 1. 1): 'Haec in praesenti iuxta numerum librorum quibus lex diuina scripta est, quinque gentium linguis unam eandemque summae ueritatis et uerae sublimitatis scientiam scrutatur et confitetur, Anglorum uidelicet Brettonum Scottorum Pictoru et Latinorum, quae meditatione scripturarum ceteris omnibus est facta communis.' The translation is my own.

[11] Gower (1899–1902: 1.20, ll. 1977–82): 'Hec humus est illa vario de germine nata, / Quam cruor et cedes bellaque semper habent: / Tristia deformes pariunt absinthia campi, / Terraque de fructu quam sit amara docet. / Non magis esse probos ad finem solis ab ortu / Estimo, si populi mutuus esset amor.' The translation is my own.

quoted above, an old man explains the varied origins of the inhabitants of the island, and while these origins have thus far led to strife and violence, they are also potentially a source of hope and future greatness. That double view, particularly tied to language, can be seen throughout Gower's long, trilingual career, as the poet frequently revisits the question of language across all three tongues. Gower is useful here because his almost obsessive concern with the proper language for poetry takes us to the very beginning of the fifteenth century, a time when, we imagine, English has clearly taken centre stage. Certainly by the time Gower writes the *Vox*, he is aware that in so doing he is addressing a particular kind of audience, the *litterati*, those who can read and write Latin. As for French, Gower's most significant French poem is the work of his early career, though he continues to write in that language as well, and there is ample evidence for the importance of French as a language of court culture in his day. His greatest poem, the *Confessio Amantis*, is presented squarely in English, written, Gower says, for England's sake. But like Gower's poetry, romance ranges across the tongues spoken on the island of Britain, so that different audiences encountered romance in different languages, and different modes, throughout the British Middle Ages.

PROLOGUE II: AUDIENCES

One of the most famous manuscript images associated with romance is the frontis-piece to Cambridge, Corpus Christi College, 61, a copy of *Troilus and Criseyde*, which apparently depicts Geoffrey Chaucer reading his poem to the court of Richard II. Much scholarship has been devoted to demonstrating conclusively that the scene reflects representational conventions of the late fourteenth and early fifteenth centuries, and must therefore not be read as in any sense a 'real' depiction of a literary event.[12] It can, however, be read as a site of imagination (both late and post-medieval), and the imagination of what it is that constitutes 'romance' is very much at issue in this essay.[13] The frontispiece's representation finds a kind of echo in book 2 of Chaucer's great poem, as Pandarus arrives at Criseyde's house:

> And fond two othere ladys sete and she,
> Withinne a paved parlour, and they thre
> Herden a mayden reden hem the geste

---

[12] See e.g. Pearsall (1977); Parkes and Salter (1978), with an essay by Elizabeth Salter, 'The "Troilus Frontispiece"', pp. 15–23. Lerer (1993) argues that the depiction reflects a desire, in the 15th cent., to confirm Chaucer's laureate status; the frontispiece, he says, 'embodies the Lydgatean fantasies of a literary past', p. 54.

[13] Elizabeth Salter suggests, 'We cannot give ourselves the pleasure of believing in the local and contemporary realism of the Frontispiece, but we can believe in its hold upon certain kinds of historical and imaginative truth', p. 22.

> Of the siege of Thebes, while hem leste.
> Quod Pandarus, 'Madame, God yow see,
> With youre book and all the compaignie!'[14]

Criseyde and her ladies are listening to a 'geste' of the story of Thebes, as one of their number reads it aloud to them. Thus one lady encounters the text in a book; the others hear it read aloud, a situation whose reality in noble households of the later Middle Ages has been thoroughly explored by Joyce Coleman.[15] The Theban story is a narrative that Chaucer recapitulates later through another female voice, as Cassandra prefaces her reading of Troilus's dream in book 5 with a summary of the story of Thebes as it appeared in Statius's *Thebaid*.[16] Thus one *roman antique* (another term for romances dealing with the classical past) provides audiences for another, in the first instance social, courtly and female, as prelude to the beginning of a new romance; and in the second, private, male, and in the context of oracular revelation. Both these realms are far from another romance context famously reflected in Chaucer's works, this time in Harry Bailey's reception of the Chaucer-pilgrim's disastrous *Sir Thopas*:

> 'Namoore of this, for Goddes dignitee,'
> Quod oure Hooste, 'for thou makest me
> So wery of thy verray lewednesse
> That, also wisly God my soule blesse,
> Myne eres aken of thy drasty speche.
> Now swich a rym the devel I biteche!
> This may wel be rym dogerel,' quod he.[17]

The Chaucer-pilgrim's romance is social in setting, as was the geste enjoyed by Criseyde and her ladies, but the social context here is, as Harry's intervention makes clear, more mixed and uproarious than either the Trojan world or the fantasy of courtly reading depicted on the *Troilus* frontispiece. Here popular opinion erupts against an example of popular romance—the matter of Britain in the broader sense, surely, though Thopas is in the traditional never-where inhabited by giants and elf-queens. The galloping tail-rhyme stanzas instantly identify this as an English verse romance,[18] a prolific category of texts, many of which, George Kane once remarked, are 'painfully bad'.[19] Other pilgrims produce other kinds of romances, from the Knight's *roman antique* concerning Theseus to the Wife of Bath's fairy-mistress tale, set in the days of King Arthur; and from the Man of Law's story of Constance, to the

---

[14] Geoffrey Chaucer, *Troilus and Criseyde*, in Chaucer (1987: 2. 81–6).

[15] Coleman (1996).

[16] Paul Strohm has explored medieval generic self-naming in a series of articles; see in particular (1971, 1977, 1980).

[17] *Canterbury Tales*, in Chaucer fragment VII, ll. 919–25.

[18] While the metre is common in Middle English romances, this is Chaucer's only use of it, and his six-line stanza is something of a departure from the usual twelve-line pattern; see Chaucer (1987: 917). For a recent reading of how MS design further aids in the recognition of this romance type (and hence of the humour attached to it), see Purdie (2005).

[19] Kane (1951: 12).

Franklin's attempt at the Breton *lai*. Thus Chaucer ranges through many of the types and audiences for romance to be found in Britain in the later Middle Ages.

Rather than add another attempt at classification to those I have described above, I move now to consider two foci, two strands of interest or emphasis, which begin to suggest ways to approach insular romance. They do not occur always together, although they can be very meaningfully linked; neither is universal or sufficient in itself to allow us to say definitively, '*this* is therefore an example of insular romance', but each is recognizable. These two threads are an interest in place, and in politics or power. Each is found in some of the most accomplished and widely read examples of insular romance (and in some of the least known as well). A survey of these emphases will not allow us to 'pick off' every last insular romance, but it may begin to suggest profitable ways to frame future inquiries.

PLACE

Some two-thirds of the way through the adventures that constitute the Middle English *Beves of Hamtoun*, Bevis enters a seven-mile horse race. The prize is a thousand pounds of gold. He trusts his marvellous steed to win the race for him:

> 'Arondel' queþ Beues þo,
> 'For me loue go bet, go,
> And i schel do faire and wel
> For þe loue reren a castel!'
> Whan Arondel herde, what he spak,
> Be-fore þe twei kniȝtes he rak,
> þat he com raþer to þe tresore,
> þan hii be half and more.
> Beues of his palfrai aliȝte
> & tok þe tresore anon riȝte:
> Wiþ þat and wiþ mor catel
> He made þe castel of Arondel.[20]

In this story Arondel the horse becomes the origin of Arundel the town, and I will return to the importance of place here and in insular romance more generally in a moment. It is worth pausing, however, to note how we arrived at this point, and what happens next. Bevis, who was sold as a child into 'paynim' lands after an attempt to avenge his father's murder (a murder arranged by his wicked mother), has returned triumphantly to his own country. The horse Arondel has come with him from Saracen lands, the gift of Bevis's love Josian, daughter to the pagan King Ermin. At this point in the narrative, Bevis's stepfather and his mother have died satisfyingly

---

[20] Kölbing (1885, 1886, 1894), ll 3531–42.

gruesome deaths; he is marshal to the English king Edgar, and he is at last wed to his
beloved Josian, now pregnant with twin boys. Josian and Arondel alike display
remarkable loyalty to Bevis throughout the tale, refusing husbands and other riders
respectively, and enduring periods of forced separation and captivity. Bevis returns
the compliment, at least as far as Arondel is concerned, immediately after this point
in the narrative. When King Edgar's son tries to steal the horse, Arondel kicks the
prince to death. Rather than hand his steed over to death, Bevis flees Edgar's wrath
with horse, wife, best friend, and servant. Ensuing plot complications see Bevis
separated from his wife (but not his horse) for many years; once reunited, they live
through more adventures in Armenia. When we pick up the story again, Bevis has
returned to England to intervene with King Edgar in a land dispute on behalf of a
friend; pursuing the king's wicked steward to London, Bevis finds himself in a
pitched battle with the burghers in the city streets:

> And after-ward, ase ʒe mai hure,
> Londegate þai sette a fure.
> Whan þai come, wiþ outen faile,
> þo be-gan a gret bataile
> Be twene Bowe and Londen ston,
> þat time stod vs neuer on.[21]

The co-ordinates of the fight include recognizable London landmarks, such as
Ludgate, Bow Street, and the London stone, a marker traditionally associated with
Brutus and at that time located in Cheapside. By the time the battle ends (with Bevis's
victory), 'So meche folk was slawe & ded, / þat al Temse was blod red'.[22] Bevis and
Edgar make peace, Edgar gives his daughter to Bevis's son Miles, and they are wed 'In
þe toun of Notinghame'.[23] Bevis and Josian return to their kingdom of Mombraunt
and live out the remainder of their days; they die (along with Arondel) on the same
day, and are buried together.

   These two incidents, and the summary that wraps them, suggests the combination
of geographical fantasy and particularity that are characteristic of *Bevis*. On the one
hand, the narrative fulfils all desire for the exotic, visiting such locales as Armenia,
Damascus, Jerusalem, Cologne, and Mombraunt—some of these places known, no
doubt, but only vaguely (and presumably not, in the case of Cologne, actually
supplied with dragons). Bevis's sojourn and travels in the East, along with his Saracen
wife and horse, create a 'troublesome hybrid...identity' which may well speak to
western anxieties about exposure to the East in the wake of the Crusades, and current
criticism has explored the resulting tensions and fantasies in *Bevis* and similar
works.[24] On the other hand are the local references: Southampton, London with its
streets and gates, and Arundel, its name explained by the story of the race. The
English adaptor adds an incident from each side of the ledger to his French original.

---

[21] Ibid. ll. 4491–6.   [22] Ibid. ll. 4529–30.   [23] Ibid. l. 4562.
[24] Rouse (2008: 126). For the role of the East in romances like *Bevis*, see Heng (2003); Wilcox
(2004); Saunders (2005); Campbell (2006).

Both the incident of the dragon of Cologne and the battle in the streets of London are apparently his additions.[25] The dragon-slaying episode has often been discussed in terms of forging an imaginative link between Bevis and St George, and the English place-names are, similarly, a means of underlining Bevis's Englishness, or (in opposition to a central English identity) his regional affiliations.[26] However they direct sympathies these names also, it seems to me, appeal to the local knowledge of readers. They are, for example, subject to variation in the English manuscript tradition: in one manuscript Josian awaits the outcome of the battle in London at 'Ledene halle',[27] while she is at 'Powntnethe'[28] in another. If Leadenhall refers to the market in Gracechurch Street, then Josian would be considerably closer to the fighting than at Putney. The marriage of Miles to Edgar's daughter takes place either in 'Notinghame'[29] or (more commonly) at the 'mynester durre' in London.[30] But of greatest interest here is the story of Arondel/Arundel, because it connects to a tradition of eponymous narrative rooted squarely in the source and ground of much English romance, the *Historia regum Britanniae* of Geoffrey of Monmouth.

Geoffrey's *Historia*, written some time around 1138, is in many ways the beginning of the insular romance tradition, because it is Geoffrey's Latin text that does the most to establish both the *Brut* traditions (in Welsh, Norman, and English) and the Arthurian story, particularly in the chronicle form often found in Britain. It recounts how refugees from the fall of Troy, led by Brutus, land on the island of Britain. The derivation of Britain from Brutus is obvious, but Geoffrey also gives us many other eponyms. Brutus's three sons, Albanactus, Locrinus, and Kamber, give their names to Albany (Scotland), Logres, and Cambria (Wales). Brutus's ally Corineus gives his name to Cornwall, after he throws the giant Gogmagog into the sea. Leicester/Kaerleir is named for Leir, Colchester for King Coel, and London, so important in *Bevis*, is provided with several stories, as Brutus names it Troia Nova, and Lud calls it Lundein. Two of the city's gates, Ludgate and Billingsgate, memorialize Lud and Belinus respectively. History is literally written across Geoffrey's British countryside, punctuated by memorials of the men who acted upon that stage. This recognition of place remains a feature of many (though by no means all) English romances, and re-emerges after the Middle Ages in the early modern practice of chorography in works like William Camden's *Britannia*. The imaginative power of these traditions is suggested by the fact that, in the eighteenth century, tourists were still visiting Arundel Castle to see Bevis's sword Morglay, and there were statues of Bevis and

---

[25] The relationship between the English and French texts is discussed in Kölbing (1885, 1886, 1894: pp. xxxiv–xxxvii); Weiss (1979); Djordjević (2008).

[26] See e.g. Fellows (1993). Turville-Petre (1996) remarks upon the expression of Englishness in the Auchinleck manuscript, which contains *Bevis* (and *Guy of Warwick*, to be discussed further below), esp. in the chapter 'Englishness in the Auchinleck Manuscript (Advocates 19.2.1)', pp. 108–41. Hanna (2005) characterizes the Auchinleck version of the romance as being 'associated strenuously with the South Coast', p. 133.

[27] Kölbing (1885, 1886, 1894), l. 4534.   [28] Ibid. l. 4241.

[29] Ibid. l. 4562.   [30] Ibid. l. 4275.

his giant servant Ascopart flanking Southampton gates.[31] Nor is *Bevis* alone in its references to known places. While insular romances, like their continental counterparts, are often vaguely located and sometimes abut on unlikely other-worlds, there is nevertheless a perceptible strand of local reference, of which a few examples must suffice.

Sir Gawain and the Green Knight sees its hero travel between a Camelot that could be anywhere, and Bertilack's castle, which may very well be nowhere. Briefly, however, he takes a route that would have been familiar to a fourteenth-century audience, as he passes through Logres (England south of the Humber)

> Til þat he neȝed ful neghe into þe Norþe Waleȝ.
> Alle þe iles of Anglesay on lyft half he haldeȝ,
> And fareȝ ouer þe fordeȝ by þe forlondeȝ,
> Ouer at þe Holy Hede, til he hade eft bonk
> In þe wyldrenesse of Wyrale; wonde þer bot lyte
> þat auþer God oþer gome wyth goud hert louied.[32]

A traveller of the later fourteenth century might well encounter the same hideous weather of freezing rain and 'hard iisse-ikkles',[33] and might even expect to fight, as Gawain does, bulls, bears, and boars; but this recognizable landscape (the forest has been identified as Inglewood Forest) is also inhabited by wodwoses (wildmen), wormes (dragons), and etayns (giants). On the other hand, whether or not Bertilack's castle is meant to suggest any real place, its function in the poem is very much to act as the traditional other-world or at the least liminal space of romance quest and testing.[34]

Like Bevis's dragon-infested Cologne, then, Gawain's landscape combines the familiar with the strange, but in the *Alliterative Morte Arthure*, there is a journey which is straightforward in both geographical and narrative terms. Mordred, hearing that Arthur in his wrath has returned to England, sets up camp by the River Tamar in Cornwall, and writes to Guenevere, urging her to flee to the wastes of Ireland with their children. Instead,

> Then sho yermes and yeyes   at York in her chamber,
> Grones full grisly   with gretand teres,
> Passes out of the palais   with all her pris maidens,
> Toward Chester in a charre   they chese her the wayes,
> Dight her even for to die   with dole at her herte;
> Sho kaires to Caerlion   and caught her a veil,
> Askes there the habit   in honour of Crist
> And all for falshed and fraud   and fere of her lord![35]

---

[31] I discuss the survival of the local histories of both Bevis and Guy of Warwick in Echard (2008: 60–96). For a recent discussion of the role of stories of heroes from the Saxon period in Middle English romance, see Rouse (2005).

[32] Tolkien and Gordon (1925), ll. 697–702.

[33] Ibid. l. 732.

[34] The notes to these lines in Tolkien and Gordon's edn. trace the place-names and take up the question of whether the castle is also meant to be identifiable (they think not), p. 94. For a more recent discussion of the geography as reflected in the works of the *Gawain*-poet, see Elliott (1997).

[35] *The Alliterative Morte Arthure*, in Benson (1994), ll. 3911–18.

This would have been a long journey, and the details are sketchy, but a traveller from York to Caerleon might well have passed through Chester, either in Arthur's real historical period, or in the fourteenth century, when (as the Gough map shows) the city was a transportation centre. Caerleon is Guenevere's traditional retreat in the *Historia regum Britanniae*, an important source for the *Alliterative Morte*, but Geoffrey does not mention Chester in describing her flight; like the local details in *Bevis*, then, it may be that place-names in the *Alliterative Morte* are intended to appeal to an audience's specific knowledge.

The *Alliterative Morte* is notable for the many British places it mentions. The poem sites action at Caerleon, Catterick, Carlisle, Cornwall, Dorset, Glastonbury, Sandwich, Wallingford, Winchester. It is tempting to read this proliferation of place-names in terms of the demands of the alliterative verse, and there are indeed lovely lines which depend on naming, such as the one expressing the relief of the Roman ambassadors when, on the evening of the seventh day since leaving Arthur's court at Carlisle, they hear 'the sound of the se and Sandwich belles' (490). It would be foolish to deny the decorative effects and rigorous requirements of alliteration, yet it is also worth noting that the bells of St Peter's Church at Sandwich were indeed rung for curfew each night, and Sandwich, as one of the Cinque Ports, is a logical place for the naval comings and goings the poem describes.[36] The Romans take Watling Street, the old Roman road, to get there. Similarly Wallingford, home to the 'wardrope' where Arthur keeps his sword Clarent, has a long history, from its Saxon origins to its important role during the war between Stephen and Matilda in Geoffrey's day. The castle was a royal residence into the fourteenth century. When Arthur sees Clarent in Mordred's hand, he knows that Guenevere has betrayed him:

> For I see Clarent uncledde   that crown is of swordes,
> My wardrope at Walingford   I wot is destroyed.
> Wiste no wye of wonne   but Waynor herselven;
> Sho had the keeping herself   of that kidd wepen,
> Of coffers enclosed   that to the crown longed,
> With ringes and relickes   and the regale of Fraunce
> That was founden on Sir Frolle   when he was fey leved. (4202–8)

The likeliness of Wallingford as a site for a royal treasury, as imagined here, adds force and poignancy to Arthur's recognition at this moment of betrayal; the personal is inextricably bound up with the realm; place and politics (understood here as power) belong together.

This connection between the person and the land is also suggested by Geoffrey's geography, here in a rare case, not of eponymous lore, but of detailed description of place. Before the famous account of Arthur's plenary Whitsun court, Geoffrey describes the city of Caerleon, where the court will take place:

---

[36] See the note to l. 490, ibid. 267.

The superior wealth of Caerleon, admirably positioned on the river Usk not far from the mouth of the Severn in Glamorgan, made it the most suitable of all cities for such a ceremony. On one side there flowed a noble river, on which could be brought by boat the kings and princes visiting from overseas. On the other, it was surrounded by meadows and woods, and so fine were its royal palaces that the gold that decked their roofs reminded one of Rome. Site of the third metropolitan see of Britain, it boasted two churches, one of which, in honour of the martyr Julius, was distinguished by a convent of devout nuns, and the other, dedicated to his companion Aaron, housed a group of canons.[37]

It is to this city, the expression of Arthur's magnificence and the site of his imperial realm—a realm invested in his person by virtue both of prowess and of direct descent from Brutus himself—that the 'transmarine' kings and princes come to witness Arthur's great court, and it is from here that the first steps towards the war with Rome are undertaken. Geoffrey's references to the site and the specific buildings are more or less accurate.[38] While he is by no means so well-informed or careful throughout the *Historia*, it seems to me significant that he should site Arthur's capital in so recognizable a place, thus placing Britain's greatest king emphatically in a familiar geography.

My final example of the significance of place in insular romance comes from another Arthurian narrative, Sir Thomas Malory's *Morte Darthur*. Malory's sources include both French and English traditions, and many of his knights quest through the undifferentiated forests of romance. Even references to recognizable locales often seem to serve tradition rather than to invoke particular geographic knowledge—for example, the insistence on Tristram's origins in Cornwall. Yet here too there are occasional glimpses of a more specific recognition of place. It is Malory who identifies Camelot with Winchester, an identification with no further detail but significant nevertheless, because it places Camelot at a site of known royal power. London also appears sporadically but importantly in Malory's text. The sword in the stone appears in the churchyard of 'the grettest chirch of London—whether it were Powlis or not the Frensshe booke maketh no mencyon'[39] at the beginning of Arthur's reign, and near the end, Guenevere takes refuge in the Tower, after fleeing Winchester and Mordred. The siege of the Tower is described:

. . . she toke the Towre of London, and suddeynly in all haste possyble she stuffed hit with all maner of vytayle, and well garnysshed his with men, and so kepte hit. And whan dir Mordred wyst thys he was passynge wrothe oute of mesure. And shorte tale to make, he layde a mighty

---

[37] Geoffrey of Monmouth (2007), c. 156, pp. 208–11: 'In Glamorgantia etenim super Oscam fluuium non longe a Sabrino mari amoeno situ locata, prae ceteris ciuitatibus diuitiarum copiis abundans tantae sollempnitati apta erat. Ex una namque parte praedictum nobile flumen iuxta eam fluebat, per quod transmarini reges et principes qui uenturi errant nauigio aduehi poterant. Ex alia uero parte pratis atque nemoribus uallata, regalibus praepollebat palaciis ita ut aureis tectorum fastigiis Romam imitaretur. Duabus autem eminebat ecclesiis, quarum una, in honore Iulii martiris erecta, uirgineo dicatarum choro perpulchre ornabatur, alia quidem, in beati Aaron eiusdem socii nomine fundata, canonicorum conuentu subnixa, terciam metropolitanam sedem Britanniae habebat.'

[38] As discussed by Tatlock (1950: 69–71).

[39] Malory (1971), *Morte Darthur*, I. 5, p. 7. The equation of Camelot with Winchester is found in X. 10, p. 624.

syge aboute the Towre and made many assautis, and threw engynnes unto them, and shotte grete gunnes. But all myght nat prevayle, for quene Gwenyver wolde never, for fayre speache nother for foule, never to truste unto sir Mordred to com in hys hondis agayne.[40]

The 'grete gunnes' are a detail specific to Malory's world, and this section of the text has been identified as suggesting a specific response to the Wars of the Roses. A rare first-person voice intrudes shortly after the siege, to reprove the English who have now (unlike Guenevere in this case) shifted their allegiance to Mordred:

Lo ye all Englysshemen, se ye nat what a myschyff here was? For he that was the moste kynge and nobelyst knyght of the worlde, and moste loved the felyshyp of noble knyghtes, and by hym they all were upholdyn, and yet myght nat thes Englyshemen holde them contente with hym. Lo thus was the olde custom and usayges of thys londe, and men say that we of thys londe have nat yet loste that custom. Alas! thys ys a greate defaughte of us Englysshemen, for there may no thynge us please no terme.[41]

The army Mordred raises around London includes 'they of Kente, Southsex and Surrey, Essax, Suffolke and Northefolke',[42] a geographical grouping which '[seems] to suggest that Malory had in mind a situation similar to that which obtained at the time of the Wars of the Roses when the strength of the Yorkists lay to a large extent in the south-eastern counties'.[43] Malory's *Morte* ends in a series of geographical references that move away from this fifteenth-century particularity to the less localized world of romance more generally. While Lancelot lands, as one might expect, at Dover and seeks news of Arthur, he soon moves on to a nameless chapel in a forest, between two cliffs. After his death, the survivors leave for the Holy Land, a territory which, as in *Bevis*, is characterized in religious terms, as the knights 'dyd many bat[y]lles upon the myscreantes, or Turkes. And there they [dyed] upon a Good Fryday for Goddes sake'.[44]

In its treatment of place, then, insular romance sometimes appeals to the local, occasionally setting it against the more general landscape of romance as if to highlight certain moments in the narrative. It would be a mistake to suggest, however, either that this habit represents 'realism' in any thoroughgoing sense, or that it is sufficient to mark out insular romance from other forms. There are romances written in England which remain squarely in the realm of faerie. Thomas Chestre's version of the story of Launfal, for example, mentions Carlisle, Glastonbury, and Caerleon (and only the first occurs in Marie de France's version of the same tale), but it is the encounter Launfal has 'toward the west' in a 'fayr forest' with Triamour, daughter of the King of Faerie, around which the story is constructed.[45] Triamour's world is characterized by the rich decoration of her pavilion and by her own unearthly beauty, and this world of supernatural excess accompanies her when, in the climax of the story, she rides through Carlisle (though the author may have meant 'Cardiff') to rescue Launfal. The narrative ends with the hero's withdrawal

[40] Ibid. XXI. 1, p. 707.   [41] Ibid. XXI. 1, p. 708.   [42] Ibid. XXI. 3, p. 711.
[43] Eugene Vinaver, ibid. 777.   [44] Ibid. XXI. 13, p. 726.
[45] *Sir Launfal*, in Shepherd (1995), ll. 219, 222.

into faerie; here the impulse is not to locate the hero, but to remove him. *Launfal* nevertheless points the way to our second strand, the concern shared by many insular romances for questions of power and politics.

POLITICS

In Marie de France's *Lanval*, we are introduced to a hero who is neglected at King Arthur's court:

[The king] apportioned wives and lands to all, save to one who had served him: this was Lanval, whom he did not remember, and for whom no one put in a good word. Because of his valour, generosity, beauty, and prowess, many were envious of him ... although he belonged to Arthur's household he had spent all his wealth, for the king gave him nothing and Lanval asked for nothing.[46]

Lanval's poverty ceases when a beautiful fairy mistress becomes his lover, but when Lanval is driven to praise her while repudiating the advances of Guenevere, his very life is threatened, as Arthur swears to have him burnt or hanged if he cannot produce the lady herself. Lanval has broken a prohibition placed on him by his mistress in speaking of her at all, and has been warned that she will abandon him, should he do so. The barons who are called together to pass judgement on Lanval know of Arthur's anger, and are constrained by their allegiance to him. The Count of Cornwall remarks, 'Only the king is accusing him, so by the faith I owe you, there ought, to tell the truth, to be no case to answer, were it not that one should honour one's lord in all things.'[47] There is considerable relief among the barons, then, when Lanval's mistress appears and all can agree that she is indeed as fair as Lanval had claimed.

I mentioned above the landscape of this story and the centrality of the other-world to which Lanval withdraws. Here I would like to dwell in the world of the court, and in particular to consider the treatment of Lanval/Launfal by his sovereign. Thomas Chestre's fourteenth-century tail-rhyme version of the story begins with a formula that draws immediate attention to the role of the king: 'Be doughty Artours dawes, / That held Engelond yn good lawes'.[48] The importance of good laws is a preoccupation that can be found in insular chronicle at least as far back as Geoffrey of Monmouth's *Historia regum Britanniae*, where the mark of many a good king is

[46] Marie de France (1952), ll. 17–23, 30–2: 'Femmes e tere departi, / Par tut, fors un ki l'ot servi: / Ceo fu Lanval, ne l'en sovient, / Ne nul de[s] soens bien ne li tient. / Pur sa valur, pur sa largesce, / Pur sa beauté, pur sa prüesce / L'envioënt tut li plusur . . . / Tut sun aveir ad despendu; / Kar li reis rien ne li dona, / Ne Lanval ne li demanda.' The translation is from Marie de France (1986: 73).
[47] Lanval, in Marie de France (1952), ll. 443–8: 'Nuls ne l'apele fors le rei: / Par cele fei ke jeo vus dei, / Ki bien en veut dire le veir, / Ja n'i deüst respuns aveir, / Si pur ceo nun que a sun seignur / Deit hum par tut fairë honur.' The translation is from Marie de France (1986: 78–9).
[48] *Sir Launfal*, in Shepherd (1995), ll. 1–2.

precisely his establishment or restoration of the rule of law. Marie's version of the story suggests a fear, among the barons, that the course of law will be perverted because of their duty to please an angry king, and Chestre's opening might lead us to expect a heightening of that emphasis. But while Marie gives no particular reason for Arthur's initial neglect of Lanval, Chestre traces the breach in their relationship to the unexplained enmity of Guenevere for the knight, an enmity that reaches its peak when Launfal rejects her advances. In this version of the story, Arthur's anger has not been preceded by the capricious neglect suggested by Marie's text, and the barons for their part place the blame squarely on the queen, whose 'maners' with respect to 'lemmannes' they know well.[49] Yet they too must agree that Launfal needs to make good on his boast, despite their clear-eyed view of Guenevere. Both versions of the story present us, albeit in slightly different ways, with the potentially negative consequences of the exercise of royal power, as each pits the king or the queen against the jury of Launfal's peers. Despite the knowledge manifested by both juries, they cannot in fact guarantee a just outcome: Launfal's safety depends on the mercy of Triamour. She, for her part, chooses not to hold to the letter of her own law, but rather to rescue Launfal, perhaps in recognition of the provocation that led to his initial breach. Fairies do not always behave in this way; fairy conditions, called *geasa*, are frequently arbitrary or mysterious, and good intentions are often irrelevant where fairy justice is concerned.[50] Here, however, the fairy mistress acts with more judgement and mercy than do the mortal rulers of either version. Chestre's Triamour further delivers a kind of poetic justice by blinding Guenevere for her transgressions (Guenevere had sworn, 'Yyf he bryngeth a fayrer thynge, / Put out my eeyn gray!'[51]). Yet although he has been vindicated and avenged, Launfal cannot remain any longer at the Arthurian court. His removal with Triamour to the kingdom of faerie is perhaps the result of the impossibility of a public relationship with an other-worldly creature, but the emphasis in both versions on the tenuous nature of justice at the court may also be at issue. Both Marie and Thomas tell us that Lanval is a perfect knight, and both show us that there is, in the end, no place for such a knight in the world of kings and courts.

The knights of romance often encounter rulers in their travels, and they sometimes become rulers themselves. Bevis begins his exile from England in service to King Ermin, and ends his days as King of Mombraunt in his own right. His occasional encounters with King Edgar suggest at least something of the same awareness concerning arbitrary royal power as that displayed in the Lanval stories. Edgar's initial impulse, after Arundel kicks to death the prince who was trying to steal him, is to kill both Bevis and his horse, and it is only the intervention of the barons that settles the sentence on Arundel alone (in the English version). But as in *Launfal*, the barons cannot completely deflect the king's anger, and only by leaving the country

---

49 Ibid. ll. 788, 791.

50 For a recent overview of the role of magic and fairies in English romance, see Cooper (2004: esp. pp. 173–217).

51 *Sir Launfal*, in Shepherd (1995), ll. 809–10.

can Bevis avoid the consequences of Edgar's wrath. In the Anglo-Norman version of the story, the barons reproach the king directly: 'They said to the king: "You wish to insult us: we saw him serving before you and coming and going with your cup. It is not right you should have him killed".'[52] This kind of direct rebuke aimed at the powerful can be found associated with Gawain, the most English of romance heroes, in both Anglo-Latin and Middle English. In the Latin prose romance known as *De ortu Waluuanii*, Gawain, his identity as Arthur's nephew unknown both to him and to the king, encounters his uncle at a ford. Arthur asks him insultingly, 'Are you a fugitive, a thief or a spy?' Gawain responds with moderation, but when Arthur attacks, Gawain unhorses him into the river, and tips Kay on top of him: 'Just in the same way, he was thrown prostrate on top of Arthur in a single heap with the first blow.'[53] Later, Gawain succeeds in routing enemies who had Arthur and his men on the run, and takes delight in taunting the king: '"Now where, o king," he exclaimed, "are your famous champions, of whom until now you have boasted that no one is their equal in strength? Lo the head of this man, the man whom I alone conquered and laid low, with all his many soldiers! This is the man by whom so many thousands of your soldiers were so often terrified and made to flee—for shame!"'[54] Marie's Arthur appears capricious and prone to irrational anger. This Arthur is boastful and apparently ineffectual, and it is Gawain in this romance who throws those qualities into relief. While the romance ends with the revelation of Gawain's identity and his being welcomed at his uncle's court, the tension of the encounter between knight and king is notable.

The tension in the Latin text finds an echo in a Middle English Gawain romance, the *Awntyrs off Arthure at the Terne Wathelyn*. In the first part of this romance, Gawain and Guenevere encounter the hideous ghost of Guenevere's mother, who draws their attention to the *memento mori* spectacle she now presents, and then urges her daughter to care for the poor. For his part, Gawain asks the ghost for a judgement on his own life:

> 'How shal we fare,' quod þe freke, 'þat fonden to fight,
> And þus defoulen þe folke on fele kinges londes,
> And riches ouer reymes withouten eny right,
> Wynnen worship and wele þorgh wightnesse of hondes?'
> 'Your king is to couetous, I warne þe sir kni3t.'[55]

---

[52] Weiss (2008: 73).

[53] *De ortu Waluuanii nepotis Arturi*, in Day (2005): 'Exulne es; predo, an insidiator?', p. 108; 'sed eodem pacto et ipse super Arturum in una congerie primo ictu prosternitur', p. 110; the translations are my own. Both this romance and the *Historia Meriadoci*, anonymous but probably by the same author, have been dated by some critics to the reign of Henry II, and by others to later in the 13th cent.; Day's new edition surveys the possibilities. For the purposes of this chapter, the dating is not as important as is the clearly insular subject-matter of both works. I discuss both at length in Echard (1998).

[54] *De ortu Waluuanii nepotis Arturi*, in Day (2005: 118): '"Quonam sunt" exclamat "O Rex, tui famosi athlete, de quibus te adeo iactabas neminem eorum parem uirtuti? Ecce capud uiri, uiri quem cum omni suorum copia militum solus uici et prostraui; a quo tot tuorum pugilium milia, tociens proh pudet fugari et eneruari".' The translation is my own.

[55] Hanna (1974), ll. 261–5.

The *Awntyrs* is in some senses a sermon dressed up as a romance—the similarity between the episode with the ghost and the Trentals of St Gregory has long been recognized.[56] The ghost's warnings and Gawain's self-condemning question can certainly be understood in terms of this exemplary context, but taken in combination with an episode in the latter part of the poem, they may also be read through the lens of insular romance's concern with the exercise (and occasional abuse) of royal power. After the incident with the ghost, the scene shifts to Arthur's court. A Scottish knight named Galeron comes to reclaim lands which Arthur has won from him with, he says, 'wrange wile'.[57] Gawain, who has been awarded the lands by Arthur, undertakes a duel with Galeron and wins, but he then restores the land to Galeron. Gawain characterizes Arthur's position here as "þe riȝt',[58] and Arthur cooperates with Gawain's plan at the end, but the ghost's comments on the Arthurians' imperial ambitions might well colour how an audience would understand this incident.

There is a similar episode in the other Latin romance written by the author of the *De ortu*. In this text, the *Historia Meriadoci*, the hero Meriadoc directly rebukes Arthur for his behaviour in another land dispute case. In this case, Meriadoc wins the battle over the disputed lands for Arthur and then, astonishingly, tells him, "'You have vexed many of your men through this matter, which I have brought to an end by my service. Lo, you have what you desired, you possess what you falsely claimed, you have settled that concerning which you disputed".'[59] It is worth noting that Meriadoc is an example of a common insular romance hero: a dispossessed king, whose adventures will culminate in his restoration to the throne. The romances of King Horn and Havelok the Dane, in both Anglo-Norman and Middle English, are perhaps the most famous examples of this type, but the Anglo-Latin story of Meriadoc suggests the spread and significance of the motif. The Latin Gawain, too, is a Fair Unknown for much of his story, and whether the unknown heroes are knights-to-be or kings in waiting, their encounters with the powerful often, in insular texts, point to the limitations of rulers.

AFTERWORD: PIETY

The threads pursued in this essay to characterize insular romance have been place and politics; they could easily be joined by a third term, piety. As the story of Gawain

---

[56] See e.g. Klausner (1972); Turville-Petre (1974); and most recently, Connolly (2006).
[57] Hanna (1974), l. 421.
[58] Ibid. l. 471.
[59] *Historia Meriadoci Regis Cambriae*, in Day (2005: 158): '"Multos tuorum" ait "huius rei examinacione uexasti, que mei est terminata obsequio. Ecce, habes quod optasti, possides quod calumpniabaris, decreuisti unde certabas".' The translation is mine; I find it important to emphasize the negative sense of *calumnio*, which normally appears only in a pejorative sense.

and Guenevere in the *Awntyrs* suggests, exemplarity is never far from certain kinds of insular romance, and as the end of Malory's *Morte* shows, a final foray into the Holy Land is often felt to be an appropriate end for a knightly hero. Two final Anglo-Norman/Middle English pairings must serve to point to this thread, however briefly. The story of Amis and Amiloun, childhood friends whose adventures lead eventually to one being stricken with leprosy, curable only by immersion in the blood of the children of the other, is one of these examples. The willingness of Amis to sacrifice his children, Abraham-like, for his friend, is rewarded by a miracle: Amiloun is cured, and the children miraculously brought back to life. The Middle English friends end their lives in a simultaneous demonstration of piety and brotherly knightly love:

> Anoon the hend barons tway,
> They let reyse a faire abbay
> And feffet it ryght wel thoo,
> In Lumbardy, in that contray,
> To senge for hem tyl Domesday
> And for her eldres also.
> Both on oo day were they dede
> And in oo grave were they leide,
> The knyghtes both twoo;
> And for her trewth and her godhede
> The blisse of hevyn they have to mede,
> That lasteth ever moo.[60]

The Anglo-Norman version of the story is even more explicit, making the heroes into saints: 'At Mortara they lie, in Lombardy, where God performs great miracles through them; the blind see, the mute speak.'[61]

Amis and Amiloun have led full lives before they die, and their religious observance is not described in detail. Our second case, however, presents a romance hero who becomes a hermit. The story of Guy of Warwick picks up many of the motifs that have been dealt with in this chapter. It is a family story, recounting the adventures of the founder of the Warwick dynasty, a story whose power in the later Middle Ages is amply testified by the willingness of the Neville family to promote the legend.[62] The eighteenth-century tourists who visited Arundel Castle might also have visited Warwick Castle and the cave at Guy's Cliff, places firmly linked to Guy's story. Politics are part of that story as well, as Guy must act as a champion for the English king Athelstan against the fearsome Danish champion. Unlike Bevis, Guy is not in conflict with his king, but there is a contrary movement of a different sort, for Guy must leave his life of penance in order to take on the climactic battle and become his nation's champion. And Guy reflects very directly, as we will see, on the proper use of power—in this case, his own.

---

[60] *Amis and Amiloun*, in Foster (1997), ll. 2497–2508.
[61] Kölbing (1884), ll. 1246–8: 'Lor corps gisent en Lombardie, / U deu fait pur eus grant vertuz, / Evegles veer e parler mutz.' The translation is from Weiss (1992: 177–8).
[62] See Richmond (1996), and the recent collection of essays edited by Wiggins and Field (2007).

The story has had two main movements. In the first, Guy, as a young man of prowess but relatively low social status, adventures far and wide to prove himself worthy of the love of Felice; the pattern suggests the Fair Unknown stories touched on above. His adventures, like Bevis's, are marked by firm friendships, dastardly betrayals, marvellous and monstrous encounters, and love. But Guy does not end his days ruling his own realm, with Felice at his side. He wins her as a wife, to be sure, but they have been married only a little while when Guy begins to question his life:

> He þouȝt wiþ dreri mode,
> Hou he hadde euer ben strong werrour,
> For Jhesu loue our saueour
> Neuer no dede he gode.
> Mani man he hadde slayn wiþ wrong;
> 'Allas, allas!' it was his song,
> For sorwe he ȝede ner wode.[63]

Guy's concern with wrongful killing suggests Gawain's concerns in the *Awntyrs off Arthure*. The rest of Guy's story sees him pursuing a life of penance, while continuing his martial pursuits, this time selflessly for others and, as noted above, as Athelstan's champion. He retires to a hermitage in a cave, and only when he feels that his death is imminent does he send word to Felice. In the Anglo-Norman and in the Auchinleck Middle English version, Guy lives long enough to see Felice before he dies, but they do not speak. By the time of the fifteenth-century English version, the lovers exchange kisses, and in the proliferation of post-medieval adaptations of the story, Guy often talks to Felice at some length, praising her pious life since his departure. What all of these have in common is the emphasis on Guy's piety and its salutary effects on those near to him. It is also important in the medieval versions that, like Amis and Amiloun, Guy may have become a saint, as his body emits sweet odours. The romance that begins in martial valour for a lady's sake, ends with witness to Christian piety.

The stories of Guy, Bevis, and Amis and Amiloun, with many others not mentioned here, occur together in the Auchinleck manuscript, and that great collection also includes biblical material, saints' lives, and exemplary and devotional texts. The range of the collection suggests the range of interests of readers of English romance. As this essay has suggested, insular romance occurs in languages other than English, and appeals to readers other than those characterized by collections like Auchinleck. But the threads of place, politics, and piety wind through many of these texts, binding many of their readers and listeners. When William Caxton printed Thomas Malory's *Morte Darthur* in 1485, the canny printer prefaced his text with a discussion of Arthur's historicity and the value of his story. Caxton's defence deftly wraps up all the themes I have outlined above, acknowledging audience, language, place, and purpose as he presents the last great medieval insular romance to its present and future audiences. He points to the many physical and geographical memorials of

---

[63] Zupitza (1883, 1887, 1891), ll. 7169–75.

Arthur's presence; he notes the prevalence of Arthurian romance in many languages, including French and Welsh; and he presents Malory's text,

to the intent that noble men may see and learn the noble acts of chivalry, the gentle and virtuous deeds that some knights used in those days, by which they came to honour; and how they that were vicious were punished and oft put to shame and rebuke; humbly beseeching all noble lords and ladies, with all other estates, of what estate or degree they be of, that shall see and read in this said book and work, that they take the good and honest acts in their remembrance, and to follow the same, wherein they shall find many joyous and pleasant histories, and noble and renowned acts of humanity, gentleness, and chivalries . . . And for to pass the time this book shall be pleasant to read in; but for to give faith and believe that all is true that is contained herein, ye be at your liberty. But all is written for our doctrine, and for to beware that we fall not to vice ne sin, but to exercise and follow virtue, by which we may come and attain to good fame and renown in this life, and after this short and transitory life, to come unto everlasting bliss in heaven.[64]

Romance, for Caxton's imagined audience of Englishmen and women of many classes, brings pleasure and spiritual profit alike. Insular romances often begin and/ or end with an appeal to God, and while such formulae certainly speak to the world beyond the romance, the lives and deaths of many romance heroes suggest such appeals are more than merely rote.

BIBLIOGRAPHY

AUERBACH, ERICH (1953), *Mimesis: The Representation of Reality in Western Literature*, tr. Willard R. Trask (Princeton: Princeton University Press).
BARRON, W. R. J. (1987), *English Medieval Romance* (London: Longman).
BEDE (1969), *Bede's Ecclesiastical History of the English People*, ed. Bertram Colgrave and R. A. B. Mynors (Oxford: Oxford University Press).
BENSON, LARRY D. (ed.) (1994), *King Arthur's Death: The Middle English Stanzaic Morte Arthur and Alliterative Morte Arthure*, rev. Edward E. Foster (Kalamazoo, Mich.: Medieval Institute Publications).
CAMPBELL, KOFI (2006), 'Nation-Building Colonialist-Style in *Bevis of Hampton*', Exemplaria, 18/1: 205–32.
CHAUCER, GEOFFREY (1987), *The Riverside Chaucer*, ed. Larry D. Benson, (3rd edn. Boston: Houghton Mifflin).
COLEMAN, JOYCE (1996), *Public Reading and the Reading Public in Late Medieval England and France* (Cambridge: Cambridge University Press).
CONNOLLY, MARTIN (2006), 'Promise-Postponement Device in *The Awntyrs off Arthure*: A Possible Narrative Model', Arthurian Literature, 23: 95–108.
COOPER, HELEN (2004), *The English Romance in Time: Transforming Motifs from Geoffrey of Monmouth to the Death of Shakespeare* (Oxford: Oxford University Press).
CRANE, SUSAN (1986), *Insular Romance: Politics, Faith, and Culture in Anglo-Norman and Middle English Literature* (Berkeley, Calif.: University of California Press).

[64] William Caxton, preface to *La Morte D'Arthur*, in Malory (1969: i. 5–6).

DAY, MILDRED LEAKE (ed.) (2005), *Latin Arthurian Literature* (Cambridge: D. S. Brewer).

DJORDJEVIĆ, IVANA (2008), 'From Boeve to Bevis: The Translator at Work', in J. Fellows and I. Djordjević (eds.), *Sir Bevis of Hampton in Literary Tradition* (Cambridge, D. S. Brewer), 67–79.

ECHARD, SIÂN (1998), *Arthurian Narrative in the Latin Tradition* (Cambridge: Cambridge University Press).

——(2008), *Printing the Middle Ages* (Philadelphia: University of Pennsylvania Press).

ELLIOTT, RALPH (1997), 'Landscape and Geography', in Derek Brewer and Jonathan Gibson (eds.), *A Companion to the Gawain-Poet* (Cambridge: D. S. Brewer), 104–17.

FELLOWS, JENNIFER (1993), 'St George as Romance Hero', *Reading Medieval Studies*, 19: 27–54.

FIELD, ROSALIND (1999), 'Romance in England, 1066–1400', in David Wallace (ed.), *The Cambridge History of Medieval English Literature* (Cambridge: Cambridge University Press), 152–76.

FINLAYSON, JOHN (1980), 'Definitions of Middle English Romance', *Chaucer Review*, 15: 161–81.

FOSTER, EDWARD E. (ed.) (1997), *Amis and Amiloun, Robert of Cisyle, and Sir Amadace* (Kalamazoo, Mich.: Medieval Institute Publications).

GEOFFREY OF MONMOUTH (2007), *The History of the Kings of Britain*, ed. Michael D. Reeve, tr. Neil Wright (Woodbridge: Boydell Press).

GOWER, JOHN (1899–1902), *Vox clamantis*, in G. C. Macaulay (ed.), *The Complete Works of John Gower*, iv (Oxford: Clarendon Press).

HANNA, RALPH (ed.) (1974), *The Awntyrs off Arthure at the Terne Wathelyn* (Manchester: Manchester University Press).

——(2005), *London Literature, 1300–1380* (Cambridge: Cambridge University Press).

HENG, GERALDINE (2003), *Empire of Magic: Medieval Romance and the Politics of Cultural Fantasy* (New York: Columbia University Press).

KANE, GEORGE (1951), *Middle English Literature: A Critical Study of the Romances, the Religious Lyrics, Piers Plowman* (London: Methuen).

KLAUSNER, DAVID N. (1972), 'Exempla and the *Awntyrs of Arthure*', *Mediaeval Studies*, 34: 307–25.

KÖLBING, EUGEN (ed.) (1884), *Amis and Amiloun* (Heilbronn: Henninger).

——(ed.) (1885, 1886, 1894), *The Romance of Sir Beues of Hamtoun*, ed. Eugen Kölbing (EETS extra ser. 46, 48, 65; London: K. Paul, Trench, Trübner & Co. for the Early English Text Society).

LERER, SETH (1993), *Chaucer and his Readers: Imagining the Author in Late-Medieval England* (Princeton: Princeton University Press).

MALORY, SIR THOMAS (1969, repr. 1986), *Le Morte D'Arthur*, ed. Janet Cowen (Harmondsworth: Penguin).

——(1971), *Works*, ed. Eugene Vinaver (2nd edn. Oxford: Oxford University Press).

MANNYNG OF BRUNNE, ROBERT (1996), *The Chronicle*, ed. Idelle Sullens (Binghamton, NY: Medieval and Renaissance Texts and Studies).

MARIE DE FRANCE (1952), *Lais*, ed. A. Ewert (Oxford: Blackwell).

——(1986), *The Lais of Marie de France*, tr. Glyn S. Burgess and Keith Busby (Harmondsworth: Penguin).

MEHL, DIETER (1968), *The Middle English Romances of the Thirteenth and Fourteenth Centuries* (London: Routledge & Kegan Paul).

PARKES, M. B., and ELIZABETH SALTER (eds.) (1978), *Troilus and Criseyde: A Facsimile of Corpus Christi College Cambridge MS 61* (Cambridge: D. S. Brewer).

PEARSALL, DEREK (1977), 'The Troilus Frontispiece and Chaucer's Audience', *Yearbook of English Studies*, 7: 68–74.

PURDIE, RHIANNON (2005), 'The Implications of Manuscript Layout in Chaucer's *Tale of Sir Thopas*', *Forum for Modern Language Studies*, 41/3: 263–74.

RICHMOND, VELMA BOURGEOIS (1996), *The Legend of Guy of Warwick* (New York: Garland).

ROUSE, ROBERT ALLEN (2005), *The Idea of Anglo-Saxon England in Middle English Romance* (Cambridge: D. S. Brewer).

——(2008), 'National and Regional Identities in *Sir Bevis of Hampton*', in J. Fellows and I. Djordjević (eds.), *Sir Bevis of Hampton in Literary Tradition* (Cambridge: D. S. Brewer), 114–26.

SAUNDERS, CORINNE (2004), *A Companion to Romance: From Classical to Contemporary* (Malden, Mass.: Blackwell).

——(ed.) (2005), *Cultural Encounters in the Romance of Medieval England* (Cambridge: D. S. Brewer).

SHEPHERD, STEPHEN H. A. (1995), *Middle English Romances* (New York, W. W. Norton).

STROHM, PAUL (1971), 'Storie, Spelle, Geste, Romaunce, Tragedie: Generic Distinctions in the Middle English Troy Narratives', *Speculum*, 46/2: 348–59.

——(1977), 'The Origin and Meaning of Middle English Romaunce', *Genre*, 10: 1–28.

——(1980), 'Middle English Narrative Genres', *Genre*, 13: 379–88.

TATLOCK, J. S. P. (1950), *The Legendary History of Britain: Geoffrey of Monmouth's Historia regum Britanniae and its Early Vernacular Versions* (Berkeley, Calif.: University of California Press).

TOLKIEN, J. R. R., and E. V. GORDON (eds.) (1925, repr. 1963), *Sir Gawain and the Green Knight* (Oxford: Clarendon Press).

TURVILLE-PETRE, THORLAC (1974), '"Summer Sunday," "De Tribus Regibus Mortuis," and "The Awntyrs off Arthure": Three Poems in the Thirteen-Line Stanza', *Review of English Studies*, 25/97: 1–14.

——(1996), *England the Nation: Language, Literature, and National Identity 1290–1340* (Oxford, Oxford University Press).

WEISS, JUDITH (1979), 'The Major Interpolations in *Sir Beues of Hamtoun*', *Medium Ævum*, 47: 71–6.

——(tr.) (1992), *The Birth of Romance: An Anthology* (London: Dent).

——(2008), *Boeve de Haumtone and Gui de Warewic: Two Anglo-Norman Romances* (Tempe, Ariz.: Arizona Center for Medieval and Renaissance Studies).

WIGGINS, ALISON, and ROSALIND FIELD (eds.) (2007), *Icon and Ancestor: The Medieval and Renaissance Guy of Warwick* (Cambridge: D. S. Brewer).

WILCOX, REBECCA (2004), 'Romancing the East: Greeks and Saracens in Guy of Warwick', in NICOLA MCDONALD (ed.), *Pulp Fictions of Medieval England: Essays in Popular Romance* (Manchester: Manchester University Press), 217–40.

ZUPITZA, JULIUS (ed.) (1883, 1887, 1891), *The Romance of Guy of Warwick* (EETS extra ser. 42, 49, 59; London: K. Paul, Trench, Truübner & Co.).

....

CHAPTER 9

A YORK PRIMER
AND ITS ALPHABET

READING WOMEN
IN A LAY HOUSEHOLD

....

NICOLA MCDONALD

In later medieval England, one book more than any other stands out for its association with women: the primer or book of hours. The primer was at once a *first* book of prayer and the layperson's *primary* devotional manual. An abbreviated form of the divine office (the cycle of daily prayer that structured religious life) designed specifically for lay use, the primer emerged in the mid-thirteenth century as a costly aide to the devotions of the elite and by Caxton's time was a runaway market success. It contained the basic prayers that all children were supposed to learn, written out in neat, easy to read letters and often accompanied by an alphabet, as well as a full programme of daily devotions, organized around the hours of the Virgin. The primer was not, of course, exclusively a women's book—easily the most popular and widely disseminated of medieval books, it was effectively everyone's, all the more so as relatively inexpensive print copies became available—but the surviving evidence points repeatedly to its *particular* affiliation with women.[1]

---

[1] Duffy (2005: 209–98) and Erler (1999) both provide excellent introductions to the primer and its cultural significance in later medieval England; Erler, in particular, focuses on its popularity with women and success in early print. For a detailed account of the make-up of the primer, see Littlehales (1895), who reproduces a representative exemplar in Middle English.

The earliest surviving English book of hours, the de Brailes Hours, was made around 1240 for an unknown laywoman; and most early books of hours, whether lavish or modest, were produced for women patrons.[2] The earliest mention of a primer in England is in Elizabeth Bacon's will of 1323 where she leaves her sister Margaret's primer to her brother.[3] Indeed, testamentary evidence like this has proved invaluable in documenting lay women's book ownership, especially in the fourteenth and fifteenth centuries, and here the primer is 'ubiquitous'.[4] More primers were owned by women than any other kind of book; more primers were bequeathed to women than any other kind of book; and more often than not women bequeathed their primers to other women. Moreover, many women testators owned more than one primer, often distinguishing them as 'my new primer', 'my best primer', or 'another primer, illuminated with gold with two gilded, worked silver clasps'.[5] Maud Clifford, Countess of Cambridge, an aristocratic Yorkshire widow who drew up her will in 1446, had at least three primers—'my green primer', 'a little black primer', and 'my biggest and best primer'—which she distributed, respectively, to her niece Beatrice Waterton, her waiting-woman Katherine Fitzwilliam, and another kinswoman Alice Montague, Countess of Salisbury.[6] As these and similar bequests suggest, the primer was more than simply a devotional tool. Often an object of material value, and no doubt as much a symbol of a woman's status as of her piety, the primer was also a site of intimate, personal history, recalling and reinforcing women's social and kinship networks. It may also have been, as Eustache Deschamps implies, something of a fashion accessory.[7]

Not surprisingly, in recent years the primer has emerged as a point of focus for scholars interested in medieval women and their books. Magnificent, illuminated books of hours and simple, work-a-day primers alike have proved invaluable in documenting women's histories and especially their rich devotional lives. The primer's function as a basic reader has also been central to the reassessment of later medieval literacy, especially its domestication and the mother's crucial role in lay education.[8] This chapter likewise takes the primer as its starting-point. It uses the evidence of the so-called Bolton Hours, a fifteenth-century manuscript associated with, in particular, the female members of a York merchant family, to trace the bookish world of the late medieval household; and it proposes that we think again about how medieval women used their ABCs.

---

[2] For the de Brailes Hours see Donovan (1991); Smith (2003) includes an overview of scholarship on women's ownership and patronage of books of hours and offers a stimulating analysis of the De Lisle, DeBois, and Neville of Horny Hours. See also Penketh (1997) and the important early work of Bell (1982).

[3] Gibbons (1888: 4).

[4] Goldberg (1994: 185).

[5] Raine (1855: 235, 156, and 144): the bequests are recorded in the wills of Agnes Bedford, Margaret la Zouch, and Hawisia Aske, respectively.

[6] BIA, ABP Reg. 19 fo. 192^r Matilda of York; printed ibid. 118–24.

[7] Raynaud (1894: 45–6, ll. 1311–19).

[8] On the domestication of literacy, see Clanchy (1993: 252); and most recently, Orme (2001: 242–6).

AT HOME WITH THE BOLTON HOURS

The importance of the Bolton Hours for thinking about laywomen and their books is already well established.[9] York, Minster Library, MS Additional 2, is a small, richly illustrated book of hours of York use that was produced, probably in York, in the early fifteenth century.[10] Its lavish programme of illumination, unmatched in extant English books of hours of this date, not only marks it out as a distinctly local production (with its provincial craftsmanship and parochial saints), but as a family anthology designed specifically with its female members in mind. Like many manuscripts of its kind, the Bolton Hours contains a series of patronal images. The first, in the current ordering of the quires, is a bourgeois family group kneeling before a Crucifix–Trinity (folio 33). The father and mother at the centre, flanked by a son on the left and a daughter on the right, represent an ideal family unit, which is no doubt informed by aesthetic and ideological criteria as much as by verisimilitude. The mother-figure is represented in two other full-page illuminations, praying to St Zita (folio 40ᵛ), the newly popular servant-saint, and St Michael (folio 123); while a young woman, her hair unbound (a sign of her maidenhood), is depicted in a three-quarter-page image kneeling before Richard Scrope (d. 1406), York's recently martyred archbishop and the focus of a local cult (folio 100ᵛ). Two historiated initials also contain lay figures: a man at prayer (folio 48) and a woman confessing to a priest (folio 78). From the evidence of its illuminations, Kathleen Scott has claimed that 'the mistress of the household was apparently the guiding hand in the production of the book', which may be an overstatement.[11] But what the images do insist upon is the association of the Bolton Hours with the women, and especially the mother, of the family for whom it was first produced.

From the entry of the obits of John and Alice Bolton into its calendar (they died in 1445 and 1472, respectively), the manuscript has long been associated with York's mercantile elite and with the Bolton family in particular. Recent work by Patricia Cullum and Jeremy Goldberg has made a compelling case for Margaret Blackburn, Alice Bolton's mother, as the book's original patron, or at least its intended recipient.[12] The Blackburns were a wealthy merchant family, prominent in civic government and generous local benefactors, who are still memorialized in their parish church of All Saints, North Street, on the west side of York's River Ouse. This side of the city, at some remove from the traditional centres of power, seems to have become something of a hub in the early fifteenth century for the ambitious householders who formed the city's new social and political elite.[13] Here the Blackburns lived in a comfortably appointed, multi-room house (comprising a hall, adjacent

[9] Cullum and Goldberg (2000); Rees Jones and Riddy (2000).
[10] The MS is described by Ker (1969–2002: iv. 786–92) and Scott (1996: ii. 119–21).
[11] Ibid. ii. 120.
[12] Cullum and Goldberg (2000: *passim*).
[13] Rees Jones and Riddy (2000: 239–44).

chamber, and separate kitchen, as well as workrooms and other outbuildings) where their wealth and status were reflected in their remarkable accumulation of stuff: silver candlesticks, spoons and goblets, a spice box and a plate for sweetmeats, an ornamental cup fashioned out of a coconut, imported fabric, painted wall hangings, bedcovers embroidered with parrots, roses, and stars, twenty-four cushions, and at least eight chests (some iron-bound, others carved or painted, one on wheels) in which to store it all.[14] In his will, Nicholas made provision for Margaret to live out her widowhood in the manner of a gentlewoman ('a gentele woman lyfelade'), complete with a servant and a priest; and, indeed, the family's aspirations to gentle status were rewarded when Alice Bolton's eldest daughter (another Margaret) married into first one and then a second local gentry family.

It is in this context of material well-being and social and spiritual ambition that we need to think about the affiliation between women and the primer that the Bolton Hours so neatly represents. A luxury manuscript, the Bolton Hours was undoubtedly a powerful symbol of its owner's prosperity; but not only on account of its substantial cost. For the Blackburns, the image of a woman with a book seems to have functioned as one of the most important markers of the family's achievements. In their parish church of All Saints, North Street, two stained-glass windows commemorating the Blackburns still survive; only one, however, is complete, with its original donor portraits intact, although it has been moved from the north aisle where the Blackburns customarily sat, to the east window.[15] In each of its three main lights a saint is depicted, from left to right, St John the Baptist, St Anne teaching the Virgin to read and St Christopher; while the lower panels of the window commemorate the donors: on the left, the younger Nicholas Blackburn (his father's heir) and his wife (yet another Margaret); and, on the right, Nicholas the elder and his wife, Margaret; in the central panel is a Crucifix–Trinity, recalling the same image in the Bolton Hours. As is conventional in donor portraits, the couples are kneeling in prayer; what is more remarkable is that both wives are depicted holding an open book. And not

[14] Throughout this chapter, I have made extensive use of the surviving wills of members of the Blackburn and Bolton families, as well as those of close friends and business associates, to try to reconstruct something of the bookish world in which they lived. The elder Nicholas Blackburn's will (BIA, Prob. Reg. 2, fo. 605) provides the detailed information on the layout of the family's residence, its workrooms, and outlying buildings, on North St, while the household goods listed here are all itemized in Margaret Blackburn's will (BIA, Prob. Reg. 3. fo. 415^v); the wills are printed in Raine (1855: 17–21 and 46–51, respectively). Throughout the chapter, I have also made use of the wills of the younger Nicholas Blackburn (BIA, Prob. Reg. 2, fo. 168^v; Joan Blackburn, the elder Nicholas Blackburn's sister-in-law (BIA, Prob. Reg. 3, fo. 141^v); John Bolton, Alice Bolton's husband (BIA, Prob. Reg. 2, fo. 107^v; as well as those of Nicholas Blackburn's executors, his brother-in-law, William Ormeshede (BIA, Prob. Reg. 3, fo. 505), fellow merchants Richard Russell (BIA, Prob. Reg. 2, fo. 439; printed in Raine (1855: 52–7)) and John Aldstanmore (BIA, Prob. Reg. 3, fo. 406) and the chaplain William Revetour (BIA, Prob. Reg. 2, fo. 137^v; printed in Raine (1855: 116–18)). Blackburn's other executors were his wife, his son Nicholas, and his son-in-law John Bolton. For a discussion of numbers of cushions owned as a 'crude barometer of wealth', see Goldberg (2008: 132).

[15] Gee (1969) remains the standard work on the remarkable collection of stained glass in the Blackburn's parish church.

just any book: a primer. The gesture is a bold one, for with their books the Blackburn women are effectively assimilated to the holy mother and daughter whose reading lesson dominates the window's composition.

Anne was a popular saint in later medieval England where she is commonly represented as an 'exemplary *materfamilias*'.[16] Married three times, with three daughters (and seven holy grandsons), she was a model of the devout bourgeois housewife and her life was a powerful confirmation of the compatibility of sanctity with marriage, motherhood, and a domestic routine. Her cult, however, was by no means the preserve of women; the 'ladi of all weddid folk', she is singled out for particular devotion by, for instance, Nicholas Blackburn.[17] The image of Anne teaching her daughter to read (also known as the education of the Virgin) is first found in English sources at the beginning of the fourteenth century, and it quickly became the dominant devotional image of the saint.[18] In the All Saints window, a gentle-faced Anne inclines protectively towards the young Virgin; her right hand cups her daughter's shoulder in a reassuring maternal embrace, while her left helps support the book from which, pointer in hand, Mary spells out her letters. This book too is a primer. Both women are dressed in sumptuous, contemporary attire and Anne's gold-trimmed red robe echoes those worn by the Blackburn wives. In the last few decades, scholars have attributed the popularity of this image to the rise of laywomen's literacy in the fourteenth and fifteenth centuries, suggesting that it at once reflected common practice in high-status households (where mothers were increasingly responsible for the education of young children and especially girls) and served as a productive role model for both mothers and daughters who could scarcely do better than to imitate not only the mother of God, but also his grandmother.[19]

The same image is found in the Bolton Hours, where the traditional iconography, Cullum and Goldberg argue, has been modified to reflect more accurately the particular circumstances of the Blackburn family, who had three daughters.[20] Here, in an innovative interpretation of the Holy Kindred, a nimbus-less Anne is depicted teaching the Virgin to read in the company of her two half-sisters, Mary Cleophas and Mary Salome; the sister who waits patiently behind the Virgin, for her instruction to start, clutches her own small, red-bound book, complete with a decorative clasp. In a manuscript that is littered with images of books, the only one whose text is intentionally legible is the one from which the Virgin reads; and the words 'Domine labia mea aperies' ('O Lord, wilt thou open my lips'), the opening versicle of Matins in the hours of the Virgin, identify it as a book of hours. The effect is powerful: the Bolton Hours is the very book from which the Virgin learns to read; while devotion, for Margaret Blackburn (who is iconographically, as well as symbolically, identified

[16] Ashley and Sheingorn (1990: 4).

[17] Ellis (1987: 467). Nicholas Blackburn the elder established a chantry in the chapel of St Anne on Fossbridge, to which he gave his 'best vestment', his 'best missal', and his 'best chalice'; his wife Margaret also left vestments, painted cloths, and curtains to the chapel.

[18] Norton *et al.* (1987: 51–3, esp. n. 99).

[19] Two seminal articles on this popular topic are: Scase (1993); Sheingorn (1993).

[20] Cullum and Goldberg (2000: 228–30).

with Anne), is construed as the education of one's daughters. In the Blackburn window in All Saints, in fact, it is no longer St Anne who is most closely identified with the book of hours' central text, but rather the elder Margaret Blackburn, on whose open book a version of the familiar words are inscribed.[21] St Anne and the Virgin, like the younger Margaret Blackburn, instead read a penitential psalm, an essential but subsidiary part of the book of hours. In a striking intervention in conventional hierarchies of representation, the elder Margaret Blackburn, exemplary *materfamilias*, confidently displays her own distinctive attribute (the Bolton Hours) and is conveniently at eye level, all the better to be seen.

ALPHABETICAL ORDER

In the Bolton Hours, as in the Blackburn window, reading is a form of religious devotion, proper to the home or parish church where it was promoted as a service to the family, whose piety, wealth, and social standing it affirmed. The conflation of reading and prayer is not, of course, peculiar to the Blackburns. Learning to read was the first step in the formation of a good Christian, and throughout the Middle Ages elementary education, facilitated by the use of the primer, was first and foremost a function of piety.[22] Although scholars disagree on the extent to which literate practice, by the later Middle Ages, extended down the social scale, there is no doubt that below the level of the greater aristocracy the teaching of basic reading skills was predominantly perceived as women's work: 'w[oman] lernyth chylde on boke', as the compiler of a list of women's occupations put it *c.*1300.[23] The domestication of literacy, its movement out of the cloister and into the lay household, did not however change its fundamental dynamic, which remained religious. Commentators who advocated women's literacy invariably did so as a safeguard for their souls—to 'knowe the perils of the sowle and her sauement'[24]—but for all children, the purpose of sounding out the alphabet was to facilitate the learning of prayers.

Indeed, the alphabet—also known as the Christ-cross or Christ-cross row, from the figure of the cross which was invariably prefixed to it—was itself a prayer. Reading the alphabet began with the words 'Christ crosse me spede' as the reader effectively sounded out the figure of the cross and, at the same time, requested Christ's help for the work ahead.[25] As alphabetic literacy became more widespread, the alphabet's opening petition, a convenient short-hand for the full prayer, became a common pious oath; we find Gawain, for instance, punctuating his 'pater and aue

---

[21] The inscription on Margaret Blackurn's book seems to have originally read 'Dñes salue mea peccatis aperies et os meum'; sometime after 1691, the window was restored and the inscription altered to the more familiar wording. Gee (1969: 156).

[22] Denley (1990).   [23] Skeat (1906: 7* (l. 146)).

[24] Tr. Caxton (1971: 122).   [25] On the medieval alphabet see Orme (2001: 246–61).

and crede' with a 'Cros Kryst me spede'.[26] In the Bolton Hours, the alphabet is laid out as the first in the series of daily prayers (including the Lord's Prayer, Hail Mary, and Creed) that precede the hours of the Virgin. It starts with a crucifix, illuminated with the bloodied body of Christ, and ends with an amen; it contains twenty-four letters, plus the variant forms of r and s encountered in written form, and is augmented by the most common Latin abbreviations (*et, con,* and *est*), reinforcing its use as both a teaching tool and a stand-alone prayer.

The 'enclosure', to borrow Marie Denley's term, of the medieval alphabet by highly charged Christian symbols, the cross and amen, works hard to delineate, for both elementary and adult readers, not only the purpose of alphabetic literacy, but its proper limits.[27] From later medieval England, there survives a remarkable amount of, especially vernacular, abecedarian verse (poems, however loosely defined, that use the alphabet as their principal structuring device) and it is here that the ideological function of the alphabet is most fully articulated. Today, Chaucer's *ABC* is the best known example, but the genre comprises a surprisingly rich body of material. Martha Rust, the first scholar to give it any sustained attention, divides the surviving verse into two broad categories: devotional *abeces* and right-conduct *abeces*, although these terms are mine.[28] Chaucer's, like other Marian alphabet poems, is a devotional ABC, as are a number of unique lyrics on the passion. These latter employ the letters of the alphabet to structure a narrative of the passion, putting flesh, as it were, on the mark of the cross with which primer alphabets invariably begin. The cross at the start of the alphabet in the Bolton Hours, complete with an image of the crucified Christ, may have been designed as an aid to precisely this kind of affective devotion. The right-conduct *abeces*, on the other hand, propose the alphabet as a suitable method for organizing moral and social precepts, and not just for mnemonic purposes. As the *Boke of Curtasye* explains, the 'croscrist' is the obligatory starting point for 'alle' of its 'werke', beginning with elementary prayers but readily encompassing advice on comportment in church, on proper familial and social relationships, and various injunctions against gambling, nose picking, and lodging in the house of a red head.[29] The most widely copied of the Middle English alphabet poems is an alliterating list of proscriptions, known as the 'ABC of Aristotle' ('Be neuer': 'A to[o] amerose, to[o] aunterose'; 'B to[o] bolde, ne to[o] bisi', and so on) that advocates measured conduct and moderate appetite, in conjunction with an acute awareness of social rank; fourteen versions of which are still extant in a diverse range of manuscript miscellanies. '*Reede ofte* on þis rolle', the prologue admonishes, 'and *rewle* ȝu eer aftir', neatly instantiating the remarkably restrictive model of literate practice that the medieval alphabet properly facilitated.[30]

[26] Ed. Tolkein and Gordon (1967), ll. 757–8, 762.   [27] Denley (1990: 226).

[28] Rust (2007: 35).   [29] Ed. Furnivall (1868), l. 144.

[30] The quotations are taken from the versions of the 'ABC of Aristotle' found in, respectively, London, British Library, Add. 36983, fos. 263[r–v] and Lambeth Palace Library, 853, pp. 30–1.

In some ways, then, the prominent images in All Saints of Margaret Blackburn, elder and younger, as readers are less audacious than they at first seem. They can be read, in fact, as confirmation of many of our assumptions about medieval women's lives and their restricted compass. The model of the devout housewife, primer in hand, satisfied secular as well as religious authorities and no doubt many women themselves. And indeed we look in vain for any overt articulation of the radical potential of alphabetic literacy to disrupt the social and sexual hierarchies that governed women's lives. There is no equivalent of Frederick Douglass's elation at learning his ABC: 'Mistress, in teaching me the alphabet, had given me the *inch* and no precaution could prevent me from taking the *ell*';[31] precisely, of course, because medieval women had nothing in common with African-American slaves. Unlike Douglass, whose reading lessons were violently interrupted by a master who recognized how they threatened the peculiar institution that was slavery, the women I am interested in here read and even owned books with institutional support and encouragement. As the example of the Blackburns demonstrates, these women's involvement in textual culture predominantly served, rather than undermined, the interests of the patriarchal family whose interests, in turn, served its female members; the Bolton Hours is explicitly a book of *family* devotion rather than that of a single individual. As Rebecca Krug emphasizes, medieval women's engagement with the written word (particularly in the guise of the Word) was not *necessarily* transgressive.[32]

MORE THAN JUST A PRETTY PRIMER

Although some medieval women's access to books may have been limited to the primer, for well-to-do bourgeois women like Margaret Blackburn and Alice Bolton (to say nothing of those of higher status), this was certainly not the case. The Bolton Hours may be the only *surviving* manuscript that has been ascribed to one or other of these women, but it was not the only book that they or their families owned. As testamentary evidence makes clear, between them the Blackburns and Boltons had a sizeable collection of books in both Latin and English, including another primer, a number of missals, a book on the Lord's prayer, a copy of the *Pricke of Conscience* in English and a large Latin roll that had an illustrated treatise on the Bible on one side and an exposition of the Lord's Prayer on the other. Moreover, in the tightly knit social world in which they moved (comprised predominantly of prosperous merchant families but including local gentry, senior members of the clergy, and the

---

[31] Douglass (1845: 38). In contrast, there *is* evidence of cultural anxiety about the dangers of teaching women how to read; the author of *Urbain le Courtois*, for instance, cautions his addressee against taking as a bride a woman who can read, because, he underlines, literate women are often deceitful; Meyer (1903: 72, ll. 57–64).

[32] Krug (2002: esp. 1–16).

occasional aristocrat) the ownership and circulation of books was remarkably common. Among the elder Nicholas Blackburn's closest associates, more than half owned one or more books, which were often passed on to close friends or family, and two had significant personal libraries: fellow merchant Richard Russell, who also helped pay for a nephew's Oxford education, had an extensive collection of liturgical books (including an Antiphoner, a Missal, three Graduals, and a two-volume Legendary) while the urbane and exceedingly well-dressed chaplain William Revetour owned at least nine, largely religious books in Latin and English, alongside, most famously, two plays, the monumental Creed Play and a shorter one about St James the Apostle.

The evidence provided by Revetour's will is especially interesting. It seems that the chaplain was in the habit of loaning out his copies of the plays (the Creed Play comprised a master copy and a set of associated books, likely containing the texts of individual episodes, while the play about St James was copied out as six separate scenes or pages[33]) and they were probably not the only texts that Revetour circulated during his lifetime. His bequests not only provide striking confirmation of the particular affinity between the Blackburn and Bolton women and books: intimate over several decades with three generations of the family, Revetour chose, at the time of his death, to articulate that intimacy through the gift of four books: two to Alice Bolton, a third to her daughter (and Revetour's goddaughter) Isabella and a fourth to Alice's husband John. They also suggest, in his careful matching of individual books with individual recipients, that his friends may have already been familiar with his collection. Alice Bolton's copy of the *Pricke of Conscience* came from Revetour, and it is unlikely that she did not make some use of it before his death. An ambitious work of popular theology, focusing on the last fifteen days of the world, the *Pricke of Conscience* held particular devotional significance for the parishioners of All Saints North Street, one of whose early-fifteenth-century windows (the gift of two wealthy mercantile families) offers a vivid rendering, unique in European art, of its apocalyptic vision.

I want to speculate further, for a moment, about the possibility that Alice Bolton had still wider access to books than has been argued so far. Margaret Blackburn's particular devotion to St Zita, the servant-saint whom she venerates in one of the Bolton Hours' patronal portraits, has already been noted. Cullum and Goldberg have conjectured that as a young woman Alice spent some time in service, as was common for adolescents from her social milieu, in the household of Maud Clifford, the aristocratic Yorkshire woman whose bequest of three primers I detailed in my introduction.[34] In her will, drawn up on the Feast of the Assumption in 1446, many years after Alice had married and was running her own household, Maud left her the extraordinarily generous sum of £20 as a marriage portion for one of her daughters, remarking that this was 'as Alice desired'. Maud must have had particular affection for the young woman; despite their social differences, she maintained contact with

---

[33] For the claim that Revetour's Creed Play was comprised of a master copy and the play texts of individual episodes, see Johnston (1975: 59).

[34] Cullum and Goldberg (2000: 234 n. 48).

her long after Alice had left her service. The daughter of Sir Thomas Clifford, one of Richard II's chamber knights, Maud was connected by birth and through two successive marriages (to John Neville, Sixth Lord Latimer, and Richard of Conisbrough, First Earl of Cambridge) to both provincial magnates and the Crown. And throughout her life she moved in powerful and, more notably, highly literate circles. Maud's own library comprised not only devotional and liturgical books (like her primers and the 'old breviary' she gave to her parish church) but substantial volumes of secular literature: she left a two-volume copy of a French romance (*Guiron le Courtois*) to Alice Montague, the same kinswoman who received her 'biggest and best primer'. Maud seems to have been particularly intimate with her younger kinswoman, whom she named as one of her executors, and from her bequest of books, reading may have been something the two women shared. Alice Montague herself came from distinctly literate stock; her father, Thomas Montague, earl of Salisbury, was a friend to Christine de Pizan and one of Lydgate's patrons and his second wife, Alice's step-mother, was Alice Chaucer, Geoffrey Chaucer's granddaughter, an inveterate reader and important literary patron in her own right.[35] With her own marriage to the Lancastrian magnate Richard Neville, Alice Montague became a sister-in-law to Cecily Neville, Duchess of York, one of the most literate and pious laywomen in later medieval England.[36] And Maud Clifford cannot have been unknown to the Duchess; on Maud's death, her waiting-woman Katherine Fitzwilliam, to whom Maud bequeathed her 'little black primer', took up service in Cecily's household.

My point is not to exaggerate Alice Bolton's literate practice. But as a woman who grew up in a family that purposefully used the image of a woman reading a book as a sign of its social and spiritual achievement, who likely spent part of her adolescence in service in a cultured aristocratic household, and who was on intimate terms with some of York's most well-read men (one of whom left her two books alongside one for her daughter, a girl whom Alice no doubt taught to read), we would be foolish to underestimate either her literacy or her familiarity with textual culture.

One Foot in the Grave

Although women only infrequently made wills, testamentary evidence has provided a rich source of information about the ownership and circulation of books by and among women, their family, and friends. At the same time, however, wills are highly selective documents whose contents were constrained by legal practice, linguistic convention, and their essentially performative nature. The snapshot that they provide of women's book ownership, to say nothing of their reading habits, is remarkably misleading. Maud Clifford's will, like those of Nicholas Blackburn, Richard

---

[35] Meale (1996).   [36] Armstrong (1942).

Russell, and William Revetour, reflects the common preoccupations, and limitations, of the genre. Death-bed giving inevitably prioritized the soul, and both material and monetary bequests privileged the testator's piety above other facets of her life. Moreover, primers and liturgical books (many of which were bound in costly fabric, decorated with expensive clasps and even outfitted with a gold or silver bookmarker) were often among a testator's more valuable possessions and so their disposal was more likely to be recorded. Nicholas Blackburn left his 'best' missal to his chantry in the chapel of St Anne's on Foss Bridge; likewise the primer Isabella Bolton was given by her godfather was a 'large' one, expensively illustrated with 'pictures' 'drawn in the Flemish style'. The predominance of religious books among those that can be attributed to the Blackburn and Bolton women and their circle is thus not surprising; but as Mary Erler cautions, we need to be careful not to equate their prominence, alongside other devotional paraphernalia, with 'extraordinary piety', nor indeed with a testator's aversion to, or unfamiliarity with other kinds of textual culture like romance, chronicle, lyric poetry, or fabliau.[37]

As Susan Cavanaugh has amply demonstrated, secular and vernacular literature, much of which circulated unbound, in booklet form, and which was of comparatively little financial value, was precisely the kind of material that was 'overlooked for the purpose of bequests'.[38] Lady Alice West, a Hampshire gentlewoman who in 1395 bequeathed a sizeable library to her daughter-in-law—'alle the bokes that I haue of latyn, englisch and frensch'—singled out only one by name, a 'masse book'.[39] Likewise, in his will of 1466, Thomas Stotevyle, a member of Lincoln's Inn, bequeathed only one book, a decretal which he gave to his parish church for tithes forgotten; an inventory, compiled in 1459–60, however, lists forty of his books including, alongside liturgical, legal, and devotional ones, books of medicine, surgery, romance, and chronicle, as well as copies of *Piers Plowman* and the *Canterbury Tales*.[40] If surviving manuscripts of *Guiron le Courtois* are in any way representative, Maud Clifford's copy of the romance, the only secular text to appear in the Yorkshire wills surveyed above, was large, fully illuminated, and enormously expensive;[41] Maud's privileging of it signals less that she perceived it as a particularly good read than that it was worth an awful lot of money.

The problem with restricting the literate practice of Margaret Blackburn and Alice Bolton to primers and other devotional material, as the evidence examined so far encourages, is not only that it is an inaccurate representation of the textual cultures to which they must have had access, but that it effectively reinforces our preconceptions about the lives that they, and women like them, lived. I have already suggested that the image of the pious mother, using the family primer to teach her daughters how to pray, reflected the fantasies of both secular and religious authorities, but it is

---

[37] Erler (1999: 495).   [38] Cavanaugh (1980: 9).

[39] The will of Lady Alice West is edited by Furnivall (1882: 5).

[40] Cavanaugh (1980: 16). TNA, PROB 11/5; PCC, 21 Godyn. Stotevyle's inventory is copied onto fo. 3ᵛ of London, British Library Add. 54233; for the full list of books, see A.J.H. (1876).

[41] Lathuillère (1966).

also a reflex of modern scholarship. In conclusion to this chapter, I want to propose a rather different, and remarkably underexploited, source of evidence for thinking about the variety of textual cultures that would undoubtedly have been available to the Blackburn and Bolton women; one that does not deny the import of devotional, or didactic, literature in shaping medieval women's lives, but rather one that puts it in dialogue with competing discourses.

USED BOOKS

'Household miscellany' is a term coined by Julia Boffey and John Thompson to refer to a disparate group of predominantly fifteenth-century, vernacular English manuscripts, united by the purposeful miscellaneity of their contents, which were designed to serve the divergent needs of a lay household: for practical information, spiritual guidance, moral instruction, and entertainment.[42] No two household miscellanies (alternatively called household books or household anthologies) are alike. They are distinguished by their methods of compilation (professional, semi-professional, amateur, or a mixture thereof), their textual make-up (some privilege pragmatic material or romance, while others have, to the modern eye, no coherence at all), their place of origin (metropolitan and provincial, they are found all across England), and the social milieu of their audiences (many of whom have been identified as either the urban, mercantile elite or the provincial gentry). Some were bound together from independently circulating booklets only after a considerable period of time and much use, whereas others were copied, sometimes piecemeal, into a conveniently available or specially purchased blank book; some can be identified with individual compilers or owners while the majority betray no signs of ownership at all; and, of course, the use to which these manuscripts were put may have changed over time, in tandem (or not) with the life-cycle of the household. Household miscellanies, in other words, resist easy generalization, but we can be sure of one thing: hybrid, vernacular, ordinary, protean, they are, in contrast to the primer, one of the least likely of household possessions to figure in a dying person's will. At the same time, however, they provide us with one of the most important resources we have for imagining the textual community, a term to which I will return below, in which Margaret Blackburn and Alice Bolton, along with the wives and daughters of other well-to-do householders in York and elsewhere, were likely to have participated.

---

[42] Boffey and Thompson (1989: 294). Representative household miscellanies, other than those discussed here, include Aberystwyth, National Library of Wales, Brogyntyn MS ii.1 (formerly Porkington 10); London, British Library, MS Cotton Caligula Aii; Cambridge University Library, MS Ff.1.6 (the so-called Findern anthology); Manchester, Chetham's Library, MS 8009; Edinburgh, National Library of Scotland, MS Advocates 19.3.1 (the Heege manuscript).

For most women, the acquisition of literacy, basic or otherwise, took place within the household; and for lay women, the household remained the place in which they experienced literate culture. As scholarship has identified, the household was 'the privileged locus for medieval women'.[43] The notion of the medieval household overlaps with that of the family, the term I have used so far in my discussion of the Bolton Hours, and indeed in Middle English the word *familie* means household.[44] The household refers both to a physical space, the house, as well as a social network; the nuclear family was at its core, but it encompassed all those living, sometimes temporarily, under its roof, bound variously by ties of kinship, service, and friendship. The household's boundaries were notoriously fluid, not only on account of the comings and goings associated with social and familial obligation, but because of the turnover in its personnel. In 1432, when her father died, Alice Bolton's household included, in addition to her husband and children (there is evidence of five daughters), at least four servants (Symkyn, Watkyn, Alison Meyke, and John Russell) and a nurse. Two years later, John Russell was still in residence (with a wife and two sons) as, in all likelihood, was Alison Meyke, and there is evidence of a sixth Bolton child, a son; but there were newcomers too, including Alice's widowed and ailing mother Margaret and her servant Joan Escrick. And there may have been more; in their wills, Nicholas and Margaret Blackburn remembered both current and former servants (of their own, their siblings, and their offspring) and a number of minor monetary bequests are probably indicative of a much larger service network; although not all servants received only small sums of money. Margaret Blackburn left Joan Escrick bed linen, wall hangings, cushions, dishes, and other household goods, along with her 'best cloak'; while her widowed sister-in-law, Joan Blackburn, left Joan Gray, her maid and one of her executors, a head of John the Baptist (a popular devotional aide) and her primer, suggesting that the affective ties of the household were by no means limited to kin. In short, the household was a place of work, devotion, and sociability, of intimacy and the everyday, where friends and neighbours, business and family converged and where social and sexual ideologies were taught in the face of life's inevitable messiness.

And it is that messiness, both material and ideological, that the household miscellany captures so effectively. Boffey, in a later discussion of manuscript taxonomy, prioritizes use as a 'household' manuscript's defining feature: 'a household book', she argues, is 'a book *in use* in a specific household.[45] Worn and often untidy, the household miscellany invariably betrays signs of its use; and in doing so it reminds us of the dynamic inherent in textual practice. No text, of course, is autonomous. Within the context of the household miscellany, the meaning of a text is produced not only by the interplay between it and the other texts that make up the manuscript but also between the text and its audience. By putting its miscellany *in use*, the household is transformed into a textual community, a concept—most closely associated with the historian Brian Stock—that over the past few decades has

---

[43] Salih (2003: 125).   [44] *Middle English Dictionary*, familie (n.).   [45] Boffey (2000: 129).

been enormously important in valorizing medieval women's experience of, in partic- ular devotional, textual culture.[46] As the iconography of the Bolton Hours demon- strates, for women like Margaret Blackburn and Alice Bolton reading was predominantly a social practice. The image of the Virgin reading alone, in the privacy of her chamber, a standard representation of the Annunciation, is conspicuously absent. The open book is designed to be shared; it is a sign of sociability, of a community of readers. Conventionally understood, however, the textual community that is produced by the practice of social, rather than solitary, reading is one that has been defined as having a shared understanding or interpretation of the text at hand, what Stock calls an 'agreed meaning'.[47] But in the context of the household (and its miscellany), we need to modify our understanding of the term to underscore not the *sharing of* (an agreed) *meaning* but rather the *sharing of texts* whose meanings may well remain contested. And this is not simply the result of the multiplicity character- istic of miscellanies which strongly militates against the achievement of a coherent, or agreed, meaning. Although we know very little about the conditions of reading in individual lay households (whether books were part of the daily routine or kept for special occasions; whether children or servants had access to them; what the effect was of factors like lighting, acoustics, and performance practice), what is readily apparent is that the make-up of the household—in terms of age, gender, and social status, to say nothing of personal disposition—was necessarily heterogeneous. We cannot assume that, as a community of any kind, the members of a household shared one seamless ideological agenda, as the example of the Pastons (the East Anglian gentry family whose well-known letter collection documents the often conflicted relations between parents and children, siblings and estate servants) demonstrates so clearly.

Arguing with Aristotle

In what follows, I have focused my discussion on the contents of a single household miscellany, Cambridge University Library, Ff.5.48, an 'undistinguished' and badly damaged paper manuscript dating from the middle of the fifteenth century that has so far received scant critical attention. It is made up of five distinct sections (which may have circulated for a short time as independent booklets) and was copied by four (possibly five) different scribes, probably in the north of England. The manuscript's audience Carole Meale has recently proposed, was 'middle-class, urban and perhaps mercantile'.[48] Although there is nothing to associate it with York's merchant families,

---

[46] Riddy (1993); Wogan-Browne (2002).   [47] Stock (1983: 91).
[48] The description of the MS and its contents in Furrow (1985) is the most complete and reliable of those published to date; although Furrow provides no information about its medieval ownership. Meale (2001) is the first to identify CUL Ff.5.48 as a household miscellany (see esp. pp. 110–17), and in

CUL Ff.5.48 is representative of the kind of hodgepodge of texts that the Blackburns and Boltons may have owned or, almost certainly, had ready access to. Its contents, more than thirty items in total, overlap suggestively with those found in other household miscellanies (including Oxford, Bodleian Library, MS Ashmole 61, associated by Blanchfield with a Leicester merchant; Cambridge University Library, MS Ee.4.35, which bears the name and merchant's mark of its East Anglian owner, Richard Calle; and Cambridge University Library, Ff.2.38, identified by Boffey and Thompson with a 'family readership'[49]) and they are, like the household itself, distinctly heterogeneous: prophetic, devotional, improving, exemplary, historical, and comic, with a whiff of the obscene.

The manuscript contains one of the fourteen surviving copies of the 'ABC of Aristotle', the abecedarian proscriptions with which I closed my earlier discussion of the proper scope of literacy. The 'ABC' is a 'rewle' of conduct that seeks to 'gouarne' the reader's impulse to push against the established limits of social, political, and sexual decorum, what 'gode maner askith' or what would please ('qweme wel') one's 'maister'.[50] That impulse is articulated as an excess—'to[o] amerows', 'to[o] aunterows', 'to[o] bolde'—and the job of the alphabet, by imposing its rigid order, is to try to contain it. The verse betrays so single-minded a fear of the unregulated, of the immeasurable ('to myche of euery thyng was neuer gode'; 'a measurable meyne wey is best for [u]s alle'), that the narrator is as determined to circumscribe excellence as he is cruelty or dullness. It is a powerfully oppressive discourse; and it can conceive of 'non argument'. But that does not necessarily mean that its hegemony was assured. The freedom to 'turne over the leef' was not the prerogative of Chaucer's readers alone;[51] the aesthetic and ideological competition that animates the *Canterbury Tales* is not very different from the principle that governs the interplay between the divergent texts that make up a household miscellany. Aristotle would scarcely have had his pupil's undivided attention; if indeed, sandwiched between advice on how to baptize a child cut from its dying mother's belly and a month-by-month account of the significance of thunder, he had it all.

Most of the limited scholarship on household manuscripts and women's reading has, to date, focused exclusively on their devotional and didactic content. For some scholars, in fact, the equation of women with domestic piety, in particular with elementary devotional instruction, is sufficiently complete that the inclusion of basic

---

doing so convincingly challenges Downing's (1969) earlier assumption that it was a clerical commonplace book. Meale's evidence, in the absence of any marks of ownership, is the suggestive overlap between the contents of CUL Ff.5.48 and a range of MSS more securely identified with later medieval lay households. There was, of course, no impenetrable divide between clerical and lay ownership, as William Revetour's bequests to the Boltons suggests; it is possible that one or more of the individual booklets that make up CUL Ff.4.58 were once owned by a cleric. What is important here, however, is that the manuscript readily represents the kinds of textual material readily available in lay households in the 15th cent.

49 Blanchfield (1991: 82–6); Boffey and Thompson (1989: 297).
50 The quotations are taken from the CUL Ff.5.48 version of the 'ABC of Aristotle' (fos. 8ᵛ–9).
51 Chaucer (1988), 'The Miller's Prologue', l. 3177.

religious texts among a miscellany's contents is itself evidence for a female readership. When Sharon Michalove posits the so-called Book of Brome (New Haven, Yale University, Beinecke Library, MS 365), a late fifteenth-century miscellany belonging to a Suffolk gentry family, as a 'spur to [women's] literacy', she uses its devotional contents—'the religious literature favoured in households'—to infer a woman reader eager to use the collection's prayers, saint's life, and catechetical material for her own edification and for the education of her household.[52] And in many ways, of course, the scholarly consensus must be right. There is no reason to think that women like Margaret Blackburn and Alice Bolton would not have been genuinely interested in the affective and penitential piety that characterizes CUL Ff.5.48's assorted religious texts: three Marian lyrics and a miracle story; copies of both the *Northern* and *Southern Passion*; a verse on the wounds of Christ as a remedy for the seven deadly sins; and two cautionary exempla (*The Adulterous Falmouth Squire* and *The Tale of the Incestuous Daughter*) preoccupied with the consequences of sexual misconduct within the household.

What we must not assume, however, is that women's interests were *restricted* to a manuscript's devotional or didactic content. What makes the household miscellany such an important site for thinking about medieval women's literate practice is that the very logic that identifies them with a manuscript's 'religious literature' demands, at the same time, that we admit them access to a much greater diversity of texts than is normally allowed. One of the most distinctive features of household books is their almost systematic inclusion of precisely the kind of material—social criticism, political complaint, vulgar comedy, and erotic verse—that we almost never imagine being read or talked about by respectable lay women. The contents of CUL Ff.5.48 are instructive. The manuscript contains, alongside its religious material, a version of the *Short Metrical Chronicle*, a series of prognostications, and a not insubstantial body of narrative that is variously comic and/or subversive. *The Tournament of Tottenham* and affiliated *Feast of Tottenham*, both of which use carnival motifs to interrogate familiar aristocratic practices and social values, are only the most well known of the manuscript's secular verse. It also includes a short fabliau, *The Tale of the Basin*, the butt of whose humour is a philandering priest; *The King and the Shepherd*, a social comedy in which a shepherd complains about the injustice of royal expenditure only to discover that his interlocutor is the king; the earliest extant Robin Hood ballad *Robin Hood and the Monk*, with its powerful celebration of outlawry; and one of a small group of extant lyrics in which a young maiden is impregnated, and abandoned, by a cleric.

To return to the 'ubiquitous' primer with which I started: although the primer was never *simply* an elementary reader, the full implications of its function as a tool for teaching women their ABCs have never been properly considered. The 'ABC of Aristotle' posits literacy as a *form of agency*, a practical method of gaining wisdom and social respect ('who so wil to be wyse / and worship desirethe / lette hym lorne oo

---

[52] Michalove (1998: 127).

lettur / and loke on a noþer / off the abc'), that has the capacity to transform people's lives: 'ful ofte þe lernyng of on lettur' 'myȝt amende a men man' 'and his life saue'. Although the verse works hard to delimit the scope of that agency (promoting knowledge of the alphabet as a means of reinforcing established cultural hierarchies), its ambivalence about its own generative potential is telling. Once a woman had mistressed the alphabet, what she could read was circumscribed only by what was available to her. As the evidence of CUL Ff.5.48 and analogous household miscellanies suggests, the literate practice of women like Margaret Blackburn and Alice Bolton was limited neither to their primers nor to the 'ABC of Aristotle' and like-minded texts. In recent years, medievalists have effectively demonstrated how adept women were at exploiting the textual communities that grew up around devotional literature as a means of self-expression, independence, and authority. We must surely credit women with no less ingenuity in using the textual community of the lay household to live out their complex lives.

BIBLIOGRAPHY

A.J.H. (1876), 'Thomas Stotevyle's Books in 1459–60', *Notes and Queries*, 5th ser. 5/124: 386.

ARMSTRONG, C. A. J. (1942), 'The Piety of Cecily, Duchess of York', in D. Woodruff (ed.), *For Hilaire Belloc: Essays in Honour of his 72nd Birthday* (London: Sheed & Ward), 73–94.

ASHLEY, KATHLEEN M., and PAMELA SHEINGORN (1990), 'Introduction', to Kathleen M. Ashley and Pamela Sheingorn (eds.), *Interpreting Cultural Symbols: Saint Anne in Late Medieval Society* (Athens, Ga.: University of Georgia Press).

BELL, SUSAN GROAG (1982), 'Medieval Women Book Owners: Arbiters of Lay Piety and Ambassadors of Culture', *Signs* 7: 742–68.

BLANCHFIELD, L. S. (1991), 'The Romances in Ashmole 61: An Idiosyncratic Scribe', in Maldwyn Mills, Jennifer Fellows, and Carole M. Meale (eds.), *Romance in Medieval England* (Cambridge: Boydell & Brewer), 65–87.

BOFFEY, JULIA (2000), 'Bodleian Library, MS Arch. Selden. B. 24 and Definitions of the Household Book', in A. S. G. Edwards, V. Gillespie, and R. Hanna (eds.), *The English Medieval Book: Studies in Memory of Jeremy Griffiths* (London: British Library), 125–34.

—— and JOHN J. THOMPSON (1989), 'Anthologies and Miscellanies: Production and Choice of Texts', in Jeremy Griffiths and Derek Pearsall (eds.), *Book Production and Publishing in Britain 1375–1475* (Cambridge: Cambridge University Press), 279–315.

CAVANAUGH, SUSAN H. (1980), 'A Study of Books Privately Owned in England: 1300–1450', doctoral dissertation, University of Pennsylvania.

CAXTON, W. (tr.) (1971), *The Book of the Knight of the Tower*, ed. M. Y. Offord (EETS SS 2; London: Early English Text Society).

CHAUCER, GEOFFREY (1988), *The Riverside Chaucer* (3rd ed.), ed. Larry D. Benson (Oxford: Oxford University Press).

CLANCHY, M. T. (1984), 'Learning to Read in the Middle Ages and the Role of Mothers', in Greg Brooks and A. K. Pugh (eds.), *Studies in the History of Reading* (Reading: University of Reading School of Education), 33–9.

—— (1993), *From Memory to Written Record: England 1066–1307* (2nd edn. Oxford: Blackwell).

CULLUM, PATRICIA, and P. J. P. GOLDBERG (2000), 'How Margaret Blackburn Taught her Daughters: Reading Devotional Instruction in a Book of Hours', in J. Wogan-Browne, R. Voaden, A. Diamond, A. Hutchinson, C. Meale, and L. Johnson (eds.), *Medieval Women: Texts and Contexts in Late Medieval Britain: Essays for Felicity Riddy* (Turnhout: Brepols), 217–36.

DENLEY, MARIE (1990), 'Elementary Teaching Techniques and Middle English Religious Didactic Writing', in H. Phillips (ed.), *Langland, the Mystics, and the Medieval Religious Tradition: Essays in Honour of S. S. Hussey* (Woodbridge: Boydell & Brewer), 223–41.

DONOVAN, CLAIRE (1991), *The de Brailes Hours: Shaping the Book of Hours in Thirteenth-Century Oxford* (London: British Library).

DOUGLASS, FREDERICK (1845), *Narrative of the Life of Frederick Douglass, an American Slave, Written by Himself* (Boston: Anti-Slavery Office).

DOWNING, J. Y. (1969), 'A Critical Edition of Cambridge University MS Ff.5.48', doctoral dissertation, University of Washington.

DUFFY, EAMON (2005), *The Stripping of the Altars: Traditional Religion in England 1400–1580* (2nd edn. New Haven: Yale University Press).

ELLIS, ROGER (ed.) (1987), *The Liber Celestis of St. Bridget of Sweden*, i (EETS OS 291; Oxford: Oxford University Press).

ERLER, MARY C. (1999), 'Devotional Literature', in L. Hellinga and J. B. Trapp (eds.), *The Cambridge History of the Book in Britain, iii. 1400–1557* (Cambridge: Cambridge University Press), 495–525.

FURNIVALL, F. J. (ed.) (1868), *The Boke of Curtasye* in *The Babees Book* (EETS OS 32; London: Kegan Paul, Trench, Trübner & Co.).

——(1882), *The Fifty Earliest English Wills* (EETS OS 78; Oxford: Oxford University Press).

FURROW, MELISSA M. (ed.) (1985), *Ten Fifteenth-Century Comic Poems* (New York: Garland).

GEE, E. A. (1969), 'The Painted Glass of All Saints Church, North Street, York', *Archaeologia*, 102: 151–202.

GIBBONS, ALFRED (ed.) (1888), *Early Lincoln Wills: An abstract of all the wills and administrations recorded in the episcopal registers of the old diocese of Lincoln* (Lincoln: James Williamson).

GOLDBERG, P. J. P. (1994), 'Lay Book Ownership in Late Medieval York: The Evidence of Wills', *The Library: Transactions of the Bibliographical Society*, 6th ser. 16 (1994): 181–9.

——(2008), 'The Fashioning of Bourgeois Domesticity in Later Medieval England: A Material Culture Perspective', in M. Kowaleski and P. J. P. Goldberg (eds.), *Medieval Domesticity: Home, Housing and Household in Medieval England* (Cambridge: Cambridge University Press), 124–44.

JOHNSTON, ALEXANDRA F. (1975), 'The Plays of the Religious Guilds of York: The Creed Play and the Pater Noster Play', *Speculum*, 50: 55–90.

KER, NEIL (1969–2002), *Medieval Manuscripts in British Libraries* (4 vols. Oxford: Clarendon Press).

KRUG, REBECCA (2002), *Reading Families: Women's Literate Practice in Late Medieval England* (Ithaca, NY: Cornell University Press).

LATHUILLÈRE, ROGER (1966), *Guiron le courtois: Ètude de la tradition manuscrite et analyse critique* (Geneva: Droz).

LITTLEHALES, HENRY (1895), *The Prymer or Lay Folks' Prayer Book* (EETS OS 105; London: K. Paul, Trench, Trübner & Co.).

MEALE, CAROL M. (1996), 'Reading Women's Culture in Fifteenth-Century England: The Case of Alice Chaucer', in Piero Boitani and Anna Torti (eds.), *Mediaevalitas: Reading the Middle Ages* (Cambridge: Boydell & Brewer), 81–101.

MEALE, CAROL M. (2001), 'Romance and its Anti-Type: *The Turnament of Totenham*, the Carnivalesque, and Popular Culture', in A. J. Minnis (ed.), *Middle English Poetry: Texts and Traditions. Essays in Honour of Derek Pearsall* (York: York Medieval Press), 103–27.

MEYER, PAUL (1903), 'Les Manuscrits français de Cambridge, III Trinity College', *Romania*, 32: 18–120.

MICHALOVE, SHARON D. (1998), 'The Education of Aristocratic Women in Fifteenth-Century England', in S. D. Michalove and A. C. Reeves (eds.), *Estrangement, Enterprise and Education in Fifteenth Century England* (Stroud: Sutton Publishing), 117–39.

Middle English Dictionary (1954–2001), ed. Hans Kurath and Robert E. Lewis (Ann Arbor: University of Michigan Press).

NORTON, CHRISTOPHER DAVID PARK, and PAUL BINSKI (1987), *Dominican Painting in East Anglia: The Thornton Parva Retable and the Musée de Cluny Frontal* (Woodbridge: Boydell & Brewer).

ORME, NICHOLAS (2001), *Medieval Children* (New Haven: Yale University Press).

PENKETH, SANDRA (1997), 'Women and Books of Hours', in L. Smith and J. M. H. Taylor (eds.), *Women and the Book: Assessing the Visual Evidence* (London: British Library), 266–81.

RAINE, J. (ed.) (1855), *Testamenta Eboracensia*, ii (Publications of the Surtees Society, 30; Durham: Surtees Society).

RAYNAUD, GASTON (ed.) (1894), *Œuvres complètes d'Eustache Deschamps*, ix (Paris: SATF).

REES JONES, SARAH, and FELICITY RIDDY (2000), 'The Bolton Hours of York: Female Domestic Piety and the Public Sphere', in Anneke Mulder-Bakke and Jocelyn Wogan-Browne (eds.), *Women and the Christian Tradition* (Turnhout: Brepols), 215–60.

RIDDY, FELICITY (1993), ' "Women Talking about the Things of God": A Late Medieval Sub-Culture', in C. M. Meale (ed.), *Women and Literature in Britain, 1150–1500* (Cambridge: Cambridge University Press), 104–27.

RUST, MARTHA DANA (2007), *Imaginary Worlds in Medieval Books: Exploring the Manuscript Matrix* (New York: Palgrave Macmillan).

SALIH, SARAH (2003), 'At Home, Out of the House', in C. Dinshaw and D. Wallace (eds.), *The Cambridge Companion to Medieval Women's Writing* (Cambridge: Cambridge University Press), 124–40.

SCASE, WENDY (1993), 'St Anne and the Education of the Virgin: Literary and Artistic Traditions and their Implications', in N. Rogers (ed.), *England in the Fourteenth Century: Proceedings of the 1991 Harlaxton Symposium* (Stamford, Lincs.: P. Watkins), 81–96.

SCOTT, KATHLEEN L. (1996), *Later Gothic Manuscripts, 1390–1490* (2 vols. London: Miller).

SHEINGORN, PAMELA (1993), ' "The Wise Mother": The Image of St Anne Teaching the Virgin Mary', *Gesta*, 31: 69–80.

SKEAT, W. W. (ed.) (1906), 'Nominale sive verbale', *Transactions of the Philological Society, 1903–06* (London): 1*–50*.

SMITH, KATHRYN A. (2003), *Art, Identity, and Devotion in Fourteenth-Century England: Three Women and their Books of Hours* (London: British Library).

STOCK, BRIAN (1983), *The Implications of Literacy: Written Language and Models of Interpretation in the Eleventh and Twelfth Centuries* (Princeton: Princeton University Press).

TOLKEIN, J. R. R., and E. V. GORDON (eds.) (1967), *Sir Gawain and the Green Knight* (2nd edn.), ed. N. Davis (Oxford: Clarendon Press).

WOGAN-BROWNE, JOCELYN (2002), 'Analytical Survey: "Reading is Good Prayer". Recent Research on Female Reading Communities', *New Medieval Literatures*, 5: 229–97.

CHAPTER 10

PERFORMING COMMUNITIES

CIVIC RELIGIOUS DRAMA

JOHN J. MCGAVIN

PERFORMING THE MEDIEVAL

In 2008 the city of Winchester put on a Passion Play.[1] It was performed in sections at different locations, progressing from an open field in the suburbs to the Great Hall at the Westgate, then through the High Street and finally to the Cathedral. It did not seek to be an authentic representation of a medieval performance; in any case, unlike York and Chester but like most other towns in England, medieval Winchester never played an extensive collection of biblically based plays.[2] Nonetheless, it had much in common with the medieval genre, not least in having to engage with civic authority, audience expectation and size, and the physical and symbolic characteristics of the available playing sites.[3] Its timing, an early and rather cold Easter, though situating the play in the liturgical year, really reflected a modern need to tie religious events to the liturgical occasion that most people, including non-Christians, would consider

---

[1] Indy Almroth-Wright and Stephen Stafford, from a text by Philip Glassborow. For further information see <http://www.bbc.co.uk/hampshire/content/articles/2007/07/12/winchesterpassion_feature.shtml>.

[2] For Winchester's playing history, see Cowling and Greenfield (2008).

[3] Medieval playing sites varied considerably in their size and nature, whether within or outside towns. See White (2000); Stokes (2003–4).

appropriate to its content. While liturgy certainly informed the content of medieval civic religious play,[4] this restrictive linking of narrative to the liturgical year was not favoured for outdoor playing of biblical history, when festivals in June or July such as Corpus Christi, Whitsuntide, or Midsummer were preferred whatever the topic. However, the sensitivity of the performance date to cultural pressure was indeed a medieval issue: shifts in a town's traditional playing time usually signified real or desired change in relative power within the community. Alexandra F. Johnston has shown, for example, how Exeter town tried to prise the Skinners' Craft play away from its episcopal connection with Corpus Christi and towards the town's Whitsun festival.[5]

The Winchester Passion's acting styles and theatrical traditions were not and could not be purely medieval: modern Winchester could have a black Christ; medieval English towns could not; Winchester had a complete acting profession to choose from, rather than simply those excellent local actors who were professional in the sense of being able to command a higher fee for their performance, mixed with participants, like musicians, whose special skills were transferable across the institutional boundaries which divided the performing communities.[6] Most obviously, the Winchester event was distinctly modern because its spectators were. Medieval spectators saw the civic religious drama as emerging from, or alluding to, a broad matrix of generically related forms of play and public ceremony which they could experience on other occasions, such as royal entries, folk play and custom, heraldic announcements, contemporary games, processions, public punishment, liturgy and religious ritual including the Mass. Modern spectators carry different generic maps in their heads, and hence one can never know how closely attempts at updating or authenticity (or mixing the two) bring us towards the experience of those in the past.

On the other hand, the Winchester event was wholly 'medieval' in many ways: in matching its scope to the capacity of the providers and the occasion; its mixed clerical and lay involvement; its processional form; its blending of biblical and imagined discourse, stylized and naturalistic acting, historical and contemporary reference, received and innovative iconography. Had it also chosen to borrow ('plagiarize' as we might now say) plays or episodes from, for example, the Manchester Passion of 2006 or the York Mystery Plays, re-established first in the Festival of Britain 1951,[7] grafting them with varying degrees of skill onto its own stock, it would have been even closer to the practice in the Middle Ages, when such cross-community transference of cultural materials seems to have been quite regular, especially in the Midlands and north of England.[8] Recent scholarship has argued persuasively for 'creative mobility'

---

[4] See e.g. King (2006).

[5] Johnston (2003: 27). For examples of the symbolic significance of playing sites and times, see Mills (1998), esp. 'Time and Space in Tudor Chester', pp. 20–38.

[6] For examples of the different categories of paid, unpaid, and paying players who might be involved in such a performance, see King and Davidson (2000: 22–3). For musical performers see Rastall (1996, 2001).

[7] For modern traditions of playing medieval see Rogerson (2007).

[8] The most significant visible borrowings link the York and Chester cycles, the remaining Coventry plays, and the Towneley collection. However, the direction, directness, dating, and motivation of borrowing are much harder to establish. See Beadle and Fletcher (2008: 133, 164–7).

rather than 'provincial isolation' as the typical cultural matrix for producing early drama, and such movement can be demonstrated at different theatrical levels from individual literary motifs to complete plays.[9] This means that play material may be judged 'local' to a community by its adoption, rather than by its creation, whether it was assimilated to existing drama or not.

In a more fundamental way, the Winchester play was a clear continuation of medieval practice: it publicly performed the identity of the town, using the corporate achievement of the plays, together with their content, to present Winchester as a commercially vibrant, regional centre of Christian ideology, and as a unified and vigorous community. Such performativity characterized medieval civic playing at all levels, and in this respect the drama was not the natural, far less inevitable, product of a pre-existing community, but one of the means by which a group constructed itself as a community in its own eyes and also persuaded others of its distinct identity. Viewed thus, the longevity of the genre appears less conservative and more like a reiterated exercise of assertion.

One can still detect in the modern event those mixed elements of Christian belief, communal celebration, aesthetic fashion, financial interest, desire for civic visibility, and institutional curiosity (once clerical, now academic) which characterized the medieval, even if their relative proportions have altered. However, historicizing this genre of socially performative drama in its original contexts is unusually difficult. The manuscripts in which the texts have come down to us vary widely: in their dates, though most now seem to belong to the period after the 1450s; in their association with a particular location (and why that might matter); in their relationship to performance, and in the various motives behind their construction. Dating the composition, or indeed performance, of the *plays* contained in the manuscripts is highly elusive. The versions which remain are, in Chester's case, the legacy of post-performance antiquarianism and reflect late revision;[10] the York texts on the other hand are closely related to mid-fifteenth-century performance. The N-Town collection seems to have been a late fifteenth- or early sixteenth-century East Anglian anthology, which fashioned historical coverage out of extended plays designed for separate performances. The Towneley manuscript's date has shifted forward by about a hundred and twenty years during the last thirty years of scholarship; its relationship to Wakefield, the traditionally assumed location of its plays, is highly arguable, and while it may carry evidence of links to performance, it is not throughout a manuscript *for* performance.[11] The famed Coventry cycle, extant in just two of its plays, can only be plausibly reconstructed in its mid-sixteenth-century form, and like the 'Norwich Grocers' Play' and the 'Newcastle Play', exists only in later transcription.[12] Many other plays, lacking texts, are known only from the traces of performance

---

[9] Palmer (2005: 292).

[10] An excellent example of close study in this area is Mills (2007).

[11] These and other difficulties are exactingly worked through by the specialist contributors to Beadle and Fletcher (2008: *passim*).

[12] King and Davidson (2000: 9); Davis (1970).

collected in the Records of Early English Drama volumes.[13] Furthermore, revision of the plays evidently took place throughout their lifespan, but where it is detectable, suggests a normative process at some times, innovation at other times, and the provision of alternative plays at others. Nor do apparent generic affinities help to fix a play's date since authors, as well as revisers, drew on existing models at the same time as adding new material. The same play can thus appear late fifteenth- or mid-sixteenth-century depending on what one looks at. For example, the iconically medieval 'Second Shepherds' Play', from a manuscript now dated to the Marian period, seems medieval when one looks at the traditional scene of the adoration of the child, but its innovatory content, the Mak and Gyl episode, fits most of the generic markers adduced for later sixteenth-century domestic comedy.[14]

Dolly Parton once said, 'it costs a lot of money to look this cheap'. It has taken a lot of dedicated scholarly work and much medieval-style enactment over the last fifty years to make the civic religious drama of the Middle Ages look as complicated as it does today. But from that process has come a more sophisticated appreciation of why communities performed it, and performed themselves through it. Views on this are extremely diverse, but all have cogency, and all can be supported from the evidence of play text or performance record, not to mention studies of how play works in contemporary societies. At one end of the spectrum is the position that medieval civic playing enabled its communities to acquire cohesion and a distinctive identity.[15] Practically, plays were known to bring financial benefit to the community and this could ensure the survival of a medieval tradition against reformation pressures.[16] But equally, they may have been intended to sustain a community emotionally over time. Clifford Davidson has suggested that the civic plays 'represent a communal project for maintaining the cultural memory of events in salvation history seen to be immensely comforting to the people'.[17] On the other hand, Rosalind Conklin Hays, looking at Sherborne in Dorset, sees diachronic *discontinuity* and opposition between clerical and lay groups, concluding that Sherborne's 'Corpus Christi festivals seem an expression of different versions of community at the different stages in the town's history.'[18] James Stokes has found evidence for both trends: while in Lincoln, guild and church cooperated in jointly sponsoring the St Anne's day play, in Somerset, drama was itself a resistance to imposed ideas of community.[19] Between these two positions, Mary A. Blackstone has argued convincingly, from the example of the town of Leicester, that performance was 'an intertextual site for the negotiation of community'.[20] All these configurations of this community drama may be true. One could argue that many were true simultaneously. A cursory glance at the records reveals that, while playing might argue for corporate convergence in an urban

[13] REED's many (and growing) publications of original source material and interpretative study can be found at <http://www.reed.utoronto.ca/index.html>.

[14] (Wall 1998) The Folger Library's 2007 colloquium on the *Second Shepherds Play* reached no final agreed date for its composition.

[15] See e.g. Clopper (2001: 137).   [16] Gibson and Harvey (2000: 219).

[17] Davidson (2006: 25).   [18] Hays (1994: 115).

[19] Stokes (2003–4: 282; 1994).   [20] Blackstone (2004: 75).

community, through the combined efforts needed to authorize, finance, and perform the same event, it was rarely uninflected by a hierarchical differentiation between groups, expressed either through the processions which were often linked to urban religious playing or through the capacity of particular groups to represent their wealth and power in the *materiel* of the performance. The author of the Chester 'Post-Reformation Banns' reveals this in a comment on the town's play of the 'Adoration of the Magi':

> And you worshippfull Mercers, though costely and fyne
> Yee tryme up your carriage as custome ever was,
> Yet in a stable was He borne, that mighty Kinge Devyne,
> Poorely in a stable betwixte an oxe and an asse.[21]

Given Chester's theological focus on signs and their interpretation, this offers fascinating insight into the paradox of expressing faith along with group identity, and, more importantly, reflects a viewer's experience of that paradox. While playing could thus be a means of visibly asserting distinctions between groups, it was also a way of ensuring some form of visibility where power was lacking. Denise Ryan's important study of the Chester Wives, who sponsored but did not play in the Assumption play, shows that involvement in the corporate enterprise, by offering support to the status quo, effectively mitigated the group's customary exclusion from power structures, and confirmed its honourable place within the community, albeit indirectly. In Ryan's view communal play here is a form of tribute to local power, and while this fits well with Chester's other public ceremonies, in which formal tributes took place, it is a salutary reminder that civic religious drama was often a site of more or less disguised compromise.[22] The coexistence of divergent, or even opposed, impulses in the putting on of play must have been an inevitable feature of communal activity, where individual and group interests could only be satisfied through a corporate effort involving others who might have different goals, let alone capacities. Once achieved, a communal event would not necessarily have had the same meaning for all the participants, and the compromises necessary to effect it probably had to continue when judging its success. Community is not a given fact; it is something which is *always* 'in the making' through the perceptions (and resulting action) of those who are its potential members.

THE SHOW MUST GO ON

Medieval civic religious drama was a show offered by and to people who were themselves on show. The actors may have had the additional pleasure of presenting

---

[21] Lines 108–11, in Walker (2000: 203). See also disputes over precedence in Scottish Corpus Christi processions in Mill (1924).
[22] Ryan (2001: 169).

themselves metamorphosed, but everyone, including the actors, knew that the event was an opportunity to be seen by others in one's 'true' colours. Before any play performance took place, communities were already performing themselves for the spectatorship of their fellows in environments where power, tradition, and chance had differentiated groups within the larger community. These were shown through the process of production in which ordering, sponsoring, supervising, and producing the plays required different degrees and kinds of power, and secondly, through the physical geography of the playing area. Attempts to vary the traditional playing sites, which have been found in the York records, were less aimed at getting a better view than at reconfiguring the visible groupings in the audience to reveal new financial power and influence, just as the traditional playing sites had made other institutions prominent.[23] Spectators declared their privileged communal identity, and fostered such a construction in the minds of others, by their physical location at the play. In large civic playing, where the same play might be performed several times through the city, local communities defined by parish or by trade or craft affinity would also have been visible at the different playing sites. Even single performances of plays, probably the more widespread practice in smaller towns, would have been marked by the distinctness of the groups involved. It is now relatively rare for spectators to come to a play already sorted by distinct affinities of origin, family, profession, or power in such predictable and visible ways as to offer opportunities for the playwright to use that knowledge, though there are exceptions. It can be safely inferred from the records that medieval audiences showed greater differentiation and, more importantly, recognized this distinctness in each other—just as at modern football matches the same large 'community' of supporters is actually made up of people who differ in their sense of communal identity, and their understanding of the grounds for their identity, but who differ most visibly in whether, and how, they perform their identity publicly before the others who are engaged in the same communal event.

Late medieval theories of vision emphasize the viewer as the potent origin of sight, and a corresponding concern for how one might be seen in real situations shows up in clerical advice literature.[24] The same anxiety is evident in the administrative records of towns and guilds, which record punishments when people refused to perform their identity publicly, for example at the events which advertised the relative power of groups within the community. The rhetoric of public 'performing' in this wider sense was almost certainly defensive as much as demonstrative. One needs no imagination to appreciate that for groups without power safety lay in obvious numbers, and for groups who felt in competition for resources, visibility was essential. Yet maintaining a successful community meant that all were, to a degree, mutually dependent, and so no one was exempt from the need to secure their

---

[23] York's *A/Y Memorandum Book* for 1417 states that play should occur 'before the doors' of those who have contributed most financially, thereby contributing more to the communal good. Johnston and Rogerson (1979: ii. 714). Normington (2009) shows the importance of play's physical contexts for judging spectator response.

[24] For a work which combines both the theoretical and practical dimensions of this issue, see Denery (2005).

position publicly. Hence, while kings did not need to take the advice they were given, they were expected to go through the motions of listening. Equally, authorities, through visibly participating in a community event, had taken the first step towards defusing any criticism of them that it might be thought to offer.

Modern spectators do not think of those who have licensed or perhaps even initiated dramatic performance as necessarily, significantly, or even willingly, present, though they do expect such attendance at high-profile sporting competitions. The proper analogy for medieval plays is with this latter group of events. Medieval spectators would have expected that the different communities in the audience, especially those differentiated by power and wealth, would be seeking to make their identity known at, and through, civic religious play. This emerges most prominently from records which show authorities, aristocratic visitors, and wealthier groups watching the outdoor theatre from reserved seating in institutional buildings, or above gateways which demarcated areas of legal jurisdiction, or merely in specially rented rooms overlooking the street performance. By making their spectatorship appear special to the rest of the medieval civic community, they both circumscribed the potential licence of the play by making visible the existing hierarchy of power and signalled that there was a limit to any potentially damaging application to them of the play's message. Their separateness was declared by their specific choice of location, their distance from the action, and their freedom to enjoy other activities, such as corporate feasting. High-status spectators thus reserved the right to increase or decrease the overtness of the patronage which their attendance implied, and depending on position, they determined whether they would choose to view the action, how it would appear to them, and also offered themselves as an alternative spectacle worthy of the spectator's gaze. The power which had permitted them to demonstrate a distinct identity within the communal event potentially distanced them from any elements in it of which they would disapprove. As a corollary, this probably helped to protect the performers from any accusation that their playing was personally directed. In a play event, public recognition that the material *might* apply to oneself is tantamount to admitting the justice of the charge, as Hamlet knew when he staged the Mousetrap. Indeed, it *creates* the charge out of what is literally a fiction—something made up. If Claudius had acted the part of the royal spectator, apparently enjoying the show, meeting any gaze from his fellow spectators unflinchingly, rewarding the players, and praising their morality, his own play might have ended better. Civic religious drama undoubtedly engaged with real community issues but whether political applications were felt, far less publicly acknowledged, depended on the local subtleties of spectatorship in a context of general public performativity.

Medieval playwrights powerfully exploited the range of potential identities and communities, which they knew were latent in their spectators, who, despite their relative invisibility to modern scholars, made up the bulk of the performing 'community'.[25] To understand how this worked, however, one has to appreciate that

---

[25] Audience response can be inferred from texts like the *A Tretise of Miraclis Pleyinge*, edited in Davidson (1993); Walker (2000: 196–200, extracts). See also Carpenter (forthcoming).

individual spectators were and are always already potential members of several different communities; that awareness of particular membership can be enhanced or repressed; and that they bring this potential to the theatrical event, which itself then creates another community.

With little access to the feelings of medieval spectators, one has to use the evidence of the play texts themselves to see how community was exploited. These texts suggest that it was the understood *responsibility* of authors, most of whom probably had clerical status or some form of clerical education, to manipulate the spectators' awareness of belonging to particular communities, by raising difficult issues, permitting fractures in society and potential fissures between communities to be glimpsed so that they could be theatrically controlled, harmonized through affect, and hopefully resolved in the authorized ideology of Christian belief. For example, Sheila K. Christie has shown how the authors of the Coventry plays used their historical subject-matter to engage with contemporary anxiety about the town's ageing government, but did so sympathetically 'by participating in a contemporary conversation about the future of Coventry's civic structure rather than didactically imposing a solution to the crisis'.[26] In this further, and more deeply literary, sense, civic religious drama 'performed community' by making it *thematically* central, strategizing its known aspects in order to achieve particular local ends which were first theatrical, but potentially constituted interventions in the community's non-theatrical life. Before embarking on specific examples, however, it is worth considering how provisional and fluctuating the spectator's sense of community can be, dependent as it often is on the spectator's sense of being seen by others. An example from contemporary experience may help.

THE SHARED EXPERIENCE

Even if most people arrived at the Winchester Passion individually or in nucleated groups, the very actions of walking together between play sites and watching in a group quickly created a sense of shared cultural work, rather than mere cultural 'consumption'. The sense of a theatrical community developed, predicated on active commitment to the event, even if the crowd and geography meant that many spectators could actually see nothing at the first site. It was the watching which made the community, not the spectacle. But awareness of even that community could fluctuate in strength. When the first play had ended, spectators moving to the next site did so notionally as members of a theatrical community but, depending on their speed of movement, the distance and route chosen, and the width of the road, physical separation from each other began to pull against this awareness. Operating

---

[26] Christie (2008: 14).

to reinforce it, however, was the surprising fact that the spectators had themselves taken on a group identity in the eyes of others: as they spilled out in their hundreds over the roads closed to traffic, they were watched by a substantial number of people standing two-deep on the pavements. For this second group, the original spectators appeared to have a common purpose; they had shared an experience (or it was believed that they had) which the second group had either missed or not sought; they were evidently 'licensed' in their communal identity by the freedom to move along carriageways. They had become a processional spectacle in their own right: apparently possessed of a communal identity, which was in reality only provisional, and probably credited by the onlooker with a more secure awareness of that communal identity than was the case. However, spectators who became conscious of themselves as the object of others' gaze by virtue of their assumed membership of a community felt their attenuating sense of that community strengthened as a consequence.

However much people may perform their identities publicly, they do not carry around with them an active sense of all the communities to which they potentially belong. Rather, awareness of belonging or of exclusion is stimulated from outside: by moments in the plays themselves, and by the performative displays, enquiring gaze, judgemental comments, or even just the community of other individuals and groups. In context a sense of particular identity can even derive from self-consciousness, without any active external prompting. A medieval visitor to York's plays would have come as one of the community of the faithful; perhaps they felt additionally intimate with the experience, having seen such plays before, or traded with the citizens. However, as soon as they recognized those who were patently inhabitants of York, membership of one community would have been overlaid by a sense of exclusion from another. Citizens could possess a secure pride of local ownership over this potentially universal Christian experience; the visitor was a 'foreigner' (in the medieval sense of being from another town), and could only feel temporarily adopted or disguised as a local. An appreciation of how one *might* be seen by other spectators can thus direct the spectator's consciousness of identity within community, and create a framework for their response to the play. This applies to all aspects of the spectator's potential identities, not just the obvious distinction between being a local or a visitor.

The fluctuations in identity which showed up in this modern performance invite its study in medieval civic theatrical contexts. It can be assumed that most medieval spectators came to such plays with at least a dormant sense of their various possible identities, and with a susceptibility to thinking of themselves as members of specific communities. The memory of these identities, which they brought into the playing space, could be subsequently activated by moments in the plays as the event progressed. Identities based on things such as their loyalty to specific forms of Christian devotion (e.g. a particular cultic piety), family, parish, craft or profession, status, allegiance, origin, gender, age, office, and so on, could all be subsequently exploited by the play. They were not discrete, but could be overlaid on each other or opposed to each other by the demands of the play, and they were all potentially inflected by the individual's most immediate sense of identity—as a spectator of the theatrical event—and membership of the most evident community: the audience. Equally, this theatrical community would have comprised spectators who felt exclusion from the non-theatrical communities of their fellows either *ab initio* or at points in the play. For example, what would children have taken from the repeated 'adult' jokes based on Joseph's doubting the Virgin Mary's honesty? How would visitors have felt about Christ's blurring York and the Holy City in the Entry to Jerusalem? How would an ordinary Cestrian have felt realizing that the town's cycle of plays contained a whole strand of scholarly textual reference which could only be enjoyed by clerics and was specifically intended for their amusement? If a Jewish merchant attended any local play with a Christian friend, which does not seem impossible given the communities of Jews who lived in or traded with England, would its content have repelled him, confirmed him in his sense of his own identity, or pleased him, or indeed done all of these things, and if all, could these sensations not have been simultaneous? Communal drama inevitably reveals the heterogeneity of community.

To understand medieval drama is therefore to look at the ways it managed audiences, moving the spectators through a range of their possible identities, sometimes to their pleasure and sometimes to their discomfiture, switching on and off their sense of the communities of which these identities made them potential members. It is through the evidence of how plays manipulated the susceptibilities of spectators that one comes closest to appreciating what made this form of playing so successful for so long. While many in medieval audiences would have taken pleasure from the biblical plays because they were Christian in ideology and authorized by tradition, one has to suppose that civic religious playing of the Middle Ages lasted as long as it did because it also had enough theatrical power to engage its audiences in a more dynamic way over a long period. One dimension of that power can be located in its exploitation of identity and community. All events are experienced differently by those who see them; the medieval drama of community had to make a virtue of this, and did.

It is easier for the modern critic to identify from the text of medieval plays their theatrical changes of mode, for example from the didactic to the affective, or of mood, for example from the comic to the penitential, than it is to acknowledge how these shifts might have been experienced by the spectators. Particularly helpful in this regard is the notion of theatrical complicity. Put simply, medieval spectators were encouraged by a range of theatrical means, such as focused or flamboyant action, risibility, direct address, visual appeal, exciting language, and so on, to concentrate on, and to enjoy, portrayals of evil behaviour so that they could feel the moral correction of subsequent shifts in tone. The *locus classicus* for this is provided by the York crucifixion play, during most of which Christ would have been invisible to those spectators standing in the street, the play's tone being established by the actions and banter of the soldiers until the moment when the cross is raised and a shift is effected towards the lyrical, devotional, and visually contemplative. While complicity is certainly an important moral force in medieval spectatorship, I feel it must be inflected by notions of community, and of the multiple identities a spectator can feel within community, if a proper balance is to be found between the moral responsibility of the individual, frequently asserted in the plays, and the reality of spectating, which contains the possibility of subversion and of finally uncontrolled responses. Didacticism has to be nuanced by the context of reception; not identified as a particular way of speaking or as an inevitably corrective sequencing of events. Plays on the biblical episode of the Slaughter of the Innocents show well how this could work in practice.

The York version is especially revealing because its theatrical strategies are so transparently designed to create specific responses. It begins with Herod challenging spectators to accept membership of a new fictive community—his subjects—and to show their membership by obediently remaining silent for fear of punishment.[27] This is in effect an invitation to backchat from the spectators and is an encouragement to them to disobey 'authority'. It promises just that turmoil for which the motif of Herod's anger was famous and which the audience would have been looking forward to. On the other hand, it immediately creates tension in the spectators' desires. As Christians they can loathe Herod, as subjects they are free to despise and reject this king's demands, as spectators they can laugh at him, but as theatre-goers who have come to hear him, they must obey his demand for silence, and implicitly become his people. York also uses this device in reverse during the Passion sequence when a later Herod demands that anyone wishing to testify against Christ should come before his criminal bar and speak. When, understandably, the spectators remain silent, Herod declares that Christ must be returned to Pilate, thereby making the audience implicitly his subjects, and responsible for the unfolding events.[28] The 'Slaughter' playwright ensures that the point is not lost: Herod's counsellor assures him that everyone is 'full fain' to know what his intentions are and no one will 'grudge' against them.[29] Everyone in the audience, of course, already knows his intentions but still wants the play to disclose them. Their mixed motives for watching the coming massacre of children are adumbrated in the mixed identities which they receive at the start. They are complicit in another sense which the playwright exploits. They have come partly to enjoy authority losing control of itself, finally proving impotent. The play thus offers a socially safe, controlled space for their emotional rebellion.[30]

The York counsellor accordingly drip-feeds Herod information about the three kings, who in his report have left, and indeed escaped Herod after locating Christ, honouring him, announcing him as king, and naming him Jesus in accordance with prophecy. It is patently a device to ratchet up Herod's rage and the audience's pleasure. But that pleasure is thus part of the same theatrical mechanism which drives the slaughter of the children. The satisfied, entertained, theatrical community which has vented its social anxieties through safe laughter at power is then

---

[27] The full text of the York cycle is available online through the University of Virginia at <http://www2.lib.virginia.edu/etext/index.html>. Good hard copy editions of the play can be found in Beadle and King (1999) and Beadle (2009).

[28] 'Christ before Herod', ll. 375–83, ibid. 190, or Walker (2000: 121–2).

[29] Ibid., ll. 25–8.

[30] The relevance of carnival theory to medieval drama studies has been recognized for some years. See e.g. Twycross (1996); Eisenbichler and Hüsken (1999).

destabilized by the wider range of responses forced on it by a killing its own spectatorship has indirectly brought about. Inevitably, some spectators will be able to cooperate imaginatively with the action so as to forget that the killed children are dolls, while some will be more conscious of artifice. But other divisions in the theatrical community are productive of social tension: between men and women; between spectators who have children and those who do not; older members of the audience who have experienced disaster and those who have not, or care less. These fissures are opened up by a play which evidently expects the community to contain widely diverse responses, because it encourages them in a rapid succession of pathos, emotional reflection, exciting action, and laughter directed both at the female victims (almost certainly played by men) as they attack the soldiers and at the aggressors. These shifts occur not because the playwright imagines that that was how the event must have occurred, or believes that that is what must be taught, but because he knows that the community of believers for which he is writing needs to feel these things, and the biblical episode can be made productive of them. In this respect a play text is as reliable a guide to the historical responses of spectators as a contemporary description.

This fracturing of theatrical community and, within the individual spectator, the paradox of enjoying horrific play, drew on real social concern with abuse of power, male violence, and the failure of generation (a confluence of issues found also in the contemporary writing of Malory),[31] and it worked on emotions already heightened by Herod's extravagant action and audience laughter. That this was a widely understood goal for dramatizing the episode is shown by the Towneley version.[32] It accompanies its protracted killing with a steady narrative of events from the participants, adding an auxiliary conflict over the soldiers' demands for silence as they kill, and mixing gendered abuse and sadistic humour: 'Dame, thynk it not yll / Thy knafe if I kyll'.[33] Explicit responses to violence from both women and soldiers mingle with pathetic reflection, and overt application to the women in the audience, 'Of wepyng who may blyn, / To se hir chylde forlorne?'[34] To represent this loss as a consequence of violence by men dressed in contemporary soldiers' gear and even mouthing platitudes about chivalry was a challenge to spectators to consider their communal affinities. The loss of children, and as a York mother puts it, of one's only child, must have been an experience which many female spectators had in common.

But the sense of community activated in the spectators by the play may not have been simply defined by gender. The soldiers were, as the York audience had been initially figured to be, Herod's maintained men. Both men and women in the audience could have felt themselves drawn together in opposition to a known source of injustice in medieval society (one explicitly commented on in the second of the two Towneley 'Shepherds' plays). This episode thus moved from a safe ridiculing of power to a much more unsettling criticism of recognizable contemporary abuse. Both dramatic versions studied here finally control the audience's

---

31 See Riddy (2000).   32 'Herod', edited in Stevens and Cawley (1994: i. 183–204).
33 Ibid., ll. 478–9.   34 Ibid., ll. 497–8.

responses—Towneley by turning again to the comic extravagance of Herod's character and York by proposing that the action is not yet over, following Herod's failure to
kill Christ—but this is theatrical control of the theatrical community.

In a genre which drew the biblical past into the spectatorial present, subtly
provisional communities linking specific characters with members of the audience
constantly appeared and faded. At one point male spectators might be reminded that,
as husbands, they were possibly cuckolds, as Joseph believed himself to be, no doubt
in company with men in the audience who had more justification for their fears.
Female spectators were confronted with the stereotypes that they might be harridans
or gossips like Noah's wife or, like the Chester Eve, wo(e)-man. More obviously
exploited than gender divisions were those between the communities of power and
the people beneath them. From Lucifer's attempted usurpation of God through the
story of Christ's Passion, plays teased the spectators by theatrically realizing hidden
fears from the non-theatrical world: making usurpation attractive for a while in the
case of Lucifer; revealing how Christ himself was judged a usurper by his opponents;
and showing the highest clerical and secular authorities at their worst: selfish,
pompous, malicious, lazy, insecure, devious. The audiences contained men who
belonged to these communities of power as well as others who might envy them or
felt injured by them. The Crucifixion plays must have been watched by men who had
authorized public executions (the genre of public action which the York version
strongly evokes), by others who had physically carried them out, and by many who
had gladly attended executions in real life as they were gladly attending this one 'in
play'. Spectators were reminded of their fear that, like the Towneley shepherds, they
were threatened by the tyranny of men above them and by larceny from those below,
or, like many of the Chester characters, that they harboured doubts about the
miraculous signs on which Christian belief was built.

The play world thus permitted the spectators to glimpse, within a realm of
theatrical control, their own potential identities and the implied communities
which went with them, intensifying theatrical effect by sometimes setting one against
another or by figuring the spectators as mere onlookers and then as participants in
the action; as enemies or supporters of particular characters; as willingly seduced by
theatre and yet as owing loyalty far beyond the event itself. Arguably, the plays were
successful not because they were 'quik' (living) books, taking the audience in a vivid
way through Christian history, or even because they updated past events with
the dress of contemporary language, reference, and iconography, though they did
these things, but because they made experiencing the past into an exploration of
the present. Medieval spectators did not only wish to be reminded that they were
Christians when they watched didactic religious drama; they already knew themselves
to be Christians and wanted the plays to bring out the many other things they were.

These performing communities did not seek to perform themselves as fragile. Nor did
they aim to release subversive genies which could not be put back in their bottles.
Nevertheless, they did not avoid performing themselves as fissile. Indeed, they seem to
have exploited this danger, and one can only assume that the different groups which
were involved in the plays, from the playwrights through the performers to the varied

subcommunities of spectators, were all content for this to happen, though perhaps with different expectations of the benefits they would receive. In the last analysis, play is driven by desire, and a performing community is one in which the desires of the different participants are all sufficiently satisfied, or appear to be satisfied, for the communal work of play to occur. For many (and not just the sponsoring authorities or playwrights), exposing the forces of potential disruption in the community, but doing so within the controlled environment of the play, would have been a welcome means of heading them off and naturalizing the status quo. However, one cannot assume that the techniques of control by which these plays recuperated the status quo within the experience of the *theatrical* community actually had this effect beyond the confines of the play itself, leading to the acceptance of social hierarchy, harmony between the sexes, improved levels of Christian belief, a penitentially informed exercise of power, and so on. Rather we should accept the likelihood that in cases such as the Slaughter plays (but not just them) memories of the disruptive, critical, politicized, gendered, emotionally confusing action, with its demonstration of fractured community and its exploitation of that in the spectators' responses, leaked out into the world of the spectators when the play was done, confirming in some the need to hold to what is good but in others the resentment they already felt. After the play all these sensations would become subject to the real constraints of the non-theatrical world.

SPECTATORSHIP

For some spectators, the plays may have satisfied a pathological need to see their anxieties performed. Some possibly even enjoyed the acting out of perverse desires within a process which was communally affirming and limited by occasion. There can be no doubt that there were those whose spectatorship was coloured by more or less ideologically sanctioned sadistic or masochistic impulses, for many plays tapped these responses knowingly, and they are undeniably present in late medieval devotional imagery. Spectators who felt morally challenged by the episodes could examine their consciences while the potential analogies between themselves and the portrayed characters were mitigated by historical distance and fictive mode. Others could use the protection of the plays freely to enjoy their prejudices or show their anger without fear of rebuke. Some aspects of medieval spectators' pleasure are no longer identifiable, having drifted out of our reach along with the identities and communities on which they were based. The attraction of miniature automata, evident in the nine small angels who are made to run about in heaven with a cord in the York 'Doomsday', still has its modern equivalent in the miniature carousels or organs displayed at local festivals.[35] But what in the modern world can help one to recover

---

[35] For this and related forms of play, see Butterworth (2005).

the emotional charge which Cain's plough and its team of 'horses' (presumably men) had in the Towneley 'Murder of Abel'?[36]

> Io furth, Greyhorne! and war oute, Gryme!
> Drawes on, God gif you ill to tyme!
> Ye stand as ye were fallen in swyme.
> What, will ye no forther, mare?
> War! let me se how Down will draw';[37]

When medieval spectators saw him enter the playing area, did they feel themselves in the presence of a mythic figure on whom their society depended for its bread, or the yeoman whom his Boy announces and who speaks as some of them might, or a comic character involved in stage 'business' driving horses which were obviously men, or a figure who was both ploughman and first murderer driving horses which were also men, or a conflation of all of these? Perhaps his entrance forced the spectator to qualify happier memories of communal plough feasts and harvest ceremonies. The play at its end makes a point of separating Cain from his plough, Cain ordering his boy to 'take yond plogh...And weynd the furth fast before'.[38] The performing community evidently needed to recuperate the process by which it got its food, through separating the core symbol of the plough theatrically from the mythic figure of the ploughman-murderer. But to set the problem up in the first place, it had tapped into sensibilities which are for the modern spectator irrecoverable. Medieval civic drama gives us evidence not so much of what everyone believed, but rather of those aspects of community they needed to see staged.

The authors of these plays evidently knew that identities brought from the non-play world could be confronted, exposed, and possibly reformulated in the world of play. Their theatrical conception of history was of just such a process working itself out through the ages to the point where identity would be fixed and community made eternal. On Corpus Christi day (16 June) 1457, Queen Margaret, having come over from her provincial court at Kenilworth, famously failed to see the Coventry 'Doomsday' play, 'which myght not be pleyde for lak of day'.[39] What she would have seen had the organization of the event not slightly buckled was the community of souls wrenched apart by divine judgement to reform as two, irretrievably separated groups throughout eternity: the true community of the saved, corporate and united in joyful worship; and the mass of individually suffering damned, unsupporting of others and unsupportable. She might even have seen the burning of the world.[40]

This episode would have been unlike the others played during the day in that it lay in the future rather than the biblical past, but it would not have been regarded as fiction. Rather, it was future fact. It offered the blessing of an ideal community promised to the Christian faithful, but it also spoke of the provisionality of earthly community and the ultimate certainty of human division, truths already revealed to

---

[36] Stevens and Cawley (1994: i. 12–25).   [37] Ibid., ll. 25–9.
[38] Ibid., ll. 454–5.   [39] Ingram (1981: 37).
[40] Detailed records of the Coventry 'Doomsday' properties only exist from a hundred years later, but suggest that during the course of the performances three worlds were burnt. Ibid. 224.

Margaret and her husband, Henry VI, in the world of *realpolitik*. They had recently fought and lost at St Albans the opening battle of what were to be the Wars of the Roses, and Henry Tudor, the man who would try to fashion a new united community of the realm, had only just been born a few months before the Coventry performance. The coming decades were to realize the many anxieties about community which civic religious drama, through its treatment of Christian history, revealed, disguised, or sought to allay. The plays provided forceful examples of attempted or feared usurpation, contention between the sexes, hatred of one brother for another, disobedience, lack of conviction, betrayal, unjust government, capricious authority, public humiliation, the killing of innocents, torture and death, all predicated on the notion of a final spiritual division between those who believe and those who do not, and a moral one between good and bad action. No community in these islands ever put on a play of the Good Samaritan, though the figure had been central to William Langland's holistic understanding of the Christian past and present in *Piers Plowman*. Probably it was avoided because it had been from its first utterance a parable rather than event. But it may also have seemed beside the point, an idealized notion of cross-community goodness, inappropriate to the more obsessive explorations of community itself which defined the genres of civic religious drama.

However much they may have given a climactic expression to community fears, the 'Last Judgement' plays also managed to assert through theatrical bravura qualities of order and control, wealth, invention, and grandeur, thus matching the future horror of what was being demonstrated with the pleasures of the demonstration itself, and thereby leaving the audience with a more reassuring communal experience to carry away in the memory. Whether this was done consciously to intensify or qualify the message of the Judgement, and whether it did either of these things in effect for an individual spectator, lies beyond the limits of the evidence, but in this paradox of mingled anxiety and pleasure, humility and grandiosity, moral message and mercantile assertiveness, one approaches the true nature of civic religious drama. The hierarchy of urban wealth, which, in fact, Doomsday would replace with a community based on goodness, was prominently on show as the guilds responsible performed themselves to their neighbours and visitors. The city of Coventry, which would be burnt in the final conflagration, asserted its genius to citizen and visitor through depicting that event. The spectator, whose future community would actually be determined by the acts of corporal mercy, also had his or her commitment to theatrical spectatorship validated by a play which made much of the revelatory opening and ominous shutting of doors.[41] The promotion of watching over doing was, and remains, the fundamental paradox of instructive theatre. It was brought to its apogee in the Chester plays, where to behold with spiritual insight is promoted as the greatest moral imperative, but it was latent in that tension between theatrical and non-theatrical community exploited by all the medieval didactic plays.

---

[41] Ibid. 217, 221, 224.

Much as one might wish to link a play with a specific historical context, the performing communities did not themselves exactly belong to a particular time. Older traditions coexist with topical issues. Older identities may be evoked when they have ceased to be active, just as one can have a passive vocabulary which one comprehends but does not use. Membership of community can be remembered tolerantly even if one is no longer a member, as no doubt some of the reformed looked back with nostalgia on unreformed times. Incomers to a town bring new configurations of community and can only 'adopt' the town's traditions, however sympathetic they are. The same play may be seen every year for ten years but it will be seen with different eyes and mean different things as time goes on. In any case, audiences include spectators from different generations: sometimes these genera-tions share ideas of what is theatrically desirable; sometimes they need to have the same anxieties performed for them; sometimes they will see the play through the same lens of external reference—but not always. One's inability to historicize this rich body of material exactly, though it is frustrating and demands even more effort, does perhaps point to a deeper truth: spectators ensured that this drama of commu-nity was always an *œuvre mouvante*. From a twenty-first-century perspective the performing communities associated with the civic religious drama of the Middle Ages must look small, homogeneous, and secure in their ideology. But if one recognizes the plays as a performing of community, not just a performance by community, a distinctive genre emerges which one simplifies at one's peril. In effect, this drama staged the *spectator* under the guise of doctrinal mimesis, and by doing so confronted its audiences with their own complex, transient, and often paradoxical desires.

BIBLIOGRAPHY

BEADLE, RICHARD, and PAMELA M. KING (eds.) (1999), *York Mystery Plays: A Selection in Modern Spelling* (Oxford: Oxford University Press).

BEADLE, RICHARD (ed.) (2009), *The York Plays: Volume I, The Text* (EETS SS 23; London: Oxford University Press).

——and ALAN J. FLETCHER (eds.) (2008), *The Cambridge Companion to Medieval English Theatre* (2nd edn, Cambridge: Cambridge University Press).

BLACKSTONE, MARY A. (2004), 'Peformance and the Intertextual Negotiation of Community: The Example of Elizabethan Leicester', *Research Opportunities in Renaissance Drama*, 43: 75–105.

BUTTERWORTH, PHILIP (2005), *Magic on the Early English Stage* (Cambridge: Cambridge University Press).

CARPENTER, SARAH (forthcoming), 'New Evidence: Vives and Audience-Response to Biblical Drama', *Medieval English Theatre*, 30.

CHRISTIE, SHELIA K. (2008), 'A Crisis of Gerontocracy and the Coventry Play', *Early Theatre*, 11/1: 13–32.

CLOPPER, LAWRENCE M. (2001), *Drama, Play, and Game: English Festive Culture in the Medieval and Early Modern Period* (Chicago: Chicago University Press).

COWLING, JANE, and PETER GREENFIELD (2008), *Monks, Minstrels and Players: Drama in Hampshire before 1642* (Hampshire Papers, 29; Winchester: Hampshire County Council).

DAVIDSON, CLIFFORD (ed.) (1993), *A Tretise of Miraclis Pleyinge* (Early Drama, Art and Music Monographs, 19; Kalamazoo, Mich.: Western Michigan University Press).

DAVIS, NORMAN (ed.) (1970), *Non-Cycle Plays and Fragments* (EETS SS 1; London and New York: Oxford University Press for the Early English Text Society).

DENERY II, DARRELL G. (2005), *Seeing and Being Seen in the Later Medieval World* (Cambridge: Cambridge University Press).

EISENBICHLER, KONRAD, and WIM HUSKEN (eds.) (1999), *Carnival and the Carnivalesque* (Ludus: Medieval and Renaissance Theatre and Drama, 4; Amsterdam: Rodopi).

GIBSON, JAMES M., and ISOBEL HARVEY (2000), 'A Sociological Study of the New Romney Passion Play', *Research Opportunities in Renaissance Drama*, 39: 203–21.

DAVIDSON, CLIFFORD (2006), 'York Guilds and the Corpus Christi Plays: Unwilling Participants?', *Early Theatre*, 9/2: 11–33.

HAYS, ROSALIND CONKLIN (1994), ' "Lot's Wife" or "The Burning of Sodom": The Tudor Corpus Christi Play at Sherborne, Dorset', *Research Opportunities in Renaissance Drama*, 33: 99–125.

INGRAM, R. W. (ed.) (1981), *Coventry* (Records of Early English Drama; Toronto: University of Manchester Press).

JOHNSTON, ALEXANDRA F. (2003), 'The Feast of Corpus Christi in the West Country', *Early Theatre*, 6/1: 15–34.

——and MARGARET ROGERSON (eds.) (1979), *York* (Records of Early English Drama; 2 vols. Toronto: University of Toronto Press).

KING, PAMELA M. (2006), *The York Mystery Cycle and the Worship of the City* (Cambridge: D. S. Brewer).

——and CLIFFORD DAVIDSON (eds.) (2000), *The Coventry Corpus Christi Plays* (Early Drama, Art, and Music Monograph series, 27; Kalamazoo, Mich.: Medieval Institute, Western Michigan University).

MILL, ANNA JEAN (1924), *Mediæval Plays in Scotland* (St Andrews: University of St Andrews; repr. New York and London: Benjamin Blom, 1969).

MILLS, DAVID (1998), *Recycling the Cycle: The City of Chester and its Whitsun Plays* (Studies in Early English Drama, 4; Toronto: University of Toronto Press).

——(2007), 'Some Theological Issues in Chester's Plays', in David N. Klausner and Karen Sawyer Marsalek (eds.), *'Bring furth the pagants': Essays in Early English Drama Presented to Alexandra F. Johnston* (Toronto: University of Toronto Press), 212–29.

NORMINGTON, KATIE (2009), *Medieval English Drama* (Cambridge: Polity Press).

PALMER, BARBARA D. (2005), 'Early Modern Mobility: Players, Payments, and Patrons', *Shakespeare Quarterly*, 56/3: 259–305.

RASTALL, RICHARD (1996), *The Heaven Singing: Music in Early English Religious Drama* (Cambridge: D. S. Brewer).

——(2001), *Minstrels Playing: Music in Early English Religious Drama* (Cambridge: D. S. Brewer).

RIDDY, FELICITY (2000), 'Middle English Romance: Family, Marriage, Intimacy', in Roberta L. Krueger (ed.), *The Cambridge Companion to Medieval Romance* (Cambridge: Cambridge University Press), 235–52.

ROGERSON, MARGARET (2007), 'REED *York*, Volume 3, The "Revivals"', in David N. Klausner and Karen Sawyer Marsalek (eds.), *'Bring furth the pagants': Essays in Early English Drama Presented to Alexandra F. Johnston* (Toronto: University of Toronto Press), 132–61.

RYAN, DENISE (2001), 'Women, Sponsorship and the Early Civic Stage: Chester's Worshipful Wives and the Lost *Assumption* Play', *Research Opportunities in Renaissance Drama*, 40: 149–75.

STEVENS, MARTIN, and A. C. CAWLEY (eds.) (1994), *The Towneley Plays* (EETS SS 13, 14; 2 vols. Oxford and New York: Oxford University Press for the Early English Text Society).

STOKES, JAMES (1994), 'Drama and the Resistance to Institutions in Somerset', *Research Opportunities in Renaissance Drama*, 33: 153–64.

——(2003–4), 'The Lost Playing Places of Lincolnshire', *Comparative Drama*, 37: 275–95.

TWYCROSS, MEG (ed.) (1996), *Festive Drama* (Cambridge: D. S. Brewer).

WALKER, GREG (ed.) (2000), *Medieval Drama: An Anthology* (Oxford: Blackwell).

WALL, WENDY (1998), '"Household Stuff": The Sexual Politics of Domesticity and the Advent of English Comedy', *ELH* 65/1: 1–45.

WHITE, EILEEN (2000), 'Places to Hear the Play: The Performance of the Corpus Christi Play at York', *Early Theatre*, 3: 49–78.

PART III

LITERATURE, CLERICAL AND LAY

CHAPTER 11

CHANGE AND CONTINUITY

THE ENGLISH SERMON BEFORE 1250

BELLA MILLETT

EARLY VERNACULAR RELIGIOUS TEXTS

The early history of the English sermon is out of step with the history of the European sermon as a whole.[1] In most European countries, very few vernacular sermons are recorded in writing from the period before 1200.[2] The skills of reading and writing in this period were normally the preserve of clerical and monastic communities, and literacy among the laity was rare. The standard written language of early medieval Europe was Latin, the international language of the Church;

---

[1] There are significant terminological problems involved in discussing sermons, particularly—as here—across periods; see e.g. the different terminologies used in Cross (2000) and Spencer (2000). Anglo-Saxonists tend to prefer the general term 'homily', but sometimes make a distinction of content between 'homilies' (expositions of the Gospel readings used in the Mass) and 'sermons' (exhortations on a general theme); scholars working in later periods usually prefer 'sermon' as a general term, but sometimes make a structural distinction between 'homilies' (the more traditional preaching method, giving a discursive commentary on a passage from scripture) and 'sermons' (the more tightly structured 'thematic' method, appearing from c.1200 onwards, dividing and subdividing a shorter theme). I will use 'sermon' as a general term throughout.

[2] See the survey by Gatch (1978), and, more generally, the chapters on sermon literature in specific areas of Europe in Kienzle (2000).

although clerics might preach in the vernacular, they worked from texts in Latin. England, however, has a substantial body of vernacular sermon literature surviving from the tenth century onwards, some of it of high literary quality.

This exceptional situation seems to have been the product of exceptional circumstances—or perhaps of one exceptional man's response to those circumstances.[3] Towards the end of the ninth century, Alfred, king of Wessex 871–99, addressed the problem of a national decline in Latin learning, accelerated by the Viking invasions of his own time, by the active encouragement of English as a written medium. Among other projects, he arranged for key Latin works, including Gregory's guide to preaching, the *Cura pastoralis* (Pastoral Care) to be translated into 'þæt geðiode ... ðe we ealle gecnawan mægen' ('the language that we can all understand') and circulated to every bishopric in his kingdom, and proposed that training in vernacular literacy, followed for potential clerics by instruction in Latin, should be made available to 'eall sio gioguð ðe nu is on Angelcynne friora monna' ('all the young freemen now in England').[4] Thomas Blount in 1656 introduced his *Glossographia*, a dictionary of 'hard words', as suitable for 'the more-knowing women and less-knowing men';[5] Alfred's programme of vernacular instruction was directed towards a similarly mixed audience of the more-educated laity and less-educated clergy, linked by their ability to read English but not Latin.

Alfred seems to have seen this programme as an emergency measure rather than a permanent remedy for the problems he described; but even when standards of clerical Latinity rose again in the later tenth century, English continued in use as an alternative written language. Successful campaigns against the Vikings and the establishment of a unified English kingdom during the first half of the tenth century were followed by a period of relative peace and stability, which provided favourable conditions for the revival of English monastic life and culture during the reign of Edgar (959–75). The 'Benedictine reform'—the establishment in England of a stricter form of monastic life based on the Rule of St Benedict—was led by Dunstan (archbishop of Canterbury 959–88), Æthelwold (bishop of Winchester 963–84), and Oswald (bishop of Worcester 961–92 and archbishop of York 971–92), following the model of earlier tenth-century continental monastic reform movements. New monasteries were founded, some older ones refounded, and an increasing number of monk-bishops combined monastic life with responsibility for the pastoral care of the laity. One product of this movement was the development of a written tradition of vernacular preaching vigorous enough to survive the second wave of Viking invasions during the reign of Æthelred (978–1016) and to maintain its influence in some institutional contexts even after the Norman Conquest.

The earliest surviving manuscripts of sermons in Old English date from the later tenth century. The 'Vercelli Book' (Vercelli, Biblioteca Capitolare 117), a collection of

---

[3] See Bately (1988); she finds little evidence for the use of vernacular prose as a literary medium before the later 9th cent., and notes that most of the prose works datable before 900 are associated with Alfred.

[4] See Alfred's preface to the translation of the *Pastoral Care* (early 890s), in Sweet (1871) i. 1–8.

[5] Blount (1656), 'To the Reader'.

religious prose and verse which includes twenty-three sermons, has been dated to the second half of the tenth century; and the collection of eighteen sermons known as the 'Blickling Homilies' (Princeton, Princeton University Library, W. H. Scheide Collection, 71) includes in one sermon a description of the time elapsed since the birth of Christ as 'nine hundred and seventy-one years in the present year'.[6] Both are compilations of material of varying age and origin, but it is uncertain how much further back the written tradition of vernacular preaching on which they draw can be traced. Donald Scragg has commented, 'Although there have been attempts to show that individual pieces were composed in the ninth century, we still have no sure means of distinguishing between homilies of the tenth century and any that are earlier.'[7] The same uncertainty applies to their audiences, whose identity is unknown and perhaps (as Milton McC. Gatch has argued) unknowable.[8] A notable feature of the Vercelli and Blickling sermons is their eclectic and sometimes highly wrought style. This is partly derived from the rhetoric of their Latin sources (as in the use of the *Ubi sunt?* theme in both collections), but there is also influence from Irish models,[9] and frequent use of techniques borrowed from the native poetic tradition, including two-stress phrases and alliteration (a description of the end of the world in Vercelli II modulates from rhythmical and alliterative prose into verse). Many of the sermons aim to engage their audience on an emotional rather than intellectual level, combining rhetorical language with sensational content, sometimes drawn from apocryphal sources (in Blickling XVI, a description of the sufferings of the damned from the apocryphal *Visio Pauli* is further enlivened with details apparently borrowed from the description of Grendel's mere in *Beowulf*).

In the later Anglo-Saxon period, the most prolific and influential writer of vernacular sermons was Ælfric, abbot of Eynsham (*c*.950–1010). Ælfric was a product of the Benedictine reform, educated under Æðelwold at Winchester. He dissociated himself from the earlier tradition of sermon-writing represented by the Vercelli and Blickling collections, explaining that he had chosen to translate Latin sermon-material into English because he distrusted the orthodoxy of much of what was currently available in the vernacular:

for ðan ðe ic geseah and gehyrde mycel gedwyld on manegum Engliscum bocum, ðe ungelærede menn ðurh heora bilewitnysse to micclum wisdom tealdon; and me ofhreow þæt hi ne cuðon ne næfdon ða godspellican lare on heora gewritum, buton ðam mannum anum ðe þæt leden cuðon, and buton þam bocum ðe Ælfred cyning snoterlice awende of Ledene on Englisc.[10]

⁶ 'Nigon hund wintra ond lxxi on þysse geare', Blickling X, in Kelly (2003) 82–3.

⁷ Scragg (1979: 223); see also Scragg (1992: pp. xxviii–xxxix), on the dating of the 'Vercelli Book' sermons ('the possibility of composition within a range from the later ninth to the later tenth centuries must remain open', p. xxxix).

⁸ See Gatch (1989).

⁹ See Wright (1989).

¹⁰ '... because I saw and heard a great deal of error in many English books, which uneducated people considered in their innocence to be great wisdom; and I regretted that they did not know and did not possess a written version of the teaching of the gospels, except for those men alone who knew the

His two series of *Sermones catholici* (Catholic Homilies), 990–5, initially of forty sermons each but later expanded further, drew on patristic sources and Carolingian homiliaries to provide more authoritative preaching material; and in a prayer at the end of the second series, he asks that the two collections should not be combined with other people's work (a hope that was not fulfilled in practice).[11] He also produced a further sermon-collection, now called the 'Lives of the Saints', towards the end of the tenth century. Ælfric's prefaces to these collections, as well as some internal evidence, suggest that they were intended for more than one type of audience. In the Latin preface to the first series of *Catholic Homilies*, he explains that both series are designed to be read aloud in church by the clergy (*a ministris Dei*) to the faithful throughout the liturgical year. But he presents this as part of a more general purpose, the instruction of those, whether readers or hearers (*legentium uel audientium*), whose only language is English,[12] and some allusions within the sermons imply more learned readers, probably in most cases monastic—although Malcolm Godden, in his discussion of the audience of the *Catholic Homilies*, points out that 'there would have been a continuous scale of Latinity and learnedness which would not always have coincided with the scale from monks through secular clergy to laity'.[13] The Latin and English prefaces to the 'Lives of the Saints', commissioned by Ælfric's learned lay patron, Ealdorman Æþelweard, seem to envisage a similarly mixed audience of readers and hearers.[14]

Ælfric's concern for doctrinal purity and correctness is matched by the purity and correctness of his prose style; but his prose nevertheless reflects, in a more controlled way, the same range of stylistic influences as the work of his predecessors. His distinctive contribution to the development of English sermon style was the development of a rhythmical and alliterative prose loosely based on the structure of Anglo-Saxon verse, linking two-stress phrases in pairs by alliteration. Introduced during the composition of the second series of 'Catholic Homilies', it is used throughout the 'Lives of the Saints', offering a medium for narrative more appealing to its listeners than ordinary prose, but simpler and more approachable in diction and syntax than Old English poetry, as in this passage from his Life of St Edmund, where Edmund's followers search for his head after his martyrdom:

---

language, and except for the books which King Alfred wisely translated from Latin into English'. Preface to the 1st series of 'Catholic Homilies', ll. 50–5, in Clemoes (1997: 174); punctuation modernized and abbreviations expanded.

[11] 'Gif hwa ma awendan wille, ðonne bidde Ic hine for Godes lufon þæt he gesette his boc onsundron fram ðam twam bocum ðe we awend habbað, we truwiað, þurh Godes diht' ('If anyone wants to translate more, then I ask him for the love of God that he should keep his book separate from the two books which we have translated, we trust, through God's will'). *Oratio* concluding the 2nd series of 'Catholic Homilies', ll. 7–9. in Godden (1979: 345); punctuation modernized. See further below.

[12] 'legentium uel audientium . . . qui alia lingua nesciunt erudiri quam in qua nati sunt'. Latin preface to 1st series of 'Catholic Homilies', ll. 10–11, in Clemoes (1997: 173).

[13] See Godden (2000: pp. xxi–xxvii).

[14] Ælfric notes that the collection deals with those saints celebrated liturgically by monks rather than the laity, but also assumes that it will be used for the instruction of the laity; see Skeat (1881: 3–7).

Waes eac micel wundor ‖ þæt an wulf wearð asend
þurh Godes wissunge ‖ to bewerigenne þæt heafod
wiþ þa oþre deor ‖ ofer dæg and niht.
Hi eodon þa secende ‖ and symle clypigende,
swa swa hit gewunelic is ‖ þam þe on wuda gað oft,
'Hwær eart þu nu, gefera?', ‖ and him andwyrde þæt heafod,
'Her! Her! Her!' ‖ and swa gelome clypode,
andswarigende him eallum, ‖ swa oft swa heora ænig clypode,
oþ þæt hi ealle becomen ‖ þurh þa clypunge him to.[15]

The other major figure in the history of late Anglo-Saxon vernacular preaching was Wulfstan, bishop of London 996–1002, bishop of Worcester 1002–16, and archbishop of York 1002–23. His heavy administrative responsibilities, which he combined with an active political career, may explain his relatively low sermon output compared with Ælfric's (the exact number is uncertain, but probably not much over twenty). Several of his sermons are eschatological, taking up a theme (the Four Last Things: death, judgement, heaven, and hell) already popular among earlier Anglo-Saxon preachers; the most well-known, Sermon XX, which has the punning title *Sermo Lupi ad Anglos* ('Sermon of Wolf to the English'), links the approaching end of the world with the Danish invasions of Æthelred's reign, which Wulfstan argues have been inflicted by God on the English for their sins. Although Wulfstan was influenced by the same range of stylistic traditions as Ælfric and the anonymous homilists, he developed an individual and highly mannered prose style, based on a sequence of two-stress (or occasionally three-stress) phrases, reinforced by rhyme, alliteration, and the pairing of words of similar or opposing meanings[16]—as in this description of the fate of the damned, who after the Last Judgement must

to helle faran mid saule and mid lichaman and mid deoflum wunian on helle witum. Ðær is ece bryne grimme gemencged, and ðær is ece gryre; þær is wanung and granung and a singal sorh . . . Ðyder sculan mannslagan, and ðider sculan manswican; ðider sculan æwbrecan and ða fulan forlegenan; ðider sculan manswordan and morðwyrhtan; ðider sculan gitseras, ryperas and reaferas and woruldstruderas; ðyder sculon þeofas and ðeodscaðan; ðyder sculon wiccan and wigleras, and hrædest to secganne, alle þa manfullan þe ær yfel worhton and noldan geswican ne wið God þingian.[17]

---

[15] 'It was also a great wonder that a wolf was sent through God's guidance to guard the head against other wild beasts both day and night. Then they went searching, and kept shouting out, as is usual for those who are often in the woods, "Where are you now, mate?", and the head answered them, "Here! Here! Here!", and went on shouting, answering them all as often as they shouted, until they all came to it because of the shouting.' 'St Edmund, King and Martyr', ll. 124–9, in Needham (1966: 51). I have laid out Needham's text as verse here to make its structure clearer.

[16] See McIntosh (1949); Orchard (1992).

[17] '. . . go to hell in soul and in body and live with devils in the torments of hell. There is endless fire fiercely stirred up, and there is endless fear; there is moaning and groaning and everlasting grief . . . There must go killers, and there must go traitors; there must go oath-breakers and the filthy fornicators; there must go perjurers and murderers; there must go misers, plunderers and robbers, and great ravagers; there must go thieves and public enemies; there must go magicians and fortune-tellers, and, to put it shortly, all those evildoers who committed sin before and would not give it up or make peace with God.' Sermon VII, *De fide catholica*, ll. 120–3, 128–34, in Bethurum (1957: 162–3).

The political and institutional changes which followed the Norman Conquest had a major impact on sermon production in English. Within a decade of the Conquest almost all of the English bishops had been replaced by Norman appointees (the longest-surviving exception was Wulfstan of Worcester, who died in 1095), and 'the abbots appointed to the great Benedictine houses were overwhelmingly Continental in origin, and generally immigrants themselves until Henry I's death [in 1135]'.[18] The displacement of English clerics and religious from the highest levels of the church hierarchy was accompanied by a sharp decline in the status of English as an alternative written language to Latin, a decline which would not be fully reversed until the later fourteenth century. There is very little evidence for the production of new written sermon-material in English in the century after the Conquest, and not a great deal for the century that follows.

TRADITION AND INNOVATION

Old English sermons, however, continued to be copied well into the post-Conquest period. Ælfric's *Catholic Homilies*, which seem to have been regarded as 'a fundamentally authoritative set of texts for use within the southern dioceses and monasteries linked by the Benedictine Reform',[19] were the source most frequently drawn on, but not always in a way of which he would have approved: post-Conquest sermon compilers preferred to combine Ælfrician content with anonymous sermon-material from the pre-Conquest or (occasionally) post-Conquest period. Wulfstan's sermons were rarely copied after the eleventh century, perhaps because they were more historically specific to his own time than Ælfric's,[20] but their manuscript tradition continues intermittently into the early thirteenth century. Some post-Conquest sermon-collections are relatively faithful copies of earlier manuscripts; but others seem to have been independent compilations from different sources, and the texts they contain have sometimes been linguistically modernized, simplified, expanded, or glossed in a way that suggests adaptation for new audiences.[21]

The post-Conquest survival of the native sermon tradition has often been explained in terms of 'reaction' and 'resistance' against the Norman regime. Some scholars have interpreted it, in M. T. Clanchy's phrase, as a 'monastic antiquarian reaction',[22] an attempt by the monks of the older Benedictine monasteries to reassert their pre-Conquest roots and preserve their vernacular literary heritage. An alternative view, recently argued by Elaine Treharne, is that it reflects an ongoing rather than backward-looking response to political change, a form of 'literary resistance' to the 'Norman hegemony', providing a corpus of English-language sermon-material which

---

[18] Thomas (2003: 203).   [19] Treharne (2006a: 214).   [20] See Wilcox (2000).
[21] See Irvine (2000).   [22] See Clanchy (1993: 211–13).

was 'dynamic, usable, and current'.[23] These readings are not necessarily mutually exclusive; either could be supported from the surviving evidence, which points to both initial resistance and continuing English resentment of the Norman hierarchy in the post-Conquest period. One of the problems faced by Lanfranc as the first post-Conquest archbishop of Canterbury (1070–1109) was the opposition of the monks of the cathedral chapter to his proposed modifications of their existing customs, liturgy, and calendar of saints; and as late as the early thirteenth century an anonymous annotator of Anglo-Saxon manuscripts in Worcester Cathedral priory (usually called, from his shaky handwriting, the 'Tremulous Hand') thought it worth copying a poem of uncertain date looking back with a mixture of nostalgia and bitterness to the bishop-saints of the pre-Conquest period:

> Þet weren þeos biscop[es] ‖ [þe] bodeden Cristendom . . .
> Þeos læ[rden] ure leodan on Englisc, ‖ næs deorc heore liht, ac hit fære glod.
> [Nu is] þeo leore forleten, ‖ and þet folc is forloren.
> Nu beoþ oþre leoden ‖ þeo læ[reþ] ure folc,
> And feole of þen lorþeines losiæþ ‖ and þet folc forþ mid.[24]

But the production of sermons in English in this period cannot be wholly explained in terms of 'literary resistance'. The relationship of English monks to their new rulers seems to have been less consistently hostile than this phrase implies; a recent study by Hugh M. Thomas argues that 'the extensive survival of the English at lower ranks in the hierarchy and . . . the good relations created between them and their immigrant superiors and peers' allowed the Church in the post-Conquest period to become 'an important venue for ethnic integration, cultural interaction, and the maintenance of English identity'.[25] The annals of the E version of the *Anglo-Saxon Chronicle* covering the period from the Norman Conquest to 1121 (of uncertain provenance, but certainly monastic in origin)[26] express dismay at the oppressiveness of William I's rule, but they also acknowledge his generous patronage of English monasteries (1087), and commemorate Lanfranc at his death in 1089 as 'se arwurða muneca feder and frouer' ('the reverend father and comfort of monks').[27] Lanfranc had been persuaded by Anselm, who was later to succeed him as archbishop of Canterbury (1093–1109), of the advantages of supporting local monastic customs and traditions rather than attempting to replace them, and R. W. Southern emphasizes Anselm's 'sympathy with the Anglo-Saxon past', noting that his 'revival of Anglo-Saxon traditions at Canterbury also influenced other centres of monastic and religious

---

[23] See Treharne (2006*b*), a collaborative anthology examining 12th-cent. uses and adaptations of pre-Conquest material, and Treharne (2006*c*).

[24] 'These were the bishops who preached the Christian faith . . . / These taught our people in English. / Their light was not dim, but shone brightly. / Now that teaching is abandoned, and the folk are lost. / Now there are other people who teach our folk, / And many of those teachers go astray, and our folk with them.' Worcester Cathedral MS F. 174, fo. 63; text (ll. 10, 16–20) from Brehe (1990: 530).

[25] Thomas (2003: 204, 214).

[26] See Clark (1970: pp. xviii–xxiv).   [27] Ibid. 17.

life, particularly at Worcester, Evesham, and Durham.'[28] The value attached by English monks to these earlier traditions did not necessarily exclude a pragmatic openness to new influences, a point which can be illustrated from two twelfth-century monastic manuscripts containing sermons in English.

The first, London, British Library, Cotton Vespasian D. xiv, was copied in the mid-twelfth century or a little later at one of two closely associated monastic houses, Rochester Cathedral Priory or Christ Church, Canterbury.[29] For most of its content it draws on sermons by Ælfric, sometimes reworked and simplified,[30] but it also contains some post-Conquest material, including two translated extracts from the *Elucidarium*, an introductory survey of theology by a member of Anselm's circle, Honorius Augustodunensis (d. *c*.1140),[31] and a translation of a sermon on Luke 10: 38, 'Intravit Jesus in quoddam castellum', by another of Anselm's associates, Ralph d'Escures, bishop of Rochester 1108–14 and archbishop of Canterbury 1114–22.[32] The translation of Ralph's sermon is workmanlike and intelligent, rendering its source sense-for-sense rather than word-for-word, and at times simplifying its content (as in the omission of some general remarks on the interpretation of scriptural words *in malum* and *in bonum*). It has no distinctive stylistic features of its own, sometimes reproducing the figures of repetition of its Latin original but making no particular effort to preserve them: where the Latin sermon praises the Virgin Mary's *humilis virginitas et virgo humilitas* ('humble virginity and virgin humility'), the English translator has *eadmede mægeðhad and cleane eadmodnysse*, preferring *mægeðhad*, his usual word for 'virginity', to the more elegant alternative *cleannysse*. An indication of its likely audience is given in the introduction to the original sermon (*c*.1100), where Ralph explains that he is writing up in Latin material which he has frequently expounded orally 'in conventu fratrum ... vulgariter'[33] (that is, in French, to his monastic community at Séez in Normandy). It is a reasonable assumption that the English translation was made for a similar audience, members of the monastic community who lacked a secure command of Latin and needed instruction in their own language, and the manuscript as a whole may have served a similar practical purpose.

The second monastic sermon-collection, London, British Library, Cotton Vespasian A. xxii, includes a set of four sermons in English (the 'Vespasian Homilies'),

---

[28] 'Anselm [St Anselm]', *ODNB* entry.

[29] The cathedral at Rochester had been founded by Lanfranc; the monastic priory attached to it was founded from Canterbury by Anselm in 1107. For the dating of the MS, see Treharne (2000*b*: 31–4). Handley (1974), examining the content of the MS in detail, argues for a Canterbury localization.

[30] See Irvine (2000: 50).

[31] On Honorius's connection with Anselm (to whom he may have been related), and more generally with the monastic cathedrals of southern England, see Valerie I. J. Flint, 'Honorius Augustodunensis', *ODNB*.

[32] For the Middle English sermon (art. 44, fos. 151ᵛ–157ʳ), see Warner (1917: 134–9); for the Latin original (which was widely disseminated because of its attribution to Anselm), see *PL* 158. 644–9. Ralph's sermon and its Middle English translation are discussed in detail by Treharne (2006*c*).

[33] 'In the community of brothers ... in the vernacular', *PL* 158. 644.

probably copied at Rochester towards the end of the twelfth century.[34] Two are drawn from Ælfric (again with some degree of simplification), but the other two items (2 and 3), in spite of the archaism of their language, seem to reflect more recent influences. Item 3, a brief development of the image of the 'whole armour of God' in Ephesians 6: 11, cannot be dated with any certainty, but its addition of a horse and spurs to the military equipment listed by St Paul suggests a post-Conquest date, and it connects its theme with the battle against the 'three enemies of man' (i.e. the world, the flesh and the devil), a sermon-topos which was not in common use before the twelfth century.[35] Item 2 can be more confidently linked with post-Conquest sources. Although it includes a borrowing from Ælfric,[36] and its style is influenced by pre-Conquest sermon prose, William Vollhardt noted over a century ago that its opening part was based on one of the similitudes in the Anselmian *Liber de humanis moribus*,[37] and Joseph Hall later identified parallels to Anselm's *Meditatio* 1 (in a description of the Last Judgement), and to the *Liber Sententiarum* attributed to Bernard of Clairvaux.[38] It also includes a charmingly affective image of Christ as a mother caring for her baby, another distinctively twelfth-century sermon-topos,[39] rounded off with an octosyllabic couplet:

Muȝe we ahct clepeien hine moder, wene we? Ȝie, muȝe we! Hwat deð si moder hire bearn? Formest hi hit chereð and blissið be þe lichte, and seþe hi dieð under hire arme oðer his hafed heleð to don him slepe and reste. Þis deð all ȝiure Drihte:

> He blisseð hus mid dȝeies licht,
> He sweueð hus mid þiestre nicht.[40]

<hr/>

[34] Fos. 54ʳ–57ᵛ. All four sermons are edited in Morris (1868: 216–45); item 2 is also edited in Hall (1920: i. 12–17, ii. 269–85). Elaine Treharne dates the hand of this section of the MS to 'the last decade or so of the twelfth century'; see Swan (2007: 414).

[35] See Wenzel (1967).

[36] See Hall (1920: ii. 278–9), and Swan (2007: 416–17).

[37] Ch. 46 in Southern and Schmitt (1969: 56–7); the parallel was first noted by Vollhardt (1888: 24). The surviving MSS date from the early 12th cent. onwards, but Southern and Schmitt think that 'the materials contained in *De moribus* must have been in existence, probably at Canterbury, at the time of Anselm's death in 1109' (p. 11).

[38] Vollhardt (1888: 24–6), and Hall (1920: ii. 281–2, 284). Scholars from Vollhardt onwards have been consistently reluctant to accept that the sermon (which contains no French loan-words but *curt* 'court', corrected back in the MS to the English *berie*) could have been composed late enough to use the Anselmian passage as a source. But the correspondences (as Vollhardt himself concluded) are so close and extensive that it is hard to see what else it could be; the further post-Conquest parallels noted by Hall provide supporting evidence; and the dating of the MS permits it. In this monastic context, the alternative possibility of deliberate stylistic and linguistic archaism should probably taken into account; compare the 12th-cent. translation of Ralph d'Escures's sermon in Vespasian D. xiv, which also includes 'only one "modern" loan-word, *cæsteľ* (Treharne 2006c: 185).

[39] See Bynum (1982: ch. 4).

[40] Hall (1920: i. 14, with modernized punctuation): 'Can we call him "mother" at all, we wonder? Yes, we can! What does the mother do for her child? First she cheers and delights it with the light, and then she cradles it in her arm or covers its head to let it sleep and rest. Our Lord does all this: "He cheers us with the light of day, / With darkness soothes our cares away."' Hall (ii. 280) cites another possible parallel from Anselm, *Oratio* 10, for this passage: 'Sed et tu, Jesu, bone domine, nonne et tu mater? Annon est mater, qui tamquam gallina congregat sub alas pullos suos? Vere, domine, et tu mater' ('But aren't you, Jesus, kind Lord, also a mother? Isn't someone a mother who like a hen gathers her chicks under her wing? Certainly, Lord, you are a mother'); but Anselm draws his image from a more traditional source, Matt. 23: 37.

The sermon addresses a general audience ('Nu, gode men, understandeð þis bis-pel'[41]), and seems to have been designed not only to teach but to entertain; Anselm's expository introduction to his similitude, 'Inter hos autem salvandos atque dam-nandos sic deus discernit, quomodo rex quidam inter fideles et infideles imperii sui', is replaced by the more immediately appealing opening: 'Hit ʒelamp þet an rice king wes, strang and mihti . . .'[42]

Both these monastic sermon-collections look back to the pre-Conquest vernacular sermon tradition, but they also show a pragmatic willingness to draw on newer Latin sources—often associated with Anselm and his circle—to meet the needs of their different audiences, and in the case of the second 'Vespasian homily', older and newer traditions are combined within the same sermon.

EARLY MIDDLE ENGLISH SERMONS

The afterlife of the Old English sermon has so far attracted considerably more scholarly attention than the beginnings of the Middle English sermon. Although editions of the three main early Middle English sermon-collections, the *Orrmulum*, the 'Trinity Homilies', and the 'Lambeth Homilies', are currently in progress,[43] most of the surviving sermon-material has not been edited—apart from extracts in undergraduate readers—since the nineteenth century, and there is not a great deal of secondary literature either. In some ways this neglect is understandable. Few early Middle English sermons survive from before 1250,[44] and most of those which do lack any literary distinction. They are still worth looking at, however, for the light they cast on the evolution of the English sermon in this period, and its relationship to broader European developments.

The late twelfth and early thirteenth centuries marked a major turning-point in the history of preaching in Europe. The late twelfth-century movement of pastoral reform which culminated in the decrees of the Fourth Lateran Council of 1215 led to a much greater emphasis on preaching to the laity, and the preaching methods evolved in the Paris schools from the 1160s onwards equipped clerics with new techniques for organizing their sermons more effectively and increasing their popular appeal. The English Church seems to have been an early adopter of these developments. Its implementation of canon 18 of the Third Lateran Council of 1179, which required

---

[41] Hall (1920: i. 13): 'Now, good people, understand this parable.'

[42] Southern and Schmitt (1969: 56): 'God distinguishes between those who are to be saved and damned as a certain king did between those who were loyal and disloyal to his rule'; Hall (1920: i. 12): 'There was once a noble king, strong and powerful . . .'

[43] By Nils-Lennart Johannesson (*Orrmulum*), Elaine Treharne ('Trinity Homilies'), and Mary Swan ('Lambeth Homilies').

[44] See O'Mara and Paul (2007), although the editors' decision to exclude any sermons containing Old English means that the listing may not be complete.

the provision of free training for cathedral clergy, was prompt and effective,[45] and clerics took an active interest in continental innovations in sermon technique. Some of the earliest aids to preaching in the new style were produced by English writers, including the *distinctio* collection *Pantheologus* (1189) by the Augustinian canon Peter of Cornwall, the preaching manual *De artificiose modo praedicandi* (*c*.1200) by another Augustinian canon, Alexander of Ashby,[46] several works by William de Montibus (d. 1213), a Paris master who became head of the cathedral school at Lincoln,[47] and the *Summa de arte praedicandi* (*c*.1215–22) by Thomas of Chobham, also a Paris master and subdean of Salisbury Cathedral.[48]

It has usually been assumed that these innovations in preaching methods had no immediate influence on the development of the Middle English sermon. Helen Spencer has said of its early stages that 'in the twelfth and thirteenth centuries...a renewed emphasis on preaching...tended to find expression in harking back to older homiliaries',[49] and most scholars have focused on those features which link the early Middle English sermon with the pre-Conquest preaching tradition.

The only early Middle English sermon-collection which is generally agreed to resist this approach is the *Orrmulum*. This collection, named after its author Orrm (or Orrmin), an Augustinian canon who addresses his dedication to a fellow-canon, his brother Walter,[50] originally included paraphrases and expositions of the Gospel readings at Mass for most of the liturgical year, although the one surviving manuscript, Oxford, Bodleian Library, Junius 1, which its author describes as the 'firrste bisne' ('original exemplar') contains only the first thirty-two—the last fragmentary—of the 242 sermons listed in its (incomplete) table of contents. Malcolm Parkes has dated the completion of the manuscript (which may have been produced over an extended period) to 'early in the last quarter of the twelfth century'.[51] The dialect of the manuscript has been localized to Lincolnshire; Parkes, noting the emphasis on St Peter and St Paul in five of the sermons, suggests that the author may have been a member of the house of Arrouaisian canons at Bourne Abbey (founded 1138), the only local Augustinian house dedicated to these saints.[52] It seems to have been designed primarily for preaching the message of the Gospels to the laity ('to læwedd follc / larspell of Godspell tellenn'), and Parkes links an allusion to hostile critics in its

---

[45] See Millett (2007: 46).   [46] Edited in Morenzoni (2004: 1–104).

[47] See the comprehensive study by Goering (1992).

[48] Morenzoni (1988); see also Morenzoni (2001), a broader survey of preaching in England in this period.

[49] Spenser (2000: 616).

[50] 'Þiss boc iss nemmnedd Orrmulum, / forrþi þatt Orrm itt wrohhte' (dedication, l. 1). For an accessible text of the author's dedication and preface, see Treharne (2000a: 273–80, where the text is laid out as alternating four- and three-stress lines). For the full text, see Holt (1878).

[51] See Parkes (1983).

[52] Ibid. 125–7. The Arrouaisians were a relatively recent order, one of the stricter independent congregations of Augustinian canons; they were favoured by churchmen with an interest in the new orders of the 'Medieval Reformation', including Alexander 'the Magnificent', bishop of Lincoln 1123–48, who was also a patron of the Cistercians and the Gilbertines, and Malachy (1094/5–1148), archbishop of Armagh, who saw the Arrouaisian customs as particularly suitable for cathedral clergy.

dedication to the twelfth-century debate on whether regular canons might engage in pastoral care,[53] but Orrm concludes his preface by asking for the prayers of both listeners and readers ('þa Crisstene menn / þatt herenn oþerr redenn / þiss boc').[54] Apart from one faint and probably indirect echo of Wulfstan's phrasing,[55] the *Orrmulum* owes no apparent debt to the pre-Conquest vernacular sermon tradition. Its Latin sources include not only works by Bede but twelfth-century scriptural commentaries.[56] Instead of the rhythmical and alliterative prose of the native sermon tradition, it uses its own distinctive metre, obsessively regular fifteen-syllable un-rhymed verse lines based on the Latin septenary; and unlike some other sermon-collections of the period, it avoids linguistic archaism, inventing instead an idiosyncratic but highly consistent phonetic spelling-system. Its uniqueness should not be overstressed—its sermon-structure follows a traditional model, and metres based on the septenary are found in other early Middle English didactic works, such as the widely distributed later twelfth-century *Poema morale*—but it does seem to occupy a no man's land all of its own between the older and newer preaching traditions discussed here.

There is some evidence, however, that continental innovations in preaching methods had reached the early Middle English sermon by the late twelfth century. The 'Kentish Homilies', close translations in Kentish dialect of five sermons from the earliest French vernacular sermon-collection, composed *c*.1170 by Maurice of Sully, bishop of Paris, survive only in a manuscript dating from *c*.1275 (Oxford, Bodleian Library, Laud 471), and cannot be dated with any certainty.[57] But new types of sermon-structure developed in the Paris schools are reflected in some of the 'Trinity Homilies', the thirty-four English sermons collected in Cambridge, Trinity College, B. 14. 52, which has been dated palaeographically to the late twelfth century.[58] The most distinctive feature of the 'scholastic' sermon of the later twelfth century was its use of division as a structuring principle. In the earlier stages, division was used to organize topics within the sermon; but towards the end of the twelfth century, it began to be used as a way of organizing the sermon as a whole—a development which led in the early thirteenth century to the emergence of the 'thematic sermon', which replaced the discursive commentary on a scriptural passage characteristic of the older 'homiletic' sermon by the schematic division and subdivision of a 'theme', a single word or scriptural verse. Although most of the 'Trinity Homilies' are traditionally 'homiletic' in form, some of them show the influence of these newer organizational techniques; several include topics divided into lists (such as the ten impediments to confession in

---

[53] See Parkes (1983: 125), and the references given there.
[54] Dedication, ll. 55–6, 329–30, ed. in Treharne (2000a: 274, 280).
[55] See Morrison (1995).
[56] The *Enarrationes in Matthaeum* formerly attributed to Anselm of Laon and the *Glossa ordinaria*; see Morrison (1983).
[57] For the French originals, see Robson (1952). All five 'Kentish Homilies' are edited in Hall (1920), and four also in Bennett and Smithers (1968).
[58] Morris (1873). I am grateful to Ralph Hanna for his advice on the dating of this MS.

Trinity XII[59]), and a few are 'quasi-thematic' in form. Six sermons (I, IV, XXV, XXVI, XXX, and XXXII) incorporate in their text unsourced Latin material, possibly from a collection of model sermons, including divisions which provide a structural basis for part or all of the English text. Trinity XXVI, for instance, on 2 Corinthians 9: 6, 'Qui parce seminat...', divides its theme through the use of a biblical *distinctio* (the commonest type of sermon-division) distinguishing three senses of *semen* 'seed' ('Sacra scriptura nomine seminis appellat tria, scilicet, hominis progenituram, Dei verbum, opus bonum'[60]), and includes under the third heading an intricately patterned four-part division on the ways in which the merit of charitable giving can be lost: 'Quatuor modis venditur elemosina, et tunc inde populi favor emitur, aut pudoris molestia deprimitur, aut recompensatio rei temporalis adquiritur, aut debiti beneficii solutio inpenditur.'[61] The institutional context of the 'Trinity Homilies' is uncertain, but the internal evidence of the sermons suggests that they were used for diocesan preaching;[62] the dialect of the two main scribes of the manuscript has been localized to the East Midlands area, on the northern borders of the London diocese, and a London origin might help to explain the early introduction of new sermon-techniques in this collection.[63]

Some of the newer sermon-material in the 'Trinity Homilies' is shared with another early Middle English sermon-collection, the 'Lambeth Homilies'. This collection of seventeen sermons survives in London, Lambeth Palace Library, 487, which has been localized by dialect to the Worcester area, and dated palaeographically to the late twelfth century or the first quarter of the thirteenth century.[64] Unlike the 'Trinity Homilies', which do not seem to have any demonstrable links with the pre-Conquest vernacular sermon tradition, the 'Lambeth Homilies' include lightly modernized material from both Ælfric and Wulfstan,[65] and most of the sermons they contain are in the older 'homiletic' style. However, they also include versions of five of the six 'quasi-thematic' Trinity sermons discussed above;[66] and the closest affinities of Lambeth V are with the popular preaching of the early thirteenth century.[67] The internal evidence of the 'Lambeth Homilies', like that of the 'Trinity Homilies',

---

[59] There is a significant overlap between this list and the ten-point list of impediments to confession in Alan of Lille's *De sex alis cherubim*, suggesting a common origin in late 12th-cent. Paris; see Millett (2007: 49–50).

[60] Morris (1873: 152): 'Holy Scripture calls three things "seed": that is, the begetting of children, the word of God, and good works.'

[61] Ibid. 156: 'Charitable giving is sold in four ways, when it is used to buy popularity, or to avoid embarrassment, or to gain worldly reward, or to pay back a favour.'

[62] See Millett (2007: 52–60).

[63] For Peter of Cornwall's description of the introduction of the new style of preaching to England by Gilbert Foliot, bishop of London, in the 1170s, see Hunt (1936).

[64] I am grateful to Malcolm Parkes and Ralph Hanna for advice on the dating of this MS. The 'Lambeth Homilies' are edited in Morris (1868).

[65] Swan (2007: 406), lists five instances: four (in Lambeth III, IX, X, and XI) draw on Ælfrician material, one (in Lambeth II) on one of Wulfstan's sermons.

[66] Trinity IV/Lambeth VII, Trinity XXV/Lambeth XVII, Trinity XXVI/Lambeth XIII, Trinity XXX/Lambeth XVI, Trinity XXXII/Lambeth XV.

[67] See the parallels to the works of Odo of Cheriton and James of Vitry cited by Hall (1920: ii. 425–7).

indicates that they were primarily intended for diocesan preaching. Christine Franzen, in her study of the 'Tremulous Hand' of Worcester, has suggested that the older native tradition of preaching was superseded in the early thirteenth century by newer fashions ('If the glossed Old English homiliaries had been intended to be used as source material for preaching, they may have fallen victim to the rapidly changing fashion in preaching in the thirteenth century... Compared with the sermons that the friars could offer, anything gleaned from these old manuscripts must have seemed old-fashioned indeed'),[68] but the two traditions seem to have been used alongside each other, at least temporarily, in the West Midlands milieu in which Lambeth 487 was produced.

ANCRENE WISSE AND THE KATHERINE-GROUP

The group of West Midlands religious prose works of which the best known is *Ancrene Wisse* ('Guide for Anchoresses') offers evidence not only for simultaneous use, but for some degree of convergence of the two traditions. They were probably produced at a rather later date than the 'Lambeth Homilies'; most of them cannot be dated with any precision, but the internal evidence of *Ancrene Wisse* points towards a date of composition in the late 1220s.[69] Some of the works of the group were composed specifically for reading by anchoresses, but three lives of virgin martyrs, *Seinte Margarete*, *Seinte Iuliene*, and *Seinte Katerine*, seem to have been designed, at least in the first instance, for public preaching ('Alle leawede men þe understonden ne mahen Latines ledene, liðeð ant lusteð þe liflade of a meiden...'[70]), and a fourth work, *Sawles Warde* ('the Custody of the Soul'), based on an Anselmian dialogue, *De Custodia interioris hominis*, may also have been used as a sermon.[71] Although none of the works of the group borrows material directly from pre-Conquest vernacular sermons, all of them make use, to a greater or lesser extent, of a rhythmical and alliterative prose which is ultimately derived from pre-Conquest models.[72] This influence is strongest in the saints' lives, least marked in *Ancrene Wisse*, but is present to some degree in all the works of the group. When the author of *Sawles Warde* is dealing with one of the favourite themes of Anglo-Saxon preachers, the pains of hell, he departs from his Anselmian source text in a highly wrought passage which looks back in style and vocabulary to late Old English sermon prose:

O helle, Deaðes hus, wununge of wanunge, of grure ant of granunge, heatel ham ant heard, wan of alle wontreaðes, buri of bale ant bold of eauereuch bitternesse, þu laðest lont of alle, þu

---

[68] Franzen (1991: 193).   [69] See Millett (2005–6: ii, pp. xi–xiii).

[70] 'All lay-people who cannot understand Latin, listen and hear the life of a virgin' (d'Ardenne 1961: 3).

[71] On English and Continental adaptations of this dialogue for use as a sermon, see Becker (1984).

[72] See Millett (1988).

dorc stude ifullet of alle dreorinesses, Ich cwakie of grisle ant of grure, ant euch ban schekeð me ant euch her me rueð up of þi munegunge ...[73]

Similarly, in *Ancrene Wisse* a description of the Last Judgement borrowed from Anselm's *Meditatio* 1 is expanded with the help of two-stress phrases linked by alliteration: *illinc terrens Iusticia*, for instance, becomes 'O þe oþer half stont Rihtwisnesse þet na reowðe is wið, dredful ant grislich ant grureful to bihalden.'[74]

There are some indications, however, that *Ancrene Wisse* was of Dominican origin,[75] and the new preaching methods of the schools are reflected in some of the works of the group. The letter on virginity *Epistel of Meidenhad* ('*Hali Meiðhad*') draws on two model sermons from the late twelfth-century *Summa de arte praedicatoria* by Alan of Lille, which may also have influenced *Ancrene Wisse*;[76] the lists of reasons for Christ's eligibility as a lover in *Ancrene Wisse* and the meditation *Þe Wohunge of ure Lauerd* are most closely paralleled in thirteenth-century Paris sermons;[77] and *Ancrene Wisse* shows the influence of the schools not only in its frequent use of division as a structuring device, but in its exploitation of the characteristic techniques of contemporary continental popular preaching, comparisons (*similitudines*) and illustrative stories (*exempla*).[78]

The accommodation of older and newer influences in the *Ancrene Wisse* group, as in some of the earlier instances cited above, suggests that the demarcation between older and newer preaching traditions in the early Middle English period may have been less sharp than has sometimes been assumed, and the transition between them less abrupt.

Pre-Conquest sermon-material continued to be copied, adapted, and imitated until the early thirteenth century, but from the mid-twelfth century onwards it coexisted with other types of homiletic writing. English writers were experimenting with new preaching materials and methods well before the Fourth Lateran Council of 1215; sometimes works reflecting both older and newer preaching traditions are juxtaposed in the same sermon-collection, indicating that they were current in the same milieu, and sometimes both traditions are integrated within a single work. The very limited evidence for Middle English sermon production in this period makes it difficult to trace the history of these interrelationships, but it may be significant that the closest links between older and newer traditions appear in collections or individual works associated either with the Worcester area or with

---

[73] 'O hell, house of Death, habitation of lamentation, of horror and execration, harsh and hateful home and dwelling of all distresses, stronghold of sorrow and abode of every bitterness, most loathsome land of all, place of darkness and haunt of dreadful griefs, I tremble with terror and dread, and every bone shudders and every one of my hairs stands on end at your memory ...' *Sawles Warde*, in Millett and Wogan-Browne (1992: 94, ll. 1–5).

[74] *Ancrene Wisse* 5. 89–91, Millett (2005–6: i. 116): 'On the other side stands Justice, which has no pity, fearful and terrifying and dreadful to see.' On the author's debt to the native tradition of rhythmical and alliterative prose, see further ibid. ii, pp. xlix–lii.

[75] Ibid., i, pp. xvi–xix.

[76] See Millett (1982: p. xlviii; 2005–6: ii, p. xxxiv).

[77] See Millett (2009).

[78] See Millett (2005–6: ii, pp. xxxvi–xliv, on division, and pp. xliv–xlix, on *similitudines* and *exempla*).

Canterbury and Rochester. The monastic cathedrals of Worcester, Canterbury, and Rochester seem to have been particularly active in the preservation of pre-Conquest sermon material,[79] and their pastoral responsibilities would have connected them to a wider episcopal network, which came under increasing pressure to extend and enhance its preaching activity during the late twelfth and early thirteenth centuries.

The coexistence of older and newer preaching traditions in the post-Conquest period was no more than temporary; by the mid thirteenth century, the language of Ælfric and Wulfstan was no longer understood, and the last direct links with the pre-Conquest sermon tradition had been broken. But the production of sermons in English in the two centuries after the Conquest reflects more than (in Celia Sisam's words) the 'last flicker' of an obsolescent tradition;[80] the variety of the material which survives to us suggests a pragmatic and sometimes creative response to political, institutional, and linguistic change.

Bibliography

Primary sources

D'ARDENNE, S. R. T. O. (ed.) (1961), Þe Liflade ant te Passiun of Seinte Iuliene (EETS OS 248; London and New York: Oxford University Press for the Early English Text Society).

BENNETT, J. A. W., and G. V. SMITHERS (eds.) (1968), Early Middle English Verse and Prose (2nd edn. Oxford: Clarendon Press).

BETHURUM, DOROTHY (ed.) (1957), The Homilies of Wulfstan (Oxford: Clarendon Press).

BLOUNT, THOMAS (1656), Glossographia (London: Thomas Newcomb).

CLARK, CECILY (ed.) (1970), The Peterborough Chronicle 1070–1154 (2nd edn. Oxford: Clarendon Press).

CLEMOES, PETER (ed.) (1997), Ælfric's Catholic Homilies: The First Series: Text (EETS SS 17; London and New York: Oxford University Press for the Early English Text Society).

GODDEN, MALCOLM (ed.) (1979), Ælfric's Catholic Homilies: The Second Series: Text (EETS SS 5 London and New York: Oxford University Press for the Early English Text Society).

——(ed.) (2000), Ælfric's Catholic Homilies: Introduction, Commentary and Glossary (EETS SS 18; London and New York: Oxford University Press for the Early English Text Society).

HALL, JOSEPH (ed.) (1920), Selections from Early Middle English 1130–1250 (2 vols. Oxford: Clarendon Press).

HOLT, ROBERT (ed.) (1878), The Ormulum: With the Notes and Glossary of Dr R. M. White (2 vols. Oxford: Clarendon Press).

KELLY, RICHARD J. (ed. and tr.) (2003), The Blickling Homilies (New York: Continuum).

MILLETT, BELLA (ed.) (1982), Hali Meiðhad (EETS OS 284; London and New York: Oxford University Press for the Early English Text Society).

[79] See Treharne (2006c: 171).   [80] Sisam (1951: 110 n. 2).

——(ed.) (2005–6), *Ancrene Wisse: A Corrected Edition of the Text in Cambridge, Corpus Christi College, MS 402, with Variants from Other Manuscripts* (2 vols. EETS OS 325, 326; London and New York: Oxford University Press for the Early English Text Society).

——and JOCELYN WOGAN-BROWNE (eds. and trs.) (1992), *Medieval English Prose for Women: Selections from the Katherine Group and Ancrene Wisse* (rev. edn. Oxford: Clarendon Press).

MORENZONI, FRANCO (ed.) (1988), *Thomas de Chobham: Summa de arte praedicandi* (*CCCM* 82; Turnhout: Brepols).

——(ed.) (2004), *Alexandri Essebiensis opera omnia*, i. *Opera theologica* (*CCCM* 188; Turnhout: Brepols).

MORRIS, RICHARD (ed. and tr.) (1868), *Old English Homilies and Homiletic Treatises . . . of the Twelfth and Thirteenth Centuries* (1st ser., EETS OS 29, 34; London: N. Trübner & Co. for the Early English Text Society).

——(ed. and tr.) (1873), *Old English Homilies of the Twelfth Century: From the Unique MS B. 14. 52 in the Library of Trinity College, Cambridge* (2nd ser., EETS OS 53; London: N. Trübner & Co. for the Early English Text Society).

——(ed. and tr.) (1874, 1876, 1880), *The Blickling Homilies of the Tenth Century: From the Marquis of Lothian's Unique MS. A.D. 971* (EETS OS 58, 63, 73; London: London: N. Trübner & Co. for the Early English Text Society).

NEEDHAM, G. I. (ed.) (1966), *Ælfric: Lives of Three English Saints* (Methuen's Old English Library; London: Methuen).

NICHOLSON, LEWIS E. (tr.) (1991), *The Vercelli Book Homilies: Translations from the Anglo-Saxon* (Lanham, NY: University Press of America).

POPE, JOHN C. (ed.) (1967–8), *Homilies of Ælfric: A Supplementary Collection* (2 vols. EETS OS 259, 260; London and New York: Oxford University Press for the Early English Text Society).

ROBSON, C. A. (1952), *Maurice of Sully and the Medieval Vernacular Homily: With the Text of Maurice's French Homilies from a Sens Cathedral Chapter MS* (Oxford: Blackwell).

SCRAGG, D. G. (ed.) (1992), *The Vercelli Homilies and Related Texts* (EETS OS 300; Oxford and New York: Oxford University Press for the Early English Text Society).

SKEAT, W. W. (ed. and tr.) (1881–1900), *Ælfric's Lives of Saints* (EETS OS 76, 82, 94, 114; London: N. Trübner & Co. for the Early English Text Society).

SWEET, HENRY (ed.) (1871), *King Alfred's West-Saxon Version of Gregory's Pastoral Care* (EETS OS 45, 50; London: N. Trübner & Co. for the Early English Text Society).

SOUTHERN, R. W., and F. S. SCHMITT (eds.) (1969), *Memorials of St Anselm* (Auctores Britannici Medii Aevi, 1: Oxford: Oxford University Press).

TREHARNE, ELAINE (ed.) (2000*a*), *Old and Middle English: An Anthology* (Oxford: Blackwell).

WARNER, RUBIE D.-N. (ed.) (1917), *Early English Homilies from the Twelfth Century MS. Vesp. D. xiv* (EETS OS 152; London: K. Paul, Trench, Trübner & Co. for the Early English Text Society).

Secondary Sources

BATELY, JANET M. (1988), 'Old English Prose before and during the Reign of Alfred', *Anglo-Saxon England*, 17: 93–138.

BECKER, WOLFGANG (1984), 'The Literary Treatment of the Pseudo-Anselmian Dialogue *De Custodia interioris hominis* in England and France', *Classica et Mediævalia*, 35: 215–33.

BREHE, S. (1990), 'Reassembling the First Worcester Fragment', *Speculum*, 65: 521–36.

BURTON, JANET (1994), *Monastic and Religious Orders in Britain, 1000–1300* (Cambridge Medieval Textbooks; Cambridge: Cambridge University Press).

BYNUM, CAROLINE WALKER (1982), *Jesus as Mother: Studies in the Spirituality of the High Middle Ages* (Berkeley, Calif.: University of California Press).

CANNON, CHRISTOPHER (2004), *The Grounds of English Literature* (Oxford: Oxford University Press).

CLANCHY, M. T. (1993), *From Memory to Written Record: England 1066–1307* (2nd edn. Oxford: Blackwell).

CROSS, J. E. (2000), 'Vernacular Sermons in Old English', in Beverly Mayne Kienzle (dir.), *The Sermon* (Typologie des sources du moyen âge occidental, 81–3: Turnhout: Brepols), 561–96.

FRANZEN, CHRISTINE, (1991), *The Tremulous Hand of Worcester: A Study of Old English in the Thirteenth Century* (Oxford English Monographs; Oxford: Clarendon Press).

GATCH, MILTON McC. (1977), *Preaching and Theology in Anglo-Saxon England* (Toronto: University of Toronto Press).

——(1978), 'The Achievement of Ælfric and his Colleagues in European Perspective', in Paul E. Szarmach and Bernard F. Huppé (eds.), *The Old English Homily and its Backgrounds* (Albany, NY: State University of New York Press), 43–73.

——(1989), 'The Unknowable Audience of the Blickling Homilies', *Anglo-Saxon England*, 18: 99–115.

GOERING, JOSEPH (1992), *William de Montibus (c. 1140–1213): The Schools and the Literature of Pastoral Care* (Studies and Texts, 108; Toronto: Pontifical Institute of Mediaeval Studies).

HANDLEY, RIMA (1974), 'British Museum MS. Cotton Vespasian D. xiv', *Notes and Queries*, NS 21: 243–50.

HUNT, R. W. (1936), 'English Learning in the Late Twelfth Century'; repr. in R. W. Southern (ed.), *Essays in Medieval History: Selected from the Transactions of the Royal Historical Society on the Occasion of its Centenary* (London: Macmillan, 1968), 106–28.

IRVINE, SUSAN (2000), 'The Compilation and Use of Manuscripts Containing Old English in the Twelfth Century', in Mary Swan and Elaine M. Treharne (eds.), *Rewriting Old English in the Twelfth Century* (Cambridge Studies in Anglo-Saxon England, 30; Cambridge: Cambridge University Press), 41–61.

McINTOSH, ANGUS (1949), 'Wulfstan's Prose', *Proceedings of the British Academy*, 35: 109–42.

MAGENNIS, HUGH, and JONATHAN WILCOX (eds.) (2006), *The Power of Words: Anglo-Saxon Studies Presented to Donald G. Scragg on his Seventieth Birthday* (Medieval European Studies, 8; Morgantown, WV: West Virginia University Press).

MILLETT, BELLA (1988), 'The Saints' Lives of the Katherine Group and the Alliterative Tradition', *Journal of English and Germanic Philology*, 87: 16–34.

——(2007), 'The Pastoral Context of the Trinity and Lambeth Homilies', in Wendy Scase (ed.), *Essays in Manuscript Geography: Vernacular Manuscripts of the English West Midlands from the Conquest to the Sixteenth Century* (Medieval Texts and Cultures of Northern Europe, 10; Turnhout: Brepols), 43–64.

——(2009), 'The "Conditions of Eligibility" in Þe Wohunge of ure Lauerd', in Susannah M. Chewning (ed.), *The Milieu and Context of the Wooing Group* (Cardiff: University of Wales Press), 26–47.

MORENZONI, FRANCO (2001), *Des écoles aux paroisses: Thomas de Chobham et la promotion de la prédication au début du XIIIe siècle* (Collection des Études Augustiniennes, Série moyen-âge et temps modernes, 30: Turnhout: Brepols).

MORRISON, STEPHEN (1983), 'Sources for the *Ormulum*: A Re-examination', *Neuphilologische Mitteilungen*, 84: 419–36.

——(1995), 'A Reminiscence of Wulfstan in the Twelfth Century', *Neuphilologische Mitteilungen*, 96: 229–34.

O'MARA, VERONICA, and SUZANNE PAUL (eds.) (2007), *Repertorium of Middle English Sermons* (4 vols. Turnhout: Brepols).

ODNB (2004), *Oxford Dictionary of National Biography* (Oxford: Oxford University Press).

ORCHARD, A. P. McD. (1992), 'Crying Wolf: Oral Style and the *Sermones Lupi*', *Anglo-Saxon England*, 21: 239–64.

PARKES, M.B. (1983), 'On the Presumed Date and Possible Origin of the Manuscript of the *Orrmulum*: Oxford, Bodleian Library, MS Junius 1', in E. G. Stanley and Douglas Gray (eds.), *Five Hundred Years of Words and Sounds: A Festschrift for Eric Dobson* (Cambridge: D. S. Brewer), 115–27.

RICHARDS, M. P. (1978), 'MS Cotton Vespasian A. xxii: The Vespasian Homilies', *Manuscripta*, 22: 97–103.

SCRAGG, D. G. (1979), 'The Corpus of Vernacular Homilies and Prose Saints' Lives before Ælfric', *Anglo-Saxon England*, 8: 223–69.

SISAM, CELIA (1951), 'The Scribal Tradition of the Lambeth Homilies', *Review of English Studies*, NS 2: 105–13.

SPENCER, HELEN (2000), 'Middle English Sermons', in Beverly Mayne Kienzle (dir.), *The Sermon* (Typologie des sources du moyen âge occidental, 81–3; Turnhout: Brepols), 597–660.

SWAN, MARY (2007), 'Preaching Past the Conquest: Lambeth Palace 487 and Cotton Vespasian A. xxii', in Aaron J. Kleist (ed.), *The Old English Homily: Precedent, Practice, and Appropriation* (Turnhout: Brepols), 403–23.

——and ELAINE M. TREHARNE (eds.) (2000), *Rewriting Old English in the Twelfth Century* (Cambridge Studies in Anglo-Saxon England, 30; Cambridge: Cambridge University Press).

THOMAS, HUGH M. (2003), *The English and the Normans: Ethnic Hostility, Assimilation, and Identity 1066–c.1220* (Oxford: Oxford University Press).

TREHARNE, ELAINE M. (2000b), 'The Production and Script of Manuscripts Containing English Religious Texts in the First Half of the Twelfth Century', in Mary Swan and Elaine M. Treharne (eds.), *Rewriting Old English in the Twelfth Century* (Cambridge Studies in Anglo-Saxon England, 30; Cambridge: Cambridge University Press), 31–4.

——(2006a), 'The Life and Times of Old English Homilies for the First Sunday in Lent', in Jon Wilcox and Hugh Magennis (eds.), *The Power of Words: Anglo-Saxon Studies Presented to Don Scragg on his Seventieth Birthday* (Morgantown, WV: West Virginia University Press), 207–42.

——(2006b), 'Categorization, Periodization: The Silence of (the) English in the Twelfth Century', *New Medieval Literatures*, 8: 247–73.

——(2006c), 'The Life of English in the Mid-Twelfth Century: Ralph d'Escures's Homily on the Virgin Mary', in Ruth Kennedy and Simon Meecham-Jones (eds.), *Writers of the Reign of Henry II* (London: Palgrave Macmillan), 169–86.

VOLLHARDT, WILLIAM (1888), *Einfluss der lateinischen geistlichen Litteratur auf einige kleinere Schöpfungen der englischen Übergangsperiode* (Leipzig: Hesse & Becker).

WENZEL, SIEGFRIED (1967), 'The Three Enemies of Man', *Mediaeval Studies*, 29: 47–66.

WILCOX, JONATHAN (2000), 'Wulfstan and the Twelfth Century', in Mary Swan and Elaine M. Treharne (eds.), *Rewriting Old English in the Twelfth Century* (Cambridge Studies in Anglo-Saxon England, 30; Cambridge: Cambridge University Press), 83–97.

WRIGHT, CHARLES D. (1989), 'The Irish "Enumerative Style" in Old English Homiletic Literature, Especially Vercelli Homily IX', *Cambridge Medieval Celtic Studies*, 18: 27–74.

CHAPTER 12

AUTHORIZING FEMALE PIETY

DIANE WATT

LIVING FOR THE DEAD: THE SPIRITUAL AUTHORITY OF WOMEN VISIONARIES

It is something of a commonplace to note that most of the relatively small corpus of writing by women in the European Middle Ages was religious in content. When we think of women authors in this period, we often think of Heloise, Hildegard of Bingen, or Julian of Norwich. Indeed, many of the more important and well-known works by medieval women are mystical texts, either written down by the visionary herself, or on her behalf by a male, or less commonly female, secretary or scribe. The reasons for this are equally commonplace: women were excluded from notions of authorship because of their perceived inferiority and thus only had access to authority as passive vessels of God's word; only aristocratic women and women religious were privileged with the education and resources necessary to write or have works written; only mystics and visionaries would benefit from the sort of patronage necessary to have their works circulated and read. While there is a certain amount of truth in these commonplaces it is important to acknowledge that the situation of religious women and women writers was not the same throughout Europe and that it changed significantly in the course of the Middle Ages. In England, for example, the negative effect of the Conquest on the wealth and autonomy of the convents and on the authority of women religious, especially abbesses, is well known, as is, towards the end of the period, the arguably more positive impact of Lollardy on heterodox laywomen, who found themselves for the first time encouraged to preach by some communities.[1] But these are, of course, only extreme examples of the sorts of transitions that took place.

In this chapter I intend to offer a broad overview of English women's authority and piety from the Anglo-Saxon period to the fifteenth century that looks at accounts of women's visions either written down by the women themselves or recorded by others. In this survey I further restrict my focus to women's visions of the dead and the dying and consider here a representative selection of texts and writers, from Bede's *Ecclesiastical History*, through *The Life of Christina of Markyate*, to the writings of Julian of Norwich, *The Book of Margery Kempe*, and an anonymous female-authored fifteenth-century text known as *A Revelation of Purgatory*. However, although the arguments here have a much broader applicability, any comprehensive discussion of medieval female piety would have to take into account not only other forms of devotional writing, but also other forms of religious cultural production and expression. Nevertheless the focus on women's visions of the dead and the dying is justified because this sort of revelation, addressing as it does that most crucial of transitions in the Christian's spiritual journey from life to afterlife, allows me to trace through the Middle Ages the impact of some key developments in female authority and piety, namely the emergence of the Blessed Virgin Mary as a female figure of authority,[2] and the 'birth' of purgatory.[3] While the significance of the cult of the Virgin Mary to women may seem self-evident (although in fact it is highly debated), the relevance of purgatory requires more explanation. In summary, purgatory mattered because intercession for the dead was a key responsibility of women, especially nuns, and visions of purgatorial suffering became widespread in the later Middle Ages.[4] Even before what Jacques Le Goff calls the 'spacialization' of purgatory in the second half of the twelfth century,[5] women's visions were often overwhelmingly concerned with testifying to the redemption or salvation of others, including of other women.[6] As Alexandra Barratt points out, women visionaries often served 'as a link between the living and the dead'.[7] To take this further, devout women might be seen to live *for* the dead, to adapt Patrick J. Geary's memorable phrase.[8] Moreover, throughout the Middle Ages, we can detect a continuity in women's visions in the attention they pay to what Mary C. Erler has called 'a bond extending beyond the grave', or more specifically 'women's friendship after death', in other words, to the connections established between living female visionaries and the deceased subjects of their visions.[9] These visions of the dead and the dying provide us with, to adapt a phrase from Carolyn Muessig, 'alternative modes of spiritual conversation' that by their very existence challenge any definition of religious authority as exclusively masculine and clerical.[10]

---

[1] For more nuanced accounts, see Hollis (1992: 1–14); McSheffrey (1995).
[2] Clayton (1990); Fulton (2002); Warner (1990).
[3] Le Goff (1984); Binksi (1996: 181–99).
[4] Newman (1995: 109–13); Wogan-Browne (2003).
[5] Le Goff (1984: 3–4).   [6] Newman (1995: 108–36).
[7] Barratt (1992: 51).   [8] Geary (1994).   [9] Erler (2007: 336).
[10] Muessig (2009: 74); Muessig's phrase is 'alternative modes of *theological* conversation'.

A DEATH IN THE CONVENT: ANGLO-SAXON VISIONARIES IN BEDE'S *ECCLESIASTICAL HISTORY*

Visions of the dying, of the afterlife, and concerning the bodies and tombs of the dead, while not unique to hagiographies of saintly women, figure prominently in Bede's narratives of abbesses and convents in the fourth book of the *Ecclesiastical History*. For example, he testifies to the great holiness of Barking Abbey, founded in the late seventh century by Eorcenwold for his sister Æthelburh. According to Bede, Abbess Æthelburh's death is predicted by a vision, witnessed by a certain solitary nun:

> One evening, at dusk, as she left the little cell in which she lived, she saw distinctly what seemed to be a human body, wrapped in a shroud and brighter than the sun, being apparently raised up from within the house in which the sisters used to sleep. She looked closely to see how this glorious visionary body was raised up and saw that it was lifted as it were by cords, brighter than gold, until it was drawn up into the open heavens, and she could see it no longer.[11]

The nun realizes that what she is seeing is a portent of death, and correctly interprets the golden cords as representing the virtuous deeds that will draw one of her sisters— the abbess as it turns out—to heaven. One striking aspect of this vision, and indeed of others that follow in the *Ecclesiastical History*, is its Marian quality. Although these visions, unlike later medieval examples (as we will see) are not explicitly concerned with the Blessed Virgin Mary, the ascension of Æthelburh resonates with the tradition of the Assumption of the Mother of God.[12] Æthelburh's exceptional piety is confirmed at the moment of her passing by the vision God gives to a member of her own convent. On this occasion, Bede identifies the visionary as Torhtgyth, a close associate of Æthelburh, who had helped the abbess maintain discipline within Barking.

The relationship between the visionary and the subject of her vision is a symbiotic one: the visionary testifies to, and thus authorizes the holiness of her subject, but in so doing she herself gains authority and her own piety becomes manifest. Furthermore, Bede anticipates the vision, and the good death of Æthelburh, by explaining that, prior to the Abbess's passing, Torhtgyth had experienced nine years of illness, which served to burn away 'any traces of sin remaining among her virtues through ignorance or carelessness' (*Ecclesiastical History*, 361). The living Torhtgyth has to be purified to prepare her to receive divine revelation, but at the same time, as becomes evident, she has to be prepared for her own good death and ascension to heaven. Three years after her vision concerning Æthelburh, Torhtgyth is herself on the verge

---

[11] Colgrave and Mynors (1969: 361). Hereafter all in-text references to the *Ecclesiastical History* are to this edn. My account here of female visions in Bede's *Ecclesiastical History* is particularly indebted to Weston (2004).

[12] Hollis (2000) points out that one model for such 'visions of ascending souls' is also the *Life of Benedict* in Gregory's *Dialogues*, book 2 (p. 260). Of particular interest here is Benedict's vision of his sister's soul rising in the form of a dove to heaven.

of death (*Ecclesiastical History*, 363). Paralysis spreads throughout her body and she remains in this state for three days and nights. The duration is significant, echoing the time between Christ's crucifixion and resurrection. At this stage in her illness, Torhtgyth has entered a liminal state between Earth and heaven, when suddenly she awakes and engages in a conversation with an invisible person. This person is, as she explains to those around her, Æthelburh herself, who has returned to call her to heaven.

The events surrounding Torhtgyth's death can be read as supporting evidence of the saintliness of Æthelburh. Yet a further point that emerges from the account of these visions is that Æthelburh's holiness and the visionary blessings surrounding her death are shared by other members of the community.[13] While her staunch supporter in the convent, Torhtgyth, is singled out for special attention, it is not only those who might be thought of as the most powerful who benefit, as even elderly nuns who may no longer have an active role to play are acknowledged. Another miracle recorded by Bede involves a disabled nun who, immediately following the abbess's death, asks to be carried to where the abbess's body lies in the church. Speaking to her 'as though she were addressing a living person', the nun petitions the abbess to intercede with Christ on her behalf, so that she can be released from her illness (*Ecclesiastical History*, 361). The nun's prayers are answered and twelve days later she dies. Nor are the miracles only experienced by those in the convent of the highest rank. While Bede tells us that the disabled nun is 'of noble family in this world' (*Ecclesiastical History*, 361), others associated with visions of death in the time of plague include a 3-year-old boy and a nun called Edith responsible for teaching him, and an anonymous nun who is summoned to God by a vision of a monk or priest (*Ecclesiastical History*, 359). Through such visions, the piety of the *whole* convent is thus recognized and authorized.

Moreover, this sequence of visions is framed in Bede's *Ecclesiastical History* by what appears implicitly to be a conflict concerning the positioning of the nuns' cemetery at Barking. As Jocelyn Wogan-Browne has noted, the nuns' cemetery clearly had great significance as the 'locus of memory and continuity and an ever-present theatre of events'.[14] Æthelburh, the founding abbess, was uncertain where to locate it, until she received divine guidance that it should be separate from that of the monks (*Ecclesiastical History*, 357–9). However, her successor at Barking, Hildelith, subsequently resolves that 'the bones of the servants and handmaidens of Christ which had been buried there should all be taken up and transferred to the church of the blessed Mother of God and buried there in one place' (*Ecclesiastical History*, 363–5). Hollis rightly contextualizes these events in terms of theological debates about the validity of double monasteries,[15] but it is important to acknowledge that *both* Æthelburh's and Hildelith's decisions receive divine authorization through visions and miracles shared by the community. This is more marked in the case of Æthelburh, because her initial hesitation is answered by a vision of light which Bede records was experienced

---

[13] On the sharing of visions within a community, see Kieckhefer (2007).
[14] Wogan-Browne (2003:179).   [15] Hollis (1992: 111).

by the nuns of Barking, who at the time were praying by the monks' graves, and which is also partially witnessed by two of their brethren, an older monk and a younger one, who are inside the oratory (*Ecclesiastical History*, 357–9). It is possible to explain away Bede's inclusion of the testimony of the two monks in terms of the gendering of authority, clerical male eyewitnesses being perceived to be more reliable than female eyewitnesses, even women religious, and therefore being necessary for the story to be convincing.[16] But, this is not the whole picture. For what emerges from this miracle is a sense of the shared nature of such revelations. This vision concerning the positioning of the cemetery radiates outwards to all parts of the community like the divine light that identifies the blessed place where the bodies of the deceased nuns are to lie. It connects the living nuns and monks, just as the souls of their companions are chastely united in death.

The significance of visions and miracles concerning the dying and the dead to the convent community are also central to two other key saintly biographies included in Bede's *Ecclesiastical History*, those of Æthelthryth and of Hild. The lives of these two important and powerful abbesses stand side by side in the *Ecclesiastical History*, and are clearly intended to be read together. Æthelthryth falls into a tradition of insular Anglo-Saxon female sanctity which is typified by the fact that the woman saint is married and has to struggle with her husband to protect her chastity.[17] The account of Æthelthryth in Bede pays far more attention to her life *and especially her death* as a woman religious than it does to her life as a devout and chaste wife (*Ecclesiastical History*, 391–401). Although we are told of Æthelthryth's great self-discipline and mortification of the flesh, once again it is the visions and miracles of death that concern Bede most, and to which he returns in his life of Æthelthryth in order to relate them in detail. Æthelthryth, like many of her nuns, is struck down by plague and buried in a wooden coffin. Sixteen years later, the decision is made to have her corpse exhumed and reburied in the church. In order to do this a new coffin has to be found, and a marble sarcophagus is discovered, miraculously provided by God, which fits Æthelthryth as if it had been carved for her. What is more, Æthelthryth's body is not only found preserved whole but actually healed: a tumour on her neck, which was lanced three days before her death, has vanished and the only mark that remains is a faint scar. Here, we have divine evidence of the perfect virginity of Æthelthryth (the body that is incorrupt in death must have been incorrupt in life), and Bishop Wilfred is named in the text as bearing witness to the truth that Æthelthryth's dead body remains whole. Indeed to Wilfred's testimony is added that of Cynefrith, the physician who had treated Æthelthryth as she lay dying.

Once again, in noticing the appearance of significant male witnesses, we should not overlook the communal aspect to these visions and miracles of death. Bede reports that Æthelthryth publicly predicted the plague that would kill her and also 'the number of those of the monastery who were to be taken from the world by the same pestilence' (*Ecclesiastical History*, 393). Through their accompanying prophecies and visions, disease

---

[16] van Houts (1999: 19–39, 41–62).
[17] Elliott (1993: 74).

and death serve to strengthen the community rather than devastate it, just as espousal to Christ overcomes the threat to Æthelthryth's virginity posed by her marriages. Furthermore, female relationships 'extending beyond the grave' figure largely in this narrative. It is Seaxburh, Æthelthryth's own sister, and successor as abbess of Ely, who decides that Æthelthryth's tomb should be moved, and who sends out the monks to look for a new coffin. Furthermore, women play a key role in attending to the corpse. While the whole community, monks as well as nuns, take part in the exhumation, it is the abbess and her sisters who open the old coffin with the intention of lifting the bones, and it is they who wash and reclothe the body and carry it to its new resting place. Æthelthryth, who, we are told, in life did not wash herself but washed her fellow nuns, is here finally physically cleansed before being returned to the ground.

What is striking about Bede's life of Hild (*Ecclesiastical History*, 405–15) is the extent to which it parallels his account of Æthelthryth. Again, as in the life of Æthelthryth, Bede is less concerned with the saintly woman's holy life than with her holy death. In fact, with the exception of a dream which Hild's mother Breguswith experienced, we are told very little at all about the first half of Hild's life beyond the fact that it was spent 'very nobly in secular habit' (*Ecclesiastical History*, 407). And, although men, whether as patrons (Bishop Aidan) or as sons of her religious house at Streanaeshalch (Whitby), are central to what he reveals of the second half of her life, once she has taken the veil, women again dominate the narrative of her death. Like Æthelthryth, Hild suffers agonizing illness for a prolonged period of time: she dies at cock-crow in the seventh year of her incapacity. The splitting of Hild's life in two parts at the age of 33, the age of Christ when he was crucified, signifies that at this perfect age Hild herself was reborn. That she struggled with ill health for seven years indicates that she achieved spiritual completion before leaving the world (seven also signifying perfection in biblical numerology). The reference to cock-crow may be to the third watch of the night in Mark 13: 35: 'Watch ye therefore: for ye know not when the master of the house cometh' rather than to Peter's denial of Christ in Matthew 26: 34–75 and John 18: 27. And again like Æthelthryth, and Æthelburh before her, her death is marked by miracles and visions that ripple through the community and bring unity and joy. Begu, a nun at Hackness, witnesses Hild's ascension in a dream. As with Æthelburh, there are strong Marian elements in this account. Sleeping in the dormitory Begu is apparently awoken by a bell toll and watches in amazement as the roof opens and light pours into the room before she sees the abbess's soul carried upwards by angels. She rushes to share what she has seen with her prioress Frigyth, who summons her nuns to gather in the church to pray for Hild. The monks who later arrive with news of Hild's death find them thus. A similar vision of the ascendance of Hild's soul was experienced by a nun at Streanaeshalch itself. As Clare A. Lees and Gillian R. Overing observe, Begu's dream, which is reiterated three times and then confirmed by another vision, is very much foregrounded in this narrative, although they also dismiss such 'visionary witnessing' for 'obscuring the real conditions of [Hild's] life'.[18]

---

[18] Lees and Overing (2001: 24).

Stephanie Hollis anticipates the argument of Lees and Overing when she contends that Bede's narratives of holy women and their communities, 'consisting of a handful of details overridingly concerned with death, burial and disease, give no encouraging impression of the preoccupations of monastic women'.[19] I argue the opposite, that Bede's accounts of the visions surrounding the deaths of Æthelburh, Torhtgyth, Æthelthryth, and Hild, whether experienced by the dying woman herself (in the case of Torhtgyth) or by her companions, serve to authorize the holiness of these women in positive terms which the women themselves would have recognized and considered important. Although not explicitly concerned with the Blessed Virgin Mary, these visions can have Marian qualities, and dying women are elevated by association with the Mother of God. Of these narratives it is Bede's life of Æthelthryth that reveals most clearly the importance of the body of the woman saint as a contested site of sin and piety, corruption and purity. This conflict is perhaps central to female religious authority more generally, but, as we have seen, it is balanced in these narratives by a concern with the convent as community and with visionary testimonies that are not singular but communal. Furthermore, in the accounts of Æthelburh and Torhtgyth, Æthelthryth and Seaxburh, Hild and Begu, particular significance is given to visionary relations between living women and their dying or dead companions.

'A WOMAN OF GREAT AUTHORITY': MARIAN VISIONS IN *THE LIFE* OF *CHRISTINA OF MARKYATE*

One of the defining and distinctive qualities of women's visions of the dying and the dead in the post-Conquest period is the increasing importance of the role played by the Virgin Mary. Although the cult of the Virgin existed in the Anglo-Saxon period, devotion to Mary intensified from the twelfth century onward.[20] A key transitional text that connects the Anglo-Saxon visionary nuns to the later medieval women mystics and visionaries is *The Life of Christina of Markyate*. Born more than four hundred years after the death of Hild, and thirty years after the Norman Conquest, Christina of Markyate was from a noble Anglo-Saxon family. Aspects of her biography echo the lives, and more specifically the deaths of Torhtgyth, Hild, and Æthelthryth.[21] Remarkably this incomplete hagiography, written by an anonymous monk of St Albans Abbey, was begun in Christina's own lifetime, and breaks off abruptly

---

[19] Hollis (1992: 260).
[20] See esp. Clayton (1990); Fulton (2002).
[21] On the influence of Hild, see also Watt (2007: 27–31).

before her death. There are, then, no accounts of visions surrounding her demise that equate with those associated with the deaths of Bede's saintly abbesses and nuns. Nevertheless, early on in *The Life of Christina of Markyate*, we are told that from the very moment that the infant Christina privately resolved to devote herself to God, she meditated on her own end and 'imagined herself lying on her deathbed (as if the future were already present)'.[22] More significantly, however, embedded within *The Life* are accounts of the terrible illnesses Christina endured for many years, following her enforced if voluntary enclosure in a cramped corner of the cell of her spiritual guide Roger, a revered hermit monk of St Albans (enforced in the sense that Christina was in hiding from her family, voluntary in the sense that she felt privileged to join Roger). After Roger's death, Christina took up residence in his hermitage, and gathered around her a community of devout women. As her fame spread, people came to her for help and guidance, including (as her biographer reports) a young woman from Canterbury, who, following Christina's intervention, was cured of the 'falling sickness' or epilepsy (*Life*, 119–21). This narrative prefaces and leads into the biographer's two accounts of Marian visions in which Christina herself is divinely healed: one from a merely physical sickness, the other from an intense spiritual as well as physical burden.

The first of Christina's Marian healing visions centres on a near-death experience, when she became paralysed down one side of her body. As with Æthelthryth, physicians intervened, but their treatments made her illness worse rather than better. Like Hild, who was sick for six years and died in the seventh, Christina was severely afflicted by paralysis for six days but cured on the seventh (Christina's biographer explains the numerology in terms of God resting on the seventh day: *Life*, 123). Nevertheless, although Christina recovered, unlike her saintly predecessors, there are further echoes of their lives in the dream of the 'woman of great authority' experienced by one of Christina's female companions (*Life*, 125). In this vision, which occurred 'in the first watch' of what was to be the final night of Christina's illness, the Virgin Mary appeared next to the bed of the apparently dying woman, and gave her a lozenge. Christina's companions tried to stop her, arguing that similar medicines had already only made her worse, but Mary continued regardless. This vision then, experienced by Christina's companion, served to confirm the miraculous nature of Christina's recovery.

The second vision concerning the curing of Christina was witnessed by Christina herself. This vision can be dated to shortly before Christina made her profession as a nun in St Albans Abbey before Alexander, bishop of Lincoln, in 1131 or thereabouts. Significantly, the vision is dated to the seventh day of the Feast of the Assumption of the Blessed Virgin Mary, that is, to 21 August.[23] As she prepared to take her vows, Christina, who had had to be released from an enforced betrothal, and who had herself struggled with reciprocated sexual desire for an unnamed cleric, experienced

---

[22] Talbot (1959: 39). Hereafter all in-text references to *The Life of Christina of Markyate* are to this edn.

[23] For a discussion of the Marian miracles that took place before Christina's birth, see Watt (2007: 28–9).

great anxiety concerning her status as a virgin and sought reassurance from the Virgin Mary. Having waited patiently for several days for a response to her prayers, she was rewarded with a vision 'about cock-crow and before dawn' on the seventh day (*Life*, 129) in a confirmation of her piety and sanctity that resonates with the Annunciation and the Assumption of the Virgin, and with Begu's dream of Hild's ascendance. Christina awoke and found her female companions still sleeping, having apparently failed to rise for nocturnes. Suddenly angels surrounded Christina, addressing her with the words 'Hail, virgin of Christ. The Lord of all, Jesus Christ Himself greets you' (*Life*, 129), and placed a crown on her head.

Thus crowned, Christina stood in the midst of the angels who had been sent to her from cock-crow until the day grew warm after the rising of the sun. Then, as the angels withdrew to heaven, she remained alone, knowing for certain from the heavenly crown that Christ had preserved her chaste in mind and body. Furthermore, she felt so strong in health that never afterwards did she feel the slightest twinge from those maladies that had afflicted her earlier on. (*Life*, 129)

While the crowning of Christina places her within the tradition of legendary virgin martyrs such as Margaret of Antioch, and the miraculous healing affirms her blessed state, the divine verification of her chastity reinforces not only her devotion to, but also her identification with, the Mother of God.

The dream vision of the crowning of Christina is, in fact, only one of a series of revelations recorded in *The Life* that serve to confirm Christina's status in heaven and that of her most significant patron Geoffrey, abbot of St Albans, on whose instructions *The Life* seems to have been written by a member of his community. However, not all of Christina's visions function to authorize the holy woman and sanction her supporters: some are critical and admonitory and it is striking that the Virgin Mary, who is so strongly associated with intercession and mercy as well as healing, does not figure in these. A particularly remarkable example is Christina's vision of a dead monk of St Albans, Alvered, who (in counterpoint to the Virgin Mary) is described as 'a certain man of great authority' (*Life*, 135) who manifested himself before Christina's eyes holding a candle 'as befits a friend of the light' and warned her against a certain unspecified action that Geoffrey of St Albans was secretly planning. When Christina let Geoffrey (who is not yet her confidant) know of her vision, his response was to dismiss it as a mere dream and to resolve to continue in the same course of action (*Life*, 137). Until, that is, 'in the first watch' of the following night he was attacked by demons, who seemed hell-bent on torturing and murdering him. Seeing Alvered, 'eyes and counte-nance blazing in anger', Geoffrey pleaded for mercy, promising to desist from his deed and to pay heed to Christina henceforth. Here the spirit of Alvered visits both the holy woman and her future mentor, confirming the former to be the vessel of divine authority and forcing the latter to pledge his obedience, thus forging a supernatural bond between them that will prove impossible to break. The vision of the dead Alvered can be contrasted with the reassurances that Christina is able to offer her dying brother Gregory, another monk of St Albans, when she reported that she had been told by a voice from heaven that the Virgin Mary was calling for him (*Life*, 141).

The Life of Christina of Markyate—written, as noted above, in Christina's own lifetime and on the instructions of Geoffrey of St Albans—does not record the latter's death either (indeed the hagiography was probably abandoned when its patron died) but just as it includes revelatory experiences surrounding Christina's illnesses, so it incorporates visions relating to the healing of Geoffrey. Twice Geoffrey is described as being on the point of death, and twice Christina receives miraculous assurances that he will live (*Life*, 141–3 and 147–9). What is particularly striking about these revelations is that Christina calls upon others to confirm them. Indeed although no visions of dying or dead nuns or lay women are recorded in Christina's *Life*, female authorization in particular plays a key role. Christina's response to prophetic knowledge was to confide it immediately to one or more of her companions; thus when a youth called Loric, who had assisted Christina in her flight from her family, appeared to her in the night and advised her not to be concerned about her own safety, from which she correctly deduced that he had recently passed away, she straightaway told the female recluse Alfwen, with whom she was living, what had occurred (*Life*, 97).

Significantly, on the first occasion when Geoffrey made an unexpected recovery, the witness to Christina's divine foreknowledge was Christina's own sister and fellow recluse Margaret. Indeed although she may not figure largely in *The Life*, Margaret plays a key role as Christina's personal confidante within the small female community at Markyate. Whereas even the biographer of the *Life* does not appear to have first-hand knowledge of many of Christina's experiences,[24] Margaret is tellingly described as the one 'who knew her secrets' (*Life*, 145). Margaret, like Geoffrey, shares some of Christina's experiences and revelations, and when Christ appears as a pilgrim he manifests himself to both Christina and Margaret, with Margaret playing Martha to Christina's Mary (*Life*, 183). Female companions do thus play an important role as confidantes of the woman visionary, able to testify to her revelations, and on occasion, as in the Anglo-Saxon lives recorded by Bede, the visionary experience is shared by other members of the community.

'TRIBULATIONS IN MY SLEEP': PURGATORY AND THE LATE MEDIEVAL TRADITION

Revelations concerning the fate of spiritual friends and members of the religious community are also typical of the writings of the late medieval women mystics and visionaries, to such an extent that their very absence becomes a matter of note, as is the case with Julian of Norwich. In both the earlier *A Vision Showed to a Devout Woman* and the longer *A Revelation of Love*, the late fourteenth-century English

---

[24] Ibid. 32–3.

woman mystic, Julian of Norwich, relates that she was denied a specific revelation concerning the spiritual destiny of a close friend or relative:[25] 'I desired of a certaine person that I loved howe it shulde be with hire. And in this desire I letted myselfe, for I was noght taught in this time' (*Vision*, 16. 13–14). Neither version of Julian's showings reveals the identity of this woman, who may have been a nun, possibly even a sister in Julian's own convent, if we accept the recently revived argument that Julian was a nun.[26] However, the anonymous woman could equally have been an anchoress, or a vowess or other pious lay woman, a relative, or a companion or servant. And even though God denies Julian this revelation, the very fact that Julian seeks to know about her friend's future indicates surely that such visions were not uncommon.

In direct contrast to Julian of Norwich, her younger East Anglian contemporary, Margery Kempe, *did* receive revelations concerning the future of her friends and the fate of the dead. And whereas Julian of Norwich was also denied a vision of hell (*Revelation*, 33. 1–8), Kempe received the divine instruction 'þu must as wel heryn of þe dampnyd as of þe sauyd'.[27] Indeed, her revelations concerning the damned caused her such distress and despair that for a time she convinced herself she was experiencing diabolic delusions. But as a result of these visions and revelations she was able to advise friends and relatives of the deceased, especially widows who had recently lost their husbands, on how the sufferings of those in purgatory could be reduced by pious acts, such as almsgiving (*Book*, 46–7). Kempe received revelations concerning the fates of the living (the sick and the healthy) as well as the dead. *The Book of Margery Kempe* records how, as she prayed before a woman's corpse on display in the Church of St Margaret in Lynn, it was revealed to Kempe that the woman's soul was in purgatory, and that the woman's husband would die imminently (*Book*, 53). While we are told little or nothing of the identity of those about whom or for whom Kempe receives revelations, it is apparent that some are close companions. Amongst those whose recovery from apparently certain death Kempe was able to predict was 'a worshepful woman & . . . an holy woman whech was a specyal frende' to Kempe herself (*Book*, 54). It is remarkable that the only mention made in the *Book* of what is evidently a close relationship between two women occurs in such a revelation.

The revelations of Julian of Norwich and Margery Kempe have to be understood in the context of both the intensifying of Marian devotion in the post-Conquest period and the emergence of a distinct subgenre of visionary literature focused on a revelation of purgatorial suffering, and often on the dreamer's or narrator's own journey through purgatory. The most famous example of this kind of text is, of course, the second cantica of *The Divine Comedy* by Dante Alighieri. However it is not the earliest. In the late twelfth-century the Anglo-Norman writer Marie de France had produced *Saint Patrick's*

---

[25] Watson and Jenkins (2006). Hereafter, all in-text references to the *Vision* or the *Revelation* are to this edn.

[26] This is the view put forward ibid. 4.

[27] Meech and Allen (1940: 144–5). Hereafter all in-text references to *The Book of Margery Kempe* are to this edn.

Purgatory, a French poetic translation of a slightly earlier Latin prose text that would go on to gain widespread currency in a number of languages.[28] One later, Middle English, example of a purgatorial vision is the fifteenth-century *Vision of William Stranton*. In this text the visionary is guided through Purgatory by the late medieval saint John of Bridlington, canonized in 1401, and, interestingly, by 'Sant Hylde of Whytby'.[29] Stranton, about whom we know little beyond his name, converses with his sister whom he wronged in life, and witnesses the sufferings of religious and lay people, including the judgement of an unnamed prioress. Women too were the recipients of such revelations. Indeed, Barbara Newman offers a necessary corrective to Le Goff's natal metaphor, which ironically is applied to a history that underplays the role of women, when she states that women writers might be seen as the 'midwives at the birth of Purgatory', citing the twelfth-century examples of Hildegard of Bingen and Elisabeth of Schönau.[30] The late fourteenth-century woman saint Bridget of Sweden, whose cult in early fifteenth-century England was fostered by the Lancastrians, famously also experienced visions of the sufferings of those in purgatory and also in hell.

Bridget of Sweden's influence on Margery Kempe, for whom she provided a model of married female sanctity, is well known, but her impact can also be seen in a text by an anonymous early fifteenth-century woman visionary and recluse, which is known simply as *A Revelation of Purgatory*. This is in fact a letter, written by the woman to one of her religious advisers. It describes a series of nightmarish visions witnessed over three nights, starting on the Feast of St Lawrence (10 August) 1422.[31] The subject of the visions is the purgatorial suffering of a nun called Margaret, and her eventual salvation. Margaret can be identified as a sister of St Mary's Winchester or Nunnaminster. As Erler has shown, the visionary herself was almost certainly a lay anchoress of Winchester.[32] Reference is made in the text to a network of four named priests, an unnamed recluse of Westminster and another monk of Westminster, which represent the author's immediate circle.[33] Mention of these figures serves once again to authorize the visions and the text, to give them the seal of masculine clerical approval, but they also testify to the visionary's own status as seer and holy woman. Indeed, there is compelling contextual historical evidence to suggest that this anonymous woman visionary had such religious standing that even before she received the revelations concerning Margaret she had been consulted by Richard Beauchamp, earl of Warwick, who sent his men to visit her, and brought her to London for three days for an extended consultation.[34]

The visionary is careful to locate her revelations, which prove to be extremely critical of ecclesiastical corruption, both within the parameters of spiritual orthodoxy and within the broader medieval tradition of the dream vision. The account in *A Revelation of Purgatory* is quite specific as to the circumstances of the visions:

---

[28] Curley (1993).
[29] 'Vision of William Stranton' (1991: 81).
[30] Newman (1995: 111).
[31] Harley (1985). Hereafter all in-text references to *A Revelation of Purgatory* are to this edn.
[32] Erler (2007: 323–6).
[33] Ibid. 327, 328–35.
[34] Ibid. 322, 325.

My der fadyr, I do 30w to witte how grete tribulacion I hadde in my slep vp-on Seynt Lorence Day at ny3t, the 3er of Our Lord MlCCCCxxij. I went to my bedde at viij of the clok and so I fel on slep. And fadyr, betwix ix and x me thoght I was rauyshed into purgatory, and sodeynly I saw al þe peynes whiche wer showed to me many tymes before—as 3e, fadyr, knew wel by my tellynge. (*A Revelation*, 59)

By giving the precise date and time, the visionary stresses the immediacy of the events, and emphasizes that this is a first-hand account. It is also apparent that the visions recorded here are by no means the first that she has received but that they are familiar in terms of general content and have already been subject to the scrutiny of her spiritual advisers.[35] She immediately goes on to stress that on this occasion she was not guided by a 'spirite' who might offer her consolation and was for that reason all the more terrified when she awoke. The implication of this claim is that previously she had been privileged with a spiritual guide, as is conventional in both religious and secular dream visions.

A number of critics have identified the influence of St Bridget in the tripartite representation of purgatory in *A Revelation*.[36] Thus, the dreamer sees 'thre grete fyres', distinct from one another, but joined together, and in the greatest fire she sees the tormented spirit of the nun Margaret (*A Revelation*, 59–60). In the final dream, Margaret is led out of the fires and into heaven. But Bridget's legacy to *A Revelation of Purgatory* extends further, and can be seen in the portrayals of the torments of the dead and of the sinfulness and sufferings of male and female religious, and in the emphasis on women and female bonds more generally.[37] The Middle English *Liber Celestis* of Bridget of Sweden notably includes a vision of a woman who 'semid on liue', her mother in hell, and her daughter in purgatory.[38] The grotesque tortures of the daughter, and especially those of the mother, resonate with those of the nun Margaret in *A Revelation of Purgatory* but, of course, only the daughter can request the prayers and deeds of alms necessary to speed her out of her pains.[39] What seems so distinct and so Brigittine about *A Revelation of Purgatory*, in comparison with the writings of the author's English women predecessors, is the emphasis on purgatory itself, the graphic depictions of the torments of those suffering there, and especially those of the men and women of religion. This emphasis is, however, completely in keeping with insular traditions of purgatorial visions extending from before Marie de France to the *Vision of William Stranton* and beyond.

As we might expect, in the text of *A Revelation of Purgatory*, as in the showings of Julian of Norwich and *The Book of Margery Kempe*, as well as St Bridget's revelations, Marian devotion is again also significant. Julian first sees the Virgin, 'a simpille maidene and a meeke, yonge of age' early in her showings (*A Vision*, 4. 22). Likewise, near the beginning of her *Book*, Margery Kempe, partly echoing St Bridget's own

---

[35] On the role of spiritual advisers, see Voaden (1999: esp. pp. 57–61); Elliot (2004).
[36] Erler (2007: 335); Harley (1985: 15–16); Hughes (1988: 342).
[37] Erler (2007: 336–7).
[38] Ellis (1987: 441–3).
[39] Ibid. 443.

visions of Christ's birth, is described as re-enacting in her meditations scenes from Mary's life, including the nativity and infancy of Christ in which she serves as Mary's handmaid (*Book*, 18–20). In contrast, the Virgin only appears in the final vision of *A Revelation of Purgatory*. There, described as a 'fayr lady' dressed in white gold decorated with gold stars, wearing a crown and carrying a sceptre, and accompanied by her Son, she orchestrates Margaret's entry to paradise (*A Revelation of Purgatory*, 84–5). However, the appearance of the Virgin is anticipated much earlier in the text. Not only are Masses of Our Lady specified in the prayers requested by Margaret to speed her through purgatory (*A Revelation of Purgatory*, 63–4), but the dreamer notes that Margaret calls out to the Virgin in her suffering, and Margaret herself explains that this is because of Mary's infinite mercy and also because of her own personal devotion to the Mother of God: 'whils I was on lyf, I fasted hyr fast' (*A Revelation of Purgatory*, 77). Later she declares 'Blessed be God and our Lady Mary þat I am here now' (*A Revelation of Purgatory*, 79) and goes on to thank the dreamer for her intervention, stating that, had it not been for the help of the dreamer and her associates, her purgatorial sufferings would have lasted much longer. As Margaret's purgatorial sufferings play themselves out, then, it becomes apparent that the visionary's role is not simply that of passive recipient but a more active one of intercessor and interme-diary. The visionary, we are told, in response to the suffering of Margaret, undertook a pilgrimage to the Marian shrine at Southwick Priory on her behalf, a pilgrimage that the nun herself had pledged but had failed to fulfil (*A Revelation of Purgatory*, 84). Similarly the prayers of the visionary's spiritual advisers helped alleviate her suffer-ing, and as a reward for their intervention they too will be granted 'ful grete mede' (*A Revelation of Purgatory*, 85). Female authority then frames this text, with the visionary herself, with the assistance of her male supporters, helping Margaret on her journey out of purgatory, and the Virgin Mary bringing Margaret to Salvation.

CONCLUSION

In the Christian Middle Ages, death was not seen as the end, and the place of the dead in the community was continually marked by rituals and memorialization. The dead continued to live alongside the living, and to communicate with them, women as well as men. Intercession for the dead was a vital aspect of women's piety. As Barbara Newman observes: 'Such prayer constituted a safe, invisible, contemplative mission that could put women's devotion and compassion to work without violating any gender taboos.'[40] In the later Middle Ages in particular, the Blessed Virgin Mary, herself a figure of compassion, offered women an important model of female religious authority, and increasingly played a significant role in their devotions,

---

[40] Newman (1995: 111).

good works, and revelations. While early medieval women's piety was certainly concerned with suffering and cleansing from sin, the post-Conquest period also saw a widespread focus in religious writings on purgatory as a third place between heaven and hell. In turn, this led to an association between female religious authority and what Newman calls women's 'purgatorial piety'.[41] Women, as witnesses to the posthumous suffering and salvation of others, were crucial intermediaries. However, perhaps unexpectedly, one crucial (and hitherto overlooked) aspect of this piety was its emphasis on relations *between* women. Women as visionaries were then not only granted authority by God to speak or even to write about what they had seen, but they were able to intervene on behalf of others who had been close to them in life, whether family, friends, or fellow religious, many of whom were indeed women.

BIBLIOGRAPHY

BARRATT, ALEXANDRA (ed.) (1992), *Women's Writing in Middle English* (London: Longman).

BINKSI, PAUL (1996), *Medieval Death: Ritual and Representation* (London: British Museum Press).

CLAYTON, MARY (1990), *The Cult of the Virgin Mary in Anglo-Saxon England* (Cambridge: Cambridge University Press).

COLGRAVE, BERTRAM, and R. A. B. MYNORS (eds.) (1969), *Bede's Ecclesiastical History of the English People* (Oxford: Oxford University Press).

CURLEY, MICHAEL J. (ed. and tr.) (1993), *St Patrick's Purgatory: A Poem by Marie de France* (Binghamton, NY: Medieval and Renaissance Texts and Studies).

ELLIOTT, DYAN (1993), *Spiritual Marriage: Sexual Abstinence in Medieval Wedlock* (Princeton: Princeton University Press).

——(2004), *Proving Woman: Female Spirituality and Inquisitional Culture in the Later Middle Ages* (Princeton: Princeton University Press).

ELLIS, ROGER (ed.) (1987), *The Liber Celestis of St Bridget of Sweden* (EETS 291; Oxford: Oxford University Press for the Early English Text Society).

ERLER, MARY C. (2007), '"A Revelation of Purgatory" (1422): Reform and the Politics of Female Visions', *Viator* 38/1: 321–45.

FULTON, RACHEL (2002), *From Judgment to Passion: Devotion to Christ and the Virgin Mary, 800–1200* (New York: Columbia University Press).

GEARY, PATRICK J. (1994), *Living with the Dead in the Middle Ages* (Ithaca, NY: Cornell University Press).

HARLEY, MARTA POWELL (ed.) (1985), *A Revelation of Purgatory by an Unknown, Fifteenth-Century Woman Visionary: Introduction, Critical Text, and Translation* (Lewiston: Edwin Mellen Press).

HOLLIS, STEPHANIE (1992), *Anglo-Saxon Women and the Church: Sharing a Common Fate* (Woodbridge: Boydell Press).

VAN HOUTS, ELISABETH (1999), *Memory and Gender in Medieval Europe, 900–1200* (London: Macmillan).

---

41 Ibid. 109.

HUGHES, JONATHAN (1988), *Pastors and Visionaries: Religion and Secular Life in Late Medieval Yorkshire* (Woodbridge: Boydell & Brewer).

KIECKHEFER, RICHARD (2007), 'Mystical Communities in the Late Medieval West', Annual Medieval Academy Lecture, International Medieval Congress, University of Leeds, 10 July.

LEES, CLARE A., and GILLIAN R. OVERING (2001), *Double Agents: Women and Clerical Culture in Anglo-Saxon England* (Philadelphia: University of Pennsylvania Press).

LE GOFF, JACQUES (1984), *The Birth of Purgatory*, tr. Arthur Goldhammer (London: Scolar Press).

MCSHEFFREY, SHANNON (1995), *Gender and Heresy: Women and Men in Lollard Communities, 1420–1530* (Philadelphia: University of Pennsylvania Press).

MEECH, SANFORD BROWN, and HOPE EMILY ALLEN (eds.) (1940), *The Book of Margery Kempe* (EETS 212; London: Oxford University Press for the Early English Text Society).

MUESSIG, CAROLYN (2009), 'Communities of Discourse: Religious Authority and the Role of Holy Women in the Middle Ages', in Anneke B. Mulder-Bakker and Liz Herbert McAvoy (eds.), *Women and Experience in Later Medieval Writing: Reading the Book of Life* (London: Palgrave), 65–81.

NEWMAN, BARBARA (1995), *From Virile Woman to WomanChrist: Studies in Medieval Religion and Literature* (Philadelphia: University of Pennsylvania Press).

TALBOT, C. H. (ed. and tr.) (1959), *The Life of Christina of Markyate: A Twelfth Century Recluse* (Oxford: Oxford University Press; repr. Toronto: Toronto University Press/Medieval Academy of America, 1998).

VOADEN, ROSALYNN (1999), *God's Words, Women's Voices: The Discernment of Spirits in the Writing of Late Medieval Women Visionaries* (Woodbridge: York Medieval Press).

'The Vision of William Stranton' (1991), in Robert Easting (ed.), *St Patrick's Purgatory* (EETS 298; Oxford: Oxford University Press for the Early English Text Society), 78–117.

WARNER, MARINA (1990), *Alone of All her Sex: The Cult of the Virgin Mary* (London: Picador).

WATSON, NICHOLAS, and JACQUELINE JENKINS (eds.) (2006), *The Writings of Julian of Norwich: 'A Vision Showed to a Devout Woman' and 'A Revelation of Love'* (Turnhout: Brepols).

WATT, DIANE (2007), *Medieval Women's Writing: Works by and for Women in England, 1100–1500* (Cambridge: Polity).

WESTON, LISA M. C. (2004), '*Sanctimoniales cum Sanctimoniale*: Particular Friendships and Female Community in Anglo-Saxon England', in Carol Braun Pasternack and Lisa M. C. Weston (eds.), *Sex and Sexuality in Anglo-Saxon England: Essays in Memory of Daniel Gillmore Calder* (Tempe, Ariz.: Arizona Center for Medieval and Renaissance Studies), 35–62.

WOGAN-BROWNE, JOCELYN (2003), 'Dead to the World? Death and the Maiden Revisited in Medieval Women's Convent Culture', in Vera Morton (tr.), *Guidance for Women in Twelfth-Century Convents*, with an Interpretative Essay by Jocelyn Wogan-Browne (Cambridge: D. S. Brewer), 157–80.

CHAPTER 13

···

VISIONS AND VISIONARIES

···

ANDREW GALLOWAY

READERS of what we call 'English medieval literature' will be aware of a large number of works presenting a *vision*—that is, an entry into another world or an encounter with a being from one, or an other-worldly perspective on this world, experienced in a dream or waking, or in some uncertain state between these. Such readers, that is, will have encountered or will readily enough encounter *The Dream of the Rood, The Wanderer*, Chaucer's dream poetry, Langland's *Piers Plowman*, and *Pearl* (if not others). But they should also venture further. For every 'literary' work of visions in English, hundreds more visionary narratives or accounts of visions survive in English that are less clearly established as serving our notion of 'literary' ends, and many thousands of others both literary and less so in all languages of the medieval period.[1]

If we include literary and non-literary, religious and secular, in our consideration of visions and vision-literature we might conclude that this form of narration unifies the Middle Ages more distinctively and pervasively than perhaps any other. It is natural to wonder why. Although it is impossible to survey the pan-European phenomenon fully here, one can seek understanding by sampling the properties, creators and uses of such writings across a wide field, charting what might be called the visionary culture of the Middle Ages at least in broad periods and emphases. Such

---

[1] General surveys or bibliographies of dream-visions in medieval English include Easting (1997); Adams (2007); Lynch (1988); Spearing (1980). Broader studies include Dinzelbacher (1981); Piehler (1971); Kruger (1992). Anthologies of Middle English dream poetry include Symonds (2004); Barr (1993); Foster (2004); anthologies of visionary literature in a range of original languages include Dinzelbacher (1989, with German translations); Ciccarese (1987, with Italian translations). Some starting points for some other traditions and languages are McCreesh (2005) (Icelandic); Green (2003) (Islamic); Idel (1999) (medieval Jewish); McClenon (1991) (medieval Chinese and Japanese).

a sampling can provide only a preface to the major English works of vision-literature rather than a careful discussion of them, for it would also need to sample some 'non-literary' materials that have received less attention than they deserve by literary scholars, as well as some of the brilliant literary works in other languages that lie around and behind the well-known English works. Those last can find some place here, but the features of all these works can be best appreciated within a wide and intensely cultivated range of visionary writings and visionary culture.

FOUNDATIONS AND SOCIAL HORIZONS: THE EARLY MEDIEVAL PERIOD

Visitors to the gloomy subterranean museum of the modern city of Bath may inspect a stone block, unearthed near present Beau Street, from the fourth century, inscribed '. . . Novanti fil[ius] pro se et suis ex visu possuit' ('the son of Novantus set this here, on behalf of himself and his family on account of a vision'). Its lost setting was probably an altar, probably dedicated to Sulis Minerva, much worshipped in Roman Bath. The inscription is not unique; a few dedications to Jupiter from Roman settlements in Asia Minor were also put up *ex visu*. In Britain, this monumental response to a vision also recalls worship of Mithras, associated with visions and symbolic deaths by which believers might attain illumination and salvation.[2]

By this date, there were schemes for dream-visions, collections of dream-visions, and exemplary books for interpreting dreams, spanning Hellenistic, late Roman, and early Christian Europe and thus touching England too.[3] But simple though it is, the Bath stone suggests one point more directly than much other evidence: the public and social implications of a vision in late antiquity and early medieval culture. The Bath stone is part of civic display, a prominent response to a *visus* (the preferred word for supernatural visions in Roman antiquity, generally dropped in favour of *visio* by later Christians), on behalf of Novantus's son's entire family.

For such public import of visions, late imperial Romans could look back to the founding text of imperial Rome, which remained centrally influential throughout the Middle Ages. In Vergil's *Aeneid* (*c*.19 BC), Aeneas, fleeing ruined Troy with no knowledge of his destiny, pauses in Thracia to offer sacrifice to his mother, Venus. A branch bleeds as he breaks it off: a *visus*[4] produced by the bush growing from the spear-intertwined body of his dead companion Polydorus, whose unquiet spirit directs Aeneas to travel further. Seeking clarification, Aeneas then goes to the birthplace of Apollo and Diana at Delos, where he asks the god where he and his

---

[2] Henig (2004: 231–2).
[3] See Miller (1997); Newman (1962: 1–128).
[4] Fairclough (1967: 3. 36).

people should settle. Apollo tells them to 'seek your ancient mother', so, travelling to the ancient Trojan home of Crete, Aeneas experiences a third kind of portent: a dream in which his household gods (small dark clay statuary penates) tell him that he must travel on to Italy, for it is there that he must raise the walls of Rome, whose traumatic, even nightmarish prehistory Vergil's poem presents. Aeneas's 'dream' (*somnia*) or 'vision' (*visus*) at Crete confronts him with a terrifyingly real power:

> talibus attonitus visis et voce deorum
> (nec sopor illud erat, sed coram adgnoscere voltus
> velatasque comas praesentiaque ora videbar;
> tum gelidus toto manabat corpore sudor)
> corripio e stratis corpus tendoque supinas
> ad caelum cum voce manus et munera libo
> intemerata focis.[5]

A vision does not simply convey information; it demands response. Vergil is explicit in showing how each of Aeneas's visions has roused him to the next step, the next revelation. The final visionary step is in book 6, when he is allowed to journey through the terrifying underworld to meet his deceased father, who shows him not only the general dead, tormented or rewarded in various ways and in various circles, but also a succession of Roman historical figures not yet born whose city, empire, and unflinching commitment to the art of governance he is destined and thereby inspired to found.[6]

In ancient and medieval culture, visions often convey public, historical, and social meanings and elicit public, social, and intellectual responses. About the same time as the Bath stone, in perhaps Roman Africa, an intellectual steeped in earlier Roman and Greek literature, Macrobius (*c.*400), contributed to the interest in this growth of virtual community by elaborately categorizing and elucidating the kinds of possible visions in his commentary on the 'Dream of Scipio' that Cicero placed at the end of his *De re publica*.[7] An encyclopedic work, Macrobius cast an even wider net than Vergil, reading in Scipio's dream a key to all political and cosmic order. The commentary is best known among modern scholars for its brief dream taxonomy,[8] which defines the kinds of appropriate responses one should take. The dreams described are the *insomnium* (wholly deceptive and useless, but mundane), the *visum* (a term Macrobius, in contrast to classical usage, uses for deceptive phantasm, the kind glimpsed between waking and sleep), the *somnium* (a dream of true prophecy, but folded into a fiction that needs explanation), the *visio* (revealing the

---

[5] Ibid. 3. 172–8. 'Awed by such a vision and the voice of gods—nor was that a mere dream, but openly I seemed to know their looks, their filleted hair, and their living faces; anon a cold sweat bedewed all my limbs—I snatch myself from my bed, raise my voice and upturned hands to heaven, and offer pure gifts upon the hearth' (Fairclough's tr.).

[6] Ibid. 6. 851–3.

[7] Eyssenhardt (1883); translation available in Stahl (1952).

[8] At 3. 1–10; see Kruger (1992: 22–3).

future by means of mundane events), and the *oraculum* (revealing the future by means of some august other-worldly figure).

Macrobius' flock of kinds of dreams, as orderly as Scipio's vision of the cosmos, certainly suggests the range of visionary materials that would have come down to a pedantically antiquarian late imperial Roman. But although Macrobius's name is mentioned by a number of late medieval poets as proof of the truth-value of dreams (from Guillaume de Lorris in the *Roman de la Rose* through Chaucer in the *Parliament of Fowls*), his distinctions do not closely reflect or influence much vision-literature, not even during the period when most surviving copies of his work were made, the eleventh and twelfth centuries.[9] Worthy of our attention is, infact, how Macrobius also comments on the social horizons involved in visions,[10] for this concern is more generally pertinent to medieval visionary culture. One kind of dream pertains to the dreamer only (*proprium*); another to some one other person (*alienum*); a third to the dreamer and another person (*commune*); a fourth to some civic or public community such as the city or the theatre (*publicum*); a fifth to everyone, on a cosmic scale (*generale*).

Thinking in terms of the social horizons that dream-visions involve is a valuable correction to our own narrowed views of dreams and visions. To most of us, a dream is almost always to be seen as a glimpse of desires and anxieties so private that we have repressed them even from our own minds. They are hardly publicly acknowledgeable means for guiding society, much less opportunities for sustaining or founding relationships and communities. The shift toward this outlook is clear by the time of Nathaniel Hawthorne's 'Young Goodman Brown', written in 1835—as happens, a decade after the 'vision' slab at Bath was discovered by builders laying the foundations of Bath's innovatively regional United Hospital.[11] Hawthorne's story offers a devastating depiction of the social and psychic blight that believing a vision literally might create. After a surreal vision of his entire community as Satan worshippers, Young Goodman Brown becomes the epitome of the sternly remote and hyper-vigilant Puritan head of family, aware of sin all around him: 'a darkly meditative, a distrustful, if not a desperate man, did he become, from the night of that fearful dream...when the family knelt down at prayer, he scowled, and muttered to himself, and gazed sternly at his wife, and turned away'.[12]

Hawthorne's satire is aimed at showing how a life-denying psychology is fostered by relatively recent Puritan visions of heaven and hell, such as the (apocryphal) *Visions of John Bunyan* (first printed in 1725, decades after Bunyan's death). There, Bunyan, who has lost his belief in God, walks into the woods and, like Goodman Brown, is rapt into a vision of the saved and the damned, including a meeting with the soul of Thomas Hobbes as a regretful atheist, and returns to lead a newly faith-filled life. But Hawthorne's view also suggests our bias against the medieval Christian

---

[9] Peden (1985).
[10] Eyssenhardt (1883: 3. 10–11).
[11] Collingwood and Wright (1995), no. 153.
[12] Pearson (1937: 1042).

vision narratives that stand in a long line behind the Puritan ones. From the earliest medieval period, these accounts often harshly separate the saved from the damned, and suggest that the waking world is a *spiritually* dangerous place. In the founding texts of this Christian tradition, the saved are often those with special access to true understanding of enigmatic or hidden meanings in obscure visions. The pattern is set by Daniel in the Hebrew Bible, but in New Testament writings the interpretations can be as obscure as the visions, keys for those who already know, as when the book of Revelation (Greek 'Apocalypsis': 'things hidden away') reuses the books of Ezekiel and Isaiah from the Hebrew Bible to describe the coming end of time; or again when Paul briefly mentions that a certain man (himself) was 'caught up into paradise and heard secret words which it is not granted to man to utter'.[13]

Such Christian visions typically became more interpretively open as soon as Christianity became an empire of its own, indeed, often functioning to found Christian identity and community as directly as Vergil's visionary journey toward Rome. The *Visio Pauli*, for instance, written in Greek in the third century, but circulated in Latin from the fifth, and quoted in English writings by the tenth, supplies the details of Paul's rapture.[14] Paul witnesses abundant torments of various kinds of sinners, but also inspects paradise and meets the patriarchs down to Moses, a communion with the dead that constitutes the core of many post-biblical visions.

Punishment is a constant feature of such early medieval foundational visions (which continued to be copied and adapted through the Middle Ages). Just as Aeneas witnesses the torments of those who seek to thwart divine wishes and the difficult paths even of those who seek to fulfil such wishes, so the early medieval Christian visions of the afterlife display through greater and lesser violence the trueness of members of the community, and especially those who, through some temporary punishment, can eventually be absolved of their errors. It is these (whose 'place' for temporary torments is later codified as purgatory) who present the most meaningful models for the living, because they show the possibility of correction and change, spurring which is often the point of the vision. This principle governs the majority of stories about sinners who nearly die and gain a glimpse of the other side then return to lead reformed lives, or those who die in some state of relatively minor sin that allows them to communicate with and be saved by the prayers of those still alive taking pity on them. The pattern is common among the many dreams collected in book 4 of Gregory the Great's *Dialogues* (*c.*594), the most influential collection of visions in medieval culture.[15] The pattern certainly informs the account in Bede's *Historia ecclesiastica* (*c.* 731) of the monk Dryhthelm. While in a near-death vision, he is led by a man in shining robes to see a staggeringly beautiful land for one group, a sobering range of discomforts for another, and a horrific set of torments for a third; yet he learns that none of these reveals the full joys of heaven or the pains of hell, but merely gradations in degrees of penance for those who are not yet ready to enter

---

[13] 2 Cor. 12: 2.
[14] Silverstein (1935).
[15] De Vogüé and Antin (1978–80).

heaven, which is perceptible to Dryhthelm only by a whiff of fragrance and blaze of light. The final truths of Heaven and hell are left to his inference; the vision is focused on the instructional punishment imposed between those extremes. Returning to earth, Dryhthelm wastes no time in striving for greater penance. Asked how he could bear the austere life he has led ever since his vision, Dryhthelm tersely answers, 'I have seen it harder.'[16]

This seems nearly Hawthornian. But Hawthorne's satire of life-denying Christian visions is itself blind to the ties of community and identity established and negotiated by medieval visions of all kinds, among the living as well as between the living and the dead. Bede concludes his account of Dryhthelm by saying, 'in his unwearied longing for heavenly bliss, he . . . led many to salvation by his words and life'.[17] As Dryhthelm himself can only imagine heaven and hell, so he becomes for others a challenge for faith and wild imagination, qualities essential to the cultural power of visionaries and vision-literature.

English 'literary' visions after Bede emphasize as strongly as the 'non-literary' visions the power of visions to define and create communities, even when the visions are solitary affairs, 'to midre nihte'. The phrase is from the *Dream of the Rood*,[18] which offers the clearest example in Old English poetry of a private experience that leads to the narrator's rededication to a new community of the holy, based on a special, almost confessional, intimacy, when the narrator hears about the equally lonely ordeal of a Cross that, with rigorous loyalty to divine will, chose to stand firm and let Jesus die as he wished. A more elaborate instance of how a long pursuit of understanding of a vision produces vast historical and social consequences is the Old English poem *Elene*. Following the Latin Acts of St Cyriacus, the poet, Cynewulf, recounts how Elene's son Constantine the Great at the brink of a battle with a vast host of Huns in the year 233 (actually, 313) dreamt of a gloriously radiant man and awoke to hear this figure tell him (more elaborately in the English than the Latin) to look at the giant vision of a cross in the sky. When Constantine carries this sign into battle and wins, he begins an investigation into just what the sign means, a process that ultimately leads him to send his mother Elene to Jerusalem to find where the Cross itself might be buried. Coercing a recalcitrant Jew to reveal the history and location of the Cross, Elene can then establish the bishopric that St Cyriac will lead. All this productive inquiry into a visionary sign's full meaning continues into the poet's labours:

> Þus ic frod ond fus, þurh þæt fæcne hus
> wordcræft wæf ond wundrum læs,
> þragum þreodude ond ʒeþanc reodode,
> nihtes nearwe; nysse ic ʒearwe,
> be ðære rode riht ær me rumran ʒeþeaht,

---

[16] Colgrave and Mynors (1992: 5. 12, p. 499).
[17] Ibid.
[18] Dickens and Ross (1963).

þurh ða mæran miht, on modes þeaht,
wisdom onwreah...[19]

Cynewulf gains his own night-time revelation, a 'larger view' that his poetic and scholarly labours finally and it seems suddenly yield. In its way his poem is thus continuous with Constantine's and Elene's empire built on a vision. It suggests too that poetic and intellectual inspiration, however quotidian they may sometimes seem, can also have a kind of visionary power.

In early English vision-poetry, *thinking things through* seems to have a special revelatory status in itself: not just true visions but also the steady pursuit of true meanings affirms and establishes communities of believers and seekers. Even an apparently 'false' dream like that in *The Wanderer*, where the solitary traveller slips into a dream of kissing and embracing his lost lord, then awakens more desolate than ever, is valuable for the further thought that it prompts in the dreamer: the vision leads him to reflect that worldly life and goods must pass. Such reflection is the Wanderer's true revelation.[20] Likewise in *The Seafarer*, the narrator's mind 'flies out beyond the breast-hoard' and surveys the earth's expanse until it returns as eager for something more as it ever was, 'gifre and grædig' ('eager and greedy'), just like the seabird that the narrator immediately turns to describe.[21] Hollow or 'false' as they might be, these are forms of 'vision' that lead to productive understanding of the human condition that is itself visionary in some sense, even, as in *The Seafarer*, yielding a 'larger view' of the true homeland in heaven.

The question of deceitful dreams and visions was, however, important because of the importance of visions in claims to authority. The need to sift visions for this reason produced the first 'psychological' dream theories. Gregory's *Dialogues* includes a range of possible causes for dreams: some from hunger or over-fullness; some from an illusion (*inlusio*) produced by the devil (that is, a sinful dream); some from a thought (*cogitatio*) along with an illusion; some from a revelation (*revelatio*); and some from a thought along with a revelation.[22] Behind the medieval categorical style, the range has a Roman legacy. The late imperial Roman poet Claudian (d. 408?) notes in his preface to a panegyric on Emperor Honorius that whatever someone desires will return to the sleeping mind: the hunter dreams of hunting, the judge of lawsuits, the lover of love's mysteries. Claudian cleverly uses this to say that he dreams of writing poetry in praise of the emperor; and lo, 'My dream has come true! It was no vain imagining; nor did the false ivory gate send forth an unaccomplished dream.'[23] Perhaps Cynewulf's epilogue to *Elene*, describing his night-time meditation followed by a successful poetic inspiration, owes something to Claudian's

---

[19] Gradon (1992: ll. 1236–42); 'Thus I, aged and about to depart hence because of this frail body, have woven the art of words and have wondrously gathered my matter, have pondered at times and sifted my thought in the anguish of the night. I knew not clearly the truth about the cross till wisdom by its glorious strength revealed to the thought of my mind a larger view.' Tr. from Gordon (1976).

[20] See Galloway 1994.

[21] Gordon (1996: ll. 62–3).

[22] De Vogüé and Antin (1980: 4. 50, pp. 172–7).

[23] Platnauer (1963: preface ll. 70–3, p. 2; compare *Aeneid* 6. 893–901.

passage. By the thirteenth century the passage was included in school-texts, and it appears in Chaucer's *Parliament of Fowls* (*c*.1380)[24] and other late medieval vision poems.[25]

MERGING STYLE AND VISIONARY FORM: THE TWELFTH CENTURY AND BEYOND

The form of the vision 'itself' and the form of the work presenting it are always closely intertwined. From the twelfth century on, though, a humanizing doubt more often shrouds the origins of visions, only partly to be explained by the new influence of Aristotelian categories of natural 'causes' in dreams, which also shifted views about inspired texts of all kinds, granting historical human agency more emphasis.[26]

This 'personalizing' of visionary authority does not mean that visions lost any claims to broad social authority. Indeed, under new conditions the opposite might occur. Both specialized community-building and powerful individual authority are clear in the life and works of the great twelfth-century visionary, the Abbess Hildegard of Bingen, who became (as her letters show) a major resource for local and distant consultation about the condition of various souls after death, even the location of buried treasure.[27] Hildegard's visionary discourse is, paradoxically, utterly distinctive because of the emphatic impersonality that she proclaims throughout her unusual literary and musical productions. As she insists in her letters and her formal visionary texts such as the *Scivias*,[28] her voice and writing often came directly from, indeed speaks directly *as*, the 'living light', inelegant Latin and all. As she told a persistently inquisitive monk in 1175 when she was over 70 years old: 'I have no knowledge of anything I do not see [in my vision], with no words of my own added. And these are expressed in unpolished Latin, for that is the way I hear them in my vision, since I am not taught in the vision to write the way philosophers do.' Yet she went on to complicate this by adding, 'the words I see and hear in the vision are not like the words of human speech, but are like a blazing flame and a cloud that moves through clear air'.[29] Such extraordinary glimpses of the continuity and discontinuity between her visions and her representation of them echo the equally unstable claims in the book of Revelation, where a 'loud voice' tells John to 'write in a book what you see', but where the Son of Man speaks with a voice 'like the sound of many waters'.[30] The contradiction of human and superhuman causes and authority somehow cohered for Hildegard; but her distinctive style, novel modes of worship, and pan-European

---

[24] At ll. 99–105.   [25] Pratt (1947).
[26] See Kruger (1992: 83–122); Minnis (1988).
[27] Baird (2006).   [28] Hart and Bishop (1990).
[29] Baird (2006), no. 70.   [30] Rev. 1: 11–12.

connections required negotiating a complex set of different realms that only a genius as well as a visionary might manage with more or less life-long success and freedom (she encountered serious opposition only early on, when there were objections not to her visions but her liturgical extravaganzas, where she gathered her group of rather socially elite nuns to sing, with loosened hair, her proto-oratorio arrangements).[31]

In the twelfth century, visions could also serve as vehicles for intimate connections: Macrobius's *communis*. A particularly delicate set of examples from England appears in the biography of another twelfth-century holy woman, Christina of Markyate, about whom we know much less directly than we do the literary powerhouse Hildegard.[32] Christina's biography is famous for her vigorous efforts to escape a marriage that her parents (Anglo-Saxons who managed to maintain social standing after the Norman Conquest) have arranged for her, and also for her escape from rape by Ranulph Flambard, chancellor of England, by slipping out of a bedroom, locking him inside as he chased her. The work's most powerful scenes of intimacy, however, are the visions later in life that Christina had of her beloved friend, Abbot Geoffrey, and that he had of her. Geoffrey first dreams of her as a tender flower from whom he can squeeze no juice if he is too forceful, but much juice if he is gentle; the next day, she greets him with a flower.[33] Their relationship flourishes through visionary sympathies. Worried about Geoffrey's salvation, she dreams of being in a chamber while he is outside, clamouring to enter; in the dream she fervently prays for his entry, and a dove flies out to him, but even then, 'she would not stop pleading until she saw the man either possessing the dove or being possessed by the dove (*vel possidere columbam vel possessum cerneret a columba*)'.[34] This is something like a version of 'courtly love', visible elsewhere in the twelfth century; but Christina's and Geoffrey's visionary intimacy is far more tender than the love depicted in those secular stories. Moreover, their visions offer only part of the phenomenon of intimate visions in this work, since it is all presented by the omniscient biographer. The *Life* is his visionary communion with them both.

Secularly oriented literature did not immediately exploit visions as a new means of love and intimacy, but when it did this it transformed literary history. Between 1230 and 1245 Guillaume de Lorris, citing Macrobius as his authorizing starting-point, presented in French a dream of a long and unresolved passion for a 'rose' to whom in the dream he dedicated his life (by way of paying homage to the God of Love, who instructs him, among other things, in writing love lyrics about unrequited love), but from which he awoke—like the Wanderer—with all the more intense longing for what he could neither obtain nor cease pursuing. This first part of the *Roman de la Rose* presents itself as recounting exactly what was to occur ('onques riens ou songe n'ot / Qui avenu tretout ne soit / Si cum li songes recontoit'[35]), a blurring of the

---

[31] Ibid. nos. 4–10.
[32] Talbot (1998); see Fanous and Leyser (2005).
[33] Talbot (1998: s. 66, p. 152).
[34] Ibid. s. 69, p. 157.
[35] Poirion (1974: ll. 28–30); tr. Dahlberg (1995).

poem's temporality with that of lived experience analogous to the poem's peculiarly 'mixed' allegory, which presents the dreamer and the God of Love as human figures, but the beloved as not only a rose but also a host of other elements given personified form. Her 'fair welcome' is a pleasant young man; her 'standoffishness' a brutal watchman. Reason is a regal woman tutor, whose elaborate and capacious arguments fail to break the dreamer's obstinate loyalty to sensual love, or rather to the lordly God of Love.

This first part of the *Rose* stands as a vastly extended dream-vision lyric of unrequited love; in that sense its irresolute ending is appropriate. Even in that form, it betrayed the Latin models that it obviously was meant to evoke and re-evaluate, especially Boethius's *De consolatione philosophiae*, the early sixth-century prose-poem dialogue between Boethius, imprisoned by Theodoric the Ostrogoth, and Lady Philosophy, who arrives to him in prison to show him how to understand the ultimate, foreknown good of all events and the ultimate ethical utility of bad as well as good Fortune. Boethius's human questioning about love and hope is drowned out as the *Consolation* goes on, and the *Rose* represents the counterargument on behalf of what is repressed.

No copies of Guillaume de Lorris's short *Rose* exist; the longer version in the later thirteenth century by Jean de Meun, however, made it the most popular vernacular poem in the Middle Ages. Jean's continuation and completion (a sexual conquest of the Rose) departs yet further from the Boethian model of a revelatory vision: Jean's part is a vehicle for satire, learning, classical *exempla*, and characters like the Old Woman (the model for Chaucer's Wife of Bath, as False Seeming is for the Pardoner) who seeks to tell her life story about deceptive men to warn the Rose. Boethian ethics reappear still more ironically; like Lady Philosophy but more experienced in sex and the ways of self-interest, the Old Lady is fully qualified in her own way to affirm the Boethian point that human beings should always be suspicious of Fortune's gifts of youth, goods, and earthly love. Jean's vision stresses other religious ethics in equally ironic ways: whereas in 1 Thessalonians 5: 21 Paul tells his listeners to 'test all things, hold fast to what is good', Jean justifies drinking many wines and having sex with many kinds of women since 'it is good to try everything in order to take greater pleasure in one's good fortune'.[36] Readers, finding the poem scandalous or allegori-cally revelatory as they might, completed and copied it in forms that reveal or carry out their own understanding of it.[37]

Ambiguity in visionary authority became itself an authorizing gesture for the late medieval courtly writers who followed the *Rose*, a way of insisting on the human skills of the poetic craftsman while keeping alive possibilities for some higher authority in their writing. The major fourteenth-century French dream-vision poet Guillaume de Machaut presented the *Fonteinne Amoreuse* (1360)—a major source for Chaucer's *Book of the Duchess*—as visionary consolation to Charles, Duke of Berry,

---

[36] Poirion (1974: l. 21542).
[37] Huot (1993).

for having to be sent to England as a hostage while the huge ransom for the captured French King John was being gathered. Just as Macrobius had described a *visum* as a phantasm arising 'between waking and full quiescence', so Machaut's narrator says, 'Ensois faisoie la dorveille, / Com cils qui dort et encor veille' ('I was half waking, like a man who sleeps yet is awake').[38] Machaut made this ambiguous state of mind fashionable for all following French and English dream-vision writers.[39] In this state, Machaut's poet-narrator overhears through a window Duke Charles lamenting (using one hundred different rhymes) his imminent departure before he has told a certain woman how much he loves her. It is a shared *visum*. Duke Charles and Machaut are both half-awake, both full of phantasms of uncertainty. In his private lament, the duke retells Ovid's tragic story of Ceux and Alcione, an indication of his own anxiety about travelling over the sea (since Ceux drowned and Juno sent his simulacrum to tell his beloved Alcione that he was dead). But in spite of the Macrobian phantasms here, a kind of prophetic power emerges from all this: Guillaume transcribes this artful lament, and when Duke Charles begs him later to write something to serve as his go-between to his beloved, Guillaume has already done so, one hundred different rhymes and all.

This is not simply pleasing a patron by anticipating his every wish (although it is that too); it is also a claim that a love-poet's craft possesses a kind of magic parallel to divinely inspired visionary writing. The parallel strengthens in the poem. The two men, falling asleep together after their night of insomnia, dream an identical dream, in which Venus presents a consolation that inverts but closely parallels the story of the dead Ceux come to tell Alcione in a dream that he is dead. In Venus's new consolation, Charles's beloved says she loves him deeply after all, and promises to wait for him, giving him a ring to remember her by. When Guillaume and the Duke awaken, the Duke finds he is wearing the ring. The vision-poem weaves a visionary intimacy between the narrator-poet, the duke, the beloved, and the reader, all of whom exit the poem with something exchanged with the others.

Chaucer's reuse of so much of this in *Book of the Duchess* shows how impressive this example was for courtly dream-poets striving to carve out secular vernacular authority; the 'Chaucerian' dream-vision poets of the fifteenth century adopted a similar range of techniques to use visionary traditions in the service of authorizing vernacular poetic craft as a key element of courtly community.[40] But in Chaucer, the key both to visionary intimacy and vernacular poetic authority is the deflation of received dream-vision authority, even that of Machaut. To recover intimacy with the rest of the living world, the Black Knight in the *Book of the Duchess* must break free

---

[38] Palmer (1993: ll. 63–4).

[39] In John Clanvowe's *Book of Cupid* (*c.*1390), the narrator is 'Not al on slepe, ne fully wakyng' (Symons 2004: l. 88); so too, Philippe de Mézières frames his 'dream of the old pilgrim' (also *c.*1390) as occurring while he was 'moitie dormant moitie veillant' (Coopland 1969: 1. 89). Hill (1978) presents other examples and traces this motif to awakening from sin, based on Augustine, but does not note the further precedents of Macrobius and Machaut.

[40] Symons (2004).

from his elegant, French-style, self-involved laments about a lost ideal woman and learn to speak plainly to a common man who does not understand courtly metaphors. Chaucer's *Parliament of Fowls* (c. 1380) opens with a brief and whimsical summary of Scipio's cosmic dream from Macrobius, but the rest of the poem offers its own 'commentary' on that by overturning any semblance of divine order in the social competitions among the bird-hierarchy for the female eagle. *The House of Fame* (c.1380), which begins with a vision of Aeneas's story, involves a journey in search of some ultimate revelation that never arrives nor is defined: 'tydings'. In search of these the narrator dutifully encounters the wise men of the literary past in a stately garden like the paradise of the *Visio Pauli*, but this grandiose realm turns out to be full of jealousy and pettiness, and the narrator finds real joy only in chasing after the 'winged wondres' that emerge from a whirling nest, 'tydinges' in which 'fals and sooth' are mingled and given life by being scattered among shipmen, pilgrims, pardoners and other lowly message-bearers.[41] Chaucer's visionary poetry deflates transcendental claims in order to scrutinize the social conventions of identity and desire.[42] His is a disenchanted vision of vision-literature, but it emphasizes, like Machaut, a kind of social magic.

Another kind of response to the *Roman de la Rose* and its followers appears in William Langland's *Piers Plowman* (written in three distinct versions, c. 1370–89), which opens into a pilgrimage as grandiose as that in the *Rose*, but through a series of interlocutors toward an elusive, and finally evanescent, spiritual and social goal. It is likely that Langland approached the *Rose* by way of the didactic mid-fourteenth-century Norman-French poems by Guillaume de Deguilleville, in his massive three dream-vision allegories of 'pilgrimage' (*Pelerinage de la Vie Humaine*; *Pelerinage de l'Ame*; *Pelerinage de Jhesu Christ*).[43] Deguileville's cheerfully doctrinal rewriting of the *Rose* is announced in the opening of his second version of the *Pelerinage de la Vie Humaine*, where his narrator falls asleep after reading the *Rose*: a display of the bookish origins of dream-visions that Chaucer exploits throughout his dream-vision poetry.[44] Langland probably took from Deguileville the idea of recasting into a Christian pilgrimage the kind of vision presented by the *Rose*, but instead of using it to pursue, like Deguileville, an allegory of personal salvation, Langland uses the visionary mode to press toward the redemption of society as a whole—economically, morally, and politically. Although the endeavour is constantly derailed, especially by the narrator's own rebelliousness and unsteady visionary authority, it nonetheless constitutes the most vigorous return to the 'public' power of visions in later medieval England, in the sense of seeking general reassessment and transformation.

---

[41] Benson (1987: ll. 2108–28).   [42] See St John (2000).
[43] Stürzinger (1893–7); see Burrow (1993: 113–18).
[44] Deguileville's second version in French is available only in translation by John Lydgate, ed. Furnivall (1899–1904).

Not surprisingly with such an agenda, Langland's poem fundamentally assails the secular ethics and elite social assumptions of a courtly vision-poem like the *Rose*. But Langland also radically revises the didactic authority of visionary literature. Langland's Pardon[45] presents the terms for salvation and damnation, doing well and doing evil; but it simply leads to more questions about what those are exactly, a questioning that the narrator keeps alive in restless and combative responses to all his teachers. The problems of understanding become the main content of the vision itself. God himself, as the allegorical figure Peace suggests at the Harrowing of Hell, has become human in order to learn what sorrow, and thus what joy, really is:

> To wite what he [Adam] hath suffred in thre sondry places,
> Bothe in hevene and in erthe—and now til hell he [God] thenkth [to go]
> To wite what alle wo is, that woot of alle joye.[46]

This shifts to a divine level the principle from the *Rose* of 'learning by contrasting experience'. It also inverts the genre of a vision: now this is God's need for learning. Either way, learning and questioning are made more important than any judgements or authority from on high, and applied this widely, the principle implies fundamental challenges to existing institutions of all kinds. There are many reasons why the lower-caste rebels in the widespread Rising of 1381 cited Piers Plowman rather than Chaucer as their companion; Langland's visions seem to demand entirely new principles for assessing as well as refounding society, though it leaves none of its own assertions undebated.

Langland's poem settles into no comfortable niche in either religious or courtly visionary literature, and it is no surprise that it generated few 'literary' followers. *Piers* may be credited with inspiring a few political dream-vision allegories in the early fifteenth century (*Richard the Redeless* and *Mum and the Sothsegger*[47]), but more generally, it points toward later writings about apocalypse during the wars of religion, especially under Oliver Cromwell, when a torrent of such writings appears.[48] By that point, the visionary form had lost its prestigious position in poetry. Only Milton—a sometime Cromwellian—could again transform the visionary tradition back into forms whose density and complexity made claims on the centrally 'canonical' poetic tradition. Yet Milton too shows a deep scepticism to literature for its own sake, in his case targeting (while invoking) classical epic. It is hard not to think that, in their similar kinds of resistance to literary conventions even while proceeding with great literary sophistication, both Langland and Milton show true visionary aspirations.

---

45 Schmidt (1995:, B, passus 7).
46 Ibid. B. 18. 222–4. For the issue, see Galloway (1998, 2006: 4, 181–2, 372).
47 Barr (1993).
48 See Firth (1979).

WOMEN'S VISIONARY AUTHORITY AND LATE MEDIEVAL VERNACULAR WRITING

Vision-literature from Boethius through the secular literature of the *Rose* and beyond focuses on powerful or dangerous feminine figures: transcendent guides or objects of desire and fear. Visionary human women, however, generally had a more difficult path to authority.[49] Even if learned, they could not claim religious, intellectual, and clerical authority equal to learned men's. And they could never allow the visionary mode to suggest directly literal erotic possibilities. Their successes as major innovators in vernacular writing in general and visionary narrative in particular are all the more remarkable.

The beguine abbess Hadewijch, writing in Middle Dutch about the time when the first *Rose* was written, uses not only exquisite rhythmic prose for her visions, but also, like the *Rose*, troubadour and Minnesang lyric forms for her declarations of love of God. Her lyrical forms' inherited capacity to express deftly deferred erotic yearning is consistent with her use of such forms to declare utterly passionate religious love, since she is in love with love itself and indeed can exuberantly claim, unlike an erotic lover, that only love exists, and for everyone, not just her: 'Die minne es al'.[50] So too the lyrical, often incantatory prose *Flowing Light of the Godhead* (*Das fließende Licht der Gottheit*) by Mechthild of Magdeburg from about the same time (c.1250) offers us, like Hadewijch's works, a vernacular literature coming into its own and in completely new forms. Mechthild mentions that she was 'warned against writing this book', but God tells her that its words 'symbolize my marvellous Godhead; / it flows continuously / Into your soul from my divine mouth. / The sound of the words is a sign of my living spirit'. She still wonders why God would build 'a golden house on filthy ooze', that is, in an unlearned and thus easily ignored woman's book, whereas 'if I were a learned religious man, and if you had performed this unique great miracle using him, you would receive everlasting honour for it'.[51]

The golden house of visionary women's literature indeed stood on unsteady foundations. In controlling their own texts, Hadewijch and Hildegard are the exceptions; Christina, whom we know about only by way of her attentive but perhaps overly imaginative biographer, the norm. We are fortunate to have the remarkable St Albans Psalter made for Christina's meditation;[52] but seeing *what* she saw and seeing *how* she saw are very different matters. Mechthild's text exists only in a High German translation; her original Low German version is lost, absorbed, like so many writings by women, into a more authoritative literary sphere. The visions of Angela of Foligno (c.1260) are part of the literary record (in Latin) only because some unknown friar

---

[49] See Newman (1989); Poor (2004).
[50] Bladel (2002); Hadewijch (1980).
[51] Tobin (1998), 2. 26, pp. 96–7; see Poor (2004).
[52] Geddes (2003).

took interest in her. Angela's visions and lyrical eloquence are captured more or less directly in the twenty 'steps' (*passus*, as in the units of *Piers Plowman*) presented at the beginning of the *Memorial* that this friar composed, followed by his more pedestrian elucidation of seven more steps, as if a kind of commentary.

This work lets us see in rare detail how a visionary text could develop as a collaboration between a visionary and sympathetic biographer. The author describes how he gradually expanded his ambitions: 'When I first began, I wrote somewhat carelessly and in summary fashion—as if I were writing a sort of memorial for myself—and I wrote on a small sheet of paper (*in una carta parvuncula*) because I thought that I would only have to write very little. But before long, after I had compelled her to speak to me, it was revealed to Christ's faithful one that I should use a large notebook (*quaternum magnum*) for writing, rather than a single small sheet'.[53] He once observes, 'when I was rereading to her, so that she could check whether I had written well, her response was that my words were "dry and without any flavour"'. Another time, she tells him that 'these words remind me of what I said to you, but your writing is very obscure'.[54] Beyond displaying modesty, these comments also seem calculated to support the view that Angela dismissed any earthly language that might seek to capture her visionary flights, a view central to how the biographer presents her. In describing 'one of her many dreams and visions' to her biographer, Angela reports that she once fell asleep pondering a passage from the Gospel. She had a Missal nearby, but, her biographer says, she fought her 'strong thirst' to open and read it because she felt it was arrogant to yield to her own 'excessive thirst and love'. Falling asleep, she dreamt that a figure asked if she wanted to *experience* the Epistle that she wished to read. She agreed, and entered a state described only as self-forgetfulness and forgetfulness of the world, a 'divine delight' of freedom so exquisite that she felt sorrow when she awoke.[55]

As the biographer shows this, she seems artfully resistant to the 'dead letter', and blessed with a visionary embrace of a text's true spirit. But the lack of detail in the vision is suspicious, as is its sentimental presentation of her distance from learning. Has the biographer retouched this vision to insist on her distance from learned culture lest, with all her theological thought and visions, she seem threatening to official clerical culture? In the remarkable scene where she toys with her own longing to read, might we glimpse something like a love of potent language that her biographer-friar does not otherwise let us see? Did Angela really dislike language so much, or just his dull Latin notebooks?

Extraordinary literary creativity is fully apparent in many of the visionary women's own writings when they can control those writings themselves. This is clear for the English anchoress Julian of Norwich, writing in East Anglia in the late fourteenth century. Julian's visions are never separate experiences from her thought or narrative: these are all continuous with her vision. The principle extends to her revisions of her

---

[53] Thier and Calufetti (1985: 166), tr. Mazzoni (1999: 37).
[54] Ibid. 38.   [55] Ibid. 31.

'shewings' (visions). After writing her first text, she revised it because she has had another explanatory vision. Its import is to clarify the first vision by displaying (as the voice offering her 'techyng inwardly' says) 'alle the propertes and the condescions that were shewed in the example': that is, in her youthful death-bed series of visions twenty years earlier.[56]

Her later vision extends both the theology and the narrative temporality of the 'short text' of her *Showings* in complex and poetic ways. A major instance of this is when she reports in the 'long version' that she sees a servant, who is Adam as well as Jesus, stumbling in front of a lord, who is God; she sees this means that as soon as Adam fell, Jesus fell to earth, for the two are identical beings.[57] This deeply incarnational vision leads to further thought with no sign of breaking off from a visionary mode: inspecting the clothing that the servant wears leads her to 'see' the flesh's humble enclosure of the spirit, thence the divine enclosure of everything, by which God is the mother of everything:[58] 'I saw no dyfference betwen God and oure substance, but as it were all God'.[59]

For Julian, revelation and thought, observation and inference, *seeing* and *seeing that*, are explicitly and quite deliberately continuous, even more than they are for Hildegard. So too, a reader's later experience of her vision, thought, narrative is also organically continuous with all these other moments of vision. At the end of her 'long version', she says, 'This boke is begonne by Goddys gyfte and his grace, but it is nott yett performyd as to my syght'.[60] The ending or fulfilment of her 'syght' and her *seeing that* is not yet in view. Its visionary moment is always unfolding in readers' continuations of her meditation.

This invitation anticipates fifteenth-century interest in guiding lay readers to formulate their own visions of sacred history, which characterizes so much of public culture in the fifteenth century. Guides to visions helped spur this trend, especially the massively popular *Meditations on the Life of Christ* translated by Nicholas Love, the English work most often listed in lay wills, which gives careful instructions for how one should visualize and understand various moments of sacred history.[61] The results are clear in cases like Margery Kempe, a mother of fourteen children, whose laboriously dictated *Book* describes her visions of 'dallying' with Jesus as part of her bid for retroactive virginity and sanctity[62] or the short narrative of the vision of Edmund Leversedge in 1465, a well-established landowner who was told in a vision to seek an education at Oxford under the humbling name William Wretch (there is no record he did so).[63] Such visions present a sense of responses to visions that break the traditional clerical–lay divide with a host of new sacred and quasi-clerical vocations. Such an efflorescence of lay visionary power both prepares for the assaults on traditional clerical authority at the Reformation, and suffers from its consequences, since there is every sign that the traditions of centuries of Church power and styles of

---

56 Baker (2005: ch. 51, p. 72).   57 Ibid. ch. 51, pp. 75–6.
58 Ibid. ch. 53, pp. 82–4.   59 Ibid. ch. 54, p. 84.
60 Ibid. ch. 86, p. 124.   61 Sargent (2004).
62 Staley (1998).   63 Nijenhuis (1991).

worship—from endorsing visual images to inciting the laity to probe their own souls in confession—were a constant and central inspiration for visionary culture.

CONCLUSION

Church traditions clearly were major causes for this long tradition, but medieval visions and vision-literature exude a power and consequence that cannot be explained away. There is nothing less real in that power than there is in our sense of dreams' ability to reveal the repressed anxieties and impulses that, we are often told, chiefly occupy them. Medieval theories of visions include those views too, but medieval vision-literature generated wide communities of readers, religious or secular, by providing guidance for political and even military decisions; surveying and seeking to change social abuses individually or as a whole; offering advice, warnings, and encouragement for personal paths to salvation or love; and, most frequently, bridging the gap between the living and the dead, providing the living a chance to commemorate the dead or even continue to commune with them after the vision, or at least, as in the case of *Pearl*, to discover that everyday religious worship has allowed communion with them all along.

We can say that the literary possibilities of all this emerged as a part of a broad social power and importance, so long as 'social' is understood to include a wider and more potent category than modern secular minds generally assume, and a much longer—indeed, eternal—span for its several modes of existence. In the claims by visionary culture on social transactions beyond death, it is pertinent that the most significant dampening of visionary writing in England occurred in the mid-sixteenth century, when prayers for those in purgatory were effectively silenced, signalled by eloquent omissions in the 1552 Book of Common Prayer and aggressively denounced by Reformist ecclesiastics generally. Communing with the distant and the dead— saintly and divine, sinful and devilish—and displaying inspired skill in doing so— may seem morbidly pathological in our post-Hawthornian world, or, again, an unfulfilled longing for our global spans of communication. But the sense of such communion was an engine for centuries of visions and vision-literature that not only affirmed but expanded community, literature, and life.

BIBLIOGRAPHY

ADAMS, GWENFAIR (2007), *Visions in Late Medieval England: Lay Spirituality and Sacred Glimpses of the Hidden Worlds of Faith* (Leiden: Brill).

BAIRD, JOSEPH (tr.) (2006), *The Personal Correspondence of Hildegard of Bingen* (Oxford: Oxford University Press).

BAKER, DENISE (ed.) (2005), *The Showings of Julian of Norwich* (New York: W. W. Norton).

BARR, HELEN (ed.) (1993), *The Piers Plowman Tradition* (London: Dent).

BENSON, LARRY (gen. ed.) (1987), *The Riverside Chaucer* (3rd edn. Boston: Houghton Mifflin).

BLADEL, FRANS VAN (ed.) (2002), *Hadewijch: Die minne es al* (Leuven: Davidsfonds/Literair).

BOLAND, PASCHAL (1959), *The Concept of Discretio Spirituum in John Gerson's 'De Probatione Spirituum' and 'De Distinctione Verarum Visionum a Falsis'* (Washington, DC: Catholic University of America Press).

'BUNYAN, JOHN' (1725, 1998), *Visions of Heaven and Hell* (New Kennington, PA: Whitaker House).

BURROW, J. A. (1993), *Langland's Fictions* (Oxford: Clarendon Press).

CICCARESE, MARIA (ed. and [Italian] trans.) (1987), *Visioni dell'Aldilà in Occidente: Fonte, modelli, testi* (Florence: Nardini).

COLGRAVE, BERTRAM, and R. A. B. MYNORS (eds.) (1992), *Bede's Ecclesiastical History of the English People* (Oxford: Clarendon Press).

COLLINGWOOD, R. G., and R. P. WRIGHT, rev. R. S. O. TOMLIN (1995), *The Roman Inscriptions of Britain*, i. *Inscriptions in Stone* (Oxford: Alan Sutton).

COOPLAND, GEORGE WILLIAM (ed.) (1969), Philippe de Mézières, *Le Songe du vieil pelerin* (2 vols. Cambridge: Cambridge University Press).

DAHLBERG, CHARLES (tr.) (1995), *The Romance of the Rose: Guillaume de Lorris and Jean de Meun* (Princeton: Princeton University Press).

DE VOGÜÉ, ADALBERT (ed.), and PAUL ANTIN (tr.) (1978–80), Grégoire le Grand, *Dialogues* (3 vols. Sources chrétiennes, 251, 260, 265; Paris: Éditions du Cerf).

DICKINS, BRUCE, and ALAN S. C. ROSS (eds.) (1963), *Dream of the Rood* (London: Methuen).

DINZELBACHER, PETER (1981), *Vision und Visionsliteratur im Mittelalter* (Stuttgart: Anton Hiersemann).

——(ed. and [German] tr.) (1989), *Mittelalterliche Visionsliteratur: Eine Anthologie* (Darmstadt: Wissenschaftliche Buchgesellschaft).

EASTING, ROBERT (1997), *Visions of the Other World in Middle English* (Annotated Bibliographies of Old and Middle English Literature, 3; Cambridge: D. S. Brewer).

EYSSENHARDT, FRANCISCUS (ed.) (1883), *Macrobius* (Leipzig: Teubner).

FAIRCLOUGH, H. RUSHTON (ed.) (1967), *Virgil* (2 vols. Cambridge, Mass.: Harvard University Press).

FANOUS, SAMUEL, and HENRIETTA LEYSER (eds.) (2005), *Christina of Markyate: A Twelfth-Century Holy Woman* (New York: Routledge).

FIRTH, KATHERINE (1979), *The Apocalyptic Tradition in Reformation England: 1530–1645* (Oxford: Oxford University Press).

FOSTER, EDWARD (ed.) (2004), *Three Purgatory Poems: The Gast of Gy; Sir Owain; The Vision of Tundale* (Kalamazoo, Mich.: Medieval Institute Publications).

FURNIVALL, F. J. (ed.) (1899–1904), *John Lydgate: The Pilgrimage of the Life of Man* (Early English Text Society, extra series, 77, 83, 92; London: Kegan Paul, Trench, Trübner for the Early English Text Society).

GALLOWAY, ANDREW (1994), 'Dream Theory in *The Dream of the Rood* and *The Wanderer*', *Review of English Studies*, 45: 475–85.

——(1998), 'Intellectual Pregnancy, Metaphysical Femininity, and the Social Doctrine of the Trinity in *Piers Plowman*', *Yearbook of Langland Studies*, 12: 117–52.

——(2006), *The Penn Commentary on Piers Plowman*, i. *C Prologue-Passus 4; B Prologue-Passus 4; A Prologue-Passus 4* (Philadelphia: University of Pennsylvania Press).

GEDDES, JANE, KRISTINE HANEY, SUE NIEBRZYDOWSKI, MARGARET JUBB, and GUNDULA SHARMAN (2003), *The St Albans Psalter Project*, <http://www.abdn.ac.uk/~lib399/english/index.shtml>.

GORDON, IDA, and MARY CLAYTON (eds.) (1996), *The Seafarer* (Exeter: University of Exeter Press).

GORDON, R. K. (tr.) (1976), *Anglo-Saxon Poetry* (London: Dent).

GRADON, PAMELA (ed.) (1992), *Cynewulf's 'Elene'* (Exeter: University of Exeter Press).

GREEN, NILE (2003), 'The Religious and Cultural Roles of Dreams and Visions in Islam', *Journal of the Royal Asiatic Society*, 13/3: 287–313.

HADEWIJCH (1980), *Hadewijch: The Complete Works*, tr. Columba Hart (New York: Paulist Press).

HART, COLUMBA, and JANE BISHOP (tr.) (1990), *Hildegard of Bingen: Scivias* (New York: Paulist Press).

HENIG, MARTIN (2004), 'Roman Religion and Roman Culture in Britain', in Malcolm Todd (ed.), *A Companion to Roman Britain* (Malden, Mass.: Blackwell), 220–41.

HILL, THOMAS D. (1978) '"Half-Waking, Half-Sleeping": A Tropological Motif in a Middle English Lyric and its European Context', *Review of English Studies*, NS 29: 50–6.

HUOT, SYLVIA (1993), *The Romance of the Rose and its Medieval Readers: Interpretation, Reception, Manuscript Transmission* (Cambridge: Cambridge University Press).

IDEL, M. (tr.) (1999), *Jewish Mystical Autobiographies: Book of Visions and Book of Secrets* (New York: Paulist Press).

KERBY-FULTON, KATHERINE (2006), *Books under Suspicion: Censorship and Tolerance of Revelatory Writing in Late Medieval England* (South Bend, Ind.: University of Notre Dame Press).

KRUGER, STEVEN (1992), *Dreaming in the Middle Ages* (Cambridge: Cambridge University Press).

LYNCH, KATHRYN (1988), *The High Medieval Dream Vision: Poetry, Philosophy, and Literary Form* (Stanford, Calif.: Stanford University Press).

McCLENON, JAMES (1991), 'Near-Death Folklore in Medieval China and Japan: A Comparative Analysis', *Asian Folklore Studies*, 50/2: 319–42.

McCREESH, BERNADINE (2005), 'Prophetic Dreams and Visions in the Sagas of the Early Icelandic Saints', in A. Harbus, and Russel G. Poole (eds.), *Verbal Encounters: Anglo-Saxon and Old Norse Studies for Roberta Frank* (Toronto: University of Toronto Press), 247–68.

MAZZONI, CRISTINA (1999), *Angela of Foligno: Memorial* (Cambridge: D. S. Brewer).

MILLER, PATRICIA COX (1997), *Dreams in Late Antiquity: Studies in the Imagination of a Culture* (Princeton: Princeton University Press).

MINNIS, ALASTAIR J. (1988), *The Medieval Theory of Authorship: Scholastic Literary Attitudes in the Later Middle Ages* (2nd edn. Philadelphia: University of Pennsylvania Press).

NEWMAN, BARBARA (1989), *Sister of Wisdom: St Hildegard's Theology of the Feminine* (Berkeley, Calif.: University of California Press).

NEWMAN, FRANCIS XAVIER (1962), '*Somnium*: Medieval Theories of Dreaming and the Form of Vision Poetry', Ph.D. dissertation, Princeton University.

NIJENHUIS, W. F. (1991), *The Vision of Edmund Leversedge: A Fifteenth-Century Account of a Visit to the Otherworld* (Middeleeuwse Studies, 8; Nijmegen: Centrum voor Middeleeuwse Studies).

PALMER, R. BARTON (1993), *Guillaume de Machaut: 'The Fountain of Love' and Two Other Love Vision Poems* (New York and London: Garland).

PEARSON, NORMAN HOLMES (ed.) (1937), *The Complete Novels and Selected Tales of Nathaniel Hawthorne* (New York: Modern Library).

PEDEN, A. (1985), 'Macrobius and Medieval Dream Literature', *Medium Ævum*, 54: 59–61.

PIEHLER, PAUL (1971), *The Visionary Landscape: A Study in Medieval Allegory* (London: Edward Arnold).

PLATNAUER, MAURICE (ed. and tr.) (1963), *Claudian* (Cambridge, Mass.: Harvard University Press).

POIRION, DANIEL (ed.) (1974), *Le Roman de la Rose* (Paris: Garnier-Flammarion).

POOR, SARA (2004), *Mechthild of Magdeburg and her Book: Gender and the Making of Textual Authority* (Philadelphia: University of Pennsylvania Press).

PRATT, ROBERT A. (1947), 'Chaucer's Claudian', *Speculum*, 22: 419–29.

SARGENT, MICHAEL (2004), *Nicholas Love: The Mirror of the Blessed Life of Jesus Christ* (Exeter: University of Exeter Press).

ST JOHN, MICHAEL (2000), *Chaucer's Dream Visions: Courtliness and Individual Identity* (Aldershot: Ashgate).

SCHMIDT, A. V. C. (ed.) (1995), *The Vision of Piers Plowman: A Critical Edition of the B Text* (2nd edn. London: Dent).

SILVERSTEIN, THEODORE (1935), *Visio Sancti Pauli: The History of the Apocalypse in Latin, Together with Nine Texts* (Studies and Documents, 4; London: Christophers).

SPEARING, A. C. (1980), *Medieval Dream-Poetry* (Cambridge: Cambridge University Press).

STAHL, WILLIAM HARRIS (tr.) (1952), *Commentary on the Dream of Scipio* (New York: Columbia University Press).

STALEY, LYNN (1998), *The Book of Margery Kempe* (Kalamazoo, Mich.: Medieval Institute Publications).

STÜRZINGER, JOHAN JAKOB (ed.) (1893), *Le Pelerinage de Vie Humaine de Guillaume de Deguileville* (London: Nichols & Sons).

——(ed.) (1895), *Le Pelerinage de l'ame de Guillaume de Deguileville* (London: Nichols & Sons).

——(ed.) (1897), *Le Pelerinage Jhesucrist de Guillaume de Deguileville* (London: Nichols & Sons).

SYMONS, DANA (ed.) (2004), *Chaucerian Dream Visions and Complaints* (Kalamazoo, Mich.: Medieval Institute Publications).

TALBOT, C. H. (ed. and tr.) (1998), *The Life of Christina of Markyate, a Twelfth Century Recluse* (Toronto: University of Toronto Press).

THIER, LUDGER, and ABELE CALUFETTI (eds.) (1985), *Il Libro della Beata Angela da Foligno* (2nd edn. Rome: College of S. Bonaventure).

TOBIN, FRANK (tr.) (1998), Mechthild of Magdeburg, *The Flowing Light of the Godhead* (New York: Paulist Press).

CHAPTER 14

....

WRITING, HERESY, AND THE ANTICLERICAL MUSE

....

MISHTOONI BOSE

Crist seiþ also þat 'Þer shal come a tyme whanne men shal seie 'Lo here, lo þere!', as þouȝ he wolde mene þat men shal seie 'Lo, here is perfeccioun at Rome!', and oþir shal seie 'Lo, here is perfeccioun or ground of christen lyuyng at Auinon!', or ellis in more special 'Lo, here among mounkis is perfeccioun, or Crist is here fair serued!' Summe seien 'Lo, here it is at þe chanouns!'; summe seien 'Lo, here at freris is Crist fairest serued!' Þus men seien now in oure daies bisili, 'Lo here, lo þere!' But what seide Crist þat trewe men shulden do in þis tyme?[1]

The English sermon *Omnis plantacio*, from which the quotation above has been taken, precisely encapsulates the central concerns of this chapter. In passages such as these, its as-yet-unidentified preacher castigates several ranks of the clergy, from the Pope to the friars. Elsewhere, he confidently translates into the vernacular a series of simplified arguments against both the wealth of endowed ecclesiastical orders, such as monks and canons ('possessioners'), and the strategies whereby the more recently founded orders of friars (or 'beggers' in his polemical lexicon) acquired alms. He goes further than this, moreover, defiantly aligning himself with 'þese þat ben callid Lollardis', by which he meant not merely reformers, but those who might have been

---

[1] Hudson (2001: 9).

considered suspect of heresy.[2] Finally, he modified the sermon's function significantly by leaving it with his audience, so that 'whoso likiþ mai ouerse it'.[3] With these final words, an audience had become a readership, and the sermon had become *writing*, situated at the centre of a newly inaugurated textual community, open for questioning, correction, and possible misunderstanding. And its preacher had become an author, at once responsible for the conditions in which it would be interpreted, and pragmatically resigned to the exercise of interpretative will by 'whoso likiþ'.[4] Writing of an earlier period in the history of literacy and heresy, Brian Stock has observed that 'wherever texts appeared, they changed relations between authors, listeners, readers, and the real or imagined public'.[5] This comment precisely maps out the trajectory of *Omnis plantacio*.

Omnis plantacio shows how a series of complex relationships were evolving between writing, heresy, and anticlericalism in late medieval England. Each of these terms requires preliminary analysis, and in the case of 'anticlericalism' strong justification. But it is sufficient for now to establish that two aspects of *Omnis plantacio*—one historical, the other textual—succinctly introduce this chapter's chief concerns. First, in targeting several clerical strata at once, the sermon shows how certain *intra*-clerical critiques, which had long been a dominant discourse of the western Church in the Middle Ages, had latterly mutated to produce a virulent and explicitly *anti*-clerical (that is, all-encompassing) strain. This important development lays the foundation for the present chapter's retention of the term 'anticlericalism' as a specific and viable historiographical category. 'Lollardy' is a notoriously imprecise term, but the preacher's defiant use of it clearly indicates his sympathies with the views of John Wyclif.[6] But just as Wycliffism (a less subjective and pejorative term) was far from being solely responsible for the development of an anticlerical mentality, so it did not monopolize it. Clerical castigation was common among both orthodox reformers and obdurate heretics, whereas on other subjects, such as the metaphysics of the eucharist, they remained sharply divided.

The chapter's second theme is the imagining of institutional—usually ecclesiastical—collapse, as figured in this sermon's relentless castigation of failing clerical ranks. This, too, was imaginative territory on which reformist and heretical mentalities often converged, as is shown by the reformist poem *Piers Plowman* and the explicitly Wycliffite poem *Pierce the Ploughmans Crede*, both of which take as their point of departure 'the inadequacies of . . . institutions and their authoritative texts'.[7] These texts, like *Omnis plantacio* and the substantial corpus of Wycliffite sermons, were the products of a period in which the vernacular was being recharged, from different ideological and institutional directions, with multiple discursive resources

[2] Ibid. 50.   [3] Ibid. 138.

[4] For a parallel discussion of a Lollard textual community centred on a suspect text, see Strohm (2006: 465–6). As Strohm acknowledges, the phrase 'textual community' comes from Stock (1983: 42–59, 90–2). For an example of an orthodox transaction 'with Lollard scripture at its centre', see Hanna (2003: 151).

[5] Stock (1983: 80).

[6] On *Lollard* as a 'meaningless' term, see Catto (1999: 160).

[7] Simpson (1990: 23).

distributed across diverse written genres from sermons to poems.[8] And thus from the spaces beyond established institutions, whether academic, ecclesiastical, curial, or legal, came a plurality of late medieval voices, some avowedly orthodox, others proudly dissenting.[9] In the early fifteenth-century English poem *De concordia inter rectores fratres et rectores ecclesie*, the Augustinian friar John Audelay would deploy a Langlandian literary idiom to argue that bribery had undermined the ability of the consistory courts to deliver restitution to plaintiffs. Some eighty or more years later, the apparent failure of a consistory court to uphold John Skelton's complaint against a hawking curate would become the pretext for his first reforming poem, *Ware the Hauke*.[10] Such pretexts were not exclusive to poets. In the decades between Audelay and Skelton, Reginald Pecock would posit an intellectually impoverished Church as the point of departure for his own programme of orthodox renewal. The critique in *Omnis plantacio* of ecclesiastical structures 'in þis tyme', as expressed so vehemently above, thus brought its author into alignment with a wide range of late medieval English writers, from Langland to Skelton, who made imaginative and textual capital out of the vacuum created when institutions, whether academic, curial, legal, or ecclesiastical, were imagined in a state of corruption or collapse.

While they envisage lay–clerical relationships in different ways, these and other texts exploited the power of written texts to sidestep the authoritative, mediating role of the clergy altogether. Hence the privileging of the term 'writing' in this chapter's title, a vestigially deconstructive gesture consonant with several recent attempts to describe important vernacular textual practices that emerged in late medieval England. This critical gesture is particularly suited to a period that saw the rise of 'non-professional' writers and readers; of 'lewed clergie' (lay learning); and, further afield, of what has been identified as the 'public intellectual', a category that includes schoolmen as disparate in intellectual temperament as Wyclif and the French theologian Jean Gerson.[11] Each of these critical formulations is an attempt to describe the blurring of institutional boundaries during this period, and the consequent hybridization of learning, as instantiated in the emergent paradoxes of 'lewed clergie' or the figure of the *laicus literatus*, and as acknowledged in the comment that *Piers Plowman* 'address[es] its matter in a context which is not specifically clerical or academic'.[12] The appearance of the unaffiliated writer is brought fully into focus in *Piers Plowman* (B XII. 16–19), in which Ymaginatif rebukes the dreamer-poet, whose social status and vocation remain undefined:

> And þou medlest þee wiþ makynges and myȝtest go seye þi sauter,
> And bidde for hem þat ȝyueþ þee bred, for þer are bokes y[n]owe
> To telle men what dowel is, dobet and dobest boþe,
> And prechours to preuen what it is of many a peire freres.

[8] On this development, see Wogan-Browne *et al.* (1999).
[9] For a reading of late medieval English literary history in these terms, see Simpson (2002).
[10] I consider these poems together in more detail in 'John Skelton and the Long Fifteenth Century' (forthcoming).
[11] Scase (1989: esp. pp. 161–73); Gillespie (2007: 403); Hobbins (2003).
[12] Hudson (1994); Simpson (1990: 19).

This passage calls into question the ethical purpose of writing that existed beyond the control of a single institution or individual, and that called all authorities into question. As the *Omnis plantacio* preacher had also recognized, the independence of writing had significant, and potentially destabilizing, implications for the relative positions of authors and readers during this period. It was one of many English texts that breached the boundaries between intra- and extramural worlds, and exuberantly translated the terms and materials of scholastic argumentation into a fledgling vernacular.[13] And whether or not particular reformist arguments were actually hereticated, the manifestation of both mentalities as *writing*—and particularly as writing in English—brought each into an arena controlled neither by the avowedly orthodox nor by the heterodox, and in which the author's voice might become one of a polyphony, or cacophony, of such voices engaged in argument and interpretation. In the following discussion, I will explore these issues through a series of comparisons and contrasts: first, between *Piers Plowman* and some Wycliffite texts; second, between the writings of two friars—the Carmelite, Thomas Netter, and the Augustinian, John Audelay; third, between the *Omnis plantacio* preacher and Reginald Pecock, bishop of Chichester; and lastly, between John Gower and John Skelton.

From Intra-Clerical Critique to Anticlericalism

When examining medieval criticisms of the clergy, we are well advised to consider the *longue durée*, since they express 'smouldering resentments directed against monks, friars, bishops, priests, and clerics who claimed this-worldly privileges by way of an other-worldly office'.[14] Criticisms of the clergy at any one time comprised a number of distinct, but often related, polemical stances and mentalities: anti-papalism, clerical self-criticism, and controversy between different clerical orders, a particularly virulent example of this latter category being anti-fraternalism (that is, hostility to the orders of mendicant friars founded during the course of the thirteenth century). Dissenters and orthodox alike were particularly haunted by the example that they believed to have been set for them by the apostolic Church. Whether emanating from rivalries between clergy and laity, or more narrowly from tensions between particular religious orders, much of what is still loosely termed 'anticlericalism' had arisen from the fundamental question as to what constituted a properly evangelical priesthood. Preoccupation with this question assumed the character of a persistent, low-grade infection liable to flare up under particular circumstances, such as the foundation of

---

[13] On this process, see Somerset (1998).
[14] Van Engen (1993: 19).

new religious orders.[15] In the first place, therefore, 'anticlericalism' might be regarded as a notoriously inexact term for what was, throughout the medieval period, an international phenomenon with multiple, and multilingual, cross-currents and points of origin.[16] Introduced into English during the nineteenth century, the term requires some critical justification before it may be retained as a viable category in the historiography and literary histories of the medieval period.[17] I have already suggested that it might be retained to describe criticisms aimed at several strata of the clergy at once, and the following phase of this discussion will provide more detailed justification for the use of the term in this sense.[18]

The rhetoric of clerical critique had been pioneered by the clergy themselves. Such a discourse was the inevitable by-product of a Church that saw itself as continually in need of institutional reform. The canons of the Fourth Lateran Council of 1215 encapsulate this preoccupation with clerical discipline and its legislative consequences. Encoding the disciplinary ambitions of Innocent III, they provide a cumulative picture of a vigilantly self-critical institution concerned not only to extirpate heresy and regulate the pastoral and internal lives of the laity, but most importantly to keep the clerical ranks in check and to standardize the disciplining of subordinate clergy by prelates. In the centuries that followed Lateran IV, a series of intra-clerical arguments would eventually mutate into a full-blown anticlerical discourse. This happened in three phases: the first typically characterized by rigorist self-criticism on the part of some mendicant thinkers; the second by anti-fraternalism, as those arguments were adapted by others beyond the fraternal orders; and the third by anticlericalism, as the resulting rhetorics proliferated in new contexts.[19] And once it became clear that arguments that the seculars, regulars, and mendicants had once used selectively against each other could be aimed at them all, something much greater was at stake. In England, this broadening of clerical critique was most clearly manifested in two parallel and independent experiments: the writings of Wyclif and his supporters, and the alliterative poem *Piers Plowman*. I will briefly consider the character of Wyclif's anticlericalism and its legacy before turning in the following section to *Piers Plowman*.

John Wyclif had established himself as a controversial academic in Oxford during the 1370s, and during his lifetime ten of his ideas were condemned as heretical, and fourteen as erroneous.[20] As it evolved after his death in 1384, the Wycliffite agenda came to centre on a core of initially well-defined theological, ecclesiastical, and

---

[15] Ibid. Van Engen goes on to list the Cluniac monks, the Roman curia, the Cistercians, village curates, mendicant friars, and the Avignon papacy as only a few examples of institutions and groups within the Church who provoked such reactions at critical points in the development of their respective jurisdictions (p. 20).

[16] For sharp criticism of the term from the perspective of Reformation historiography, see Haigh (1983).

[17] *OED*, anticlerical (*a.* and *n*). See further Georgianna (2000: 148–9).

[18] In this I concur with the use of the term in Scase (1989).

[19] This necessarily succinct account of some extremely complex developments in intellectual life is indebted to the following: Scase (1989); Dawson (1983); Dipple (1994); Clopper (1997); Szittya (1986).

[20] For a succinct summary with timeline, see Hudson (1978).

political issues, including criticism of the validity of the sacramental system, of the use of images and pilgrimages, of the role of the papacy, the material wealth of the Church, the taking of oaths, and the killing of men in war. But most germane to the present argument is the fact that, in Wyclif's thought, an initial attraction to mendicant rigorism had subsequently given way to anti-mendicant feeling, a change resulting from the friars' opposition to his later views concerning the metaphysics of the eucharist.[21] From this point, a significant broadening of Wyclif's ideas took place: 'once [he] sought to impose [a] model of poverty and meekness upon the clergy as a whole—from parish priest to archbishop and pope...he became a dangerous man'.[22] Furthermore, Wyclif's theory of predestination brought him significantly nearer to the imagining of a 'radically de-institutionalized Church'. Because it was impossible to know whether or not individual members of the clergy had been predestined to salvation, it could no longer be assumed that they were members of the true Church. And since 'no ecclesiastical office or institution [could] constitute the membership of the Church...the legal structure of the Church had effectively crumbled. Wyclif attributed all the authority ascribed previously to priests, rectors, bishops and popes to Christ alone'.[23]

The subsequent controversies over Wyclif's ideas that generated texts such as *Omnis plantacio* are best understood as 'one episode, admittedly the most extreme, in a long series of controversies' in a period in which heresy was a sporadic but inevitable by-product of religious orthodoxy.[24] Legislation gradually deprived Wycliffism of its academic and political support. The 1401 statute *De heretico comburendo* made it possible for relapsed heretics to be handed over to the secular powers for burning. Archbishop Thomas Arundel's anti-heretical *Provincial Constitutions* of 1407–9 could be seen as the antithesis of the catechetical ambitions that had marked the statutes of his predecessors. Consolidating the achievements of earlier legislation, the *Constitutions* were intended to curb the spread of heretical ideas by outlawing certain literate and academic practices, such as the unauthorized translation of the scriptures into the vernacular. But extant records of heresy trials from the fifteenth and early sixteenth centuries show that some of the different emphases apparent in earlier examples of Wycliffite discourse continued to play themselves out in closely knit communities investigated for heresy. First, they show the survival of ideas recognizably derived from earlier phases of the controversy, as in the Norwich heretic John Skylan's confession (1430) that he believed that 'aftir the sacramental wordis said at messe of ony prest ther remayneth oonly pure material bred'.[25] Second, they show the evolution of views more popular among later Lollards, such as Skylan's

---

[21] Levy (2006) points out that Wyclif 'had a special affinity for those strictly observant Franciscans' but 'then took the radical step of demanding that this principle be applied to the entire clergy' (p. 317).

[22] Ibid. 294.

[23] Shogimen (2006: 216–17). Lahey (2009), however, gives a somewhat more moderate account of Wyclif's ecclesiology, pointing out his arguments for the retention of an episcopate (pp. 220–1).

[24] Pantin (1955: 123).   [25] Tanner (1977: 147).

belief that 'all Cristis puple is sufficiently baptized in the blood of Crist and nedeth noo other baptem'.[26] Third, they show something that the ecclesiastical inquisitors, armed with lists of topics on which to examine suspects, may not have expected: divergences from the central core of orthodox belief that nevertheless had little or nothing to do with Wycliffism and more to do with a less easily classified self-reliance. Thus, among the charges of heresy made against Robert Clerke of Coventry (1489/90) was the claim that he had 'instructed that it is damnable to say the Our Father and Hail Mary, because the whole efficacy of prayer is in the Creed'.[27] What appears to have been transmitted to him is a selective distrust of the standard formulae through which orthodox religion expresses itself, together with a sense of entitlement to improvise with those formulae in a way that seemed authentic to him.

Orthodox reformist criticisms of the clergy typically arose from concern about the impact on the 'care of souls' (*cura animarum*) of clerical abuses such as the non-residence of priests in their parishes, or the lax administration of sacerdotal duties such as the sacrament of confession. Crucially, orthodox reformers avoided fundamental questions about the status of the material, institutional Church. What made Wycliffite anticlericalism distinct from the clerical castigation typical of reformist orthodoxy was the wholesale rejection of the authority of the institutional Church and its individual representatives. This arose out of its fundamental preoccupation with the nature, origins, and remit of clerical dominion (*dominium*), or lordship. Questions regarding the Church's temporal wealth, and arguments for and against its disendowment, had long featured in intra-clerical disputes and, as will be observed below, this preoccupation was far from distinctively Wycliffite; but the topic assumed a distinctive role in Wyclif's thought because of the importance he accorded to the apostolic poverty of Christ, and to the *lex Christi* (law of Christ) by which, he believed, the Church should be governed.[28] By instituting these absolute standards as those by which the Church should be measured, Wyclif made it possible to imagine a Church divested of temporal wealth and thereby freed to concentrate on pastoral care and the saving of souls. And this was a pressing necessity for a contemporary ecclesiastical hierarchy which, according to Wyclif's vision, was 'riddled with disease'.[29]

LANGLAND'S VAGUENESS

Like Wyclif, Langland was the beneficiary of well-established debates concerning ecclesiastical disendowment that had in turn arisen from disputes over the nature,

---

[26] Ibid. 146.   [27] McSheffrey and Tanner (2003: 96).

[28] This phase of my discussion is indebted to the lucid exposition of *dominium* in Lahey (2009: 199–221).

[29] Ibid. 196.

origins, and remit of clerical dominion. But *Piers Plowman* shows how this tradition of intra-clerical dispute could be taken in a different and more radical direction. *Piers Plowman* not only bears the imprints of previous intra-clerical controversies, but also conducts an independent, fluid refiguring of ecclesiastical breakdown conducted from the distinctive vantage-point of a poem of uncertain authorship, addressed to no patron, and affiliated to no single institution, whether academic, legal, curial, or ecclesiastical. The radical implications and character of the poem originate precisely in this lack of affiliation, which is ably characterized by the phrase 'vagrant poetics'.[30] The modern adjective *vague* is derived, via the intermediate French thirteenth-century adjective *vague*, from the Latin *vagus*, meaning 'wandering, inconstant, uncertain'.[31] It is also related to the ME *vagaunt*, ultimately derived from Latin *vagans* and meaning 'wandering', or 'idle'.[32] Wandering and uncertainty were necessary aesthetic and epistemological principles in a poem that exploited its potential as an arena of religious exploration that went well beyond the institutional Church's catechetical agenda, or the discursive remit of conventional satire. For example, individual passages in the poem might appear to collude with such conventions, such as the depiction in B III. 35–63/C III. 38–67 of a friar who hears the confession of 'Mede the mayde' in return for material gifts. Nevertheless, the poem's fundamentally vagrant aesthetic principles prohibit it from ultimately finding satisfaction with any single rank of the clergy, as figured in an explicit contrast between 'Clerkes' that 'haue no knowyng' and the greater insight enjoyed by 'Piers þe Plowman, *Petrus id est christus*' (B XV. 198, 212). And it invests more in the reformist potential of malleable abstractions such as Patience, Reason, Conscience and, of course, the Will.[33]

Given that both Langland and Wyclif drew on earlier phases of intra-clerical controversy, it is not surprising that they should have been thinking, in certain cases, along parallel lines. What they have in common is that the thought of one and the imagination of the other led each to imagine a deinstitutionalized Church, Wyclif arriving at that point via his theories concerning dominion and predestination, and Langland's objective correlative being the charismatic figure of Piers the Plowman. What divides them absolutely, however, is that Langland is, to use J. A. Burrow's pregnant phrase, 'thinking in poetry'.[34] This is the heart of his radicalism. Wyclif confined himself to sermons and polemical treatises, the latter being an offshoot of established academic literary genres, and the medium of choice for the emerging public intellectual.[35] But the poetic frame within which *Piers Plowman* situates the topic of disendowment enacts something yet more radical: while Wyclif and other non-fictional writers were embroiled in the controversies, Langland's imagination dramatized them without being encompassed by them.

---

[30] Some of the implications of the poem's vagrant aesthetic are discussed in Scase (1989: 125–36, 169, 161–73); Middleton (1997: 208–317).

[31] *OED*, vague (*a., adv., and n*).

[32] *MED*, vagaunt (*adj.*).

[33] Compare Scase (1989: 119), '[I]t is conscience which becomes the site of truth'.

[34] Burrow (1993).

[35] On the tract, see Hobbins (2003).

The *passus* is his equivalent not only of a scholastic disputation, but also of a literary genre, the late medieval tract, which contemporary and later theologians would find useful not only for the exploration but also for the dissemination of ideas. B XV, for example, is a forum (analogous to the romance, or the *quodlibet*) in which Langland made it possible to try out solutions to pressing questions, in his case concerning the Church's temporal wealth. It is here that he replays a stock element in the critique of endowment, namely the story concerning the Emperor Constantine's donation of the Lateran in Rome to Pope Sylvester, and the angel's condemnation of the endowment with its assertion that '*Dos ecclesie* this day hath ydronke venym' (l. 558). Both in the B-text and C-text versions of this moment, the poem comes strikingly close to positions that Wyclif would have found congenial ('Taketh hire landes, ye lordes'), and in particular the claim that:

> If possession be poison, and inparfite hem make,
> Good were to deschargen hem for Holy Chirches sake. (B XV. 563–4)

The poet even emphasizes this compelling and provocative speculation by articulating it as a rhyming couplet (a formal choice rejected in C XVII. 2297–31, the equivalent passage).[36] So it is important to note that Wyclif did not enjoy exclusive ownership of this topic, whether at this or at subsequent points in English literary history. It is certainly a subject that Wycliffite writers treated energetically; but it also received attention from Gower in *Vox clamantis* and, later, from Pecock in *The Repressor of Over-Much Blaming of the Clergy*, a text in which he condemns the Donation as a forgery.[37] The pervasiveness of this particular topic powerfully exemplifies the way in which reformist discourses continued to flourish alongside, and after, the distinctive and disruptive contributions of Wyclif and his supporters.

PROFITABLE *PROCUTOURS*: LAITY AND CLERGY IN DIALOGUE

'Explicit hic dialogus petri plowman': the colophon to the B-text of *Piers Plowman* in Cambridge, Trinity College, B. 15. 17, precisely justifies a recent interpretation of the poem as 'a *social text*, a *corporate poem*'.[38] In its use of the capacious alliterative line to open up multiple spaces for the mooting of unresolved theological and pastoral topics, the poem interpellates its readers as participants in an ongoing sequence of

---

[36] For a succinct discussion of Wyclif's position in this respect, see Lahey (2009: 218).
[37] Levine (1973).
[38] Kelly (2007: 548).

debates. But in the broader context of medieval engagements between laity and clergy over pastoral and sacerdotal issues, *Piers Plowman* was hardly an isolated venture.[39] One of the most fertile literary genres in late medieval England was the dialogue between lay and clerical interlocutors which tested the latter's ability to pre-empt doctrinal confusion in the former.[40] In such cases, no less than in *Piers Plowman*, the vernacular text had become an arena in which relationships between the laity and the clergy could be imagined, projected, tested, and refined. There was also a minor renaissance in fifteenth-century England in the production of writings featuring visions of the other world, a genre whose principal purpose was to affirm the moral and institutional accountability of the clergy as a continuing and fundamentally acceptable topic for discussion within the capacious frame of orthodox discourse. One such example of this genre is *The Vision of William of Stranton*, in which the recently canonized St John of Bridlington shows William the tormented souls of bishops, prelates, and curates of the Church, who should have preached the law of God to the people, and given them an example of good living.[41] Such textual engagements were hardly determined by the course and remit of the Wycliffite controversies. Rather, those controversies appear to have sharpened appetites on all sides for a profound and practical formulation of the duties and behaviour of a good priest. In the 1420s, intellectual Wycliffism had gone into decline, but this period also produced two writers with much to tell us about the state of both intra-clerical and lay-clerical relations in the wake of the Wycliffite controversies.

Thomas Netter, a distinguished Carmelite and committed anti-heretic who ultimately became prior provincial, produced his *Doctrinale antiquitatum fidei*, the most substantial response to Wycliffite views, in instalments throughout the 1420s.[42] Netter's method throughout this volume is generally uniform: he subdivides major topics, such as the eucharist, into separate chapters, and in each chapter lists a number of Wycliffite propositions regarding the theme. He sets out to reconstruct Wyclif's views by quoting copiously from his writings, or by summarizing views attributed to him or to his followers. He then refutes each proposition, point by point, sometimes by turning Wyclif's authorities (notably St Augustine) against him, or by quoting at length from other, largely patristic, sources in order to demolish Wyclif's position.[43] But in one section of this long work, he departs from this method to present his views in the form of a dialogue between *clericus*, a secular priest, and *religiosus*, a member of a regular order.[44] The tenor of the dialogue is established with the general call to humility with which it begins. Netter evokes an image of himself in the cloister with his *confrères*, not hearing about matters that are transacted in public. Rather, what preoccupies those in the claustral life is their derelictions of duty, and

---

[39] On dialectic and dialogue in this context, see Graus (1993).

[40] For a preliminary discussion of some of these texts, such as *Dives and Pauper*, see Bose (2003: 231–3).

[41] See Easting (1991); Scase (1994); Erler (2007).

[42] Netter (1757–9), hereafter *Doctrinale*. References to this edn. will be by volume, column, and letter. On its composition and dissemination, see Harvey (1992).

[43] See Ghosh (2001: 174–208).

[44] *Doctrinale*, III. 512B ff.

the extent to which they fall short of the standards of perfection that might be expected of them. Thus, Netter opens his dialogue not with an assumption of fraternal superiority, but rather with the words of St Paul in Philippians 2: 3: 'Alter alterum sibi superiorem existimet' ('Let each judge another to be better than himself'). Likewise, using the authority of St Augustine, Netter argues that one should consider what one lacks in the way of virtue, rather than what one possesses. This serves not only as the moral but also as the aesthetic principle on which the ensuing dialogue is grounded. In the exchange that follows, the clerical interlocutors compete to praise one another.[45] Thus, the *religiosus* praises the *clericus* for his public work, which includes the administering of the sacraments, daily prayers, an exemplary life, and preaching. One of the authorities appealed to by both interlocutors is Pseudo-Dionysius's *The Ecclesiastical Hierarchy*, with the *religiosus* making his case on the strength of Dionysian statements such as the following: '[T]he order of monks does not have the task of leading others, but . . . it follows the clerical orders, and as an attendant it is obediently uplifted by them to the divine understanding of the sacred things of their order.'[46] The charitable disputation revolves around the *religiosus*'s contention that the *gradus* (status, rank) and *officium* (roster of duties) of the secular priest make him innately superior, and the *clericus*'s response that *gradus* does not automatically confer superiority: the title of priest (*sacerdos*) is the title of an office, not a merit. Where the *religiosus* is awed by the practical difficulties that naturally accrue to the office of secular priest, the *clericus* praises the asceticism and discipline of regular life, together with chastity, poverty, and the *religiosus*'s courageous commitment to facing spiritual demons. They similarly tussle over claims to teaching authority (*magisterium*), with the *religiosus* claiming that he, the disciple, is not above his master and the *clericus* countering this with the argument that he, the preacher, is not always to be preferred to his auditor.

To read the avowedly orthodox Netter on intra-clerical relations and then to pass to the vernacular poetry of John Audelay, his Augustinian contemporary, on the same theme is to become forcibly aware of the resilience of clerical castigation in England at this time. Netter's dialogue can justifiably be called reformist because of the way in which both of the interlocutors have introjected conventional critical topics regarding their respective orders and voice them in an extended autocritique, as when, for example, *clericus* chastizes the hypocrisy of priests who preach at others and neglect to scrutinize their own conduct.[47] But Audelay's vernacular poetics unravel the neatness of Netter's self-consciously authoritative picture, and show how a reinvented Langlandian idiom could be brought to bear creatively on a new phase of concern with lay-clerical and intra-clerical relations. A sequence of poems from Oxford, Bodleian Library, MS Douce 302 (the only surviving manuscript of Audelay's works) shows how such concerns, dating from the time of the Council of Constance and its aftermath, could be articulated in a passionate but subtle idiom

---

[45] I give an alternative discussion of this dialogue in 'Netter as Critic and Practitioner of Rhetoric: The *Doctrinale* as disputation' (forthcoming).

[46] *Doctrinale*, III. 514D. The translation is from Pseudo-Dionysius (1987: 246).

[47] *Doctrinale*, III. 516A.

mimetic of the unresolved nature of the disputes themselves.[48] The colophon to this sequence, numbered 1–18 in Ella Keats Whiting's edition, dates it as complete in 1426. It also suggests two titles for the sequence (here referred to as *liber*, a book): 'concilium conciencie aut scala celi et vita salutis eterni': 'the council of conscience, or ladder of heaven and way of eternal life'. Audelay thus offers up this sequence as a poetic counterpart to the Council, signalling its reformist aspirations. The colophon also states that the sequence was written 'for the example of others in the monastery of Haughmond' ('ad exemplum aliorum in monasterio de Haghmon'): thus, like Netter, Audelay was writing in the first instance for his *confrères*; but, unlike Netter, Audelay may not have aimed at a wider audience.

One of the principal reformist characteristics of Audelay's poetry is a roving attentiveness to ecclesiastical and lay duties expressed in poetry that operates, both thematically and idiomatically, in ways clearly derived from Langland's purposeful vagueness. The second poem in this sequence, *De concordia inter rectores fratres et rectores ecclesie*, is more subtle than a sequence of dialogues could be. The poem's perspectives shift from stanza to stanza as the attention of its speaker, Marcol the fool, moves restlessly between secular priests, friars, and the laity. The idiom that Audelay uses here deliberately keeps in play multiple perspectives, but its chief concern, as the rubric suggests, is to broker a 'loveday' (*concordia*) between friars and secular priests (ll. 392–3) because both are accountable to the laity, and lay perceptions of clerical failings amplify the social instabilities and uncertainties that allow false accusations of heresy to be bandied about. This poem, which brilliantly evokes the paranoia and rumour-mongering attendant on the breakdown of trust between ranks of the clergy, and between clergy and laity, has received more critical attention than others in the sequence.[49] However, notwithstanding the subtleties achieved through its complex syntax and thematic mobility, much of what it achieves deliberately resonates with what happens later in the sequence, and demands to be read in that context. One of Marcol's claims is that secular priests are obliged through shame to disassociate themselves from speaking the truth:

> And ȝif þe secular say a soþ anon þai ben e-schent,
> And lyen apon þe leud men and sayn hit is lollere ... (ll. 669–70)

The collocation of the verb *shenden* and the noun *soþ*, and thus the association between speaking the truth and being destroyed, marks out a theme of considerable importance for Audelay. Forms of *shenden* appear regularly throughout the first poem in the sequence, but in the relatively uncomplicated context in which the priest-poet castigates clearly identifiable wrongdoers. But Poem 18, with which the sequence closes, enters into an implied dialogue with Poem 2, the only poem in the sequence that can match its complexity. Here the speaker reprises the role of prophet and visionary that Marcol had formerly occupied. As in Poem 2, it is argued that no one pays attention to preaching and teaching, but that an individual's deeds

---

[48] Audelay (1931).
[49] Simpson (2005); Green (2001).

'deem' him, a claim that implicitly puts pressure on the perceptions of those who scrutinize such deeds. As in Poem 2, the work of a consistory court is imperilled because of corruption, and the ecclesiastical hierarchy is suffering from a chronic lack of discipline, as bishops are failing to correct their curates. Nevertheless, although painfully aware of the multiplicity of clerical transgressions, the speaker exhorts the laity to participate in the sacraments, such as the making of oral confession to a priest. In a manner not unlike the situation in *Piers Plowman*, Conscience emerges as the greatest authority in this poem: once again, an abstraction has more charisma than material institutions and their workings. Things come to a head in the stanza beginning at l. 258, which reprises the earlier poem's collocation between the necessity of truth-telling and the debilitating risk of being destroyed by it, amid false perceptions of an undefined 'lollardre'. Christian men, the speaker complains, risk accusations of Lollardy if they keep the commandments and do God's will. In answer to this, the speaker asserts that:

> Here is non error ne lollardre,
> Bot pistil and gospel, þe sauter treuly; (ll. 257–8)

His taking refuge in the authority of 'þe treue clargy', however, cannot entirely dispel questions that the poem itself has raised concerning perception, through the speaker's own attentiveness to the difficulty that many clearly have in distinguishing between zeal and error, and thus in locating and trusting what is 'treue'. Thus, the poetic voice created in this sequence articulates a complex clerical subjectivity, at times taking refuge in simple, dichotomous thinking regarding good and bad conduct (as in Poem 1), but at others simultaneously transfixed and energized by intra-clerical conflict and the ill-defined threat of 'Lollardy'. The 'Council of Conscience' sequence boldly offers itself up as a parallel, poetic arena in which the Church's agitated conversation with itself at Constance concerning reformation and the extirpation of heresy is endowed with a distinctively Langlandian character, baffled and compelled in turn by its internal tensions and contradictions.

ADULTEROUS TEXTS

Audelay and Netter were motivated by a similar concern to improve intra-clerical relations, but the different choices they made regarding language, genre, imagined audience, and, above all, their very different projected relationships to institutional authority (the powerful Netter confidently and expansively international, the obscure Audelay cryptically parochial) make for a distinctly polychromatic picture of those relationships. Such a picture is complicated even further if we compare the voices of the *Omnis plantacio* preacher and Reginald Pecock, an avowedly orthodox reformer from a later generation who was, nevertheless, arraigned for heresy and deposed from the see of Chichester.[50] Pecock is an isolated but eloquent witness to the way in which concerns regarding intra-clerical and lay-clerical relations continued to play themselves out in Archbishop Chichele's time and beyond.[51] As he would have been well aware, the autocritical elements in his defence of the clergy drew on long-established traditions of fraternal correction and self-castigation. In *Piers Plowman*, Clergie, who appears at the feast in B XIII. 122–4, models clerical humility—or at least diffidence—in his admission that institutionally sanctioned learning is no match for the extramural charisma figured by Piers:

> 'I am unhardy', quod he, 'to any wight to preven it,
> For oon Piers the Plowman hath impugned us alle,
> And set alle sciences at a sop save love one . . .'

This is not so very far from Pecock's disarmingly frank admission that '[The laity know that] the clergie may faile and erre as weel as thei . . . sith, as thei seien, the clergie is not worthie be visited by eny special inspiracioun or revelacioun fro God more than thei hem silf ben worthi.'[52] But in Pecock's English writings we see an attempt, not to collude with Clergie's self-castigation, but rather to renew fruitful relations between *scientia* and *caritas*, clergy and laity, vernacular and argumentation. These aspirations are encapsulated in Pecock's explicit desire to be a 'profitable procutoure' to the laity and in the rhetorical disposition of some of his works as 'dialogazacioun', quite possibly to give them something analogous to the provisional, discursive, exploratory atmosphere invited by Langland's capacious alliterative lines, with their persistent, implied invitation to readers to collaborate with him in thinking, imagining, and arguing.[53]

On one hand, Pecock attempted to distinguish his vernacular voice from the textual polyphonies (and, indeed, the dissonance) of the Wycliffite controversies. On the other, he displayed an apparently irresistible compulsion to replay some of the lexical and argumentative strategies of those controversies.[54] Thus, at times, his textual voice and that of the *Omnis plantacio* preacher can seem to bleed into one another, to be fundamentally entangled and enmeshed—even adulterated—in the same narrow discursive space. Their familiarity with the same canon of literary authorities provides a straightforward reason for this, and furthermore explains why vernacular prose theology from this period can seem like an echo-chamber.[55] But, as the *Omnis plantacio* preacher had been aware, the competition for vernacular discursive space threatened to rebound against the writers of particular texts, creating a polyphony of writings open for interpretation beyond the control of individuals. This can be seen at the level of specific lexical choices. For example, Pecock was

---

[50] Scase (1996).
[51] On the distinctive reformism of the Chichele era, see Gillespie (2007).
[52] Pecock (1909: 110).
[53] Pecock (1921: 8; 1909: 122).
[54] See Bose (2003) for further discussion.
[55] This is an effect enhanced—and consciously striven for—by the anonymity of Wycliffite writings, on which see Von Nolcken (1995).

hardly the first writer to muse in English on the role of priest as *procutoure*. The *Omnis plantacio* preacher had arrived there long before him, with his awareness that Christ 'tauʒte hise prestis to be procuratours for nedi peple and pore at þe riche men', and his succinct identification of 'þe office of presthod' with this role.[56] Even this small example has two important aspects: first, it establishes that both men were caught up in a long-standing and difficult reformist conversation about the office of priesthood and the role of clerical mediation; but it also shows how a shared conceptual vocabulary could serve as a point of divergence. Thus, the *Omnis plantacio* preacher assertively pushed the role of 'procuratour' in the direction of a discourse about poverty that Wycliffism had partly appropriated, whereas Pecock was trying to reinvent the role of the clergy as honest brokers of doctrine and interpretation to the laity.

A further and more substantial example of this competition for discourse is provided by a comparison between the *Omnis plantacio* preacher's discussion of 'goostly lecherie' and a passage from the 'entre', or introductory material, to Pecock's *Reule of Cristen Religioun*, in which the author describes a vision of the truths of philosophy appearing before him as the daughters of God, who instruct him to write the ensuing work.[57] The Egerton preacher offers a commentary on what St Paul calls 'auoutrie' (adultery) against the word of God: 'as a woman þat doiþ auoutrie aʒens her husbonde leueþ þe seed of his husbonde, bi þe which she shulde bringe forþ [lawful] fleschly children, and takiþ to hir alien seed, wherof she bryngiþ forþ bastardis unlawful and mysborun children'.[58] The preacher's concern here is to distinguish between what he considers to be legitimate and illegitimate bodies of knowledge. It is clear that this is an implicit distinction, familiar in Wycliffite writings, between scripture and what he elsewhere calls 'heuenli kunnyng' more generally, and 'ungroundid' texts, typically including mendicant sermons with their interpolated 'talis'.[59] The imagery of 'alien seed' derives directly from the theme of the sermon itself, Matthew 15: 13 (*Omnis plantacio quem non plantauit pater meus celestis eradicabitur*: 'Every plant which my heavenly Father hath not planted, shall be rooted up'). The Wycliffite controversies had made this scriptural passage contested ground. As well as providing this preacher with the theme of 'bastard braunchis', a pervasive metaphor in this context, the text had also been chosen by John Sharpe, an anti-Wycliffite writer, as the theme for a tract on topics such as the efficacy of saints' intercessory prayers.[60] The distinction between 'lawful goostli children' and the seed of 'bodily spousebrekers' would prove tenacious, showing how established theological topics could not be definitively appropriated by either side in this debate. For in Pecock's *Reule*, the daughters of God complain that the clergy, who should be the 'sones of God', have been seduced by the 'douʒtris

[56] Hudson (2001: 102, 132).
[57] Pecock (1927: 31–4). I discuss different aspects of this passage in Bose (2000, 2003).
[58] Hudson (2001: 15).
[59] The reference to 'heuenli kunnyng' is on p. 2.
[60] Sharpe's text is in Oxford, Merton College, MS 175, fos. 263ʳ–275ᵛ. On 'bastard braunchis', see Bose (2003: 225–6).

of men', namely 'worldly trouthis, oolde rehercellis, strange stories, fables of poetis, newe invencious'. For this reason, the daughters of God lack their 'goostlie progenye'. The passage is provocative for its minimalist withholding of authority from any source except 'oure fadir and modir, that is to seie . . . resoun and scripture', and in the daughters' recoiling from the inauthenticity of 'additamentis or . . . eny bastard braunchis'.

It is not that Pecock had passively allowed his opponents to shape his polemical and discursive world. Rather, what had been released into the vernacular by both men was a thickly textured theological discourse that was not easily amenable to the more rigid forms of thinking encoded in ecclesiastical legislation.

Voices in the Wilderness

Audelay and Pecock had in different ways registered their fraught awareness that clerical authority was vulnerable to misconstruction by the laity. This awareness was ultimately replayed to particularly unsettling effect in the poetry of Skelton, which is as much the creation of fifteenth-century reformism as it is innovative. For the successful imitation of Langland, two things were required. The first was a mobile, febrile, essentially recursive imagination simultaneously invigorated and haunted by an inability, or unwillingness, to narrow its field of vision and thus incapable of taking refuge in the univocal view. The second was a poetic idiom sufficiently skilful and idiomatic to communicate this provisional, recursive vision. No poet writing after Langland would possess both, although Spenser would later offer himself as a promising candidate for consideration. Skelton, the most consummate Langlandian after Audelay, took the ingenious route of refashioning polyvocality from scratch, learning from Langland's vague poetics in his multiplication of liminally clerical personae, but wisely honing a new poetic idiom, the Skeltonic, which enabled him to achieve something as distinctive and uncomfortable as *Piers Plowman* whilst keeping his poetry free from the fustian tinge of old controversies. A useful way to make sense of Skelton in this context is to contrast the poetic and prophetic roles he assumed with that modelled by John Gower in *Vox clamantis*. This poem presents London as New Troy, beset by the Peasants' Revolt, burnt and despoilt. Books 3 and 4 recycle entrenched elements of protest against the shortcomings of the clergy in general (thus easily qualifying for the label 'anticlerical' as I have used it here): the corrosive effects of temporal possessions, the evils of simony, the time-wasting of unbeneficed priests who set a bad example to the laity, and the host of vices to which those in private religion, whether monks or friars, fall prey. And above all, the critique of the clergy in book 3 opens with a damning assertion of failure of authority in the Church. Gower imagines his role as a reformist prophet with confidence, presenting himself as a latter-day Isaiah, the poem's title alone conflating Old and New Testaments.[61] The dedication of this poem to Archbishop Arundel is, therefore, paradigmatic of an imagined role for prophetic reformism, vehemently critical of clerical institutions and practices, within a spectrum of beliefs and literate practices that could nevertheless be described as orthodox.

But where Gower had conflated the voice of the poet with the prophetic role of the *vox clamantis*, Skelton ironizes this position, populating his various poetic wildernesses with introjected and projected voices that assimilate, recycle, parry, or parody clerical castigation. An important dimension of Skelton's poetry is its essentially occasional nature, animated as it is by local hostilities from the transgressions of the hawking priest at Diss in the early sixteenth century (*Ware the Hauke*) to the heresies of Bilney and Arthur in the late 1520s, as assailed in *A Replycacion*. But it is important to note that instabilities of the kind registered in Audelay's poetry, whereby complaint can rapidly mutate into exhortation, and whole octaves of insight can be abruptly and dramatically blunted, consistently resurface in Skelton's works. He could reprehend the hawking priest in *Ware the Hauke* for his blasphemous parody of the liturgy:

> Thys fawconer then gan showte,
> 'These be my gospellers,
> These be my pystyllers,
> These be my querysters
> To helpe me to singe,
> My hawkes to mattens rynge!' (ll. 120–4)[62]

and then unleash comparable blasphemies in *Phyllyp Sparowe*:

> And Robyn Redbrest
> He shall be the preest,
> The requiem masse to singe,
> Softely warbelynge,
> With helpe of the red sparrow
> And the chattrynge swallow
> This herse for to halow. (ll. 399–405)

Thus, reading Skelton's poetry in the context of medieval anticlericalism allows us to hear him in a critically underappreciated way, namely as a writer whose works had partly been produced by the pressures that had built up in the Church's internal, disciplinary rhetorics. The self-castigatory modes that had resonated through Langland, Netter, Audelay, and Pecock, in even earlier phases of intra-clerical controversy, and in the literature and institutions generated by the Church's vigilance against both heresy and clerical transgression, are provocatively exposed and reduced to verbal rubble in the Skeltonic, whose goliardic energies imply the exhaustion of more expansive, and more clearly accountable, modes of discourse. Even as it gathers satirical energy to itself, Collyn Clout's image of himself as a 'clerkely hagge' (l. 52)

---

[61] The *vox clamantis in deserto* passages are Isaiah 40: 3 and Mark 1: 3.
[62] Quotations are taken from Skelton (1983).

encapsulates this compulsion to turn the vulnerability of the clergy, and of ecclesiastical institutions in general, into a grotesque spectacle.[63]

CONCLUSION

As Skelton well knew, the sacraments and other priestly offices and institutions should render poems—and particularly poems by priests—unnecessary. Such an insight returns us to Ymaginatif's stern rebuke about 'bokes enow', with which this chapter began. But in conclusion I would emphasize that what we see in this period is often the reverse: poetry bypassing the control of institutions, a process that has described in terms of the literary usurpation of clerical *dominium*.[64] The third of Arundel's Constitutions seeks to establish firm boundaries between preaching *clero* (to the clergy) and preaching *populo* (to the people), insisting that preachers confine themselves to castigating clerical vices before an audience of the clergy, and lay vices when preaching to the laity.[65] It will be immediately apparent that, of the texts considered in this chapter, even those that appeared after 1409 were in breach of this Constitution. There is a simple explanation for this: the Constitution specifically addresses preaching, and our texts are examples, as our title reminds us, of writing. It was the transformation of *Omnis plantacio* into writing, as described at the beginning of this chapter, that considerably amplified its potential for transgression against the third Constitution. If Pecock was right in his insistence that written theology was a better vehicle than preaching for doctrinal instruction, it was equally true that writing could exacerbate the transgressions of heretical preaching simply by documenting them.[66] The texts considered in this chapter, and many others, show how new kinds of intra-clerical and lay-clerical relationships were being imagined through a dynamic interaction between clerical subjectivity and literary experimentation.

BIBLIOGRAPHY

AUDELAY, JOHN (1931), *The Poems of John Audelay*, ed. Ella Keats Whiting (EETS OS 184; London: Oxford University Press for the Early English Text Society).

---

[63] I am grateful to Kantik Ghosh for pointing out the importance of this line to me in the present context, and for his suggestion that a parallel Scottish lineage for this disendowment of clerkly authority might be traced through the writings of Dunbar, Henryson, and Douglas.

[64] Scase (1989: 173). Compare Simpson (1990): '[A]pparent deference is shown to sets of authoritative institutions, whose very existence should render a truth-teller, and his poem, unnecessary. But the inadequacy of their responses generates the need for a discourse without institutional backing' (p. 23).

[65] *Concilia Magnae* (1737: iii. 316).   [66] Pecock (1924: 88).

BOSE, MISHTOONI (2000), 'The Annunciation to Pecock: Clerical Imitatio in the Fifteenth Century', *Notes and Queries*, 47: 172–6.

——(2003), 'Reginald Pecock's Vernacular Voice', in Fiona Somerset, Jill C. Havens, and Derrick G. Pitard (eds.), *Lollards and their Influence in Late Medieval England* (Woodbridge: Boydell Press), 217–36.

——(2009), 'Netter as Critic and Practitioner of Rhetoric: The Doctrinale as Disputation', in John Bergström-Allen and Richard Copsey (eds.), *Thomas Netter of Wealden* (Faversham: St Albert's Press), 233–50.

——(forthcoming), 'John Skelton and the Long Fifteenth Century', in Shannon Gayk and Kathleen Tonry (eds.), *Form and Reform in the Long Fifteenth Century*.

BURROW, J. A. (1993), *Thinking in Poetry: Three Medieval Examples. The William Matthews Lectures* (London: Birkbeck College).

CATTO, JEREMY (1999), 'Fellows and Helpers: The Religious Identity of the Followers of Wyclif', in Peter Biller and Barrie Dobson (eds.), *The Medieval Church: Universities, Heresy, and the Religious Life. Essays in Honour of Gordon Leff* (Woodbridge: Boydell Press for the Ecclesiastical Society), 141–61.

CLOPPER, LAWRENCE (1997), *'Songes of Rechelesness': Langland and the Franciscans* (Ann Arbor: University of Michigan Press).

CONCILIA MAGNAE (1737), *Concilia Magnae Britanniae et Hiberniae ab Anno MCCCL ad Annum MDXLV*, ed. David Wilkins (London).

DAWSON, JAMES DOYNE (1983), 'Richard FitzRalph and the Fourteenth-Century Poverty Controversies', *Journal of Ecclesiastical History*, 34: 315–44.

DIPPLE, GEOFFREY L. (1994), 'Uthred and the Friars: Apostolic Poverty and Clerical Dominion between FitzRalph and Wyclif', *Traditio*, 49: 235–58.

EASTING, ROBERT (ed.) (1991), *St. Patrick's Purgatory: Two Versions of Owayne Miles and The Vision of William of Stranton together with the Long Text of the Tractatus de Purgatorio Sancti Patricii* (EETS OS 298; Oxford: Oxford University Press for the Early English Text Society).

ENGEN, JOHN VAN (1993), 'Late Medieval Anticlericalism: The Case of the New Devout', in Peter A. Dykema and Heiko A. Oberman (eds.), *Anticlericalism in Late Medieval and Early Modern Europe* (Leiden: Brill), 19–52.

ERLER, MARY C. (2007), '"A Revelation of Purgatory" (1422): Reform and the Politics of Female Visions', *Viator*, 38: 322–47.

GEORGIANNA, LINDA (2000), 'Anticlericalism in Boccaccio and Chaucer: The Bark and the Bite', in Leonard Michael Koff and Brenda Deen Schildgen (eds.), *The Decameron and the Canterbury Tales: New Essays on an Old Question* (Madison, NJ: Associated University Presses), 148–73.

GHOSH, KANTIK (2001), *The Wycliffite Heresy, Authority and the Interpretation of Texts* (Cambridge: Cambridge University Press), 174–208.

GILLESPIE, VINCENT (2007), 'Vernacular Theology', in Paul Strohm (ed.), *Middle English: Oxford Twenty-First Century Approaches to Literature* (Oxford: Oxford University Press), 401–20.

GRAUS, FRANTISEK (1993), 'The Church and its Critics in Time of Crisis', in Peter A. Dykema and Heiko A. Oberman (eds.), *Anticlericalism in Late Medieval and Early Modern Europe* (Leiden: Brill), 65–81.

GREEN, RICHARD FIRTH (2001), 'Marcolf the Fool and Blind John Audelay', in Charlotte C. Morse and Robert F. Yeager (eds.), *Speaking Images: Essays in Honor of V. A. Kolve* (Asheville, NC: Pegasus Press), 559–76.

HAIGH, CHRISTOPHER (1983), 'Anticlericalism and the English Reformation', *History*, 68: 391–407.

HANNA, RALPH (2003), 'English Biblical Texts before Lollardy and their Fate', in Fiona Somerset, Jill C. Havens, and Derrick G. Pitard (eds.), *Lollards and their Influence in Late Medieval England* (Woodbridge: Boydell Press), 141–53.

HARVEY, MARGARET (1992), 'The Diffusion of the Doctrinale of Thomas Netter in the fifteenth and sixteenth centuries', in Lesley Smith and Benedicta Ward (eds.), *Intellectual Life in the Middle Ages: Essays Presented to Margaret Gibson* (London and Rio Grande, Ohio: Hambledon Press), 281–94.

HOBBINS, DANIEL (2003), 'The Schoolman as Public Intellectual: Jean Gerson and the Late Medieval Tract', *American Historical Review*, 108: 1308–37.

HUDSON, ANNE (1978), *Selections from English Wycliffite Writings* (Cambridge: Cambridge University Press).

——(1994), 'Laicus Litteratus: The Paradox of Lollardy', in Peter Biller and Anne Hudson (eds.), *Heresy and Literacy, 1000–1530* (Cambridge: Cambridge University Press), 222–36.

——(ed.) (2001), *The Works of a Lollard Preacher* (EETS OS 317; Oxford: Oxford University Press for the Early English Text Society).

KELLY, STEPHEN (2007), 'Piers Plowman', in Peter Brown (ed.), *A Companion to Medieval English Literature and Culture c.1350–c.1500* (Oxford: Blackwell), 537–53.

LAHEY, STEPHEN E. (2009), *John Wyclif* (Oxford: Oxford University Press).

PANTIN, W. A. (1955), *The English Church in the Fourteenth Century* (Cambridge: Cambridge University Press).

LEVINE, JOSEPH M. (1973), 'Reginald Pecock and Lorenzo Valla on the Donation of Constantine', *Studies in the Renaissance*, 20: 118–43.

LEVY, IAN CHRISTOPHER (2006), 'Wyclif and the Christian Life', in I. C. Levy (ed.), *A Companion to John Wyclif: Late Medieval Theologian* (Leiden: Brill), 293–363.

McSHEFFREY, SHANNON, and NORMAN TANNER (ed. and tr.) (2003), *Lollards of Coventry, 1486–1522* (Cambridge: Cambridge University Press).

MIDDLETON, ANNE (1997), 'Acts of Vagrancy: The C Version "Autobiography" and the Statute of 1388', in Steven Justice and Kathryn Kerby-Fulton (eds.), *Written Work: Langland, Labor and Authorship* (Philadelphia: University of Pennsylvania Press), 208–317.

NETTER, THOMAS (1757–9), *Doctrinale Antiquitatum Fidei*, ed. B. Blanciotti (Venice; repr. Farnborough: Gregg Press, 1967).

NOLCKEN, CHRISTINA VON (1995), 'A "Certain Sameness" and our Response to it in English Wycliffite Texts', in R. Newhauser and John Alford (eds.), *Literature and Religion in the Later Middle Ages: Philological Studies in Honor of Siegfried Wenzel* (Binghamton, NY: Medieval and Renaissance Texts and Studies), 191–208.

PECOCK, REGINALD (1909), *Reginald Peacock's Book of Faith*, ed. J. L. Morison (Glasgow).

——(1921), *The Donet*, ed. E. V. Hitchcock (EETS OS 156; London: Oxford University Press for the Early English Text Society).

——(1924), *The Folewer to the Donet*, ed. E. V. Hitchcock (EETS OS 164; London: Oxford University Press for the Early English Text Society).

——(1927), *The Reule of Cristen Religioun*, ed. W. C. Greet (EETS OS 171; Oxford: Oxford University Press for the Early English Text Society).

PSEUDO-DIONYSIUS (1987), *The Complete Works*, tr. Colm Luibheid, ed. Paul Rorem *et al.* (New York: Paulist Press).

SCASE, WENDY (1989), *Piers Plowman and the New Anticlericalism* (Cambridge: Cambridge University Press).

——(1994), '"Proud Gallants and Popeholy Priests": The Context and Function of a Fifteenth-Century Satirical Poem', *Medium Ævum*, 63: 275–86.

SCASE, WENDY (1996), 'Reginald Pecock', *Authors of the Middle Ages*, iii, ed. M. C. Seymour (Aldershot: Variorum), 69–146.

SHOGIMEN, TAKASHI (2006), 'Wyclif's Ecclesiology and Political Thought', in I. C. Levy (ed.), *A Companion to John Wyclif: Late Medieval Theologian* (Leiden: Brill), 199–240.

SIMPSON, JAMES (1990), 'The Constraints of Satire in "Piers Plowman" and "Mum and the Sothsegger"', in Helen Phillips (ed.), *Langland, the Mystics and the Medieval English Religious Tradition: Essays in Honour of S. S. Hussey* (Cambridge: D. S. Brewer), 11–38.

——(2002), *Reform and Cultural Revolution: The Oxford English Literary History*, ii. *1350–1547* (Oxford: Oxford University Press).

——(2005), 'Saving Satire after Arundel's Constitutions: John Audelay's "Marcol and Solomon"', in Helen Barr and Ann M. Hutchison (eds.), *Text and Controversy from Wyclif to Bale: Essays in Honour of Anne Hudson* (Turnhout: Brepols), 387–404.

SKELTON, JOHN (1983), *The Complete English Poems*, ed. John Scattergood (Harmondsworth: Penguin).

SOMERSET, FIONA (1998), *Clerical Discourse and Lay Audience in Late Medieval England* (Cambridge: Cambridge University Press).

STOCK, BRIAN (1983), *The Implications of Literacy: Written Language and Models of Interpretation in the Eleventh and Twelfth Centuries* (Princeton: Princeton University Press).

STROHM, PAUL (2006), 'Writing and Reading', in Rosemary Horrox and W. Mark Ormrod (eds.), *A Social History of England 1200–1500* (Cambridge: Cambridge University Press), 454–72.

SZITTYA, PENN R. (1986), *The Antifraternal Tradition in Medieval Literature* (Princeton: Princeton University Press).

TANNER, NORMAN (1977), *Heresy Trials in the Diocese of Norwich, 1428–31* (London: Royal Historical Society).

WOGAN-BROWNE, JOCELYN, NICHOLAS WATSON, ANDREW TAYLOR, and RUTH EVANS (eds.) (1999), *The Idea of the Vernacular: An Anthology of Middle English Literary Theory 1280–1520* (Exeter: University of Exeter Press).

....

CHAPTER 15

ACQUIRING WISDOM

TEACHING TEXTS AND THE LORE OF THE PEOPLE

....

DANIEL ANLEZARK

THE concept of wisdom is not easily defined. It cannot be equated simply with either knowledge or experience—an individual can experience a great deal, or know quite a lot, without acquiring wisdom. The word has survived unchanged into Modern English from Old English, a linguistic durability pointing to the enduring cultural value placed on wisdom as a concept. The active nature of wisdom as a power of the mind is signalled by the word's etymology: 'knowing-judgement'. For the individual, wisdom consists of understanding the relationship between an inherited body of lore, the experiences life presents, and the reactions of the heart. The wise person is able to 'judge' future courses of action based on this understanding, though often an inherently conservative wisdom tradition teaches resignation to events beyond one's control.

The distinction in the Middle Ages between the few who were literate and the many who were not did not mean that the unlettered were ignorant of the traditional knowledge of their society. A store of wisdom was preserved and transmitted in memorable sayings, proverbs, and maxims offering a guide to people on how to live life, rear children, and find success and happiness. This shared traditional knowledge travelled across the generations, at times crossing cultural and linguistic boundaries, often entering the written record. In the early Middle Ages the oral and the literate transmission of wisdom coexisted in an easy relationship in a society with a profoundly conservative approach to knowledge and social norms. From the Old English epic poem *Beowulf* to Geoffrey Chaucer's *Miller's Tale*, proverbial wisdom offered the medieval reader a measure of common sense with which to understand the chaos of human existence.

The most famous collections of wisdom in the Middle Ages were found in two Old Testament books attributed to King Solomon, Proverbs and Ecclesiastes, containing aphorisms, often arranged around themes, at times profoundly enigmatic in style.[1] Essentially conservative in outlook, proverbs present truisms about life, society, and nature. Old English literature reveals a taste for proverbs; some surviving texts are wholly gnomic in character, while others incorporate proverbs and aphorisms into narratives.[2] The Old English poem *Maxims I* owes little direct debt to the biblical tradition, but its form echoes the crafting of wisdom collections into more meaningful wholes:

> Frige mec frodum wordum.   Ne læt þinne ferð onhælne,
> degol þæt þu deopost cunne.   Nelle ic þe min dyrne gesecgan,
> gif þu me þinne hygecræft hylest   ond þine heortan geþohtas.
> Gleawe men sceolon gieddum wrixlan.
>
>   Beam sceal on eorðan
> leafum liþan,   leomu gnornian.
> Fus sceal feran,   fæge sweltan
> ond dogra gehwam   ymb gedal sacan
> middangeardes.   Meotud ana wat
> hwær se cwealm cymeþ,   þe heonan of cyþþe gewiteþ.[3]

The link between human experience and the natural world is more than metaphoric, and the cycle of life and death is perceived to be part of the ordering of the world, a recurrent theme in wisdom literature. The unidentified speaker invites the reader into dialogue with a playful inversion of the conventional beginning of the Old English narrative poem, *Ic gefrægn* ('I have found out by asking'), implicitly offering an active engagement with how words mean, rather than simply what they say. This dialogic element is an important aspect of wisdom itself: the acquisition of wisdom demands an active search for meaning.[4]

---

[1] Solomon was also the supposed author of the Song of Songs, and considered by some as the author of Wisdom and Ecclesiasticus (Sirach).

[2] See especially *Maxims I*, in Krapp and Dobbie (1936: 156–63); *Maxims II*, in Dobbie (1942: 55–7); Cox (1972).

[3] Lines 1–4a, 25b–30. 'Interrogate me with wise words. Do not let your mind be concealed, or hidden what you understand most deeply. I will not explain my mystery to you if you hide from me your intelligence and your heart's thoughts. Wise men must exchange meaningful utterances.... The tree must shed its leaves on the earth, the branches mourn. The ready one must travel, the fated one must die and each day struggle about the departure from this middle-earth. The Creator alone knows where the killing will come, who will depart hence from knowing.'

[4] The enigmatic first-person address suggests affinities with the riddle genre, many examples of which are found beside *Maxims I* in the Exeter Book, which similarly draw attention to the way words develop meaning.

Maxims I addresses a range of topics, emphasizing God's rule over the world, which is thematically linked to the ordering of human society. The society represented is an idealized version of the traditional Germanic life in the aristocratic hall:

> Cyning sceal mid ceape   cwene gebicgan,
> bunum ond beagum;   bu sceolon ærest
> geofum god wesan.   Guð sceal in eorle,
> wig geweaxan,   ond wif geþeon
> leof mid hyre leodum,   leohtmod wesan,
> rune healdan,   rumheort beon
> mearum ond maþmum,   meodorædenne
> for gesiðmægen   symle æghwær
> eodor æþelinga   ærest gegretan,
> forman fulle   to frean hond
> ricene geræcan,   ond him ræd witan
> boldagendum   bæm ætsomne.[5]

The proscriptive nature of the passage and its poetic form suggest a debt to the oral tradition, though the inclusion of the passage in the poem suggests the reception of older traditions into a learned literary milieu, a movement continued in the inclusion of the poem into the Exeter Book. Nevertheless, the timeless concern with understanding the underlying order of the world, and the organization of human experience into gnomic utterance, remain the major concerns of the wisdom poet.

THE WORLD AND *BEOWULF*

The Old English epic poem *Beowulf* offers a complex insight into the Anglo-Saxons' understanding of their place in the world, most clearly in the life of the young Geatish prince Beowulf. The hero presents the Anglo-Saxon aristocratic audience with a mirror reflecting the process of maturity, from intemperate young man, to faithful warrior, to wise old king. The narrative presents a theme found across the western tradition in conduct books and wisdom collections designed to teach the young how to grow into useful members of society, and to teach those with power how to use it wisely.[6] *Beowulf*, however, is more than a *Fürstenspiegel* for the Christian prince, presenting as it does a fantastic mix of aristocratic life in the pre-Christian Germanic

---

[5] Lines 81–92. 'A king must procure a queen with exchange, with cups and rings; both must be first in the giving of gifts. War and warfare must be fostered in the man, and the woman prosper as one loved among her people, be gentle, keep confidences, be generous of heart with horses and with treasures, in counsel over the mead before the troop always and everywhere greet first the leader of princes with the brimming cup, into the lord's hand, and must know wise counsels for the two of them together, for the custodians'.

[6] See Anton (1968).

North and the dark world of monstrous creatures threatening human society and psyche. Woven into the poem's fabric is a proverbial commentary, with observations on the workings of fate beside advice for the young warrior:[7]

> Swa sceal geong guma   gode gewyrcean,
> fromum feohgiftum   on fæder bearme,
> þæt hine on ylde   eft gewunigen
> wilgesiþas,   þonne wig cume,
> leode gelæsten;   lofdædum sceal
> in mægþa gehwære   man geþeon.[8]
>
> Swa mæg unfæge   eaðe gedigan
> wean ond wræcsið   se ðe Waldendes
> hyldo gehealdeþ![9]

It is difficult to tell whether the poet is presenting the Anglo-Saxon audience with familiar utterances, or using proverbial style to convey generally held truths, but in these and comparable passages, a range of analogues can be found in Latin and medieval vernacular literatures.[10] Such statements can seem simplistic and sententiously moralizing to modern readers; however, they offer an insight into what made wisdom wise to the early medieval mind. Such aphorisms are not true simply because a poet utters them, or because they represent a felicitous turn of phrase, but rather because his authoritative voice speaks within a long tradition in which the truth of such statements has been verified through shared experience.

The Danish king Hrothgar represents *par excellence* the wise pagan who is able to discern divinely established order in human experience, a wisdom he shares with the young hero in a 'sermon' advising him how to live wisely. In a paternal voice, Hrothgar discerns the workings of God—the giver of wisdom—in human life, and warns the hero against the excesses of power:

> 'Wundor is to secganne,
> hu mihtig God   manna cynne
> þurh sidne sefan   snyttru bryttað
> eard ond eorlscipe;   he ah ealra geweald.
> Hwilum he on lufan   læteð hworfan
> monnes modgeþonc   mæran cynnes,
> seleð him on eþle   eorþan wynne
> to healdenne,   hleoburh wera,
> gedeð him swa gewealdene   worolde dælas,
> side rice,   þæt he his selfa ne mæg
> his unsnyttrum   ende geþencean.

---

[7] Fulk *et al.* (2008); Liuzza (2000).

[8] Lines 20–5, 2291–3a. 'So a young man should do good, with worthy gifts in his father's capaciousness, so that later in old age loyal companions will stand fast, when battle comes, the people will support him; with praiseworthy deeds one will prosper among his kinfolk everywhere.'

[9] 'So may the unfated one easily endure woe and exile, he who possesses the Ruler's protection!'

[10] See Deskis (1996).

Bebeorh þe ðone bealonið,   Beowulf leofa,
secg betsta,   ond þe þæt selre geceos,
ece rædas;   oferhyda ne gym,
mære cempa!   Nu is þines mægnes blæd
ane hwile;   eft sona bið,
þæt þec adl oððe ecg   eafoþes getwæfeð,
oððe fyres feng,   oððe flodes wylm,
oððe gripe meces,   oððe gares fliht,
oððe atol yldo;   oððe eagena bearhtum
forsiteð ond forsworceð;   semninga bið,
þæt ðec, dryhtguma,   deað oferswyðeð.'[11]

Hrothgar addresses the familiar themes of wisdom literature in all times and places: the dangers of pride, the transitory nature of life, and the need to choose what is right to avoid falling into folly. Beowulf must understand the nature of, and limits on, his power if he is to use it well, for the benefit of his own people and for his own happiness. Inseparable from this wisdom is the acknowledgement of God's power over all things (compare Proverbs 9: 10–12).

DIALOGUES AND WISDOM

The idiosyncratic Old English dialogue poem *Solomon and Saturn II*, dating from the beginning of the tenth century, touches on a range of popular philosophical and moral questions of the early Middle Ages. Saturn, a Chaldean prince whose characterization recalls the pagan god, has travelled the world in search of wisdom, finally arriving at the court of King Solomon. The two engage in a verbal duel with features of two related literary forms: the dialogue and debate. In a debate a proposition is usually at stake, with characters presenting arguments around this idea. In the dialogue, popular from the time of Plato, the form is more often a vehicle for instruction, with an authoritative speaker asked a series of questions, often by an uncomprehending interlocutor. The dialogue is intrinsically less speculative than the debate, where two contending, and often equally plausible, points of view can be placed before the reader. The resolution of many debates is not to be found in authority, but in the mind of the reader, if at all.

---

[11] Lines 1724–34, 1758–68. 'It is a wonder to describe, how mighty God through his broad being distributes land and lordship among the human race; he has the rule of all. At times he allows the thoughts of a man of mighty race to move in delights, gives him earthly joys in stewardship in his homeland, the stronghold of men, gives to him worldly goods to wield, a broad kingdom, so that he himself in his un-wisdom cannot imagine an end of it.... Protect yourself from malice, dear Beowulf, best of men, and choose the better, the eternal counsels; do not care for vanity, great champion! Now is the might of your glory for a brief moment; soon afterwards it will be that illness or sword will weaken your might, or fire's grasp, or the current's surge, or the sword's grip, or the spear's flight, or terrible old age; or the light of your eyes will diminish and darken; suddenly it will happen, O warrior, that death will overwhelm you.'

In consequence, the debate format can problematize questions of epistemology, and ultimately undermine the very notion of objectively knowable truth. Any proposition debated by Solomon and Saturn has been lost with a missing leaf from the unique manuscript, but their contest is more than a simple exchange of information, and has some affinities with the Old Norse mythological poem *Vafthruþnismal*, where a disguised Odin seeks out the secret knowledge of the giants about the creation and end of the world.[12] Solomon and Saturn also discuss eschatology, beside more popular topics, ranging from the origin of evil to the nature of fate. One of the striking elements of the dialogue is its emphasis on books:[13]

> Salomon cuæð:
> Bec sindon breme,   bodiað geneahhe
> weotodne willan   ðam ðe wiht hygeð,
> gestrangað hie ond gestaðeliað   staðolfæstne geðoht,
> amyrgað modsefan   manna gehwylces
> of ðreamedlan   ðisses lifes.
> Saturnus cwæð:
> Bald bið se ðe onbyregeð   boca cræftes,
> symle bið ðe wisra   ðe hira geweald hafað.
> Salomon cuæð:
> Sige hie onsendað   soðfæstra gehwam,
> hælo hyðe,   ðam ðe hie lufað.[14]

In his travels, Saturn has visited many nations famous for their learning, including Greece and India. It comes as something of a surprise that the people most frequently associated with learning in the poem are the Philistines:

> Saturnus cwæð:
> Full oft ic frode menn   fyrn gehyrde
> secggan ond swerian   ymb sume wisan,
> hwæðer wære twegra   butan tweon strengra,
> wyrd ðe warnung,   ðonne hie winnað oft
> mid hira ðreamedlan,   hwæðerne aðreoteð ær.
> Ic to soðon wat   —sægdon me geara
> Filistina witan,   ðonne we on geflitum sæton,
> bocum tobræddon   ond on bearm legdon,
> meðelcwidas mengdon,   moniges fengon—
> ðæt nære nænig manna   middangeardes
> ðæt meahte ðara twega   tuion aspyrian.[15]

---

[12] See Larrington (1993).

[13] Menner (1941); Shippey (1976: 86–103). Lineation follows Shippey's edn.

[14] Lines 60–74. Solomon said: 'Books are famous, they abundantly proclaim the ordered mind to the one who thinks at all. They strengthen and establish resolute thought, make merry the mind of each man against the mental oppressions of this life.' Saturn said: 'Bold is he who tastes of the power of books, he will always be the wiser who has control of them.' Solomon said: 'They present victory to each of the righteous, a harbour of safety for those who love them.'

[15] Lines 247–57. Saturn said: 'Very often of old I heard wise men speak and avow concerning a certain matter, whether without doubt either of two things was stronger—fate or foresight—when they struggle

The problem of fate and foresight is inseparable from two other philosophical questions—free will and the experience of time—and the poet does not attempt to resolve their difficulties beyond promising the Last Judgement, a known future that will end time and judge the expressions of human freedom. Why the poet chooses to emphasize the role of the Philistines remains a mystery, but Saturn's reminiscence presents for us an insight into the conduct of a learned dispute in the early Middle Ages, where books provided topics and evidence for debate. Saturn is clearly an advanced student, travelling from school to school much in the way many scholars, most famously the Irish, travelled across Europe in the early Middle Ages.[16]

Saturn's journeying leaves him dissatisfied until he reaches Solomon, whose divinely inspired wisdom satisfies the quest of the Chaldean prince, and allows him to return happy to his homeland:

> Hæfde ða se snotra   sunu Dauides
> forcumen ond forcyðed   Caldea eorl.
> Hwæðre was on sælum   se ðe of siðe cwom
> feorran gefered.   Næfre ær his ferhð ahlog.[17]

Solomon has resolved Saturn's intellectual difficulties with reference to the problem of sin, stemming from Lucifer's proud rebellion. The reversion to divine revelation to address questions emerging from human reason is unsurprising in an early medieval text, but as the distinction between philosophy and theology grew across the medieval period, such reversions to authority lost their appeal. Later medieval authors, especially those trained in universities, are often more confident in the power of reason, but also pessimistic about the mind's ability to know truth.

EDUCATION IN THE MIDDLE AGES

In the early Middle Ages, western European education had been conducted in monastic and cathedral schools, and in this regard Anglo-Saxon England was no exception.[18] In the century after the Norman Conquest changes taking place across western Europe also spread to England: the growth of the towns and the rise of the merchant class; the birth of the universities, and the introduction into them of new

---

often with each other, with their mental oppression, which of the two becomes tiresome first. I truly know (the wise men of the Philistines told me formerly, when we sat in debate, we opened up books and put them in our laps, we exchanged speeches, seizing on many matters) that there is not any man in this middle-earth who is able to apprehend the ambiguities of these two.'

16 See Bayless and Lapidge (1998).

17 Lines 333–6. 'The wise son of David had then overcome and rebutted the nobleman of the Chaldeans. Nevertheless, he was joyful, he who had come on the journey, travelled from afar; never before had his heart laughed.'

18 See Orme (2006).

learning and new philosophical method. Both the revolution in educational form and content, and the linguistic and literary changes instigated with the arrival of a French-speaking aristocracy, are evident in the thirteenth-century poem *The Owl and the Nightingale*. This superficially light debate between two birds begins as a dispute over the relative merits of their songs, but extends to include many of their differing habits:[19]

> Ich was in one sumere dale,
> In one suþe diȝele hale:
> Iherde ich holde grete tale
> An hule and one niȝtingale.
> Þat plait was stif & stark & strong,
> Sumwile softe & lude among;
> An aiþer aȝen oþer sval,
> & let þat vole mod ut al;
> & eiþer seide of oþeres custe
> Þat alre worste þat hi wuste;
> & hure & hure of oþeres songe
> Hi holde plaiding suþe stronge.[20]

Rhetoric and disputation took on great importance in medieval universities and schools, but neither bird is very good at it. For the thirteenth-century reader, the introductory frame serves to emphasize the comic defectiveness of the dispute, as the birds' method is established from the outset as grounded in emotion rather than skill: each attacks her opponent in a quest for victory, rather than a search for resolution, let alone for truth.

It is likely that these defects were not limited to birds, and in its playfulness with the triumph of form over content, *The Owl and the Nightingale* presents a disruption in the traditional assumptions surrounding the desire for knowledge and wisdom in an age when rhetorical skill promised social advancement for poorer clergy. An important feature of the poem is its self-conscious attention to rhetorical form; the birds constantly pause over their arguments, considering their style and effectiveness:

> Þe nyhtegale in hire þouhte
> Atheold al þis, & longe þouhte
> Hwat heo þarafter myhte segge:
> Vor heo ne myhte noht alegge
> Þat þe vle hedde hire iseyd,
> Vor ho spak boþe riht & red.
> & hire ofþuhte þat heo hadde
> Þe speche so feor uorþ iladde,

---

[19] Cartlidge (2001).

[20] Lines 1–12. 'I was in a summer-valley, in a really out-of-the-way retreat, when I heard an owl and a nightingale having a huge dispute. This controversy was fierce and ferocious and furious, sometimes calm and sometimes noisy; and each of them swelled up against the other and vented all her malicious feelings, saying the very worst thing they could think about their antagonist's character; and about their songs especially, they had a vehement debate.'

& wes aferd þat hire answare
Ne wurþe nouht ariht ivare.
Ac noþeles heo spak boldeliche,
Vor heo is wis þat hardeliche
Wiþ his fo berþ grete ilete,
Þat he for arehþe hit ne forlete:
Vor suych worþ bold if þu flyhst,
Þat wile fleo if þu ne swykst;
If he isihþ þat þu nart areh,
He wile of bore wurche bareh.
& forþi, þey þe nyhtegale
Were aferd, heo spak bolde tale.[21]

That the owl has spoken *riht and red* is a problem challenging the nightingale's skill; that she has herself been convinced by her opponent's 'truth and sense' is irrelevant. The poet's easy use of proverbial style—and perhaps popular proverbs about courage—echoes the ancient search for wisdom; however, they are here applied superficially to the conduct of the argument. The nightingale must overcome fear not to gain wisdom, but to avoid being argued down by her opponent. It is in the crassness of the birds' approach and the baseness of their arguments that much of the ironic humour of the poem is developed. For this humour to work, both poet and reader must share an awareness of how such a dispute might be better conducted. The proposition debated in *The Owl and the Nightingale* is essentially frivolous, and neither speaker is able to gain objectivity in a dispute over their relative merits. The ultimate deferral of resolution at the end of the poem leaves the reader in a comparable position, as the birds agree to submit their case to Master Nicholas of Guildford—a clergyman seeking a better income. While most readers will happily laugh at the difficulty of determining which is the superior bird, such an ending invites the suggestion that even in trivial matters, objective truth is hard to grasp, an insight further suggested by the foolish birds' inability to appreciate any other truth than the one each sees.

The Owl and the Nightingale suggests a debt to a range of French and Anglo-Norman debate poems circulating at the same time.[22] However, the one debt that is repeatedly, and perplexingly, signalled in the poem is to a work known as the *Proverbs of Alfred*, cited repeatedly by both birds. This is all the more striking because the *Proverbs of Alfred* accompany *The Owl and the Nightingale* in the manuscript Oxford, Jesus College 29 (II). This miscellany contains texts designed for moral edification

---

[21] Lines 391–410. 'The nightingale turned all this over in her mind and thought for a long time what she could say after that, for she could not refute what the Owl had said to her, since she had spoken both truth and sense. Now she regretted that she had allowed the debate to progress so far and was afraid that her answer might not come out right. But nevertheless, she spoke confidently, for it's prudent to be assertive and put up a brave front against one's enemy, so as not to abandon the matter out of cowardice. Indeed, he will grow bold if you run away, but he'll run away himself if you don't let up. If he sees that you're no coward, he'll change from a boar to a barrow-pig—and therefore the Nightingale spoke bravely, despite her fears.'

[22] Cartlidge (2001: pp. xxxi–xxxv).

and entertainment, probably for a lay owner fluent in French and English. However, the birds' attempted citations bear little resemblance to the text of the *Proverbs of Alfred*. The 'Alfred' of the proverbs is the West Saxon king, Alfred the Great (d. 899), who was responsible for a revival of English fortunes after a century of sustained Viking attacks. The centrepiece of Alfred's subsequent reform project was a revival in education, which saw a rapid growth in vernacular literary production. While it seems certain Alfred had a direct hand in the translation of Pope Gregory the Great's *Pastoral Care* from Latin, his relationship to the Old English versions of Boethius's *On the Consolation of Philosophy* and Augustine of Hippo's *Soliloquies* is less certain. Both texts are philosophical dialogues modified for an Old English readership under the influence of the commentary tradition current in Carolingian schools around the beginning of the tenth century. It is evident, especially in the case of the Old English Boethius, that the vernacular rendering did not necessarily imply a dumbing down for a monolingual audience, but included an active engagement with contemporary philosophical questions. Whatever Alfred's relationship to these works, most English vernacular prose written around the year 900 came to be attributed to him by the end of the tenth century, and his reputation as a wise ruler lasted well beyond the Conquest, as the works supposedly by him continued to be copied.

PROVERBIAL WISDOM

The *Proverbs of Alfred* are a post-Conquest addition to the 'Alfredian' corpus, probably composed around the middle of the thirteenth century. The collection of wise sayings begins as a discourse on wisdom by the king to his assembled nobles:[23]

> At Seuorde
> sete þeynes monye,
> fele Biscopes
> and fele bok-ilered,
> Eorles prute,
> knyhtes egleche.
> þar wes þe eorl Alurich,
> of þare lawe swiþe wis,
> and ek Ealured, englene hurde,
> Englene durlyng,
> on englene londe he was kyng.
> Heom he bi-gon lere,
> so ye mawe i-hure,
> huu hi heore lif lede scolden.[24]

---

[23] Arngart (1942–55); the text cited is from Jesus 29 (II).

[24] No. 1, ll. 1–13. 'At Seaforth sat many noblemen, many bishops and many book-learned men, proud princes, warlike knights. There was the prince Alfric, very wise in law, and also Alfred, the guardian of the

The setting is not maintained throughout the proverbs, as Alfred later directly addresses only his 'son', an echo of the style of the opening chapters of the book of Proverbs. Alfred is presented in the persona of King Solomon throughout, giving the benefit of his wisdom on a range of conventional subjects. One shared feature of the wisdom of both Solomon and Alfred is their interest in the role of women:

> þus queþ Alured:
> Ne wurþ þu neuer so wod,
> ne so wyn-drunke,
> þat euere segge þine wife
> alle þine wille.
> For if þu iseye þe bi-vore
> þine i-vo alle,
> And þu hi myd worde
> i-wreþþed heuedest,
> Ne scholde heo hit lete,
> for þing lyuyinde,
> þat heo ne scholde þe forþ vp-breyde
> of þine balue-syþes.
> Wymmon is word-wod,
> and haueþ tunge to swift.
> þeyh heo wel wolde,
> ne may heo hi no-wiht welde.[25]

It is normal for traditional wisdom to adopt a masculine, and often antifeminist, point of view; however, as has been seen in the Old English poem *Maxims I*, not all traditional wisdom is necessarily critical of women. Indeed, in *Maxims I* the ideal queen is praised as a trustworthy confidante and adviser to her husband, rendering the attribution to Alfred of this kind of antifeminism strikingly anachronistic. The suspicion of female sexuality and deceptive speech which characterizes much medieval proverbial writing reflects not only the continued and growing influence of certain biblical attitudes, but also the effect of contemporary social transformations. The figure of Adam's tempting wife Eve loomed large, and the more stridently antifeminist aspects of biblical wisdom gained cultural weight over time. Proverbs warns against the danger of loose women and their tongues:[26]

Conserva fili mi praecepta patris tui et ne dimittas legem matris tuae; liga ea in corde tuo iugiter et circumda gutturi tuo; cum ambulaueris gradiantur tecum cum dormieris custodiant

---

English, England's darling, in England he was king. He began to teach them, as you can hear, how they should lead their life.'

[25] No. 17, ll. 280–95. Thus said Alfred: 'Don't ever become so crazy, nor so drunk with wine, that you ever tell your wife all that is your will. For if she saw you before all your foes, and you angered them with words, she would not omit for anything living to reprove you for your wicked doings. Woman is word-crazy, and has a swift tongue; even if she really wanted to, she couldn't control it at all.' Compare Eccles. 25: 35: '[mulier] confundet te in conspectu inimicorum' ('a wife will confound you in the presence of your enemies'); see Arngart (1942–55: 171).

[26] Weber (1994); punctuation has been supplied.

te et evigilans loquere cum eis; quia mandatum lucerna est et lex lux et via vitae increpatio disciplinae, ut custodiant te a muliere mala et a blanda lingua extreneae.[27]

It is apparent, however, that the biblical tradition in itself is not sufficient explanation for the hardening of antifeminist attitudes in popular wisdom, as this had been available to the Anglo-Saxons since their conversion, and indeed Proverbs (31: 26) praises the perfect wife as one who teaches wisdom. Undoubtedly an important factor was the rise of the universities—exclusively male communities—at a time when clergy were being forbidden to marry, a new requirement for priests in western Europe. This development increased both the sense of threat presented by female sexuality, and confirmed prejudices against the intellectual capabilities of women who cannot easily have known as much as their male contemporaries.

In this light *The Owl and the Nightingale* appears to be more than a harmless amusement playing with conventional literary forms. The two speakers are most definitely female, each attempting to justify her way of life by attacking the other. Neither reveals any interest in truth, as both pursue victory through verbal assault, while both are clearly temperamental. The nightingale is indifferent to women's marital infidelity, and after all, sex can be fun:

> 'Þah sum wif beo of nesche mode—
> Vor wymmen beoþ of softe blode—
> Þat heo, vor summe sottes lore
> Þe ȝeorne bit and sykeþ sore,
> Misrempe & misdo sumne stunde,
> Schal ic þarvore beo ibunde?
> ȝif wymmen luuieþ for unrede,
> Hwitistu me hore misdede?
> ȝef wymmon þencheþ luuie derne,
> Ne ne may ic mine songes werne.
> Wummon mai pleye under cloþe,
> Weþer heo wile wel þe wroþe,
> & heo mai do bi mine songe,
> Hweþer heo wile wel þe wronge.'[28]

The nightingale's defence of her own song is contradictory: is it men's pleas which cause women to go astray, or their own weakness of nature and desire for such affairs? The ignorance of the two birds is one of the poem's most striking

---

[27] Prov. 6: 20–4. 'My son, keep your father's precept and do not disregard your mother's law; bind them always in your heart and put them around your neck; when you walk they will lead you, when you sleep they will guard you, and when you wake you will converse with them; because the decree is a lamp at the law light, and the corrections of discipline are the way of life, to guard you against the evil woman and the smooth tongue of the adventuress.'

[28] Lines 1349–62. 'Even though a woman might occasionally be of such a delicate temperament (for women are made of delicate material), that, because of some idiot flattering and beseeching her urgently with pitiful sighs, she rushes astray and does wrong once in a while, should I be held responsible for that? If women love ill-advisedly, do you blame me for their misdeeds? If women are bent on secret affairs, I can't withhold my singing. A woman can enjoy herself under the sheets whether her intentions are good or bad, just as she can make use of my song whether her intentions are good or bad.'

characteristics, and their appeal to Alfredian authority may in itself be a demonstration of their intellectual feebleness. It is hard to imagine Alfred's English works being used in scholarly disputation in the thirteenth century, and in any case it may well be that the birds are to be perceived as making up the wisdom they attribute to the wise king, or are persistently guilty of deliberate misattribution in a misguided attempt to strengthen their arguments.

The Nature of Wisdom

Also important for understanding *The Owl and the Nightingale* is the medieval bestiary tradition, descended from the late antique *Physiologus*, an approach to nature underpinned by a principle articulated by the twelfth-century poet Alan of Lille: 'Omnis mundi creatura quasi liber et pictura nobis est speculum' ('Everything created in the world is for us like a book, a picture, and a mirror').[29] In this way of seeing the world, animals gathered symbolic and allegorical associations with a moral or religious significance. No less an authority than Solomon had suggested nature as a source of wisdom and understanding (compare Proverbs 6: 5–8). Medieval bestiary collections, usually illustrated, described a range of animals—both mythical and real, though the distinction could not easily be appreciated—and the qualities they represent. The tradition might seem arbitrary to the modern reader, but in the medieval imagination nothing in the created world was without meaning, nothing random. A seminal work in this tradition is the *Hexaemeron*, a commentary on the six days of creation by St Basil, transmitted to the Latin West by St Ambrose of Milan. For the medieval Christian, the 'book of nature' presented a symbolic order teaching human beings about God and themselves. All creatures were made by God for man, and all had meaning for him, and the allegories of nature could teach moral lessons. The validity of this approach is confirmed for the medieval Christian by Christ himself, who uses nature to teach trust in God:

Et de uestimento quid solliciti estis? Considerate lilia agri quomodo crescunt: non laborant neque nent. Dico autem uobis, quoniam nec Salomon in omni gloria sua coopertus est sicut unum ex istis. Si autem foenum agri quod hodie est, cras in clibanum mittitur, Deus sic uestit, quanto magis uos modicae fidei.[30]

Both the owl and the nightingale had conventional associations within this tradition: the owl represented those whose knowledge is limited to the worldly and so see in the

[29] Cartlidge (2001: pp. xxxvi–xxxvii).
[30] Matthew 6: 28–30. 'And why be worried about clothing? Consider how the lilies of the field grow: they do not work nor spin. Yet I say to you, even Solomon in all his glory was not arrayed like one of these. If therefore God clothes in this way the grass in the field which is here today, and thrown into the stove tomorrow, how much more you of little faith?'

dark, but are blinded in the light of faith; the nightingale sings sweetly, but is preoccupied with sex, representing human carnality. While these associations are drawn on in the poem, the poet also develops new ideas around the 'book of nature'. Indeed, he playfully reverses the mirror, as the birds contemplate human conduct in an attempt to understand their own. The owl compares the nightingale's sexual energy with men's:

> Vor sumeres-tyde is al wlonk,
> & doþ mysreken monnes þonk:
> Vor he ne rekþ noht of clennesse,
> Al his þouht is of golnesse:
> Vor none dor no leng nabideþ,
> Ac euerich vp oþer rideþ:
> Þe sulue stottes yne þe stode,
> Beþ boþe wilde and mare-wode.
> & þu sulf art þar-among,
> Vor of golnysse is al þi song.[31]

The poet is not dismissing the idea of nature as book or mirror, but rather pointing out that the image seen can depend on how you look at it. It is readily apparent that the attitudes to love, life, and morality presented by the birds are a vehicle for the discussion of human mores. Nevertheless, the poet playfully extends this tradition. If the 'book of nature' can teach human beings about themselves, and its order can teach them about God, then it is inescapably ironic when the birds read human activity as an explanation of their own animal behaviour. Part of the humour is, of course, that animal sounds such as those made by birds, cannot contain or convey the rational aspect of human speech. This joke about animal wits is best summed up in the poet's own image:

> On ape may on bok biholde,
> & leues wende and eft folde:
> Ac he ne con þe bet þarvore
> Of clerkes lore top ne more.[32]

The *Beowulf* poet also interprets nature as a form of revelation and source of wisdom. Immediately after Beowulf has severed the head of the monster Grendel, the blade of the mysterious sword is dissolved by the monster's poisonous blood:

> Þa þæt sweord ongan
> æfter heaþoswate   hildegicelum,
> wigbil wanian;   þæt wæs wundra sum,
> þæt hit eal gemealt   ise gelicost,

---

[31] Lines 489–98. 'For summertime is far too splendid, and it disturbs a man's mind—for he doesn't think about clean living: he sets his mind on lechery. Indeed, there's not an animal able to wait, but each of them climbs upon the next; and even the draught-horses in the paddock go wild in their madness for mares! And there you are among them, for your song is all about lechery.'

[32] Lines 1325–8: 'An ape can look at a book, turn the leaves and shut it again, but it by no means makes him any more advanced in scholarly knowledge.'

ðonne forstes bend   Fæder onlæteð,
onwindeð wælrapas,   se geweald hafað
sæla ond mæla;   þæt is soð Metod.[33]

The appeal to the 'book of nature' reveals an appreciation of this way of viewing creation: in it the wise might read the workings of the divine, and the righteous pagan come to a realization of the truth of the Creator in the creation bearing his imprint. The belief that God arranged time gave special status to the science of reckoning time in the Middle Ages, with the mathematics of the calendar, or *computus*, providing an insight into the principles of divine order. At the beginning of the eighth century the Anglo-Saxon schoolmaster Bede produced a text for understanding and calculating the movement of the heavenly bodies which remained the standard text till the fifteenth century.[34] The science of *computus* could easily lead into a fascination with prognostics, the 'science' of lucky and unlucky days, in an attempt to gain a degree of mastery over time. Manuscripts associated with the Anglo-Saxon class-room reveal this overlapping interest; one example is London, British Library, Harley 3271 (of the mid-eleventh century), which for the most part contains texts for teaching Latin grammar, but also contains *computus* notes, and lists of auspicious and inauspicious days.[35]

WISDOM BY LEARNING

The worlds of book learning and popular wisdom frequently collide in Chaucer's *Canterbury Tales*, completed in the 1390s.[36] University students (or clerks) feature frequently, often entangled with women, and in one case practising the relatively new science of astrology. The description of the pilgrim Clerk in the General Prologue is the most memorable of a medieval university student:

A clerk ther was of Oxenford also,
That unto logyk hadde longe ygo.
As leene was his hors as is a rake,
And he nas nat right fat, I undertake,
But looked holwe, and therto sobrely.
Ful thredbare was his overeste courtepy;
For he hadde geten hym yet no benefice,
Ne was so worldly for to have office.

---

[33] Lines 1605b–11: 'Then the sword began to waste away from the combat-blood in battle-icicles; that was a kind of wonder, that it completely melted, most like ice, when the Father releases the bonds of frost, a pool's ropes; he has power of times and seasons—that is the true Creator.'

[34] See Wallis (1999).

[35] See Chardonnens (2007).

[36] Chaucer (1987).

> For hym was levere have at his beddes heed
> Twenty bookes, clad in blak or reed,
> Of Aristotle and his philosophie,
> Than robes riche, or fithele, or gay sautrie.
> But al be that he was a philosophre,
> Yet hadde he but litel gold in cofre;
> But al that he myghte of his freendes hente,
> On bookes and on lernynge he it spente,
> And bisily gan for the soules preye
> Of hem that yaf hym wherwith to scoleye.
> Of studie took he moost cure and moost heede,
> Noght o word spak he moore than was neede,
> And that was seyd in forme and reverence,
> And short and quyk and ful of hy sentence;
> Sownynge in moral vertu was his speche,
> And gladly wolde he lerne and gladly teche.[37]

The Clerk apparently has no interest in the carnal pursuits characterizing other clerks who appear elsewhere in the collection, and his love of books and learning keeps him poor. His attempts at the 'science' of alchemy ('he was a philosophre') have borne no result; neither alchemy nor Aristotle had been available to the Anglo-Saxons, as both had come into the West later through contact with Islamic scholarship. In the Prologue to the *Wife of Bath's Tale*, the *Miller's Tale*, and the *Reeve's Tale*, we find poor university students whose interest in learning is minimal, but whose interest in women is overpowering. In all three instances the dangers presented by women for clerks, and by clerks for women, are explored. The Clerk's own *Tale*, a version of the legend of Griselda, presents what for him is a feminine ideal: the woman who is seen and not heard, and who obeys her husband in all things. The Wife of Bath takes a different view, and her fifth husband Jankyn is a clerk, whom she marries not for money, but for love. The marriage is not harmonious, as Jankyn berates Alisoun with readings from his antifeminist anthology:

> By God! He smoot me ones on the lyst,
> For that I rente out of his book a leef,
> That of the strook myn ere wax al deef.
> Stibourn I was as is a leonesse,
> And of my tonge verray jangleresse,
> And walke I wolde, as I had doon biforn,
> From hous to hous, although he had it sworn;
> For which he often tymes wolde preche,
> And me of olde Romayn geestes teche;
> How he Symplicius Gallus lefte his wyf,
> And hire forsook for terme of al his lyf,
> Noght but for open-heveded he hir say
> Lookynge out at his dore upon a day.
> Another Romayn tolde he me by name,

---

[37] Lines 285–308.

> That, for his wyf was at a someres game
> Withouten his wityng, he forsook hire eke.
> And thanne wolde he upon his bible seke
> That ilke proverbe of Ecclesiaste
> Where he comandeth, and forbedeth faste,
> Man shal nat suffre his wyf go roule aboute.[38]

The Wife's destructive reaction to this learned discourse leads to a physical assault causing her permanent partial deafness. Chaucer's dark metaphor of the Wife's refusal to hear plays with medieval stereotypes derived from popular and learned traditions: the garrulous wife would rather talk than listen, command rather than obey. And indeed, the Wife goes on to explain how she used her sexual power to achieve a reversal in the marriage, forcing Jankyn to throw his book into the fire, and turning him into a perfectly submissive husband, the mirror image of a perfect wife. This is no feminist victory however, but a moral tale for fools like Jankyn who choose marriage, when all authorities warn against involvement with women.

In the *Miller's Tale* we find another clerk entangled with a woman. Here it is a carpenter and not the clerk who marries, but the story is set in Oxford, and the foolish carpenter has a student lodger in his house:

> Whilom ther was dwellynge at Oxenford
> A riche gnof, that gestes heeld to bord,
> And of his craft he was a carpenter.
> With hym ther was dwellynge a poure scoler,
> Hadde lerned art, but al his fantasye
> Was turned for to lerne astrologye,
> And koude a certeyn of conclusiouns,
> To demen by interrogaciouns,
> If that men asked hym in certein houres
> Whan that men sholde have droghte or elles shoures,
> Or if men asked hym what sholde bifalle
> Of every thyng; I may nat rekene hem alle.
> This clerk was cleped hende Nicholas.
> Of deerne love he koude and of solas;
> And therto he was sleigh and ful privee,
> And lyk a mayden meke for to see.
> A chambre hadde he in that hostelrye
> Allone, withouten any compaignye,
> Ful fetisly ydight with herbes swoote;
> And he hymself as sweete as is the roote
> Of lycorys, or any cetewale.
> His Almageste, and bookes grete and smale,
> His astrelabie, longynge for his art,
> His augrym stones layen faire apart,
> On shelves couched at his beddes heed . . .[39]

---

[38] Wife of Bath's Prologue, ll. 634–53.
[39] Lines 3187–3211.

Nicholas's learning is far from praiseworthy, and he has clearly strayed in his obsession with astrology. The desire to know the future was universally condemned as futile in the Middle Ages, and attempts to discern future events through astrology (another introduction from the Arab world) sometimes condemned as necromancy. Nevertheless, it was generally held that the science of time was greatly enhanced, and with astrology it seemed possible to predict the future.[40]

As the story unfolds, however, we find that Nicholas is not much wiser than his landlord, John the Carpenter, who is treated by him as a fool. This is not to say John isn't foolish. As the Miller points out, John violates a fundamental precept of popular wisdom:

> This carpenter hadde wedded newe a wyf,
> Which that he lovede moore than his lyf;
> Of eighteteene yeer she was of age.
> Jalous he was, and heeld hire narwe in cage,
> For she was wylde and yong, and he was old,
> And demed hymself been lik a cokewold.
> He knew nat Catoun, for his wit was rude,
> That bad man sholde wedde his simylitude.
> Men sholde wedden after hire estaat,
> For youthe and elde is often at debaat.
> But sith that he was fallen in the snare,
> He moste endure, as oother folk, his care.[41]

The *Distichs of Cato* are a late antique collection of proverbial wisdom often attributed to Cato the Elder, or the Younger, but written by neither. Their store of common sense formed a common feature of the school curriculum read by Chaucer at St Paul's Cathedral school in London, and Benjamin Franklin in Puritan New England.[42] It is against this cultural store of proverbial wisdom that John the Carpenter's folly is measured, with ludicrously disastrous results.[43]

Nicholas, inevitably, lusts after the carpenter's wife, and she is happy to oblige as long as she is not caught. Allaying her fears, the clerk assumes his intellectual superiority:

> 'Nay, therof care thee noght,' quod Nicholas.
> 'A clerk hadde litherly biset his whyle,
> But if he koude a carpenter bigyle.'[44]

Nicholas's scheme is unnecessarily complicated, and designed as much to demonstrate his great intelligence as to enable him to satisfy his desire. He uses astrology to deceive her husband:

---

[40] See Juste (2007).   [41] Lines 3221–32.

[42] Franklin published James Logan's *Cato's moral distichs, Englished in couplets* (Philadelphia, 1735).

[43] The Miller's attribution, however, is mistaken, giving an ironic twist to his dismissal of the carpenter's 'rude' wit.

[44] Lines 3298–3300.

'Now John,' quod Nicholas, 'I wol nat lye;
I have yfounde in myn astrologye,
As I have looked in the moone bright,
That now a Monday next, at quarter nyght,
Shal falle a reyn, and that so wilde and wood,
That half so greet was nevere Noes flood.
This world,' he seyde, 'in lasse than an hour
Shal al be dreynt, so hidous is the shour.
Thus shal mankynde drenche, and lese hir lyf.'
This carpenter answerde, 'Allas, my wyf!
And shal she drenche? allas, myn Alisoun!'
For sorwe of this he fil almoost adoun,
And seyde, 'Is ther no remedie in this cas?'
'Why, yis, for gode,' quod hende Nicholas,
'If thou wolt werken after loore and reed.
Thou mayst nat werken after thyn owene heed;
For thus seith salomon, that was ful trewe,
Werk al by conseil, and thou shalt nat rewe.—
And if thou werken wolt by good conseil,
I undertake, withouten mast and seyl,
Yet shal I saven hire and thee and me.'[45]

The carpenter's concern for his wife's welfare is in touching contrast to the clerk's lust, but this tenderness does not redeem his folly. The clerk mocks the carpenter, whose 'owene heed' has no wisdom in it, and with profound irony offers the wisdom of Solomon (compare Ecclesiasticus 32: 24), advising the old fool to listen to advice. The carpenter is as ignorant of scripture (which promises no further flood, Genesis 8: 21) as he is of common sense, and is convinced. What Nicholas forgets, however, is that female sexuality, especially potent in the young Alisoun, presents as great a danger to him as it does to the old man, a fact also neglected by the parish clerk Absolon, who is also drawn to the siren. The climax of the tale leaves the carpenter brought low and the laughing-stock of the town, the squeamish Absolon with more than mud on his face, and Nicholas aptly branded with a hot iron for his intellectual pride.

In the *Miller's Tale*, Chaucer's sympathy for the vital character of Alisoun is apparent, but the logic of the disasters she causes for her husband and suitors is firmly grounded in both popular and learned wisdom about the dangers women present to men. The *Tale's* end could be predicted more easily by the wisdom warning men about women, than by any illusion of foresight offered by astrology. The popularity of proverbs across the Middle Ages implies a confidence that the wisdom they conveyed was essential for a happy life. However, many authors point to the invincibility of folly, which is, of course, more entertaining. In *The Owl and the Nightingale* and Chaucer's *Tales* the inevitability of folly is signalled by frequent reference to proverbial wisdom, only for this to be ignored. The desire for mastery,

---

[45] Lines 3513–33.

the attractions of wealth, and the pressing demands of sexual desire, all conspire in human nature to frustrate the search for wisdom. An enduring question in scholarship on *Beowulf* concerns the old king's demise, killed by a fire-breathing dragon, whose strength he cannot possibly match. He wins for his people great wealth from the dragon's hoard, which they cannot use. Questions about Beowulf's motivation often focus on his moral character, but we might more accurately ask whether or not contemporary readers might have considered him a fool. Not all examples teaching wisdom are positive, and the use of humour in texts as diverse as *Solomon and Saturn II, The Owl and the Nightingale* and *The Canterbury Tales*, suggest that wisdom is often best learnt through laughter at fools who present readers with a mirror of their own folly.

BIBLIOGRAPHY

ARNGART, O. S. (ed.) (1942–55), *The Proverbs of Alfred* (2 vols. Lund: C. W. K. Gleerup).

BAYLESS, M., and M. LAPIDGE (eds.) (1998), *Collectanea pseudo-Bedae* (Dublin: Dublin Institute for Advanced Studies, School of Celtic Studies).

CARTLIDGE, NILE (ed.) (2001), *The Owl and the Nightingale: Text and Translation* (Exeter: University of Exeter Press).

CHARDONNENS, L. S. (2007), 'London, British Library, Harley 3271: The Composition and Structure of an Eleventh-Century Anglo-Saxon Miscellany', in P. Lendinara, L. Lazzari, and M. A. D'Aronco (eds.), *Form and Content of Instruction in Anglo-Saxon England in the Light of Contemporary Manuscript Evidence: Papers Presented at the International Conference Udine, 6–8 April 2006* (Turnhout: Brepols), 3–34.

CHAUCER, GEOFFREY (1987), *The Riverside Chaucer*, ed. Larry Dean Benson (Boston: Houghton Mifflin).

COX, R. S. (1972), 'The Old English *Dicts of Cato*', *Anglia*, 90: 1–42.

ANTON, H. H. (1968), *Fürstenspiegel und Herrscherethos in der Karlolingerzeit* (Bonner historische Forschungen, 32; Bonn: L. Röhrscheid).

DESKIS, S. E. (1996), *Beowulf and the Medieval Proverb Tradition* (Tempe, Ariz.: Medieval and Renaissance Texts and Studies).

DOBBIE, E. V. K. (ed.) (1942), *The Anglo-Saxon Minor Poems* (Anglo-Saxon Poetic Records, 6; New York: Columbia University Press), 55–7.

FULK, R. D., R. E. BJORK, and J. D. NILES (eds.) (2008), *Klaeber's Beowulf and The Fight at Finnsburg* (Toronto: University of Toronto Press).

JUSTE, DAVID (2007), *Les Alchandreana primitifs: Étude sur les plus anciens traités astrologiques latins d'origine arabe (Xe siècle)* (Leiden: Brill).

KRAPP, G. P., and E. V. K. DOBBIE (eds.) (1936), *The Exeter Book* (Anglo-Saxon Poetic Records, 3; New York: Columbia University Press), 156–63.

LARRINGTON, CAROLYNE (1993), *A Store of Common Sense: Gnomic Theme and Style in Old Icelandic and Old English Wisdom Poetry* (Oxford: Clarendon Press).

LIUZZA, R. M. (2000), *Beowulf: A New Verse Translation* (Peterborough, Ontario: Broadview).

MENNER, ROBERT J. (ed.), (1941), *The Poetical Dialogues of Solomon and Saturn* (New York: Modern Language Association of America; London: Oxford University Press).

ORME, NICHOLAS (2006), *Medieval Schools: From Roman Britain to Renaissance England* (New Haven: Yale University Press).

SHIPPEY, T. A. (ed.) (1976), *Poems of Wisdom and Learning in Old English* (Cambridge: D. S. Brewer; Totowa, NJ: Rowman & Littlefield).

WALLIS, FAITH (tr.) (1999), *Bede: The Reckoning of Time* (Liverpool: Liverpool University Press).

WEBER, R. (ed.) (1994), *Biblia sacra iuxta vulgatam versionem* (4th edn. Stuttgart: Deutsche Bibelgesellschaft).

PART IV

....

LITERARY
REALITIES

....

CHAPTER 16

THE YORKSHIRE PARTISANS AND THE LITERATURE OF POPULAR DISCONTENT

ANDREW PRESCOTT

ROSSELL HOPE ROBBINS AND 'THE YORKSHIRE PARTISANS'

It is a common misapprehension that the ordinary people of medieval England were excluded from documentary culture by virtue of their illiteracy, so that their voice is effectively missing from our history. As G. K. Chesterton put it in his poem *The Secret People*: 'We are the people of England, that never have spoken yet'. The medieval clerical elite frequently presented ordinary people as subhuman beings, to whom the written word was a mystery. The St Albans monk Thomas Walsingham described the rebels of 1381 as bare-legged ruffians who sought to destroy every written document they could find, so that property rights and the law would be destroyed.[1] However, as recent

---

[1] Taylor *et al.* (2003: 415–17). I am grateful to Susan Mitchell Sommers, Paul Strohm, and Elaine Treharne for their comments on earlier versions of this chapter.

discussion by scholars such as Susan Crane and Steven Justice has emphasized,[2] the depiction of the ordinary people as illiterate brutes was a deliberate ideological distortion, designed to help keep the lower classes in their place. Everyday life in the later Middle Ages was permeated by texts of many different types, and people of all social levels had a number of routes by which they could engage with literate culture.

Among the most evocative and intriguing of the surviving texts connected with the life of everyday people of the Middle Ages are the various Middle English poems and verses commenting on contemporary events, scattered through a variety of manuscript collections, administrative records, and other texts. A convenient collection of some of this material is the section headed 'Popular Struggles' in the edition of *Historical Poems of the XIVth and XVth Centuries* published in 1959 by the American-based scholar and critic Rossell Hope Robbins.[3] This selection of poetry includes some verses dating from 1392 to which Robbins gave the title *The Yorkshire Partisans*.[4] Robbins's invented title, which suggests a ballad concerning the adventures of some men from Yorkshire or a song about some other subject connected with the county, is unhelpful. Although the verses are from Yorkshire and do express a strong sense of camaraderie, their message seems much more general and wide-ranging.

The verses begin by stating that there had been reports that officials ('schrewes') would be coming to the area ('oure soken') to carry out an inquiry ('with al for to bake'—to fix things up). Doubtless, the verses declare, the friars and the other religious orders would look after themselves, covering up as necessary and supporting one another as brothers.[5]

In þe contre herd was we	)
	) With al for to bake
Þat in oure soken schrewes shuld be	)
Among þis Frers it is so	)
	) Whether þei slepe or wake
And other ordres many mo	)
And þet wil ilkan hel vp other	)
	) Bothe in wrong and right
And meynten him als his brother	)

The laymen who wrote these verses were determined to follow the example of the religious orders and stick up for their neighbours, supporting each other through

---

    [2] Crane (1992); Justice (1994).
    [3] Robbins (1959: 54–63).
    [4] Ibid. 60–1.
    [5] The verses are printed here for the first time from The National Archives, KB 9/144 m. 31, which, as is explained below, is probably the earliest version of these verses. In addition to the major differences noted below to the enrolled version in The National Archives, KB 27/528 *rex* m. 16 (printed in Sayles 1971: 84–5), there are a number of small differences in orthography between the file and enrolled versions. All MS citations are to documents in The National Archives unless otherwise stated.

thick and thin with all their might. While they would not obstruct or hinder anyone, they would nevertheless not tolerate any mocking or mischief ('hethyng wil we suffre non'). They would not be mucked about by anybody ('Neither of hobbe ne of Iohan')

And so[6] wil we in stond and stoure	)
	) With al oure myght
Meynten oure negheboure	)
Ilk man may come and goo	)
	) I say yow sikerly
Among vs both to and froo	)
But hethyng wil we suffre non	)
	) With what man he be
Neither of hobbe ne of Iohan	)

The authors of these verses declared that it was unnatural for a man to accept mockery from any person, whether great or small. If punishment was meekly accepted, the certain consequence was further punishment and misfortune. The motto of these comrades was 'One for All and All for One'. Any injustice perpetrated against one of their number was done to them all.

For vnkynde we ware	)
	) Any vilans hethyng
ȝif we suffird of lesse or mare	)
But it were quit double agayn	)
	) To byde oure dressyng
And a corde and be ful fayn	)
And on þat purposȝet we stand	)
	) In what plas it falle[7]
Who so dose vs any wrang	)
Yet he myght als wel	)
	) Do a geyn vs alle
Als haue i hap and sel[8]	)

Despite what Scattergood calls their 'colloquial vigour and directness',[9] these verses as presented by Robbins appear slightly baffling, even perplexing. They clearly express discontent and a determination to fight against injustice, but the exact nature of the grievances is not clear. Who were these 'shrews' who would 'bake up' this area of northern England? Why were they such a threat? And who were the 'partisans' who stuck so firmly

---

[6] 'also' in KB 27/528 *rex* m. 16.

[7] Not now legible in KB 27/528 *rex* m. 16, but given as 'Fall' by Powell and Trevelyan (1899: 20), and 'Falle' by Sayles (1971: 85).

[8] 'hel' in KB 27/528 *rex* m. 16.

[9] Scattergood (1972: 356).

together? Concerned to emphasize the intrinsic poetic qualities of the verses, Robbins printed only these Middle English lines. For Robbins, the fact that these lines are in Middle English, and rhyme, was sufficient to make them of interest. In Robbins's presentation, these lines stand proudly on their own, hewn out of their textual context. Determined to present these verses in isolation as a poem with some inherent literary quality, Robbins robbed them of meaning, reducing them to the level of a linguistic curio.

Robbins's notes provide little further elucidation.[10] The verses occur in two legal records from the Court of King's Bench compiled in 1392–3, but Robbins took his text from London, British Library, Stowe 393, folio 99. The use of the Stowe manuscript as the base text for this edition is eccentric, to say the least. Stowe 393 dates from the seventeenth century, but Robbins justified using this manuscript on the grounds that the verses had not previously been printed from this source and that this manuscript was 'interesting for its late preservation of a popular song'.[11] This would be reasonable if the Stowe manuscript was a literary collection, but in fact it consists of extracts from legal records, and simply shows that an early-modern legal antiquary came across these lines in the records of the King's Bench and thought the verses (or, more likely, the case containing them) sufficiently curious to be worth copying out. There is no evidence that these verses had continued currency in medieval England after 1393. The transcription of the Middle English verse in the Stowe manuscript is extremely unreliable. Among the many errors is a misreading of the first line, given as 'you fryers', suggesting wrongly that the poem was addressed directly to members of religious orders. Some of the readings are completely garbled in the Stowe manuscript, with the line 'With what man he be' being given as 'with what may he mery be'. In this case, Robbins corrects the Stowe manuscript from the King's Bench records, but this again raises the question of why Robbins preferred to use Stowe.

Robbins was determined to demonstrate the literary qualities of historical poems such as these, declaring that 'The present anthology of historical poems reveals literary qualities that bear comparison with those of similar collections of religious and secular lyrics.'[12] It is difficult to escape the impression that Robbins thought that the appearance of *The Yorkshire Partisans* in a manuscript volume in the British Library enhanced its literary quality. He refers almost dismissively to the appearance of these lines in the King's Bench records, stating merely that they 'occur also' in a roll of the court.[13] For historians, Robbins's procedure is surprising, since historians usually give priority to administrative records which are (rightly or wrongly) construed as more reliable because of their 'official' status. Evidently, for literary scholars different hierarchies apply, with a greater emphasis given to manuscripts which suggest the aesthetic judgement of the connoisseur. There is an unspoken sense in Robbins's treatment of these verses that he felt their appearance in a British Library manuscript more significant than their occurrence in an administrative record. Despite the fact that Robbins's edition inherently dealt with political themes, he

---

[10] Robbins (1959: 277).   [11] Ibid.
[12] Ibid. p. xvii.   [13] Ibid. 277.

seems to have been concerned that overt treatment of politics undermines literary quality, commenting that 'where the historical and political poems reflect only the interests of a special class, they seldom make for great poetry'.[14] Thus, if a poem is found in a manuscript in a great cultural institution such as the British Library, it is more likely to have some literary merit; if it occurs only in an administrative record, it has a merely functional value. There is a range of (largely Victorian) cultural assumptions about the role of literature in society on display here which have played a powerful role in the academic articulation of the accepted literary canon.

By seeking to illustrate that the lines of *The Yorkshire Partisans* had a separate life of their own and were appreciated for their own sake, Robbins robbed them of a rich context which can only be recovered by grappling with those administrative records which Robbins effectively ignored. Far from detracting from the literary quality of these verses, an investigation of their immediate textual environment reveals a complexity and depth which is not apparent in the Stowe manuscript or in Robbins's edition. Moreover, as we explore the appearance of this text in three different contexts, first in the formal roll of the King's Bench, then in the files of presentments made to the King's Bench by local juries, and finally in local records and traditions, these verses assume various aspects which suggest differing connections with wider popular literacy and discontent. As we pursue *The Yorkshire Partisans* through these vellum rolls and files, the text becomes increasingly unstable and its apparent cultural connections more complex. As presented by Robbins, these lines are an inert dead specimen, pinned to the board of a formal anthology. Pursued through their original textual environment of legal and local records, the verses begin to display complex layers of meaning, which shift and interact with each other.

The Yorkshire Partisans in the King's Bench Rolls

After Parliament, the Court of King's Bench was the most powerful of the royal courts, where litigation most closely associated with the Crown was heard and which had authority to correct the errors of other courts (except for the Exchequer and the court of the Cinque Ports).[15] Its most authoritative record was the formal series of King's Bench rolls compiled for each legal term which summarized proceedings in the various cases heard by the court and are preserved in The National Archives in London. In 1880, a young barrister, Maurice Henry Hewlett, who was afterwards to

---

[14] Ibid. p. xlv.
[15] For an overview of King's Bench, see Musson and Ormrod (1999: 17–20); Powell (1989: 54–6); Sayles (1959).

become a well-known historical novelist, was searching through the King's Bench rolls and noticed in the King's Bench Roll for the Easter Term of 1393 the case containing *The Yorkshire Partisans*. Hewlett reported his discovery in the recently established 'magazine devoted to the study of the past', *The Antiquary*, providing a very inaccurate transcription of the lines.[16] Hewlett noted that the verses dated from the age of Chaucer but was dismissive of this 'poetical effort', suggesting that the lines were the work of a band of 'lawless youths' in Beverley and Hull. For Hewlett, the verses were a historical curiosity, appropriate to the rag bag of diverting historical information and anecdotes in the pages of *The Antiquary*.

In 1899, the rising young star of Cambridge history, G. M. Trevelyan, published with the records scholar, Edgar Powell, a small volume of documents from the public records under the title *The Peasants' Rising and the Lollards*, as a supplement to his *England in the Age of Wycliffe*. Trevelyan was the great-nephew of the celebrated historian Thomas Babington Macaulay and *England in the Age of Wycliffe* was in many respects an echo of the literary history written by Macaulay. The publication of *The Peasants' Rising and the Lollards* as a documentary appendix to a separate volume can be seen as a cursory acknowledgement by Trevelyan of the increasing emphasis of historians on documentary criticism. Powell and Trevelyan's volume, while still useful, is an eccentric production. Trevelyan was less interested in accurate manuscript scholarship than in extolling his central theme that the reign of Richard II was a crucial period in the growth of individual liberty. The selection of documents in *The Peasants' Rising and the Lollards* is serendipitous and, in attempting to exclude 'much repetition and mere legal phraseology' from the documents,[17] Powell and Trevelyan also omitted much substantive information, such as some of the names of the accused and details of dates and places.[18] Powell and Trevelyan printed the Yorkshire verses from the King's Bench roll, much more accurately than Hewlett, but, like Hewlett, only published a very small section from the whole case, stating that the rhymes had been publically recited at Beverley on 21 July 1392 and at Hull on the following Sunday by John Berwald the younger of Cottingham, a large village near Hull, and others.[19] This information, which provided a dating for the verse and suggested a possible author, was reported by Robbins in his notes and indeed the verses have as a result generally been ascribed to Berwald himself.[20] Although they only printed part of the case containing the 1392 verses, Powell and Trevelyan were more enthusiastic about these verses than Maurice Hewlett, comparing this poem to

[16] Hewlett (1880).   [17] Powell and Trevelyan (1899: p. v).

[18] e.g. in printing the file of indictments from west Kent against the insurgents of 1381 which is now The National Archives, KB 9/43, Powell and Trevelyan omitted details of goods stolen and, where individuals are frequently mentioned, they only printed a selection of the charges against them. As a result of Powell and Trevelyan's highly selective editing methods, one of the few direct references in the judicial records to Wat Tyler, declaring that 'Walter Tyler of Colchester, John Abel of Dartford, Walter Appledore of Malling and William Heneke were leaders of the revolt', was omitted from their edn. of this file: KB 9/43 m. 12.

[19] Powell and Trevelyan (1899: 19–20).

[20] e.g. Patterson (1991: 261).

the letters circulated during the revolt of 1381, and declaring that 'the rioters of 1392 were not merely bent on plunder and arson, but were inspired by an ideal of independent manhood which could not tamely endure slavery or wrong'.[21]

The formal record of the case in the King's Bench roll for Easter 1393 containing *The Yorkshire Partisans* was only finally printed in full in 1971 by G. O. Sayles, who also for the first time provided a reliable edition of the verses.[22] It is ironic that, despite the attempt of Robbins to establish the poetic quality of these Middle English lines, the first accurate printing of them was in a volume published by the Selden Society, an organization for the publication of editions of legal texts. The complete entry on the King's Bench roll contains an indictment which describes in full the charges brought in connection with the verses. This reads (in Sayles's translation) as follows:

Yorkshire. It is presented that John Berwald the younger of Cottingham, Thomas Rawlinson of Cottingham, Edmund Howden of the same, John Slater of the same, John Tyndale, formerly the servant of Robert Bulmer of the same, Andrew Crauncewick of the same, Robert Green of Cottingham, farrier, William Barker of Hessle, William Marshall of Cottingham, Stephen Thomson of the same, Richard Johnson of the same, John Berwald the elder of the same, John Watson of Dunswell, William Brotelby of the same, William Steven the elder of the same, William Mageson of Newland, John Webster of the same, John Ricall of the same, Patrick Gesede of the same, Thomas Rayner of the same, John of Skidby, flesher, of the same, Thomas son of Richard of Holme, Richard Johnson of Cottingham, Thomas Cartwright of the same, John Navendyke, flesher, of the same, Robert son of Steven Malynson of the same, Simon son of Steven Malynson of the same, John Rayner the younger of Newland, Thomas King of Hullbank, John King son of the said Thomas, and Robert Stevenson of Hullbank, together with other malefactors of their covin to the number of eighty, whose names they do not know, were dressed for the last six years in one livery of a single company by corrupt allegiance and confederacy, each of them in maintaining the other in all plaints, true or false, against whosoever should wish to complain against them or any one of them, in breach of the terms of the statute etc. And they were dressed and assembled in such aforesaid livery of a single company in various places in the county of York, namely at Beverley and Benning-holme, on the Saturday after the Feast of the Nativity of St John the Baptist in the tenth year of the reign of King Richard, second after the Conquest [30 June 1386]. And they assaulted William, a former servant of John of Garton, at Beverley with force and arms, namely with swords etc., and there they beat, wounded and ill-treated him so that his life was despaired of, in breach of the king's peace. And they say that no sheriff of the county of York, escheator or any other royal minister of whatsoever rank he is can at any time do anything that is his duty within the domain of Cottingham, and that Robert Bulmer of Buttercrambe and William, his son, are the chief maintainers and leaders of all the aforesaid malefactors, in breach of the terms of the statute promulgated thereon and in breach of the peace, etc.

The indictment then goes on to describe how Berwald the younger and the others had publicly recited the verses in 1392. On 21 May 1393, Robert and William Bulmer appeared together with William Barker of Hessle in the King's Bench while it was at

[21] Powell and Trevelyan (1899: p. x).
[22] Sayles (1971: 83–5), from KB 27/528 *rex* m. 37d.

York. They presented pardons for these offences dated 19 March 1393.[23] The pardons added additional information which included an accusation that they had attacked William Hulme, the royal escheator responsible for collecting money owed to the king, while he was going about his duties. These pardons were duly checked and recorded by the court, and Robert and William Bulmer and William Barker were allowed to go *sine die*.

John Berwald, the supposed reciter of *The Yorkshire Partisans*, was a member of a large group of alleged malefactors drawn almost entirely from the village of Cottingham near Hull and its constituent hamlets such as Newland and Dunswell. This group, allegedly, had been members of a corrupt fraternity which had promoted false lawsuits and had used fictitious testimonies and other fraudulent strategies to impede any attempts to prosecute them. Over a long period, they had threatened royal officials, so that they could not carry out their duties. The company had affirmed its collective identity by wearing distinctive hoods as a uniform. They seem to have been a fulcrum of lawlessness in east Yorkshire. In this context, the verses read at Beverley and Hull appear not so much as a spontaneous expression of discontent but rather more like a formal declaration by a group which had terrorized the county for years and was already very well known there. This Cottingham fraternity was a substantial body of men—at least eighty—and would have appeared imposing and even intimidating as they read their verses to the Sunday crowds, presumably leaving or going to church, at Beverley and Hull.

Given the large size of this group, we cannot be confident that the verses were necessarily the work of Berwald the younger; they may have been produced by various members of the fraternity. It is evident that most members of the fraternity were relatively humble. The group includes two fleshers, who were engaged in the butchery trade, and a farrier. However, Robert and William Bulmer were more substantial. The manor of Cottingham had formed part of the estates of the Black Prince, which had passed to the Duchess of Kent, the king's mother, and on her death in 1385 descended to her son Thomas Holland, Fifth Earl of Kent, a close and rather hot-headed associate of Richard II.[24] Bulmer was a tenant of the Earl of Kent at Cottingham and also held property in another of the earl's manors at Buttercrambe, close to York.[25] The indictment states that the Bulmers were the 'chief maintainers and leaders' of the fraternity, and it is tempting to suggest that the Bulmers may themselves have played a part in the composition of *The Yorkshire Partisans*. The Bulmers had most to lose from these accusations, and it is striking that it was the Bulmers, together with William Barker of Hessle, slightly to the south of Cottingham on the banks of the Humber, who went to the trouble and expense of having their

---

[23] *Calendar of Patent Rolls 1391–6*, pp. 249–50.

[24] Allison (1979: 68).

[25] Page (1923). It is tempting to identify the Ralph Bulmer of the indictment with Sir Ralph Bulmer who died in Apr. 1406: *Calendar of Inquisitions Post Mortem, 7–14 Henry IV*, pp. 129–30. Both owned property in north and east Yorkshire. However, there is no record of Sir Ralph owning property in Cottingham or Buttercrambe or that he had a son named William.

pardons processed formally by the court of King's Bench, while the Cottingham participants in the band, although they obtained pardons, did not have them registered by King's Bench.

Were the verses recited at Beverley and Hull a generic song which the fraternity had used throughout its career? Probably not. Indeed, the context of the King's Bench record indicates the identity of the 'schrewes' who were going to 'bake' the lawlessness prevalent in Humberside. The 'schrewes' were the officials of the Court of King's Bench itself. Sessions of King's Bench were not invariably held at Westminster.[26] During the reign of Edward III, King's Bench frequently held sittings away from Westminster in order to try to impose law and order throughout the country. The superior jurisdiction of King's Bench meant that it was able to summon local juries to make presentments relating to crimes in the county in which the court was sitting. Under Richard II, such provincial sittings of the King's Bench were rarer, but nevertheless still occurred from time to time, particularly when parliament sat outside London. On 30 May 1392, the King's Bench, Court of Common Pleas, the Exchequer, and the Chancery were all ordered to hold their sittings at York from the end of June.[27] This has generally been interpreted as a consequence of Richard II's quarrel with the City of London. However, for Yorkshire, the arrival of the King's Bench meant that a powerful court would be scrutinizing lawlessness and disturbances in the area, and it is possible that concern about northern unrest may have been another factor in the decision to hold court sessions in Yorkshire.

Certainly, Berwald and his comrades from Cottingham seem to have thought that the move of royal courts and officials to Yorkshire would have serious consequences for them personally. It appears to have been news of the arrival of the main offices of the royal government in Yorkshire which prompted the Cottingham fraternity to make its proclamations at Hull and Beverley. The advent of the King's Bench, with its county-wide criminal jurisdiction, would have particularly alarmed them, and their anxieties proved well-grounded, since it was during these sessions of King's Bench at York during the Michaelmas Term of 1392 that Bulmer, Berwald, and the others were indicted by Yorkshire juries. By the end of 1392, Richard had instructed his courts and officials to move back south, but the King's Bench was sufficiently concerned by the problems it had found in Yorkshire to return the following year.[28] In March 1393, aware that the King's Bench was shortly coming back to Yorkshire, Bulmer, Berwald, and the others took the precaution of obtaining pardons. When King's Bench held its Easter 1393 sessions at York, the Bulmers and William Barker both appeared to have their pardons processed. The process designed to force the other Cottingham malefactors to appear in court, which resulted ultimately in their outlawry, proved ineffectual, as was generally the case with proceedings to persuade defendants to

[26] Musson (2001: 141, 145–6); Powell (1989: 173–94); Sayles (1971: pp. xxvii–xxviii).

[27] Barron (1971: 181–2); *Calendar of Close Rolls 1389–92*, pp. 466–7. The orders on the Close Rolls do not specifically include the King's Bench, but its movements at this time are recorded on its rolls: Sayles (1971: p. lvi).

[28] Sayles (1971: p. lvi).

appear in medieval courts. Having obtained a pardon, the other members of the band apparently felt no need of the extra reassurance of appearing in King's Bench so that the case could be formally concluded. Nevertheless, it is easy to see why the verses of *The Yorkshire Partisans* suggest that dealings with courts could only lead to trouble and further punishment. The indictments before King's Bench caught up the Bulmers, Berwald, and the others in a lengthy legal process which could only result in expense, difficulty, and perhaps even danger.

As they appear in the record of the case against the Bulmers and Barker in the King's Bench Roll for Easter 1393, the verses known as *The Yorkshire Partisans* are presented largely as an expression of contemporary reactions to concerns about livery and maintenance. Late medieval English aristocratic society was still fundamentally based on the noble household. Noblemen acquired power and influence by granting offices, land, and wages to a retinue of followers, who would wear a uniform known as a livery. During the fourteenth century, liveries became increasingly commonplace and the social conventions which regulated their issue were undermined. Richard II's reign saw an upsurge of anxiety about the indiscriminate distribution of liveries and widespread concern that unsuitable people were giving and receiving them.[29] The growth of liveried retinues was seen as precipitating violent incidents in the country at large. Above all, there were constant complaints that these social networks were being used to promote false lawsuits by a process known as maintenance, preventing justice being dispensed by the royal courts. As commentators such as Paul Strohm and Elliot Kendall have recently emphasized, these anxieties were reflected in the works of poets such as Geoffrey Chaucer and John Gower. In the *Confessio amantis*, Gower complains:

> That of here large retenue
> The lond is ful of meintenue
> Which causith that the commune right
> In fewe countrees stant upright (8. 3011–12)

Parliament repeatedly attempted to act against the growth of liveries and the various abuses given the collective label of maintenance, but they were not so much concerned to act against the principle of liveried retinues as to ensure that liveries were issued only by noblemen of a suitably elevated rank. The use of distinctive hats and badges was one means by which the gentry and merchants could cheaply and quickly establish liveries. In 1377, a statute was passed against liveries of hats, and in 1384 parliament protested against the growth of badge liveries. In 1388, the Cambridge Parliament again demanded action against such novelties as the distribution of badges and protested vehemently at the growth of maintenance, declaring that not only were individuals bringing false lawsuits but also assemblies of retainers and riotous gatherings were preventing the effective operation of justice. The Cambridge Parliament further instituted an inquiry into guilds and fraternities, apparently reflecting concern that these might have been a vehicle for manipulating lawsuits.

[29] Storey (1971); Strohm (1992: 57–74); Given-Wilson (2003: 123–8); Kendall (2008: 9–27, 173–93).

Another parliamentary petition in 1390 demanded that a lord should only distribute livery to the 'familiars of his household, his kin and kin by law, his steward, his counsel, or to his bailiffs on their manors'.[30] As Elliot Kendall has observed, 'This petition and the more numerous ones which target badges are especially concerned to exclude recipients of less than aristocratic status unless they are connected to a household by a secure tie. Divisions are drawn and redrawn at about the level of "vadletz" and (lesser) esquires, at the base of the armigerous strata.'[31] The resulting statute of 1390, described as the first major attempt to regulate and control retaining, restricted the right to give liveries to the most senior nobles—dukes, earls, barons, and bannerets—and stipulated that such liveries could be given only to the immediate household of such noblemen together with knights and esquires retained by them for life on indenture.

It was this 1390 statute that the Bulmers, Berwald, and the other men from Cottingham were accused of breaching. It is difficult to imagine a more striking illustration of the way in which the use of liveries had spread beyond a noble milieu than their adoption by the fleshers and farriers of this Yorkshire village. However, in this area of Yorkshire, the adoption of distinctive hats and caps conveyed a distinctive message beyond the simple adoption of noble behaviour by common folk. The Yorkshire towns of Scarborough, Beverley, Hull, and York had all suffered serious disturbances during the Peasants' Revolt of 1381, reflecting class tensions among the tradesmen and wealthy merchants in these towns.[32] Men from Cottingham had been accused of taking part in the riots in Beverley in 1381 and 1382.[33] In both York and Scarborough, factions within the town distributed liveries in the form of distinctive hoods and caps at the time of the rising.[34] The use of liveries by the men of Cottingham may have been interpreted by those who saw them at Beverley and Hull as a reference not so much to noble use of such devices as to the earlier urban disturbances and unrest in Yorkshire. In this sense, the Cottingham activities might perhaps have been perceived as an echo of the urban discontent in 1381 and a reflection of continuing social tensions in towns such as Hull and Beverley, as well as an expression of wider problems created by the growth of livery and maintenance. Moreover, the link between maintenance and insurgency was one that had already been made by juries making presentment in relation to the urban riots in Yorkshire in 1381. In Scarborough, for example the jurors of Dickering and Buckrose described how in 1381 the insurgents in the town had 'formed a mutual confederacy and bound themselves by oath . . . to maintain each of their individual complaints in common',[35] words that anticipate the allegations against the Cottingham group.

In this context, Paul Strohm sees *The Yorkshire Partisans* as emulating insurgent strategies by annexing a form of discourse associated with other, more elevated, social groups.[36] He points out that *The Yorkshire Partisans* stands in a line of literary

---

[30] Kendall (2008: 190).   [31] Ibid.   [32] Dobson (1984).
[33] SC8/225/11233; SC8/225/11235; SC8/225/11238; SC8/225/11239; SC8/225/11242, partly printed in Flower (1905).
[34] Dobson (1983: 289–94).   [35] Ibid. 291.   [36] Strohm (1992: 180–2).

complaint about livery and maintenance reaching back to the early fourteenth century. *The Yorkshire Partisans* verses echo many of the wider criticisms of livery and maintenance: everybody did it; the friars and other religious orders stick up for each other; they cover up for each other regardless; there was no point in appearing in court, it would only lead to further trouble. However, as Strohm emphasizes, the remarkable feature of *The Yorkshire Partisans* was the conclusion drawn: since everybody else was engaged in maintenance and corruption, Berwald and his colleagues would join in. In Strohm's words, 'The poem's central strategy is simply to embrace what everyone already knew about maintainers: that they stick up for each other, right or wrong. The poem is, in other words, produced within a matrix of mainly negative comments about maintenance, and its ingenuity is to stand these criticisms on their heads, to embrace them unapologetically.'[37] Strohm points out that the poem seems to be written for accessibility in a metre and rhyme similar to that parodied by Chaucer in *Sir Thopas*, and he sees the poem as 'an element in a highly successful program of self-representation to the people of the countryside'.[38] The discourse of livery and maintenance is thus sequestrated to support a popular movement against a corrupt system of justice. It is ironic that a movement which in this reading reflects popular anxieties about maintenance ends up by being prosecuted for breaching statutes against liveries and maintenance.

Strohm suggests that a sign of the success of the Cottingham band was that they 'unaccountably' received pardons, but the grant of a pardon in return for payment and maybe some special pleading was at this time not unusual: one need only think of the pardons given to some of the most notorious insurgents in 1381. Moreover, in view of the involvement of Robert and William Bulmer, and the fact that it was their pardons which were eventually processed by the King's Bench, it is difficult to see the pardons as reflecting widespread popular sympathy for the Cottingham group. Given Robert Bulmer's position as a tenant of the Earl of Kent, a half-brother of Richard, it is likely that it was Bulmer's influence with the Earl of Kent which was primarily responsible for the pardons. Indeed, the Cottingham group as described in the case from the King's Bench rolls printed by Sayles looks suspiciously like a retinue developed by Bulmer, a man who was definitely 'at the base of the armigerous strata'. Viewed in this way, the Cottingham case appears to be a textbook illustration of the way in which the distribution of liveries by the lowest ranks of the gentry had undermined the operation of the legal system, precisely the kind of problem that parliament had complained so vociferously about.

However, this does not satisfactorily explain the tension between the rhetoric of the verses and the reported actions of the Cottingham band. The verses do indeed protest vehemently against the maintenance practised by the friars—presumably the Austin Friars of Hull and the Black Friars of Beverley, where the verses were read—while declaring that what was sauce for the Beverley friar was also sauce for the Cottingham butcher. But this raises a broader difficulty, namely that it is unclear

---

[37] Ibid. 182.   [38] Strohm (1992: 182 n. 4).

what legal function the inclusion of the verses performed in the record of the case of the King's Bench roll. An indictment was a very tightly defined form of text. In order for an indictment to be valid, it had to include certain set pieces of information such as the name of the accused, the date of the offence, and the place where it occurred. There were very specific rules governing how each offence should be described, with certain essential pieces of information being required, such as a statement that the offence occurred 'against the king's peace', which was necessary to establish that the case could be heard in a royal court, or a declaration of the value of goods stolen, required to establish whether or not a theft was a felony. Failure to include any of these key elements of an indictment frequently resulted in the charges being dismissed.[39] Moreover, the risk of an indictment failing on such formal grounds was sufficiently high that it was inadvisable to include unnecessary information. The English verses in this King's Bench case were unnecessary to establish the case against Bulmer and the others. The Latin indictment describing the activities of the group in distributing liveries and manipulating lawsuits was sufficient to establish a prima facie case that there had been a breach of the 1390 statute. The information concerning the verses adds nothing further to the indictment. Indeed, this section of the case is hardly in the form of an indictment—an essential part of an indictment was the declaration of the nature of the offence. Berwald and the others are simply accused of reading the verses aloud at certain times and certain places. There is no statement as to what offence they had committed, what statute they had broken, and why such activities were held to be unlawful.

There is a puzzle at the heart of the record of this case on the King's Bench roll. Robert Bulmer and the others are accused of contravening the 1390 statute against livery and maintenance. This part of the indictment is drawn in the correct form. The verses are intriguing because of the way in which they echo and relate to the current debate on livery and maintenance, but they are unnecessary to the indictment, which does not state that the reading of the verses was an offence. It might be suggested that the verses further illustrated the culpability of the Cottingham men, but indictments were formal statements of the charges, not reviews of evidence; a discussion of the verses was more suitable for the court hearing. At no point in the case as it appears in the King's Bench roll is there any statement that the verses were used in any treasonable fashion to rally popular discontent or, by exploiting the rhetoric of protest against maintenance, to promote a popular rising. The appearance of sections of text in Middle English in the King's Bench records is unusual, one reason why it was noticed by the compiler of Stowe MS 393. *The Yorkshire Partisans* would not have been included accidentally or casually in the King's Bench rolls, which were highly professional productions by experienced clerks of the court, but the reasons for the poem's inclusion are unclear. In order to investigate this conundrum further, it is necessary to explore the file documents from which the roll was compiled, and these present a completely different set of contexts for the verses.

[39] Musson (2001: 152–3).

THE YORKSHIRE PARTISANS IN
THE ANCIENT INDICTMENTS

The formal plea rolls of the King's Bench were highly professional scribal productions.[40] Each roll contained dozens of long membranes sewn strongly together at the
top and protected by a vellum flap with an elaborately written label specifying the
contents and date of the roll. These imposing artefacts were the end product of a long
process of collecting, collating, and summarizing information from large numbers of
vellum documents relating to many different cases. The working documents of the
King's Bench were kept in a series of files.[41] One contained the various writs relating
to particular lawsuits sent to the court (the *Brevia* file). Another consisted of writs
relating specifically to Crown litigation (*Brevia Regis*). Details of the names of jurors
were placed on the *Panella* files. Hundreds of these files survive, each containing
dozens of scraps of vellum strung together on a vellum thong securing them to an
external wrapper. For many centuries, these files languished in sacks in such reposi-
tories as the Tower of London or the Chapter House at Westminster. Following the
building of the Public Record Office in London in the nineteenth century, the sacks
were placed in vaults in such out-of-the-way parts of the record office as the Clock
Tower or the basement beneath the Round Reading Room. The recovery of this
material from centuries of accumulated dust and filth and the recreation of the
medieval file series, one of the most heroic archival endeavours of the last century,
was largely the work of one Assistant Keeper of Public Records, C. A. F. Meekings.

The most fascinating of these series of King's Bench files are the *Recorda* files,
which contain the working documents used in drawing up the accusations against
individuals which appear in the final roll. Since so many cases failed to come to trial,
full details of them were not recorded on the final roll, but copies of the accusations
nevertheless survive on the *Recorda* files. The King's Bench *Recorda* files for the
years immediately after the Peasants' Revolt include, for example, details of the
proceedings of a commission against the rebels in Essex containing much information about the early development of the revolt not recorded elsewhere, the complete
appeal of the Suffolk rebel leader John Wraw, of which there are only extracts on the
final roll, and a confession relating to a resurgence of the troubles in the autumn of
1381, also not copied elsewhere.[42] The King's Bench *Recorda* files are perhaps the
single greatest cache of unexplored documentary materials relating to late medieval
England. By about 1382 the *Recorda* files had become unmanageably bulky and it was

---

[40] A large number of images of the King's Bench rolls from 1272 onwards are available on the
Anglo-American Legal Tradition (www.aalt.law.uh.edu/AALT.html), a website established by Professor
Robert Palmer of the University of Houston in Jan. 2007, and maintained by the O'Quinn Law Library of
that university.

[41] Meekings (1978). The National Archives has also produced a useful research guide entitled *The
Records of the Court of King's Bench, c. 1200–1600*. See <www.nationalarchives.gov.uk>.

[42] Prescott (1998: 12, 16); KB 145/3/5/1; KB 145/3/6/1.

found more convenient to keep the indictments made directly by juries in the county in which the King's Bench was sitting separate from records summoned by other courts. These term indictment files were recovered from the great deposit of King's Bench sacks and files in the late nineteenth century. The term indictment files have been available to scholars since the end of the nineteenth century, having been given the misleading and, in Meekings's view, rather *fin-de-siècle* designation of Ancient Indictments. However, the process of recovering the Ancient Indictments from the mass of King's Bench files was not performed very systematically: choice documents were removed from file series; dates were assigned wrongly; and coverless files mixed up.

Despite these problems, the availability of the Ancient Indictments made scholars aware that the information in the King's Bench rolls was drawn from various other preliminary documents preserved in files. In 1931, Magdalene Weale, in an appendix listing manuscripts containing Middle English in the public records to Chambers and Daunt's *Book of London English 1384–1425*, noticed that the term indictment file for Michaelmas 1392 in the Ancient Indictments contained another version of *The Yorkshire Partisans*, which she described as a 'rebel proclamation and song'.[43] Since this was the document from which the trial record on the King's Bench roll was prepared, it represents an earlier state of the text than the version printed by Sayles. Although Weales's entry was noted by Sayles[44] and by Boffey and Edwards in their *New Index of Middle English Verse*,[45] this earliest version of the text, given above, has never previously been printed.

The term indictment file for Michaelmas 1392 contains working documents relating to the presentments made by Yorkshire juries when the King's Bench visited the county. The indictments were the result of a complex iterative process of discussion and interrogation between juries, justices, and clerks, with a number of bystanders and local bigwigs probably intervening at various points.[46] The juries did not initially produce a final polished Latin indictment. They probably made a series of informal accusations in English or French and clerks noted down details on wax tablets or scraps of vellum. On the basis of these initial exchanges, the clerks produced a rough draft of an indictment in Latin. An example of such an early draft indictment can be seen in accusations of theft, burglary, and counterfeiting against Giles Brewer and others on the Michaelmas 1392 term indictment file.[47] The names of the accused are written in a separate list in the top left-hand corner of the membrane, and annotations show that this list was used to check whether the accused had already been arrested or not. The indictment covered a number of offences and not all of those in the list were accused of participating in every incident, so the clerk cross-checked with the jurors to establish who was involved in what,

---

[43] KB 9/144 m. 31; Chambers and Daunt (1931: 276).
[44] Sayles (1971: 84 n. 3).
[45] Boffey and Edwards (2005: 106; no. 1543).
[46] Prescott (2008: 15–21).
[47] KB 9/144 m. 39.

adding some names to particular offences, and scratching out others. The clerk tinkered with the legal form of the indictment, again probably checking with the juries. One accusation related to burglary, which had to take place at night, so the clerk has inserted the word 'noctanter'. In the section of the indictment relating to the counterfeiting of money, there had not surprisingly been difficulty establishing exactly where the false money had been produced, so a place-name has been scratched out and another name substituted, with an additional catch-all interlineation 'et alibi'. Forgery was treason, so the necessary word 'proditorie' has been added to the description of the offence.

The indictment containing *The Yorkshire Partisans* was gradually pieced together in just such a fashion by the King's Bench clerks from information provided by the jury. The accusations containing the lines of *The Yorkshire Partisans* occur on the term indictment file in the midst of a long document containing the presentments of the grand jury at York which would perhaps have represented the most serious of the allegations gathered by the King's Bench during its stay in Yorkshire. The file version of the presentment comprises three membranes sewn together and is close to its final form—possibly earlier working documents may survive separately on the relevant *Recorda* file. Some final adjustment of the form of the indictment was still, however, being undertaken by the clerk, so that some essential technical phrases, such as 'with force and arms' (necessary to establish the breach of the king's peace) and 'with swords' (required to establish the seriousness of the attack) in respect of the attack on William, the servant of John Garton, were inserted at the last minute. The clerk who compiled this original indictment was the same clerk who was responsible for the section of the King's Bench rolls recording the trial of the Bulmers and Barker.

There is one immediately striking and significant difference between the file version of this case in the York grand jury indictment and the presentment as it was finally recorded in the King's Bench roll, namely that there is an additional, and very serious, indictment. The Cottingham band was accused in a separate additional indictment of trying to foment a revolt.[48] The York grand jury stated that William Bulmer, John Berwald the younger, and all the others had on 31 January 1392 with force and arms, arrayed in a war-like fashion, armed with shields, 'brestplattes', plate armour, swords, bows, and arrows, assuming royal power, against their allegiance to the Crown, had newly risen up 'de nouo insurrexerunt', a term that was used in indictments after 1381 to refer to attempts to revive the rising of that year. Interestingly, the phrase 'newly risen up', which was used in indictments to help establish that the rising was treasonable under the terms of legislation introduced after 1381,[49] is interlineated, suggesting late discussion between justices, juries, and clerks as to the exact nature of the offence. The Cottingham band were said to have had one particularly grisly standard of rebellion which harked directly back to 1381: they carried a long lance on which had been sewn a head—exactly whose head is not clear. Bearing this gruesome standard, they rode to the village of Benningholme,

[48] This incident is noted from KB 9/144 m. 31 by Bellamy (1964–5: 259; 1970: 106).
[49] Bellamy (1970: 105).

about six miles from Hull, where, treasonably arrayed as an army, they attacked the house and property of Sir Peter Buckton, the steward of Henry, Earl of Derby's household and a friend of Chaucer, to whom Chaucer later dedicated an *envoi*.[50] The Cottingham insurgents violently assaulted one of Sir Peter's servants and besieged Sir Peter's house, so that his household did not dare leave for fear of their lives. The indictment concludes by declaring that John Berwald the younger, Thomas Rawlinson, Edmund Howden, John Slater, John Tyndale (formerly Bulmer's servant), Andrew Crauncewick, William Barker, William Marshall, Steven Thomson (the first ten names in the indictment containing *The Yorkshire Partisans*), and the appropriately named John Hardlad (who did not appear in the case in King's Bench roll, but is named in the pardon) were the chief leaders of this new and treasonable insurrection. A further indictment against the same group states that three years previously, on 2 February 1389, they had attacked William Hulme, the royal escheator, while he was trying to hold a session at Hessle, so that he had been unable to collect money owing to the Crown in the lordship of Cottingham. This is then followed by the indictment containing *The Yorkshire Partisans*, in the form in which it appears in the King's Bench roll.

The initial accusations against the Cottingham band thus did not simply concern breaches of the 1390 statute against livery and maintenance but were much more serious: nothing less than rebellion, a treasonable offence. Moreover, the presenting jury goes out of its way to suggest parallels with the rising of 1381. The detail of the head sewn to the lance recalls such notorious aspects of 1381 as the procession in which the decapitated head of the archbishop of Canterbury was carried around London stuck to a pole or the incident at Bury St Edmunds in which, following the execution of John Cavendish, the Chief Justice of the King's Bench, and John Cambridge, the Prior of Bury, the Suffolk rebels, according to Thomas Walsingham, 'bore the head of the prior high on the end of a lance in full view of the townspeople, as if they were going round in a procession, until they reached the pillory. When they arrived there, to signify the friendship that had existed previously between the prior and John Cavendish, and to deride each of these persons, they most shamefully brought the heads together in turn at the tops of the lances, first as if they were whispering to each other, then as though kissing.'[51] The jury and the clerk who drew up the Cottingham indictment apparently took a lot of trouble in arriving at the precise form of words describing the detail of the lance with the mysterious head sewed to it, since there is a long erasure after this point in the indictment, suggesting that this detail was considered of importance. Memories of 1381 would have been fresh in this area of Yorkshire, since there had been major disturbances in York, Scarborough, Beverley, and Hull. Indeed, Sir Peter Buckton, whose house was attacked by the Cottingham insurgents, had been a member of a commission appointed the deal with the disturbances in Scarborough in 1381.[52]

[50] Rawcliffe (1993).
[51] Taylor *et al.* (2003: 483).
[52] Rawcliffe (1993).

In this context, it is understandable why William and Ralph Bulmer and William Barker were so anxious to have their pardons formally recorded by the King's Bench. However, the pardons issued to the Bulmers only covered the offences connected with livery and maintenance. They were pardoned for various trespasses against the peace, sworn conspiracies, assemblies, taking of fines and ransoms, issues of liveries of hoods, and assaults on royal officials such as William Hulme. The pardon did not cover treason or rebellion. William Bulmer consequently appeared separately in King's Bench to answer the allegations of treason and rebellion and pleaded not guilty to the charge of treason, as well as to a further allegation that he and his father had illegally released a man accused of murder from the stocks at Cottingham.[53] He was acquitted by the trial jury and allowed to go free. William Barker also surrendered himself to King's Bench and was also found not guilty of treason.[54] Once these charges of treason were dealt with, Bulmer and Barker were able to present their pardons for the less serious accusations concerning livery and maintenance.

The trial records in the King's Bench rolls, by dealing with these indictments separately, uncouple the lines of *The Yorkshire Partisans* from the accusations of rebellion and treason. Reunited with these allegations in the context of the original return of the York grand jury in term indictment file, the verses look far more like an insurgents' chorus. The verses' affirmation of comradeship, of all for one and one for all, appear less like an appropriation of noble discourses relating to maintenance and more as a declaration of a determination to fight to the last man against injustice. However, the York presenting jury did not link the English verses to the indictments of treason and rebellion but rather to the accusations of livery and maintenance. This may perhaps be explained by looking at the way in which these indictments were pieced together by the King's Bench clerk. The indictment concerning livery and maintenance by the Cottingham band occurs at the foot of one of the three membranes containing the presentments by the York grand jury. It breaks off just before the section describing how Berwald and the others recited the verses. The section of the indictment accusing Berwald of proclaiming the verses at Hull and Beverley begins on a new membrane. Moreover, the part of the indictment containing the verses is written on a separate piece of vellum, much smaller than the others. It looks very much as if the King's Bench clerk had separately collected the information about the verses from the jury, thought that it was in some way important, but was uncertain where it actually belonged—whether it should be placed with the indictment concerning rebellion or the indictment concerning maintenance. In the end, he decided it was best placed at the end of the indictment about the alleged maintenance, possibly because a proclamation urging an offence was considered tantamount to committing that offence. The verses were sewn to the end of the indictment accusing Bulmer and the others of breaching the 1390 statute against livery and maintenance, and the two became inextricably linked in subsequent

---

[53] KB 27/528 *rex* m. 28d.
[54] KB 27/528 *rex* m. 29d.

discussion. The original connection with allegations of treasonable insurrection was forgotten.

Did *The Yorkshire Partisans* only exist as oral verse? Were they simply a kind of gang chant which was only finally written down when the indictment was prepared? It is impossible to be certain. Since the verses and details of the circumstances of their proclamation were entered on a separate scrap of parchment when the indictment was prepared, it seems possible that they were copied by the clerk from a different note to the rest of the indictment. It is feasible that the verses had been drawn to the court's attention because somebody had handed the jurors or court officials a written copy of them. This copy may have been made from memory or may have been a copy posted as a broadside—again, there is a possibility that some further preliminary documents might yet be found on the *Recorda* file which might shed some light on this.

An open proclamation, similar to the circumstances under which *The Yorkshire Partisans* were recited at Hull and Beverley, was one of the chief means by which word of the rebellion was spread in 1381. During the 1381 rising, for example, proclamations were made in Kent ordering that no one should perform labour services and inciting attacks against particular individuals.[55] In Essex, jurors who made presentments before a commission led by the Earl of Buckingham against the rebels reported that proclamations were made at an early stage of the disturbances in many villages in southern Essex threatening those who did not join the rising with death and the burning of their property. These proclamations were accompanied by signals such as the ringing of a bell at St Osyth or the spreading of rumours such as that knights were coming to kill the villagers of Great and Little Wakering.[56] In Norfolk, proclamations were made demanding that two justices of the peace should be handed over to the rebels.[57] In Cambridgeshire, the rebel leader John Hauchach had proclamations inciting burning and destruction made across the county,[58] and in Cambridge itself a proclamation was made commanding the townsfolk to attack Barnwell Priory,[59] while at Ely, Richard Leicester, probably a butcher, entered the pulpit of Ely Abbey and proclaimed what measures he thought the rebels should take against those who had betrayed the realm.[60] In Yorkshire, the insurgents in the city of York 'made a new ordinance declaring that whenever the bells on the bridge sounded "aukeward", whether by day or night', all the commons of the city should rise together and have proclaimed various ordinances newly composed by them'.[61]

The open proclamation in 1392 of the verses protesting against the arrival of the King's courts in Yorkshire can be seen as a similar act of insurgency. Moreover, some of the lines in *The Yorkshire Partisans* may also be taken as a direct reference to

[55] JUST 1/400 mm. 1–2, printed in translation in Flaherty (1860: 71–2).
[56] KB 145/3/6/1.
[57] KB 9/166/1 m. 68.
[58] JUST 1/103 m. 4, summarized in Palmer (1895–6: 101).
[59] JUST 1/103 m. 12.
[60] JUST 1/103, m. 10, summarized by Palmer (1895–6: 212).
[61] Dobson (1983: 286).

literature associated with 1381. The phrase 'Neither of hobbe ne of Iohan' for example recalls the line in the letters attributed to the chaplain John Ball, one of the leaders of the 1381 rising in London, 'chastise wel Hobbe þe Robbere, and takeþ wiþ yow Iohan Trewman, and alle his felawes'.[62] As Barrie Dobson has commented of *The Yorkshire Partisans*, 'Hobb makes another appearance ..., and their love of "trewth" and hatred of "traytors" forms a common bond' with the rebels of 1381.[63] Indeed, the condemnation of religious orders in *The Yorkshire Partisans* makes more sense if seen as an echo of the rebellion of 1381, in which the disendowment of the Church was demanded. Although the Church figured in debates about livery and maintenance, the main focus was on the misdemeanors of the gentry and their followers, who do not figure at all in *The Yorkshire Partisans*. The message of the Yorkshire Partisans is in many ways closer to the complaints in the rebel letters of 1381 that 'falsnes and gyle haviþ regned to longe' and that 'falnes [*sic.*] regneth in everylk flokke'[64] than the protests of the parliamentary petitions against livery and maintenance.

Anxieties about popular rebellion appear to have been a particular concern of the King's Bench as it undertook investigations in Yorkshire and the East Midlands during 1392 and 1393. While it was in Derbyshire in 1393, King's Bench heard an isolated case relating to the outbreak of disturbances in 1381 at the Priory of Breadsall Park.[65] Most striking is the way in which treasonable rebellion was linked by the King's Bench and presenting juries in Yorkshire in 1392 and 1393 to public proclamations in English. The same grand jury that made the accusations against the Cottingham group also alleged that, in January 1392, more than 300 men from the lordship of Hatfield near Doncaster in South Yorkshire, arrayed and armed in a warlike fashion, rose against their allegiance, the Crown and royal estate of the king, and proceeded like traitors to Doncaster.[66] The precise legal drafting of the indictment and its close relationship to the Cottingham allegations is evident from the way in which the warlike character of the South Yorkshire insurgents is described in almost exactly the same words as for Cottingham: the Doncaster insurgents were also said to have borne shields, breastplates, plate armour, swords, bows, and so on. Once at Doncaster, these insurgents also allegedly made a proclamation in English:

We cry and comaunde on þe kynges be halue of Ingland on þe Dukes of Lancastre on þe Dukes of York and on þe lords of þis towne þat þar be noman so hardy of þis towne be vertue of any patente of þe kyng of panage grauntyd to þis towne to take any costume panage or toll of þe tenauntz of ye Dukes of Lancastre or of þe Dukes of York of payn of lesyng of hys lyf and if any man of þe foresayde towne had any panage or tolle takyn of þe te nauntz of þe Dukes forseyde þat þai schulde giffe it þaim agayn of þe peryle of þe payne be forsayde[67]

[62] Taylor *et al.* (2003: 549).   [63] Dobson (1983: 380).
[64] Martin (1995: 222).   [65] Crook (1987: 11–12).
[66] Sayles (1971: 85–7); Powell and Trevelyan (1899: 20); Bellamy (1964–5: 258–9); Bellamy (1970: 106).
[67] This is the file version of the proclamation: KB 9/144 m. 31, which has not previously been printed. Sayles (1917) and Powell and Trevelyan (1899) both printed the proclamation from the version on the King's Bench roll at KB 27/528 *rex* m. 16.

Again, just as in the Cottingham case, the indictment links this proclamation to an accusation concerning interference with royal officials. The leaders of the group who made the proclamation at Doncaster were indicted for seizing a bailiff who in 1390 attempted to execute a royal writ at Thorne. The hapless bailiff had been assaulted and imprisoned for the night in the house of the constable, where the bailiff was treated as if he was a common thief, being kept awake all night with singing and the sound of horns. Pardons were issued to the South Yorkshire insurgents for the assault on the bailiff, but the outcome of the treason allegations is not known. The Doncaster indictment again has echoes of 1381, not only in the formal use of proclamations, but also in the claim that the insurgents were acting on the king's behalf, a distinctive feature of the rebel actions in 1381. Attacks on unpopular grants of tolls and monopolies had been another prominent theme of the 1381 rising, as at Great Yarmouth in Suffolk, where an unpopular charter granting a monopoly on the sale of fish was torn in half, with one part being sent to the rebel leader Geoffrey Lister in Norfolk and the other to his Suffolk counterpart, the chaplain John Wraw.[68]

Recent discussion of the revolt of 1381 has stressed the complex relationship between the rebels and the written word. The chronicle accounts of the rising portray the burning and destruction of documents as one of the most characteristic actions of the rebels. The Anonimalle chronicle describes how, furious at the King's attempts to fob them off with a written bill containing inadequate concessions, the rebels announced throughout London 'that all men of law, and all those of the chancery and exchequer, and all who knew how to write a brief or a letter, should be beheaded wherever they might be found'.[69] As they swarmed through the chambers of lawyers in the Inns of Court in London, rebels broke open chests containing documents and smashed the seals of the records they found.[70] The ritual burning of manorial records and other documents by rebels was so widespread and distinctive that it is one means by which the mass of private litigation against the rebels in the courts of Common Pleas and King's Bench can be traced. In Essex, Ralph Wood of Bradwell took royal documents from the house of Edmund de la Mare, the king's admiral, and carried it as a trophy, impaled on a pitchfork, to Mile End.[71]

Yet, as Steven Justice has observed, 'the rebels aimed not to destroy the documentary culture of feudal tenure and royal government, but to re-create it; they recognized the written document as something powerful but also malleable, something that, once written, could be rewritten'.[72] The rebels communicated by letters written in English, and the text of some of these letters are preserved in the chronicles. Indeed, it is possible that these letters were themselves used as the basis of proclamations. Moreover, when the king finally acceded to the demands of the rebels, they demanded confirmation in writing. Charters of manumission were issued by the king

---

[68] KB 9/166/1 mm. 47, 55, 62, 76, 83–6; Holmes (1975: 114–18).
[69] Dobson (1983: 160).
[70] Thorne, Hager, Thorne and Donohue (1996: 180–3).
[71] The National Archives, KB 27/484 rex m. 1d. Extracts printed in Sparvel-Bayley (1878: 217).
[72] Justice (1994: 48).

to the rebels, which were carefully preserved even after they were cancelled. The sealed charter given to the Kentish rebels was for example kept as a memento of the revolt by a member of the local gentry.[73] It follows the same form as similar letters given to rebels from Hertfordshire and to draft letters prepared for Somerset:[74]

Richard by the grace of God King of England and France, and lord of Ireland, to all his bailiffs and faithful men to whom these present letters come, greetings. Know that by our special grace we have manumitted all our liegemen, common subjects and others of the county of Kent and have freed and quitted each of them from all bondage by the present letters. We also pardon our said liegemen and subjects for all felonies, trespasses and extortions performed by them or any one of them in whatsoever way. We also withdraw sentences of outlawry declared against them or any of them because of these offences. And we hereby grant our complete peace to them and each of them. In testimony whereof we order these letters of ours to be made patent. Witnessed by myself at London on 15 June in the fourth year of my reign.

These letters of manumission were in a correct and up-to-date legal form. A royal clerk would have been involved in their production, but in order to demand letters such as these and understand the written concessions which were offered to them, the insurgents required access to a literate culture. Some could understand the basic formulae of a legal document; others were fully literate; others relied on friends who could interpret these documents for them. This insurgent access to literacy is further illustrated by an incident on 25 June 1381, by which time the letters of manumission had been withdrawn and the suppression of the revolt was in full swing.[75] A judicial commission against the rebels was sitting at Chelmsford in Essex. John Preston of Hadleigh in Suffolk presented to the justices a petition on behalf of the commons repeating the demands which the rebels had made at Mile End. Preston was either stupid, naïve, or incredibly badly informed in repeating these demands in the midst of the bloody repression of the revolt. Preston was hauled before the justices and asked who had drawn up the petition and if anyone had assisted him. Preston said that he had drafted the petition himself and delivered it personally to the court. He was immediately executed. Preston, of course, may have been seeking to protect others when he said that he wrote this petition, but nevertheless his case demonstrates how the insurgents had access to advanced forms of literacy and were capable of operating within the framework of the documentary culture of royal law and administration. Insurgent engagement with the textual apparatus of government is also apparent at other stages of the suppression of the rising. Thus, for example, John Bettes, also known as Creek, of Wymondham, one of the most notorious rebels in

---

[73] London, British Library, Cotton Charter iv. 51, which consists of a letter written on paper in an early 15th-cent. hand addressed to Richard Bere. The transcript of the letters of manumission for Kent is followed by a series of brief notes of dates of such events as the Black Death and the Great Earthquake. According to the author of this letter, the sealed Kentish letters of manumission was at the time of writing in the possession of Henry Apoldrefeld, presumably to be identified with the associate of the Kentish sheriff William Septvanz: C 241/168/32.

[74] Taylor *et al.* (2003: 440–3); Harvey (1965).

[75] Prescott (1998: 13–15).

Norfolk who was excluded from the general amnesty to the rebels, was able to pay for the production of a petition, elegantly written in the most up-to-date hand, insisting that the charges against him had been procured by his enemies.[76]

The love–hate relationship between the insurgents and the written word is not only apparent in 1381. Rosamond Faith has described how a widespread misapprehension that peasants could secure their freedom by obtaining exemplifications of entries in Domesday Book created consternation among landowners in the 1370s.[77] In Cottingham itself, the tenants of the Princess of Wales in about 1375–6 presented to her council a petition in which they complained about the parson of Cottingham, who was attempting to interfere with the terms under which they held their land.[78] They declared that an inquisition had found that the tenants were able to alienate or sell their lands without paying any dues, but that the parson claimed that they held these lands at will and made grievous distraints upon them contrary to what was found by the inquisition. Throughout the late fourteenth and early fifteenth centuries, texts became more and more familiar and pervasive in everyday life. As they became more familiar, texts also became increasingly vehicles for protest. The Lollards were pioneers in this respect. John Aston had disseminated his views on the eucharist in London in 1392 by distributing flysheets, while in the same year Willliam Repingdon and Nicholas Hereford nailed a list of their beliefs to church doors in London.[79] In 1387–8, Lollard broadsides were again nailed to the doors of St Paul's Cathedral and Westminster Hall.[80] Such activities were not restricted to Oxford academics; in 1430 Lollard craftsmen were distributing written criticisms of the Church in Somerset and Wiltshire.[81] But, as Steven Justice notes, broadsides were also used for political and other purposes: following John of Gaunt's attack on the liberties of the City of London, broadsides in verse were posted around the city claiming that Gaunt was the illegitimate son of a Ghent butcher.[82]

The indictments describing verses of *The Yorkshire Partisans* and the proclamation made at Doncaster must be seen in the context of increasing peasant and artisan access to literacy and the social anxieties generated by this. The York presenting juries were alarmed by the way in which increasing numbers of people had access to literate means of communication and they saw this as an engine of social unrest and insurgency. The use of English proclamations, fraternal songs, and broadsides expressing discontent was seen by the jurors as a matter of particular concern. Literacy was for the jurors apparently tantamount to insurgency. 1381 casts a long shadow here, but it may be more than a shadow. The parallels between the activities of the Cottingham group and reports of the disturbances in Yorkshire towns in 1381 have already been

---

[76] SC8/262/13099. On Bettes, see further Prescott (2004: 319).
[77] Faith (1984).   [78] SC 8/333/E1025.
[79] Justice (1994: 29).   [80] Ibid.
[81] KB 9/227/2 mm. 1–2.   [82] Justice (1994: 29).

noted. There may be a more direct link. The troubles in Scarborough and Beverley took a long time to subside: Barrie Dobson suggests that 'Beverley in the later middle ages was never free from internal discord',[83] while the leaders of the 1381 disturbances in Scarborough were not finally pardoned until 1386, the very year in which the Cottingham livery was said to have been first distributed.[84] In short, it seems as if the disturbances which generated the riots in Yorkshire in 1381 perhaps never fully abated, and the Cottingham and Doncaster disturbances may be regarded as a continuation of the events of the Peasants' Revolt. By contrast, J. G. Bellamy has suggested that the activities of the Cottingham band and the disturbances at Doncaster were generated by local political conditions, and in particular by the attacks of William Beckwith on Lancastrian officials, caused by his annoyance at his failure to secure the office of Constable of Knaresborough Castle.[85] However, this is unconvincing, since the activities of the Cottingham band, at least, were said to have begun before Beckwith and his followers began their operations. Bellamy sees the Beckwith episode as a noble 'feud of the old sort which was allowed to persist in the absence of the Duke of Lancaster by officials who were disinclined or unable to compose it on their own account'.[86] Seen in the perspective of the documents in the term indictment files, the activities of the Cottingham band appear more as a social rising, reflecting many of the same tensions and themes that had been evident in 1381.

The Yorkshire Partisans in this context appears as a rebel song, from the same stable as the rebel letters of 1381. It is tempting to see these verses as another direct record of a rebel voice. However, just as with the letters attributed to John Ball, our engagement with *The Yorkshire Partisans* is heavily mediated. We only know about John Ball's letters because they were copied by chroniclers. This means that we do not know why they were composed or what use they were put to and even if they were really composed by John Ball. The chroniclers sought to portray the rebels as simple, credulous folk, possibly led astray by Lollard heretics. The inclusion of mysterious English letters bolstered such a presentation. Likewise, we only know about *The Yorkshire Partisans* because they occur in an indictment pieced together by a clerk of the King's Bench in a complex fashion from some vague allegations made by local juries. We do not know how the jurors or the clerk came by the text of the verses. We cannot even be sure that these were the verses which were proclaimed at Beverley and Hull. It was not unknown for juries to put invented words in the mouths of defendants, and it is possible that these lines were intended to convey the sort of things that the defendants might have said. *The Yorkshire Partisans* might appear in some ways to be a very direct declaration by rebels from 1392, but the text only comes to us through a heavily mediated source which may have subjected it to many profound distortions.

---

[83] Dobson (1984: 129).   [84] Ibid. 138.
[85] Bellamy (1964–5: 254–60).   [86] Ibid. 261.

THE YORKSHIRE PARTISANS AND
THE ANTIQUARIES OF HULL

As presented in the formal rolls of the King's Bench, *The Yorkshire Partisans* forms part of the literature of livery, an expression of the anxieties of the 1380s and 1390s about the disruptive impact of new forms of social relationship. Traced back into the files of the King's Bench, *The Yorkshire Partisans* appears as a song of revolt, with strong connections to the insurgency of 1381. The text of *The Yorkshire Partisans* also however descends to us by a third route, hitherto unnoticed by scholars of medieval literature, and in this context it appears in a further distinct guise, with a completely different set of cultural connections.

Thomas Gent was born in Ireland in 1693 and, having served an apprenticeship in London, became a jobbing printer in London, Dublin, and York.[87] He managed eventually through marriage to secure his own business in York. He immediately realized that local history was a good market, and his first substantial publication was *The Antient and Modern History of the Famous City of York*, which appeared in 1730. This was followed in 1734 by a similar volume on Ripon, and in the following year by his *Annales Regioduni Hullini*, a history of Hull. These were the first published histories of these Yorkshire cities. Gent's histories were aimed at the general visitor, but were not mere compilations of earlier works, and included a great deal of original research and personal observation by Gent. In his history of Hull, under his entry for Peter Steeler, the mayor in 1392, Gent adds the following note:

In the Spring Time, near a thousand Persons, belonging to Cottingham, Woolferton, Anlaby and other neighbouring Towns, being offended, that the inhabitants of *Hull*, had, by cutting the Earth, drawn some fresh Water from them; they bound themselves, with a terrible Oath, to stand by one another whilst they were able to shed their last Drops of Blood. Then, having ordained the most rustical Leaders, they appear'd in the like Sort of Arms, ransacking Houses, and abusing such Owners, who would not as madly confederate with them. Soon they did lay siege to Hull, vowing the utter Destruction of it. Being strangely poetically given too, they made such inspid Rhimes, to encourage the Seditious, as indeed would dishonour the Flights of Antiquity, should such ridiculous Stuff be publickly set forth. The Canals, which had been made at a vast Expence, they quickly fill'd up, almost as they had been before. But tho' by these Means they had spitefully deprived the Town of fresh flowing Streams, and stopt Provisions that were sent to the valiant Inhabitants; yet these ill-advised Wretches found themselves too much deluded, and withal too impotent, to prevail against them. Upon which, withdrawing to *Cottingham*; and afterwards, through Fear dispersing; some fled quite away; others, taken, and sent to *York*, were executed; and about 30 obtain'd pardon, upon their Penitence, and faithful Promise, never to attempt the like again.[88]

In 1788, an East India Company officer named George Hadley was staying in Hull. Hadley had previously published a novel and a book on oriental dialects and he was

---

[87] Tedder and Barr (2004).
[88] Gent (1735: 93–4).

approached by a Hull printer called Thomas Briggs, who asked Hadley if he was willing to put his name to a history of Hull currently being prepared for the press. Published authors were presumably thin on the ground in Hull at this time and Briggs apparently thought that Hadley's appearance on the title-page would boost the credibility of his project. Hadley's *New and Complete History of the Town and County of the Town of Kingston-upon-Hull* was published by Briggs between 1788 and 1791. Rosemary Sweet points out that Hadley's work 'is manifestly not the work of a single author, since the prose style and mode of narration show striking variation, but it is not known who else was involved in the project'.[89] This history is a work of almost aggressive urban patriotism and suffused with a partisan Whig triumphalism. Published cheaply in parts, it was aimed at the middling merchants and tradesmen of Hull. To quote Sweet again: 'Hadley, or whoever the author was, was a popularizer, deliberately going against the dry as dust tradition of local antiquarianism. He made a great point of the fact that he had not the assistance of literary gentlemen or been granted access to the manuscripts of noblemen.'[90]

The sensational story of the siege of Hull in 1392 by inhabitants of the surrounding villages was worth repeating and Hadley duly reported it as follows:

This year was revived the quarrel between the Town, and *Cottingham, Anlaby*, and the other circumjacent villages, on the subject of the fresh water canal. A number of persons, to the amount of almost a thousand of the inhabitants of those villages, being irritated by the draft of fresh water from their reservoirs, associated in a league, offensive and defensive, against the Town's-people of *Hull*, binding themselves, by the most solemn oaths, to act with fidelity to the cause, and to each other; they appointed leaders and furnishing themselves with such weapons as they could get, they invested the Town.[91]

Like Gent, Hadley notes the appearance of verses ascribed to the Cottingham insurgents, but he describes them in eighteenth-century terms as a lampoon, suggesting the kind of pamphlet that might have been found in coffee houses or taverns. This contrasts with Gent's treatment of the verses as illustrating the rusticity and backwardness of the Cottingham men. Hadley goes on to give a copy of the verses, the first time that they were printed:[92]

COPY OF VERSES.

YN the cuntre hard was wee,
Yat in our soken shrews shud bee
    with alle for to bake
Amang you ffriers yt yo so
And othur Ordurs many mo
    whether ya slep or wak
And yet will Ilk and help up othur
And maintain him als his Brother
    both in wronge and ryght:
And also will yn stond and stower

89 Sweet (1997: 243).   90 Ibid. 248.
91 Hadley (1788–91: 54).   92 Ibid.

Mantayn oure neighbour
　　　with alle our myghte
Ylk man may com and go
Amang us both to and fro
　　　say you sickerly
But hethning will wee suffer none
Neither of Hob or Johne
　　　with what may merry be
Ffor unkind wee ware
If suffur'd less or mare
　　　ony villain Hethning
But yt wer quit duble agaiane
And accoured and be full fain
　　　to byde dressing
And on yat purpose yat wee stande
Wo sal do us ony wrang
　　　in what place ih fall
Yat hee had alse weel
Alse have I hap and heel
　　　do against us elle

Although the verses as given by Hadley correspond closely to the lines in the King's Bench records, there are sufficient verbal differences to suggest that Hadley was working from a separate transcription of these verses. Hadley goes on to give a slightly different account of the conclusion to this incident to Gent:

Finding at length they were so strongly opposed, to carry their projects into execution, they retreated to Cottingham, where they encamped, and remained some time, till being dispersed by the sheriff of the county, and the *posse comitatus*, the ringleaders were taken, and some executed at *York*, at the Easter assizes following; and the rest, to the number of twenty, on their submission were pardoned.[93]

Shortly after the publication of Hadley's *History*, another much more elaborate history of Hull was published, compiled by John Tickell, a clergyman who came from Hedon, about eight miles from Hull, but who does not seem to have played an active part in Hull society.[94] Tickell's *History of the Town and County of Hull* was published in 1796 by a consortium of Hull printers and booksellers. In contrast to Hadley's work, it was aimed at the most prosperous strata of Hull society, and was handsomely printed with a flowery dedication to William Wilberforce, the local member of parliament and a native of Hull, many engravings and a subscription list of nearly 400 names, chiefly drawn from Hull itself, and apparently representing the cream of late eighteenth-century Hull. Tickell describes the 1392 siege of Hull in the most rumbustious tones yet adopted by any of the Hull antiquaries, denouncing the Cottingham insurgents as 'banditti' and declaring that they threatened to raze Hull to the ground.[95] Tickell adds that 'to prevent their ardour from subsiding, and

---

[93] Ibid. 55.　　　[94] Sweet (1997: 243).
[95] Tickell (1796: 76–8).

to encourage others to join them, they composed verses in which they magnified the glorious cause they were engaged in, and dispersed their seditious songs through the country'.[96] Tickell also reproduces the verses, in a slightly more modernized form than that given by Hadley, and adds the detail that the verses were openly sung at Beverley and elsewhere. Tickell's account of these disturbances has been repeated by Yorkshire antiquarians down to the present day, although the verses are generally not mentioned.[97] The incident was considered sufficiently serious to be included in William Grainge's chronology of battles and battlefields in Yorkshire published in 1854.[98]

These antiquarian publications suggest a completely different context for *The Yorkshire Partisans*. The incident emerges not as a reflection of wider social tensions in the late fourteenth century but rather as an expression of a local dispute about water supplies. These had been a contentious matter on Humberside for some time.[99] Hull was built on salt soil and since the thirteenth century it had been necessary for fresh water to be brought from a distance. In 1376, an inquiry was ordered into a proposal to cut a ten-foot-wide canal from Anlaby, to the south of Cottingham.[100] It appears to have been an attempt by the men of Hull to dig just such a canal which prompted the disturbances in 1392. Those engaged with the butchery trade such as John of Skidby and John Navendyke, the two fleshers named in the King's Bench indictment, would have found these fresh-water channels particularly inconvenient because they would have restricted their ability to dispose of offal and waste meat. Gent, Hadley, and Tickell drew their information about this dispute from the Bench Books of Hull, where a copy of the verses was apparently preserved. The issue of Hull's water supply continued to be a contentious one for many years. In 1402, the construction of a dyke running from a spring called Julian Well in Anlaby was authorized, provoking more protests from the inhabitants of Anlaby, Cottingham, and other nearby villages, who, according to Hadley, filled up the canal as it was dug and threw every obstacle they could in the way of the works, 'breeding a riot, beating the labourers, and doing a good deal of mischief'.[101] The protestors were seized and imprisoned in Hull and only released when they agreed to perform a penance, which included processing to the Church of the Holy Trinity with uncovered heads and bare feet, bearing wax candles which they were to present to the altar of the church. They also had to give £5 to the vicar of the church, £10 to the town chamberlain for the repair of the walls, and give sureties for their future good behaviour. Even this did not prove sufficient to prevent attacks on the canal, and in 1412 the mayor and burgesses complained to the Pope about the constant attempts to fill in the canal and poison the water supply and asked him to excommunicate the malefactors.[102] Following a papal exhortation, the attacks on the water supply seem finally to have abated.

---

[96] Ibid. 77.   [97] e.g. Sheahan and Whellan (1856: 27); Overton (1861: 25).
[98] Grainge (1854: 133).   [99] For the following, see Allison (1969: 371).
[100] *Calendar of Patent Rolls 1374–7*, pp. 324–5.
[101] Hadley (1788–91: 56).   [102] Allison (1969: 371).

In this context, disturbances associated with *The Yorkshire Partisans* appear to have been generated by specifically local concerns. This may to some extent reflect the outlook of the antiquarians who report these incidents. As Rosemary Sweet has illustrated, Hull was at the end of the eighteenth century a particularly insular and inward-looking society, with very little interest in the surrounding area.[103] The histories of Harvey and Tickell were written for local consumption and their readers would have found the story of the digging of the Julian Dyke, which was still the main source of fresh water for Hull in the eighteenth century, of more immediate interest than concerns about livery and maintenance. However, there appears to be no doubt about the severity of the disputes over Hull's water supply, and this certainly appears to be part of the cultural milieu which produced *The Yorkshire Partisans* which has not previously been noticed by commentators on these verses.

Does this mean that these verses should be dismissed as reflecting purely local concerns? This would be an overhasty conclusion. The way in which these verses connect with concerns about livery and maintenance in the late fourteenth century is evident from the context of the King's Bench case and from the direct references in the verses themselves to neighbours sticking up for each other. Likewise, the references in the verses to Hobbe and Johan do seem to point back to 1381, and even in the eighteenth century the verses were seen very much as a rebel song. Rather, the various guises which these verses assume, first in the King's Bench rolls, then in the King's Bench files, and finally in the Hull antiquarian tradition, seem to reflect the way in which the discontents of the late fourteenth century were frequently a heady mixture of general, local, and personal discontents. This can be seen in the events of 1381 in London. While the insurgents made general demands for a reform of land-holding and personal freedom in the meetings with King Richard at Mile End and Smithfield, many insurgents took the opportunity to pursue local and personal grievances. On 14 June 1381, the day when King Richard met the rebels at Mile End, Robert Allen, a city fishmonger, was said to have persuaded some Kentish rebels to destroy all the documents held by Hugh Ware, another fishmonger, relating to the disputed lease of a property near Billingsgate.[104] Allen presumably hoped that the destruction of these documents would disadvantage Ware in their litigation over this property. Walter Key, a London brewer, was said to have attempted to destroy a book known as the Jubilee Book which contained ordinances for the city government granted in 1376 to which the victualling trades objected.[105] The way in which wider political grievances became fused with local grievances at London in 1381 is succinctly demonstrated by the destruction of John of Gaunt's magnificent palace of the Savoy. While Gaunt was seen as encapsulating the failed and treacherous government which was demanding more and more taxes for an ineffective campaign against the French, he was also resented by Londoners for the allegation that in 1377 he had attempted to overthrow the city's liberties and an attempt had been made to attack the Savoy at that time.[106] This coalescence of political, social, and local grievances in 1381 was not

---

[103] Sweet (1997: 241–52).   [104] Prescott (1981: 136).
[105] Ibid. 133.   [106] Holmes (1976: 190).

restricted to the London participants in the rising. One of the largest contingents in the attack on the Savoy from outside London came from Ware in Hertfordshire, a town which had a bitter rivalry with Hertford, dominated by Gaunt's recently refurbished country residence, Hertford Castle. Before marching on London, the Ware insurgents had already ransacked Hertford Castle.[107]

The way in which medieval discontents frequently fused political, social, local, and personal grievances is also vividly illustrated in the way in which there was during 1381 a resurgence of long-standing social grievances in many different towns across the country, ranging from York and Scarborough in the north to Winchester and Bridgwater in the south. In short, the varying political and social contexts in which the verses of *The Yorkshire Partisans* appear as we pursue then from the King's Bench rolls back to the files and then to the works of the Hull antiquaries should not be surprising. The mix of political, social, and local anxieties is a characteristic late medieval brew. The potency and complexity of that brew is vividly illustrated by the rich layers of connections and contexts revealed by the different archival appearances of *The Yorkshire Partisans*.

BIBLIOGRAPHY

ALLISON, K. J. (ed.) (1969), 'The City of Kingston-upon-Hull', *The Victoria History of the Counties of England: York, East Riding*, I (Oxford: Oxford University Press for the Institute of Historical Research).

——(1979), 'Cottingham', in K. J. Allison (ed.), *The Victoria History of the Counties of England: York, East Riding*, 4 (Oxford: Oxford University Press for the Institute of Historical Research), 61–84.

BARRON, CAROLINE M. (1971), 'The Quarrel of Richard II with London 1392–7', in F. R. H. Du Boulay and Caroline M. Barron (ed.), *The Reign of Richard II: Essays in Honour of May McKisack* (London: Athlone Press), 173–201.

BELLAMY, J. G. (1964–5), 'The Northern Rebellions in the Later Years of Richard II', *Bulletin of the John Rylands Library*, 47 (1964–5), 254–74.

BELLAMY, J. G. (1970), *The Law of Treason in England in the Later Middle Ages* (Cambridge: Cambridge University Press).

BOFFEY, JULIA, and A. S. G. EDWARDS (2005), *A New Index of Middle English Verse* (London: British Library).

CHAMBERS, R. W., and MARJORIE DAUNT (1931), *A Book of London English 1384–1425* (Oxford: Clarendon Press).

CRANE, SUSAN (1992), 'The Writing Lesson of 1381', in Barbara A. Hanawalt (ed.), *Chaucer's England: Literature in Historical Context* (Minneapolis: University of Michigan Press), 201–21.

CROOK, DAVID (1987), 'Derbyshire and the English rising of 1381', *Historical Research*, 60: 9–23.

DOBSON, R. B. (1983), *The Peasants' Revolt of 1381* (2nd edn. London: Macmillan).

---

[107] Prescott (1981: 129).

——(1984), 'The Risings in York, Beverley and Scarborough 1380–1381', in R. H. Hilton and T. H. Aston (ed.), *The English Rising of 1381* (Cambridge: Cambridge University Press), 112–42.

FAITH, ROSAMOND (1984), 'The "Great Rumour" of 1377 and Peasant Ideology', in R. H. Hilton and T. H. Aston (ed.), *The English Rising of 1381* (Cambridge: Cambridge University Press), 43–73.

FLAHERTY, W. (1860), 'The Great Rebellion in Kent of 1381 Illustrated from the Public Records', *Archaeologia Cantiana*, 3: 65–96.

FLOWER, C. T. (1905), 'The Beverley Town Riots, 1381–2', *Transactions of the Royal Historical Society*, NS 19: 79–99.

GENT, THOMAS (1735), *Annales Regioduni Hullini: or, the History of the Royal and Beautiful Town of Kingston-upon-Hull* (York: Thomas Gent).

GIVEN-WILSON, CHRIS (2003), 'Richard II and the Higher Nobility', in Anthony Goodman and James L. Gillespie (ed.), *Richard II: The Art of Kingship* (Oxford: Oxford University Press), 107–28.

GRAINGE, WILLIAM (1854), *The Battles and Battle Fields of Yorkshire from the Earliest Times to the End of the Great Civil War* (York: A. Hall).

HADLEY, GEORGE (1788–91), *A New and Complete History of the Town and County of the Town of Kingston-upon-Hull* (Kingston-upon-Hull: T. Briggs).

HARVEY, B. F. (1965), 'Draft Letters Patent of Manumission and Pardon for the Men of Somerset in 1381', *English Historical Review*, 80: 89–91.

HEWLETT, MAURICE (1880), 'Two Political Songs of the Middle Ages', *The Antiquary*, 2: 202–4.

HOLMES, GEORGE (1975), *The Good Parliament* (Oxford: Clarendon Press).

JUSTICE, STEVEN (1994), *Writing and Rebellion: England in 1381* (Berkeley, Calif.: University of California Press).

KENDALL, ELLIOT (2008), *Lordship and Literature: John Gower and the Politics of the Great Household* (Oxford: Clarendon Press).

MARTIN, G. H. (1995), *Knighton's Chronicle 1337–1396* (Oxford: Clarendon Press).

MEEKINGS, C. A. F. (1978), 'King's Bench Files', in J. H. Baker (ed.), *Legal Records and the Historian* (London: Royal Historical Society), 97–139.

MUSSON, ANTHONY (2001), *Medieval Law in Context: the Growth of Legal Consciousness from Magna Carta to the Peasants' Revolt* (Manchester: Manchester University Press).

——and W. M. ORMROD (1999), *The Evolution of English Justice: Law, Politics and Society in the Fourteenth Century* (Basingstoke: Macmillan).

OVERTON, CHARLES (1861), *The History of Cottingham* (Hull: J. W. Leng).

PAGE, WILLIAM (1923), 'Bossall', in W. Page (ed.), *The Victoria History of the Counties of England: History of the County of York North Riding*, 2 (London: Constable).

PALMER, W. M. (1895–6), 'Records of the Villein Insurrection in Cambridgeshire', *The East Anglian*, NS 6: 81–4, 97–102, 135–9, 167–72, 209–12, 234–7.

PATTERSON, LEE (1991), *Chaucer and the Subject of History* (Madison: University of Wisconsin Press).

POWELL, EDWARD (1989), *Kingship, Law and Society: Criminal Justice in the Reign of Henry V* (Oxford: Clarendon Press).

POWELL, E., and G. M. TREVELYAN (1899), *The Peasants' Rising and the Lollards* (London: Longman).

PRESCOTT, ANDREW (1981), 'London in the Peasants' Revolt: A Portrait Gallery', *London Journal*, 7/2: 125–43.

——(1998), 'Writing about Rebellion: Using the Records of the Peasants' Revolt of 1381', *History Workshop Journal*, 45: 1–27.

——(2004), '"The Hand of God": The Suppression of the Peasants' Revolt of 1381', in N. J. Morgan (ed.), *Prophecy, Apocalypse and the Day of Doom: Proceedings of the 2000 Harlaxton Symposium* (Harlaxton Medieval Studies, 12; Donington: Shaun Tyas), 317–41.

——(2008), 'The Imaging of Historical Documents', in Mark Greengrass and Lorna Hughes (ed.), *The Virtual Representation of the Past* (Aldershot: Ashgate), 7–22.

RAWCLIFFE, C. (1993), 'Sir Peter Buckton', in J. S. Roskell, L. Clark, and C. Rawcliffe (eds.), *The History of Parliament: The House of Commons 1386–1421* (Woodbridge: Boydell & Brewer), i. 404–7.

ROBBINS, ROSSELL HOPE (1959), *Historical Poems of the XIVth and XVth Centuries* (New York: Columbia University Press).

SAYLES, G. O. (1959), *The King's Bench in Law and History* (Selden Society lecture; London: B. Quaritch). Repr. in *Scripta Diversa* (London: Hambledon Press, 1982).

——(ed.) (1971), *Select Cases in the Court of King's Bench under Richard II, Henry IV, and Henry V* (Selden Society, 88; London: B. Quaritch).

SCATTERGOOD, V. H. H. (1972), *Politics and Poetry in the Fifteenth Century* (London: Blandford Press).

SHEAHAN, J. J., and T. WHELLAN (1856), *The History and Topography of the City of York, the Ainsty Wapentake and the East Riding of Yorkshire*, (Beverley: John Green).

SPARVEL-BAYLEY, J. A. (1878), 'Essex in Insurrection, 1381', *Transactions of the Essex Archaeological Society*, NS 1: 205–19.

STOREY, R. L. (1971), 'Liveries and Commissions of the Peace 1388–90', in F. R. H. Du Boulay and Caroline M. Barron (eds.) *The Reign of Richard II: Essays in Honour of May McKisack* (London: Athlone Press), 131–52.

STROHM, PAUL (1992), *Hochon's Arrow: The Social Imagination of Fourteenth-Century Texts* (Princeton: Princeton University Press).

SWEET, ROSEMARY (1997), *The Writing of Urban Histories in Eighteenth-Century England* (Oxford: Oxford University Press).

TAYLOR, JOHN, WENDY CHILDS, and LESLIE WATKISS (2003), *The St Albans Chronicle 1376–1394: The Chronica Maiora of Thomas Walsingham* (Oxford: Clarendon Press).

TEDDER, H. R., C. BERNARD and L. BARR (2004), 'Thomas Gent (1693–1778)', in *The Oxford Dictionary of National Biography* (Oxford: Oxford University Press; http://www.oxforddnb.com/view/article/10519, accessed 29 Mar. 2009).

THORNE, SAMUEL E., MICHAEL HAGER, MARGARET MCVEGH THORNE, and CHARLES DONOHUE JR. (1996), *Year Books of Richard II: 6 Richard II 1382–3* (Cambridge, Mass.: Ames Foundation).

TICKELL, JOHN (1796), *The History of the Town and County of Kingston upon Hull* (Hull: Thomas Lee).

CHAPTER 17

THE GOTHIC TURN AND TWELFTH-CENTURY ENGLISH CHRONICLES

THOMAS A. BREDEHOFT

In the twelfth-century Anglo-Norman kingdom, history *mattered*. Whether one's heritage and cultural affiliations lay with the Normans, the Saxons, or the Welsh, the spirit of the times seems to have encouraged reflections on place and time—and on one's place in time—that led to a magnificent flowering of literary works that can be gathered under the generous umbrella of the historical. Such historical works span from vernacular chronicles like the *Anglo-Saxon Chronicle* on the one hand to the romance-inflected histories of King Arthur told by Geoffrey of Monmouth and his followers Wace and Layamon on the other. Somewhere in between lie a host of serious Latin historians like William of Malmesbury, Henry of Huntingdon, John of Worcester, and Gerald of Wales, to name only the most famous, as well as compilers of historically organized cartulary-histories like the *Liber Eliensis*. Modern historians and literary readers may sometimes be dubious about the varying degrees of adherence to factuality exhibited in some of these works, but in the ways all of these various authors and texts re-presented the past for their more contemporary audiences, they were all engaged in the project of historical writing.

This flowering of historical writing was roughly contemporaneous with an equally notable blossoming of book culture and literary culture in the twelfth century, as well as with the growth of what has come to be called Gothic culture more generally. It is a striking conjunction: at the same time as we see such careful attention to the past, as a key source for narratives of all sorts, we also see the long-held standard forms of the Carolingian script being actively replaced by Gothic innovations, just as we see Romanesque churches being rebuilt along Gothic lines. And while it may be impossible to prove whether or not the two twelfth-century developments were truly interdependent or not, my purpose in this essay is to at least attempt to trace ways in which they seem to be intertwined. It may well be the case that the twelfth-century historical imagination was caught up, in its own unique way, with the developments of twelfth-century Gothicism. The central link, I shall suggest, lies in the twelfth-century's seeming fascination with reproduction and reproducibility.

REPRODUCING HISTORY

In a letter to the Empress Matilda prefaced to Troyes, Bibliothèque Municipale 294 bis, William of Malmesbury suggests: 'It is true that in the old days, books of this kind were written for kings or queens in order to provide them with a sort of pattern *exemplum* for their own lives, from which they could learn to follow some men's successes, while avoiding the misfortunes of others.'[1] The notion that histories might contain models of behaviour to both emulate and avoid goes back at least to Bede's prefatory letter to Ceolwulf in his eighth-century *Historia ecclesiastica*, but in William's twelfth-century context (as I will argue), the notion of a textual 'exemplum' for a king, queen, or indeed empress to follow must have had an especially timely resonance. Interestingly, William uses another familiar trope for the purpose of historical writing in his separate prefatory letter to Earl Robert, preserved in other branches of the *Gesta Regum*'s textual history: 'Receive, therefore, most distinguished of men, a work in which you can see yourself as in a mirror; for you will understand and will agree that you were imitating the actions of the greatest princes before you even heard their names.'[2] Strikingly, both prefatory letters implicitly contextualize such modelling or mirroring in terms of genealogy: the genesis of the *Gesta Regum*, William tells Empress Matilda, lay in her own mother's interest in her more remote ancestor St Aldhelm; in the case of Earl Robert, on the other hand, 'There is no one for whom patronage of the liberal arts is more appropriate than yourself, in whom

---

[1] 'Solebant sane huiusmodi libri regibus siue reginis antiquitus scribi, ut quasi ad uitae suae exemplum eis instruentur aliorum prosequi triumphos, aliorum uitare miserias' (Mynors 1998: 6–9).

[2] 'Suscipe ergo, uirorum clarissime, opus in quo te quasi e speculo uideas, dum intelliget tuae serenitatis assentus ante summorum procerum imitatum facta quam audires nomina' (Mynors 1998: 10–13). Mynors 1998 also offers some clarification of the textual history of these letters.

combine the noble spirit of your grandfather, your uncle's generosity, your father's wisdom, whose pattern (*liniamentis*) you reproduce as their rival in activity.'[3]

To the degree that both letters draw an analogy between genealogical reproduction and the textualized mirroring or modelling of the actions of historical figures, they engage in a set of concerns that I think we can understand as characteristic of the twelfth century; the term that we ought to apply to such concerns, I shall suggest, is 'Gothic'. Specifically, William of Malmesbury's concerns with human reproduction (both genetic and behavioural) are implicitly linked in both letters to the very process of the *Gesta Regum*'s textual production and reproduction. We can see this linkage not only in William's story of Matilda's mother and her interest in Aldhelm, or in the discussion of Earl Robert's lineage, but also in the very fact that William addresses three prefatory letters to three separate parties (King David, Empress Matilda, Earl Robert): from an early stage, William imagines his audience as multiple and he imagines his book as multiplied. As we shall see, William's awareness of his work's multiple audiences, as well as the process of textual reproduction that allowed such multiple audiences to flourish, should probably be seen in the context of the twelfth century as 'the last great age of monastic book production', characterized (as Derolez suggests) by increases in both numbers of books produced and a 'spread in centres of production'.[4] Textual reproduction was a current concern, it seems, and William appears to understand the patterning or mirroring that he anticipates in his readers as imaginatively linked to the processes of both textual and human reproduction.

Though literary works had certainly been published in multiple copies before the twelfth century (one thinks immediately of King Alfred's *Pastoral Care* and the other books in his translation programme in the decade before the turn of the tenth century), Derolez's observations confirm the degree to which textual production and reproduction seem to have surged in the twelfth century. For Derolez, this phenomenon cannot be separated from the twelfth century's increasing development of a recognizable Gothic style: 'the so-called Renaissance of the Twelfth Century ... represented the birth of a new age with new religious, intellectual and aesthetic concerns'.[5] It will be one strand of my argument in this essay that the chronicle form in particular (and one should here recall the prominence of *The Anglo-Saxon Chronicle* among William of Malmesbury's sources) exhibits such powerful structural and formal parallels to the developing Gothic style that we should probably understand the chronicle form in the twelfth century as a prototypically Gothic genre.[6]

---

[3] 'Nullum enim magis decet bonarum artium fautorem esse quam te, cui adhesit magnanimatis aui, munificentia patrui, prudentia patris; quos cum emulis industriae liniamentis representes' (ibid. 10–11).

[4] Derolez (2003: 56).

[5] Ibid.

[6] I use the term 'chronicle' with an intentional ambiguity: on the one hand, our modern understanding of a chronicle as a historical text structured by an annalistic framework remains very powerful. But I include other, less annalistic histories as well, as does Chris Given-Wilson, who suggests

Although it continues to have some currency in the fields of palaeography and architecture the term 'Gothic' is currently out of fashion in literary circles, perhaps because of an anxiety that its use may call to mind the vampires and haunted cloisters of more recent literary works. Yet, as I hope to suggest here, there remains a real usefulness to the term, perhaps especially in relation to recent efforts in the literary criticism of medieval works to take into account aspects of codicology and palaeography as meaningful elements of books and texts, precisely because the term 'Gothic' seems to capture a relevant and powerful aspect of visual culture under development in the twelfth century. To the degree that the Gothic aesthetic involves visual iteration, boundedness, pointedness, compactness, and reproducibility, it is intertwined with the literary form of chronicles and chronicle manuscripts in just such a way as to generate and reflect literary developments centred on questions of translation, vernacularity, and authority with which the twelfth-century chroniclers, historians, and poets discussed here were themselves concerned.

My argument's second strand, by contrast, will focus on a seemingly divergent dynamic in twelfth-century historiography: the development of non-annalistic histories of Britain, from Geoffrey of Monmouth to Layamon. To the degree that modern scholars often refer to such histories of Britain as chronicles (through such familiar terms as 'Brut chronicle'), we implicitly see such texts as connected somehow to the tradition of annalistically organized chronicles. As I shall suggest, such a linkage is implicit in the 'history of Britain' genre from Geoffrey's time onward, and even winkingly acknowledged in Geoffrey's famous postscript, with its references to William of Malmesbury and Henry of Huntingdon, both of whom rely so heavily on chronicle sources for their own histories. Though the separate strands of my argument might seem to have little enough connection, what draws them together is the relation of each to the developing Gothic aesthetic, its investment in issues of reproduction and reproducibility, and its textual implications. This is not to say that all literary (or other) productions of the period were determined by a Gothic aesthetic, but rather that twelfth-century Gothicism involved an interesting set of homologies across various forms and genres, and that those homologies, especially as they manifest themselves in chronicles and histories, demand our attention.

THE GOTHICISM OF THE CHRONICLE FORM

In *The Palaeography of Gothic Manuscript Books*, Albert Derolez takes a position that he acknowledges has often been approached with scepticism:

that most medieval historians 'would not have quibbled at being described as chroniclers, and there is no very good reason for us to desist from describing their works as chronicles' (Given-Wilson 2004: p. xix).

the similarities between full-grown Gothic script and Gothic codicological features, on the one hand, and Gothic architecture on the other, are too numerous to be fortuitous, and each must be considered an expression of the same aesthetic, of a 'Gothic taste' or 'Gothic mood'. It is expressed in verticality, compactness, angularity, pointedness, closedness and framing, and uniformity. It is a systematic and intellectual approach that sacrificed clarity for style.[7]

Indeed, as Derolez notes, 'the changes in script predate those in architecture', taking place in the twelfth century, and likely originating in 'the Anglo-Norman kingdom',[8] perhaps with a specific contribution from earlier Anglo-Saxon script and practice. These changes in script, then, must be virtually simultaneous with the work of Anglo-Norman historians like William of Malmesbury, Henry of Huntingdon, John of Worcester, and even Geoffrey of Monmouth, all of whom were working in the third and fourth decades of the twelfth century.[9] Although Gothic script developments were far from instantaneous, the synchronicity of these authors' interest in historical writing and chronicles and the development of the Gothic script is notable. And it is striking that chronicles, in particular, are characterized by formal issues that seem to have anticipated Gothic developments.

We can begin our examination of the aesthetic connections between twelfth-century chronicles and the Gothic style through careful consideration of a single manuscript. Chronologically, Oxford, Bodleian Library, Laud Misc. 636, the Peterborough manuscript of the *Anglo-Saxon Chronicle*, must have been copied soon after 1122.[10] This manuscript is, of course, the poster child for the continuation of the Old English *Chronicle* into the twelfth century, though at least two other centres besides Peterborough must have had their own traditions of early twelfth-century chronicling in Old English.[11] The annals on most pages of Laud Misc. 636 are written in a single column across the width of the page, with annal numbers (each placed at the beginning of a new line) written in red and extending into the left-hand margin (by the width of 'A' in 'Anno' up until the year 1000, when it is replaced by the 'M' of 'Millesimo'). The text of each new annal usually begins almost half-way across the writing space, often a noticeable distance to the right of the end of the annal number itself; blank space also often usually appears at the end of individual annals. Most annals begin with a small capital letter which has often been infilled with red. Each annal, then, is clearly demarcated from the others in spatial terms, the look of the page (and indeed of the book itself) dominated by the repeated presence of red

[7] Derolez (2003: 70).   [8] Ibid.

[9] Indeed, one of Derolez's earliest examples of 'Praegothica' script (his pl. 4) is from a text by William of Malmesbury, copied at Malmesbury before 1137.

[10] The Peterborough (E) MS of the *Anglo-Saxon Chronicle* has been most recently edited by Irvine 2004. See also the facsimile edited by Whitelock (1954).

[11] Besides the Peterborough *Chronicle* itself, a single leaf (labelled manuscript H by Plummer) survives containing parts of Old English annals for the years 1113 and 1114 in London, British Library, Cotton Domitian ix, fo. 9. Of course, the 1121 *Chronicle* copied in Peterborough must have also been a living chronicle: 'the archetype of E on which the Peterborough scribe drew existed as a single exemplar' (Irvine 2004: p. lxxxv). Irvine 2004 also notes that copies identical to or very close to the immediate exemplar of E appear to have been used by the Waverly Annals, Henry of Huntingdon, and probably John of Worcester as well.

annal numbers and accompanying blank spaces. In Derolez's terms, each annal thus has a remarkably uniform presentation, one characterized by its cohesiveness or compactness and its presence within a visual frame; the extension of the annal indicators into the left-hand margin adds a pointed, projecting effect to the beginning of each entry.[12] If we see in the Gothic aesthetic a tendency towards visual iteration and repetition (familiar at the levels of both architecture and script, I believe, though not among the specific characteristics listed by Derolez), the annalistic form of the *Anglo-Saxon Chronicle* (as it appears here and in its other manuscripts) corresponds to what we know of the Gothic visual style to a remarkably high degree. Indeed, the Gothic fascination with iteration and repetition also underlies the focus on reproduction and mirroring or modelling seen in William of Malmesbury's prefatory letters.

The page layout used in Laud Misc. 636, of course, has a long series of antecedents in earlier manuscripts of the *Anglo-Saxon Chronicle*, including the Parker manuscript, Cambridge, Corpus Christi College, 173, dating from the late ninth or early tenth century; the close correspondence between the visual style of the *Chronicle* and the Gothic aesthetic may be only fortuitous.[13] On the other hand, it is at least suggestive enough to raise the possibility that the continuing popularity of the Old English *Chronicle* so far into the Norman period may derive from its very compatibility with the Gothic aesthetic.[14] It is probably not out of place to recall, in this context, that William of Malmesbury, Henry of Huntingdon, and John of Worcester all used the *Anglo-Saxon Chronicle* fairly extensively in their Latin works, and that, at the moments they made use of the *Chronicle*, it was anything but a mere archaic curiosity: Henry of Huntingdon, writing in the late 1120s, seems to have used a *Chronicle* manuscript extending at least to 1121 (possibly the immediate ancestor of the Laud manuscript); William of Malmesbury and John of Worcester were apparently working even earlier in the 1120s, and both made use of *Chronicle* manuscripts, as Plummer's edition made clear over a century ago. Whatever else we say, with at least two branches apparently surviving into the 1120s (with another making it at least to 1114) and with three such prominent historians as readers, the *Anglo-Saxon Chronicle* must have continued to exert a palpable cultural presence, one possibly enhanced by the *Chronicle*'s compatibility with the developing Gothic aesthetic. Though the case is almost surely impossible to prove, one begins to wonder whether the *Anglo-Saxon Chronicle*'s formal boundedness, the vertical, visual iterations of its structure, and the boxy uniformity of the individual annals all may have themselves contributed to the twelfth century's developing aesthetic trends even if the

---

[12] The emphasis on verticality can be seen, perhaps, in the sparse early annals of fos. 1^v to 7^v, where a dual-column layout is employed.

[13] On the layout of the *Anglo-Saxon Chronicle* manuscripts, see Bately (1988).

[14] Recent work on the 12th-cent.'s investment in Old English literature, however, suggests that we need offer no special explanation for the 12th-cent. continuations of the *Chronicle*, which take their place alongside numerous other Old English texts copied and composed in the century and more after the Norman Conquest. See the essays collected in Swan and Treharne (2000); Swan (2006); Treharne (2006).

Peterborough manuscript itself does not seem to have been especially well used in the decades following its production.

Certainly, some of the most Gothic aspects of the *Anglo-Saxon Chronicle*'s form and even content were adapted and furthered by John of Worcester in his Latin *Chronicle*. This chronicle effectively integrates material from the *Anglo-Saxon Chronicle* into a world chronicle compiled on the Continent by Marianus Scotus around 1076 (Darlington and McGurk 1995: ii, p. xviii); in its conception, then, John of Worcester's chronicle evidences a taste for accretion and augmentation that might itself be seen as Gothic in its effects.[15] Even more remarkable, however, is the opening of Oxford, Corpus Christi College 157 (which is plausibly John's own book, as it seems to include a continuation in his own hand to 1140). The chronicle itself, as Darlington and McGurk's summary of this manuscript's contents indicates, begins only on p. 77 of this 396-page book. The initial sections of the book include a large number of texts and lists relevant to establishing chronology: genealogies, consular tables, lists of popes and bishops, and computistical materials. Importantly, however, the Anglo-Saxon genealogical material includes items such as the one Darlington and McGurk describe as a 'Genealogical tree from Adam to the sons of Woden, six of whom are named as ancestors of the royal dynasties of Kent, East Anglia, Mercia, Deira, Wessex (with Bernicia) and Lindsey'.[16] At least part of this information (specifically, the genealogical material from Adam to Woden) probably derives from the *Anglo-Saxon Chronicle* itself (or, possibly, from Asser), where it always appears in narrativized form. The visual structuring of genealogies into trees (and, more generally, into tabular or columnar form) must have also appealed to the developing Gothic mindset in the early twelfth century (a similar process operated in the *Textus Roffensis*), and the use of textual space on many of the initial pages of OCCC 157 (and other copies of John's *Chronicle*) offers numerous examples of the Gothic tendencies towards boundedness, compactness, verticality, and visual iteration.[17]

Given these examples, one cannot help but think of the later twelfth-century example of Richard Fitzneal's now-lost *Tricolumnis*, which Andrew Prescott describes as 'a work on Henry II arranged in three columns, one describing the affairs of the English Church, another the deeds of Henry and the third other events of interest' (Prescott 1998: 255). This work, which was apparently structured as a chronicle, also must have made striking use of the Gothic penchant for verticality (its three columns

---

[15] These tastes, again, appear to be implicit in the chronicle form itself, at least as reflected in English chronicles.

[16] Darlington and McGurk (1995: II, xxvi).

[17] To be precise, narrativized genealogies and tabular or columnar genealogies usually occupied somewhat separate spaces in Anglo-Saxon culture, with the narrativized genealogies closely associated with historical texts, as in the *West Saxon Regnal Table* (ed. Dumville 1986) and the *Anglo-Saxon Chronicle*. The so-called Anglian collection of genealogies in London, British Library, Cotton Vespasian B. vi was presented in tabular form, as were the lists in Cambridge, Corpus Christi College, 183. Such a presentation may have influenced the scribe of London, British Library, Cotton Tiberius B. v, who also uses a columnar layout, though he (like John of Worcester) also de-narrativized some genealogies (in this case, from the *West Saxon Regnal Table*; fo. 22ʳ, col. 4) to put them into a proto-Gothic tabular form. For recent discussion of the lists in this MS, see Stodnick (2006).

echoing the increasing Gothic predilection for writing Latin in multiple columns on the page) and boundedness (in this case, relegating three types of historical data to three separate physical areas on the page).[18] If nothing else, the example of the *Tricolumnis* suggests just how radically the Gothic approach could reconfigure the activity of chronicling itself.

It is useful, however, to return to a consideration of some of the differences between the *Chronicle* of John of Worcester and the *Peterborough Chronicle*. Specifically, we must attend to the obvious linguistic differences: John's *Chronicle* is in Latin, while the *Peterborough Chronicle* is in English. This linguistic dynamic, far from being a mere curiosity or accident, is almost certainly also implicated in the emergent Gothicism of the twelfth century.

Crucially, the Englishness of the *Peterborough Chronicle* is surely aligned with its other most striking feature: the inclusion of a number of (generally spurious) local Peterborough charters.[19] These added charters powerfully assert the localization of this particular copy of the *Anglo-Saxon Chronicle*, with the resulting implication of the *Peterborough Chronicle*'s localized audience: it was written not only at Peterborough, but for Peterborough. The linkage between local chronicling activity and the recording of charters or the production of cartularies is, in fact, somewhat of a twelfth-century commonplace; Sarah Foot has recently written, for example, that 'English abbeys, such as Abingdon in Berkshire or Ramsey and Ely in Cambridgeshire, produced texts that so fused historical account with copies of records concerning lands and rights that these have been called "monastic cartulary-chronicles"'.[20] But in both its Englishness and its conspicuous localization, the *Peterborough Chronicle* must be understood as clearly exemplifying a set of linked twelfth-century concerns about place and time.[21] More importantly for my argument here, the specific configuration of these concerns, in the case of the Old English *Peterborough Chronicle* (and to a lesser degree in Latin books like the *Liber Eliensis*), operates primarily in regard to a local (rather than national or international) audience.

The *Chronicle* of John of Worcester (like the *Gesta Regum* of William of Malmesbury), on the other hand, appears to have been designed with just such a national or international audience in mind. Just as William's prefatory letters and the number of copies of the *Gesta Regum* suggest a broad audience for that work, Gransden suggests that 'Soon after 1130, copies of [John of Worcester's] chronicle to the end of 1130 were made for the abbeys of Abingdon, Bury St Edmunds, Peterborough and Gloucester.'[22] A further copy apparently made its way to Durham, where it was used in the

---

[18] For another notable and familiar 12th-cent. example of columnar layout and bounding, see Eadwine's Psalter.

[19] The *Peterborough Chronicle*, of course, is far from a monolingual document, including a number of Latin annals as well as using the Latin chronological framework employed throughout the *Anglo-Saxon Chronicle*. The Peterborough Chronicle manuscript became trilingual in the later 13th cent. with the addition of a French chronicle to the margins of fos. 86^v to 90^v.

[20] Foot (2006: 43–4); see also Barrow (2006).

[21] Sheppard (2004: 146–53).

[22] Gransden (1974: 148).

production of the *Historia Regum* attributed to 'Simeon' of Durham.[23] Though Gransden identifies a small amount of local Worcester material in John's *Chronicle*, she acknowledges that 'up to the early twelfth century the focus is kept pretty well on national events';[24] the reproduction and dispersal of copies of John's *Chronicle* and its national focus presumably go hand-in-hand, just as with William of Malmesbury's *Gesta Regum*.

Importantly, as I suggested above, it appears to be the case that the very immediate proliferation of manuscript copies, for both William of Malmesbury's *Gesta Regum* and John of Worcester's *Chronicle*, is itself a manifestation of the twelfth-century Gothic aesthetic, in which the iterative duplication of texts and books echoes the iterative qualities of Gothic script and architecture.[25] These are works always intended to be presented to the public in multiple physical books. Indeed, the coexistence of local productions like the *Peterborough Chronicle*, on the one hand, and 'publications' like John of Worcester's *Chronicle*, on the other, appears to reflect the existence of two distinct ideologies of manuscript textuality. One of these ideologies sees the making of a physical book as an act of production, undertaken for a singular (often local) audience, while the other, contrastingly, understands the making of a physical book as an act (at least in potential) of reproduction. Presumably, then, the *Peterborough Chronicle*'s use of English and its use of local charters both relate to its status as a (singular) production, and (of course) there is no evidence that it was itself ever copied (reproduced) in the Middle Ages: although the *Peterborough Chronicle*'s visual appearance may have had similarities to the developing Gothic style, the *Peterborough Chronicle* never partook of the Gothic penchant for reproducibility, precisely because of its local purpose and function. Contrastingly, John of Worcester's *Chronicle*, in its Latinity and its general focus on national events, was eminently suitable (and, indeed, probably intended) for widespread reproduction, a fact that seems clearly reflected in the fact of its actual dissemination. Both models of textuality—the model of book-as-production and the model of book-as-reproduction—were current throughout the Middle Ages, but it is my contention in this chapter that the twelfth century's developing Gothic aesthetic had an especial affinity for the book-as-reproduction model. The very success of Gothic script, we might note, must probably be connected to the widespread and rapid dissemination of manuscripts in the twelfth century.

In the light of the 'book-as-reproduction' ideological model, William of Malmesbury's prefatory letters, with their linkages of notions of mirroring, modelling, and genetic descent come into sharper focus as crystallizing a set of paradigmatically Gothic concerns. As far as William's letters are concerned, the publication of his work

---

[23] Ibid.

[24] Ibid. 147.

[25] In the 13th cent., Gothic iterativeness would result in the development of the *pecia* system of manuscript reproduction (Derolez 2003: 30), which emphasized (in its dismantling effects) the mechanical aspects of copying and the constructed nature of books (as Gothic script itself powerfully organized the constructed nature of individual letters). The rapid multiplication of 12th-cent. chronicles, especially works organized annalistically, might plausibly be seen as contributory towards the *pecia* system's understanding of texts and books as separable and composite.

is a matter of textual reproduction, and the mirroring, modelling, and copying of *exempla* that will take place in his readers clearly involves a further sort of imaginative reproduction of his text in the minds or characters of his readers. To the degree that twelfth-century chronicles and histories reflected the *Anglo-Saxon Chronicle*'s effect as a family chronicle (thus implicitly concerned with genealogy and lineage), such a concern also marks much (although not all) twelfth-century history writing and chronicling as almost overdetermined in its Gothicism.[26]

GOTHIC REPRODUCTION AND THE HISTORY OF BRITAIN

Although they were widely and quickly disseminated, as we have seen, it is nevertheless interesting to recall that one of the earliest readers of both William of Malmesbury's *Gesta Regum Anglorum* and Henry of Huntingdon's *Historia Anglorum* was Geoffrey of Monmouth. Both authors are directly referenced in an epilogue of Geoffrey's *Historia Regum Britanniae*:

The Saxon kings [I leave] to William of Malmesbury and Henry of Huntingdon; however, I forbid them to write about the kings of the Britons, since they do not possess the book in British which Walter, archdeacon of Oxford, brought from Brittany.[27]

The existence or non-existence of Geoffrey's British book has long been a matter of debate and dispute, as has been the overall import of Geoffrey's reference here to William and Henry. Valerie I. J. Flint's assessment provides a compelling reading of Geoffrey's knowledge of (and reliance upon) both William and Henry, and her comment about Geoffrey's relationship to William is especially revealing: 'William of Malmesbury's work was used by Geoffrey in a manner that closely resembles deliberate teasing abuse, and teasing abuse directed at least in part at William's monastic sources'.[28] Clearly, what lies at the heart of Geoffrey's claim about the British book is the issue of its status as a source: William and Henry, Geoffrey suggests, should steer clear of British history because they do not have the British book that Geoffrey has, even if they implicitly do have Geoffrey's own putatively reliable translation of it in his 'rustic style'.[29] William's and Henry's lack of access to the key information on British kings is simultaneously supported by their not possessing the British book and utterly undermined by Geoffrey's own claim to translate that very book in a simple, rustic style.

---

[26] See Sheppard (2004).
[27] 'Reges uero Saxonum [permitto] Willelmo Malmesberiensi et Henrico Huntendonensi, quos de regibus Britonum tacere iubeo. cum non habeant librum illum Britannici sermonis quem Walterus Oxenefordensis archidiaconus ex Britannia aduexit' (Reeve and Wright 2007: 280–1).
[28] Flint (1979: 454).
[29] 'Agresti . . . stilo'; Reeve and Wright (2007: 4–5).

Another way of describing the opposition that structures this aspect of Geoffrey's claims regarding the British book is to note that the distinction is drawn between a singular, localized vernacular book, on the one hand, and a widely distributed and reproduced Latin book, on the other. Thus Geoffrey thematizes the current twelfth-century Gothic dynamics of textual production and reproduction in a fashion quite different from William's deployment of those very issues in his own prefatory letters. Surely, however, Geoffrey would have approved of William's own words in the prologue to the first book of the *Gesta Regum*: 'let [the reader] be warned that I guarantee the truth of nothing in past time except the sequence of events; the credit of my narrative must rest with my authorities' (Mynors 1998: 17).[30] Chief of these authorities for the period between Bede and Eadmer, as William admits, is a vernacular authority, the *Anglo-Saxon Chronicle*: 'some records in the form of annals in the mother tongue'.[31] Surely one of the effects of Geoffrey's claims about the British book is to call our attention to the degree that a work like William's *Gesta Regum* demands of its readers a great deal of trust, in that the reader may well not have access to the sources that allow an estimation of their reliability. Our own knowledge of the manuscript tradition of the *Anglo-Saxon Chronicle* reminds us that no one manuscript contains a complete record, but that knowledge, of course, is made available to us precisely through the modern reproduction of *Chronicle* texts and the acts of collation that that reproduction makes possible. In the twelfth century, as Geoffrey seems to have understood, few of William's readers would have been able to collate the *Gesta Regum* with its sources in order to evaluate William's reliability, if only because manuscripts of the *Anglo-Saxon Chronicle* were not as widely distributed as the *Gesta Regum* itself.[32] And if readers were not literate in Old English (or, worse yet, Welsh or British, in the case of Geoffrey's readers), collation would be ruled out even if they did have a relevant manuscript at hand. Despite William's claim that his text rests on the authority of his sources, most readers of the *Gesta Regum* were forced to rely as heavily on the authority of William himself as the readers of the *Historia Regum Britanniae* had to rely on Geoffrey's authority for the accurate reporting of the content of his source.

In this sense, the question about whether or not Geoffrey's ancient British book ever existed or not is a red herring, since the crucial issue for Geoffrey's readers is that they were unlikely to have had access to it under any circumstances. For modern readers and medieval readers alike, separate access to Geoffrey's British book would be useful only to assess the degree to which his translation of it is faithful: even if we had it in hand today, it would not make the events reported in the *Historia* any more or less historically plausible, especially if the translation is accurate. That is,

---

[30] 'Sciat me nichil de retro actis preter coherentiam annorum pro uero pacisci; fides dictorum penes auctores erit' (Mynors 1998: 15–16).

[31] 'Uetustatis inditia cronico more et patrio sermone' (Mynors 1998: 14).

[32] Although simple numbers do not attest to the complexities of the MS tradition, Mynors 1998 lists some thirty-six MSS in the list of sigla (xxix–xxx), seventeen of which appear to date from before 1200, compared to the eight surviving MSS of the *Anglo-Saxon Chronicle*.

Geoffrey's British book would be valuable for the purposes of history only if Geoffrey is not a faithful translator; the paradox here is that the more reliable Geoffrey (or, by implication, William) is, from a historian's perspective, the more the source becomes unnecessary, because the historian's own authority guarantees the quality of the translated text; only when the translation is unreliable does the separate authority of the source make a difference, and it can manifest that authority only through the act of collation. In this sense, Geoffrey's invocation of the ancient British book simply points up the degree to which William's readers (and readers of Henry of Huntingdon and John of Worcester, of course) were physically (and perhaps linguistically) cut off from the sources that supposedly granted all of these historical texts their authority. The truth claim is of value only if readers trust the person who makes it, and the very inaccessibility of Geoffrey's book is what brings that dynamic into its clearest focus.

In other words, Geoffrey of Monmouth's *Historia Regum Britanniae*, from this perspective, interrogates the developing twelfth-century Gothic aesthetic and its concerns with reproduction and iteration, and it does so by pointing out the paradoxical effect of treating Latin translations of vernacular texts as reproductions, rather than productions. That the *Historia* itself seems to have been intended for rapid dissemination in fact reveals the degree to which the source itself is irrelevant for the Gothic machinery of textual reproduction.[33] The fact that Geoffrey's own book was, in relatively short order, translated into the major vernaculars of England, first by Wace and then, ultimately, by Layamon, allows us to trace an especially intriguing strand of the impact of Geoffrey's ideas about sources and translations as the effects of this Gothic perspective gained momentum.

Wace's Anglo-Norman translation of Geoffrey's *Historia*, the *Roman de Brut*, is interesting in this context for the way it almost entirely avoids the questions of translation, reproduction, and authority that occupy Geoffrey. Apparently completed in 1155,[34] Wace's long poetic translation dives right into its matter with only the briefest introduction:

Whoever wishes to hear and to know about the successive kings and their heirs who once upon a time were the rulers of England—who they were, whence they came, what was their sequence, who came earlier and who later—Master Wace has translated it and tells it truthfully.[35]

---

[33] Geoffrey's book was an enormous and immediate success; over 200 MSS of the *Historia Regum Britanniae* survive, 'perhaps a third of them written before the end of the [twelfth] century' (Reeve and Wright 2007: p. vii). Notably, one MS, London, British Library, Royal 13 D. II, contains especially correct 12th-cent. copies of both Geoffrey's *Historia Regum Brtanniae* and William of Malmesbury's *Gesta Regum* (Reeve and Wright 2007: p. xvi).

[34] Weiss (2002), l. 14865.

[35] 'Ki vult oïr e vult saveir / De rei en rei e d'eir en eir / Ki cil furent e dunt il vindrent / Ki Engleterre primes tindrent, / Quels reis i ad en ordre eü, / E qui anceis e ki puis fu, / Maistre Wace l'ad translaté Ki en conte la verité' (Weiss 2002: ll. 1–8).

Obviously, this introduction is largely a summary of the contents of the poem that follows. Like Geoffrey, Wace announces his status as translator and asserts the truthfulness of his own version, but he fails to offer even the briefest comment on what exactly he is translating. Possibly, this choice results simply from the great popularity of the *Historia Regum Britanniae*, which presumably meant that Wace's source would have been obvious to all but the most obtuse readers.

Even so, it seems likely to be the case that Wace's disengagement from the tactics and topics raised by Geoffrey's introduction and its claims to rely on the British book may relate to Wace's use of a vernacular language. Likewise, we should probably note that while the *Roman de Brut* had a notable medieval popularity, of the twenty-nine surviving manuscripts and fragments listed in Weiss's edition, only one manuscript and one fragment date from the twelfth century; the *Roman de Brut*'s popularity seems greatest in the thirteenth and fourteenth centuries, but not the twelfth. If, as in the case of the *Peterborough Chronicle*, the vernacularity of Wace's text suggests that its twelfth-century context was a small and localized one, it may well have had the character of a production rather than a reproduction, and the Gothic concerns of Geoffrey's own prologue would have been out of place, precisely because such vernacular productions lay outside the conceptual domain of Gothic reproduction. If Layamon is correct that Wace's poem was presented to Eleanor of Aquitaine,[36] it may never have been intended for any wider audience at all.

But, as is clear, Wace's *Roman de Brut* did eventually find an audience in Layamon, who translated it into an English poem around the end of the twelfth century.[37] Remarkably, Layamon's introductory section, unlike Wace's, does, in fact, provide us with a Geoffrey-esque truth claim about his reliability as a translator and the nature of his sources:

Layamon journeyed widely among the people and acquired the noble books that he took as exemplars. He took the English book that Saint Bede made; he took another book in Latin that Saint Albin and the fair Augustine (who brought baptism here) made. He took a third book and put it between them that a French clerk made. He was named Wace, who could write well.[38]

Layamon's claim to have compiled these three books into one,[39] however, has proved to be a challenge for modern readers. Not only has there been a great deal of difficulty in identifying precisely what these three books might have been, but a collation of Layamon and Wace shows pretty conclusively that Wace was the only source Layamon used for the bulk of the contents of his narrative, although Layamon

---

[36] *Brut*, Caligula manuscript, Brook and Leslie (1963–78, ll. 22–3).

[37] Françoise Le Saux, in her review of previous opinions, inclines towards the view that Layamon's *Brut* 'was written between 1185 and 1216' (1989: 10).

[38] 'Laȝamon gon liðen.~ wide ȝond þas leode. / & bi-won þa æðela boc.~ þa he to bisne nom. / He nom þa Englisca boc.~ þa makede Seint Beda. / An-oþer he nom on Latin.~ þe makede Seinte Albin. / & þe feire Austin.~ þe fulluht brohte hider in. / Boc he nom þe þridde.~ leide þer amidden. / þa makede a Frenchis clerc.~ / Wace wes ihoten.~ þe wel couþe writen' (Brook and Leslie: Caligula manuscript, I, ll. 14–21; my tr.).

[39] *Brut*, Caligula manuscript, Brook and Leslie (1963–78: l. 28).

occasionally also used other sources not listed in his introductory section, including Geoffrey of Monmouth and possibly the *Anglo-Saxon Chronicle*.[40]

As such, Layamon's claim to use three sources (by four authors) in three different languages must be more important, in some sense, than the actual sources he did or did not use. To put Layamon's claim into the terms of my discussion here, Layamon claims his poem is a kind of de-production, in which he reverses the effects of multiplicative textual reproduction, collapsing three books, three languages, and four authorities all into one. That he does so in a poem that displays so clearly its 'antiquarian sentiments' (to use E. G. Stanley's phrase) as an aspect of its vernacularity serves to indicate, I think, how clearly Layamon is aware of the very contemporary issues of Gothic textuality raised by Geoffrey's prologue.

And, of course, Layamon's poem never achieved anything like the popularity of Geoffrey's *Historia* or even Wace's *Roman*: all that survive of Layamon's work are two thirteenth-century manuscripts, preserving two quite distinct versions. One text, preserved in London, British Library, Cotton Caligula A. ix, is usually seen as the better version, closer to Layamon's original, while the text in London, British Library, Cotton Otho C. xiii, partly damaged in the Cotton fire of 1731, is 'inferior to the Caligula text both in terms of material conservation and literary value'.[41] The opinion about literary value rests largely upon the fact that the Otho scribe is understood to both abbreviate and update the language of the poem; his possible work as an abbreviator can be seen in the Otho version of the preliminary passage printed above from Caligula, which reads:

Layamon travelled as widely as was the land, and took the English book that Saint Bede made. He took another that Saint Albin made. He took a third book, and put it between them, that Augustine made, who first brought baptism here.[42]

Certainly, the Otho version is shorter than the Caligula version, but the change in its effect is notable. Le Saux implies (apparently following Madden's logic) that the elimination of Wace as a source here derives from confusion on the Otho scribe's part, but surely it makes more sense to see that the Otho version claims three sources, none of which is actually a source for the poem in any straightforward sense, and none of which is easily identifiable. The non-appearance of Wace as a claimed source serves to radically hinder any attempt at collation or source evaluation on the reader's part; in that sense, the Otho version of this introductory section more closely mirrors the effects of Geoffrey's original prologue.

However our literary tastes respond to the Otho version on the whole, the radical differences between the Otho and Caligula versions do make one thing abundantly clear: at least one of the scribes—and probably both—saw his or her job as producing

---

[40] See Bredehoft (2005: 115–20) Le Saux (1989: ch. 5).
[41] See Le Saux (1989) referencing A. C. Gibbs, 13.
[42] 'Loweman gan wende. so wide was þat londe. / and nom þe Englisse boc. þat makede Seint Bede. / Anoþer he nom of Latin. þat makede Seint Albin. / Boc he nom þan þridde. an leide þar amidde. / þat makede Austin. þat follo[s]t bro[s]te hider in' (Brook and Leslie 1963–78: ll. 14–19; my tr.).

a text, rather than reproducing one. Layamon's *Brut*, with its abundant archaisms and difficulties, as well as its vernacularity, was always unlikely to have been designed for a widespread and multiple audience, and in both the rarity of surviving copies and their treatment by their scribes, we can see that it always remained in the realm of a literary production, one that perhaps never aspired to the status of a widely reproduced and published text. Layamon's Geoffrey-esque prologue, with its implicit interrogation of the nature of sources and translation, was ahead of its time for an English text, and ultimately perhaps in conflict with the *Brut*'s own existence as a textual production and not a reproduction. The heyday of Gothic vernacularity, in England at least, would not begin in earnest until the thirteenth century; the evidence of Layamon's *Brut* seems to suggest that the vernacular text was still not really suitable for widespread publication as a Gothic reproduction, even well into the thirteenth century.

Conclusions

In the Epilogue to his *Historia Anglorum*, finished, as he put it, in 'the 135th year of the second millennium [1135]' ('secundo millenario . . . centesimo tricesimo quinto anno',[43] Henry of Huntingdon includes a remarkable address to his potential future readers:

Now I speak to you who will be living in the third millennium, around the 135th year . . . I, who will already be dust by your time, have made mention of you in this book, so long before you are to be born, so that if—as my soul strongly desires—it shall come about that this book comes into your hands, I beg you, in the incomprehensible mercy of God, to pray for me, poor wretch.[44]

Following closely upon the heels of Henry's *ubi sunt* discussion of those living a thousand years before his time, this passage suggests that Henry hopefully imagines at least a possibility of lasting renown unachieved (and, perhaps, unachievable) by the 'archdeacons of that time', a thousand years before his own ('illius tempore archidiaconi').[45]

And while Henry, here, does not make explicit use of the logic of reproduction invoked by William of Malmesbury, it is difficult not to suspect that Henry's imagining his book might well come to third-millennium readers' hands is predicated precisely upon Henry's understanding that his book will be a reproduction in the

---

[43] Greenaway (1996: 494–5).

[44] 'Ad uos igitur iam loquar qui in tercio millenario, circa centesimum tricesimum quintum annum, eritis. . . . Qui tanto tempore antequam nascamini de uobis mentionem iam uestro tempore puluis in hoc opere feci, si contigerit—quod ualde desiderat anima mea—uestras ut in manus hoc opus meum prodeat, precor ut Dei clementiam inexcogitabilem pro me miserrimo exoretis' (ibid. 496–7).

[45] Ibid.

Gothic mode, not merely a local and unitary production. Surely, Henry's reference to the *Historia* as his 'opus' (as opposed to 'liber') signals his understanding of the *Historia* as a textual entity reproducible in many different physical books. His textual legacy rests not upon the chance survival of a single textual production through a millennium (exactly the sort of flukish circumstance which supposedly preserved Geoffrey of Monmouth's British book!), but rather on the imagined reproduction of his work. In this sense, Henry seems clearly to be possessed of a Gothic imagination.

Even so, it is important to recall that the Gothicism of the twelfth century was not a totalizing force, obliterating other aesthetic or textual practices and styles, even if there nevertheless seems to have been a real shift in textual and architectural practice that we can usefully label 'Gothic'. Likewise, the Gothic concerns I have discussed here were neither confined to the chronicle genre nor limited to the twelfth century, but I have tried to suggest that they do cluster and develop around twelfth-century chronicles in crucial and interesting ways. Specifically, an understanding of Gothic concerns allows us to see more clearly the divergent trajectories of historical writing by authors such as William of Malmesbury and John of Worcester on the one hand, and works like Geoffrey of Monmouth's *Historia* and Layamon's *Brut* on the other hand, especially in their various attitudes towards textual reproduction and vernacularity. To a surprising degree, the logic of Gothicism and Gothic reproducibility seems to help sort out the relationship between Latin and vernacular manuscripts in this period, at least to the degree that the distinction between textual productions and textual reproductions can be a useful heuristic for thinking about the cultural function and presence of individual texts as following or countering the Gothic paradigm. Part of the achievement of thirteenth- and fourteenth-century English writers (both in the realm of chronicles and elsewhere), of course, was to move English letters more centrally into the realm of textual reproduction previously dominated by Latin. The twelfth-century chronicles I have examined ultimately serve as a mirror in which we can see the Gothicism of medieval texts under development, and the number of writers who found a model to emulate or to avoid in these exemplars emphasizes the degree to which these texts demand our attention today.

BIBLIOGRAPHY

BARROW, J. (2006), 'William of Malmesbury's Use of Charters', in E. M. Tyler and R. Balzaretti (eds.), *Narrative and History in the Early Medieval West* (Turnhout: Brepols), 67–89.

BATELY, J. (1988), 'Manuscript Layout and the Anglo-Saxon Chronicle', *Bulletin of the John Rylands University Library of Manchester*, 70: 21–43.

BREDEHOFT, T. A. (2005), *Early English Metre* (Toronto: Toronto University Press).

BROOK, G. L., and R. F. LESLIE (eds.) (1963–78), *Laȝamon: Brut* (EETS OS 250, 257; London: Early English Text Society).

DARLINGTON, R. R., and P. McGURK (eds.) (1995), *The Chronicle of John of Worcester*, ii. *The Annals from 450 to 1066*, tr. J. Bray and P. McGurk (Oxford: Oxford University Press).

DEROLEZ, A. (2003), *The Palaeography of Gothic Manuscript Books from the Twelfth to the Early Sixteenth Century* (Cambridge: Cambridge University Press).

DUMVILLE, D. (ed.) (1986), 'The West Saxon Genealogical List: Manuscripts and Texts', *Anglia*, 104: 1–32.

FLINT, V. I. J. (1979), 'The *Historia Regum Britanniae* of Geoffrey of Monmouth: Parody and its Purpose. A Suggestion', *Speculum*, 54: 447–68.

FOOT, S. (2006), 'Reading Anglo-Saxon Charters: Memory, Record, or Story?', in E. M. Tyler and R. Balzaretti (eds.), *Narrative and History in the Early Medieval West* (Turnhout: Brepols), 39–65.

GIBBS, A. C. (1962), 'The Literary Relationships of Laȝamon's Brut', doctoral dissertation, University of Cambridge.

GIVEN-WILSON, C. (2004), *Chronicles: The Writing of History in Medieval England* (Hambledon and London: Palgrave Macmillan).

GRANSDEN, A. (1974), *Historical Writing in England* (Ithaca, NY: Cornell University Press).

GREENAWAY, D. (ed. and tr.) (1996), *Henry, Archdeacon of Huntingdon, Historia Anglorum, The History of the English People* (Oxford: Oxford University Press).

IRVINE, S. (ed.) (2004), *MS E. The Anglo-Saxon Chronicle: MS E* (Cambridge: D. S. Brewer).

LE SAUX, F. (1989), *Layamon's Brut: The Poem and its Sources* (Arthurian Studies, 19; Cambridge: D. S. Brewer).

MYNORS, R. A. B. (ed. and tr.) (1998), *William of Malmesbury: Gesta Regum Anglorum*. Completed by R. M. Thomson and M. Winterbottom (Oxford: Oxford University Press).

PLUMMER, C. (ed.) (1892–9), *Two of the Saxon Chronicles Parallel* (2 vols.), with a chronological note by Dorothy Whitelock, 1952 (Oxford: Clarendon Press).

PRESCOTT, A. (1998), 'The Ghost of Asser', in P. Pulsiano and E. Treharne (eds.), *Anglo-Saxon Manuscripts and their Heritage* (Aldershot: Ashgate), 255–91.

REEVE, M. D. (ed.), and N. WRIGHT (tr.) (2007), *Geoffrey of Monmouth: The History of the Kings of Britain* (Arthurian Studies, 69; Woodbridge: Boydell Press).

SHEPPARD, A. (2004), *Families of the King: Writing Identity in the* Anglo-Saxon Chronicle (Toronto: University of Toronto Press).

STODNICK, J. (2006), '"Old Names of Kings or Shadows": Reading Documentary Lists', in C. E. Karkov and N. Howe (eds.), *Conversion and Colonization in Anglo-Saxon England* (Tempe, Ariz.: ACMRS), 109–31.

SWAN, M. (2006), 'Old English Textual Activity in the Reign of Henry II', in R. Kennedy and S. Meecham-Jones (eds.), *Writers of the Reign of Henry II: Twelve Essays* (New York: Palgrave Macmillan), 151–68.

——and E. TREHARNE (eds.) (2000), *Rewriting Old English in the Twelfth Century* (CSASE 30; Cambridge: Cambridge University Press).

TREHARNE, E. (2006), 'The Life of English in the Mid-Twelfth Century: Ralph D'Escures Homily on the Virgin Mary', in R. Kennedy and S. Meecham-Jones (eds.), *Writers of the Reign of Henry II: Twelve Essays* (New York: Palgrave Macmillan), 169–86.

WEISS, J. (ed. and tr.) (2002), *Wace's Roman de Brut: A History of the British. Text and Translation* (rev. edn. Exeter: University of Exeter Press).

WHITELOCK, D., ed. (1954), *The Peterborough Chronicle* (EEMF 4; Copenhagen: Rosekilde & Bagger).

CHAPTER 18

....

ANTI-SOCIAL REFORM

WRITING REBELLION

....

STEPHEN KELLY

I

....

On his knees—this is how Jean Froissart is pictured presenting his *Chroniques* to King Richard II (Paris, Bibliotheque Nationale, FR 2646, folio 194^v and London, British Library, Harley 4380, folio 23^v). Images designed to authorize the chronicle account by invoking royal sanction, they also confess that texts must submit to power.[1] Narratives of rebellion in medieval culture, whether by self-conscious, cosmopolitan writers such as Froissart or monastic chroniclers such as Walsingham or Knighton, will, by needs, consider dissent to be an affront to royal sovereignty.[2] And, while the chronicles consider baronial rebellion as at least comprehensible within the philosophical purview of aristocratic politics,[3] the rebellion of the third estate—pre-eminently in the Peasants' Revolt of 1381—borders on the apocalyptic. In common with much political theory in fourteenth-century England, the social imaginary of historiographical writing has not yet caught up with the extraordinary transformations of social reality after the Black Death. Whether in the form of

---

[1] Such images are typical iconographically; see, among others, Hoccleve's presentation of the *Regement of Princes* to Henry V. London, British Library, MS Arundel 38, fo. 37^r.

[2] For the reader's convenience, all quotations from the chronicles are taken from Dobson (1983).

[3] Valente (2003: 44–8).

mercantile self-confidence in London, Bristol, York, or Lynn, which accumulated wealth on a par with the aristocracy, or in the new social mobility of tenants and the gradual disappearance of serfdom, 'plebeian' aspiration violates a social order modelled as natural in political theory. *Piers Plowman* illustrates powerfully and repeatedly that while the model of the three estates is no longer materially coherent, the poet's wistful desire for its philosophical stability frequently overwhelms his simultaneous recognition of its inherent injustice. The figure of Mede (B. II–V) functions as the crux of Langland's anxieties about the new cash-based mechanism of social relations, her moral ambiguity undercutting the idealism of the justice of the King's Bench (a justice which, it seems, has little basis in reality given the myriad poems of complaint concerning the corruption of Westminster, as will be seen below). And while the moral radicalism of Piers himself issues in the dangerous destruction of Truth's pardon (B. VII: 115) and repudiation of clerical authority (B. VII: 116–39), his refusal to accept the submission of the Knight in the Ploughing of the Half-Acre (B. VI: 24–5) reasserts a now nostalgic preference for feudal relationships.

But at least Langland *worries*. For writers such as Gower and Chaucer, as for the monastic historians of the 1381 Revolt, the assertion of plebeian self-determination is an embarrassment.[4] Gower presents us with braying monsters;[5] Chaucer sets his petty bourgeois Miller and Reeve at one another's throats (internecine conflict the destiny of any plebeian project). The Miller himself, with his wheezing pipes and drunken intervention disruptive of the transfer of (narrative) authority from aristocracy to Church, is the very model of indecorous 'peasant' culture,[6] reminiscent of the *Anominalle Chronicle*'s account of the insolent Wat Tyler before Richard. And, of course, suppressed in Chaucer's version of the late medieval commonwealth is the extent of his own profit from the economic upheavals of post-Plague England.

The Peasants' Revolt of 1381 represents the most acute articulation of plebeian aspiration in medieval English history. If historians have been reluctant to identify coherent objectives for the rebellion, arguing that motives vary at the level of county and town, we can at least propose recurrent concerns, which regularly cluster in chronicle accounts and trial records subsequent to the Revolt. The objective of the Revolt is, simply, reform (*not* revolution). The aims of the rebels seem to coalesce around the desire to disentangle local affairs from an increasingly complex, overbearingly bureaucratic manorial law. The assault in Essex, Suffolk, Norfolk, and Kent on gentry, lawyers, escheators, abbots, and secular clergy involved in local government[7] and the destruction of documentary culture associated with the machinery of government and law seeks to root out corruption and abuse, bringing those responsible to justice for 'common profit'.[8]

The final straw was the application of the December 1380 Poll Tax, which was three times the level of the tax demanded in 1377.[9] It was widely evaded and early in 1381 the government had no choice but to dispatch commissioners to collect arrears; they

---

4 Blamires (2000).   5 Stockton (1962: 66).   6 Patterson (1991: 244–79).
7 Prescott (1981); Dyer (1994).   8 Robertson (2006: 55–8, 89–93).
9 Harriss (2005: 447).

found a third fewer returns than in 1377.[10] The political disinterest of the magnates and the self-service of county and town officials, the application of the Statute of Labourers, and the 'servile obligations' enforced 'through the manorial courts'[11] fomented plebeian resentment, which spilled over in the summer of 1381. But the dissatisfaction expressed by the rebellion had a long history and must not be misunderstood as emerging *sui generis*. As Christopher Dyer has demonstrated with reference to Suffolk, tensions between the inhabitants of Mildenhall and the great abbey of Bury St Edmunds had rumbled throughout the fourteenth century. 'In October 1320 Roger son of William Hervy of Mildenhall brought an action . . . against the abbot, alleging that as Robert was a tenant in an ancient demesne, the abbot was not entitled to services beyond certain labour services . . . The case was tried in 1321. Domesday Book was consulted.'[12] Trouble between the abbot and the people of Mildenhall recurs in 1323, 1327, and 1341; a continuing 'series of small-scale incidents illustrates the constant frictions between lords and peasants'[13] through the 1360s and 1370s. As Dyer argues, 'the essential prerequisite for the events of 1381 was provided by the combination of actions by landlords and by the royal government to create a universal sense of grievance among all sections of Suffolk's rural society including bailiffs, chief pledges and other members of the village élites, and even some gentry and clergy'.[14] That the Revolt involved all layers of plebeian society is illustrated in the litigation brought by John of Gaunt after the rebellion. According to Andrew Prescott, the rebels who assaulted Gaunt's interests in the Home Counties and in London included 'a very prosperous element'.

Some of them were described as rich and another had goods worth 400 marks . . . They were inspired by the depredations of Thomas Harding in their locality . . . Harding had manipulated food prices and arranged avoidance of customs dues. He harassed his neighbours through unfair tactics in litigation and extorted money from them. Some of those who turned on him in 1381 had suffered directly from his racketeering.[15]

I will not repeat here Prescott's findings about the 'socially cogent' affinities among lower gentry rebels, which pre-dated the Revolt. Suffice to say that the social constitution of the rebels is indicative of the extent and variety of popular resentment toward the structures of manorial law and the exercise of royal prerogative through the commissions and statutes which succeeded the Black Death.

The chronicles, of course, work to suppress the legitimacy of such grievances. In a classic reading of chronicle ideology, Paul Strohm reminds us that 'the chronicles employ a broad range of strategies designed to discredit the social standing, judgement, and objectives of the rebels at every level of representation'.[16] Walsingham cannot resist the story of John (or Geoffrey) 'Littestere', a Norwich dyer. He records how Littestere (or Lister) appropriates the sheriff's office and jail of Norwich Castle and sets himself up as 'the "King of the Commons"', forcing knights 'to be tasters of his food' who 'drink and knelt to him in deference as he sat at meals'.[17] But the rebels' self-

---

[10] Ibid. 229.   [11] Ibid.   [12] Dyer (1994: 226).   [13] Ibid. 228.   [14] Ibid. 231.
[15] Prescott (1981: 127).   [16] Strohm (1992: 34).   [17] Dobson (1983: 258).

perception as a 'true commons' is key throughout, contrasting their own sense of *communitas* with that of parliamentary representation. There are myriad other examples where the carnivalesque inversion of social hierarchy reported in the chronicles reveals political dissatisfaction on the part of the rebels. What is constructed as definitively anti-social action on the part of the rebels should be seen as reformism rooted in a plebeian culture which monastic historiography sought to erase.

II

Among the chronicles' most successful derogatory strategies is, of course, the presentation of the rebels' attitude to texts. As Steven Justice has suggested, 'their narratives of the rising are black fantasias about the victimization of written culture and its agents at the hands of those who could not coherently speak (much less think or write)'.[18] Again, other records report that the destruction of documents was more pointed, if not strategic: in August 1381 Thomas Orgrave and others are paid for recollecting and repairing 'diverse rolls of pleas and records of both benches and other records of diverse kings in the king's treasury in Westminster Abbey' which had been destroyed in the rebellion.[19] The *Anominalle Chronicle* reports that 'commons of Essex'[20] sacked Lambeth Palace and 'destroyed a great number of the archbishop's goods and burnt all the register books and chancery remembrancers' rolls they found there'.[21] So widespread and systematic is the assault on documentary culture that, according to Justice, 'manorial courts in the years following sometimes dated events of 1381 with the phrase *tempore rumoris et combustionis rotulorum cure*—"during the uproar and the burning of court rolls"'.[22] As Justice makes clear, whenever the rebels destroyed texts 'they did so with a specificity that shows their familiarity and competence with the forms of literate culture'.[23] We must treat Walsingham's account of their textual vandalism with suspicion and note, with his ink-pot in view, the morbid *frisson* of cloistered excitement in his account:

What else did they do? They strove to burn all records; and they butchered anyone who might know or be able to commit to memory the contents of all or new documents. It was dangerous enough to be known as a clerk but especially dangerous if the ink-pot should be found at one's elbow: such men scarcely or ever escaped from the hands of the rebels.[24]

---

[18] Justice (1994: 17).   [19] Ormrod (1990: 5).
[20] In the view of the Monk of Westminster (Dobson 1983: 199) Lambeth Palace is sacked by rebels from Kent.
[21] Dobson (1983: 155).   [22] Justice (1994: 40).   [23] Ibid. 41.   [24] Dobson (1983: 364).

III

'The rebels aimed not to destroy the documentary culture of feudal tenure and royal government, but to re-create it.'[25] The temptation to believe the characterization of the rebels as categorically excluded from literate culture[26] or to seek a rebel 'voice' in order to counterpoint written and oral cultures and their antagonized politics risks eliding the extent to which, as Justice infers, the writing of rebellion was not just the prerogative of monastic chronicler or judicial clerk. The quest to discover how 'those excluded from the dominant institutions and cultures of discourse made themselves heard'[27] risks implying that dissent belongs to the 'lewed'—to those outside the bounds of literate culture. But literate culture is by the late fourteenth century enormously complex and diverse, both within and without metropolitan contexts, a fact missed when we focus on the chronicle as our premier form of 'evidence'. As Wendy Scase has recently pointed out, 'if we concentrate on these sources as evidence for the rebels' literary achievements, we neglect a good deal of evidence for the quantity and nature of the rebels' textual outputs'.[28] We must remember that the prerogative of writing rebellion in the later Middle Ages belongs, more broadly, to a new and internally diverse class. It is institutionalized and, because of its relation to power, it enjoys the privilege of political and historical decision, although its agency is often disguised by its seemingly secretarial and administrative relationship to power. The enormously complex culture of bureaucracy which emerges in the later Middle Ages provides us with the stage upon which the Peasants' Revolt will be both made and reported. The rebellion is, as Andrew Prescott reminds us, 'recorded in more detail than any other uprising in the middle ages'.[29] It must be assumed that bureaucratic culture helped articulate the objectives of the revolt and frame its actions; and that it provided disparate expressions of local resentment with what looks like collective political and juridical intent. The focus on the rebels' assault on documentary culture ignores the fact that the grievances and sentiments which issue explosively across England in the summer of 1381 themselves enjoy a range of textual articulations. In other words, it is insufficient to rely for our sense of rebellious (as opposed to homologously rebel) 'ideology' on the famous Letters recorded by Walsingham and Knighton. Rather, a gamut of complaint writing, bills, petitions, doggerel, and theological and political speculation which arises out of bureaucratic culture is the background noise in which we should seek signals of Justice's 'insurgent literacy'. However, it will also be this self-same bureaucratic culture which most effectively crushes the aspirations of the rebellion in the trials which succeed its suppression.

Bureaucratic culture has been of interest to literary historians for some time, but usually in the context of metropolitan textual production. Studies of reception of *Piers Plowman*,[30] the textual environment of Thomas Hoccleve,[31] and, most recently,

---

[25] Justice (1994: 48).   [26] Crane (1992).   [27] Aers (1999: 432).   [28] Scase (2007: 84).
[29] Prescott (1998: 5).   [30] Justice and Kerby-Fulton (1997).   [31] Knapp (2001).

the scribal milieu of Adam Pinkhurst[32] have drawn our attention to the symbiotic relationship of literary production and bureaucratic culture in later medieval England.[33] Bureaucratic culture should also be seen to subsume the chronicle evidence so readily deployed by historians of the Peasants' Revolt (indeed, the extent of borrowing, interpolation, and intertextuality generally in the chronicles is indicative of how porous chronicle as a genre is). But bureaucratic culture is best understood as being rather more amorphous, intersecting with civic and ecclesiastical institutions while not being determined by them. If writers such as Hoccleve are instruments of a governmental 'secretariat',[34] there is a burgeoning class of clerks, unbeneficed clerics, and freelance scribes who work as textual functionaries for mercantile and gentry households, county courts, and town plutocracies both in and outside London. The common or town clerk, too long ignored by literary historians, facilitates power as an instrument of judicial culture but can also be assumed to be a conduit for 'insurgent literacy'. Indeed, in a brilliant assessment of the cultural agency of the town clerk, Andrew Butcher has argued that, 'far from being expressive only of a single domain of urban government, a narrowly defined genre of legal, administrative, or financial writing', the social and cultural significance of the writings of town clerks

needs to be understood within the locally determined field of text and speech which constitutes the community. The 'speech/text' community of the town is a multi-ethnic complex involving a network of discursive interrelationships of personal, collective, and institutional kinds, and the writings themselves are to be regarded as performative of economic, social, religious, moral, and civic practices and processes, and not merely representative of a narrowly defined 'pragmatic' literacy . . . The individual contribution of the clerk(s) in the processes of interpretation, in editorial practice, and in the development of distinctive characteristics of textual form, and of script, plays a crucial part in the construction of collective consciousness.[35]

Crucially, 'the relationship between the clerk/text and the persons for whom and of whom these texts are produced is, in significant part, a relationship of social control in the performance of their construction, a relationship which embodies obligation and reciprocity'.[36] Indictments, pardons, and trial records after the Revolt allow us to see the fine grain of such relationships of 'obligation and reciprocity': clerks, whether at the urban or county level, determine the social narratives of their communities by memorializing individual and collective history, and they record the negotiation of law in maintaining fealty to local gentry and magnate culture, as well as to the Crown. Thus the cry of Margery Starre, 'Away with the learning of the clerks, away with it' as she cast up the ashes of documents burnt in the revolt at Cambridge.[37] But clerks, we must assume, are similarly active participants in the emergence of a recognizably common idiom of insurgent politics in the events of the Revolt, whether they are clerically trained or civic or county functionaries. When Steven Justice seeks rebel disgust for bureaucratic culture and their subsequent appropriation of the rhetoric of

---

[32] Mooney (2006).   [33] Also, see Lindenbaum (1999); Steiner (2003).
[34] Harriss (2005: 41–7).   [35] Butcher (2004: 169).   [36] Ibid. 170.   [37] Justice (1994: 72).

complaint in the shire-moot,[38] he ignores the fact that, like the priest who is so completely a villager,[39] the clerk who records the dealings of gentry, peasantry, magnate, and Crown must also live among his disgruntled neighbours and that, while the 'construction of collective consciousness' might serve power when government is strong, it might also be deployed on behalf of irate members of rural society in times of uprising. Walsingham reports that John Bocher, clerk of the church of Thanet, 'by commission' of Wat Tyler and other leaders of the rebellion in Kent, used the Church of St John as the location for their proclamation of revolt.[40] If we are to believe the chronicles that 'clerkly' members of the community were subject to particular malice during the Revolt, we must assume that they also played an active role not only in mobilizing dissent, but in the production of what Wendy Scase has recently called the 'literature of clamour'.[41]

That insurgent ideologies emerge to compensate for the misapplication of draconian taxation and other coercive policies on communities whose social realities are no longer adequately represented under law[42] chimes with Scase's findings in her account of complaint in later medieval culture. '"Complaint,"' she says, refers 'to the expression of a grievance as a means of obtaining a judicial remedy'.[43] The theatricality of the rebels' meeting with King Richard II lies in its appropriation and relocation of the procedures of complaint, as Wat Tyler lists his demands not to a judge but directly to the King (see particularly the *Anominalle Chronicle*[44]). The chronicles report myriad attempts by the rebels to present their objections, reaffirming that a primary motive for rebellion was that the instruments of complaint, from manorial and ecclesiastical courts to Westminster itself, had been fatally compromised. According to Mark Ormrod, the rebellion 'represented a serious loss of public confidence in the central administrative and legal departments located in Westminster Palace and the city of London'.[45] As the macaronic poem entitled 'On the Times' by Thomas Wright puts it:

> At Westmynster halle
>   leges sunt valde scienties (there are men most learned in law)
> Noght ellys before thayme all
>   ibi vincuntur jura potentes. (there the powerful laws are chained)
> That never herd the case,
>   juramento mediabit, (will arrange things with an oath)
> That mater wylle he face
>   et justum dampnificabit, (and will condemn the just)
> And an obligacion
>   de jure satis valitura (that would be valid in law)
> Throgh a fals cavelcoun
>   erit effectu caritura (will be emptied of its force)

---

[38] Ibid. 55–66.   [39] Ibid. 54.   [40] Dobson (1983: 147).
[41] Scase (2007).   [42] Rigby (1995).   [43] Scase (2007: 1).
[44] Tr. in Dobson (1983: 164–7).   [45] Ormrod (1990: 2; see also 17).

His own cause mony mon
    nunc judicat et moderatur. (now judges and oversees)
Law helpis nott then,
    ergo lex evacuator (for alas, the law is eviscerated)[46]

The representation of the corruption of law in such poetry resonates, we can assume, with both literate and illiterate experience of legal process. When seeking remission from extraneous new laws and their abuse by agents in the community, it is inevitable that legal discourse should be appropriated and parodied. As Scase comments, the rebels 'articulated their oppression in the judicial form of the petition or plaint that listed grievances and requested remedy'.[47] Prior to submitting to meet the rebels, Richard receives, according to the *Anominalle Chronicle*, a petition from them naming the main culprits to be put to death in satisfaction of their demands. We must assume that such a petition is written by someone who is deeply familiar with the rhetorical structures of petitionary writing. As Scase suggests,

presumably they were imitating the methods used by the crown to publicise legislation and other matters, sending out documents whose contents were to be proclaimed in English . . . The rebels rallied support by sending letters to Kent, Norfolk, and Suffolk. Possibly the letters communicated the lists of grievances for proclamation. After the revolt, some lawyers claimed they had been coerced into supporting the rebels.[48]

The prosecution of the leadership of the rebellion likely led to the destruction of myriad textual materials which circulated among the protagonists of the Revolt. Ball's Letters are remembered because of the extent to which they mystified conformist world-views such as those of the chroniclers. But we should imagine that the rebels achieve textuality in more diffuse and *ad hoc* ways: in what Justice calls 'broadsides', in bills and parodic petitions and poems of complaint.[49] The confidence with which we might imagine them writing rebellion is licensed, I want to suggest, by a reformist consensus convulsing fourteenth-century society.

IV

The internal tensions and contradictions within reformist politics, as well as a general hunger for reform, is best illustrated in Langland's *Piers Plowman*. But it is likely that Langland's poem had not meaningfully escaped London reading circles by the time of the Revolt (which has implications for Ball's Letters, as we shall see below). *Piers Plowman* is but the most sophisticated articulation of a register of reform which finds expression in myriad forms in the later fourteenth century. Justice reminds us that plebeian literacy

---

[46] Dean (1996: 142).   [47] Scase (2007: 84).   [48] Ibid. 84–5.
[49] I forego discussion of these texts thanks to their superb discussion in Scase 2007; see particularly chs. 2 and 3.

might be evidenced in the distribution and consumption of broadsides.[50] Texts such as the *Twelve Conclusions of the Lollards*, although produced later, evidence the broadside as a genre of hortatory political announcement, whose conventions are clearly understood by consumers. Might it be safe to assume that such documents, regardless of ideological orientation, ebb and flow across public spaces—churchyards, village squares, taverns—as part of the performance of political life? Itinerant priests such as John Ball are a nexus for such texts and for their distribution, whether they help 'publish' them or simply incorporate them into homiletic performance. The circulation of Ball's Letters speaks to textual networks of contestation and resistance which presumably pre-exist the rebellion; the notion that such conduits emerge overnight, as the clamour for revolt takes hold, makes no sense. In turn, the view of the chronicles that Ball was a Lollard suggest that varieties of non-conformist thought intersect with and cross-pollinate one another throughout the period. Hudson warns that 'disclaimers of Wyclif's involvement' in the Revolt 'have gone too far'[51] and in a recent study Andrew Cole reinforces this view.[52] Conversely, in his latest reflection on the Uprising, Justice argues that 'since not a whit of compelling evidence has been successfully adduced in support of any direct relation' between Wycliffitism and the Rebellion[53] the case for Lollardy permeating rebel ideology remains unconvincing. But literary history has too neatly packaged dissent in the late Middle Ages, insisting on the internal coherence of non-conformist trends—particularly in the case of Lollardy. Recent work, such as that of Kathryn Kerby-Fulton,[54] has demonstrated the difficulty of unravelling normative from dissenting religious and political currents in fourteenth-century cultural life. Indeed, as Justice argues, orthodox religious practices 'exhibited an almost alarming plasticity';[55] it would not be difficult to find scriptural justification for the rebellion's aims, and no doubt preachers found and used precisely such materials. Whatever the case, whether informed by intellectual currents of dissent or sponsored by orthodox practice, there emerges what we might term a reformist consensus in fourteenth-century England.[56] The frustrations unleashed by the Uprising of 1381 leave superficial and distorted traces in the chronicle and judicial accounts; we forget at our peril that the purpose of such accounts is to suppress dissent and even out the historical narrative.

V

And yet we have the Letters. These are surely some of the most treacherous documents in English literary history, as 'full of enigmas' (as Walsingham characterizes them) for the modern critic as the fourteenth-century chronicler. The temptation to

---

[50] Justice (1994: 29–30).   [51] Hudson (1988: 68).   [52] Cole (2008:197).
[53] Justice (2007: 205).   [54] Kerby-Fulton (2006).   [55] Justice (2007: 215).
[56] On the 'reformist' character of late medieval cultural practice in England, see Simpson (2002).

find in the Letters echoes of rebel ideology has been irresistible. Furthermore, the potential relationship between the Letters and the text they apparently quote—none other than *Piers Plowman*—has licensed extraordinary claims for the intelligibility of rebel ideology.

The Letters certainly provide the best evidence for the influence of bureaucratic culture on the organization and promotion of the rebellion.[57] They 'borrow the official salutations of legal documents, ranging from the simpler notifications of broadsides or pamphlets . . . to . . . more elaborate imitation of an official patent'.[58] But their intentions remain frustratingly opaque:

> Johon Schep, some tyme Seynte Marie prest of York, and now of Colcestre, greteth wel John Nameles, and John the Mullere and Johon Cartere, and bideth hem that thei bee war of gyle in borugh, and stondith togidre in Godes name, and biddeth Pere Ploughman go to his werk, and chastise wel Hobbe the Robbere, and taketh with yow Johan Trewman and alle his felawes, and no mo, and schappe you to on heved, and no mo.[59]

This excerpt from the *Chronicon Angliae* likely provides the basis for Walsingham's version in the *Historia Anglicana*. 'Schep' is a pseudonym for John Ball and the other generic names are clearly pseudonymous as well. The Letter clearly implies a distinction between rural and urban culture, modelling the town or city as a space of dissimulation: 'bee war of gyle in borugh'; there is also the promotion of rebel collectivity sanctioned by God: 'stondith togidre in Godes name'. But it is in its supposed references to *Piers Plowman* that Ball's Letter has been most seductive. 'For though they invoke Piers Plowman among their own company, they treat him as having the malleability of a fictional creation, available for the creation and elaboration of other fictions, and indeed for his own re-creation: their Piers is their own Piers.'[60] Justice is circumspect enough to frame his discussion of the relationship between the poem and the Letters with numerous caveats concerning access to Langland's text. But others make more ingenious claims. For Emily Steiner, the Letters

> capitalize on the documentary process by which vernacular allegorical poetry becomes a mode of public address. *It is as if these letters are the ones that Piers might carry on his person, if he were really as sympathetic to labor as his name suggests* . . . In this respect they are following the lead of *Piers Plowman*: it is precisely Langland's fictionalizing of documentary culture that provides a viable model for public writing, one that is indebted to—but ultimately goes beyond—real documents.[61]

We have entered a Borgesian realm of uncanny and fortuitous intertextuality, where vastly complex cultural processes are shown to enjoy a simple, secret logic. Carlo Ginzburg has warned us of the methodological risks of such an approach: 'the historian reads into [artistic documents] what he has already learned by other

---

[57] Justice (1994: 117).   [58] Steiner (2003: 171–2).
[59] Dean (1996: 135). Dean reproduces the Letter from the *Chronicon Angliae* in British Library, Royal MS 13.E.ix, fo. 287ʳ. The Letter is also reproduced in Dobson (1983: 381) and Justice (1994: 14–15).
[60] Justice (1994: 121).   [61] Steiner (2003: 173–5; my emphasis).

means, or what he believes he knows, and wants to "demonstrate".[62] But what if the Letters did not know Langland's poem at all?

Steven Justice was not the first to comment on the association of the 1381 Revolt with the feast of Corpus Christi; but his account reminds us of the complex rural culture within which the rebellion is conceived. Just as they exploit bureaucratic culture to achieve textuality, the rebels draw on the festive calendar to imbue their actions with a cultural logic to which *all* participants have access:

Ascension week with its rogation processions, 20–26 May in 1381, preceded the initial assault on Brentwood; the Bocking oath was taken on Whitsunday—Pentecost, the feast of the church's founding; court rolls were burned on Trinity Monday; and of course the rising reached its climax around the greatest of all these feasts, Corpus Christi, the celebration of community, body and food.[63]

In these festivities, Justice argues, 'we can catch rural communities in the act of self-description'.[64] But the substance of such acts, based in oral performance and folk culture, is all but lost to us. In a brilliantly suggestive essay rarely referenced by literary historians, the folklorist Thomas Pettit takes us as close as is possible to such a culture. Rebel ideology emerges, Pettit argues, out of 'pre-existing official systems of organization available in medieval or pre-industrial society. Such use of "every-day" channels would be more likely the more the revolt attracted the support and participation of the gentry and local administrative officials.'[65] Such '"everyday" channels' might help explain the Letters' cryptic use of pseudonyms. As Pettit argues:

there is every likelihood that 'Jack Straw' was the traditional name of a figure from seasonal folk revelry. In the early sixteenth century this was the name assigned to the 'king' of the Christmas revels at Lincoln Inn, an order of 1517 noting damage caused in connection with the revels and concluding 'that Jack Straw and all his adherents be from henceforth utterly banyshed and no more to be used in Lincolles Inne.' There is also an obscure reference to 'Iacke Strawe' in connection with rural holidays in Ben Jonson's masque of 1621, *The Gypsies Metamorphos'd*. Norman Simms associates Jack Straw with a heterogeneous cluster of figures from seasonal custom, 'Jack in the Green,' 'Jack o' Lent,' Robin Hood, and other figures in 'the many variants of the spring-time games of death-and-resurrection played in England,' but such vague equivalences are misleading, and the important specific connection, surely, is with the straw-clad figures common in the folk drama of many countries.[66]

Furthermore, the figure of Piers the Plowman is also, likely, a creation of folk culture, exploited for its familiarity by Langland and his successors: 'Piers, like the "Erle of the Plo," may be a pseudonym adopted by a rebel leader. For if we read the letters literally, that is what Piers Plowman is, and we find unexpected support in the *Chronicle of*

---

[62] Ginzburg (1989: 35).

[63] Justice (1994: 157). Compare Pettit (1984: 6: 'Corpus Christi was still a fairly new feast in the 1380's, however, and the occasion of civic, rather than rural customs, and it may be more significant that the disturbances in Essex which triggered the revolt started at Whitsun, a much more important feast for country customs, with its ales, morris dancers, summer king and queen, Robin Hood plays, and other forms of folk drama, perhaps like Perdita's "Whitsun pastorals" (*Winter's Tale*, IV, iv).'

[64] Justice (1994: 157).   [65] Pettit (1984: 6).   [66] Ibid. 8.

Dieulacres Abbey, written in the first decade of the fifteenth century, which lists the leaders of the revolt as "Iohannis B., Iak Strawe, Per Plowman et ceteri".[67]

We thus have a situation in which *Piers Plowman* and the Letters draw on a common idiom of rural myth. If we are to believe that Langland's excision of the Tearing of the Pardon in his C-version of *Piers Plowman* is a response to the Revolt of 1381, we might ask, if Piers the Plowman was himself thought to be an agent of the revolt, why a more radical revision did not take place. It is likely because Piers was such a well-known figure in the folk tradition. Indeed, it might be argued that the intelligibility of Langland's myriad allegorical figures relies on their prior circulation in popular drama and folk narrative.

If the quest for a rebel 'voice' has often been undertaken at the expense of rebel textualities, we might conclude that the excavation of rebel ideology must begin by recognizing the desire for reform across all levels and institutions of fourteenth-century English society. We must not underestimate the radical expansion of cultural horizons enabled by the collapse of serfdom after the Black Death: in the midst of a kind of Gramscian 'interregnum', English culture was in the process of remaking itself. We are best not to historicize the rebellion of 1381 as the beginnings of English radical non-conformism; it is all too tempting to recruit the Revolt to the history of popular radicalism, pursuing its 'egalitarian' energies through the modern socialist tradition, culminating in the muddled notion of 'multitude' with which philosophy on the postmodern left has sought to challenge globalization.[68] But might we safely see the demand for reform articulated by the Revolt as expressing a more fundamental desire for human self-determination? As the novelist and critic John Berger reminds us in a reflection on the return of religion to post-Communist Europe, 'the human imagination . . . has great difficulty in living strictly within the confines of a materialist practice or philosophy. It dreams, like a dog in the basket, of hares in the open.'[69]

BIBLIOGRAPHY

AERS, DAVID (1999), '*Vox Populi* and the Literature of Dissent', in David Wallace (ed.), *The Cambridge Companion to Medieval English Literature* (Cambridge: Cambridge University Press), 432–53.

BERGER, JOHN (2001), 'The Soul and the Operator,' in Geoff Dyer (ed.), *The Selected Essays of John Berger* (London: Bloomsbury), 570–5.

BLAMIRES, ALCUIN (2000), 'Chaucer the Reactionary: Ideology and the General Prologue of *The Canterbury Tales*', *Review of English Studies*, 51: 523–39.

BUTCHER, ANDREW (2004), 'The Functions of Script in the Speech Community of a Late Medieval Town, c.1300–1550', in Julia Crick and Alexander Walsham (eds.), *The Uses of Script and Print, 1300–1700* (Cambridge: Cambridge University Press), 157–70.

[67] Ibid. 10.   [68] Hardt and Negri (2004).   [69] Berger (2001: 572).

COLE, ANDREW (2008), *Literature and Heresy in the Age of Chaucer* (Cambridge: Cambridge University Press).

CRANE, SUSAN (1992), 'The Writing Lesson of 1381', in Barbara Hanawalt (ed.), *Chaucer's England: Literature in Historical Context* (Minneapolis: University of Minnesota Press), 201–21.

DEAN, JAMES M. (ed.) (1996), *Medieval English Political Writings* (Kalamazoo, Mich.: Medieval Institute Publications).

DOBSON, R. B. (ed.) (1983), *The Peasants' Revolt of 1381* (London: Macmillan).

DYER, CHRISTOPHER (1994), 'The Rising of 1381 in Suffolk: Its Origins and Participants', in *Everyday Life in Medieval England* (London: Hambledon Press), 221–40.

GINZBURG, CARLO (1989), *Clues, Myths and the Historical Method*, tr. John and Anne Tedeschi (Baltimore: Johns Hopkins University Press).

HARDT, MICHAEL, and ANTONIO NEGRI (2004), *Multitude: War and Democracy in the Age of Empire* (London: Hamish Hamilton).

HARRISS, GERALD (2005), *Shaping the Nation: England 1360–1461* (Oxford: Oxford University Press).

HUDSON, ANNE (1988), *The Premature Reformation: Wycliffite Texts and Lollard History* (Oxford: Oxford University Press).

JUSTICE, STEVEN (1994), *Writing and Rebellion: England in 1381* (Berkeley, Calif.: University of California Press).

——and KATHRYN KERBY-FULTON (1997), 'Langlandian Reading Circles and the Civil Service in London and Dublin, 1380–1427', in Rita Copeland, David A. Lawton, and Wendy Scase (eds.), *New Medieval Literatures*, i (Oxford: Oxford University Press), 59–83.

KERBY-FULTON, KATHRYN (2006), *Books Under Suspicion: Censorship and Tolerance of Revelatory Writing in Late Medieval England* (Ind.: University of Notre-Dame Press).

KNAPP, ETHAN (2001), *The Bureaucratic Muse: Thomas Hoccleve and the Literature of Late Medieval England* (Pennsylvania: Penn State University Press).

LINDENBAUM, SHEILA (1999), 'London Texts and Literate Practice', in David Wallace (ed.), *The Cambridge Companion to Medieval English Literature* (Cambridge: Cambridge University Press), 284–309.

MOONEY, LINNE R. (2006), 'Chaucer's Scribe', *Speculum*, 81/1: 97–138.

ORMROD, MARK (1990), 'The Peasants' Revolt and the Government of England', *Journal of British Studies*, 29: 1–30.

PATTERSON, LEE (1991), 'The Miller's Tale and the Politics of Laughter', in *Chaucer and the Subject of History* (London: Routledge), 244–79.

PRESCOTT, ANDREW (1981), 'London in the Peasants' Revolt: A Portrait Gallery', *London Journal*, 7: 125–43.

PRESCOTT, ANDREW (1998), 'Writing about Rebellion: Using the Records of the Peasants' Revolt of 1381', *History Workshop Journal*, 45: 1–27.

RIGBY, S. (1995), *English Society in the Later Middle Ages: Class, Status and Gender* (Basingstoke: Macmillan).

ROBERTSON, KELLIE (2006), *The Laborer's Two Bodies: Labor and the 'Work' of the Text in Medieval Britain, 1350–1500* (Basingstoke: Palgrave).

SCASE, WENDY (2007), *Literature and Complaint in England, 1272–1553* (Oxford: Oxford University Press).

SIMPSON, JAMES (2002), *The Oxford English Literary History: 1350–1547: Reform and Cultural Revolution* (Oxford: Oxford University Press).

STEINER, EMILY (2003), *Documentary Culture and the Making of Medieval English Literature* (Cambridge: Cambridge University Press).

STOCKTON, ERIC W. (1962), *The Major Latin Works of John Gower* (Seattle: University of Washington Press).

STROHM, PAUL (1992), '"A Revelle!": Chronicle Evidence and the Rebel Voice', in *Hochon's Arrow: The Social Imagination of Fourteenth-Century Texts* (Princeton: Princeton University Press), 33–56.

VALENTE, CLAIRE (2003), *The Theory and Practice of Revolt in Medieval England* (Aldershot: Ashgate).

CHAPTER 19

SECULAR MEDIEVAL DRAMA

ELISABETH DUTTON

THE NATURE OF MEDIEVAL DRAMA

The medieval Mystery Cycles, with their vibrant presentation of scriptural narrative, dominate discussion of medieval drama. Together with the Morality Plays, which do not tell scriptural stories but which consider the human soul as it falls into sin and is then redeemed, and the Saints' Plays, which stage a similar narrative in the life of a named saint, the cycles contribute to a picture of medieval drama as fundamentally religious—until, that is, the 1490s, when Henry Medwall wrote *Fulgens and Lucres*, the first secular play in English, and the first of a string of 'secular' Tudor interludes. But, as James Simpson argues, the development of the secular theatre is not, as has often been thought, 'a moment of liberation from a religious theatre governed by an oppressive Church'—this liberation had already largely occurred in the Mystery Plays, through a presentation of scriptural narrative which critiqued royal and episcopal abuse of power.[1] The presentation of ecclesiastical power in the cycles is strategically anachronistic and aligned with the oppressive power of biblical tyrants like Herod: regimes ecclesiastical and secular, biblical and contemporary are thus exposed all together. In addition, the Mystery Cycles' dependence for their performance on the firm power of civic authority has long been recognized.[2] It is difficult to exclude the 'secular' from medieval drama.

---

[1] Simpson (2002: 518).
[2] See, most recently and eloquently, King (2006).

It is difficult, too, to exclude the religious from the secular. *Fulgens and Lucres* may be claimed as the 'earliest surviving purely secular play in English' by virtue of its humanist roots and classical theme:[3] Lucres, the daughter of a senator, must choose between two suitors—Cornelius, a man of great fortune and ancestry, and Gayus, a man of low birth and moderate fortune who has trained himself in virtue and service to the State. To choose her husband, Lucres must decide whether nobility lies in wealth and birth or in virtue. Medwall's play is based on a 1428 Latin treatise by Buonaccorso de Montemagna, the *Controversia de vera nobilitate*, which was popular in Italy; Duke Philip the Good had the treatise translated into French and it was quickly also popular at the Burgundian court. But Buonaccorso's characters are heavily allegorized: for the humanist reader, Lucres, the reward, is secular power, but Fulgens, her father, is a figure of divine ordinance. Thus religious allegory informs the sources of *Fulgens and Lucres*, which is furthermore a profoundly moral work, by a cleric.

Nonetheless, Medwall's play is predominantly secular: his treatment of his characters is not allegorical, and his classical theme is good conduct in this world as opposed to preparation for the life hereafter. John Tiptoft translated the *Controversia* into English as *The Declamacion of Noblesse*, which in 1481 was popular enough to become one of the first products of Caxton's new press. In the 1490s, in the early years of Henry VII's reign, Medwall dramatized its nobility debate in a new, very particular, context: it is possible that the first performance of *Fulgens* was associated with negotiations for the proposed marriage of Prince Arthur and Katherine of Aragon; it is certain that *Fulgens*'s 'nobility debate' would have had strong resonance at the court of Henry VII and his 'new men', the gentry-born counsellors whom the king preferred above the established nobility.[4] The circumstances of the play's production are thus also fundamentally secular, as are the material circumstances of its dissemination on the page: not only was its source disseminated through the secular press, but *Fulgens* itself survives only in a printed edition by Rastell of between 1512 and 1516.[5] While the cycle plays are preserved only in manuscript, Medwall's play was printed and marketed commercially.[6]

SECULAR DRAMATURGY

Does this secular narrative—moral, certainly, and the work of a cleric, but concerned with worldly morality—exhibit also a distinctively secular dramaturgy? This will be the central

---

[3] See Walker (2000: 305). Subsequent line references to *Fulgens and Lucres* are to the edn. in this anthology.

[4] Lexton (2008) engages the play in its historical context.

[5] STC 17778; the single surviving complete copy is held in the Huntington Library, San Marino, Calif. (Huntington Library 62599).

[6] Walker (1998) discusses the printing of secular drama; see esp. ch. 1.

question explored in this chapter. Of course, dramaturgy cannot be entirely separated from a play's themes, nor from the circumstances of production: perhaps for this reason James Simpson chooses to categorize medieval drama principally as 'amateur' or 'professional':

One [dramatic] form is non-metropolitan, amateur, played in the street, and as critical of its own exercise of power as it is of royal and episcopal power; Tudor household drama is, by contrast, metropolitan, professional, played indoors, and extremely cautious under the eyes of its powerful patrons.[7]

Simpson's study of dramatic literature takes him to 1547, which is some years beyond the scope of this book, but he makes a strong case for the continuities between one type of Tudor 'interlude'—the instructional and comic—and the 'medieval morality play': while the content of the interlude may differ from that of the morality, the interludes often exhibit a comic structure of rise–fall–recovery taken directly from the moralities, 'from a medieval theatre of instruction, which is also a professional troupe theatre'.[8] Simpson notes further that, whereas most types of literature exhibit 'total rupture' at the Reformation, drama is marked more by its post-Reformation continuities:[9] he articulates a common scholarly difficulty with the categorization of drama within the boundaries of the 'medieval' and the 'early modern' as defined by historical events or in relation to other forms of writing.

Thus the title of this chapter is fully problematized: neither the 'secular' nor the 'medieval' in 'secular medieval drama' can be decisively defined. This chapter will, by focusing on *Fulgens and Lucres*, occupy the fifteenth century as far as possible, but it will also make reference to plays of the sixteenth century, since it is from the sixteenth century that most household drama survives. This chapter will also invoke some plays which, though treating religious rather than secular subject-matter, share with *Fulgens* its status as printed text, or small troupe play, or household drama.

The comic instructional mode does not characterize *Fulgens and Lucres*: rather, Medwall's play falls into Simpson's alternative subsection of Tudor interlude, the debate. Both instructional and debate interludes are produced by and addressed to 'coterie' audiences 'whose consciousness is never far from the business of gaining royal favour'.[10] The appeal to royal favour may be a rather cynical gloss on the enquiry into moral living in this world, though it seems a likely one: an audience is, however, unlikely ever to be uni-conscious. Nonetheless, an audience preoccupied even in part with ambition and sycophancy would certainly contribute to the 'claustrophobic' sense which Simpson finds in the debate plays and attributes to their concern with 'promotion within closely defined institutional spaces'.[11] While the claustrophobia may be in the mind of the audience, the institutional spaces are figurative but also literal, since interludes like *Fulgens and Lucres* were performed in the great halls of great men, on great occasions.[12]

---

[7] Simpson (2002: 553) See also Emmerson (2005: 53) and Simpson (2005: 117).
[8] Simpson (2002: 554) 554.   [9] Ibid.   [10] Ibid. 549.   [11] Ibid.
[12] Emerson (2005: 55) restates the traditional view that *Fulgens* was staged at Lambeth Palace, under the patronage of Cardinal Morton: See 'Dramatic History', p. 55. However, there is no solid evidence to support this view.

My consideration of medieval secular dramaturgy will focus on dramatic manipulations of place, and also of time. Both are curiously compromised in *Fulgens and Lucres*. The play opens with a direct address to the audience from a character, nominated simply 'A', who appears to be a member of the household and who draws attention to the feast which the household/audience have just been enjoying—for *Fulgens and Lucres* is written to be performed as the accompaniment to a meal.

> A, for Goddis will,
> What meane ye, syrs, to stond so still?
> Have not ye etyn and your fill
> And payd no thinge therfore? (ll. 1–4)

A comments that the audience falls still, and also silent—'I mervayle moche . . . there is no wordes amonge this presse' (ll. 14–17)—while apparently oblivious to the fact that it is he, by speaking as an actor, who has silenced the household, according to conventions of audience behaviour. A does not know he is an actor, and he is therefore also unaware that the household are an audience—to him they are still diners in the great hall. He knows that there is going to be a play, however, and, when another man, 'B', enters, he incorrectly assumes that he is part of the play. Since B is not one of the diners, his entrance into a playing-space suggests he must be an actor (the Latin stage direction is the theatrically conventional 'Intrat B'), an impression reinforced by the way B is dressed:

> Ther is so myche nyce array
> Amonges these galandis now aday
> That a man shall not lightly
> Know a player from a nother man. (ll. 53–6)

Although B's entrance into the playing-space seems to A to be part of the action, the space is still 'here', the hall, and the time is still 'now', a present in which gallants dress as finely as players. B is native to the time but perhaps not the place, which he seems to differentiate from 'the parish where I abide' (l. 169). The actual play, he explains, will be set at the time of the Roman Empire's flowering (l. 170); its place will be Rome, and B argues that this fact should forestall any objection to the action of the play from the audience:

> I trow here is no man of the kyn or sede
> Of either partie, for why they were bore
> In the cytie of Rome (ll. 178–80)

A's confusion as to the moment at which 'the play' begins is later mirrored in his uncertainty as to the moment of its ending: 'Why then, is the play all do?' (l. 2305). A's doubts indicate that a play may not begin and end where expected, but nonetheless assert an audience's expectation of a play's having a beginning and an end which contain it within a distinct—artificial—space and time. It is all the more intriguing, then, that when B wishes to assert that nobody 'here', that is, among the diners in the hall, has any reason to object to the action of the play, he takes as his defence not the fictionality of the play's action, but its remoteness of place.

Perhaps the remoteness of fiction would prevent A and B getting involved in the play—the remoteness of time does not. The two talk their way into the employment of Lucres's two suitors, and are soon involved in carrying messages between the Ancient Romans, and in competing over the hand of Lucres's Ancilla—by way of subplot, the first in English drama: this competition takes the form of a singing contest, a wrestling match, and a round of 'farte pryke in cule', a parody of a joust in which the combatants are bound into a squatting position with poles tied between their legs to serve as spears.[13] Medwall thus incorporates, in his humanist Roman debate, scripted enactments of a range of popular entertainments which are very much of his own time and place, and far from learned or noble.

A and B continue to be aware that they are in a dining hall, performing a play, with an audience in the here and now: the Ancient Romans simultaneously occupy a very different reality but apparently do not mind the gap. At one elusive moment, A apparently tries to draw Gayus's attention to the reality outside the play:

> A . . . some tyme ye knewe me,
> Though it be now oute of youre remembraunce (ll. 604–5)

A seems here to allude to his pre-play acquaintance with the Gayus actor, but Gayus's reaction seems at once uncomprehending and untroubled:

> Gayus: By my fayth it may well be,
> But never the lesse I thanke thee. (ll. 606–7)

The situation is reversed when Lucres questions A about his name and the identity of his master. The questions apparently require A to answer with relation to Lucres's time and space, Ancient Rome, in which, as B has already pointed out, no one in the dining hall has any part. Consequently, A cannot answer:

Et scalpens caput post modicum intervallum dicat:[14]

> 'By this light, I have forgotten!' (l. 1780).

The stage direction gives charming detail, and, in calling for a brief interval before A's speech, echoes an earlier stage direction indicating Lucres's response to Fulgens's injunction that she should resolve the question of her marriage herself:

Et facta aliqua pausatione, dicat Lucres:[15]

> Lucres: I wyll not dysclaunder nor blame no man,
> But nevertheless, by that I here saye,
> Pore maydens be dissayved now and than.
> So greate dyssemblynge now a daye
> There is . . .
> (ll. 471–6)

---

[13] For further details of this curious game, see Meredith and Twycross (1984).
[14] 'And, scratching his head, let him a little later say'.
[15] 'And after a certain pause, Lucres shall say'.

Possibly, Lucres is considering the plight of the Ancient Roman virgin, but her 'now a daye' recalls the 'nowadays' of A's comment on the dress of the modern-day gallant: the impression that Lucres is in fact addressing the situation of maidens contemporary with, perhaps among, her audience is reinforced by the fact that she appears to be speaking directly to the audience at this point. The 'brief pause' before Lucres speaks, like A's brief pause and head-scratching, is a significant interval: for all its brevity, it carries the actors between the age of imperial Rome and the age of the Tudor household drama.

The apparently peaceful but sometimes self-consciously problematized coexistence of two temporal settings is matched by an unruffled spatial bilocation. A tells Gayus that he has no more friends 'within this hall' (l. 631): Gayus, thirty lines later, reflects that there is no one better born than Cornelius 'within all this cyte' (l. 660). The city in question is Rome, and Cornelius is sure of the setting for the speech proclaiming his nobility—'all this londe Of Italy' (ll. 1954–5): A, on the other hand, is definitely in England, and declares himself able to sing 'As well as ony man in Kent' (l. 1106). B continues to be aware of the audience: he is ashamed that the Ancilla beats him 'Before as many as here be present' (l. 1329), and also assures Gayus that 'this honorable audyence' will be present at his debate with Cornelius (l. 1313)—as indeed the audience will be, though not in Ancient Rome. What are the implications of this curious sense of time and space to a staging of the play?

The fluidity which *Fulgens and Lucres* seems to require in its use of space might suggest the *locus and platea* staging which Robert Weimann found to be characteristic of medieval theatre, and which, he argues, exerted profound influence on the use of space on the early modern stage.[16] Janette Dillon writes:

The two terms denote two interconnected ways of using space. While the place or *platea* is basically an open space, the *locus* can be literally a scaffold, but can also be any specifically demarcated space or architectural feature [which] . . . can represent a particular location, such as a house, a temple, a country, heaven or hell . . . whereas a *locus* always represents, for a given stretch of time, a specific location, the *platea* is essentially fluid and frequently non-representational. It is not tied to the illusion, to the fictional places where the drama is set, but is often predominantly an actors' space . . . in which performance can be recognised as performance rather than as the fiction it intermittently seeks to represent.[17]

As an example, Dillon discusses the Croxton *Play of the Sacrament*, a play which is neither Mystery nor Morality, which may or may not be early Tudor (it was written some time between 1461 and 1520), and which Simpson considers as like the Tudor interlude and unlike the cycle drama in that its focus is on correct belief, not good works.[18] In this play, a Jewish merchant, Jonathas, pays a Christian merchant, Aristorius, to steal the eucharistic wafer from church: Jonathas and his fellow Jews then stab the wafer and subject it to various forms of torture to test the doctrine that it is Christ's body. The wafer bleeds, and an apparition of the crucified Christ appears, whereupon the Jews are converted and Aristorius repents. There are a number of fixed, defined locations—the

---

[16] See Weimann (1978, 2000).   [17] Dillon (2006: 4–5).   [18] Simpson (2002: 557).

church, from which the wafer is stolen and into which the converted Jews process, Aristorius's house, Jonathas's house, all of which are part of the conversion narrative which, we are told, took place in Eraclea, Aragon, in 1461: between these locations, however, the *platea* is occupied by a comic doctor, Master Brundycche of Brabant, who lives 'a little beside Babwell Mill', near Bury St Edmunds, and who talks to the audience about the ailments of the 'grete congregacyon' who are 'here' (l. 521)[19]—the contemporary, Croxton audience.

Clearly this is in many ways similar to the temporal and spatial duality of *Fulgens and Lucres*, in that A and B parallel both Master Brundycche's participation in the time and space of the audience and his capacity to talk to characters in an alternative time and space of 'the play'. Nonetheless Medwall's interlude does not seem entirely to function as a *locus* and *platea* play, because the *locus* is too vague to be given the necessary visual focus. Publius and Cornelius are in Ancient Rome, but that's too big for a play. There is no house nor church nor other fixed location established within the city of Rome, and the action happens generally 'in the city', as generally 'in the hall'. When Fulgens meets Cornelius, he asserts that 'this is the oure that ye and I Apoyntid here to mete' (ll. 296–7)—the time and place are correct, but, for the audience, unnominated: deixis can be at once precise and ambiguous. A tells B that Lucres has made an appointment to meet Cornelius 'here Sone, in the evynyng aboute suppere' (ll. 1359–60): the meeting must certainly be in Ancient Rome, but is clearly appointed to coincide with mealtime in the Tudor great hall, where it will be witnessed. Furthermore, apart from these two fixed meetings, all the Romans in *Fulgens and Lucres* seem only to appear in the playing space on their way somewhere else. Fulgens leaves Cornelius and goes off to talk to Lucres (ll. 343–4); Cornelius then goes off to find himself a serving man (l. 359); Fulgens leaves Lucres to attend to his 'bysynes at whome' (l. 466); the Ancilla encounters B as she is on her way to find Gayus (ll. 861–3); A overhears news about Cornelius 'as I brought my mayster on hys way' (l. 1354), and so on. There is of course nothing unusual, for a modern audience, in a character making an exit because, within the narrative of the play, he needs to go to another place: this is, however, very different from the *locus* and *platea* staging of *Croxton* in which locations are realized and movement between them is scripted as part of the action—sometimes within the lines, as when the Clericus goes to seek a rich merchant and narrates: 'Now wyll I walke by thes pathes wyde' (l. 65), and sometimes in the stage directions: '*Here shall the Jewe merchaunt and his men come to þe Cristen merchaunte*' (l. 185 s.d.). *Locus* and *platea* staging shows the audience fixed points, and incorporates into its action the movement between them; *Fulgens and Lucres* does not show the audience the destinations of its characters, and dramatizes only a tiny portion, a few moments, on each of their journeys back and forth.

This indeterminacy of location is perhaps the reason for Lucres's astonishment when Gayus finds her: 'How wyste he For to fynde me here?' Gayus seems to assert that he finds her not because he knows where to look, but because he is dedicated:

---

[19] Line references are to the edn. of the play in Walker (2000).

'He that lysteth to do his dylygence.... At the laste he may come to your presence' (ll. 485–7). Because he loves her, he will find her 'wher so ever ye go' (l. 484). It is not places but people who are sought in *Fulgens and Lucres*. Asked where he dwells, A replies that he lacks a master—a reply which both reflects the reality of the servant who is dependent on a master for shelter, and indicates a definition of space according to the people occupying it. Unsurprisingly, then, Gayus tells A to 'Go thy waye unto Lucres' (l. 674), not Lucres's house, or a particular place where she might be found: A later realizes guiltily that he should have gone 'to Lucres... Thetherwarde I was bent' (ll. 807–9), and 'thetherwarde' demonstrates a conflation of person and location.

Place and Time in *Magnyfycence*

What is the purpose of *Fulgens*'s curious dramaturgy of place and time? Dillon states that a metonymic identification of person with place is a common aspect of *locus* and *platea* staging: a scaffold can represent, for example, 'the place of Covetousness', 'which is a conceptual rather than a properly physical place'.[20] Of course, Covetousness is an allegorical figure; possibly this aspect of the presentation hints at the allegorical roots of Medwall's narrative—and this impression is reinforced by comparison with the explicitly allegorized *Magnyfycence* of John Skelton. *Magnyfycence* was written, probably, in 1519–20 and, probably, as veiled advice to King Henry VIII about his treatment of the French minions who were seen as corrupting his court. The prince, Magnyfycence, is tricked by Fansy into admitting a series of Vice figures into his court: the Vices persuade Magnyfycence to ignore the advice of his trusted counsellor, Measure, and the prince is brought to ruin, only to be rescued and restored by Good Hope. Like *Fulgens*, it is small-troupe, household drama, also disseminated in print (it was printed by William Rastell around 1530): although its structure is that of the instructional morality, its secular, political intent is clear from the character of its Vices, who are not the Seven Deadly Sins but rather more specific and satirical personifications of Courtly Abusyon, Clokyd Colusyon, and so on.

Magnyfycence does not explicitly display bilocation, but it has, like *Fulgens*, a curiously double sense of time and place. In *Magnyfycence*, this stems from the play's double identity as political satire and moral allegory. The palace of Magnyfycence constitutes an important conceptual location, but it is never presented, and what happens there is narrated to the audience by the Vices, who seem always to be on their way somewhere: usually they are going to the Palace, or heading from it for a wild night on the tiles. It is this sense of motion which defines place in

[20] Dillon (2006: 4).

Magnyfycence—but only for the Vices. The Vices appear to be 'in the street', a street which leads to and from the palace, and which separates the prince from the publican. Presumably, when the play was staged in a Tudor hall, the Vices would consistently exit through the same door when going to the palace: the sense of motion is accelerated by the fact that cast doubling (if, as is thought, there were five actors playing all the different roles) would necessitate the same actor passing repeatedly through the door in different roles.

But that door never becomes fully a *locus* representing an entrance to the palace, because the staging of characters other than the Vices resists the sense of 'street' outside it. When Welthfull Felycyte meets Lyberty, Lyberty declares that the meeting was 'apoynted', but says nothing about the time or place appointed for the meeting (ll. 24–5).[21] The two, soon joined by Measure, conduct a philosophical discussion about the correct relationships among measure, wealth, and liberty, with reference to Horace: the scene is not one of street-talk. These characters discuss the abstractions which they simultaneously represent: because they are allegorical figures, their presence or absence, proximity to or distance from each other, carry at least as much meaning as the words they speak. 'Where wonnys Welthe?', asks Welthfull Felycyte (l. 22): 'whens come ye?', asks Felycyte of Lyberte (l. 29). No place is ever named in response: the answer is not spoken, but enacted, for the grouping of Lyberty, Welthfull Felycyte, and Measure onstage together is itself the answer, and the non-specificity of place carries the general nature of the teaching that these three things of necessity come together.

The Vices in *Magnyfycence* are sometimes comically confused and directionless, as when Counterfet Countenaunce, eager to look busy about getting rid of Measure, demands 'my botes and my spores' (l. 570). Crafty Conveyaunce's puzzled question 'In all this hast whether wyll ye ryde?' meets the unsatisfactory response: 'I trowe it shall not nede to abyde' (ll. 570–1). Similarly, Fansy is 'Bysy, bysy, and ever bysy' (l. 1038). But this is busy-ness without moral direction, not the generalized location which characterizes moments of virtue. The Vices invoke specific times and places— contemporary 'Tyburn', especially, and the local taverns, but also Pountesse, Calais, Cockermouth, everything from the Tyne to the Trent—and these invocations root them in the here and now of contemporary satire.

Specificity of location seems an aspect of Vice in late medieval drama. Aristorius, the corrupt Christian merchant, in the speech which opens the Croxton *Play of the Sacrament* offers a loosely alphabetical list of all the places in the world in which his fame has spread: and place and profit are connected, for his fame is based on his wealth—'of all Aragon I am most mighty of sylver and of gold' (l. 7), and his ultimate expression of wealth is that he would unhesitatingly buy a whole country—'and yt wer a counter to by now wold I nat wond!' (l. 8). The speech is chillingly suggestive of the Mystery Cycle's scene of Christ's temptation by Satan. In N-Town the same

---

[21] Line references are to the edn. of the play in Walker (2000).

connection is made between place and corrupt profit as Satan tempts Christ with everything he can give him:

> Turne thee now and this syde, and se here Lumbardye,
> Of spycery ther growth many an hyndryd balys;
> Archas and Aragon and grett Almonye;
> Parys and Portyngale and the town of Galys;
> Pownteys and poperynge and also Pycardye... (ll. 170–4, Play 23)[22]

Satan tells Christ to 'see' these places: it is as if he is trying to assert a series of rich and exotic *loci* all of which 'longyth to' him (l. 178). But Christ resists temptation by asserting the generalized *platea*, or *'plas'*:

> Go abak, þu flowle Sathanas!
> In Holy Scrypture wretyn it is,
> Thi Lorde God to wurchipp in every plas (ll. 183–5)

In the Mystery Cycles, the capacity of the *platea* to signify the here and now has heavy theological significance. The *locus* would keep a historical Christ remote in time and place from his audience—it has been shown that, in *Fulgens*, B argues that an audience can have no vested interest in action performed in a remote place. But in cycle drama, Christ can step into the *platea*, and Christ in the *platea* is Christ in the same time and place as the audience, offering the audience contact with a present divinity.

Because *Magnyfycence* shares an allegorical mode with the Morality Plays, the broader action of *Magnyfycence* takes place 'in a virtual space, for the most part outside of time and geography',[23] as Walker has written of the Morality Play: at the same time, if the Moralities display, through the appearance of Vices such as 'Nowadays', a 'theologically grounded distrust of the modern',[24] *Magnyfycence* displays a secular, politically grounded distrust of the modern through its carefully located Vices. The political grounding is important, however, because it is what makes the dramaturgy of space and time in *Magnyfycence* distinctive.

Magnyfycence and *Fulgens and Lucres* offer political comment by staging antique or allegorical fables in the halls of the politically powerful.[25] The halls—whether royal halls, noblemen's halls, or guild halls—are not incidental. They are not merely empty spaces, in which a scaffold or stage, or even just a character's assertion of location, creates an alternative space for the period of the play; they are themselves the set. The audience must be led to respond to all of the space in the hall in the same way: if one area or feature of the hall were established as a separate *locus*, then action which occurred there might appear to differ in its significance from other action, when in fact the political message depends on everything signifying equally within the great hall. So, when the Vices in *Magnyfycence* try to assert specific, *other* locations, they are seeking to defeat the play's method of instruction, and indeed the instruction itself. Even the

---

[22] Line references are to Spector (1991).
[23] Walker (2000: 210).
[24] Ibid.
[25] For examples of discussion see Scattergood (1993); Evershed (2005).

urgency of their movement to and from the 'offstage' palace of Magnyfycence undermines the truth of the political allegory, that the drama is actually what is happening in the great hall. In *Fulgens*, A and B, like Vices, also allude to specific, other, contemporary locations (York, Kent) and engage in contemporary folk games. But most importantly, by their discussion of 'the play', they try to assert the separation of the play from life in the great hall, and thus, Vice-like, defeat instruction.

The hall in which A has no more friends is the same as the city in which no one is nobler born than Cornelius: the audience must realize this for the play's political message to get across. The play is concerned with the definition of virtuous behaviour in a political and social context, and with the nature of the contract between the nobleman and the man who serves him. It is vital that the great hall audience—of the served and the serving—do not feel, as B suggests at the beginning of the play, that they need not object to the action of *Fulgens and Lucres* because it happened somewhere else: rather, the audience must see, as B states much later, that the play involves and concerns them. B, as aching member, realizes that the play and the audience are one, and the play will only end when he and A leave, when the audience/household leave the playing-space/dining hall: 'and we were ons go It were do straight wey' (ll. 2306–7).

Bibliography

DILLON, JANETTE (2006), *The Cambridge Introduction to Early English Theatre* (Cambridge: Cambridge University Press).

EMMERSON, R. K. (2005), 'Dramatic History: On the Diachronic and Synchronic in the Study of Early English Drama', *Journal of Medieval and Early Modern Studies*, 35, 39–66.

EVERSHED, ELIZABETH (2005), 'Meet for Merchants? Some Implications of Situating Skelton's Magnyfycence at the Merchant Tailors' Hall', *Medieval English Theatre*, 27: 69–85.

KING, PAMELA (2006), *The York Mystery Cycle and the Worship of the City* (Cambridge: D. S. Brewer).

Lexton, Ruth (2008), 'Henry Medwall's Fulgens and Lucres and the Question of Nobility Under Henry VII', in Linda Clark (ed.), *The Fifteenth Century*, viii. *Rule, Redemption and Representations in Late Medieval England and France* (Woodbridge: Boydell Press), 163–82.

MEREDITH, PETER, and MEG TWYCROSS (1984), '"Farte Pryke in Cule" and Cockfighting', *Medieval English Theatre*, 6: 30–9.

SCATTERGOOD, JOHN (1993), 'Skelton's Magnyfycence and the Tudor Royal Household', *Medieval English Theatre*, 15: 21–48.

SIMPSON, JAMES (2002), *Reform and Cultural Revolution: The Oxford English Literary History*, ii. *1350–1547* (Oxford: Oxford University Press).

—— (2005), 'Not the Last Word', *JMEMS*, 35, 111–19.

SPECTOR, STEPHEN (ed.) (1991), *The N-Town Play* (2 vols. EETS SS 11; Oxford: Oxford University Press for the Early English Text Society).

WALKER, GREG (1998), *Politics of Performance* (Cambridge: Cambridge University Press).

——(ed.) (2000), *Medieval Drama: An Anthology* (Oxford: Blackwell).

WEIMANN, ROBERT (1978), *Shakespeare and the Popular Tradition in the Theater: Studies in the Social Dimension of Dramatic Form and Function* (Baltimore: Johns Hopkins University Press).

——(2000), *Author's Pen and Actor's Voice: Playing and Writing in Shakespeare's Theatre*, ed. Helen Higbee and William West (Cambridge: Cambridge University Press).

CHAPTER 20

'SWEIT ROIS...DELYTSUM LYLLIE'

METAPHORICAL AND REAL FLOWERS IN MEDIEVAL VERSE

GILLIAN RUDD

THE LANGUAGE OF LOVE

'Sweit rois of vertew and of gentilnes' begins Dunbar's evocative lyric, continuing

> Delytsum lyllie of everie lustynes,
> Richest in bontie and in bewtie cleir
> And euerie vertew that is deir,
> Except onlie that ȝe ar mercyles.
>
> In to ȝour garthe this day I did persew.
> Thair saw I flowris that fresche wer of hew,
> Baithe quhyte and rid moist lusty wer to seyne,
> And halsum herbis vpone stalkis grene,
> ȝit leif nor flour fynd could I nane of rew.
>
> I dout that Merche with his caild blastis keyne
> Hes slayne this gentill herbe that I of mene,

Quhois petewous deithe dois to my hart sic pane
That I wald mak to plant his rute agane,
So confortand his levis vnto me bene.[1]

Ostensibly speaking of two flowers, we know immediately that this poem addresses one woman, and that in terms not entirely benign. The courtly overtones of 'virtew', 'gentilnes', 'bontie', and even of 'lustynes' with its more basic associations encourage us to move swiftly on from the flowers invoked into the metaphorical world where all ladies are flowers, beautiful, idealized, and for the most part harsh in their treatment of lovers, badly in need of the rue which as both herb and quality (pity) would make this lady more tolerable to and indeed tolerant of her poetic suitor. The wit of the poem lies in Dunbar's deployment of the familiar metaphorical tropes, which allows a certain risqué tone as well as one of decorous courtship and perhaps sardonic disillusion. The 'garth' into which the poet strays in the second verse is suggestive to say the least, especially to those familiar with *The Romance of the Rose* and its prevailing *double-entendre* of private garden and female body. The insistence on the flowers and herbs found or not in this garth serves to keep the poem clean and courtly, but also ensures the plants are read metaphorically. Within that metaphor there are two spheres of reference in play: the courtly and the medical, with the latter being most evident in 'halsum' (wholesome), but also present in 'vertew' as indicating a healing property or power, and 'confortand' with its connotations of making comfortable as well as comforting. Many of the words are thus equally available to courtly and medical lexis, which should be no surprise, given how much the language of love revolves around ideas of wounds, illness, and succour. Added to these are the religious undertones: the cluster of 'vertew', 'gentilnes', and 'bontie' in such close proximity to the rose and lily, which are both associated with Mary, allows the poem to sound like a devotional lyric until we hit the fourth line and even after it religious tones still resonate in the poem as the secular lady is tacitly compared to the divine as well as to a more sympathetic ideal woman of this world.

None of this is new; amongst others, Bawcutt neatly refers to the garden as 'hover [ing] between the literal and allegorical',[2] while Reiss, who reads 'lustynes' in the second line as referring specifically to sexual desire rather than the broader possible sense of attractiveness, remarks that 'the traditional significations of the two flowers are reversed: lily would be more appropriately associated with virtue and rose with lustiness'.[3] This is clearly a poem that rejoices in inverting expectations and in witty transpositions, but here I want to discuss its use of the natural world and to highlight the extent to which other available facts about the plants pressed into service here as vehicles for metaphor contribute to the meaning of the poem. Horticultural understanding of the flowers is operating in this lyric, and underpinning the whole are the actual plants, so obvious as to be customarily overlooked, but there nonetheless and also worth our attention.

[1] Bawcutt (1998).
[2] Bawcutt (1992: 298).
[3] Reiss (1979: 101).

In what follows I will be focusing in detail on the flowers in a selection of lyrics to show how familiar tropes and typical passages contain elements of the material world as it is in fact rather then just in literary conception. Paying due attention to these aspects not only reinvigorates our reading of even the most familiar literary devices, but requires us to admit that the non-human natural world is not secondary, but integral to us in ways which we rarely acknowledge, or too easily take for granted: our reaction and relation to it informs our language. Such an assertion necessarily borders on larger questions of what 'nature' is: how far is it a social construct which defines what we see, or recognize, how far an unalterable fact.[4] Much of what follows shows that words and images slide across the boundary between real and symbolic, so much so that we might question how much there is indeed a boundary; perhaps we would do better to think of the terms as part of a continuum. Better still we could shed the image of a straight line that 'continuum' implies and instead try to think in terms of moving fluidly among a wealth of signification, association, and description. We press flowers, animals, even the weather into service almost without thought and the result is that within our apparently thoroughly human constructs of metaphor, image, or description, the actual remains, beleaguered, overwritten perhaps, overlooked almost certainly, but nonetheless there. This discussion will focus on the flowers named in Dunbar's poem, but the broad terms of the argument will be applicable to almost any element of the natural world that is found in literature.

ROSES, LILIES, AND RUE

Isidore of Seville places roses and lilies in close proximity to each other as he defines them in sequence in the ninth section of book 17 of his widely popular and influential *Etymologies* (*c*.615–30).[5] This book deals with Rural Matters (*de rebus rusticis*) and the entries read as follows:

17. The rose (*rosa*) is so called from the appearance of its flower, which blushes (*rubere*) with a red (*rutilans*) color. 18. The lily (*lilia*) is a plant with a milk-white (*lacteus*) flower, whence it is named, as if it were *liclia*. Although its petals are white, a glitter of gold appears within it.[6]

Isidore moves between plant and human points of reference as he seeks to pin down not what the plants are, but what the words mean. The result is a mixture of latent

---

[4] For 'nature' as a construct see Evernden (1992). A good collection of essays indicating the variety of ways medievalists are currently thinking about nature is Hanawalt and Kiser (2008).

[5] Isidore, bishop of Seville, began composing his *Etymologies* in Latin *c*.615, leaving it unfinished at his death in 636. It remained an influential book of reference for a thousand years and was well enough known for Chaucer, amongst many others, to refer to 'Isidore' without need for further explanation.

[6] Isidore (2006: 351).

anthropomorphism and objective description. There is a humanizing subtext in the blushing rose *rubere*; flowers of course do not blush, nor do many animals (humans and octopuses are in the minority), yet we easily accept Isidore's use of the word as adding a level of precision to the colour of the rose. Likewise in his choice of 'milk' as a descriptive term, he uses a potentially human, certainly mammalian referent for the lily's whiteness. *Lacteus* is here translated as the colour milk-white, but *lacteus* also means 'milky, full of milk', which offers a sense of the petals containing liquid which in turn introduces a tactile element entirely apt for the thick, almost fleshy feel of the petals of *Lilium candidum*, still commonly known as the Madonna Lily. Whether we translate the word as colour or state, the root word is *lac*, which is milk itself and that is what carries the animalizing if not indeed anthropomorphic element which the lily shares with the blushing rose.

Here, as elsewhere, Isidore somewhat stretches his etymology as *lilia* is not *liclia*; he has to create that possibility in order to clinch his derivation, but his careful observation of the actual flowers continues with the mention of gold, which is indeed a part of the open lily bloom. In Isidore's definition, however, gold is not just the colour, it is also the mineral which we humans value so highly. As intended, that creates a further connection with Mary, Mother of God, whose high religious status is frequently indicated in pictures by the use of gold. This trend of moving from the natural world to the human continues in the definitions of violet and acanthus that complete this paragraph in the *Etymologies*. The description of the violet refers to the three different colours of flower that occur in the plant as well as its scent:

19. The violet (*viola*) gets its name from the strength (*vis*) of its scent (cf. *olere*, 'be fragrant'). There are three kinds of violet: purple, white and quince-yellow.[7]

Again, Isidore, or his sources, is showing direct acquaintance with the plant, but the choice of information is significant as although only the fact of its strong scent is necessary for the derivation of its name, he also includes the range of colours associated with the flower, which happen to be liturgical, as if the latent reference to Mary in the lily entry is affecting what is included under violet. Finally the paragraph ends with the acanthus, which begins entirely within the plant world and is the kind of entry we might expect in botanical lists, with its area of origin and brief description of the physical plant:

20. Acanthus (*acanthus*) is an evergreen Egyptian plant, full of thorns and with supple shoots. 21. Clothing artfully decorated with an acanthus pattern is called *acanthinus*. It is also called *acanthis*.

Isidore refrains from an overt reference to the crown of thorns, but he does move swiftly from the plant's attributes into clothing, which is so clearly human that it merits an entry to itself. This betrays not only the way we use the plant world for decoration but also perhaps our inability to maintain focus exclusively on that world;

---

[7] Ibid.

we seem to be compelled to relate any information and perhaps any experience back to ourselves.

As a whole then, this paragraph from the *Etymologies* invites symbolic connections and arguably such symbolic and therefore entirely human reference is entirely proper for a volume which is, after all, dealing with what we humans call things and why. More interestingly, the trend is also evident in tomes purporting to offer only objective information, such as John Trevisa's popular translation of Bartholomew Anglicus's encyclopedia *De proprietatibus rerum*.[8]

Trevisa is most informative about roses. As is the case with most of his entries on plants, the bulk of the material is horticultural and medical, reflecting the way plants were valued for their medicinal and culinary uses more than as simple decorative objects. Thus, his opening, brief botanical description swiftly yields to comments on the rose's curative power or 'vertu'. This medicinal aspect is important enough to merit immediate repetition to ensure the reader understands which bits of the plant are most effective:

Rosa 'þe rose tree,' as Plius [Pliny] seiþ, is a litil tree with prikkes, and most vertu þerof is in þe flour and þe secounde in þe leues and in þe seed, for þe tree is medicynable in flour, leues, and seed.[9]

Having thus established that the flowers, the leaves, and the seed all have some medicinal qualities, Trevisa goes on to mention that there are two kinds of rose, the wild and the tame.[10] The tame grows in gardens and is trained like a vine; lack of such training will result in the plant reverting to its wild state. The wild rose is less potent as a medicine, has fewer petals and those it has are broader and, significantly, less red ('whytisshe ymedlid wiþ litel rednesse'). They also have a fainter scent. The point about the colour is noteworthy in the light of Isidore's definition and of the literary use of the rose. It seems that the type of rose which springs to mind with the word 'rose' is inevitably red and cultivated. In short, it is the kind we expect to find in gardens, not the one scrambling wild in hedges or woods. This automatic association is not in fact right, as a moment's reflection will tell us, and indeed Trevisa enacts this reflection as he swiftly counters the presumption that roses are red in his description of the tame rose, which is 'alle rede oþer al most white' (completely red, or almost white). The 'oþer' reveals that the recollection of the almost white rose is a counter to the red rose which sprang most immediately to mind.

It is only after a long paragraph establishing the medicinal powers of the plant, its growing habits, and details on how the flower-buds emerge, that Trevisa provides a passing sentence in the next paragraph on how the rose is regarded and valued in

---

[8] John Trevisa completed *On The Properties of Things*, an English translation of Bartholomew's Latin text, in 1398/9. Bartholomew compiled his work in the mid-1200s drawing on other authorities such as Aristotle and Pliny for his material. It and Trevisa's translation remained influential into the 15th cent.

[9] Trevisa (1975: 1029).

[10] Trevisa's use of 'leues' moves between 'leaves' and 'petals'. When 'leues' appears with 'flour' it indicates the whole bloom; later, when, differentiating between the colour of the wild and cultivated rose, 'leues' means 'petals'.

more general terms. Here we are told that the rose is the chief flower of the world, and for that reason it is used to make crowns, as these roses then sit on the most important part of the human body, the head. Fleetingly it seems that its elevated status results from its power to please the senses as it delights the eye, the nose, and the touch, but then within the sentence it becomes apparent that its really important aspect is its curative virtue against 'many siknesses and yueles'.[11] There then follows a third and final long paragraph detailing various medicinal properties and offering recipes for cures for specific ailments. As with Isidore's definition, the overall effect is of sliding off the actual physical flower into its uses and attributes for humans. Value comes with proven effectiveness, it seems, and simple pleasures, such as the sight or smell of a rose, are not allowed to be as important as what a concoction of rose-petals and honey can do for you.

Much the same can be said of the first paragraph of Trevisa's entry on the lily. As before, a brief physical description is soon followed by a longer list of the plant's virtues, particularly in curing boils, sores, and sundry other swellings. Interestingly, the lily is reputed to be next to the rose 'in worþiness and nobilite'[12] and while the rest of the sentence makes it clear that worth and nobility are here, too, measured in curative terms, yet the words themselves suggest a more innate quality that fleetingly draws these plants into the human sphere of reference not as mere ingredients, but as entities (almost people?) respected in themselves. Worthiness and nobility are character attributes and hint at the possibility of equality between human and flower. Perhaps it is this latent acknowledgement of the plant as a something with its own integrity which allows Trevisa to continue into a longer and more detailed description of the plant itself. We are told exactly what the stalk looks like, how the flower hangs and where the seeds are carried. Next we learn of the root, which (being a bulb) has cloves like garlic and how, according to Aristotle, the stalk has many 'knottes' (joints) on it and that if the stalk is pegged down before the plant goes to seed, each knot will root. By now we are in truly botanical territory, and significantly it is at this point that a tone of simple appreciation for the plant enters, as the propagation tip from Aristotle is concluded with 'and þat is wonder'.[13] More lore from Aristotle follows about the effects of cutting lilies at particular times of their growth and here another nice horticultural detail is included: if a lily stalk is cut clean from the root before the flower opens, the goodness of the stalk is fully contained in the pith of the cut bloom; this is then digested as the flower opens and makes the flower itself white. This somewhat arcane process is credited as being the reason why 'versifours likned þe lilye to mannes inwitte þat is besy atte laste to þenke on þinges þat euer schal laste'.[14] Trevisa does not tell us which poets or versifiers make this connection between the lily and a person's conscience, but it is another mark of the wonder the flower has engendered in others now, as well as himself, that such an analogy should be made and be based on such precise observation of the plant.

---

[11] Ibid. 1030.   [12] Ibid. 981.   [13] Ibid.   [14] Ibid.

READING THE REAL

What does all this information add to our reading Dunbar's lyric? One thing it might do is allow us to see an unexpected and perhaps unconscious level of precision in the choice of words. The rose is sweet (sweit)—an allusion to its smell, which also tells us that this rose is a tamed one, since, as we now know from Trevisa, the wild rose has less scent than the cultivated. The 'gentilnes' with which it is attributed could also be a reflection of its tamed state and decorous growth, as opposed to the wild and tangled rambling of its wild cousin. The lily, however, is 'delystum' a more general word which might reflect this flower's broader range of appeal while maintaining the hierarchy in which lily comes second to rose. Of course the first stanza primarily refers to the lady who is alluded to in familiar courtly and allegorical terms, but it is worth noting that such specifics of the actual flowers are to be found here as well. In other words the metaphor works best when we pause to give space to the real flower, not just the generic 'rose' or 'lily' that serves to create the connection to an equally generic idealized lady. As we move through the poem this becomes even more the case. It is accurate, not just typical, to say that the blooms in the garden are white and red; these are the two colours of the rose, but, we might recall, red is the default colour of rose, and the lily is mainly thought of as white, despite Trevisa's initial mention of its colours as white, yellow, or 'purpre' (probably a crimson or red colour rather than what we think of as purple today). 'Lusty' is a deliberate pun on 'flourishing' and lusty in the sexual sense, and so blends the human and plant world, but 'halsum herbis upon stalkis grene' can now be seen to be particularly appropriate to the lily, whose stalks attract particular comment.

Isidore and Trevisa offer further pertinent information on rue (*rota*). It was known to guard against snake's venom (as did the lily), it forms part of a cure for nasal polyps, and also helps mitigate if not actually cure lechery in men, while, contrari- wise, it acts against coldness in women.[15] This adds a rather different dimension to the poem as the lack of pity (rue) in the lady is bemoaned by the poet who conventionally begs mercy in the hope it will lead to the fulfilment of his desire, yet it appears that if rue (the herb) is administered to him, then his desire will indeed be cured. On the other hand, if she takes it, there might be some hope that his desire would be reciprocated. This fits perfectly with the amused, sardonic undertone of the verse and also demonstrates how amorous and medical discourses intertwine, but still detracts attention from that third sphere of reference, the horticultural. Yet this, too, has something to add, for Trevisa, again drawing on Aristotle, tells us that rue is a very fertile plant, being capable of springing from seed, stalk, spray, and root:

And virtue seminatyf of rue is in þe seed, in the stalk, in spray, and in roote, for sprayes þerof ybent dounward in toward þe grounde taketh roote anon an nought druyeþ soone.[16]

---

[15] Isidore (2006: 357); Trevisa (1975: 1038–40).   [16] Ibid. 1039.

Given which the new rooting desired in the final lines, introduced through the deft word-play on 'ru(t)e', should not prove difficult, despite the tone whose longing implies it is beyond the poet's powers. A different poem is being revealed, one which lies under and also underpins the one we encounter first. Rather than the subject being a lady who is allegorized through flowers and who is the one to cure the poet's lovelorn state by taking pity on him, it is the actual flowers who not only offer the immediate delights of scent and beauty, but, through their medicinal properties, can cure his longing permanently, offering comfort as good health rather than emotional support. The fact that an alternative poem exists within the surface one is typical of our human response to the world around us: even though we know this other, natural world exists, we overlook it without exactly denying it. My latent poem does not really counteract this habit, as it too talks about the plants in terms of what they can do for the poet. It does, however, offer the plants a place as plants rather then solely as vehicles for human emotions or characteristics.

The above demonstration is intended to highlight our readerly habit of focusing on the allegory, examining its development and explicating its meaning without pausing to admire the actual entities (in this case flowers) involved in the allegory. This does not alter the fact that the poem weaves together the allegorical, courtly rose, lily, and rue and the medical ones; indeed they are brought together with greatest force in the word 'vertew'. The horticulture theme is foregrounded from the second verse, but we are expected to be reading metaphorically throughout. However, my alternative reading suggests that the full depth of the metaphor works best if we retain the actual plants in our mind. That in turn implies that often we do not retain this depth of meaning and that is due to our habitual overlooking of the physical nature around us. In literature, as in life, humanity exploits the natural world without much thought; now, however, with the rise of environmentalism and green awareness, we are being exhorted to focus our attention more on that world which we have previously taken for granted, and that refocusing rightly includes literary critical attention as well as more hands-on endeavours.[17]

The emphasis on healing, cures, and benefit to the spirit as well as the body, makes it tempting to say that medical discourse is the site where the allegorical or spiritual meets the factual; however, given the hints on growing and propagation that are often intermingled with the other information, there is an equal temptation to term that discourse horticultural. These temptations spring from a very post-medieval categorization of knowledge. As is clear from the above quotations from Isidore and Trevisa, the medicinal and botanic were not regarded as clearly distinct categories. Knowledge of any kind, including allegorical and spiritual, is all part and parcel of what defines both word and plant, and that knowledge in turn reveals how humans tend to regard the non-human world. This mingling of what we now regard as distinct spheres of reference can also be found in the herbals and bestiaries, of which the latter in particular were highly popular. Much work has been done on the bestiary

[17] Examples of such attention being devoted to medieval texts and studies, some more consciously 'green' than others, are: Howes (1997); Kiser (2001); Rudd (2007); Salisbury (1993). See also n. 18 below.

tradition, on the role of animals and birds, and the tension surrounding the question of where the line can or ought to be drawn between human and animal; I will not repeat such discussions here, but it is worth noting that a good deal of the references to non-human animals function to make human habits and institutions proper or natural.[18] Rather, let us stay within the world of flowers and in particular that of roses and lilies and see how the mingling of discourses is used in poems that feature these blooms.

'THER IS NO ROSE'

The Trinity College carol 'ther is no rose of swych virtu' is allegorical from the start. The familiar reading of 'rose' as Mary is suggested in both the immediate assertion that the rose referred to here is exceptional (there is none other like it), further endorsed by the phrase 'swych virtue', with its customary reference to Mary's purity, and finally made clear in the second line as only Mary, the metaphorical rose, could be said to give birth to Jesus, assuming this is how we read 'bare'. The 'alleluia' that is both the third line and the word of recognition and acclamation familiar to all from the introduction of the Gospel in the weekly Mass confirms this association and in doing so also recognizes how the rose is operating here. Bearing in mind that carols were songs sung by a wide section of the community, not just restricted to those who could read or those in religious orders, the way this carol moves through its images and its languages implies, and indeed presumably helped create, a widespread familiarity with this kind of metaphor: a kind that invokes visual image, the medicinal power of plants, and the expectation that the purpose of an image is to interpret it. At the end the carol collapses the invoked world of the nativity into the literal one of the singer who walks out of the church (or hall) at the end of the song, enacting the final call 'let's go' (*transeamus*). The first three verses are the ones relevant here:

> Ther is no rose of swych virtu
> As is the rose that bare Jesu.
> *Alleluia.*
>
> For in this rose conteyned was
> Heven and erthe in lytyl space.
> *Res miranda.*
>
> Be that rose we may weel see
> That he is God in personys thre.
> *Pari forma.*[19]

---

[18] For discussions of the use of animals and birds in literature see: Crane (2007); Fudge (2000); Fudge *et al.* (2000); Flores (2000); Salter (2001).

[19] Saupe (1998: 68).

The language of the rose here is as macaronic as the English and Latin of the verse in general; we move between the rose as rose, its medicinal use (invoked but not developed through the word 'virtue'), and its symbolic meaning as Mary. However, familiar as this reading is, this carol is not as fixed in its use of the symbol as the lyric 'Of on that is so fayr and briht' in which Mary is explicitly the rose without thorns ('Leuedi flour of alle thing / rosa sine spina'). Without that specific pinning of rose to lady it is possible to say that the rose is not in fact Mary, but Christ himself, which makes the 'rose' of the first line the rosebush, which allows Jesus to be a flower, rather than rosehip or seed. This fits with Isidore's inclusion of 'flos' (flower) as one of the names attached to Christ; according to Isidore, it is appropriate because flowers exist to be picked (a point to which we will return later). Moreover, reading the whole rosebush as Christ fits with Trevisa's information that the rose has medicinal powers in its three areas of flower, leaf, and seed. Suddenly we are not sure if we are looking at just the bloom here or the bush as a whole: the word 'rose' serves for both. However, the likelihood is that we have the flower in our mind's eye and that is in part because of the word 'conteyned' which summons up or perhaps relies upon the shape of a rosebud before it is fully open. While it is important to expunge from our modern minds latter-day complicated hybrids and cabbage roses and consider only the simpler form of the flower with fewer petals which open flat, as wild and many shrub roses still do,[20] it is still true that in bud form the petals curl round to enclose the small space of the centre of the flower. This, in the carol's terms, is surely the little space that contains heaven and earth. One could go on, chasing details and pondering exactly how closely the flower is being used in this carol, but the point is that no one does. We do not feel the need because the image is so easily present in our minds. It is in fact an example of what Isidore calls using 'types of names from other lesser things so that he [Christ] might more easily be understood'.[21] The point of interest is how far the actual, individual, and material rose survives, withstanding being subsumed into a typical notion of a rose and the use humans have for the plant either medically or as metaphor. Although it has been the habit in the past to assume there is indeed no rose in the carol (as a punning misreading of the first line suggests), only the symbolic one, perhaps closer attention has revealed that there is indeed a rose in this text.

This suggestion concurs with Pavord's and Collins's separate observations on the marked change that occurs in the kinds of illustration provided for herbals from the fourteenth century on. Previous pictures were copies of classical and Arabic illustrations, reproduced without reference to what the actual plant looked like. Pavord posits a habit of stylization that 'impelled medieval illustrators to turn plants into formal abstractions, patterns rather than living things'.[22] In such a world, words

---

[20] Medieval illustrations show roses with neat petals, evenly spaced; the open flower is flat, buds, tightly furled. A fine example of such drawings may be found in Collins (2003: fo. 83^r), where, interestingly, the rose begins the 'r' section, presumably in recognition of the flower's high status. For discussion of the development of MS illustration see Collins (2000).

[21] Isidore (2006: 157).

[22] Pavord (2005: 134).

became more reliable vehicles for description than pictures, but the fact that this stylistic compulsion was shaken off during the Middle Ages (as proved by the remarkably handsome herbal, London, British Library, Egerton MS 747, which was produced in southern Italy c.1300) indicates a counter-impulse to restore accurate observation to these reference books, even if such splendour would be found only in the libraries of a privileged few. Similar attention to detail and direct observation of the actual rather than conceptual natural world can be found in literature.

Offering just such attention and so a contrast to the Trinity carol is the following Harley lyric which seems to include roses and lilies just as flowers in its opening lines. The plants mark a particular point in the seasonal year and simple, stark juxtaposition is used to enable the poem to move swiftly on to the now familiar blend of courtly and religious tropes.

> Nou skrinkeþ rose ant lylie-flour,
> þat whilen ber þat suete sauour
>   in somer, þat suete tyde;
> ne is no quene so stark ne stour,
> ne no leuedy so bryht in bour
>   þat ded ne shal by glyde.
> Whose wol fleysh lust forgon
>   ant heuene blis abyde,
> on Iesu be is þoht anon,
>   þat þerled was ys side.[23]

This is the first stanza of a longer lyric that develops the theme of Mary as provider of cures rather than being the medicine itself. This becomes clear in stanza 4 where Mary is referred to a 'leche' (leech in the sense of physician) and that stanza begins with a reference to the remedies she offers:

> Betere is hire medycyn
> þen eny mede or eny wyn;
> Hire erbes smulleþ suete;

The Mary offered here can be read as someone who grows or perhaps supplies plants for use in remedies; 'erbes' covers any plant, though usually indicates one which is used in either cookery or medicine. It is worth remembering that gardens provided food, remedies, and pleasure all at once and that the efficacy of a plant as a remedy might well rest in its scent, not just in a concoction made from it, as we have seen in Trevisa's entries on roses and lilies. That said, it is clear that the lyric is not really attending to whatever plants Mary may be growing; 'hire erbes' are surely intended to be allegorical, better than any other medicine because spiritual, not bodily. We do not expect to be told which flowers we should grow to cure the distress which afflicts this poet.

The lyric does not make clear whether that distress stems from remorse for sin in general, or for sexual sin specifically, nor whether the speaker of the poem is male or

---

[23] Brook (1956). A text of this lyric may also be found in Saupe (1998: 149–50).

female. While it works as a generalized exhortation to reform, it is also possible to read this as the song of a pregnant woman, anxious about her condition, if not also about what has led her to it and even the possibility of death in childbirth it entails. This reading adds point to the first stanza's insistence that no matter how noble the lady, she will die and to the urging that whoever wishes to merit heaven should avoid fleshly lust. It also adds meaning to the reference to Mary as the one woman who was both mother and virgin and adds poignancy to the use of the word 'shoures' in the final verse:

> For he þat dude is body on tre,
> Of oure sunnes haue piete
> þat weldes heouene boures!
> Wymmon, wiþ þi iolyfte,
> þou þench on Godes shoures!
> þah þou be whyt ant bryht on ble,
> Falewen shule þy floures.

The primary meaning of 'shoures' in this verse must be 'pain', but it also carries connotations of the pains of childbirth.[24] The fading of the archetypal flowers of a lady's complexion thus also marks the end of her life as a carefree young woman and her entry into the world of mother, unless, as the poem darkly hints, it is into the next world altogether. Perhaps this interpretation is too particular; perhaps it is better read as a lyric of frustrated love, in the mode of 'Lenten ys come wiþ loue to toune' but with a religious rather than secular final sphere of reference.[25] In either case, courtly, religious, and medical terms interact and blend as the poem moves through the several arenas that make up the human world. Thus heaven is made up of bowers and the garden image continues in the 'whyt and bryth' which pick up the rose and lily of the first line, but become the flowers of ladies's complexions. This may also carry symbolic meanings, indicating female virtue, which is sharply contrasted with the women's jollity through the juxtaposition which leads into the command to think on God's suffering. The inevitability of mortal passing is foregrounded here, but by now the only mortality that matters is human: the specific rose and lily seem to have passed out of the lyric, replaced by symbolic, anonymous, and generic flowers. Except that in order for the allegory to work we must maintain a sense, even a clear image of the shrinking and fading blooms with which the lyric started. These real flowers contribute to the heavenly bowers, allow the falling of the metaphorical flowers of the women, and presumably take part in honouring Jesus, just as all the world does. So the rose and lily are still there, albeit latent.

---

[24] See MED 'shour' (n.) 4. Interestingly, the citations offered in the MED suggest a development of physical pain from the discomfort suffered in harsh weather.

[25] In his elegant reading of 'Lenten ys come with loue to toune' (pp. 66–73), Reiss (1972) summarizes the lyric as 'relating the activity of nature to the feelings of man in general and of the narrator in particular' (p. 67), adding that the 'particular flowers and birds mentioned do more, however, than provide a certain kind of imagery' (p. 69). His reading offers many insights pertinent to anyone interested in ecocriticism and its precursors.

Nevertheless, this poem, which began with the actual, observed natural world of those fading roses and lilies, can be seen as reintroducing that world again in the two final lines which simultaneously attest that all the world honours Jesus, and that this poem at least honours all the world:

> Iesu, haue merci of me,[26]
> þat al þis world honoures.

The form that honour takes could be, I suggest, the simple but rarely deployed one of paying attention to the world around us and allowing it intrinsic worth rather than immediately making it into something else, anthropomorphizing it or rendering it into a symbol. If we focus on the natural world a further reading of 'shoures' appears.

Could there be subtextual rain in 'shoures'? Taken out of context, our first instinct would be to read it as 'showers', as in, most famously, Chaucer's opening to the *Canterbury Tales* with its 'shoures soote'. Chaucer's showers happen in April, where those of the Harley lyric occur after summer, but the word is arguably at work here. If so, the image becomes one not just of flowers fading at the end of the season, but perhaps of being damaged by rain. The image is still natural, but now contains fuller realism than the conventional and possibly more romanticized, inevitable fading suggested by the opening line. God's showers in this reading are literal rains which mark the passing of the year and will indeed contribute to the fading of the rose and lily, but were also necessary to their blooming. With this latent return to the non-human natural world, the lyric ends on a rhyme which links the action of honouring with the rain which both sustains and destroys. Women are still flowers, as the courtly language of the previous lines assert, but now, as flowers, they needs must fade, just like the rose and lily. The lyric thus ends on a note in which flourishing, fading, joy, pain, God, and the rain are part and parcel of a whole, which can be honoured if not fully understood.

There is a similarity, then, between Dunbar's poem and this Harley lyric. Both make use of metaphor while retaining an awareness of the material plant on which that metaphor is founded; moreover, in each case the actual plant remains present, albeit not always to the fore, and prevents us moving explicitly and wholly into the symbolic. To end, let us briefly look at a short passage where the lily and the rose are explicitly symbolic, the description of Emelye in The Knight's Tale:

> ... Emelye, that fairer was to sene
> Than is the lylie upon his stalke grene,
> And fresher than the May with floures newe—
> For with the rose colour stroof hire hewe,
> I noot which was the fyner of hem two.[27]

---

[26] Brook's emendation of 'me' for the MS 'us' is adopted here, but 'us' works equally well for this reading, as the 'us' would be made up of those readers who have learnt from the poem and join in the poet's attention to nature.

[27] Chaucer (1988), 'The Knight's Tale', ll. 1035–9.

These lines occur when Palamoun and Arcite see Emelye in the enclosed garden of Theseus's court; a setting and a narrative point which make it inevitable that she be described in floral terms. Chaucer gives us lilies and roses in due order: the lily's green stalk is commented upon, as it is by Trevisa, while the comparison with the rose rests solely on the detail of colour. Yet when we look carefully at Chaucer's words, the flowers themselves are absent. Rose and lily exist only as comparative terms, not as physically present plants as Emelye's presence prevents them entering the text. The lily exits immediately as Emelye is straight away fairer than that and the flower is dismissed without more ado. In the case of the rose a brief struggle is enacted as woman's complexion vies with the flower's shade, but the term 'stroof' which accompanies the reference to rose's colour reminds us of Isidore's definition of the rose as blushing: a seemly maidenly response and also one of a human rather than a flower. Thus the rose is both bested in the contest and anthropomorphized to boot.

The inevitability of this comparison rests on the established courtly tradition of describing women as flowers. Add to this Emelye's position as a typical lady of courtly romance, not quite imprisoned, but certainly contained within her brother-in-law's household and here seen wandering in the courtyard garden which is thus surely her rightful place, and it is no wonder that she is presented as a combination of rose and lily: the complete, idealized courtly heroine as seen by two young knights of romance. It is a skilful deployment of the trope and one which hardly needs the actual flowers to be present in our minds at all. Indeed the less scrutiny we give it the better perhaps, as we are being given here a view of womanhood as mediated by the male, romanticizing eyes of Palamon and Arcite, as well as by the pilgrim Knight, as teller of this Tale.[28] Here, if anywhere, we find literary lilies and roses that have almost no connection with the flowers of the real world. Except perhaps one: as mentioned already, in book 8 of his *Etymologies* (on God, angels, and saints) Isidore lists some of the names of ordinary things which are used to refer to Christ, offering the following gloss on why Jesus is called a flower: 'Flower (*Flos*) because he was picked'.[29] No further elaboration is required; in Isidore's world flowers exist solely to be picked and indeed his gloss may reflect what is perhaps the most common, most unremarked, and most automatic human reaction to flowers: to pick them. Moreover, this is exactly what we see Emelye doing as she walks up and down in the enclosed garden:

> And in the gardyn, at the sonne upriste,
> She walketh up and doun, and as hire liste
> She gadereth floures, party white and rede,
> To make a subtle garland for hire hede.[30]

These lines and Isidore's passing remark might lead us to reassess how the analogy between Emelye and the lily and rose works. It appears that Emelye is most like a

---

[28] Howes (1997: 87–95) provides a detailed reading of the kind of garden Emelye is in and why. See also Crane (1994: 80–1, 170–4).

[29] Isidore (2006: 157).

[30] Chaucer (1988), Knight's Tale ll. 1051–4.

flower not in her appearance, nor in her happening to be in a garden, nor even in the implied need to keep her walled and trained, like a cultivated rose, lest she turn into the rambling wild rose her desire to devote herself to Diana suggests she herself would prefer to be, but because she exists in order to be picked. Her story bears this out, as does Diana's refusal or inability to answer the first part of Emelye's petition that she be allowed to remain single. Such picking is, of course, the fate in store for all those other allegorical flower-women, whether they be the secular archetype, the Rose of *The Romance of the Rose*, Emelye, or the anonymous women of Dunbar's poem or the Harley lyrics. The same could also be said of the actual flowers encountered in this discussion. They, too, exist in order to be picked and be put to use whether socially, medically, or in religious terms. It seems it is difficult to remain a flower and be left alone. Paradoxically then, perhaps the only way to avoid being pressed into service and to hold on to independent existence is to allow one's material existence to be supplanted by the analogies, metaphors, and allegories that surround one. This may incur the risk of being overlooked, but maybe that is not after all such a bad result. As the readings offered here have shown, actual flowers may indeed continue to exist within the texts that interpolate them into the human world, but their existence will be latent, require an effort of attention, and may indeed be tenuous. Nevertheless, the material flower constantly underpins all its uses to the human world. Although we will inevitably destroy the physical plant as we pick it for use as medicine, food, or for the aesthetic pleasure it brings as decoration, we do not have to destroy or overlay it in order to use it figuratively. As long as we are willing to seek and see the actual within the metaphorical, we can return from the interpretation of the text to its words and see that metaphor and allegory are most fully understood when we hold a specific flower in mind in its actual detail, not just a generic one with its familiar points of comparison. Such a return may turn us once again to the natural world with renewed appreciation of it and a willingness to value it anew.

BIBLIOGRAPHY

BAWCUTT, PRISCILLA (1992), *Dunbar the Maker* (Oxford: Clarendon Press).

——(1998), *The Poems of William Dunbar* (Glasgow: Association of Scottish Literary Studies, 27, 28).

BROOK, G. L. (1968), *The Harley Lyrics: The Middle English Lyrics of MS Harley 2253* (4th edn. Manchester: Manchester University Press).

CHAUCER, G. (1988), *The Riverside Chaucer*, ed. Larry Benson *et al.* (3rd edn. Oxford: Oxford University Press).

COLLINS, MINTA (2000), *Medieval Herbals: The Illustrative Tradition* (London and Toronto: British Library and University of Toronto Press).

——(2003), *A Medieval Herbal: A Facsimile of British Library Egerton MS 747*, with introd. by MINTA COLLINS (rev. edn. London: British Library).

CRANE, SUSAN (1994), *Gender and Romance in Chaucer's 'Canterbury Tales'* (Princeton: Princeton University Press).

CRANE, SUSAN (2007), 'For the Birds', *Studies in the Age of Chaucer*, 29: 21–4.

DUNBAR, WILLIAM (1998), *The Poems of William Dunbar*, ed. Priscilla Bawcutt (2 vols. Glasgow: Association for Scottish Literary Studies, 27, 28).

EVERNDEN, NEIL (1992), *The Social Creation of Nature* (Baltimore and London: Johns Hopkins University Press).

NONA FLORES (ed.) (2000), *Animals in the Middle Ages* (New York and London: Routledge).

FUDGE, ERICA (2000), *Perceiving Animals: Humans and Beasts in Early Modern English Culture* (Basingstoke and London: Macmillan Press).

——RUTH GILBERT, and SUSAN WISEMAN (eds.) (2000), *At the Borders of the Human: Beasts, Bodies and Natural Philosophy in the Early Modern Period* (Basingstoke and London: Macmillan).

HANAWALT, BARABARA, and LISA KISER (eds.) (2008), *Engaging with Nature: Essays on the Natural World in Medieval and Early Modern Europe* (Notre Dame, Ind.: University of Notre Dame Press).

KISER, LISA (2001), 'Chaucer and the Politics of Nature', in Kathleen Wallace and Karla Armbruster (eds.), *Beyond Nature Writing: Expanding the Boundaries of Ecocriticism* (Charlottesville, Va.: University Press of Virginia), 41–59.

LAURA L. HOWES (1997), *Chaucer's Gardens and the Language of Convention* (Gainsville, Fla.: University Press of Florida).

ISIDORE OF SEVILLE (2006), *The 'Etymologies' of Isidore of Seville*, ed. Stephen Barney, W. J. Lewis, J. A. Beach, and Oliver Berghof (Cambridge: Cambridge University Press).

PAVORD, ANNA (2005), *The Naming of Names: The Search for Order in the World of Plants* (New York: Bloomsbury).

REISS, EDMUND (1972), *The Art of the Middle English Lyric: Essays in Criticism* (Athens, Ga.: University of Georgia Press).

——(1979), *William Dunbar* (Boston: Twayne Publishers).

RUDD, GILLIAN (2007), *Greenery: Ecocritical Readings of Late Medieval English Texts* (Manchester: Manchester University Press).

SALISBURY, ELIZABETH (ed.) (1993), *The Medieval World of Nature: A Book of Essays* (New York and London: Garland Publishing).

SALTER, DAVID (2001), *Holy and Noble Beasts: Encounters with Animals in Medieval Literature* (Cambridge: D. S. Brewer).

SAUPE, KAREN (ed.) (1998), *Middle English Marian Lyrics* (TEAMS Middle English Text Series, Kalamazoo, Mich.: Medieval Institute Publications).

TREVISA, JOHN (1975), *On the Properties of Things: John Trevisa's Translation of Bartholomaeus Anglicus De Proprietatibus Rerum. A Critical Text*, ed. M. Seymour (3 vols. Oxford: Clarendon Press).

PART V

COMPLEX
IDENTITIES

CHAPTER 21

....

AUTHORITY, CONSTRAINT, AND THE WRITING OF THE MEDIEVAL SELF

....

KATHRYN KERBY-FULTON

GENRES OF THE SELF IN THE MIDDLE AGES

....

Autobiography, in our modern sense of writing about the self for its own sake, is a rare species in the Middle Ages. Despite the great late antique models offered by such diverse texts as Augustine's *Confessions*, Boethius's *Consolatio*, or, among women authors, the *Passio* of St Perpetua, the culture of the Middle Ages did not encourage autobiography that stood alone. Traditional monastic culture, though introspective to the core, also taught stark humility. Thomas à Kempis wrote in his *Imitatio Christi* that the 'highest and moste profitable' way was by:

veri knowynge and despisinge of a mannes self. A man *noþing to accompte of himselfe*, but euermore to fele welle and highe of oþer folks, [is] souerayne wysdame and perfeccioun . . . Alle we be frayle, but þou shalte *holde no man more frayle þenne thiselfe*.[1]

There is not much room here for literary self-indulgence: one should not only know but *despise* the self, account it as nothing in relation to others, and always, always be on guard since 'no man is more frayle þenne thiselfe'. Given the massive popularity of the *Imitatio* (it was the most copied book of fifteenth-century Europe) such sentiments cannot have been very wide of the mark for many medieval readers, and it is perhaps no wonder that the genre of autobiography did not flourish on such comparatively stony ground. But the great late antique models mentioned above did have many imitators, most of whom used other genres as umbrellas under which to slide their self-revelatory writing. So, for instance, the *Vita* of Christina of Markyate, written or redacted by an anonymous monk of St Albans, unmistakably echoes Perpetua's first-person *Passio*; Petrarch was so taken with Augustine's *Confessiones* that he wrote his *Secretum* as a dialogue not with God but with Augustine himself; and Abelard snatched—or more likely created—the opportunity of writing his turbulent life history, the *Historia calamitatum*, by claiming to offer a *consolatio*, ostensibly Boethian, to an unnamed friend.[2]

Such snatched or generically contrived opportunities to write about the self are rampant in the period: Guibert de Nogent unfolded his own famous personal story as part one of a longer history of his monastery and important current events, calling the entire book the *Monodies*. This title, meaning 'Odes for One Voice', suggests perhaps a conscious harking back to classical models for writing about the self—too often lost on modern translators, however, who usually call it something like *A Monk's Confession: The Memoirs of Guibert of Nogent* or *Self and Society in Medieval France: The Memoirs of Abbot Guibert of Nogent*,[3] even though our modern concept of 'memoirs' or 'autobiography' has no exact medieval counterpart. Rather, genres such as the *consolatio*, the *confessio*, the *historia*, the *apologia*, and even the *visio* (the *Book of Margery Kempe*, after all, is the first autobiography in English) were most often employed when medieval people wrote about themselves. Apart from these, more fragmentary self-comment appears all over in medieval texts: in prologues, letters, retractions, petitions, annotations, inquisitorial materials—and of course, most elusively, in poetry.[4]

From Colin Morris's foundational study, *The Discovery of the Individual in the Twelfth-Century* (1972) to John Burrow's rehabilitation of autobiography in his unmasking of the 'conventional fallacy' in 1982, to the critical studies that deconstructed interiority (take, for instance, James Simpson's treatment of Langland's narrator as 'an unstable analogy' in 1990), to A. C. Spearing's recent treatment of 'autography' (writing in the first person that implies no self, whether real or fictional), the last fifty

---

[1] My emphasis, quoting in the Middle English translation, Biggs (1997), ch. 2, ll. 16–19 (with omissions).

[2] For Christina's *Vita*, see Talbot (1998); for Petrarch's *Secretum*, ed. Doti (1993); for Abelard, *Historia*, ed. Monfrin (1959).

[3] Archambault (1995); Benton (1970).

[4] In addition to the examples below, see, for instance, for prologues: Wogan-Browne *et al.* (1999); for letters Hildegard of Bingen's *Epistolarium*; for petitions Burrow (1981); for inquisitional accounts, William Thorpe in (Hudson 1978: no. 4).

years of scholarship have offered a broad array of approaches to this complex subject. Scholars of medieval literary theory have elucidated the role of the author or 'I speaker' in scholastic biblical commentaries (Minnis), in the vernacular prologue (Wogan-Browne *et al.*), and even in modern psychoanalysis of the 'pre-modern text' (Strohm). These formalist approaches for studying the medieval self—all differently profitable—are now being supplemented by methodologies from history, codicology, and reception study, some of which will appear in this chapter.[5]

The editors of the present volume, then, were right, I believe, at this juncture, to ask for a chapter on 'writing the self' in relation to medieval issues of constraint and authority. Both secular and ecclesiastical authorities (the latter equally political) had an impact on the evolution of medieval ideas of selfhood: the subjectivities shaped in largely feudal, or at least socially non-equalitarian, worlds of patronage networks and autocratic powers on the one hand, and interiorities structured by devotional discourse and clerical views of reality on the other, are virtually inseparable. A walk along the Thames in modern-day Westminster abundantly dramatizes these realities: on the west side, in the shadow of the Victorian Houses of Parliament, lies what remains of the nerve centre of medieval royal and governmental power, the Palace of Westminster (most visibly, Westminster Hall and the nearby fortification known as the Jewel Tower). In full view across the river is Lambeth Palace, the home of the archbishop of Canterbury, still looking more like a fortress than a manse, not far from what remains of the bishop of Winchester's palace (his medieval prison, 'The Clink', now a morbid tourist attraction). This was the balance of power in the medieval world. These two powers were custodians of a different, more intangible kind of balance, that between constraint on freedom of expression and tolerance of freedom of expression (evidence of which, like the good news of the day in most modern media, too often goes unnoticed). In the short space I have here, I will examine both male and female writers, both clergy and laity, for all were trying to make their way as medieval selves in an age that valorized interiority and devotion more than materiality and pragmatism—though, of course, it had plenty of both—even as writers stumbled to create new literary genres to bear the weight of these things.

THE 'POETIC AND EMPIRICAL "I"' IN MEDIEVAL LITERATURE: A BRIEF HISTORY OF SCHOLARSHIP

The care of the self, which also meant, as we saw at the outset of this chapter, the guarding of the self, was, in one sense, the entire *raison d'être* of medieval religious

---

[5] In addition to the examples below, one might site the stunning additions to our knowledge of both Hoccleve's and Chaucer's lives revealed in the historical documents recently uncovered by Linne Mooney (2006, 2007).

orders and movements.[6] Care of the self has been linked to all kinds of devotional writings and practices, and the real watershed of its development can perhaps be pinpointed to twelfth-century philosophical and legal developments, such as Abelard's 'ethic of intention' (which perhaps first solidified the idea that what matters is intentions, not acts), and Gratian's insistence that marriage was valid only in cases of mutual consent.[7] Medieval canon law defined adulthood—which must in some sense be a definition of the mature self—as the state of being capable of showing guile.[8] This complex cocktail of high medieval attitudes toward the self, simultaneously interiorist, respectful, and fallen, may account for some of the inherent complexities of the literary self throughout the period.

While outright autobiography may be scarce, of literary self-revelation or its representation, both experiential and fictional, there is virtually no end in medieval texts. So, for instance, in the *Roman de la Rose*, Jean de Meun creates 'I' speaking characters, such as Faus Semblant, who ostensibly 'tell all' to a fascinated and shocked audience. Langland used the same dizzying slippage for his 'I' speaking monologues of the Seven Deadly Sins, and for many of his personifications that come nearer the narratorial voice. Chaucer may have imitated both writers, but certainly Jean de Meun, in creating his own self-revealing characters like the Wife of Bath and the Pardoner. But these are not stable 'selves': they perform this gripping confessionalism, all the while sequentially transforming from one persona to another to another.[9] These are all clearly fictional characters; less clear is how we should read the 'I' speaker who narrates the *Canterbury Tales* (the one whom Chaucer calls 'me' in the prologue to 'Sir Thopas', or, even more bewilderingly, the one Chaucer calls 'I' in the 'Retractions'), or who narrates the 'autobiographical' passage in C. V of *Piers Plowman*. Scholarship has given us many choices for interpretation of such instances of self-naming, which include regarding these interventions as literary persona, as autography, or as autobiography—that is, as meta-discursive moments. A short history of these choices is in order.

Reviewing the literary scholarship on writing the self in the Middle Ages one cannot help but notice what a profound effect a single scholar, Leo Spitzer, has had on studies of medieval 'self-naming'.[10] Spitzer, along with Ernst Robert Curtius, Erich Auerbach, Roman Jacobsen, and the other Second World War giants of formalism, shaped a literary Middle Ages for us that is still recurrently seductive. So, for instance, Robert Meyer-Lee reminds us that the 'I' of *Elene* 'signifies both the poet . . . and the traditional medieval universal "I", a grammatical placeholder occupiable by the listener and standing for the condition of all humanity'. In a footnote he says, 'Here I am especially paraphrasing the view of Leo Spitzer's "Note on the Poetic

---

6 Van Engen (2008).
7 For Abelard, see Marenbon (1997); for marriage issues, Brundage (1987).
8 Van Engen (1998)
9 For a nuanced recent study, see Geltner (2004).
10 Spitzer (1946).

and the Empirical 'I' in Medieval Authors".[11] In this seminal essay, Spitzer had written:

> According to Augustine, it is the personality of God which determines the personal soul of man...whose characteristic is its God-seeking quality....Thus Dante must take care to establish his own personality in the *Commedia*....It is only for this reason that we find, in this objective work of art, the insertion of autobiographical material. (p. 417)

The characterization of the *Commedia* as 'this objective work of art', however comforting this thought must have been during the bewildering year after the defeat of Hitler when this essay was published, is no longer a truth we all find to be self-evident. But we can trace it in all the literary critics of the late 1940s, and for decades beyond: this view that art is timeless, that real literary art rises above history, above particularity, above pathology, above difference—and most importantly here—above autobiography. In this view, great literary art is only touchable by other (earlier) great literary art—Dante, Spitzer insists, is only autobiographical to the extent he was because Augustine was. While no one would question Augustine's influence on Dante, by Spitzer's methodologies, for instance, Chaucer's self-naming in the *House of Fame* would be only a reflection of Dante's, whereas now, for instance, it might be seen as a hint of coterie joking, or a whimsical way of creating an authorial signature in a manuscript culture laden with false attributions and appropriations.

Of course, modern scholarship no longer inhabits Spitzer's aesthetic world, but this tendency towards detachment from history and flattening of the autobiographical is a powerful recurring motif, and even today scholarship regularly feels the pull of this aesthetic. A recent instance might be C. David Benson's study of *Piers Plowman* as a 'public' poem, a conscious response to previous scholarship emphasizing Langland's historical particularities.[12] Similarly, Robert Meyer-Lee expresses agreement with Gregory Stone's argument,

> for a general late medieval poetic resistance to the newly elevated status of the idea of the singular, self-determining ego. Chaucer, Gower, and Langland, each in their own way, grapple with the full import of this idea, but their ultimate aim is to find their way through it, *back to the homogeneous subject of traditional Christianity*.[13]

While these are valid readings, and this kind of pressure to move 'back to the homogeneous subject' does indeed exist all over medieval culture (we will see some examples shortly), we can never just assume it. Writing the self in a manuscript culture, as we are about to see, was surprisingly complex.

---

[11] Meyer-Lee (2000); see also Meyer-Lee (2007).
[12] Benson (2004).
[13] Meyer-Lee (2000; my emphasis).

AUTHORIAL DISCOURSE OF THE SELF AND THE 'COHERENT DISCURSIVE EGO' IN A MANUSCRIPT CULTURE

Attractive as Spitzer's tenacious characterization of the medieval 'I' may be, is it even historically accurate? In fact, reception evidence now tells us it often isn't. In a 1998 award-winning essay also published in *Traditio*,[14] Linda Olson examined the reception of Augustine in the fourteenth century and found it to be passionately autobiographical in interest. So, for instance, among the marginalia of Bishop John de Grandisson's own copy of the *Confessions* a note appears, written in Grandisson's student hand, beside a troublesome passage: '*Ego inscius non bene intelligo*' (I, ignorant, do not understand it well). In later years, when bishop of Exeter, he returned to the passage and inserted into the comment his episcopal name, leaving the passage to now read, 'I, *John of Exeter*, ignorant, do not understand . . .'). There is something poignant in the admission of an ageing bishop that he still, even as a privileged member of the clerical establishment, cannot grasp Augustine's meaning; this is other side of the coin of medieval *humilitas*, and it tells us that we may not always be looking in the right places for penetrating evidence of the medieval self. In another essay on the reception of Augustine, Olson uncovers an abridgement of the *Confessions* made for Benedictine novices in which all the philosophy and non-personal material is stripped away, reducing the book to a gripping, fast-paced autobiography.[15] Olson's work is just one instance of how reception study is changing the map that Spitzer and his colleagues—or even Foucault and his colleagues—assumed.[16] We now have a wealth of material ranging across author and reader annotations, corrections, directives to illustrators, variant readings, and documentary records—in short, a vast body of evidence that suggests that the later Middle Ages had a highly developed sense of the autobiographical—and that poets were as much aware of this as they were of the literary precedents that previous scholarship has illuminated.

Chaucer's medieval annotators, for instance, were divided on whether to use the word *auctor* to designate Chaucer's 'I' speaker in *Troilus* or the word *actor* (that is, whether to designate Chaucer's 'I' as empirical, rather than poetic, in Spitzer's terms).[17] Chaucerian annotators of the *Canterbury Tales* will often write 'auctor' beside any use of the apostrophe in a tale—a move that really unhinges modern senses of author/narrator distinctions.[18] Take the following example from the Ellesmere Manuscript version of the 'Nun's Priest's Tale' (VII. 3050), which identifies the narrator's interjection as Chaucer's:

---

[14] Olson (1997), which won the Medieval Academy's Van Courtlandt prize for that year.
[15] Olson (2002).
[16] Foucault (1979).
[17] Benson and Windeatt (1990).
[18] Ellesmere Manuscript.

'Auctor' (written at VII. 3050)   'O blissful God, that art so just and trewe,
                                    Lo, how that thou biwreyest mordre alway!'

Sylvia Huot, in her studies of annotations to the *Romance of the Rose*, finds a similar phenomenon:

Specifically, 'l'Amant' is used whenever the protagonist speaks lines addressed to other characters within the fictional world, as well as for narrative accounts of actions that befall the protagonist or that he directly witnessed. 'L'Aucteur,' in turn, narrates action that the protagonist could not have witnessed, such as the conversation between Bel Aceuil and la Vieille within the tower, or narrative digressions unrelated to the action of the dream, such as the account of the death of Adonis.[19]

Even though this is coming closer to modern understanding than what we find in Chaucerian manuscript annotations (or, as we'll see below, in Langland), the 'I' speaker in medieval literary texts, then, is a complex and unstable phenomenon, taking in a much broader spectrum of referents than even the 'postmodern' world can boast. At one extreme on this spectrum, medieval editors were prone to tear out, root, and branch, anything that smacked of the autobiographical or the idiosyncratic; at the other extreme, editors and annotators could literally create 'autobiography' or 'biography' where absolutely none was intended. Nor is there any consistency in the behaviour of authors and editors: they could fabricate 'autobiographical' detail out of whole cloth in ways that modern autobiographers would never dare; alternatively, they could flatten all vestiges of autobiography into the 'homogenous subject of traditional Christianity'. To illustrate the one extreme, one need look no further than the Berlin redaction of Hildegard of Bingen's letters, in which an editor has silently removed all the names and particulars of her correspondents, and given each letter a moral title.[20] In another kind of move that defies modern sensibilities about the autobiographical, Hildegard herself—or an editor working with her collusion—altered factual elements of her personal correspondence to maximize her importance for posterity: letters sent to her were attributed to clerics of higher rank; other letters were conflated or revised to represent more august interventions in moral or political events than she actually made.[21] Were we to sit her down before a judge and jury to ask why she did this, she would likely be puzzled by our concern with—as she might see it—mere quotidian accidentals or *minutiae*, which apparently paled for her in relation to the goal of enhancing the glory of God in all her actions. Something we need to accept about medieval representations of the self is that they do not always share the same goals as modern writing.

Similarly, the scribe of the manuscript of *Piers Plowman*, Oxford, Bodleian Library, Douce 104, stripped the poem's narrator of whatever meagre elements of individuality he had in his humiliating encounter with Elde. In all other manuscripts of the poem, Elde renders Will bald, toothless, and impotent in this episode. The Douce scribe, however (or the scribe of his now lost exemplar), altered the whole passage to reflect a *universal*

---

[19] Huot (1993: 45). I would like to thank Nicole Eddy for bringing this to my attention.
[20] *Epistolarium*, i (1991), pp. xxx–xl. See also the appendix to Dronke (1984).
[21] See Van Acker's introduction ('Einleitung') to *Epistolarium*, i (1991).

experience of old age, simply by revising 'me' to 'men' (or a grammatical variation thereof):

> And Elde after hym: and ouer me*nnes* hedeszede
> And made men balled be for: and bare on þe crone
> So herd heʒede ouer men*es* heuedys: hit wold be sene euer.
> (MS Douce 104, folio 109ʳ)

> And Elde aftur hym; and ou*er* myn heuedʒede
> And made me balled before and baer on þe crowne;
> So harde heʒede ou*er* myn heued hit wol be sene eu*ere*.
> (Russell and Kane, C.XXII. 183–5)

But at the other end of this broad spectrum, a B-Text annotator of London, British Library, Additional 10574 (Bm)[22] simply assumed that the poem's 'I' speaker was the author, writing at XV. 152: 'Nome*n* auctor*is* / {h}ui*us* lib{r}i e*st* longe wille' (The name of the author of this book is Long Will: (folio 62ᵛ)). This assumption is even more revealing in a prior note of his, written beside the waking episode where the dreamer wanders in a semi-mad and anti-social state:

{n}ota de condicionibus compila ⎮ {to}ris huius libri (Note the condition of the compiler of this book: written at line XV. 5 in Add. 10574, folio 60ᵛ)

> And so my wytt wex and wanyed til : y a fool wer*e*
> And sume lackid my lif : allowid it fewe
> And leten me for a lorel: and loþ to reverence Lordis or ladies: or eny lif ellis—
> Þat folk held me a fool: and in that folie I raved.
> (B. XV. 3–10, from Add. 10574, folio 60ᵛ)

Not only are author and narrator conflated here, and not only is Will is also called a 'compiler',[23] but whatever the use of this descriptor for the author of *Piers Plowman* may say of contemporary views of the poem's genre, the annotator's assumption that Will's state of madness describes the real-life condition of the poet is rather alarming. We can scoff at this as naïve reading of persona, but in a period when Hoccleve can describe himself in his poetry as suffering from madness and mean what he says (so far as we can establish from documentary evidence), what does this assumption on the part of the annotator really mean—an annotator learned enough to compose and write in Latin?[24] It is clear that the distinctions between author and persona are lost on him, and that he was not alone.[25]

---

[22] The manuscript is only a B-Text from Passus III to the end. Bm is in a government hand.

[23] The term *compilator* (compiler) can have a very specific meaning in the Middle Ages, as Alastair Minnis has shown (see Minnis 1988: ch. 5). This is what Chaucer is called in the *explicit* of the Ellesmere manuscript: 'Heere is ended the book of the tales of Caunterbury, compiled by Geffrey Chaucer, of whos soule Jhesu Crist have mercy. Amen.' See *Riverside Chaucer*, 328.

[24] See Burrow (1982), and for the newest documentary evidence of Hoccleve's illness, see Mooney (2008: 313ff.).

[25] In addition to the examples below, one could note that many scribes and medieval editors of Chaucer and those authors in his literary circle show a passionate interest in the personalized details of their lives. In copying these writers, the famous bookman, John Shirley, tried to offer specific occasions

The annotator of the single extant Margery Kempe manuscript, almost certainly a member of the Carthusian priory of Mount Grace, not only highlights nearly every available piece of autobiographical information about Kempe ('14 childer' he notes in astonishment at one point), but he also directly names recent members of his community; for instance, in relation to Kempe's roaring outbursts of tears he writes 'So did prior Norton in his excess' (folio 51ᵛ).[26] This is about as far away from the formalist sense of the homogeneous subject as one can get. We can find specific, personalized historical reference even before the Ricardian period in manuscripts like the *Omne bonum* (whose author-compiler, James le Palmer, directly rebukes his fellow Exchequer clerks by name in marginalia), as does Hoccleve, who teases his fellow clerks by name within his verse itself—breaking down all boundaries between discursive and meta-discursive self-reference.[27] Hoccleve, that 'spectacular' self-namer, as Meyer-Lee rightly says, looks much less eccentric when one reads all these Ricardian and Lancastrian writers in their manuscript contexts—and this is an important dimension for our understanding of authorial and readerly concepts of the self. Hoccleve, a writing office clerk by profession and a literary scribe by moonlight, managed to maintain unusual textual control over the dissemination of his work, and did so not only by his carefully prepared holographs, but by narrative repetition of his name at moments of self-naming to give, one can only assume, future copyists the best shot at getting it right.[28] But there is a still more important reason for us to look at Hoccleve: as John Burrow showed in his 1982 British Academy address, and Linne Mooney has just confirmed by bringing to light new sources from the Public Record Office (2008), the evidence that survives in the shape of civil service documentation for the life of Hoccleve matches almost exactly the 'autobiographical' elements in his poetry. This vastly complicates not only Spitzer's view of the 'empirical "I"', but also Foucault's 'author function' and ought, therefore to complicate ours. The question, then, for modern critics, who are highly unlikely to go back to the kind of reading of persona assumed by the Bm annotator, and are equally unlikely to go all the way back to Spitzer or even Foucault at this stage in our professional history, would seem to be this: how might our medieval authors have *exploited* such a broad range of possible 'I' speaker reception? The question, perhaps, becomes most pressing when writers were negotiating complex political territory or even working under adverse political conditions.

and other information for works by Chaucer, Scogan, Lydgate, and others. In these annotators we see the coterie or even personalizing impulse, which runs counter to the 'homogenizing I'. For a recent treatment of close historic connections among these writers, see Nuttall (2007), esp. her 'Conclusion'.

26 See Parsons (2001) for a complete transcription of the Kempe marginalia.

27 On both passages, see Kerby-Fulton (1997) and, more recently on Hoccleve, see Nuttall (2007).

28 Discussed in Kerby-Fulton (1997).

WRITING THE AUTHORIAL SELF
IN TROUBLED TIMES

It appears that Langland was actually dissatisfied with the 'homogeneous subject' of the B-text by the time he wrote the C-text—but that he left his 'autobiographical' intervention vague enough to serve in part as a convenient shield behind which to dodge political and ecclesiastical censure when he felt the heat of 1381. His 'autobiographical passage' is startlingly specific in places: among prominent English works, only William Thorpe's testimony regarding his inquisition before Arundel, as Anne Hudson has pointed out, records an early life history comparable with Langland's.[29]

We still, however, do not really know for certain who Langland was. Among historically identifiable writers, as Perkins, Nuttall, and other recent scholars have shown, Hoccleve is a remarkable example of a poet who negotiated the dangerous waters of a politically constrained environment, using the discourse of the self with great originality and to sophisticated effect. Moreover, the documents written in Hoccleve's own hand that Mooney has recently listed in calendar format show, if read carefully, that Hoccleve was drafting or copying some of the most politically sensitive instruments of Henry IV's young and paranoid regime. It was, for instance, apparently Hoccleve himself who made sure that Chaucer was paid at the end of his life.[30] We have long known that Hoccleve worked to ensure that Chaucer's memory was preserved after his death. None of this could have been easy: Chaucer had been one of Richard's men. Hoccleve's own treatment of the self in poetry went far beyond Chaucerian self-deprecatory conventions in order to pull this off. The fact that Hoccleve's poetry, ostensibly 'autobiographical' though it was, was widely anthologized in fifteenth-century collections, points perhaps to growing tolerance for the autobiographical. He was also in the vanguard of the turn-of-the-century move towards personalized portraiture.[31] An even earlier, if less adept, exploiter of the written self was Thomas Usk, also, like Hoccleve, part of London vernacular reading circles (these were still very small circles, especially in Usk's time). Usk is among those who found themselves on the wrong side of the law, and we will thus reserve him for the last section of this chapter. But in these literary circles there is much evidence that authorial self-reference occurred at particular moments for particular reasons, and not simply because, for instance, there was literary precedent. The conscious intrusion of what I have elsewhere called 'bibliographic ego' *within* the narrative framework of the text itself occurs for at least six reasons (and there may well be more):

---

[29] Excerpted in Hudson (1978: no. 4).
[30] Mooney (2008).
[31] Pearsall (1992: appendix I).

(1) to reveal authorial identity

(2) to appeal for patronage and protection for publication

(3) to explicitly placate offended readers

(4) to represent the author laying claim to his own text (in the fluid and unstable medium of manuscript publication)

(5) to highlight awareness of a learned tradition of monastic *apologia*, or other literary traditions

(6) to overtly enact literary mendicancy (explicit requests for payment or for prayers).[32]

This is a sophisticated set of strategies for writing (and begging) in delicate times.

As scholars who study French and Italian writers have shown, meta-discursive autobiographical allusion occurs in continental precedents as well. James Nohrnberg, for instance, tracks the complex intersection of the eschatological, the autobiographical, and the literary in Beatrice's arresting injunction, 'Dante, because Virgil leaves you, do not weep, do not weep yet, for you must weep for another sword'.[33] Only a multi-faceted concept of the authorial self and its historical context can unravel lines like this, as Nohrnberg shows. And it is just this kind of multi-faceted reading that Kevin Brownlee brings to his study of 'Discourses of the Self' in Christine de Pizan's daring contributions to the *Romance of the Rose* debates. Speaking of three of her early works in relation to these debates, Brownlee asks:

What kind of identity and authority must be assumed in order for these three works to be viewed as the products of a coherent discursive ego? For the act of reading in early fifteenth-century France presupposed this kind of causal relationship between writer and text; and Christine strategically exploited this presupposition for her own polemical ends.

Brownlee traces the evolution of her 'discourse of the self' from the *Epistre au Dieu d'Amour* (1399) to her *Epistres sur le Debat du 'Roman de la Rose'* (1401–2), in which, he says, Christine speaks, 'entirely in her own voice, dispensing with fictional frames and constructs altogether'.[34] And in so doing, he uncovers virtually all six aspects of what I would call 'bibliographic ego' at work in the complex of literary, intertextual, historical, autobiographical, and polemical uses of the 'I' speaker in Christine's voice. This is the kind of cross-section we need to *really* understand the writing of the self in a medieval context fraught with polemic. Many of the recent scholars cited here give us a good vantage point from which we can see more—more, I hope, than Spitzer could in 1946, even if he was the giant upon whose shoulders we still sit.

[32] Kerby-Fulton (1997).
[33] Nohrnberg (2003).
[34] Brownlee and Huot (1992: 235).

CONSTRAINTS REAL AND IMAGINED:
REPRESENTING THE SELF UNDER DURESS

Some of the most unusual descriptions of the medieval self arise in contexts in which writers find themselves in *actual* conflict with medieval authorities—or, at the very least, represent themselves as such—and this will be the topic of our final section. One of the most striking examples of traumatized 'bibliographic ego' in Ricardian England arises in the *Opus arduum*, a reformist Apocalypse commentary written from prison in 1389 by an unknown author. This intriguing author remains a puzzle: he exhibits Wycliffite leanings, though not some of the more extreme theological positions of the movement, and he exhibits a much more pan-European perspective than many identifiable English Wycliffite writers.[35] He compares himself to St John in a fascinating autobiographical outburst in which he claims even to *surpass* John in one crucial regard:

[John] suffered persecution under the tyrant Domitian, I, he says, am persecuted by Antichrist...He shaped his book [looking] toward the correction of the church of Asia; I... toward the reformation of the universal church.

Ille a Domiciano tyranno [*sic*], ego ab Anticristo tollero persecucionem...Ille librum suum edidit ad correccionem ecclesie Asyane, ego quod scripturus sim intendo ad reformacionem universalis ecclesie[36]

Whoever wrote the *Opus*, he writes as one who sees himself as central to a large ecclesiastical reformist programme, even calling himself a *campiductor* at one point.[37] Perhaps this is why the authorities saw fit to hold him for a lengthy period, perhaps at times in shackles, though also with—so far as we can tell—full access to pen and parchment, enough to write a lengthy work.

As I have shown elsewhere, ecclesiastical officials both feared and respected claims to higher inspiration, and allowed and even sometimes encouraged those who made such claims to write from prison or while awaiting trial. Such claims could arise as gifts of private understanding, apparent in writers such as the mystic Marguerite Porete (tragically burnt at the stake in 1310); the radical Franciscan, John of Rupescissa (imprisoned, sometimes in tortuous conditions, for most of his adult life); or Walter Brut (under inquisition for a complex set of beliefs, not by any means all Wycliffite, 1391–3).[38] Such claims could also arise via oblique identification with the

---

[35] Kerby-Fulton (2006: ch. 5), for a full, recent discussion of the *Opus*.

[36] As transcribed by Bostick (1988: 50 n. 6). For Hereford's history abroad, and the theory that he was the author of the *Opus Arduum*, see Hudson (1985: 43–66); for discussion of the continental apocalypticism of the *Opus*, see Bostick (1988: ch. 4).

[37] The identity of the author is unknown, but he is someone who lays little stress on the more radical theological elements of Wycliffism that characterized its heretical profile, but who sees Wycliffism as still having a hope within the established Church (he tells us he writes *ad reformacionem universalis ecclesie*).

[38] See Kerby-Fulton (2006).

self-confessional moments of a biblical figure such as John of Patmos, the apostle Paul, the patriarch Joseph, or any other august imprisoned or exiled figure who had found him (or her)self on the wrong side of the law.[39] In Christian history, being on the wrong side of the law was not necessarily a bad place to be—in fact, it was often just the right place.

Perhaps this is why one of the best known tropes of Langlandian constraint writing came to be so often imitated: the poet's habit of implying that truth or justice does not lie with the authorities, but with the poet and like-minded audience members. In fact, Langland's narrator often appears to bait or tantalize the authorities. Sometimes he simply likes to give the impression of testing the limits of tolerance for the controversial, as when the dreamer mutters after Scripture's sermon, that '*if lewede men hit knewe*' (that is, what scripture preached) 'Þe lasse . . . louye thei wolde . . . that lettrede men techen'. This is a practised *rhetoric* of constraint in Langland, and it is all over his poetry. Some of these passages he must have considered more disturbing than others, since he felt it necessary to revise out a few in C, like the following one implicating the ecclesiastical authorities emphasized here:

> Ac of þe Cardinals at court þat kauȝte of þat name,
> And power presumed in hem a pope to make
> To han þe powere þat Peter hadde—impugnen I nelle—
> . . . Forþi I kan & kan nauȝt of court speke moore.
>   (*Piers* B Prol. 107–11)

A similar passage, which, however, withstood the scythe of the C revision, is a political one, spoken after the tale of the rat parliament:

> What þis metels bymeneþ, ye men þat ben murye,
> Deuyne ye, for I ne dar, by deere god in heuene.
>   (*Piers* B Prol. 209–10)

This is the tone—constructed out of audacious representation of secrecy and self-constraint—that Langlandian imitators like Thomas Usk, John But, the *Richard the Redeless* author, the *Mum and Sothsegger* author, and others all seem to imitate. This tendency to 'conspire' with the good-willed reader in making more meaning than can be said, and simultaneously to bait the disapproving authorities, is vintage Langland. The authorities are thereby *implied* into his very audience, whether academic, ecclesiastical, or political (and we have just seen an instance of each, respectively) in a stunning rhetorical gesture.

It is a gesture that trumpets a sense of constraint. But how much constraint was there in reality, and how many authorities were really listening (or reading)? Scholars are still working to answer this question, but the fragmentary evidence we have so far suggests that some readers with real clout (including Walter de Brugges, the financial

---

[39] Rita Copeland has rightly noted the tendency of Wycliffite writers like Wyche and Thorpe to identify with Paul's imprisonment (see Copeland 2001: 143). She also notes there that Boethius is the 'literary precedent of choice for [prison] writers whose religious orthodoxy is never in question', citing Thomas Usk among others.

adviser to the Appellants) were among the earliest owners of *Piers Plowman* manuscripts, along with many in legal, pastoral, and civil service positions.[40] Many of these people, however, were, so far as we know, friendly readers. Some who undertook various inquisitorial roles during their lifetimes may also be associated with poem via ownership, though this is far less certain: the Benedictine John Wells, and the friar William Jordan, who is also possibly alluded to in an unflattering way in the poem, were members of the York Austin convent that likely owned the poem.[41] Be that as it may, as James Simpson and others have shown, Langland had good reason to be nervous in relation to some official legislation or acts of confiscation, both ecclesiastical and political, legislation that was also *pre*-Wycliffite or simply *non*-Wycliffite.

More study of reception and historical context can also add to our knowledge of the sense of constraint *around* Langland. The work perhaps closest to *Piers* itself, the 'John But' passus ostensibly redacted or composed to 'finish' the A text of the poem by an admirer, and appearing in three manuscripts as Passus XII of A, offers a good example. Here a quotation from St Paul's own autobiographical experience appears as part of a complex network of biblical allusions to enforced silence—all on the theology of salvational generosities. The quotation, *Audivi archana verba que non licet homini loqui* (I have heard secret words which are not licit for a man to utter), Langland had originally put in the mouth of Christ after the Harrowing, perhaps as a hint of inclusive salvation; in the But passus, it appears linked to a series of quotations on silence, and a Langlandian 'I dare not say' trope:[42]

> And (P)oul precheþ hit often, prestes hit redyn:
> *Audivi archana verba que non licet homini loqui*
> 'I am not hardy,' quod he, 'þat I herde with erys
> Telle hit . . . to synful wrecches.
> ('But' Passus, ed. Kane, XII. 22–4)

In fact, it is the reception of both Langland and Chaucer in the 1380s and 1390s that really highlights for us how importantly the constraint issues played to their immediate audiences. This is when Usk was writing, when the 'John But' passus was composed to salvage the closure of Langland's A text, and when other Langlandian imitators began to work. The Z text, too, which, given its borrowings from B and C, was likely to have been written about this time, also underlines a sense of wariness about speaking out.[43] All these writers have or show Westminster civil service or legal connections, and this, too, has to be a factor in their parallels on constraint issues and rhetoric.[44]

---

[40] Kerby-Fulton (2000).

[41] Based on codicological evidence, in neither case conclusive, but in both cases plausible: John Wells, whose name appears in the ex libris MS Bodley 851, was a key Benedictine spokesman at the Blackfriars Council; William Jordan, the friar accuser of Uthred de Boldon, came from the York convent that, as Ian Doyle has shown, likely owned MS Cambridge University Library, Dd.1.17. Both cases are discussed in Kerby-Fulton (2006), case Studies 3 and 1 respectively.

[42] Kerby-Fulton (2006: ch. 10), for a fuller study of this issue.

[43] Rigg and Brewer (1993: 101).

[44] Kerby-Fulton and Justice (1998).

Thomas Usk was also connected with these circles, and his history as a writer under constraint is perhaps best documented of all. Although not held on theological charges, Usk was a literal prison writer when he wrote his *Appellum* from house arrest. His Boethian *Testament of Love* was written, so far as we know, sometime after this and probably before his last imprisonment and execution in 1388. Usk was a controversial member of the London scrivening community we know to have been involved in copying the works of Chaucer, and apparently Langland as well, during the lifetimes of both authors.[45] His writing faithfully reflects their poetic language of the self, their preoccupation with issues like destiny, predestination, and verbal constraint or coded or strategically 'displaced' forms of visionary writing.[46] Usk portrays himself as commissioned by love in a vision to write:

and I charge thee, in vertue of obedience that thou to me owest, to wryten my wordes and sette hem in wrytinges, that they mowe, as my witnessinge, ben noted among the people. For bookes written neyther dreden ne shamen, ne stryve conne; but only shewen the entente of the wryter, and yeve remembraunce to the herer. (I. ii)

And he makes repeated reference to both literal and verbal imprisonment held in:

derk prison, caitived from frendshippe and acquaintaunce, forsaken of al that any word dare speke (I. i)
Depe in the pyninge pitte with wo I ligge y-stocked . . . with chaynes linked of care and tene (I. i)[47]

Even though there is no known reason to believe that Usk was physically in prison by the time he wrote the *Testament*, there is a Gramscian sense of destiny about the work, for instance in his poignant appeal to the untainted clarity and durability of literary witness ('For bookes written neyther dreden ne shamen, ne stryve conne; but only shewen the entente of the wryter, and yeve remembraunce to the herer')—surely in implied contrast with legal and political testimony. Usk shared many topics with both Chaucer and Langland,[48] but in a more Langlandian move, he, too refers explicitly to much that is coded in the book, and 'baits' or tantalizes his readers with what they will *not* find:

In this boke be many privy thinges wimpled and folde; unneth shul leude men the plites unwinde. (III. ix)

---

[45] Mooney (2007), and references there to previous scholarship on 'Scribe B'.
[46] Usk seems to have known Langland's C text, as well as Chaucer's *House of Fame*, *Troilus*, and *Boece*, evidence of which appears throughout his *Testament of Love*. What all these texts have in common (and this is not the first thing a modern audience would think of) is that all are concerned with predestination (see Kerby-Fulton and Justice 1998). And all these texts—i.e. if we take the final scene of the *Troilus* as a metonymy for the whole—are or end in visionary experience.
[47] Usk, *Testament of Love*, cited here from Skeat (1897), the edn. to which virtually all previous scholarship on the Langlandian allusions refers. There is also a new TEAMS reading edn. by A. Shoaf (Usk, 1998).
[48] Usk wrote at length about free will, predestination, and salvation, translating large chunks of Anselm on these topics, borrowing directly from Chaucer and, at least imitatively, from Langland.

Although the problem of Langland's influence on Usk, or the intertextualities they may have shared, still needs further study (and this is not the place to do it), we can observe that this kind of passage in Usk is not Chaucerian in either tone or tenor.[49] In fact, this Langlandian trope of constraint even reached as far as the Dublin civil service (often staffed from Westminster). Here is James Yonge, whose adulation for Langland led to borrowing from *Piers* to the point of petty plagiarism.[50] At the end of a very Langlandian passage on fear of truth-telling he writes that he is afraid to name the 'dyuers Englyshe captaynys of Irland that haue bene and now byth, whose neclygence' has caused havoc (like that in the *exempla* he has just borrowed from Langland) 'leste y sholde be shente' (160/40).

The most spectacular of the Langlandian imitators on constraint, however, is, of course, *Mum and the Sothsegger*, as the careful attention of James Simpson and others to this aspect of this text has firmly established.[51] This visionary text, all about the political advantages of keeping 'mum' while truth-tellers are cast into the streets, tracks a narrator whose quest for the courage to speak out against corruption is rendered possible by a dream. In the dream a wise figure clothed in white (the 'wye' in the white clothes of line 1294) gives the dreamer a commission to write: 'Though thou slepe now my soon, yit whenne thou seis tyme,/Loke thou write wisely my wordes echone' (1267–8). In advice modelled closely on Leute's legal counsel to Will in *Piers Plowman* on how to avoid being charged with slander, the beekeeper also manages to reverse Imaginatif's disapproval of Will's poetic activities:

> He chargid me cleerly to change not myn intent
> Til the matire of Mvm were made to th'ende,
> And that I shuld seye sothe and sette no dreede
> Of no creature of clay, for *Criste so hym taughte.*
> And though sum men of sweuenes sauery but lite[.] (1305–9)

His advice about the legalities of publishing dangerous poetry is so minute that we even hear how a poem, given the right patronage, can circulate freely beyond its safe audience,

> And furst feoffe[52] thou therewith the freyst of the royaulme,
> For yf thy lord liege allone hit begynne,
> Care thou not though knyghtz copie hit echone'. (1284–6)

In fact, the poem is a remarkable document on dangerous book production in the period. The models are overtly biblical, St John (in the commission to write) and, in

---

[49] Among critics who accept the idea of Langland's influence on Usk are Skeat, Kane, Pearsall, Middleton; among those who have disagreed, John Bowers and Allan Shoef. See Kerby-Fulton and Justice (1998: 73–6, esp. n. 47), and the introduction to A. Shoef, ed., Usk's *Testament*, for summaries of recent discussion and bibliography.

[50] He borrows whole lines verbatim, and borrows extensively from Langland's exempla. See Kerby-Fulton and Justice (1998: 81–2). Quotations here are from the edn. by Steele (1898).

[51] In addition to Simpson (1990*a*), see the detailed annotations provided by Helen Barr (1993). All quotations from *Mum* are from this text.

[52] Meaning 'to put in legal possession'.

the long *exemplum* that follows, Joseph, whose story prompts this declaration of courage: 'And therefore my doute and dreede is the lasse/To do that the burne bade' (1334–5). This is the poem's turning point, and in an embryonic rewriting of the last allegory of Langland's poem, the 'saluing' of festering wounds, the poet declares that his intent is to apply 'a newe salue

> That the sothe-sigger hath sought many yeres
> And mighte not mete therewith for Mvm and his ferys
> That bare a-weye the bagges and many a boxe eeke. (1339–42)

These bags and boxes are full of episcopally confiscated books, and these books are the 'salve' itself. Mum, as Barr points out, has already twice previously been portrayed in the poem as a bishop; however, these lines need not necessarily refer to Arundel's Constitutions, since there were other earlier, non-Wycliffite confiscations during this period, as the *Opus* author himself tells us.[53] The narrator then begins to open secret verse ('pryue poyse'), from books 'vnbredid':

> Now forto conseille the king vnknytte I a bagge
> Where many a pryue poyse is preyntid withynne
> Yn bokes vnbredid in balade-wise made. (1343–5)

The poem is a remarkable work for understanding the genres of political book production (and their physical formats), as well as issues of libel, sedition, and silence. Mum advises taciturnity, reappears constantly as a kind of figure of surveillance, advises the dreamer of his legal rights on libel, sneers, tantalizes and brilliantly personifies the sceptic's view of survival in a hyper-political world. But the poem's complex portrayal of *tacit toleration* on the part of the authorities in this poem is also sophisticated, and still underappreciated by modern scholarship; it advocates, after all, the writing and circulation of controversial poetry, and even gives some guidance as to how this may be safely done. Also underappreciated is the fact that the *Mum* author portrays his dreamer as receiving a divine commission to write, which is *not* very Wycliffite—or 'maverick' Wycliffite at best.[54] Whether *Mum* is *as* Lollard a work as one of its most recent editors has suggested is difficult to say, because so many of the poem's bids for authority come from *visionary* tradition, rather than Wycliffite modes of construction of authority; these rarely involved the invocation of vision, with the exception of two early 'prison' narratives (the *Opus* author's and Brut's affidavit). Jenni Nuttall, moreover, has recently illuminated the highly political (as distinct from religiously heterodox) influences in the poem, offering yet another new direction for research on this complex narrative of tacit and not-so-tacit constraint and toleration in early Lancastrian England.[55]

That there was a climate of constraint in Ricardian vernacular texts, a range of areas, not all of which relate to Wycliffism, and a string of which relate to visionary,

---

[53] See Barr's note to 1341; Kerby–Fulton (2006) 403.
[54] Kerby-Fulton (2006: ch. 5).
[55] Nuttall (2007).

salvational, or entirely secular political issues is clear. Examining the role that both revelatory theology and—to coin a phrase—revelatory politics play in the establishment of a kind of 'free space', even in some instances a 'site of resistance', to discuss the undiscussable, then, is an ongoing task before us, as scholars of the late medieval self and its socio-literary representation.

Bibliography

Manuscripts Cited

London, British Library, Additional 10574

Oxford, Bodleian Library, Douce 104

Oxford, Bodleian Library, Bodley 851

Cambridge, University Library, Dd.i.17

The Ellesmere Manuscript, in *The Canterbury Tales: the New Ellesmere Chaucer Facsimile (of Huntington Library MS EL 26 C 9) / by Geoffrey Chaucer*, ed. Daniel Woodward and Martin Stevens. (Tokyo: Yushodo Co; San Marino, Calif.: Huntington Library Press, 1995).

Printed Sources

ABELARD, PETER (1959), *Historia calamitatum*. Critical edn. with introd. J. Monfrin (Paris: J. Vrin).

ARCHAMBAULT, PAUL (1995), *A Monk's Confession: The Memoirs of Guibert of Nogent* (University Park, Pa.: University of Penn State Press).

BARR, H. (ed.) (1993), *The Piers Plowman Tradition.* (London: Dent).

BARRON, C. (2004), *London in the Later Middle Ages: Government and People, 1200–1500* (Oxford: Oxford University Press).

BENSON, C. DAVID (2004), *Public Piers Plowman: Modern Scholarship and Late Medieval English Culture* (University Park, Pa.: Penn. State University Press, 2004).

——and BARRY WINDEATT (1990), 'The Manuscript Glosses to Chaucer's *Troilus*', *Chaucer Review*, 25: 33–53.

BENTON, JOHN (ed.) (1970), *Self and Society in Medieval France: The Memoirs of Abbot Guibert of Nogent* (Toronto: University of Toronto Press).

BIGGS, J. H. (1997), *The Imitation of Christ* (Oxford: Oxford University Press).

BOSTICK, CURTIS (1988), *The Antichrist and the Lollards: Apocalypticism in Late Medieval and Reformation England* (Leiden: Brill).

BROWNLEE, KEVIN (1992), 'Discourses of the Self: Christine de Pizan and the *Romance of the Rose*', in K. Brownlee and S. Huot (eds.), *Rethinking the Romance of the Rose* (Philadelphia: University of Pennsylvania Press).

BRUNDAGE, JAMES (1987), *Law, Sex, and Christian Society in Medieval Europe* (Chicago: University of Chicago Press).

BURROW, J. (1981), 'The Poet as Petitioner', *Studies in the Age of Chaucer*, 3: 61–75.

——(1982), 'Autobiographical Poetry in the Middle Ages: the Case of Thomas Hoccleve', *Proceedings of the British Academy*, 68: 389–412.

——(1994), *Thomas Hoccleve* (Aldershot: Ashgate Publishing).

CHAUCER, G. (1988), *The Riverside Chaucer*, ed. L. Benson (Oxford: Oxford University Press).

CLANCHY, M. (1993), *From Memory to Written Record: England 1066–1307* (2nd edn. Oxford: Blackwell Publishers).

COPELAND, RITA (2001), *Pedagogy, Intellectuals and Dissent in the Later Middle Ages* (Cambridge: Cambridge University Press).

CROW, M., and C. OLSON (eds.) (1996), *Chaucer Life-Records* (Oxford: Clarendon Press).

DRONKE, PETER (1984), *Women Writers of the Middle Ages* (Cambridge: Cambridge University Press).

FOUCAULT, M. (1979), 'What is an Author?', tr. J. Harari, in J. Harari (ed.), *Textual Strategies: Perspectives in Post-Structuralist Criticism* (Ithaca, NY: Cornell University Press), 141–60.

GALLOWAY, A. (2000), 'Authority', in P. Brown (ed.), *A Companion to Chaucer* (Oxford: Blackwell Publishers), 23–39.

GELTNER, GUY (2004), 'Faux Semblants: Antifraternalism Reconsidered in Jean de Meun and Chaucer', *Studies in Philology*, 101: 357–80.

GREEN, R. (1999), *A Crisis of Truth: Literature and Law in Ricardian England* (Philadelphia: University of Pennsylvania Press).

HANNA, R. (2005), *London Literature, 1300–1380* (Cambridge: Cambridge University Press).

HILDEGARD (1991), *Hildegardis Bingensis Epistolarium*, i, ed. Lievan Van Acker (Corpus Christianorum CC, 91; Turnhout: Brepols).

HOCCLEVE, T. (1970), *Hoccleve's Works: The Minor Poems*, ed. F. Furnivall and I. Gollancz, rev. A. Doyle (EETS ES 61 and 73; London: Oxford University Press).

——(1999), *The Regiment of Princes*, ed. C. Blyth (Kalamazoo, Mich.: Medieval Institute Publications).

——(2002), *Thomas Hoccleve: A Facsimile of the Autograph Verse Manuscripts*, ed. J. Burrow and A. Doyle (EETS SS 19; Oxford: Oxford University Press).

HUDSON, ANNE (1985), 'A Neglected Wycliffite Text', in A. Hudson, *Lollards and their Books* (London: Hambledon), 43–66.

——(ed.) (1997), *Selections from English Wycliffite Writings* (Cambridge: Cambridge University Press, 1978; repr., University of Toronto).

HUOT, SYLVIA (1993), *The Romance of the Rose and its Medieval Readers* (Cambridge: Cambridge University Press).

JUSTICE, S. (1994), *Writing and Rebellion: England in 1381* (Berkeley, Calif.: University of California Press).

KERBY-FULTON, K. (1997), 'Langland and the Bibliographic Ego', in S. Justice and K. Kerby-Fulton (eds.), *Written Work: Langland, Labor, and Authorship* (Philadelphia: University of Pennsylvania Press), 65–141.

——(2000), 'Professional Readers of Langland at Home and Abroad', in Derek Pearsall (ed.), *Harvard New Directions in Manuscript Studies* (Cambridge: Brewer), 101–37.

——(2006), *Books Under Suspicion: Censorship and Tolerance of Revelatory Writing in Late Medieval England* (Notre Dame, Ind.: University of Notre Dame Press).

——and S. Justice (1998), 'Langlandian Reading Circles and the Civil Service in London and Dublin, 1380–1427', *New Medieval Literatures*, 1: 59–83.

KNAPP, E. (2001), *The Bureaucratic Muse: Thomas Hoccleve and the Literature of Late Medieval England* (University Park, Pa.: Pennsylvania State University Press).

LANGLAND, W. (1886), *Piers the Plowman in Three Parallel Texts*, ed. Walter Skeat (Oxford: Clarendon).

——(1960), *Piers Plowman: The A Version*, ed. George Kane (London: Athlone).

——(1975), *Piers Plowman: The B Version*, ed. George Kane and E. T. Donaldson (London: Athlone).

——(1998), *Piers Plowman: The C Version*, ed. George Russell and George Kane (London: Athlone).

MARENBON, JOHN (1997), *The Philosophy of Peter Abelard* (Cambridge: Cambridge University Press).

MEYER LEE, ROBERT (2000), 'Self-Naming in Medieval Literary Texts', Paper given at MLA conference, in a session organized by Seeta Chaginti.

——(2007), *Poets and Power from Chaucer to Wyatt* (Cambridge Studies in Medieval Literature, 61; Cambridge: Cambridge University Press).

MINNIS, A. (1988), *Medieval Theory of Authorship: Scholastic Literary Attitudes in the Later Middle Ages* (2nd edn. Aldershot: Scolar Press).

MOONEY, L. (2006), 'Chaucer's Scribe', *Speculum*, 81: 97–138.

——(2007), 'Some New Light on Thomas Hoccleve', *Studies in the Age of Chaucer*, 29: 293–340.

MORRIS, COLIN (1972), *The Discovery of the Individual, 1050–1200* (Toronto: University of Toronto Press; repr. 1987; originally publ. by the Society for Promoting Christian Knowledge).

NOHRNBERG, JAMES (2003), 'The Autobiographical Imperative and the Necessity of "Dante" in *Purgatorio* 30. 55', *Modern Philology*, 111: 1–47.

NUTTALL, J. (2007), *The Creation of Lancastrian Kingship: Literature, Language and Politics in Late Medieval England* (Cambridge: Cambridge University Press).

OLSON, LINDA (1997), 'Reading Augustine's *Confessiones* in Fourteenth-Century England: John de Grandisson's Fashioning of Text and Self', *Traditio*, 52: 201–57.

——(2002), 'Untangling the Thread: Reading Augustine in Medieval Norwich', *Studies in Medieval and Renaissance History*, 1 (2002), 41–80.

PARSONS, KELLY (2001), 'The Red Ink Annotator in *The Book of Margery Kempe* and his Lay Audience', in K. Kerby-Fulton and M. Hilmo (eds.), *The Medieval Professional Reader at Work: Evidence from Manuscripts of Chaucer, Langland, Kempe and Gower* (Victoria, BC (Canada): English Literary Studies), 143–216.

PEARSALL, DEREK (1992), *The Life of Chaucer* (Oxford: Blackwell Publishing).

PERKINS, N. (2001), *Hoccleve's 'Regiment of Princes': Counsel and Constraint* (Cambridge: D. S. Brewer).

——(2007), 'Thomas Hoccleve: *La Male Regle*', in P. Brown (ed.), *A Companion to Medieval English Literature and Culture, c.1350–c.1500* (Oxford: Blackwell Publishing), 585–603.

PETRARCA, FRANCESCO (1993), *Secretum/Francesco Petrarca*, ed. Ugo Dotti (Rome: Archivio Guido Izzi).

PORETE, MARGUERITE (1986), *Le mirouer des simples âmes / Marguerite Porete*, ed. Romana Guarnieri (Turnhout: Brepols). *Margaretae Porete Speculum Simplicium Animarum*, ed. Paul Verdeyen and Romana Guarnieri (Corpus Christianorum, 969; Turnhout: Brepols).

RIGG, A. G., and CHARLOTTE BREWER (eds.) (1993), *Piers Plowman: The Z Version* (Toronto: PIMS).

RUSSELL, G. H. (1969), 'Some Aspects of the Process of Revision in *Piers Plowman*', in S. S. Hussey, *Piers Plowman Critical Approaches* (London: Methuen), 27–49.

SCASE, W. (2007), *Literature and Complaint in England, 1272–1553* (Oxford: Oxford University Press).

SIMPSON, JAMES (1990a), 'Constraints of Satire in *Piers Plowman* and *Mum and Sothsegger*', in H. Phillips (ed.), *Essays in Honour of S. S. Hussey* (Cambridge: Brewer), 11–41.

——(1990b), *Piers Plowman: An Introduction to the B-Text* (London: Longman).

SPEARING, A. C. (2004), 'Textual Performance: Chaucerian Prologues and the French Dit', in Marianne Børch (ed.), *Text and Voice: The Rhetoric of Authority in the Middle Ages* (Odense: University Press of Southern Denmark).

——(2005), *Textual Subjectivity: The Encoding of Subjectivity in Medieval Narratives and Lyrics* (Oxford: Oxford University Press).

——(2007), 'Medieval Autographies: The "I" of the Text', The Conway Lectures, University of Notre Dame.

SPITZER, LEO (1946), 'Note on the Poetic and the Empirical "I" in Medieval Authors', *Traditio*, 4: 414–22.

STEINER, E., 'Authority', in P. Strohm (ed.), *Middle English* (Oxford: Oxford University Press, 2007), 142–59.

STROHM, P. (1992), *Hochon's Arrow: The Social Imagination of Fourteenth-Century Texts* (Princeton: Princeton University Press).

——(2000), *Theory and the Pre-Modern Text* (Minneapolis: University of Minnesota Press).

TALBOT, C. H. (1998), *The Life of Christina of Markyate* (Toronto: University of Toronto Press).

USK, THOMAS (1897), *Testament of Love*, ed. W. W. Skeat, in *Chaucerian and other Pieces* (Oxford: Clarendon).

——(1998), *The Testament of Love*, ed. R. A. Shoaf (Kalamazoo, Mich.: Medieval Institute Publications, TEAMS ed.).

VAN ENGEN, JOHN (1998), 'Religious Profession: From Liturgy to Law', *Viator*, 29: 323–43.

——(2008), *Sisters and Brothers of the Common Life: The Devotio Moderna and the World of the Later Middle Ages* (Philadelpia: University of Pennsylvania Press).

WOGAN-BROWNE, NICHOLAS WATSON, ANDREW TAYLOR, and RUTH EVANS (1999), *The Idea of the Vernacular: An Anthology of Middle English Literary Theory, 1280–1520* (University Park, Pa.: Pennsylvania State University Press).

YONE, JAMES (1898), *Three Prose Versions of the Secreta Secretorum*, ed. Robert Steele (EETS, OS 74; London: Longman).

....

CHAPTER 22

COMPLEX IDENTITIES

SELVES AND OTHERS

....

KATHY LAVEZZO

CONTEMPORARY cultures in many respects appear to have a special claim on complex subject positions. Such factors as the emergence of densely populated global cities, new transportation and communication technologies, and an increasing moral relativism have made manifest, as never before, the fragility, contingency, and ambiguity inherent to identify formation. Medieval western society may seem starkly opposed to modern life, in large part due to its dominance by a universal Christian Church. But as recent work on the problem of difference in medieval literature has made clear, notions of identity in the Middle Ages are hardly straightforward and unproblematic. Rather, the period's hegemonic identity—male, Christian, and, in the case of England, increasingly English—was imagined during the period in uneasy relation to images of a whole host of 'others', among them: animals, children, devils, the disabled, heretics, monsters, Jews, pagans, the poor, Saracens, sodomites, Tartars, and women. For all its seemingly monolithic power in the medieval West, patriarchal Christian identity is, it turns out, as fragile as any other identity formation, and depends for its production on the creation of imagined identities from which it differs. A crucial arena in which we can glean the complex workings of medieval identity formations is indisputably literary production. Arguably more than any other area of medieval culture, literary texts play a fundamental role in the creation and dissemination of notions of selfhood, community, and alterity. By carefully considering representations of difference in medieval texts, we gain a powerful means of appreciating how, then as now, identity is contingent, iterative, layered, fluid, vulnerable, and contradictory.

In what follows, I consider the complexities of medieval identity formation by surveying the depiction of Jews and Saracens in English texts produced throughout the medieval period, from the time of Bede (c.673–735) to the second half of the fifteenth century. As the chapters covered in this section well demonstrate, there are many ways to approach productively the question of identity and medieval literature, and it is futile to posit any claims about a 'primary' other during the period. The relationships between the selves and others imagined by medieval texts are far too multiple, fraught, and unstable. That said, insofar as, among all possible identificatory characteristics, it was a religious trait—Christianity—that claimed primacy during the period, the problem of how Christians imagined their religious others is surely well worth pursuing. Images of Jews and Saracens have provided fertile ground for scholars interested in medieval identity formation, in large part due to the fact that Jews and Muslims constituted the foremost religious others to Christianity. Indeed, those religious and ethnic outsiders came to be lumped together, along with Satan himself, as prime enemies of the universal Church. At the same time, though, by closely looking at representations of Jews and Saracens in medieval texts, we discover their association with other forms of alterity (for example, women and sodomites) and moreover learn that even the most fiercely demonized others of the medieval West were imagined, at times, to be not altogether different from the Christians themselves.

EARLY MEDIEVAL REPRESENTATIONS
OF SARACENS AND JEWS

Although the emergence of the Anglo-Saxon period coincided with the appearance of Islam at the start of the seventh century,[1] early English writers generally demonstrate neither an informed conception of Islam nor the notably hostile and fantastic attention that western writers would devote to Saracens in later centuries.[2] But, as Katherine Scarfe Beckett recently has made clear, those Anglo-Saxon representations of the Islamic world that exist are nevertheless worth examining for several reasons, among them their introduction of ideas that would continue to inform literary depictions of Saracens into the Middle Ages and beyond. The 'earliest surviving

---

[1] Augustine of Canterbury arrived in England in 597; and Islam is believed to have been revealed to Muhammad in 610.

[2] Revising the position of Kedar, who claims that information about Islam was widely available before 1100 even in the far western reaches of Europe, Scarfe Beckett asserts that informed opinions were 'exceptional' (p. 7).

Anglo Saxon description of the Arab conquests' appears in Bede's early eighth-century commentary on Genesis.[3] A Benedictine monk, historian, and scholar, Bede alludes to Muslim conquest in his interpretation of the angelic prophecy to Hagar in Genesis 16: 12 regarding her birth of a son named Ishmael, who 'will be a wild man' (*erit ferus homo*):

It means that [Ishmael's] seed is to live in the wilderness—that is to say, the wandering Saracens of uncertain abode, who invade all those living beside the desert, and are resisted by all. But this is how things used to be. Now, however, to such an extent is '[Ishmael's] hand against everyone and everyone's hand against him' that they oppress the whole length of Africa under their authority and, moreover, inimical and full of hate towards everybody, they hold most of Asia and a considerable part of Europe.[4]

Bede demonstrates in the passage his knowledge of the remarkable expansion of Muslim civilization, an awareness that prompts the scholar to stress the changing geographic identity of the Saracens, who once were wanderers 'of uncertain abode' in the desert, but now control most of the known world. The colossal territorial power that Bede allots the Saracens exemplifies how pre- and early modern European representations of Saracens do not demonstrate, in Nabil Matar's words, 'the authority of possessiveness or the security of domination which later gave rise to what Edward Said has termed "Orientalism".[5] While the British Empire would enjoy global dominion during the period analyzed by Said (an era spanning the eighteenth to early twentieth centuries), it is Muslim power that looms over the world during Bede's time. The sheer might of Islam is not simply recognized but indeed exaggerated by Bede.

This is not to say, however, that Bede's account of the Saracens does not support other aspects of Said's theory of Orientalism, namely his identification of a Western European desire to master intellectually and criticize the Eastern other through stereotypes. For Bede situates the fact of Muslim expansion in a fictitious biblical context that reflects how early English writers deployed scripture and patristic exegesis as a means of comprehending and denigrating Arabs and Muslims. First, by identifying the Saracens as Ishmael's descendants, Bede associates the Muslims of his own time with the people whom Jerome (d. 420) three centuries earlier linked to Ishmael and his mother Hagar.[6] Possibly following an earlier Christian source, Jerome claims in his commentaries on the narrative of Abraham and his wife Sarah[7] that 'Saracen' denotes the name that the descendants of Ishmael took on as

---

[3] Scarfe Beckett (2003: 129).

[4] 'Significat semen eius habitaturum in eremo, id est Saracenos uagos, incertisque sedibus. Qui uniuersas gentes quibus desertum ex latere iungitur incursant, et expugnantur ab omnibus. Sed haec antiquitus. Nunc autem in tantum manus eius contra omnes, et manus sunt omnium contra eum, ut Africam totam in longitudine sua ditione premant, sed et Asiae maximam partem, et Europae nonnullam omnibus exosi et contrarii teneant'; Bede (1967: 201); tr. Scarfe Beckett (2003: 18).

[5] Matar (1998: 11). See also Scarfe Beckett (2003: 198–9) and, more generally, Gellner (1993).

[6] On the etymology of the term 'Saracen', Jerome's etymology and its wide influence, see Scarfe Beckett (2003: 93–104).

[7] Gen. 16, 21: 1–21.

a means of both denying Ishmael's actual, if illegitimate, status as the offspring of Abraham and the slave woman Hagar, and asserting a false but respectable descent from Abraham and his wife Sarah.[8]

A fiction generated by Christians (no Arab peoples referred to themselves as Saracens) and widely promoted via Jerome,[9] the notion of the Saracens situates deceit at the core of Arab and/or Muslim identity: the Saracens are frauds and are in reality Ishmaelites (or, alternately, Hagarenes from Hagar). At the same time, the idea of the Saracen assures Christians that they know the 'correct' bloodline of an Eastern people and can understand them further through recourse to biblical authority. Hence, Bede can acknowledge historical change (the spread of the Muslim world) but also affirm continuity in terms of the history of Saracen behavior as outlined in the Bible. As Scarfe Beckett puts it, 'Bede presents the Islamic conquests in such a way as to affirm that, far from being a new phenomenon, they demonstrate what has been known all along about the Saracens',[10] and what is known is hardly complimentary. The reference in Genesis to Ishmael's 'hand against everyone and everyone's hand against him' has only intensified in its applicability to the contemporary Saracens, whom the monk stereotypes as 'inimical and full of hate towards everybody'.[11] As Scarfe Beckett observes, to the extent that Bede designates an 'everyone' against which the hostile Saracens contend, he exhibits an 'us' versus 'them' attitude that accords with 'the idea that Orientalism consists largely in the implicit boundary which separates the necessarily different and very often dangerous, threatening "Orient"—the "Other"—from the western writer who describes it'.[12] Utter enemies of universal Christendom, the Saracens occupy in Bede's writings the same position inhabited by other perceived enemies of the Church, such as the devil, heretics, and Jews.

While early English literature offers relatively few images of Saracens, texts from that period frequently offer representations of Jews. This hardly means, to be sure, that the Anglo-Saxons had much if any personal experience of Jews. We have no evidence of a Jewish presence in Anglo-Saxon England, and Jews only began to enter the island after the Norman Conquest. But from the inception of Christianity, the intertwining of Jews and Judaism in Christian thinking was so thorough as to ensure that Christian writers, regardless of their personal experience with Jews, would represent them and their religion. As Lisa Lampert puts it, 'one cannot conceive . . . [of] Christianity without Judaism';[13] thanks to their own immersion in a Christian perspective, Anglo-Saxon

---

[8] See Jerome (1964: 335).

[9] Scarfe Beckett (2003: 94–5).

[10] Ibid. 20.

[11] Wallace-Hadrill has suggested that Bede's hostile representation of Saracens here and elsewhere represents a shift in the monks' texts, which initially exhibited a more 'neutral' stance that eroded due to Muslim expansion into Spain and Aquitaine (1994: 77–8). While recent scholars such as Tolan have adopted Wallace-Hadrill's theory (2002: 75–6), Scarfe Beckett qualifies it by pointing out Bede's reliance upon sources in the earlier texts as well as his ongoing reading of hostile patristic accounts of Saracens by Jerome and others (2003: 137).

[12] Ibid. 19–20.   [13] Lampert (2004: 2).

writers frequently would depict Jews in their texts. One telling example of those early English representations of Jews appears in the sermon by Ælfric, abbot of Eynsham (*c.*950–1010), on the last two books in the Vulgate Old Testament, Maccabees I and II, which narrate the lengthy guerrilla war that the Jewish family of the Maccabees waged against their pagan Syrian oppressors between 175 and 134 BC.[14] Ælfric's text offers an early instance of how, throughout the medieval period, English writers both overcame imaginatively the historical and theological problems that Jews posed to Christianity and deployed constructions of Jews as a means of engaging with the weaknesses and potentials of English Christian society.

Ælfric touches on two of the main dilemmas Jews presented to Christians when the monk comments on the curious fact that 'five angels from heaven, riding on horses with golden apparel' (*fif englas of heofonum, ridende on horsum mid gyldenum gerædum*) assist the Maccabees during their conflict.[15] 'If any one now should wonder how it might happen that angels should ride on saddled and bridled horses, then let him know', Ælfric explains,

that truly everywhere tell us the holy books of God (which may not be false) that angels often came to men truly as if riding upon horses, even as we have here related. The Jews were the most dear to God in the old law, because they alone honored the Almighty God with worship continually; until Christ, God's son, was Himself conceived of human nature, of the Jewish kin, of Saint Mary the virgin, without human father.

Then some of them would not believe that He was the Very God, but laid snares for His life, even as He Himself permitted. There were however many good men of that nation, both in the old law, and also in the new, patriarchs and prophets, and holy apostles, and many thousands that follow Christ (although some remain froward until now). They shall, however, all finally believe; but there shall perish too many, in the period between, for their hardheartedness against the heavenly Savior. (ll. 508–29)[16]

Ælfric points to an issue at the heart of the intertwining of Jews and Christians in Christian writing: the manner in which Christianity grew out of and was based upon Judaism. Jesus, as Ælfric points out, was Jewish. The priority of the Jews in the history

[14] On Ælfric's method of translating the Maccabees books, his own originality, and the monk's sense of audience, see Wilcox (1993).

[15] Ælfric (1966), ii, ll. 490–1; Ælfric (1999), ll. 434–6. Translations are based upon Skeat with minor changes unless indicated; citations of the Old English follow Lee's web edn., with slight alterations in punctuation and expansion of some abbreviations. Citations of line numbers in Skeat will hereafter appear in the text; citations of the Old English will cite line numbers in Lee.

[16] 'Gif hwa nu wundrige hu hit gewurþan mihte þæt englas sceoldon ridan on georædedum horsum, þonne wite he to soþan þæt us secgað gehwær ða halgan Godes bec (þe ne magon beon lease) þæt englas oft comon cuðlice to mannum, swilce on horse ridende, swa swa we her rehton. Þa Iudeiscan wæron ða dyreste Gode on ðære ealdan æ, forðan þe hi ana wurðodon þone ælmihtigan God mid biggencgum symle, oþþæt Crist, Godes sunu, sylf wearð ascenned of menniscum gecynde of þam Iudeiscum cynne, of Sancta Marian þam mædene, butan menniscum fæder. // Þa noldon hi sume gelyfan þæt he soð God wære, ac syrwdon embe his lif swa swa he sylf geðafode. Waeron swaþeah manega of þam cynne gode, ge on ðære ealdan æ ge eac on þære niwan—heahfæderas and witegan, and halige apostolas, and fela ðusenda þe folgiað Criste (þea þe hi sume wunian wiðerwerde oþ þis). Hi sceolon swaðeah ealle on ende gelyfan; ac ðær losiað to feala on þam fyrste betwux, for heora heardheortnysse wið þone heofonlican hælend' (ll. 449–68).

of Christianity posed a problem of belatedness for Christians that was exacerbated by the exalted status of the Jews as God's chosen people, a privilege that explains the seemingly outrageous idea of angels on earth. Precisely because they were 'dearest to God in the old law' (*dyreste Gode on ðaere ealdan ae*) the Jews were blessed with divine assistance in the form of angelic warriors.

Coupled with the problem of their prior privilege was that of the ongoing Jewish rejection of the Christian faith. Paradoxically, many of the very people whom God first chose upon witnessing Christ did not acknowledge him as their God and 'some remain froward until now' (*sume wunian wiðerwerde oþ þis*), Ælfric admits. Ælfric only exacerbates the vexed relationship of the Jews to Christ when he states that the Jews murdered Christ or, in Ælfric's words 'laid snares for his life' (*syrwdon embe his lif*).[17] Points of origin yet consummate others, perceived enemies of the faith who are nevertheless located deep within Christian history, a people who 'were from God and... were not from God' (*wæron fram gode and... næron fram gode*), the Jews constituted highly charged and fraught figures for Anglo-Saxon writers like Ælfric.[18]

Obviously, the Jews' rejection of the Christian message seriously challenged the authority of that religion, and Ælfric draws on his patristic heritage as a means of dealing with the dilemma. The monk especially relies upon the work of Augustine, who 'established', as Andrew Scheil points out, 'the paradigm for the Christian understanding of Jews in the early Middle Ages'.[19] According to his 'remainder' theory, Augustine posited that God retained the Jews as witnesses to Christ's presence as revealed in the Old Testament, witnesses who were destined to participate in the final episode in salvation history, at the Second Coming. Thus Ælfric affirms of the Jews that 'They shall, however, all finally believe' (*Hi sceolon swaðeah ealle on ende gelyfan*). When the monk goes on to write that many Jews shall die for their *heardheortnysse* or 'hardheartedness', he also draws on Augustine, who claimed that the Jews possess a stubborn literalism. The idea that the Jews obstinately adhere to a carnal and literal point of view—and, conversely, the notion that Christians embrace a spiritual and more figurative perspective—served to overcome imaginatively many of the dilemmas Jews and Judaism presented to Christianity and would powerfully inform English writing on Jews throughout the Middle Ages. By elevating the spirit over the letter (compare Paul's famous dictum, 'The letter kills, but the spirit gives life', in 2 Corinthians 3: 6), Christian writers could qualify the Jews' divine election by subordinating them to Christian history. The Jews of the Old Testament were, to be sure, a heroic and admirable people, but those achievements existed on a literal, worldly register that was always superseded by the spiritual nature of Christian history.

Ælfric's approach to the theme of his Maccabees sermon suggests as much. The bulk of the sermon relates the heroism and faith of the Jewish warriors, and above all

---

[17] On the myth of deicide, see Cohen (1985).
[18] Scheil (2004: 233).
[19] Ibid. 10; see also Cohen (1999:: 19–65).

that of Judas Maccabeus, whose brave battles against seemingly overwhelming odds dominate the text. But, as Scheil has observed, 'admirable as Judas's deeds are, according to Ælfric they designate a Jew who cannot move beyond the literal level of interpretation... The ultimate servant of God, according to Ælfric, is not a worldly warrior, but rather a spiritual one.'[20] Thus the monk writes of Judas:

> Manifold were his great battles; and he is as holy, in the Old Testament, as are God's elect ones, in the Gospel preaching, because he ever contended for the will of the Almighty... But Christ, at His coming, taught us another thing and entreated us to hold peace and truthfulness ever; and we ought to strive against the cruel enemies, that is, the invisible ones, and the deceitful devils, that wish to slay our souls with vices. Against them we should fight with spiritual weapons... The ancient people of God had to fight then with weapons, and their contest had the signification of holy men who drive away vices and devils from them in the New Testament, that Christ Himself appointed. (ll. 680–704).[21]

Ælfric's discussion of Judas Maccabeus culminates in a politicized reading of the Old Testament in relationship to the New Testament: the Old Testament Jews' battles with real weapons against pagan aggressors have the 'signification' (getacnunge) of Christian clerics who battle 'with spiritual weapons' (mid gastlicum wæpnum) against 'invisible' (ungesewenlican) enemies in the New Testament. The literal battles, that is, of heroic Jews like Judas carry within them another prophetic meaning that looks toward the history of Christians and their spiritual warfare against evil. 'Fully revers (ing)', as Jonathan Wilcox puts it, 'the glorification of physical battle implicit in the narrative which he is translating', Ælfric subordinates the literal warfare waged by the Maccabees to the holy battles of Christian history.[22]

The figurative, or typological, mode of interpretation the monk employs was vital to Christian thinking on Jews, and enabled Christians to read Jewish history as an imperfect version of episodes within Christian history.[23] Furthermore, typology proved to be a powerful political tool for Christian writers concerned with problems inherent to their particular communities. Ælfric closes his Maccabees sermon by turning to the ordering of his own Anglo-Saxon community under the three estates,[24] and particularly the relationship between its clerical and martial orders:

> Now toils the field-laborer for our subsistence, and the worldly warrior must fight against our enemies, and the servant of God must always pray for us, and fight spiritually against invisible

---

[20] Scheil (2004: 323).

[21] 'Menigfealde wæron his micclan gefeoht, and he is eallswa halig on ðære ealdan gecyðnysse, swa swa Godes gecorenan on ðære godspelbodunge, forðan þe he æfre wan for willan þæs ælmihtigan Godes... Ac Crist on his tocyme us cydde oðre ðincg, and het us healdan sibbe and soðfæstnysse æfre, and we sceolon winnan wið þa wælhreowan fynd; þæt synd ða ungesewenlican, and þa swicolan deofla, þe willað ofslean ure sawla mid leahtrum, wið ða we sceolon winnan mid gastlicum wæpnum... þæt ealde Godes folc sceolde feohtan þa mid wæpnum, and heora gewinn hæfde haligra manna getacnunge, þe todræfað þa leahtras and deofla heom fram, on ðære niwan gecyðnysse þe Crist sylf astealde' (ll. 600–24).

[22] Wilcox (1993: 9).

[23] Auerbach (1984); Cohen (1999); Robbins (1991: 1–10).

[24] On the medieval notion of three feudal orders, see Duby (1985). On Ælfric's notion of the three estates in his Maccabees sermon, see Godden (1990).

enemies. Greater therefore is now the struggle of the monks against the invisible devils that lay snares around us, than may be that of the worldly men that struggle against fleshly [foes], and visibly fight against the visible [enemies]. Then the worldly soldiers ought not to the worldly battle compel the servants of God, away from the spiritual struggle; because it will profit them more that the invisible enemies may be overcome than the visible ones. (ll. 819–30)[25]

Ælfric's concern in the passage with 'worldly soldiers' and 'the servants of God' reflects two key aspects of his own immediate tenth-century context: the recurrent Viking invasions and the ongoing Benedictine reform movement to which his homiletic project contributed. Ælfric's words suggest that the warriors defending England from northern aggressors pressured the monks dedicated to correcting England's spiritual ills to join the thanes' 'worldly battle'. By appending his elevation of the spiritual battles of his own clerical order over the physical battles of England's secular order to the Maccabees sermon, Ælfric deploys typology as a means of fortifying his own ideological program. As Scheil puts it, 'the insufficient values of the Jews in Maccabees are superimposed on the *bellatores* of Anglo-Saxon England; the thanes defending England from Vikings are incomplete without the spiritual complement of the Benedictine reform'.[26] At stake in most Anglo-Saxon representations of Jews, in other words, is not always the Jews or Judaism *per se*, but the manner in which fictions of Jews speak to problems facing English society. The Jewish 'other' in Ælfric's sermon finally isn't strange at all, but analogous to the aristocratic warriors of the monk's own English society.

HIGH MEDIEVAL REPRESENTATIONS OF SARACENS AND JEWS

William the Conqueror brought Jews from Rouen into England shortly after 1066, and within one hundred years a textual and visual culture geared especially towards Christian discussion of Jews would be 'firmly in place' in England.[27] As the increasing production of English artifacts mainly concerned not with biblical Jews but with the question of their continued existence suggests, the physical presence of Jews in England informed those textual and cultural representations. But this is hardly to say that such texts provide us with any reliable access to the lived experience of Jews

---

[25] 'Nu swincð se yrðlincg embe urne bigleofan, and se woruldcempa sceall winnan wið ure fynd, and se Godes þeowa sceall symle for us gebiddan and feohtan gastlice wið þa ungesewenlican fynd. Is nu forþy mare þæra muneca gewinn wið þa ungesewenlican deofla þe syrwiað embe us, þonne sy þæra woruldmann þe winnað wiþ ða flæsclican and wið þa gesewenlican feohtað. Nu ne sceolon þa woruldcempan to þam woruldlicum gefeohte þa godes þeowan neadian fram þam gastlican gewinne; forðan þe him fremað swiðor þæt þa ungesewenlican fynd beon oferswyðde þone ða gesewenlican...' (ll. 730–41).

[26] Scheil (2004: 327).   [27] Bale (2006: 16).

during their colonization of England after 1066. Rather, what we primarily witness in Anglo-Christian (and indeed, most Euro-Christian) images of Jews is what Anthony Bale describes as 'a process of fictionalization' whereby historical phenomena 'were overlaid and redetermined in fantastical (or "chimerical") terms'.[28] Bale offers an excellent example of how Christians endeavored to layer their own cultural constructions over contemporary Jews in his discussion of the effects of one of the most notorious canons of the Fourth Lateran Council of 1215, which orders that Jews and Saracens 'of either sex in every Christian province and at all times shall be distinguished from other people by the character of their dress in public'.[29] England would be the first site to introduce the law, by requiring Jews to don white badges shaped like the two tablets of the Ten Commandments. As Bale points out, the badges might 'be seen as a way of turning real Jews into symbols or signs', signs that, among other things, ignored the actual heterogeneity of the Jews by subjecting them 'to a collective alterity'. The badge as well demonstrates the historical effects of the Christian constructions of the Jews, insofar as Jewish people literally had to wear those symbols on their bodies.[30]

Of all the medieval anti-Semitisms circulating in the Middle Ages, surely one of the most potent emerged in the English legends of Jews murdering Christian children.[31] Those stories represented 'a technology of power with the ability over time to bring about the legal State execution of English Jews on the basis of a cultural fiction'.[32] In 1255 nineteen Jews thought to be associated with the death of Hugh of Lincoln were executed, and the expulsion of Jews from Bury St Edmunds in 1190 probably resulted partly from the allegation ten years earlier that Robert of Bury St Edmunds was killed by Jews. Those stories of the supposed martyrdom of young Christian boys by Jews were related to a larger genre of defamatory narratives of Jewish criminality against Christians, myths that often imagine Jews using Christian blood for ritual purposes. A disturbing transhistorical significance is, to be sure, suggested by such narratives (compare the role of the ritual murder accusation in Nazi Germany); but, as Miri Rubin, Bale, and other scholars have stressed, it is crucial also to attend to the individual contexts in which such tales emerge, the various and contradictory ways in which Jews were imagined, and the particular historical needs those anti-Semitic representations addressed.[33]

An early Latin homiletic *exemplum*, written by a Norman who would become the first bishop of Norwich, suggests the various uses to which anti-Semitic constructions of Jews could be put in high medieval England. At the close of a sermon that he

---

[28] Bale (2003: 138).   [29] Lateran IV, canon 68, tr. in Rothwell (1975).

[30] Bale (2003: 132; 2006: 15).

[31] Despite its modern origins, I employ the term anti-Semitism to describe medieval texts, because, as Bale observes, 'the fact that the label did not exist does not mean that antisemitism was absent; it simply had not yet been categorized' (2003: 129). Following Bale and like-minded scholars, I will use 'anti-Jewish' to designate attacks on 'those who identify as Jews' and Jewish faith and culture (ibid.).

[32] Heng (2007: 252).

[33] Compare Rubin's critique of Langmuir's view of the 'eternal, unchanging' nature of narratives of abuse (1999: 1) and Bale (2003: 129).

wrote for Christmas Day, Herbert de Losinga (d. 1119), relates a version of the widely circulated story of the Jewish boy who accompanies his Christian playmates to an Easter Mass, where the child takes communion. The boy relates his deed to his mother who, 'stirred with a woman's fury', tells her husband and 'kindled in the father of the child madness and cruelty. Whereupon', Losinga continues, 'this most unnatural father heated a furnace, and threw his son into the midst of it, into the live coals and raging flames, and in his madness sealed up the mouth of the furnace with stones and cement.'[34] The mother goes on to relate her husband's crime to her Christian friends, who pry the furnace open to discover the child unharmed. The boy tells the Christians that 'The Lady who sitteth above the Altar of the Christians, and the Little One Whom she cherishes in her bosom, stood around me, and stretching forth their hands hedged my body round, and protected me from the flames and fiery coals.'[35] The story ends with the 'most just vengeance' for those Jews who refuse conversion, who are incinerated in the same furnace used by the father.

The story of the Jewish boy condenses a host of anxieties and desires within the local, national, and international communities that Losinga inhabits—far more concerns than I can adequately cover in this survey. In what follows I sketch out three, interrelated issues to which the tale speaks: the problem of female alterity, doctrinal controversies over the Virgin Mary, and discord between the English natives and Norman rulers of post-Conquest England. As Lampert has made clear, woman presented a problem for the medieval and patriarchal Christian community very similar to that posed by Jews. As Lampert puts it, both 'are not simply the Other for the Christian exegetical tradition; they also represent sources of origin'.[36] The fraught standing of both Jews and women as 'insiders and outsiders to Christian society' leads to their mutual constitution in many anti-Semitic narratives, and Losinga's sermon is in many respects as much about demonizing woman as it is about demonizing Jews. Jewish monstrosity—the father's 'unnatural' effort to incinerate a child he should properly protect—is all the more perverted in the sermon due to its 'kindling' by an angry, emotional woman. Christian patriarchal ideology dictated that a husband should control his wife, due largely to the female gender's supposedly heightened susceptibility to carnal desires and feelings. With her 'woman's fury' the Jewish mother exemplifies woman's presumed vulnerability to emotions. But instead of being controlled by her husband, she influences his behavior.

At the same time that Losinga's construction of Jewish alterity speaks to anxieties produced in Christian patriarchy by its female population, it also addresses medieval Christian discord over one woman in particular: the Virgin Mary. Many medieval

[34] 'Tunc mater femineo furore commota maritum adiit factum retulit patremque parvuli in amentiam et crudelitatem exasperavit. Hinc nefandissimus pater clibanum succendit et in ejus prunas et sevientes flammas filium suum introrsus projecit atque os clibani lapidibus et cemento insaniens obturavit' (Losinga 1868: 30–1).

[35] 'Domina inquit quae super aram christianorum sedet et paulus quem fovet in sino suo circumsteterunt me et porrectis manibus suis corpus meum vallaverunt atque a flammis et prunis estuantibus defenderunt' (ibid. 32–3).

[36] Lampert (2004: 2).

anti-Jewish narratives feature the Virgin Mary, a pattern that, as critics such as Joan Young Gregg and Lampert have pointed out, demonstrates how constructions of the Jewish other emerge from doctrinal conflicts within Christian society. The extraordinary qualities ascribed to Mary—her persistent virginity, her immaculate conception, her intercessory role, etc.—were the subject of heated debate. Imaginatively resolving such doubts about Mary, anti-semitic Marian tales depict her miraculous triumph over Jews, who were particularly associated with skepticism about the Virgin. In the case of Losinga, by representing Mary as the miraculous caretaker of the boy—indeed as a figure who serves a protective function similar to that of God—Bishop Herbert supports her elite standing in the Christian hierarchy. With this move, Losinga circles back to a theme he introduced earlier in the sermon, whose opening moves include the affirmation of Mary's immaculate conception and virginity.[37] But the bishop's return to the topic of Mary carries with it the added ideological charge provided by the inclusion of a fantasized Jewish alterity: by opposing Mary specifically to the abusive Jewish father, the sermon suppresses Christian–Christian dissent about the Virgin's standing with a spectacularly gruesome and fiery Christian–Jewish conflict.

Bishop Herbert's anti-Semitic production of Marian authority may also have addressed issues particular to England, which occupied a distinctive role in the history of Marian devotion. As Mary Clayton has made clear, the Anglo-Saxons underwent two lengthy waves of devotion to the Virgin, the second of which was still under way when the Normans arrived on the scene in 1066. The Normans, through the agency of Archbishop Lanfranc of Canterbury (1005–89), engaged in a reform of the native Church, including the abolition of many of the feast days that were unique to Anglo-Saxon England. The apparent inclusion of two Marian feast days among those abolished suggests how the cult of the Virgin so important to Anglo-Saxon spirituality separated the native English from their Norman conquerors. Marian piety, of course, was just one of many divisive issues in Anglo-Norman England. As Jeffrey Jerome Cohen has pointed out with respect to eleventh-century Norwich, a variety of factors separated the English and Normans, factors including different vernaculars (English and French), different estates (the English were by and large poor and disempowered, the Normans wealthy and dominating), and different geographies and architectures (the Normans tended to occupy stone edifices in urban centers, the English lived on the urban periphery and countryside). We might speculate that the mutual construction of Jews and Mary in Losinga's sermon served to address such divisions, and particularly that of Norman–English division over Mary. The elevation of Mary by Losinga, a Norman, in the tale of the Jewish boy and elsewhere in the sermon suggests an effort to join his fellow Normans to the native English. While some native auditors may well have viewed Losinga's sermon as part of a Norman program bent on eradicating the Marian practices unique to England, Losinga opposes Mary to the monstrous Jewish father. More generally,

[37] Losinga (1868: 5).

the host of issues dividing the Christian inhabitants of post-Conquest England may have dissolved for Losinga's audience when faced by the Jewish threat depicted in the bishop's *exemplum*. That threat was made all the more palpable by the fact that the urban environment of the story of the Jewish boy—a city where 'Christians and Jews dwelt mingled with one another. Thence sprang familiarity and common dealings' — applied not only to the fictitious Greek town in which the bishop sets the sermon but also to a post-Conquest England into which Jews had been newly introduced.

As the aforementioned canon from Lateran IV on distinctive clothing demonstrates, along with Jews, Saracens were the focus of increased anxieties and desires on the part of Christians during the high Middle Ages. A crucial factor behind that heightened interest in Saracens was the Crusades, which placed the idea of the Saracen at the forefront of Christian occidental imaginations as never before. Launched first by Pope Urban II in 1096, the Crusades licensed Christian warfare against the Muslim possessors of Jerusalem and other Middle Eastern territories perceived to be the rightful property of Christendom. England's 'royal family and ruling caste' assumed a prominent role in the Crusades from the start, and their contribution had literary correlatives.[38] From the twelfth century onward, a variety of literary genres in England—most famously *chansons de geste* and romances—would feature Saracens. Those representations, to be sure, were as divorced from the historical features of the distant Islamic world as their anti-Semitic counterparts were separated from the life of Jews living within England. And yet in the same way that anti-Semitic narratives, however fanciful, could have historical effects, constructions of Saracens could intersect with real violence against Muslims.

Most obviously, negative stereotypes of Saracens as unclean, evil, licentious, etc. could 'function in crusading propaganda . . . as both a call to arms and an uncomplicated antithesis to Christian identity'.[39] But as Cohen, Heng, and other scholars have taught us, constructions of Saracens could also function in a more complicated manner, one that spoke to historical issues that included but were not limited to the Crusades. Consider the case of *Richard Coer de Lyon*, a romance that likely emerged in the thirteenth century in Anglo-Norman, and would be rewritten and elaborated in Middle English over the fourteenth and fifteenth centuries. *Richard Coer de Lyon* recounts the exploits of its eponymous English hero, King Richard I, while leading the Third Crusade against the Muslim military leader, Saladin. *Richard Coer de Lyon* is an unabashedly outrageous text featuring over-the-top battle scenes and, of course, King Richard devouring the still-pulsing heart of a lion, down whose throat he had just thrust his arm. But by far the most shocking and repellant aspect of this extravagant romance is its depiction, no less than three times, of Saracens as food fit for a king. I will examine the first of those episodes, which occurs when an ailing Richard expresses an impossible craving for pork, a food that is unavailable in Acre. Unbeknownst to the king, his men feed him instead an elaborately prepared roast

---

[38] Heng (2007: 256–7).   [39] Cohen (2001: 114).

made from a Saracen youth. Richard recovers and later demands the head of the 'pig'
that was served to him, and finds himself confronted by a Saracen man's head:

> Hys swarte vys whenne þe kyng seeþ,
> Hys blacke berd, and hys white teeþ,
> Hou hys lyppys grennyd wyde.
> 'What deuyl is þis?' the kyng cryde,
> And gan to lauȝe as he were wood.
> What, is Sarezynys flesch þus good?'[40]

> When the king saw his black visage,
> His black beard, and his white teeth,
> And how his lips bore a wide grin,
> 'What devil is this?' cried the king,
> who began to laugh as if he were mad.
> 'What, is Saracen flesh this good?'

As Heng points out, the head upon which Richard (and the reader) gaze is unques-
tionably marked along biologically racial lines, in terms of its swarthy skin: 'color is
the first thing which we, and Richard, are forced to see, in acknowledging the
victim'.[41] The blackness of the Saracen's visage reflects, as Heng, Cohen, and others
have demonstrated, that 'race' is a category of identity that signified during the
Middle Ages.[42]

In the case of *Richard Coer de Lyon*, the raced construction of the Saracen, on the
one hand, reinforces negative stereotypes. Richard's claim that the head belongs to a
devil reflects how, from the First Crusade onward, Saracens became '*the* enemy of
Christendom'.[43] Reinforcing the demonization of the Saracen is the manner in which
its lips widely 'grennyd', insofar as 'grennen' was used in Middle English to refer to
the gaping mouth of hell, as well as the menacing grimace of the devil. The grinning
lips on the head also reflect the tendency of Christian-identified texts to render
the religious other animalistic, bestial, and generally less than human.[44] The primary
meaning of *grennen* refers to the snarl of an animal: insofar as it suggests a growl,
the Saracen's mouth thus reinforces moments elsewhere in the romance when the
Saracens are stereotyped as 'hounds'. Because it houses the mind, the head is the body
part that most sets men apart from animals and renders them closest to God.[45] But in
this scene of cannibalism or, to use a more historically accurate term, anthropophagi,[46] a Saracen head becomes thoroughly embodied, nothing more than meat,
a face whose mouth utters no words but memorializes the growl of a 'beast' fiercely
resisting with bared teeth its own death.

---

[40] Brunner (1913: ll. 3211–16).
[41] Heng (2003: 76).
[42] Cohen (2001); Hahn (2001); Heng (2003, 2007); Lampert (2004); Sponsler and Clark (1999).
[43] Mastnak (2002: 127–8).
[44] Shell (1993).
[45] Isidore (2006: 11. 1. 11, 11. 1. 25).
[46] McDonald (2004: 125).

But as is so often the case with constructions of a racialized other, the denigration of the Saracen merges with fascination, envy, and desire in this episode.[47] To return to the grin, the open mouth represents a charged site of enjoyment and sensual pleasures, thus reflecting how carnal excesses—whether in terms of eating habits or sexuality—were attributed to Saracens. Further support for the status of the grin as a sign of Saracen enjoyment comes from its representation in a scene of Christian cannibalism. The pleasures associated with Saracens, in other words, prove so enticing in *Richard Coer de Lyon* as to prompt their incorporation by the English King himself. Far from recoiling in horror from the severed head, Richard wonders over the delectability of Saracen flesh, and even carves up another head in the final scene of cannibalism in the romance. The open mouth of the Saracen, with its suggestion of sensual desires, thus mirrors Richard's own appetites, whether for food or 'territorial digestion', that is, the king's military programme.[48] The ostensible division of self and other proves markedly unstable in the romance, whose scandalous hero strays very, very far from notions of proper Christian identity. Richard's incorporation of Saracens suggests the presence of the other deep within the self. If we are what we eat, the Christian king is also part Saracen.

As Heng has made clear, humor is fundamental to our understanding of the curious representation of English cannibalism in *Richard Coer de Lyon*. Taken seriously, Richard's cannibalism is unthinkable and barbaric. But by tapping 'conventions of humor that make the transgression of taboos acceptable', the romance licences the representation of royal English barbarism.[49] The historical problems to which that barbarism may speak are manifold and include animosity toward the French during the Hundred Years War[50] and ongoing debates regarding the doctrine of transubstantiation. But perhaps the clearest issue addressed by Richard's taboo eating practice is, as Heng has brilliantly made clear, the alimentary habits of actual Christian crusaders. During the First Crusade, the unthinkable occurred in a northern Syrian city, when crusaders, in the words of eyewitness Fulcher of Chartre, 'cooked and chewed, and devoured with savage mouth' dead Muslims.[51] An act that inverted the binary of Christian purity and heathen contagion central to Crusade propaganda, Crusader cannibalism was a monumental trauma that *Richard Coer de Lyon* shockingly transforms into something celebratory, albeit in a humorous register. Audaciously and jocularly, the poem even attempts to transform anthropophagi into a badge of honor, as a penchant for Saracen meat becomes emblematically English. 'Þer is no fflesch so norysschaunt / Unto an Ynglssche Cristen-man', according to Richard, 'As is þe flessche of a Sarazeyn'.[52]

We have no evidence that Richard himself engaged in anthropophagi while on crusade, but the king's behavior in the romance may speak to other taboos breached by the historical monarch. Medieval chronicles allude to the erotic nature of Richard

---

[47] Cohen (2001).   [48] Heng (2003: 73).   [49] Ibid. 74.
[50] Ambrisco (1999).   [51] Heng (2003: 22).
[52] Brunner (1913: ll. 3548–52); compare Ambrisco (1999); Heng (2003).

I's relationships with other men, including Philip Augustus of France.[53] Insofar as it constituted the worst kind of sin, that is, a sin against nature, sodomy was utterly condemned by the Church and, eventually, the State as well.[54] Like cannibalism, sodomy was a highly transgressive act that was associated with Christianity's enemies, such as heretics and Muslims. It is possible, then, that in its brashly funny depiction of the transgressive nature of Richard's alimentary habits, the poem also creates a safe means of acknowledging the problem of the king's sexual appetite. The forbidden pleasure of Saracen 'meat' in *Richard Coer de Lyon* thus suggests other illicit urges in which the king indulges, desires that the romance elsewhere registers through, as Heng has demonstrated, multiple joking references to English 'tails'.[55]

Late Medieval Representations of Saracens and Jews

By the late Middle Ages, a major shift in terms of Western Christian relations with Islam had occurred. While a succession of military Crusades into Muslim-occupied lands took place during the high Middle Ages—from the eleventh century well into the thirteenth century—no major Western expeditions would be launched during the rest of the medieval period. And although those high medieval crusades at times enjoyed some success, with the creation of Crusader states and the Christian occupation of Jerusalem, those martial enterprises ended in failure, with the loss of the last Crusader colony of Acre in 1291.[56] This hardly meant, however, that the idea of overcoming the presence of Islam (a presence, indeed, that was ever encroaching upon Western Christendom, with the rise of the Ottoman Turks in the fourteenth century) disappeared. Rather, the period witnessed the proliferation of treatises speculating on modes of subduing the perceived Muslim threat—most famously, Philippe de Mézière's *Songe due Vieil Pèlerin*.[57] The late medieval period also gave rise to a preponderance of literary texts depicting Saracens, such as the popular romances contained in the Auchinleck book.[58] One of Chaucer's *Canterbury Tales*—that told by the Man of Law—offers a late fourteenth-century example of both kinds of texts. In the Man of Law's Tale (*c*.1390–5), the prospect of overcoming the problem of Islamic difference hinges not on warfare of the kind that appears in *Richard Coer de Lyon*, but on the religious conversion of a people through marriage.[59]

---

[53] Heng (2003: 91–2).   [54] Karras (2005).   [55] Heng (2003: 94–8).
[56] Madden (2005: 187–222).   [57] Kedar (1984).   [58] Calkin (2005).
[59] Heng (2003: 186–9).

Set in a sixth-century Syria that is anachronistically Muslim,[60] the tale opens with the hopeless love of the Sultan of Syria for the Roman princess, Custance. Smitten by a woman he has never met but has heard praised by Syrian merchants, the Sultan determines to convert himself and legislate his people's conversion from Islam to Christianity in order to wed Custance. But the marriage never happens, thanks to the machinations of the Sultan's mother. By far the most memorable and extensively characterized Syrian depicted in the Man of Law's Tale, the Sultaness exemplifies how the question of alterity in the Man of Law's Tale is a matter of not simply religious and ethnic difference, but also gendered difference.[61] In a move that manifests the dangers posed to Christian patriarchy by the East, Islam, *and* woman, the Sultaness leads a resistance effort that entails the Syrians first feigning conversion but then murdering the Sultan and all other converts at a feast hosted by the Sultaness in Custance's honor. Regarding the question of why the killings should occur, the Sultaness points to her Muslim faith, a claim that the Man of Law tells us is only a cover for the Sultaness's plan to govern Syria herself.[62] But, as Heng recently has suggested, yet another reason may account for the failure of the Syrian–Roman marriage in the tale, and that rationale is hinted at in the following words spoken by the Sultaness regarding the imminent violence:

> '...I shal swich a feeste and revel make,
> That, as I trowe, I shal the Sowdan quite.
> For thogh his wyf be cristned never so white,
> She shal have need to wasshe awey the rede,
> Though she a font-ful water with hire lede'.[63]

The striking interplay of skin color, religion, and blood in the Sultaness's words (the blood that will stain Custance's white skin) not only stresses the violent nature of the Sultaness's actions but also suggests a discourse of racial alterity at work in the tale, one in which the racial difference of the Syrians precludes their union with the Romans in the tale. As Heng puts it, 'for though Constance's Sultan has been converted to Christianity, and the marriage would not in this instance transgress religious boundaries, conversion to Christianity is insufficient *in and of itself* to cancel out differences of race and color'.[64] In the deep structure of the tale, we find an insurmountable color line that divides East from West, one that infuses Syria with 'a penultimate alienness, an alienation beyond the pale'.[65]

---

[60] Set in the 6th cent., the tale pre-dates the divine revelations that, according to Islamic tradition, Muhammad received in the following century.

[61] On the intertwining of misogynistic and Orientalist discourse in the Man of Law's Tale, see Schibanoff (1996); Heng (2003); Davis (2000).

[62] Chaucer (2000), Man of Law's Tale, ll. 330–40, 432–4.

[63] Ibid., ll. 353–7.

[64] Heng (2003: 232). Heng develops her case regarding the racism at work in the Man of Law's Tale by analysing a similar dynamic in one of its analogues, the *King of Tars* (2003: 226–37).

[65] Heng (2003: 233).

This is not to say, however, that the binaries of self and other are not destabilized in the Man of Law's Tale. As Kathryn Lynch has observed, the Roman princess who survives the slaughter orchestrated by the Sultaness—and thus is in a sense 'rescued' from miscegenation—emerges nevertheless as 'contaminated . . . as the Sultaness predicts gruesomely, "She shal have need to wasshe awey the rede"'.[66] Moreover, as many critics have noted, further similarities between East and West emerge when we consider the Man of Law's representation of Britain, the place where Custance lands after having been exiled from Syria on a rudderless boat. Britain is distinguished from Syria insofar as the former site successfully converts to Christianity, thanks to Custance's marital union with a Northumbrian king. But a host of parallels with the Syrians link the far western territory of Britain and its eastern counterpart. The evil Sultaness finds her western double in the Northumbrian queen mother, Donegild, who similarly plots against her son, whose name, 'Alla', uncannily echoes the Arabic word for God.

What are we to make of such slippages that muddy the line between East and West, slippages that in many ways make Britain as strange a site, as alien a territory, as Syria is in the Man of Law's Tale? As was the case in *Richard Coer de Lyon*, such destabilizations can serve as a means of engaging problems in Chaucer's homeland. One such problem, as I have suggested elsewhere, is Britain's own long-standing status as a strange and isolated land. On many of the world maps that were created in the medieval West, England appeared as an outlying territory situated far from cultural centers. Thus from the perspective of an inhabitant of Rome such as Custance, Britain was nearly as foreign as Syria.[67] Syrian alterity, then, becomes in the Man of Law's Tale a tool for addressing and thinking through the problem of Britain's standing as a global backwater, a problem that intersected with such issues as the paganism of the early English and the low standing of the English vernacular in which Chaucer wrote.[68] But the eliciting of parallels between Syria and Britain for national ends has its limits: for all their similarities, Syria and Britain enjoy no fellowship of any kind, and are in fact virtually ignorant of the other's existence throughout the tale. Such separations return us to the fundamental ethnic and indeed racial alterities to which the tale subscribes.

Like Muslim–Christian interactions, those between Christians and Jews underwent a radical shift during the late Middle Ages in England. From 1290 onwards, Jews officially were banned from the country they had inhabited for over two centuries. The first such forced expulsion in medieval Europe, the events of 1290 were preceded by a number of contributing factors, among them: the anti-Jewish feeling demonstrated by repeated acts of violence; the decline of the Jews' legal and economic status; and heightened aggression toward Jews on the part of the post-Gregorian reform

[66] Lynch (1999: 418).
[67] On the manner in which the three territories of the Man of Law's Tale—Syria, Rome, and Britain—can be analysed productively in a contrapuntal manner, see Ingham (2003: 59–67).
[68] On the problem of writing authoritative literature in English, see Wallace (2004: 48–61); Salter (1988).

Church.[69] As we have noted, the relationship between the history of Jews in England and the representation of Jews in medieval Christian texts is complex. Prior to the expulsion, medieval Christians rarely if ever offered accurate literary accounts of contemporary Jews, but instead constructed fictions about those religious others. Thus the many images of contemporary Jews that populate late medieval English literature in many respects elaborate themes that pre-date the expulsion of historical Jews, even as those constructions speak to historical problems specific to the moment of their production. One text that has served as a kind of touchstone for literary critics concerned with late medieval representations of Jews is the late fifteenth-century Croxton *Play of the Sacrament*. The only extant medieval English host desecration drama, the *Play of the Sacrament* purports to portray events that occurred in 1461, in the Spanish city of Heraclea.[70] In the play, Jonathas, the most powerful of Jewish merchants, successfully negotiates the purchase of a consecrated host from the leading Christian merchant in Spain, Aristorius. Eager to test the doctrine of transubstantiation, which testifies to the real presence of Christ's body in the eucharistic wafer, Jonathas and his companions take the host to his home, where they stab the wafer in imitation of the tortures of the Passion. The host proceeds to bleed, and a frightened Jonathas then tries to carry it to a cauldron of hot oil, but finds his hand permanently attached to the bread. When his companions nail the host to a post, Jonathas's arm becomes detached from his body. After further torments—involving the oil and later an oven—Jesus miraculously appears as a wounded and bleeding child, restores Jonathas's hand, and effects the conversion of all Jews present.

As Lampert has pointed out, by staging the severing of Jonathas's hand, the play represents the divine punishment of a body part that epitomizes the problematic carnality and literalism attributed to the Jews from Augustine onward. As Lampert puts it, 'the hand, which can touch, grasp, and interact with the world, concretely symbolizes carnality',[71] a literalism that Jonathas and his companions manifest in both their lack of faith in the host's divine presence and their efforts to test whether the host 'haue eny blood'.[72] In the case of Jonathas, the interpretive failings accorded to his people become inscribed on his body, so that the severing of his hand physically manifests the extent to which he is 'hermeneutically handicapped'. And when, after converting to Christianity, Jonathas regains his hand, 'the healing of his soul is mirrored in his bodily restoration'.[73]

By spectacularly embodying the interpretive failings that separate Jews from Christians, Jonathas's bodily fragmentation contributes to the play's demonization of the Jews, who, in their attacks on the host, perform their stereotyping as ongoing

[69] On the causes of the expulsion as well as the continuing presence of certain Jews in England after 1290, see Wolf (1928, 1934); Stacey (1988, 1995, 2003); Mundhill (1998).

[70] Myths of Jews desecrating the host began to circulate from the 1280s onwards. The definitive scholarly work on host desecration narratives and their various historical contexts is Rubin (1999).

[71] Lampert (2004: 102).

[72] Davis (1970: l. 452). See also Nisse (2005) and Kruger (1992) on Jonathas's body.

[73] Lampert (2004: 103).

enemies of Christendom. But that process of othering is complicated in the Croxton play insofar as the Jews are hardly the only *dramatis personae* guilty of a certain lack of faith. Indeed, the crime of stealing the host is enabled by both the greedy Christian merchant Aristorius, who sells the host at a profit to Jonathas, and the gluttonous Presbyter Isoder, who is seen indulging in 'a drawte of Romney red' and 'a lofe of light bred' instead of guarding the sacrament closely.[74] Jews in the Croxton play, in other words, are not clearly separated from the Christians that populate the drama but instead offer only the most severe example of spiritual decay. As Ruth Nisse has suggested, we can understand that 'confusion of Christian and Jew' in terms of the scene of the play's probable East Anglian provenance.[75] East Anglian cities such as Norwich and Bury St Edmunds were notably mercantile, and the play may serve to criticize the spiritual corruption to which such commercial ventures led through the thin disguise of an urban Spanish setting.[76]

Interestingly, however, the identity of Christian and Jew in the Croxton play emerges not only in terms of the similitude between sinful Jews and sinful Christians, but also extends in the opposite moral direction as well: Jonathas bears certain striking resemblances to none other than Christ. Claire Sponsler and Robert Clark have laid stress on the manner in which 'Jonathas grotesque[ly] blend[s] with the bleeding host as his hand becomes so strongly attached to the host that it is actually ripped from his body'.[77] The physical welding of Jonathas's hand to the host suggests a kind of unity between persecutor and persecuted. That identification of Jonathas and Christ intensifies when we consider how the hand becomes 'crucified' along with the host; how both the host and the severed hand constitute bloody and abject entities; and how Jonathas's dialogue gains Christic resonance when he states 'Ther ys no more; I must enduer!' after his body is detached from his crucified hand.[78]

Complicating the question of how the *Play of the Sacrament* imagines identity is the manner in which the scene of the severing of Jonathas's hand from his body, and that of its crucifixion alongside a bleeding host, after all, comprise part of a series of sensational scenes featuring violent special effects and gory props. Robert Homan has suggested that such moments 'could have been taken quite seriously by the original audience, both because of the skill with which they are written and because they incorporate devotional sensibilities popular in the art and prose of the fifteenth century'.[79] A successful effort to stage, with earnest piety, the grotesque union of Jonathas and the eucharist may have produced in its audience a kind of terrified wonder, an awe that could have transitioned into pious joy upon the restoration of Jonathas's hand and his conversion to Christianity. The play might then have reaffirmed the faith of its auditors in Christ, in transubstantiation, and in the supersession of Christianity over Judaism.

On the other hand, the sensationalism of the scenes also risks multiple unorthodox responses. The audience possibly could experience a revulsion that could be directed

---

[74] Davis (1970), ll. 340, 342.   [75] Nisse (2005: 114).   [76] Compare Beckwith (1992).
[77] Sponsler and Clark (1999: 72).   [78] Davis (1970: l. 520); Homan (1987: 332).
[79] Homan (1987: 328).

at Jonathas or even the gory host. Perhaps the most disturbing prospect is the possibility that audience members could have felt—and even voiced—a malicious glee over the spectacular violence endured by Jonathas, a sinister pleasure that could contribute to a fervent stereotyping that trumps those aspects of the play that trouble divisions between Jew and Christian. Sensationalism as well could lead to humour or even slapstick. Audience laughter may have acknowledged the artificial nature of the identities on stage—the linked facts that the severed hand is not real, but only a ludicrous prop; that the Jew who loses that hand is no Jew at all, but a Christian actor impersonating a Jew; and that the bleeding host is not really Christ, but a special effect, an illusion.[80] That self-conscious theatricality could, in turn, lead to the contestation of religious and ethnic identities. For example, audience members may become attuned to how the threat posed by Jews to Christian ritual (their theft of the host) in the Croxton play is presented by means of another threat, that is, the threat posed by the Christian stage, whose actors 'steal' Christian eucharistic ritual, a theft that hints at the theatricality (and possibly, then, the fraudulence) of Christian ritual itself.[81] I have listed here only a few of the myriad possible responses the play may have produced in its auditors; suffice it to say that the element of performativity essential to drama renders the question of its perspective on issues of selfhood and alterity all the more iterative, contingent, and unstable.

I would like to close by emphasizing a couple of the lessons on identity formation indicated by this brief survey of Christian images of Jews and Saracens. First, I would like to stress how indispensable—and, in fact, central—constructions of others are to notions of selfhood in the medieval West. As recent scholarship by Lampert and Bale, for example, has demonstrated, binaries of minority versus majority, margin versus centre are in many respects unhelpful in thinking about identity formation, insofar as they suggest that notions of Jews, Saracens, women, foreigners, etc. play only a negligible part in conceptions of hegemonic identity. Rather, such 'others' serve a fundamental role in fantasies of both Christian identity and, as national tendencies become more operative in the late medieval period, a specifically English identity. We cannot, in other words, gain a full understanding of Christianity and, later on, Englishness, in the Middle Ages without including consideration of Christianity and England's others in our analyses.

Secondly, I would like to emphasize that inquiry into the problem of alterity is anything but conventional and straightforward. One complaint that critics have lodged against recent work on race and ethnicity in medieval literary texts (and indeed, against work on race and ethnicity in other periods as well) is its predictability. According to such scholars, critics on alterity simply apply to primary texts widely recognized theories—such as the psychoanalytic notion that we project onto

---

[80] On the manner in which the theatricality and grotesque physicality of the Croxton play may destabilize the legitimacy of both the Mass and its clerical actors, as well as how such destabilizations complement Lollard critiques of the Church, see Beckwith (1992). On the manner in which role-playing troubles identity formation and enables the questioning of Christian doctrine, see Lampert (2004) and Sponsler and Clark (1999).

[81] Beckwith (1992).

others our own disavowed antagonisms and appetites—that lead to predetermined outcomes and arguments. But the examples analysed above should suggest otherwise. In the Croxton play, the Man of Law's Tale, and *Richard Coer de Lyon*, Jews and Saracens appear in unexpected association with other groups, including members of the Christian community (priests, even Jesus) and members of an emerging English community (even English kings and queens). Binary models prove insufficient to characterize the triangulation or even greater multiplicity of identity in texts such as *Richard Coer de Lyon*, where the English's enemies are not only Saracen but also French, or Ælfric's Maccabees sermon, where Christian priests contrast with both ancient Jewish and contemporary Anglo-Saxon warriors. The question of what particular historical problems images of alterity address is always open and leads to many possible avenues of inquiry.

BIBLIOGRAPHY

ÆLFRIC (1881–1900, repr. 1966), *Ælfric's Lives of Saints*, ed. W. W. Skeat (EETS OS 76, 82, 94, 114, 2 vols. London: Oxford University Press).

——(1999), *Ælfric's Homilies on Judith, Esther, and the Maccabees*, ed. Stuart Lee (ed.), http://users.ox.ac.uk/~stuart/kings/main.htm

AMBRISCO, ALAN (1999), 'Cannibalism and Cultural Encounters in *Richard Coeur de Lion*', *Journal of Medieval and Early Modern Studies*, 29/3: 499–528.

AUERBACH, ERICH (1984), *Scenes from the Drama of European Literature* (Minneapolis: University of Minnesota Press).

BALE, ANTHONY PAUL (2006), *The Jew in the Medieval Book: English Antisemitisms, 1350–1500* (Cambridge: Cambridge University Press).

——(2003), 'Fictions of Judaism in England before 1290', in Patricia Skinner (ed.), *The Jews in Medieval Britain* (Woodbridge: Boydell & Brewer), 129–44.

BARTLETT, ROBERT (2001), 'Medieval and Modern Concepts of Race and Ethnicity', *Journal of Medieval and Early Modern Studies*, 31/1: 39–56.

BECKWITH, SARAH (1992), 'Ritual, Church and Theater', in David Aers (ed.), *Culture and History 1350–1600: Essays on English Communities, Identity and Writing* (Detroit: Wayne State University Press).

BEDE (1967), *Commentarius in Genesim*, ed. C. W. Jones (CCSL 118A; Turnhout: Brepols).

BRUNNER, KARL (ed.) (1913), *Richard Coer de Lyon: Der Mittelenglische Versroman Richard Löwenherz* (Leipzig: Wilhelm Braunmüller).

CALKIN, SIOBAHN BLY (2005), *Saracens and the Making of English Identity: The Auchinleck Manuscript* (New York: Routledge).

CHAUCER, GEOFFREY (2000), *The Canterbury Tales*, ed. Larry D. Benson (Boston and New York: Houghton Mifflin Co.).

COHEN, J. J. (2001), 'On Saracen Enjoyment: Some Fantasies of Race in Late Medieval France and England', *Journal of Medieval and Early Modern Studies*, 31/1: 113–46.

——(2006), *Hybridity, Identity, and Monstrosity in Medieval Britain: On Difficult Middles* (New York: Palgrave Macmillan).

COHEN, J. (1999), *Living Letters of the Law: Ideas of the Jew in Medieval Christianity* (Berkeley, Calif., and London: University of California Press).

——(1985), 'The Jews as Killers of Christ in the Latin Tradition, from Augustine to the Friars', *Traditio*, 59: 1–17.

DAVIS, KATHLEEN (2000), 'Time Behind the Veil: The Media, the Middle Ages, and Orientalism Now', in J. Cohen (ed.), *The Postcolonial Middle Ages* (New York: Palgrave).

DAVIS, NORMAN (ed.) (1970), *Non-Cycle Plays and Fragments* (EETS SS 1; London: Oxford University Press).

DUBY, GEORGES (1980), *The Three Orders: Feudal Society Imagined*, tr. Arthur Goldhammer (Chicago and London: University of Chicago Press).

GELLNER, ERNEST (1993), 'The Mightier Pen? Edward Said and the Double Standards of Inside-Out Colonialism', review of *Culture and Imperialism* by Edward Said, *Times Literary Supplement* (19 Feb.), 3–4.

GODDEN, MALCOLM (1990), 'Money, Power and Morality in Late Anglo-Saxon England', *Anglo-Saxon England*, 19: 41–65.

HAHN, THOMAS G. (ed.) (2001), 'Concepts of Race and Ethnicity in the Middle Ages', special issue, *Journal of Medieval and Early Modern Studies*, 31.

HENG, GERALDINE (2003), *Empire of Magic: Medieval Romance and the Politics of Cultural Fantasy* (New York: Columbia University Press).

——(2007), 'Jews, Saracens, "Black Men", Tartars: England in a World of Racial Difference', in P. Brown (ed.), *A Companion to Medieval English Literature and Culture, c.1350–c.1500* (Malden, Mass.: Blackwell), 247–70.

HOMAN, RICHARD L. (1987), 'Devotional Themes in the Violence and Humor of the Play of the Sacrament', *Comparative Literature*, 20: 327–40.

INGHAM, PATRICIA (2003), 'Contrapuntal Histories', in Patricia Ingham and Michael R. Warren (eds.), *Postcolonial Moves: Medieval through Modern* (New York: Palgrave Macmillan).

Isidore of Seville (2006), *The Etymologies of Isidore of Seville*, ed. Stephen A. Barney *et al.* (Cambridge: Cambridge University Press).

JEROME (1964), *Commentarii in Ezechielem*, ed. F. Glorie (CCSL 75; Turnhout: Brepols).

KEDAR, BENJAMIN Z. (1984), *Crusade and Mission: European Approaches to the Muslims* (Princeton: Princeton University Press).

KRUGER, STEVEN F. (1992), 'The Bodies of Jews in the Late Middle Ages', in James M. Dean and Christian K. Zacher (eds.), *The Idea of Medieval Literature: New Essays on Chaucer and Medieval Culture in Honor of Donald R. Howard* (Newark, Del.: University of Delaware Press).

LAMPERT, LISA (2004), *Gender and Jewish Difference from Paul to Shakespeare* (Philadephia: University of Pennsylvania Press).

——(2004), 'Race, Periodicity, and the (Neo-) Middle Ages', *Modern Language Quarterly*, 65: 391–421.

LANGMUIR, GAVIN (1990), *Toward a Definition of Antisemitism* (Berkeley, Calif.: University of California Press).

LAVEZZO, KATHY (2006), *Angels on the Edge of the World: Geography, Literature, and English Community, 1000–1534* (Ithaca, NY: Cornell University Press).

LOSINGA, HERBERT (1868), *The Life, Letters, and Sermons of Bishop Herbert de Losinga*, ed. Edward M. Goulburn and Henry Symonds (Oxford and London: James Parker & Co.), ii.

LYNCH, KATHRYN L. (1999), 'Storytelling, Exchange, and Constancy: East and West in Chaucer's *Man of Law's Tale*', *Chaucer Review*, 33/4: 409–22.

McDONALD, NICOLA (2004), 'Eating People and the Alimentary Logic of *Richard Coeur de Lion*', in N. McDonald (ed.), *Pulp Fictions of Medieval England: Essays in Popular Romance* (Manchester: Manchester University Press), 124–50.

MADDEN, THOMAS F. (2005), *The New Concise History of the Crusades* (Lanham, Md.: Rowman & Littlefield Publishers).

MASTNAK, TOMAŽ (2002), *Crusading Peace: Christendom, the Muslim World, and Western Political Order* (Berkeley, Calif.: University of California Press).

MATAR, NABIL (1998), *Islam in Britain 1558–1685* (Cambridge: Cambridge University Press).

MUNDILL, ROBIN R. (1998), *England's Jewish Solution: Experiment and Expulsion, 1262–1290* (Cambridge and New York: Cambridge University Press).

NISSE, RUTH (2005), *Defining Acts: Drama and the Politics of Interpretation in Late Medieval England* (Notre Dame, Ind.: University of Notre Dame Press).

ROBBINS, JILL (1991), *Prodigal Son/Elder Brother. Interpretation and Alterity in Augustine, Petrarch, Kafka, Levinas* (Chicago: University of Chicago Press).

ROTHWELL, HARRY (ed.) (1975), *English Historical Documents, 1189–1327* (London: Eyre & Spottiswoode).

RUBIN, MIRI (1999), *Gentile Tales: The Narrative Assault on Late Medieval Jews* (New Haven and London: Yale University Press).

SAID, EDWARD (2003), *Orientalism* (25th anniversary edn. New York: Vintage).

SALTER, ELIZABETH (1988), *English and International: Studies in the Literature, Art, and Patronage of Medieval England* (Cambridge and New York: Cambridge University Press).

SCARFE BECKETT, KATHARINE (2003), *Anglo-Saxon Perceptions of the Islamic World* (Cambridge: Cambridge University Press).

SCHEIL, ANDREW P. (2004), *The Footsteps of Israel: Understanding Jews in Anglo-Saxon England* (Ann Arbor: University of Michigan Press).

SCHIBANOFF, SUSAN (1996), 'Worlds Apart: Orientalism, Antifeminism, and Heresy in Chaucer's *Man of Law's Tale*', *Exemplaria*, 8/1: 59–96.

SHELL, MARC (1993), *Children of the Earth: Literature, Politics, and Nationhood* (Oxford and New York: Oxford University Press).

SPONSLER, CLAIRE, and ROBERT L. A. CLARK (1999), 'Othered Bodies: Racial Crossdressing in the *Mistere de la Sainte Hostie* and the Croxton *Play of the Sacrament*', *Journal of Medieval and Early Modern Studies*, 29: 61–87.

STACEY, ROBERT C. (1995), 'Jewish Lending and the Medieval English Economy', in Richard H. Britnell and Bruce M. S. Campbell (eds.), *A Commercialising Economy: England 1086 to c.1300* (Manchester: Manchester University Press), 78–88.

——(2003), 'The English Jews under Henry III', in P. Skinner (ed.), *The Jews in Medieval Britain: Historical, Literary and Archaeological Perspectives* (Woodbridge: Boydell), 41–54.

——(1988), '1240–1260: A Watershed in Anglo-Jewish Relations?', *Historical Research*, 61: 135–50.

TOLAN, JOHN VICTOR (2002), *Saracens: Islam in the Medieval European Imagination* (New York: Columbia University Press).

WALLACE, DAVID (2004), *Premodern Places: Calais to Surinam, Chaucer to Aphra Behn* (Malden, Mass.: Blackwell).

WALLACE-HADRILL, J. M. (1994), 'Bede's Europe', in Michael Lapidge (ed.), *Bede and his World: The Jarrow Lectures* (Aldershot: Variorum), i.

WOLF, LUCIEN (1928), 'Jews in Elizabethan England', *Transactions of the Jewish Historical Society of England*, 11: 1–91.

——(1934), 'Jews in Tudor England', in Cecil Roth (ed.), *Essays in Jewish History* (London: Jewish Historical Society of England), 71–90.

WILCOX, JON (1993), 'A Reluctant Translator in Late Anglo-Saxon England: Ælfric and Maccabees', *Proceedings of the Medieval Association of the Midwest*, 2: 1–18.

CHAPTER 23

THE CHOSEN PEOPLE

SPIRITUAL IDENTITIES

SAMANTHA ZACHER

IT is striking that the majority of literature produced on the subject of Jews in medieval England survives from those periods where there were no Jews living in the British Isles. There are no records of Jewish inhabitants or visitors from the earliest Anglo-Saxon period; it is in fact not until after the Norman Conquest that Jews made their way to the island as Norman imports.[1] At the other end of the chronology, the expulsion of the Jews from England in 1290 limits their extraordinarily brief presence in medieval England to precisely that period of time from which the fewest collective productions of English literature survive.

Apparently, the absence of living, breathing Jews in England during the majority of the medieval period did not curtail writings about them. Authors culled their ideas from a host of sources—from the writings of the Church Fathers, from contemporary continental materials, from widespread cultural stereotypes, and of course from their own imaginations.[2] Such literary representations were not radically different

---

[1] The scholarly consensus has been that the Jews came to England only after the Norman Conquest. For this view, see Michelson (1926: 12–21); Roth (1964: 2), Hyams (1996: 174), and Golb (1998: 112–14). On the possible presence of Jews in Roman Britain, see Applebaum (1951–2).

[2] Studies on the literary representations of Jews in pre-Conquest England include those by Howe (1989), Estes (1998), Scheil (2004), and Fleming (2006). For studies of Jews in post-Conquest medieval English literature, see esp. Rubin (1999), Finkielkraut (1994), Delany (2002), Bale (2006), and Kruger (2006).

from those produced elsewhere in Europe. As has often been argued, the Jew in medieval literature served primarily as a textual construct,[3] formulated around a series of shifting, but nevertheless common topoi.[4] One trend that bleeds across geographical and chronological divides is the attempt at separation between the biblical Hebrew, who could be lauded as belonging to the original *populus dei* (the people to whom were given the very laws, rituals, and theology upon which Christianity was founded), and the (contemporary) Jew, who was often constructed as a sign of willful, even obstinate, otherness. Though such divisions could be gleaned from early Christian writings, in general they were neither coherently constructed nor rigorously maintained.[5] While Jews in these texts sometimes occupied the ritualistic space of the hated other, they were also, on other occasions, venerated as the original chosen nation of God and the original guardians of God's law.

Even though Anglo-Saxon England was a land without Jews,[6] it produced its share of writings on the subject of Jews and Jewishness.[7] While Jews in these texts necessarily occupied purely imaginary positions, they nevertheless served as objects for continued identification and repudiation. Anglo-Saxon depictions of Jews reveal more than simply the mechanisms by which Anglo-Saxon authors constructed ideas of 'otherness'; they also elucidate the self-understanding of early English nationhood and the religious community. One pervasive and lasting theme that emerged from these writings was the interpretation of the 'English' as the New Israel and chosen elect.[8] Bede, generally acknowledged as the English architect of this theme, cast migration-age Germanic invaders in the role of the conquering Israelites who overcame the sinful and unruly Britons (a view he himself proclaims to have inherited from the British writer Gildas).[9] Bede also extended this allegory to his eighth-century *gens Anglorum*, when he argued that the Old Testament paradigm of Israel

---

[3] Several terms have been suggested to explain the 'hermeneutical' status of Jews in medieval texts. These include the 'hermeneutical Jew' (Cohen 1999: 2–4), the 'imaginary Jew' (Finkielkraut 1994), the 'spectral Jew' (Kruger 2006), and the 'virtual Jew' (Tomasch 2002). For a review and summary of these terms, see Bale (2006: 20) and Scheil (2004: 7).

[4] An emphasis upon shared hermeneutic constructions of Jews, of course, does not replace the need to acknowledge the temporal specificity of certain genres, such as the Jewish blood libels that emerged in 12th-cent. England. See Rubin (1999) and Bale (2006: 105–44).

[5] On the use of such divisions in early patristic writings, see Cohen (1999: 1–20).

[6] Wasserstein argues the presence of a single Jew at the court of King Athelstan in England, on the basis of a questionable reference to an *Israel* (also identified as a *Iudeus Romanus*, or a 'Roman Jew'), in a text known as the *Alea euangelii* ('Gospel Dice'), which survives only in a 12th-cent. MS in Oxford, Corpus Christi College 122 (written c.1140). This interpretation, however, is summarily dismissed by Lapidge (1993: 89), who argues that the *Israel* in question reflects a botched reference to the famed Breton scholar Israel the Grammarian.

[7] Scheil (2004: 6) makes the crucial point that Jews and Judaism are neither 'static motifs' launched from within patristic and Anglo-Saxon imaginations, nor are they 'an unchanging, universally despised, unproblematic "Other"'.

[8] As Harris (2003: 131–56) argues, the self-fashioning of the English as a chosen people (cast in the footsteps of Israel) was a theme that continued well into the post-Conquest era, at which point it competed with other Norman ethnogenetic myths that claimed special descent from the Trojans.

[9] For Gildas, it was of course the Britons who represented the chosen peoples. For discussions of Bede's use of this theme of chosenness, see especially Wormald (1994: 1, 12–16; 1983: 121–5), Scheil (2004: 111–42), and Harris (2003: 45–82).

as a nation operating under a single (and divinely inspired) covenant provided a model for Anglo-Saxon claims to a unified political, cultural, and religious identity that had not yet been successfully established.[10] Drawing on the examples of the great biblical kings, such as David and Solomon, Bede constructed his *gens Anglorum* as 'a people who, like the Israelites, were internally divided, but were being guided towards the true God in the land they had invaded' (McClure 1983: 96).

Bede's comparison provided a productive paradigm for numerous Anglo-Saxon authors. For instance, Alfred self-consciously fashioned his own laws after the decrees of Moses. In so doing, he invited the Anglo-Saxons 'to remodel themselves as a new Chosen People', unified under one Christian law (Foot 2002: 55). Such political metaphors could also be shaped to more localized ideological ends: several West Saxon genealogies laid claim to rightful and divinely sanctioned rule by tracing Wessex ancestry back not just to Woden but also to Noah, thus assigning these kings a separate holy pedigree.[11] Broader literary expressions of Jewish 'chosenness'[12] can also be identified, for example, in the Old English poem *Exodus* (based loosely upon parts of the Old Testament narrative), which arguably aligns the experience of the exiled Hebrews seeking their homeland with the trials of the sea-borne Germanic tribes who first inhabited Britain.[13] In addition to providing a positive vehicle for Anglo-Saxon self-fashioning, the theme of Old Testament chosenness could be used to forecast calamity. The historical model of inheritance and loss of God's favour proved an apt theme for writers such as Wulfstan; in several of his sermons (including 'Gifts of the Holy Spirit') Wulfstan expressed the view that, just as the Israelites were handed over to their enemies on account of their sins, the Viking attacks upon the English in the late tenth century could be seen as a scourge sent by God to punish the English for their sins.[14]

Of course, the English appropriation of Jewish chosenness as a means of describing a political cycle of inheritance and loss was hardly unique. Bede's model was anticipated by a host of Christian writers who, beginning already in Roman times, laid claim to an elect status and rule by divine right.[15] Whether the earliest English authors inherited their models of chosenness from classical texts, or from later Frankish paradigms, has been the matter of a lengthy and still inconclusive debate.[16] In the following, I will focus on literary rather than merely historical evidence, and

[10] As Wormald explains, Bede cultivated the ideal of a united 'English people' far in advance of any such political reality (Wormald 1983: 105).

[11] Anlezark (2002) provides a full account and textual stemma for these genealogies where possible.

[12] I use the term 'chosenness' hereafter without quotations.

[13] See esp. Howe (1989: 72–107).

[14] See Harris (2003: 180). On the appearance of similar tropes in the writings of Ælfric, see Godden (1991: 225).

[15] For the adoption of the entwinement of the theme of Old Testament election with genealogies going back to Trojan ancestry, see Tanner (1993).

[16] According to Wallace-Hadrill (1962; 1971: 48–50), the Frankish kings began to cultivate a view of themselves as inheriting the divine right to rule as early as the 7th cent. in the reign of Clovis. On the potential influence of Frankish model upon English expressions of chosenness (beginning with Bede), see Wormald (1994: 11–15).

concentrate on moments when the claim to special election is used on the basis of an explicit transference. The chapter begins with a brief discussion of the theme of election in the Old and New Testaments—both works present obvious intertexts for all subsequent claims to chosenness. I analyse a passage from Bede's *Historia eccle-siastica* that uses a densely layered comparison to highlight both the positive and negative options for the representation of the chosen Israelites. I contrast Bede's highly allusive mode with the more straightforward strategy employed in the Old English poem *Daniel*. As my analysis indicates, this text assigns particular relevance to the expansion of election, so that it is transferred from the righteous Hebrew to the devout Christian, and even to the moral pagan, who functions as a precursor of, and placeholder for, the pious Christian.

By staging a comparison between Bede and *Daniel*, my purpose is to highlight the continued currency of the theme of chosenness within Anglo-Saxon literature (and beyond) and also to foreground chosenness and election as a potent literary theme worthy of study in its own right. Since medieval depictions of Jews are often depressingly negative, it is of some consequence that *Daniel* provides a model that appears to celebrate Jewish election on its own terms, even as it is expanded to include devout non-Jewish individuals in the process.

Old and New Testament Election and the Principle of Transference

Israel is first proclaimed a 'chosen people' in Deuteronomy 7: 6–10. The passage is usually read in isolation as presenting an ethnocentric claim to privileged and elite status (I quote from the Vulgate text here and below):[17]

(6) quia populus sanctus es Domino Deo tuo te elegit Dominus Deus tuus ut sis ei populus peculiaris de cunctis populis qui sunt super terram (7) non quia cunctas gentes numero vincebatis vobis iunctus est Dominus et elegit vos cum omnibus sitis populis pauciores (8) sed quia dilexit vos Dominus et custodivit iuramentum quod iuravit patribus vestris eduxitque vos in manu forti et redemit de domo servitutis de manu Pharaonis regis Aegypti (9) et scies quia Dominus Deus tuus ipse est Deus fortis et fidelis custodiens pactum et misericordiam diligen-tibus se et his qui custodiunt praecepta eius in mille generationes (10) et reddens odientibus se statim ita ut disperdat eos et ultra non differat protinus eis restituens quod merentur.

(6) Because thou art a holy people to the Lord thy God. The Lord thy God hath chosen thee, to be his peculiar people of all peoples that are upon the earth. (7) Not because you surpass all nations in number, is the Lord joined unto you, and hath chosen

---

[17] Unless otherwise stated, all translations of the Vulgate Bible are cited from the Douay-Rheims version as revised by Challoner (1749–50; 1956 edn.).

you, for you are the fewest of any people: (8) But because the Lord hath loved you, and hath kept his oath, which he swore to your fathers: and hath brought you out with a strong hand, and redeemed you from the house of bondage, out of the hand of Pharaoh the king of Egypt. (9) And thou shalt know that the Lord thy God, he is a strong and faithful God, keeping his covenant and mercy to them that love him, and to them that keep his commandments, unto a thousand generations: (10) And repaying forthwith them that hate him, so as to destroy them, without further delay immediately rendering to them what they deserve.

The Latin terms designating special election are *sanctus* ('holy'), *electus* ('elect'), and *peculiaris* ('peculiar' with the additional sense of 'private' or 'special'). The latter designation, *peculiaris*, comes closest to the Hebrew *segullah*, which can mean either 'specific' or even 'treasured'. In Hebrew, this term highlights the special value placed upon the people in question and participates in the pervasive rhetoric of growth, health, and abundance associated with Israel's status of election. Thus, in the remaining passages of Deuteronomy 7, God promises to increase the nation, to provide an abundant harvest, to remove sickness, and to enable Israel to 'destroy and consume' all other peoples (which is to say the seven nations mentioned in 7: 1). Assigning this unique status to Israel, the passages in Deuteronomy also insist on the otherness of the surrounding nations who practise idolatry and are therefore cut off from the blessings of Israel. This distinction between Israel and its others is then reinforced by the emphatic injunction to refrain from intermarriage in 7: 2–3. While the entire passage does not specify whether Israel has deserved its elect status, it is made abundantly clear that nations who hate God merit (*merentur*) the twin punishments of exclusion and destruction.

An important correlative to this passage appears in Deuteronomy 26: 16–19, which states that the status of Israel's election is contingent upon the strict observance of God's command (including ceremonial laws and religious customs) and is therefore subject to annulment, at least in theory:

(16) hodie Dominus Deus tuus praecepit tibi ut facias mandata haec atque iudicia et custodias et impleas ex toto corde tuo et ex tota anima tua (17) Dominum elegisti hodie ut sit tibi Deus et ambules in viis eius et custodias caerimonias illius et mandata atque iudicia et oboedias eius imperio (18) et Dominus elegit te hodie ut sis ei populus peculiaris sicut locutus est tibi et custodias omnia praecepta eius (19) et faciat te excelsiorem cunctis gentibus quas creavit in laudem et nomen et gloriam suam ut sis populus sanctus Domini Dei tui sicut locutus est.

(16) This day the Lord thy God hath commanded thee to do these commandments and judgements: and to keep and fulfil them with all thy heart, and with all thy soul. (17) Thou hast chosen the Lord this day to be thy God, and to walk in his ways and keep his ceremonies, and precepts, and judgements, and obey his command. (18) And the Lord hath chosen thee this day, to be his peculiar people, as he hath spoken to thee, and to keep all his commandments: (19) And to make thee higher than all nations which he hath created, to his own praise, and name, and glory: that thou mayst be a holy people of the Lord thy God, as he hath spoken.

This passage, in contrast with the previous one, stresses that Israel must choose the Lord and his ways in order to be chosen.[18]

It should be said that the Deuteronomic conception of election presents only one formulation of Old Testament chosenness. As internal political and religious structures changed, the conditions of election shift markedly over the course of the period covered by Old Testament narratives. One such redefining moment (cited frequently by New Testament authors) is the split of Israel into the northern kingdom of Israel and the southern kingdom of Judah. The 'new' Israel, having fallen into the sin of idolatry, against which Deuteronomy 7 states a clear injunction, is depicted as being cut off from election. Thus, 2 Kings 17: 18, states: 'And the Lord was very angry with Israel, and removed them from his sight, and there remained only the tribe of Judah.' While the people of Judah likewise go on to break 'the commandments of the Lord their God', they are nevertheless spared because they continue to observe 'the customs that Israel had introduced' (2 Kings 17: 19–20).[19] It is the tribe of Judah (eventually joined by the tribe of Benjamin) that came to inherit the status of the Lord's chosen people.

New Testament authors quite naturally cited this fissure between the old and new Israel as sufficient grounds for further reinterpretation of the concept of chosenness. If special election could be lost through sin, it would only seem logical that it could also be transferred to true believers. Thus, for Paul the newly chosen 'people' included only the remnant of Jews who believed in Christ in addition to the new gentile believers (whom he called 'the circumcised' and 'the uncircumcised', respectively). The rhetoric of transference, however, becomes more totalizing elsewhere in the New Testament. Peter explains to his formerly gentile readers (in 1 Peter 2: 9–10): '(9) But you are a chosen generation, a kingly priesthood, a holy nation, a purchased people: that you may declare his virtues, who hath called you out of darkness into his marvellous light: (10) Who in time past were not a people: but are now the people of God. Who had not obtained mercy; but now have obtained mercy.' Citing and co-opting the language of Deuteronomy 7: 6–10, Peter also extends the range of chosenness to universal proportions.

[18] The change in rhetoric in Deut. 26: 16–19 is reflected in the passage's inverted structure: while Deut. 7: 6 states that 'quia *populus sanctus es Domino Deo tuo te elegit Dominus Deus tuus ut sis ei populus peculiaris* de cunctis populis qui sunt super terram' ('Because thou art *a holy people to the Lord thy God. The Lord thy God hath chosen thee, to be his peculiar people of all peoples that are upon the earth*'), the chiastic statement in Deut. 26: 18–19 stipulates that '*et Dominus elegit te hodie ut sis ei populus peculiaris*... ut sis *populus sanctus es Domino Deo tuo* sicut locutus est' ('And the Lord hath chosen thee this day, to be his peculiar people,... that thou mayst *be a holy people of the Lord thy God*, as he hath spoken').
[19] 2 Kings 17: 19–20: '(19) But neither did Judah itself keep the commandments of the Lord their God: but they walked in the errors of Israel, which they had wrought. (20) And the Lord cast off all the seed of Israel, and afflicted them and delivered them into the hand of spoilers, till he cast them away from his face.'

BEDE AND HIS CHOSEN PEOPLE

While the New Testament conception of transferred election presented a clear model for Anglo-Saxon conceptions of election, one may well argue that Old Testament narratives of chosenness had an equal share in their construction. Patrick Wormald, for one, has pointed out that Old Testament depictions of Jews as the chosen people of God provided a persistent template and intertext for Bede's *Ecclesiastical History*:

The pattern of God's dealing with his original Chosen People [i.e. the Israelites] remains Bede's underlying theme. Thus the *Ecclesiastical History* begins with a geographical survey of Britain as effectively another land of milk and honey. Its opening chapters are thereafter devoted to an account of how the land's original inhabitants, the Britons, proved unworthy of the Roman and Christian civilizations that were brought to them. Once the Romans had withdrawn, the unbridled wickedness of the Britons had been faithfully chronicled by Gildas, 'their own historian' (as Bede had revealingly called him). Contemptuous alike of his warnings and of a first 'scourging' by Anglo-Saxon invaders, they were eventually abandoned by God, who transferred their heritage to a new favourite. Rome came again to Kent, in the person of Augustine, not Julius Caesar. The English fell heirs to what the Britons had lacked the grace to deserve. (Wormald, 1994: 14)

Embedded in this dense summary of Bede's project are several important assertions that deserve to be laid out in detail. The first is that Bede viewed the experience of the post-exile Israelites who established a homeland for themselves as presenting a *type* for the experience of the earliest Germanic peoples who migrated to England. The second is that Bede envisioned the Germanic invasion as following the scheme of *translatio imperii*. He saw the divine right to rule as being passed from the sinful Britons to the virtuous invaders.

Despite the generally acknowledged pervasiveness of this *type* in the *Historia ecclesiastica*, it is nevertheless difficult to pinpoint precise textual instances where Bede identifies his *gens Anglorum* as a New Israel. In fact, there are only a few examples in the whole *Historia ecclesiastica* where Bede cites the Hebrew nation as a model for direct emulation. (Comparable associations are far more frequent in his homilies and commentaries.) Nevertheless, Wormald is undoubtedly correct in asserting Bede's pervasive employment of this very theme. In Bede's *History*, the type operates largely through the use of veiled biblical allusion.[20] For example, in

[20] One frequently quoted passage can be found at the beginning of the *Historia ecclesiastica* as Bede likens the five languages of Britain to the five books of the Pentateuch: *Haec in praesenti iuxta numerum librorum quibus lex diuina scripta est, quinque gentium linguis unam eandemque summae ueritatis et uerae sublimitatis scientiam scrutatur et confitetur, Anglorum uidelicet Brettonum Scottorum Pictorum et Latinorum, quae meditatione scripturarum ceteris omnibus est facta communis* ('At the present time there are five languages in Britain, just as the divine law is written in five books all devoted to seeking out and setting forth one and the same kind of wisdom, namely the knowledge of sublime truth and of true sublimity. These are the English, British, Irish, Pictish, as well as the Latin languages; through the study of the scriptures, Latin is in general use among them all'.) By asserting Latin as a common biblical language, Bede integrates the separate identities of the other languages and nations into a single hypothesized 'Britain', and furthermore, under a single hypothesized biblical episteme: since the

1. 22, Bede summarizes his view that the earliest Germanic invaders of Britain were sent by divine decree to replace the sinful and fallen nation of the Britons (Colgrave and Mynors 1992: 68–9; emphasis mine):

Qui inter alia inenarrabilium scelerum facta, quae historicus eorum Gildus flebili sermone describit, et hoc addebant, ut numquam genti Saxonum siue Anglorum, secum Brittaniam incolenti, uerbum fidei praedicando committerent. *Sed non tamen diuina pietas plebem suam, quam praesciuit*, deseruit, quin multo digniores genti memoratae praecones ueritatis, per quos crederet, destinauit.

To other unspeakable crimes, which Gildas, their own historian describes in doleful words, was added this crime, that they [the Britons] never preached the faith to the Saxons or Angles who inhabited Britain with them. *Nevertheless God in his Goodness did not reject the people whom he foreknew*, but He had appointed much worthier heralds of the truth to bring this people [that is, the *gens Anglorum*] to the faith.

In this passage, Bede performs a double act of ventriloquism. On the one hand he alludes to Gildas, the sixth-century British writer, who, in his *De excidio et conquestu Britanniae* explained the Germanic victory over his people as a divine transfer of favour (a view endorsed by Bede). While Bede names Gildas, he actually quotes, either directly or through some intermediary Latin text, from a different and hitherto neglected source, namely, Paul's Epistle to the Romans 11: 1–5. In these passages, Paul laments the plight of the Jews who have not accepted Christ, though he allows that not every Jew has been cut off from election. It is highly relevant that Paul counts himself as a Jew and a believer, who has been saved as part of the elect (emphasis mine):

(1) *dico ergo numquid reppulit Deus populum suum absit nam et ego Israhelita sum ex semine Abraham tribu Beniamin* (2) *non reppulit Deus plebem suam quam praesciit* an nescitis in Helia quid dicit scriptura quemadmodum interpellat Deum aduersus Israhel (3) Domine prophetas tuos occiderunt altaria tua suffoderunt et ego relictus sum solus et quaerunt animam meam (4) sed quid dicit illi responsum diuinum reliqui mihi septem milia uirorum qui non curuauerunt genu Baal (5) *sic ergo et in hoc tempore reliquiae secundum electionem gratiae factae sunt.*

(1) *I say then: Hath God cast away his people? God forbid. For I also am an Israelite of the seed of Abraham, of the tribe of Benjamin.* (2) *God hath not cast away his people, which he foreknew.* Know you not what the scripture saith of Elias; how he calleth on God against Israel? (3) Lord, they have slain thy prophets, they have dug down thy altars; and I am left alone, and they seek my life. (4) But what saith the divine answer to him? I have left me seven thousand men, that have not bowed their knees to Baal. (5) *Even so then at this present time also, there is a remnant saved according to the election of grace.*

five books of Moses are all held to seek out and deliver 'the knowledge of sublime truth and of true sublimity', the people of Britain, by virtue of their 'study of scriptures', are likewise imbued with 'one and the same kind of wisdom' that is offered in those books (though Bede's proposed unity with regard to knowledge is as fantastic as his claim to social and political unity in this period). The deictic tag 'at the present time' (*Haec in praesenti*) is likewise of central importance because it resists what might have been an easy association between the Old Testament and pre-conversionary England on the one hand, and the New Testament and post-conversionary England on the other: Bede's model forges an association between the textual history of the original people of the book, the *populus Israhel*, and that of Bede's *gens Anglorum*.

Paul's passage in turn contains a series of literary echoes. It splices together passages from 1 Kings 19: 10, in which the prophet Elijah complains that he alone of all of the Israelites has remained faithful to God's covenant, and also from 1 Kings 18, in which God answers Elijah, stating that there are seven thousand who will be spared because they resisted the idolatrous worship of the Canaanite god Baal. Since (as seen in the previously quoted passage from 2 Kings 17) idolatry presents sufficient grounds for the forfeiture of divine election, Jews who continue to be monotheists remain among the elect. Paul's emphasis on his descent from the tribe of Benjamin, the only tribe that joined Judah after the split between the kingdoms of the North and South, is thus an implicit, yet potent claim to the status of chosenness.

In citing Paul—note the verbatim quotation *plebem suam quam praesciit*—Bede casts the pagan Angles and Saxons, the founding peoples of the *gens Anglorum*, in the role of the Jews whom God *praesciuit* ('foreknew'), and thereby extends to them Paul's hope of salvation.[21] Moreover, Bede also casts himself in the role of Paul, but with an important difference: while Paul takes a universalist approach (the terms of election are expandable), Bede resists this internationalist discourse, using Paul's words instead to establish difference between the conquered and conquering groups.

Though generally favourable, Bede's comparison to the Jews is nevertheless complicated by a second Pauline echo that can be found in Bede's castigation of the British who fail to preach to the Angles and Saxons. The possible source for this section is Romans 10: 14–15, where Paul cites the ignorance of the Jews and their need for learned preachers, asking: '(14) quomodo ergo inuocabunt in quem non crediderunt aut quomodo credent ei quem non audierunt quomodo autem audient sine praedicante (15) quomodo uero praedicabunt nisi mittantur' ('(14) How then shall they call on him, in whom they have not believed? Or how shall they believe him, of whom they have not heard? And how shall they hear, without a preacher? (15) And how shall they preach unless they be sent?'). For Paul, the necessary instruction comes from within his own community of preachers, while for Bede, the *digniores praecones ueritatis* represent those who came with the Augustinian mission from Rome to educate the ignorant Germanic settlers.

Even a cursory review of the textual layers of Bede's passage makes clear that the comparison of Angles and Saxons to the chosen Jews is complex: if the Germanic conquerors are likened to the Jews, then their later, converted selves must represent a perfected Christian elect people that has no equivalent in the original figural paradigm. For Bede, the idea of the 'foreknown' Jews thus simultaneously presents a model to be imitated and transcended. Because here (and throughout) Bede's work, Jewish chosenness is presented as a status already in transition, it provides an apt vehicle for Bede's discussion of emergent English nationhood, however mythical and imaginary that totalizing status may be in eighth-century England.

---

21 The verb 'to foreknow' (*praescere*) occurs five times in the New Testament at Acts 26: 5; Rom. 8: 29, 11: 2; 1 Pet. 1: 20; 2 Pet. 3: 17. The nominal form 'foreknowledge' (*praescientia*) appears an additional two times in Acts 2: 23 and 1 Pet. 1: 2.

THE THEME OF *TRANSLATIO ELECTIONIS*
AND THE OLD ENGLISH *DANIEL*

In the cited passage from the *Historia ecclesiastica*, Bede's type of Old Testament election presents a vehicle for promoting both a united English Church and an integrated English people. It also functions as an expression of *translatio imperii* (a theme which inscribes the double inheritance of Holy Roman rule and Old Testament election), since Bede uses the concept of chosenness to claim the legitimate and rightful rule of the conquering Angles and Saxons. In contrast, the tenth-century Old English poem *Daniel* offers a markedly different and less obviously politicized use of this scheme of transferred election. It comes closer to the Pauline scheme of expansion—rather than replacement—of election. For the purpose of distinguishing this use of the theme of chosenness, I propose a different coinage—namely, *translatio electionis* ('the transfer of election or chosenness')—that highlights the assumption of the mantle of the Jews as the religious chosen elect.

The biblical book of Daniel is often seen to epitomize the theme of *translatio imperii*. This topos is expressed most clearly in the first dream of Nebuchadnezzar (Daniel 2), which prophesies the successive rise and fall of four kingdoms (each of which is lost through sin), and also the ultimate rightful and permanent victory of an almighty Israel. Scholars of the tenth-century Old English poem have argued that a similar theme of *translatio imperii* pervades the entire text, since it describes the rise and fall of three sovereign entities in succession: the nations of the Israelites, the Babylonians, and the Chaldeans.[22] One significant argument brought against this interpretation has been the observation that many of the geographical and imperial details that frame this political allegory in the biblical book are absent from *Daniel*.[23] But rather than suppose that the poet has banished this theme altogether from the poem, I would suggest that he has shifted his emphasis in order to focus on the appropriation of divine election. While the Hebrews at the beginning of the poem collectively lose their earthly sovereignty *and* their divinely chosen status, the poet's view of Jews cannot be reduced to a purely negative statement. Rather, like Bede and Paul before him, the *Daniel*-poet preserves the idea of the 'elected Jew', namely, through the figures of Daniel and the three youths, who remain both Hebrew *and* chosen throughout the text. At the same time, the poet expands his usage of divine election. He extends the status of chosenness to other pious individuals, both heathen and Christian. Nebuchadnezzar becomes an important figure in this respect: although he is a heathen, who learns to embrace the Hebrew God, the description of his conversion relies heavily on Christian terminology. In this case, the poet adopts a universalist Pauline conception of chosenness, one which presumably incorporates the poet's contemporary Christian English audience.

[22] On the theme of *translatio imperii* in *Daniel*, see esp. Anderson (1987).
[23] For this counterargument, see Remley (1996: 248–52).

The poet establishes his theme of divine election in the first few lines of *Daniel* (ll. 1–16):[24]

Gefrægn ic Hebreos eadge lifgean	1
in Hierusalem, goldhord dælan,	
cyningdom habban, swa him gecynde wæs,	
siððan þurh metodes mægen on Moyses hand	
wearð wig gifen, wigena mænieo,	5
and hie of Egyptum ut aforon	
mægene micle. Þæt wæs modig cyn!	
þenden hie þy rice rædan moston,	
burgum wealdon; wæs him beorht wela.	
Þenden þæt folc mid him hiera fæder wære	10
healdan woldon, wæs him hyrde god,	
heofonrices weard, halig drihten,	
wuldres waldend. Se ðam werude geaf	
mod and mihte, metod alwihta,	
þæt hie oft fela folca feore gesceodon,	15
heriges helmum, þara þe him hold ne wæs...	

I have heard tell of the Hebrews living blessedly in Jerusalem, controlling their gold-hoard, maintaining their kingdom, as was natural for them; since, through the might of the Creator, an army was delivered into Moses's hand, a company of warriors; and they went out of Egypt with great strength. That was a courageous people! For a while they were allowed to govern their kingdom, to manage their strongholds; they had brilliant prosperity. For a while that people wished to keep their Father's covenant among them; God was a shepherd to them, the Guardian of the heavenly kingdom, the Holy Lord, the Wielder of Glory. He, the Creator of all things, gave to that company courage and strength, so that they often destroyed the lives of many people, (and of) the protectors of the army, of those who were not loyal to Him...

Following the terms of election outlined in Deuteronomy 7 and 21, the *Daniel*-poet explains Israel's blessedness as being contingent upon the observance of *hiera fæder wære* ('their father's covenant'; in line 10b).[25] The righteousness of the Israelites is rewarded with economic and political sovereignty: they are permitted to live blessedly in Jerusalem, to hold their kingdom, to wield its treasures, and to gain victory over all those who are not *hold* (or 'loyal') to God. The poet even describes this state of chosenness as being 'natural' or 'rightful', as indicated by the phrase *swa him gecynde wæs* ('as was natural for them'; in line 3b).

But the tenuousness of this state of election is clear from the outset, even when the poet seems most complimentary about Israel. For example, in line 7, seemingly in

---

[24] All quotations from the Old English *Daniel* are from Farrell's edn. of the poem (1974); translations are mine.

[25] On the importance of the theme of the covenant in *Daniel*, see Bjork (215). Bjork shows that just as the covenant is broken by the Hebrews at the beginning of *Daniel* (an act that results in the scattering of the Jews throughout the world (l. 300) and a life of slavery (ll. 302a–7a)), it is renewed by means of the *Song of Azarias* (ll. 315–25), since the youths exhort God to keep his promise to Israel and expand their nation. The fulfilment of the theme occurs as Nebuchadnezzar returns the remnant of the Jewish captives to the youths (ll. 452–3).

terms of praise the poet tells us that *Þæt wæs modig cyn!* (a phrase that recalls the thrice repeated, and not always positive, *Beowulf*-ian *þæt was god cyning*). Since *modig* can mean 'courageous' or 'proud', the phrase either compliments Israel's valour (see the positive use of *mod* in 14a) or else it berates the Israelites' vainglory (reinforced by the parallel interjection *Þæt wæs weorc gode!;* 'that was a pain for God!', in line 24).[26]

The anticipated negative turn comes in line 17, when Israel is shown to slip into sin:

> ... oðþæt hie wlenco anwod   æt winþege
> deofoldædum,   druncne geðohtas.
> Þa hie æcræftas   ane forleton,
> metodes mægenscipe;   swa no man scyle   20
> his gastes lufan   wið gode dælan!
> Þa geseah ic *þa* gedriht in gedwolan hweorfan,   [MS *þe*]
> Israhela cyn   unriht don,
> wommas wyrcean.   Þæt wæs weorc gode!
> Oft he þam leodum   lare sende,   25
> heofonrices weard,   halige gastas,
> þa þam werude   wisdom budon.
> Hie þære snytro   soð gelyfdon
> lytle hwile,   oðþæt *hie* langung beswac   [MS *me*]
> eorðan dreamas   eces rædes,   30
> þæt hie æt siðestan   sylfe forleton
> drihtnes domas,   curon deofles cræft.

... until pride invaded them at their banquets, drunken thoughts with devilish deeds. Then they at once abandoned their expertise in law and the might of the Creator; so must no man cut off his spirit's love from God! Then I saw that company, the people of Israel, turn to error, (and) perform acts of unrighteousness and sin. That was a pain for God! Often He, the Guardian of heavenly kingdom, sent his teaching to that people (and) holy spirits, those who preached wisdom to that company. They believed the truth of that wisdom for a little while, until longing for the joys of the earth seduced them away from eternal counsel, so that they themselves abandoned the judgements of the Lord, (and) chose the Devil's craft.

The sudden shift from blessedness to wretchedness is marked by the rhetorical *oðþæt* ('until') in line 17a. While the Israelites were once *gecorene* ('chosen'), they have lost that privilege as a community, for they *curon deofles cræft* ('chose the devil's craft').[27]

This important rhetorical turn is followed by another in line 22, when the narrator perplexingly inserts himself into the text as an eyewitness. Though the narrator generally gathers information by hearing it (he uses the phrase *gefrægn ic*, 'I have heard', four times in the poem at lines 1a, 57a, 458a, 738a), here he explains *Þa geseah ic þa gedriht in gedwolan hweorfan* ('then I saw that company turn to error'). The

---

[26] Several scholars have commented on the poem's thematic attention to the sin of pride. For a review of this scholarship, see Bjork (1980: 221–3). Also see Caie (1978: 1–9), who reads the poem in general as an *exemplum* that warns against pride.

[27] The sins in this passage have received much commentary. Bjork (1980: 214–17), Anderson (1987: 9) remark extensively on the patterns of feasting and drunkenness in the poem.

change is important: while *hearing* implies the narrator's temporal and (possible) spatial dislocation from events in the poem, his status as an eyewitness closes that distance. The speaker's function as a spectator is highlighted by other elements that have generally been emended in modern translations (and treated as scribal errors): for example, in line 22, Farrell's edition substitutes the more logical deictic *þa* ('then') for the manuscript's second person accusative *þe* ('you'), while in line 29 Farrell substitutes the first person plural *hie* ('they') for the manuscript's first person singular *me* ('me'). This last example is interesting, since the manuscript reads: *oðþæt [me] langung beswac* ('until longing seduced me'), as if to indicate that the narrator himself has absorbed the sins of Israel (much as the narrator in *The Dream of the Rood* professes to share in the pain of the Cross by stating that: *eall ic wæs mid sorgum gedrefed*, 'I was all stirred up with sorrow').[28] In the *Daniel* passage, the speaker both connects himself to and distances himself from the experiences of the fallen Israelites. The narrator's *geseah ic* ('I saw') is furthermore unique to the Old English *Daniel*, when compared with the poem's putative biblical sources.[29] Though in the Vulgate, Nebuchadnezzar introduces each of his dreams by saying 'I saw' (in Latin *vidi* or *videbam*), in the Old English, both dreams are conveyed through third-person narration.[30] By transferring the language of dream-visions to the narrator, the poet sets him up as a visionary figure in his own right, and one qualified to comment on the sins of Israel.[31]

Though the opening passages of the poem depict the corruption of Israel, they also set up an important difference between the demoted Israelites and the continued

[28] There are still further verbal and thematic connections between *The Dream of the Rood* and *Daniel*, e.g. the phrase in *Daniel* 122b–3 *hwæt hine gemætte,/þenden reordberend reste wunode* which parallels *The Dream of the Rood* 2–3 *hwæt me gemætte to midre nihte,/syðþan reordberend reste wunedon!* Several further and hitherto unnoticed parallels have been cited by Orchard (forthcoming).

[29] The relationship of the Old English *Daniel* to various biblical versions is still unclear. The case has been made for the poem's dependence upon several versions, including: two distinct Greek versions (the Theodotian and the Septuagint versions), two distinct Old Latin versions, and the Vulgate. A still excellent study of the poem's relationship to the Old Latin texts can be found in Hofer (1889). For a comprehensive summary of all previous scholarship on the issue, and a meticulous consideration of the verbal correspondences between *Daniel* and these biblical versions, see Remley (1996: 287–333). Remley concludes that the *Daniel*-poet probably had direct knowledge of the Vulgate, access to a continuous Old Latin exemplar, and indirect knowledge of the Septuagint. Since the poem shows the most sustained correspondences with the Vulgate, I use this as the base text for my comparison. For a list of the poem's departures from the Vulgate text of Daniel 1–5, see Bjork (1980: 214).

[30] On the rhetorical impact of the poem's omniscient narration of the dreams, see Harbus (1994: 499–504).

[31] The phrase *geseah ic* forms a signature mode of telling dreams within Old English poetry. In *The Dream of the Rood*, this phrase appears four times in close proximity (and one further time with some variation) as follows (these examples are from Orchard forthcoming): 'Geseah ic wuldres treow . . . wynnum scinan' ('*I saw* the tree of glory . . . joyfully shine'; *The Dream of the Rood*, 14b and 15b); 'Geseah ic þæt fuse beacen/wendan wædum ond bleom' ('*I saw* that eager beacon change its coverings and colours'; ll. 21b–22a); 'Geseah ic þa frean mancynnes/efstan elne mycle' ('*I saw* the lord of mankind hasten with great zeal'; ll. 33b–34a); 'þa ic bifian geseah/ eorðan sceatas' ('Then I saw the corners of the earth tremble'; ll. 36b–37a); 'Geseah ic weruda god/þearle þenian' ('*I saw* the god of hosts cruelly stretched out'; ll. 51b–52a).

'chosen' status of the three youths and Daniel. By establishing this contrast, the poet adds to the biblical text, since the word 'chosen' does not appear anywhere in Daniel 1–5 (arguably a primary source for the poem). In fact, there are only three uses of the word 'chosen' in all of the biblical Daniel, in the Vulgate at 11: 15, 11: 35, and 12: 10. The first example from Daniel 11: 15 is irrelevant in this context, as it refers to selected troops of warriors, while the remaining two occurrences in 11: 35, and 12: 10 are questionable since they depart from the parallel text in the original Hebrew. In these verses, the Vulgate imprecisely translates *eligantur* ('they may be chosen'; 11: 35) and *eligentur* ('they shall be chosen'; 12: 10) for the Hebrew *ulivarer* ('they may be purified'; 11: 35) and *yitbararu* ('they will be purified'; in 12: 10). In both cases, the Latin text mistakes (or perhaps deliberately misreads) the Hebrew root *barer* ('purified') for *barar* ('chose').[32] Since the poet only seems to have relied upon some version of Daniel 1–5 it is not at all clear whether he might have used these passages to establish the chosenness of the youths.

In fact, the past participle *gecoren* 'chosen' appears three times in the Old English *Daniel*, and each time it refers to the Hebrew youths. In line 90, we are told that the youths were *ginge and gode in godsæde . . . metode gecorene* ('young and good in God-seed' [*godsæd*] . . . chosen by God'). This special interpretation of the youths' role was possibly inspired by the Hebrew etymologies embedded in their names—*Hannania* means 'the mercy of God', *Azarias*, 'the help of God' and *Mishael* (possibly) 'who is like God'.[33] These names remain the same throughout the poem, whereas in the Vulgate they are changed (possibly to reflect the names of Babylonian gods) once the youths arrive at Nebuchadnezzar's court.

The poet's theme of chosenness also explains the nonce compound *godsæd* (literally 'God-seed' in line 90b). The term has posed problems for translators—the *Dictionary of Old English* suggests that it might mean 'divine progeny', with the sense of 'among God's children', though the exact meaning is uncertain. In fact, the compound renders imprecisely a phrase in Daniel 1: 3–4 (emphasis mine):

(3) et ait rex Asfanaz praeposito eunuchorum suorum ut introduceret de filiis Israhel et *de semine regio* et tyrannorum (4) *pueros in quibus nulla esset macula* decoros forma et eruditos omni sapientia cautos scientia et doctos disciplina et qui possent stare in palatio regis ut doceret eos litteras et linguam Chaldeorum

(3) And the king spoke to Asphenez the master of the eunuchs, that he should bring in some of the children of Israel, and *of the king's seed* and of the princes, (4) *Children in whom there was no blemish*, well favoured, and skilful in all wisdom, acute in knowledge, and instructed in

---

[32] The full passages from the Vulgate are as follows: Dan. 11: 35 *et de eruditis ruent ut conflentur et eligantur et dealbentur usque ad tempus praefinitum quia adhuc aliud tempus erit* ('And some of the learned shall fall, that they may be tried, and may be chosen, and made white even to the appointed time, because yet there shall be another time'); and 12: 10 *eligentur et dealbabuntur et quasi ignis probabuntur multi et impie agent impii neque intelligent omnes impii porro docti intelligent* ('Many shall be chosen, and made white, and shall be tried as fire: and the wicked shall deal wickedly, and none of the wicked shall understand, but the learned shall understand').

[33] On the order and spelling of the names of the youths in *Daniel*, see Remley (1996: 305, n. 194).

science, and such as might stand in the king's palace, that he might teach them the learning, and the tongue of the Chaldeans.

The term *godsæd* translates the Latin *de semine regio*, which in the Vulgate refers to human rather than divine rule. In citing divine lineage, the poet may have associated the physical perfection of the youths with that of the priestly class, the 'chosen' of God, who are described in Leviticus 21: 17–23 as being *de semine Aaron sacerdotis*. The Aramaic text of Daniel 1: 3 further supports the double sense in the Old English, since the parallel phrase *mizerah hamlucha*, 'of royal seed or offspring' may refer either to God or to earthly nobles. Both options were apparently familiar to patristic exegetes, since as Jerome points out in his commentary on Daniel (a text that some have supposed the poet knew intimately),[34] the Septuagint and Aquila translated the phrase *de semine regio* as simply 'the chosen ones'.[35]

The word 'chosen' appears twice more in the Old English *Daniel*. First, in line 145, when Daniel comes to Nebuchadnezzar's court to interpret the king's initial dream (lines 145–57); this dream, we are told, exceeded the interpretive abilities of even the wisest men at the Babylonian court (emphasis mine):

> Ne meahte þa seo mænigeo   on þam meðelstede   145
> þurh witigdom   wihte aþencean
> ne ahicgan,   þa hit forhæfed gewearð
> þætte hie sædon   swefn cyninge,
> wyrda gerynu,   *oðþæt witga cwom,*
> *Daniel to dome,   se wæs drihtne gecoren,*   150
> *snotor and soðfæst,   in þæt seld gangan.*
> Se *wæs* ordfruma   earmre lafe   [MS *þæs*]
> þære þe þam hæðenan   hyran sceolde.
> Him god sealde   gife of heofnum
> þurh hleoðorcwyde   haliges gastes,   155
> þæt him engel godes   eall asægde
> swa his mandrihten   gemæted wearð.

Then the multitude in the meeting place could not reflect at all or consider through prophecy, since it was denied to them that they might have told the dream to the king, the mysteries of fates, *until Daniel the prophet, wise and steadfast in truth, chosen by the Lord, came entering the hall to pass judgement.* He was the leader of the wretched remainder, of those who had to obey the heathens. To him God gave a gift from the heavens, so that an angel of God told him everything as his earthly lord had dreamed it.

Although Daniel is introduced together with the three youths in the Vulgate, he makes a separate entrance in the poem. His arrival provides a remedy for the

---

[34] See Jerome's *Commentarii in Danielem*, PL 25 col. 496D.
[35] The poet's use of the compound *godsæd* may also reflect an interpretation the poet could only have been aware of through other biblical commentaries: since the Aramaic *zerah* refers both to offspring and seeds to be eaten. In the Aramaic text, the youths shun the food of the king, and instead ask to be given *min-hazroim vinochlah omayim vinishta* (legumes/seeds to eat and water to drink), so maintaining the dietary restrictions of *kashrut* (a detail otherwise omitted from the Old English). The youths are thus in multiple senses *gode in godsæd* ('good in God-seed').

people—the *oðþæt* that appeared in line 17 to introduce the downfall of the people of Israel is used here (line 149b) to show a reversal of fortune. In the Vulgate, Daniel (having been endowed with the gift of interpreting all visions and dreams—*vision[es] et somni[a]*) takes it upon himself to interpret Nebuchadnezzar's dream. In the poem, by contrast, Daniel is chosen by God to render interpretation and is granted the means to do so. Through this change in emphasis, Daniel's election is choreographed to mirror that of the three youths. As their names inscribe their relationship with God, so does that of Daniel—his Hebrew name means 'judgement of God', an etymology that is reflected in the Old English collocation *Daniel* and *dom* ('judgement').[36]

Lines 149–51 of the previous passage are repeated almost verbatim at the end of the poem, when Daniel is called upon to read the writing on the wall in the hall of Balshazzar. This is the final occurrence of the word 'chosen' in *Daniel*. We are told that no one could interpret the characters, *oðþæt Daniel com, drihtne gecoren,/snotor and soðfæst, in þæt seld gangan* ('until Daniel came entering the hall, chosen by the Lord, wise and steadfast in truth'). In the Vulgate, the Queen invites Daniel to construe the writing. By contrast in the poem, Daniel is described as being *drihtne gecorene*. Here, Daniel's election and wisdom stand in contrast to the limited knowledge of the *runcræftige men* (who ironically cannot read these divine 'runes', if this is indeed the intended meaning of the simplex).

It would seem, then, that each time the word *gecoren* appears in *Daniel* it is always presaged by the allocation of divine wisdom. By citing the Deuteronomic observance of law as the precondition for chosenness, and by adding to it the reception of God's wisdom, the poet employs a recognizable Christian hermeneutic shift that privileges the spirit over letter.

I would argue, however, that the scheme of *translatio electionis* is not complete. We encounter a further layer as Nebuchadnezzar becomes not just a convert, but also a spokesman for God.[37] Though he is not described as *gecoren* (for he is not a Hebrew), he takes on the properties of the elect youths in the poem, since he too becomes endowed with divine wisdom. The emphasis on knowledge in the process of his conversion is clear: whereas the Israelites were said 'to turn to error' (*in gedwolan hweorfan*), we are told that Nebuchadnezzar 'turned again (*eft onhwearf*) from the madness of his intellect' so that eventually 'his spirit turned (*ahwearf*) to the memory of God'. As he recovers his kingdom, he reverses the pattern of the 'fall' established by the sinful Hebrews—he regains control of his *gestreona* ('treasure') and *rice* ('kingdom'). The crowning moment of *translatio electionis* occurs in lines 640–60a:

> Þa wæs eft geseted   in aldordom   640
> Babilone weard,   hæfde beteran ðeaw,

---

[36] On the poet's formulaic and repeated use of the Hebrew etymology for Daniel, see Frank (1972: 216–17).

[37] As Remley has pointed out (1996: 283 and 319–20), Nebuchadnezzar's conversion is unusual; his role as a evangelist, however, does resemble parts of the Septuagint, and the theme in *Daniel* may reflect its debt to this source. For a thematic reading of Nebuchadnezzar's conversion (in the context of the poem's emphases on pride and sin), see Overing (1984).

leohtran geleafan   in liffruman,
þætte god sealde   gumena *gehwilcum*   [MS *gehwililcum*]
welan swa wite,   swa he wolde sylf.
Ne lengde þa   leoda aldor   645
witegena wordcwyde,   ac he wide bead
metodes mihte   þær he meld ahte,
siðfæt sægde   sinum leodum,
wide waðe   þe he mid wilddeorum ateah,
oðþæt him frean godes   in gast becwom   650
rædfæst sefa,   ða he to roderum beseah.
Wyrd wæs geworden,   wundor gecyðed,
swefn geseðed,   susl awunnen,
dom gedemed.   Swa ær Daniel cwæð,
þæt se folctoga   findan sceolde   655
earfoðsiðas   for his ofermedlan.
Swa he ofstlice   godspellode
metodes mihtum   for mancynne,
siððan in Babilone   burhsittendum
lange hwile   lare sægde,   660
Daniel domas.

Then the guardian of Babylon was set up again in governance; he held to a better custom, a clearer belief in the Lord of Life—namely that God gave to every man prosperity and punishment, as he himself wished. He, the prince of the people, did not delay in the utterances of his wise men, but he preached widely (with?) the might of the Creator where he had the power of proclamation, he told of his journey to his own people, the wide wanderings he took with wild beasts, until a sensible thought of the Lord God came upon him, into his spirit, when he looked up to the heavens. Fate was cast, the miracle made known, the dream fulfilled, the torment overcome, the judgement deemed, just as Daniel before said that the leader of people should meet with miserable journeys on account of his pride. So he (?) zealously brought good tidings, (with?) the powers of the Lord before mankind, after Daniel for a long time had uttered teachings and judgements to the citizens of Babylon.

The subject of the passage is unclear—who is this bringer of 'good tidings'—Daniel or Nebuchadnezzar? I would argue that the grammatical subject 'he' refers to Nebuchadnezzar, since we are told in the Vulgate that he preached the glory of the Lord, and in the poem that *he wide bead* ('he preached widely'). But the poet has left this and other elements ambiguous—perhaps deliberately. According to the *Dictionary of Old English*, *godspellian* generally takes the accusative of thing and dative of person. However, line 658a seems to imply that the subject has spoken 'by means of' the powers of the Lord (*metodes mihtum*), since the feminine noun *miht* appears as an instrumental plural (see further line 647a). The passage implies a transfer of status—just as Daniel interpreted through God's intercession, so now Nebuchadnezzar carries on the *domas* ('the judgements') of Daniel through the powers of God. The word-choice *godspellian* is striking. Either the poet intends the neutral sense 'bringing good tidings', or else he wishes to highlight evangelical activity. While the poet used the terms *spelboda* ('messenger'; 229b, 464b, 532a, 742a) and *þa[] þe his spel berað* ('those who bear his tidings'; 478b) for Daniel and the youths, he chooses this different (and more acutely Christianized) term for Nebuchadnezzar.

If the reception and proclamation of divine wisdom functions as a stable indication of divine chosenness in the poem, then we come back to the point I made earlier about the narrator, who claims to have 'seen' the Jews fall into sin. As both an eyewitness and reporter, the narrator becomes part of the process of *translatio electionis*. As we saw above, it is difficult to assess the narrator's temporal relation to the poem. If he is indeed speaking as a Christian looking back to a biblical past, then the extension of the pattern of 'conferred election', beyond the biblical communities in *Daniel*, has been accomplished. Through the cycle of transference, the poem leaves open a space for the chosenness of its English audience beyond the pale of the poem.

Though the theme of chosenness in *Daniel* differs markedly from the model found in Bede's *Historia ecclesiastica*, it nevertheless employs a similar trajectory of expansion from a closed model of chosenness to one that is reframed within a more porous Christian context. In *Daniel*, as the poet inscribes his new theme of chosenness, he suppresses details in the biblical Daniel that earmark the Jews as being restrictively 'special' or 'peculiar' (such as the emphasis on the observance of Jewish dietary laws),[38] and instead emphasizes the service of faith as the main criterion for chosenness—thus embracing another important facet of the Pauline ideal.

CONCLUSIONS

The above comparison of the passages from Bede's *Historia ecclesiastica* and *Daniel* makes clear that while 'the Jew' continues to occupy a largely ambivalent and even imaginative space in Anglo-Saxon texts, the 'chosen' Old Testament Hebrew provided a potent and malleable model for Christian and English self-identification. Anglo-Saxon authors naturally turned to Germanic heroic and legendary models as a means of shaping ideas of nationhood. But in addition they found a powerful model in the Old Testament paradigm of a divinely chosen nation.

Focusing especially on Bede's comparison of the emergent 'English' nation to a New Israel, Patrick Wormald has argued that this rhetoric was not merely descriptive. Rather, Bede's influential textual descriptions of the English in these terms had the effect of shaping Anglo-Saxon reality. As Wormald contends, the 'unrivalled

---

[38] It may also be significant that the poet de-emphasizes the special status of Jews in the text: while the composite Hebrew and Aramaic 'original' includes references to both Jews (Aramaic *yihudaiye*; Latin *Iudaeos*; in Dan. 3: 8 and 12) and Israelites (Hebrew *b'nai yisrael*; Latin *filios Israhel*), the poet writes of Israelites or Hebrews in every instance but one, when he speaks of the *blæd Iudea*—either the 'glory of Judah' or 'the glory of the Jews' (707b–708a). I would like to thank Peter Gilgen for numerous conversations on conceptions of nationhood and religious community; they helped me clarify several important aspects of the present chapter.

longevity and durability of the English state' may well be based on 'the fact that it was the first European political organism to exploit with complete success the model of obligatory coherence supplied by the Old Testament in the history of Israel and its relations with its Maker' (1994: 1). For Wormald, the association of the *gens Anglorum* with the chosen Israelites had the effect of projecting a stable identity that eventually translated into greater political unity.

As I have argued in this chapter, Bede's identification of the emergent 'English' nation as the rightful inheritors of biblical chosenness provided a potent model for the continued expression of this theme in Old English poetry. In the Old English *Daniel*, we find a similar dynamic of transference, though it is recast as a far more personalized venture: though the nation of Israel is depicted collectively as having forfeited its divine right to special election, individual pious Israelites are nevertheless numbered with those pagans and Christians who rise to the status of the chosen through their exemplary faith in God. As enacted in *Daniel*, the paradigm of *translatio electionis* thus comes closer to the early Pauline conception of universality, which extends the status of the elect to all devout individuals. This model importantly leaves more space for the acceptance of Jewish chosenness as a foundational principle of spiritual perfection.

It would of course be a vast exaggeration to claim that the view of Jews in *Daniel* is thoroughly positive. In fact, the *Daniel*-poet in many ways continues the vexed dialectic initiated by Bede that seeks both identification with the biblical Hebrews and repudiation of the Jews. But while Bede uses biblical allegory primarily to tell a story of national and political identity (with the express aim of setting apart his *gens Anglorum* as a unique people), the *Daniel*-poet is primarily interested in how conceptions of chosenness served to construct idealized religious and spiritual communities. As such, the poem underscores the central notion that medieval writings about Jews did not merely present opportunities to comment on otherness. Rather, discussions of Jews served performatively to elucidate the self-understanding of early English nationhood and, inextricably linked with it, the religious community.

BIBLIOGRAPHY

ANDERSON, E. R. (1987), 'Style and Theme in the Old English *Daniel*', *English Studies*, 68: 1–23.

ANLEZARK, D. (2002), 'Sceaf, Japheth and the Origins of the Anglo-Saxons', *Anglo-Saxon England*, 31: 13–46.

APPLEBAUM, S. (1951–2), 'Were there Jews in Roman Briton?', *Transactions of the Jewish Historical Society of England*, 17: 189–205.

BALE, A. (2006), *The Jew in the Medieval Book: English Antisemitisms, 1350–1500* (Cambridge and New York: Cambridge University Press).

BJORK, R. E. (1980), 'Oppressed Hebrews and the *Song of Azarias* in the Old English *Daniel*', *Studies in Philology*, 77: 213–26.

CAIE, G. D. (1978), 'The Old English *Daniel*: A Warning against Pride', *English Studies*, 59: 1–9.

COHEN, J. (1999), *Living Letters of the Law: Ideas of the Jew in Medieval Christianity* (Berkeley, Calif.: University of California Press).

COLGRAVE, B., and R. A. B. MYNORS (ed. and tr.) (1992), *Bede's Ecclesiastical History of the English People* (Oxford: Clarendon Press, repr. from 1969).

DELANY, S. (ed.) (2002), *Chaucer and the Jews: Sources, Contexts, Meanings* (New York: Routledge), 69–85.

ESTES, H. (1998), 'Lives in Translation: Jews in the Anglo-Saxon Literary Imagination', Ph.D. dissertation, New York University.

FARRELL, R. T. (1968), 'The Structure of Old English *Daniel*', *Neuphilologische Mitteilungen*, 69: 533–59.

——(1969), 'A Possible Source for Old English *Daniel*', *Neuphilologische Mitteilungen*, 70: 84–90.

——(ed.) (1974), *Daniel and Azarias* (London: Methuen; New York: Harper & Row).

FINKIELKRAUT, A. (1994), *The Imaginary Jew*, tr. K. O'Neill and D. Suchoff (Texts and Contexts, 9; Lincoln, Neb.: University of Nebraska Press), 295–321.

FLEMING, D. (2006), '"The Most Exalted Language": Anglo-Saxon Perceptions of Hebrew', Ph.D. dissertation, University of Toronto.

FOOT, S. (2002), 'The Making of *Angelcynn*: English Identity before the Norman Conquest', in R. M. Liuzza (ed.), *Old English Literature* (New Haven: Yale University Press), 51–78. Repr. from *Transactions of the Royal Historical Society*, 6 (1996): 25–49.

FRANK, R. (1972), 'Some Uses of Paronomasia in Old English Scriptural Verse', *Speculum*, 47: 207–26.

GODDEN, M. (1991), 'Biblical Literature: The Old Testament', in M. Godden and M. Lapidge (eds.), *The Cambridge Companion to Old English Literature* (Cambridge: Cambridge University Press), 206–26.

GOLB, N. (1998), *The Jews in Medieval Normandy: A Social and Intellectual History* (Cambridge: Cambridge University Press).

HARBUS, A. (1994), 'Nebuchadnezzar's Dreams in the Old English *Daniel*', *English Studies*, 75: 489–508.

HARRIS, S. J. (2003), *Race and Ethnicity in Anglo-Saxon Literature* (Studies in Medieval History and Culture, 24; London and New York: Routledge).

HOFER, O. (1889), 'Ober die Entstehung des ags Gedichtes *Daniel*', *Anglia*, 12: 158–204.

HOWE, N. (1989), *Migration and Mythmaking in Anglo-Saxon England* (New Haven: Yale University Press).

HYAMS, P. R. (1996), 'The Jews in Medieval England: 1066–1290', in A. Haverkamp and H. Vollrath (eds.), *England and Germany in the High Middle Ages* (New York: Oxford University Press), 173–92.

KRUGER, S. (2006), *The Spectral Jew: Conversion and Embodiment in Medieval Europe* (Minneapolis: University of Minnesota Press).

LAPIDGE, M. (1993), 'Israel the Grammarian in Anglo-Saxon England', in *Anglo-Latin Literature 900–1066* (London and Rio Grande: Hambledon Press), 87–104.

MCCLURE, J. (1983), 'Bede's Old Testament Kings', in Patrick Wormald (ed.), *Ideal and Reality in Frankish and Anglo-Saxon Society: Studies Presented to J. M. Hadrill* (Oxford: Blackwell), 76–98.

MICHELSON, H. (1926), *The Jew in Early English Literature* (Amsterdam: H. J. Paris).

NELSON, J. L. (1994), 'Kingship and Empire in the Carolingian World', in R. McKitterick (ed.), *Carolingian Culture: Emulation and Innovation* (Cambridge and New York: Cambridge University Press), 52–87.

ORCHARD, A. (forthcoming), 'The Dream of the Rood: Cross-References', in S. Zacher and A. Orchard (eds.), *New Readings on the Vercelli Book* (Toronto: University of Toronto Press).

OVERING, G. R. (1984), 'Nebuchadnezzar's Conversion in the Old English *Daniel*: A Psychological Portrait', *Papers on Language and Literature*, 20: 3–14.

REMLEY, P. G. (1996), *Old English Biblical Verse: Studies in Genesis, Exodus, and Daniel* (Cambridge Studies in Anglo-Saxon England, 16; Cambridge and New York: Cambridge University Press).

RUBIN, M. (1999), *Gentile Tales: The Narrative Assault on Late Medieval Jews* (New Haven: Yale University Press).

ROTH, C. (1964), *A History of the Jews in England* (3rd edn. Oxford: Clarendon Press).

SCHEIL, A. P. (2004), *The Footsteps of Israel: Understanding Jews in Anglo-Saxon England* (Ann Arbor: University of Michigan Press).

TANNER, M. (1993), *The Last Descendant of Aeneas: the Hapsburgs and the Mythic Image of the Emperor* (New Haven: Yale University Press).

TOMASCH, S. (2002), 'Postcolonial Chaucer and the Virtual Jew', in S. Delany (ed.), *Chaucer and the Jews: Sources, Contexts, Meanings* (New York: Routledge), 69–85.

WALLACE-HADRILL, J. M. (1962), 'The Work of Gregory of Tours in the Light of Modern Research', in J. M. Wallace Hadrill (ed.), *The Long-Haired Kings* (London: Methuen).

——(1971), *Early Germanic Kingship in England and on the Continent* (Oxford: Clarendon Press).

——(1983), 'The New Israel and its Rulers', in *The Frankish Church* (Oxford: Clarendon Press; New York: Oxford University Press).

WASSERSTEIN, D. J. (2002), 'The First Jew in England: "The Game of the Evangel" and a Hiberno-Latin Contribution to Anglo-Saxon History', in M. Richter and J.-M. Picard (eds.), *Ogma: Essays in Celtic Studies in Honour of Próinséas Ní Chatháin* (Dublin: Four Courts Press), 283–8.

WORMALD, P. (1983), 'Bede, the *Bretwaldas* and the Origins of the *Gens Anglorum*', in P. Wormald (ed.), *Ideal and Reality in Frankish and Anglo-Saxon Society: Studies Presented to J. M. Hadrill* (Oxford: Blackwell), 99–129.

——(1992), 'The Venerable Bede and the "Church of the English"', in G. Rowell (ed.), *The English Religious Tradition and the Genius of Anglicanism* (Wantage: Icon), 13–32.

——(1994), '*Engla Lond*: The Making of an Allegiance', *Journal of Historical Sociology*, 7: 1–24.

——(1995), 'The Making of England', *History Today* (Feb.): 26–32.

CHAPTER 24

INDIVIDUALITY

ALCUIN BLAMIRES

IN the fourteenth-century English romance *Sir Gawain and the Green Knight*, Gawain finds himself fending off the eager attentions of a married lady who persistently invokes his alleged reputation as a paragon of eligible knightliness. In response, Gawain attempts to extricate himself from her glamorizing version of his identity. He comments, picking his monosyllables carefully, 'I be not now he that ye of speken'.[1]

Although his disclaimer can be construed as polite flotsam, just a way of preserving a proper modesty, the poem's extreme concentration on Gawain's dedication to a web of behavioural ideals supports a more psychologically attuned reading: he, the aspirational Gawain in front of the lady, is to be differentiated from a shallower 'Gawain' of popular acclaim. Perhaps he is even to be read as an 'individual' possessing what we would now call a self-concept. His individuality is being defined antithetically, in opposition to external assumptions. This befits Lee Patterson's suggestion that the medieval idea of selfhood emerges from 'the dialectic between an inward subjectivity and an external world that alienates it . . . from itself'.[2] Individuality arising through alienation will be a recurrent topic in the present chapter.

DEFINING THE INDIVIDUAL

'Individuality' was a prominent criterion of evaluation among medieval scholars of various disciplines in the 1960s and 1970s, at a time when the phenomenon was

---

[1] Andrew and Waldron (1978: l. 1242).
[2] Patterson (1991: 8).

understood to signify 'a self-aware consciousness', and an 'executive will' exerting itself through behaviour assumed to be 'freely chosen rather than socially or historically determined'.[3] While a definition of individuality within literature had always been a contentious matter, the bottom line was the text's capacity to project persons as though they 'exist as independent people'.[4] Yet individuality has lately lost credibility in academic discussion and has been overtaken by terms such as 'identity' and 'subject'. The reasons for the current reign of 'identity' and 'the subject' are quite complex but may be put simply. An 'identity' is a recognizable pre-existing external matrix that can be *adopted* by, or indeed *conferred upon* a person; it does not inhere in that person as a supposedly private possession, as 'individuality' was presumed to inhere. And the ambiguity of the word 'subject' again acknowledges what the term 'individuality' does not. One who is a 'subject' is not solely a sovereign consciousness ready to initiate action like the grammatical subject which theoretically controls a verb, but is at the same time *subject to* formation by a mass of subtle encompassing cultural and linguistic systems.[5]

Given that 'individuality' has lost ground to new academic terminology, a long-standing debate about when it was 'discovered' has necessarily been reshaped. Formerly, the issue was whether the post-classical '(re)discovery of the individual' was the prerogative of medieval culture, or the prerogative of Renaissance Europe. That turf war has simply carried on under a new guise. Latterly, it has been a question of whether 'subjectivity' makes its first appearance in English writing with (say) *Hamlet*, or originates further back in the Middle Ages.

David Aers is one medievalist who has challenged Renaissance partisans in this ongoing debate. He emphasizes that 'interiority' and 'self-scrutiny' already contributed to 'individual subjective consciousness' in medieval literature in such areas as mystical and confessional writing, and insists that it is not anachronistic to talk of 'competitive forms of individualism' in the Middle Ages.[6] Previous challenges from medievalists had already claimed the emergence of 'individuality' in twelfth-century European culture, a culture which displayed what Caroline Walker Bynum sums up as a 'new concern with self-discovery and psychological self-examination, an increased sensitivity to the boundary between self and other, and an optimism about the capacity of the individual for achievement'.[7] Such concerns would suggest that, in that part of the Middle Ages at least, there was an anticipation of key elements in modern individualism—defined by Colin Morris as 'the sense of a clear distinction between my being, and that of other people', and 'confidence in the individual's value'.[8]

---

[3] Ibid. 3.

[4] Mann (1973: 189), within a concluding chapter which identifies the difficulty of defining individuality. Examples of other discussions of that difficulty are Shanahan (1992); Harré (1998: esp. pp. 1–9); Logan (1986).

[5] A useful summary is in Ganim (2005).

[6] Aers (1992).

[7] Bynum (1982: 83). Landmark arguments for emergent individualism in the period were: Southern (1970); Dronke (1970); Morris (1972); Hanning (1977).

[8] Morris (1972: 3).

Bynum herself, however, would substitute 'discovery of the *self*' for 'discovery of the *individual*' as the phenomenon seen in the central Middle Ages. What was discovered was not what we now mean by 'the individual'. We mean 'a particular self, a self unique and unlike other selves', whereas the insight into oneself (*seipsum*) most written about at that time was essentially the discovery 'within oneself of [shared] human nature made in the image of God'.[9]

We can begin to see that it may be somewhat easier to locate such phenomena as 'interiority' (the *homo interior*), 'self-scrutiny', 'the self', and even 'subjectivity' in medieval writing than to locate individuality. Individuality—which refuses to go away despite the objections of theorists—is actually a more demanding concept. Medievalists often sweepingly dismiss it as unmedieval. The present chapter takes up the challenge, testing out the category of individuality on the literature. Does the literature show that individuality was anathema to the Middle Ages? How far did the period's pervasively Christian culture in the West suppress individuality, in favour of personal obedience to the institution of the Church, and self-effacement before God?

MEDIEVAL INDIVIDUALITY: REAL OR IMAGINED?

It seems logical to begin by studying the vocabulary available (especially, for present purposes, in Latin and English) in the Middle Ages that might approximate to 'individuality'. *Individualis* itself existed as a medieval Latin coinage based on earlier Latin *individuum*. The sixth-century philosopher Boethius defined the latter in terms of its root meaning, 'something which cannot be divided', but also in terms of 'something whose designation is not applicable to anything of the same kind', as for example 'Socrates' is a designation not applicable to another human.[10] Here we have the beginnings of the meaning, 'a distinct person', but that meaning does not evolve in a neutral or laudatory sense. Rather, before the eighteenth century, *individualis* and 'individual' either simply pointed to the smallest (indivisible) unit within a general group, or pointed pejoratively to eccentricity, a deviation from the norm. Not until the nineteenth century did the idea of the individual being a unique representative of the species emerge. From there develops the generally positive modern sense concerned with human individuality as a fulfilment and expression of a person's particular aptitudes and characteristics.

---

[9] Bynum (1982: 87), citing reservations about the term 'individuality' raised by John F. Benton in a 1977 paper later published as Benton (1991).

[10] *In Porphyrium commentarium liber secundus*; see Williams (1983: 161–5), to which I am indebted for the following summary. How to define individuation was a technical problem intricately chewed over by the 12th-cent. scholastic mind; see Benton (1991: 343).

It is interesting to notice how hostile John Donne still was in the seventeenth century to individuality, for which in common with medieval writers his nearest word was *singularity*. God, he often claims in his sermons, never loved singularity. Similarly, in the poem *First Anniversarie* he attributes the dissolution of social coherence to the human conceit of uniqueness:

> For euery man alone thinkes he hath got
> To be a Phoenix, and that then can be
> None of that kinde, of which he is, but he.[11]

Donne is here echoing a classic medieval assumption about 'singularity': that it is wrong to identify oneself as unique, as if one could stand out from one's species. Somewhat the same point is a complex focus of the Middle English poem *Pearl*. The dreamer there is right to assert the Virgin Mary's unique, Phoenix-like status (so called because of the 'synglerty o hyr dousour [singularity of her sweetness]' and because she 'fereles fleʒe of hyr Fasor [flew unequalled from her Creator]'.[12] But he is wrong to suppose that Pearl's achievement of heavenly rewards must have come about by an individualistic assertion of herself over competitors. Pearl is obliged to explain, on the contrary, her harmonious assimilation into the corporate fellowship of innocents.

The whole poem therefore emphasizes the submergence of competitive selfhood within Christian communality or 'compaynye',[13] realigning the dreamer's understanding of what might truly be 'singular' about Pearl: not, that is, the combative social climbing he attributes to her, not the uniqueness he formerly ascribed to 'his' particular human gem ('I sette hyr sengeley in synglure'[14]), but the singularity or special oneness of the pearl signifying heaven, which paradoxically becomes a livery to all those who share its properties. Nevertheless it is very important for our purposes that *Pearl* so clearly acknowledges the existence of a mindset ruled by an individualistic ethos even while seeking to repudiate it. If the Church was so busy inhibiting this 'singularity', individuality (of a kind) was evidently a force to be reckoned with in that society. But what was the semantic range of 'singularity' itself?

The root meaning of the noun is the grammatical one: singularity as against plurality.[15] Depending on context, however, this may already carry evaluative innuendo. In a group of religious recluses or a community of nuns, single-ness is out of order. As the adviser writes to his female charges in the thirteenth-century *Ancrene Wisse*, there should be no 'singularite' or egotistical deviation ('anful frommardschipe') among them, for that would disrupt the unanimity of their way of life.[16]

---

[11] Donne (1621: ll. 216–18).   [12] Andrew and Waldron (1978: ll. 429–31).
[13] Ibid. l. 851.   [14] Ibid. l. 8.
[15] *MED* gives separate entries for three different spellings of the noun: *singularite, singulerte, singlerte*, which seem however not to carry differentiated meanings.
[16] Millett (2005: pt. 4, 1082–8, an injunction repeated at 1093–9). M. B. Salu translates *singularite* in terms of making oneself an 'exception': Salu (1955: 113). Anglo-Norman *singulerté* and its variants appear more limited in meaning; *AND* offers only the senses 'quality of being indivisible' and 'individual power'.

Tracking an analogous usage, we would find that the medieval ideological preoccupation with what Chaucer calls 'common profit' tends in theory to demonize the idea of singular (private, personal) advantage.[17] But the dominant resonance of *singularitas* in the Middle Ages, enshrined in moral doctrine in the ubiquitous preachers' confessional manuals from the thirteenth century onwards, concerned the type of arrogance that asserts uniqueness. Singularity was a branch of pride: 'the fourth branch occurs when someone despises other people and wants to appear unique (*appetit singulariter videri*)'.[18] Linked with presumption, 'syngulertee' is synonymous with 'only-hede' and is seen when 'þe proude man . . . ne wole not don as oþere doþ þat ben bettere þan he, but wole be soleyn, þat is only, in his doynges' (here 'onlyhood' and 'soleyn' are interesting vernacular alternatives).[19] Langland harnesses these and other moral perspectives on assertive singularity in his representation of Haukyn, the complacent Active Man in passus XIII of the 'B' version of *Piers Plowman*. The narrator judges Haukyn to be someone who sets himself apart in clothes and manner;

> And so singuler by himself as to sighte of the peple
> Was noon swich as hymself, ne noon so pope holy;
> Yhabited as an heremyte, an ordre by hymselve.[20]

The key element in such accounts of pride is the claim to uniqueness—the presumption that there can be 'none of that kinde, of which he is, but he'.[21]

'Singularity' was not without positive possibilities, as we are about to see, but it has seemed to me necessary to acknowledge the doctrinal hostility to uniqueness in the period. Burckhardt famously claimed that at that epoch 'man was conscious of himself only as a member of a race, people, party, family or corporation—only through some general category'.[22] Our discussion suggests, however, that it is not true that people were not 'conscious of themselves' as having potential singularity. It is rather that they were ideologically conditioned to see some expressions of the self's uniqueness as incipiently sinful. Not all expressions, certainly. For example it has recently been pointed out that personal seals, increasingly adopted during the Middle Ages, amounted to residual statements of individuality.[23]

So, too, 'singular' privileges or qualities or aspirations could sometimes be acceptable. Writers of courtly poetry were liable to celebrate their courtly heroines by appropriating the phoenix analogy. It was shorthand for 'this lady is special'. Moreover, superlative human love for Christ could be described as singular the more it attained an exclusive focus. 'Singular' love was the second-highest form of spiritual love in a fourfold

[17] *AND* shows that this pejorative meaning is paralleled in the Anglo-Norman adjective *singuler*.
[18] Wenzel (1989: 38–9).
[19] Francis (1942: 17).
[20] Langland (1978: XIII. 282–4). In the C-text the passage is incorporated into the confession of Pride ('C' passus VI. 36ff.).
[21] For another representative example, see Pride's self-exposition in Henry (1985: ll. 4041–4).
[22] Burckhardt (1965: 143). More recently it is still asserted that e.g. 'one's life was viewed as part of a whole—the family—rather than as an autonomous entity'; Johnson (1991: 13–14).
[23] Bedos-Rezak (2000); discussed by Clanchy (2003: 296); and see Mooney's discussion of Hoccleve's seal (2007: 315–18).

categorization ('insuperable', 'inseparable', 'singular', and 'insatiable') that was disseminated by the theologian Richard of St Victor (d. 1173).[24] Perhaps more telling in relation to the evolution of individuality, however, are examples of renowned figures accorded enthusiastic or at least neutral singularity. Lydgate writes of Xerxes that he constructed a mighty bridge over the Great Sea 'to shewe a special syngulerte'.[25] This is ambiguous, a sign of magnificent ambition that also bespeaks presumption. But another fifteenth-century text, a chronicle, celebrates more unambiguously the unique charisma of King Alfred, universally commended 'for his dedes and singularitee'.[26]

These are quite late writings. More representative of the fraught attitude to singularity in the Middle Ages, perhaps, is the ambivalence of Dante at the start of the fourteenth century, writing his account of Ulysses in *Inferno*, canto 26. Dante was acutely conscious of individual ambition and of its cost in his own case as a political exile. He consigns ambitious Ulysses to a deep circle in hell reserved for 'false counsellors'.[27] Here Ulysses gives a celebrated account of his last fatal voyage, on which he urged his crew to sail beyond the ultimate human bounds of the pillars set by Hercules, on the grounds that they 'were not born to live as brutes, but to follow virtue and knowledge'.[28] Ulysses's spirited exhortation sounds ethical but is really 'false counsel' for he is inciting his men to see themselves, as he sees himself, as somehow special, unique, capable of passing beyond 'what men should not pass beyond' ('che l'uom più oltre non si mettra'[29]). He registers the ambivalent appeal of *singularitas* as he charismatically pursues an idea of self-exception from common humanity. It is a temptation personally felt by Dante the pilgrim-poet, who recalls that this was the division of hell in which he felt the most precarious.[30]

Having established, then, that certain aspects of individuality were deeply problematic in the Middle Ages, the second part of this chapter will consider growth points for representation of individuality in medieval writings. We shall attend particularly to descriptive conventions, and to the 'voicing' of the self through complaint and dissent, as we examine evidence for an evolving interest in individual human consciousness.

REPRESENTING THE INDIVIDUAL

The early medieval rhetoricians transmitted formulae for the positive or negative description of various categories of persons. Such formulae provided familiar

---

[24] *De Quattuor Gradibus Violentiae Caritatis, PL* 196. 1213ff.

[25] Bergen (1924:, iii. 2258).

[26] *MED, singularite*, 1(c), 'excellence in thought or deed', citing Hardying, *Chronicle 'B'* (1812).

[27] XXVI. 44–5, 69. The edn. and translation used is Sinclair (1949).

[28] Ibid. ll. 97–8, 112–20.

[29] Ibid. l. 109.

[30] Ibid. ll. 44–5.

paradigms for eulogy or for satire. Most routine, and sometimes exasperating from a modern perspective, were the rhetorical conventions for describing women who were love-objects in lyric or romance—or for not describing them—as indescribably beautiful. Fénice in Chrétien's *Cligès* is a case in point. What, indeed, justifies her name and makes her phoenix-like, that is, 'unique'? Not anything that we could now fully interpret in terms of modern 'individuality'. Initially it is a matter of a generalizing declaration that she is peerless in beauty.

Fénice was the maiden's name, and for this there was good reason: for if the Phoenix bird is unique as the most beautiful of all the birds, so Fénice, it seems to me, had no equal in beauty. She was such a miracle and marvel that Nature was never able to make her like again. In order to be more brief, I will not describe in words her arms, her body, her head and hands . . .[31]

Subsequently Fénice fulfils further implications of her name by the contrivance she uses to escape an unwanted marriage. She feigns death then secretly 'resurrects' herself, in imitation of the Phoenix's legendary act of self-renewal. The trick is extraordinary, and the heroine is courageous—or reckless—in being prepared to carry it through; yet while it 'individualizes' her story (or shall we say, unexpectedly conforms her life with specific models from bestiary lore and the life of Christ) it does not 'individualize' her. At most it aligns her with a subcategory of heroine, the 'forward' or bold-spirited heroine driven to take unusual risks on behalf of her love.

To that extent, it is true, she is more autonomous than the woman commemorated in Chaucer's *The Book of the Duchess* by her knight-husband. Duchess Blanche, too, is asserted to have been unique. To the knight, she would have stood out among ten thousand; she was 'the soleyn fenix of Arabye'.[32] Yet in this elegy to—it is presumed—a real woman, little individualizing detail is allowed to disturb the traditional rhetorical compendium of feminine beauty, physical and moral. Daringly, the poem's narrator risks remarking to the knight that doubtless any who saw the lady with *his* eyes would have considered her a paragon.[33] Chaucer here exposes traditional description to a cross-light of gentle scepticism, hinting that existing conventions rely on subjective idealizing hyperboles.

Chaucer went on to probe individualizing possibilities further, as we shall see. Before his time, this chapter will argue, any impulse towards representation of individuality in literature emerges rather less through objective description (though there are salient exceptions)[34] than through two interrelated modes of discourse in which the self protests at what it perceives itself to have become, and analyses the circumstances which have brought this about. The two modes are 'complaint' and confession. We shall discuss complaint first.

---

[31] Chrétien de Troyes (1975; 1987: ll. 2725–60).   [32] Ibid. ll. 971–5, 982.   [33] Ibid. ll. 1048–51.
[34] e.g. Guibert of Nogent (12th cent.) individualizes his childhood tutor thus: 'because he did not say what he meant and what he tried to express was not at all clear to himself, his talk rolled on and on ineffectively in a circle, trundling along without direction, and could not arrive at any conclusion, let alone be understood'; cited by Morris (1972: 85–6).

Complaint was in some respects a form fraught with artifice; not a promising context for locating expressions of individuality. Yet the survival into the Middle Ages of Ovid's *Heroides*, constructed as a series of letters ostensibly written (mostly) by abandoned heroines, supplied a model for the voicing of intense private emotion arising out of particular narratives of betrayal.[35] True, the predicaments are not *very* distinct; the voices in these 'letters' share a common rhetoric of lament and reproach as they contemplate their loss. Many of the women are also alike in being trapped between the instinct to condemn faithless partners and the imperative of a perversely unstoppable love for them. Moreover they all express themselves with an 'Ovidian' penchant for paradox and epigram.

Nevertheless the voices are incipiently individualized. Take Oenone (*Heroides* 5): we hear the voice of a spirited nymph conscious of her own status, who was previously the young soul-mate and spouse to Paris when he was a mere shepherd. Now she finds herself usurped by Helen whom Paris, as King Priam's son, has brought back by ship arrayed in royal purple. While Oenone still pleads to be 'his own' once again, her complaint is distinctive for being fraught with class-consciousness and with jealous scorn for her rival (a 'Greek heifer', a 'runaway'[36]). In Oenone, indignation and consciousness of her own rejected worth vies with nostalgia for her lost adolescent romance.

Reacting against the specific perceived injustices inflicted upon them, Ovid's heroines individualize themselves; but not strikingly, because their predicaments converge, and also because the rhetorical arts of pleading a case will always, for Ovid, take precedence over the impulse towards individualization (something that might be said about many medieval writers also). Nevertheless, here was one important growth point for expressing individuality in literature.

The second growth point was confession. The *Heroides* themselves are fitfully confessional in that their speakers reflect introspectively on their errors of judgement, but of course confession is particularly associated with Christian writing. St Augustine set a stunning early precedent in his *Confessions* by plotting the twists and turns of his moral and intellectual struggle towards Catholic doctrine and faith.[37] This was the book 'that most eloquently demonstrated to the postclassical world that Christianity could provide both a reason and a method for examining one's personal history, the collection of unique though mundane experiences that make up an individual life'.[38] His personality does appear partly through individuating mundane recollections; for instance, how he gave his clinging mother the slip when he embarked from Carthage (5. 8); or how along with some teenage pals he stole pears (2. 4–6). However, the individuality that primarily emerges is that of a powerful analytical mind (thus the motivation for pear-stealing is subjected to ferocious moral/psychological interrogation). This is a mind determined to arrive at truth, and arrogant enough to suppose that it will. Indeed, in 'hating to be wrong' Augustine discloses a 'capacity to upset people' (1. 20, 3. 12).

[35] Ovid (1986).   [36] Ibid. 5. 91, 117–18.
[37] Sheed (1949).   [38] Georgianna (1981: 1).

At the same time, the talents of this towering intellect are not attributed to himself or (much) to his upbringing, but are found to be God-given and to be directed towards God. Augustine measures his conspicuous early success as a public rhetorician against his eventual conviction that the single human being is 'nothing'—nothing but an infant suckled on God's milk (4. 1). The *Confessions*, then, is shot through with the impression of a formidable individual in whom faith nevertheless threatens to nullify individuality itself. This is the paradox of Christian 'confessional' writing. It creates the sense of an individual by expressing the self-aware mind of one who struggles against specific forces that impede spiritual improvement (in Augustine's case, libido, arrogance, and Manichaeism): but while the spiritual destiny of the individual soul matters, the progress is inevitably *away* from that 'confidence in the individual's *value*' which, for Morris, characterizes individuality.

This is a simplification, of course. That the very suppression of individual will can paradoxically constitute someone's individuality seems to me to be demonstrated by the tale of Griselda, as Chaucer's Clerk tells it. Here is a person who wishes to subsume her own will into the will of her husband. Yet her insistence that she left her will behind when she married her marquis husband, and that she would do his will in advance if she knew it (IV. 655–61); and the assurance that there is only one will between them because what he wishes she too wishes (IV. 715–17), do not so much empty her of individuality as assert the individuality of strenuous suspension of personal will. She becomes individualized precisely in the extremity of her desire not to be individual.

Griselda is perhaps the exception that proves the rule. Many of the medieval writings which have especially been claimed to project individuality express personal protest, often in combination with confession. They are both confrontational and self-analytical. That is most dramatically the case with Abelard and Heloise, whose passionate lives interacted in early twelfth-century France. The philosophical position which Abelard developed was one which (though not totally hostile to universals) promoted individualization: 'Although people say that Socrates and Plato are one in their humanity', he wrote, 'how can that be accepted, when it is obvious that all men are different from each other both in matter and form?'[39] This interest in differentiation is consistent with the continuous thread of independence in his life. One example would be the name he gave to the remote 'oratory' in Troyes to which he retreated at a time of despair.[40] When students flocked to his retreat and it became an impromptu community, Abelard named it the 'Paraclete' (the 'Comforter'). This was a novel name—'unknown to general custom'—for a religious foundation, but adopted as a personal tribute to the oratory's role in comforting him in his own distress (*Historia calamitatum* 30–2). Heloise later emphasized her husband's unique role as its 'sole founder', 'sole builder', 'sole creator' (letter 2. 49); but Abelard's uniqueness is most apparent in the provocative naming, which he found himself obliged to defend.

[39] Wade (1963: 165).
[40] Radice (2003: rev. Clanchy). Page references are to this edn.

Abelard's account of his 'calamities' everywhere attests the stridently assertive personality of a hugely talented, idealistic public figure who exercised his intellect self-consciously and with no great sensitivity. His *Historia*, disguised as a letter of consolation to a 'friend', is in fact one long complaint against the blows of misfortune—the alleged 'injustice' of the opposition and persecution which he provoked. It is intertwined with confessional analysis of his motives and faults.[41] Heloise's letters in response also appropriate postures of complaint. Like an Ovidian heroine she accuses her lover-husband of 'forgetfulness' and injustice, in his failure to console her in her misery and thus repay the 'debt' he owed her after, in the boundlessness of her love, she took the veil at his bidding (letter 2. 50–1, 53–4). She begs him to let her feel his presence, if only by writing. Disclosing haunting personal preoccupations with sensual memories, she expresses her utter misery at their separation, how close she is to 'raging' against God in 'complaint' (letter 4. 64–5). Here is individualization in terms of strength, confidence, logic, and emotions still smarting at the mistrustful way her husband hurried her into the cloisters. Abelard is obliged to answer what he calls her 'old perpetual complaint' about this (*veterem illam at assiduam querelam tuam*, letter 5. 72).[42] He resorts to trying to *redirect* her emotion into protest at the injustices committed against Christ. In a way, this is tantamount to an attempt to de-individuate her sense of her situation (R. 152–3).

Complaint and confession emerge, then, as two medieval conventions of utterance which nourish literary projections of individuality. At least, they do so when allied with convincing personal circumstance. Giovanni Boccaccio is an example of a writer who strenuously fictionalizes the conjoined possibilities of complaint and confession, but on a flimsy scaffold of circumstance, in *The Elegy of Lady Fiammetta* (1343–5).[43] With the *Heroides* and other classical precedents very much in mind, Boccaccio creates a 'modern' high-status heroine, amicably married but overwhelmed with love for an admirer ('Panfilo'), who soon disappears. Fiammetta pours out her complaint partly as an exemplary warning to other women not to allow passionate love to enslave them mentally and emotionally. Although there are moments when a 'local' specificity grounds her story—at one point she is held back from a headlong rush to suicide because her skirts become entangled on a nail[44]—the element of individuality arises primarily from her expression of her inner life. Feeding her mind obsessively on what the prolonged absence of her lover implies, she is hyper-aware of every twist of the emotions stirred in her by her heated imagination; an imagination which deceives and undeceives itself, endlessly configuring both the best and worst interpretations of her developing predicament of abandonment. While *Fiammetta's* experiment in expressing the psychology of hope and despair is overprotracted, it

---

[41] In one view the confessional dimension merely underlines Abelard's conforming of his life to 'the story of the rise and fall of a type; the philosopher'; Bynum (1982: 96). For other reservations about the extent of 'individuality' in Abelard, see Hanning (1977: 19, 25); Logan (1986: 259, 263–4); Bagge (1993); Clanchy (2003).

[42] Muckle (1953: 83).

[43] Boccaccio (1990).

[44] Ibid. ll. 123–4; perhaps ironic: a lady's elaborate clothes save her from a mortal sin.

has been hailed with some justice as 'an early attempt at creating an image of a self becoming conscious of its uniqueness, ambivalence, and multiplicity' (Causa-Steindler Boccaccio 1990: p. xvii).

Beside this we might set a short confessional protest-poem from the next century, again expressive of fraught individual emotion, namely Thomas Hoccleve's *Complaint* (*c.* 1419–21).[45] Here we hear the voice of a clerk who has recovered from a period of mental illness (a 'wylde infirmitee'[46]) but finds that former acquaintances barely credit his recovery. Their suspicion (so he alleges) that his illness will return any time, their surveillance of his every bodily gesture for signs of continuing aberration, draw from the Hoccleve of the poem a mood which is by turns indignant, gloomy, and resigned. Whatever he does, he feels in his incipient paranoia, is likely to be disparagingly construed. There is nothing in medieval literature that quite matches the mingling of self-aware humour with bitter pathos as he describes himself checking a mirror at home for reassurance, practising what appears to him to be a normal expression[47] that ought to shore up his public credibility. True, certain facets of the *Complaint* draw it away from individuality. It resorts to biblical *dicta* to articulate its speaker's profound sense of alienation; and the speaker absorbs his fate into the universal principle that God sends such trouble as a deserved corrective: a 'bone' for him to 'gnaw' on as he puts it.[48] But the dominant impression remains that of an individual responding to personal crisis with strategies that include traditional moralizing; not that of traditional moralizing dressed up with touches of individualization.

The same might be said of *The Book of Margery Kempe*, produced a little later in the fifteenth century. Kempe's reminiscences, as mediated by her amanuenses, evoke formulae from the medieval saint's life (persecution, interrogation, conquest of sin, and disputation with unenlightened authorities) as well as the formulae of the mystic's account of the way to God. Her self-representation is therefore forged with reference to pre-existing narrative matrices. Yet Kempe's account strikes most readers for its idiosyncrasy; for its projection of an assertive personality, whose clamorous evangelizing impulse and convulsive bouts of devotional tears make her uniquely challenging. While there were precedents for holy tears and for the missionary calling of a strong woman, her individuality is especially constituted by her nagging self-doubt with regard to her role. She is perennially anxious for recognition and validation by authoritative clerics. Above all she is haunted by the thought that as a married woman who has had many children, she does not qualify as an inspirational female mystic, because she perceives virginity as a criterion for the highest spiritual status.

Significantly, Kempe alludes to this eccentricity in her role as her 'singularity'. Pondering her lack of virginity, she gains Christ's reassurance that she is a 'singular'

[45] The dating is J. A. Burrow's in his 1999 edn., to which my discussion refers.
[46] Ibid. l. 40.
[47] Ibid. ll. 155–68.
[48] Ibid. ll. 398–9.

lover to him, and will therefore gain a 'singular' grace in heaven.[49] As for her troublesome outbursts of tears, they amount to a 'synguler and special gift' from God.[50] It is tempting to make a connection here with something we have already observed, the classification of 'singular' love as one of the highest forms of mystical love. (It was propounded in English by Richard Rolle, a fourteenth-century English mystic with whose ideas Kempe was familiar.[51]) However, the contexts show that she is primarily thinking of the *unusualness* of her candidacy for spiritual perfection and of her involuntary weeping. She is acutely aware of her individuality, and of its cost in a society which readily confuses individuality with deviance.

With Kempe, thanks to her self-doubt and alienation, we come close to individual autobiography. According to John Burrow, Hoccleve's *Series* (of which the 'Complaint' is the first part) also verges on autobiography.[52] In fact Burrow sees Langland, Gower, Chaucer, and Hoccleve as a group of late medieval English writers who purposefully incorporate their own 'names and identities' and 'distinctive voices' in their work. If there was a 'discovery of the individual' in French and Latin culture in the twelfth century, that 'discovery' was delayed in English writings, he suggests, until the fourteenth century.[53]

By definition, Burrow cannot include the unnamed *Gawain*-poet in his grouping. Yet we saw at the beginning of the chapter that the idea of an individual self-concept is glimpsed within that poet's work, in the character of Sir Gawain. Picking that point up now, it is interesting to note that it would actually be difficult to speak confidently of an 'individualized' Gawain. He solemnly avows a constellation of Christian and chivalric virtues, hardly distinctive except in the interdependence he claims for them. When he errs in promise-keeping and is confronted with this by his tester, the narrative becomes thick with a conventional language of confession. It has been suggested that what really makes the situation special in medieval romance and what potentially individualizes Gawain is his enormous embarrassment and sense of humiliation—going beyond the normal public associations of Middle English 'shame'—when he not only realizes he has been found out, but finally has to live with that realization. Derek Pearsall sees here 'a new art of the interior self'. The connection between embarrassment and the private self is such that Gawain is rendered solitary: what he discovers in himself is 'the quality in individuals [i.e. the self-concept capable of embarrassment] that we have become accustomed to believe constitutes them in their essential individual humanity'.[54] It is perhaps in this

---

[49] Windeatt (2000: bk 1, ch. 22, ll. 1617–29, 1679–82); tr. Windeatt (1985: 86, 88).

[50] '. . . dowtyr, drede the nowt, for it is a synguler and special gift that God hath yovyn the', Windeatt (2000: bk 1, ch. 41, ll. 3267–9); tr. Windeatt (1985: 136).

[51] See Windeatt (2000: 135 n. to 1628). Rolle describes the highest form of love for God as 'synguler' because it has no equal; Rolle (1988: 16–17).

[52] Burrow (1989).

[53] Burrow (1982: 40, 43).

[54] Pearsall (1997: 361). An argument that shame might not really be 'individual', however, if it primarily registers a sense of unwanted removal from a public community to which one wants to belong, is developed by Logan (1986) in relation to Abelard's *Historia*, pp. 263–4.

respect, more than in the test of mettle and morality he undergoes, that he is individualized. The romance quest in its heyday amounts, Hanning has proposed, to a strenuous exercise in self-realization for the hero.[55] Arguably, however, such self-realization remains generic—what *all* knights achieve—rather than the realization of individual humanity to which Gawain approximates.

Whether this distinction is accepted or not, it is interesting that, as in the case of Hoccleve and Kempe, so in Gawain a focus on flawed humanity has an isolating effect, which releases a phenomenon which we might want to label 'individuality'. Is it only the phenomenon of isolation that generates exceptional instances of individuality in the Middle Ages? Would Chaucer's pilgrims in the *Canterbury Tales* embody a development away from that?

In approaching this we should note that Chaucer is rather more concerned than his contemporaries to find terminology for the process of identifying individual traits. One word that he tries using is 'circumstances', a term borrowed from confessional discourse. In 'The Knight's Tale' it is a collective noun for the particular qualifications ascribed to Palamon for possible marriage to Emelye.[56] It is logical that a word which was especially deployed to indicate the 'how, what, where', of sin could be adapted to the purpose of suggesting the make-up of an individual.[57]

However, Chaucer's preferred term was 'conditions'. The moral attributes forming part of the rhetorical coding of literary portraiture were usually called 'condiciouns' by him, and occasionally by other English writers. We are told, for instance, in 'The Physician's Tale' that the heroine Virginia lacks no praiseworthy 'condicion'—and there duly follows a rehearsal of these conditions; chastity, humility, moderation, discretion in speech, etc.[58] More interestingly, the *summation* of someone's behavioural traits can also be called their *condicioun* in Chaucer's vocabulary. The narrator of 'The Man of Law's Tale' remarks on the fate of Custance, sent away to face marital subjection to a foreign ruler whose 'condicioun' she 'knoweth nat'.[59] 'The Clerk's Tale' ponders how certain people can be 'of swich condicion' that, once embarked on a course of action, they become obsessed with it.[60] The last two significations come interestingly close to the modern word 'character', and put us in mind of the individuality of the persons concerned.[61]

Virtue and vice did not constitute the only arena in Chaucer for identifying the components of a person's *condicioun*. There were also the more learned formative constituents from physiological and astrological learning. A person might be

[55] Hanning (1977: 4 and 194–233).

[56] Knight's Tale, I. 2788.

[57] See Parson's Tale, X. 959–78; and examples from earlier confessional writings in Georgianna (1981: 99–100, 116–17). The qualities actually attributed to Palamon are quite conventional, but that is not the point.

[58] VI. 41–71.

[59] II. 268–71.

[60] IV. 701–3.

[61] In my view this is clearly what is meant by the narrator's intention to tell 'al the condicioun' of each of the pilgrims (*Canterbury Tales*, General Prologue, ll. 38–9), though editors are coy about the meaning.

reckoned to manifest a predominant 'complexion' or bodily humour, or to manifest the specific influence of a planetary configuration prevailing at their birth. 'Venus me yaf my lust . . . And Mars yaf me my sturdy hardynesse':[62] so speaks the Wife of Bath, pleading a justification for what we might call her individualizing drives—to her they are external drives, but still *hers*; '*myn* inclinacioun' and '*my* constellacioun'.[63]

However, Chaucer's pilgrims disclose their varying shades of individualization especially by reference to the intertwined occupational and moral realms they inhabit. Here again, impulses of protest and alienation play their part. Chaucer is keenly interested in role alienation. A delicately worldly prioress lives in elegant friction with her vocation: she 'counterfeits' court manners; draws attention to her face and lips in her dainty eating; and pours out charity upon pets. A monk with incongruously 'supple' boots and jingling horses not only emulates lordly equipage but actually justifies his protest against cloistered discipline by dismissing received monastic rules as antiquated. The Prioress and Monk are selves defined against the grain of vocation. It is 'as if subjectivity itself were the result of conflict', as Ganim puts it.[64]

Jill Mann authoritatively demonstrated in 1973 how normative in estates satire are the pilgrims' deviations from the respective ideal standards for their vocations. Chaucer works with received negative stereotypes. But Mann also saw the way in which the ostensibly non-judgemental use of selective detail in the 'General Prologue' imparts the illusion that each pilgrim is autonomous in the way they inhabit their social roles. The technique seems to allow the personae to be projected almost from their own point of view, to 'give us an extraordinarily vivid *impression* of [their] existence as individuals'.[65]

The Reeve, for example, is projected in terms of his meticulous control over the manor's produce and the comfortable position he has achieved in his lord's estate. The satirical social model here would be the astuteness and exploitation associated with manorial officials; but his spindly legs and a clerically cropped head unforgettably sharpen the impression of a cheerless man whose tight surveillance has isolated him, even while it has elevated him. So he emerges as individual through his anti-social alienation from the manorial community which he oversees, and from which he screens himself in a house set apart on a heath.[66] In a very different representation, the Franklin's gregarious individuality emerges as that of a host and *bon viveur* preoccupied with the quantity and delicacy of the food 'snowing' in his house. There is a whiff of a gluttony caricature, and of a stereotype of venal shire officialdom, but the Franklin is differentiated away from such simplification by the way his hospitality complicatedly invokes altruistic generosity (he is a 'St Julian'), as well as defensive self-justification (Epicureanism). In a different vein again the virtuous,

---

62 III. 611–12.
63 III. 615–16.
64 Ganim (2005: 233).
65 Mann (1973: 16).
66 Ibid. 163–7

honourable Parson gains individuality through differentiation. In his case, his energetic performance of parish duties is expressed in serial opposition to failings endemic in the job, as if he were driven on by an urgent and overt determination to distinguish himself at every point from negative parsonhood.

Chaucer's best-known candidates for 'individuality' are the Wife of Bath (in her Prologue), and Criseyde. In both cases, subtle forms of differentiation simultaneously entangle them with, and distinguish them from, literary forebears and prospective role models (especially that of 'widow'). In both, the spaces which especially nourish development as individuals are created by dialectic. The Wife of Bath both revels in and protests against negative stereotypes of women. She both desires autonomy and gives it away. Criseyde is (and plays) the victim of predatory masculine intrigue when Troilus's love is urged upon her; but she discloses that she responds knowingly. In both cases the impression of 'individuality' is created partly because a figure is in active dialogue with itself, if it is not indeed a figure torn by dual imperatives. There is no doubt that the dialectical monologues revealing Criseyde's thoughts, even if they owe much to 'pro' and 'con' conventions of medieval debate, take us to unprecedented levels of subjectivity. Boccaccio's Fiammetta had remarked, as does Criseyde, on her sense of being 'her own woman' and not wanting to endanger that,[67] but Fiammetta never convinces us of her individuality to the same degree as Criseyde—primarily because Fiammetta becomes too predictable, too knowable.

What Chaucer seems to have intuited is that human personality may exert particular fascination by virtue of an element of unknowability, especially through self-contradiction. The Wife of Bath and Criseyde strike many readers as finally unknowable. The pilgrim descriptions in the 'General Prologue' achieve in cameo something of that enigma also: they invite but defy simplification into caricature, they invite but defy censure, they engage us in the creative subtlety of trying to understand people who seem 'individuals' precisely because they elude straightforward labelling.[68]

It would be perverse not to credit Chaucer with making discoveries about individuality, even if he did so from a standpoint that still owed much to a schematic habit of mind in defining people.[69] This chapter has given some sense of a trajectory leading towards him, and beyond him to the examples of Hoccleve and then Margery Kempe. Kempe might stand as epitome of the 'arrival' of a form of individualistic self-projection 'new' in the early fifteenth century. The social shake-up caused by the Black Death, the sensitization of individual religious practice prompted by the spread of Wycliffism, and the influence of Ockham's championship of particularities as against universals, are examples of phenomena which could be taken to support a neat chronology of a late medieval 'ascent of individualism' in England. To me the picture seems more confused than that. Across Europe there is an ebb and flow throughout the Middle Ages on the matter of individualization. The reason for the

---

[67] Boccaccio (1990: 8 and 28; *Troilus and Criseyde*, II. 750).
[68] Emphasized by Mann (1973: 189).
[69] See Fisher (1992: 96).

ebb and flow is that doctrinal hostility towards 'singularity' was never easily budged. As we have said, that hostility also implies that there was indeed an impulse to be reined in. Individuals appeared—but not in a neat chronological evolution—who in writing about themselves or others could project an individuality that we think we recognize. They did not yet let it loose into rampant defiance of an ideology of commonality.

BIBLIOGRAPHY

AERS, DAVID (1992), 'A Whisper in the Ear of Early Modernists; or, Reflections on Literary Critics Writing the "History of the Subject"', in David Aers (ed.), *Culture and History 1350–1600: Essays on English Communities, Identities and Writing* (London: Harvester Wheatsheaf), 177–202.

ALIGHIERI, DANTE (1949), *The Divine Comedy of Dante Alighieri*, ed. John D. Sinclair (rev. edn. London: John Lane).

ANDREW, MALCOLM, and Ronald Waldron (eds.) (1978), *The Poems of the Pearl Manuscript* (London: Arnold).

AUGUSTINE (1949), The *Confessions of Augustine*, tr. F. J. Sheed (London: Sheed & Ward).

BAGGE, SVERRE (1993), 'The Autobiography of Abelard and Medieval Individualism', *Journal of Medieval History*, 19: 327–50.

BEDOS-REZAK, BRIGITTE (2000), 'Medieval Identity: A Sign and a Concept', *American Historical Review*, 105: 1489–1533.

BENTON, JOHN F. (1991), 'Consciousness of Self and Perceptions of Individuality', in *Culture, Power and Personality in Medieval France* (London: Hambledon Press).

BOCCACCIO, GIOVANNI (1990), *The Elegy of Lady Fiammetta*, tr. Mariangela Causa-Steindler and Thomas Mauch (Chicago: University of Chicago Press).

BURCKHARDT, JACOB (1965), *The Civilization of the Renaissance in Italy* (London: Phaidon).

BURROW, J. A. (1982), *Medieval Writers and their Work: Middle English Literature and its Background 1100–1500* (Oxford: Oxford University Press).

——(1989), 'Autobiographical Poetry in the Middle Ages: The Case of Thomas Hoccleve', in J. A. Burrow (ed.), *Middle English Literature: British Academy Gollancz Lectures* (Oxford: Oxford University Press for the British Academy), 223–46.

BYNUM, CAROLINE WALKER (1982), 'Did the Twelfth Century Discover the Individual?', in *Jesus as Mother: Studies in the Spirituality of the High Middle Ages* (Berkeley, Calif.: University of California Press), 82–109.

CHRÉTIEN DE TROYES (1975), *Cligès*, ed. Alexandre Micha (Paris: Champion).

——(1987), *Arthurian Romances*, tr. D. D. R. Owen (London: Dent).

CLANCHY, MICHAEL (2003), 'Documenting the Self: Abelard and the Individual in History', *Historical Research*, 76: 293–309.

DONNE, JOHN (1621), *The First Anniversarie: An Anatomie of The World* (London: A. Matthewes for Thomas Dewe).

DRONKE, PETER (1970), *Poetic Individuality in the Middle Ages* (Oxford: Clarendon Press).

FISHER, JOHN H. (1992), 'Chaucer and the Emergence of the Individual', in *The Importance of Chaucer* (Carbondale and Edwardsville, Ill.: Southern Illinois University Press), 71–103.

Francis, W. Nelson (ed.) (1942), *The Book of Vices and Virtues: A Fourteenth Century English Translation of the 'Somme le Roi' of Lorens D'Orléans* (EETS OS 217; London: Oxford University Press).

Ganim, John M. (2005), 'Identity and Subjecthood', in Steve Ellis (ed.), *Chaucer: An Oxford Guide* (Oxford: Oxford University Press), 224–38.

Georgianna, Linda (1981), *The Solitary Self: Individuality in the 'Ancrene Wisse'* (Cambridge, Mass.: Harvard University Press).

Hanning, Robert W. (1977), *The Individual in Twelfth-Century Romance* (New Haven: Yale University Press).

Hardying, John (1812), *The Chronicle of John Hardying*, ed. H. Ellis (London).

Harré, Rom (1998), The *Singular Self: An Introduction to the Psychology of Personhood* (London: Thousand Oaks, Calif.).

Henry, Avril (ed.) (1985), *The Pilgrimage of the Lyfe of the Manhode*, i (EETS OS 288; Oxford: Oxford University Press for the Early English Text Society).

Hoccleve, Thomas (1999), *Thomas Hoccleve's Complaint and Dialogue*, ed. J. A. Burrow (EETS OS 313; Oxford: Oxford University Press).

Johnson, Penelope D. (1991), *Equal in Monastic Profession: Religious Women in Medieval France* (Chicago: University of Chicago Press).

Langland, William (1978), The *Vision of Piers Plowman: A Complete Edition of the B-Text*, ed. A. V. C. Schmidt (London: J. M. Dent).

Logan, Richard D. (1986), 'A Conception of the Self in the Later Middle Ages', *Journal of Medieval History*, 12: 253–68.

Lydgate, John (1924), *Lydgate's Fall of Princes*, ed. Henry Bergen, part ii (EETS ES 122; Oxford: Oxford University Press for the Early English Text Society).

Mann, Jill (1973), *Chaucer and Medieval Estates Satire: The Literature of Social Classes and the 'General Prologue' to the Canterbury Tales* (Cambridge: Cambridge University Press).

Millett, Bella (ed.) (2005), *Ancrene Wisse, a Corrected Edition of the Text in Cambridge, Corpus Christi College, MS402*, i (EETS OS 325; Oxford: Oxford University Press).

Mooney, Linne R. (2007), 'Some New Light on Thomas Hoccleve', *Studies in the Age of Chaucer*, 29: 293–340.

Morris, Colin (1972), *The Discovery of the Individual, 1050–1200* (London: Society for Promoting Christian Knowledge).

Muckle, J. T. (ed.) (1953), 'The Personal Letters between Abelard and Heloise', *Mediaeval Studies*, 15: 47–94.

Ovid (1986), *Heroides and Amores*, tr. Grant Showerman (2nd edn), rev. G. P. Goold (Cambridge, Mass.: Harvard University Press).

Patterson, Lee (1991), *Chaucer and the Subject of History* (London: Routledge).

Pearsall, Derek (1997), 'Courtesy and Chivalry in Sir Gawain and the Green Knight: The Order of Shame and the Invention of Embarrassment', in Derek Brewer and Jonathan Gibson (eds.), *A Companion to the Gawain-Poet* (Cambridge: D. S. Brewer), 351–62.

Radice, Betty (tr.) (2003), *The Letters of Abelard and Heloise*, rev. M. T. Clanchy (London: Penguin).

Rolle, Richard (1988), *The Form of Living* in S. J. Ogilvie-Thomson (ed.), *Richard Rolle, Prose and Verse* (EETS os 293; Oxford: Oxford University Press for the Early English Text Society), 16–17.

Salu, M. B. (tr.) (1955), *The Ancrene Riwle* (London: Burns & Oates).

Shanahan, Daniel (1992), *Toward a Genealogy of Individualism* (Amherst, Mass.: University of Massachusetts Press).

SOUTHERN, RICHARD W. (1970), 'Medieval Humanism', in *Medieval Humanism and Other Studies* (New York: Harper & Row), 29–60.

WADE, F. (1963), 'Abelard and Individuality', in Paul Wilpert (ed.), *Die Metaphysik im Mittelalter* (Berlin: De Gruyter), 165.

WENZEL, SIEGFRIED (ed. and tr.) (1989), *Fasciculus Morum: A Fourteenth-Century Preacher's Handbook* (University Park, Pa.: Pennsylvania State University Press).

WILLIAMS, RAYMOND (1983), *Keywords: A Vocabulary of Culture and Society* (rev. edn. London: Fontana Press).

WINDEATT, B. A. (tr.) (1985), *The Book of Margery Kempe* (Harmondsworth: Penguin).

——(ed.) (2000), *The Book of Margery Kempe* (Harlow: Longman).

....

CHAPTER 25

EMERGENT ENGLISHNESS

....

JACQUELINE FAY

EMERGENT ENGLISHNESS?

....

The word *Englishness* reveals much about the nature of the quality it designates. Although it is a modern term, used for the first time in the early nineteenth century, the word is composed of elements that date back to Old English. *English*, or *Englisc* as it was originally spelled, was used adjectivally in Old English to characterize individuals or groups of people, and, most commonly, to refer to the language itself. In fact, the modifier *Englisc*, without any need of a noun such as *geðeode*, meaning *language*, was already in Old English sufficient to refer to the vernacular. The affixed ending of *Englishness* is also an Old English element (*-nyss*), and represents an enduringly useful way to form abstract nouns from adjectives. Among numerous other examples, *menniscnyss* connoted *humanity*, a state of being among the mennish race; *grænnysse* described the quality of being green; and *forgifenysse* and *rihtwisnysse* had meanings equivalent to their modern English forms *forgiveness* and *righteousness*. While the usefulness (another -ness word) of this suffix to Anglo-Saxon speakers seems limitless—allowing them to qualify a wide variety of physical and emotional states, as well as ethical and spiritual positions that an individual could take up—it was not used to classify the distinctive qualities of an ethnic group, English, French, Danish, or otherwise.

It is not sufficient, however, to conclude from the absence of a medieval reflex of the word *Englishness* that the quality itself is an exclusively modern property.[1] The ambivalent modernity of the term, composed of elements that simulate an overall impression of antiquity, in fact points to one of the ways that *Englishness*, like other group identities based on national or ethnic terms, is given content. As Benedict Anderson puts it, '[i]f nation-states are widely conceded to be "new" and "historical," the nations to which they give political expression always loom out of an immemorial past'.[2] In other words, the viability of *Englishness* relies on it being both new and old at the same time, simultaneously resting on a time-worn inevitability while also necessitating constant performance in order to rein-scribe its boundaries and assert its presence. Like the word *Englishness*, the antiquity that underpins national identity is, in some sense, inauthentic: a patched-together affair, the elements of which add patina only through their reiteration in the present. Common to almost all commentary on nationality and ethnicity is a sense that this fundamental paradox, or difference, both maintains the identity, and also haunts it from within by a sense of its own potential dissolution. The necessity for this differential explains nationalism's intimate relation with imperialism and with patri-archal authority, since both structures offer the nation an encounter with otherness, whether defined in racial, sexual, or linguistic terms. In this way the nation's problematic relation to an origin, and the complex notion of past and present on which it is founded, becomes imbricated in concerns about other types of difference more immediate and more capable of manipulation; for example, the adoption or rejection of certain female dress codes.[3]

Given this outline of the form of national and ethnic identity, two related ques-tions arise when we consider the project of writing about 'Emergent Englishness' in the medieval context. How to conceptualize this period as possessing a notion of Englishness when it generally serves either as the immemorial past from which national identity looms, or as the field of alterity against which nationalism is defined? And, given the necessity for national or ethnic identity constantly to be performed, is it valid to speak of certain periods during which it is 'emergent', or is it not rather constantly emergent in some sense? Both questions originate in the same basic problem: the extent to which it is valid to think of a category such as Englishness in historical terms, and thus as a quality that appeared at a definite point in time, when these are the precise terms upon which the identity Englishness serves to replicate itself.[4] It is a concern for the scholar writing about the history of Englishness that our discourse not become complicit with the aims of nationalism

---

[1] Middle English does contain the noun *English(e)rie*, which connotes the quality of being English, or being of English descent. Both the French-derived suffix of this noun, and its frequent use in the context of references to Ireland, highlight the essentially hybrid nature of such ethnic designations: they emerge *in distinction* to qualities designated as other, while being far from pure in themselves.

[2] Anderson (1991: 11).

[3] For consideration of the role of gender in medieval political community, see Davis (2004). For post-colonial and national investment in the veil, in particular, see Davis (2000).

[4] Much excellent work on ethnic and national identity in medieval culture has informed my thinking here, including: the essays in Forde *et al.* (1995); Davis (1998); Harris (2003); (2008); Lavezzo (2004); Kabir and Williams (2005); Cohen (2000); Ingham and Warren (2003); Turville-Petre (1996).

itself, and particularly with its striving for an uncomplicated and early origin. Such an origin is attractive to nationalist movements because it lends coherence and authority to the nation as a social formation; it holds capital in scholarly circles because it functions as one way to overcome charges that early periods are irrelevant to and disconnected from contemporary concerns. This chapter will begin, then, not with the differences between medieval and later notions of Englishness, although many of these will become evident in the course of the analysis, but with the strategic relation between ethnicity and the past. Rather than arguing for the newness of English identity during the medieval period, I will claim that Englishness, during this period as in others, resists any characterization as emergent, instead being found in association with the antique.

This is not to deny the significant changes that Englishness undergoes during this lengthy period of some one thousand years between the mid-fifth and the late fifteenth centuries. Numerous events could be identified as significant to its development: the writing of the first history of the English people in 732, the late ninth-century Alfredian translation programme, the requirement from 1215 for yearly confession, King Henry III's 1258 open letter to his subjects upholding the Provisions of Oxford, the Peasant's Revolt, the Crusades, the introduction of the printing press, early fifteenth-century controversy over the Wycliffite Bible, to mention but a few important moments. In other words, as Kathy Lavezzo puts it, '[i]nstead of parsing out the cultural from its perceived others, it is crucial to consider how a variety of phenomena worked in conjunction to make it possible to imagine an English nation in the late Middle Ages'.[5] Historical, political, legal, and literary discourse combine in complex ways during this period to cement the idea of the English as a distinctive group bound by a common language, history, religious practice, and economic structure. That a massive extension of the bureaucratic function of the English language occurred during the latter part of the medieval period is also well-recognized.[6] In fact, textual references to an English-language community increase exponentially after the Norman Conquest, until the discourse of Englishness is hegemonic in a way it is arguably not during the pre-Conquest centuries. On the other hand, late Anglo-Saxon literary culture is also marked by a significant interest in the vernacular, which was routinely used alongside Latin for pedagogical, religious, and legal purposes. Nor can the explosion of vernacular writing in the late medieval period be imagined as occurring free from the influence of dominant Latin and French models, which to a certain extent determined the syntax, vocabulary, and genre of English-language texts. To proffer a narrative of Englishness that emphasizes a gradual and incremental increase in its potency throughout the medieval period would, based on this evidence, be misguided.

[5] Lavezzo (2004: p. xviii).
[6] See e.g. Stock (1983); Clanchy (1993). The question of language is central to thinking about ethnic or national communities, and the multilingual and elite nature of medieval textual culture is often cited as a restriction on the development of certain types of communal identity during this time period. Benedict Anderson, for instance, notes that medieval readers formed 'tiny literate reefs on top of vast illiterate oceans' (1991: 15).

In order to take as its object the entire medieval period, while remaining attentive to subtle differences of context, therefore, this brief chapter will focus on an investigation of Englishness in one genre common to both pre- and post-Conquest literary culture, and a privileged site for the staging and investigation of a relationship to the past: hagiography.[7] Saints' lives are a compelling venue for an investigation of Englishness because they bring into proximity a set of considerations and concepts the association of which has been seen as essential to the formation of ethnic community: history, place, language, gender, and the relationship between the local and the universal. First, the life, death, and afterlife of saints afforded medieval authors multiple opportunities to thematize the relation of past to present, and to dramatize what is basically a revisionist impetus, or an urge to rewrite the past, within a spiritually sanctioned environment. Second, the intimate relation between history and place in hagiography also makes it a rich venue for ethnic and national imaginings, since it allows for the association of a people with their environment. Third, because saints' lives are often translated from Latin into English, questions of linguistic authority and mediation are always near the surface. These linguistic questions open onto a broader concern with literacy, and the bilateral status of hagiography as both a highly literate and popular genre, which was written by clerics but was accessible in its elements to a wide swath of people in oral form. Fourth, since certain routes to sanctity are restricted only to male saints, gender is by necessity an important organizational category in hagiography, and frequently works to refract questions of sovereignty and self-determination, as it does in modern national discourses. And fifth, the genre of hagiography is deeply and predictably governed by universal narrative patterns while, at the same time, it typically bears a special relation to its context of production because it serves to celebrate and authorize local saints. The capability to seat the local within the universal makes hagiography a suitable field for the promotion of ethnic or national community, because such identity positions rely on being able to demonstrate the trans-local meanings of local experience. Finally, saints offer their audience what could be described as a domesticated encounter with alterity, by which this audience may sound the constituent bounds of its own identity. Saints are, in this respect, akin to monstrous beings, in that their prodigious abilities and even their appearance mark their difference from ordinary society; some saints, like St Christopher, are in fact members of exotic races. At the same time, however, saints are men and women whose lives, in the case of native saints, would be in some sense familiar to their audiences, and whose actions their readers are often encouraged to emulate. Occupying a position that is both other and not other in relation to worshippers, saints bring the question of boundaries and definition to the fore. By examining texts associated with two early medieval saints, Æthelthryth and Erkenwald, this chapter will argue that hagiography works to transmit ideas about communal integrity by investigating and instantiating the relation between bodily incorruption and the past.

---

[7] Essential general reading on medieval hagiography includes: Brown (1981); Heffernan (1988).

SAINT ÆTHELTHRYTH: THE SCARRED BODY

Bede's life of Æthelthryth, given in book 4 of the *Historia ecclesiastica*, is the earliest narrative associated with the saint and was to become paradigmatic for all subsequent retellings of her story.[8] As Bede tells us, Æthelthryth was a seventh-century East Anglian princess married, for the second time, to Ecgfrith of the Northumbrians in order to cement a dynastic alliance between these two kingdoms. Despite her two marriages, Æthelthryth remained a virgin and, after twelve years, Ecgfrith finally granted her wish to enter the monastery at Coldingham; a year later, she founded and became abbess of a dual monastery at Ely. While Æthelthryth showed mild signs of sanctity during her life, especially in her austere mode of life and in predicting the date of her own demise, Bede's narrative is really focused on those events occurring after her death, which serve retroactively to reveal the signifi-cance of what went before. When the new abbess, her sister Seaxburh, raises Æthel-thryth's body after sixteen years in the grave, it is found to be incorrupt. Of particular import to Bede is the healing of a wound made shortly before her death when her physician lanced a large neck tumour, which Æthelthryth herself believed to be God's punishment for the youthful vanity of wearing many necklaces. Both her original coffin and burial clothes subsequently perform healing miracles, while her body is rehoused in a white marble coffin fortuitously discovered by the monks.

Bede describes Ely in such a way as to make obvious its metonymic relation to the larger island of Britain. The *Historia ecclesiastica* begins, as scholars are fond of noting, with the observation that, 'Brittania Oceani insula' (Britain is an island of the ocean, *HE* 1.1). Ely, like Britain, is also an island, necessitating the monks to take to boats when they leave in search of the stone for Æthelthryth's new coffin, 'ipsa enim regio Elge undique est acquis ac paludibus circumdata' ('for the district of Ely is surrounded on all sides by waters and marshes', *HE* 4.19). As Ely is to Britain, so Æthelthryth is to her new sarcophagus, which exactly replicates the contours of her body: '[m]irum uero in modum ita aptum corpori uirginis sarcofagum inuentum est, ac si ei specialiter praeparatum fuisset, et locus quoque capitis seorsum fabrefactus ad mensuram capitis illius aptissime figuratus apparuit'.[9] Bede's attention to the rewrapping and contain-ment of Æthelthryth's body restates the microcosmic relation between Ely and Britain itself, and provides a way to think about her as simultaneously a local and an insular saint. Such an association is furthered by the juxtaposition of Æthelthryth's story with that of John the Archcantor's visit to Wearmouth-Jarrow, given in the previous chapter.

---

[8] All quotations from the *Historia* in both Latin and English translation are drawn from Colgrave and Mynors (1969), and are cited by book and chapter number. Much scholarship has been dedicated to Æthelthryth, including: Blanton (2007); Blanton-Whetsell (2002a, 2002b); Gretsch (2005: esp. pp. 157–231); Griffiths (1992); Karkov (2005); Otter (1997); Pulsiano (1999: 1–42).

[9] 'This sarcophagus was found to fit the virgin's body in a wonderful way, as if it had been specially prepared for her; and the place for the head, which was cut out separately, seemed to be exactly shaped to its size' (*HE* 4.19). For the ways that the representational containment of female saints relates to the enclosure of Anglo-Saxon female monastics, see Horner (2001: esp. 1–6 for a discussion of Æthelthryth).

Invited to Britain by Benedict, John's visit provides an occasion to question to what degree the identity of the English Church is contained by its relationship to Rome, since John is charged not only with the responsibility of teaching liturgical chant to the English but also with bringing back to Rome a report about the English stance on the Monophysite heresy.[10] Bracketing Æthelthryth's narrative, this chapter mirrors its concern with a synecdochic notion of regionality that asserts the symbolic value of the part in relation to the whole.

Bede's investment in Æthelthryth—not only does he dedicate a lengthy chapter to her life, but he also composes a Latin hymn in praise of her virginity—is part of this need to assert a likeness between the English and Roman Churches. The abecedarian hymn makes clear that Æthelthryth is to Bede's age what the virgin saints Agatha, Eulalia, Thecla, Euphemia, Agnes, and Cecily were to theirs:[11] as Ælfric will describe her in his own version of her life written two hundred and fifty years later, Æthelthryth is 'þam engliscan mædene'.[12] For both Bede and Ælfric after him, Æthelthryth's preservation of her virginity through two marriages proves God's continuing presence in history, and asserts that the contemporary English context is no different, in this respect, from Rome during the age of persecutions: 'Nec diffidendum est nostra etiam aetate fieri potuisse, quod aeuo praecedente aliquoties factum fideles historiae narrant, donante uno eodemque Domino, qui se nobiscum usque in finem saeculi manere pollicetur.'[13] Like *translationes* in general, the story of how Æthelred is unearthed and rehoused serves to refract some of these overt concerns with the potentially alienating effects of history, and especially with the position of contemporary communities seeking self-definition in reference to a past that threatens to vanish. Frequent and often spectacular translation of a saint's body, as in the case of Æthelthryth, was a material practice that quite literally brought the past into the present; the narration of such translations in texts captured this process and allowed for its infinite repeatability by a general readership. While the performance of miracles asserts that saints are never entirely of the past, translations specifically allowed for the iteration and reordering of the historical narrative associated with each saint.

These concerns about history are particularly obvious in Æthelthryth's translation not only because of its focus on the miraculous healing of her neck wound, but also for the way that Bede builds his exegesis of the scar's meaning specifically as a retrospective. In contrast to Ælfric's later version of the saint's life, in which events are given in the chronological order in which they occurred, Bede does not report the existence of the neck wound until after Æthelthryth's death and exhumation, when her doctor, Cynefrith, is provoked to deliver an explanatory speech when he sees that the wound has healed. Only at this point do we read that, 'mirum in modum pro

[10] For John the Archcantor's visit and the Monophysite heresy, see Ó Carragáin (2005: 223–8).
[11] Bede, HE 4. 20: 'the English virgin'.
[12] All quotations in the original from this text are taken from Skeat (1881–5), and are cited by page and line number. I have removed Skeat's pointing and italics throughout. Translations are my own.
[13] 'Nor need we doubt that this which often happened in days gone by, as we learn from trustworthy accounts, could happen in our time too through the help of the Lord, who has promised to be with us even to the end of the age' (HE 4.19). Ælfric repeats this statement, and attributes it directly to Bede (432. 24–434. 30).

aperto et hiante uulnere, cum quo sepulta erat, tenuissima tunc cicatris uestigia parerent'.[14] For Bede, this miracle of healing, along with the incorruption of her body, is the material sign of her virginal status.[15] That the narrative of medical penetration thus works to cathect concerns about other types of bodily violation seems relatively obvious, and has been well-explored by scholars. As interesting, however, is the relation between the postposition of the narrative of the wound and the symbolic significance of the wound itself as a historical marker. Incorrupt saints like Æthelthryth have, of course, particular value for the ways that their bodies resist the ravages of time and thus offer reassurance about the potency of identifications based on history. Æthelthryth's scar, however, both complicates and intensifies the solace extended by her incorrupt body as a sign of perfection. That her body has healed after death serves to demonstrate, and thus to encourage a reassessment of, the truth of her life. This is not to say that the fact of Æthelthryth's virginity was ever seriously challenged, although it very well may have been. Rather it is to argue that the burden of proving, quite literally, that nothing happened (nothing, that is, to change the status quo of virginity) forces hagiographers into a direct engagement with the problem of historical representation more generally: how to make present a disappearing field of ephemeral events. In this reading, Æthelthryth's scar doubly refers to an absence—the 'aperto et hiante uulnere' (open gaping wound)—not only in the sense that virginity itself is negatively defined as an absence of sexual contact, but also because these particular non-events occurred in the past. The scar itself serves to cover over, or to suture, but not to eradicate these double absences, since the presence of the scar is necessary to provoke an iteration of the narrative of its own creation, which, in turn, authenticates the existence of virginity and affirms the connection between past and present. Without the scar, the perfection of Æthelthryth's body could not be made manifest; with the scar, the reader is reminded that historical revision requires a type of intervention, and that it leaves a mark. In this respect, the scar is that which both heals and underscores the divide between past and present.

Although Ælfric's Æthelthryth is demonstrably less interesting than Bede's for not being scarred, a detail that Ælfric omits in his translation, the connection between the saint's uncorrupted body and a sense of English identity is overt in the later text.[16] In his life of St Edmund, another saint inflicted with a fatal neck wound that heals after death, Ælfric is provoked to observe how fortunate the English are in their saints:

---

14 '... instead of the open gaping wound which she had when she was buried, there now appeared, marvellous to relate, only the slightest traces of a scar' (HE 4.19).

15 He writes at the beginning of the chapter that, 'Nam etiam signum diuini miraculi, quo eiusdem feminae sepulta caro corrumpi non potuit, indicio est quia a uirili contactu incorrupta durauerit' (And the divine miracle whereby her flesh would not corrupt after she was buried was token and proof that she had remained uncorrupted by contact with any man).

16 Ælfric notes that, when the coffin was opened, '[þ]a wæs seo wund gehæled þe se læce worhte ær' (then was the wound healed that the doctor had made).

Nis angel-cynn bedæled drihtnes halgena
þonne on engla-landa licgaþ swilce halgan
swylce þæs halga cyning is and cuþberht se eadiga
and sancte æþeldryð on elig and eac hire swustor
ansunde on lichaman geleafan to trymminge
Synd eac fela oðre on angel-cynne halgan
þe fela wundra wyrcað swa swa hit wide is cuð.[17]

This catalogue of uncorrupted English saints, interwoven as it is with references to the English people and land (as well as, in the following part, anti-Semitic rhetoric), expresses the coherence of English identity, a nebulous and shifting concern, through the wholeness of the saintly body. To be English, according to Ælfric, is to have joint possession of a body of undecayed saints, the perfection of each of which embodies the finitude of the community in general and grounds its unique relationship to history and to the territory it occupies.

ST ERKENWALD: THE DISAPPEARING BODY

Drawing a comparison between Anglo-Saxon narratives of the life of Æthelthryth and the late fourteenth-century text St Erkenwald, and focusing especially on the ways that both invoke and produce the discourse of Englishness, might seem farfetched. While the texts concerned are in many respects very different, most problematic for the comparison would seem to be the lengthy period of time separating their composition. This long span is, however, explicitly addressed, indeed erased, by the Erkenwald-poet, who sets his narrative in late seventh-century Anglo-Saxon England, the moment and place inhabited also by St Æthelthryth. In fact, St Erkenwald was the direct contemporary of Æthelthryth, becoming bishop of London at almost exactly the time that she herself founded the monastery at Ely.[18] Although Erkenwald was an Anglo-Saxon, and his holiness was briefly recognized in Bede's Historia ecclesiastica, his saintly capital was not realized until the later medieval period, when he became an important figure associated with the influential cathedral church of St Paul's.[19] Whereas Æthelthryth was an Anglo-Saxon saint

---

[17] 'The English people is not deprived of God's saints, when in English-land lie such saints as this holy king and Cuthbert the blessed and Saint Æthelthryth in Ely and also her sister, whole in body as a confirmation of the faith. There are many other saints among the English people also who work many miracles, just as is widely known.'

[18] Erkenwald became bishop of London in 675/6 and died in 693 (Morse 1975: 13), whereas Æthelthryth founded the monastery at Ely in 672–3 and died in 679 (for a useful timeline of Æthelthryth's life, see Blanton 2007: 6).

[19] Bede's brief narrative of Erkenwald is given in HE 4. 6, and refers to the extraordinary holiness of his life; the miracles performed by the wood of the horse litter on which he used to be carried; and his founding of monasteries at Chertsey and Barking.

who was important to Anglo-Saxons, while Erkenwald was effectively a late medieval Anglo-Saxon saint, the episode related in *St Erkenwald* resonates with events in the life of Æthelthryth: both feature a miraculously preserved corpse that provokes its audience to meditate on the difficult role that the past plays in the instantiation of communal identity. While the similarity might seem to end at this point, the distinctive differences between the two post-mortem encounters are of equal interest in establishing how each configures this relation between the English and their past, and the role of sanctity in holding together this relation. By investigating these differences, the final section of this chapter will argue that *St Erkenwald* uses the uncorrupted body to provoke and model the experience of belonging to a group, first by offering a form of community in which collective reactions and behaviours are mediated by strong ecclesiastical leadership, and, second, by situating its protagonist within a uniquely English founding narrative that also functions as a commentary on an important current theological debate.

The plot of *St Erkenwald* needs little rehearsal. Despite its title, the text is more accurately to be described as a *miraculum* or *inventio* than a *vita*, revealing the sanctity of its protagonist through events that ostensibly occurred while he was alive.[20] During the renovation of St Paul's minster, dated in this text to the seventh century although it actually occurred during the mid-thirteenth to mid-fourteenth, workers find a remarkable marble tomb containing the incorrupt body of a strange man of aristocratic appearance. Despite consulting remembered and recorded history, authorities are unable to identify the man, and the subsequent mystery throws the public into a state of excited turmoil. Returning from a pastoral visit, Bishop Erkenwald prays all night for guidance and, in the morning, directly questions the corpse about its origins. Surprisingly, the bishop receives an answer and, in a long dialogue, learns that the body is that of a pagan judge who had lived during the reign of Belyn and Berynge, Geoffrey of Monmouth's Belinus and Brennius.[21] Because of the man's exceptional honesty and fairness during his life, the Lord caused his body to endure undecayed, even though his soul remained in hell since he had no knowledge of Christ and thus no possibility of salvation. In expressing how much he wished that the judge could achieve redemption, Erkenwald lets a tear fall upon the corpse's face, through which act his baptism becomes effective. The body then decays and crumbles away.

Unlike the life of Æthelthryth, then, the body at the centre of *St Erkenwald* is not that of the saint himself, even though everything about its discovery recalls the hagiographical genres of *inventio* and *translatio*.[22] The description of the marvellous

---

[20] For discussion of *St Erkenwald*'s position within the *miraculum* genre, see Whatley (1986: 330–1).

[21] Belinus and Brennius ruled some time after the founding of Rome, although Geoffrey of Monmouth provides no exact date. For background on these figures, see Morse (1975: 71–2). Whatley (1986: 349) dates the judge's lifetime to the first half of the 4th cent. BC.

[22] Otter (1996: 21–57) provides a helpful introduction to the medieval genre of *inventio*. As she observes, *inventiones* are often subsumed under the category of *translationes*, and thus have lacked specific attention from scholars (p. 21). While her study amply demonstrates the rewards of treating *inventiones* in particular, it is nonetheless the case that the first translation of saints inevitably muddies

tomb, with its close-fitting lid and archaic inscription, is reminiscent of the concern typically expressed in these genres with containment and labelling. Just as in Æthel-thryth's translation, the housing of the body in *St Erkenwald* is thus of especial importance, as is its incorrupt state when it is finally revealed:

> & als freshe hyn þe face & the fflesh nakyd
> Bi his eres & bi his hondes þat openly shewid,
> Wyt ronke rode as þe rose & two rede lippes
> As he in sounde sodanly were slippid opon slepe.[23]

In both texts, then, a 'mysterious tomb' is 'metonymically related ... to the unde-cayed body' it contains.[24] The body's accoutrements are described as 'unwemmyd' (ll. 96, 266), immaculate or untainted, just as Æthelthryth was herself preserved 'un-gewemmed mæden' (line 107, with variations of the word also used in 13, 18, 24 of Ælfric's version of her life) through the trial of her two marriages. In short, this scenario, in which an undecayed corpse is found encased in a well-appointed and labelled container, at first seems to ask its audience to respond as they would to such an encounter in a hagiographical context, where the incorruption of the body would be thought of as the material demonstration of sexual purity. Even the mixed characteristics of the corpse's appearance—with the crown and sceptre signifying a king, and the coif and miniver trim a judge (ll. 78–84)—does not preclude this reaction, since so many of England's early saints were of royal descent.

The excitation of the crowd in *St Erkenwald* mirrors the genre confusion provoked in the reader: the heightened mystery of the corpse positions both audiences as information-hungry onlookers, testing the boundaries of their preconceived notions about the meaning of preserved bodies. As with reactions to the much later 'freaks' of travelling shows, the 'meruayle' that is the corpse engenders a desire both to see and to know in its audience, a desire that acts centrifugally to unite the diverse compo-nents of the populace by bringing them together in space and time:

the boundaries between these two genres, since it is not always clear that a given individual is considered to be a saint before they have been unearthed. When Seaxburh orders Æthelthryth to be exhumed, for example, it seems likely that she hoped to find evidence of sanctity; the confirmation of this hope constituted a new discovery which, in turn, changed Æthelthryth's status. While Otter discusses how later accounts based on Bede's worked 'to approximate ... her successive *translations* to *inventions*' (pp. 31–2), it could be argued that such approximation was inherent in the details of Æthelthryth's narrative from its inception. The model for the *inventio* genre, as Otter explains (pp. 26–9), was the finding of St Stephen's body, as recorded in the *Revelatio Sancti Stephani*. While Bede knew this text (p. 29), Otter notes that 'it is not clear if the *Revelatio* was known to the English of the late Anglo-Saxon period' (p. 29). A brief account based on the *Revelatio*, however, appears under the entry for St Stephen in the *Old English Martyrology*, which was copied at least twice during the 11th cent., although it was composed much earlier (Rauer 2000).

[23] Lines 89–92: 'And his face, and the naked flesh that openly showed by his ears and hands, was completely fresh, with health as red as a rose and two red lips as if he, in a swoon, were suddenly slipped into sleep'. All quotations from the poem are drawn from Morse (1975), and are cited by line number. All translations are my own. The poem's metaphors of 'unlocking' and 'opening' have been noted and examined by Peck (1974: 16–17).

[24] Otter (1994: 410).

Quen tithynges token to þe toun of þe toumbe wonder
Mony hundrid hende men highid þider sone:
Burgeys boghit þerto, bedels and other,
& mony a mesters mon of maners dyuerse...
þer commen þider of all kynnes so kenely mony
þat as all þe worlde were þider walon wytin a honde quile.[25]

The discovery of the body thus breaks down social boundaries (although, interestingly, not gender divisions, since this audience is overwhelmingly masculine) to produce a wondering community, or quite literally a group whose differences are overwhelmed by a shared attitude of questioning: 'Bot þen wos wonder to wale on wehes þat stoden, / That myt not come to knowe a quotyse strange'.[26] As a number of commentators have observed, such unity in ignorance comes close to provoking civic discord, causing the cessation of work and, as men report it to Bishop Erkenwald, 'troubull in þe pepul' (l. 109).[27] While the conclusion of the poem, as Gordon Whatley has cogently argued, conservatively asserts the necessity of strong ecclesiastical leadership to discover the truth of the corpse and to restore social harmony, the text is nonetheless equally committed to exploring the potential of wondrous bodies to de- and then reinstall communal boundaries.[28] Importantly, this transgressive experience is also available to the reader, who experiences genre trouble of their own in response to the mixed signals surrounding the finding of the body.

Moreover, the spectacle involved in finding and interrogating the corpse is ultimately of the same type as that surrounding the cult of saints, which had a central function in testing and confusing boundaries of all kinds—for instance, those separating human and divine, the living and dead body, heaven and earth. As Christine Chism puts it, '[t]his corpse in its lovely and loving entombment at first bespeaks a forgotten past of wondrous alterity but grows increasingly and disquietingly familiar in the course of the conversation, eventually adumbrating to the bishop his own posthumous career as foundational relic'.[29] The startling originality of such a narrative move, which allows the relationship of relic and community to be explored discursively and at length, should be contrasted with Æthelthryth's life, in which she may speak 'after' her death only in words reported second-hand (when, in Bede's

[25] Lines 57–64: 'When news of the tomb wonder was taken to the town, many hundred noble men went there soon. Burgesses went there, messengers and others, and many a master's man of diverse modes of life... there came there of all kinds so very many that it was as if all the world were gathered there within a moment.' As Morse (1975: 39) observes, the 'crowd is a most important "character" in "St. Erkenwald"', and is depicted as an active participant in the encounter with the corpse. Morse also notes the significance of the words 'meruayle' and 'wonder', both of which could describe miracles and non-religious wonders (p. 40). As Morse describes it, the corpse is interpretatively assimilated from the latter to the former in the exchange between the Dean and Bishop in ll. 143–76.
[26] Lines 73–4: 'But then was wonder in abundance among the men that stood, who might not come to know a strange thing.' Morse translates these lines as, 'But then there was a wonder to think about for the men that stood there, who were not able to understand this strange thing' (1975: 67–8).
[27] Chism (2002: 47), for instance, notes that 'the Londoners lose their powers of speech and argument, dwindling from articulate unity to an avid mob desperately in need of governance'.
[28] Whatley (1986).
[29] Chism (2002: 41).

narrative, it is revealed that she welcomed her neck tumour as a punishment for the necklaces she wore during her life). At the same time, the movement that Chism describes—from extreme alterity to familiarity—marks the process of communal dis- and reintegration that is regularly effected by an encounter with a bodily relic.

In marked contrast to the life of Æthelthryth, the body in *St Erkenwald* does not endure past the conclusion of the text itself. Ostensibly, the disintegration of the judge's material form is connected to his salvation: 'ffor assone as þe soule was sesyd in blisse / Corrupt was þat oþir crafte þat couert þe bones' (for as soon as the soul was possessed of happiness, corrupt was that other structure that covered the bones). As much of the scholarship on *St Erkenwald* has explored, however, the disappearing body is also part of the work's lengthy investigation of the community of St Paul's relationship to its own past.[30] The poem begins with a statement that locates events securely in place, while communicating an ambiguous and overlapping sense of the time at which they occurred: 'At London in Englond not full long sythen, / Sythen Crist suffrid on crosse & Cristendome stablyd' (At London in England not very long ago, since Christ suffered on the cross and established Christendom; lines 1–2). The reference to the ultimate origin of the Christian faith is followed in lines 12–36 by a more specific articulation of how Augustine brought the religion to England, turning all the temples to churches and the idols to saints. This section ends by explicitly linking Augustine and Erkenwald, now the bishop of Augustine's former district (lines 33–6). Underpinning this specifically English narrative of religious origin is Gregory's famous injunction, reported in Bede's *Historia ecclesiastica*, that Augustine should superimpose Christianity on the existing structure of pagan observance, rather than making an entirely new beginning. This text makes a further super-imposition of its own, however, since the account of Erkenwald's meeting with the unbaptized pagan judge alludes to, even retells, that of Gregory's encounter with Trajan. This narrative—which itself seems to have been of English invention, first appearing in the Whitby life of Gregory—became the paradigmatic scenario by which to explore the question of the virtuous pagan during the Middle Ages. As Gordon Whatley has shown in a detailed study, the Middle English *St Erkenwald* conservatively suggests that redemption is possible for the pagan only if he is saved by ecclesiastical intervention of an almost accidental variety: Erkenwald apparently does not intend to baptize the judge, but mouths the formula and allows his tear to drop as he wishes that such an outcome were possible.[31] Importantly, therefore, Erkenwald does not believe that he could effect the baptism, which, in other versions of the legend, lent a problematic agency to the character of Gregory. Nor do the judge's own acts alone win him salvation, a possibility that is suggested in the *Piers Plowman*

---

[30] Longo (1987: 36), for instance, considers how 'the Londoners' confrontation with the body of the pagan judge and the chaos to which it leads form a kind of parable about the wages of historical ignorance', arguing that the poem as a whole is a working through of 'the recurrent thematic and ideological preoccupations that shape the British historiographical tradition'. Faigley (1978: 382) also addresses the poem's take on history, arguing that 'the anachronistic details in *St. Erkenwald* facilitate the blending of the specific historical foreground with the timeless background of providential design'.

[31] Whatley (1986).

version of the story. Instead the baptism is represented as resulting from God's mercy, properly channelled through the ministers of his Church: according to Gordon Whatley, 'the poet of *St. Erkenwald* has neatly turned Gregory's famous act of saintly individualism and defiance of orthodoxy into a canonical gesture of humility and dependence on liturgical access to divine aid and inspiration'.[32]

Erkenwald's meeting with the pagan judge at the centre of the poem therefore makes material, writes as a bodily encounter, what the narrative itself implicitly performs: an assimilation of the past as distinctively English. Erkenwald geographically and narratively occupies the place of Augustine and Gregory, the two most significant figures in the conversion of the English. His own treatment of the judge brings the pagan past of the island into the present and allows it to be claimed through retroactive baptism. At the same time, Erkenwald, in acting the part of Gregory, is presented as a more perfect emissary of God's will, and the text as a whole therefore redeems and disambiguates, from an ecclesiastical perspective, this paradigmatic account of the status of the virtuous pagan. That it does so by setting the narrative on English soil and by giving it an English protagonist is a statement of the significance of the island's religious history, and its imbrication in contemporary theological debates. But, as Christine Chism observes, the disappearance of the pagan's body is but one sign that such assimilation of the past, especially in the construction of an ethnic history, can never be entire: as she puts it, the absence of the corpse marks 'the gaping fissure of a still not quite known past'.[33] Like Æthelthryth's scar, another type of 'gaping fissure', the judge's disappearing body thus references the problematic necessity of continuously rehearsing the past in the construction of an identity like Englishness.

ÆTHELTHRYTH AND ERKENWALD: LOCAL OR ENGLISH SAINTS?

As Monika Otter points out, *inventiones*, and indeed *translationes*, are generally produced in periods of stress or growth for monastic communities, since such texts work to verify (or rather provide) the historical origins of contemporary institutional relationships and structures.[34] Both saints that I have examined here are firmly embedded in such local contexts of production. Monika Otter, Mechtild Gretsch, and, most recently and comprehensively, Virginia Blanton, have provided detailed analyses showing that St Æthelthryth's popularity was largely a product of the Benedictine reform period, when Bishop Æthelwold reinvigorated the cult at

---

[32] Ibid. 340.
[33] Chism (2002: 65).
[34] Otter (1996: 21).

Ely.[35] Christine Chism, in her work on *St Erkenwald*, has similarly elucidated the ties between that work and its late fourteenth-century context, arguing that the poem 'works to quell assertions of civic and religious agency from London laity'.[36] The veneration of both saints is therefore limited in distinctive ways, and especially by geographical and ecclesiastical context. Even though the texts associated with Æthelthryth seem to have had a much wider readership during the Anglo-Saxon period than that later garnered by *St Erkenwald*, the many material artefacts associated with the female saint, which have been catalogued by Virginia Blanton, are still of limited geographical extent.[37] Legitimately, then, it should be asked to what degree texts associated with these saints can be thought of as promoting Englishness, rather than the regional or ecclesiastical identities with which they are most closely associated.

Even though their immediate energies may be being harnessed by their authors in the service of local identity formation, these texts bear a fascinating relation to Englishness precisely because they promote and develop the type of thinking necessary to uphold such a concept. The urge to produce discourse about particular saints will likely be, as Otter observed, contingent on local circumstances, but the significance of such discourse is not solely constrained by those circumstances. Narratives of incorrupt saints, in particular, serve to triangulate concerns with history and with integrity that are of import in the formation of English, and not just local, community. The authors of these narratives often intimate the broader import of what they are writing, as, for example, in the nationalistic diversion—or perhaps more aptly, outburst—that I described in Ælfric's life of Edmund above. For Ælfric, writing about St Edmund inevitably recalls Æthelthryth, her sister, Cuthbert, and all the glory of England's undecayed saints, their wholeness embedded in, and metonymic of, the integrity of the English themselves. Although *St Erkenwald* makes no such explicit tie between the body of the judge and England's incorrupt saints, much of the interest of the text is drawn from the challenge that it poses to previous insular narratives of incorrupt saints, its affinity with which the reader must recognize in order fully to understand *Erkenwald*. Undecayed saints—like, but perhaps more so than, other types of saints—therefore provoke a type of canonical thinking that is advantageous to the production of community because it specifically fuses the historical and geographical register. As a group, incorrupt saints recall each other, and thus the passage of time between their lives; but they also, in their affinity and their endurance in certain places, supersede their temporal location and insist on the present-ness of any community identification that they call forth. The question of presence and absence, which I have repeatedly returned to here in the figure of Æthelthryth's scar and the judge's disappearing body, relates to this friable nature of any group identification based upon a common history, which must continuously be rehearsed

---

[35] Otter (1997); Gretsch (2005); Blanton (2007).   [36] Chism (2002: 42).

[37] Whatley (1986: 361) notes of *St. Erkenwald* that, 'the poet was moving against the tide. The poem was by no means a popular success, and it had no discernible impact on the cult literature of St. Erkenwald. There is only one manuscript copy, and little indication that many intermediate copies separate it from the original.' Blanton (2002) catalogues medieval representations of St Æthelthryth.

in order for its valence to be felt. The impresarios of such saints' cults thus adeptly manipulated visual access to the bodies in their keeping, knowing that this was the only way for such bodies to keep their promise and to remain always emergent.

BIBLIOGRAPHY

ANDERSON, BENEDICT (1983, 1991), *Imagined Communities: Reflections on the Origin and Spread of Nationalism* (rev. edn. London: Verso).

BLANTON, VIRGINIA (2007), *Signs of Devotion: the Cult of St. Æthelthryth in Medieval England, 695–1615* (University Park, Pa.: Pennsylvania State University Press).

BLANTON-WHETSELL, VIRGINIA (2002*a*), 'Imagines Ætheldredae: Mapping Hagiographic Representations of Abbatial Power and Religious Patronage', *Studies in Iconography*, 23: 55–107.

——(2002*b*), 'Tota Integra, tota incorrupta: The Shrine of St. Æthelthryth as Symbol of Monastic Autonomy', *Journal of Medieval and Early Modern Studies*, 32: 227–67.

BROWN, PETER (1981), *The Cult of the Saints: Its Rise and Function in Latin Christianity* (Chicago: University of Chicago Press).

CHISM, CHRISTINE (2002), *Alliterative Revivals* (Philadelphia: University of Pennsylvania Press).

CLANCHY, M. T. (1993), *From Memory to Written Record: England 1066–1307* (2nd edn. Oxford: Blackwell).

COHEN, JEFFREY JEROME (ed.) (2000), *The Postcolonial Middle Ages* (New York: Palgrave).

COLGRAVE, BERTRAM, and R. A. B. MYNORS (eds.) (1969), *Bede's Ecclesiastical History of the English People* (Oxford: Clarendon Press).

DAVIS, KATHLEEN (1998), 'National Writing in the Ninth Century: A Reminder for Postcolonial Thinking about the Nation', *Journal of Medieval and Early Modern Studies*, 28: 611–37.

——(2000), 'Time Behind the Veil: The Media, the Middle Ages, and Orientalism Now', in Jeffrey Jerome Cohen (ed.), *The Postcolonial Middle Ages* (New York: Palgrave), 105–22.

——(2004), 'Hymeneal Alogic: Debating Political Community in *The Parliament of Fowls*', in Kathy Lavezzo (ed.), *Imagining a Medieval English Nation* (Minneapolis: University of Minnesota Press), 161–87.

FAIGLEY, LESTER (1978), 'Typology and Justice in *St. Erkenwald*', *American Benedictine Review*, 29: 381–90.

FORDE, SIMON, LESLEY JOHNSON, and ALAN V. MURRAY (eds.) (1995), *Concepts of National Identity in the Middle Ages* (Leeds: Leeds Studies in English).

GRETSCH, MECHTHILD (2005), *Ælfric and the Cult of Saints in Late Anglo-Saxon England* (Cambridge: Cambridge University Press).

GRIFFITHS, GWEN (1992), 'Reading Ælfric's Saint Æthelthryth as a Woman', *Parergon*, 10: 35–49.

HARRIS, STEPHEN (2003), *Race and Ethnicity in Anglo-Saxon Literature* (New York and London: Routledge).

——(2008), 'An Overview of Race and Ethnicity in Pre-Norman England', *Literature Compass*, 5: 740–54.

HEFFERNAN, THOMAS J. (1988), *Sacred Biography: Saints and their Biographers in the Middle Ages* (Oxford: Oxford University Press).

HORNER, SHARI (2001), *The Discourse of Enclosure: Representing Women in Old English Literature* (Albany, NY: State University of New York Press).

INGHAM, PATRICIA CLARE, and MICHELLE R. WARREN (eds.) (2003), *Postcolonial Moves: Medieval through Modern* (New York: Palgrave Macmillan).

KABIR, ANANYA JAHANARA, and DEANNE WILLIAMS (eds.) (2005), *Postcolonial Approaches to the European Middle Ages: Translating Cultures* (Cambridge: Cambridge University Press).

KARKOV, CATHERINE (2005), 'The Body of St Æthelthryth: Desire, Conversion and Reform in Anglo-Saxon England', in Martin Carver (ed.), *The Cross Goes North: Processes of Conversion in Northern Europe, AD 300–1300* (Woodbridge: Boydell), 397–411.

LAVEZZO, KATHY (ed.) (2004), *Imagining a Medieval English Nation* (Minneapolis: University of Minnesota Press).

LONGO, JOHN (1987), 'The Vision of History in St. Erkenwald', *In geardagum*, 8: 35–51.

MORSE, RUTH (ed.) (1975), *Saint Erkenwald* (Cambridge: D. S. Brewer).

Ó CARRAGÁIN, ÉAMONN (2005), *Ritual and the Rood: Liturgical Images and the Old English Poems of the* Dream of the Rood *Tradition* (London and Toronto: British Library and University of Toronto Press).

OTTER, MONIKA (1994), ' "New Werke": *St Erkenwald*, St. Albans and the Medieval Sense of the Past', *Journal of Medieval and Renaissance Studies*, 24: 387–414.

——(1996), *Inventiones: Fiction and Referentiality in Twelfth-Century English Historical Writing* (Chapel Hill, NC: University of North Carolina Press).

——(1997), 'The Temptation of St. Æthelthryth', *Exemplaria*, 9: 139–63.

PECK, RUSSELL (1974), 'Number Structure in St. Erkenwald', *Annuale mediaevale*, 14: 9–21.

PULSIANO, PHILLIP (1999), 'Blessed Bodies: The Vitae of Anglo-Saxon Female Saints', *Parergon*, 16: 1–42.

RAUER, CHRISTINE (2000), 'The Sources of the *Old English Martyrology*: Stephen', *Fontes Anglo-Saxonici: World Wide Web Register*, <http://fontes.english.ox.ac.uk/> (accessed Nov. 2008).

SKEAT, WALTER W. (ed.) (1881–5), *Ælfric's Lives of Saints* (EETS OS 82; London: Oxford University Press).

STOCK, BRIAN (1983), *The Implications of Literacy: Written Language and Models of Interpretation in the Eleventh and Twelfth Centuries* (Princeton: Princeton University Press).

TURVILLE-PETRE, THORLAC (1996), *England the Nation: Language, Literature, and National Identity, 1290–1340* (Oxford: Clarendon Press).

WHATLEY, GORDON (1986), 'Heathens and Saints: *St. Erkenwald* in its Legendary Context', *Speculum*, 61: 330–63.

PART VI

....

LITERARY PLACE, SPACE, AND TIME

....

CHAPTER 26

REGIONS AND COMMUNITIES

HELEN FULTON

A SINGLE NATION?

If there is one century we can point to as the time when the idea of England began to take on its modern form, it would be the thirteenth. Though a centralized monarchy emerged in the late Anglo-Saxon period, impelled by the ambitions of the West Saxon dynasty and its powerful kings, the notion of a politically unified territory called England, with Wales, Scotland, and Ireland as its subaltern states, assumed an identifiable shape in the thirteenth century.

This manifestation of what might be called the consciousness of nationhood began with the loss of Normandy in 1204 and an inevitable reconsideration of what 'England' now meant, cut off from many of the French and Norman territories to which it had been seamlessly joined for a century and a half. Later in the thirteenth century, the wars of Edward I with Wales and Scotland precipitated revisions to these political boundaries, along with a growing acknowledgement of Scotland's claim to be an independent kingdom. In the person of the king, buttressed by an evolving system of central bureaucracy and taxation, England had a figurehead whose wars with the 'other'—whether Welsh, Scottish, or French—served to define what was 'England' and what was 'foreign'. A dramatic increase in the number of towns during the thirteenth century, most of them new foundations initiated by local magnates, resulted in improved communication and transport systems, by road and river, which brought different parts of the country into greater contact with each other. The rise of parliament, with its centralized meetings and control of supply to the royal budget, brought barons, knights, and merchants together to speak on behalf of the *communitas regni*, the 'community of the realm', as a single unit.[1]

Developments such as these helped to create the idea of England as a single nation, geographically, politically, and cognitively. More than that, by the end of the thirteenth century England was defined as the place where English people—as opposed to Welsh or Scottish people—lived. Across the borders of Wales and Scotland, there arose 'a defensive sense of identity that was embedded in history and myth, and in a lingering hostility to England and the English'.[2] Yet the English Crown used ancient tradition, codified by historians such as Geoffrey of Monmouth, to claim authority over the whole island, and over much of Ireland, equating the kingdom and nation of England with the geographical map of Britain and Ireland, as if the two things were the same. Edward I was the first of a series of medieval English kings to use the figure of Arthur as a symbolic ancestor whose reign over a single kingdom of Britain could be used to justify royal claims to a nation of England which stood for the whole of Britain. Pierre de Langtoft, that well-known apologist for English nationalism, wrote in about 1300, following the success of Edward I against the Scots in 1296, 'Ore sunt les insulanes trestuz assemblez / Et Albanye rejoynte' (Now are the islanders all joined together, and Albany reunited),[3] eliding cultural, political, and linguistic divisions which were still very much in place. He went on to assert that 'Arthur ne avayt unkes si plainement les fez' (Arthur never held the fiefdoms [of Britain, Scotland and Ireland] as fully [as Edward]).[4] But, as Max Lieberman has pointed out, 'What Edward I presided over towards the end of his reign was an English empire in the British Isles'—that is, an English state which exerted a colonial rule over its possessions in Wales, Scotland, and Ireland.[5]

Paradoxically, those same developments towards a central state apparatus in England worked to entrench the existence of local communities, which made the medieval map of Britain into a jigsaw of interconnecting regions. These regions, many of them based on the old Anglo-Saxon kingdoms, maintained their own identities, articulated through linguistic diversity, local administration, and feudal ties to local magnates. The rapidly growing towns, with their protectionist legislation excluding non-citizens and 'aliens' from even a few miles away, fostered a keen sense among their inhabitants of a primary identification with a town rather than with a nation. Towns, especially the larger and more prosperous boroughs, attracted a hinterland of rural settlements to form an economic community within a shire. Parliament itself, though part of the centralized administration, was an assembly of local representatives who spoke for their region or town. The entire system of central administration operated by the Crown was inseparable from the processes of regional

---

[1] Wickson (1970: 3).
[2] Griffiths (2003: 181).
[3] Wright (1866–8: ii. 264).
[4] Ibid. 266.
[5] Lieberman (2008: 85).

government managed by local officials who were in constant (if reluctant) dialogue with the centre.

What this indicates is that, although a growing sense of nationalism relating to England can undoubtedly be traced from at least the thirteenth century, it is just as true that a sense of regionalism in England, Wales, and Scotland remained a powerful source of political and cultural identity throughout the Middle Ages and well into the period of the nation-state in Europe. Throughout Britain, the region pre-dated the kingdom as a unit of socio-political organization and identity, and as the English monarchy grew ever more autonomous, only nominally answerable to either pope or emperor, its power continued to rest on its economic and administrative relationships with the regions. To the concept of region we should add that of community, as an equally significant aspect of the medieval—and indeed the modern—social order. Whereas 'region' defines a geographical area, 'community' refers to a sense of common social and cultural identity which resists the territorialism of either nation or region. Communities can be based on place, but also on class, occupation, age, gender, religion, language, or a combination of any of these. The communities of the shires, towns, and manors formed the bedrock of the community of the realm.

WALES AND SCOTLAND AS 'REGIONS' OF THE ENGLISH KINGDOM

The definition of England as a geographical and territorial space was cemented in the thirteenth century by the fixing of its borders with Wales and Scotland. England was defined not only in terms of itself—its shires, manors, towns, and cities—but also in terms of what was 'other' than itself, the quasi-nations to its west and north. The cartographic borders of Scotland and Wales are effectively modern creations, designed to separate economic and political jurisdictions within a state-based government. In the Middle Ages, the borders were fluctuating areas of land, the 'Marches', which were linked on both sides by manorial estates whose Anglo-Norman owners scarcely thought of themselves, let alone their land, as English, Welsh, or Scottish. Early maps of the island of Britain, such as those drawn by or for Matthew Paris as part of his Latin chronicles, the *Chronica Majora*, the *Historia Anglorum*, and the *Abbreviatio Chronicorum*, mark the border between England and Scotland as being virtually the same as its modern political border along the Solway–Tweed line. Wales is less clearly distinguished; in one map, 'Wales, which lacks a convenient eastern boundary, is cunningly cut off by a four-line rubric giving the dimensions of England'.[6] Scotland, with its own line of kings, was eventually granted independent

---

[6] Turville-Petre (1996: 2).

territorial status, while the status of Wales, problematic since the Anglo-Saxon settlements, remained unresolved until the Acts of Union in the reign of Henry VIII.

Under the Normans, the Marches of Wales and Scotland enjoyed considerable autonomy from central royal control, but the price of independence was the political instability and constant warfare of a frontier zone. A specifically English ideology constructed through the discourses of history and chorography, from Gerald of Wales through Ranulph Higden's *Polychronicon* of *c*.1340 to William Camden's *Britannia* of 1586, regarded Scotland and Ireland as countries which were outlying regions of the English kingdom, even though Scotland at any rate had its own monarchy. For Tudor historians such as Raphael Holinshed (d. *c*.1580), Wales and Cornwall had little more status than English counties; the former having been formally incorporated into England by the Act of Union of 1536; Holinshed's famous chronicle of 1577 was called *Chronicles of England, Scotland and Ireland*, with Wales included as part of England.

Regionalism in medieval Scotland was shaped by border warfare, by the system of sheriffdoms (borrowed from the English shire system), by urban centres, or 'burghs',[7] and by the survival of a Gaelic and British tribalism combined with Norman manorialism. But there was another aspect of regionalism in Scotland which was more profound than the impact of warfare or urbanism, and that was the distinction between the 'highlands' and 'lowlands'. Retaining a significant linguistic and political legacy from its Gaelic and Norse past, much of the highland zone, above the Clyde–Forth line, was relatively unaffected by Norman settlement and its attendant urbanization. While the whole of Scotland had been involved in the wars of independence in the late thirteenth and fourteenth centuries, the recognition of Scottish independence by the English Crown failed to create a single national identity, but rather entrenched a growing awareness of cultural separation between the two regions. By the fourteenth century, Gaelic was losing status against English which, as in England itself, was gaining prestige over French and Latin. At around the same time, the Highlanders began to be perceived, by the Scots themselves, as a lawless and violent people: in 1369 the Scottish parliament decreed that 'for the pacification and rule of the higher regions' the major landowners in the Highlands should take responsibility for keeping the peace within their estates.[8]

To Scottish writers of the fourteenth and fifteenth centuries, the Highlanders seemed uncivilized, with their Gaelic speech, rural economy, and unpolished behaviour. The first surviving coherent history of Scotland, the *Chronica gentis Scotorum*, 'Chronicles of the Scottish People', written by John of Fordun and completed by *c*.1387, reiterates the independence of Scotland from the very beginning of its history.[9] Yet, even while celebrating Scottish freedom and cultural identity through anti-English rhetoric, Fordun also separates out the Highlanders as a race apart:

[7] Ewan (1990); Whyte (1995).
[8] Grant (1984: 203).
[9] Broun (2007: 215).

The people of the coast [that is, the lowlands] are of domestic and civilized habits, trusty, patient, and urbane, decent in their attire, affable, and peaceful, devout in Divine worship, yet always prone to resist a wrong at the hands of their enemies. The highlanders and people of the islands, on the other hand, are a savage and untamed nation, rude and independent, given to rapine, ease-loving, of a docile and warm disposition, comely in person, but unsightly in dress, hostile to the English people and language, and, owing to diversity of speech, even to their own nation, and exceedingly cruel.[10]

This colonialist portrait of the Highlanders as unsophisticated natives needing the government of a superior power is echoed by other writers, such as the poet William Dunbar (*c*.1460–1515). In the 'Dance of the Seven Deadly Sins', the sleeping poet sees a vision of hell, presided over by 'Mahoun' (Muhammad) who is a synonym for the devil:

Than cryd Mahoun for a heleand padyane:
Syne ran a feynd to feche Makfadyane,
    Far northwart in a nuke.
Be he the correnoch had done schout
Erschemen so gadderit him abowt,
    In hell grit rowme thay tuke.
Thae tarmegantis with tag and tatter
Full lowd in Ersche begowth to clatter
    And rowp lyk revin and ruke.
The devill sa devit wes with thair yell
That in the depest pot of hell
    He smorit thame with smuke.[11]

Then Mahoun called for a highland pageant: Sin sent a fiend to fetch Macfadyean, far northwards in a corner. When the call had gone out, Highlanders gathered around him, taking up a lot of room in hell. Those termagants in rags and tatters began to clatter in Erse and to croak like ravens and rooks. The devil was so deafened by their yelling that in the deepest pit of hell he smothered them with smoke.

The name 'Macfadyean' represents a sort of generic, and somewhat comic, High-lander, but it is also the name of a fictional traitor celebrated in the 1470s minstrel poem about William Wallace and his campaign against the English in 1297–1305.[12] By association, then, Highlanders are implicitly targeted as traitors to Scotland, a crime only intensified by their barbaric speech, the 'Erse', or Gaelic, which sets them apart from the English-speaking lowlanders: 'Was thou noucht of oure Inglisch all the lycht?' ('Were you not the leading light of our English?'), says Dunbar of Chaucer.[13]

Even more than Scotland and England, medieval Wales was a country of regions and communities. Lacking any kind of centralized government or political autonomy (unlike Scotland with its line of kings), its people nevertheless sustained a powerful sense of national identity based on a quasi-mythological history of Welsh sovereignty held by their British ancestors over the whole of the island of Britain. It was precisely

[10] Skene and Skene (1872: 2.9).
[11] Tasioulas (1999: 308).
[12] Brown (2004: 188); Tasioulas (1999: 738).
[13] Tasioulas (1999: 529).

this ancient tradition of a pre-Saxon British sovereignty that the medieval Norman and English kings appropriated to create a hybrid British-English nationhood. In tandem with their acute sense of Welshness, located in their language and in their common British past, the Welsh people identified themselves most strongly with their local region, the ancient territorial lands of independent kings and princes whose dynasties were constantly at war. The main territorial divisions of Wales were Gwynedd in the north, Powys to the east, and Deheubarth in the south; within these provinces, as Gerald of Wales described in his *Itinerary* of 1188, were smaller regions such as Dyfed and Ceredigion in the south-west and Morgannwg and Brycheiniog in the south-east. Each region had its own origin myths, its own traditional ancestors and dynasties, its own sense of place in the early history of Britain.

The most significant, and symbolically potent, border between Wales and England was Offa's Dyke. Motivated by military defence strategy, the eighth-century king of Mercia built an earthwork boundary stretching 150 miles along the eastern edge of Wales, from the Wye estuary to the Dee estuary, and although the exact length of Offa's Dyke in its original form is a matter of debate,[14] both Welsh and English regarded it as the *de facto* Welsh border, at once topographical and symbolic. Gerald of Wales recognized it as such in the twelfth century when he wrote in his *Description of Wales*: 'King Offa . . . by a long and extensive dyke separated the British from the English'.[15] Medieval Welsh law texts refer to 'Clawdd Offa' (Offa's Dyke) as the acknowledged boundary between Wales and England,[16] and it formed the basis of the political border between Wales and the western counties of England when this was officially determined by the Act of Union of 1536.[17] In modern Welsh usage Clawdd Offa continues to signify an entire set of historical, cultural, and political mythemes about relations between Welsh and English.[18]

Apart from Offa's Dyke, the borders between Wales and England were marked by traditional topographical features, mainly rivers: the Dee estuary in the north, bordering with Cheshire, the River Severn in the south, and the River Wye in the south-east. Moreover, the formation of shires and hundreds in Mercia and Wessex during the tenth century helped to establish jurisdictional and quasi-political borders with Wales. But, despite these topographical and conventional boundaries, the March of medieval Wales remained a contested territory more or less until the Acts of Union in the early sixteenth century. The possibility of fixing a definitive political boundary between Wales and England was dependent on a clear sense of unitary nationhood emanating either from the Welsh or from the English, and before 1066 such a sense was not clearly formulated in either country. Wales may have had an awareness of a shared history and language but it was politically very fragmented and internally quarrelsome. On the other side of the border, the central authority of the

---

[14] Lieberman (2008: 77).
[15] Thorpe (1978): *Description*, 2. 7.
[16] Davies (1987: 3).
[17] Fox (1940).
[18] Jones and Fowler (2007); Rosser (2008).

late Saxon kings was undermined by the presence of the Scandinavians and the ensuing power struggles. Any hopes of further progress towards a more clearly articulated English nationalism were postponed by the arrival of the Normans.

Awarded large grants of land along the Welsh borders by William I, the first generation of Norman barons lost no time in expanding their estates into Wales while removing them, as far as possible, from the central control of the English Crown. What they created were virtually independent Marcher lordships, straddling the two countries and answerable to their Norman rulers. By the middle of the thirteenth century, despite some successful challenges by the Welsh in the previous century, about forty of these Marcher lordships had been established along the eastern border of Wales and right along the south coast into Pembrokeshire.[19] As the central apparatus of the English kingdom became institutionalized during the thirteenth century, the Marcher lordships held on to their political autonomy, exercising what they claimed to be a traditional right to fiscal and judicial independence.[20] The Marcher lords sometimes adopted the machinery of English administration—Glamorgan, for example, functioned as a shire with its own sheriff from 1102—but any such county officials reported to the seigneurial lord and not, as elsewhere in England and Scotland, to the King.[21] A reference in the Magna Carta to the Marcher lordships as separate jurisdictions reveals the extent to which their independence was accepted as a traditional right by the Anglo-Norman kings.[22]

After 1284 and the Edwardian conquest of north Wales—that is, the non-Normanized areas of *pura Wallia*, or native Wales—there was no further expansion of the Marcher lordships. Between 1284 and the Acts of Union, Wales was divided between the Marcher lordships to the south and east, and the Principality to the north and west, comprising the native Welsh regions of Gwynedd, Anglesey, Meirionydd, and most of Ceredigion. (It is intriguing to note that following the Welsh Assembly elections of May 2007, the area held largely by the Plaid Cymru national party can be mapped almost exactly onto the area of the medieval Principality.[23]) In the Principality, now wholly under the rule of the English Crown, the system of shires and hundreds, already adopted by the Marcher lordships, was formally imposed and the border areas became increasingly multicultural. English colonists settled on the Welsh side of the border to populate the newly established towns in north Wales, ensuring the economic marginalization of the native Welsh, while sizeable numbers of Welsh continued to live in the areas around Hereford, Shropshire, and Cheshire. The geographically wild and mysterious landscape traversed by Sir Gawain in *Sir Gawain and the Green Knight* represents an English view of the Welsh side of the border, to the west of Chester.

[19] Lieberman (2008: 1).
[20] Davies (1978: 217 ff.).
[21] Ibid. 200.
[22] Lieberman (2008: 61).
[23] BBC News website (2007).

The March lived on as a hybrid territory, politically anomalous, whose identity and autonomy, according to Max Lieberman, merely delayed the development of the English kingdom into a unified state.[24] This transition was finally achieved with the Acts of Union passed in 1536 and 1542. Conventionally regarded by modern historians of Wales as anti-Welsh legislation, the main effect of the Acts was to destroy the Marcher lordships and therefore to unify Wales into something close to a single nation (albeit one subordinate to England), for the first time in its recorded history. The old Marcher lordships in the east were absorbed into the existing English counties along the border; the southern lordships were reconfigured as the new counties of Pembrokeshire, Glamorgan, and Montgomeryshire. Wales had become a nation, but not a state.

Medieval Wales was primarily a land of identifiable regions and communities, many of them based on ancient land divisions which long pre-dated the English system of shires and hundreds. While Welsh chroniclers and poets celebrated the land of Wales as the remnant of British sovereignty, it was the region—*gwlad*, 'country', or *bro*, 'local district'—which was most consistently evoked as the source of patriotism and identity. In the twelfth century, the court poet Hywel ab Owain Gwynedd (d. 1170), himself a prince of north Wales, celebrated his region in a triumphant listing of its virtues:

> Caraf ei milwyr a'i meirch hywedd,
> A'i choed a'i chedyrn a'i chyfannedd.
> Caraf ei meysydd a'i mân feillion anaw
> Myn yd gafas ffaw ffyrf orfoledd.
> Caraf ei brooedd, braint hywredd,
> A'i diffaith mawrfaith a'i marannedd.[25]

I love its soldiers and its trained horses, and its forests and its brave men and its homesteads. I love its fields with their covering of little clover, where honour was given a firm triumph. I love its regions, entitlement of valour, and its wide wastelands and its wealth.

These words were echoed in the late fifteenth century by Guto'r Glyn who, introducing a praise-poem to Sir Rhys ap Tomas of Abermarlais (Carmarthenshire), a man who fought with Henry Tudor on Bosworth field, commends the *gwlad*, the 'country' or region which produced him:

> Caraf urddol Caerfyrddin,
> Cerir gwalch caer aur a gwin.
> Cerais (Paham nas carwn?)
> Cariad deheuwlad yw hwn.[26]

I love distinguished Carmarthen, its hawk, castle, gold and wine are loved. I loved it, and why wouldn't I? It is the love of the southern region.

---

[24] Lieberman (2008: 82).
[25] Parry (1962: 26).
[26] Williams (1939: 263).

SHIRE AND PARISH

On the eve of the Norman Conquest, 'England was one of the best-developed monarchies and probably the wealthiest in Western Europe',[27] financed by various forms of land tax, the *geld*, levied on estates throughout the country. In addition to the centralized tax system, there was a parallel system of devolved administrative and judicial authority initiated by the West Saxon kings as early as the seventh century and rolled out steadily across the country as the centralized monarchy emerged. Taken over by William the Conqueror and his sons and strengthened by the medieval kings, this essentially Anglo-Saxon system of organization has survived in a recognizable form up until the present day. This is the system of shires, with the shire defined variously as 'a unit held together by proximity, by local feeling and above all by common living traditions and common responsibilities',[28] or more functionally as 'manageable units of local administration for military, fiscal and judicial purposes'.[29]

The shire, or county, was one of the most significant building blocks of regional and cultural identity in medieval Britain. As West Saxon political power grew, former kingdoms, including Kent, Sussex, and Essex, were reconfigured into shires. The kingdom of Mercia was subdivided into the counties of Gloucester, Hereford, Worcester, Warwick, Shropshire, and Cheshire. The former kingdom of East Anglia reverted to its older subdivisions of Norfolk and Suffolk. The counties of Leicester, Nottingham, Derby, and Lincoln were restructured from areas of the Danelaw, whose *burhs* became the administrative centres of the shires, while Bedford, Cambridge, Huntingdon, Northampton, and Buckingham emerged around borough towns fortified during the Anglo-Saxon campaigns against the Danish.[30] Further north, the shires of York, Lancashire, Westmorland, and Cumbria were less clearly defined until the twelfth century, when Henry II mapped out the shires and strengthened them as the basic units of government. In 1157, he retrieved the northern counties of Cumbria, Westmorland, and Northumberland from the Scots and thus fixed the boundary between England and Scotland.

Governed by *ealdormen* in the tenth and early eleventh centuries, the shires were taken over by William the Conqueror as earldoms for his most powerful followers. Administrative management of each shire was devolved to a royal official, the sheriff (from 'shire-reeve'), who was appointed by the King and was in constant communication with central government, so that a 'web of bureaucracy stretched from Westminster throughout the land'.[31] Each shire was subdivided into hundreds and vills (small settlements), with borough towns emerging from the tenth century as royal estates managed by a reeve. It was these units of space—the shires, hundreds,

---

[27] Loyn (1991: 75).
[28] H. Cam, cited in Genet (1981: 19).
[29] Loyn (1991: 79).
[30] Jewell (1972: 43).
[31] Turville-Petre (1996: 8).

vills, and boroughs—which William I accounted for in his Domesday Book, so that he would know exactly where his revenues were coming from, and how much they should be. Of the participants who gave evidence to the Domesday commissioners, by far the largest number were 'men of the hundred'.[32]

Within each shire, the sheriff and his staff were directly answerable to the King, financially and judicially. Before 1066, the *geld* was levied on each shire as a sum accumulated from its hundreds. After the Conquest, the sheriff was responsible for collecting rents and taxes for the whole shire on behalf of the King.[33] County courts, established in the tenth century, continued to hold local sessions after the Norman Conquest, supplemented by circuits made by royal justices as a higher court or court of appeal. Most importantly, the county court, held in a magnate's castle or in the leading borough town of the region, was a meeting point for the local population, the place where assemblies were held, local officials appointed and representatives to parliament elected.

The growth of parliament during the thirteenth century was one of the most significant factors in the entrenchment of regional identities in England and Wales. When the King summoned a parliament, he requested a number of 'discreet knights' and citizens from each county to attend the court at Westminster, as in this writ of 1275 for the first parliament of Edward I:

Edward, by the grace of God king of England, lord of Ireland, and duke of Aquitaine, to the sheriff of Middlesex greeting. Whereas, for certain particular reasons, we have prorogued our general parliament at London with our prelates and other magnates of our realm until the morrow of the Sunday after Easter next; we command you that you summon to the same place, on the morrow of the Sunday after Easter aforesaid, four knights from your county of those more discreet in the law, and likewise from each city, borough and trading town of your bailiwick six or four citizens, burgesses, or other good men, to consider, along with the magnates of your kingdom, the affairs of the said kingdom.[34]

The business of electing the county representatives to attend parliament was devolved to the sheriff of each county, and later to the mayor of borough towns. Magnates, owners of large manorial estates in particular counties, represented royal authority in their regions and influenced the appointment of the permanent staff of county officials, particularly the sheriff, escheator (responsible for lands which had escheated to the King due to failure of heirs or forfeit), and commissioners of the peace.

These county offices were generally filled by members of the local gentry, including 'knights of the shire', who were clients of particular magnates; appointments to county offices were based on patronage and the exercise of power on a number of levels, from Crown to magnates to gentry. Although administrative power was devolved to the shires, the King and his magnates could impose their authority on any region through the appointment of suitable county officials.[35] Thus the

<hr>

[32] Fleming (1998).
[33] Jewell (1972: 44).
[34] Stubbs (1913: 441–2); tr. Stephenson and Marcham (1937: 153–4).
[35] Virgoe (1981: 73).

magnates, representatives of feudal authority, were part of the 'community of the realm' but were not necessarily regarded as part of the 'community of the shire'. The gentry, on the other hand, had to navigate the geopolitical terrain of the shire while remaining mindful of the need to retain the patronage of the upper aristocracy—a preoccupation constantly in the minds of the Paston family of the fifteenth century and articulated in their letters.

Parallel to the secular divisions of the shires and hundreds lay another system of regional organization, that of the parish. Organized by the institution of the Church, the parish, with its central church and cemetery, came to represent feudal power on its home ground. Like the counties, the parishes were already taking shape in the Anglo-Saxon period and were largely established by the early thirteenth century, with an estimated 8,500 distinct parishes identified.[36] In terms of their boundaries, the parishes were often co-extensive with the older vills or with manors, the estates owned by particular lords, as is evident from the Domesday Book. However, this mapping of space was not seamless and parishes might occupy their own traditional borders, which might extend across a number of adjacent manors.[37] To some extent parishes can be regarded as homologies of manorial space, both of them cutting across the secular spaces of hundred and shire. The issue of territory was important because it determined who would pay tithes in any particular parish, and the tithe—a tax on each household in the parish—was its major source of income, used to support the parish priest, to maintain the fabric of the church, and to provide relief for the needy. The ancient tradition of 'beating the bounds' was encouraged by the Church as a means of reminding each generation of parishioners of the exact limits of the parish borders, and through such rituals the parish bounds became 'to the small, closely knit communities of pre-industrial England almost as important as international boundaries today'.[38]

The function of the parish, which contributed to its significance as an aspect of social identity, was not merely ecclesiastical but commemorative. Through its officers, the births, marriages, and deaths of all parishioners were recorded and preserved, so that in a very real sense individual identity resided most powerfully with the parish. The poor and the sick, ignored by the larger state apparatus, were wholly dependent on their families or on the parish. In addition, the parish undertook some secular duties, including the maintaining of roads, boundary markers, and bridges, and it had its own network of officials headed by the rector, the priest attached to the parish church. In the later Middle Ages the manorial system weakened, and '[i]n so far as village and parish did not entirely coincide with the extent of the manor, then the significance of the manor tended to be eroded'.[39] The manorial courts, in particular, began to lose their authority, partly due to absentee lords, and judicial functions in local areas were increasingly devolved to the parish. Thus the duties of

[36] Pounds (2000: 3).
[37] Morris (1989: 229–30).
[38] Pounds (2000: 76).
[39] Goldberg (2004: 33).

the constable, for example, originally a manorial official, were gradually transferred to the parish.[40] With the decline of the manor as a stable system of administration, the central state found that the parish was a more reliable unit to support local government.

The importance of the shire as a unit of identity is recognized by an anonymous fifteenth-century poem which neatly summarizes the 'properties' of every shire, creating a list that could be memorized:

The propyrte of every shyre
I shal you telle, and ye will here.   [*if*]
Herefordshire sheeld and spere,
Worsetershire wryngpere.   [*a pear-press, for making juice*]
Gloucetershire sho and nayle,   [*shoe*]
Brystowe shippe and sayle.
Oxenfordshire gyrde the mare,   [*spur the horse*]
Warwykshire bynde bere.   [*chain a bear*]
London resortere,   [*a place to return to*]
Sowtherey gret bragere.   [*braggart*]
Esex ful of good hoswyfes,
Middelsex ful of stryves...   [*quarrels*][41]

The striking inclusion of Cornwall and Wales, not to mention Holland, further on in this list indicates that this poet, at least, recognized very little distinction between a county and a country. William Langland and Geoffrey Chaucer, among others, use the word 'contree' to mean 'county' ('And so seiden sixty of the same contree', *Piers Plowman*, B-Text, 20.224; '...and famulier was he [the Friar] / With frankeleyns over al in his contree', General Prologue, ll 215–16), suggesting that the county, rather than a country in the modern sense, was still the primary unit of identity in fourteenth-century England.

MANOR AND TOWN

The administrative system of shires and hundreds, developed in Anglo-Saxon England and extended into the lowlands of Scotland in the twelfth century and throughout Wales after 1284, was only one of the ways in which the regions of medieval Britain could be mapped. Cutting across these geographical regions were

---

[40] Pounds (2000: 4).
[41] Hearne (1711: v, pp. xxvi–xxvii). The poem is also printed in T. Wright and J. O. Halliwell, *Reliquiae Antiquae* (London, 1841 and 1843), i. 269–70, ii, 41–2. See also Boffey and Edwards (2005: no. 3449) for manuscript copies.

cultural communities based on class, manorial divisions, urban practices, and language. I have already mentioned the role of the magnates, the upper aristocracy, in forming a bridge between central government, the royal court, and county administration, using their power and influence to ensure that the 'right' people were placed in key offices. These are the kinds of people satirized by Chaucer in *The House of Fame*, men who sought advancement ('fame') by royal patronage and who passed that patronage downwards to their own regional clients.

Upon the basic structure of the shire and its smaller hundreds and vills, the manorial estates of the Norman aristocracy imposed themselves as an alternative division of space. Representing land held from the Crown and managed by a lord, secular or ecclesiastical, great or small, the manor can be defined as 'the extent of the jurisdiction of the lord as exercised through the manorial court'.[42] Held every few weeks in the manor house, the manorial court dealt with the customary rights and obligations of the tenant farmers and labourers who worked the land on behalf of the lord. Each manor was its own economic unit, accounting for income generated by rents, land transfers and charges for the use of communal facilities such as the mill or bread-oven, and for expenditure such as the hire of labour or the cost of livestock and farming equipment. The most significant manorial officials were the steward, who ran the manor in the absence of the lord, the bailiff, responsible for the economic production of the manor, and the reeve, usually elected by the tenant farmers, who managed the workforce. At the regional level, manorial boundaries within each county complemented the administrative subdivisions of hundreds and vills, though some functions of the manor, such as the raising of feudal armies from honours and fees, cut across county and hundred divisions. For those who worked the land or were fully engaged with agricultural production in some way, the manor was the basis of their social identity.

The magnates, the upper stratum of the feudal nobility, were united not by geography, since their estates were often located all over the country and abroad, but by a strong sense of class identity, their proximity to the King and royal power, and by allegiances of marriage and family. Theirs was a particular kind of community, one that transcended geographical region and depended on a status determined mainly by birth. Sir Thomas Malory, no magnate himself but rather a 'knight of the shire' in Warwickshire,[43] captured precisely this concept of a class-based community in his depiction of Arthur's round-table society in the *Morte Darthur*, a world whose exact geography, relative to the map of Britain, is often obscure and even unimportant. What counts, in Malory's diegetic construction of Arthur's world, are the bonds between the King and his feudal lords, and between the members of noble families, related by blood or marriage.[44]

[42] Goldberg (2004: 30).
[43] Field (1993).
[44] Radulescu (2003).

To audiences of gentry families, like Malory himself, the Arthurian world he depicted captured an essential reality of late medieval society, the spatial difference between the mobile upper aristocracy, moving from royal court to estate to castle, and the earth-bound gentry tied to local lands and county offices. Medieval adventure stories addressed to the gentry, the 'romances' such as *Havelok* or *Bevis of Hamtoun*, emphasized exotic travel and far-flung countries, not simply as allusions to military expeditions with which gentry audiences may have been familiar, but as aspirational markers of a global mobility which was by and large the privilege of the upper aristocracy.

Even more significant than the feudal manors as a type of regional community were the borough towns, which spread over England, Wales, and Scotland in ever-increasing numbers during the twelfth and thirteenth centuries.[45] Many were based on earlier Roman, Anglo-Saxon, or Danish foundations; others were new towns founded by local magnates. The boroughs, or *burhs*, of Anglo-Saxon England had all been possessions of the Crown, founded by kings on their own land. Administration of these towns followed the pattern of other royal estates, with a reeve responsible for collecting the rents and tolls from each town.[46] Following the Norman Conquest, the new lords of England, both secular and religious, realized the financial advantages of establishing towns on their own estates as guaranteed sources of revenue, and as institutions of conquest. The Norman towns established in the Marches of Wales, to the east and south-west of the country, such as Monmouth, Chepstow, Pembroke, and Cardigan, acted as agents of Norman control in these areas. During his Scottish and Welsh campaigns in the latter half of the thirteenth century, Edward I used town-foundation as a critical post-conquest strategy, founding boroughs such as Flint, Conwy, and Denbigh and populating them with English migrants charged with keeping the king's peace against rebellious natives.[47]

Whether ancient settlements or post-Norman foundations, royal, feudal, or episcopal, the ambition of most of the larger towns was to achieve particular privileges, or 'liberties', which would free them from both feudal rule and the control of central government operated via the shire system. Borough towns were technically those which had received a 'charter' of such privileges from their founder, either the King or feudal lord (though charters bestowed by feudal lords also had to be ratified by the King).[48] The most common 'liberty' was the right of the borough to hold regular markets, and perhaps fairs as well. Citizens could trade in the town for free, while non-citizens had to pay tolls and customs taxes which were, along with rents for burgages (plots of land in the town), the main source of the town's revenue.

Another basic liberty granted to most towns was the right to elect their own executive officers, who were therefore outside the county system. From the early thirteenth century, the chief executive officer of the borough town was the mayor, supported by a fixed number of aldermen (usually twenty-four) and other officers such as reeves,

---

[45] Reynolds (1977); Swanson (1999); Palliser (2000).
[46] Jewell (1972: 52).
[47] Beresford (1967); Griffiths (1978).
[48] Ballard and Tait (1923); Tait (1936).

bailiffs, and coroners.[49] A more desirable liberty was the borough's right to have its own court, which again removed it from both the feudal system of manorial courts and the central system of county courts. The most sought-after liberty, not always granted, was the right to 'farm' the borough—that is, to collect all its rents, tolls, and judicial fines—on behalf of the King or feudal lord. The town paid an annual fixed sum and was able to keep the rest of the revenue, providing an income stream which supported its independence from both sheriff and Crown.

The story of the borough towns in England, Wales, and Scotland during the thirteenth and early fourteenth centuries is one of steady population growth (halted by the Black Death of 1346) and increasing independence. A number of the larger cities were eventually reconfigured as counties in their own right, the first being Bristol, awarded county status in 1373, followed by York in 1396, and Newcastle in 1400. However, as Helen Jewell reminds us, 'borough self-government did not entail independence from central government... boroughs were neither independent of the Crown nor democratic in constitution'.[50] If a town failed to keep the king's peace, to run its administration and judicial systems efficiently or to deliver a steady stream of revenue to the cash-strapped Crown, then the King had the power to cancel its privileges, as happened a number of times in London, for example in 1392, under Richard II.[51] The 'taking of the city into the king's hand' meant the appointment of a warden to replace the mayor and the suspension of all the city's privileges, a severe economic punishment.[52] In France and Italy, where there was limited central government at national level, the cities achieved far greater independence, with self-governing *communes* in France and the great city-states such as Florence, Pisa, and Venice in Italy.[53] In Britain, however, with its strong monarchy and well-organized system of government devolved from the centre to the shires and boroughs, the towns had to accept that there were limits to their self-governing powers.

The city of London, adjacent to the centre of royal power in the city of Westminster and essential to the royal economy, had a privileged position. Henry I had granted the citizens of London judicial and mercantile privileges in 1131, including the right to have its own court and the right to farm the borough on behalf of the King, rights which were granted in perpetuity, making London the first borough to have its privileges recognized by royal charter. These privileges removed London entirely from the structure of the shire. It began to elect its own sheriffs, but after 1215, when it acquired the right to elect a mayor, the sheriffs gradually declined in power. In London, as in many of the larger boroughs of Britain, there developed a marked separation between the structure of the shire and the new structures of urban government.

[49] Campbell (2000).
[50] Jewell (1972: 55).
[51] Barron (2003).
[52] Bird (1949).
[53] Waley (1988).

In terms of the development of what might be called an urban identity, the evidence of both literary and functional texts indicates that townspeople saw very little common ground between themselves and the feudal world, and indeed that a large part of their urban identity was shaped by their difference from that world, however much economic factors might have tied them together at a supra-urban level. Burgesses did not necessarily aspire to become knights: in fourteenth-century London, attempts by the Crown to force the wealthier citizens to assume knighthoods in order to supply military assistance were generally unsuccessful.[54] By the same token, the feudal nobility claimed a clear distinction between their own cultural traditions and hierarchies and those of the towns and cities, even though in practice knights could also be merchants, and mercantile incomes were in many cases larger than those of county gentry dependent on agricultural revenues.[55]

Urban identity was vested in both citizenship and membership of a guild; the former was a prerequisite for the latter. Citizenship was conferred by birth, or by length of residence within a city, typically a year and a day. Apprentices who served a master craftsman, like the flighty young protagonist of Chaucer's Cook's Tale, could be eligible for citizenship at the end of their apprenticeship. It is important to remember that urban communities were not homogeneous: within each town, citizens, non-citizens, aliens, women, members of parish, craft, and mercantile guilds, all rubbed shoulders and lived and worked alongside each other, acutely aware of the different sets of rights and privileges which shaped their identity and their relationship to the town.

REGIONAL IDENTITIES

The significance of shire, parish, manor, and town as the interlocking units of regional community and identity is everywhere in evidence throughout medieval English and Welsh literatures. In particular, the differences between 'city' and 'country' were significant in terms of cultural stereotypes and expectations. The honest Kentish ploughman who complains in the poem 'London Lickpenny' (c.1400) that he has been cheated and robbed in that avaricious city cannot wait to get back to the more familiar world of the local manor. William Langland's 'fair feeld of folk' in the Prologue to Piers Plowman represents a binary opposition of regional identities, where the agricultural workers of the manor, engaged in honest toil, occupy the high moral ground compared to the merchants, street entertainers, friars, and beggars who throng the towns. Broad distinctions between the provincial north and west of England on the one hand and the more powerful south on the other

---

[54] Thrupp (1948: 276).
[55] Nightingale (2000).

hand, including the magnet of London, were recognized not only linguistically but in terms of social and cultural differences. The author of the fourteenth-century alliterative poem *Wynnere and Wastoure* cautions against men of the west sending their sons southward in troubled times, in case they never return:

> Dare neuer no westren wy while this werlde lasteth   *western man*
> Send his sone southewarde to see ne to here
> That he ne schall holden byhynde when he hore eldes.[56]

For the fourteenth-century Welsh poet Dafydd ap Gwilym, the parish church at Llanbadarn is the obvious meeting-place for bashful young men and giggling young women:

> Ni bu Sul yn Llanbadarn
> Na bewn, ac eraill a'i barn,
> Â'm wyneb at y ferch goeth
> A'm gwegil at Dduw gwiwgoeth.[57]

There was no Sunday in Llanbadarn when I was not—and others will criticize it—with my face towards a pure girl and the back of my neck towards God, the truly pure.

In contemporary Wales, the village of Llanbadarn has become a suburb of the larger borough town of Aberystwyth, but in the fourteenth century it was the centre of a thriving parish whose fine church—still in use—was a focal point for the surrounding countryside.

If we look at the description of the pilgrims in Chaucer's General Prologue to the *Canterbury Tales* from the perspective of regional organization, it is immediately obvious that they all belong to one or more of the regional communities of Britain—the manor, shire, parish, or borough town. At the beginning of the Prologue, Chaucer tells us that in early summer people feel like going on pilgrimages: 'And specially from every shires ende / Of Engelond to Caunterbury they wende', affirming the status of the shire as a primary unit of organization and identity. The first trio of pilgrims, the Knight, his son the Squire, and their retainer the Yeoman, represent the manorial way of life as a benign form of active service, both military and agricultural, on behalf of Crown and community. But the manor does not escape criticism. Later in the Prologue, the Reeve (employed by the steward or lord of a manor) reminds us of the economic and exploitative aspects of the manorial system; his enemy, the Miller, stands for the tenant farmers who were under the thumb of the reeve. The Parson and his brother the Plowman suggest the close administrative relationship between the parish and the manor, while the figures of the genteel and possibly aristocratic Prioress and the Monk,[58] with his obvious wealth and his delight in expensive clothing and horses, signify not only their identification with manorial interests but also the substantial monastic incomes derived from local parish churches.[59]

The Franklin is to the shire as the Knight is to the manor: a leading figure in shire politics, the Franklin was 'lord and sire' at the county court, he had served as 'knight of the shire', representing his county at parliament, and had even been the 'shirreve' or sheriff of the county, appointed by the Crown. The Merchant symbolizes the town as commercial centre, peopled by characters such as the Cook, the Shipman, the Doctor, the Clerk, the Friar, the Pardoner, and the Wife of Bath, while the Five Guildsmen stand for particular kinds of urban communities, the guilds who policed their own crafts and ran the urban administration through the office of 'alderman' (General Prologue, line 372). The legal characters, the Serjeant-at-law, the Manciple, and the Summoner, represent a fraction of the numerous procedures of the judiciary, secular and ecclesiastical, which invariably took place in the larger towns but whose impact reached out into the shires. It is no surprise that the majority of Chaucer's pilgrims owe at least some part of their identity to the borough town, given that Chaucer himself was part of the royal bureaucracy centred on London. Yet even Chaucer, writing as an urban poet, could not elide the network of social, economic, and political bonds which connected urban life with those other communities of shire, manor, and parish. Describing the Manciple, the steward or buyer of provisions for one of London's Inns of Court, Chaucer says that at least some of the trainee lawyers could aspire to become another kind of steward, that is, the financial manager of a manorial estate who could help his lord live within his means, 'And able for to helpen al a shire / In any caas that myghte falle or happe' (General Prologue, ll. 584–5). The town, the manor, the shire—they are all connected, all interdependent in the medieval economy.

LINGUISTIC COMMUNITIES IN MEDIEVAL BRITAIN

For the whole of its recorded history, Britain has been a multilingual country. In the eighth century, Bede identified 'five languages and four nations—English, British, Scots and Picts',[60] with 'Scots' meaning Gaelic and Latin as the fifth language. In the fourteenth century, Ranulph Higden noted in the *Polychronicon* the various languages of Britain and his translator, John of Trevisa, commented that 'there were so many diversites of langages in that londe as were diversites of nacions'.[61] Cultural identity, then as now, depended to a large extent on which one or more of the available languages were used, and in which contexts. In the centuries between 1100 and 1500,

---

[59] Pounds (2000: 50–3).
[60] Sherley-Price (1968: 38).
[61] Babington (1869: 157).

English, French, and Latin were the major languages of Britain, with Welsh, Gaelic, and Cornish on the margins and migrant languages such as Flemish adding to the variety. Scots, known as 'Inglis' until the fifteenth century,[62] a version of the Anglian dialect spoken in northern and central Britain during the Anglo-Saxon settlements, was the first language of most lowland Scottish people and became a prestige literary language during the fifteenth century, when poets such as William Dunbar and Robert Henryson entertained the royal court.[63]

Throughout Norman Britain and Ireland, French was the language of courtly literature, while the Celtic vernaculars of Wales (Welsh) and Scotland and Ireland (Gaelic) maintained their own traditions of court poetry, prose tales, histories, and religious writing. Latin remained the language of record, though French was beginning to take over this function from the middle of the thirteenth century.[64] By the fourteenth century, particularly in the latter half following the Black Death, English had reasserted itself as both a literary and normative language, one that was taught in schools and regularly used by the urban middle classes.[65] The availability of several languages for both speech and writing created a number of overlapping linguistic communities whose status and occupations were marked by language choice: Latin for clerics and record-keepers, French for lawyers and court society, English for merchants and urban gentry. Most French speakers were bilingual, using English or French in different contexts, like Chaucer's Prioress who spoke French 'ful faire and fetishly / After the scole of Stratford atte Bowe' (General Prologue, ll. 124–5).

As English became more acceptable as a first language during the fourteenth century, coinciding with the war with France, the idea that the English language was a particular indicator of the English nation took hold. The author of *Cursor Mundi*, writing as early as 1300, declared there was no point in writing in French, which was the language of Frenchmen, when he wanted to address the people of England, who spoke English:

> This ilk bok es translate
> Into Inglis tong to rede
> For the love of Inglis lede.
> Inglis lede of Ingland,
> For the commun at understand.[66]

This same book is translated to be read in the English language, for love of the English language. English language of England, for the common people to understand.

Derek Pearsall rightly cautions that contemporary examples such as this 'are evidence only of fragmentary, sporadic, regional responses to particular circumstances, not of a wave of English nationalism sweeping the country'.[67] What the literary evidence

---

[62] Smith (2006: 129).
[63] McClure (1995).
[64] Knowles (1997: 49).
[65] Fennell (2001: 121).
[66] Morris (1874: 20).
[67] Pearsall (2006: 29); see also Thompson (1998: 8–10).

does show, however, is that different linguistic communities in Britain were clearly identified and (as in modern multilingual communities) were often perceived to be in competition for status and resources.

Yet the English language, certainly in its written form and almost certainly in its spoken form as well, was by no means a uniform entity across the country, as Higden himself noted.[68] Even as late as the fourteenth century, as James Milroy says, 'the English nation still had not reached agreement on a single supralocal standard variety for use in literary texts'.[69] The transition from Old English (itself a regionalized language) to Middle English resulted in a pattern of Middle English dialects and subdialects distinguished by phonological, syntactic, and lexical differences. The major Middle English dialects are Northern (that is, north of the Humber, including Cumbria, Northumbria, and Yorkshire); West Midland (Herefordshire, Shropshire, and Cheshire, that is, the areas of the Anglo-Saxon kingdom of Mercia not in contact with Scandinavian settlements), East Midland (the areas of Mercia south of the Humber which were in contact with Scandinavian settlement, including East Anglia); Southern, more or less corresponding to the old West Saxon kingdom, including Dorset, Devon, and Cornwall; and Kentish (or South-Eastern), derived from the Anglo-Saxon dialect spoken in Kent and Sussex.[70]

These dialect differences, mapped on to the administrative structure of shires, made an important contribution to the distinctive regional identities of medieval Britain. Already in the twelfth century, William of Malmesbury was commenting on the rough speech of northerners: 'The speech of the Northumbrians, especially that of the men of York, grates so harshly upon the ear that it is completely unintelligible to us southerners',[71] a piece of southern propaganda repeated almost verbatim by Higden in the fourteenth century.[72] Chaucer, too, was well aware of dialect differences, though his concern was more to do with maintaining the integrity of his own writing against the copying habits of scribes using a different dialect. Towards the end of *Troilus and Criseyde* he expresses a wish that the poem is copied faithfully:

> And for ther is so gret diversite
> In Englissh and in writyng of oure tonge,
> So prey I god that non myswrite the,
> Ne the mysmetre for defaute of tonge.
> (*Troilus and Criseyde*, ll. 1793–6)

As well as these regional variations in English, there were other kinds of linguistic communities which had their own particular characteristics, including the discourses of law, commerce, and royal bureaucracy. The 'chancery English' used for official documents in the fourteenth and fifteenth centuries made an important contribution

---

[68] Babington (1869: 156–8)   [69] Milroy (1992: 158).
[70] Ibid. 174–7; Corrie (2006). For examples of these Middle English dialects, see Baugh and Cable (2002: 409–21).
[71] Preest (2002: 139).   [72] Babington (1869: 163).

to the development of a standard written language,[73] while London itself formed a distinctive and influential linguistic community.[74] On the dialect map of medieval Britain, London (both City and Westminster) occupies a central place on the linguistic borders of the East Midland, Southern, and Kentish dialects. Its multilingual and multicultural environment, as the centre of trade, business, and royal administration, ensured a constant linguistic variety, but the East Midland dialect, representing a large and economically powerful region, was the predominant ingredient in what became London English, which 'began as a Southern and ended as a Midland dialect'.[75] The political and economic pre-eminence of London, already known to the fourteenth-century poet of *St Erkenwald* as the 'metropolis and the master town' of England (line 25), ensured that its written English became the standard form against which other dialects were measured as provincial. By the time Caxton set up his printing press in London in 1476, using London English as his standard, regional differences in written English (though certainly not in spoken English) had almost disappeared.

THE 'DESCRIPTION OF BRITAIN'
AND THE CONSTRUCTION OF NATION

The descriptive map of medieval Britain which I have outlined here, made up of a mosaic of interlocking and overlapping units which include shires, hundreds, manors, parishes, towns, and linguistic communities, is one which medieval writers themselves recognized. What might be called an entire literary genre of the 'description of Britain' is exemplified in a wide range of medieval texts, many of them, like Bede's introductory description of the island of Britain, drawing on classical models of geography and topography. In these 'descriptions', the island of Britain, mapped and subdivided, its borders and regions identified, is stealthily reinterpreted as the nation of England.

Because of the political and economic significance of the regions and territories of Britain, various institutions, including the Church, manorial lords, local government, and the Crown, made a point of listing the areas of land to which they staked a claim and in which they had a financial interest. In these 'descriptions', the shires and sees (dioceses) are listed, often the hidages (family landholdings) as well, and occasionally the major towns, all units of financial return. As with the Domesday Book, the function of such texts (for example, the 'Red Book of the Exchequer',

---

[73] Machan (2003: 97).
[74] Chambers and Daunt (1931).
[75] Baugh and Cable (2002: 194).

produced during the reign of Henry I) was mainly administrative and economic, in that the 'descriptions' itemized the territories owned or 'farmed' (in the sense of collecting revenue) by particular landowners, whether religious or secular.

As the genre developed, however, the motivation became less administrative and more nationalistic. Henry of Huntingdon (c.1080–1150), as part of his *Historia Anglorum*, 'History of the English People', produced a historical description of the Anglo-Saxon kingdoms of England, along with the major towns, thirty-five shires, and their dioceses, topping it off with an account of the customs, marvels, languages, and major roads of Britain, by which he meant England.[76] Henry's description influenced a number of similar texts, most importantly the *Polychronicon* of Ranulph Higden. A genuine 'universal history', covering the whole of the known world, Higden's book includes a geographical and topographical account of Britain drawn mainly from Bede, Geoffrey of Monmouth, William of Malmesbury, and Gerald of Wales, covering its location, resources, marvels, political divisions, counties, shires, languages, and, most importantly, its Roman past. Hugely popular, the British section of the *Polychronicon* was translated into English by John Trevisa in 1387, becoming a national history for the emerging English-speaking people. A century later, in 1480, William Caxton printed his own selection of Trevisa's work under the title *The Description of Britain*, shaping it to produce a mixture of history, geography, and legend which appealed to the late medieval English search for authentic origins. The listing of shires, sees, and towns which had begun as an administrative tool had become an implement for inscribing a national history in which England and Britain were invisibly stitched from the same cloth.

CONCLUSION

Just as there is no 'denotative' text devoid of ideological positioning, so there is no 'empty space' devoid of meaning. Notional regions, or areas of territory, are mapped onto land which has already been divided and subdivided into different configurations, so that the landscape, like a linguistic text, is always already a signifying element, constantly read and interpreted by the people who move through it. Regions, like nations, are as 'imaginary' as communities;[77] they do not pre-exist the social meanings that are made for them and by which they are defined.

Significantly, this sense of regionalism is currently enjoying something of a revival. In today's globalizing economy, the nation-state is on notice as a form of political organization. As national boundaries buckle and stretch under the pressure of multinational movements of capital and labour, national identity itself becomes

---

[76] Greenway (1996).
[77] Anderson (1983).

problematic. What is emerging, or re-emerging, in a post-national world is the salience of the region as a site of cultural and economic production. Cultural geographers refer to this as the 'new regionalism', a movement focusing on the consequences of reconfigurations to our understanding of the nation-state.[78]

But, if this is 'new regionalism', we should not forget the 'old regionalism', itself a product of a pre-nation-state world. During the centuries when the nation-state was dominant in the Western world—roughly the sixteenth to the twentieth centuries—the region as a cultural and economic unit was, by definition, subaltern to the nation. With the waning of the nation-state, we see a revival of the political order that prevailed before it came into being, namely a hierarchy of regions, some of which were organized into nations or into larger entities called empires. This was the geopolitical order which characterized the Middle Ages.

BIBLIOGRAPHY

ANDERSON, BENEDICT (1983), *Imagined Communities: Reflections on the Origins and Spread of Nationalism* (London: Verso).

BABINGTON, CHURCHILL (ed.) (1869), *Polychronicon Ranulphi Higden, monachi Cestrensis: Together with the English Translations of John Trevisa and of an unknown writer of the fifteenth century*, ii (Rolls Series; London: Longman).

BALLARD, ADOLPHUS, and JAMES TAIT (eds.) (1923), *British Borough Charters, 1216–1307* (Cambridge: Cambridge University Press).

BARRON, CAROLINE (2003), *London in the Later Middle Ages: Government and People 1200–1500* (Oxford: Oxford University Press).

BAUGH, ALBERT C., and THOMAS CABLE (2002), *A History of the English Language* (5th edn. London and New York: Routledge).

BBC NEWS WEBSITE (2007), 'Welsh Assembly Election'.<http://news.bbc.co.uk/1/shared/bsp/hi/vote2007/maps/wales_constituencies/html/wales_constituencies_map.stm, accessed 28 Jan. 2009.

BERESFORD, M. W. (1967), *New Towns of the Middle Ages: Town Plantation in England, Wales and Gascony* (London: Lutterworth).

BIRD, RUTH (1949), *The Turbulent London of Richard II* (London: Longman, Green & Co.).

BOFFEY, JULIA, and A. S. G. EDWARDS (2005), *A New Index of Middle English Verse* (London: British Library).

BOWDEN, MURIEL (1973), *A Commentary on the General Prologue to the Canterbury Tales* (London: Souvenir).

BROMWICH, RACHEL (1982), *Dafydd ap Gwilym: A Selection of Poems* (Llandysul: Gomer).

BROUN, DAUVIT (2007), *Scottish Independence and the Idea of Britain, from the Picts to Alexander III* (Edinburgh: Edinburgh University Press).

BROWN, MICHAEL (2004), *The Wars of Scotland, 1214–1371* (Edinburgh: Edinburgh University Press).

[78] Entrikin (2008).

CAMPBELL, JAMES (2000), 'Power and Authority 600–1300', in David M. Palliser (ed.), *The Cambridge Urban History of Britain*, i. *600–1450* (Cambridge: Cambridge University Press), 51–78.

CHAMBERS, RAYMOND W., and MARJORIE DAUNT (1931), *A Book of London English 1384–1425* (Oxford: Clarendon Press).

CORRIE, MARILYN (2006), 'Middle English: Dialects and Diversity', in Lynda Mugglestone (ed.), *The Oxford History of the English Language* (Oxford: Oxford University Press), 86–119.

DAVIES, R. R. (1978), *Lordship and Society in the March of Wales 1282–1400* (Oxford: Clarendon Press: Oxford).

——(1987), *Conquest, Coexistence and Change: Wales 1063–1415* (Oxford: Oxford University Press).

ENTRIKIN, J. NICHOLAS (ed.) (2008), *Regions: Critical Essays in Human Geography* (Aldershot: Ashgate).

EWAN, ELIZABETH (1990), *Town Life in Fourteenth-Century Scotland* (Edinburgh: Edinburgh University Press).

FENNELL, BARBARA A. (2001), *A History of English: A Sociolinguistic Approach* (Oxford: Blackwell).

FIELD, P. J. C. (1993), *The Life and Times of Sir Thomas Malory* (Cambridge: D. S. Brewer).

FLEMING, ROBIN (1998), *Domesday Book and the Law* (Cambridge: Cambridge University Press).

FOX, CYRIL (1940), *The Boundary Line of Cymru* (Proceedings of the British Academy 26; London: British Academy).

GENET, J. P. (1981), 'Political Theory and Local Communities in Later Medieval France and England', in J. R. L. Highfield and R. Jeffs (eds.), *The Crown and Local Communities in England and France in the Fifteenth Century* (Stroud: Alan Sutton), 19–32.

GOLDBERG, P. J. P. (2004), *Medieval England: A Social History 1250–1550* (London: Arnold).

GRANT, ALEXANDER (1984), *Independence and Nationhood: Scotland 1306–1469* (Edinburgh: Edinburgh University Press).

GREENWAY, DIANA (ed. and tr.) (1996), *Henry, Archdeacon of Huntingdon: Historia Anglorum, the History of the English People* (Oxford: Clarendon Press).

GRIFFITHS, RALPH ALAN (ed.) (1978), *Boroughs of Mediaeval Wales* (Cardiff: University of Wales Press).

——(2003), 'The Island of England in the Fifteenth Century: Perceptions of the Peoples of the British Isles', *Journal of Medieval History*, 29: 177–200.

HEARNE, THOMAS (1711), *The Itinerary of John Leland the Antiquary* (9 vols. Oxford).

JEWELL, HELEN M. (1972), *English Local Administration in the Middle Ages* (New York: Barnes & Noble).

JONES, RHYS, and CARWYN FOWLER (2007), 'Where is Wales? Narrating the Territories and Borders of the Welsh Linguistic Nation', *Regional Studies*, 41/1: 89–101.

KNOWLES, GERALD (1997), *A Cultural History of the English Language* (London: Arnold).

LIEBERMAN, MAX (2008), *The March of Wales 1067–1300: A Borderland of Medieval Britain* (Cardiff: University of Wales Press).

LOYN, H. R. (1991), *The Making of the English Nation: From the Anglo-Saxons to Edward I* (London: Thames & Hudson).

McCLURE, J. DERRICK (1995), *Scots and its Literature* (Amsterdam and Philadelphia: John Benjamins).

MACHAN, TIM WILLIAM (2003), *English in the Middle Ages* (Oxford: Oxford University Press).

MILROY, JAMES (1992), 'Middle English Dialectology', in Norman F. Blake (ed.), *The Cambridge History of the English Language*, ii. *1066–1476* (Cambridge: Cambridge University Press), 156–206.

MORRIS, RICHARD (1874), *Cursor Mundi: A Northumbrian Poem of the Fourteenth Century*, i (EETS OS 57; Oxford: Oxford University Press).

—— (1989), *Churches in the Landscape* (London: J. M. Dent).

NIGHTINGALE, PAMELA (2000), 'Knights and Merchants: Trade, Politics and the Gentry in Late Medieval England', *Past and Present*, 169: 36–62.

PALLISER, DAVID M. (2000), 'The Origins of British Towns', in David M. Palliser (ed.), *The Cambridge Urban History of Britain*, i. *600–1450* (Cambridge: Cambridge University Press), 17–24.

POUNDS, N. J. G. (2000), *A History of the English Parish* (Cambridge: Cambridge University Press).

PREEST, DAVID (tr.) (2002), *William of Malmesbury, Deeds of the Bishops of England* (Woodbridge: Boydell).

RADULESCU, RALUCA (2003), *The Gentry Context for Malory's Morte Darthur* (Woodbridge: D. S. Brewer).

REYNOLDS, SUSAN (1977), *Introduction to the History of English Medieval Towns* (Oxford: Clarendon Press).

ROSSER, SIWAN (2008), ' "Ynom mae y Clawdd?" Croesi ffiniau llenyddol', *Transactions of the Honourable Society of Cymmrodorion 2007*, 14: 188–212.

SHERLEY-PRICE, LEO (tr.) (1965), *Bede, A History of the English Church and People* (Harmondsworth: Penguin).

SKENE, WILLIAM FORBES (ed.), and FELIX JAMES HENRY SKENE (tr.) (1872), *John of Fordun's Chronicle of the Scottish Nation* (Edinburgh: Edmonston & Douglas).

SMITH, JEREMY J. (2006), 'From Middle to Early Modern English', in Lynda Mugglestone (ed.), *The Oxford History of the English Language* (Oxford: Oxford University Press), 120–46.

STEPHENSON, CARL, and FREDERICK GEORGE MARCHAM (ed. and tr.) (1937), *Sources of English Constitutional History: A Selection of Documents from A.D. 600 to the Present* (New York: Harper).

STUBBS, WILLIAM (1913), *Select Charters and Other Illustrations of English Constitutional History from the Earliest Times to the Reign of Edward I* (Oxford: Clarendon Press).

SWANSON, HEATHER (1999), *Medieval British Towns* (New York: Macmillan).

TAIT, JAMES (1936), *The Medieval English Borough* (Manchester: Manchester University Press).

TASIOULAS, J. A. (1999), *The Makars: The Poems of Henryson, Dunbar and Douglas* (Edinburgh: Canongate).

THOMPSON, JOHN J. (1998), *The Cursor Mundi: Poem, Texts and Contexts* (Oxford: Society for the Study of Medieval Languages and Literatures).

THORPE, LEWIS (tr.) (1978), *Gerald of Wales, The Journey through Wales and the Description of Wales* (Harmondsworth: Penguin).

THRUPP, SYLVIA L. (1948), *The Merchant Class of Medieval London* (Ann Arbor: University of Michigan Press).

TURVILLE-PETRE, THORLAC (1996), *England the Nation: Language, Literature, and National Identity, 1290–1340* (Oxford: Clarendon Press).

VIRGOE, ROGER (1981), 'The Crown, Magnates and Local Government in Fifteenth-Century East Anglia', in J. R. L. Highfield and Robin Jeffs (eds.), *The Crown and Local Communities in England and France in the Fifteenth Century* (Stroud: Alan Sutton), 72–87.

WALEY, DANIEL PHILIP (1988), *The Italian City-Republics* (London: Longman).

WHYTE, IAN D. (1995), *Scotland before the Industrial Revolution: An Economic and Social History c.1050–c.1750* (London: Longman).

WICKSON, ROGER (1970), *The Community of the Realm in Thirteenth-Century England* (London: Longman).

WRIGHT, T. (ed.) (1866–8), *The Chronicle of Pierre de Langtoft in French Verse* (London: Longman, Green, Reader, & Dyer).

CHAPTER 27

THE CITY AND THE TEXT

LONDON LITERATURE

ALISON WIGGINS

The story of London literature is unwieldy and sprawling. As Peter Ackroyd observes, as he contemplates the challenge of producing a summary portrayal of the city's literary life: the literature of London 'to a large extent also represents the literature of England'.[1] An exploration of Middle English London literature must therefore begin by considering the definition and methods necessary to capture a meaningful sense of the distinctiveness of the city's literary culture—if, indeed, such distinctiveness is to be had. One issue concerns where the primary focus of such a study should lie: should a definition of London literature be focused around writers, or should it prioritize dialect, books, texts, scribes, or readers, or perhaps a combination of these? A second issue concerns the construction of these categories: how it is possible to define and distinguish what is and what is not a 'London' writer, book, text, scribe, or reader? Over and above these questions of focus and categorization, a third issue concerns how geography should be related to literary culture: in what ways does locality engage with issues of literary interpretation or interact with methods and modes of reading? The purpose of this chapter is to reflect upon and explore these related and overlapping questions.

---

[1] Ackroyd (2000: 782–3).

POETS AND WRITERS

The nature of the issues raised can be illustrated by considering, first of all, the implications of defining London literature around poets and writers. There are a number of cases where biographical information is available and indicates a writer's consistent affiliations with the city of London, such as London scribe, administrator, politician, and author of *The Testament of Love* Thomas Usk, and poet, copyist, and clerk of the privy seal Thomas Hoccleve.[2] However, more often than not, where it is available, biographical information emphasizes fluidity and flux. Geoffrey Chaucer was a city man: a citizen, born into a merchant vintner family, living for many years over Aldgate, who often wrote for other citizens, and who used a London dialect. Yet his marriage and his career as a civil servant brought him regularly within the sphere of the court and much of his writing is distinguished by its courtliness. His career provided him with opportunities to travel and he had contact with the European literary cultures of Italy and France. He also spent time living outside the city and may well have composed some of his most famous works whilst living in the provinces.[3] That is, Chaucer's shifting and versatile career, what Marion Turner has called his 'chameleon nature',[4] above all emphasizes the reality of the interrelated status of city, court, and provinces, and his urban identity, as much as anything, reflects his internationalism and his courtliness.

The other founding figures of English poetry are no less ambiguous in terms of their affinities with London. William Langland was living and writing in London and his masterwork *Piers Plowman* is richly infused with imagery and knowledge of the city. London features vibrantly and at many levels: in the density of topographical references, the prominence of the city's sites and setting, and in the awareness of issues of governance, labour legislation, and craft disputes.[5] However, while Langland is in many senses, and perhaps most distinctively, a London poet, he also seems certainly to have been a native of the West Midlands, was familiar with the Malvern hills, used a West Midland dialect, and his pseudonym presents him as an 'opelond' (provincial) poet. Other examples of such ambiguity can be cited. There is the case of John Gower, who lived and worked, spoke and wrote, in London but whose family connections were in Kent and Suffolk and who retained Kentish and Suffolk features in his dialect.[6] Ambiguity can again be found in the case of Benedictine monk and poet John Lydgate, whose writings include those for the citizenry, for city guilds and civic occasions, for the mercers, goldsmiths, and sheriffs, and for London-based gift-giving occasions, processions, pageants, royal entries, and mummings. All these literary activities mean that Lydgate is, in many ways, the premier city poet of the

---

[2] Burrow (2004); Waldron (2004).
[3] Pearsall (1992).
[4] Turner (2007: 29).
[5] Barron (1992); Clopper (1992).
[6] Gray (2004a); Smith (2004).

fifteenth century, yet he was born and lived most of his life in the area around Bury St Edmunds and manuscripts of his work continued to be produced there after his death.[7] Chaucer, Langland, Gower, and Lydgate, in various ways, incline toward but also resist definition as London poets.

Another problem with focusing on writers and poets, in terms of the definition of London literature, is the lack of any sort of stable medieval concept of authorship and the pervasive anonymity of Middle English literature. A second, alternative option, therefore, would be to select and prioritize those literary texts which feature images of the city. To analyse the city through its literary representations relates to the approach of cultural historians such as Michael de Certeau, who believe spaces acquire meaning—become *places*—through the stories associated with them. Landscapes and locales are 'made' through the narratives attached to them, and these take readers along unknown pathways and imaginatively represent aspects of the city and experiences of its populace invisible elsewhere in the historical record. *Piers Plowman* has already been mentioned in this respect, but there are several examples of anonymous and non-canonical medieval texts that directly depict London. The romance of *Athelston* incorporates a series of London landmarks: 'Charynge-cross' (l. 335), 'Flete-strete' (ll. 336, 498), 'Loundone-brygge' (ll. 340, 385), 'Westemynstyr' (ll. 407, 755), 'Saint Powlys heyghe awtere' (ll. 592, 616), 'the Brokene-cros of ston' (l. 546), and 'the Elmes' (l. 805). The alliterative *St Erkenwald* recounts a miracle of salvation performed by Erkenwald, the seventh-century bishop of London: an elaborately carved tomb is uncovered by builders in St Paul's Cathedral and this archaeological discovery becomes an opportunity to celebrate the London saint and the city's layered history. And the cacophonous venality satire *London Lickpenny* evokes the dizzying bustle and hubbub of London street life: the sounds of court summonses merge with the music of minstrels and both compete with the noise of clattering piles of pewter pots and the cries of street traders hawking felt hats, fine cloths, sheep's feet, ripe strawberries, spices, and a multitude of goods.

London features prominently in these narratives and action and incident are embedded within and revolve around the city's famous landmarks and locations. More difficult to distinguish and identify are texts that include metaphorical or oblique images of the city, or texts which do not explicitly mention London but seem to ring with its sounds and speech. This is the case with many of Chaucer's writings. Chaucer most extensively and elaborately imagined London through the image of Troy: the ancient city provided a culturally specific symbol that was common to London readers and writers and through which their own city could be constructed as a 'New Troy'.[8] Only rarely does Chaucer provide direct or explicit glimpses of the city, such as in the reference to the Peasants' Revolt in the Nun's Priests Tale, the setting of the Man of Law in an urban context through the mention of St Paul's porch, or the fragment of lively street narrative that is the Cook's Tale. Yet critics have argued that Chaucer's works should be more closely read and understood within a

---

[7] Gray (2004*b*); Scott (1982).
[8] Federico (2003); Turner (2007).

London social and political context and as echoing with the language and voices of the city. London is present everywhere in Chaucer's writings through his rich engagement with political culture and persistent depiction of a conflicted, antagonized society. This method of reading sees Chaucer's works against contemporary legal and administrative texts, with his writings shown to be reliant upon and interwoven with political and documentary discourses.[9] The validity of such an approach has been reinforced by the identification of Chaucer's scribe Adam Pinkhurst, copyist of two important early manuscripts of the *Canterbury Tales* known as the Hengwrt and Ellesmere Manu-scripts.[10] That Pinkhurst's career had a legal and administrative capacity, and included copying documents such as the Mercer's Petition, further situates the production of Chaucer's works within the same textual environment as contemporary discourses of metropolitan political and documentary culture.

Pinkhurst is undoubtedly an important figure for understanding the London affinities of Chaucer's works, although it is important to remember that Pinkhurst came from a Surrey family and might have shuttled between London and Surrey;[11] and, indeed, works such as the *Canterbury Tales* subsequently came to circulate in other manuscripts, copied by a great variety of scribes, both within and outside of London, and for a range of reading occasions. Here, in these manuscripts, the immediacy and original function of the London context is often loosened or dis-appears altogether. That is to say, where multiple manuscript copies exist, the geography and reception of a single literary work is itself highly fragmented, distributed, and plural. Thus the presence of London in any such single literary work is, itself, unstable as it is inflected through the dynamics and imperatives of manuscript culture.

MANUSCRIPTS AND THE BOOK TRADE

The issue of manuscript transmission relates to a third option according to which London literature could be focused and defined; that is, in terms of the manuscripts produced as part of the London book trade. There are examples of literary manuscripts produced in the capital where both the text and the scribe are associated with London and both use a London dialect. This is the case of Pinkhurst copying Hengwrt and Ellesmere. But here, even in this relatively clear-cut case, comparison of Hengwrt and Ellesmere reveals substantial variation at the levels of language, texts, and visual and material presentation and is a reminder that the situation is in no way monolithic. In fact, Middle English manuscript books produced in late medieval London constitute a wide and heterogeneous spectrum. Books copied in London contain texts that vary in

---

[9] Strohm (1992); Turner (2007).

[10] Mooney (2006).

[11] Mooney (2006: 116–19).

terms of theme, genre, provenance, and regional origin, such as miscellaneous volumes like the manuscript Manchester, Chetham's Library 8009.[12] There is also diversity in terms of language: both local and immigrant scribes working in London, regardless of the forms of their exemplars, retained the individualism of their own dialect.[13] On the other hand, some scribes working in London were respectful and tolerant of the authorial status of provincial spelling forms in exemplars transmitting texts by poets such as Gower and Langland.[14] The diversity of scribal copying practices and attitudes to different dialects indicates the complexity and fluidity of the linguistic situation in London. It is a situation that involves a jostling range of lects and texts continually in play. This can make it difficult to distinguish a book produced in London from one copied in the provinces and it means a 'London book' cannot be identified simply by dialect criteria or text type alone 'since people from many different regions moved in and out of the city, complicating our understanding of the linguistic situation.

Further to these issues of language variation, there is the important adjacent question of whether the conceptualization of the London book trade should be extended to include not only books copied in the city but also those that passed through the capital or were owned and read there. There is the case of John Paston II who, writing to his family in Norfolk from his London lodgings, the George 'at Powles Wharff', in 1474, asks for books to be sent 'hyddre by the next messanger'; if he is away he asks they 'be delyueryd to myn ostesse' at the inn saying that she 'wolle kepe them saffe'; and he subsequently, in 1479, describes a book of romance and chronicle material which was 'had off myn ostesse' at the George.[15] London's inns, halls, and households flowed with textual traffic, including books and letters transmitted both in and out of London. In the reverse direction, there is the example of the copy of the *Siege of Thebes* mentioned by John Paston III, writing from Norfolk in 1472 to his brother John II in London. He says that the book belongs to his sister Anne, was lent to 'my lord the Erle of Arran', who has it at his lodging 'at the George in Lombard Streete', and he asks his brother to ensure it is returned with 'Portlond' who is lodged at the same inn.[16] It illustrates how a book could pass in and out of different social and regional communities, and it encapsulates, in miniature, the ready circulation of books between court, country, and city. Just as Chaucer's life, works, and career veered between city, court, and provinces, so did many English books continue to move in and out of these different social and geographical orbits. The question remains as to how this textual traffic—books exchanged, gifted, and temporarily borrowed, books that moved quickly through the capital, carried with visitors, exchanged in packages along with letters, passed over the bar at the George at Powles Wharff, or the George at Lombard Streete, or other such locales, transmitted in and out of households and communities—can be captured and incorporated into a distinctive sense of London literature.

[12] Meale (1984); Sánchez-Martí (2003).
[13] Samuels (1985, 1988).
[14] Horobin (2005); Smith (2004).
[15] Davis (1971: 477, 481, 517).
[16] (Ibid. 574–6); Doyle (1983: 197).

As this discussion and these examples begin to indicate, in studies of literary geography, a central methodological tension exists between location and transition. On the one hand, there is a need to link specific authors, books, and texts to particular regional communities in order to anchor precise analyses of particular local literary cultures. Yet, on the other hand, there is a requirement to capture the mobility and flux of literary culture, to map the traffic in books, texts, and people, and to acknowledge the dynamics of inter-regional networks.[17] In the case of late medieval England, the situation is further complicated by the unstable, informal, and individualistic nature of medieval manuscript culture. Each manuscript book is unique and each of its component processes (composition, compilation, copying, production of materials such as ink and vellum, decoration, binding, etc.) represents a web of geographically and historically precise production and reception circumstances.[18] Any understanding of geography and regionalism in relation to medieval literature must fully acknowledge and take account of the essentially dynamic and unstable nature of the manuscript culture within which that literature was produced and consumed. This is particularly so in relation to London, which is remarkable for its social dynamism: a large centre for trade and exchange with a high population turnover, the city was constantly reinventing and replenishing itself in terms of language, population, and textual cultures.[19] Any analysis must strive to replicate, as far as possible, these shifts and reinventions.

An Experiment in Literary Geography: Mapping the Auchinleck Manuscript

In order to consider these issues in more detail, and to demonstrate and explore the implications of the dynamics of literary geography in relation to late medieval London's manuscript culture, for the rest of this chapter one manuscript book will be discussed: the 'Auchinleck' manuscript (Edinburgh, National Library of Scotland, Advocates' 19.2.1, available at http://www.nls.uk/auchinleck). Auchinleck is an appropriate choice to start exploring London literature. Dating from the 1330s, it is the first example of a book produced in London of what we would now call English literary texts. Auchinleck is anonymous and, as yet, we have no names or direct biographical information about its scribes, artists, patrons, or owners. There is no doubt it is an ambitious book, staggering in its richness, density, variety, and polyvocality. Included among its wide range of verse texts are a social satire, a chronicle, a comedy, a debate,

---

[17] Thompson *et al.* (2006).
[18] Scase (2004: 1).
[19] Ackroyd (2000); Ekwall (1956).

texts of basic doctrinal instruction, a psalm paraphrase, a poem in praise of women, and several saints' lives. In addition to these is the impressive array of romances that dominate the collection and include the adventures, exploits, and life stories of heroes of England including Guy of Warwick, Bevis of Hampton, Richard I, Horn Childe, and Sir Orfeo (here uniquely relocated to Winchester); of Britain there is the romance of Arthur and Merlin; from France there are Roland and Verague and Otuel; and from the East Floris and Blanchflour and King Alisaunder. The great narratives of past saints, soldiers, kings, and leaders are not by any means a feature peculiar to London literature: they are a preoccupation of medieval literature more generally. But this does not mean that Auchinleck's texts should be dismissed as merely conventional. It is the particular realization of these narratives in this volume— their specific codicological, palaeographical, linguistic, and literary materialization— that reciprocates with late medieval London. This analysis is concerned to emphasize the way that Auchinleck exposes a continually varying and mutating literary and linguistic environment, and reveals London's literary culture to be part of a reticulated network of textual production and reception.

In terms of 'species' of book, Auchinleck represents an assimilation of different preexisting traditions of literary manuscript production. On the one hand, there are many resemblances between Auchinleck and the manuscripts of Anglo-Norman romance which had been produced and circulated in England for over a century and were a prominent feature of the libraries of the wealthy nobility, aristocracy, and gentry. Although differing in language (Anglo-Norman rather than Middle English) these manuscripts resemble Auchinleck visually and in terms of content and likely owners. For example, the layout and presentation of booklet 4, containing Auchinleck's central text, *Guy of Warwick*, resembles manuscripts of its Anglo-Norman counterpart *Gui de Warewick*. There is New Haven, Yale University, Beinecke Library, MS 591, a single-text manuscript of *Gui de Warewic* copied in the early fourteenth century, in double columns of thirty-six lines, with red and blue capitals and divided initials, and which was owned by the Cholmondeley family. Or, Cologny-Geneva, Bibliotheca Bodmeriana 168, copied at the end of thirteenth century, in double columns of forty-two lines, with red and blue capitals, that compiles *Waldef, Gui de Warewic,* and *Otinel,* and was owned by the Grey family.[20] Auchinleck booklet 4, the *Guy* booklet, similarly, is copied in double columns of around forty-four lines, with red and blue capitals, and divided first initials. Its surrounding booklets compile chronicle, saints' lives, and romance materials, including the Middle English *Otuel,* of the kind found in books of Anglo-Norman romance.

It is important to acknowledge these continuities with earlier and concurrent Anglo-Norman romance manuscripts, although Auchinleck does differ in certain crucial respects. First, Auchinleck differs from Anglo-Norman romance manuscripts in terms of range and number of texts. Auchinleck has a total of forty-four texts across twelve booklets that include a number of translations of short Latin texts (basic doctrinal staples such as *David the King*, the *Pater Noster,* and the *Seven Deadly*

---

[20] Ailes (2007).

Sins) as well as verse texts from the native English tradition. These latter originate from established centres of English literary production outside London, most notably Yorkshire and the South-West Midlands. They include *The Thrush and the Nightingale*, *Alphabetical Praise of Women*, and the *Anonymous Short English Metrical Chronicle*, which Auchinleck has in common with earlier provincial (South-West Midland) trilingual collections, Oxford, Bodleian Library, Digby 86; London, British Library, Harley 2253; and London, British Library, Royal 12 c. xii. This range of texts reflects the availability of provincial exemplars to the Auchinleck compilers in London. Secondly, and in addition to its range of texts, Auchinleck diverges from Anglo-Norman romance manuscripts in terms of scale and certain features of layout and presentation, including its decorative scheme of miniatures. In these respects comparison has usefully been made between Auchinleck and large Anglo-Norman and Latin legal and administrative books being produced in London, such as those compiled by Andrew Horn, Chamberlain of the City 1320–8. The close similarities between Auchinleck and Horn's books, in terms of mode of production, size, layout, type, and style illumination, as well as thematic continuities, make it very likely their scribes and illuminators were drawn from the same pool of craftsmen.[21] Here we have, then, in Auchinleck, an assemblage of texts ranging in origin, that relate to Anglo-Norman, Latin, and Middle English traditions of literary manuscript production. These are presented in a visual and material format that was familiar to London scribes and craftsmen accustomed to producing large legal and administrative books in the capital. London had the proximity to both aristocratic Anglo-Norman and administrative and legal cultures, the inter-regional connections and the means of production in terms of scribes and artists that resulted in such a book.

The extent of Auchinleck's indebtedness to polyglot and regional cultures is further reflected in aspects of its language. One of Auchinleck's poems (*The Sayings of the Four Philosophers*) is macaronic, several are interspersed with Latin or French headings or segments (*The Harrowing of Hell, Short Metrical Chronicle, David the King, The Desputisoun Bitwen the Bodi and the Soule*) and, more generally, there is a macaronic quality to much of the English of this manuscript. Two of Auchinleck's scribes (Scribes 1 and 3) use London dialects, but other sections of the book are copied in provincial dialects: Scribes 2 and 6 use South-West Midland dialects while Scribe 5 uses an Essex dialect. It indicates tolerance of linguistic variety—including usages with a regional bias—within a single, high-status, London book. Auchinleck is often described as being remarkable for its 'Englishness'. That is, both for its extensive use of the English language at such an early date, and for its expression of a burgeoning sense of 'English national identity' through its assemblage of stories recounting English history and heroism. But it is important to remember that neither its language nor its brand of national identity is monolithic. Both are expressed as a fragmented spectrum of regional varieties. And just as the English identities of Auchinleck's romance heroes are complicated by their regional affiliations—with Warwick, Southampton,

21 Hanna (2005: 54–82).

Winchester, and Yorkshire[22]—so too is the English of Auchinleck's scribes and texts marked by regional forms.

In terms of codicology and language, then, Auchinleck can only be understood in relation to its inter-regional connections and as a series of translational procedures texts underwent as they moved between manuscripts, languages, and locales. A comparable set of translations and transformations occurred at the literary level. While Auchinleck's histories and heroes of England are generally characterized by their regional affinities, two of its texts also incorporate depictions of London: *The Anonymous Short English Metrical Chronicle* and *Bevis of Hamtoun*. In both cases, these representations of London are accretions or additions gathered as these texts moved in and out of different regional and linguistic spheres. The instability of medieval literary culture means that images of London can literally appear and disappear in and out of texts, interpolated or excised, expanded or contracted, at different moments, in response to production and reception scenarios. The relationship between city and text is reciprocal: just as it is possible to locate Auchinleck in London, so it is also possible to locate London in Auchinleck. Just as the book was made by the city—using London's scribes, craftsmen, and inter-regional networks—so the city is made by the book. The particular images of the city correspond to different but well-known ways of imagining London so it is worth examining these in more detail here.

THE ANONYMOUS SHORT ENGLISH METRICAL CHRONICLE

The Anonymous Short English Metrical Chronicle (SMC) originated in the West Midlands before 1307 and the earliest version functioned as a historical summary: little more than a list of kings and events, designed for the basic instruction of the local community.[23] The Auchinleck copy of the *SMC*, compared to the West Midland branch of the textual tradition, is substantially longer: 2,370 lines compared to just over one thousand lines of the West Midland original. The additions consist of a prologue; a continuation that updates the chronicle to the beginning of the reign Edward III in 1327 or 1328; and a series of interpolated stories and narrator's interjections which amplify the rather sparse list of events by comparison with the earlier West Midland version. A number of these stories and interjections are unique to the Auchinleck version and several are specifically concerned with the history of London and offer incidental local and topographical details.

[22] Rouse (2008).
[23] O'Rourke (2005: 52); Zettle (1935).

Threaded throughout the unique passages is an interest in the history of the naming of London. There is the scene which features Hengist, where he renames the capital 'Hengisthom' (line 738) and reflects on its previous appellations as 'Newe Troye' by Brutus (line 734) and 'Luddesburgh' by Lud (line 736). The reader is subsequently told that the city remains known as Hengisthom until it is conquered by Julius Caesar, who 'London þe cite he dede clepe,/& so it schal be cleped ay/Til þat it be domesday' (ll. 960–3). Another unique passage provides an account of the consecration of Westminster Abbey and the naming of Charing Cross following a miraculous encounter between a Thames fisherman and St Peter (ll. 1139–1254). In another unique passage the story of St Edward is recounted, as he prays for and receives a miracle at Westminster (ll. 1939–68). There are also other, shorter, unique passages that offer topographical knowledge of the city, such as in the information that Brutus and his son are buried near the Thames where Westminster is founded (ll. 481–4, 493); the mention that Lud and Bladud are buried outside Ludgate (ll. 531–4, 595); and the directions to specify the exact location of the 'tower of Eldwerk' that is 'opon Houndesdiche/Bitvene Algat & þe Tour' (ll. 605–8). The cumulative result of these additions is partially to reroute the nation's history through London in order to feed an interest in marvellous stories pertaining to the urban environment. Often in texts involving a journey of some kind a description of a marvellous landmark or object will be followed, as means of authentication, by a comment from the narrator stating that the object can still be seen there or that pilgrims who have travelled there will tell you of its existence.[24] One of the unique passages in the Auchinleck *SMC* contains a version of this formula: after reporting on the miraculous 800-year-old relic of King Seberd's body at Westminster, the narrator states that: 'ife wil nout leue me/Go to Westeminster &e may se' (ll. 1261–2). The reader is invited to journey through the city and to read the text as a visitor to the locales. Auchinleck's description of the city thus makes the city text and, by attaching stories to its landmarks and locations, imagines the city archaeologically and historically.

It is not possible to know who is responsible for these passages unique to the Auchinleck *SMC*, but the rhyme words indicate they were not written in the same West Midland dialect as the original thousand lines. And whereas the original thousand lines contain a number of West Midland forms carried over into the Auchinleck copy, along with a number of rhyme-destroying forms due to the difference between the original West Midland dialect and Auchinleck Scribe 1's Type II London dialect (for example, ll. 154, 1174 *mon* 'man', 1721 *wes* 'was', 1600 *[swon]* 'swan'), there are none of these in the sections that are unique to Auchinleck. That is, the unique passages have the appearance of additions made by a redactor writing in a dialect that did not diverge drastically from the language of Auchinleck Scribe 1. It is possible the additions were made by Scribe 1 himself, especially for this manuscript, and a number of commentators have accepted this theory based on the observation of certain similarities of wording with the Auchinleck *Richard Coer de*

[24] Ganin (1998: 88).

Lyon. The similarities may suggest sharing of material between the two texts, which would suggest that revision took place at the Auchinleck stage of production.[25] Either way, whether the passages were added at this or at an earlier stage, the Auchinleck *SMC* it is an example of the mobility of medieval literary culture and of the dynamic relations between readers, regions, and texts.

BEVIS OF HAMTOUN

In the case of the *SMC*, images of London enter and exist as the text circulates between different geographical regions and between urban and provincial contexts. In the case of the romance of *Bevis of Hamtoun*, comparable shifts occur as part of the translational process from Anglo-Norman into Middle English. The Middle English *Bevis* contains three scenes which were added by an early redactor of the romance and which do not appear in the Anglo-Norman *Boeue*; they include the climactic London street battle at the end of the romance (ll. 4110–4384). Bevis returns to England to find that his lands around Southampton have been taken by King Edgar. He goes to court to demand the lands are reinstated, but the king's steward, who hates Bevis, warns Edgar that Bevis presents a danger and the request is denied. Angrily, Bevis leaves court and goes to his lodgings in London. Meanwhile, the steward goes to Cheapside and, in the king's name, makes a cry 'among þe peple' (l. 4154). He activates the populace, telling them to defend themselves against an enemy of the king who, he tells them, is 'inour cite' (l. 4158). In the battle that ensues Bevis slaughters thousands of London residents, kills the steward, is almost killed himself by a Lombard, before being rescued from the angry mob by his two sons. King Edgar then offers his daughter in marriage to Bevis's son Miles and thus, after the violent purging of the city, Bevis's inheritance is regained and social harmony is restored.

A remarkable feature of the episode—especially given romance's reputation for bland, stereotyped settings—are the detailed references to actual London locations. Precise details are given of movements into, out of, and around the city: after leaving Josian outside the city at Putney ('Potenhiþe', line 4114), Bevis meets the King at 'Westmenster' (line 4119), enters the city by crossing 'Temse flode' (line 4118), and lodges in 'Tour strete' (line 4144). The battle moves from Cheapside ('Cheap', line 4219) to Gose lane ('Godes lane', line 4221) back into Cheapside (line 4247) then from 'Londen gate' (line 4307) to the area 'Betwene Bowe and Londen ston' (line 4319). Finally, Bevis and his entourage celebrate victory at the 'Ledenhalle' (line 4358). There is an insistent concern to fully integrate description of the city—its spaces, locations, and boundaries—with the events of the battle. The physical locations and material constituents of the city become, as it were, participants in the action. The people shut

---

[25] Zettl (1935: xcvi); Turville-Petre (1996: 112).

'eueri gate' with 'barres' (ll. 4167–8); the city 'wal' is defended by people with bows and catapults (ll. 4169–70); 'everi gate and eueri strete' is barricaded with 'chaines gret' (ll. 4171–2); repeated cries are heard to go up 'boþe of lane and of strete' (l. 4263). The 'chynes held [Bevis] faste' at the end of Gose lane (l. 4244) and Gose lane becomes a kind of urban pass of Roncevalles, so narrowly built that it prevents Bevis from defending himself and stops his horse Arundel from turning (ll. 4221–38).[26] Bevis is imagined to be fighting against the city itself and the narrator states that this was 'þe grete bataile/Of sire Beues . . . /þat he dede aenes þat cite' (ll. 4257–9). At the conclusion of the battle 'So meche folk was slawe & ded/þat al Temse was blod red' (ll. 4353–4) and King Edgar grieves 'for is borgeis in is cite' (l. 4365). The repeated references to the streets, city gates, and walls create a realistic stage for the battle which, elsewhere in romance, is rivalled only by the portrayal of the streets of Lincoln in *Havelok*.

The graphic and realistically topographic nature of this episode may suggest that an actual historical revolt lies at its core. Judith Weiss,[27] for example, suggests similarities with the revolt of 1263 which began against, and then turned to be for, Simon de Montfort, and was underpinned by the kind of pro-baronial, anti-royalist sentiments which can be detected here in Bevis's triumph. However, without a date of composition it is difficult to confirm or build on this point. Moreover, it may be more appropriate to think in terms of a layered process of transmission. That is, it is possible that, while the 1263 revolt may have provided the Middle English redactor with the original inspiration for the episode, subsequent events may inflect later individual manuscript versions. Cheapside, the main stage of Bevis's battle and London's most important public space, was the site of a number of rebellions and mob-led executions of hated authority figures in the late medieval period. These include, for example, the lynching and decapitation of Bishop Walter Stapleton, chancellor to Edward II. His execution by a mob of Londoners in October 1326 occurred after the coup of Isabella and Mortimer, in the place of those deemed traitors.[28] An association with this 1326 revolt would certainly explain the otherwise puzzling location, unique to Auchinleck, of the wedding of Miles and Edgar's daughter in Nottingham, as Nottingham was subsequently, in 1330, the site of Isabella and Mortimer's capture before the full restoration of Edward III.

Ultimately, whether or not a specific historical event can be identified, the street battle speaks to a perception of threats to local governance over contested spaces such as Cheapside. Not only a market area, Cheapside was a place for publicity, celebration, validation, and political affirmation through display, pageantry, and public punishment.[29] Bevis's London street battle presents a graphic awareness of these links between control and the occupation of civic space. It also expresses a fear of revolt and factionalism, perhaps most vividly apparent, amid the topographical realism, in the figurative fantasy of London as hell. When Bevis's sons Guii and Miles hear that their father is dead they proclaim 'be him þat herwede helle/We scholle his deþ wel dere selle' (ll. 4293–4). They descend into the city as Christ into hell. The image of Christ prising open the gates of hell is figured through Guii and Miles at 'Londen gate' (l. 4307); they fight their way through 'Londen gate' which is guarded by 'Mani man . . . /Wel i-armed to þe teþ' (ll. 4308–9) and which they then set on fire (l. 4316). This gateway to the city is imagined as a flaming hell-mouth and the mob the force of evil which the rescuers must defeat. The description is at once an actual image of London and a literary, typological fantasy of the city turned upside-down and become a type of Babylon. The scene imagines London as a city capable of sudden and dramatic transformation. It is no coincidence that it is a 'Lombard' who comes closest to killing Bevis—a member of one of London's most well-known immigrant communities—the scene speaks to a fear of those outside of regulatory structures, the unstable mob, aliens, foreigners, and incomers.

Whereas the *SMC* presents London historically and archaeologically, in *Bevis* London is imagined through its contested spaces, as a violent, volatile city, and as characterized by its immigrant population. They do not present any kind of coherent or consistent view. The extent to which they should be regarded as prominent or defining features of the manuscript, or of its particular expression of English or metropolitan identity, indicates the extent to which reading is itself an unstable act, never final, fixed, or conclusive. Whereas earlier critics related Auchinleck's texts to the expression of a distinctive and unified 'mercantile identity', the disassembling of this view has opened up the book and its texts to new, more provocative and imaginative readings.[30] Chaucer's *Sir Thopas* provides one London reader's response to Auchinleck-type texts, but there is no reason to restrict interpretation of Auchinleck along these lines. This is especially so given that, although Auchinleck was produced in London, it is uncertain how long it remained in the capital. Upon completion, Auchinleck may, perhaps, have been swiftly dispatched to a provincial patron in East Anglia or Yorkshire where it may have remained, at some as yet undisclosed location, until it reached Scotland in the eighteenth century. It raises the question of whether the physical movement of the book itself, or its readers, in and out of London, makes Auchinleck any more or any less a London book. Or whether the presence of London resides inscribed within its pages (in its language, texts, and form) and exists conceptually and imaginatively in the minds of its readers.

CONCLUSIONS

This analysis of Auchinleck has shown that it needs to be understood in terms of its regional links and affiliations. Auchinleck illustrates that, while London was

[30] Hanna (2005); Rouse (2008); Turville-Petre (1997); Lindenbaum (2006).

important as a centre for manuscript and literary culture, it was not just as a place of production, of output, but a nexus point and a site of cultural exchange: more Samarkand than Stalybridge. Middle English London literature, like the city, is complex and dynamic. London literature cannot be fixed to a narrow canon. Nor can it be strictly defined or characterized as representing a coherent or unified urban identity. London continually reinvents itself, linguistically, architecturally, and demographically. It is a moving concept, a mass of lives and experiences, a meeting place of diverse traders and communities. Like the city, London's medieval literary culture is a fluid phenomenon. It is porous, protean, and animate. It cannot be narrated, experienced, or grasped as a whole and to tell its story involves several intertwined, disjoined, and partly overlapping historical narratives. No single account can capture London literature and anyone wishing to explore the subject would be advised to read widely and diversely among biographies and historiographies, summary overviews and close-up encounters and perspective from different disciplines.

This chapter has explored the methodological dilemma that an examination of 'London' literature presents; that is, the need for location and to ground examination in relation to texts, books, poets, and readers that can be securely geographically situated, against the necessity to capture London's fluid and mobile literary culture. In order to explore the tension between fixity and flux in manuscript culture, this chapter has focused on the example of the Auchinleck manuscript. But it is worth emphasizing that other books could have been chosen, such as the literary collections copied by Scribe D or by the Hammond Scribe;[31] the poetic anthology Oxford, Bodleian, Fairfax 16;[32] the heterogeneous miscellany Oxford, Bodleian Library, Rawlinson C. 86;[33] the manuscripts circulated by the bibliophile John Shirley;[34] or the commonplace book compiled between 1517 and 1539 by London merchant John Colyns, now London, British Library, Harley 2252.[35] Each of these books presents literary and linguistic realizations of texts that are specific to and were accommodated within London's literary culture. A fragmented approach, manuscript by manuscript, is appropriate because it mimics and mirrors the unstable, piecemeal, bespoke nature of manuscript culture. Just as the city reinvented itself, so was it reinvented in each of its manuscripts. Each of these would have provided an equally fascinating 'Rough Guide'; each would have offered different routes through and insights into the city. Anyone interested to know more about London literature would do well to read more about each of these individual manuscripts.

---

[31] Doyle and Parkes (1978); Smith (2004).
[32] Boffey and Thompson (1989).
[33] Boffey and Meale (1991).
[34] Boffey and Thompson (1989).
[35] Meale (1983).

BIBLIOGRAPHY

ACKROYD, P. (2000), *London: The Biography* (London: Chatto & Windus).

AILES, M. (2007), '*Gui de Warewic* in its Manuscript Context', in A. Wiggins and R. Field (eds.), *Guy of Warwick: Icon and Ancestor* (Studies in Medieval Romance, 4; Cambridge: Brewer), 12–26.

An Anonymous Short English Metrical Chronicle (1935), ed. E. Zettl (EETS OS 196; London: Oxford University Press).

The Auchinleck Manuscript (1977), ed. D. Pearsall and I. C. Cunningham (London: Scolar Press).

The Auchinleck Manuscript (5 July 2003), ed. D. Burnley and A. Wiggins (National Library of Scotland Digital Library,<http://www.nls.uk/auchinleck>, accessed 17 December 2008).

BARRON, C. M. (1992), 'William Langland: A London Poet', in B. A. Hanawalt (ed.), *Chaucer's England: Literature in Historical Context* (Minneapolis: University of Minnesota Press), 91–109.

——(2000), 'London 1300–1540', in D. M. Palliser (ed.), *The Cambridge Urban History of Britain, i. 600–1540* (Cambridge: Cambridge University Press), 395–440.

BEADLE, R. (1994), 'Middle English Texts and their Transmission, 1350–1500: Some Geographical Criteria', in M. Laing and K. Williamson (eds.), *Speaking in our Tongues* (Cambridge: Brewer), 69–91.

BOFFEY, J. and C. MEALE (1991), 'Selecting the Text: Rawlinson C.86 and Some Other Books for London Readers', in F. Riddy (ed.), *Regionalism in Late Medieval Manuscripts and Texts* (Cambridge: Brewer), 143–69.

——and J. J. THOMPSON (1989), 'Anthologies and Miscellanies: Production and Choice of Texts', in J. Griffiths and D. Pearsall (eds.), *Book Production and Publishing in Britain 1375–1475* (Cambridge: Cambridge University Press), 279–315.

BURNLEY, J. D. (1983), *A Guide to Chaucer's Language* (London: Macmillan).

BURROW, J. A. (2004), 'Hoccleve, Thomas (*c.*1367–1426)', *Oxford Dictionary of National Biography* (Oxford: Oxford University Press), <www.oxforddnb.com/view/article/13415>, accessed 12 Sept. 2008.

BUTTERFIELD, A. (ed.) (2006), *Chaucer and the City* (Chaucer Studies, 37; Cambridge: Brewer).

CLOPPER, L. M. (1992), 'Need Men and Women Labor? Langland's Wanderer and the Labor Ordinances', in B. A. Hanawalt (ed.), *Chaucer's England: Literature in Historical Context* (Minneapolis: University of Minnesota Press), 110–29.

DAVIS, ISABEL (2007), *Writing Masculinity in the Later Middle Ages* (Cambridge: Cambridge University Press).

DE CERTEAU, MICHEL (1984), *The Practice of Everyday Life*, tr. S. Rendall (Berkeley, Calif.: University of California Press).

DOYLE, A. I. (1983), 'English Books In and Out of Court from Edward III to Henry VII', in V. J. Scattergood and J. W. Sherborne (eds.), *English Court Culture in the Later Middle Ages* (New York: St Martin's Press), 163–81.

DOYLE, A. I., and M. PARKES (1978), 'The Production of Copies of the *Canterbury Tales* and the *Confessio Amantis* in the Early Fifteenth Century', in M. Parkes and A. G. Watson (eds.), *Medieval Scribes, Manuscripts and Libraries: Essays Presented to N. R. Ker* (London: Scolar Press), 163–210.

EKWALL, E. (1956), *Studies on the Population of Medieval London* (Stockholm: Almkvist & Wiksell).

FEDERICO, S. (2003), *New Troy: Fantasies of Empire in the Late Middle Ages* (Medieval Cultures, 36; Minneapolis and London: University of Minnesota Press).

GANIN, JOHN M. (1998), 'The Experience of Modernity in Late Medieval Literature: Urbanism, Experience, and Rhetoric in Some Early Descriptions of London', in J. J. Paxson, L. M. Clopper, and S. Tomasch (eds.), *The Performance of Middle English Culture: Essays on Chaucer and the Drama in Honor of Martin Stevens* (Cambridge: Brewer), 77–96.

GRAY, D. (2004a), 'Gower, John (d. 1408)', *Oxford Dictionary of National Biography* (Oxford: Oxford University Press),<www.oxforddnb.com/view/article/11176>, accessed 18 Dec. 2008.

GRAY, D. (2004b), 'Lydgate, John (c.1370–1449/50?)', *Oxford Dictionary of National Biography* (Oxford: Oxford University Press), <www.oxforddnb.com/view/article/17238>, accessed 12 Sept. 2008.

HANNA, R. (2005), *London Literature 1300–1380* (Cambridge: Cambridge University Press).

HARDING, V. (2008), 'Cheapside: Commerce and Commemoration', *Huntington Library Quarterly*, 71: 77–96.

HOROBIN, S. (2005), ' "In London and Opelond": The Dialect and Circulation of the C Version of *Piers Plowman*', *Medium Ævum*, 74: 248–69.

LANCASHIRE, A. B. (2002), *London Civic Theatre: City Drama and Pageantry from Roman Times to 1558* (Cambridge: Cambridge University Press).

LINDENBAUM, S. (1999), 'London Texts and Literate Practice', in D. Wallace (ed.), *The Cambridge History of Medieval English Literature* (Cambridge: Cambridge University Press), 284–309.

London Lickpenny (1996), J. M. Dean (ed.), *Medieval English Political Writings* (TEAMS; Kalamazoo, Mich.: Medieval Institute Publications; also available at http://www.lib.rochester.edu/camelot/teams/dean1.htm).

MEALE, C. M. (1983), 'The Compiler at Work: John Colyns and BL MS Harley 2252', in D. Pearsall (ed.), *Manuscripts and Readers in Fifteenth Century England* (Cambridge: Brewer), 82–103.

——(1984), 'THE MIDDLE ENGLISH ROMANCE OF IPOMEDON: A LATE MEDIEVAL "MIRROR" FOR PRINCES AND MERCHANTS', *READING MEDIEVAL STUDIES*, 10: 136–91.

MOONEY, L. R. (2006), 'Chaucer's Scribe: New Evidence of the Identification of the Scribe of the Hengwrt and Ellesmere Manuscripts of Chaucer's *Canterbury Tales*', *Speculum*, 81: 97–138.

O'ROURKE, J. (2005), 'Imagining Book Production in Fourteenth-Century Herefordshire: The Scribe of British Library, MS Harley 2253 and his "Organizing Principles" ', in S. Kelly and J. J. Thompson (eds.), *Imagining the Book* (Medieval Texts and Cultures of Northern Europe, 7; Turnhout: Brepols), 45–60.

Paston Letters (1971) *Paston Letters and Papers of the Fifteenth Century: Part I*, ed. N. Davis (EETS SS 20; Oxford: Clarendon Press).

PEARSALL, D. (1992), *The Life of Geoffrey Chaucer: A Critical Biography* (Blackwell Critical Biographies, 1; Oxford and Cambridge, Mass.: Blackwell).

ROUSE, R. A. (2008), 'For King and Country? The Tension between National and Regional Identities in *Sir Bevis of Hampton*', in J. Fellows and I. Djordjevic, *Sir Bevis of Hampton in Literary Tradition* (Studies in Medieval Romance, 9; Cambridge: Brewer), 114–26.

SAMUELS, M. L. (1963), 'Some Applications of Middle English Dialectology', *English Studies*, 44: 81–94. Repr. with some revisions in M. Laing (ed.), *Middle English Dialectology: Essays on Some Principles and Problems* (Aberdeen: Aberdeen University Press, 1989), 64–80.

——(1985), 'Langland's Dialect', *Medium Ævum*, 54: 232–47. Repr. in J. J. Smith (ed.), *The English of Chaucer and his Contemporaries* (Aberdeen: Aberdeen University Press, 1998).

——(1988), 'Dialect and Grammar', in J. A. Alford (ed.), *A Companion to Piers Plowman* (Berkeley, Calif.: University of California Press), 201–22.

SÁNCHEZ-MARTÍ, J. (2003), 'The Scribe as Entrepreneur in Chetham's Library MS 8009', *Bulletin of the John Rylands University Library of Manchester*, 85: 13–22.

SCASE, W. (ed.) (2007), *Essays in Manuscript Geography: Vernacular Manuscripts of the English West Midlands from the Conquest to the Sixteenth Century* (Medieval Texts and Cultures of Northern Europe, 10; Turnhout: Brepols).

SCOTT, K. L. (1982), 'Lydgate's Lives of Saints Edmund and Fremund: A Newly-Located Manuscript in Arundel Castle', *Viator*, 13: 335–66.

SMITH, J. J. (2004), 'John Gower and London English', in S. Echard (ed.), *A Companion to Gower* (Cambridge: Brewer), 61–72.

STROHM, P. (1992), *Hochon's Arrow: The Social Imagination of Fourteenth-Century Texts* (Princeton: Princeton University Press).

Thompson, J., with S. KELLY, *et al.* (2006–), AHRC Geographies of Orthodoxy Project, <www.qub.ac.uk/geographies-of-orthodoxy>, and AHRC Imagining History Project, <www.qub.ac.uk/imagining-history/wordpress/>, both accessed 20 Dec. 2008.

THRUPP, S. (1948), *The Merchant Class of Medieval London: 1300–1500* (Chicago: Chicago University Press).

TURNER, M. (2006), 'Politics and London Life', in C. Saunders (ed.), *A Concise Companion to Chaucer* (Oxford: Blackwell).

——(2007), *Chaucerian Conflict: Language of Antagonism in Late Fourteenth-Century London* (Oxford: Clarendon Press).

TURVILLE-PETRE, T. (1996), *England the Nation: Language, Literature, and National Identity, 1290–1340* (Oxford: Clarendon Press).

WALDRON, R. (2004), 'Usk, Thomas (*c.*1354–1388)', *Oxford Dictionary of National Biography* (Oxford: Oxford University Press), <www.oxforddnb.com/view/article/28030>, accessed 12 Sept. 2008.

WALLACE, D. (1992), 'Chaucer and the Absent City', in B. A. Hanawalt, *Chaucer's England: Literature in Historical Context* (Minneapolis: University of Minnesota Press), 59–90.

WEISS, J. (1979), 'The Major Interpolations in *Sir Beues of Hamtoun*', *Medium Ævum*, 48: 71–6.

CHAPTER 28

....

READING
COMMUNITIES

....

WENDY SCASE

IN the modern western world reading is considered to be a silent, solitary, individual, and private activity. Occasions when reading is communal—the poetry reading, the book group, the primary school story-time—are viewed as exceptions to the norm. The typical modern book—for example, the 'paperback original'—is marketed as an individual purchase; its format enables it to be carried around by the individual reader, and to be used in a multitude of settings: in the home, on public transport, in the airport, in the doctor's surgery, on the beach, in bed. It is not generally designed as an investment purchase, or as an item to be shared, or as a product that can be customized to the needs of specific communities. It is perhaps not going too far to say that medieval reading was, by contrast, always a community activity. In this chapter I shall illustrate this claim by drawing on some of the vast range of evidence of reading cultures in medieval England, starting with literary and visual representations— the most accessible, but also the most problematic evidence—and then turning to more material forms of evidence. At the end of the chapter I shall briefly discuss some current developments in research on this topic, and identify some possible directions for the future.

IMAGINED READING COMMUNITIES

Perhaps the earliest description of a medieval reading community occurs in Bede's *Ecclesiastical History of the English People* (completed 731). Bede tells the story of how the poet Cædmon became the centre of community reading of Bible stories. In Bede's account, Cædmon was a simple cowherd at Whitby Abbey in the late seventh century, when Hild was abbess. Members of the community used to recite poetry to the accompaniment of a harp during feasts. Cædmon never joined in, because he did not know how to sing. One night, having gone out to the cowshed to avoid the embarrassment of having to sing, he had a vision in which he was given the gift of composing poetry, and he composed a short hymn about the creation of the world. Hearing his poem, the abbess and members of the order judged that Cædmon's ability to compose poetry was given by God. After that, monks would read the Bible to him, and he would go home and translate what he had heard into poetry, returning the next day to recite his poems to the community:

> In the morning . . . he was bidden to describe his dream in the presence of a number of the more learned men and also to recite his song so that they might all examine him and decide upon the nature and origin of the gift of which he spoke; and it seemed clear to all of them that the Lord had granted him heavenly grace. They then read to him a passage of sacred history or doctrine, bidding him to make a song out of it, if he could, in metrical form. He undertook the task and went away; on returning next morning he repeated the passage he had been given, which he had put into excellent verse. The abbess, who recognized the grace of God which the man had received, instructed him to renounce his secular habit and take monastic vows. She and all her people received him into the community of the brothers and ordered that he should be instructed in the whole course of sacred history. He learned all that he could by listening to them and then, memorizing it and ruminating over it, like some clean animal chewing the cud, he turned it into the most melodious verse: and it sounded so sweet that his teachers in turn became his audience.[1]

We should not expect Bede to give us a documentary account of 'real-life' vernacular reading culture in an Anglo-Saxon monastery. Rather, Bede's narrative explores through fiction the place of vernacular poetry in a community where Latin texts are the usual reading material. The story of Cædmon epitomizes an event in vernacular literary history, when traditional poetry intersects with Latin literature. That being said, for the modern reader, the story of Cædmon serves as an introduction to the extent to which the production and the reception of literature were grounded in community. It demonstrates how vernacular literate culture was necessarily a product of community, and how it generated community around it. The reading community created by Cædmon shares written texts by reading them aloud, and by hearing translations of Latin writing in traditional poetry. The monks of the community provide Cædmon with his source material, and with an audience for his vernacular poetry. In Bede's narrative, the composition of poetry depends on

---

[1] Colgrave, and Mynors (1969: 417–19).

community reading, and the reception of Cædmon's poems is also a community activity. That community, moreover, is socially diverse. It comprises men and women (the head of the monastery is a woman) and both those in religious orders and lay-people (Cædmon only becomes a monk once his gifts are discovered). Its distinctive cultures are not merely functional, but also deeply meaningful and formative of individual and communal identity. The characteristics of this imagined reading community have much in common with those of the later communities discussed in this chapter.[2]

Bede's story of the enjoyment of poetry during feasts has many later analogues. Romance literature is often associated with reading in a convivial setting. The idea that romance would be enjoyed by a community of well-born, discerning listeners is so conventional that it is inscribed in many romances. French romances frequently suggest the reading aloud of romance to an audience.[3] The convention is also found in English texts. In Chaucer's *Troilus and Criseyde*, when Pandarus goes to visit Criseyde at her house, he finds her with two companions listening to a romance read aloud by a maiden:

> Withinne a paved parlour, and they thre
> Herden a mayden reden hem the geste
> Of the siege of Thebes, while hem leste.[4]

Other texts suggest a convivial circumstance for their own delivery. The first fitt (division) of *Winner and Waster*, for example, closes with a call to provide the poet/ performer with refreshment:

> And he þat wilnes of this werke to wete any forthire
> Full freschely and faste for here a fitt endes.[5]

A very different reading community is depicted in *Westerne Wyll, vpon the debate betwyxte Churchyarde and Camell*, a pamphlet printed in London in the mid-sixteenth century.[6] This text depicts a scene in a printer's shop near St Paul's in London. Three sailors from Essex, unable to sail home because there is no wind, visit the shop in search of 'newes'. The printer offers them the text of a prophecy called *Dauy Dycars Dreame*, together with several texts by Thomas Churchyard and an opponent called Camell that comment upon and debate the prophecy. Seeing that the sailors are illiterate, the printer starts to read the texts to them, and an extremely comic debate takes place as the sailors discuss the texts. Herman, for example, is very suspicious of the credentials of the commentator Camell: if a camel cannot pass

---

[2] My phrase 'imagined reading community' is indebted to Anderson (1983), though I do not agree with Anderson's thesis concerning the medieval period.

[3] Coleman (1996: 83); for a deconstruction of this image and its meanings for contemporary critics see Wogan-Browne (2002: 240–1).

[4] Chaucer (1988), II. 82–4.

[5] Trigg (1990), ll. 216–17 ('And he who wishes to know anything further of this work, let him fill up [my cup] promptly and quickly, for this is the end of a fitt.').

[6] For discussion of the text and its contexts see Scase (2007*a*).

through the eye of a needle, as the Bible says, how on earth could one speak and write? Reading and discussion come to a halt when the wind gets up and the sailors must leave. They buy the verses for a groat and take them away, meaning to ask a literate sailor to finish reading the texts to them. *Dauy Dycars Dreame* was a real publication, a prophecy loosely based on prophecies in *Piers Plowman* printed and sold as a broadside (a single sheet). *Westerne Wyll* comically engages with mid-sixteenth-century concerns about how the printing of cheap books and pamphlets might bring reading material to communities lacking in learned interpretative skills.

Artists often represented reading communities in conventional images of poets and their patrons or audiences. One of the most common images is that of the poet presenting his work to a patron. For example, a manuscript of Hoccleve's *Regiment of Princes*, composed for Henry, Prince of Wales, includes a dedicatory verse to the 'Hye, noble and myȝtty Prince excellent' from the poet ('I humble seruant and obedient') beneath a miniature in which the poet, kneeling, presents a book to the prince.[7] In this image the book is closed with clasps. Other images depict the poet performing his work to an audience. One of the most famous is an image on the frontispiece of a manuscript of Chaucer's *Troilus and Criseyde*.[8] This miniature depicts Chaucer addressing a company of male and female courtiers in an idealized landscape, while behind them, in a separate space, other courtiers seem to pass to and fro on a road to a castle. The poet is depicted in the stance of an orator or preacher. He addresses his audience standing in a raised dock. Though his mouth is shut, he gestures, and some members of the audience look on attentively (while others look away or talk privately in small groups). Presumably the viewer is meant to understand that this is Chaucer delivering his poem from memory to an audience of lovers who discuss it. Of course, this image illustrates only one of the audiences imagined in the poem, that of experienced and knowledgeable lovers. It does not represent the audience to whom the poem is addressed at the end of the fifth book, 'moral Gower' and 'philosophical Strode',[9] readers whom the poet knew personally.[10]

The observation that the *Troilus* frontispiece is more idealized than reflective of reality points to a need for caution when using visual materials and literary texts as evidence for reading communities. Daniel Wakelin's painstaking recent analysis of *The Book of Noblesse* by William Worcester (1415–c.1483) illustrates this point powerfully. Wakelin suggests that Worcester's ideal is a 'commonweal of readers' and that he sets out to 'draw the reader into an imaginary readership of people familiar with certain literary and historical materials' which shares 'certain forms of literary and historical culture, certain rhetorical forms'.[11] Wakelin argues that Worcester is not reflecting any real reading community that was devoted to humanist ideals, but rather is creating an imaginary readership or community of readers. As a check on the veracity of the impression the reader gains from Worcester's *Boke*, Wakelin looks to material evidence: the manuscript record. Only one manuscript of

[7] London, British Library, Arundel 38, fo. 37, reproduced in Scattergood and Sherborne (1983), pl. 7.
[8] Cambridge, Corpus Christi College, 61, frontispiece.
[9] V. 1856–7.   [10] Compare Strohm (1989: 57).   [11] Wakelin (2007: 124–5).

the *Boke of Noblesse* survives. This gives weight to the suspicion that Worcester's reading community is an imagined community, for a text that survives in only one copy is unlikely to have enjoyed much of a community of readers. Due caution and a critical perspective should be applied to all of the representations of reading communities that we have encountered above. Each representation has its own agenda and, while it no doubt corresponds to some degree with contemporary culture, it may say as much about what reading in community might have meant, or have been desired to mean, as about what actually occurred. We must endeavour to triangulate evidence of this kind with other kinds of evidence and careful scrutiny of the material books themselves.

COMMUNAL READING

In the medieval period, illiteracy, together with the high cost of book production and lack of infrastructure for obtaining books meant that reading must often have been a group activity involving a reader and an audience. Those who were illiterate—an uncertain but no doubt relatively large proportion of the population—and those who had little or no personal access to books obviously relied on hearing texts read or recited aloud by someone else. But reading was very often an auditory activity anyway. Well into the later medieval period, even when they were alone, readers of vernacular texts would customarily read aloud.[12] With regard to recreational reading, public readings in company were the preference even among those who possessed books and were literate.[13]

Mealtimes, when there was a place to sit, leisure from work or other duties, and an environment warm enough to keep still in, were common occasions for communities to gather and participate in both devotional and recreational reading. There are many instances of communities gathering at mealtimes to hear devotional reading. A late thirteenth-century Anglo-Norman book of saints' lives that belonged to Campsey Priory (Suffolk) bears the inscription 'this book [is] given to Campsey Priory to read during meals'.[14] In the early fifteenth century a certain layman was advised to arrange for reading during dinner, 'now by one, now by another, and by your children as soon as they can read'.[15] Perhaps this guidance was modelled on the practice in religious communities. The purpose seems partly to have been to prevent idle discussion. (The same layman is also enjoined, while hearing mass, to 'look at

---

[12] Saenger (1982).   [13] This is the thesis of Coleman (1996).
[14] London, British Library, Additional 70513, fo. 265^v, quoted in Wogan-Browne (2001: 7); my translation.
[15] Pantin (1976: 399).

the books of the church' instead of engaging 'in talk with other people'.) Later in the century Cecily, duchess of York and mother of Edward IV, listened during mealtimes to readings from saints' lives, meditative material, and writings of women visionaries, and at supper-time repeated what she had heard earlier to her companions.[16]

Henry Scogan's 'A Moral Balade', the scribe John Shirley tells us, was written for the four sons of Henry IV (whose tutor he was) and was read publicly to its addressees at a supper arranged by some London merchants:

Here foloweth next a Moral Balade, to my lord the Prince, to my lord of Clarence, to my lord of Bedford, and to my lord of Gloucestre, by Henry Scogan; at a souper of feorthe merchande in the Vyntre in London, at the hous of Lowys Johan.[17]

The statutes of New College, Oxford, provided for scholars and fellows to remain in hall after dinner for the purposes of entertainment with singing and the enjoyment of secular literature such as poems and chronicles.[18]

Lollards—adherents to heterodox beliefs centred on Bible-reading—gathered in secret 'conventicles' (schools) to read, study, and discuss doctrine, sometimes in private houses. One gathering took place in the early sixteenth century at the house of Edward Walker in Maidstone. William Baker testified that he read 'a booke of Mathewe, where yn was conteyned the gospellis in Englisshe' aloud to John Bampton, William Riche, Edward Walker, and a young man who was an acquaintance of Walker's. Evidently the gathering discussed the text read by Baker, and concluded that it was 'ayenst the sacramentis of thaulter, baptisme, Matrimony, and preest-hode'.[19] A Lollard sermon on mendicancy concludes with a message that the preacher will leave the text with his audience for anyone who wishes to read it:

Nou siris þe dai is al ydo, and I may tarie ȝou no lenger, and I haue no tyme to make nou a recapitulacioun of my sermon. Neþeles I purpose to leue it writun among ȝou, and whoso likiþ mai ouerse it.[20]

The preacher says he will return at a later date to receive any corrections from his audience.

Probably many authors, if not all, belonged to and were sustained by reading communities. Many texts found in medieval manuscripts were composed by authors unknown, and often long dead when the manuscripts were made. However, we can sometimes glimpse the role of the living author in the reading community. 'Lenvoy de Chaucer a Bukton' is a balade on the topic of marriage addressed by the poet to 'my maister Bukton'. We are not completely sure who Bukton was, but the epistolary address implies that he was an acquaintance of the poet and familiar with at least some of his works: he is advised to read 'The Wyf of Bathe' for more on the topic of marriage. Another courtly epistle, 'Lenvoy de Chaucer a Scogan', appears to be

[16] Riddy (1993: 110).
[17] Quoted by Coleman (1996: 133), from the edn. by W. W. Skeat.
[18] Ibid. 136.
[19] McSheffrey (1995: 50).
[20] Hudson (1978: 96).

addressed to a fellow poet, possibly the courtier Henry Scogan. Poems such as this were probably circulated round a small coterie audience to whom the poet was known.[21]

COMMUNITIES AND THEIR BOOKS

Medieval books were often made by and for specific communities. In the century or so after 1066, religious communities set about building up libraries for their houses or remedying deficiencies in their existing collections. In some cases they imported books from the Continent, but houses also had their own scriptoria, where either monks or paid scribes copied books; sometimes local decorators worked on the volumes also. Between c.1100 and c.1150 many communities made libraries of core or standard works. This intensive activity of book making within religious houses gave rise to the development of distinctive 'house styles' which can be detected in surviving volumes.[22]

Many later vernacular devotional manuscripts whose provenance we can identify are associated with religious communities (often communities of women).[23] Since members of religious orders were not generally allowed private property, the readers of these books were perforce reading them as part of reading communities. The nuns at Syon, a Bridgettine community founded in 1415, were taught to view their private devotional reading within the context of their membership of a community dedicated to following the example of St Bridget.[24] Some of these religious reading communities were convents and monasteries, but others were perhaps more informal, such as the group of three anchoresses (women recluses) for whom the Early Middle English text *Ancrene Wisse* (Guidance for Anchoresses) was first composed by a spiritual adviser, probably in the early thirteenth century.[25]

The contents of medieval books were often shaped by the communities for whom they were made. Books were often compiled to address the interests of specific communities—whether a religious community, a household, or a guild, for example. This customization was enabled by bespoke methods of book production. Until the advent of printing, it is believed, books were normally copied to order, rather than

[21] Chaucer (1988: 655–6); Strohm (1989: 47–83). Trigg (2002) comments perceptively on the meanings and implications of this identification of Chaucer's audience; see esp. pp. 29–39.

[22] Thomson (2008: 137–53).

[23] The data in Ker (1964) amply support this claim about the gendering of English texts. For a very full survey of recent work on female reading communities see Wogan-Browne (2002).

[24] Krug (2002: 153–206); Erler (2002: 43–4).

[25] Millett (2005–6). For discussion of dating see pp. xi–xiii and for the audience see pp. xix–xxiv. Millett notes that, despite passages that specifically refer to the circumstances of the three women, there are signs that the author anticipated a wider audience also (p. xxiii).

being produced speculatively in the hope of finding a buyer. Bespoke book production enabled the patron or purchaser to choose the contents of a book, insofar as the availability of exemplars allowed. While religious houses aimed to build up a library of standard reading material, there are emphases which speak to local interests and agendas. For example, the continued copying of Old English material during the decades surrounding the Norman Conquest may be associated with particular centres and even individual bishops, such as Leofric at Exeter.[26]

Later manuscripts often seem to have been copied with the needs of a particular household in mind. In the mid-fifteenth century, Robert Thornton, a member of the gentry, appears to have tried to cater for every need, practical and spiritual, of the members of his Yorkshire household, copying alliterative and metrical romances, the prose *Alexander*, ethical and moral material (*Winner and Waster* and the *Parliament of the Three Ages*), work by the mystic Richard Rolle, medical recipes, and perhaps a herbal.[27] The Findern manuscript, a later fifteenth-century miscellany that includes romances, lyrics, and shorter verse by Chaucer and Lydgate, may have been compiled by and for the members of a Derbyshire household. It includes material copied in many different hands, some of them very unpractised, as well as family names and annotations.[28]

Some books may originally have been compiled by an individual scribe for personal use, later being used by a circle of readers. Oxford, Bodleian Library, Digby 86 might fit into this category. This manuscript, containing romances, devotional texts, recipes, and other recreational and functional materials, has been described as 'a layman's common-place book or miscellany'.[29] What gives it the character of a commonplace book is that the main scribe appears to have made additions to the texts after copying the main body of the material, for example, writing additional material in the lower margin. But the nature of the contents of the manuscript, diverse, trilingual (it includes texts in Latin, French, and English), and speaking to a multiplicity of human needs, creates the suspicion that, while the book may have been compiled by one person, it was intended for social use, perhaps by a household. It includes 'Ragemon le bon', for example, a game in which participants were allocated stanzas that told their character and fortune, and the comic dialogue *Dame Sirith* with the initials of the speakers marked, as if cues for reading aloud to an audience.[30] And whether or not this manuscript was originally intended for a community of readers, it is clear that a community began to use it. Obits in the Calendar record the deaths of members of two families who seem to have lived in close proximity, the manuscript passing from one family to another, and the manuscript includes materials in a hand other than that of the main scribe. The main

---

[26] Treharne (2007).

[27] Lincoln Cathedral, Dean and Chapter Library, 91, and London, British Library, Additional 31042; See Thompson (1987); Keiser (1996).

[28] Cambridge, Cambridge University Library, Ff.i.6; for a facsimile see Beadle and Owen (1977).

[29] Tschann and Parkes (1996: p. xi).

[30] Fos. 162^r–163^v and 165^r–168^r.

scribe may have been some kind of professional clerk whose employment—perhaps in estate administration—gave him a skill he could transfer to book making and proximity to a circle of families who could use his work.[31]

Medieval books that were produced to a costly standard are often far more eager to tell us about their patrons and their patron's households than about those (perhaps often members of the same community) who composed, copied, decorated, and assembled them. Many books of hours include depictions of their patrons or intended users, often in attitudes of adoration or prayer before Christ or the Virgin Mary. Images or other records of the scribes and artists are rare. The Luttrell Psalter is a good example of the ways in which a book can evoke one part of its community while suppressing other parts. A lavishly decorated book of Psalms made for a Lincolnshire lord *c.*1320–40, this manuscript includes a half-page miniature that depicts Sir Geoffrey Luttrell, commissioner of the volume, mounted, in full armour, accompanied by his wife and daughter-in-law.[32] In the margins of the volume are idealized depictions of community, including images of members of reading communities. In one margin a female grotesque—half woman in extravagant headdress, half bird—holds a closed book.[33] In an initial a cleric reads from an open book to a grotesque who looks the other way.[34] In another initial a group of lavishly dressed tonsured clerics gather around a book of music singing a psalm.[35] These images jostle for attention with images of those who are depicted as workers rather than readers, those whose labours sustain the privileges of the readers in their midst: a ploughman, a sower, harvesters, musicians, even a dentist. There is, though, no image of a scribe. Above the picture of Sir Geoffrey is the caption *Dominus Galfridus Louterell me fieri fecit* ('Sir Geoffrey Luttrell arranged for me to be made'). This method of announcing the origins of the volume reinforces the invisibility of those who enabled Sir Geoffrey and others to read their community in its pages: its scribe and decorators.[36]

It is, however, by no means always the case that we can readily identify the communities for whom expensive manuscripts were made or how they might have used them. A case in point is the Vernon manuscript, Oxford, Bodleian Library, Eng.poet.a.1. With 700 pages written in two or three columns (there were originally more pages, but some have been lost), the Vernon manuscript is the largest surviving Middle English manuscript. It is an extremely fine volume, written on good-quality vellum. The hand of the main scribe is clear and careful, and several artists have provided decorated initials and borders. The volume includes homilies, saints' lives, biblical narrative, lyrics, religious prose, and an A-text of *Piers Plowman*. A table of contents at the beginning of the volume records that the book contains material for

[31] Tschann and Parkes (1996: pp. lvii–lix (ownership), xxxviii–xxli (hands); lviii–lix n. 6 (profession of main scribe)).

[32] London, British Library, Additional 41230, fo. 202ᵛ, reproduced in Camille (1998), pl. 29, and discussed pp. 49–53.

[33] Fo. 192ᵛ, reproduced ibid., pl. 141.

[34] Fo. 158ᵛ, reproduced ibid., pl. 57.

[35] Fo. 147ʳ, reproduced ibid. pl. 41.

[36] See however ibid. 344–6, where Camille suggests that one of the marginal heads is a self-portrait by one of the artists; he also suggests that 'Geoffrey probably never noticed' (p. 344).

'salus anime' (spiritual well-being). The great size and weight of the volume mean that it cannot have been intended for private reading and that it almost certainly must have been intended to be read in a permanent place rather than being easily portable. These properties also suggest that it was made to be read aloud to an audience, probably from a standing position.[37] Yet not all of its materials could have been used in such a way. An elaborate table in which the Pater Noster is linked diagrammatically with the vices and virtues has to be seen to be understood, could not have been read in linear fashion (the table demands reading vertically and horizontally), and could not have made any sense to an audience who could not see it. The relations of the Vernon texts with texts in other volumes, its language, and some other features suggest that it comes from the Warwickshire/Worcestershire region, but we have no firm evidence to identify the community for whom it was made. Possibilities include a community of women religious, or a household with connections to a religious community, perhaps of Cistercians.[38]

LITERACY AND THE PROVISION
OF READING MATERIAL

Reading communities enlarged and sustained themselves through education in literacy, formal or informal. Elementary education—for both boys and girls—must often have taken place within the household. The first book was the 'primer', a book of prayers, psalms, and sometimes an abc. Well-to-do families engaged tutors or chaplains to educate their children in reading, but many children must have been taught to read the primer more informally. The image of the Virgin Mary being taught to read by St Anne, her mother, is ubiquitous in later medieval England. The fact that it is so common suggests that the Church sought to promote and endorse the transmission of religious literacy from parents to children, within the household.[39] For those (usually only boys) who progressed to more advanced reading of Latin, grammar schools offered formal education in Latin. Their syllabuses were built around a remarkably stable and uniform collection of 'set texts' drawn from classical authors. Probably often only the schoolmaster had use of a textbook; his pupils heard him read aloud and translated and imitated the texts they heard on wax tablets, though there are images of classrooms in which both teacher and pupils have books.[40]

A growth in the proportion of the population that was literate and an increase in the composition of vernacular reading material in later medieval England coincide with

---

[37] Robinson (1990); for a new facsimile of the manuscript, see Scase (forthcoming (a)).
[38] Doyle (1987: 14–15); see also Scase (forthcoming (b)).
[39] Scase (1993); Clanchy (1993) is an indispensable history of literacy.
[40] Reynolds (1996: 7–27); Woods and Copeland (1999). A sculpture at Chartres depicts Lady Grammatica wielding her birch over two dozing pupils; teacher and pupils all have open books before them.

the development of infrastructure designed to educate and provide books for communities of readers beyond the religious house or the family. In the fifteenth century John Shirley was at the heart of a community of readers which he seems to have facilitated by copying and loaning out books. Shirley compiled shorter poems by Chaucer, Hoccleve, and Lydgate, as well as anonymous work, in several volumes which he appears to have lent out among members of noble households.[41] The evidence for his lending of books includes short verse compositions in which he requests the return of books he has lent, for example, the 'bookplate stanza' which survives in two of his manuscripts:

> Yee þat desyre in herte and haue plesaunce
> Olde storyes in bokis for to rede
> Gode matiers putte hem in remembraunce
> And of oþer ne take yee none hede
> Beseching yowe of youre godely hede
> Whane yee þis boke haue over redde and seyne
> To Johan Shirley restore it ageyne.[42]

There is no direct evidence as to the identities of the borrowers of his books and critics have put forward a variety of suggestions. However, the tone of Shirley's verses is that of a respectful retainer to his social equals or superiors, suggesting that he expected to lend the volumes he copied to members of the noble household with which he was associated.[43]

Testamentary schemes, in which books were left in wills, suggest a community constituted through personal links that extended beyond the lives of its individual members. One example was planned by a chaplain of Coventry, William Wilmyncote, who left a collection of seven books to John Morele, with the stipulation that on his death they were to pass to a poor clerk and then to other poor chaplains until they wore out.[44] The will specifies that the beneficiaries are not to have absolute ownership of the books. This scheme is in this and other respects similar to a 'common-profit' scheme for book circulation in fifteenth-century London. Several books survive bearing 'common-profit' inscriptions which record that they were made with proceeds from estates and were entrusted to readers on condition that they were to be lent to others when not in use. One inscription records that the book is to be 'delyuered and committed fro persoone to persoone man or woman', suggesting circulation of reading matter around informal and inclusive reading communities.[45]

Other innovative charitable schemes relate to the founding of libraries to serve communities of readers. Some of the larger parish churches and some hospitals had libraries.[46] A library at Guildhall, London, was founded on the initiative of John Carpenter, Common Clerk of the city, using the estate of Richard Whittington (d. 1423) for whom

---

[41] Connolly (1998).

[42] Ibid. 192; the stanza appears in Oxford, Bodleian Library, Ashmole 59, and Cambridge, Trinity College, R.3.20.

[43] Connolly (1998: 191–5) discusses previous views and puts forward this suggestion.

[44] Scase (1992: 263).

[45] Ibid. for discussion of this scheme, and p. 261 for the quotation.

[46] Thrupp (1989: 162).

he was chief executor. Merchants contributed to the collection by leaving books to the library in their own wills.[47] A possible relative of John Carpenter of London, John Carpenter, bishop of Worcester, founded two libraries in his diocese at Bristol and Worcester. In each case a chaplain was appointed to run the library and take responsibility for explaining scripture or preaching.[48] These schemes were probably aimed at providing books for poor clerics who could not afford their own material, or who might have come by reading material the Church did not approve of. The Church authorities were acutely concerned during this period about Lollard communities, and in particular about their secret reading of heretical books, and it is possible that these schemes were set up in some measure in response to the threat of heresy.

Lollards followed the teachings of John Wyclif which were condemned as heretical by the Church in 1382. At the heart of their ideology was the idea that the Bible should be made available to all in English, and to this end they fostered the production of Bible translations and vernacular interpretative materials, such as sermons, glosses, and treatises. Because Lollardy was punishable by burning, and possession of Lollard books could be evidence towards a conviction, activity of this kind had to be conducted in secret. In late medieval Coventry a conventicle flourished whose fourteen members were exclusively female. At least five of the group were literate, and many possessed and exchanged books. The leader of the group, Alice Rowley, loaned and borrowed books from other Lollards, and was said to have put some in a hiding-place described as her 'chapell chambre'.[49]

Other reading communities feared by the authorities were those associated with the production and transmission of seditious and libellous texts. The tradition of posting clandestinely produced matter in public places incited nervous imaginings of how such material could spread rapidly from person to person. For example, a proclamation issued by the Crown in mid-fifteenth-century London forbids 'any man to read, pronounce, publish, deliver, or shew, copy, or cause to be copied or impart to any man secretly or openly any seditious schedule or bill or one subversive of the peace, or any infamous libel which has come to his hands'.[50]

COMMUNITIES AND NETWORKS

Reading communities did not operate in isolation; there is much evidence that they were sustained by larger networks. In the period before and immediately after the Conquest, local production and provision of books by and for religious communities took place within broader social networks. Networks developed and grew as monks

---

[47] Ibid.   [48] Scase (1992: 269).
[49] McSheffrey (1995: 29–37); quotation at p. 35.
[50] Quoted from Scase (1998: 229).

moved from a religious house to establish a new community, or abbots from several houses became members of a confraternity association. Networks could facilitate the movement of books and the material for making books. And books seem sometimes to have been made for use in networks. Manuscripts containing Old English material written after the Conquest hint at some of these relationships among readers centred on Worcester and other houses with which there were connections.[51]

In the case of women readers in particular, the transmission and exchange of reading material seems to have been enabled by family and social networks, whether the readers were professed religious or pious laywomen.[52] Krug's recent study, *Reading Families*, suggests that the family was the most important enabling condition of women's literate practice. One example from later in the period is a reading community associated with Anne Stafford, mother-in-law of Margaret Beaufort, who in turn was mother to Henry VII. Anne, Margaret, and Anne's own daughter Anne de Vere formed a reading community that exchanged books in the 1460s. Anne Stafford was the dedicatee of *The Nightingale*, a religious poem whose poet imagines Anne calling her household to listen to the poem.[53] Mary Erler's study of female book owners suggests that, while female readers were 'strongly dependent on membership in a community of readers', those communities could take varied forms and could be mixed as well as all female.[54]

Aristocratic and gentry households provided nodes or nexuses where complex lines of social relation intersected. Ryan Perry has suggested that they might also have provided ways in which the exemplars for a new manuscript could be found and borrowed, and that a manuscript assembled in this way might have had particular social associations and symbolic meaning for its commissioner and readers. His example is the Clopton manuscript, a fifteenth-century volume that originally included *Piers Plowman*, *Mandeville's Travels*, and various vernacular religious texts. The manuscript is closely related textually to other manuscripts from the same Warwickshire/Worcestershire area. Perry suggests that its compilation may have depended on the social networks in the region, and well beyond, that were associated with the Beauchamp family, and that the constant travel and communication among members of the Beauchamp affinity might have also sustained a community of readers and the production of reading materials for them.[55]

Heretical and seditious material also travelled along geographical networks from community to community. There is much evidence for connections among geographically scattered Lollard reading communities.[56] Seditious and libellous bills were thought to be (perhaps actually were) thrown onto highways for transmission by travellers, or distributed in geographically separate places by travelling rebels or heretics.[57] A bill against the enemies of Lord Protector Somerset, issued in 1550, for

---

[51] Swan (2007).   [52] See Wogan-Browne (2001: 11–12); and for the later period, Riddy (1993).
[53] Krug (2002: 76–80).   [54] Erler (2002: 136–7).
[55] Perry (2007). The volume is now in three separate parts: Washington, Folger Library, V.b.236; Princeton, Princeton University Library, R.H. Taylor 10; and London, University of London, Senate House Library, Sterling V.17.
[56] For a subtle analysis of the evidence see Hudson (1988: 137–42).
[57] Scase (1998: esp. p. 238).

example, carries the endorsement 'Rede it and give it ffurth'.[58] Much like today's chain letters, or even email spam, such texts were designed to make use of existing social and communications networks for their means of transmission.

FUTURE STUDY

Study of medieval reading communities is relatively recent, and is still very much in its early stages. Study of the subject requires work with a variety of kinds of evidence, including literary texts, manuscripts, and library catalogues, but also less obvious sources such as wills and inventories, letters, and even court records. Researchers are still identifying and analysing the evidence and our state of knowledge is at the level of the case study rather than the synthesis. Much remains to be done before it will be possible to write a comprehensive history of medieval reading and its place in communities. Every manuscript, potentially, has evidence to offer to the bigger picture, and manuscripts need to be studied in sufficiently large numbers to enable scholars to move beyond the case study towards generalization. Researchers are attempting to tackle the huge task of the description and analysis of manuscripts in large numbers by working cooperatively and creating computerized databases.[59] But assembling the data is not enough. Researchers also need to decide what counts as relevant data, and how the data collected can be analysed and understood. This search for productive theoretical frameworks is also in its infancy. Some scholars have experimented with an 'ethnography of reading' and similar concepts borrowed from social history and anthropology.[60] Others are invoking the term 'knowledge network' to inform research on reading communities, drawing on work in mathematics (network theory) and information technology, social policy, and business studies (knowledge networks, social network analysis).[61] Perhaps new models too

[58] Scase (2007b: 161–2 and pls. 16–17).

[59] E.g. *The Production and Use of English Manuscripts, 1060–1220*, at the universities of Leicester and Leeds (<http://www.le.ac.uk/ee/em1060to1220/index.html>) and *Manuscripts of the West Midlands: A Catalogue of Vernacular Manuscript Books of the English West Midlands, c.1300–c.1475*, at the University of Birmingham (<http://www.mwm.bham.ac.uk>).

[60] Coleman (1996: 76) uses the term 'ethnography of reading'. McSheffrey (1995) defines *community* as 'a complex of social relations', following social historian C. J. Calhoun (p. 17). Other researchers describe their work as 'cultural mapping', a term commonly used in the fields of development studies and public arts and heritage planning (see e.g. the project *Geographies of Orthodoxy: Mapping Pseudo-Bonaventuran Lives of Christ 1350–1550* (http://www.qub.ac.uk/geographies-of-orthodoxy/discuss/). Stock's (1983) use of the term 'textual community' to denote a group to whom the interpretation of a particular text is central, has proved productive and influential. Wogan-Browne (2002: 229–31), reflects on the uses, resonances, and dangers of the term 'community' in recent medieval scholarship.

[61] The Australia-based Network for Early Europe Research project Knowledge Networks and Reading Communities 'aims to draw together Australian and international researchers, across a broad range of cognate specialised areas, to develop collaborative projects on researching the nature of knowledge networks in late medieval England and the reading communities consequent on and sustained by those networks; see <http://confluence.arts.uwa.edu.au/display/KNOW/Home>

will derive from the interactive reading communities that are emerging, and becoming subjects of study, in the internet age. Social computing networks such as Facebook that translate real communities into cyberspace, and the virtual reading communities enabled by interactive media such as blogs and wikis might give us new frameworks for investigating and understanding the reading communities that produced, and were produced by, medieval books.

Knowledge networks in late medieval England and the reading communities consequent on and sustained by those networks; see <http://confluence.arts.uwa.edu.au/display/KNOW/Home>

BIBLIOGRAPHY

ANDERSON, BENEDICT (1983), *Imagined Communities: Reflections on the Origin and Spread of Nationalism* (London: Verso).

BEADLE, RICHARD, and A. E. B. OWEN (1977), *The Findern Manuscript, Cambridge University Library MS Ff.1.6* (London: Scolar Press).

CAMILLE, MICHAEL (1998), *Mirror in Parchment: The Luttrell Psalter and the Making of Medieval England* (London: Reaktion Books).

CHAUCER, GEOFFREY (1988), *The Riverside Chaucer*, ed. Larry D. Benson (3rd edn, Oxford: Oxford University Press).

CLANCHY, M. T. (1993), *From Memory to Written Record: England 1066–1307* (2nd edn, Oxford: Blackwell).

COLEMAN, JOYCE (1996), *Public Reading and the Reading Public in Late Medieval England and France* (Cambridge Studies in Medieval Literature, 26; Cambridge: Cambridge University Press).

COLGRAVE, BERTRAM, and R. A. B. MYNORS (eds.) (1969), *Bede's Ecclesiastical History of the English People* (rev. edn. Oxford Medieval Texts; Oxford: Clarendon Press).

CONNOLLY, MARGARET (1998), *John Shirley: Book Production and the Noble Household in Fifteenth-Century England* (Aldershot: Ashgate).

DOYLE, A. I. (1987), *The Vernon Manuscript: A Facsimile of Bodleian Library, Oxford, MS. Eng. Poet.a.1* with intro. by A.I. Doyle (Cambridge: D. S. Brewer).

ERLER, MARY C. (2002), *Women, Reading, and Piety in Late Medieval England* (Cambridge: Cambridge University Press).

HUDSON, ANNE (ed.) (1978), *Selections from English Wycliffite Writings* (Cambridge: Cambridge University Press).

——(1988), *The Premature Reformation: Wycliffite Texts and Lollard History* (Oxford: Clarendon Press).

KEISER, GEORGE R. (1996), 'Reconstructing Robert Thornton's Herbal', *Medium Ævum*, 65: 35–53.

KER, N. R. (ed.) (1964), *Medieval Libraries of Great Britain: A List of Surviving Books* (2nd edn. London: Royal Historical Society).

KRUG, REBECCA (2002), *Reading Families: Women's Literate Practice in Late Medieval England* (Ithaca, NY: Cornell University Press).

McSHEFFREY, SHANNON (1995), *Gender and Heresy: Women and Men in Lollard Communities, 1420–1530* (Philadelphia: University of Pennsylvania Press).

MILLET, BELLA (ed.) (2005–6), *Ancrene Wisse: A Corrected Edition of the Text in Cambridge, Corpus Christi College, MS 402 with Variants from other Manuscripts*, drawing on the uncompleted edn. by E. J. Dobson, with a glossary and additional notes by Richard Dance (2 vols. Early English Text Society, OS 325, 326; Oxford: Oxford University Press for the Early English Text Society).

PANTIN, W. A. (1976), 'Instructions for a Devout and Literate Layman', in J. G. Alexander and M. T. Gibson (eds.), *Medieval Learning and Literature* (Oxford: Clarendon Press), 398–422.

PERRY, RYAN (2007), 'The Clopton Manuscript and the Beauchamp Affinity: Patronage and Reception Issues in a West Midlands Reading Community', in Wendy Scase (ed.), *Essays in Manuscript Geography: Vernacular Manuscripts of the English West Midlands from the Conquest to the Sixteenth Century* (Turnhout: Brepols), 131–59.

REYNOLDS, SUZANNE (1996), *Medieval Reading: Grammar, Rhetoric and the Classical Text* (Cambridge Studies in Medieval Literature, 27; Cambridge: Cambridge University Press).

RIDDY, FELICITY (1993), ' "Women Talking about the Things of God": A Late Medieval Sub-Culture', in Carol Meale (ed.), *Women and Literature in Britain, 1150–1500* (Cambridge Studies in Medieval Literature, 17; Cambridge: Cambridge University Press), 104–27.

ROBINSON, P. R. (1990), 'The Vernon Manuscript as a "Coucher Book"', in Derek Pearsall (ed.), *Studies in the Vernon Manuscript* (Cambridge: D. S. Brewer), 15–28.

SAENGER, PAUL (1982), 'Silent Reading: Its impact on Late Medieval Script and Society', *Viator*, 13: 367–414.

SCASE, WENDY (1992), 'Reginald Pecock, John Carpenter, and John Colop's "Common-Profit" Books: Aspects of Book Ownership and Circulation in Fifteenth-Century London', *Medium Ævum*, 61: 261–74.

——(1993), 'Saint Anne and the Education of the Virgin: Literary and Artistic Traditions and their Implications', in Nicholas Rogers (ed.), *England in the Fourteenth Century: Proceedings of the 1991 Harlaxton Symposium* (Stamford, Lincs.: Paul Watkins), 81–96.

——(1998), ' "Strange and Wonderful Bills": Bill-Casting and Political Discourse in Late Medieval England', *New Medieval Literatures*, 2: 225–47.

——(2007a), '*Dauy Dycars Dreame* and Robert Crowley's Prints of *Piers Plowman*', *Yearbook of Langland Studies*, 21: 171–98.

——(2007b), *Literature and Complaint in England, 1272–1553* (Oxford: Oxford University Press).

——(ed.) (forthcoming (a)), *The Vernon Manuscript: A Digital Facsimile Edition* (Bodleian Digital Texts, Oxford: Bodleian Library).

——(ed.) (forthcoming (b)), *The Making of the Vernon Manuscript: The Production and Contexts of Oxford, Bodleian Library, MS Eng. poet. a. 1* (Texts and Transitions: Studies in the History of Manuscripts and Printed Books 6; Turnhout: Brepols).

SCATTERGOOD, V. J., and J. W. SHERBORNE (eds.) (1983), *English Court Culture in the Later Middle Ages* (London: Duckworth).

STOCK, BRIAN (1983), *The Implications of Literacy: Written Language and Models of Interpretation in the Eleventh and Twelfth Centuries* (Princeton: Princeton University Press).

STROHM, PAUL (1989), *Social Chaucer* (Cambridge, Mass.: Harvard University Press).

SWAN, MARY (2007). 'Mobile Libraries: Old English Manuscript Production in Worcester and the West Midlands, 1090–1215', in Wendy Scase (ed.), *Essays in Manuscript Geography: Vernacular Manuscripts of the English West Midlands from the Conquest to the Sixteenth Century* (Turnhout: Brepols), 29–42.

THOMPSON, JOHN J. (1987), *Robert Thornton and the London Thornton Manuscripot: British Library MS Additional 31042* (Cambridge: D. S. Brewer).

THOMSON, RODNEY M. (2008), 'Monastic and Cathedral Book Production', in Nigel J. Morgan and Rodney M. Thomson (eds.), *The Cambridge History of the Book in Britain*, ii. *1100–1400* (Cambridge: Cambridge University Press), 137–67.

THRUPP, SYLVIA L. (1989), *The Merchant Class of Medieval London*, with rev. introd. (Ann Arbor: University of Michigan).

TREHARNE, ELAINE (2007), 'Bishops and their Texts in the Later Eleventh Century: Worcester and Exeter', in Wendy Scase (ed.), *Essays in Manuscript Geography: Vernacular Manuscripts of the English West Midlands from the Conquest to the Sixteenth Century* (Turnhout: Brepols), 13–28.

TRIGG, STEPHANIE (ed.) (1990), *Wynnere and Wastoure* (Early English Text Society, OS 297; Oxford: Oxford University Press for the Early English Text Society).

——(2002), *Congenial Souls: Reading Chaucer from Medieval to Postmodern* (Medieval Cultures Series, 30; Minneapolis: University of Minnesota Press).

TSCHANN, JUDITH, and M. B. PARKES (1996), *Facsimile of Oxford, Bodleian Library, MS Digby 86* (Early English Text Society, supplementary series, 16; Oxford: Oxford University Press for the Early English Text Society).

WAKELIN, DANIEL (2007), *Humanism, Reading, and English Literature 1430–1530* (Oxford: Oxford University Press).

WESTERNE WYLL (*c.*1550), *Westerne Wyll, vpon the debate betwyxte Churchyarde and Camell* (London: William Powell, STC 25668.5).

WOGAN-BROWNE, JOCELYN (2001), *Saints' Lives and Women's Literary Culture c.1150–1300: Virginity and its Authorisation* (Oxford: Oxford University Press).

——(2002), 'Analytical Survey 5: "Reading is Good Prayer": Recent Research on Female Reading Communities', *New Medieval Literatures*, 5: 229–97.

WOODS, MARJORIE CURRY, and RITA COPELAND (1999), 'Classroom and Confession', in David Wallace (ed.), *The Cambridge History of Medieval English Literature* (Cambridge: Cambridge University Press), 376–89.

CHAPTER 29

SCOTTISH WRITING

....

ELIZABETH ELLIOTT

A passage from *The Flyting* of Dunbar and Kennedy offers a provocative illustration of the role of cultural nationalism in the construction of Scottish literary history. Within this poetic exchange of insults, Walter Kennedy (*c*.1455–*c*.1518), whose association with the Gaelic-speaking region of Carrick suggests fluency in both of the vernacular languages of late medieval Scotland, responds to William Dunbar's derisive attack on 'Sic eloquence as thay in Erschry vse', and on himself as an 'Iersche brybour baird' ('Irish' or 'Gaelic-speaking beggar bard'):[1]

> Thou lufis nane Irische, elf, I vnderstand,
> Bot it suld be all trew Scottis mennis lede. [*language*]
> It was the gud langage of this land,
> And Scota it causit to multiply and sprede
> Quhill Corspatrik, that we of treson rede,
> Thy forfader, maid Irisch and Irisch men thin,
> Throu his treson broght Inglise rumplis in. [*tails*]
> Sa wald thy self, mycht thou to him succede.[2]

Kennedy's allusion to the potent origin myth ascribing the foundation of Scotland to Scota, daughter of Pharaoh, invokes a tradition of Scottish historiography that sought to establish Scotland's right to self-determination against English hegemonic claims based in part on the mythic foundation of Britain by the Trojan Brutus. His invective implies a racial difference between the English and the Scots, in an allusion to the enduring legend

---

[1] Bawcutt (1998: no. 65, ll. 107, 49).
[2] Ibid. ll. 345–52.

that the English bore tails as a punishment for having mocked St Augustine of Canterbury, and it seeks to establish an authentic version of Scottish identity through an
insistence upon Scotland's past as a politically autonomous and linguistically homogeneous whole. Yet Kennedy's polemical appeal to a clearly delimited, authentic model of
Scottish culture inevitably exposes the impossibility of any singular definition of
Scottish identity. In common with the historiographic tradition upon which it depends,
Kennedy's vision reveals the complexity of Scotland's past in its own hybrid construction. As Katherine Terrell argues, such attempts to delineate Scotland's cultural boundaries are inescapably compromised by their origins as responses to English imperialist
claims, and by their engagement with the sources invoked to legitimize those claims.
Dialogic in nature, such narratives expose the function of the border as a site of
interaction as well as of exclusion, as a space where identity is negotiated through
contact with the Other.[3] Kennedy's ideal of linguistic unity is palpably subverted both by
its conditional expression and because, like all Kennedy's surviving poetry, the *Flyting* is
not written in Gaelic, but in the language then termed 'Inglis', the ancestor of modern
Scots. The *Flyting* illustrates the complex cultural negotiations taking place within
Scottish writing in the Middle Ages, yet it also offers a playful image of the prejudices
and strategies of exclusion entailed in certain perspectives that have influenced the
formation of a Scottish literary tradition.

   This chapter does not attempt to offer a comprehensive account of Scottish writing,
but instead seeks to explore the tensions at issue in the development of particular
models of a Scottish national tradition and their implications for our reading practice:
first, by tracing the influence of the history of Scottish literary studies on the modern
reception of early literature, and then through analysis of a particular conjunction in
that history, between the Bannatyne Manuscript and the Bannatyne Club.[4] A third
section will examine the ways in which the extended model of the Scottish canon
developed in recent criticism troubles received ideas of a national tradition. Finally,
the poets conventionally, if problematically, designated as Scottish Chaucerians will be
considered in their role as makers of the received canon of Scottish literature.

A NATIONAL TRADITION?

In his insistence upon a common language, on an unisonance located within a
mythologized past, as the mark of cultural authenticity, Kennedy anticipates modern
critics such as Edwin Muir, whose reading of literary history influenced the development of the established canon of Scottish literature in the twentieth century. For

---

[3] Terrell (2008).

[4] Recent comprehensive surveys of early literature in Scotland include Clancy and Pittock (2007);
Crawford (2007: 21–113); and, for the 14th cent. onwards, Bawcutt and Hadley Williams (2006); Gray
(2008: 441–566). Still especially valuable is Jack (1988).

Muir 'the prerequisite of an autonomous literature is a homogeneous language', and he concurred with Hugh MacDiarmid and others in regretting a perceived 'disintegration' of Scots, the natural 'language of Scottish literature', during the sixteenth century.[5] The effects of such interpretations upon literary history have been examined by Gerard Carruthers (1999) and R. D. S. Jack (1993, 1997a), who highlight the residual influence of anachronistic and essentialist notions of a national tradition within the main current of Scottish criticism. Building on Jack's analysis, Sarah Dunnigan has drawn attention to the part played by such cultural and aesthetic assumptions in obscuring the literature of the pre-Reformation era, which resists incorporation within any unitary narrative of Scottish literature.[6] More recent anthologies and literary histories attest to a resurgence of interest in the neglected literature of the early period, in a revival encompassing both academic publications, such as the first volume of the new *Edinburgh History of Scottish Literature* (2007), and paperbacks aimed at the general reader. These include Thomas Owen Clancy's pioneering anthology of Scottish poetry down to 1350, *The Triumph Tree*, first published by Canongate in 1998 and reprinted by Birlinn in 2009; and the *New Penguin Book of Scottish Verse*, which includes a substantial selection of pre-modern literature.[7] Since republished as the *Penguin Book of Scottish Verse* (2006), it is indicative that its companion volume, *Scotland's Books*, was conceived as an unprecedented attempt: 'the first time anyone had tried to encompass the extended history of Scottish literature in all the languages of Scotland'.[8] The lasting influence of reductive conceptions of a coherent literary tradition, like that developed by Muir, renders further examination of their effect on Scottish literary studies useful.

Muir's identification of Scots as the authentic language of Scottish literature depends upon the perception of Scots and English as a contrastive pairing, yet the evidence suggests that it was only at the end of the fifteenth century that speakers began to use the term 'Scotis', rather than 'Inglis', to designate Lowland speech. Rather than being a reflection of the linguistic heritage of the early modern period, the sense of a dichotomy between Scots and English, and the idea that Scots as a literary language had suffered a historic collapse, owe more to Scotland's role in shaping the growth of English literature as an institutionalized discipline. Eighteenth-century Scots have been credited with the invention of English literature as a subject for tertiary study, as they attended courses of lectures in order to assimilate their modes of expression to an English model.[9] As Cairns Craig has demonstrated, however, Scottish writing remained central to the new discipline, since the rediscovery of the shared Anglo-Saxon origins of English and Scots in the early nineteenth century endorsed a conception of English literature that encompassed Scottish writing in these languages. Within this model, Henryson and Dunbar occupied key positions

---

[5] Muir (1936: 18–19).
[6] Dunnigan (2004, 2005).
[7] Crawford and Imlah (2000).
[8] Crawford (2007: p. x).
[9] Crawford (2000, 1998).

within the canon, as Chaucer's heirs, and as precursors to the literature of sixteenth-century England. The influence of this version of literary history contributed to the institutionalization of the study of Gaelic literature within departments of Celtic studies, limiting the vision of Scotland's literary heritage.[10] Scottish literature gained recognition as a separate national tradition only as the decline of the British Empire saw the emergence of a more exclusive conception of English identity and of the English canon, and its development as a discipline was inevitably circumscribed by the historically constituted perception of Scottish tradition. Thus, the earliest modern narratives of Scottish literary history, like that developed by Gregory Smith, retrospectively interpret the history of Scottish writing as a long and regrettable process of Anglicization, not 'a theory of an independent Scottish literature but of its defeat'.[11]

It is symptomatic of the tendency to identify Scottish literature with writing in Scots that most literary-historical narratives of the medieval period begin with John Barbour's *The Bruce*, the earliest substantial work extant in Scots. Barbour's position at the head of a Scottish tradition has been further reinforced by nationalistic conceptions of Scottish literature, which respond to the *Bruce*'s treatment of key events in Scotland's self-determination, and its role as 'arguably the most impressive work of national ideology produced in Scotland before the novels of Sir Walter Scott'.[12] As the editors of the *Edinburgh History of Scottish Literature* argue, however, 'such a starting point disenfranchises languages and communities from the nation's literary story', privileging the cultural heritage of Lowland Scotland and neglecting the diversity of a literature that also encompasses works surviving in Latin, Gaelic, Norse, French, and Welsh.[13] Yet, the expanded sense of the canon of Scottish literature articulated in such new literary histories is contentious, because it poses fundamental questions about the nature of Scotland and a Scottish literary tradition. The earliest texts predate Scotland's emergence as a nation-state, and an acknowledgement of the full variety of the literary heritage of what is now Scotland entails the partial appropriation of texts that also occupy a place in the canons of other national literatures, such as the *Gododdin*. This problem is compounded in the case of works in Gaelic and Norse, since these traditions looked to cultural centres beyond Scotland, to Scandinavian and Irish homelands.

To paraphrase Ernest Renan's analysis of the relationship between historical enquiry and nationalism: if nations are communities whose cohesion depends in part upon the collective memory of shared experience and upon a selective amnesia that draws a veil over their heterogeneous and often violent origins, then the enlargement of Scottish literary studies threatens the myth of national unity as it acknowledges the diverse communities contributing to Scotland's literary heritage.[14] In unsettling the concept of a fixed national identity, projects such as the *Edinburgh*

[10] Craig (2007*a*, 2007*b*).
[11] Smith (1919); Craig (2007*b*: 29).
[12] Goldstein (1993: 141).
[13] Brown *et al.* (2007: 8).
[14] Renan (1990: 11).

History enable a critical re-examination of the idea of culture like that proposed by Edward Said, which envisages cultures as permeable boundaries, rather than mono-lithic forms. He contends that, 'to see Others not as ontologically given but as historically constituted would be to erode the exclusivist biases we so often ascribe to cultures, our own not the least'.[15] Such a re-examination facilitates reflection upon the tradition of Scottish writing, and on Scotland itself, as 'embodied argument', the expression of an ongoing debate between a multitude of conflicting voices, both past and present.[16] Against this background, critical analysis of the historical context that informs a particular conception of the national tradition offers a means to explore the interplay between past and present reflected within that model. An examination of two related examples that have attracted attention as being in some sense attempts to fashion an image of a national tradition, the Bannatyne Manuscript and the work of the Bannatyne Club, will serve as illustration.

THE BANNATYNE MANUSCRIPT
AND THE BANNATYNE CLUB

The most celebrated of Middle Scots manuscript miscellanies, the Bannatyne Manu-script[17] was completed in 1568 by George Bannatyne (1545–1607/8). Although late in date, it includes numerous medieval works, and bears witness to the eclectic tastes of its compiler in the remarkable diversity of its contents. The fivefold arrangement of the Main Manuscript by genre is especially distinctive, and has no close parallel. An excellent facsimile exists, and the manuscript has deservedly attracted much critical interest.[18] Nevertheless, it is significant that other important Scottish miscellanies, such as the group associated with Sir Richard Maitland of Lethington (1496–1586), have been oddly neglected. As Priscilla Bawcutt argues, although the Bannatyne Manuscript is 'perceived as unique . . . few have questioned this unique status, or made much attempt to relate it to other manuscript miscellanies'.[19] Bawcutt identi-fies the enduring influence of Sir Walter Scott as the source of a number of preconceptions surrounding this manuscript, and an examination of Scott's vision of Bannatyne offers an insight into the construction of a Scottish literary tradition.

In characterizing Bannatyne as a man with 'the courageous energy to form and execute the plan of saving the literature of a whole nation', Scott presents a version of

[15] Said (1989: 225).
[16] Craig (1999: 9–36).
[17] National Library of Scotland, Adv. MS 1. 1. 6.
[18] Fox and Ringler (1980).
[19] Bawcutt (2005).

the past that mirrors his own concerns.[20] His work, with that of several Scots who collected folk materials, is described in intriguing terms by Robert Crawford: 'Writing in a culture under pressure, each sought to bind that culture together, to preserve it and celebrate it through anthology, which was closely bound up with creative endeavour.'[21] Confronted with the Bannatyne Manuscript, 'writtin in Tyme of Pest', Scott and his contemporaries cast it in the image of their own enterprise, and this conception of Bannatyne and his work was perpetuated in the foundation of the Bannatyne Club in 1823, as a society for the publication of 'Works, illustrative of the History, Topography, Poetry and Miscellaneous Literature of Scotland in former times'.[22] Recent work attests to the patriotic motivations of the Bannatyne Club and to the diverse ways of conceiving the past represented by its collective endeavours.[23] In certain respects, the Bannatyne Club encouraged the conceptualization of the writing of the past as commodity and as fetish: as one member wryly commented, 'Very few of us can read our books, and still fewer can understand them; yet type, morocco, and the corporation spirit make us print on, and this quite independently of the temptation arising from the marketable worth of what we get being far beyond what we pay.'[24]

Yet, as Ina Ferris argues, the desire to print an illegible past also reflects a concern with authenticity, since it counteracts the nostalgic impulse that sought to transform ballads and other literary 'relics' into foci for collective memory. In common with other antiquarian societies, the Bannatyne Club valued marginalized works precisely because they had the power to unsettle received versions of literature and history. If their publications seek to allow an authentic past to speak, however, they also enact an alteration, as the process of citation inevitably transforms text and context by bringing the two into juxtaposition.[25] The printing of the past works to define the community that the Bannatyne Club represents, bringing it into contact with a distinctive Scottish tradition and thus counteracting the homogenizing influence of the Union, yet it also reinvents that tradition in the process. Bannatyne himself emerges from this intersection recast as a version of Scott, a patriotic antiquarian whose manuscript is a repository of national tradition, but if it would be 'critical hindsightism' to accept this image, it nevertheless represents a response to the functions of the manuscript itself.[26]

The Bannatyne Manuscript may be said to incarnate a national tradition insofar as it enacts a debate taking place within society at the time of its production. It transmits an inheritance from the past and shapes a course for that tradition's future development because it embodies a definition of the ends towards which such a tradition should move. The logic of this conception of a national tradition is borne

[20] Scott (1829: 11).
[21] Crawford (2000: 113).
[22] Bannatyne Club minutes, quoted in Ray Murray (2007: 279).
[23] Ray Murray (2007); Ferris (2005).
[24] Cockburn (1874: 39).
[25] Ferris (2005).
[26] Bawcutt (2005: 207).

out in the treatment of frequency of transmission as evidence of canonical status,[27] since the reproduction of an individual text effects a judgement as to which elements of literary culture are worth preserving. This model is one that has been used to describe the affinity between the novel and national tradition,[28] and it is significant that the manuscript anthology shares common features with the novel. Both are composite forms uniting diverse elements within borders, and this aspect of the novel has been seen as a key factor in the rise of the modern nation-state, since it induced people to imagine a national community.[29]

The cohesive effect produced by such forms is dependent upon their circulation: in the case of the Bannatyne Manuscript, the possibility that its contents were intended for print is still the subject of controversy,[30] but Bannatyne's inclusion of addresses to 'The Redar' and to his 'freindis' invoke a literate community, and suggest the plausibility of scribal publication. Harold Love defines one function of this form of transmission as 'bonding groups of like-minded individuals into a community … with the exchange of text in manuscript serving to nourish a shared set of values and to enrich personal allegiances'.[31] Such a community has been identified by Theo van Heijnsbergen, whose study of the prosopographical context locates the Bannatyne Manuscript in relation to a social group whose 'contrasting yet not mutually exclusive cultural, political and religious identities' reflect its poetic content, and traces its connections to a 'humanist "republic of letters" that considered literature to be a vital component of a national heritage'.[32] The manuscript also articulates aspects of the religious and political controversies of the period leading up to its completion, which saw the deposition of Mary, Queen of Scots, as Bannatyne censors the poems in his collection, excising references to the queen and revising poems alluding to Catholic devotion. In this respect, the manuscript is in dialogue with the recent past, and it offers an illustration of the ways in which post-Reformation tastes have shaped the surviving corpus of early religious literature.[33] Like the novel, or the folk anthology, the form and content of the Bannatyne Manuscript invoke and produce a particular experience of community as they give shape to tradition.

It is also significant that the contents of the Bannatyne Manuscript anticipate the matter of a national literary tradition as conceived by Scott and his contemporaries to a greater extent than is usually recognized. The manuscript's substantial English component, including poems by Chaucer, foreshadows the nineteenth-century perception of English literature as a tradition to which Scottish writing was central. This is no accident, but reflects the ways in which the Middle Scots poets participate in the construction of Chaucer as authority, the father of a tradition.[34] In each case, the

---

[27] e.g. in MacDonald (2003: 67).
[28] Craig (1999).
[29] Brennan (1990).
[30] Most recently in MacDonald (2003) and Bawcutt (2005).
[31] Love (1993: 177).
[32] Heijnsbergen (1994: 186, 224).
[33] MacDonald (1983).
[34] Lerer (1993); Craig (2007b: 18).

relationship between past and present versions of tradition is not a simple fabrication: each instance is in dialogue with what has gone before, and the transmission of the past coincides with its redefinition. The interlinked examples of the Bannatyne Manuscript and the Bannatyne Club draw attention to the need to examine the historical construction of such traditions, in order to avoid reinscribing them as being ontologically given in critical reception. Manuscript studies play a significant part in this enterprise, as Priscilla Bawcutt's comment on the need for a holistic approach to the manuscript suggests: 'silent selectivity, whether inspired by nationalism or some other motive—extracting merely the plums, like little Jack Horner—may lead to distortion and falsification, not only of a manuscript's character but of a society's literary and musical culture'.[35] The publication of new work illuminating the circumstances of textual production, circulation, and reception in medieval and early-modern Scotland will greatly advance understanding of how such ideas of tradition were constructed and developed; most notable are the forthcoming volume I of *The Edinburgh History of the Book in Scotland: From the Earliest Times to 1707*,[36] and a DVD of digitized facsimiles of the Chepman and Myllar prints (*c*.1508), early products of Scotland's first press.[37]

THE EXTENDED CANON

The relationship between literature and conflicting notions of a national tradition is also at issue in study of the texts of the early period, as conceived within the extended model of the canon.[38] In itself, this model brings questions surrounding the 'national' aspects of a literary tradition into sharp focus: the earliest surviving texts are Latin compositions, associated with the ecclesiastical centres established by an influx of Gaelophone clergy from Ireland, who gradually diffused outwards from Scottish Dál Riata, part of an Irish overkingdom encompassing Antrim. The most famous of these is the monastery of Iona, founded by St Columba (Colum Cille, *c*.521–97), who sailed from Ireland in 563. A key intellectual centre, Iona's significance to Irish tradition is reflected in the status of its records as the main source for the early Irish annals, and the life of its founder written by the ninth abbot, Adomnán of Iona, offers evidence of the extent to which such communities defined themselves through their affiliation with Ireland.

Adomnán's role as the voice of a community is signalled in his repeated allusions to 'noster Columba' and 'nostra insula', and he identifies this community as Irish in

---

[35] Bawcutt (2005: 192).   [36] Mann and Mapstone (2011).
[37] Mapstone (2008).
[38] This account of early medieval Scottish writing is most indebted to Clancy and Pittock (2007). See also articles and bibliography in Koch (2006) and, for accessible translations of the poetry, Clancy (1998).

speaking of 'nostram Scotiam', 'our Ireland', although the *Vita Columbae* suggests that the monastery at Iona also housed Pictish, British, and Anglo-Saxon brethren.[39] Moreover, within the *Vita*, spiritual and didactic purposes are concurrent with political intent: Adomnán became abbot in 679, at a time when Iona's stance on the Easter controversy had prompted attempts to cast doubt on Columba's sanctity, most notably at the Synod of Whitby (664), and the text is in part a response to such slights. Drawing on a body of traditions relating to Columba, both oral and written, its central concern is to inspire reverence for the saint, rather than to provide a biography in the modern sense. Adomnán presents his materials in tripartite form, addressing Columba's prophecies, miracles, and visions, and he alludes to key works of European hagiography in establishing Columba's place alongside the pre-eminent saints of the day, in the company of the apostles and prophets. As a powerful affirmation of Columba's sanctity, the *Vita* serves Adomnán's own community in commemorating the life of their patron, yet it also bespeaks an irenic purpose, in reminding a potential Northumbrian audience of their historic debt to the saint, and supplying an image of a wider monastic community united in reverence for Columba.[40]

The *Vita Columbae* and the career of Adomnán also reflect the extent to which monastic communities like Iona were affiliated to the Irish nobility, in a manner typical of the early Church, 'where monasteries function partly as the royal court, and partly as royal family property'.[41] As a member of the Cenél Conaill ('Conall's kindred'), Columba had close ties to the ruling Uí Néill dynasty, which traced its ancestry back to the semi-legendary king, Níall of the Nine Hostages, and most of his successors to the abbacy, including Adomnán, were drawn from the same aristocratic lineage. The development of the cults of Columba and Adomnán was thus bound up with dynastic piety and patronage.[42] Furthermore, the Latin and Gaelic poetry associated with this milieu suggests a taste shaped by courtly literature: the idiom of much early Christian verse is essentially aristocratic, and it assimilates the reper-toire of allusion associated with secular praise poetry. Thus, poems devoted to Columba, such as the sixth-century *Amra Choluimb Cille*, often imagine the saint in heroic terms and combine praise with appeals for personal protection, conceiving the relationship between saint and devotee on the model of the reciprocal bond between lord and retainer.[43] The *Vita Columbae* reflects a similar cross-fertilization of Gaelic and Latin traditions in the conception of the saint's character,[44] and Adom-nán depicts the saint in heroic terms, as possessing a special influence over victory and defeat granted to him as 'victoriali et fortissimo propugnatori' ('triumphant and

---

[39] Picard (1982: 166); Anderson and Anderson (1991: 232–3).
[40] Stancliffe (2007: 113).
[41] Wormald (1978: 58).
[42] Lynch (1992: 35–6).
[43] Márkus (2007).
[44] Picard (1982: 79).

powerful champion').[45] Moreover, the *Vita* envisages a distinctive relationship between Church and secular aristocracy, as Adomnán invokes biblical models to present an ideology of kingship whereby kings owe their status to divine providence, with the Church as its intermediary.[46]

The emphasis on Columba as a saint of particular importance to kings is not simply political, however, but reflects the theological belief that the Church has a crucial role in establishing divine law within society at large.[47] Adomnán's involvement with canon law shows this principle in practice: *Cáin Adomnán* (Adomnán's law), promulgated at the Synod of Birr in Ireland (697), sought to protect non-combatants from the effects of war.[48] A continuing interest in canon law at Iona is indicated by the citation of the monk and poet Cú Chuimne (d. 747) as one of the compilers involved in the transmission of the *Collectio canonum hibernensis*, an important Irish collection of legal tradition. The example of Adomnán and Iona thus serves to underline the point that if the texts associated with such monastic communities are part of Scotland's literary heritage because they were produced within the area delimited by its modern borders, they are nonetheless the product of a world that was profoundly involved with Ireland, and that was itself instrumental to the making of Irish tradition.

Another key text linked with early Scotland presents an acute example of the particular methodological challenges associated with the early period, and of their implications for the construction of a national tradition. A single late-thirteenth-century manuscript compiled in Wales preserves the body of poetry known as the *Gododdin*, which has been called the oldest Scottish poem.[49] The Gododdin was a tribal kingdom, whose people spoke the Cumbric dialect, part of a family of Brythonic languages of which only Breton and Welsh survive, and which would have been mutually intelligible in the early period. *The Gododdin* comprises a series of elegies, both individual and collective, for a war-band who set out from Din Eidyn (Edinburgh) and suffered a terrible defeat at Catraeth (identified with Catterick). Its narrative component is limited, and the battle of which it speaks is not attested elsewhere. The manuscript ascribes the *Gododdin* to Aneirin, named in a ninth-century text with Taliesin and three other poets famed for their skill in British verse during the latter half of the sixth century, and it is known as *Llyfr Aneirin* (*The Book of Aneirin*). Nonetheless, the status of the surviving text is contentious: the manuscript preserves two incomplete variant versions, called A and B, copied by two scribes, and it is predominantly in Middle Welsh, although the B scribe also worked from an exemplar in Old Welsh orthography. Modern critical consensus favours the theory that the *Gododdin* is based on an older composition in Cumbric that can be plausibly attributed to Aneirin, yet this raises many questions about the process and

---

[45] Anderson and Anderson (1991: 14–15).
[46] Enright (1985).
[47] Sharpe (1995: 61–3).
[48] O'Loughlin (2007: 2).
[49] Cardiff, South Glamorgan City Library, 1.

effect of transmission. A rubric in the manuscript indicates the status the *Gododdin* acquired in Welsh poetry as part of a bard's mnemonic repertoire: 'No more than a man ought to go to combat without arms should a poet go to a competition without this poem.'[50] The extant text shows signs of deliberate embellishment for poetic effect, as in conflicting claims that there were three survivors, and only one. There are also accidental interpolations, such as the cradle song 'Dinogad's Coat' (*c*.650), and a stanza celebrating a victory for the Britons against the forces of Dál Riata at the battle of Strathcarron (642).[51] The inclusion of the latter in both A and B texts of the *Gododdin* suggests that the poem might have been transcribed in the kingdom of Dumbarton at a relatively early stage in its transmission. J. T. Koch in particular has made attempts to recover a putative original text, but the extent to which the surviving poem can be described as Scottish remains debatable, while it is certainly a mainstay of the Welsh canon.[52]

A similar intersection between what are now usually treated as separate national literary traditions is indicated by the runic inscriptions in the Northumbrian dialect carved into the early eighth-century Ruthwell Cross in Dumfriesshire. These preserve fragments of a version of *The Dream of the Rood*, an Anglo-Saxon poem which otherwise survives only in the Vercelli book, a manuscript usually dated to the second half of the tenth century and of south-eastern English origin. The relationship between cross and manuscript text thus indicates a long and complex process of transmission.[53] Nonetheless, an amalgamation of Latin theology with the imagery of the native heroic tradition is visible in both versions, and is in sympathy with the early Christian poetry produced at Iona. The disparate geographical and temporal origins of the inscriptions and the manuscript text offer a further illustration of the complexities elided by attempts to construct clearly delimited national literary traditions.

Other literary traditions present in medieval Scotland are equally resistant to incorporation within any unitary narrative of Scottish literary history. The Norse literature associated with the Orkney Earldom, established following Viking raids in the eighth century and especially significant as a cultural hub in the twelfth century, is for the most part recorded only in Icelandic manuscripts dating from the thirteenth century onwards. With the exception of what is now called skaldic verse, which typically preserves the name of the poet, the Icelandic context of transmission presents obstacles to the identification of literature of Scottish origin. Moreover, the key literary figures associated with Orkney, such as Earl Rögnvaldr Kali Kolsson (*c*.1103–58) and Bishop Bjarni Kolbeinsson (d. 1223), had Norwegian origins and associations. The texts that originated within this milieu belong to a pan-Scandinavian tradition, and refuse narrow categorization as part of any one literature conceived along national lines.[54]

---

[50] Koch (2006: 354).
[51] Clancy (1998: 94, 114).
[52] Koch (1997).
[53] Wilcox (2001: 56–7).
[54] Jesch (2007); Clancy (1998: 40–3).

Gaelic presents a similar case and, while evidence for the earliest period of literary production in Scotland is sparse, later literature attests to the influence of the twelfth-century revolution in poetic practice emanating from Ireland, inaugurating what is termed the Classical tradition. During this period, the monasteries were displaced as the primary centres of literary production, and the twelfth century saw a formalization of relations between poets and other literary practitioners, such as historians, and their secular patrons. Ruling families from this time forward down to the seventeenth century maintained hereditary lines of professional poets (*filidh*), and such poets acquired their craft through years of training, primarily in the bardic schools of Ireland, although there is also some evidence of instruction taking place in Scotland.[55] As the product of intensive training, the poetry of the classical tradition is 'uncannily consistent' throughout the period, conforming to standards of metre and language established in twelfth-century Ireland, and often drawing on a common repertoire of images and themes.[56] The extent to which such literature is the product of a pan-Gaelic culture centred on Ireland is borne out in evidence of a mutual traffic between the learned orders of Scotland and Ireland, although, in recent years, Wilson McLeod has questioned previous assumptions about the frequency with which trained poets travelled across the North Channel in search of patronage.[57] In Scottish historiography too, there is evidence that learned Scots conceived themselves as part of Gaeldom, regarding their history as an adjunct to Irish history, even after Irish historians had begun to conceive Ireland's history as a more distinct narrative.[58]

The oft-noted hostility to Gaelic culture manifested in the later Middle Ages obscures the particular prestige attached to vernacular poetry within the Gaelic world.[59] Alongside the legal, medical, and clerical professions, the poet held a distinguished place in Gaelic society as a member of the learned orders, and the height of his profession was the position of *ollamh*, official poet to the head of a noble house, an appointment that carried with it an allocation of land.[60] The *ollamh* was responsible for the production of panegyric verse endorsing his lord's position and, while other forms of poetry survive, the function and status of these official compositions are reflected in their dominance within the surviving corpus. A further indication of the status of these master-poets is their entitlement to a retinue, including apprentice poets, harpists to supply accompaniment, and reciters to declaim compositions on their behalf.[61] The extent of contact with this model of literary production in the Lowlands is difficult to gauge, but language distribution provides one indication. In the twelfth century, Gaelic was the dominant language north of the Forth–Clyde area, and while it declined in eastern Scotland during the Middle Ages, this was a gradual process during which Gaelic and Scots coexisted,

---

[55] McLeod (2004: 84).
[56] Gillies (1988: 247).
[57] Thomson (1968: 72); McLeod (2004: 83–5).
[58] Broun (1997: 9).
[59] Goldstein (1999: 253).
[60] Thomson (1968); Koch (2006: 1004).
[61] Gillies (1978: 67).

with Gaelic surviving in some Lowland areas, even as late as the nineteenth century.[62] The fourteenth-century chronicler John of Fordun's account of the inauguration of Alexander III in 1249 suggests the longevity of Gaelic's official role in court culture: the ritual concludes with the recitation of the king's genealogy in Gaelic, by a figure who has been persuasively identified as the *ollamh ríg*, or king's poet.[63] This genealogy is extended back to Scota and her husband, Gaedel Glas, evoking mythic origins in pronouncing the king's right.

It is significant that the authority of Gaelic culture became crucial to the ideological construction of Scotland as a distinct polity, as the source of the origin myth used to legitimize the claim to national autonomy. In appealing to the myth of Brutus in support of his claim to suzerainty over Scotland, Edward I's letter to the papal court of Boniface VII shaped the course of Scottish historiography,[64] yet this nationalist tradition is also in dialogue with Ireland. Initially a legend of Ireland's origins, the myth of Scota was adapted by Scottish writers, who recast the predestined homeland of the *Scoti* as Scotland, with the first surviving account to do so being Baldred Bisset's Latin *Processus* of 1301.[65] The attempt to establish Scotland's historic right to self-determination thus depends upon the appropriation of Ireland's legendary past: where Bisset demotes Ireland to the status of temporary anchorage, the account of the mythic peregrinations of the Scots offered in the Declaration of Arbroath (1320) suppresses all mention of Ireland.[66] The continuing importance of such versions of the legend is manifested in the historiographical romance Barbour's *Bruce* (*c*.1375), where the myth underwrites Barbour's influential projection of a 'Brucean ideology' defining loyalty to Bruce and his cause as the hallmark of Scottish identity.[67] In extending the narrative beyond the high water mark of Bannockburn to encompass Edward Bruce's ill-fated campaigns in Ireland and the death of Sir James Douglas, crusading in Spain with the Bruce's heart, the structure of the *Bruce* retraces the mythic journey of Scotland's founders to Spain, Ireland, and finally, Scotland.[68]

THE 'SCOTTISH CHAUCERIANS'

If the first extant work in Scots endorses a distinctive identity for Scotland and its tradition of historical writing, later poets appeal to an alternative model of literature in declaring their affiliation to Chaucer, both explicitly, through panegyric, and in

---

[62] McDonald (2006: 71–3).
[63] Bannerman (1989).
[64] Goldstein (1993: 64); Terrell (2008).
[65] Broun (1997).
[66] Ibid. 14.
[67] Goldstein (1993: 82, 195).
[68] Jack (1997*b*: 229).

adopting elements of his style. The traditional critical designation of these poets as
'Scottish Chaucerians' recognizes these qualities, yet, like its fellow label, 'English
Chaucerians' (albeit to a lesser extent), it has sometimes encouraged the treatment of
this response to Chaucer as a passive mode of reception.[69] As Denton Fox argues, the
encomia of the Middle Scots poets conceive Chaucer as 'the father of modern English
poetry, the man who purified, regularised, and clarified English, and so made it
possible for highly civilised and highly wrought poetry to be written in the vernacular', however, this praise is not disinterested.[70] It is a strategic gesture contributing to
an ongoing literary dialogue informed by the model of *translatio studii et imperii*,
that seeks to define English as a language of textual authority in relation to Latin and
the more prestigious vernaculars.[71] In endorsing the image of Chaucer as the father
of English poetry, these Scottish writers at once supply a precedent for their own
literary activities, and shape the development of a literary tradition.

   The earliest instance of such an appeal to Chaucer's authority in Scottish literature
is in the envoy to the *Kingis Quair* (*c*.1424), which Seth Lerer has interpreted as a
meditation on John Lydgate's aspirational vision of Chaucer as both ideal and ideally
situated poet, writing in a lost golden age of literary patronage. In the context of the
Quair, as a thinly disguised narrative of James I of Scotland's experience of imprisonment in England, the allusion to Gower and Chaucer as the king's 'maisteris dere'
and 'poetis laureate' authorizes these vernacular writers, by conferring on them this
most prestigious form of a title still principally reserved for the classical *auctoritates*,
yet it also asserts James's own authority in the field of literature as the image of an act
of patronage befitting a prince.[72] This simultaneous acknowledgement and appropriation of authority is characteristic of the *Quair*: the poem stages the reading of its
major Latin source, Boethius's *Consolation of Philosophy*, in a context that evokes the
conventional device whereby reading serves as a cue for dreaming, and dreaming is a
shorthand for the process of mnemonic invention that produces new compositions.[73] Within the *Quair*, the act of composition is explicitly presented as a conscious response to the authoritative text, yet James does not seek to justify this
vernacular composition by presenting it as an exegetical supplement to Boethius,
in the manner of Chaucer and Gower.[74] Instead, he claims that his 'scole is ouer yong'
to 'declare' Boethius, stating 'Therfore I lat him pas'.[75] The allusion to Boethius
authorizes a narrative based on James's own experience, against the background of a
medieval reception history that positioned the *Consolation* as a source of wisdom
with special relevance for princes, who must risk misfortune in fulfilling their
political duty. In identifying the experience of imprisonment and love as the source
of an increase in 'lore' that brought him to the ideal state of sufficiency, James

---

[69] Lerer (1993: 4).
[70] Fox (1966: 169).
[71] Evans *et al.* (1999).
[72] Norton-Smith (1971: ll. 1373, 1376); Lerer (1993: 52–3).
[73] Carruthers (1998: 171–220).
[74] Copeland (1991).
[75] Norton-Smith (1971), ll. 46, 47.

participates in a continuing effort to translate Boethian wisdom into the context and idiom of contemporary politics, also manifested in texts such as Jean Froissart's *Prison amoureuse* and Thomas Usk's *Testament of Love.*[76] The *Quair* thus works to establish vernacular writing as a medium capable of supplanting Latin authority, and as the product of an officially sanctioned tradition.

Writing in the latter half of the fifteenth century, Robert Henryson combines praise for 'worthie Chauceir glorious' with a subtle treatment of vernacular authority in the *Testament of Cresseid.*[77] Like the *Quair*, the *Testament* plays on the conventional link between reading and dreaming, in an opening that positions Chaucer as *auctor.* Rather than writing, however, the narrator takes 'ane vther quair', a substitution that not only evokes the circulation of competing versions of the Cressida legend, but also suggests that this 'quair' is the *Testament* itself.[78] Questioning Chaucer's authority, Henryson intimates the existence of a community of poets, possessing the capacity to invent new material. As the implied author of the 'vther quair', his words also function as a comment on his own vernacular poetic practice:

> Quha wait gif all that Chauceir wrait was trew?
> Nor I wait nocht gif this narratioun
> Be authoreist, or fenyeit of the new
> Be sum poeit, throw his inuention
> Maid to report the lamentatioun
> And wofull end of this lustie Creisseid.
> And quhat distress scho thoillit, and quhat deid.[79]

As Tim William Machan and Rita Copeland argue, Henryson's treatment of textual authority indicates a significant shift in the status of the vernacular.[80]

While Henryson is far from typical in this respect, the figure of Chaucer continues to serve as the means to define and validate the idea of a vernacular tradition in later Scots poetry, in company with Gower and Lydgate. This trio are invoked as the precedent for a national literary tradition in Gavin Douglas's *Palice of Honour* (*c.*1501), where the poets 'of Brutus Albion' are matched with three 'Of this Natioun': Kennedy, Dunbar, and, lastly, Quintine, whose works are not now known.[81] They appear again as prelude to the list of twenty-one poets 'of this cuntre' in Dunbar's 'I that in heill wes and gladnes' (*c.*1505),[82] and to a similar catalogue in David Lyndsay's *Testament of the Papyngo* (*c.*1530). Lyndsay underlines the significance of this trio in a series of charged questions:

> The bell of rethorick bene roung
> Be Chawceir, Goweir, and Lidgate laureate.
> Quho dar presume thir poetis tyll impung,
> Quhose sweit sentence throuch Albione bene soung?
> Or quho can, now, the workis cuntrafait

76 Ibid. ll. 1265, 1281. For a pioneering new study of amatory discourse in political and advisory Scots poetry, including the *Quair*, see Martin (2008).

77 Henryson (1981: l. 41).

78 Ibid. l. 61; McKim (2006: 112).

79 Henryson (1981: ll. 64–70).

80 Machan (1992); Copeland (1991: 228–9).

81 Bawcutt (2003: ll. 918, 922).

82 Bawcutt (1998: no. 21, l. 55).

> Of Kennedie, with termes aureait,
> Or of Dunbar, quhilk langage had at large,
> As maye be sene in tyll his *Goldin Targe?*[83]

The vernacular poets of England and Scotland are conceived as part of two interlinked traditions whose authority derives from the inimitability of their past expo-
nents, and from the assured status of the canonical trio. Emphatic reference to the
'dull intellygence' of contemporary poets serves to confirm the importance and
longevity of this literary past.[84] In both unifying and distinguishing English and
Scottish literature, this model of tradition anticipates the Scoto-English canon of
English literature prominent in the nineteenth century.

In Scotland, however, the endorsement of a coherent tradition of vernacular
English carries an additional political charge. Dunbar's claim that, before Chaucer,
Gower, and Lydgate, 'This ile . . . was bare and desolate/Off rethorike or lusty fresch
endyte' stands in sharp contrast to Kennedy's assertion that Gaelic was the authentic
language of 'this land'.[85] The classical tradition of Gaelic is remarkable, as a courtly
vernacular literature already conscious of a long history by the late Middle Ages, in
possession of an established metrical and linguistic repertoire, and whose practitioners commanded high status within their own culture. As such, it presents a
challenge to retrospective attempts to construct a stable tradition in vernacular
English dating back no further than the fourteenth century, and the particular
virulence of some of the Scots responses to Gaelic literature suggests not only the
hostility arising from political contact, but also an anxiety focused on the position of
the poet in Gaelic culture. Richard Holland's satirical depiction of a 'bard owt of
Irland' in his bird fable, *The Buke of the Howlat* (*c.*1448), displays some understanding
of Gaelic language and literary culture: it includes some recognizable, if broken,
Gaelic speech, and parodies the practice of genealogical recitation.[86] The bard, who
appears as a rook, threatens to 'ryme' those who do not afford him due respect, a
threat that finds a precedent in Gaelic culture, where satire was conceived as possessing the supernatural properties of a curse.[87] In punishment for his 'lesings', the bard
is humiliated and befouled by the lapwing and the cuckoo.[88] The episode appeals to a
taste for farce and scatological humour, but its satisfaction also lies in the way it
stages the exclusion of the Gaelic poet from the aristocratic community at the feast.

That such an exclusion had not taken place at the court of James IV is suggested by
records of payment for entertainment by harpists and bards in the accounts, and by
the claim of one visitor to James's court, Pedro de Ayala, that the king could speak
Gaelic. Louise Fradenburg also draws attention to the hermeneutic function of Gaelic
culture in the courtly entertainments of James's reign, such as the tournament of the
wild knight and the black lady (1507/8).[89] The unique manuscript miscellany, *The
Book of the Dean of Lismore*,[90] compiled *c.*1512–42 in Perthshire, offers later evidence

---

83 Hadley Williams (2000: ll. 10–18).   84 Ibid. l. 9.
85 Bawcutt (1998: no. 59, ll. 269–70).   86 Bawcutt and Riddy (1987: l. 795, and notes).
87 Ibid. ll. 797, 815.   88 Ibid. ll. 807, 810.
89 Fradenburg (2003: 525).   90 National Library of Scotland, Advocates MS 72. 1. 37.

of intercultural contact in its contents and orthography. Although dominated by Gaelic verse, the manuscript also contains poetry by Henryson, Dunbar, and Lydgate, and is written in a highly unusual orthography based on Middle Scots, rather than traditional Gaelic spelling.[91] The tensions generated through such cultural contact are played out in the *Flyting* of Dunbar and Kennedy, lending impact to the poets' rival attempts to establish 'authentic' traditions by devaluing Irish eloquence or invoking the Gaelic past. Kennedy's insistence on Gaelic as being 'all trew Scottis mennis lede', and as an inheritance from the mythic past, exposes a fault line in striking at the relative youth of the English vernacular tradition. The consciousness of such a fault line, identified in serious jest, provides an added impetus for the fascination of the 'Scottish Chaucerians' with English poetry as a technology of the word.[92] Dunbar's aureate style and Douglas's enlargement of the Scots language through the translation of Virgil's Latin authority are strategies for the creation of a Scots to challenge not only the authority of the classical languages, but also the longevity and formidable technique of Gaelic poetry.

In approaching particular ideas of a national literary tradition as historical constructions, as the expression of debates taking place within a particular temporal and cultural context, it becomes possible to explore the ways in which such traditions, and the assumptions upon which they depend, work to shape our perceptions of the literatures of the past. This chapter has sought to analyse a series of attempts to define a model of national tradition, in light of recent efforts to renegotiate the canonical boundaries delimiting Scotland's early literature. Within this ongoing critical project in Scottish Studies, the recovery of a sense of national tradition as being like the *Flyting* of Dunbar and Kennedy, an embodied argument within borders, works to acknowledge the full range of voices at play within Scottish literary history, beyond the constricting desire for a unitary tradition, and for named, canonical authors.

BIBLIOGRAPHY

ADOMNÁN OF IONA (1995), *Life of St Columba*, tr. R. Sharpe (Harmondsworth: Penguin).

ANDERSON, ALAN O., and MARJORIE O. ANDERSON (ed. and tr.) (1991), *Adomnán's Life of Columba*, rev. M. O. Anderson, (Oxford: Oxford University Press).

BANNERMAN, JOHN (1989), 'The King's Poet and the Inauguration of Alexander III', *Scottish Historical Review*, 68: 120–49.

BAWCUTT, PRISCILLA (ed.) (1998), *The Poems of William Dunbar* (2 vols. Glasgow: ASLS).

—— (ed.) (2003), *The Shorter Poems of Gavin Douglas* (Edinburgh: Scottish Text Society).

—— and Felicity Riddy (eds.) (1987), *Longer Scottish Poems*, i. *1375–1650* (Edinburgh: Scottish Academic Press).

—— (2005), 'Manuscript Miscellanies in Scotland from the Fifteenth to the Seventeenth Century', in Sally Mapstone (ed.), *Older Scots Literature* (Edinburgh: John Donald), 189–210.

——and JANET HADLEY WILLIAMS (eds.) (2006), *A Companion to Medieval Scottish Poetry* (Cambridge: D. S. Brewer).

---

[91] Clancy and Pittock (2007: 209–25).   [92] Shuffleton (1975).

BRENNAN, TIMOTHY (1990), 'The National Longing for Form', in Homi K. Bhabha (ed.), *Nation and Narration* (London: Routledge), 44–70.

BROUN, DAUVIT (1997), 'The Birth of Scottish History', *Scottish Historical Review*, 76: 4–22.

BROWN, IAN, THOMAS O. CLANCY, SUSAN MANNING, and MURRAY PITTOCK (2007), 'Scottish Literature: Criticism and the Canon', in Thomas O. Clancy and Murray Pittock (eds.), *The Edinburgh History of Scottish Literature*, i. *From Columba to the Union (until 1707)* (Edinburgh: Edinburgh University Press), 3–15.

CARRUTHERS, GERARD (1999), 'The Construction of the Scottish Critical Tradition', in Neil McMillan and Kirsten Stirling (eds.), *Odd Alliances: Scottish Studies in European Contexts* (Glasgow: Cruithne Press), 52–65.

CARRUTHERS, MARY J. (1998), *The Craft of Thought: Meditation, Rhetoric, and the Making of Images, 400–1200* (Cambridge: Cambridge University Press).

CLANCY, THOMAS OWEN (ed.) (1998), *The Triumph Tree: Scotland's Earliest Poetry AD 550–1350*, (Edinburgh: Canongate).

COCKBURN, HENRY (1874), *Journal of Henry Cockburn: Being a Continuation of the Memorials of his Time. 1831–1854* (Edinburgh: Edmonston & Douglas).

COPELAND, RITA (1991), *Rhetoric, Hermeneutics, and Translation in the Middle Ages: Academic Traditions and Vernacular Texts* (Cambridge: Cambridge University Press).

CRAIG, CAIRNS (1999), *The Modern Scottish Novel* (Edinburgh: Edinburgh University Press).

——(2007a), 'The Making of a Scottish Literary Canon', in Bill Bell (ed.), *The Edinburgh History of the Book in Scotland*, iii. *Ambition and Industry 1800–80* (Edinburgh: Edinburgh University Press), 266–77.

——(2007b), 'The Study of Scottish Literature', in Thomas O. Clancy and Murray Pittock (eds.), *The Edinburgh History of Scottish Literature*, i. *From Columba to the Union (until 1707)* (Edinburgh: Edinburgh University Press), 16–31.

CRAWFORD, ROBERT (ed.) (1998), *The Scottish Invention of English Literature* (Cambridge: Cambridge University Press).

——(2000), *Devolving English Literature* (2nd edn. Edinburgh: Edinburgh University Press).

——(2007), *Scotland's Books: The Penguin History of Scottish Literature* (London: Penguin).

CRAWFORD, ROBERT, and MICK IMLAH (eds.) (2000), *The New Penguin Book of Scottish Verse* (London: Allen Lane).

DUNNIGAN, SARAH M. (2004), 'The Return of the Repressed', in Gerard Carruthers (ed.), *Beyond Scotland: New Contexts for Twentieth-Century Scottish Literature* (Amsterdam: Rodopi), 111–32.

——(2005), 'A New Critical Cartography: Pre- and Post-Union Scottish Renaissance', in Marco Fazzini (ed.), *Alba Literaria: A History of Scottish Literature* (Venice: Amos Edizioni), 99–119.

ENRIGHT, MICHAEL J. (1985), 'Royal Succession and Abbatial Prerogative in Adomnán's Vita Columbae', *Peritia*, 4: 83–103.

EVANS, RUTH, ANDREW TAYLOR, NICHOLAS WATSON, and JOCELYN WOGAN-BROWNE (1999), 'The Notion of Vernacular Theory', in J. Wogan-Browne, N. Watson, A. Taylor, and R. Evans (eds.), *The Idea of the Vernacular: An Anthology of Middle English Literary Theory, 1280–1520* (Exeter: University of Exeter Press), 314–30.

FERRIS, INA (2005), 'Printing the Past: Walter Scott's Bannatyne Club and the Antiquarian Document', *Romanticism*, 11(2): 143–60.

FOX, DENTON (1966), 'The Scottish Chaucerians', in D. S. Brewer (ed.), *Chaucer and Chaucerians: Critical Studies in Middle English Literature* (London: Nelson), 164–200.

FOX, DENTON, and WILLIAM A. RINGLER (1980), *The Bannatyne Manuscript: National Library of Scotland Advocates, MS. 1. 1. 6* (London: Scolar Press).

FRADENBURG, L. O. (2003), 'Scotland: Culture and Society', in S. H. Rigby (ed.), *A Companion to Britain in the Later Middle Ages* (Oxford: Blackwell), 521–40.

GILLIES, WILLIAM (1978), 'Gaelic and Scots Literature Down to the Reformation', in Jean-Jacques Blanchot and Claude Graf (eds.), *Actes du 2e colloque de langue et de littérature écossaises* (Strasbourg: Institut d'études anglaises de Strasbourg et l'Association des médieévistes anglicistes de l'enseignement supeérieur).

——(1988), 'Gaelic: The Classical Tradition', in Ronald D. S. Jack (ed.), *The History of Scottish Literature*, i. *Origins to 1660 (Medieval and Renaissance)* (Aberdeen: Aberdeen University Press).

GOLDSTEIN, R. JAMES (1993), *The Matter of Scotland: Historical Narrative in Medieval Scotland* (Lincoln, Neb.: University of Nebraska Press).

——(1999), 'Writing in Scotland 1058–1560', in David Wallace (ed.), *The Cambridge History of Medieval English Literature* (Cambridge: Cambridge University Press), 229–54.

GRAY, DOUGLAS (2008), *Later Medieval English Literature* (Oxford: Oxford University Press).

HADLEY WILLIAMS, JANET (ed.) (2000), *Sir David Lyndsay: Selected Poems* (Glasgow: ASLS).

HENRYSON, ROBERT (1981), *The Poems*, ed. Denton Fox (Oxford: Oxford University Press).

JACK, RONALD D. S. (ed.) (1988), *The History of Scottish Literature*, i. *Origins to 1660 (Mediæval and Renaissance)*, gen. ed. Cairns Craig (Aberdeen: Aberdeen University Press).

——(1993), 'Of Lion and of Unicorn: Literary Traditions at War', in Ronald D. S. Jack and Kevin McGinley (eds.), *Of Lion and of Unicorn: Essays on Anglo-Scottish Literary Relations in Honour of Professor John MacQueen* (Edinburgh: Quadriga), 67–99.

——(1997a), 'Critical Introduction:"Where Stands Scottish Literature Now?"', in Ronald D. S. Jack and P. A. T. Rozendaal (eds.), *The Mercat Anthology of Early Scottish Literature 1375–1707* (Edinburgh: Mercat), pp. vii–xxxix.

——(1997b), 'The Language of Literary Materials: Origins to 1700', in Charles Jones (ed.), *The Edinburgh History of the Scots Language* (Edinburgh: Edinburgh University Press).

JAMES I OF SCOTLAND (1971), *The Kingis Quair*, ed. John Norton-Smith (Oxford: Clarendon).

JESCH, JUDITH (2007), 'Norse Literature in the Orkney Earldom', in Thomas O. Clancy and Murray Pittock (eds.), *The Edinburgh History of Scottish Literature*, i. *From Columba to the Union (until 1707)* (Edinburgh: Edinburgh University Press).

KOCH, JOHN T. (ed.) (1997), *The Gododdin of Aneirin: Text and Context from Dark-Age Britain*, (Cardiff: University of Wales Press).

——(ed.) (2006), *Celtic Culture: A Historical Encyclopedia* (5 vols. Santa Barbara, Calif.: ABC-Clio).

LERER, SETH (1993), *Chaucer and his Readers: Imagining the Author in Late-Medieval England* (Princeton: Princeton University Press).

LOVE, HAROLD (1993), *Scribal Publication in Seventeenth-Century England* (Oxford: Clarendon).

LYNCH, MICHAEL (1992), *Scotland: A New History* (rev. edn. London: Pimlico).

MACHAN, TIM WILLIAM (1992), 'Textual Authority and the Works of Hoccleve, Lydgate, and Henryson', *Viator*, 23: 281–99.

MÁRKUS, GILBERT (2007), 'Saving Verse: Early Medieval Religious Poetry', in Thomas O. Clancy and Murray Pittock (eds.), *The Edinburgh History of Scottish Literature*, i. *From Columba to the Union (until 1707)* (Edinburgh: Edinburgh University Press), 91–102.

MACDONALD, ALASDAIR A. (1983), 'Poetry, Politics, and Reformation Censorship in Sixteenth-Century Scotland', *English Studies*, 64(5): 410–21.

——(2003), 'The Cultural Repertory of Middle Scots Lyric Verse', in G. J. Dorleijn and H. L. J. Vanstiphout (eds.), *Cultural Repertoires: Structure, Function and Dynamics* (Louvain: Peeters), 59–86.

MCDONALD, RUSSELL ANDREW (2006), 'The Western *Gàidhealtachd* in the Middle Ages', in Bob Harris and Alan R. MacDonald (eds.), *Scotland: The Making and Unmaking of the Nation c.1100–1707*, i. *The Scottish Nation: Origins to c.1500* (Dundee: Dundee University Press), 65–89.

McKim, Anne (2006), 'Orpheus and Eurydice and The Testament of Cresseid: Robert Henryson's "fine poeticall way"', in Priscilla Bawcutt and Janet Hadley Williams (eds.), A Companion to Medieval Scottish Poetry (Cambridge: D. S. Brewer).

McLeod, Wilson (2004), Divided Gaels: Gaelic Cultural Identities in Scotland and Ireland, c.1200–c.1650 (Oxford: Oxford University Press).

Mann, A. J., and Sally Mapstone (eds.) (2011), The Edinburgh History of the Book in Scotland, i. From the Earliest Times to 1707, gen. ed. Bill Bell (Edinburgh: University of Edinburgh).

Mapstone, Sally (ed.) (2008), The Chepman and Myllar Prints: Digitised Facsimiles with Introduction, Headnote and Transcription, DVD, Scottish Text Society and National Library of Scotland, Edinburgh.

Martin, Joanna (2008), Kingship and Love in Scottish Poetry, 1424–1540 (Aldershot: Ashgate).

Muir, Edwin (1936), Scott and Scotland: The Predicament of the Scottish Writer (London: Routledge).

O'Loughlin, Thomas (2007), Adomnán and the Holy Places: The Perceptions of an Insular Monk on the Locations of the Biblical Drama (New York: T&T Clark).

Picard, J. M. (1982), 'The Purpose of Adomnán's Vita Columbae', Peritia, 1: 160–77.

——(1985), 'Structural Patterns in Early Hiberno-Latin Hagiography', Peritia, 4: 67–82.

Ray Murray, Padmini (2007), 'Antiquarianism', in Bill Bell (ed.), The Edinburgh History of the Book in Scotland, iii. Ambition and Industry 1800–80 (Edinburgh: Edinburgh University Press), 278–85.

Renan, Ernest (1990), 'What is a Nation?', tr. Martin Thom, in Homi K. Bhabha (ed.), Nation and Narration (New York: Routledge), 8–22.

Said, Edward (1989), 'Representing the Colonized: Anthropology's Interlocutors', Critical Enquiry, 15: 205–25.

Scott, Sir Walter (1829), 'Memoir of George Bannatyne', in Memorials of George Bannatyne MDXLV–MDCVIII (Edinburgh: Bannatyne Club).

Shuffleton, Frank (1975), 'An Imperial Flower: Dunbar's The Goldyn Targe and the Court Life of James IV of Scotland', Studies in Philology, 72: 193–207.

Smith, G. Gregory (1919), Scottish Literature: Character and Influence (London: Macmillan).

Stancliffe, C. (2007), 'Adomnán of Iona and his Prose Writings', in Thomas O. Clancy and Murray Pittock (eds.), The Edinburgh History of Scottish Literature, i. From Columba to the Union (until 1707) (Edinburgh: Edinburgh University Press), 110–14.

Terrell, Katherine (2008), 'Subversive Histories: Strategies of Identity in Scottish Historiography', in Jeffrey Jerome Cohen (ed.), Cultural Diversity in the British Middle Ages: Archipelago, Island, England (New York: Palgrave Macmillan), 153–72.

Thomson, Derick S. (1968), 'Gaelic Learned Orders and Literati in Medieval Scotland', Scottish Studies, 12: 57–78.

van Heijnsbergen, T. (1994), 'The Interaction between Literature and History in Queen Mary's Edinburgh: The Bannatyne Manuscript and its Prosopographical Context', in A. A. MacDonald, Michael Lynch, and Ian Borthwick Cowan (eds.), The Renaissance in Scotland: Studies in Literature, Religion, History and Culture Offered to John Durkan (Leiden: Brill), 183–225.

Wilcox, Johnathan (2001), 'Transmission of Literature and Learning: Anglo-Saxon Scribal Culture', in Elaine Treharne and Phillip Pulsiano (eds.), A Companion to Anglo-Saxon Literature (Oxford: Blackwell), 50–70.

Wormald, Patrick (1978), 'Bede, Beowulf, and the Conversion of the Anglo-Saxon Aristocracy', in Robert T. Farrell (ed.), Bede and Anglo-Saxon England: Papers in Honour of the 1300th Anniversary of the Birth of Bede, Given at Cornell University in 1973 and 1974 (British Archaeological Reports, 46; Oxford), 32–95.

CHAPTER 30

....

PLACES OF THE IMAGINATION

THE *GAWAIN*-POET

....

THORLAC TURVILLE-PETRE

ALLITERATIVE poets are particularly good at visualizing a scene in precise detail. A characteristic example is the description of poaching that opens the *Parlement of the Thre Ages* as a prelude to the dream-debate. Here the narrator goes into the woods one lovely May morning:

> The cukkowe, the cowschote kene were þay bothen,
> And the throstills full throly threpen in the bankes,
> And iche foule in that frythe faynere þan oþer
> That the derke was done and the daye lightenede.[1]

Intent on poaching, he hides himself and spots a magnificent stag accompanied by a younger animal guarding it, but they are nervous and the poacher waits immobile while 'gnattes gretely me greuede and gnewen myn eghne'.[2] Once the deer have been reassured they are not in danger, the huntsman draws his crossbow and shoots, hitting the great stag behind the left shoulder, and it rushes in its death throes thrashing through the undergrowth. When the poacher and his dog reach the hart, it is 'dede als a dore-nayle'.[3] He dismembers it with care and skill; the twenty-five-line

---

[1] Turville-Petre (1989: ll. 13–16).
[2] Ibid., l. 50.   [3] Ibid., l. 65.

description[4] is as detailed as the account of a similar scene in *Gawain*.[5] Then he hides the carcass and settles down in the warm sun waiting for night to fall so that he can take home his prize without fear of the forester discovering him. And so he sleeps and dreams of a debate between the Three Ages.

The sights and sensations of an English wood are admirably captured by the poet, and the dream-vision structure encourages the reader to look further for correspondences between the experience of the narrator awake and dreaming. In this case we may reflect that Youth's preoccupation with sensual pleasures is adumbrated by the poacher's concentration on the physical activities of his stalking, a correspondence reinforced by Youth's own detailed description of the joys of hawking.[6] Elde's reflections on mortality find a parallel in the death agonies of the stag and then its butchering, and Middle Elde's obsession with material gain has its counterpart in the poacher's determination to profit from his morning's work and carry home his winnings.[7] These are thematic links whereby the arguments of the Three Ages are obliquely prefigured in the introduction to the dream. There are also, as we should expect from a dream, psychological links, to the extent that the poacher's anxieties are expressed in the conflicting opinions of the Ages. 'Nightmares', wrote Macrobius, 'may be caused by mental or physical distress, or anxiety about the future: the patient experiences in dreams vexations similar to those that disturb him during the day'.[8]

These are the standard features of a dream-vision. The narrator is alone; the dream is his own personal revelation, even though he chooses to communicate it later. The fact that the narrator of the *Parlement* is operating outside the forest laws and has thus isolated himself from the normal social constraints has the effect of further concentrating attention on this enigmatic figure and his dream. The three scenes from the *Gawain*-poet that I shall look at here similarly feature protagonists who are, for one reason or another, as isolated from society as this poacher is. Jonah's only episode of human contact is so disastrous that the sailors have no option but to tip him into the whale's mouth, and his interior experience is described in an extraordinary account. Gawain, struggling through the solitary dangers of his wintry journey, desperately misses the familiar comforts of companionship, of a knightly society that defines and sustains him, until a wonderful castle appears to him as if by magic. The dreamer in *Pearl* has responded to the death of his daughter by immersing himself in grief, rejecting the consolation of man and of God, yet the coruscating dream-landscape through which he walks so enraptures him that it lifts him from his self-absorption and prepares him for contact with his beloved daughter.

Though isolation is a significant link between the central figures of the *Gawain*-poet and the dreamer of the *Parlement*, there is an important difference. The poacher remains just that; the scene in the woods tells the reader nothing more about him; as he carries his trophy home at dusk, we are left to wonder about his reaction, if any, to his dream. This technique of leaving the narrative open to the reader's interpretation is a familiar one in the dream-vision form. In contrast, by revealing how Jonah,

---

[4] Ibid., ll. 67–91.   [5] Andrew and Waldron (2007: ll. 1328–61).
[6] Turville-Petre (1989: ll. 208–45).   [7] Waldron (1972).   [8] Stahl (1952).

Gawain, and the bereaved father react to what they observe around them, the *Gawain*-poet explores the psychological and spiritual condition of his three protagonists when they are at their most vulnerable and alone. The three scenes I shall analyse are not static but all involve progression, a physical movement that mirrors a psychological development towards some sort of reintegration. The emotions of the three change in response to the surprise of what they see. There is nothing to match this subtle use of description of place in the *Parlement* or for that matter in *Cleanness*, though we shall see that the latter is a useful point of comparison.

INSIDE THE WHALE

Patience, though closely following the narrative of the Old Testament Book of Jonah, adds five scenes that are fully realized from mere hints in the Bible, all of which function to highlight aspects of the theme of patient endurance. The first two demonstrate man's vulnerability in the face of divine power: the description of the proud ship as it leaves the port of Joppa and the magnificent evocation of the storm at sea summoned by God. The three other scenes reveal the psychology of Jonah. Most remarkable of them all is the description of Jonah inside the whale, expanded from the simple statement in the Old Testament, 'And Jonah was in the belly of the fish three days and three nights'.[9]

In *Patience* the whale swallows Jonah while the sailors are holding onto his feet and swims with him to the depths of the sea. The poet describes how Jonah slips past the gills through muck and slime, tumbling through an intestine into the whale's stomach which stinks like hell, looking all around for a place of refuge; and how, after offering a brief prayer for mercy, he finds a nice, clean corner where he sits safe and sound for three days and nights.

The account begins with an outrageous simile to express the size of the whale. Jonah enters its mouth 'As mote in at a munster dor, so mukel wern his chawlez' (l. 268).[10] The illustrator of the manuscript, ignoring this image, paints the traditional scene of Jonah being dunked by the sailors into a very average-sized whale, shown more clearly, for example, in the miniature from the Lampeter Bible chosen by Putter[11] for his cover-illustration. The poet's imagination has been fired by a different pictorial motif, the Last Judgement, with devils pitchforking the damned into the mouth of Leviathan, which is at the same time a door about to be locked by an angel, as illustrated for example in the Winchester Psalter Doom.[12] This opening simile makes it immediately clear to the reader that the whale is more a symbolic than a

---

[9] Jonah 2: 1.
[10] All quotations from the *Gawain*-poet are from the edn. by Andrew and Waldron (2007).
[11] Putter (1996).
[12] Wormald (1973), frontispiece.

natural creature, and indeed the poet has already called the whale *warlowe*, 'monster' (l. 258),[13] used as an epithet for the Devil.[14] The fantastic nature of the description is surely reinforced rather than dissipated by the poet's acknowledgement that the account would be incredible if it were not for the authority of Holy Writ (l. 244), since the reader knows very well that the description is entirely invented.

We see everything from Jonah's point of view (and, of course, there was no one else to see it or vouch for it). In this alien place Jonah processes everything he sees in terms of objects with which he is familiar in the world outside the whale. He tumbles along an intestine 'that seemed like a road to him' (l. 270), and comes to an abrupt halt in a *blok*, 'closed space' (l. 272), and there he establishes his 'bower' (l. 276). Though he looks round for *le best*, 'the best shelter' (l. 277), he can find no place of rest or succour until he prays to God for mercy. At that moment he finds his *hyrne*, 'enclosure' (l. 289), where he can sit in safety for three days and nights.

In his attack on political quietism written at the outbreak of war, George Orwell comments on Henry Miller's fantasy of being inside a whale. For Miller, he says,

there are many worse things than being swallowed by whales, and the passage makes it clear that he himself finds the idea rather attractive.... The whale's belly is simply a womb big enough for an adult. There you are, in the dark, cushioned space that exactly fits you, with yards of blubber between yourself and reality, able to keep up an attitude of the completest indifference, no matter *what* happens.... Short of being dead, it is the final, unsurpassable stage of irresponsibility.[15]

It is improbable that Orwell had read *Patience*, but his comment works very well as an analysis of the poet's description. For Jonah, being inside the whale is indeed an escape rather than an imprisonment. He finds a corner clear of filth and sits there in comfort, troubled by nothing other than the darkness (ll. 289–91). 'A storm that would sink all the battleships in the world would hardly reach you as an echo', writes Orwell.[16] Absolutely so. Ensconced in his submarine, Jonah has no contact with the elemental battle that he can hear raging around him:

> Ande as sayled þe segge, ay sykerly he herde
> Þe bygge borne on his bak and bete on his sydes. (ll. 301–2)

But the comfort inside the whale's belly is only relative, for it 'sauoured as helle' (l. 275). Indeed it is not just like hell; Jonah eventually acknowledges that it *is* hell, that state of sin in which man is separated from God:

> Careful am I, kest out fro þy cler yȝen
> And deseuered fro þy syȝt. (ll. 314–15)

It is in his great psalm of repentance, closely translated from the Old Testament, that Jonah at last recognizes that his physical location denotes his spiritual state; he is, he sees now, 'in hellen wombe' (l. 306). He has, in another image from his prayer, reached rock bottom: 'To laste mere of vche a mount, man, am I fallen' (l. 320).

---

[13] Andrew and Waldron, 1.258.
[14] See *MED* 2(b).   [15] Orwell (1962: 42–3).   [16] Ibid. 43

Jonah's prayer has verbal parallels with Psalm 68, *Salvum me fac*, which begins 'Save me, O God, for the waters are come in even unto my soul. I stick fast in the mire of the deep'. The artistic scheme used in psalter sequences recognized this with an illustration of Jonah emerging from the whale's mouth and God gazing at him beneficently, as in the Ranworth Antiphonal.[17]

Sarah Stanbury[18] observes how Jonah moves from one enclosure to another within the whale, seeing just one bit at a time, and she comments that this signifies his lack of overall perception. He gropes (l. 273), he sees (l. 277), he smells (l. 274), he hears (l. 301), but it is not until he starts *thinking* (l. 294) that he comes to recognize his Lord and can reach sufficient self-awareness to be released from his own hell. This self-recognition takes place in an enclosure whose only characteristic is darkness; in this place of stillness, Jonah finds God.

In his *hyrne* Jonah is remarkably comfortable and content, and, for such an impatient man, accepts his strange situation with equanimity. The fact is that Jonah is a claustrophile, only happy in enclosed spaces. The poet draws a parallel with the previous scene; Jonah was as comfortable in the whale 'As in þe bulk of the bote þer he byfore sleped' (l. 292). In the Old Testament the behaviour of Jonah in the ship is inexplicable, and biblical commentators reached for an allegorical interpretation. As the tempest rages, 'Jonah went down into the inner part of the ship and fell into a deep sleep' (1:5). In *Patience* we recognize that Jonah's characteristic reaction to a threat is to hide. When first commanded to travel to Nineveh, Jonah had supposed that, by taking the boat to Tarshish instead, he could escape from God. The poet comments on his folly in attempting to hide from God's sight (ll. 113–16). So when faced with the danger of the storm at sea, Jonah lay asleep in his hiding place ('jowked in derne', l. 182). To medieval commentators Jonah's deep sleep symbolized moral torpor; the *locus classicus* of this association is the parable of the wise and foolish virgins.[19] Yet, while not excluding the allegorical interpretation, the poet asks us to take Jonah's sleep on a naturalistic level, as is underlined by the description of his dribbling and snoring, 'sloberande he routes' (l. 186). He sleeps entirely comfortably in his enclosure. How could this be so, with the world in turmoil around him, the storm raging terrifyingly, the sailors desperately casting out their bags and feather-beds, praying to Vernagu, Diana, Neptune, Mahoun, and Mergot? The answer is that Jonah is magnificently solipsistic; he exists entirely within himself for himself. He is part of no society, has no fellow-feelings, regards charity as a weakness and a danger to himself, and consequently denounces God's compassion, using French terms to suggest that it is mere courtly affectation:

> Wel knew I þi *cortaysye*, þy *quoynt soffraunce*,
> Þy *bounté* of *debonerté*, and þy *bene grace*. (ll. 417–18)

God mischievously exploits Jonah's pathological need to hide from the open when he causes the ivy to grow over him, then destroys it and exposes him. In *Patience* Jonah

---

[17] Scott (1996: i, pl. 447, and ii. 378–9).
[18] Stanbury (1991: 80–1).   [19] Matt. 25: 1–13.

has gathered the few ferns and grasses he can find to make himself a *bour* to huddle under as he watches to see what will happen to Nineveh and wakes in wonder the next morning. God in the Old Testament covers Jonah with a *hedera*; the poet gives Jonah a veritable house of leaves:

> Such a lefsel of lof neuer lede hade,
> For hit watz brod at the boþem, boȝted on lofte,
> Happed vpon ayþer half, a hous as hit were,
> A nos on þe norþ syde and nowhere non ellez,
> Bot al schet in a schaȝe þat schaded ful cole. (ll. 448–52)

In Jonah's eyes this gift of the Almighty is a man-made structure, complete with a *nos*, interpreted by *MED* as 'a projecting doorway'. His reaction is ecstatic; once in his shelter, the world outside is forgotten:

> Þenne watz þe gome so glad of his gay logge,
> Lys loltrande þerinne lokande to toune;
> So blyþe of his wodbynde he balteres þervnder. (ll. 457–9)

So completely has this become *his* space, that he imagines himself living within it in his own country on 'Ermonnes hillez' (l. 463). The destruction of the *wod-bynde* causes extravagant despair and fury; the prophet calls out in anger at the removal of his *cumfort* and asks for death.

The three scenes of Jonah in enclosures are verbally linked: the poet comments that in the whale he sat as comfortably as previously in the ship (ll. 291–2), and like a fieldmouse whose first instinct is to build a protective nest, Jonah constructs a makeshift *bour* in the whale as also on the hill above Nineveh (ll. 276, 437). Jonah's open space is the great city of Nineveh. This may seem surprising. A poet who can so well evoke the buildings and streets of the Heavenly Jerusalem in *Pearl* here resists the opportunity to expand the biblical narrative:

And Jonah arose and went to Nineveh, according to the word of the Lord. Now Nineveh was a great city of three days' journey. And Jonah began to enter into the city one day's journey. (3: 3–4)

This is exactly translated:

> To Niniue þat naȝt he neȝed ful euen;
> Hit watz a ceté ful syde and selly of brede,
> On to þrenge þerþurȝe watz þre dayes dede.
> Þat on journay ful joynt Jonas hym ȝede. (lines 352–5)

For Jonah the city is a place of danger and exposure, an open space with nowhere to hide. Here he must announce God's warning of destruction and, as he envisages, will incur torture, eye-gouging, and crucifixion (ll. 79–80, 96). In fact, of course, the king and his people repent immediately in sackcloth and ashes. Jonah makes no human contact, there are no interiors; where the poet might have described the royal palace, it is not even mentioned. Instead, the king leaves his *chayer*, strips off his robes, and leaps onto a pile of ashes, presumably in the open (ll. 378–80). Jonah's one brave action is heightened by his sense of danger, and even here the danger is entirely in Jonah's head.

For anyone else, being swallowed by a whale would surely be a much more frightening experience, but for Jonah the safety of enclosure far outweighs his fear of exposure. God asks him to open himself to suffering and endurance, to learn that even in the whale there is no final escape from the world. But it is a lesson he is unable to learn, and an experience which, in the long run, does not bring him any self-knowledge.

THE CASTLE OF ROMANCE

Riding alone through the wilderness of the Wirral on Christmas Eve, Gawain prays to the Virgin that he might find somewhere to attend Mass. At once there appears a castle so exquisitely elaborate that it seemed to be 'pared out of papure', cut out of paper (l. 802). We must suspend our post-Romantic attachment to natural beauty and our distrust of artifice: Gawain experiences wild nature as threatening, both in the Wirral and at the Green Chapel.

The road that Gawain follows through Wales up to the north-west is carefully mapped, with Anglesey on his left and a crossing at the Holy Head. From there he plunges into the Wirral, where, like Dante, he finds himself in a dark wood with no direct path. He meets no one who has heard of the Green Chapel. Though an errant knight might expect to find a hermit here and there to give him shelter for the night, very few of the inhabitants of the Wirral have any good in them, and Gawain must spend his nights in the cold, sleeping in his armour, and his days fighting those who try to block his way, battling with wodwoses and giants. It is the cold and sleet that afflict him worst of all; the misery of the birds piteously piping is an expression of his own distress.

The contrast with the castle that suddenly appears could not be sharper, for Gawain sees before him a supreme example of the civilizing of the wilderness (ll. 763–806). It is demarcated from the tangled forest trees by an encircling palisade enclosing the park, whose carefully positioned 'schyre okez' direct the eye to the shimmering castle itself. Nature has been regulated to create order out of chaos, so that the castle-name that Bertilak later reveals could not be more apt: Hautdesert, 'high lonely place', the courtly French title keeping at bay the surrounding *klyf*, *knarrez*, and *heȝe felle*. The castle is an expression of cultural hegemony not military might, for like John of Gaunt's rebuilt castles of Tutbury and Kenilworth, Hautdesert is a palace built for display, not a stronghold for defence, designed to ward off the forces of wild nature, 'wyndez blaste', rather than hostile incursion.

The castle is described from Gawain's perspective as he moves closer and closer towards it and sees more and more detail.[20] It isn't wholly true to say that the castle is described from Gawain's point of view, for only Bertilak and the poet could have known that the circumference of the palisade was more than two miles. Nevertheless,

---

[20] Cockcroft (1978).

the poet's epithets of commendation also convey Gawain's wonder and delight at what he *auysed*. The castle is 'þe comlokest', the walls below the battlement are designed 'in þe best lawe', the turrets are 'ful gaye', the windows 'luflych'. That Gawain does indeed share these impressions is confirmed at the end by the statement that 'þe fre freke . . . hit fayr innoghe þo3t'. Having first caught sight of a general view of the castle, Gawain's gaze is drawn forward to what must lie within the *cloyster*, the enclosed space, and what it promises a cold, hungry, and lonely knight. But promise is not fulfilment, and Gawain cannot yet be assured of the 'bone hostel' for which he anxiously beseeches Jesus and St Julian, the patron of travellers. Reining in Gringolet at the drawbridge, he looks down at the water in the moat, and from there his gaze is carried upward to the cornices, the turrets, the windows, and on inwards to the hall with its towers and pinnacles. Though he is waiting outside the building, his thoughts are directed inside to the warmth and companionship of the hall.

Such a sophisticated descriptive technique had been used previously to similar effect by Chrétien de Troyes.[21] There is close parallel with *Perceval*:

On that rock, situated on a slope that ran down towards the sea, was a magnificent, strong castle. Where the river opened into a bay, the youth turned to the left and saw the castle towers (*torz*) springing up; for it seemed to him they were shooting up and emerging from the rock. Rising in the centre of the castle was a high, strong keep (*tor*). A massive barbican (*barbacane*) faced the bay, challenging the sea, which broke against its foot. At the four corners of the wall with its hard stone blocks were four strong, handsome, low turrets (*torneles*). . . . In front of the round gatehouse (*chastelet*) was a bridge over the water, built of stone, sand and lime. The bridge was strong, high and completely battlemented. In the middle of it was a tower (*tor*) and in front of it a drawbridge (*pont torneïz*). . . . The youth made his way towards this bridge.[22]

As in *Gawain*, so here the castle is described in great architectural detail from the changing perspective of the young knight as he approaches.

The sudden appearance of the castle deep in the Wirral in answer to Gawain's prayer is also reminiscent of the appearance of the Grail Castle in *Perceval*. Perceval goes through a fissure in the rock, but at first finds nothing. Then 'he saw the top of a tower appear. You could not have found one so splendid or well situated this side of Beirut.'[23] After spending the night there, Perceval wakes to find all the inhabitants have disappeared, and a lady he meets in the forest tells him there is no habitation anywhere nearby. There is always a suspicion that Hautdesert, appearing as mysteriously and seemingly 'pared out of papure', is equally insubstantial. Admittedly, the Green Knight invites Gawain to return after their encounter, but of course he refuses.

Any reader of romance would expect the knight errant to come across a fine castle, and would anticipate that this would lead to some *aventure* which, as the word suggests, involves risk. It is sometimes argued that we (and Gawain) should be alerted by the extravagant architecture to the court's misplaced valuation of artifice for its own sake and to the dangers that await Gawain within.[24] Such suspicion might be reinforced by some striking echoes in *Cleanness*. But this is to misunderstand, I think,

---

[21] Putter (1995: 31–6).   [22] Owen (1993: 392).   [23] Ibid. 414.

[24] Wilson (1976: 124) confesses to a 'vague disquiet aroused by the castle's architecture'.

the poet's ironic intertextual reference to the castle architecture in *Cleanness* (which implies, though certainly doesn't prove, that *Cleanness* was written after *Gawain*). The vainglorious Balthazar prepares a banquet at his 'palayce of pryde' (l. 1389), and drunkenly conceives the blasphemous notion of bringing on the holy vessels looted from the Temple. They include:

> Couered cowpes foul clene, as casteles arayed,
> Enbaned vnder batelment with bantelles quoynt,
> And fyled out of fygures of ferlylé schappes.
> Þe coperounes of the couacles þat on þe cuppe reres
> Wer fetysely formed out in fylyoles longe;
> Pinacles py3t þer apert þat profert bitwene. (ll. 1458–63)

The first line alerts us to the extraordinary artifice of these vessels, cups in the form of castles. Like Hautdesert itself, which is 'Enbaned vnder þe abataylement in þe best lawe' (l. 790), the cups have fancy projecting coursing below a crenellated top.[25] The vessels have 'fylyoles longe', like the 'fayre fylyolez . . . ferlyly long' (l. 796) of Hautdesert. Both vessels and castle are adorned with *coperounes*, 'ornamental tops', and *pinacles*. The poet has already drawn attention to the artifice of this feast and has made what appears to be a reference to Hautdesert by remarking that the table decorations included miniature buildings 'Pared out of paper' (l. 1408). The point of these precise parallels is to demonstrate the vainglorious show of the banquet with its inappropriate display, compounded by Balthazar's grotesque impropriety in drinking from the holy vessels. There is no suggestion that artifice is improper in itself, or that Gawain should have been alerted to impending danger by the glorious castle architecture. What may, however, be true is that the safety of even such a splendid enclosure may prove illusory. The dangers of the exposed landscape are obvious enough, and Gawain can cope with them, but Jonah discovered that the relative comfort of the enclosed space can be deceptive and short-lived. The warmth of the fire, the food and drink, the civilized companionship of his own kind, present Gawain with a far more complex test, which takes place in an enclosure (the curtained bed) within an enclosure (the bedroom) within an enclosure (the castle).

THE EARTHLY PARADISE

Lying in misery on the grave-mound, the narrator of *Pearl* falls asleep and his spirit travels 'on a quest where marvels happen' (l. 64). The extraordinary scene of his dream is often traced back to the *Roman de la Rose*. E. V. Gordon, for example, writes that 'the

---

[25] The suggestion by Thompson (1997: 121) that *enbaned* and *bantelle* should be transcribed as *enbaued* (*MED embouen* v.(1)) and *bautelle* (*MED boutel*) is attractive.

influence . . . is clear in the general conception of the heavenly region in which the dreamer finds himself', although he goes on to caution that 'the direct influence of the *Roman* is neither so clear nor so extensive as has sometimes been claimed'.[26] Yet this association might be thought especially inappropriate in the light of the end of the *Roman* where the enclosed garden of *amour courtois* is revealed as the false paradise.

The true source of the poet's description was long ago identified by P. M. Kean in a study that has been unjustly neglected.[27] She points to the widely known account of Alexander's visit to the Earthly Paradise, in which so many of the elements of *Pearl's* description are prefigured. For purposes of this comparison it is appropriate to refer, as she does, to the *Wars of Alexander*,[28] a fine poem composed in the same tradition as the *Gawain*-poems, using the same alliterative line as *Gawain* and *Patience*, and with many close parallels of vocabulary.[29] It is very probable that one poet drew directly upon the other.[30] The *Wars* is translated with elaborations from the prose *Historia de Preliis*, and presumably the Latin account was the source for the conception of the Earthly Paradise in *Pearl*.

The story as retold in the *Wars* relates that Alexander was forced to turn back from impassable mountains and went into a plain where 'all was brettfull of bowis & blossoms so swete' (l. 4995). He and his men journeyed north for many days till they reached a cliff 'of adamand stanes' with 'rede gold cheynes' and climbed its 2,500 steps set with sapphires (ll. 5003–7). Having made offerings to the gods, Alexander and his followers climbed further up to the 'grete lawe' touching the clouds, where they found a palace with twelve gates and seventy windows all of gold, carved and 'clustrid with gemmes' (ll. 5021–3). In the east was a golden minster which was bejewelled as richly as the dream-paradise of *Pearl*:

> Vmbegildid with a garden of golden vynes
> Was chatrid full of chefe frute of charbocle stanes,
> Withouten mesure emaunge of margarite grete. (ll. 5026–8)

This is the House of the Sun; there was nothing to equal it 'bot paradyse selfe' (l. 5032). In the temple Alexander came across a lovely man wearing a blue *bleant* covered with golden angels, his bed-head adorned with angels 'with trimaballand wingis' and with silk curtains and 'knopis of perle' (ll. 5039–44). This guide led them through the wood where the trees with aromatic gums measured 100 feet, and passing the Dry Tree with its phoenix they came to the Trees of the Sun and Moon. Alexander questioned them about his fate, and then returned to the plain, where he set up a marble memorial to mark the extent of his travels.

Descriptions of the Earthly Paradise generally represent it as an enclosed space which no one may enter. So in *Mandeville's Travels* it is situated at "the highest place of erthe" where the Flood could not reach it:

---

[26] Gordon (1953: p. xxxii).

[27] Kean (1967: 89–113); Spearing (1970: 118–20) discusses Kean's observations, but maintains that the *Roman* is a major source.

[28] Ed. Duggan and Turville-Petre (1989).

[29] Mabel Day in Gollancz (1940: pp. xiii–xviii).   [30] Duggan and Turville-Petre (1989: p. xliii).

And this Paradys is enclosed alle aboute with a walle, and men wyte not wherof it is, for the walles ben couered alle ouer with mosse, as it semeth.[31]

Indeed 'paradise' is probably derived from a Persian word meaning 'enclosed park'. John Trevisa, translating Ranulph Higden's universal history, was not so far wrong when he wrote: 'Þis name Paradys i-turned out of Grew into Latyn is to menynge an orcheʒerde'.[32] This tradition of enclosure has, I think, misled Kean into identifying the Earthly Paradise as the place situated across the river where the Pearl Maiden stands, and the Dreamer's location as lying outside its walls. 'It is not likely that, at this stage, the Dreamer expects to see Heaven itself, the actual New Jerusalem, the abode of the Lamb', she writes.[33] But this is exactly what he expects to see, and indeed does so. In the Alexander story the Earthly Paradise is a region through which Alexander travels and sees wondrous sights. There is no insurmountable wall; indeed there is a contrast between mountains that he cannot pass:

> He flitt may na ferre, ne his fokke nouthire:
> Þare was so hedous and so hoge hillis þam beforn,
> Cloʒes at was cloud-he, clyntirand torres. (ll. 4988–90)

and the adamantine cliffs conveniently set with steps 'for gomes vp to wynde' (l. 5005), up which they ascend to the clouds, and discover the palace of the sun.

It is therefore important to distinguish between *Pearl*'s enclosed *erber* which the narrator *entred* at the start of the poem, the open landscape of the Earthly Paradise at the outset of his dream, and the enclosed Heavenly City of his final vision. It is the first of these that is indebted to the garden of the *Roman de la Rose* with its little wicket-gate, and behind the *Roman* lies the *hortus conclusus* of the Song of Songs. It is this enclosure, the *spot*, which figures the narrator's absorption with his loss and his inability to see any escape from his obsessive grief. In the Earthly Paradise, by contrast, he is assailed by so many new experiences that his mood is inevitably lifted. The beauty of the scene

> Bylde in me blys, abated my balez,
> Fordidden my stresse, dystryed my paynez. (ll. 123–4)

This points to the real difference between the *Wars* and *Pearl*: the former is an extraordinary travelogue of Alexander's adventures; the latter is an exploration into the developing mood and understanding of the Dreamer, and a prefiguration of the central issues of the poem. This is *his* dream, his experience.[34]

His first comment is 'I ne wyste in þis worlde quere þat hit wace' (l. 65). Editors point out that this is ambiguous, for he might merely be saying idiomatically 'I didn't know where on earth I was'. The fact is, though, that the Earthly Paradise was thought of as having a physical location somewhere in the Orient, and this is where he supposes he is in his dream. He says a little later:

---

[31] Seymour (1967: 220, ll. 21–3).   [32] Trevisa (1865–6: 1. 75).
[33] Kean (1967: 91).   [34] Spearing (2005: 147–73).

> I þo3t þat paradyse
> Was þer, oþer gayn þo bonkez brade. (ll. 137–8)

This is always emended to 'Was þer-ouer', referring to the opposite side of the river, but perhaps it might instead be taken as another expression of the Dreamer's uncertainty: 'Paradise was there where I was, or else was near those broad hills'. The passage is difficult in any case: he is looking for a *mote*, that is, a castle or a city, but all the verbs express uncertainty as to where it might be or whether it exists: *I þo3t, I hoped, I hoped* (ll. 137, 139, 142).

His uncertainty is understandable, given that the biblical paradise has two locations. It is 'paradys greue' on earth (*Pearl* l. 321), that is, the Garden of Eden from which Adam was expelled: 'Et emisit eum Dominus Deus de Paradiso voluptatis';[35] it is also the paradise where Christ will wait[36] and into which St Paul was raptured to hear words that are not given to man to utter.[37] The Dreamer's reference to the Pearl Maiden living in 'paradys erde' (l. 248) refers to the second of these, not to the Earthly Paradise: *erde* has nothing to do with 'earth' in this context, but means 'region', as in Orm's use of the phrase 'Paradisess ærd' as a synonym of 'heoffne' in the previous line.[38]

The unearthly features of the Earthly Paradise are drawn from the same stock in *Pearl* and the *Wars*, and both develop the description of *paradisi dei* as a list of precious stones in Ezekiel 28: 13. This list is repeated in the description of the Heavenly City in the Apocalypse, closely followed in *Pearl* (ll. 999–1018). The crystal cliffs and pearls underfoot in *Pearl* ll. 66–74 and 81–2 are similar to the cliff of adamant with steps of sapphires of *Wars* ll. 5002–8; with the birds 'of flaumbande hwez' (*Pearl* l. 90), compare the phoenix 'with frekild pennys/Of gold graynes and of goules' (*Wars* ll. 5115–16). Most striking of all in both accounts are the trees of the Earthly Paradise. In the *Wars* the Sun Tree is 'clethid/ With feylour as of fine gold þat ferly faire lemes', the Moon Tree is 'loken ouire with leues as it ware li3t siluir' (ll. 5130–2). The Sun Tree shakes when Alexander asks about his fate:

> Þan schogs hire þe son tree and schoke hire schire leues
> And with a swe3and swo3e þis sware scho him 3eldis (ll. 5145–6)

So, too, in an exquisite description, the silver leaves of the trees in *Pearl* shimmer in the breeze:

> As bornyst syluer þe lef on slydez,
> Þat þike con trylle on vch a tynde;
> Quen glem of glodez agaynz hem glydez
> Wyth schymeryng schene ful schrylle þay schynde. (ll. 77–80)

Unlike the flowers that spread over the burial mound in the enclosed garden, the silver and gold foliage cannot decay. It is this point that the maiden makes when she reproves her father for his grief at losing something transitory when he has gained something eternal:

---

[35] Gen. 3: 23.   [36] Luke 23: 43.
[37] 2 Cor. 12: 4.   [38] *Ormulum*, ll. 8412–13.

> For þat þou lestez watz bot a rose
> Þat flowred and fayled as kynde hyt gef;
> Now þurȝ kynde of þe kyste þat hyt con close
> To a perle of prys hit is put in pref. (ll. 269–72)

In this way the landscape of the Earthly Paradise contributes to the central symbolism of the pearl as eternal perfection.

Though unchanging, the scenery of the Earthly Paradise is far from static. Everything is movement: the leaf slides, gravel grinds, birds fly and wings beat, water sweeps. And through all this movement the Dreamer is on the move 'In auenture þer meruaylez meuen' (l. 64), heading towards the forest, walking on further where the meadows rise, reaching a river, following it down in search of a crossing-point. This is a very different figure from the mourner who falls upon the flowery turf in the garden, immobilized by grief. The Dreamer is receptive, open to experience, full of wonder and excitement, 'bredful my braynez' (l. 126) as each new scene comes into view. It will be evident that I disagree with Gregory Roper, who argues that the dreamer is too caught up in the sensual beauty of the scene and that it represents a projection of his disordered world,[39] for this interpretation would mean that the beauty was deliberately deceptive, since we see it only through his senses and in his words. Instead it is a necessary prologue to his encounter with the Maiden, when his brains will be crammed even more with new concepts and emotions. His earthly self-knowledge is inevitably limited, so that in the end he is dragged back from his wild attempt to cross the river. And yet as he wakens from his dream his words signal his resigned acceptance of what must be: 'Now al be to þat Pryncez paye' (l. 1176).

PLACES OF THE IMAGINATION

These descriptions of the whale's interior, the castle of romance, and the Earthly Paradise, all describe imaginary places that the poet cannot possibly have visited. Two of them draw on well-established literary traditions, but it appears that Jonah's journey through the whale is entirely original. The poet, in pointing out that the story would be difficult to believe if it were not the word of God, is surely saying: 'The Bible tells us that it happened, so let's try to imagine the experience and what the prophet felt about it.'

Would a description of an actual place, rather than an imaginary one, be any less a work of the imagination? Not in the slightest. To demonstrate this, we may

---

[39] Roper (1993).

suppose—I think it probable in any case—that the Green Chapel is a real place in north Staffordshire on the border with Cheshire, a notable rock-fissure called Ludchurch.[40] A local author and audience would undoubtedly have seen it or known of it. So the poet's description would have an added interest for readers in the region, and would have spoken to them in the same way as the regional dialect and vocabulary of the poem. Nevertheless, the fact that it might be an actual place makes no difference at all to the character or significance of the scene, which the poet handles in the same way as the three scenes I have been examining, for it is not essentially a view of Ludchurch that he presents but of Gawain's mistaken conception of the spot. There are two sources for Gawain's mistake: one is the guide's terrifying but false warning that it is inhabited by a gruesome murderer who kills all who ride by; the other is the name by which the Green Knight refers to the place of their appointment, from which Gawain naturally infers that it is some sort of church. With his fear of death and, no doubt, a certain amount of guilt buried in his conscience, Gawain concludes that what to all appearances is 'nobot an olde caue/Or a creuisse of an olde cragge' (ll. 2182–3) is in fact the church of the Devil who has summoned him to destroy him. So Gawain's imagination makes something quite different of the Green Chapel. We see it through his heightened apprehension, just as we see the castle in terms of his hopes of refuge, and the inside of the whale through Jonah's fears and his recognition of wrongdoing, and the paradisaical landscape through the Dreamer's consciousness of grief and its temporary alleviation.

For each of these protagonists, their view of the scene alters as they move through it. They have no overall vision, but see the scene bit by bit as each new aspect appears to them. This is the key image in Salman Rushdie's *Midnight's Children* of the 'perforated sheet' through which Dr Aziz is obliged to examine his patient (soon to be his wife) bit by bit, and which is symbolically inherited by his grandson, the narrator, and 'condemned me to see my own life—its meanings, its structures—in fragments also'.[41] In just this way Jonah, Gawain, and the Dreamer have fragmentary understanding and lack that whole vision that might save them from foolishness and disappointment. Jonah lives for the moment only, never accepting that actions have consequences, and that he who tears up his clothes in a rage will have to sit down and sew them up again (ll. 526–7). Gawain has no insight that can prepare him to encounter the fate that awaits him in the castle; subsequently he fails to foresee the consequences of accepting the Lady's girdle. And the Dreamer, entranced by the loveliness around him, has to learn the hard way that for him it is just a dream from which he must awake to mourn again in his dungeon of sorrow (l. 1187). It is the nature of our human condition that condemns us to see existence through a sheet with a hole in it.

---

[40] Elliott (1984: 34–72); Turville-Petre (2008).   [41] Rushdie (1995: 143).

BIBLIOGRAPHY

ANDREW, MALCOLM, and RONALD WALDRON (eds.) (2007), *The Poems of the Pearl Manuscript* (5th edn. Exeter: Exeter University Press).

COCKCROFT, ROBERT (1978), 'Castle Hautdesert: Portrait or Patchwork?', *Neophilologus*, 62: 459–77.

DUGGAN, HOYT N., and THORLAC TURVILLE-PETRE (eds.) (1989), *The Wars of Alexander* (EETS SS 10; Oxford: Oxford University Press for the Early English Text Society).

ELLIOTT, R. W. V. (1984), *The Gawain Country* (Leeds Texts and Monographs, NS 8; Leeds: University of Leeds).

GOLLANCZ, SIR ISRAEL (ed.) (1940), *Sir Gawain and the Green Knight* (EETS OS 210; London: Oxford University Press for the Early English Text Society).

GORDON. E. V. (ed.) (1953), *Pearl* (Oxford: Oxford University Press).

KEAN, P. M. (1967), *The Pearl: An Interpretation* (London: Routledge & Kegan Paul).

ORWELL, GEORGE (1962), *Inside the Whale and Other Essays* (Harmondsworth: Penguin).

OWEN, D. D. R. (tr.) (1993), *Chrétien de Troyes: Arthurian Romances* (2nd edn. London: J. M. Dent).

PUTTER, AD (1995), *Sir Gawain and the Green Knight and French Arthurian Romance* (Oxford: Oxford University Press).

——(1996), *An Introduction to the Gawain-Poet* (London: Longman).

ROPER, GREGORY (1993), '*Pearl*, Penitence and the Recovery of the Self', *Chaucer Review*, 28: 164–86.

RUSHDIE, SALMAN (1995), *Midnight's Children* (London: Vintage).

SCOTT, KATHLEEN L. (1996), *Later Gothic Manuscripts 1390–1490* (2 vols. London: Harvey Miller).

SEYMOUR, M. C. (ed.) (1967), *Mandeville's Travels* (Oxford: Clarendon Press).

SPEARING, A. C. (1970), *The Gawain-Poet* (Cambridge: Cambridge University Press).

——(2005), *Textual Subjectivity* (Oxford: Oxford University Press).

STAHL, W. H. (1952), *Macrobius: Commentary on the Dream of Scipio* (New York: Columbia University Press).

STANBURY, SARAH (1991), *Seeing the Gawain-Poet* (Philadelphia: University of Pennsylvania Press).

THOMPSON, MICHAEL (1997), 'Castles', in Derek Brewer and Jonathan Gibson (eds.), *A Companion to the Gawain-Poet* (Cambridge: D. S. Brewer), 119–30.

TREVISA, JOHN (1865–86), *Polychronicon Ranulphi Higden*, ed. C. Babington and J. R. Lumby (9 vols. Rolls Series; London: Longmans).

TURVILLE-PETRE, THORLAC, (ed.) (1989), *Alliterative Poetry of the Later Middle Ages* (London: Routledge).

——(2008), 'The Green Chapel', in O. J. Padel and David N. Parsons (eds.), *A Commodity of Good Names* (Donington: Shaun Tyas), 320–9.

WALDRON, R. A. (1972), 'The Prologue to *The Parlement of the Thre Ages*', *Neuphilologische Mitteilungen*, 73: 786–94.

WILSON, EDWARD (1976), *The Gawain-Poet* (Leiden: E. J. Brill).

WORMALD, FRANCIS (1973), *The Winchester Psalter* (London: Harvey Miller & Medcalf).

PART VII

LITERARY
JOURNEYS

CHAPTER 31

PILGRIMAGES, TRAVEL WRITING, AND THE MEDIEVAL EXOTIC

JEFFREY JEROME COHEN

A fictional account of an English knight's voyage to the Holy Land and the alien realms beyond, the *Book of John Mandeville* was a medieval bestseller, and possibly the most popular travel narrative ever composed. A kind of fourteenth-century *Fodor's Guide to Imagined Places*, the book is not the record of a historical traveller's sojourn, but a compendium of cultural details, pious histories, marvels, and exotica culled from an array of sources. Unflaggingly congenial yet quietly treacherous, the *Book of John Mandeville* masks its recalcitrance beneath what postcolonial theory calls a 'sly civility'.[1] Bearing a reassuring resemblance to traditional accounts of pilgrimage and travel, as well as to classical ethnography (descriptions of customs and peoples), the text seems companionable enough. Its easygoing narrative of foreign marvels and distant travels lure readers into enthusiastic encounter . . . but

I thank the audience at the Southeast Medieval Association meeting in St Louis for their enthusiasm for this project. My colleagues Jonathan Hsy and Robert Hakan Patterson of Washington University gave valuable feedback.

[1] 'Sly civility' is a concept borrowed from Homi Bhabha, who describes the phenomenon as a 'native refusal to satisfy the colonizer's narrative demand' through what appears to be polite agreement. On closer inspection such assent turns out to be a deflection or rejection of any attempt at assimilation or coercion. See Bhabha (1994: 93–101).

then leaves them to wonder if the motion-filled and unsettled world it brings into being won't erode the stability of their own. The *Book of John Mandeville* is, in a word, unsettling. Its volatility derives from the fact that, strictly speaking, it does not exist: there is no *Book* of John Mandeville, no single or originary version, no 'complete' source from which textual variants sprang, just a volatile multiplicity of texts masquerading as a unity.[2] The nonexistence of the *Book* as object, as thing, has serious consequences for its analysis. We'll always be chasing after what was supposed to remain where we placed it, something that keeps moving just beyond that skyline where *terra cognita* curves to harbour incalculable islands.

In honour of its peripatetic subject, this chapter follows a meandering path. But I don't want to lose you. Here is the rough itinerary we'll use to pursue this ever-in-transit collection of texts filled with wonders, miracles, and motion. This chapter will attempt to map:

1. How the work transforms itself from a typical account of Holy Land pilgrimage based upon William of Boldensele's *Liber de quisbusdam ultramarines partibus* (an account of the German knight's journey through Constantinople to Palestine in 1332–3) to a boundary-defying ethnography capable of almost circling the round earth.

2. How the Book populates its worlds with bodies in motion—so much so that things that ought to be utterly immobile (rocks, ruins, graves) are possessed of magnetism and motility, alluring or radiative effects that medieval writers called *virtus*.

3. How the constant forward motion of the text never arrives at its destination (the globe is circumnavigable only in theory; the world cannot in the end be contained within a circle's enclaspment).

4. How for all the *Book*'s dreams of a cosmos where bodies constantly move, impediments ('lapidary narratives') nonetheless serve to interrupt the text's restless itinerary, transfixing the *Book* to small identities like *English*. Even if imaginary or fictive, these identities are nonetheless a powerful counterweight to the embrace of otherness found elsewhere in the work.

5. Finally, how the Book is ultimately less of a text than an event: how it performs its own content, becoming itself a marvel, a body in perpetual motion.

Though numerous editions of the *Book of John Mandeville* exist in French and in English, I will be quoting from the version known as Defective, an appellation this group earned because 'missing' a section known as the Egypt Gap. The Defective version possesses the best claim to be 'the English Mandeville',[3] and Mandeville's potential national identity will be one of my themes. This supposedly 'unfortunate name' of *Defective* also captures something profound about the text's openness, about why the *Book* should possess such enduring vitality.[4] Several versions of the

---

[2] The Book's multiplicity is well-stressed throughout Iain Macleod Higgins's magisterial book (1997; see also 1998).

[3] Hanna (1984: 123).

[4] Kohanski and Benson (2007: 13). All quotations in Middle English are from this text.

Defective text are extant. I have chosen the recently edited London, British Library, Royal 17 C. xxxvii, a 'highly individualistic' treatment that, even if 'somewhat compressed', nonetheless contains most of the richest material found in other versions.[5] This version also contains some fine illustrations, especially of buildings and mountains. As enduring markers along the pilgrimage trail or as marvels in themselves, such rocky architectures, monuments, ruins, and fragments of stone populate the narrative throughout, providing the *Book* with its sturdiest and yet its most strangely mobile substance.

In the Myddel

The *Book of John Mandeville* narrates a miraculous journey during which a traveller might encounter professional virgin deflowerers (the *gadlybyriens*, p. 87), or hermaphrodites who know the enjoyments of both sexes (p. 71), or an island where a lady still awaits the kiss that will free her from her dragon's flesh and reward with wealth, title, and lands the man so brave as to brush his lips against hers (Hippocrates's transfigured daughter, pp. 29–30). Travel narratives, like medieval bestiaries and romances, allow their readers to enjoy pleasures ordinarily withheld, to consume fantasies otherwise precluded.[6] Early in the *Book* Mandeville reaches Satalia, a 'greet cité' that 'sanke adoun' when one of its residents could not resist opening a 'grave of marble' and being with his beloved one last time. Just as subterranean Satalia renders the paths that cross above its buried towers 'parolous passages' (p. 31), so the *Book of John Mandeville* likewise possesses its own perilous passages, marble tombs that when opened could divert pilgrims from their certain and orthodox roads. Pilgrimage is supposed to be a journey towards a known and reverenced destination, not an errantry that enables haphazard encounter with the inexplicable, the dangerous, and the obstinately exotic.

For despite the salacity of some of its eventual destinations, the *Book of John Mandeville* begins as a personalized version of a venerable genre: a conventional account of pilgrimage to the Holy Land.[7] Labelled *itineraria* ('accounts of journey' or 'verbal roadmaps'), this genre of Christian writing traces its history back to at least AD 333, when an anonymous pilgrim from Bordeaux composed a laconic report of his voyage to Jerusalem, the *Itinerarium Burdigalense*. Based upon Roman models, Christian *itineraria* tend to be terse records, providing some information on how to

---

[5] Ibid. 14–15.

[6] On the bestiary as delectation of the forbidden, see Cohen (2008). The culturally normalizing function that fantasies of the exotic other could serve are thoroughly examined by Geraldine Heng in her impressive *Empire of Magic* (2003).

[7] The initial destination of Jerusalem is, in other words, wholly orthodox. The place is known in advance: if we've read even a fraction of what the book's author has, we have already in a way been there. We are led to expect no surprises on this pilgrimage that all serious medieval tourists eventually take.

get to the Holy City and a catalogue of sites to behold upon arrival. Visited locations and encountered objects are tied through scriptural citation to whatever biblical event gives the building, well, town, mountain, altar its significance. Thus the Pilgrim of Bordeaux writes of some artefacts he beholds:

> Here is also the corner of an exceeding high tower, where our Lord ascended and the tempter said to Him, 'If thou be the Son of God, cast thyself down from hence'... There is a great corner-stone, of which it was said, 'The stone which the builders rejected is become the head of the corner.'[8]

Even when a crumbled ruin is all that remains of the structure that provided the setting for a biblical story, that narrative nonetheless comes fully to present life by invocation. An 'exceeding high tower' suddenly looms in a place where a pilgrim beheld its only extant corner. The bodies that once moved across these stages might have perished or risen heavenward long ago, but stones abide the silent centuries to offer lasting testament to the histories that unfolded nearby.

To journey through this revered landscape is to traverse sacred time: a pilgrim arrives at the rock of Calvary, and there meditates upon the Passion as if Jesus and the two thieves were still hanging on their crosses. Pilgrimage is a kind of time travel, the terminus of which is absolution at the site of the resurrection. Travellers might partake of some side excursions (Jericho, the river Jordan, Bethlehem), they might immediately return home, but in a way the pilgrim is forever stuck at that place of revelation and redemption. There is no compelling story to tell afterwards, because the *itinerarium* was never about its narrator in the first place. The Holy Land persists in its timelessness as the traveller (whose soul is now similarly wrenched from the temporal) quickly ends the tale.[9] Pilgrimage is a one-way movement. Even if the sketch of a homeward journey is provided, doctrinally speaking there is no return from Palestine.

Although known for its peregrination without certain destination, the *Book of John Mandeville* likewise almost becomes transfixed here in the middle of the world.

THE ROCK IN THE MYD OF THE ERTHE

John Mandeville, the knightly narrator of the book that bears his name, provides his readers with several options for arriving in the Holy Land, both by land and by sea.

---

[8] 'Ibi est anglus turris excelsissimae, ubi dominus ascendit et dixit ei is, qui temptabat eum, et ait ei dominus: non temptabis dominum deum tuum, sed illi soli seruies. Ibi est et lapis angularis mangus, de quo dictum est: lapidem, quem reprobauerunt aedificantes, hic factus est ad caput anguli'; *Itinerarium Burdigalense* 590, http://www.christusrex.org/www1/ofm/pilgr/bord/10Bord01MapEur.html

[9] This general observation has its obvious exceptions: the pilgrim of Bordeaux e.g. acknowledges that Emperor Constantine has built a basilica 'at present' to commemorate the site of the Holy Sepulchre. Yet such acknowledgement of a present tense in the Holy land—of the living, contemporaneous inhabitation of its expanses—tends to be both rare and marginal to the pilgrimage itself.

He also details some unanticipated sights to enjoy along the way, including that princess in dragon form and the city sunk below the earth for its necrophiliac resident mentioned earlier.[10] Bodily presence is foregrounded from the start. The Holy Land, we are told, was 'y-halwed' by the corporealization and physical touch of Christ ('In the which londe hit liked Hym to take flesh and blood of the Virgyn Marie and to honoure that lond with His blessed foot', p. 21). Why it pleased him to take body in this particular place is also explained. Palestine is best among geographies because '"vertu of thynges is in the myddel"' and Jerusalem is 'in the middel of the worlde' (p. 22). At the very centre of this centre is the Church of the Holy Sepulchre, within which is enclosed the rock of Calvary, upon which was set the cross of Christ, atop which Abraham attempted to sacrifice Isaac, under which was found in a crack the head of Adam. A sign in Latin and in Greek announces that we have arrived 'in the myd of the erthe' (p. 38). Ground zero—the middle of the middle—is to be found nearby, 'in the myddel of this cherche', within a 'compass' (circle) drawn by Joseph of Arimathea. Here was placed the corpse of 'Oure Lord' after he was taken down from the cross: 'And that compass, men seyn, hit is in the myddel of the world' (p. 39).

The pivot of the earth, Jerusalem is central geographically, theologically, and historically—a place where the literal and the metaphorical are indistinguishable, where sign is thing. We find ourselves within the Holy Land, within the walls of Jerusalem, within the church of the tomb, within Joseph's compass: within, that is, a series of ever shrinking concentric circles that announce, once we can get to no more medial a site, that we have arrived at the locus where time and space are one. For just as we can move no further geographically, so temporality itself seems arrested: we are witnesses with Mandeville of events that occurred thirteen or fourteen hundred years before, a living history caught in eternal loop. Thus not only can we glimpse the red stains of Christ's blood upon the mortice that secured his cross, but the chains that held him to a pillar when he was scourged. Not far from Joseph's compass was the cross itself entombed, placed 'under a roche' by Jews. Almost every step of this sacrosanct expanse brings to mind a story from the Bible, brings sacred narrative into the present to unfold once more. The centre of the earth would seem a place of profound stasis, inscribed with a history so holy that the very stones retain its crimson imprint.

Except that these precincts are inhabited, and not by Joseph of Arimathea or Abraham or the Virgin Mary. 'This lond of Jerusalem hath y-be in hond of diverse nacions', Mandeville observes, providing an extensive list of the peoples who have come and (in most cases) gone: 'Jewes, Cananeus, Assirienes, Perces, Medoynes, Massydoyns, Grecis, Romayns, Cristen men, Sarasyns, Barbaryns, and Turkes, and many other naciouns with hem' (p. 37). The Church of the Holy Sepulchre is

---

[10] Unanticipated, at least, in the *Liber de quibusdam ultramarines partibus* of the German Dominican William of Boldensele, the foundation text for the Book's narratives of Constantinople and travel to Palestine. Higgins (1997: 83) writes of the Hippocrates's daughter episode and the necrophilia at Satalia (neither found in William) that they have in common a theme of 'eros gone awry', that they derive from 'the shadowy world where romance couples with folklore,' and that—since they seem so out of place within the didactic narrative—they have a 'crepuscular quality').

Constantinople's addition to the Levantine landscape. A Muslim Sultan now owns the building, and he has built a fence around the tomb of Jesus to prevent pilgrims from chiselling souvenir pebbles. Godfrey of Bouillon, Baldwin, and other crusaders who held but could not keep the city are buried nearby. The cross of Christ and the nails that secured him to its wood were long ago discovered and carried away, the latter now possessed by 'paynems and Sarasyns'. Within the church that has engulfed this sacred region in stone, the priests who say the masses do not use a familiar liturgy. Rocks and tombs that once held secrets—subterranean or stonework spaces that had enclosed bodies and relics and kept them transfixed—have all been opened, emptied. In the middle of the world, history carries on. Clergy go about their business indifferent to Roman changes to the mass, colonizers and tourists of various faiths come and go, the Sultan who owns the place remodels with his own architectural additions.

THREE TOMBS

We immure bodies beneath or within stone because we possess no weightier material. Lithic heaviness keeps the body in its place, marks the hope that some trace will there endure even as the dead are lost to us. Christ rose because he could not be kept by such stone; death could not still his divine body. The Church of the Holy Sepulchre is in Jerusalem, not Satalia—Satalia, that suddenly subterranean metropolis where a mysterious and unnamed 'yong man' loved so ardently that he opened the marble tomb withholding the body to which he was devoted. Nine months later a voice commanded 'Go to the tumbe of that womman and opene the tumbe and byhold what thow hast gyte on here' (pp. 30–1). The youth unseals the stone for a second time, and a flying head swoops out, restless progeny of a corpse not surrendered to mortuary immobility. The airborne head circles his habitation, and 'anoon the cité sanke adoun': the earth swallows Satalia in its entirety.[11] The marble grave here was not empty but too full: with a body not yielded to stillness, with forbidden pleasure, with the monstrous product of a passion that transgressed the limit of death.

Compare a tomb that comes just a bit earlier in the narrative, that of St John the Evangelist, interred at Ephesus (p. 29). We are told two irreconcilable stories about this apostle's resting place: either John's body was translated to heaven and the grave filled with manna; or that he entered the tomb while still alive, where he still remains, awaiting the Day of Judgement. 'Men may se', asserts Mandeville, 'the erthe of the

---

[11] According to M. C. Seymour, Satalia or Adalia is modern Antalya, whence Paul sailed to Antioch. Seymour sees the story as a version of the Gorgon's head myth combined with that of Callimachus and Drusinia of Ephesus, but writes that 'the immediate source is unknown' (Seymour 2002: 141). Though the tale does bear elements of both these narratives, it stands alone: this is not a story the Mandeville-author took wholesale from another known text.

tumbe many tymes stire and meve, as ther were a quyk thing ther under' (p. 29). What has the unholy passion of the young man at Satalia to say to this tomb of restless occupant? Or to the narrative of Christ's Passion in the book of Mark, where the three women coming to anoint the body of Jesus find that the great rock sealing his tomb has been rolled away?[12] A mysterious young man (*iuvenem*) has already entered the tomb, and he decrees the vacancy of the place: 'Be not affrighted; you seek Jesus of Nazareth, who was crucified: he is risen, he is not here, behold the place where they laid him.'[13] The Holy Sepulchre is empty, and the message of the untenanted tomb is that death itself has perished. Necrophiliac Satalia sinks to the underground; Jerusalem, a place to which every approach is (in Mandeville's account) uphill, remains the earth's pinnacle. Could the contrast be more stark? Three tombs, three possibilities: revelation, mystification, boundary-crossing exploration. The tomb of Jesus enjoins the pilgrim who has reached the earth's *omphalos* to return home, the trajectory of a conventional *itinerarium*. Who can blame the tourist who wants to chip a piece off the grave to remember its revelations? But the Sultan who regulates the church no longer allows its rocks to be transported.

The tombs at Satalia and Ephesus, tombs that interrupt the journey to the Holy Land, hint at perilous routes and dangerous dalliances. They suggest in advance that Mandeville will not be content to turn back after reaching Jerusalem. Mandeville's movement beyond the city does not necessarily take away from its centrality. I don't think that we witness here, as Stephen Greenblatt argued, 'the abandonment of the dream of a sacred centre'.[14] As Iain Macleod Higgins has shown, the Mandeville-author stresses Jerusalem's middleness more than any other medieval writer, a literal as well as symbolic placement of the city that permeates the *Book*.[15] This world orientation and its consequences are not going to be abandoned by leaving Jerusalem behind—and indeed, the *Book* will return to its status as centre much later, when Mandeville details the sphericity of the earth. Yet at that point of return, as Mandeville describes the potential circumnavigability of the globe, Jerusalem seems to be the top of the world rather than its centre. The flatness of a mappa mundi possesses a middle: Jerusalem, source-city of history, can be emplaced like the umbilicus of the body of Christ.[16] Yet the *Book of John Mandeville* repeats, obsessively, that the world is not a disc but a globe: the people of the Isles of Prester John walk beneath English feet ('they ar under the erthe to us', p. 92), but so far away that their patter is impossible to discern. A dedicated and God-protected traveller could, by always moving forward, 'come right too the same countrees that he wer come of and come fro, and so go aboute the erthe' (p. 92).

Spheres do not, of course, possess physical middles. The best to which a globe can aspire would be a conceptual middle, but that is not quite the same thing. If

---

[12] *et respicientes vident revolutum lapidem erat quippe magnus valde*, Mark 16: 4.   [13] Mark 16: 6.
[14] Greenblatt (1991: 29).   [15] Higgins (1998).
[16] Though, as Higgins notes, there are some *mappaemundi* that do not orient the world around Jerusalem. Matthew Paris e.g. centres his map of Palestine around Acre, and puts Jerusalem off to the side in his world map as well (ibid. 49).

Jerusalem is the world's centre, then that fixed point exists only on maps and timelines that cannot capture the fullness of the world, cannot capture the perpetual curve that gives to lands and waters their unattainable horizons.

LAPIDARY MANDEVILLE

The errant trajectory of the *Book of John Mandeville* was suggested early on, when the narratives of Hippocrates's daughter and the monstrous flying head of Satalia erupted into a pilgrimage narrative, the Mandeville-author's additions to a source containing neither. The *Book* gains so much velocity in its narration that it escapes the theology-saturated landscapes of the Holy Land to boomerang through heterodox India, Egypt, Africa, China, Sumatra, Hungary, Amazonia, a multiverse that in its proliferations trades sacred histories for secular multiplicities.[17] Mandeville's travels are in fact the motions of a body transported by reading, encountering its other worlds in books and fashioning new realms from dynamic textual convergence. The *Book of John Mandeville* is a literary pastiche, an alchemical experiment concocted of perhaps three dozen sources, from encyclopedias and *itineraria* to religious tracts, traveler's tales, and histories.[18] 'John Mandeville' seems to have been a fiction, no more likely to have existed than the incubus-begotten Merlin in Geoffrey of Monmouth's *History of the Kings of Britain*. Yet the *Book of John Mandeville* never intended to give us the best routes or the most dogma-soused accounts of sacred sites. An energetic meditation upon the exotic, upon the genre of travel narrative, upon the nature of the world we inhabit, the *Book of John Mandeville* (in all of its multifarious manifestations) is constitutionally incapable of offering anything but a cosmos where change and movement are constants, and geographies where bodies are caught in perpetual motion, where even the inanimate stirs with a kind of desire-soaked life.

The *Book* opens by providing those anchoring bits of biography that have propelled readers to locate a real person as the text's narrator. Born in St Albans, John Mandeville is possessed of a nonchalant Englishness, seen most often as he quietly interprets the foreign from an Anglocentric point of view. A knight who 'travelide

---

[17] Here I am arguing against Iain Macleod Higgins's influential account of the Mandeville's achievement and ambitions in Higgins (1998). Higgins observes that the *Book* 'is virtually unique among medieval travel writings in expanding the pilgrims' guide with a survey of the world beyond the Holy Land' (p. 40). He ties this movement somewhat counter-intuitively to a desire to make Jerusalem the centre of the entire text ('a consolation offered to a much shrunken Christendom and a challenge laid down to those Christians who, as the prologue puts it, have the wherewithal to undertake a holy voyage overseas', p. 45, as well as 'to remind them of how much they had lost with the failure of the Crusades', p. 51).

[18] For a thorough consideration of the Mandeville-author's sources see Deluz (1988: 39–93), as well as the extensive table at 428–91.

aboute in the world' (p. 21), Sir John possesses a thorn from the crown placed on Jesus at the Passion; served in the Sultan's army and was offered a wife; drank from the fountain of youth; hates Jews; is a specialist in exotic alphabets; knows good wine and balm and diamonds from bad. These attributes act as truth-effects, attaching the story to what seems a historical personage with lived experience, securing the narrative to a bulwark, a seeming veridicality. The text sutures itself at the same time to a specific chronology: Mandeville's year of departure is in the Defective Version 1332; his year of return 1366; his circuit through the world the accomplishment of thirty-four years in total.

Mandeville's attachment to home serves as an effective brake upon his nomadism, the guarantee that, despite not having turned back after attaining Palestine, he will nonetheless eventually reappear at his point of departure.[19] And indeed it is upon native soil ('my contré', p. 95) that we last glimpse him, composing the book we now read. An enduring pull within Mandeville's identity strives to keep him bound in place, to keep him attached to specific designation. This adhesiveness can go under many names, but its best designation might be *Englishness*. Whether the lost "original" version of the *Book* was composed by an author who would have self-identified as English or French is not only impossible to decide, it is ultimately not all that relevant. No matter who the actual author, no matter what collective identity that author would in life have embraced, the *Book of John Mandeville* is strewn with allusions to its narrator's nationality, affixing him in history and to place. Some references are trivial, giving the Mandeville-persona a patina of casual Englishness: thus in detailing the Saracen alphabet, he writes that just as they have 'extra' letters in their alphabet, so do 'we' English possess thorn and yogh (p. 58). Like most medieval English writers, Mandeville glibly conflates 'England' and 'Britain', as if the Welsh and Scots did not share the island (Constantine is called 'kyng of Ingelond that was that tyme called the Greet Brytayne', p. 25). The knight's birthplace is St Albans, not far from London; his name is by the fourteenth century sufficiently Anglophone, and given the polyglot nature of his contemporary homeland, his Englishness is in no way attenuated when his words sound like this: 'ieo Johan Maundeuille, chiualer . . . neez et norriz Dengleterre de la ville Seint Alban, qi y passay la meer'.[20]

The English Mandeville is a smaller circle within the wider compass drawn by the pilgrim Mandeville whose initial destination is Jerusalem. Just as within the Christian compass, a Jewish presence inheres within the English circle as well: most famously in Mandeville's fantasy that a large population of Jews has been immured behind remote hills, ready to mingle with their brethren when freed in the time of Antichrist. Mandeville asserts that Jews living among contemporary Christians study Hebrew so as to welcome in their ancient tongue these enclosed people when they are freed. They will join with them 'for to destruye men of Cristendom' (p. 83). Having detailed the Mandeville-author's tendency never to miss an opportunity to demonize the Jews, and having stressed his anti-Jewish innovations, Benjamin Braude labels the

---

[19] On the circularity of the text, see Heng (2001: esp. 152).

[20] Warner (1889: 2–3); cited by Higgins (1997: 31).

passage about the enclosed Jews 'blood-curdling' and 'a warrant for genocide'.[21] Just the opposite configuration of space is closer to the truth: having expelled its Jewish population in 1290, England inhabits an island rather like the enclosed regions where these distant Jews supposedly dwell. Late medieval Englishness is a national identity precipitated through the exclusion of Jewishness.[22] A tiny minority at best, pre-Expulsion Jews in England had been under frequent threat from both their neighbours and from the nation. Their wholesale removal from the island did nothing to reduce English anti-Jewish fantasies. Just the opposite: once gone, they loomed as more of an imagined danger than ever. The *Book of John Mandeville* is widely regarded for its extensive tolerance, a generosity extended even to the distant Mongols and the Muslims who hold the Holy Land.[23] Ian Higgins observes:

No other religious community . . . is so badly served in *The Book* as the Jews, who inhabit only the past and the future, and are depicted with a hostility bordering on paranoia.[24]

Rather than a puzzling lapse in an otherwise tolerant persona, this paranoia may be no more than yet another signifier of Mandeville's recalcitrant, immobilizing Englishness— an Englishness that cannot be wholly disentangled from the Jewishness it abjects.

In *The Jew in the Medieval Book*, Anthony Bale maps the narrative turbulence coursing through Chaucer's Prioress's Tale, intermixing as it does both Christian and Jewish identities.[25] Its flux and instability are counteracted by a 'lapidary vocabulary' of tombs and gems, metaphorical petrifications that strive to impede the text's roiling. Like the description of the *litel clergeon* as a jewel,

the 'tombe of marbul stones' into which the boy's body is placed (VII: 680) is an attempt to contain the expansive landscape and soundscape envisioned in the tale, a reassertion of the Christian community's faith in the fixity of signs . . . The tomb stands for morbid permanence and closure . . . The solid stone tomb repudiates the bodily rupture with which the Prioress is fascinated.[26]

In a story filled with blood, tears, and songs in constant and boundary-smashing movement, the marble tomb strives to demarcate, contain, and immobilize. The monument of stone fails, however, to still what it immures. The closing stanzas of the tale transport the scene to Lincoln and conflate ancient Syrian Jews with more recent English ones. 'The little boy', Bale writes, 'wanders out of his distant Asian tomb into the Prioress's England and the pilgrimage group.'[27] Of the three tombs we've seen in Mandeville's *Book*, one has been emptied of the body that once occupied it, while the other two are too full: a restless apostle in fitful slumber, awaiting a distant future; the

---

[21] Braude (1996). Braude explains this hatred through reference to Christian crusade and a desire to attain a Holy Land without co-claimants.

[22] On this point see esp. Tomasch (2000).

[23] See, most notably, Campbell (1988: 122–61). Campbell describes Mandeville as a 'hedonist of knowledge' with an 'aesthetic attitude towards fact' (p. 141), leading him to stress 'tolerance and understanding' (p. 155), especially as compared to his source (in this case, Ordoric of Pordenone).

[24] Higgins (1997: 42).   [25] Bale (2006).

[26] Ibid. 85.   [27] Ibid. 86.

monstrous progeny of illicit union.[28] Given his fascination with such bodies that remain filled with uncanny life even in the grave, shouldn't John Mandeville likewise be able to escape lapidary capture, to leave the Holy Land to its scriptural eternities?

BODIES IN MOTION

The Book of John Mandeville records how a traveller once journeyed the earth's roundness, only to turn back at that point where his relentless forward motion had *almost* conveyed him to the place of his departure. This story, overheard by Mandeville in his youth, exerts a peculiar grip upon his imagination: the narrator describes the tale as one 'Y have y-thought man tymes.' A 'worthy man of oure countré' decides to leave England—and not for pilgrimage, not for redemption, but for no other reason than 'to se the worlde' (p. 67). Having passed through India and the five thousand isles that lie beyond its shores, he arrives at an island where 'he herde his owen speech' in the exhortations of men driving cattle. The traveller takes the familiar language to be a marvel rather than a marker of return. Mandeville, however, insists that the man had come so far in his journey that he had arrived 'into his owen marches'—England's borders, the edge of the known world abandoned so long ago. Finding no transportation forward, the traveller 'turned agayn as he com, and so he hadde a gret travayl'. After having finally arrived home and (apparently) too restless to long remain, the man sails to Norway. Storm-driven to an island in the North Sea, he encounters an eerily familiar scene:

And when he was ther, hym thoughte that hit was the yle the which he hadde y-be on byfore, where he hurde speke his owen speche as the men drof beestys. And that myght ryght wel be. (p. 67)

A man circles the world to meet a place intimate and strange at once, to meet in a way his own past, his own self, but from an unanticipated perspective.

According to Mandeville, any traveller can potentially arrive home again by remaining ever in motion. But 'the erthe is gret' and 'ther beth so many wayes': Mandeville never states that anyone has successfully circled the earth to arrive at his departure, to attain home via an endlessly curving route. Yet if the man who *almost* circuited the world has any regrets about not completing the compass, he never voices them. The traveller who so inspired Mandeville as a young man is never witnessed returning to the England of his birth. He is glimpsed only upon the road or the sea, never since his initial departure within 'oure countré.' What would happen if this traveller really had circumambulated the globe? Would he then have settled into sedentary life? Or must he turn back before he arrives because, having so filled his life

---

[28] A slightly earlier tomb held the body of 'Hermogenes the wise man'. Disinterred at the building of St Sophia in Constantinople, this 2,000-year-old corpse was clutching a golden plaque on which was inscribed (in Hebrew, Greek, and Latin) that man's faith in messiah to come (p. 27).

with motion, the stillness of a homeland—the stasis of an English identity—no longer proves able to satisfy? Mandeville, Defective: always open to the future, never to arrive comfortably at home.

Mandeville's boyhood imagination is captured by a traveller who nearly circles the world but abandons the journey at the borders of home. He does not fully recognize the familiar, perhaps because he himself has become in his wandering strange. Maybe that is why the traveller's story is so alluring to Mandeville: the man must never return, the voyage must never be completed, for the only way to keep a body in motion is to prevent its coming home. Mandeville, of course, does return. He writes his *Book* while resident in the England from which he had been long absent. Yet in the Defective version, that return is not wholly satisfying: no sooner is the book completed than Mandeville is in transit to Rome. He totes his volume to the Pope, who gives the narrative his papal seal of approval. As the story comes to a close, Mandeville is travelling again . . . this time (according to the *Book*'s narrative fiction) in his memory, his mind, his armchair. Rather like medieval readers of the *Book*, rather like us, his 'partyners' (p. 95).

Would Mandeville's fellow pilgrims, his medieval readers, his *partyners*, have recognized the limits of their companion's tolerance? Would they have realized the brake that Mandeville's Englishness places upon his restless trajectory? Would they have realized that Mandeville's failure was perhaps to have *almost* circled the world, but to have returned before he could arrive home by a route that would have changed his perspective, that would have queered his orientation, that would have made him see what remains stubbornly in place when a voyager who wants to 'se the world' carries with him and transports back the failings of his home?

Mandeville is sometimes confined by the compass of his own Englishness, by the limits of his own devotional circuit, as if these were (following Bale) lapidary narratives, marble tombs. Yet the *Book* is also *geological*, in the rocky triple meaning of that word: sedimentary (an accretion of histories and texts into new forms), igneous (hardened after long movement into settled contours), metamorphic (ever changing, open to the future, circling the world to meet and no longer recognize oneself). Each text of the *Book* can be seen as a crystallization, a hardening, a gem created from an ever-fluid narrative that does not ever cease to be a body in motion, ready for metamorphoses to come.

GEOLOGICAL MANDEVILLE

In the Church of the Holy Sepulchre, if we look just off to the side of the vacant compass that Joseph of Arimathea drew, we will find ourselves confronted not only with the stone of an ancient tomb, but with a scattering of other rocks: the 'rooch' of Calvary, its whiteness forever stained by the dripping of divine blood (p. 38); four rocks near the pillar at which Jesus was scourged, continually dropping water in an endless act of terrestrial mourning (some versions, though not Defective); the 'roche' under which the

Jews hid the cross for St Helena to exhume. Such stones commemorate the past by standing in for it: the relics they hid were long ago removed, the death for which they shed their endless tears vanquished by a bodily return to life. Yet these lithic monuments might activate in a careful reader a wider chain of associations, for the *Book* offers a story told through stones.

Sir John Mandeville is widely known for his geographical obsessions, but these unfold beside, along with, and through passions best described as geological. To give some highlights: in Tyre one can see the stone on which Jesus sat to preach (p. 32). Not far from Jerusalem is the Fosse Ynone (Ditch of Memnon), where an eternal supply of undulating gravel can change suddenly into glass (p. 32). This oceanic expanse of rock may be a gulf of the Gravel Sea. The Sultan built his great city 'upon a rooch,' and nearby are stones left for St Katherine by angels (p. 33). Not far from Damascus a voyager can see the ground from which Adam was fashioned, and the rock-hewn cave inside which he dwelt with Eve once expelled from paradise (p. 35). The Dead Sea casts forth chunks of asphalt, big as horses (p. 45). By its shores spreads the barren plain upon which a fasting Jesus was tempted to transform stones into bread. In the river Jordan, the Children of Israel left enormous stones 'in the myddel of the water' when through a miracle they passed over its bed dryshod (p. 46). On the rock outside of Nazareth where some Jews attempted to hurl Jesus to his death can still be viewed his footprints, impressed forever upon the stone when he vanished from his would-be assassins (p. 49). The Saracen paradise features homes wrought of precious stones (p. 54). Diamonds have a gender, as well as a sexuality: male and female come together to spawn even more of the glistening and libidinous rocks:

They groweth togodres, the maule and the femaule. And they beth noryshed with the dew of hevene, and they engendreth comunely and bryngeth forth other smale dyamaundes, that multeplieth and groweth all yeres. (p. 62)

Engendering 'comunely' renders diamonds, with their lithic promiscuity, rather like the soon-to-be-encountered nudist communist cannibals of Lamoria, the ultimate test of Mandeville's tolerance (successfully passed; in some versions he even comments on the vaunted sweetness of the flesh of children). The Lamorians, like diamonds, keep all women 'in commune' (p. 65). Mandeville avers that he knows from experience feeding your diamonds with May dew makes them increase in size. Diamonds of either sex can overcome poison, prevent strife, banish evil dreams. They can also heal lunatics . . . and Englishmen, we are told, are 'lunar', rendering them like Mandeville incessant travellers (p. 62).

Some of the world's heaving seas obscure magnetic stones ('roch of the adamaund', p. 62) in their depths, pulling to oblivion any ship manufactured with metal nails. A sea without bottom has reeds that float its surface; their roots entangle 'many precious stones of vertu' that protect their bearers from bodily harm (p. 69). The beastly men of Tracota covet a stone called 'traconyghte', not because it possesses any innate virtue but simply because it comes in forty attractive colours (p. 70). Cyconcephali carry foot-long rubies around their necks as a sign of kingly office (p. 70). The Great Khan prefers his accoutrements of daily living to be fashioned from jewels. Rubies and garnets worked into grapevine designs seem his household favourite. Even the steps to his throne and the chair itself are hewn from gems and bordered in gold (p. 73). The Khan also possesses a radiant carbuncle that serves as a palace nightlight (p. 77).

For no reason other than a seemingly innate animus, Alexander the Great attempts to enclose the Jews 'of the kynde of Gog Magog' (p. 82) in far-off hills. When human labor proves insufficient to the task, Alexander seeks God's assistance, and is rewarded by divine imprisonment of these people: 'God herd his prayer and enclosed the hilles togedre so that the Jewes dwelleth ther as they were y-loke in a castel.' The gates that confine the homicidal race are wrought of 'great stones wel y-dight with sement'. A barrier that will not be overcome until the time of Antichrist, these rocks keep the Jews removed from the stream of time, just as their ancient Hebrew locks them in a perpetual premodern (p. 83). Submarinal 'roches of adamaundes' not far from the lands of Prester John, meanwhile, freeze matter in place. Like underwater magnets they bind to themselves ships with iron fittings. Mandeville tells us he once went to see the expanse, and in a rare moment of poetry he describes a forest fashioned of naval masts: 'Y say as hit had y-be a gret ile of trees growing as stockes. And oure shipmen sayde that thilke trees were of shippes mastes that sayled on see, and so abode the shippes ther thorgh vertu of the adamaund' (p. 84).

Prester John's domain is home to the Gravel Sea, where rocks and sand 'ebbeth and floweth with gret wawes as the see doth. And it resteth never' (p. 84). This billowing sea of stone sports fish 'of good savour and good to ete'. Prester John, like the Great Khan whose daughter he weds, prefers housewares, eating utensils, and furniture made of gleaming gems, for jewels and precious metals betoken 'his nobley and his might' (p. 85). The Vale Perilous is strewn with gems, gold, and silver to lure covetous men to their deaths. In the middle of this terrible place is a rock on which is engraved the 'visage and the heed of the devel boylich, right hydous and dredful to se' (p. 86). His eyes stare, colours swirl, fire erupts from mouth and nostrils. An island exists in which women have 'stones in her eyen'. When enraged they can slay men with their vision (p. 87). On an island so distant that few stars shine and the moon is viewed only in its last quarter dwell ants ('pismeres') as large as hounds. They gather the abundant gold into great heaps. Local men use clever tricks to rob the insects of their hoards (p. 91). East of the land of Prester John are only 'great roches', their stony lifelessness the mark of impassable wilderness. Paradise is hidden behind immobile rocks (p. 92).

In his meditation on stone as a radiantly beautiful material and a durable spur to philosophy, John Sallis writes of stone's 'peculiar temporality':

Stone is ancient, not only in the sense that it withstands the wear of time better than other natural things, but also in the sense that its antiquity is of the order of the always already. Stone comes from a past that has always been present, a past inassimilable to the order of time in which things come and go in the human world; and that nonbelonging of stone is precisely what qualifies to mark and hence memorialize such comings and goings, such births and deaths. As if stone were a sensible image of timelessness, the ideal material out on which to inscribe marks capable of visibly memorializing into an indefinite future one who is dead and gone.[29]

---

[29] Sallis (1994: 26).

Such everlasting stones are certainly part of the landscape of the *Book*. They mark tombs and discoveries and great events. Stone is the perfect material to use to think about that which cannot be transported or transmuted. Thus in the wilderness outside Bethany Mandeville relates the biblical story of the temptation of Jesus by the 'devel of Helle' (p. 45). The fiend commands the fasting savior 'Dic ut lapides isti panes fiat', or 'Say that these stones ben maked bred' (p. 45). Only divine power can perform such transubstantiation. For a human to contemplate such volatility in lapidary substance would be extreme folly.

Yet the transmutation of rock through words is precisely what the Mandeville-author accomplishes. In the *Book*, stone is a strangely mobile, even itinerant material. Though rocks never do become bread, we watch as they billow into waves, as they offer us the miracle of fish from a pebble sea, as they exude rays of light and virtue. Rocks pull metals towards their embrace. They mate licentiously and engender baby gems. The stones that mark the Mandevillian landscape are of two kinds: those that affix history to place, and those that act like bodies in motion.[30] The former anchor the narrative, the latter unmoor the *Book*, alluring and mobile rocks that are indistinguishable from flows of water or lava. Anchoring stones—the igneous accretions left behind by molten flow—include inert wealth, lonely ruins, rock-hewn gates that bar paradise or seclude Jews, empty tombs. These are historical residua, depositories of ancient stories, unmoved markers of vanished time. Metamorphic or nomadic stones serve not as suture points but as spurs to constant motion: the endless pull of 'adamaund', the restless roil of the Gravel Sea, living practice that unfolds within inhabited space (the Sultan reconfigures a church, diamonds mate and reproduce and are traded by the wayfarers they ward).

Undulating, magnetic, lovemaking stones: despite the lapidary effects of religious and national identities, within the *Book of John Mandeville* even the most static of bodies are spurred into motion.

Seismic Mandeville

What I have been calling for convenience the *Book of John Mandeville* is in reality not a singular thing but a diffuse and volatile concatenation. There is no '*The*' *Book of John Mandeville*, only a proliferation of *Books* of Mandeville, few of which have a historically identifiable author, redactor, or translator, all of which vary in major or minor ways from their apparent siblings, parents, cousins, queer friends, assorted

[30] The same could be said of identities in the *Book*: so long as Mandeville is the name given to a unsettled forward motion (a motion that is Mandeville's travels, and *Mandeville's Travels*, a literary peregrination *and* a historical event), so long as the trajectory of his wandering does not trade its love of mobility for the ardour of a destination, it is difficult to say exactly who 'Mandeville' is: like his *Book*, he seems more a phenomena than a persona anchored in a geography or time.

hangers-on. Developing a vocabulary adequate to capturing the *Books* has proven a difficult critical task (as my foray into kinship metaphors just proved; other critics turn to chemistry or biology for their taxonomic metaphors). The text refuses to settle down into some well-delimited identity. Is it a reinvented *itinerarium*, a spur to pilgrimage, a Crusading substitute, an armchair travel guide, a romance, a heretical tract, a paean to orthodoxy, a proto-novel, an imaginative delectation of the exotic and the monstrous, a compilation, an encyclopedia? Yes. And because it is all these things at once it breaks generic boundaries and cannot be sorted neatly for library filing. No wonder Stephen Greenblatt called the *Book* a 'hymn to mobility'.[31] Though a bricolage of materials drawn from a dizzying array of texts (mainly French and Latin), the *Book of John Mandeville* seems almost *sui generis*. Nothing quite like it exists.

Iain Macleod Higgins, the critic who has studied the dynamic and dispersed existence of the Mandeville manuscripts most closely, describes the *Book* as a 'multi-text':

> *The Book* can be regarded not as a single, invariant work, but as a multinodal network, a kind of rhizome, whose French 'radical' gave rise to a discontinuous series of related offshoots in several languages, each of which can vary considerably from the others while being *The Book* itself to certain readers... Clearly, *The Book* is more than several books at once, both in its origins and generically; it is textually multiple as well.[32]

Critical consensus holds that the *Book* was first composed in French (and likely continental rather than insular French), though no original exists. No text inhabits the centre of the compass away from which speed two continental and one Anglo-French versions, away from which scatter a plethora of English variants with Egypt gaps or in rhyme or in close sympathy with French forebears, away from which are propelled at further and further removes German, Latin, Irish, Italian, Danish, and Spanish redactions. At the centre of this Big Bang that sent Mandevilles careening through Latin Christendom is only... the Postulated Archetype, an *Ur*-Book that we assume must have been in existence at some point. When the Postulated Archetype abandoned its sepulchre in Palestine to retreat to that heaven where perfect texts reside, it left no earthly trace of its having been here, only the lingering textual ripples that suggest its inherent volatility, and perhaps indicate that it never intended to be transfixed like a glossed and reverenced Bible.[33]

The *Book of John Mandeville* is therefore more of an event than an object. It moves through the world, leaving behind various versions of itself that bear witness to the form it took in a certain place under some influential and typically indeterminable conditions. It would be a mistake to look at any one of these precipitates as if it were the *Book* itself rather than a record of the *Book*'s passing, just as a lava flow cannot be reconstituted from one of the igneous rocks into which it hardened and then abandoned in its onward rush. The *Books of John Mandeville* are best seen as a

---

[31] Greenblatt (1991: 28).   [32] Higgins (1998: 32–3).
[33] My discussion of the Mandeville manuscripts is based on the overview in Higgins (1997: 20–5).

performance of their own narrative structure, as a *textual flow* that crosses linguistic and national boundaries in a directionless quest to remain in motion, to circle the world by pressing forward and yet never to return home. This flow might leave in its wake certain crystallizations (manuscript attestations that we read today, but cannot assemble into some singular entity). Like Mandeville's diamonds these crystals will always copulate with others and form strange new progeny. The *Books of Mandeville* amount to a body ever in motion, because structurally defective, open, reaching forward not to assimilate but to embrace, to touch and to change. In their proliferation, dispersal, and constant mutation, the *Books of John Mandeville* display an irreducible surplus not diminishable into the small contours of historical context or local determination. That thing in the *Books of Mandeville* which renders them ever restless over time, that surplus that can take a body outside of itself and scatter it across a suddenly more capacious world: that exorbitance in Mandeville so tied to an ardor for the lithic, that thing is art, restless and nomadic art.

Unleashed by books that wander the world to vanish into varying forms is an art no more human, no more ours alone, than are marble tombs containing manna or missing bodies or monsters, diamonds that yearn for copulation and increase, the heave of Gravel seas, or any other beauty we share with stone.

BIBLIOGRAPHY

BALE, ANTHONY (2006), *The Jew in the Medieval Book: English Antisemitisms, 1350–1500* (Cambridge: Cambridge University Press).

BHABHA, HOMI (1994), *The Location of Culture* (London: Routledge).

BRAUDE, BENJAMIN (1996), 'Mandeville's Jews among Others', in Bryan F. Le Beau and Menachem Mor (eds.), *Pilgrims and Travelers to the Holy Land* (Omaha, Neb.: Creighton University Press), 133–58.

CAMPBELL, MARY B. (1988), *The Witness and the Other World: Exotic European Travel Writing, 400–1600* (Ithaca, NY: Cornell University Press).

COHEN, JEFFREY J. (2008), 'Inventing with Animals in the Middle Ages', in Barbara A. Hanawalt and Lisa J. Kiser (eds.), *Engaging with Nature: Essays on the Natural World in Medieval and Early Modern Europe* (Notre Dame, Ind.: University of Notre Dame Press), 39–62.

DELUZ, CHRISTIANE (1988), *Le Livre de Jehan de Mandeville: Une 'géographie' au XIVe siècle* (Louvain-la-Neuve: Institut d'Études Médiïvales de l'Université Catholique de Louvain).

GREENBLATT, STEPHEN (1991), *Marvelous Possessions: The Wonder of the New World* (Chicago: University of Chicago Press).

HANNA, RALPH (1984), 'Mandeville', in A. S. G. Edwards (ed.), *Middle English Prose: A Critical Guide to Major Authors and Genres* (New Brunswick, NJ: Rutgers University Press), 123.

HENG, GERALDINE (2003), *Empire of Magic: Medieval Romance and the Politics of Cultural Fantasy* (New York: Columbia University Press).

HIGGINS, IAIN MACLEOD (1997), *Writing East: The 'Travels' of Sir John Mandeville* (Philadelphia: University of Pennsylvania Press).

HIGGINS, IAIN MACLEOD (1998), 'Defining the Earth's Center in a Medieval "Multi-Text": Jerusalem in the Book of John Mandeville', in Sylvia Tomasch and Sealy Gilles (eds.), *Text and Territory: Geographical Imagination in the European Middle Ages* (Philadelphia: University of Pennsylvania Press), 29–53.

KOHANSKI, TAMARAH, and C. DAVID BENSON (eds.) (2007), *The Book of John Mandeville* (Kalamazoo, Mich.: Medieval Institute Publications).

LOMPERIS, LINDA (2001), 'Medieval Travel Writing and the Question of Race', *Journal of Medieval and Early Modern Studies*, 31: 149–64.

SALLIS, JOHN (1994), *Stone* (Bloomington, Ind.: University of Indiana Press).

SEYMOUR, M. C. (ed.) (2002), *The Defective Version of Mandeville's Travels* (EETS OS 319; Oxford: Oxford University Press for the Early English Text Society).

TOMASCH, SYLVIA (2000), 'Postcolonial Chaucer and the Virtual Jew', in Jeffrey Jerome Cohen (ed.), *The Postcolonial Middle Ages* (New York: Palgrave), 243–60.

WARNER, GEORGE F. (ed.) (1889), *The Buke of John Maundeuill* (Westminster: Roxburghe Club).

....

CHAPTER 32

'BRITAIN'

ORIGINARY MYTHS
AND THE STORIES
OF PEOPLES

....

ANKE BERNAU

Wondrously ornate is the stone of this wall, shattered by fate: the precincts
of the city have crumbled and the work of giants is rotting away.[1]

When to begin? All narratives begin some time, as well as somewhere, and the stories
of the origins of peoples are more concerned than most with the questions of when,
where, who, and why. Such stories, though not necessarily constituting a discrete
generic category, were ubiquitous in a range of medieval writings, attesting to their
widespread and persistent popularity. Susan Reynolds notes that myths of descent
'are first recorded in sources of the sixth and seventh centuries' and increased
exponentially in following centuries.[2] These stories clearly fulfilled a need—or rather,
multiple needs—which changed over time and in response to a range of political,
religious, and cultural shifts. Located in the distant past, inaccessible to living
memory and often based on dubious or even invented sources, stories of origins
also signal the intimate relationship between beginnings and language. As D. Vance
Smith argues in his study of medieval literary beginnings, the narrative opening was
'a principle that all medieval writers in the West knew well: that beginnings are
inseparable from language, that the Word was there at the beginning'.[3] Thus,

---

[1] 'The Ruin', tr. Bradley (1991: 402, ll. 1–2).
[2] Reynolds (1983: 389).   [3] Smith (2001: 8).

medieval accounts of the beginnings of peoples are found not in a singular kind of narrative or source; Patrick Geary reminds us of this as well as of the numerous versions and diversity of such stories when he states that 'origin stories are embedded in other sorts of texts, and origins can take a wide variety of forms'.[4] Focusing on Britain and drawing on texts considered 'historical', this chapter will consider a range of different origin stories that circulated, were appropriated, and reworked between the fifth and the fifteenth centuries. Some of the names of listed founders will perhaps still be familiar to readers today: Aeneas, Noah, Arthur. Others have largely disappeared from common knowledge, and certainly from more recent historical writings, even though their influence was considerable and often long-lasting: Brutus, Scota, Albina. As indicated above, the uses to which such stories were put were manifold: they proclaimed a people's glorious ancestry; they justified invasion and conquest; they narrated continuity where there was rupture, unity where there was strife and fragmentation. They provided a means of understanding or creating, as well as a paradigm for, communal and national self-understanding and cohesion. They were potent stories.

The Myths of Origins

In his study *Myths and Memories of the Nation*, Anthony D. Smith distinguishes two broad types of communal origin myth. On the one hand, there are those which 'cite *genealogical* ancestry', tracing origin back to 'a hero, a founder, or even a deity' through an 'unbroken bloodline'; on the other there are those that Smith calls myths of '*ideological* descent', which anchor the community's identity in the continuation of shared custom and belief—their 'spiritual kinship'.[5] This spiritual kinship is presented as stemming from an idealized past, and three of the most important elements that contribute to its flourishing are a shared law, language, and religious belief. Medievalists have identified further characteristics of medieval stories of peoples, which frequently combined genealogical and ideological motifs, resisting clear categorization. One theory was that the three sons of Noah founded the peoples of Asia, Africa, and Europe, while another, as Robert Bartlett notes, was 'that there were a total of 72 races, paralleling the 72 apostles sent out by Jesus according to chapter 10 of the Gospel of Luke in the Vulgate version'.[6] While genealogy was undoubtedly of fundamental importance when medieval thinkers conceptualized the past and its connection to the present, both for individuals and for communities, it was often merged with other concerns. Bartlett pinpoints what he calls 'ideas of environmental

---

[4] Geary (2006: 18). See also Reynolds (1983: 375).
[5] Smith (1999: 58).
[6] Bartlett (2001: 45).

influence' and the 'emphasis on the cultural and social components of ethnic identity'—akin to Smith's concept of 'ideological descent'.

Different forms or versions of origin stories in the medieval context resulted from divergent views of historical framework. Mary Garrison points out two prevalent understandings which informed the work of medieval writers: firstly the idea of 'Christian universality' and, secondly, the 'particularist' view which, while it acknowledged the elect status of all Christians, held that 'the notion of election would be privatized in successive appropriations'.[7] The claim that a particular people were the chosen ones of God was widespread, and made by many. The earliest surviving narrative to focus on 'Britain', the sixth-century *De excidio Britanniae* (*Concerning the Ruin of Britain*) by Gildas, uses a biblical framework in a lament for what Gildas sees as the sinful condition of his country and countrymen. Though critical of the Britons, he also casts them in the role of a chosen people, like the Israelites. Having 'frequently pondered', with a 'bewildered' mind and 'remorseful' heart, the reasons for the Britons' decline in the face of invasions by Germanic tribes, Gildas searches for an answer in the Old Testament:

For (I said to myself) when they strayed from the right track the Lord did not spare a people that was peculiarly his own among all nations, a royal stock, a holy race . . . *When then will he do with* this great black blot on *our* generation?[8]

Gildas goes on to present his readers with two originary moments. The first is local and specific: 'Ever since it was first inhabited, Britain has been ungratefully rebelling, stiff-necked and haughty.'[9] The second is universal and Gildas refers to it only to add immediately that he will not talk about it: 'I shall not speak of the ancient errors, common to all races, that bound the whole of humanity fast before the coming of Christ in the flesh.'[10] Gildas' narrative of a chosen, if deeply flawed, people, is echoed by the writings of his successors.

A more sustained and elaborate combination of the particularist and universalist models can be found in the ninth-century *Historia Brittonum* (*The History of the British*) usually attributed to Nennius. Here the reader is offered an intricate account of interconnected origin stories that do not restrict themselves to the foundation of Britain but reach back ever further in time, to Adam and God Himself, in order to account for the diversity of peoples found in the world, especially in Europe. As mentioned above, medieval writings joined a tripartite division of the world to the story of Noah's three sons in order to explain the dispersal of humanity, which originally sprang from shared parents: Adam and Eve. This idea is based on biblical evidence found in Genesis: 'These are the generations of the sons of Noe: Sem, Cham, and Japheth: and unto them sons were born after the flood . . . These are the families of Noe, according to their peoples and nations. By these were the nations divided on the earth after the Flood.'[11] Nennius elaborates on this by explaining that 'Sem

---

[7] Garrison (2000: 116).   [8] Gildas (1978: 15, 1. 13).
[9] Ibid. 17 (4. 1).   [10] Ibid. 17 (4. 2).   [11] Gen. 10: 1, 32.

extended his boundaries in Asia, Ham in Africa, Japheth in Europe'[12] and goes on to relate that Japheth sired seven sons who went on to become the founders of different peoples, including the Britons.[13] Alanus, Brutus' grandfather, was the 'first man who came to Europe',[14] and also fathered three sons. Apart from Brutus' father, Hessitio, there were Armenon and Negue. These three sons all founded different peoples, who are now 'subdivided throughout Europe':

> From Hessitio derive four peoples, the Franks, the Latins, the Albans and the British; from Armenon five, the Goths, the Walagoths, the Gepids, the Burgundians, the Langobards; from Negue four, the Bavarians, the Vandals, the Saxons and the Thuringians.[15]

All of these lineages participate in the genealogical mode familiar from Genesis and trace individual peoples' origins as well as their shared '*Ur*'-origin.[16] The *Historia Britonnum* combines several models medieval writers used to account for the beginnings of peoples: the genealogy of Alanus, the biblical descent from Japheth, and descent from Trojan ancestors.

It is evident, therefore, that multiple—at times even conflicting—models for narrating the stories of peoples coexisted.[17] Referring to the different models of identity available in an Anglo-Saxon context, for instance, Clare Lees and Gillian Overing contrast the Germanic (emphasizing name, kinship, and location) and the Christian (emphasizing religious faith).[18] The various elements then survived in succeeding origin stories, with varying emphases, so that biblical, classical, and folkloric motifs and themes all mingled. There is no clear distinction that can be drawn; no stable or straightforward categorization or development that can be traced.

One writer who clearly privileged a Christian worldview in his story of a people is the Anglo-Saxon cleric Bede, whose influential *Ecclesiastical History of the English People* was written before Nennius' history, in the early eighth century. Bede's account differs in interesting ways from both Gildas' and Nennius', showing how attempts to determine origins are often motivated by contemporary agendas and concerns. Bede begins, as do Gildas' and Nennius', with the Britons, but does not privilege them as a people: 'To begin with, the inhabitants of the island were all Britons, from whom it receives its name; they sailed to Britain, so it is said, from the land of Armorica, and appropriated to themselves the southern part of it.'[19] Bede's opening is actually not properly concerned with the origin of a people so much as the first settlement of a land. The Britons are, in this account, merely the first to arrive. Whereas in other accounts, as we will see, precedence confers a powerful legitimacy and is central to claims to ownership of a territory, in Bede's text it does not fulfil this function. Even before he recounts the arrival of the Britons, Bede outlines the present

---

[12] Nennius (1980: 22 (17)).   [13] Ibid. 22 (18).
[14] Ibid. 22 (17).   [15] Ibid. 22 (17).
[16] For more on the various models medieval writers based their myths of descent on, see Reynolds (1983: 377) and Patterson (1987). For more on the Trojan model, see Waswo (1995).
[17] See also Butterfield (2005: 51).
[18] Lees and Overing (2004: 9).   [19] Bede (1969: 17).

situation of Britain, an island in which different languages spoken by different peoples coexist:

At the present time, there are five languages in Britain, just as the divine law is written in five books, all devoted to seeking out and setting forth one and the same kind of wisdom, namely the knowledge of true sublimity. These are the English, British [Welsh], Irish, Pictish, as well as the Latin languages; through the study of the scriptures, Latin is in general use among them all.[20]

The scriptural framework Bede highlights here provides a common ground, presumably counteracting the fragmentation threatened by such diversity. The precedence of Latin over all other languages signals Christianity's precedence over temporal custom—its universal *langue* subsuming particularist *paroles*—and, to some extent, counteracting the heteroglossic outcome of the destruction of the Tower of Babel. Bede also relates the successive arrival of these peoples: after the Britons come the Picts, who are told by the Irish to settle in the northern part of Britain before the Irish themselves come to the same region, intermarrying with and ultimately conquering them. Bede speaks of the arrival of 'three very powerful Germanic tribes, the Saxons, Angles, and Jutes'[21]—the ultimate enemy for both Gildas and Nennius.[22] While Bede openly acknowledges their non-Christian status, referring to them as 'heathen',[23] he nonetheless presents them as God's divine instrument, sent to purify and punish the Britons: 'To put it briefly, the fire kindled by the hands of the heathen executed the just vengeance of God on the nation for its crimes.'[24] While this account is reminiscent of Gildas', which also presents the Saxons as a trial sent by God, for Gildas it is, importantly, a trial of love: God is testing his 'family',[25] the Britons. As Garrison notes, for Gildas 'the British status as the elect was imperilled, but not lost'.[26] Gildas refers to the Saxons in terms of unequivocal enmity, calling them a foreign 'sprig of iniquity' that 'sprouted in our soil with savage roots and tendrils'.[27] Here, Britain is God's 'sanctuary', his 'holy temple' that the invading Saxons have 'burned' and 'polluted'.[28] Even during his powerful lament over the Britons' intractability, Gildas makes it clear that his focus is 'the final victory of our country that has been granted to our times by the will of God'.[29]

For Bede, writing from a perspective modified by two centuries and as their descendant, it is the Anglo-Saxons who are God's chosen ones, despite the fact that they arrive as pagans. God's favour shifts from the Britons to the 'English'. This transferral heralds, as Patrick Wormald points out, a return of sorts, for 'Rome came

---

[20] Ibid.   [21] Ibid. 51.

[22] Bede's details concerning the different Germanic tribes are often identified as his 'most important historical contribution'; ibid. 51 n. 1. Bede also notes that the Angles' first leaders, Hengist and Horsa, trace their ancestry back to the pagan god Woden, 'from whose stock the royal families of many kingdoms claim their descent' (p. 51). The note to the text adds that '[w]ith the exception of Essex all genealogies of the English royal families which have been preserved go back to Woden' (p. 51 n. 2). For a further example of this, see the oldest extant manuscript of the *Anglo-Saxon Chronicle* (late 9th-cent.), which includes a genealogy of King Alfred that goes back to Woden.

[23] Ibid. 53.   [24] Ibid.   [25] Gildas (1978: 25 (22. 1)).

[26] Garrison (2000: 157).   [27] Gildas (1978: 26 (23. 4)).

[28] Ibid. 27 (24.2).   [29] Ibid. 16 (2).

again to Kent, in the person of Augustine, not Julius Caesar'.[30] The English are read as the 'heirs to what the Britons lacked the grace to deserve'.[31] We can see here how the same theme or motif—that of the elect people—is used to promote antithetical agendas; the politics might change, but the form remains familiar. This ongoing stability of form—despite variations in detail or emphasis—confers an authority on the claims being made. In a sense, this formal continuity works along similar lines as Bede's image of different languages united through Latin: here the biblical model of God's chosen people accommodates different ideologies or versions of history. In their discussion of Bede's particularist vision, Lees and Overing note that it has given rise to 'intense debate' among scholars in the field, due to its 'creation ... of one important trajectory for England and the "English", and its concurrent forgetting of what might have comprised Britain and the "British"'.[32] It is with Bede's *Ecclesiastical History* that we are presented with 'one beginning of the historical process whereby *Britannia* becomes identified with England and the English'.[33]

BEGINNINGS AND RETURNS

Two aspects of origin stories and narratives of beginning stand out as a result of such a comparison: the role of forgetting and the prevalence of return, or repetition. In their brief but illuminating discussion of narrative beginnings, Andrew Bennett and Nicholas Royle discuss several of various several functions and characteristics. Discussing Milton's famous opening to *Paradise Lost*, they point out that it introduces a beginning (Adam and Eve's transgression in the Garden of Eden), as well as referring to 'a return to a time before that beginning', which lies in the future. This 'restoration' is thus simultaneously 'the beginning of a new age and the repetition of a previous state'.[34] This is in turn related to the impossibility of 'absolute beginnings'—there are, they argue, 'only strange originary middles'.[35] While this is evident in medieval narratives of beginnings, medieval thinkers still closely and powerfully associated beginnings with an idealized, pristine condition. Origins—of 'words and of their users'—were singular and pure;[36] history multiple and plural. At the same time, it was recognized that meaning developed 'within a diachronic system of correspondences' as well as

---

[30] Wormald (1994: 14).
[31] In the 10th cent., the Saxons also claimed descent from the Macedonian hero, Alexander the Great. For more on this, ibid. 11. Garrison (2000: 158) points to the power of such narratives to project or even construct a unity that does not, in fact, exist.
[32] Lees and Overing (1994: 14).
[33] See also Davis (1998) and Foot (1996).
[34] Bennett and Royle (2004: 2).   [35] Ibid. 3.
[36] Stephens (1989: 63). Stephens refers to this when he argues that, in medieval thought, 'origin is privileged as the moment of essence and purity for both words and their users'.

through 'semantic accretion', creating a tension between the fall from grace associated with time and movement, which is necessary for meaning even as it destabilizes it, and the unity of a pure origin, desirable but static. The temporality of beginnings is therefore always indeterminate, even as origin stories aim to locate a specific moment in time. That the uneasiness over this temporal uncertainty extended to that which came *before* the beginning is evident in attempts to erase it from the historical record. Such deliberate 'forgetting' is, however, never fully or finally achievable.

Gildas' 'beginning' is founded on an explicit disavowal of what Bennett and Royle call the 'time before th[e] beginning'.[37] Gildas tells us that he will not only *not* speak of the universal origin of humanity, but that he will also be silent about the 'devilish monstrosities of my land . . . some of which we can see today, stark as ever, inside or outside deserted city walls'. Indeed, he 'shall not name the mountains and hills and rivers . . . on which, in those days, a blind people heaped divine honors'. Furthermore, he 'shall be silent on the long past years'.[38] *His* 'proper' beginning, then, lies with 'the time of the Roman emperors'[39] and the arrival of Christianity 'to an island numb with chill ice and far removed, as in a remote nook of the world, from the visible sun'.[40] For Gildas, then, the pagan past is unmentionable while being referred to; shrouded in darkness and distance, yet 'as stark as ever'. Ruins, which signal decay and ending, lie paradoxically at the beginning. Yet at this moment the ruins of the past are necessary to the new beginning, as well as offering a warning to the future: a sinful people must mend its ways in order to avoid replicating the downfall symbolized by ruins. Ruins are a reminder of past greatness come to naught.

Two frameworks coexist in such a beginning: one is historical, with references to invasion, conquest, destruction, and exile; the other is divine and eternal, for the light that Christianity brings to Britain is 'not from the temporal firmament merely, but from the highest citadel of heaven, that goes beyond all time'.[41] As Matthew Innes points out, 'the past was not merely conceived in linear, chronological terms', but also according to a 'typological mode of thought', in which historical events rendered their full and proper meaning only in relation to biblical ones.[42] In this sense, then, beginnings are never absolute, or even singular, but can simultaneously refer to specific moments in time, especially within a linear narrative, and reflect or repeat other, previous moments, either biblical or historical. And while in some instances the narrative account of a beginning self-consciously echoes accounts of other and others' beginnings, they also, as the example of Gildas shows, attempt to erase 'what came before'.

Edward Said states in his famous study of beginnings that it is this simultaneous presence of the new and the old (even if that past referred to is disavowed) which marks all new, historical beginnings.[43] One particularly prevalent and persistent example of this illustrates the complexities involved in forgetting as well as repetition. Giants, either secular or religious in character, abound in medieval origin narratives.

---

[37] Bennett and Royle (2004: 2).   [38] Gildas (1978: 17 (4. 2–3)).
[39] Ibid. 17 (4. 4).   [40] Ibid. 18 (8).   [41] Ibid.
[42] Innes (2000: 6).   [43] Said (1997: 34).

In Britain, giants are integral to what was to become the most successful and influential of foundation narratives: Geoffrey of Monmouth's twelfth-century *Historia regum Britanniae* (*The History of the Kings of Britain*), which provided the most coherent and sustained account of the history of the Britons, from their beginning to the death of Cadwallader and their defeat by the Saxons. Geoffrey also provided a highly detailed account of the life and deeds of King Arthur, which was to influence English politics and literature for many centuries. In Geoffrey's account, Brutus is the original founder of Britain, just as in Nennius' work. However, in Nennius' account Brutus is first said to be 'a Roman consul'; only later does Nennius offer three separate explanations for Brutus' lineage. In contrast, Geoffrey highlights Brutus' Trojan ancestry and, as Christopher Baswell points out, 'also connects later British kings, Arthur's ancestors, to the Roman imperial line', thereby consolidating and expanding on the 'widely held notion of the westward movement of world power—*translatio imperii*—from Troy to Greece to Rome, and now to Britain'.[44] This motif was not particular to British historiography, nor was it new when Geoffrey used it. Indeed, as Hugh MacDougall explains, 'the dignifying of one's own history by associating its beginnings with an earlier civilization or even with the gods' was a motif already familiar to classical writers.[45]

In Geoffrey's history, Britain enters the text as the subject of a prophecy, when the goddess Diana evokes it to Brutus as the homeland he is seeking for his people. In a temple on the deserted island of Leogetia, which he has reached after leaving Greece, Brutus is told by Diana:

> [B]eyond the setting of the sun, past the realms of Gaul, there is an island in the sea, once occupied by giants. Now it is empty and ready for your folk. Down the years this will prove an abode suited to you and your people; and for your descendants it will be a second Troy. A race of kings will be born there from your stock and the round circle of the whole earth will be subject to them.[46]

Diana's words recall some of the characteristics of origin stories discussed so far: Brutus' predicted foundation will be a beginning, but also a repetition. It offers a version of the future ('A race of kings will be born') that is a renewed version of the past (a 'second Troy'). This prediction bears within it all the promise of glory as well as the warning of destruction that the past story of Troy can offer. Yet the island that Diana speaks of also turns out to have a prehistory: it was 'once occupied by giants'. It is at this point that Diana appears to make a mistake, for when Brutus arrives at the promised isle not only does he find that it is still very much inhabited, but that it has also been named: 'At this time the island of Britain was called Albion. It was uninhabited except for a few giants.' This conjunction of motifs, original inhabitants (though they are monstrous and few in number), and a named territory, suggests evidence of a territorial consciousness. It is reasonable to conclude that the giants

---

[44] Baswell (2005).   [45] MacDougall (1982: 8).

[46] Geoffrey of Monmouth (1966: 65). These details of Diana's prophecy are not recounted by Nennius. He merely states that the 'British came to Britain in the Third Age of the world' (Nennius 1980: 21 (15)). It could be inferred from this that the island was empty before their arrival, since he emphasizes that it was '[f]rom that day' that 'Britain has been inhabited until the present day' (p. 18 (7); my emphasis).

have consciously given their home a name and, by bringing it into language in this way, are expressing their understanding of it as a specific place with which they have a specific relationship. This, in turn, raises questions about the kind of beginning Brutus represents, as he and his men are turned from original settlers to latecomers—even invaders.

Since names of countries were often etymologically linked to founding figures in medieval origin myths, the connection between the name, 'Albion', and the giants poses an intriguing mystery, which Geoffrey does not explain. That the importance of names is evident to Geoffrey becomes clear shortly after he has narrated Brutus' arrival and his dispersal of the giants to 'caves in the mountains':

> Brutus then called the island Britain from his own name, and his companions he called Britons. His intention was that his memory should be perpetuated by the derivation of the name. A little later, the language of the people, which had up to then been known as Trojan or Crooked Greek, was called British, for the same reason.[47]

The founder's name acts as a powerful link, connecting him to a territory, a people and the language that they share. It is also an expression of legitimate ownership: the land, thus named, seems an extension of the leader's person and qualities. Names are also important to historiography, for it is through the written memorial that the founder ensures that he, and what he stands for, are remembered, suggesting continuity and triumph over the ravages of time.

That the giving of names is a way of exerting dominance emerges not only from Geoffrey's account of Brutus, but also in the slightly later text of a cleric named Wace, whose Anglo-Norman verse history of the British people based on Geoffrey's work, the *Roman de Brut*, is the first known vernacular chronicle of British history. Unlike the *History*, however, the *Roman* expresses this interest most insistently in its concern with the 'English'. Picking up on Geoffrey's account of the African king, Gormund, who allegedly helped the Saxon invaders conquer Britain, Wace adds telling details of his own to this episode. The 'son of a heathen king', Gurmunt invades Britain along with many 'pagans and enemies', who together 'caused the destruction through which Britain lost its name'. Gurmunt annihilates the land, erasing almost all traces of the Britons' Christian civilization:

> Gurmunt destroyed many cities and many old castles, many churches, many groups of clergy, many a bishopric and abbey which were not restored or inhabited thereafter. The ruins, waste land and wilderness can still be seen which Gurmunt made in many places, in order to rob the British of their domains.[48]

Once he has done this, Gurmunt hands over the kingdom to the Saxons. It is at this point—not before—that, together with the takeover by the Saxons, the name-change which signals a profound rupture in the Britons' history occurs:

> After the name of that race who first received the land, they called themselves 'English', in order to recall their origins, and called the land given to them 'England'; the name means 'land

---

[47] Geoffrey of Monmouth (1966: 72).   [48] Wace (1999: 337).

of the English', that is its explanation. From the time Brutus arrived from Troy, Britain always retained its name and acquired new inhabitants, new kings and new lords. These wished to keep their customs: they had no wish to use another language. They altered the names of the towns and renamed them in their own language.[49]

It would be difficult to find a clearer account of the relationships that were perceived to exist between names, origins, territorial ownership, and a people's identity. 'England' becomes a commemorative term, just as Brutus intended 'Britain' to be: it recalls the people's origin, as well as signalling their belonging to the land that bears the same name. A new name replaces—*erases*—a previous name, just as the conquest has erased the landscape of familiar landmarks and has destroyed the culture and claims of the previous inhabitants. New names follow violent destruction—'the destruction through which Britain lost its name'.

How does this insight influence our reading of Geoffrey's story of the Trojan origins of Britain? What do the giants signify? By the time the *History* was being written, there was a long and established tradition that associated giants with sinfulness, and Geoffrey does not try to elicit his audience's sympathy for them. Indeed, Brutus and his men only kill the giants in self-defence, once they have been attacked by them in an ambush. Their leader, Gogmagog, is described as 'particularly repulsive'.[50] 'Gogmagog' was a semantically loaded term in the Middle Ages, often appearing as two separate figures, 'Gog' and 'Magog', or used to refer to different races or territories. The Apocalypse of St John the Apostle associates the names with the nations 'seduced' by the devil at the end of the world:

And when the thousand years shall be finished, Satan shall be loosed out of his prison, and shall go forth, and seduce the nations, which are over the four quarters of the earth, Gog and Magog, and shall gather them together to battle, the number of whom is as sand of the sea. And they came upon the breadth of the earth, and encompassed the camp of the saints, and the beloved city.[51]

Victor Scherb shows that the names functioned as 'typological metaphors, names that could be appropriated to whatever was alien, threatening, or actively hostile'.[52] While they were associated with beginnings, as well as with a 'distant past', they were also figures of return and ending.[53] Read within this context, Brutus and his men arguably represent the 'camp of saints' and Brutus himself could even be read as a type of David: 'Did he not kill the giant [Goliath], and take away reproach from his people?'[54] Does Brutus' destruction of the giants reveal him to be 'chosen', a leader who can redeem his exiled people and show his military prowess and virtue? In one sense that is surely the case—yet, as we have seen, Geoffrey's account is not overtly religious in tone, and gestures towards a wide range of other sources and genres. The wrestling match that follows the Trojans' battle with the giants is, after all, between

49 Ibid. 343.   50 Geoffrey of Monmouth (1966: 72).
51 Rev. 20: 7–8.   52 Scherb (2002: 61)
53 For the relationship between narrative beginnings and endings, see also Nuttall (1992).
54 Ezek. 47: 2–4.

one of Brutus' men, Corineus, and Gogmagog. Furthermore, its depiction suggests an equivalence or similarity between the two combatants, rather than emphasizing their difference. Finally, the qualities usually associated with giants, such as pride or quarrelsomeness, are shown by Geoffrey (and many other medieval writers) to mark the Britons and their history.[55]

In Geoffrey, such ambivalence is also present in less explicit ways. On the one hand the Britons are shown to cultivate the land, and to 'build homes, so that in a short time you would have thought that the land had always been inhabited'.[56] This suggests that, before their arrival, the land was *as if* empty, even though we know that there were at least some inhabitants. Habitation and the founding of a homeland tend to be associated with certain marks of civilization: the practice of agriculture, the building of cities, the presence of a hierarchically organized society. Hence the ubiquitous motif of ruins, those melancholy remains of past cultures and great civilizations. These giants, however, leave no ruins as they live in caves and forests. On the other hand, it is not possible simply to equate life in the wilderness with savagery, for we have also been told by Geoffrey that Brutus and his men themselves lived in the wild during their war with King Pandrasus, in keeping with the 'purity of their noble blood'. They would rather live 'as though they were wild beasts, and have their liberty, rather than remain under the yoke of your slavery, even if pampered there by every kind of wealth'.[57] The crucial difference between these Britons-to-be and the giants of Albion is, then, that the former choose to live in the wilderness as a last resort, in preference only to a life of ignominious subjection. The giants, however, appear to have chosen such a life freely, even though they have a homeland and its plentiful resources are available to them. The giants, it seems, thus reveal themselves to be unworthy of that land.

In Geoffrey, the idea is put forward (though it is also evident in earlier accounts, such as Bede's) that a people can win or lose a land according to their merits. Brutus and his Trojans *deserve* Albion. Such a view suggests that subsequent peoples who conquer and win the land—such as, for instance, the Normans in the eleventh century—also win control over a territory because they *deserve* it. Thus, Geoffrey states clearly that

Britain is inhabited by five races of people, the Norman-French, the Britons, the Saxons, the Picts and the Scots. Of these the Britons once occupied the land from sea to sea, before the others came. Then the vengeance of God overtook them because of their arrogance and they submitted to the Picts and the Saxons.[58]

It is at this precise moment in his narrative that Geoffrey sets out the purpose of the whole following work: 'It now remains for me to tell how they came and from where, and this will be made clear in what follows.'[59] The *History* is presented as an extended

---

[55] It is interesting that, according to Scherb (2002), the biblical tradition places Magog and his descendant, Gog, in the line of Noah's son Japheth, which is the same ancestry of which, according to Nennius, Brutus partakes. See also Gen. 10: 1–2.

[56] Geoffrey of Monmouth (1966: 72).   [57] Ibid. 56.

[58] Ibid. 54.   [59] Ibid.

story concerning with the origins of the Britons, about whom we have been told that they have been vanquished, their time of glory past. Nonetheless, the reader is encouraged to identify with their history—or at least to learn something from it— even if no single, unproblematic continuity is offered. In fact, quite the opposite is the case: there are, after all, 'five races of people' living in Britain in Geoffrey's time, even though the Britons continue to possess symbolic importance as the first, having arrived 'before the others came'. As MacDougall shows, Geoffrey offered his Norman patrons a story that connected them to the Britons by suggesting that they were the worthy inheritors of a mighty kingdom—an empire that stretched across the globe and usurped the position even of Rome. This association between Britons and Normans is further gestured towards by yet another prophecy, made by the magician Merlin to the British king, Vortigern.[60] As MacDougall points out, '[t]he prophecies are filled with imagery of dragons in conflict—the white dragon (Saxons) is initially victorious, but ultimately vanquished by the red dragon (Britons) through the assistance of a people dressed in wood and iron corselets (Normans in their ships and coats of mail)'.[61] What links Britons and Normans is not blood (or genealogy) but land and worthiness.[62]

While invasion and conquest, as Wace's account of Gurmunt's attack vividly demonstrates, are certainly ruptures—violent caesuras in the history of a people— continuity is suggested either through shared, idealized qualities, the continuation of law and custom, or a shared religious faith. The giants of Albion, in contrast, are associated with entirely different qualities, externalized and rendered visible in their excessive physiology. Yet these qualities also threaten to irrupt into the future: the inheritance of the giants cannot be erased entirely and crops up in place names, customs, and the seemingly indefatigable tendency of the British to sinfulness and internecine conflict. Nevertheless, some writers try to present such ruptures as violent-yet-neat waves of succession, with each wave constructed as a 'new' beginning. Wace, for example, offers a concise summary of the series of conquests of the

---

[60] Ibid. 171–3.   [61] MacDougall (1982: 9–10).

[62] Turville-Petre (1996: 6–7) supports such a reading with his claim that Geoffrey's history provided a version 'based on homeland that the Normans chose to attach themselves to, rather than to the alternative version emphasizing race'. This was due to the fact that such a version allowed them to overcome some of the disruptive elements that threatened their claim to legitimate rule. Being 'English' in this version meant not being of a particular race by virtue of descent, but by virtue of participating in the established laws of the land. Turville-Petre notes that there was also a counter-narrative to this one: 'The rather obvious flaw in this facade could be exposed by those with a different agenda, that of distinguishing the Norman lords as the oppressors of native-born English people unjustly deprived of their ancestral rights.' Thus, two versions worked against one another: the former, basing itself primarily on ideology, the other on genealogy. Weiss (1999: pp. xvii–xviii) notes that 'Geoffrey created for his Norman patrons a quite new history of their adopted country. Using the *Historia Brittonum*, he elaborated on the Britons' valiant Trojan origins; with little or no information about British history before the Romans came, he produced a long line of named kings . . . and, again drawing on the *Historia Brittonum* and on Gildas, constructed for the British past a pattern of rise, decline and final loss tightly connected to moral strength and weakness. His history was not a formless account of past events; it had to answer the question: why did British dominion over the island end?'

island in a manner that suggests that each succeeding dominant people erase those who came before, allowing them to 'begin' with something like a clean slate:

When the land was cleansed of giants and their race, the Trojans felt secure. They built houses, ploughed lands, constructed towns and cities, sowed corn and reaped it. The country was called Albion, but Brutus changed its name, calling it after his own, and he had it called Britain. . . . But English has since altered it. . . . [The English] drove out all the Britons, who never returned.[63]

Wace's passage, which fantasizes the successful prevention of return in its insistence on the absolute nature of the new beginning, indicates an anxiety about the rather messier and more complex realities that are being recounted. The diversity of peoples living in Britain as related to us by Geoffrey is momentarily elided here in favour of a more singular, linear representation, in which the newcomers are only 'secure' when those whom they have vanquished are utterly annihilated or displaced. Arguably, the concurrence of ending and beginning that Scherb[64] identifies as being associated with giants, as well as the violence that inheres in such ending-beginnings, are indicated by Geoffrey in his account of Brutus' arrival on Leogetia, the ruined and deserted island which is marked by the depredations of pirates. That this place should be the very location in which Brutus receives the prophecy about his people's future homeland is telling. The violence of the past, visible still in the remains of the now-lost civilization of Leogetia, provides the setting for a vision of the future and a new beginning for the Trojans.

Lees and Overing discuss the violent nature of medieval accounts of new beginnings in the light of Homi Bhabha's well-known disquisition on the necessary forgetting inherent in beginnings:[65] what he calls the 'minus in the origin'.[66] They conclude that '[t]he violence and division involved in the establishment and origins of nations must be elided, forgotten'. While such 'forgetting' is certainly at work in many of such accounts medieval stories of origins do not necessarily or insistently forget the violence of beginnings. At times, quite the opposite happens. Thus, in the first quarter of the fourteenth century, there appeared a new foundation narrative which seemed to amend the 'minus in the origin'. It offers, instead, a sustained attempt to *augment* Geoffrey's account, by narrating its prequel. This was the story of Albina and her sisters, which is also the story of Albion and its original inhabitants, the giants. Initially circulating as an independent narrative, composed in Anglo-Norman under the title *Des Grantz Geanz*, it was soon translated into English, Welsh, and even Latin (as *De origine gigantum*), which suggests its cultural importance. It soon became incorporated—often in the form of a prologue – in the immensely popular and influential English prose *Brut* chronicle, through which it reached a wide audience.[67]

There were two versions of the Albina story, one of which begins in Syria, the other in Greece. While further details, such as the exact number of sisters, varies, the thrust

---

[63] Wace (1999: 31).   [64] Scherb (2002).   [65] Lees and Overing (2004: 5).
[66] Bhabha (1994: 160). See also Davis (1998).   [67] For more in this, see Matheson (1998).

of the story is as follows. A powerful king, who has subjugated all neighbouring kingdoms, and his beloved wife decide that the time has come to marry off their beautiful daughters, the eldest of whom is called Albina. The husbands they choose for their daughters are the kings of the realms that have been vanquished. Albina and her sisters are outraged at the thought of marrying men of lower status than themselves and set out to defy them in every possible way. The husbands, having tried to 'tame' their wives first with gifts and then with physical violence, and finding both means equally unsuccessful, finally appeal to their father-in-law for help. He berates his wayward daughters and they, their hatred of their husbands inflamed yet further, agree to Albina's suggestion that they should all murder their spouses, thus freeing themselves from the despised marital yoke. When the plan is discovered—in one version only after the murders have been committed, in the other just before—the livid king wants to put his daughters to death for treason. His barons convince him to send them into exile instead, in a rudderless boat. The boat eventually washes up on the shores of an empty and beautiful island, which the sisters claim in the name of the eldest, calling it Albion. They live here harmoniously, dwelling in caves, trapping animals for food and collecting wild herbs. Soon, however, they begin to miss the company of men. As their desire grows ever greater, the devil becomes aware of it and comes (or sends demons) to impregnate them, and they give birth to giant offspring. In later versions the giants are usually presented as living peacefully on the island until Brutus' arrival; in earlier versions they are depicted as incestuous and violent.[68]

THE AUTHORITY OF BEGINNINGS

The Albina story draws on a wide range of narrative genres and motifs familiar to medieval writers and audiences.[69] The origin that the Albina story related is thus a beginning that cleverly combines novelty with authority; it conformed to known literary modes and registers, which made it seem instantly familiar. It offers, in relation to the Brutus story, an account of the time before *that* beginning, thereby confirming the impossibility of absolute beginnings, even as it claims to relate Britain's prehistory from the very moment it was first inhabited. The fact that it is most commonly presented as a prologue, textually located *before* the history of Britain 'proper' begins, is also suggestive, raising questions about the function and

---

[68] Scherb (2002: 62) refers to a late medieval tradition in English writing in which 'the races of Gog and Magog practice incest and free love'.

[69] Carley and Crick (1995: 48 n. 26). Cohen (1992: 197) sees this dense web of associations as being made up from 'biblical, classical, folkloric and ecclesiastical sources'.

meaning of different origin stories, the relationship between them, as well as about how they were received or understood.

The Albina story once again highlights the unstable temporality of openings which are heavily invested in the present, and (sometimes are in relation to a imagined, desired or feared future), even as it articulates this instability in terms of the exemplary potential of the inaccessibly distant past (see Bernau (2009)). Unsurprisingly, critics and scholars have tended to read Albina as an attempt to offer an explanation for the presence of those giants as well as for the name, Albion, both of which arguably detracted from Geoffrey's claims to have started at the beginning (though he does, of course, offer the beginning of 'Britain'). It has also been read as a response to, or comment on, contemporary political contexts, particularly Anglo-Scottish hostilities. Here we can see how seriously origin stories were taken (even if it was acknowledged that they might not be entirely credible, or based on authoritative sources); how they were used as tools in ongoing conflicts over land and dominion. As James P. Carley and Julia Crick point out in relation to the thirteenth-century Anglo-Scottish context: 'Scottish and English circles were nurturing competing traditions about the historical foundations of their respective kingdoms.'[70]

In his *History*, Geoffrey relates the division between England, Wales, and Scotland that occurs after Brutus' death. Britain, he explains, is divided between Brutus' three sons, with the eldest, Locrinus, receiving 'Loegria' (England), Kamber receiving Wales, and the youngest, Albanactus, receiving Scotland.[71] They reign their respective territories in harmony; when the King of the Huns kills Albanactus, however, his people 'flee to Locrinus' for protection.[72] Edward I (crowned 1272) vigorously asserted the English king's right to overlordship of Scotland which Geoffrey's account implicitly justifies by associating England with the eldest son and Scotland with the youngest. In a letter to Pope Boniface, written c.1301, the English king makes explicit the legitimacy of his 'rights in the realm of Scotland', which, he begins by saying, are 'graven upon the tablets of our memory with an indelible mark, that our predecessors and progenitors, the kings of England, by right of lordship and dominion, possessed *from the most ancient times*'.[73] Edward then traces this 'most ancient' right through history until the present moment, beginning with Geoffrey's account, according to which the 'dignity of the inheritance should go to the first born'. He faithfully repeats Geoffrey's account of the arrival of the Trojans in Albion, the defeat of the giants and the construction of London. Then, he writes, Brutus 'divided his realm among his three sons', with 'the royal dignity being reserved for Locrine, the eldest'.[74] This claim to overlordship was reasserted, Edward's letter continues, by successive English kings, including the famous Arthur, who subdued 'rebellious Scotland', after which 'all the kings of Scotland have been subject to all the kings of the Britons'.[75] The response by the papal court was not favourable to Edward's claim,

---

[70] Carley and Crick (1995: 55).
[71] Geoffrey of Monmouth (1966: 75).   [72] Ibid.
[73] 'Sanctissimo patri Bonifacio', in Stone (1965: p. 96; my emphasis).
[74] Ibid. 97   [75] Ibid. 98.

as a subsequent report, sent to Edward by one of his officials, shows. Edward's version of the relationship between the three sons of Brutus is challenged, and yet another story of origins is drawn on by the Scots to bolster their claim to independence. The sources Edward bases his claims on are contradicted by the 'true facts', these being supported with different 'chronicles and narratives'. According to these sources, Brutus' sons were all 'peers', with 'none of them...subject to another'. Furthermore, the Scots show that they are the descendants of an entirely different people, originating with an illustrious foundress called Scota, who came to Scotland after Brutus and his sons:

Afterwards came a woman named Scota, daughter of Pharaoh of Egypt, who came via Spain and occupied Ireland, and afterwards conquered the land of Albany, which she had called, after her name, *Scotland*, ... and they drove out the Britons, and from that time the Scots, as a new race and possessing a new name, had nothing to do with the Britons, but pursued them daily as their enemies, and were distinguished from them by different ranks and customs and by a different language.[76]

The important markers medieval writers used to categorize peoples are here evident once again: genealogy, custom, and language. In this instance, the differences in these markers for the Britons and the Scots serve also to distinguish between their polities. Thus, while the Brutus story serves the designs of, as Carley and Crick put it, the '[e]xpansionist kings of England',[77] who could use it to claim the legitimacy conferred by ancient law and precedent, the Scota myth allowed the Scots to fight such English claims. Furthermore, the Scots accuse the English of 'remov[ing] by force the muniments and writings and chronicles that they had in Scotland, in order to deprive them of defence and of evidence of the truth'.[78] Such a removal implies that the English recognized the power of competing narratives, especially those that related a competing origin myth.

The story of Scota, in many of its narrative features similar to those of Brutus and Albina, also forms the beginning of the famous Declaration of Arbroath, in which the Scots formalized their claims of independence, and which remains an important and treasured national document for Scots to this day.[79] Written in 1320, in the form of a letter addressed to Pope John XXII, it opens: 'Most Holy Father and Lord, we know and from the chronicles and books of the ancients we find that among other famous nations our own, the Scots, has been graced with widespread renown.' It then continues, to relate the travails and long journey undertaken by them, from 'Greater Scythia', via Spain, where they lived 'among the most savage tribes' without, however, being 'subdued by any race, however barbarous'. Eventually, 'twelve hundred years after the people of Israel crossed the Red Sea', they arrive at 'their home in the west where they still live today'. They fight hard, repeatedly and successfully, for this

---

[76] 'L'Apostoille et le droit d'Escoce', in Stone (1965: 112–13). For an overview of the development and influence of the Scota myth, see Matthews (1970).

[77] Carley and Crick (1995: 42).

[78] Stone (1965: 116).

[79] 'The Declaration of Arbroath', at http://www.geo.ed.ac.uk/home/Scotland/arbroath_english.html

homeland, driving out first the Britons, then the Picts, and defending it against 'the Norwegians, the Danes and the English'. Thus, 'as the historians of old times bear witness, they have held it free of all bondage ever since. In their kingdom there have reigned one hundred and thirteen kings of their own royal stock, the line unbroken by a single foreigner.' Battle and the witness of historians together here form the most authoritative evidence for a people's claims to their land and right to self-rule.

By claiming an origin that is utterly separate and distinct from that of the Britons, and by their resounding martial victory over them and all others who 'assail' them, the Scots are expressing the irrelevance of Brutus' heritage for their people. Just as Brutus emptied the land of giants, thereby making it his own—his success proving his worthiness—so Scota and her people drove out the Britons and Picts, claiming *their* homeland. Their ongoing right to it is made evident by their successful defence of it against all invaders and would-be newcomers. Unlike the Britons or the English, the Declaration appears to suggest, the Scots have been continuously worthy of their homeland. Furthermore, they can boast of a line of kings 'unbroken by a single foreigner'. If accounts of British history had to find ways of negotiating the ruptures of repeated conquest and internal conflict, this version of Scottish origins presents a model of genealogical and ethnic continuity and purity with which to counter—and trump it.

The question of whether and how the Albina story fits into this battle of origin myths is one that is still being explored. As Carley and Crick note, it is suggestive that the *De origine gigantum* began circulating 'within twenty years of the Declaration [of Abroath]'.[80] Yet the story was not, it seems, used in official exchanges, such as that between Edward I and Pope Boniface. The dubious character of these female founders, while not unusual in medieval representations of what Geary terms 'women at the beginning',[81] did perhaps serve as a riposte to the Scota myth, reminding audiences that foundation and genealogy, as well as political order, were ultimately and properly men's business. Albina, in such a reading, allows Brutus to emerge even more emphatically as an ideal founder figure, worthy of representing the 'proper' beginning. Yet other readings of the Albina story are also possible, and it has been noted that it cannot be read simply as a negative foil to the Trojan origin.[82] Whether the Albina story was regarded primarily as an entertaining prequel to the 'serious' history that followed it and began with Brutus, or whether it was, in fact, an attempt to augment Geoffrey's incomplete story of origins, its appearance, its relation to the Scota legend, its various forms, and its subsequent narrative variations testify to the ongoing desire for origins, or desire for narratives of origins, in late medieval Britain.

Medieval stories of the beginnings of peoples—as the British examples discussed show—complicate one of Said's main distinctions: that between a *beginning*, which he defines as resulting from an individual's deliberate, willed act, and ascribed 'retrospectively to a founding figure', and an *origin*, which comes about as the result of 'purely circumstantial' factors.[83] Or, as Paul Ricoeur concisely sums up: 'the

---

[80] Carley and Crick (1995: 43).   [81] Geary (2006).
[82] See Johnson (1995).   [83] Said (1997: 32).

beginning is historic, the origin is mythic'.[84] According to such a distinction, Brutus' founding could be termed a 'beginning', while Albina's and Scota's appear initially to be 'origins'. Yet such oppositions or distinctions (as with Smith's, between genealogical and ideological origin myths) are difficult to sustain. The question of intentionality as well as that of circumstance is complicated by such issues as the role that God's omniscience, or 'fate', play in relation to human agency and free will. Does Diana's prophecy to Brutus reveal his subsequent founding act to be due to circumstance, or does his intention to find a homeland and his appropriation of Britian counteract that with its evidence of intentionality? Do the ocean waves that wash Albina and her sisters ashore detract from their highly self-conscious claiming of the land? What the origin stories repeatedly suggest is, in fact, a complex and nuanced coexistence of circumstance with intentionality; human responsibility and the inexorable, untidy, multiplicity that is history as it is narrated.

The textual presentation of the Albina story, as prologue, also poses questions: where and when does 'history' begin? How and why is the story of Brutus more credible than that of Albina, when both are located in an unrecoverable past? (After all, Geoffrey had his detractors from the moment the *History* first circulated.) That such questions occupied medieval writers is evident as early as Gildas' account. As he makes clear, reliable information about beginnings is hard to come by, for sources—especially indigenous ones—are lacking, 'having been burnt by enemies or removed by our countrymen when they went into exile'.[85] The absence of such records troubled British historiographers throughout and beyond the Middle Ages. Eventually, the medieval versions of origin myths, such as the story of Brutus, or Albina, or Scota, began to decline in influence and drew down the scorn of more 'modern' historiographers who in part defined their own modernity by reading them as signs of medieval ignorance, obtuseness, credulity, and fancy—though this was by no means a straightforward or uncontested development. In succeeding centuries, other types of histories that claimed to relate the beginnings of peoples emerged, and in the Middle Ages often feature prominently as a point of origin.[86]

Stories of beginnings allowed writers and audiences to conceptualize and imagine 'Britishness' in multiple ways, for multiple purposes. These were complex stories, offering flexible narratives of identity that could be adapted to a range of contexts and needs. Importantly, they were also *pleasurable*: the events they related were heroic, exciting, scandalous—full of action, drama, and affective power. Motivated by present, and future, concerns, origins were *relevant*, legitimizing colonization as well as claims to independence. Medieval writers understood that truth and fable are not always—or even necessarily—distinguishable. As Wace notes judiciously about the life and stories of King Arthur: 'they have become the stuff of fiction: not all lies, not all truth, neither total folly nor total wisdom'.[87]

---

[84] Ricoeur (2004: 140).   [85] Gildas (1978: 17 (4. 4)).
[86] See, for instance, Frantzen (1990) and Geary (2002).   [87] Wace (1999: 247).

Bibliography

Primary Sources

BEDE (1969), *Bede's Ecclesiastical History of the English People*, ed. B. Colgrave and R. A. B. Mynors (Oxford: Clarendon Press).

BRADLEY, S. A. J. (ed. and tr.) (1991), 'The Ruin', in S. A. J. Bradley (ed. and tr.), *Anglo-Saxon Poetry: An Anthology of Old English Poems in Prose Translation* (London: J. M. Dent & Sons), 401–2.

Geoffrey of Monmouth (1966), *The History of the Kings of Britain*, tr. and introd. L. Thorpe (London: Penguin Books).

GILDAS (1978), *Gildas: The Ruin of Britain and Other Works*, ed. and tr. M. Winterbottom (London: Phillimore & Co.).

NENNIUS (1980), *Nennius: British History and Welsh Annals*, ed. and tr. J. Morris (London: Phillimore & Co.).

STONE, E. L. G. (ed. and tr.) (1965), *Anglo-Scottish Relations, 1174–1328: Some Selected Documents* (London: Thomas Nelson & Sons).

WACE (1999), *Wace's Roman de Brut*, ed. and tr. J. Weiss (Exeter: University of Exeter Press).

Secondary Sources

BARTLETT, R. (2001), 'Medieval and Modern Concepts of Race and Ethnicity', *Journal of Medieval and Early Modern Studies*, 31(1): 39–56.

BASWELL, C. (2005), 'England's Antiquities: Middle English Literature and the Classical Past', in Peter Brown (ed.), *A Companion to Medieval English Literature and Culture, c.1350–c.1500* (Oxford: Blackwell), 231–46.

BENNETT, A., and N. ROYLE (2004), 'The Beginning', in Bennet and Royle, *An Introduction to Literature, Criticism and Theory* (3rd edn. Harlow: Pearson Education), 1–8.

BERETON, G. DE (ed.) (1937), *Des Grantz Geanz: An Anglo-Norman Poem* (Medium Ævum Monographs, 2; Oxford: Basil Blackwell).

BERNAU, A. (2009), 'Beginning with Albina: Remembering the Nation', *Exemplaria* 21(3): 247–73.

BUTTERFIELD, A. (2005), 'Nationhood', in S. Ellis (ed.), *Chaucer: An Oxford Guide* (Oxford: Oxford University Press), 50–65.

CARLEY, J. P., and J. CRICK (1995), 'Constructing Albion's Past: An Annotated Edition of *De origine gigantum*', in J. Carley and F. Riddy (eds.), *Arthurian Literature*, xiii (Cambridge: D. S. Brewer), 41–114.

COHEN, J. J. (1992), 'The Tradition of the Giant in Early England: A Study of the Monstrous in Folklore, Theology, History and Literature', Ph.D. dissertation, Harvard University.

——(1999), *Of Giants: Sex, Monsters, and the Middle Ages* (Medieval Cultures, 17; Minneapolis: University of Minnesota Press).

DRUKKER, T. (2003), 'Thirty-Three Murderous Sisters: A Pre-Trojan Foundation Myth in the Middle English Prose *Brut* Chronicle', *Review of English Studies*, NS 54/216: 449–63.

EVANS, R. (1998), 'Gigantic Origins: An Annotated Translation of *De origine gigantum*', in J. P. Carley and F. Riddy (eds.), *Arthurian Literature*, xvi (Cambridge: D. S. Brewer), 197–211.

——(2002), 'Devil in Disguise: Perverse Female Origins of the Nation', in L. H. McAvoy and T. Walters (eds.), *Consuming Narratives: Gender and Monstrous Appetite in the Middle Ages and the Renaissance* (Cardiff: University of Wales Press), 182–195.

FOOT, S. (1996), 'The Making of *Angelcynn*: English Identity before the Norman Conquest', *Transactions of the Royal Historical Society*, 6th ser. 6: 25–49.

FRANTZEN, A. J. (1990), *Desire for Origins: A New Language, Old Engliksh, and Teaching the Tradition* (New Brunswick, NJ: Rutgers University Press).

GARRISON, M. (2000), 'The Franks as the New Israel? Education for an Identity from Pippin to Charlemagne', in Y. Hen and M. Innes (eds.), *Uses of the Past in the Early Middle Ages* (Cambridge: Cambridge University Press), 114–61.

GEARY, P. J. (2002), *The Myth of Nations: The Medieval Origins of Europe* (Princeton: Princeton University Press).

——(2006), *Women at the Beginning: Origin Myths from the Amazons to the Virgin Mary* (Princeton: Princeton University Press).

INNES, M. (2000), 'Introduction: Using the Past, Interpreting the Present, Influencing the Future', in Y. Hen and M. Innes (eds.), *The Uses of the Past in the Early Middle Ages* (Cambridge: Cambridge University Press), 1–8.

JOHNSON, L. (1995), 'Return to Albion', in J. P. Carley and F. Riddy (eds.), *Arthurian Literature*, xiii (Cambridge: D. S. Brewer), 19–40.

LEES, C. A., and G. R. OVERING (2004), 'Signifying Gender and Empire', *Journal of Medieval and Early Modern Studies*, 34(1): 1–16.

MACDOUGALL, H. A. (1982), *Racial Myth in English History: Trojans, Teutons, and Anglo-Saxons* (London: University Press of New England).

MARVIN, J. (2001), 'Albine and Isabelle: Regicidal Queens and the Historical Imagination of the Anglo-Norman *Brut* Chronicles', in Keith Busby (ed.), *Arthurian Literature*, xviii (Cambridge: D. S. Brewer), 143–92.

MATHESON, L. M. (1998), *The Prose Brut: The Development of a Middle English Chronicle* (Tempe, Ariz.: Medieval and Renaissance Texts and Studies).

MATTHEWS, W. (1970), 'The Egyptians in Scotland: The Political History of a Myth', *Viator*, 1: 289–306.

NUTTALL, A. D. (1992), *Openings: Narrative Beginnings from the Epic to the Novel* (Oxford: Clarendon Press).

PATTERSON, L. (1987), *Negotiating the Past: The Historical Understanding of Medieval Literature* (London: University of Wisconsin Press).

REYNOLDS, S. (1983), 'Medieval *Origines Gentium*', *History*, 68/224: 375–90.

RICOEUR, P. (2004), *Memory, History, Forgetting*, tr. K. Blamey and D. Pellauer (Chicago: University of Chicago Press).

SAID, E. W. (1997), *Beginnings: Intention and Method* (London: Granta).

SCHERB, V. I. (Winter 2002), 'Assimilating Giants: The Appropriation of Gog and Magog in Medieval and Early Modern England', *Journal of Medieval and Early Modern Studies*, 32(1): 59–84.

SMITH, A. D. (1999), *Myths and Memories of the Nation* (Oxford: Oxford University Press).

SMITH, D. V. (2001), *The Book of the Incipit: Beginnings in the Fourteenth Century* (Medieval Cultures, 28; Minneapolis: University of Minnesota Press).

STEPHENS, W. (1989), *Giants in Those Days: Folklore, Ancient History, and Nationalism* (London: University of Nebraska Press).

SWANTON, M. J. (ed. and tr.) (1996), *The Anglo-Saxon Chronicle* (London: J. M. Dent).

TURVILLE-PETRE, T. (1996), *England the Nation: Language, Literature, and National Identity, 1290–1340* (Oxford: Clarendon Press).

WASWO, R. (1995), 'Our Ancestors, the Trojans: Inventing Cultural Identity in the Middle Ages', *Exemplaria*, 7: 269–90.

WORMALD, P. (1994), '*Engla Lond*: the Making of an Allegiance', *Journal of Historical Sociology*, 7(1): 1–24.

....

CHAPTER 33

MAPS AND MARGINS

OTHER LANDS, OTHER PEOPLES

....

ALFRED HIATT

W‌HAT is a margin? The term derives from the Latin noun *margo*, whose primary meaning is 'an edge, brink, or border'.[1] In a textual sense—and particularly in the context of the book—a margin is a space peripheral to a main or central body of text. As such, it performs a number of functions. The margin borders text; over time, it protects text from decay. More nebulously, a margin helps to define text by showing the reader its boundaries. Of course, the margin also offers a space *for* text. The margin is a site in which scribes, illustrators, and readers may intervene in, or simply alongside, a text—supporting, supplementing, adjoining, or opposing it. In the Middle Ages, as in post-medieval eras, the variety of material that could be located within the space of the margin was considerable. Marginalia included images, ranging from elaborate illumination to simple sketch, and decorative borders, rubrics, headings, glosses, ranging from a single word to lengthy disquisition, 'notae bene', scribal marks and symbols, separate texts. Such material was usually intended to have direct or tangential relevance to the main text on the page, but some marginalia were irrelevant to the central text, inserted into a conveniently free space. Margins were—in the Middle Ages as now—frequently left blank.

---

[1] Lewis and Short (1879), s.v. *margo.*

A number of extended meanings have accrued to the space of the margin. Marginal space has come to be associated with exclusion from societal (and textual) norms; and at the same time, with transgression and subversion of those norms. Studies of marginality in medieval society have taken as their subjects groups living on the geographical or legal peripheries of society, such as the mentally or physically ill, prostitutes, Jews, heretics, or the 'temporarily marginalized', such as hermits and anchorites.[2] Marginal status has been extended to women, rural folk, the geographically remote, convicted criminals, the unemployed, and members of 'non-respectable' professions, such as minstrels. In textual studies perhaps the most powerful and provocative exploration of marginality has been Michael Camille's *Image on the Edge: The Margins of Medieval Art*, from which the margin emerged as a site for radical cultural inversion. According to Camille's reading, the playful, obscene, and occasionally disturbing imagery contained in Gothic manuscripts was integral to the period's dominant textual culture: rather than a position of exclusion, the margin interacted with the central text, animating, playfully subverting, but never entirely undermining it.[3]

However attractive and provocative it is, Camille's hypothesis cannot be taken as a definitive statement on medieval marginalia.[4] Studies of verbal, rather than visual, marginalia have tended to find evidence of scribal and readerly engagement with texts along established paradigms.[5] Marginal glosses were frequently not spontaneous responses to text on the part of scribes and readers, but more often represented long-standing traditions, with commentaries on classical or biblical texts themselves copied from manuscript to manuscript, in some cases over the course of several centuries. Margins were frequently used for pedagogical ends, providing a location for critical apparatus: scribes of manuscripts of the works of Virgil, for example, were far more likely to use the margin to copy the commentary of the late antique scholar Servius than to insert their own thoughts on the text. The margin, in other words, could be a place in which tradition was conserved and transmitted, rather than flaunted. That said, it was very frequently a space in which difference—temporal, functional, textual—was articulated: the difference between antique or medieval commentary and classical text, biblical commentary and scripture, image and word, scribe and author, reader and scribe, paratext and text.

The concept of the margin is relevant to medieval maps and mapping in two ways. First, it was literally in the margins of manuscripts that maps first appear in the Middle Ages, as part of the great late antique/early medieval attempts to codify classical antiquity. Simple cartographic diagrams, and occasionally more elaborate maps, were used to help readers comprehend texts such as Isidore of Seville's *Etymologiae* (see Figure 1). From those seeds grew the great artefacts of medieval

---

[2] See e.g. Goodich (1998).   [3] Camille (1992).

[4] Note also the rather different findings regarding Gothic sculpture in Kenaan-Kedar (1995).

[5] e.g. Reynolds (1996: esp. 31): 'Reader response is replaced by the notion of mediation; the glossator or expert reader painstakingly mediates the text for a specific purpose... shaped by the needs of a particular set of learners.'

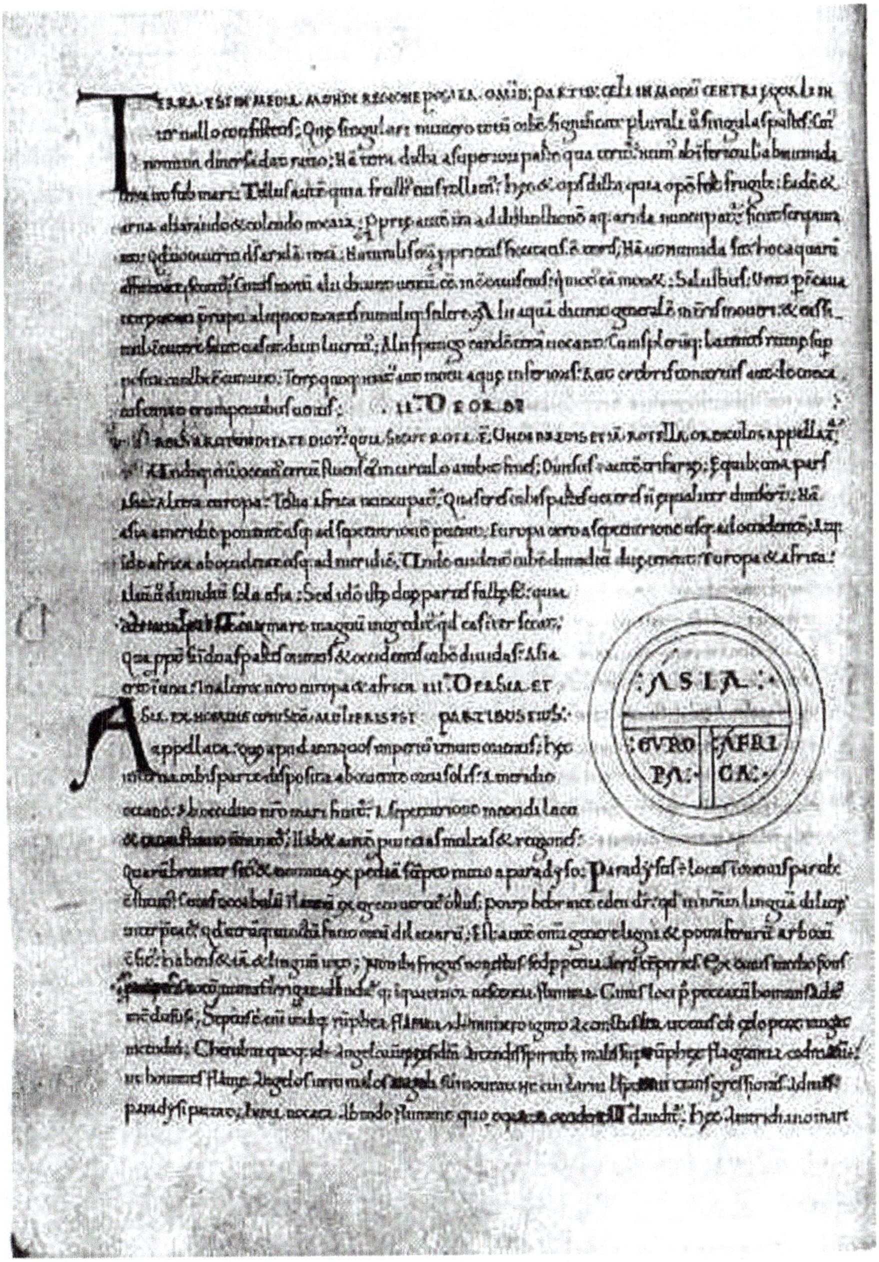

Figure 1 T–O map in Isidore of Seville's *Etymologiae*. London, British Library, MS Royal 6.c.1, fol. 108ᵛ. © British Library Board. All Rights Reserved.

cartography, the *mappae mundi*. So it might be said that, in textual terms, in the early Middle Ages maps themselves were literally marginal: not only were they relatively rarely produced by comparison with other forms of text, they were peripheral to the verbal geographical description which they illustrated.[6] Second, the literal meaning of the Latin *margo* had, in classical and medieval formulations, topographical/ cartographical applications—*margo terrarum* signifies a shore, *margo imperii* a political boundary.[7] In Isidore of Seville *margo*, a border, 'is a part of every place', but it is particularly associated with the sea (*mare*), 'after which it is also named'.[8] Thinking of the margin in terms of boundaries, edges, and shores has an obvious application to the function performed by maps of demarcating and defining borders and ends of the earth. Medieval maps that depicted a world space inevitably represented lands and peoples foreign to the maps' makers and audiences. They expressed in visual form regions that were attested but not directly known to medieval Europeans. The combination of the peripheral status of the map as a border form in medieval textual culture—between word and image, experience and authority, representing both time and space—and the presence of geographical and ethnographical borders and edges within the map raises a number of questions, which will be addressed in the following pages. What was shown at the margins of medieval maps? How do these margins of maps correspond with literary descriptions of travel to and encounter with marginal spaces and peoples? And how might maps help us to understand the nature of the margin as a textual space in the Middle Ages?

MAPPING MARGINS

The medieval world image was inherited from classical antiquity, though with significant adaptations and alterations. Classical texts such as Pliny the Elder's *Natural History* taught that the shape of the earth was spherical, that the known world was divided into the three *partes* of Europe, Asia, and Africa, and that these three parts were encircled by Ocean. This image of the ecumene was depicted on medieval *mappae mundi*, as well as in other, more schematic maps. The *mappae mundi* depicted not only space but also time, from the fall of Adam and Eve to the

---

[6] See further Gautier Dalché (1994).

[7] Ovid, *Metamorphoses* 1. 12–15: 'nec circumfuso pendebat in aere Tellus / ponderibus librata suis nec bracchia longo / margine terrarum porrexerat Amphitrite' (nor was Earth hanging in the surrounding air, balanced by its own weight, nor had Amphitrite [Ocean] stretched a long arm around the shores of the earth). Ovid, *Tristia* 2. 199–200: 'haec est Ausonio sub iure novissima vixque / haeret in imperii margine terra tui' (This land is the very last to come beneath Ausonian law, and it clings with difficulty to the very edge of your empire).

[8] Isidore of Seville (1911), 14. 8. 42: 'Margo est pars cuiuslibet loci, utputa maris; unde et nomen accepit'; 2006: 300; tr. Stephen A. Barney, W. J. Lewis, J. A. Beach, Oliver Berghof.

present, and even looked forwards towards the end of time, implicit in some maps in the presence of the tribes enclosed by Alexander the Great in the north-east part of the world, believed to be destined for release on the Day of Judgment. One function of ecumenical maps was, then, to represent Christian history. In this context the ends of the earth took on a special significance: they represented the furthest extent to which knowledge of Christ had spread as a result of the preaching of the Apostles.[9]

The medieval image of the world was not restricted to the northern hemisphere: it was also possible to conceive of parts believed to exist beyond Asia, Europe, and Africa. Standard cosmological theory taught that the earth was divided into climatic zones: two frigid zones at the far north and far south, a central zone of extreme heat at and around the equator, and two temperate zones, one in the northern hemisphere (including, obviously, the known world) and one in the southern hemisphere, theoretically habitable, but unknown.[10] Two vast oceans, one running from pole to pole and the other equatorial, were thought to divide the world, and, along with the frigid and torrid zones, to make passage across the zones impossible.[11] This theory was frequently expressed in the form of a diagram which appeared in a number of widely disseminated works, from late antique classics such as Macrobius Ambrosius Theodosius' *Commentarii* on Cicero's 'Dream of Scipio', Martianus Capella's *De nuptiis Philologiae et Mercurii* (On the Marriage of Philology and Mercury), and Calcidius' commentary on Plato's *Timaeus*, to twelfth-century scholastic treatises such as William of Conches' *Philosophia*. More elaborate forms of the zonal diagram, such as the world image that illustrates Macrobius' *Commentarii*, represent an opposition between the known world of Europe, Asia, and Africa and the hypothe- sized temperate zone of the southern hemisphere (see Figure 2).[12] In fact, antipodal theory held that the known world was but one of four separate land masses, divided from each other by the vastness of the encircling Ocean, by the heat of the torrid zone, and by the freezing cold of the far north and south of the earth. As several medieval scribes of Macrobius' work pointed out, belief that lands in other parts of the world could be inhabited ran counter to the position on the antipodes clearly stated by Augustine of Hippo in *De civitate dei*.[13] There, as an addendum to his discussion of monstrous births and races, Augustine had considered the question of the antipodes and concluded that, since the word of God could not have reached putative people on the other side of the earth, then they would not have been redeemed by Christ; since all humanity was redeemed by Christ, any beings at the

[9] For a survey of medieval representation of the ends of the earth see von den Brincken (1992).

[10] The origins of zonal theory seem to lie in classical Greek science, apparently originating with Parmenides: Strabo, *Geography* 2. 2. 2, but it was widely disseminated and adapted in classical and medieval Latin literature. In the Middle Ages a standard exposition was contained in Macrobius' *Commentarii in Somnium Scipionis* 2. 5.

[11] Macrobius, *Commentarii in Somnium Scipionis* 2. 9.

[12] See Hiatt (2007).

[13] e.g. Paris, BNF MS lat. 6622, fo. 59ᵛ, where a 15th-cent. hand has added to the 'temperate zone of the antoikoi' on a zonal map in Macrobius' *Commentarii* the words 'that there may be men living here Augustine rejects, Book 16, *De civitate dei*' (quod hic sint homines habitantes reprobat Augustinus 16 libro de ciuitate dei).

antipodes could not be human.[14] Augustine's statements did not disable debate and commentary on spaces beyond the known world, as over 150 surviving copies of Macrobius' world map attest. To represent the 'temperate zone of the antecians' or 'antipodeans' on a map was to allow the medieval reader to view the theory of classical science and literature, without necessarily affirming belief in all its elements. It provided a representation of lands and (perhaps) peoples not at the ends of the known world, but opposite and equal to it.[15] If the margin is a border, the antipodal unknown might, then, be seen as its very antithesis—what lies beyond the border. In fact, the unknown acts to decentre the known world—showing that there are other worlds. But it does not do so by asserting a new centre: it inverts and multiplies the image of the known world, making the notion of centrality difficult to sustain. So might we see the margin as a space not in terms of centre and periphery, but in terms of transition and remaking—in terms, that is, of movement rather than stasis?

Two examples of detailed *mappae mundi*, both produced in England, demonstrate the range of material—geographical, historical, legendary, and literary—that could be deployed by mapmakers at the ends of the earth. The Cotton world map (sometimes referred to as the 'Anglo-Saxon world map') dates from *c.* 1000 (Figure 3). The circumstances of its composition are not known, although a number of possible contexts have been suggested.[16] The manuscript in which the Cotton map appears contains a wide variety of material which may be plausibly regarded as having some connection with the map, including the *Marvels of the East* (an illustrated conspectus of mirabilia associated with Asia, another copy of which is found in the *Beowulf* manuscript), an account of Archbishop Sigeric's journey to Rome, Priscian's translation of the *Periegesis* of Dionysius, a variety of computistical material, and Ælfric's *De temporibus anni*. The map has been regarded as a descendant from a classical Roman world map, an argument perhaps supported by its emphatic division of Roman provinces.[17] At the same time, the Cotton map contains material of direct significance to a Christian audience: it shows the tribes of Israel; the cities of Jerusalem, Tarsus, Constantinople, Babylon, Alexandria, and Rome are (among others) prominently displayed; the Ark of Noah is given particular prominence in Armenia. The British Isles may, on one reading, be said to be marginal to this image: they appear at the far north-west (the map's lower left corner), far from the Holy Land and the Mediterranean, which might be said to constitute the map's centre. On another reading, however, they constitute an alternative centre: disproportionately large, detailed (the cities of London, Winchester, and 'Arthm', that is, Armagh, in Hibernia, appear), and poised amidst a web of implicit regional interconnections—with 'Brigancia', with the 'Suðbryttas' (Bretons, significantly marked in the vernacular), with Scandinavia ('Island', and two peoples, the 'Scridefinnas' and 'Neronorroen') and with 'Sleswic'

[14] *De civitate dei* 16. 9.
[15] I discuss this point at greater length in *Terra Incognita* (2008: 65–95).
[16] See in particular McGurk (1983); Edson (1997: 74–80); Englisch (2002: 245–58, 590–1); Barber (2006: 4–8). For the map as an example of the hyperreal see Foys (2007: 110–58).
[17] See Harvey (1991: 21–5).

Figure 2 Zonal map in Macrobius, *Commentarii in Somnium Scipionis*. London, British Library, MS Harley 2772, fol. 70ᵛ. ©British Library Board. All Rights Reserved.

and the 'Sclaui' of northern continental Europe.[18] This space includes regions and peoples unknown or at best poorly known to classical geography, but apparently of significance to the map's maker and audience. Moving eastwards around the periphery, one departs from areas of direct Anglo-Saxon knowledge, and therefore enters classically derived and/or biblically informed regions. Scythia, the Tanais (Don) river, and the Rhipaean mountains constitute the northernmost limits of Europe. In north Asia are marked 'griphorum gens', 'Turchi', Gog and Magog (thought to be part of the enclosed tribes), the Caspian sea, an anonymous 'flumen', and forty-three tribes ('Gentes xliii'), presumably those enclosed by Alexander.[19] In east Asia (top of the map) the periphery continues to reveal features of natural historical, ethnographic, and historical/mythographical interest: the inscription 'hic abundant leones' (here lions abound) above a large, richly maned lion, 'mons aureus' (Golden Mountain), 'India inqua sunt gentes xliiii' (India in which there are forty-four peoples), the island of Tabrobana, noted for its ten cities and its fecundity, Media, the Red Sea, the Arabian desert, and the 'mons super ardens'.[20] The space of southern Africa is demarcated by the Nile, beneath which appear a number of inscriptions marking Ethiopia ('ethiopica deserta', 'Libia Ethiopum' twice, 'Hic Ethiopes', 'Hic oberrant gangines Ethiopes'), as well as other peoples, including the cinocephales (dog-heads). The Atlas mountain(s) and 'hisperidum civitates et promontorium' (cities and promontory of the Hesperides) are the westernmost toponyms in Africa; the two columns of Hercules between Europe and Africa, just to the right of 'Ispania citerior', and opposite to Taprobana (usually identified as Sri Lanka) at the far east of the known world act as a kind of punctuation mark at the base of the map. It is worth pausing to note the richness of knowledge on display on the Cotton world map. The range of places, from India to Spain, and Scythia to Ethiopia seems to contradict stereotypical notions of a closed and limited medieval worldview. The material here as in other parts of the map derives from the accretion of information derived from various authorities, principally Paulus Orosius' geographical introduction to his *Histories in Seven Books against the Pagans*, but supplemented by later texts such as the *Cosmographia* attributed to Æthicus Ister and other authors, probably including local sources for the British Isles. The ends of the earth are the product of neither pure fantasy nor empiricism, but of the transmission and distillation of verbal descriptions into visual form.

The edges of the earth on the Cotton world map are predominantly secular, with natural features taking precedence over mirabilia and features of explicitly Christian significance. This balance shifted somewhat in later medieval *mappae mundi*. The twelfth-century Sawley map is located at the beginning of a copy of Honorius Augustodunensis' *Imago Mundi* (Figure 4), and may be a copy of a large *mappa*

---

[18] For a list of toponyms see McGurk (1983: 86–7). On the importance of the British Isles on the map see Michelet (2006: 142–57).

[19] McGurk (1983: 83) identifies *The Cosmography of Æthicus Ister*, chs. 31–2, as the most likely source for the race of griffins, Turks, and Gog and Magog. For the tribes enclosed by Alexander see Orosius (1882, ed. C. Zangemeister), 1. 2. 43–7, and compare Æthicus Ister (1993, ed. Otto Prinze), ch. 33.

[20] The source for Tabrobana seems to be Orosius, *Historiarum adversum paganos libri VII* 1. 2. 16.

Figure 3 The Cotton or 'Anglo-Saxon' world map. London, British Library, MS Cotton Tiberius B.V, fol. 56ᵛ. © British Library Board. All Rights Reserved.

mundi known to be at Durham during the time that Hugh de Puiset was bishop.[21] It depicts essentially the same space as the Cotton map, but it is framed by four angels, is ovoid rather than four-sided, probably following the form proposed in Hugh of

---

[21] Harvey (1997).

St-Victor's *De arca Noe mistica*, and contains an increased number of toponyms.[22]
Many of the features of the ends of the earth on the Cotton map are replicated on the
Sawley map: the extensive stretch of Ethiopia beneath the Nile, the Atlas mountain(s)
and the columns of Hercules in the far west, the 'mons ardens', Red Sea and
Taprobana in the east, Gog and Magog and the Caspian sea in the north. Yet there
are several significant differences: most strikingly, Paradise now appears at the top of
the map, in the far east. Rather than in southern Africa, the 'cynocephales' appear in
the far north of Europe, where they seem to form part of a series of remarkable
peoples, including the 'Griffe' (described as 'homines nequam', worthless people), the
Anthropophagi (that is, human-eaters), and the Hyperboreans ('beatissima sine
morbo et discordia', most blessed without disease or discord), secluded and to the
north of Amazonia and west of the enclosed races ('Gens imunda').[23] In the north-
west, the British Isles notably appear in significantly less detail than on the Cotton
map. They in fact can be read as part of a northern archipelagic periphery, extending
from unnamed islands in the far west, through the Orcades (Orkneys), 'Island' and
'Ganzmir', 'Taraconta insula', 'Rapharrica insula', and 'Albatia insula', 'Tiles insula'
(i.e. classical Thule, here unusually located in the far north-east, rather than north-
west), as far as the earthly paradise.[24] Again one may discern a primarily secular,
natural historical, and mythographical focus to the periphery, but features such as
the terrestrial paradise, Gog and Magog, the 'monasteria Sancti Antonii' located
south of Egypt, and the framing angels, indicate the potential for a Christian reading
of these uncertain and shifting spaces.

LITERATURE AT THE MARGINS OF THE EARTH

The preceding discussion of the ends of the earth on medieval maps has established
that representation of the ends of the earth and the antipodes responded to debates
about the extent of the known world, and therefore the extent of Christianity. On a
mappa mundi representation of peoples and places at the earth's periphery also could
serve a historiographical function, showing what had been at the ends of the earth as
well as, or instead of, what was still there. Such land was neither literally nor
metaphorically *terra incognita* for a medieval audience: it was known, even if not
experienced directly, since it fell within the conspectus of natural and biblical history.
Medieval literary texts that stage encounters with peoples and places at and beyond

[22] Lecoq (1990: 162) counts 215 toponyms.
[23] For further discussion ibid. 181–7.
[24] Lecoq (ibid. 199–200) suggests that Island and Ganzmir are probably distortions of the
Scandinavian peninsula, derived from book 4 of Adam of Bremen's *History of the Archbishops of
Hamburg-Bremen*, while Tarraconta, Rapharrica, and Albatia islands all derive from Æthicus Ister's
Cosmographia, 3. 32, 37, 64.

the limits of the known world may similarly be understood to broach complex theological and natural philosophical questions. At the same time, literary texts could approach the representation of the ends of the earth from a perspective and with a license quite different to those of the medieval world map.

The voyage beyond the western ends of the earth is the central theme of one of the earliest and most popular narratives of travel in the Middle Ages, the *Navigatio Sancti Brendani*. The *Navigatio* survives in 125 manuscripts; it was copied throughout Europe, and translated into several vernacular languages, including Middle English.[25] It seems to have emerged from the cult of Brendan in Ireland, and perhaps represents a fusion of hagiography (the *Vita Brendani*, a more standard account of the saint's life and miracles, albeit with an account of his travels to the west, appears to pre-date the *Navigatio*) with Irish genres of travel narrative, the *immrana* ('rowings'), or *echtrae* ('outings').[26] According to the *Navigatio*, Brendan is inspired to travel west by the account of St Barrind, who arrives in Clonfert and tells of two islands in the western ocean that he has visited, one ('deliciosa') populated by many monks, and another which, after some days of wandering and an encounter with an angel, he and a companion realize is the Promised Land of Saints.[27] Brendan's journey reaches its climax with his own discovery of the promised land and encounter with the angel, but the process of voyaging rather than its destination emerges as the more important focus of the story.

Spatial description is undoubtedly an important means to the spiritual ends of the *Navigatio Sancti Brendani*. The text is initially quite precise about duration of time, and about directions. Barrind says that he and a companion, the Abbot Mernoc, set out on a journey 'to the far west to the island which is called the promised land of saints' (*contra occidentalem plagam ad insulam que dicitur terra repromissionis sanctorum*).[28] Brendan and his monks begin to sail 'towards the summer solstice' (*contra solsticium estiuale*),[29] presumably in the same direction as Barrind, but they quickly lose any sense of where they are, and from which direction the wind is blowing. Subsequently hell is clearly described as being in a northerly direction, and the voyagers travel east for forty days to reach the promised land from an island of birds.[30] However, for the most part orientation remains vague: we are told that 'sometimes they had a wind, but they did not know from which direction it came or where the boat was carried' (*aliquando uentum habebant, sed tamen ignorabant ex qua parte ueniret aut in quam partem ferebatur nauis*), and later that Brendan and his followers 'were tossed here and there through the ocean sea for three months' (*per oceani equora huc atque illuc agitabatur per tres menses*).[31] An episodic structure develops, punctuated by the formulaic 'on a certain day they saw' (*quadam die*

---

25 See the collection in Barron and Burgess (2002).
26 For discussion of source material see Strijbosch (2000: 125–65); Dumville (1988).
27 Brendanus (1959: 3–9).
28 Ibid. 5.
29 Ibid. 12.
30 Ibid. 78: 'Erat ... nauigium eorum contra orientalem plagam quadraginta dierum'.
31 Respectively, ibid. 12, 28.

uiderunt). The mixture of precision and vagueness seems calibrated.[32] The islands encountered by Brendan and his men are (just) reachable from Ireland, itself towards the westernmost extent of the known world,[33] but they are at a great distance. As a result, in a culture in which hypothetical cartography was permissible, the places described by the *Navigatio* could be mapped. On the Hereford Map (*c*.1300), the six islands are depicted alongside north-west Africa with the inscription 'Fortunate insulee sex sunt insule Sancti Brandani' (the six fortunate islands are the islands of St Brendan).[34] The inscription thus connects the Fortunate Islands recorded at the far west of the known world in classical sources such as Pliny with the early medieval Brendan legend. 'St Brendan's Island(s)' appeared on numerous subsequent medieval and early modern maps, eventually fuelling theories of the Irish discovery of the Americas.[35]

This position, poised between the known and other worlds, is wholly appropriate for a text which is, in large part, a meditation upon monasticism. Brendan initially sets out with fourteen monks, as well as three men who approach the boat as it is about to set sail and request to travel with them. One strand of the narrative concerns the fates of these supernumeraries: one turns out to have a demon inside him (he dies after Brendan exorcizes it), another is seized by demons and dragged to hell, the third is left on the island of three choirs, which is populated with anchorites. For the original crew, spared these fates, the voyage becomes a circular affair, one of routine more than discovery. They follow the same pattern each year for seven years (following the instructions and prophecy of interlocutors, rather than their own instincts and inclinations): at Easter they spend Maundy Thursday (Cena Domini) on a remarkably fertile island, occupied by a single penitent and a large number of sheep, before moving on Holy Saturday to celebrate masses and vigils on what at first appears to be a barren island, but subsequently is revealed to be the fish, Jasconius. After Easter Sunday they travel west (*contra occidentalem plagam*) to another island, populated by birds, one of which informs Brendan that the birds are angels who have wandered the skies and the earth, alienated from the faithful as a result of Lucifer's fall, but that God gives them bodies on holy days and Sundays.[36] Christmas is spent on the island of St Ailbe, where monks follow a strict rule of silence. If Ailbe represents an ideal of monastic life, so too does Brendan's boat. The brothers agree to follow Brendan because, they say, 'your own will is also ours. Have we not left our parents behind?' (*Abba, uoluntas tua ipsa est et nostra. Nonne parentes nostros dimisimus...*).[37] There is a strong emphasis on the liturgy, on singing (the 'island of three choirs' provides a spectacular musical interlude), as well as silence, fasting, and other restraints. Structured around a calendrical cycle (the birth and death of Christ), the *Navigatio* is punctuated by encounters with marvels and

---

[32] See Morison (1971–4: i. 13–31).
[33] Orosius, *Historiarum adversum paganos libri VII*, Isidore, *Etymologiae* 14. 6. 6.
[34] *The Hereford Map*, ed. and trans. Westrem (2001: 389).
[35] See amongst a sizeable literature, the discussion in Morison (1971–4: i. 13–31).
[36] Brendanus (1959: 24). See the discussion by Jacobsen (2006).
[37] Brendanus (1959: 9).

wonders (remarkably sustaining fruit, griffons, a vast crystal pillar reaching to the sky), as well as emblematic figures from Christian history.

Most strikingly, near to the confines of hell (evident from an encounter with particularly aggressive blacksmiths and demons) the travellers encounter Judas seated on a rock. He reveals that he is on day-release from hell, where he is tortured with Herod, Pilate, Annas, and Caiphas; despite the desolate nature of his perch on the rock, he assures Brendan that it is preferable to his normal surrounds. Moved, Brendan quells the demons who demand Judas's return to hell, and allows him to remain for the night on the rock. An unsettling dialogue ensues between Brendan and the demons, in which they re-enact the temptation of Christ ('Are you the Lord of all, so that we should obey your words?' *Numquid Dominus es omnium, ut tuis sermonibus obediamus?*), and state that Judas will suffer double punishment to compensate for Brendan's protection of him.[38] Brendan and companions sail on, leaving Judas to be reclaimed by the demons 'with great force and howling' (*cum magno impetu et ululatu*).[39] Perhaps equally thought-provoking for monastic readers of the *Navigatio* is the subsequent meeting with Paul the hermit, in which the simple life of a former monk of St Patrick who has dwelled alone on a barren island for thirty years causes Brendan to question his own virtue, and dramatizes the tension between monasticism and asceticism.[40] Through encounters of this kind the *Navigatio* stages fundamental Christian debates about mercy and charity, community and solitude, action and contemplation. But the *Navigatio*, where geography meets *vita* meets Christian psychojourney, is also a story of the preparation for death. Both Barrind and Brendan are fated to die shortly after their return to Ireland from the promised land. The voyage west is, in this way, a journey to the margins of life.

Roughly a century after the *Navigatio Sancti Brendani* was first written and circulated within Ireland[41] the court of King Alfred received detailed accounts of the far north-west of Europe. The narratives of Ohthere and Wulfstan were incorporated within the Old English translation of Orosius' *Historiae*, where they emerge from and significantly expand the author's description of Germania. Little can be known of the identities of the two men, although much has been conjectured. Linguistic evidence tends to support the theories that Ohthere was a Norwegian (he describes himself as living 'northern-most of all the Northmen', and in the region of Hålogaland), and that Wulfstan was probably an Anglian.[42] The translation of Orosius, once attributed to Alfred himself but now of uncertain authorship, can be considered to be part of an attempt to transmit and update a specifically, at times polemically, Christian understanding of history. Orosius' history is prefaced and underpinned by his description of the world's geography, and it is this opening section of the text that the narratives of Ohthere and Wulfstan infiltrate and enliven. Their travel accounts rupture the Old English translation of Orosius' geography in more ways than one. Ohthere's account begins without warning following the

---

[38] Ibid. 69.   [39] Ibid. 70.   [40] Ibid. 70–6.
[41] On the dating see Dumville (1988); Orlandi (2006: esp. 227–8); Zelzer (2006).
[42] Fell (1984); Townend (2002: 90–3).

translation of Orosius' description of 'Sweon'—'Ohthere told his lord, King Alfred, that he lived northern-most of all the Northmen'[43]—and after Wulfstan's account we return without comment to Orosius on eastern Europe. Further, the mode of spatial description introduced by the two narratives differs significantly from that of Orosius. Orosius locates peoples and places by reference to cardinal directions, and the Old English supplement to his description initially retains this mode:

Þonne wið norþan Donua æwielme & be eastan Rine sindon Eastfrancan, & be suþan him sindon Swæfas, on oþre healfe þære ie Donua, & be suþan him & be eastan sindon Bægware, se dæl þe mon Regnesburg hætt, & ryhte be eastan him sindon Bæme, & eastnorþ sindon Þyringas, & be norþan him sindon Ealdseaxan, & be norþanwestan him sindon Frisan.

The Eastfrancan are situated north of the source of the Danube and to the east of the Rhine; to their south are the Swæfas [Swabians], on the other side of the Danube, and to the south-east are the Bægware [Bavarians], the region that is called Regensburg, directly to the east the Bæme [Bohemi], to the north-east the Þyringas [Thuringians], to the north the Ealdseaxan ['Old Saxons'], and to the north-west the Frisan [Frisians].[44]

By contrast, the accounts of Ohthere and Wulfstan introduce an element of personal experience. While they at times operate in the mode of depersonalized description, at others they construct a linear narration of their movement through space. Most significantly, the accounts of Ohthere and Wulfstan describe an area beyond the knowledge of classical geography. Ohthere in particular declares his ambition to travel as far north as possible, and indeed the tone of his account indicates that many of the peoples and places he finds were hitherto unknown to him as well as to Alfred and his court.

Þa for he þa giet norþryhte swa feor swa he meahte on þæm oþrum þrim dagum gesiglan. Þa beag þæt land þær eastryhte, oþþe seo sæ in on ðæt lond, he nysse hwæðer, buton he wisse ðæt he ðær bad westanwindes & hwon norþan & siglde ða east be lande swa swa he meahte on feower dagum gesiglan.[45]

Then he travelled further directly northwards, as far as he could get in another three days' sailing. Then the land turned directly east, or the sea (entered) into the land, he did not know which, but he knew that he waited for the west wind there, and a little from the north, and sailed then east along the coast as far as he could sail in four days.

It has been argued plausibly that in his account Ohthere is clearly responding to questions (presumably from members of Alfred's court or the king himself); as in this passage, the uncertainties articulated ('he nysse hwæðer, buton he wisse') seem likely to be responses to unrecorded demands, though they may also register difficulties of translation from Old Norse to Old English.[46] As well as individual experience, then, Ohthere's narrative stands as testimony to collective Anglo-Saxon interest

[43] Orosius (1980, ed. Janet Bately, p. 13): 'Ohthere sæde his hlaforde, Ælfrede cyninge, þæt he ealra Norþmonna norþmest bude'.
[44] Ibid., p. 12. My translation, with peoples supplied according to Bately's commentary (pp. 167–8). On the interrelationship between the Old English *Orosius* and its Latin source see Gilles (1998).
[45] Orosius (1980: 14).
[46] See Townend (2002).

in a fairly precise account of the far north, with details of distances (measured in days travelled) and direction carefully monitored. Wulfstan's account of his sea-journey from Hedeby in Denmark through the land belonging to the Sweon, to the mouth of the Vistula, and to the land of the Ests is not portrayed in such boundary-breaking terms, but its topographic and ethnographic detail is clearly presented as exploratory and novel. In expanding upon available classical and early medieval spatial descriptions, the texts of Ohthere and Wulfstan can be considered to fulfil Orosius' own interests in the ends of the earth as the extent of Christian society and history. At the same time, their descriptions are at least on the surface resolutely secular. As well as giving precise details of duration and direction of journeys from place to place, Ohthere describes local industries (whale and walrus hunting, fishing, hunting of land animals including reindeer, fowling); hostilities and trade between the peoples; linguistic difference and likeness (the *Finnas* and *Beormas* speak nearly the same language); and local economies. Wulfstan also supplements spatial description with details of social custom: the kings and the richest men in Estland drink mare's milk, while the poor and servile drink mead; bodies lie unburied for as many as six months before being cremated; an elaborate horse race is staged to claim the dead man's possessions.[47] Only by implication can this commentary on non-Christian practices be seen to have relevance to Anglo-Saxon England. It is certainly tempting to read the accounts of Ohthere and Wulfstan, and indeed the entire project of the Old English *Orosius*, alongside maps such as the Cotton world map, a text that also attempts to subjoin an unusually detailed picture of the north-west to a representation of the entire ecumene, from Scythia to Ethiopia.[48] The project of expanding the margin, and of integrating border territories to the north, seems to be one shared by a number of texts from ninth- and tenth-century Anglo-Saxon England. Poems such as *Widsið* and *Deor* exuberantly weave European and indeed world history and geography into personal or quasi-personal narratives. *Deor* refers fleetingly and elliptically to the Maering city of Theodoric, Eormanric's Gothland, while sketching what is apparently the speaker's career as a *scop* in the companies of great men. By contrast *Widsið* (literally: the widely travelled one) deploys a more extensive territorial repertoire. The poem's dizzying conspectus of rulers and peoples includes a blizzard of personal names and ethnonyms, ranging from Alexander the Great to Wod, ruler of the Thurings, and from the *Finnas* of the north to the Indians of the East.[49] Ostensibly a display of experience, *Widsið* is in fact a display of knowledge, and its effect is to intertwine narratives of the far north and west—of Scandinavia, of Gothia and Germania, and of Anglo-Saxon England—into the staple narratives of southern Europe: the story of Alexander, the Roman empire, Greece, the far east, and the land of the Israelites. *Widsið*, in other words, defies marginality because in its dazzling movement centre and periphery can no longer be discerned.

[47] Orosius (1980: 16–18).   [48] See Michelet (2006: 142–57).   [49] Malone (1962).

MARVELS, MONSTERS, WONDER:
MARGINS EAST AND SOUTH

In the imaginations of many medieval Europeans the east was a vast and hetero-geneous space. Asia was, so most authorities concurred, half the known world, the size of both Europe and Africa combined.[50] In it, it was often asserted, the origins of European cultures and peoples could be located: Troy, the Tower of Babel, paradise itself—all were, geographically speaking, Asian. And of course the Holy Land was to be found on the Asian side of the Mediterranean. The far east was the site of mirabilia, including not only animals and nations, but also commercial items such as spices and silk. Asia was the origin of pepper as well as people.[51] Was such a space marginal? There are times when Asia's size and wealth, and the extent of power wielded by its rulers must have made Europe seem to be on the margins. But again, from a Christian perspective, Asia had received the word of God. In the later Middle Ages—in part as an offshoot of the Crusades—interest grew in the possibility that Christian communities, above all those converted by St Thomas, could be found in parts of Asia. The figure of Prester John—a Christian king possessed of a vast army, willing to deploy it to retake the Holy Land from the Saracens—began to develop a vigorous literary life from the twelfth century. The Latin 'Letter of Prester John', addressed to the Emperor of Byzantium, conjured a wondrous realm of monstrous races, extraordinary wildlife, rivers flowing with precious stones, the fountain of youth, a palace with crystal walls and twenty-four gold columns.[52] Even as the letter was copied and translated throughout Europe, serious attempts were being made to contact Christians in Asia, and to convert non-Christians. The Franciscan friars John of Plano Carpini, William of Rubruck, and Odoric of Pordenone all wrote accounts of their travels to the Mongol kingdom in the thirteenth and early fourteenth centuries on missions of conversion.[53] Such reports enjoyed nothing like the popu-larity of Marco Polo's account of political, social, and economic life in the Mongol empire and beyond, but all attest to the urgency with which many Europeans attended to narratives of travel to the east.

On the Hereford map, the largest extant medieval world image (1.59 × 1.30 m), the wealth, history, and wonder of the far east and the far south are represented in impressive detail (Figure 5). At the top of the map, at its easternmost point, a small but detailed circular representation of the earthly paradise shows its four rivers, Adam, Eve, the serpent, and the gates of paradise. Beyond, just to the right, the expulsion of Adam and Eve is depicted.[54] In northern Asia (Figure 6) detailed inscriptions include the Ganges and the size of India; monoculi (described as people

[50] Isidore, *Etymologiae* 14. 1. 2.
[51] See Freedman (2005).
[52] Zarncke (1879); Gosman (1982).
[53] For introduction and translation of the accounts of John and William see Dawson (1980).
[54] Westrem (2001: 35–7). For detailed commentary see Scafi (2006: 145–9).

Figure 4 The Sawley Map. Cambridge, Corpus Christi College, MS 66, p. 2.
By permission of the Master and Fellows, Corpus Christi College, Cambridge.

Figure 5 The Hereford Map. Dean and Chapter of Hereford and the Hereford Mappa Mundi Trust.

with a single leg, who use their very large foot to shade themselves); the peoples enclosed by Alexander, said to be cannibals and 'accursed sons of Cain' (*fili Caim maledicti*), who will burst forth at the time of Antichrist; the blessed Hyperboreans, as in the Sawley map a people that live without discord and grief; the Essedones, who consume their parents' bodies after their death; the Scythians, who are warlike and drink out of the skulls of their enemies; the altars of Alexander; the wicked Griste who use the skin of their enemies for clothes and saddles; and dog-headed people

Figure 6 The Hereford Map (detail of northern Europe and Asia).

(Cynocephales). The knowledge assembled here is, in many senses, traditional, but it would be wrong to see it as static. The very act of transmission and reproduction is a dynamic one: careful choices have been made about where and how to depict information. Within the map itself, the inscriptions and images seem to emphasize interaction, albeit often of a violent kind, rather than stasis: the edges of the earth are temporally and ethnically heterogeneous, filled with signs of the past (Alexander), future (enclosed races), and with peoples virtuous and vicious whose significance may be to induce not only wonder, but also contemplation.

Beneath the Nile (Figure 7), in the space devoted to Ethiopia on other world maps, the Hereford map is well known for its series of 'monstrous races', represented visually as well as by a label: these include the four-eyed Marmini Ethiopians, the Blemmyae (head in chest), an island full of Sirens, the Himantopods (people who creep rather than walk), hermaphrodites, a people with a sealed mouth who consume

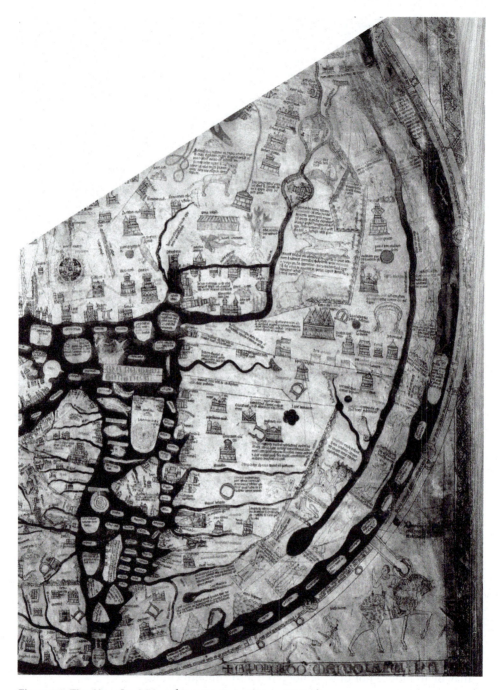

Figure 7 The Hereford Map (detail of southern Africa).

food through a straw, one-legged Sciapods, and a people without ears.[55] Clearly the presence of such peoples is a departure from and development of trends evident on earlier *mappae mundi*. The marvellous races are grouped (though others appear elsewhere on the map) and illustrated. They are connected to the natural world around them, and at the same time cut off from it by the Nile and the surrounding ocean.[56] At the ends of the earth—particularly, but not exclusively, in the far south—are located marvellous varieties of human form and human custom. It is difficult to discern the effect these images and their inscriptions were supposed to have on their medieval viewer, but they would seem to include wonder, disapproval (the anthropophagi), horror or at least surprise, and amusement. The dynamic does not seem to have been one of exclusion or rejection, however. Consistent with the precepts of Augustine, the monstrous races can be considered within the ambit of human nature and therefore history; they too may be judged by Christ.[57] This position is made most explicit on the monumental Ebstorf map (*c*.1300), where the crucified Christ, whose body is depicted underlying the world image, reaches his right hand to encompass the monstrous races. The monstrous races on medieval *mappae mundi* are marginal in the sense that they occupy a border zone, an edge, but they remain part of the world and its knowledge.

The expansion of European knowledge of parts east in the thirteenth and fourteenth century had perhaps its most curious and most popular expression in the *Book of Sir John Mandeville*.[58] Here too the representation of mirabilia at the ends of the earth is complex. Mandeville's *Book* is a composite of several different texts. Its principal sources are the works of two friars, William of Boldensele's *Liber de quibusdam ultramarinis partibus* of 1336, a narrative of pilgrimage to Egypt and the Holy Land, and Odoric of Pordenone's *Relatio*, used particularly for description of lands in the further east, including India and Cathay. Amongst an impressive variety of additional sources, the Mandeville author drew on other pilgrimage and travel literature, histories such as Hayton of Armenia's early fourteenth-century *Flos historiarum terrae Orientis*, encyclopedists such as Vincent of Beauvais, hagiography (Jacobus de Voragine's *Golden Legend*), accounts of non-Christian beliefs (William of Tripoli's *Tractatus de Statu Sarracenorum*), and scientific treatises (John of Sacrobosco's *De sphaera*).[59] Surprisingly, this multitude of texts is melded together into a relatively supple narrative, guided by the insistent presence of 'Mandeville', a self-proclaimed English knight, who has to date defied all scholarly attempts to identify conclusively his actual identity and nationality. The *Book* seems likely to have been

---

[55] Westrem (2001: respectively pp. 385, 383, 381, 379, 377, 375).

[56] We see a similar grouping of peoples on the 13th-cent. Psalter Map (British Library, Additional MS 28681, fo. 9ʳ), and on the contemporary Ebstorf *mappa mundi*. There are too many differences to suggest copying, but map makers were clearly using the same principle of spatial organization. On the Ebstorf map see Kugler (2007).

[57] Augustine (1955, ed. Dombart and Kalb), 16. 8. For discussion see Flint (1984); Cohen (1996); Bynum (1997).

[58] Deluz (1988: 271) counts 262 MSS, including 15 fragments.

[59] On Mandeville's sources ibid. 39–72.

first composed in Anglo-French, though whether in England or the Continent remains a matter of debate.[60] A fundamentally open text, subject to interpolation and correction, the work was quickly translated into continental French, Latin, English and several other European vernaculars. The *Book* begins as a description of the ways from the north-west of Europe to Jerusalem, with lengthy descriptions of Constantinople, the cross and crown of Christ, the Sultans and Babylon, Egypt, and the Holy Land itself. But gradually the descriptions move further and further east, and Christian history is supplemented by chapters on the beliefs of the Saracens, the Amazons, the customs of India (including evidence of the enduring presence of St Thomas), Java, Cathay, and the lands beyond, before returning to the familiar tropes: Prester John, Alexander, and the earthly paradise. Some sense of the rapid and often disconcerting movement of this text can be given by a summary of the contents and most obvious sources of a chapter towards the end of the *Book*,[61] ostensibly describing the areas beyond Cathay:

- the kingdom of Cadhilne (or Caldilhe), 'a fulle fair contre', where a large fruit is found to contain an animal like a lamb without wool (Odoric of Pordenone, *Relatio*, ch. 27, 'Cadeli');
- Mandeville tells the people of Cadhilne that barnacle geese grow from a tree; they marvel (Vincent of Beauvais, *Speculum naturale*, 16. 40);[62]
- the kingdom also contains long apples, trees bearing spices, and large bunches of grapes (Jacques de Vitry, *Historia orientalis*, 1099);
- within the hills of the Caspian in this land are the ten lost tribes of Jews, called Gog and Magog, shut up by Alexander (Vincent of Beauvais, *Speculum historiale*, 4. 43);
- the Caspian sea is in fact a lake, barring escape for the Jews (no known source);
- the Jews have no land, but pay tribute to the Queen of the Amazons, who prevents them from crossing her hills, though one occasionally escapes (no known source);[63]
- a man-made path called Clyrem (or Clyron) does lead out of the enclosure, but snakes, dragons, and desert make exit possible only in winter (Brunetto Latini, *Li Livres dou Tresor*, 1. 122);
- the Jews speak only Hebrew, and will attack Christian men in the time of Antichrist; other Jews learn Hebrew so as to be able to converse with the enclosed tribes at the time of Antichrist and realize prophecies of Jewish domination of Christians (*Speculum historiale*, 4. 43);
- a fox will precipitate the exit of the Jews and the destruction of the gates of Alexander at the time of Antichrist by tunnelling into the enclosure, causing the

---

[60] Ibid. 3–24; and recently Bennett (2006: 272–92).

[61] Ch. 29 in M. C. Seymour's edn. of the Cotton version (1967: 191–4). For the sources for this section see Deluz (1988: 482–3).

[62] Seymour (1967: 254); the story is a Celtic myth, told also by Gerald of Wales, *Topographia Hibernica* 1. 15.

[63] Higgins (1997: 182–3), suggests Hugh Ripelin of Strasbourg's *Compendium theologicae veritatis* as a possible source.

Jews to marvel at it, and by then being chased out by them through the tunnel (*Mirabilia mundi*);[64]

- in nearby Bactria there are evil people and trees that bear wool like that of sheep, man-eating hippopotami (*ipotaynes*), half-man half-horse, bitter rivers and waters, griffons in great number, capable of carrying a horse (Jacques de Vitry, *Historia orientalis*, 1100; *Letter of Alexander to Aristotle*);
- men make cups out of the talons of griffons, and bows from their ribs and their feathers (*Letter of Alexander to Aristotle*; *Speculum historiale*, 4. 53–60);
- the land of Prester John, Emperor of India, is many days' journey from Bactria.

Is there an organizing principle at work here? In part the discourse is one of undermining wonder. The marvels of the east are met with marvels or mundanity of the west (for every animal-fruit a goose; for every griffon talon a bull's horn). In part too there is a spatial logic at work in which legend—the enclosed tribes/ Gog and Magog/Amazons/Alexander/Prester John—is located alongside classical and medieval geography (Bactria, the Caspian, and the more recent addition of Cadhilne). There is the interest in language, a persistent theme of the *Book*, here woven into an account of Jewish identity that unambiguously links Jews to Antichrist, in contrast to the apparently more tolerant attitude to Saracens and other non-Christians shown elsewhere in the book. Jews in this chapter of the *Book* are marginal in several senses: at the ends of the earth, isolated, monoglot, and incomprehensible to others, simultaneously past (the moment of enclosure) and future (the destined release). The incongruous detail of the fox is typical of the enigmatic quality of Mandeville's *Book*. Is the fox slanderously associated with the Jews because of its fabled cunning and connection with heresy?[65] And yet 'they will marvel at him greatly', for they have no foxes. Is it an inversion of Alexander ('they will break down these gates')? A parody of Christ (they will pursue him until they come to the hole whence he came out)? It is the fox that seems to characterize Mandeville's *Book*: a composite text, unoriginal, yet memorable, multivalent, unassimilable.

MARGINS ON THE MOVE

By the second decade of the fifteenth century it had become clear to certain learned observers that the boundaries of the known world were expanding. As texts such as Marco Polo's *Devisement dou monde*, the *Book of Sir John Mandeville*, and the reports

---

[64] See Burnett and Gautier Dalché (1991: 162), where the *Mirabilia mundi*, a 13th-cent. text describing the marvels of the world, is suggested as the likely source for the story of the fox and the escape of the enclosed races.

[65] Higgins (1997: 185); compare Burnett and Gautier Dalché (1991: 162 n. 48).

of William of Rubruck and other missionaries testify, from the thirteenth century onwards the traditional basis of European knowledge of the far east had been supplemented by new information. In the fourteenth century, European economic and political expansion developed in the opposite direction as well. In the 1330s and 1340s the discovery of the Canary Islands in the Atlantic attracted the attention of several European monarchs, knights, and the papacy. The reports of the indigenous populations of the islands drew comments from Francis Petrarch in his *De vita solitaria*, and even induced Giovanni Boccaccio to translate from Italian into Latin a letter describing an expedition to the islands in 1341.[66] The fifteenth century saw Portuguese exploration along the west coast of Africa, gradually providing evidence to support earlier conjectures that the 'torrid zone' was habitable, and passable. To the north, accounts of human settlement in polar regions (beyond even the peoples already reported in the late ninth century by Ohthere) further unsettled notions of an uninhabitable 'frigid zone', and helped to supplement classical and antique mappings of Scandinavia and northern Europe.[67] Intimately connected with these various accounts of hitherto unknown places and peoples was the question of the legal and moral rights of non-Christian peoples, and in some cases the legitimacy of the claims of Europeans to their lands and resources.[68] These questions remain with us still.

Representation of the ends of the earth in the fifteenth century had changed too. It was not the case that old knowledge was jettisoned to make way for new. The mode of the accretion of information persisted. It is true that new models for the world map were available: most notably, the translation of Claudius Ptolemy's *Geography* into Latin in the first decade of the fifteenth century, and the dissemination of the maps that accompanied that text, provided a significantly different image of the world, one based upon the principles of projection. Yet the most important aspect of Ptolemy's work was initially perceived to be the lists of toponyms he provided, rather than the maps, and it was also the case that many map makers immediately saw the need to supplement Ptolemy's images of the world and its regions with additional information, and in some cases to debate the utility of his projections.[69] Perhaps the most significant change in the conceptualization of the ends of the earth (assisted both by Ptolemy and by exploration and contacts) was the notion that unknown parts of the world were contiguous and reachable from the known parts. Many remained uncertain whether there were parts of the world beyond Europe, Africa, and Asia. But the oceanic and climatic barriers to travel no longer seemed as daunting. On the world maps of the fifteenth century, then, one finds many of the old features, but also debate, uncertainty, and *terrae incognitae*.

[66] See further Bouloux (2002: 249–65).
[67] See Björnbo and Petersen (1909: 145).
[68] For an overview of these matters with regard to the late medieval expansion of European polities see Muldoon (1979).
[69] Gautier Dalché (2007).

Already in fourteenth-century English cartography, revision of traditional boundaries was starting to take place. The maps that illustrated Ranulf Higden's *Polychronicon* in the fourteenth and throughout the fifteenth centuries maintain much of the
traditional *mappae mundi* format and features at the ends of the earth: monstrous
races in Africa beneath the Nile, the columns of Hercules in the far west and the
earthly paradise in the far east, Scythia in the far north, and an encircling ocean filled
with islands. Yet contemporaneous with versions of Higden's *mappae mundi* was the
Aslake map fragment (*c*.1360), part of a large, now lost world map, possibly produced
for North Creake Abbey, Norfolk. Some of the material on the fragment is familiar:
a dragon threatens a child-hugging woman of the Psylli, inscriptions record the
Ganfanstantes and lion-killing Leontophona in Numidia. At the same time, three of
the Canaries appear on the Aslake map fragment, along with toponyms on the North
African coast line which were presumably ultimately derived from a nautical chart.
Such information certainly circulated in fourteenth- and fifteenth-century England.
Amongst the multifarious material relating to English history and institutions
contained in the *Itineraries* of William Worcester is a careful list of Atlantic islands,
made in 1478. Worcester's list includes the Azores, the Canaries, the Cape Verde isles,
and several islands off the west coast of Africa, information derived 'from the book of
Christopher Baldement clerk, who laboured in several of the said 80 islands'.[70]
Worcester's purpose in recording the list cannot be stated with certainty, but it attests
to a level of interest and knowledge about Atlantic exploration. Just twenty years after
Worcester made his notes, John Cabot would lead an expedition to North America
from Bristol, charged by Henry VII with 'full and free authority . . . to sail to all parts,
regions and coasts of the eastern, western and northern sea . . . to find, discover and
investigate whatsoever islands, countries, regions or provinces of heathens and infidels, in whatsoever part of the world placed, which before this time were unknown to
all Christians'.[71] Any towns, castles, cities, and islands discovered by John and his sons
were to be conquered, occupied, and possessed 'as our vassals and governors lieute-
nants and deputies therein', with one-fifth of capital gained from the voyage to be paid
to the Crown.[72] English colonization of the Americas, spearheaded by Venetian
navigators, was under way.

What was a margin? A comparison of two modes of representation—maps and
literary texts—indicates that marginal space in medieval English textual production
was a site for the reception of tradition. The margin was a limit, but a permeable one.
The ends of the known world were spaces where Christian encountered non-Christian
practices (Ohthere, Wulfstan; monstrous races; Mandeville). But paradoxically—
perhaps—they were also spaces at which the most intense expressions of faith could
be found: the search for the promised land of saints (Brendan), the lingering present-
absence of the earthly paradise, the trace of the apostolic spread of Christianity
throughout the world's human populations. Beyond? There certainly was much
discussion throughout the Middle Ages about what lay beyond the margin, and a

---

[70] Worcester (1969: 372–3).   [71] Williamson (1962: 204).   [72] Ibid. 205.

variety of answers, ranging from the secular (antipodal populations) to the spiritual (paradise, inferno, purgatory) could be given. The reception of tradition was not, then, an act of unthinking copying: reception also meant transformation, debate, questioning. These were mental processes, rather than the physical ones of exploration practiced, glorified in the later Middle Ages and thereafter. Margins receded quickly in the late fifteenth and sixteenth centuries: many other lands and other peoples gradually became known to Europeans. Writers responded, as always, but the utopias and travel narratives, factual and fictional, that flourished in post-medieval literature had their bases in texts such as the *Navigatio Sancti Brendani*, the voyages of Ohthere and Wulfstan, and the *Book of Sir John Mandeville*. Paradigms of encounter—of self and others—had been shaped.

BIBLIOGRAPHY

AUGUSTINE (1955), *De civitate dei*, ed. B. Dombart and A. Kalb (Corpus Christianorum, Series Latina, 47–8; Turnhout: Brepols).

BARBER, PETER (2006), 'Medieval Maps of the World', in P. D. A. Harvey (ed.), *The Hereford World Map: Medieval World Maps and their Context* (London: British Library), 1–44.

BARRON, W. R. J., and GLYN S. BURGESS (eds.) (2002), *The Voyage of St Brendan: Representative Versions of the Legend in English Translation* (Exeter: University of Exeter Press).

BENNETT, MICHAEL (2006), 'Mandeville's Travels and the Anglo-French Moment', *Medium Ævum*, 75: 272–92.

BJÖRNBO, AXEL ANTHON, and CARL S. PETERSEN (1909), *Der Däne Claudius Claussøn Swart, der älteste Kartograph des Nordens, der erste Ptolemäusepigon der Renaissance* (Innsbruck: Wagner'schen Universitäts Buchhandlung).

BOULOUX, NATHALIE (2002), *Culture et savoirs géographiques en Italie au XIVe siècle* (Turnhout: Brepols).

BRENDANUS (1959), *Navigatio Sancti Brendani Abbatis, from Early Latin Manuscripts*, ed. Carl Selmer (Notre Dame, Ind.: University of Notre Dame Press).

BRINCKEN, ANNA-DOROTHEE VON DEN (1992), *Fines Terrae: Die Enden der Erde und der vierte Kontinent auf mittelalterlichen Weltkarten* (Monumenta Germaniae Historica Schriften, 36; Hanover: Hahnsche Buchhandlung).

BURNETT, CHARLES, and PATRICK GAUTIER DALCHÉ (1991), 'Attitudes towards the Mongols in Medieval Literature: The XXII Kings of Gog and Magog from the Court of Frederick II to Jean de Mandeville', *Viator*, 22: 153–67.

BYNUM, CAROLINE WALKER (1997), 'Wonder', *American Historical Review*, 102: 1–27.

CAMILLE, MICHAEL (1992), *Image on the Edge: The Margins of Medieval Art* (London: Reaktion).

COHEN, JEFFREY JEROME (ed.) (1996), *Monster Theory: Reading Culture* (Minneapolis: University of Minnesota Press).

DAWSON, CHRISTOPHER (ed.) (1980), *Mission to Asia* (Toronto: University of Toronto Press in Association with the Medieval Academy of America).

DELUZ, CHRISTIANE (1988), *Le Livre de Jehan de Mandeville: Une 'géographie' au XIVe siècle* (Louvain-la-Neuve: Université Catholique de Louvain).

DUMVILLE, DAVID (1988), 'Two Approaches to the Dating of *Navigatio Sancti Brendani*', *Studi medievali*, 3rd ser. 29: 87–102.

EDSON, EVELYN (1997), *Mapping Time and Space: How Medieval Mapmakers Viewed their World* (London: British Library).

ENGLISCH, BRIGITTE (2002), *Ordo orbis terrae: Die Weltsicht in den Mappae mundi des frühen und hohen Mittelalters* (Berlin: Akademie Verlag).

FELL, CHRISTINE E. (1984), *Two Voyagers at the Court of King Alfred*, tr. and ed. Niels Lund (York: William Sessions Ltd).

FLINT, VALERIE I. J. (1984), 'Monsters and the Antipodes in the Early Middle Ages and Enlightenment', *Viator*, 15: 65–80.

FOYS, MARTIN K. (2007), *Virtually Anglo-Saxon: Old Media, New Media, and Early Medieval Studies in the Late Age of Print* (Gainesville, Fla.: University Press of Florida).

FREEDMAN, PAUL (2005), 'Spices and Late-Medieval European Ideas of Scarcity and Value', *Speculum*, 80: 1209–27.

GAUTIER DALCHÉ, PATRICK (1994), 'De la glose à la contemplation: Place et fonction de la carte dans les manuscrits du haut Moyen Age', *Settimane di studio del Centro italiano di studi sull'alto medioevo*, 41: 693–771.

——(2007), 'The Reception of Ptolemy's Geography (End of the Fourteenth to Beginning of the Sixteenth Century)', in David Woodward (ed.), *The History of Cartography*, iii. *Cartography in the European Renaissance* (Chicago: University of Chicago Press).

GILLES, SEALY (1998), 'Territorial Interpolations in the Old English Orosius', in Sylvia Tomasch and Sealy Gilles (eds.), *Text and Territory: Geographical Imagination in the European Middle Ages* (Philadelphia: University of Pennsylvania Press), 79–96.

GOODICH, MICHAEL (ed.) (1998), *Other Middle Ages: Witnesses at the Margins of Medieval Society* (Philadelphia: University of Pennsylvania Press).

GOSMAN, MARTIN (ed.) (1982), *La Lettre du Prêtre Jean: Les Versions en ancien français et en ancien occitan, textes et commentaires* (Groningen: Bouma's Boekhuis).

HARVEY, P. D. A. (1991), *Medieval Maps* (London: British Library).

——(1997), 'The Sawley Map and Other World Maps in Twelfth-Century England', *Imago Mundi*, 49: 33–42.

HIATT, ALFRED (2007), 'The Map of Macrobius before 1100', *Imago Mundi*, 59: 149–76.

——(2008), *Terra Incognita: Mapping the Antipodes before 1600* (London: British Library; Chicago: University of Chicago Press).

HIGGINS, IAIN MACLEOD (1997), *Writing East: The 'Travels' of Sir John Mandeville* (Philadelphia: University of Pennsylvania Press).

Isidore of Seville (1911), *Etymologiarum sive originum libri xx*, ed. W. M. Lindsay (2 vols. Oxford: Clarendon Press).

——(2006), *The Etymologies of Isidore of Seville*, tr. Stephen A. Barney, W. J. Lewis, J. A. Beach, and Oliver Berghof (Cambridge: Cambridge University Press).

ISTER, ÆTHICUS (1993), *Die Kosmographie des Æthicus*, ed. Otto Prinze (Munich: Monumenta Germaniae Historica).

JACOBSEN, PETER CHRISTIAN (2006), 'The Island of the Birds in the *Navigatio Sancti Brendani*', in Glyn S. Burgess and Clara Strijbosch (eds.), *The Brendan Legend: Texts and Versions* (Leiden: Brill), 99–116.

KENAAN-KEDAR, NURITH (1995), *Marginal Sculpture in Medieval France: Towards the Deciphering of an Enigmatic Pictorial Language* (Aldershot: Scolar Press).

KUGLER, HARTMUT (ed.) (2007), *Die Ebstorfer Weltkarte* (2 vols. Berlin: Akademie Verlag).

LECOQ, DANIELLE (1990), 'La Mappemonde d'Henri de Mayence ou l'image du monde au XIIe siècle', in Gaston Duchet-Suchaux (ed.), *Iconographie médiévale: Image, texte, contexte* (Paris: Éditions du Centre national de la recherche scientifique), 155–207.

LEWIS, C. T., and C. SHORT (1879), *A Latin Dictionary* (Oxford: Clarendon Press).

McGurk, Patrick (1983), 'The Mappa Mundi', in P. McGurk, D. N. Dumville, M. R. Godden, and Ann Knock (eds.), *An Eleventh-Century Anglo-Saxon Illustrated Miscellany (British Library Cotton Tiberius B.V. Part I)* (Copenhagen: Rosenkilde & Bagger), 79–86.

Malone, Kemp (ed.) (1962), *Widsið* (rev. edn. Anglistica, 13; Copenhagen: Rosenkilde & Bagger).

Michelet, Fabienne L. (2006), *Creation, Migration, and Conquest: Imaginary Geography and Sense of Space in Old English Literature* (Oxford: Oxford University Press).

Morison, Samuel (1971–4), *The European Discovery of America: The Northern Voyages* (2 vols. New York: Oxford University Press).

Muldoon, James (1979), *Popes, Lawyers, and Infidels* (Philadelphia: University of Pennsylvania Press).

Orlandi, Giovanni (2006), 'Brendan and Moses', in Glyn S. Burgess and Clara Strijbosch (eds.), *The Brendan Legend: Texts and Versions* (Leiden: Brill), 221–40.

Orosius, Paulus (1882), *Pauli Orosii Historiarum adversum paganos libri VII*, ed. C. Zangemeister (Vienna: C. Geroldi).

——(1980), *The Old English Orosius*, ed. Janet Bately (EETS SS 6; London: Oxford University Press for the Early English Text Society).

Reynolds, Suzanne (1996), *Medieval Reading: Grammar, Rhetoric and the Classical Text* (Cambridge: Cambridge University Press).

Scafi, Alessandro (2006), *Mapping Paradise* (London: British Library).

Seymour, M. C. (ed.) (1967), *Mandeville's Travels* (Oxford: Clarendon Press).

Strijbosch, Clara (2000), *The Seafaring Saint: Sources and Analogues of the Twelfth-Century Voyage of Saint Brendan*, tr. Thea Summerfield (Dublin: Four Courts Press).

Townend, Matthew (2002), *Language and History in Viking Age England: Linguistic Relations between Speakers of Old Norse and Old English* (Turnhout: Brepols).

Westrem, Scott D. (ed. and tr.) (2001), *The Hereford Map: A Transcription and Translation of the Legends with Commentary* (Turnhout: Brepols).

Williamson, James A. (1962), *The Cabot Voyages and Bristol Discovery under Henry VII* (Cambridge: Cambridge University Press).

Worcester, William (1969), *Itineraries*, ed. John H. Harvey (Oxford: Clarendon Press).

Zarncke, Friedrich (1879), *Der Priester Johannes* (Leipzig: Hirzel).

Zelzer, Michaela (2006), 'Philological Remarks on the So-Called *Navigatio S. Brendani*', in Glyn S. Burgess and Clara Strijbosch (eds.), *The Brendan Legend: Texts and Versions* (Leiden: Brill), 337–50.

....

CHAPTER 34

MONSTERS AND THE EXOTIC IN MEDIEVAL ENGLAND

....

ASA SIMON MITTMAN

SUSAN M. KIM

INTRODUCTION

....

Societies, medieval as well as modern, define themselves not only through introspection but through an outward gaze to what they perceive as other cultures, other races, other genders, or other species. Through representation of and comparison to these 'others', societies and the subjects who comprise them can attempt to establish those qualities by which they wish to be defined.[1]

In the English Middle Ages, the producers of dominant culture—male, European, and Christian—often represented themselves through comparison to exotic, fantastic beings, monsters, and monstrous humans. So pervasive was this fascination with and reflexive identification through the literally monstrous other that when experientially real and known cultural and religious others, such as Jews and Muslims, were

---

[1] See Cohen (2006: ch. 1, 'Acts of Separation: Shaping Communal Bodies').

evoked in Christian European literature, they were often rendered in precisely the language of the monstrous.

In the use of the language of the monstrous in the depiction of medieval Jews and Muslims, but also in the use of such language at the very heart of constructions of the medieval hero, or the Christian saint, we can see clearly the contradiction integral to the construction of the monstrous 'other' in the English Middle Ages: the monstrous 'other' is not absolute, stable, or firmly outside the boundaries of the normative: on the contrary, the 'other', like the monsters who so often embody it, remains recognizable, strange yet familiar, a possible version of oneself.

In this chapter, we will discuss some of the textual sources relied upon by medieval English authors and artists, and we will survey some of the most widely read medieval texts dealing with the monstrous.

WHY A LITERATURE OF THE MONSTROUS AND EXOTIC?

Before our discussion of backgrounds, sources, texts, and readings, we begin with the question: *why* a literature of the monstrous and exotic in the English Middle Ages? That is, we ask why such a literature might have developed, but also how that development is distinctive: how, that is, the literature of the monstrous in the Middle Ages is different from that of the present day.

Among possible reasons for the development of what we might call a genre of the monstrous and exotic we locate first a body of mythological material we can assume is, in broad strokes, shared among Germanic peoples, among them the Anglo-Saxons and Scandinavians. This mythological material, articulated, for example, in Snorri Sturluson's *Gylfaginning*, contains not only a vast array of giants and hybrid creatures, but also a cosmogony in which the human world is created from the spectacular dismemberment of the body of the giant Ymir. The literature of the monstrous develops in medieval literature thus in part as a reflection of this native body of tradition. This tradition also perhaps gives at least the early medieval literature of the monstrous some aspects of its distinctive character: as the broken body of Ymir creates the world, the monstrous in medieval literature is associated not simply with that which threatens human civilization, but also with that which creates and sustains it.

Because the medieval West is dominantly Christian, however, and because, especially in the early period, textual production occurs in a monastic context, this body of native tradition can be summoned via allusion, but remains associated with a repudiated paganism. As Jacques Le Goff has argued with respect to the broad European context, '[t]he roots of the marvellous are almost always pre-Christian. The traditions in question being continuous, medieval Christianity was obliged to confront them throughout its history'.[2] This confrontation can take the form of repression or erasure, but also can include incorporation. Of course, Christianity has its own monstrous, the beasts and giants we will discuss below. Hence we find in some early medieval explicitly Christian texts at once extension of Christian monstrous figures and striking incorporations of the pagan monstrous figure in, for example, the Old English Life of St Christopher, a giant with the head of a dog.

The dominance of Christianity in the production of texts provides yet another motivation for the development and persistence of literature of the monstrous and exotic. Anglo-Saxon England is converted to Roman Christianity through the mission of Augustine of Canterbury at the end of the sixth century. In the narrative he provides of Augustine's journey to convert the Anglo-Saxons, the Venerable Bede explains that Augustine, setting out from cosmopolitan Rome, becomes overwhelmed with fear at the idea of a journey to a barbarous people at the edges of the known world.[3] In Augustine's fear, at that originary moment for Christianity in England, we can see clearly how the position of Anglo-Saxon literate Christians might lend itself to the development of a literature of the monstrous: literate, Christian Anglo-Saxons found themselves at once part of a powerful Christian culture, and also identified as those dwellers at the very fringes, margins, or borderlands of that culture, *against* whom Christian culture defined itself; that is, literate Christian Anglo-Saxons found themselves, within that culture, in the position of the monstrous.

In addition, from the first migrations, England was a territory of dramatically shifting and contested borders: from the instability of the early kingdoms to the Scandinavian invasions, settlement in the Danelaw, West Saxon expansion, renewed hostilities, and Danish rule, the Norman Conquest, and the dramatic changes of the Hundred Years War, territorial borders, and with them conceptions of what it means to dwell within them, as 'English' men, are under nearly constant renegotiation. As Jeffrey Jerome Cohen has argued for the early period, '[b]ecause of its diversity and because of its permeable, perpetually transgressed borders, Anglo-Saxon England was relentlessly pondering what it means to be a warrior, a Christian, a hero, a saint, an outlaw, a king, a sexed and gendered being'.[4] Hence, Cohen concludes, 'It is not surprising, then, that the monster became a kind of cultural shorthand for the problems of identity construction, for the irreducible difference that lurks deep within the culture-bound self'.[5]

It is conventional to divide the medieval period in England into two periods, the Anglo-Saxon period and the later medieval, or post-Conquest period. In the

---

[2] Le Goff (1985: 28).

[3] Bede (1969), 1. 23: 'Qui cum iussis pontificalibus obtemperantes memoratum opus adgredi coepissent, iamque aliquantulum itineris confecissent, perculsi timore inerti redire domum potius quam barbaram feram incredulamque gentem, cuius ne linguam quidem nossent' (In obedience to the pope's command, they undertook this task and had already gone a little way on their journey when they were paralysed with terror. They began to contemplate returning home rather than going to a barbarous, fierce, and unbelieving nation whose language they did not even understand.)

[4] Cohen (1999: 4–5).   [5] Ibid. 5.

literature of the monstrous, the period following the Conquest reflects the dramatic social and linguistic changes that justify such a division, changes brought about in part by the establishment of Norman rule. The literature in the generations immediately following the Conquest also reflects changes in the broader Western self-understanding brought about by the institution of the Crusades.

As George Garnet has articulated, the Normans, '[l]ike many totalitarian regimes in the twentieth century,... seem to have realized that control of the past was a prerequisite for mastery of the present, and set about propagating an official version of history'.[6] Garnet is concerned with 'official' histories, like the Bayeux Tapestry, but the post-Conquest emphasis on the reinvention of the past extends to other forms of history, including texts such as Geoffrey of Monmouth's *The History of the Kings of Britain*, which provide the framework for the reintroduction of yet another body of tradition for the literature of the monstrous: the Celtic mythologies, here focused in Arthurian narratives.[7] This post-Conquest association of Arthurian texts with the 'matter of Britain' rewrites the history of England, constructing a continuity between Anglo-Norman and continental dynasties and a Celtic prehistory, and eliding the Anglo-Saxon period. Yet the giants, dragons, and transformed humans in the new Arthurian narratives remain strikingly familiar: if they appear to confirm rupture from the Anglo-Saxon past, they also provide continuity with that past.

Within thirty years of the Conquest, Urban II's call for the First Crusade established the possibility for Western contact with an East which had, until then, appeared in Christian texts, and pilgrimage narratives, and in fictional stories of exotic lands and monstrous races. This contact was explicitly hostile: early Crusaders slaughtered indigenous populations as they carved out the Outremer states. The Outremer states were relatively short-lived, but the impact of the violence of Crusader incursions in the East resonates throughout the later Middle Ages and afterward. In the literature of the monstrous, we see not surprisingly the introduction of the figure of the vilified yet often problematically chivalrous Saracen, a new hostility in the representation of Jews, and a new and explicit anxiety about the proximity of such figures to Christian Europeans, anxiety articulated in the Fourth Lateran Council's requirement of marked clothing for Jews, Saracens, and prostitutes, and represented in courtly literature perhaps most clearly in the generic cloaking of the body of the courtly lady in 'Saracen silk'.[8]

'Real' Western contact with the 'exotic' East becomes increasingly possible, not only with the ongoing Crusades, but also in the expansion of Western trade and travel routes, as evidenced both by the eastern journeys documented in the late thirteenth century, and by the literary narratives of those journeys, the most famous among them being Marco Polo's *Travels* (*Divisament dou Monde*). Yet the durability of the literature of the monstrous and exotic remains so pervasive that as late as the mid-fourteenth century, texts like *The Book of Sir John Mandeville* reproduce many of

⁶ Garnett (1997: 61–2).   ⁷ See Cohen (2006: 65–9).   ⁸ See Burns (2002: ch. 6).

the narratives of earlier, clearly fictional texts. Dramatic evidence of the real power of these texts, and the truths their readers believed they contained is provided by the role of these texts in subsequent exploration: explorers like Columbus and Frobisher consulted not only navigational charts and maps, but also *The Book of Sir John Mandeville*.

Why a medieval literature of the monstrous and exotic? Because the foundational cultures of medieval England—Germanic, Celtic, and Christian—relied on such figures; because the conditions of literacy made such figures intensely relevant; because, throughout the period, political and social conditions warranted the representation both of a hybrid 'body' of the state and of an externalized embodiment of what that state excluded; and because, in the course of this period, these fabulous narratives acquired the status of truth, truth as least as powerful as empirical observation.

THE MONSTERS AND 'THE EAST'

While many cultures in the Middle Ages believed that there were monsters of various sorts living in the forests and fens just outside of their towns, medieval texts tend to focus their attention on a semi-mythical region referred to as 'the East'. In the Middle Ages, particularly in the early portion of the period, concepts of the East did not extend into East Asia, but rather, encompassed the so-called Near East. Although geographically closer to England, this territory was distant enough to ensure that few European travellers would visit it. This distance thus provided a certain measure of safety for the readers of such texts. An uncrossable distance protected the reader or viewer from direct contact with the monstrous, and protected accounts of the monstrous from debunking by first-hand observation. Although the location of the wonders was not likely chosen to disallow empirical verification, their remoteness did serve to assist in the persistence of these accounts.

However, the wonders were not as tied to their locations as their geographically focused texts might lead us to believe. As the so-called Age of Exploration began, and European contact with the Near East and North Africa became more routine, the wonders moved. Accounts returned to Europe from the first expeditions to the Americas, claiming that this land was peopled with the very same beings once claimed to exist in the exotic East.[9] Christopher Columbus reported, for example, that the island of Bohio was said to be inhabited by people with 'but one eye and the face of a dog'.[10]

The mobility of the wonders (and the free blending thereof, such as the fusion of the Cyclops and the Cynocephalus in Columbus's account) tells us a great deal about

---

[9] MacKie (1891: 173).   [10] de las Casas and Columbus (1989: 74).

their function. Their importance often lies not in their specific location, but rather, in their position at the very edge of our knowledge. Less vital than that they were said to be found in 'the East' was their location on the periphery, beyond the pale, at the edge of the world. When this edge shifted westward in the fifteenth century, the wonders shifted with it.

Sources: Biblical Monsters

Biblical Giants

In the Middle Ages, the Bible was taken to be literally accurate in its details. Jerusalem, for example, is identified as being in the centre of the world, and so it was literally believed to be, as represented on many medieval maps of the world.[11] This biblical worldview is essential to an understanding of monsters in medieval culture. Unlike in most modern readings, the Bible in medieval readings is brimming with monsters, and thereby lent the most powerful authority to medieval beliefs about such beings.

Perhaps the most common of biblical monsters are giants, the most famous of which is Goliath.[12] However, in addition to the Philistine champion, we find a host of antediluvian giants, appearing as early as Genesis 6: 4: 'There were giants on the earth in those days'. In addition, we read of races of giants, such as the Anakim:

And they have slandered the land they had examined, saying to the sons of the house of Israel, 'The land which we have inspected devours its inhabitants. Its people, whom we have seen, are of great stature. There we have seen certain monsters who are the sons of Anak, of the race of Giants, by whom we were seen as if we were locusts'.[13]

There are also other named giants, such as Og, King of Bashan, who 'remained from the stock of the giants. Has it not been seen that his bed is of iron, which is in Rabbath, of the sons of Ammon? It is nine cubits long and four wide by the measure of a human cubit'.[14]

---

[11] Vulgate, Psalm 73 and Ezek. 5: 5: 'This the Lord God said: I have placed Jerusalem in the middle of the peoples, and around her the lands'.

[12] For a selection of giants from the Jewish Bible, see the following Vulgate passages: Gen. 6: 4; Num. 13: 33; Deut. 2: 11, 2: 20, 3: 11, 3: 13; Josh. 12: 4, 13: 12, 15: 8, 17: 17, 18: 16; 2 Sam. 21: 16, 18, 20, 22; 1 Chron. 20: 4, 6, 8.

[13] Vulgate, Num. 13: 33–4: 'Detraxeruntque terrae quam inspexerant apud filios Israhel dicentes terram quam lustravimus devorat habitatores suos populum quem aspeximus procerae staturae est. Ibi vidimus monstra quaedam filiorum Enach de genere giganteo quibus conparati quasi lucustae videbamur'.

[14] Deut. 3: 11: 'Solus quippe Og rex Basan restiterat de stirpe gigantum monstratur lectus eius ferreus qui est in Rabbath filiorum Ammon novem cubitos habens longitudinis et quattuor latitudinis ad mensuram cubiti virilis manus'.

Modern readers might be tempted to read these passages as either metaphorical or, if literal, as if referring to humans of moderately large stature, though based on the size of his bed, Og would easily be somewhere around twelve feet tall. St Augustine, bishop of Hippo, one of the leading authorities of the Middle Ages, confirmed the veracity of these accounts, noting in *The City of God*:

Following the canonical scripture, Jewish and Christian, there is no doubt many giants existed before the flood, and were citizens of the earthly society of men, while the sons of God, who are descended from the flesh of Seth, having deserted righteousness, declined into this society. Nor is it to be marvelled at, that those [descended] from the same were able to be born giants.[15]

Augustine lent the authority of personal experience to this scriptural argument, describing not only a giant Goth he had heard was recently living in Rome, but also a relic of a giant:

I have seen, myself, not alone, but with several others with me, on the beach at Utica, the molar tooth of a man, so huge that, if it were cut up into small pieces, it could be seen to be able to make one hundred of our standard teeth. Indeed, I would believe it to have been from a giant, for, the giants of old exceeded by far the bodies of all the others back when others were bigger than we are.[16]

In these three instances, one of the foremost authorities of the Middle Ages verified the existence of ante- and, most importantly, *post*-diluvian giants through scriptural commentary, second-hand, and first-hand accounts. We can also note that at least 'the giants of old' were not moderately larger than ordinary humans, but a hundred times their size.

Contemporary giants come, owing to their outlandish size, to frequently stand for excess in all its forms. Their unnatural size—which was according to Augustine owing to their 'having deserted righteousness'—came to be associated with sinful behaviour. As will be common for medieval monsters, a flawed or deviant body was assumed to be the result of a flawed or deviant mind and soul. Indeed, Gerald of Wales, writing around 1200, informs his readers that Ireland contained 'so many born blind, so many lame, so many with imperfect bodies, deprived of the beneficence of nature' because the Irish are 'an adulterous race, an incestuous

---

[15] Augustine (1981: 15. 23, p. 112): 'Igitur secundum scripturas canonicas Hebraeas atque Christianas multos gigantes ante diluvium fuisse non dubium est, et hos fuisse cives terrigenae societatis hominum; Dei autem filios, qui secundum carnem de Seth propagati sunt, in hanc societatem deserta iustitia declinasse. Nec miranda est, quod etiam de ipsis gigantes nasci potuerunt. Neque enim omnes gigantes, sed magis multi utque tunc fuerunt, quam post diluvium temporibus ceteris'.

[16] Augustine (1981: 15. 23, p. 109, and 15. 9, p. 75. Stephens (1989: 91) explains Augustine's reference to times when men were larger: 'Since Homer and Pliny had both maintained that human stature is steadily declining, it did not require much imagination to see that the Giants of old stood in the same statistical relation to their contemporaries as modern physical deviants'. He refers to Pliny's *Natural History* 7. 73–4 and Homer's *Illiad* 7. 155 and 7. 211.

race, a race of illegitimate birth and conception, a race outside of the law, foully ravishing nature herself with hateful and hostile craft'.[17] In this case, genuine human beings living with what modern sensibilities would define as medical conditions, are blamed and condemned based on the assumption that outer difference matches inner deformity, a notion that bears ramifications for all of the monstrous beings discussed here.

Other Biblical Monsters

In addition to the Bible's giants, we also find a number of references to dragons, basilisks, unicorns, Behemoth, Leviathan and, of course, the Beasts of the Apocalypse.[18] There was and is considerable debate over the meaning of many of these passages, and of the nature of the creatures they describe, but their very profusion makes an implicit argument about the nature of God's world: it is, at least in part, monstrous. That such creatures were not only present in the Middle Ages (considered to be long after humanity's golden age in the distant past), but also in the days of the prophets, indicated that they were, in fact, part of God's divine plan.

Some of the most well-respected exegetes and scholars of the Middle Ages treated this notion. The two most widely cited are Augustine and Isidore, bishop of Seville. Both verified at least the possibility of the reality of monsters, though they came to different conclusions about their origins and functions. Augustine traced the Latin *monstra*, 'monster', to *monstrare*, 'to show' declaring that monsters were a de*monstration* of God's powers. Isidore also traced it to *monere*, 'to warn', suggesting that they were a warning from God against deviation from righteousness.[19] While there are differences between these accounts, as Lisa Verner writes, for both Augustine and Isidore monsters served the overarching purpose of allowing 'the contemplation of the glorious superabundance of God's creation, in a word, wonder. Blemmyeas and Pygmies and all the other monstrous races signify His power, wisdom and presence in all of creation'.[20] In the medieval worldview, therefore, while monsters and other marvels were exotic, nonetheless they were natural parts of creation.

---

[17] Gerald of Wales (1867: 181).

[18] For a selection of dragons from the Jewish Bible, see the following Vulgate passages: Deut. 32: 33; Neh. 2: 13; Job 30: 29; Psalms 44: 19, 74: 13, 91: 13, 148: 7; Isa. 13: 22, 27: 1, 34: 13, 35: 7, 43: 20, 51: 9; Jer. 9: 11, 10: 22, 14: 6, 49: 33, 51: 34 and 37; Ezek. 29: 3; Mic. 1: 8; Mal. 1: 3. Nigg (1999: 97–101) provides references to all of the biblical passages mentioning these monsters.

[19] These passages are widely cited. See e.g. Cohen (1999: p. xiv); Verner (2005: 2–5).

[20] Verner (2005: 36).

SOURCES

···

Classical Monsters

The presence of so many monsters in the Bible, a text considered to be the word of God, lent veracity to accounts of such creatures found in other texts. Most notable among these were a series of classical texts containing accounts of the wondrous sites, plants, animals, and peoples of India and Ethiopia—two regions often viewed as somewhat analogous in classical and medieval sources and grouped together more generally as 'the East'. These works would eventually serve at the models for one of the most noteworthy monster-compilations of the Middle Ages, the *Wonders* or *Marvels of the East*, discussed below. Each of the classical texts draws heavily on the preceding work, with authors excising and embellishing freely. The earliest of the surviving passages are found in Herodotus' *History* of the fifth century BCE.[21] Herodotus was influential on two works which would, in turn, impact many others, Ktesias' 'Ινδιχά of c.400 BCE, which caused India to be 'stamped as the land of marvels' and a now-fragmentary treatise by Megasthenes of c.300 BCE which survives in the works of Strabo, Aelian, and Pliny, among others.[22]

This body of classical knowledge would be transmitted to the patristic period largely though Pliny's *Natural History*, completed in 77 CE, and Solinus' *Collectanea rerum memorabilium*, c.200, and then onward into the Middle Ages by Isidore's encyclopedic *Etymologies*, c.620. These works vary in their style and approach to monsters, but share common features. Most present the monsters and other marvels in the form of a list, in which each entry provides the same stock information: name, location, size, brief physical description and, for some, behaviour. For example, we read in book 7 of Pliny's *Natural History*:

At the extreme boundary of India to the East near the source of the Ganges, [Megasthenes] puts the Astomi tribe, that has no mouth and a body hairy all over; they dress in cottonwool and live only on the air they breathe and the scent they inhale through their nostrils; they have no food or drink except the different odours of the roots and flowers and wild apples, which they carry with them on their longer journeys so as not to lack a supply of scent; he says they can easily be killed by a rather stronger odour than usual.[23]

In this highly typical passage we learn the marvel's name (Astomi, from the Greek for 'Without Mouth'), their location (eastern India), their appearance (mouthless, hairy), and behaviour (sniffing food). This basic pattern is followed throughout,

---

[21] Wittkower (1942: 159). Wittkower provides the earliest serious discussion of this tradition, and includes extensive commentary on the earlier sources and their transmission into the Middle Ages. His text will be relied on here. Also invaluable to the study of the medieval monstrous is Friedman (1981).

[22] Wittkower (1942: 160–2).

[23] Pliny the Elder (1942, repr. 1969), 7. 2. 25–6: 'Ad extremos fines Indiae ab oriente circa fontem Gangis Astomorum gentem sine ore, corpore toto hirtam, vestiri frondium lanugine trahant; nullum illis cibum nullumque potum, radicum tantum florumque varios odors et silvestrium malorum, quae secum portant longiore itinere ne desit olfactus; graviore paulo odore haut difficulter exanimari'.

and repeated in most of the sources. Embedded as these passages are amidst more mundane accounts of the natural world, these beings were considered as part of the natural world.

Medieval Incarnations

The Wonders of the East

The *Wonders of the East* is among the most striking of the early medieval English works with monstrosity as a theme. The earliest copy survives in the same codex as *Beowulf*, a poem also deeply concerned with monstrosity (London, British Library, MS Cotton Vitellius A. xv, the *Beowulf* manuscript, *c.*1000). Unlike its sources, outlined above, and related texts to be covered below, the *Wonders* does not contain any narrative framework for its discussion of the monsters and marvels of 'the East'. Instead, it presents a series of texts and images, loosely connected through vague geographic references ('At the beginning of the land', 'as you go towards the Red Sea', 'between these two rivers', 'in the same place', etc.). Each discrete section informs the reader, generally in imprecise or otherwise baffling terms, of the location, appearance, and habits of the wonders. While these wonders include the oil-producing balsam tree and vines that grow enormous berries and jewels, most of the accounts focus on wondrous animals and peoples, though the line dividing these categories is most pointedly blurred by their physical composition. Many of the wonders are hybrids, consisting of the parts of disparate creatures. The Cynocephalus, for example, has a horse's mane, a boar's tusks, and a dog's head (from which it derives its name). Likewise, the Lertices are 'wild beasts' possessing donkey's ears and sheep's wool and bird's feet. While the Lertices is explicitly bestial, the Cynocephalus is more transgressive, not clearly fitting into one category or another. Indeed, in the Old English text they are called 'healfhundingas' or 'half-hounds', emphasizing their equally divided nature.

Other wonders, though, are not cobbled together from the parts of multiple known creatures. Rather, they deviate from the norm through excess or lack. The Blemmyes, for example, are men without heads, but with their eyes and mouth on their chests. Similarly, the Sciopod (not found in the earliest *Wonders* manuscript, but common in subsequent versions and related texts) has only one foot. On the other hand, the Homodubii are fifteen feet tall and have two faces on one head, and the Panoti have ears so large that they use them to cover themselves at night. In all of these cases, the wonders are not hybrid beings, but rather, are composed exclusively of human parts, though they deviate from normative standards in their arrangements thereof.

Finally, there are human wonders whose mark of difference is not bodily, at all, but rather, a matter of behavior, such as the 'generous men' who give women to passing travellers and the people who live on raw meat and honey. These people are, according to the accounts, no different, except in these matters of diet and custom, from 'normal' people (in this case, the English readers). As a result, this final category underscores the destabilizing notion that these wonders are possible versions of the viewers and readers of the text. Both the hybrid monsters and the human composites are wonders because they displace, conflate, and strangely juxtapose categories of species, anatomy, and culture; but their very strangeness is comprehensible because they are constructed from familiar elements. We recognize the bird's feet, the ass's hindquarters, the man's features, even if we do not expect these elements to be so conjoined. This familiarity in strangeness is further emphasized by wonders like the 'generous men': these wonders, even as they seem to mark off a boundary of the normative (the exchange of women between men in Western Europe is subject to aggressive cultural regulation), also represent the permeability of any such boundary. If the monstrous cannot be *simply* a matter of being elsewhere, or possessing a monstrous body, anyone has the potential to become one of the monsters.

Liber monstrorum

Like the *Wonders of the East* discussed above, the *Liber monstrorum* contains a series of accounts describing distant monsters.[24] The earliest of the four surviving manuscripts of the *Liber monstrorum* can be dated to the early tenth century, but like the somewhat later *Wonders*, the *Liber monstrorum* draws from a range of materials available in Pliny, Augustine, and Isidore.[25] As L. G. Whitbread has observed, twenty-one of the sections of the *Wonders*, including the descriptions of the half-hounds, the Donestre, and the giant women with ox tails, clearly overlap with materials in the *Liber*.[26] The *Liber monstrorum* differs from the *Wonders*, however, in that it contains framing devices indicating authorship and audience. The narrator introduces himself, and the materials he describes, and justifies his project:

You have asked about the hidden parts of the orb of the earth, and if so many races of monsters ought to be believed in which are shown in the hidden parts of the world, throughout the deserts and the islands of the ocean, and are sustained in the most distant mountains... and that I ought to describe the monstrous parts of humans and the most horrible wild animals and innumerable forms of beasts and the most dreadful types of dragons and serpents and vipers.[27]

---

[24] Butturff (1969).

[25] Whitbread (1974: 434–71). Whitbread acknowledges that 'the range of guesses' about the dating of the Liber 'extends from the sixth through the tenth century', but notes, 'Of the four known manuscripts, Leiden Voss. Lat. Oct. 60, in a hand of ca. 900, is the earliest; the others belong to the tenth century' (pp. 448–50).

[26] Ibid. 446–7.

[27] London, British Library, Royal 15. B. xix. For a transcription and translation of this text, see Orchard (1995: 255–317).

The author casts doubt on some of the accounts, claiming to organize book 1 in descending order of commonness and verifiability, and later writing 'if it were possible to fly with wings, exploring, one might prove [these tales] to be seen as fictions, despite so much talk'.[28] This measure of scepticism is not found in the frameless *Wonders* text.

The *Liber monstrorum* also presents more directly the concept that an 'ordinary' person might become 'monstrous' through actions. The first of the common and verifiable human monsters it describes, for example, is a person who looks like a man from the waist up, but 'loves feminine occupations'. The narrator concludes, 'but this has happened often among men'. By introducing this catalogue of monsters with a figure the narrator himself considers not monstrously strange, but proximate and familiar, the *Liber monstrorum*, like the *Wonders*, reminds us that the very categories by which we read these text and the worlds we inhabit—male/female, self/other—are blurred and crossed even as we employ them.

Beowulf

The *Liber monstrorum* intersects not only with the *Wonders of the East*, but also with perhaps the most famous of early English poems, *Beowulf*. In the *Liber* appears a King Higlacus, ruler of the Getae. Although this king is a sort of giant, a man so big that no horse can carry him, he is also perhaps recognizable as the Hygelac of the Geats, of the epic poem, uncle to the great hero Beowulf.[29]

Beowulf is in obvious ways concerned with monsters and the exotic: in the poem, the hero fights first Grendel then Grendel's mother, two ambiguously human monsters, and then a dragon. Less obviously, perhaps, Beowulf also presents the inextricability of the monstrous from human life. Grendel, the first of the monsters, is described in terms strikingly equivalent to those which describe Beowulf: Grendel kills thirty men in a single stroke; Beowulf has the strength of thirty men in his handgrip; both Beowulf and Grendel are larger than other men; Grendel has no known father; Beowulf is anomalous among Germanic heroes in the fact that his name does not alliterate with his father's. As several critics have noted, in Beowulf's physical fight with Grendel, the bodies of hero and monster, joined by their handgrips, become indistinguishable to the readers: during the climactic struggle, the text renders it impossible to tell who is doing what to whom.[30] Similarly, when Beowulf departs to Grendel's mere to kill Grendel's mother, he travels to a place 'not far in miles' from Hrothgar's court. The possibility of litotes in that description suggests that Grendel's mere may be understood in some senses as a *version* of Hrothgar's court, at *no* literal distance from the hall.[31] Certainly, both Grendel and his mother are creatures of the *mearc*, the borderland, contiguous to but just outside the world of Heorot. Beowulf's struggle with these monsters is thus also a struggle against the ductility of those borders. Hence the final triumph of the poem, after the slaying of

28 Ibid. 256.
29 Ibid. 258–9, I. 2.
30 O'Brien O'Keeffe (1981: 484–94, esp. 487–90). Kroll (1986: 117–29, esp. 125–6).
31 Orchard (1995: 258–9); Kim (2005: 4–27).

the dragon, is the posthumous erection of the tomb of Beowulf at the headland, the border, a final stand in which Beowulf, as hero, marks off, and reinforces with his body, a difference from the monstrous which the poem itself has demonstrated to be an impossibility.

The monsters of *Beowulf* explicitly evoke those of the Old Testament: Grendel occupies the 'fifelcynnes geard', 'the place of the race of giants', who are the 'kin of Cain', a place from which 'all the evil brood arose, giants and elves, and monsters, and likewise giants, who fought against God'.[32] Yet as many critics have argued, these monsters also link *Beowulf* to the body of Norse literature and mythology, a link which is unsurprising, given the shared Germanic linguistic and cultural back-grounds, but which also emphasizes the strong pre-Christian traditions and mythol-ogies informing the poem. Andy Orchard, in his chapter, 'Grettir and Grendel Again', surveys the structural and thematic similarities between the Norse saga, *Grettis saga Asmundarsonar*, and *Beowulf*.[33] In both texts, the hero's fights against a series of monsters end with the hero both victorious against those monsters and identified with them. Orchard concludes: 'This is the shared tragedy of such essentially heathen heroes whose tales are retold in a Christian world, who must begin with proud hope and bravado, and end haunted with melancholy, defeated but not diminished.'[34]

Seth Lerer has argued that perhaps less obvious connections between *Beowulf* and Norse literature may bespeak equally powerful commonalities. In 'Grendel's Glove', Lerer reminds us that Beowulf's reference—in his own account of his fight—to the magical dragon-skin glove is an innovation in the story: we have no mention of the glove at any point in the narrator's description of the action. This innovation alludes at once to Norse mythological material, presented in Snorri Sturluson's *Gylfaginning*, in which Thor and Loki themselves become lost in the giant Skrýmir's glove, and to the function of narratives of monstrosity and dismemberment in both *Beowulf* and Norse mytholo-gy.[35] Lerer suggests that, '[m]ore than a relic of a Northern legend, and more than a piece of narrative exotica, Grendel's glove comes to symbolize the very meaning of the monster and the very resources of literary making that articulate that meaning'.[36] For

---

[32] *Beowulf*, ll 104b–107a: 'fīfelcynnes eard / wonsǣlī wer weardode hwīle, / siþðan him Scyppend foscrifen hæfde / in Cāines cynne...' (the place of the kin of giants, the unhappy man occupied for a while, / after the Creator had condemned him in the kin of Cain). Continued at 111–114a: 'Þanon untȳdras ealle onwōcon, / eotenas ond ylfe ond orcnēas, / swylce gīgantas, Þā wið Gode wunnon / lange prāge' (from there an evil brood was born, giants and elves and monsters, likewise giants, who fought against God for a long time). Unless otherwise indicated, we have used Klaeber's edn (Fulk et al. 2008) and our own translation. See also Klaeber (1950). We have translated both 'eotenas' and the Latin borrowing 'gigantes' as 'giants', though 'eotenas' has a broader semantic range, suggesting monsters not only of great size but perhaps also, as Heather Blurton has recently argued, monsters of consumption—cannibals. See Blurton (2007: esp. ch. 2). For representative readings of *Beowulf* in this context, see Williams (1982); Kaske (1971); and, more recently, Orchard (1995).

[33] Orchard (1995: 140–68). Fjalldal (1998) argues strongly against any except the most distant of genetic relationships between the two texts. His arguments need not devalue the significance of the allusion in *Beowulf* to traditions like those represented in *Grettis saga* which position the poem clearly in a period of equivalence and transition between Germanic and Christian traditions.

[34] Orchard (1995: 168).

[35] Lerer (1994: 721–51).   [36] Ibid. 722.

Leher, thus, in Beowulf's retelling of his adventures with Grendel, the emphasis on the glove, by linking the story to the Norse material, at once evokes the violence of the threat which Grendel poses to Hrothgar's hall, and to Beowulf's own body, and makes explicit reference to the process of the story-telling, and thus of the means by which humans transform the horror of real violence through the power of culture, or artifice, into the reassuring performance of a narrative.

Alexander

Such self-consciousness in literary performance as Lerer argues for in *Beowulf* is the premise of the fictional *Letter of Alexander to Aristotle* with which *Beowulf*, as well as the *Wonders of the East*, is bound, in Cotton Vitellius A. xv. The *Letter of Alexander to Aristotle* takes the form of a fictional letter written by Alexander the Great to his teacher, Aristotle, detailing Alexander's journeys through the East, a penetrative exploration, in Alexander's terms, 'lest anything in that land was hidden or concealed from me'.[37] Its narrative is given in the first person, and the encounters with the monstrous and exotic (many of the figures of which—jeweled vines, pestilential serpents, water monsters—are familiar from the *Liber Monstrorum* and the *Wonders*) are represented directly as phenomena encountered or witnessed by the narrator, and crafted by the narrator for reading by his intended audience, his teacher, Aristotle. Alexander's description of the exotic East thus becomes inextricable from his epistolary self-presentation. It is for this reason that Orchard, for example, reads Alexander, through this self-presentation of his conquest of the East, as 'a monstrous figure of pride'.[38] The context of *Beowulf* and the *Wonders of the East*, as well as the *Liber Monstrorum*, suggests that whatever moral condemnation might accompany the figure of Alexander, the *Letter* picks up a consistent thread in the early literature of the monstrous: the troublesome relationship between the representation of the self *through* movement through or conquest of monstrous and exotic worlds, but at the same time the recognition of the threat that the monstrous or exotic worlds pose to any self thus represented. If in *Beowulf* we can read the hero's transformation of the horror of violence into a socially affirming narrative, in the *Letter of Alexander*, which ends with the promise of Alexander's death in Babylon, the heroic narrator closes his text with the promise that he himself, for all his glory, will be absorbed by the East against which he has battled.

---

[37] Orchard (1995) provides an edn. and tr. of the Letter, pp. 224–53. This passage occurs in Orchard's s. 26: 'On ic þa ða wynstran dælas Indie wolde geondferan þy læs me owiht in þæm londe beholen oððe bedegled wære' (And I then wished to travel through the left-hand parts of India, lest anything in that land was hidden or concealed from me). Unless otherwise indicated, we will use Orchard's edn. and our own translation.

[38] Ibid. 139.

Monstrous Saints

Given that the monstrous embodies the 'other', it is to be expected that many of the lives of the saints depict the saint in conflict with, and victorious over, a monstrous figure. St Margaret, for example, battles a dragon in her prison cell, bursting him from within by making the sign of the cross in his belly. St George, in later legends, famously battles a similar dragon. As we have been arguing, secular literature of the monstrous often dwells on the problem that the figure which opposes the monstrous again and again becomes identified with it. As Friedrich Nietzsche writes in *Beyond Good and Evil*, 'Whoever fights with monsters should see to it that he does not become one himself'.[39] While one might read Margaret, swallowed into the belly of the dragon, literally incorporated within it, as in that moment congruent with the monstrous, we need not work so hard: in the figure of another saint, Christopher, we find the explicit embodiment at once of the figure of the saint and the representation of the monstrous. The St Christopher of the later Middle Ages was a giant, and the saint known to the Anglo-Saxons was, even more dramatically, a giant with the head of a dog. The literal monstrosity of St Christopher emphasizes the resonance between the literature of the monstrous and the lives of the saints: the saints, like the monsters, have extraordinary bodies, and extraordinary relationships to those bodies. The saint, as s/he bridges heaven and earth for man, at once body, material, human, and spirit, an extension of the divine, also like the monster, is in a sense both a hybrid creature and, as such, a kind of border-dweller. If, as in the case of Margaret or George, the saint evidences sanctity in the possession of miraculous power against a fabulous beast like the dragon, at the same time, the positioning of the saint beside or within the body of the beast reminds us of the similarity the saint bears to that creature.

The Exotic and the Matter of Britain

The Arthurian literature which in many ways has come to represent all of medieval literature in the contemporary imaginary comes late into English. There are no Anglo-Saxon stories of Arthur and his knights, despite the fact that, if any historical Arthur existed, he would have lived at the very beginning of the Anglo-Saxon period. Arthuriana enters into English literature only after the Conquest, as part of a reinvention of the idea of England, with roots in the Classical past, continuity through Celtic Britain, and re-emergence, after the Anglo-Saxon period, in Norman England.[40] The twelfth-century Geoffrey of Monmouth, one of the earliest chroniclers of the history of the Britons, writes that 'Britain is inhabited by five races of people, the Norman-French, the Britons, the Saxons, and the Picts and Scots. Of these the Britons once occupied the land from sea to sea, before the others came.'[41] Geoffrey's historical project is thus to present the history of the Britons, retrieving it from obscurity and Welsh sources, and granting force to the Norman appropriation of that history as its own.

---

[39] Nietzsche (2002: 69).
[40] Cohen (2006: 65–9).   [41] Geoffrey of Monmouth (1966: 54).

It is in Geoffrey's Latin *History of the Kings of Britain* that we encounter some of the earliest depictions of Arthur and Merlin, and hence of the monsters against whom Arthur fights, and the dragons and other fabulous beasts of Merlin's prophecies. Among the giants whom Arthur fights, perhaps most memorable are the monster of Mont-Saint-Michel and, because his narrative is embedded in that of the monster of Mont-Saint-Michel, the giant Retho. The giant Retho, who collects men's beards and wears a cloak sewn from them, taunts Arthur with a request that the king send his own beard for the collection. Arthur predictably responds with violence, kills the giant, and takes the giant's beard as well as his cloak as a trophy. Retho's strength, according to Arthur, is nearly equaled by that of the man-eating rapist monster of Mont-Saint-Michel, whose club blows resound from sea to sea, but whom Arthur brains and then orders beheaded. Yet for all that, Geoffrey's Arthur, fighting Romans and monsters and thereby making the world safe for the Britons, embodies the prehistory of England; Geoffrey does not include the now-famous references to Arthur's return after his death. Instead, Arthur, for Geoffrey, is 'mortally wounded' and taken to have his wounds treated, and then vanishes from the history.[42]

Of course, Arthuriana remains, in the Lais of Marie of France, in romances like Heldris of Cornwall's *Silence*, and, later in English, in *Gawain and the Green Knight*, and Chaucerian texts like the Wife of Bath's Tale. And, even in these later texts, Arthur's court, while it epitomizes chivalry and civilization, continues to be associated with marvels, monsters, and the very exotic against which it defends itself. In *Gawain and the Green Knight*, for example, the green giant who challenges Arthur to the beheading game appears in the midst of the young Arthur's court, summoned as if part of the courtly feasting ritual.

Gerald of Wales

Gerald of Wales likewise dwells on the exotic nature of the British Isles, though his perspective differs from that of the other authors discussed here, and so his interpretations likewise vary. His most remarkable work is the *Topographia Hibernica* (*Topography of Ireland*), composed, expanded and edited from around 1185 until the end of his life some forty years later.[43] The text is primarily historical and geographical in nature, but woven all throughout its accounts of natural features and rulers are miracle stories and marvels, ranging from oxmen, bearded ladies, and werewolves, to speaking crosses and eternally burning hedges. Perhaps owing to its exotic tales, the *Topography* was quite popular, and survives in dozens of manuscripts. Several of these are richly illuminated with a series of direct illustrations of the text that may have been designed by Gerald himself.[44]

---

[42] Ibid. 261.   [43] Bartlett (1982: 145).

[44] These MSS include: London, British Library, Royal MS 13 B.VIII; Dublin, National Library, MS 700; Oxford, Bodleian Library, Laud. Misc. 720; and Cambridge, University Library, Ff. 1. 27 (hereafter Royal, Dublin, Bodleian, and Cambridge). These are all 13th-cent. MSS, and their production is generally believed to have been interconnected. See Brown (2002: 34–59, Morgan (1982: number 59 a–b), Morgan (1988: number 11b). Knight (2001: 60) argues against Gerald's participation.

While much Arthuriana places the emphasis on the monstrosity of Britain, formerly the land of giants, Gerald pushes that monstrosity further outward from the normative centre of the world. In moving outward from the perfection of Jerusalem, one risked increasing dangers and horrors, as shown on many medieval world maps, such as the thirteenth-century Hereford Map (London, British Library Add. 28681, folio 9ʳ, figures 4 and 6).[45] Here, along the left (or southern) edge of the world, we find a host of marvels and monsters, each carefully bound by a tight-fitting frame. Lest we assume such monstrosity to be a southern characteristic, the map balances out this concentration with the prominent depiction to the north of the wall enclosing the monstrous hordes of Gog and Magog.

On this map, and many others, England appears at the edge of the *ecumene*, the inhabitable world.[46] This border region is the land of monsters, but also for many English writers and artists, it is home. Gerald, though, was not English, at least by medieval standards. He was the son of a Welshman, William de Barri, and a Norman, Angharad (daughter of a mistress of Henry I). As a result, he was an outsider to the power structure of England, but also to Wales. As he wrote, 'Each people considers me to be a stranger to them and not one of their own, always looking at me with eye of a stepmother, the one harboring suspicion against me and the other hating me.'[47] Perhaps as a consequence of his hybrid identity, and the resultant prejudice he experienced, Gerald turned his fertile imagination to the only land more marginal than England: Ireland. Here, his attention is focused on its exoticism, expressed through physical, religious, cultural, and dietary oddities.

Gerald's descriptions of the wonders he claims to have observed in Ireland are varied not only in the nature of their exoticism, but also in his attitude toward them. The population of Ireland, he tells us, includes 'so many born blind, so many lame, so many with imperfect bodies, deprived of the beneficence of nature'.[48] In this case, Gerald concludes that the Irish are deformed because they are 'an adulterous race, an incestuous race, a race of illegitimate birth and conception, a race outside of the law, foully ravishing nature herself with hateful and hostile craft'.[49] This outlook, in which individuals are blamed for their condition, was characteristic of the Middle Ages. On the other hand, Gerald shows surprising sympathy for the Oxman, who:

[45] This popular map has been discussed in most publications on medieval cartography, including Harvey (1991: 30); Mittman (2006: 12–58).

[46] Campbell (1988: 65); Lavezzo (1999: 11).

[47] Gerald of Wales (1868: p. lviii): 'Ut uterque populus me sibi tanquam alienum reputans et non suum semper oculo respexerit novercali, alter ob hæc suspectum habens et alter exosum'.

[48] Gerald of Wales (1867: 181): 'tot caecos natos, tot claudos, tot corpore vitiatos, et naturae beneficio destitutos'.

[49] Ibid.: 'Nec mirandum si de gente adultera, gente inceta, gente illegitime nata et copulata, gente exlage, arte invida et invisa ipsem turpiter adulterante naturam, tales interdum contra naturae legem natura producat'.

had the complete body of a human, except for the extremities, which were those of an ox. From the joint where the hand meets the arm, and where the feet meet the legs, extending out, he exhibited the hooves of an ox. His head was completely without hair, deformed by baldness, more so in the back of the head than in the front part. Here and there in places, he merely had soft down instead of hair. He had swollen eyes, which were round, and like an ox's in roundness and colour. His face down to his mouth was flat; for a nose, instead of nostrils he had two holes, but no projection.[50]

This emotive and sensitive description, which evokes images of human deformity as much or more than the monsters of fantasy, is accompanied in several manuscripts by images equally poignant.[51] The episode concludes grimly: the Oxman was killed by a group of youths living in the Norman castle of none other than Gerald's own relatives, the fitzGeralds. Gerald tells us that 'he did not deserve their wickedness and envy'.[52]

For Gerald, Ireland is a land of deeply conflicted emotions. Its position further from the centre of the world allowed him to describe it as a land of even greater monstrosity than England, and thereby to render England as more central and normative than is common in previous works. On the other hand, perhaps resulting from his own status as a 'self-conscious hybrid', Gerald seems to feel an uncommon sympathy with these monsters.[53] Through his *Topography*, then, Gerald's outsider view moves England closer to the world's center, while he simultaneously identifies with the marginal.

Sir Gowther and Bisclavret

While Gerald's sometimes sensitive depictions bespeak self-consciousness and identification not only against, but also with the monstrous, increasingly, depictions of the monstrous and exotic in later medieval literature explore the intimacy of the monstrous with the human, the exotic with the emergency of proto-national identity. Marie de France's *Bisclavret*, and the later anonymous *Sir Gowther* both explore notions of monstrosity as it appears in the very centre of court life. In *Bisclavret*, a werewolf, trapped by his wife's deception in his wolf body, after a marvellous performance of courtly obeisance, lives submissively at the court of the king. In *Sir Gowther*, the monstrous giant, in an act of penance, lives like a dog under the table of the emperor, eating only food from the mouths of hounds and forsaking speech. In

---

[50] Ibid. 108: 'Habebat enim totum corpus humanum praeter extremitates, quae bovinae fuerant. A juncturis namque quibus et manus a brachiis, et pedes a tibiis porriguntur, ungulas bovis expessas praeferebat. Caput ei sine crine totum, tam in occipite, quam anteriori parte, calvitio deforme; raras tantum lanugines per loca pro capillis habens. Oculi grossi; tam rotunditate quam colore bovine. Facies oretenus subinde plana; pro naso, praeter duo narium foramina, nullam eminentiam habens'.

[51] For a reproduction, see Mittman (2003: 100).

[52] Gerald of Wales (1867: 108). O'Meara (1982: 11) notes that Gerald was a cousin to the fitzGeralds, who were the children of his grandmother, Nest, mistress of Henry I. See also Mittman (2003); Cohen (2006: ch. 3).

[53] Bynum (2001: 151).

both texts, as Jeffrey Jerome Cohen has argued, the central figures, Bisclavret and Gowther, pass through the monstrous as household intimates: for Bisclavret, 'learning to be a proper dog (that is, by submitting with an absolute love to his allotted place within the masculine hierarchy)' enables the hybrid to emerge as 'a proper man'; for Gowther, similarly, life as if a dog becomes 'training', in Cohen's term, in the 'functional symbolic of the court'.[54] In both texts, then, the monstrosity of the central figures becomes less timelessly aberrant, external, or abject than *developmental*, a phase in the development of courtly masculinity rather than a clearly defined and externalized other against which that masculinity defends itself.

Sir Gawain and the Green Knight

The much anthologized late-fourteenth-century *Sir Gawain and the Green Knight* demonstrates continuity both with Geoffrey's association of Arthuriana and its monsters with narratives of proto-national identity and with the significant shift in the literary representation of monstrosity articulated in *Bisclavret* and *Sir Gowther*. *Gawain and the Green Knight* focuses on the adventures of one of the knights of the Round Table in the youth of Arthur's court, but it begins not with the court itself, but with the founding of Britain by Brutus. The subsequent confrontation between Gawain and the green giant thus emerges in the immediate context of foundational myth. The association of the confrontation with the giant with both the narrative of proto-national origin and the representation of the monstrous with developing masculinity becomes all the more striking given the insistent description of Arthur and his court as 'young', 'boyish', 'in the flower of life'.[55] The giant appears most literally in answer to Arthur's demand for a marvel before his supper. That is, it is the young Arthur who seems to summon the giant's presence. But it is the giant, with his full beard and aggressively adult male body, who issues the challenge to the identity of Arthur—'Where is the noblest of all of this crowd?'[56]—and who seems to control the subsequent events. As Jeffrey Jerome Cohen argues, '[t]he Green Knight plays the role of the traditional giant of romance, that catalyst to the formation of an adult identity, but with some important modification to that monstrous body'.[57] For Cohen, the Green Knight, the giant in this romance, has moved significantly from the realms of the exterior, the wilderness, the conquerable 'other' to the interior, the domestic spaces of court life.[58] Hence, the challenge to the beheading game, in which the Green Knight vows to stand still for a single blow with an axe from one of Arthur's knights, in exchange for the opportunity to return the blow in a year's time, is issued *within* the court, and Gawain's trials a year later, on the way to receive the

---

[54] Cohen (1999: 129).   [55] O'Donoghue (2006), ll. 59–89.
[56] Ibid., ll. 224–5.   [57] Cohen (1999: 144).
[58] Ibid. 146–7: 'Unlike the romances that *Sir Gawain and the Green Knight* cites in the development of its narrative, the locus of mastery will not be the vast, psychological landscape of the wilderness, where the giant seems to represent everything exterior to the law, but will be postponed instead for the familiar, domestic spaces of the court, where the giant is revealed as abiding at that law's secret interior'.

'nick' on his own neck occur in oppressively internal space—not only inside Berci-lak's castle, but in a curtained bed, in an inner chamber of that castle.

The contracts in this romance appear to be between men, or between men and monsters: between the Green Knight, Arthur, and Gawain, between Bercilak and Gawain. Yet in the central episodes of the romance, the contract, that Gawain and Bercilak will exchange what they gain during the day, Gawain lying in Bercilak's home, in bed, and Bercilak out hunting, replaces a direct and physical confrontation between man and giant (like the exchange of axe blows) with prolonged testing, over three days, of a man by a courtly lady, in this case Bercilak's wife.[59] While Bercilak hunts for animals, that is, Bercilak's wife entices Gawain to respond to her sexualized advances with at least a kiss, and finally by accepting a token, a green silk girdle, both a love token and a magical defence against the impending axe blow. When Bercilak returns from the hunt each day, he gives Gawain his catch; Gawain, in exchange, kisses Bercilak as many times as the lady has kissed him. The poem brilliantly emphasizes the substitution of the lady for the giant by framing the seduction scenes with graphically violent depictions of hunting and butchery, scenes which both echo and amplify the violence of the decapitation of the Green Knight. Not surprisingly, when Gawain goes finally to receive the axe blow from the Green Knight, he discovers that Morgana, not the Green Knight himself, has set the plot in motion, and that the threat is directed not against Arthur so much as against Guenevere, whom Morgan wished to terrify. What Cohen has recognized as 'important modification to [the] monstrous body' of the figure of the giant we might also consider as articulated here in the possibility of the substitution of the *courtly lady* for that monstrous body, or at the least the supplementation of the courtly lady to the monstrous body of the giant.[60]

As E. Jane Burns has argued, the courtly lady in medieval literature, increasingly recognizable by her costly silk clothing, signifies at once male aristocratic dominance, and an alterity, or hybridization, at the very focal point of that dominance.[61] As Burns argues, given that high-quality silk is not produced in Europe until the end of the Middle Ages, the ostentatious cloaking of aristocratic bodies and spaces in silk in courtly literature marks those spaces and bodies with the evidence of European conquest of the East, from which all high-quality silk is imported. But at the same time, by bringing the exoticized East, in textiles still identified with places like Constantinople, or Damascus, into the very centre of European aristocratic domestic space, and in particular, by marking the body of the courtly lady by her clothing of 'Saracen silk', this literature creates at its centre a figure both European and Eastern, both normative and exotic, both intimate and strange.[62] In *Gawain and the Green Knight*, as the green silk girdle passes from the lady's body to Gawain's, and, as we

---

[59] For a compelling reading of the erotics and homoerotics of *Sir Gawain and the Green Knight*, see Dinshaw (1997).

[60] Cohen (1999: 144).

[61] This discussion draws deeply on Burns (2002: ch. 6).

[62] Cohen (1999: pp. xi–xii), examines this figure of the 'intimate stranger' as precisely the figure of the giant.

later learn, has passed already from Bercilak's to the lady's, the dangerous ductility of this association of the aristocratic body with its silken clothing becomes all the more transparent: if the body marked by this clothing is at once normative and exotic, it is also at once possibly male and female. As *Gawain and the Green Knight* plays with homosocial desires, kissing games, and the underlying violence between men, this late romance also draws the figure of the monster all the more inextricably into its innermost spaces, representing alterity, and with it not tacit but controlling power, at the pivotal point in male aristocratic European culture, in the figure of the courtly lady.

Alexander and 'The Book of Sir John Mandeville'

Medieval interest in the figure of Alexander, evident in the early *Letter of Alexander to Aristotle*, continues after the Conquest. As Gerrit H. V. Brunt notes, as early as 1170 the Anglo-Norman poem, *Le roman de toute chevalerie*, written by Thomas of Kent, details the life of Alexander, incorporating materials from the continental Alexander romance as well as familiar source materials such as Solinus' *Collectanea rerum memorabilium* and the Latin version of the *Letter of Alexander to Aristotle*.[63] *Le roman de toute chevalerie* in turn becomes a significant source for the fourteenth-century Middle English *King Alisaunder*.[64] The Alexander material is preserved, and proliferates, moreover, not only in romances like *King Alisaunder* or the *Prose Life of Alexander*, but also in historical treatments like Vincent of Beauvais' *Speculum Historiale*, one of the sources for *The Book of Sir John Mandeville*.[65] As Brunt notes, by the later Middle Ages the figure of Alexander is so widely recognizable that Chaucer's Monk introduces him as 'so commune/That every wight that hath discrecioun/Hath herd somewhat or al of his fortune' ('so well known that every man who has judgement has heard something or all of his fortunes').[66] For Chaucer's Monk, Alexander, like Nero, Holofernes, Antioch, Julius Caesar, and Croesus, who surround him in the Monk's catalogue, is in essence a great man who falls and thus simply typifies the tragic. Yet the Monk's encapsulated Alexander also emphasizes an aspect of the Alexander narratives consistent from the earliest versions in English, and increasingly evident in later versions: Alexander, conqueror of the East, is killed not by an outsider, not even by a sword, but by poison, and by his own people. As the Monk puts it, 'O worthy, gentil Alisandre, allas,/That evere sholde fallen swich a cas!/ Empoysoned of thyn owene folk thou weere...' ('O worthy, noble Alexander, alas that such a case should ever occur! You were poisoned by your own people').[67] That is, even as, in the later romances especially, Alexander becomes not only a Western conqueror, but also, as the Monk labels him, 'of knyghthod and of fredom flour' ('the flower of knighthood and nobility'),[68] the epitome of Western European aristocratic

---

[63] Brunt (1994: 19–20).   [64] Ibid. 21.   [65] Ibid. 36.
[66] Ibid. 44; The Monk's Tale, ll. 2631–4. Quotations from Chaucer are from Benson (1987); translations are our own.
[67] Benson (1987), The Monk's Tale, ll. 2658–60.
[68] Ibid., The Monk's Tale, l. 2642.

values, Alexander remains so inextricably bound up with the territories he has
conquered that the reversal of fortune which makes his death tragic in the medieval
sense is not that he is oppressed by those he has oppressed, but rather that he is killed
by his own people: in his death Alexander, the 'flower of knighthood', is memorialized, in the East, as a *victim* of his own conquering power.

It is not surprising, then, both that the Alexander materials are substantial sources for
The Book of Sir John Mandeville and that the figure of Alexander appears in episodes of
Mandeville's re-examination of the exoticized East as a critique of Western practices and
values. *The Book of Sir John Mandeville*, written as early as the mid-fourteenth century,
becomes quickly and widely popular in Europe, appearing in vernaculars including
English, Spanish, and Dutch, and remaining an authoritative source of information on
the East for at least two centuries.[69] Although it clearly relies on sources familiar to
readers of the literature of the monstrous and the medieval exotic—the Alexander
materials, Isidore, Orosius, the Bible—*The Book of Sir John Mandeville* represents a
significant departure from most of the literature in that it presents itself as a first-person
narrative of actual observation, not by a legendary hero but by a real traveller.[70] The
identity of Sir John Mandeville, however, has not been confirmed, and especially given
the familiarity of many descriptions from extant sources, the likelihood that the
narrative reflects much actual travel is extremely low. Yet, as Suzanne Conklin Akbari
has noted, the 'extraordinary popularity'[71] of the text over several centuries, and
reception not as fiction or legend, but as a narrative with significant truth value well
into the Age of Exploration shifts the generic identity of this text: it is both literature of
the monstrous and exotic, and *travel* literature. It is perhaps then less striking that, as
Iain Macleod Higgins observes, among the many sources located and cited for *The Book
of Sir John Mandeville*, 'conspicuously absent' is the book of Marco Polo's travels, the
Divisament dou Monde.[72] Macleod suggests that *Mandeville* may function as a 'critical
response' to Polo's representations, at once extending and correcting, recontextualizing
and revising.[73]

The reception of *The Book of Sir John Mandeville* thus underscores a significant
tension between contemporary and medieval understandings of the literature of the
monstrous. Caroline Walker Bynum has demonstrated clearly that the medieval
literature of wonder is predicated on belief, or an assumption of truth: 'You can
only marvel at something that is, at least in some sense, there'.[74] One might extend
Bynum's insight to much medieval literature of the monstrous. Hence, discussions of
the monstrous races in Isidore are part of an encyclopedic description and explanation of the earth and its inhabitants, not a fictional aside, and, similarly, depictions
of these monstrous beings appear on the *mappae mundi* with claims to reality equal
to those of Adam and Eve, Noah, or the English. If one contemporary reflex is to

[69] Higgins (1997: 6): '[W]ithin about fifty years of 1356 The Book was circulating widely on both sides
of the English Channel in a total of eight languages—French, Czech, Dutch, English, German, Italian,
Spanish, and Latin—and within about fifty years more it would be available in another two: Danish and
Irish'.
[70] Ibid. 8–9.   [71] Akbari (2004: 156).   [72] Higgins (1997: 12).
[73] Ibid. 12–13.   [74] Bynum (2001: 73).

read the literature of the monstrous as an explicitly fictional mirror to a medieval reality, the reception of *The Travels* reminds us that for the medieval and even early modern reader, this literature was not only significant because it provided real insights into the nature of the world, and one's place within it: much of the literature of the monstrous was significant also because it was understood to be true.

Encountering Others: Jews and Saracens

Real and true as the representations of the monstrous in much of the literature we have surveyed were understood to be, such representations also extended to language and images used to describe experientially real religious and cultural 'others' in the dominantly Christian West, perhaps most clearly the communities of Jews within Europe, and the Islamic peoples who occupied much of Spain and against whom European Crusaders fought throughout much of the High Middle Ages. As Mary B. Campbell has noted, 'eerily charming' as many literary representations of the monstrous may be, the power of those representations can also be articulated in their extension to living people, and to real violence done to those people.[75]

Jews formed a distinct subaltern group in Medieval Europe, separated from their Christian neighbours by 'ethical, bodily, and cultural deviance that would be so well established by the close of the Middle Ages'.[76] In England, the presence of a Jewish community was restricted to the period between the Norman Conquest and the Expulsion in 1290, allowing Jews to be somewhat more mythical before and after than they were on the Continent. The newness of the Jews to England may have been a factor in the locality of the origin of the Blood Libel claims, and the ignominious and persistent claims of an international Jewish conspiracy 'every year [to] sacrifice a Christian in some part of the world to the Most High God in scorn and contempt of Christ'.[77] The earliest extant tale clearly working to constitute these claims is the twelfth-century *Life and Miracles of St William of Norwich* by Thomas of Monmouth. In this account, the ritual murder of a young boy sets the Jews in wilful and violent opposition to the Christian community, and thereby allows this exotic group to serve the same function fulfilled by the monsters discussed above, helping the dominant culture to define itself at their explicit expense.[78]

It should therefore not be surprising to find Jews depicted in texts and images as distorted and caricatured to the point of monstrosity. Perhaps the most famous visual example is the image of Isaac of Norwich from the Rolls of the Issues of the Exchequers, depicting Isaac, the wealthiest Jew in England, with three faces.[79] He is surrounded by Jews with caricatured profiles and devils. While in this case the

---

[75] Campbell (1988: 86).   [76] Cohen (2006: 141).

[77] Thomas of Monmouth (1896: 2. 11).

[78] See Ruben (2004); Bale (2006). Many thanks to Debra Higgs Strickland for these and other references.

[79] Rolls of the Issues of the Exchequers, 1233, Roll 87, Kew, National Archives E.401/1565. For an illustration, see Felsenstein (1995: 27).

monstrous figure is an identifiable individual, in most cases the Jew is simply that—
an iconic representation of a people.

Although anti-Semitism is integral to much medieval Christian thinking, an
escalation of violence, both literal and figurative, against European Jews parallels
the onset of the crusading movements at the end of the eleventh century. While the
motivations for such violence are extremely complex, it cannot be coincidental that
large-scale military mobilization against peoples identified as religiously and culturally dangerous to Christianity in the Holy Lands is accompanied by violence to
peoples identified as religiously and culturally dangerous to Christianity also within
Europe.[80]

Crusading literature, from historical accounts to romances, establishes the Islamic
peoples of both Islamic Spain and the Holy Lands, referred to as Saracens, as not only
enemies to European Christianity, but enemies depicted explicitly in the language of
the monstrous. John Block Friedman has detailed 'a fairly widespread connection of
Saracens and Cynocephali in the Middle Ages, in both East and West, as the Muslims
were often described by Christians as a 'race of dogs' and argues for the popularity of
the figure of the 'dog-headed Saracen' in its appearance in both literary and visual
contexts.[81] Of course, as Jeffrey Jerome Cohen points out, this literature also contains
images of Saracens, like images of Jews, which are not necessarily monstrous, and
which, in episodes of 'passing' for example, emphasize not difference but a permeability of identity for European and Saracen alike, a permeability which haunts
English medieval literature at some of its very foundations.[82] Certainly vilified figures
persist in the literature: consider, for example, the treacherous Sultaness in Chaucer's
Man of Law's Tale, or the blood-drinking and violence in The Sultan of Babylon. Yet,
as Cohen observes, foundational texts like Geoffrey of Monmouth's History of the
Kings of Britain contain narratives that imagine that the Saxons act in league with and
merge with African or Saracen forces to defeat the Britons, thus justifying 'Anglo-
Norman claims to difference and superiority'[83] but also positioning the figure of the
Saracen at the moment of the origin, however denied, of an idea of England.

Visual Counterparts

Monstrosity is not only a prevalent literary theme, but, rather a theme that appears
frequently in all aspects of medieval culture. Medieval art is overflowing with images
of monsters. They appear all throughout the period, in every sort of manuscript and
architecture. Among the most significant early images of monstrosity are those which
appear in manuscripts of the Wonders or Marvels of the East. The three English

[80] For a brief discussion of the violence against Jews associated with the First Crusade, see Richard
(1999: 38–40).
[81] Friedman (1981: 67–9). White (1991: 67–8) surveys such representations; see also Monaño (2002:
esp. 124–6).
[82] Cohen (2003: 199, 220–1). See also Uebel (1996).
[83] Cohen (2003: 219).

manuscripts of this monster-cycle are all heavily illustrated, and while the style shifts dramatically from the earliest (London, British Library, MS Cotton Vitellius A. xv, the *Beowulf* manuscript, *c.*1000) to the latest (Oxford, Bodleian Library, MS Bodley 614, *c.*1125), nonetheless all three are clearly connected and share many features.

A few features are dominant in these images. First is the collective quality of the images. Individually, each is like an illustration in a biological field guide, presented as if to assist in the identification of the marvel. However, when viewed in series, page after page, the collective effect is of a fearsome sea of monstrosity, a hideous aggregate. Just as the human body came to serve 'as a figure for the Christian community united in the body of Christ as the body of the church',[84] as early as Paul's writings, so too, the monstrous body can be seen as a figure for the monstrous 'community', united by their collective exclusion from the body of the church. Monsters do not, of course, form a coherent and unified body politic; nonetheless (and it might be argued that in the early Middle Ages, no group was really such), they function collectively, rather than individually. A reader does not contemplate the features and habits of a single monster (for example, the dog-headed Cynocephalus, the one-footed sciopod, etc.) and from this single interaction draw conclusions about his identity as a human. Rather, it is through contemplation of the mass of monstrosity that fills not only the *Wonders* and *Marvels* manuscripts, but which can likewise be found bundled together in the margins of sacred texts such as the Lutrell Psalter, at the edges of world maps, in the crypt of Canterbury Cathedral and the corbels of Durham Cathedral, and so on, that the reader/viewer is able to establish fundamental elements of his own identity. Indeed, this is likely the reason that monsters rarely appear singly, in any medieval context.

The second characteristic element of the images of monstrosity is aggressive interaction. This interaction might be with the frames that struggle (often unsuccessfully) to contain them, with the text adjacent to them (which they lick, claw, and bite), or with the viewer, directly addressed through eye contact that can be of the most unsettling nature. This aggression creates tension between the location and the monsters—they are often characterized as distant, but are self-evidently present in the immediate space of the reader/viewer.

Mappae Mundi

Among the most common loci for the appearance of monsters in medieval materials are the *mappae mundi*, or maps of the world. Few with significant details survive from the early Middle Ages, though increasing numbers appear around 1050, and these numbers grow throughout the rest of the period. These complex documents contain information as both text and image, and so in some cases, we find names and narratives for monsters, while in others, we have images; some contain both. The earliest detailed medieval map to survive is bound with the second copy of the

---

[84] Blurton (2007: 63).

Wonders of the East in London, British Library, Cotton Tiberius B. v, known as the Cotton or Anglo-Saxon map (figure 2). This manuscript, *c*.1050, is a miscellany of scientific materials including charts for the dating of Easter, astrological materials such as the *Aratea*, a zonal map, and Priscian's verse translation of Dionysius Periegetes' geographical poem, *Periegesis*.

The Cotton map contains a series of wonders or marvels, some monstrous and all exotic. They reside, in this case, exclusively at the outer edge of the continents of the world, forming a ring in this liminal zone. The wonders included here are: monstrous people (the Cynocephalus, the 'Barbaric People', the Ethiopians—often included in accounts of the *Wonders of the East*, and described alternately as burned black by the hot African sun or having the snouts of pigs—and the Griffin People, perhaps derived from Æthicus Ister's Cosmographia,[85] as well as the biblical hordes of Gog and Magog); exotic animals (lions, the only marvel to have an image on this map); geographical features (the Pillars of Hercules, the Mountains of Gold and of Extreme Heat); and wonder-filled regions (Zeugis and Africa, described as 'wild . . . full of beasts and plentiful of serpents').

The location of these wonders is not incidental. Rather, it is intricately tied to their basic definition as figures of the exotic. They are, in their bodies and habits, strange and different from their readers, and so their location is outlandish, in the most literal way. They serve to mark the boundaries of humanity, in their bodies and their cultural norms, and so they are relegated to the periphery of the world. Since this world was considered to be the reflection of a divine plan and order, their location was purposive; these liminal creatures served to elucidate the meaning of the universe, and so their inclusion on world maps and elsewhere was far from incidental and though images of monsters are often mischaracterized as drolleries, they are far from droll.

Critical Approaches to Monstrosity

The study of medieval monstrosity has been ongoing at least since J. R. R. Tolkien's study 'Beowulf: The Monsters and the Critics', published in the *Proceedings of the British Academy*, in 1936, followed by Rudolf Wittkower's seminal article, 'Marvels of the East: A Study in the History of Monsters'. The former was a call, in essence, to acknowledge the monsters roiling throughout Old English literature. The latter is a masterful articulation of the sources that lie behind medieval accounts and images of monsters, tracing these stories back well beyond the usual citations to classical authors such as Pliny and Herodotus to more ancient sources like the *Mahabhar-*

---

[85] Prinz (1993: 118): 'Griphas gentes proximam oceani partem, unde ait vetusta fama processisse Saxonum subolem et ad Germaniam proeliorum feritate peraccessisse, gentes stultissimas, velut ferarum et strutionum vel curcodrillium et scurpionum genera sunt'. Our thanks to Teresa Hooper for this reference.

ata.[86] This influential and often cited article was typical of the approaches that dominated the study of monsters in the twentieth century.

In more recent years, the study of monstrosity has made increasing use of theoretical approaches. Perhaps the most common of these have been rooted in psychoanalytical and post-colonial theories, with their stresses on abjection (as explored by Julia Kristeva[87]) and disgust (articulated by William Ian Miller[88]), and on the power relations between central and marginal groups (most clearly indebted to Michel Foucault,[89] but also to Edward Said[90] and more recently to Homi Bhabha[91]). The range of approaches brought to medieval monsters indicates their complexity as subjects of inquiry, their difficulty but also their richness. The majority of these recent efforts have been directed not at figuring out the origins of these creatures, literary or 'real', but rather, at determining what they can tell us about the cultures that produced, reproduced, and consumed them in texts and images.

CONCLUSIONS

As we have surveyed medieval literature of the monstrous, we have emphasized the function of the monstrous and exotic in the definition of the normative, even as that definition shifts, and shifts dramatically in the roughly eight hundred years that make up the long Middle Ages. We have also argued that medieval depictions of giants, dog-headed men, and other monstrous creatures explore not only the ways in which these creatures are not men, but also the ways in which the strangeness of the monstrous is inextricably part of the English, the Christian, the human experience.

BIBLIOGRAPHY

AKBARI, SUZANNE CONKLIN (2004), 'The Diversity of Mankind in *The Book of John Mandeville*', in Rosamund Allen (ed.), *Eastward Bound: Travel and Travellers 1050–1550* (Manchester: Manchester University Press), 156–76.

AUGUSTINE (1981), *De Civitate Dei Libri XII*, ed. A. Kalb and B. Dombart (Bibliotheca Scriptorum Graecorum et Romanorum Teubeneriana; Stuttgart: Teubner).

BALE, ANTHONY PAUL (2006), *The Jew in the Medieval Book: English Anti-Semitism, 1350–1500* (Cambridge: Cambridge University Press).

BARTLETT, ROBERT (1982), *Gerald of Wales 1146–1223* (Oxford: Clarendon Press).

BEDE (1969), *The Ecclesiastical History of the English People*, ed. Bertram Colgrave and R. A. B. Mynors (Oxford: Clarendon Press).

---

[86] Wittkower (1942: 164).   [87] Kristeva (1982).   [88] Miller (1997).
[89] Foucault (1999).   [90] Said (1979).   [91] Bhabha (1994).

BENSON, LARRY D. (ed.) (1987), *The Riverside Chaucer* (3rd edn. Boston: Houghton Mifflin).

BHABHA, HOMI (1994), *The Location of Culture* (London: Routledge).

BLURTON, HEATHER (2007), *Cannibalism in High Medieval English Literature* (New York: Palgrave Macmillan).

BROWN, MICHELLE (2002), 'Marvels of the West: Giraldus Cambrensis and the Role of the Author in the Development of Marginal Illustration', in A. S. G. Edwards (ed.), *English Manuscript Studies*, x (London: British Library), 34–59.

BRUNT, GERRIT H. V. (1994), *Alexander the Great in the Literature of Medieval Britain* (Mediaevalia Groningana, 14; Groningen: Egbert Forsten).

BURNS, E. JANE (2002), *Courtly Love Undressed: Reading through Clothes in Medieval French Culture* (Philadelphia: University of Pennsylvania Press).

BUTTURFF, DOUGLAS ROLLO (1969), *The Monsters and the Scholar: An Edition and Critical Study of the Liber Monstrorum* (Latin text with English translation), Ph.D. dissertation, University of Illinois (Ann Arbor: University Microfilms).

BYNUM, CAROLINE WALKER (2002), *Metamorphosis and Identity* (New York: Zone).

CAMPBELL, MARY B. (1988), *The Witness and the Other World: Exotic European Travel Writing, 400–1600* (Ithaca, NY: Cornell University Press).

COHEN, JEFFERY JEROME (1999), *Of Giants: Sex, Monsters, and the Middle Ages* (Medieval Cultures, 17; Minneapolis: University of Minnesota Press).

——(2003), *Medieval Identity Machines* (Medieval Cultures, 35; Minneapolis: University of Minneapolis Press).

——(2006), *Hybridity, Identity and Monstrosity in Medieval Britain: On Difficult Middles* (New York: Palgrave Macmillan).

DE LAS CASAS, BARTOLOMÉ, and CHRISTOPHER COLUMBUS (1989), *The Journal of Christopher Columbus*, tr. Lionel Cecil Jane (New York: Random House).

DINSHAW, CAROLYN (1997), 'Getting Medieval: Pulp Fiction, Gawain, Foucault', in Dolores Warwick Frese and Katherine O'Brien O'Keeffe (eds.), *The Book and the Body* (Ward-Phillips Lectures in English Language and Literature, 14; Notre Dame, Ind.: University of Notre Dame Press), 116–63.

FELSENSTEIN, FRANK (1995), *Anti-Semitic Stereotypes: A Paradigm of Otherness in English Popular Culture, 1660–1830* (Baltimore, Md.: Johns Hopkins).

FJALLDAL, MAGNÚS (1998), *The Long Arm of Coincidence: The Frustrated Connection between Beowulf and Grettis Saga* (Toronto: University of Toronto Press).

FOUCAULT, MICHEL (1999), *Abnormal: Lectures at the College de France, 1974–1975*, tr. Graham Burchell (New York: Picador).

FRIEDMAN, JOHN BLOCK (1981), *The Monstrous Races in Medieval Art and Thought* (Cambridge: Harvard University Press).

FULK, R. D., ROBERT BJORK, and JOHN NILES (eds.) (2008), *Klaeber's Beowulf* (4th edn. Toronto: University of Toronto Press).

GARNETT, GEORGE (1997), 'Conquered England 1066–1215', in Nigel Saul (ed.), *The Oxford Illustrated History of Medieval England* (Oxford: Oxford University Press), 61–101.

Geoffrey of Monmouth (1966), *The History of the Kings of Britain*, tr. Lewis Thorpe (London: Penguin).

Gerald of Wales (1867), *Opera*, v. *Topographia Hibernica et Expugnatio Hibernica*, ed. James Dimock (London: Longmans, Green, Reader, & Dyer).

——(1868), *Opera*, viii. *In librum de principis instructione præfatio prima*, ed. James Dimock (London: Longmans, Green, Reader, & Dyer).

HARVEY, P. D. A. (1991), *Medieval Maps* (Toronto: University of Toronto Press).

HIGGINS, IAIN MACLEOD (1997), *Writing East: The 'Travels' of Sir John Mandeville* (Philadelphia: University of Pennsylvania Press).

KASKE, R. E. (1971), '*Beowulf* and the Book of Enoch', *Speculum*, 46(3): 421–31.

KIM, SUSAN M. (2005), '"As I Once Did with Grendel": Boasting and Nostalgia in *Beowulf*', *Modern Philology*, 103(1): 4–27.

KLAEBER, FREDERICK (ed.) (1950), *Beowulf and the Fight at Finnsburg* (3rd edn. Lexington, Ky.: D. C. Heath & Co.).

KNIGHT, RHONDA (2001), 'Werewolves, Monsters, and Miracles: Representing Colonial Fantasies in Gerald of Wales's *Topographia Hibernica*', *Studies in Iconography*, 22: 55–86.

KRISTEVA, JULIA (1982), *Powers of Horror: An Essay on Abjection*, tr. Leon S. Roudiez (New York: Columbia University Press).

KROLL, NORMA (1986), '*Beowulf*: The Hero as Keeper of Human Polity', *Modern Philology*, 84(2): 117–29.

LAVEZZO, KATHY (1999), 'Angels on the Edge of the World: The Geography of English Identity from Ælfric to Chaucer', Ph.D. dissertation, University of California, Santa Barbara.

LE GOFF, JACQUES (1985), *The Medieval Imagination*, tr. Arthur Goldhammer (Chicago: University of Chicago Press).

LERER, SETH (1994), 'Grendel's Glove', *ELH* 61(4): 721–51.

MACKIE, CHARLES PAUL (1891), *With the Admiral of the Ocean Sea: A Narrative of the First Voyage to the Western World, Drawn Mainly from the Diary of Christopher Columbus* (Chicago: C. McClurg).

MILLER, WILLIAM IAN (1997), *The Anatomy of Disgust* (Cambridge, Mass.: Harvard University Press).

MITTMAN, ASA SIMON (2003), 'The Other Close at Hand: Gerald of Wales and the "Marvels of the West"', in Robert Mills and Bettina Bildhauer (eds.), *The Monstrous Middle Ages* (Cardiff: University of Wales Press), 97–112.

——(2006), *Maps and Monsters in Medieval England* (New York: Routledge).

MONAÑO, JESUS (2002), 'Sir Gowther: Imagining Race in Late Medieval England', in Albrecht Classen (ed.), *Meeting the Foreign in the Middle Ages* (New York: Routledge), 118–32.

MORGAN, NIGEL (1982), *Early Gothic Manuscripts*, i. *1190–1250* (London: H. Miller).

——(1988), *Early Gothic Manuscripts*, ii. *1250–1285* (London: H. Miller).

NIETZSCHE, FRIEDRICH (2002), *Beyond Good and Evil*, tr. Judith Norman, ed. Rolf-Peter Horstmann and Judith Norman (Cambridge: Cambridge University Press).

NIGG, JOSEPH (ed.) (1999), *The Book of Fabulous Beasts: A Treasury of Writings from Ancient Times to the Present* (Oxford: Oxford University Press).

O'BRIEN O'KEEFFE, KATHERINE (1981), '*Beowulf*, Lines 702B–836: Transformations and the Limits of the Human'. *Texas Studies in Literature and Language*, 23(4): 484–94.

O'DONOGHUE, BERNARD (tr.) (2006), *Sir Gawain and the Green Knight* (New York: Penguin).

O'MEARA, JOHN (trans.) (1982), *Gerald of Wales, The History and Topography of Ireland* (Atlantic Highlands, NJ: Humanities Press).

ORCHARD, ANDY (1995), *Pride and Prodigies: Studies in the Monsters of the Beowulf-Manuscript* (Cambridge: D. S. Brewer).

Pliny the Elder (1942; repr. 1969), *Natural History*, ed. and tr. H. Rackham (Cambridge, Mass.: Harvard University Press).

PRINZ, OTTO (1993), *Die Kosmographie des Æthicus* (Monumenta Germaniae Historia, 14; Munich: Monumenta Germaniae Historia).

RICHARD, JEAN (1999), *The Crusades, c.1071–1291*, tr. Jean Birrell (Cambridge Medieval Textbooks, Cambridge: Cambridge University Press).

RUBIN, MIRI (2004), *Gentile Tales: The Narrative Assault on Late Medieval Jews* (Philadelphia: University of Pennsylvania Press).

SAID, EDWARD (1979), *Orientalism* (New York: Vintage Books).

STEPHENS, WALTER (1989), *Giants in Those Days: Folklore, Ancient History, and Nationalism* (Lincoln, Neb.: University of Nebraska Press).

THOMAS OF MONMOUTH (1896), *The Life and Miracles of St. William of Norwich*, ed. and tr. Augustus Jessopp and Montague Rhodes James (Cambridge: University of Cambridge Press).

UEBEL, MICHAEL (1996), 'Unthinking the Monster: Twelfth-Century Responses to Saracen Alterity', in Jeffrey Jerome Cohen (ed.), *Monster Theory: Reading Culture* (Minneapolis: University of Minnesota Press), 264–91.

VERNER, LISA (2005), *The Epistemology of the Monstrous in the Middle Ages* (New York: Routledge).

WHITBREAD, L. G. (1974), 'The *Liber Monstrorum* and *Beowulf*', *Mediaeval Studies*, 36: 434–71.

WHITE, DAVID GORDON (1991), *Myths of the Dogman* (Chicago: University of Chicago Press).

WILLIAMS, DAVID (1982), *Cain and Beowulf: A Study in Secular Allegory* (Toronto: University of Toronto Press).

WITTKOWER, RUDOLF (1942), 'Marvels of the East: A Study in the History of Monsters', *Journal of the Warburg and Courtauld Institutes*, 5: 159–97.

CHAPTER 35

···

SPIRITUAL QUEST AND SOCIAL SPACE

TEXTS OF HARD TRAVEL FOR GOD ON EARTH AND IN THE HEART

···

MARY BAINE CAMPBELL

THANKS to protracted international attention to travel of many kinds, travel writing, and 'boundaries' over the last quarter century or so, not to mention new theoretical models for examining space both geographical and social, critical interest in pilgrimage on the part of literary scholars, social historians, and anthropologists has crossed the boundaries of history of religion and Church history to which it was once 'proper'.[1] In particular, historical work in English on Islamic and Jewish pilgrimage is now more available, though most (not all) relevant original texts in Arabic and

[1] The literature is vast: see for a start the journals *Studies in Travel Writing; Journey; Society and Space; Journal of Borderland Studies*, and the inaugural contemporary classics of Tuan (1977); Smith (1991); Appadurai, guest editor of the special issue (Feb. 1988) 'Place and Voice in Anthropological Theory', of *Cultural Anthropology*; Said (1979); Clifford and Marcus (1986); Turner and Turner (1978). The field continues to be exceptionally lively across the world, with international conferences (in locations from Derry to Bucharest to Hong Kong) coordinated by *Studies in Travel Writing*, as well as in France by the Centre de Recherche sur la Littérature des Voyages at the Sorbonne, and innumerable other organizations. See also Hulme and Youngs (2002); Friedman and Figg (2000).

Hebrew remain untranslated into English.[2] The 'general passages' of the Crusades (*c*.1095–1272), considered a form of highly meritorious pilgrimage from the time of their first polemicist, Pope Urban II, are due for further analysis in the new context of the Palestinian intifadahs and the events and consequences of 11 September 2001. Consequences include, to the sorrow of most scholars in the humanities, a renewed sense of the medieval 'clash of civilizations', first emphasized in the *Historia transmarina* of William of Tyre (*c*.1130–85), Jerusalem-born historian of the First Crusade, apprehended with dismay by Matthew Paris (1200–59), and reified as theory in the 1990s and subsequently by Samuel P. Huntingdon's *Clash of Civilizations*.[3] That the Crusades were economic and colonialist in their conduct and the motives of their military leadership goes without saying: *cui bono?* after all. But they were also in fact a form of pilgrimage and as such inspired such major literary works as Bishop Fulcher of Chartres' eyewitness account of the First Crusade (1095–9) and William of Tyre's somewhat later chronicle, and those of aristocratic leaders Joinville and Villehardouin written during and after the Fourth (1199–1204); the basically fictional pre-Crusade genre of the *chanson de geste* (and later Spanish *cantar de gesta*) expanded to include the legendary exploits of major pilgrim-warriors. Pilgrimage, that is, contains militarist as well as devotional and individually pious motives and expressions.

As a form of travel, pilgrimage need not be conducted in space at the geographical scale: the *chemins de Jerusalem* on high and late medieval church floors and walls permitted virtual Holy Land pilgrimage on foot within one's local church or cathedral for the stay-at-home, and even by finger for the lame.[4] But however earnestly we may long for a delicious 'Voyage around my Room' from such a spiritual journey, it does not exist: only the crossing of political and ecclesiastical boundaries motivated the extant medieval texts, and it was the long-distance pilgrimage 'beyond the seas', or *outremer*, which also crossed major linguistic and cultural boundaries, that stimulated the largest corpus.[5] The word *peregrinus* meant, for a long time, stranger or foreigner: it is not always easy to tell whether a given peregrine is a pilgrim or not.[6]

The practice of pilgrimage covers such a huge historical time-span and variety of geographical itineraries that discussion of the delimitation of the 'social spaces' it traversed can only be hinted at here. What pilgrimages had in common for many centuries was the requirement of permission to leave home for this purpose from one's local bishop, community, and family (the latter particularly for women); for lengthy or overseas pilgrimages such as those to Rome, Compostela, and the Holy

---

[2] Even the number of collections, series, and bibliographies is vast, in translation as well as original languages, online as well as in print. Those I have cited in this article are useful; more can be found in the bibliographies of the reliable critical and reference works cited here.

[3] Huntington (1996).

[4] See Matthews (1922: 60–7).

[5] Of the published collections of medieval Christian texts from this archive, Anglophone readers are still well served by 13 vols. of translations of the *Library of the Palestine Pilgrims Text Society* (1887–97) (hereafter *PPTS*). For medieval Jewish religious travels, Adler (1930) remains the most convenient and widely accessible translated collection. It has an excellent bibliography of sources.

[6] Webb (1999: 7).

Land the making of a last will and testament was also customary, as well as the settling of debts and various parish rituals of leave-taking. Margery Kempe, for instance, 'preyd the parysch preste of the town ether sche was dwellyng [Norwich] to sey for hir in the pulpyt that, yf any man or woman that claymed any dette of hir husband or of hir thei xuld come & speke with hire er sche went, & sche, with the help of God, xulde makyn aseth to ech of hem that their schuldyn heldyn hem content. & so sche dede'.[7] In wartime such permissions were more difficult to get (particularly because they took money out of Christendom), as they increasingly were under later medieval ecclesiastical disapproval of the practice in general. The infrastructure of the major pilgrimage routes, to shrines and relics at Canterbury, Walsingham, Tours, Mont St Michel, Loretto, and countless other European sites as well as to the bigger shrines, was elaborate (though providing little creature comfort by modern standards) and eventually included the great hostels of the Knights Templar and Hospitaller in the Holy Land as well as innumerable inns, docks, shipping companies, victuallers, maps, caravanserai, guides, and guidebooks for both 'the way thither' and the destinations.[8]

This chapter will provide a very selective survey of spiritual travel in its major prose forms, concentrating especially on pilgrimage. But some attention will be paid as well to mystic and poetic texts that engage the form of the quest in romance, allegory, and the *vidas* and confessions of mystics. I will draw mainly on texts available in English translation, for the benefit of Anglophone students and teachers. These always include bibliographical information on the Latin or vernacular originals, and some are printed in bilingual format.

In the theoretical and critical language of our time, 'quest' may be one of the least fashionable of all terms (with the possible exception of 'spiritual'), while analysis of matters that could be aggregated under the heading of 'social space' has seen an unprecedented vitality and accomplishment. I was thus intrigued by the title afforded me by the editors of this volume. Guided by it, I have considered the primary corpus of pilgrimage and crusade as subsets of a large (indeed impossibly diverse) corpus devoted (in more than one sense) to spiritual travel in both physical and inward—or between-ward—spaces. From this point of view the magnificent late medieval poem in which both terms of my title make identical and clear claims on our reading, Chaucer's *Canterbury Tales* (1387–1400), feeds as much from allegorical and mystical usage of the tropes of journey as from accounts of actual pilgrimage and a knowledge of its social practices. Dante's *Commedia* (1308–21), while clearly based on the

---

[7] Kempe (1940: chs. 26, 60). In 1309, the Sire of Joinville describes at great length his own such preparations. After a week of feasting and banqueting given for his friends, Jean says to them all: '"My friends, I'm soon going oversea, and I don't know whether I shall ever return. So will any of you who have a claim to make against me come forward..." Since I did not wish to take away with me a single penny to which I had no right, I went to Metz in Lorraine, and mortgaged the greater part of my land.' (Jean de Joinville and Geoffroi de Villehardoun 1963: 192).

[8] Among many works on the circumstances and documentation of medieval European pilgrimage I have found especially useful Webb (1999, 2000); Birch (1998); Morrison (2000). For Muslim and Jewish religious travel, ch. 2 of Elad (1995); and chs. 1 and 2 of Weber (2005).

widespread visionary tradition of voyages to hell and purgatory (and occasionally heaven, including Arabic mystical poems of North Africa), is based for the drama of its encounters on an overturning of hierarchies of social space as he knew them, and as we know them still.[9] And as pilgrimage supposedly effaced them.[10]

Not only is 'quest' old-fangled, it is also in our context somewhat new-fangled: for most of its meanings in English, French, and Catalan a fourteenth- and even fifteenth-century word, with origins in words for alms, tax collection, inquest/ inquiry, and later in hunting jargon for hunting with dogs or for their baying especially. It is through the connection with hunting that it enters the language of romance, where it remains until fairly late a hunting term (as in Malory's fifteenth-century 'Questing Beast'). Thus it harks, so to speak, back to more and less violent pursuits of prey, whether animal or human, physical, economic, or legal: it is linked to *quarere*, but in the vernaculars in these contexts.

Bearing this loaded term always in mind, I will include under the rubric of 'quest' all effortful travel, actual, fictional, and metaphorical, towards a goal imagined in spiritual terms. (This means leaving out the Celtic sources and instances of the quest romances, which conceive their goals in magical and martial terms.) Neither medieval pilgrims nor medieval crusaders saw themselves as 'questing'. But they were searching, even (especially but not exclusively Jewish pilgrims) searching for knowledge. For as Roger Bacon says in *Opus Majus* (1267): 'Not only philosophy requires this, but also theology, of which the whole sequence deals with places in the world. Whence the literal sense rests on a knowledge of the places of the world, so that by means of suitable adaptations and similitudes taken from things the spiritual meanings may be elicited.'[11]

PILGRIMAGE

Jewish pilgrimage took the form at first, under seriously constricting Roman regulations (no Jews, for example, were to live in Aeolia Capitolina after 70 CE), of visits to an annual ritual of mourning on the Mount of Olives, renewed after the Christian conquest of Jerusalem as the Church's means of emphasizing the Jews' loss of proper claim to Jerusalem. Later some Jews—the Karaites of Iran in particular but in the thirteenth century also, according to the Spanish codifier Nachmanides, Jews living in Europe under rabbinic law—came under the requirement of making aliyah. There was a Yeshivah at Jerusalem, which moved after the Muslim conquest of 638 CE to

---

[9] Several (mostly Irish, English, and French) visions of purgatory and hell are collected in translation in Gardiner (1993, 2008).

[10] On the 'flow' of group pilgrimage experience see Turner and Turner (1978).

[11] Bacon (1928), 1. 4, 'On Mathematics', 320.

Tiberius, and again after the Fatayid conquest in 970 to Tyre: scholars congregated there, and as it moved so did the centre of gravity for Jewish travellers. The relation to memory was largely a relation to the loss of Eretz Israel as a Jewish homeland, as opposed to the Christian memorializing of biblical sites and anticipation of Christ's Second Coming.[12] After the conquest of Jerusalem by the Ommayeds in 638, the practice of *ziyarah* brought Muslim pilgrims from the east to Jerusalem and environs, to visit the tombs of the great sages—a Jewish and Christian practice as well, but never the chief goal of either sort of pilgrim. I will include the journey of Rabbi Benjamin of Tudela as an example of this kind of spiritual travel, but as I do not read Arabic I can do no more than point to the difference between the *ziyarah* and the more religiously central motive of Christian Holy Land pilgrimage. (Jerusalem was not comparable to Mecca, for Muslim pilgrims. And neither Jerusalem nor Rome was a required pilgrimage for Christians, as was the *hejira* to Mecca, which is outside of our purview.[13]) Although Christians also visited the tombs of sages (Abraham, David, St Jerome), their central concern was the experience of visiting the scene of Christ's Passion: the tomb of Christ was not that of a sage, as it was for Muslims (or of a false Messiah, as it was for Jews), but that of the Incarnate God himself. It is easy to imagine what blasphemy this must have seemed to Jewish and Muslim residents and religious travellers, but towards the end of our period and afterwards there were occasional interfaith dialogues and conferences.[14]

The late fourth-century Galician nun Egeria left us the first first-person narrative account of Christian Holy Land pilgrimage, in the form of a (truncated) letter to her convent back home, although the experiences of the earlier female pilgrims of later antiquity, Paula and Eustochium, were summarized and quoted in the letters of St Jerome, to whose side they had travelled.[15] They are not medieval pilgrims, and Paula and Eustochium intended to settle in the desert of Sinai, but they laid down a basic pattern for later Christian pilgrims of using the biblical sights as opportunities for heightened memory—for 'remembering', in the first person, scenes of sacred history and events known to them from scripture before they arrived (Egeria notably tells her sisters to look up the details of a certain site in Numbers—'It was too much . . . to write down each one individually'[16]—when she is too pressed for time to describe a certain biblical site).[17] Egeria relates a few details of the present tense countries she travelled in (Egypt, Palestine, and Syria), as St Jerome's redactions of the letters of Paula and

[12] See Friedman (1996).

[13] For more on Muslim travel to Jerusalem, see Elad (1995: ch. 2); for Muslim spiritual travel in general see El-Shibabi (1998).

[14] See Hoerder *et al.* (2003), esp. chs. 1 and 2.

[15] The letters of Paula and Eustochium are translated by Aubrey Stewart, from Jerome's redactions, listed under his name in the *Patrilogia Latina*, Series Latinae, in *PPTS* 1 (1889).

[16] Egeria (1958), v, 8.

[17] I quote Egeria in my own translations from the *Itinerarium Egeriae* (1958). For a complete translation see Egeria 1970 (ed. and tr. George E. Gingras). For more on Egeria's (and Paula's) readings of the Holy Land, see Limor (2001); Campbell (1988: ch. 1, 'Egeria, Arculf and the Written Pilgrimage').

Eustochium do not: as she admits frequently, she is 'satis curiosa'. She makes frequent reference to the pauses for prayer that ritualized her access to many biblical sites, particularly Mt Zion (which are recapitulated by Dante on Mt Purgatory) and in Jerusalem, which also narrativize her journey. But the fullest of the early medieval pilgrimage texts of Europe recounts the experiences of the Merovingian bishop Arculf, written down a few years later by the famous Irish abbot of Colona, Adamnan (679–704), who interviewed him at length after a shipwreck. It is lengthy, complete, and even illustrated.[18] It was widely circulated, and quoted as late as the fifteenth century by the loquacious Felix Fabri of Zurich.[19] Both the pilgrim and Adamnan were well-educated and important ecclesiastical figures, and Adamnan added many bits of cross-reference and commentary to his interlocutor's narrative: while for Arculf it was mostly a religious observance, for Adamnan it was a source of data, to be collated with such texts as the *Onomasticon* of Bede: he titled the work *De locis sanctis*, de-emphasizing whatever narrative quality it may have had in Arculf's own relation. While Egeria seemed to want to provide occasion for holy meditation, Adamnan, like the later Roger Bacon, is interested in the spiritual fibre of knowledge.

De locis sanctis has been increasingly important since Denis Meehan's scholarly text and translation of 1958, especially to historians of religion and the early medieval church. Adamnan edited his interviews with Arculf, and concentrates intensively on architecture and place description: there is almost no narrative content in the text, unlike Egeria's letter, although one can detect the overall trajectory of his travels, which led him on his homeward journey to the last place described by Adamnan, Mt Vulcan, which thunders 'more on Friday and Saturday . . . With the hearing of his own ears he [Arculf] heard its thunderous noise when he was lodged for some days in Sicily.'[20]

The emphasis on architecture—whether of churches, tombs, or occasionally ruins—would prove to be common throughout the early and high Middle Ages, as the significant Holy Land sites grew closer together and churches and basilicas spread around and connected them (it was also of course important to more local pilgrimage to shrines and churches that held holy relics). By the high Middle Ages, texts such as the *Libellus de locis sanctis* of Theodorich are describing the places and their proximity in terms of paces, hands-breadths, and feet: one could easily build models of them ('as we return from the chapel by the same door, on the left hand, beneath the jamb of the door, there is a place five feet in length and breadth on which our Lord stood . . .').[21] But Arculf seems already to be a bit of a measurer: 'in this spot as the holy Arculf . . . relates, a huge bronze circular structure has been set up, levelled

---

[18] Adamnan (1958, ed. and tr. Denis Meehan). I give Latin and English page numbers of this bilingual edn. Meehan arrives at 679–82 CE as the year's of Arculf's voyage, and 683–6 for the rough date of Adamanan's composition. See also Campbell (2004).

[19] For Felix Fabri's expansive text see the translation in *PPTS* 7–10.

[20] Adamnan (1958: 3. 6, para. 1, pp. 120/121).

[21] Theodoricus, *Libellum de locis sanctis* 1. 16 (quoted from the *PPTS* 5 translation by Aubrey Stewart). For more on this tendency see Campbell (1991). For relevant texts in translation from the earlier Middle Ages, see Wilkinson (1977).

out on top, the height of which measures up to the chin'.[22] The overall impression of these accounts is distant from Egeria's intermittent sense of sublime landscape ('we came to a certain place where these mountains among which we were going opened and made an endless valley, vast, exceedingly flat and beautiful, and across the valley appeared the holy mountain of God, Sinai'[23]) and overwhelming decoration ('could the number or weight moreover of the candelabra and candles or lamps and divers sacred vessels be guessed or written?'[24]), and tends to leave out even so much attention as she had paid to the physical difficulties of Holy Land travel. One has the feeling of watching a grand collective memory palace under construction, in which even Egeria's and Arculf's scant attention to present-day Palestine has no place. Jewish 'pilgrims' went to visit living Jewish communities, or to meet each other at the ritual of mourning on the Mount of Olives or at the Yeshivah. Christian pilgrims, whatever their experience, seem to have felt the pressure, first to build up devotionally useful images of the sites and rituals of memorialization, and second, to confirm their continued existence, and offer guides to other pilgrims coming in their tracks ('then you come to a declivity of Mount Olivet, two furlongs eastward, to Bethphage').[25] The places must stay the same, the present must not impinge on them, the 'general passages' of the Crusades must make them once again accessible for spiritual purposes to Christian pilgrims.

For Christian pilgrims, the Holy Land was largely what we would now call a museum or even a theme park, and the corpus of *peregrinationes* is best described as one of itineraries—occasionally fleshed out by first-person references to eyewitness experience that gives readers access to a sense of imaginative journeying themselves: 'In the solitude where John [the Baptist] used to live our friend Arculf saw a very small type of locust, the body being small and short like one's finger. As their range of flight is very short, like the leaping of light frogs, they are easily captured in the grass. When cooked with oil they provide meagre sustenance.'[26] Such details give the religious reader a more intimate *connaissance* of John the Baptist's desert diet, of his daily hardships in the service of God. Arculf's own are not mentioned, not pertinent.

The 'social spaces' traversed by Egeria and Arculf, three centuries apart, were quite different. Egeria travelled well after the conversion of Constantine and Helena's construction of churches on the holy sites, in a period before Islam came to Palestine and the wider Judeo-Christian landscape. Arculf travelled during the reign of the first Omayyed caliph, at a time when Christian and Jewish pilgrims had to travel with Muslim escorts: a kind of religious tourist industry was set up that helped to rigidify the itinerary, at least of Christians.

---

[22] Adamnan (1958: 66–7).
[23] Egeria (1958: 1. 1).
[24] Ibid. 25. 9
[25] Anonymous *Guidebook to Palestine* (1971: para. 78).
[26] Adamnan (1958: 92–3).

After the First Crusade, a Latin Christian administration preserved and augmented this industry, while discouraging Jewish travel, introducing another kind of text, the first-person Crusade chronicle most memorably exemplified by Fulcher of Chartres at the end of the eleventh century and Geoffroi Villehardouin and Jean, Sire de Joinville, in the early thirteenth and early fourteenth respectively.[27] The one thing all these Christian pilgrim texts have in common is that they have been composed by travellers (or their scribes) in religious or military orders; Jewish records of travel were composed by rabbis. Individual travel of ordinary (if still well-to-do) lay persons awaits the later development of vernacular literacy: Margery Kempe knew no Latin, and seems even to have been illiterate, though not unread: a priest transcribed her dictation in English. Protestant vernacular accounts of pilgrimage constituted another major shift in the corpus, but that is not part of our story.[28]

Many books about the geographical region and physical infrastructure of these lands so important to people who did not live in them do not take the form of itineraries or *peregrinations*: Jerome's late fourth-century *Liber locorum* (a Latin expansion of Eusebius of Caesarea's Greek *Onomasticon*, written sixty years earlier) was only one account of the holy places, and indeed even Arculf's pilgrimages goes, as text, by the title *De locis sanctis*. Although Egeria's late fourth-century text intentionally provides a narrative of travel for devotional reading, the genre ossified in the high Middle Ages into the form of guidebook: distances in space are crucial— no place description lacks information on how many days' journey (or in Jerusalem and Bethlehem, how many paces) one place was from the next, and the fixity of the itinerary—'from there you go to X'—reflects the systematization of the experience by successive Roman, Islamic, and Christian administrations of Palestine in particular. That long-distance travel in the Middle Ages was arduous and dangerous no one needs reminding, and periods of armed struggle for political control made it all the more arduous, at different times, for travellers of all three Abrahamic faiths. Jews suffered particularly under Roman and Christian control, Muslims under Christian control, and the difference made by the existence of various faith communities in Jerusalem, Tyre, Acre, Alexandria, Damascus, and Constantinople varied the difficulties still further. But the difficulties do not interest most Christian writers of *peregrination* or even of guidebooks; the more lively writings of Jewish travellers and pilgrims, where they are concerned with troubles, are concerned with the difficulties endured by Jewish residents and communities in the wider region in which they travelled—largely to meet and talk with their fellow Jews. Rabbi Petachia of Ratisbon (who travelled widely in the Middle East from his second home in Prague, c.1174–87) 'then went to Jerusalem. The only Jew there is Rabbi Abraham, the dyer, and he pays a heavy tax to the king to be permitted to remain there.'[29]

The Jewish 'pilgrims' of Europe consistently attended to the present—to Jewish persons and especially communities located in the cities of the Middle East, through

---

[27] For translations see Foucher (1941); and Jean de Joinville and Geoffroi de Villehardouin (1963).
[28] On early modern Protestant pilgrims see Williams (1999, 2009).
[29] Adler (1930: 41).

which they travelled more extensively than the Jerusalem-focused memorializing and/or messianic Christians. They are messengers and knowledge-seekers of a far-flung diasporic community—they speak of Tibet and China long before any Christian traveller-writer does, and occasionally missionize a bit among resident communities of Karaites (Petachia tells of teaching the ritual prayers after meals to the Karaite community of Kedar in the region of Ararat[30]). They too describe distances and the tombs of patriarchs and prophets, but their focus is on Jewish communities and the larger social and political context of the Islamic and Christian polities in which they are embedded. The constant travel of diasporic rabbis is not a particularly medieval phenomenon, but their medieval texts make more valuable sources for medieval historians because their travels are more reports on the present conditions of the Asian diaspora than guidebooks for a contingent of devotional readers and prospective pilgrims.

The fourteenth-century text of Isaac b. Joseph ibn Chelo, however, a Kabbalist from Aragon, is known as the *Shebile Jerusalem*, and seems to show some influence from the high medieval Christian texts in its focus on Jerusalem and its memorial sites. Jerusalem in 1334 is more visitable thanks to the presence of a 'quite numerous' Jewish expatriate community there, mostly 'working day and night at the study of the Holy Law and of the true wisdom, which is the Kabbaleh'.[31] From Jerusalem he describes the sites and communities along seven routes leading outward towards other centres of Jewish life and learning—Jaffa, Schechem, Acre, Tiberias, Dan, and from Tiberius to Safed. The interest in locating sites of biblical Israel or Talmudic reference in contemporary Palestine meets obstacles in Ramallah and Jaffa (more or less modern Haifa), which do not readily find such identifications: 'Several persons have assured me that *Ramleh* was *Modin*, others maintain that it is *Thimira*. In one author I have found that this city is called *Palestine*, in another writer that its name is *Rama*. God alone knows what the truth of the matter is.'[32]

The author of *Mandeville's Travels* (c.1354) may have had access to some of the more anecdotal texts of the French rabbis; he certainly depended on the texts of Christian pilgrimage and especially of Franciscan and Dominican missionaries to the lands beyond Palestine and Syria. His famous text is of course not a *peregrinatio*, though the first portion is based on his readings in that genre and, perhaps, a pilgrimage of his own. It is fundamentally fictional, but draws on and even plagiarizes the accounts of historically verifiable pilgrim and missionary writers, and contributes to a developing genre of travel writing an unusually present, if imaginary, first-person.[33] In the most prominent versions of this multiply-redacted, expanded, contracted, fragmented, and even versified text, the trope of 'I, John Mandeville' is pervasive—nowhere more richly than at the gates of 'Paradise', which the narrator poignantly cannot enter. But it is not a religious or devotional work in any version. It is a secular account of travel for its own sake, dependent not only or even mainly on

---

[30] Ibid. 66.   [31] Ibid. 133.   [32] Ibid. 138.
[33] On this narrator see ch. 4 of Campbell (1988); on the history of the book and its many variations, see the definitive study by Higgins (1997).

the *peregrinationes* or guidebooks but also on a growing body of travel to the 'East',
mercantile as well as missionary, and is relatively worthless to historians because of
its fictionality, though it was not widely understood as a fiction for several centuries
(Columbus carried a copy with him on his first voyage to the New World).[34] There is
nothing of the quest in the structure of this early masterpiece of French and English
vernacular prose, and despite its influence and its enormous charm, we cannot linger
with it, except to say that at least in its prominent English versions it constitutes a
marvellous antidote to the outward- and inward-directed violence both of the
general passage and the cloistered mystic. For if it has a goal, it is the propagation
of a message that undermines the Christian geography of faith and its ascetic
decorum, decentring Jerusalem and inviting the European reader to imagine the
wealth, civilization, and sensible beauty of a round and diverse world. The 'social
space' of Mandeville's round earth is that of a utopian planet, impossibly open
(except at the gates of Paradise) to all the curious who would widen the space of
their own *Weltanschauung*. Might it be in part from Benjamin of Tudela's account of
Baghdad that he learnt to imagine respectfully the great society of a Muslim caliph-
ate? At any rate, his text betokens, along with the widely translated chronicle of the
Armenian Christian diplomat Heytoun (*c*.1307), a growing interest in the history,
geography, and proto-sociology of the lands east of Latin Christendom. (Heytoun,
for many reasons, ends his chronicle rhetorically with a call for a new 'general
passage', but his text is no more devotional than the Mandeville author's, nor is it
the account of a journey.[35])

For an account of something closer to a quest in the genre of the chronicle, we
might turn to the hagiography-cum-Crusade chronicle of Jean, sire of Joinville in
Champagne, *La Vie de Saint Louis*, composed in the thirteenth century in the wake
not only of many such chronicles but of the romances inspired partly by them. The
second part of this work, on the *gestes* of his friend the Crusader-king Louis IX, is an
extremely lively eyewitness account of the consequence of Louis's decision in 1248,
made at the moment of his miraculous recovery from a state near death, to 'take the
cross' and recover Jerusalem, which had fallen in 1244 to the Turks. The action takes
place in Egypt, Acre, Caesarea, Jaffa, and Saida, and there is little or no mention of
the *locis sanctis*, but the military adventure is narrated not only as a 'pilgrimage' (in
the sense of a 'general passage') but as the religiously inspired quest of its pious

---

[34] The missionary travels, mostly Italian and francophone, are not discussed here: though effortful
indeed, they are not journeys undertaken for spiritual motives, but tasks performed under ecclesiastical
orders: the missionaries did indeed hope to convert some of those they met, but their voyages were
mainly those of reconnaissance. Particularly important are those, published in translations in various
volumes of the Hackluyt and Roxburghe Societies, of the 13th- and 14th-cent. Franciscan and Dominican
missionaries to Asia, ODeric of Pordenone, Jordanus Catalini (bishop of Columbia), John de Piano di
Carpini, John of Montecorvino, and William of Rubruck, far the most interesting and intelligent of all.
Original Latin texts are published in the *Historia Missionum Ordinis Fratrum Minorum* (1967); most are
among those conveniently issued together in translation in Dawson (1955). See Camps (2000); for
missions to northern Europe, see Addison (1936).

[35] Glenn Burger has published, with extensive commentary, a 16th-cent. English translation (Hetoum
1988).

subject. It begins with a promise to God, and ends with Louis's canonization. The chivalric romance of its action (nonetheless wonderfully detailed and useful to historians) is contained within the expanded pilgrimage frame as the tale of a quest to regain Christian control of the Holy City that was the object of the highest goal of medieval pilgrim travel. It is a bloody story, relishing violence to Jews and 'Saracens' and unlikely to have moved the Mandeville author, but its climactic narrative is nonetheless that of a spiritual quest, which encounters the most difficult of all obstacles in 'social space', the defended boundaries of religious war.

I will conclude this section on pilgrimage, as a transition to the internal and experiential focus of the literary and mystical texts we turn to next, by mentioning another and later important prose book of a life, in this case of the writer's own, the famous *Book of Margery Kempe* (after 1438). The married mystic and frequent pilgrim, whose lifetime overlapped with Chaucer's, has left vivid accounts of the personal difficulties of her many pilgrimages (*c*.1413–33), to Canterbury, Rome, Assisi, Aachen, Compostela, and Palestine, but they do not belong in the tradition of *de locis sanctis* texts or pilgrimage guidebooks any more than Joinville's *Vie de Saint Louis*. They belong to the first English-language work of autobiography—a work focused on Margery's mystical relationship with Jesus and the trials of her attempt to live as his bride rather than her husband's, after the birth of several children and a nervous breakdown from which she, like St Louis, was rescued by a vision of Christ in her sickroom. Her *Book* is the account, written during the era of 'affective piety' in Britain, of an almost life-long quest for union with Christ, hampered but not defeated by the givens of her sex and marital status—though she was lucky in a husband who gave up early on the struggle to prevent her from living as a married celibate, and who permitted her many travels. It is studded with detailed episodes of her internal dialogues with a mystically present Jesus, as her accounts of travel are with moments of intense religious grief and ecstasy (the grief in particular a difficulty for her fellow-pilgrims, as she was given to frequent and boisterous weeping): her first pilgrimage, to the Holy Land, was forecast 'be reuelacyon yerys a-forn'.[36] 'And whan this creatur saw Ierusalem, ryding on an asse, sche thankyd God wiyth al hir hert, preying hym for hys mercy that lych as he had browt hir to se this erthly cyte Ierusalem he wold grawnten hir grace to se the blysful cite Ierusalem a-bouyn, the cyte of Heuyn . . . Than, for joy that sche had & the swetenes that sche felt in the dalyawnce of owyr Lord, sche was in point to a fallyn of hir asse, for sche muth not beryn the swetenes & grace that God wrowt in hir sowle.'[37] Here we find no attention to architecture or to physical space, but the visit is measured in terms of imitative and identificatory passion: 'whan this creatur with hir felawship came to the grave wher owyr Lord was berijed, a-non, as sche entryd that holy place, sche fel down with her candel in her hand as sche xuld a deyd for sorwe . . . Than sche thowt sche saw owyr Lady in her sowle, how sche mornyd & how she wept her Sonys

---

[36] Kempe (1940: 26. 60).
[37] Ibid. 28. 67.

deth...'[38] Margery's cataphatic mysticism welcomed the stimulus of actual travel. We will turn now to some of the imagined and metaphorical responses to the corpus of religious travel.

THE QUEST OF THE IMAGINATION: ROMANCE, ALLEGORY, MYSTIC ASCENT

The quest romances of France, England, Italy, Germany (not to mention translations and adaptations in most other European languages—including Hebrew!) were well established in the growing vernacular literature of Europe by the time of Joinville's stunning account (*c*.1309) of the Seventh Crusade (1248–54) and especially by the time of Margery's path-breaking autobiographical work—which recounted a private life seen and felt as a kind of quest, as well as specific overseas pilgrimages. Personal pilgrimage itself was losing ecclesiastical favour in Western Europe after the first few crusades, as it encouraged a destabilizing mobility, contact with non-Christians, and a kind of literalism of belief that was increasingly seen as theologically dubious. Not to mention the freedom that travel might provide for licentious enjoyments of all kinds, rendered unforgettably by Margery's contemporary, Geoffrey Chaucer, in the ironic structure of his *Canterbury Tales* of mostly secular and scandalous story-telling, all devised and 'governed' (in his fiction but also at times in reality) by a supremely literal-minded inn-keeper.

Linguistically, as I have said, the word 'quest' in the Arthurian canon belonged to the aristocratic practice of hunting. As early as the late twelfth century, however, in the *Perceval* of Chrétien de Troyes, the *Joseph d'Arimathe* of Robert de Boron, and the slightly more pagan *Peredur ab Efeawg*, it was transferred metaphorically to what became known in the huge French Vulgate and Post-Vulgate Cycles of the first half of the thirteenth century as the 'Quest of the Holy Grail', the various narratives of which led its protagonists to the 'Saracen' Middle East, where their earlier violent participation in worldly power, militarism, and conquest dissolved in an entirely spiritual fulfilment, crowned for the best by death. This is seen as a good thing in the Cistercian-inspired *Quest* text of the prose *Lancelot* (by which name the Vulgate Cycle is also known), which entirely eschews the values of the more secular Arthurian narratives, and is linked to an allegorical and mystical tradition. The Grail (originally a dish most likely to bring various fish to table during feasts) becomes a symbol of a symbol—the Eucharist—and its quest a personal and mystical one for ecstatic union with God. It leads, however, in Thomas Malory's abbreviated English redaction at the end of our period (*Le Morte d'Arthur*, *c*.1470), to the dissolution of an idealized image

---

[38] Ibid. 29. 71.

of social space, Arthur's utopian Britain, whose best knights are drawn off to this personal spiritual quest, breaking the fellowship of the Round Table and thus leading to the fall of the just kingdom of the Christlike 'once and future king'. The spiritualizing of the militaristic knightly genre of Arthurian romance's quest for *aventur* has been very influential in the development of the semantic sphere of the modern English word: we idealize a 'quest' as something both morally admirable and practically more or less unachievable. Those who quest for the Holy Grail are described as wanting to 'achieve' the Grail, but the verbal accounts of its achievement leave the physically conceived object behind: the achievement is almost simultaneous, for both continental and English romance, with the bodily death of the quester. In the case of the Galahad of the prose *Lancelot* 'Returning then to the table [where the Grail is housed in an "ark" of gold and gems] he prostrated himself on hands and knees before it; and it was not long before he fell face downwards on the flagged floor of the palace, for his soul had already fled its house of flesh and was borne to heaven by angels'.[39] The grail and those who seek it become entirely spiritual: the grail becomes a disposable symbol, the questers' bodiless souls—thus dead, to the world if not in body. Words can only hint at achievement: Dante dramatizes his own arrival at the object of his spiritual goal as literally indescribable, sublimely so. The consciousness of this spiritual traveller blacks out: 'Thenceforward my vision was greater than speech can show, which fails at such a sight, and at such excess memory fails' (*Da quinci innanzi il mio veder fu maggio/che 'l parlar mostra, ch'a tal vista cede,/e cede la memoria a tanto oltraggio*).[40]

This fulfilment of goal-oriented activity harks back to the goal-less understanding of the early Irish pilgrims. They wander, by *aventur*, fully conscious the whole time that social and physical space holds no teleological value and only physical death can grant them sight of their desideratum: the face of God, the Beatific Vision seen in a dream and instantly forgotten by Dante-pilgrim. Such images are very much opposed to the more common intention of later medieval pilgrimage, which became so unpopular with the Church.

Allegorical poetry is a perfect literary medium for such a problematic, especially in the hands of a mystic, and beside the allegorical dreams and events embedded in the French Quest romances, we have the inward pilgrimages of allegory, often imaged as ascents in the winding pit and high mountain of Dante's *cammin del nostra vita*, Islamic poetry's mystical ladders (which have been noted as a source for Dante's vision via Brunetto Latin's soujourn in North Africa) and that of Walter Hilton's *Ladder of Perfection*; Philippe de Mezière's long prose allegory, *Le Songe du Vieil Pélerin* (1389, 'The Dream of the Old Pilgrim') is in part a kind of 'Mirror for Princes', essentially reformist in its motives but structured around a physical and spiritual journey, as is William Langland's fourteenth-century narrative poem *Piers Plowman*. Travel was a fact of life for some of the great Renaissance mystics it is not my brief to discuss here, such as Teresa d'Avila, but this was also true for the twelfth-century

---

[39] Matarasso (1969: 283).
[40] Alighieri (1975), *Paradiso* XXXIII. 55–7.

mystic and ecclesiastical administrator Hildegard von Bingen, poet, composer, painter, and saint (1098–1179).

Several songs in Hildegard's great liturgical song cycle, the *Symphonia Harmonia Celestium Revelationum*, are devoted to the voyage and martyrdom of the legendary saint Ursula and her 11,000 virgins (after which the Virgin Islands were named by Columbus).[41] Twenty-seven out of its sixty-nine songs are devoted to women and children—to the Virgin (16), to widows, virgins and children (5), and to St Ursula and her companions (6)—but only the songs of Ursula concern us here, as in some sense narrating and celebrating a religious journey, a pilgrimage to Rome after which the virgins' ships were arrested and the virgins slaughtered by Attila the Hun at Cologne. The legend was 'authenticated' and recorded in the visionary nun Elisabeth of Schoenau's twelfth-century *Book of Revelations concerning the Sacred Army of Virgins of Cologne*, though it had been earlier narrated in a tenth-century *passio* and by Geoffrey of Monmouth (as the virgins were supposed to have set sail for Cologne from Britain).

As Hildegard expects the narrative kernel of the legend to be widely known, the narrative element is relatively scant: the songs are largely typological and allusive, relating Ursula to Abraham ('she left the land of her fathers/like another Abraham' (*unde ipsa patriam suam/sicut Abraham reliquat*, 'Spirituo Sancto', ll. 7–8), to the Garden of Eden and Paradise, to the Song of Songs, to Abel and to Moses and the burning bush. But this of course is the mental space, the devotional space, of pilgrimage, particularly Holy Land pilgrimage, in which the pilgrim is himself or herself a type of the earlier scriptural personage whose experience s/he shares at a given site. If her purported pilgrimage was to Rome, it was *ad liminum apostularum*, as the pilgrimages to Rome were often designated: to Rome as the home of so many relics of the Apostles and early martyrs of the Holy Land, and as replica of the holy cities of Jerusalem and the Celestial Jerusalem. And blood is here, pervasively, as in the quests of the romances and the Holy Grail, both sacrificial and typological (the Blood of the Lamb), and as in so many historical pilgrimages and above all the 'general passages' (compare the 'Sacred Army of Virgins') real and meritorious. 'By the red of this blood,/let praise be sung in Jerusalem' (*Laus sit in Ierusalem/per ruborem huius sanguinis*, 'Cum vox sanguinis', st. 4).

Despite the landscape of scripture in the imagery of the six poems, and the structural motif of journey or general passage, Hildegard is clear from the outset about the space in which the events take place, the mystic's favoured space of the mind. The sequence begins, 'Hail to the Holy Spirit!/In the mind of Ursula,/maiden, a flock/of maidens gathered like doves./From whence she left the land of her fathers' (*Spiritui sancto/honor sit,/qui in mente Ursule virginis/virginalem turbam/velut columbas/collegit./Unde ipsa patriam suma/... reliquat*, 'Spiritui sancto', ll. 1–8). The prevalence of pilgrimage as a narrative

---

[41] Typical of Columbus's self-glorifying naming practice over the course of his exploratory voyages, one notes the following lines from one of Hildegard's Ursula lyrics: 'This virgin, who on earth is called Ursula,/is named in the heights Columba' (*Symphonia* 65, 'Cum vox sanguinis', st. 7). I will quote Hildegard from the bilingual critical edn. Hildegard (1998, ed. and tr. Barbara Newman). I have occasionally altered Newman's beautiful translations for a more literal rendering.

structure in the culture and literature of the high and late Middle Ages permitted a shadow corpus of allegorical poetry and mystical prose that could lean on the expectations created by this fundamental spiritual practice and its textual reports, as well as on the somewhat later romance corpus. Imagery itself was usually eschewed by the mystics of the *via negativa*, as too rooted in the body it was their quest to transcend. But even Marguerite Porete, who achieved her desire to escape the body as a victim of the Inquisition's fire (1310), could begin her *Speculum simplicium animarum* with an analogy to a wordly tale of love for a distant king, to whom she could only come near by means of a representation— not the physical replicas of Jerusalem, Rome, or 'Sarras', to which the pilgrims and Grail knights made their way, but in the fictional vehicle in a painting of the great explorer and conqueror Alexander, loved by a damsel in 'a distant land', and in the tenor of her narrative, the 'Mirror of Simple Souls', itself: 'I heard tell of a most mighty king, who through his graciousness and his most gracious nobility and generosity was a noble Alexander; but he was so far away from me and I from him that I could find no comfort for myself; and to remind me of him, he gave me this book, which in some rites represents the love of him. But even though I have his picture, still I am in a distant land, and far from the palace where the most noble loved ones of this lord dwell'.[42]

The hardships, physical, social, and bureaucratic, of pilgrimage and 'general passage' in an era whose infrastructure left a great deal to be desired, even when Europe and the Middle East were not especially dangerous to traverse because of war, and which were especially onerous for women, produced a large corpus of works by both men and women for the stay-at-home—those mental travellers whose circumstances made books accessible in one way or another. The situation of religious mystics was normally even more constrained to physical immobility by ideology and commitments to the cloister and other forms of social isolation. Ecclesiastical and theological disapproval of the literalism of religious travel was raised to a level of ecstatic rejection of the body's adventures by mystical aspiration to a purely spiritual consciousness. But even so, the pervasive tropes of pilgrimage, quest, and ascent provided a carapace of meaning for writing that ranged from the historical, geographical, and polemic to the fictional, allegorical, mystical, and even frankly erotic (the love poetry of the troubadors and *trouvières*, first composed by Crusaders and their wives and lovers, is another genre we have not touched upon). Much of the surviving vernacular literature especially is dependent on the tropes and experiences of spiritually motivated journey that this chapter has attempted to survey. For an entire continent, over the course of a millennium, the search for truth, significance, and memorable experience in places (or persons, divine and human) far from home could be said to undergird the practice of non-theological writing, and Roger Bacon makes the case that theology itself was dependent on the textual relics of much of the actual travel involved. Perhaps it was the very constrictions that rendered 'spiritual quest' so difficult that account for the massive production of medieval writing of these kinds. When religion declares that home is never where the heart is truly, the

---

[42] Porete (1999). Though written in French, it was widely circulated in Latin translation, for which see Porete (1986, ed. Paul Verdeyen).

imagination of what is elsewhere is irradiated with yearning, ardent and often violent, and writers of every kind and every nation responded, as writers do, to the magnet of collective desire.

BIBLIOGRAPHY

ADAMNAN (1958), *Adamnan's De locis sanctis*, ed. and tr. Denis Meehan (Dublin: Dublin Institute for Advanced Studies).

ADDISON, JAMES THAYER (1936), *Medieval Missionary: A Study of the Conversion of Northern Europe, AD 500–1300* (New York and London: International Missionary Council).

ADLER, ELKAN NATHAN (ed.) (1930; repr. n.d.), *Jewish Travelers of the Middle Ages: Nineteen First-Hand Accounts* (New York: Dover Books).

ALIGHIERI, DANTE (1975), *The Divine Comedy: Paradiso*, i, tr. Charles Singleton (Bollingen Series, 40; Princeton: Princeton University Press).

APPADURAI, ARJUN (ed.) (1988), 'Place and Voice in Anthropological Theory', *Cultural Anthropology*, 3(1): 16–20.

BACON, ROGER (1928), *The Opus Majus of Roger Bacon*, tr. Robert Belle Burke (2 vols. Philadelphia: University of Pennsylvania Press; London: Oxford University Press).

BIRCH, DEBRA J. (1998), *Pilgrimage to Rome in the Middle Ages* (Woodbridge: Boydell Press).

CAMPBELL, MARY BAINE (1988), *The Witness and the Other World: Exotic European Travel Writing, 400–1600* (Ithaca, NY, and London: Cornell University Press).

——(1991), ' "The Object of One's Gaze": Landscape, Writing and Early Medieval Pilgrimage', in Scott Westrem (ed.), *Discovering New Worlds: Essays on Medieval Exploration and Imagination* (New York: Garland), 3–15.

——(1999), 'Adamnan', in John Friedman and Kristen Moss Figg (eds.), *Medieval Trade, Travel, and Exploration: An Encyclopedia* (New York and London: Garland), 3–4.

CAMPS, ARNULF (2000), *Studies in Asian Mission History 1956–1998* (Studies in Christian Mission, 25; Leiden: Brill).

CLIFFORD, JAMES, and GEORGE E. MARCUS (eds.) (1986), *Writing Culture: The Poetics and Politics of Ethnography* (Berkeley, Calif.: University of California Press).

DAWSON, CHRISTOPHER (ed.) (1955; repr. 1980), *Mission to Asia* (Toronto and Buffalo, NY: University of Toronto Press).

EGERIA (1958), *Itinerarium Egeriae*, ed. E. Franceschini and R. Weber (Corpus Christianorum, Series Latina, 175; Turnhout and Paris: Brepols).

——(1970), *Egeria: Diary of a Pilgrimage*, ed. and tr. George E. Gingras (Ancient Christian Writers: The Works of the Fathers in Translation, 38; New York: Newman Press).

EL-SHIBABI, FATHI (1998), 'Travel Genre in Arabic Literature: A Selective Literary and Historical Study', dissertation, Boston University.

ELAD, AMIKAM (1995), *Medieval Jerusalem and Islamic Worship* (London: E. J. Brill).

FRIEDMAN, JOHN, and KRISTEN MOSS FIGG (eds.) (2000), *Medieval Trade, Travel, and Exploration: An Encyclopedia* (New York and London: Garland).

FRIEDMAN, MARK (1996), 'Jewish Pilgrimage after the Destruction of the Second Temple', in Nita Rosovsky (ed.), *City of the Great King* (Cambridge, Mass., and London: Harvard University Press), 136–46.

FOUCHER DE CHARTRES (1941), *Chronicle of the First Crusade (Fulcheri Carnotensis Historia hierosolymitana)*, tr. Martha E. McGinty (Tranlations and reprints from the original sources of history, 3rd ser. 1; Philadelphia: University of Pennsylvania Press).

GARDINER, EILEEN (1993), *Medieval Visions of Heaven and Hell: A Sourcebook* (Garland Medieval Bibliographies, 11; New York and London: Routledge).

——(2008), *Visions of Heaven and Hell before Dante* (New York: Italica Press).

Guidebook to Palestine (1894; repr. 1971), tr. J. H. Bernard (Library of the Palestine Pilgrims' Text Society, 6; New York: AMS Press).

HETOUM (1988), *Hetoum: A Lytell Cronycle: Richard Pynson's Translation (c.1520) of La Fleur des histoires de la terre d'Orient (c.1307)*, tr. Glenn Burger (Toronto: University of Toronto Press).

HIGGINS, IAIN (1997), *Writing East: The 'Travels' of Sir John Mandeville* (Philadelphia: University of Pennsylvania Press).

HILDEGARD (1998), *Symphonia: A Critical Edition of the Symphonia armonie celestium revelationum*, ed. and tr. Barbara Newman (2nd edn. Ithaca, NY, and London: Cornell University Press).

Historia Missionum Ordinis Fratrum Minorum (1967) (2 vols. Rome: Secretarius missionum).

HOERDER, DIRK, CHRISTIANE HARZIG, and ADRIAN SHUBERT (eds.) (2003), *The Historical Practice of Diversity: Transcultural Interactions from the Early Modern Mediterranean to the Postcolonial World* (Oxford and New York: Berghahn Books).

HULME, PETER, and TIM YOUNGS (eds.) (2002), *The Cambridge Companion to Travel Writing* (Cambridge and New York: Cambridge University Press).

HUNTINGTON, SAMUEL P. (1996; repr. 2002), *The Clash of Civilizations and the Remaking of the World Order* (New York: Simon & Schuster).

JEAN DE JOINVILLE and GEOFFROI DE VILLEHARDOUIN (1963), *Joinville and Villehardouin: Chronicles of the First Crusades*, tr. M. R. B. Shaw (Harmondsworth: Penguin).

KEMPE, MARGERY (1940; repr. 1960), *The Book of Margery Kempe*, ed. and introd. Sanford Brown Meech with Emily Hope Allen (London: Oxford University Press for The Early English Text Society).

Library of the Palestine Pilgrims Text Society (1887–97; repr. 1971) (13 vols. New York: AMS Press).

LIMOR, ORA (2001), 'Reading Sacred Space: Egeria, Paula, and the Christian Holy Land', in Yitzhak Hen (ed.), *De Sion exibit lex et verbum domini de Hierusalem: Essays on Medieval Law, Liturgy and Literature in Honour of Amnon Linder* (Turnhout: Brepols), 1–15.

——(2004) 'Pilgrims and Authors: Adomnán's *De locis sanctis* and Hugeburc's *Hodoeporicon Sancti Willibaldi*', *Revue Bénédictine*, 114: 253–75.

MATARASSO, P. M. (tr.) (1969), *The Quest of the Holy Grail* (Hammondsworth: Penguin).

MATTHEWS, W. H. (1922; repr. 1970), *Mazes and Labyrinths: Their History and Development* (New York: Dover Books).

MORRISON, SUSAN SIGNE (2000), *Women Pilgrims in Late Medieval England* (London and New York: Routledge).

PORETE, MARGERET (1999), *The Mirror of Simple Souls*, tr. and introd. Edmund Colledge, J. C. Marler, and Judith Grant (Notre Dame, Ind.: University of Notre Dame Press).

——(1986), *Speculum Simplicium Animarum*, ed. Paul Verdeyen (Corpus Christianorum, Continuatio Mediaeualis, 69; Turnhout: Brill).

SAID, EDWARD (1979), *Orientalism* (New York: Pantheon Books).

SMITH, NEIL (1991), *Uneven Development: Nature, Capital and the Production of Space* (London: Blackwell).

TUAN, YI-FU (1977), *Space and Place: The Perspective of Experience* (Minneapolis: University of Minnesota Press).

TURNER, VICTOR, and EDITH TURNER (1978), *Image and Pilgrimage in Christian Culture* (New York: Columbia University Press).

WEBB, DIANA (1999), *Pilgrims and Pilgrimage in the Medieval West* (London and New York: I. B. Tauris).

——(2000), *Pilgrimage in Medieval England* (London and New York: Hambledon and London).

WEBER, ELKA (2005), *Traveling through Text: Message and Method in Late Medieval Pilgrimage Accounts* (New York and London: Routledge).

WILKINSON, JOHN (1977), *Jerusalem Pilgrims before the Crusades* (Warminister: Aris & Phillips).

WILLIAMS, WES (1999), *Pilgrimage and Narrative in the French Renaissance: 'The Undiscovered Country'* (Oxford: Clarendon Press).

——(2009), 'Dangers and Friends: Forms of Narrative Witness in Renaissance Pilgrimage', in Palmira J. Brummett (ed.), *The 'Book' of Travels: Genre, Ethnography, Pilgrimage, 1250–1650* (Leiden: Brill).

··

WHEN DID 'THE MEDIEVAL' END?

RETROSPECTION, FORESIGHT, AND THE END(S) OF THE ENGLISH MIDDLE AGES

··

GREG WALKER

BOUNDARIES are always problematic. Difficult to agree upon and almost impossible to trace accurately over long distances without ambiguity or disputation; the closer you look at them, the vaguer they seem to become. At a local level, a national frontier disappears into a contested patch of desert, a mountain range or the flux of a body of water; looked at through a microscope, the atoms of our own skin seem hard to distinguish from those of the clothes we are wearing or the air that surrounds us. Chronological periods have boundaries of this sort: we think we know where they are, but as soon as we look at them more closely, certainty ebbs away in a miasma of qualifications, exceptions and inconsistencies. What, then, should we do with them? A decade or two ago it would have been tempting to use these observations as a way of deconstructing concepts such as the nation-state, human identity or chronological periodicity *per se*. If their edges could not be defined, then clearly the things themselves had no stable essence, no existence outside the always already politicized language we use to describe them. Such claims seem rather less alluring today. It is, perhaps, an index of how far we have returned to historical ways of thinking that they seem merely reminders that we need to think carefully, and be sure of our evidence, before we attempt to address a question such as 'When did the medieval period end?': a question which, while it is as much political as it is chronological or metaphorical, nonetheless addresses a real and potentially very significant issue.

All period boundaries are political, of course, but some are more political than others. And the long, vulnerable and intensely contested border between 'the medieval' and 'what came after' is probably the most political of them all. The shifting terminology that has defined the competing positions since their inception is itself an index of the intensity and durability of the struggle. A change of name can often have profound effects on the nature of a struggle, of course, especially if it is one's enemy one is renaming. And medievalists have for some time made useful capital from the claim that they have always been at a special disadvantage in the periodization disputes, since they have usually been forced to muster under names not of their own making.[1] Whether the term in question is 'the Dark Ages', 'The Middle Ages', or 'The Medieval', the implication, it is claimed, is always pejorative. Each is a name coined by scholars of the Renaissance and designed to do their cultural work for them. Without the dark ages to precede it, the star of the Renaissance would not shine so brightly; without 'a Middle Ages'—a long period of unalloyed mediocrity—to separate them from the classical past, the products of the early Renaissance might not look so obviously like a golden reawakening of the glories of Athens and Rome. And, as for 'the medieval period' itself, what fledging epoch would *not* look bright and enticing when standing next to something so obviously associated with backwardness, superstition, ignorance and brutality: all those things of darkness that the light of the Renaissance was supposed to have swept away? Indeed, of all the terms used to describe this period, 'the medieval' is probably the least flattering. At least the other two offer that consoling plural, 'Ages', acknowledging a degree of diversity to the long period from the fifth to the sixteenth century, whereas 'the medieval' simply throws them all together into a single unregenerate lump. What hope, we might think, for a period born under so inauspicious a star?

A moment's reflection might, however, give us pause. If medievalists have laboured thanklessly under flags of inconvenience all these years, what of our more modern colleagues? They too are currently locked in something of a crisis of terminological confidence, torn between the attractions of the traditional rallying point 'the Renaissance' with its positivist agenda (not to mention its bold, exclusivist definite article) and the lure of the more understated, but seemingly more progressive 'early-modern', borrowed initially from the historians, but increasingly favoured among literary scholars. The shift of emphasis has potentially profound implications for the way in which the post-medieval is conceived. What had once seemed a period characterized by a great enabling act of retrospection, a looking back over the *longue durée* of the deep, dark 'middle ages' to the distant monuments of Classical civilization, is now being rethought as a period with its eyes set resolutely forward, towards a

---

[1] Patterson (1990); Aers (1992).

coming modernity of which it is only the earliest phase. That which was categorized by 're'—revisiting, revival, rebirth—is now to be thought of as 'pre-'; no longer mature and fully formed, but incomplete and still striving towards. What was a rehearsal *of* things already completed is now a rehearsal *for* things yet to come.[2] In each case, however, the key term, like 'the Middle Ages', is defined by—and in terms of—something else: a thing beyond itself, and by implication a thing more interesting, towards which it can only gesture, Janus-like, from the threshold. Whether that more interesting thing is the Classical past, which it seeks by some implausible gynaecological intervention to 're-birth', or the modern future, which it—equally problematically—ushers in, the post-medieval period is also seemingly carrying the bags of another, more complete and confident period beyond it.

And, if the Renaissance clearly needs 'the medieval' against which to define itself, so too, it must not be forgotten, does the medieval need the idea of a Renaissance if its own foundational myths are to have any cultural capital. For the medieval story is itself founded on narratives of progress not unlike those which drive its post-medieval counterpart, in which western civilization, after the collapse of the Roman empire, falls into decay and obscurity until a range of diverse political, spiritual, social, and economic phenomena contrive to revive it and point it onward. The paradigm argues, whether implicitly or explicitly, for a movement upwards and outwards from the singularity of the fall of Rome, through which light is gradually restored to the dark corners of the western world, across the fields of learning, government, religious belief and practice, art, craft, and economic prosperity.

Far from denying the need for a Renaissance on first principles, then, medievalists frequently try to claim its glories for themselves. Trumping the assertions of their later colleagues with the counterclaim that the early-modernists are always already too late, the *real* Renaissance has already happened, centuries earlier, as they would have known if only they had the initiative (and the scholarly training) to look beyond the parameters of their own period-bounded ghetto. The modern medievalist can thus appear rather like the predictable Anglo-Indian patriarch in the BBC comedy show *Goodness Gracious Me!*, who, when shown any aspect of world culture from Superman to the British royal family, immediately claims its origins to be Indian. Ask a medievalist to identify the origins of multi-cultural tolerance, and they will point confidently to the medieval period (did not Islamic Spain enjoy centuries of peaceful, productive coexistence between Muslims, Christians and Jews?). Ask who were the first protestants, and they will talk about the Hussites and Lollards. Humanism? Medieval. The discovery of the Individual? Medieval. The high point of women's economic and social independence before the twentieth century, or the finest triumphs of female spirituality, or of representative art? All medieval.

The historiography of the medieval period is thus littered with premature Renaissances (not to mention premature reformations, agrarian and industrial revolutions), all of which predate and redefine the traditional chronology. A brief survey of the

---

[2] Hattaway (2005: 6).

scholarly literature of the last half-century throws up a tenth-century scholarly and religious Renaissance; an eleventh-century scholarly Renaissance; a full-blown twelfth-century Renaissance in religion, art, and culture; a thirteenth-century philosophical and spiritual Renaissance; and a fourteenth-century musical Renaissance, each one being used by its advocates to pre-empt aspects of the more familiar events of the later fifteenth and sixteenth centuries.[3] All of which gives rise to the conclusion that, despite the anguished cries of many a recent writer to the contrary, if the Renaissance did not, infuriatingly, already exist, it would be necessary for medievalists to invent it. And they would have to conceive it, not as a sudden, unexpected irruption in late-fourteenth-century Italy, based on the rediscovery of a long-dead ancient past, but as an ongoing process of renewal running through—and giving meaning to—an extended period of cultural renovation stretching from the tenth to the sixteenth centuries. The Renaissance, it seems, has always been with us, and the medieval period, as a consequence, would barely seem to begin before it has to cede precedence to its successor.

This is not to argue, of course, that periodization is of no consequence, nor that modern descriptions of period boundaries bear no relation to past experience. Notwithstanding all those attempts to find evidence of 'modernity' (Renaissances, agrarian and industrial revolutions, discoveries of individual subjectivity) before the fifteenth century (and indeed to find evidence of 'medieval' attitudes and practices after the sixteenth), it would be perverse to deny that the medieval period did, at some point, give way to something (an epoch? A culture? A sensibility?) which was in crucial respects quite different. Indeed, in what follows I will follow those scholars who have argued that it is vital that we recognize that crucial aspects of the medieval world did end, abruptly and violently, at a particular moment in the mid-sixteenth century, giving way to a new and quite distinct dispensation imposed by central government.[4] This process marked a fundamental change in the nature of English culture and society, and its effects are as evident in English literature as they are in other aspects of elite and popular culture.

Is This the Promised End?

When the early Tudor poets Stephen Hawes and John Skelton looked back to the age of the great late-medieval triumvirate of Chaucer, Gower, and Lydgate, they did so with an affectionate, playful, familiarity. For Skelton, this trio were the master craftsmen of his own writerly trade, brother poets who had laboured to make the English language—his language—smooth, sweet and potent.[5] In his *Garland or Chaplet of Laurel* (published in 1523), he imagines them approaching him, arm in arm, and inviting him to join their brotherhood.

---

[3] Lapidge (2002); Bolgar (1958: 72–7); Swanson (1999); Thomson (1983); Burns (1985); Wathey (1993).
[4] See Simpson (2002); Wallace (1997); Walker (2005).
[5] Lerer (1993).

> I saw Gower, that first garnished our Englysshe rude,
> And maister Chaucer, that nobly enterprysyd
> How that our Englysshe myght fresshely be ennewed;
> The monke of Bury then after them ensuyd,
> Dane John Lydgate. Theis Englysshe poetis thre,
> As I ymagenyd, repayrid unto me,
>
> Togeder in armes, as bretherrn, enbrasid,
> There apparel farre passynge beyonde that I can tell . . .[6]

Duly appreciative of their poetic achievements, clearly impressed by their modish clothing and seemingly unaware of any linguistic barrier to hamper their convivial conversation, the Tudor poet greets his medieval precursors with fraternal affection, quipping familiarly that 'Thei wantid nothynge but the laurell'[7]—the laureate degree that Skelton himself possessed—to make their greatness complete.

When the next generation of English writers, John Leland and John Bale, and their successors, Philip Sidney, George Puttenham, John Stow, and William Camden, looked back to that same late medieval period, they did so as if to an age lost in the mists of time and barbarism—a foreign country in which they did things very, indeed indefensibly, differently.[8] They saw not stylish poets inhabiting a courtly world much like their own, but something akin to noble savages, toiling instinctively against the superstitious ignorance of their age to produce a pale pre-figuration of the truths which their Tudor critics held to be self-evident. Even Chaucerian English, the tongue that seemed so sweet and smooth to Skelton, appeared to his Elizabethan editors to be rather rough and awkward—or so they said. In part, of course, this was Protestantism talking. Although the philological experiments of the later sixteenth century also played their part, Chaucer's alleged linguistic rudeness was seen primarily as a product of the doctrinal backwardness of his times. A good man in a catholic age,[9] he could achieve only so much before running up against the limitations of his culture, and thus had to wait patiently, like the pious pagans in Limbo, for the light of a later age to redeem his understandable blindness. The Elizabethan commentators said the same about Skelton and Hawes' own language, then still only sixty years old.[10] But that did not stop one of the most modish of them, Edmund Spenser,

---

[6] Skelton (1983), ll. 387–94.

[7] Ibid., l. 397.

[8] Simpson (2002: 24–6). The precedent was set early in the Henrician reform process in the preface to William Thynne and Sir Brian Tuke's edn. of Chaucer's Works, printed in 1532, which noted that 'it is much to be marvelled how in this time when doubtless all good letters were laid asleep throughout the world [that] . . . such an excellent poet in our tongue should, as it were nature repugning, spring and arise'. Chaucer (1532), fo. Aiii.

[9] See Sidney (1973: 133): 'Chaucer undoubtedly did exceedingly in his *Troilus and Criseyde*; of whom, truly I know not whether to marvel more, either that he in that misty time could see so clearly, or that we in this clear age walk so stumblingly after him. Yet he had great wants, fit to be forgiven in so reverent an antiquity.'

[10] See e.g. Whigham and Rebhorn (2007: 173): 'Such were the rhymes of Skelton (usurping the name of a poet laureate), being indeed but a rude, railing rhymer, and all his doings ridiculous.'

admiringly pastiching their aureate, alliterating diction to great acclaim in his *Shepherd's Calendar* and *The Faerie Queene*.

What divided Spenser, Sidney, Bale, and Camden from Skelton, Hawes, Chaucer, and Gower was, of course, the Reformation and the cultural revolution that it ushered in during the tumultuous middle third of the sixteenth century. As the recent work of James Simpson, Brian Cummings and others has suggested, the consequences of this 'violent fissure' in British cultural life provoked by Henry VIII's break with Rome can be detected as readily in the literary production of the period as in its religious practice or human geography.[11] Unlike those other phenomena that have been used to date the end of the medieval period—the rise of humanist learning, 'the discovery of the individual' or the advent of a 'new monarchy' under Henry VII—the Reformation was no abstract concept but a series of all too real events, violent and terrifying in their impact, and almost universal in their consequences across the social, economic, and cultural fabric of the realms they affected, principally England and Wales from the mid-1530s and Scotland from 1560—although, like all social and cultural changes, they were felt to different degrees and within a different timescale in different parts of the realm.

The Dismantling of Catholic Culture

The crucial markers of incipient 'modernity' which a previous generation of sixteenth-century historians saw as the definitive 'revolutionary' achievements of the Tudors: a more impersonal, bureaucratic style of government, a clear division between the royal household and the public administration, a stronger and more independent House of Commons: each of these has been shown to have been either a short-lived or largely illusory achievement.[12] Both Henry VII and his son remained personal monarchs, gathering and exercising political power in their own persons, and their courts remained the crucial arena for both social and governmental activity. If by the end of the sixteenth century the central administration was larger, then this was because it was being given more business to do by the Crown, not because it was growing on its own initiative as a counterweight to the monarch in the running of the State. And most of that increased business was itself a consequence of the Reformation. The Middle Ages, it is now accepted, were not killed of by administrative reforms or the rise of modern, more representative institutions of government.

It was Henry VIII's monumental, unprecedented decision to break with Rome, to 'nationalize' control of the Church in England in his own hands, and enforce the imposition of changes of religious belief and practice upon each and every one of his

---

[11] Cummings (1999: 851); Cummings (2002); Simpson (2002), (2007); Walker (2005).
[12] Elton (1953); Coleman and Starkey (1986); Starkey *et al.* (1987); Gunn (1995).

subjects that was the decisive event of the sixteenth century, and the crucial factor which convinced Leland and Camden that they were living in a radically different world to that inhabited by their predecessors Chaucer and Skelton. Over the course of a decade, Henry redrew the cultural landscape of the realm by dissolving the English monasteries, priories, abbeys, and nunneries, removing their highly visible denizens—monks, friars, and nuns in their distinctive habits—from the social fabric of towns and countryside alike. Similarly, he overturned the belief systems that had sustained generations of English men and women when he dismantled the 'idolatrous' shrines, reliquaries, images, and icons that had been a fundamental focus of popular piety in both cathedrals and parish churches, banned pilgrimages, and hedged prayers to saints around with strict injunctions against particularism, literalism, and the kind of local cults that saw more efficacy in praying to a saint in one place than in another. And what was not reformed out of existence by Henry was removed by the administration of his son, the 'godly imp' Edward VI.

Henrician policy did not destroy these things at a single stroke; rather, it was careful to do so only by stages, criticizing abuses before moving on to attack the practice itself in a manner that has prompted at least one scholar to see the king as motivated by a consistently 'Erasmian' reforming spirit.[13] But beneath the liberal rhetoric one might suspect a rather more determined and fundamentalist intention. Thus the Ten Articles, the set of religious protocols issued in 1536, while appearing simply to clarify the reasons why it remained laudable to pray to saints, actually cut away the foundations of the culture which prompted folk to do so, declaring,

it is very laudable to pray to saints in heaven everlasting living, whose charity is ever permanent, to be intercessors, and to pray for us and with us unto Almighty God . . . so be it done without any vain superstition, as to think that any saint is more merciful, or will hear us sooner than Christ, or that any saint doth serve for one thing more than another, or is patron of the same.[14]

Thus the kinds of local identification with—and affection for—particular saints or sites of miraculous events that were at the heart of saintly cults and provided the motivation for pilgrimages were quietly but firmly removed, even as the practices themselves were seemingly authorized and commended. And, later that same year, the Injunctions issued by Thomas Cromwell, Henry's vicegerent-in-spirituals, glossed the Articles in a still more positively reformist fashion, instructing bishops and preachers that,

to the intent that all superstition and hypocrisy, crept into divers men's hearts, may vanish away, they shall not set forth or extol any images, relics or miracles [of any saint] for any superstition or lucre, nor allure the people by any enticements to the pilgrimage of any saint, otherwise than is permitted in the articles . . . as though it were proper or peculiar to the saint to give this commodity or that, seeing all goodness, health and grace ought to be both asked and looked for only of God, as the very author of the same, and of none other.[15]

---

13 Bernard (2005).
14 Williams (1971: 803–4).
15 Williams (1971: 806).

Thus criticism of the notion of patron saints and local cults quickly gave way to criticism of praying to saints more generally. Rather than promote their cults, all preachers should,

Exhort as well their parishioners as other pilgrims, that they do rather apply themselves to the keeping of God's commandments and fulfilling of His works and charity, persuading them that they shall please God more by the true exercising of their bodily labour, travail or occupation, and providing for their families, than if they went about to the said pilgrimages, and that it shall profit more their soul's health if they do bestow that on the poor and needy which they would have bestowed upon the said images or relics.[16]

A second set of Injunctions, issued in 1538, ratcheted up the critical rhetoric a further notch, instructing the clergy to,

Exhort your hearers to the works of charity, mercy and faith, specially persuaded and commanded in Scripture, and not to repose their trust or affiance in any other works devised by men's [f]antasies besides Scripture, as in wandering to pilgrimages, offering of money, candles or tapers to images or relics, or kissing or licking the same, saying over a number of beads, not understood or minded on, or in such-like superstition; for the doing whereof ye not only have no promise of reward in Scripture, but contrariwise, great threats and maledictions of God, as things tending to idolatry and superstition.[17]

Such images that a priest or bishop knew 'to be so abused with pilgrimages or offerings ... ye shall, for the avoidance of that most detestable sin of idolatry, forthwith take down and destroy'.

These instructions were reiterated in a proclamation of 31 July 1547, one of the first issued on the authority of Edward VI, with the additional injunction that the clergy should now go further and,

Take away, utterly extinct and destroy all shrines, covering of shrines, all tables, candlesticks, trundles or rolls of wax, pictures, paintings, and all other monuments and feigned miracles, pilgrimages, idolatry and superstition, so that there remain no memory of the same in the walls, glasses, windows or elsewhere within the church or houses, and they shall exhort all their parishioners to do the like within their several houses. And that the churchwardens, at the common charge of the parishioners, in every church shall provide a comely and honest pulpit to be set in a convenient place within the same, for the wise preaching of God's word.[18]

Thus in little over a decade, an official religious culture in which saints might be prayed to with royal approval was replaced by one in which all material traces—all memories—of such practices were ordered to be destroyed. The nation was being asked collectively to forget things that had sustained belief and practice for centuries: effectively to dismantle both the physical and the mental architecture of medieval religious culture and to believe that its existence had been an aberration, built on superstition and ignorance.

Along with this assault upon the cult of the saints, came the erosion of royal endorsement of the idea of Purgatory, that 'third place' between Heaven and Hell to

---

[16] Ibid.   [17] ibid., p. 812.   [18] Hughes and Larkin (1964: 401).

which the vast majority of fallen human beings, too sullied by sin to ascend directly to heaven, but saved by grace and the merits of their faith and works from condemnation to eternity in Hell, were believed to go to atone for their sins and await their eventual redemption. Again, the process of reform began with a qualification, but swiftly gave way to outright rejection.

The last and most far-reaching of the Ten Articles of 1536 began with the declaration that, since there was good evidence for doing so in the Book of Maccabees, in the works of diverse ancient doctors, and in the long and continual practice of the Church,

> it is a very good and charitable deed to pray for souls departed, and ... also to cause other[s] to pray for them in masses and exequies, and to give alms to other[s] to pray for them, whereby they may be relieved and holpen of some part of their pains: but forasmuch as the place where they be, the name thereof, and kind of pains there, also be unto us uncertain by Scripture, therefore this with all other things we remit to Almighty God, unto whose mercy it is meet and convenient for us to commend them, trusting that God accepteth our prayers for them, referring the rest wholly to God, to whom is known their estate and condition.[19]

As a consequence of this, however, 'it is necessary that such abuses be clearly put away, which under the name of Purgatory hath been advanced, as to make men believe that through the bishop of Rome's pardons souls might clearly be delivered out of Purgatory', or that masses or prayers said in particular places had greater efficacy to aid the souls of the dead.

A similar process of softening up followed by expropriation brought about the dissolution of the chantries, those chapels founded to provide prayers and masses for individual donors or the members, living and dead, of collective bodies such as the trade and religious guilds and confraternities. In 1545, an Act of Parliament required that a survey be made of all chantries, reporting to the Court of Augmentations, the new body established by the Crown to deal with the property seized for the king from the dissolution of the monasteries, with a view to appropriating the assets of any of them discovered to be guilty of financial malpractice or in the process of being wound up independently by their founders.[20] Henry died before the survey could be completed, but in the first year of his son's reign, a new act launched a more fundamental assault upon the entire institution. The Chantries Act of 1547 provided for the dissolution of all such institutions, citing in justification, the 'great point of superstition and errors ... brought into the minds and estimation of men ... by devising and [f]antasising of vain opinions of Purgatory and masses satisfactory to be done for them which be departed, the which doctrine and vain opinion by nothing more is maintained and upholden than by the abuse of trentals, chantries and other provisions made for the continuance of the said blindness and ignorance'. Henceforth such revenues attached to the chantries should be appropriated by the Crown to be spent on 'goodly and godly uses, as in erecting of grammar schools to the

---

[19] Williams (1979: 804–5).
[20] Scarisbrick (1984: 65–6, 113–19).

education of youth in virtue and godliness, the further augmenting of the universities and better provision for the poor and needy'.[21]

Alongside the chantries themselves, and the metaphysical communion with the generations of the dead in Purgatory which they represented and facilitated, went the social bodies which funded, serviced and benefited from those bodies, the 'associational' groupings seen by David Wallace as so fundamental a part of the cultural fabric of late medieval society.[22] The same Act of 1547 empowered the King to 'direct his ... commissioners under the Great Seal of England to such persons as it shall please him ... to survey all and singular lay corporations, guilds, fraternities, companies and fellowships of mysteries or crafts incorporate and every of them ... and all the evidences, compositions, books of accompts and other writings of every of them, to the intent thereby to know what money and other things was paid or bestowed to the funding or maintaining of any priest or priests anniversary, or obits, or other like thing, lights or lamps' And, from 'the feast of Easter next coming, have and enjoy to him, his heirs, successors for ever, all fraternities, brotherhoods or guilds being within the realm of England and Wales, and other the King's dominions, and all manors, lands, tenements and other hereditaments pertaining to the said corporations.' In total, as Wallace notes, some 2,374 fraternities, guilds and chantries were dissolved and their wealth transferred to the Crown as a consequence of this process.[23]

The stated aim was, as we have seen, to convert such 'barren' endowments to more productive uses: to fund schools and schoolmasters and other good works. Cultural resources that had been directed towards the past, to help the souls of the dead and so to provide for the future of the souls of the living when they themselves came to die, were now redirected to look exclusively forward, toward the young and their education: retrospection would seemingly give way to forward thinking. As Wallace notes, 'the 1540s acts ... were following a semi-conscious economic logic in seeking to free up the capital invested, or buried, in the support of perpetual chantries'.[24] And what the Act also sealed was an end to those spiritual continuities that had hitherto bound the generations of the living and the dead together in mutually supportive collaboration, and tied both to the mediation of the saints in heaven: the kind of fellowship indeed, celebrated in the opening lines of Chaucer's *Canterbury Tales*, with their evocation of the collective springtime urge to journey 'from every shires ende / Of Engelond to Caunterbury' (ll. 15–16) to pray to St Thomas, who had helped them in their sickness—a mediator newly declared by a proclamation of 1538 to be no saint at all but a rebel and a traitor to his prince.[25]

What this legislation also engineered, as Wallace and Simpson have argued, was a centralization and simplification of the channels available for religious expression

[21] Williams (1979: 775).
[22] Wallace (1997: pp. xiv–xv, 2, 83–9).
[23] Ibid. 103; Scarisbrick (1984: 85–8); Duffy (1994: 277–447).
[24] Wallace (1997: 92).
[25] Hughes and Larkin (1964: 276).

and practice, and an increased focus on the parish as the centre of local religious and social life. From this point onwards people who had previously provided for their spiritual welfare—and constituted their spiritual identities—through numerous collective associational forms which cut across the traditional boundaries of the parish and diocese, were reduced primarily to a single institutional body (the parish) which would form the focus of their spiritual identity, and a single diocesan disciplinary structure which would ensure their conformity.[26] A popular religious culture hitherto characterized by a mild form of self-regulatory anarchy was reduced to a new simplicity and order, just as within the churches themselves a colourful diversity of images and polyphony of sound was to give way to whitewashed walls and a focus on the biblical word. From one perspective, of course, this was progress, a necessary purging of spiritual functions for which (as the Articles and Injunctions asserted) there was no demonstrable biblical warrant, and their replacement by activities of manifest cultural utility: a tidying up of the doctrinal furniture. But the spiritual and cultural impact of the loss of the kind of numinous, mutually affective links between the living and the dead attested to not only in such grand literary works as Dante's *Divine Comedy* but on a more modest scale in texts such as *Pearl*, *St Erkenwald*, Chaucer's *Second Nun's Tale* or *The Book of Margery Kempe* remains almost impossible to calculate.[27]

WINDOWS IN MEN'S SOULS

The doctrinal and practical changes of the mid-sixteenth century were made all the more significant by the way in which they were carried out. For, unlike other reforming monarchs before him, Henry VIII insisted not only that his subjects acquiesced in his reforms, but that they actively subscribed to them, swearing oaths to uphold the new regime, support the Royal Supremacy in the Church and reject the usurped authority of the Pope—now downgraded in official rhetoric to merely 'the bishop of Rome'.

This unprecedented intrusion into the thoughts and beliefs of his subjects claimed numerous direct victims among those men and women who were unwilling to subscribe to the legitimacy of his demands—whether because they thought those demands were too radical, as they were for catholic martyrs such as Sir Thomas More and Bishop John Fisher of Rochester, or because they thought they were not radical enough, as they seemed to evangelical martyrs such as Robert Barnes and Anne Askew. One measure of Henry's tyranny can thus be found in the cartloads of victims

26 Wallace (1997: 84); Simpson (2002: 1).
27 See Andrew Galloway's chapter in this volume for the effects on dream-vision writing of this severing of the links with the dead through the assault upon purgatory.

taken to their deaths at Smithfield, Tyburn, or the Tower of London in the last fifteen years of his reign, or executed in the northern counties in the aftermath of the Pilgrimage of Grace of 1536, the first large-scale popular reaction against the Reformation. More subtle, but perhaps more far-reaching, however, were the less visible changes brought about by those same demands in the habits of thought and expression among Henry's subjects. At a popular level one can detect a new anxiety to avoid the public expression of contentious opinions, a wariness of the kind of outspoken criticism of government policies, which brought unprecedented numbers to the attention of Thomas Cromwell in the later 1530s for speaking unwisely in the streets or alehouses.[28] At a higher social level, among scholars and writers, there was a still more marked turn towards discretion, evident in the adoption of new forms and modes of writing more suitable for living under tyrannical scrutiny.[29] The literary genres through which a previous generation of courtly writers had conventionally expressed their political aspirations and contributed to the intellectual culture of the court, genres based upon the concept of 'counsel'—the giving of honest, critical advice to the monarch—began to die away in the course of the later 1530s, withering in the face of Henry's unwillingness to countenance anything that did not conform to his demands for absolute public and private obedience. In their place, poets and prose writers turned to genres forged in earlier periods of political oppression, chief among them the stoic poetry, prose and dramatic works of Horace, Plutarch, and Seneca, which advocated the withdrawal of the virtuous man from the political centre, and lauded the virtues of the life of the mind and of rural contemplation.[30] These, and the savage satires of courtly life which grew from them, purporting to describe events in the distant past, but in reality commenting on experiences much nearer to home, were the forms that attracted courtier poets such as Thomas Wyatt, Henry Howard, earl of Surrey, and Sir Francis Bryan, and prose writers such as Sir Thomas Elyot in the last decade of Henry's reign: forms that allowed them to explore contemporary politics, freed from the need to address the sovereign as the idealized 'first reader' of any new work.

If, then, we are looking, for simplicity's sake, for a single date on which it might be said that the Middle Ages were brought to an end, 1547 has probably a stronger claim to that distinction than any other single year in the long sixteenth century. It was then that a spiritual dispensation that had underwritten social and cultural life in England for generations was officially erased from the nation's cultural memory, and beliefs that had been central to official and popular culture for centuries were declared definitively to be false, after a decade of official criticism and circumscription. Of course, epochs do not end so quickly or conveniently. And indeed, things would not have looked quite so clear-cut even at the time. The process of reform took much longer to take hold in some places than in others, and many contemporary observers would probably have rejected the notion that the reforms imposed were either as

[28] Elton (1973), *passim*; Simpson (2002: 150).
[29] Lerer (1997); Walker (2005).
[30] Burrow (1999); Walker (2005), *passim*.

pressing or as permanent as they were actually to prove. It might well have been possible as late as 1560, and certainly during the brief reign of the catholic Mary Tudor (1554–58), to hope—even to assume—that the Henrician and Edwardian reforms were merely a passing aberration, part of an ongoing renegotiation of jurisdiction and authority between the English Crown and Rome that would eventually be settled, returning things more or less to the *status quo ante*. But by the mid-1560s it would probably have been clearer to most informed observers that a point of no return had already been passed, and such things as the chantries, the cults of the saints and the fraternities and guilds that sustained them would never return to the heart of English cultural life. In these respects at least, the medieval dispensation had passed, certainly in the south of England and in the major towns and cities of the realm, and with it had gone many of the beliefs and practices which are the subject of chapters in this book. What had taken their place is rather less clear. Was it the Renaissance, the Protestant world, early modernity, or a mixture of all three? Such questions will no doubt form the basis of further boundary disputes and definitional debates among scholars for many decades to come.

BIBLIOGRAPHY

AERS, DAVID (1992), 'A Whisper in the Ear of Early Modernists: Or Reflection on Literary Critics Writing the "History of the Subject"', in David Aers (ed.), *Culture and History, 1350–1600: Essays on English Communities, Identities, and Writing* (Detroit: Wayne State University Press), 177–202.

BERNARD, G. W. (2005), *The King's Reformation* (New Haven: Yale University Press).

BOLGAR, R. R. (1958), *The Classical Heritage and its Beneficiaries* (Cambridge: Cambridge University Press).

BURNS, ROBERT I. (1985), *The Worlds of Alfonso the Learned and James the Conqueror* (Princeton: Princeton University Press).

BURROW, COLIN (1999), 'The Experience of Exclusion: Literature and Politics in the Reigns of Henry VII and Henry VIII', in David Wallace (ed.), *The Cambridge History of Medieval English Literature* (Cambridge: Cambridge University Press), 793–820.

CHAUCER, GEOFFREY (1532), *The Workes of Geffray Chaucer newly Printed*... (London: Thomas Godfray).

COLEMAN, CHRISTOPHER, and DAVID STARKEY (eds.) (1986), *Revolution Reassessed; Revisions in the History of Tudor Government and Administration* (Oxford: Oxford University Press).

CUMMINGS, BRIAN (1999), 'Reformed Literature and Literature Reformed', in David Wallace (ed.), *The Cambridge History of Medieval English Literature* (Cambridge: Cambridge University Press), 821–51.

——(2002), *The Literary Culture of the Reformation: Grammar and Grace* (Oxford: Oxford University Press).

DUFFY, EAMON (1994), *The Stripping of the Altars* (New Haven: Yale University Press).

ELTON, G. R. (1953), *The Tudor Revolution in Government* (Cambridge: Cambridge University Press).

ELTON, G. R. (1973), *Policy and Police: the Enforcement of the Reformation in the Age of Thomas Cromwell* (Cambridge: Cambridge University Press).

GUNN, S. J. (1995), *Early Tudor Government, 1485–1558* (Basingstoke: Palgrave Macmillan).

HATTAWAY, MICHAEL (2005), *Renaissance and Reformations: An Introduction to Early Modern English Literature* (Oxford: Blackwell).

HUGHES, P. L., and J. F. LARKIN (eds.) (1964), *Tudor Royal Proclamations*, i (New Haven: Yale University Press).

LAPIDGE, MICHAEL (ed.) (2002), *Anglo-Latin Literature, 900–1060*, ii (London: Hambledon Press).

LERER, SETH (1993), *Chaucer and his Readers* (Princeton: Princeton University Press).

——(1997), *Courtly Letters in the Age of Henry VIII: Literary Culture and the Arts of Deceit* (Cambridge: Cambridge University Press).

PATTERSON, LEE (1990), 'Critical Historicism and Medieval Studies', in Lee Patterson (ed.), *Literary Practice and Social Change in Britain, 1380–1530* (Berkeley, Calif.: University of California Press), 1–14; adapted and expanded from Patterson, 'On the Margin: Postmodernism, Ironic History, and Medieval Studies', *Speculum*, 65 (1990): 87–108.

PUTTENHAM, GEORGE (2007), *The Art of English Poesy by George Puttenham: A Critical Edition*, ed. Frank Whigham and Wayne A. Rebhorn (Ithaca, NY: Cornell University Press).

SCARISBRICK, J. J. (1984), *The Reformation and the English People* (Oxford: Blackwell).

SIDNEY, SIR PHILIP (1973), *An Apology for Poetry*, ed. Geoffrey Shepherd (Manchester: Manchester University Press).

SIMPSON, JAMES (2002), *Reform and Cultural Revolution, 1350–1547* (Oxford English Literary History, 2; Oxford: Oxford University Press).

——(2007), *Burning to Read: English Fundamentalism and its Reformation Opponents* (Cambridge, Mass.: Belknap).

SKELTON, JOHN (1983), *John Skelton: The Complete English Poems*, ed. John Scattergood (Harmondsworth: Penguin).

STARKEY, DAVID, NEIL CUDDY, D. A. L. MORGAN, JOHN MURPHY, KEVIN SHARPE, and PAM WRIGHT (1987), *The English Court from the Wars of the Roses to the Civil War* (London: Longman).

SWANSON, R. N. (1999), *The Twelfth-Century Renaissance* (Manchester: Manchester University Press).

THOMSON, R. M. (1983), *England and the Twelfth Century Renaissance* (Aldershot: Ashgate/Variorum).

WALKER, GREG (2005), *Writing under Tyranny: English Literature and the Henrician Reformation* (Oxford, Oxford University Press).

WALLACE, DAVID (1997), *Chaucerian Polity: Absolutist Lineages and Associational Forms in England and Italy* (Stanford, Calif.: Stanford University Press).

WATHEY, ANDREW (1993), 'The Motets of Philippe de Vitry and the Fourteenth-Century Renaissance', *Early Music History*, 12: 119–50.

WILLIAMS, C. H. (ed.) (1971), *English Historical Documents*, v (London: Eyre & Spottiswoode).

INDEX OF MANUSCRIPTS

INDEX

....

Lightning Source UK Ltd.
Milton Keynes UK
UKOW05f1226210817

307550UK00007B/5/P

9 780198 798088